IMPORTANT.

S0-BAS-608

HERE IS YOUR REGISTRATION CODE TO ACCESS YOUR PREMIUM McGRAW-HILL ONLINE RESOURCES.

For key premium online resources you need THIS CODE to gain access. Once the code is entered, you will be able to use the Web resources for the length of your course.

If your course is using **WebCT** or **Blackboard**, you'll be able to use this code to access the McGraw-Hill content within your instructor's online course.

Access is provided if you have purchased a new book. If the registration code is missing from this book, the registration screen on our Website, and within your WebCT or Blackboard course, will tell you how to obtain your new code.

Registering for McGraw-Hill Online Resources

TO gain access to your McGraw-Hill web resources simply follow the steps below:

1. USE YOUR WEB BROWSER TO GO TO: **www.mhhe.com/strong5**

2. CLICK ON **FIRST TIME USER**.

3. ENTER THE REGISTRATION CODE* PRINTED ON THE TEAR-OFF BOOKMARK ON THE RIGHT.

4. AFTER YOU HAVE ENTERED YOUR REGISTRATION CODE, CLICK **REGISTER**.

5. FOLLOW THE INSTRUCTIONS TO SET-UP YOUR PERSONAL UserID AND PASSWORD.

6. WRITE YOUR UserID AND PASSWORD DOWN FOR FUTURE REFERENCE. KEEP IT IN A SAFE PLACE.

TO GAIN ACCESS to the McGraw-Hill content in your instructor's **WebCT** or **Blackboard** course simply log in to the course with the UserID and Password provided by your instructor. Enter the registration code exactly as it appears in the box to the right when prompted by the system. You will only need to use the code the first time you click on McGraw-Hill content.

REGISTRATION CODE

xpvgi-c5qf-gcsd-e3e6

Thank you, and welcome to your McGraw-Hill online Resources!

 Mc Graw Hill **Higher Education**

Mc Graw Hill **Higher Education**

0-07-296409-X T/A **STRONG: HUMAN SEXUALITY, 5E**

Human Sexuality

Human Sexuality
Diversity in Contemporary America

BRYAN STRONG
University of California, Santa Cruz

CHRISTINE DeVAULT
Cabrillo College

BARBARA W. SAYAD
California State University, Monterey Bay

WILLIAM L. YARBER
Indiana University

Boston   Burr Ridge, IL   Dubuque, IA   Madison, WI   New York   San Francisco   St. Louis
Bangkok   Bogotá   Caracas   Kuala Lumpur   Lisbon   London   Madrid   Mexico City
Milan   Montreal   New Delhi   Santiago   Seoul   Singapore   Sydney   Taipei   Toronto

The McGraw-Hill Companies

Higher Education

Human Sexuality: Diversity in Contemporary America
Published by McGraw-Hill, a business unit of The McGraw-Hill Companies, Inc., 1221 Avenue of the Americas, New York, NY 10020. Copyright © 2005 by The McGraw-Hill Companies, Inc. All rights reserved. No part of this publication may be reproduced or distributed in any form or by any means, or stored in a database or retrieval system, without the prior written consent of The McGraw-Hill Companies, Inc., including, but not limited to, any network or other electronic storage or transmission, or broadcast for distance learning.

Some ancillaries, including electronic and print components, may not be available to customers outside the United States.

1 2 3 4 5 6 7 8 9 0 WCK/WCK 0 9 8 7 6 5 4

Vice president and editor-in-chief: *Thalia Dorwick*
Publisher: *Stephen D. Rutter*
Senior sponsoring editor: *John Wannemacher*
Developmental editor: *Barbara Armentrout*
Supplements development editor: *Jane Acheson*
Marketing manager: *Melissa Caughlin*
Senior project manager: *Christina Gimlin*
Media producer: *Ginger Bunn*
Design manager: *Kim Menning*
Cover and interior designer: *Susan Breitbard*
Art editor: *Cristin Yancey*
Illustrator: *Patrick Lane*
Manager, photo research: *Brian Pecko*
Senior production supervisor: *Richard DeVitto*
Senior supplements producer: *Louis Swaim*
Print supplements producer: *Mel Valentin*
Compositor: *GTS-LA*
Printer: *Quebecor World, Versailles*
Cover Art: © 2003 *Gayle Kabaker*

Psychology Advisory Group
Sherree D'Amico
Stephen Day
Myron Flemming
Tim Haak
John Kindler
James Koch
Don Mason
Jeff Neel
Robert Edward Oakley
Dan Pellow
Terri Rowenhorst
Kathy Shackelford
Emily Sparano

The text was set in 9.5/12 Palatino.

The credits for this book begin on page C-1, a continuation of the copyright page.

Library of Congress Cataloging-in-Publication Data

Human sexuality: diversity in contemporary America.—5th ed. / Bryan Strong ... [et al.]
    p. cm.
Includes bibliographical references and index.
ISBN 0-07-286049-9 (acid-free paper)
1. Sex.   2. Sex customs.   3. Hygiene, Sexual. I. Strong, Bryan.

HQ21.S8126 2005
306.7—dc22   2003069117

www.mhhe.com

Brief Contents

Contents

3

Female Sexual Anatomy, Physiology, and Response   76

4

Male Sexual Anatomy, Physiology, and Response   109

5

Gender and Gender Roles 128

6

Sexuality over the Life Span   163

7

Love, Intimacy, and Sexuality   215

8

Communicating About Sex   *247*

Sexual Expression   *276*

12

Conception, Pregnancy, and Childbirth   *391*

The Sexual Body in Health and Illness   436

14

Sexual Difficulties, Dissatisfaction, Enhancement, and Therapy *486*

Sexually Transmitted Infections   529

16

HIV and AIDS   566

17

Sexual Coercion: Harassment, Aggression, and Abuse 607

Sexually Explicit Materials, Prostitution, and Sex Laws   650

About the Authors

Bryan Strong

Christine DeVault

Barbara W. Sayad

William L. Yarber

BRYAN STRONG AND CHRISTINE DEVAULT were married to each other when they wrote the first and second editions of *Human Sexuality*. Sadly, at the young age of 53, Bryan died of melanoma. Bryan received his doctorate from Stanford University and taught at the University of California, Santa Cruz. His fields of expertise included human sexuality, marriage and the family, and American social history. Christine DeVault is a Certified Family Life Educator, educational writer, consultant, and photographer. She received her degree in sociology from the University of California, Berkeley. Christine is the mother of three children and grandmother of two.

BARBARA W. SAYAD is a full-time faculty member at California State University, Monterey Bay. She has been teaching and mentoring at the university level for nearly twenty years and currently teaches courses in human sexuality, women's health, marriage and family, and foundations of wellness, with a focus on service learning. In addition to co-authoring the last three editions of *Human Sexuality*, she has co-authored the 8th edition of *The Marriage and Family Experience* with Bryan Strong and Christine DeVault and has contributed to a variety of other texts. Barbara has served as a health and sexuality educator in both university and organizational settings. She received her master's degree in public health and is currently pursuing her doctoral degree in health and human services, with a focus in human sexuality. Barbara is married and has three teenage children.

WILLIAM L. YARBER is professor of applied health science and professor of gender studies at Indiana University, Bloomington. He is also senior research fellow at The Kinsey Institute for Research on Sex, Gender, and Reproduction and senior director of the Rural Center for AIDS/STD Prevention at Indiana University. He has authored or co-authored over 100 scientific reports on sexual risk behavior and AIDS/STD prevention in professional journals. He also authored the country's first secondary school AIDS prevention curriculum. Bill, who received his doctorate from Indiana University, is past president of The Society for the Scientific Study of Sexuality (SSSS) and past chair of the board of directors of the Sexuality Information and Education Council of the United States. He has received $3 million in federal and state grants to support his research and AIDS/STD prevention efforts. His awards include the 2002 SSSS Award for Distinguished Scientific Achievement, the 2002 Research Council Award from the American School Health Association, the 1991 President's Award for Distinguished Teaching and the 2002 Graduate Student Outstanding Faculty Mentor Award at Indiana University. He regularly teaches undergraduate and graduate courses in human sexuality. He has presented papers at numerous national and international conferences. He was previously a faculty member at the University of Minnesota and Purdue University, as well as a public high school health science and biology teacher. Bill is married and is the father of two adult daughters.

To the trailblazers in human sexuality and other fields who have the courage and conviction to do what is right, and to my family and friends, who provide me with the support and love I need to pursue this vision.

—B. W. S.

To my wife, Margaret—thanks for being my loving companion as we journey through the seasons of life. To my daughters, Brooke and Jessica—may the brightness of life shine upon you.

—W. L. Y.

Preface

LANGUAGE   JUST AS WE use language to communicate our ideas and intentions, language can also set a tone, establish a precedent, or alter a way of thinking. In this edition, we have carefully and thoroughly examined our use of language in order to ensure that it represents the most current and nonjudgmental terminology in our field. For example, when discussing women who are homosexual, we intentionally replace the term "lesbian" with "lesbian women" to underscore the fact that women who are attracted to the same gender are more than their sexual orientation. In our desire to bring less value-related and more contemporary vocabulary into the text, we also include terms such as "extrarelational sex" (instead of "affairs" or "adultery"), "sexual attractions" (instead of "impulses"), and "sexually transmitted infections" (instead of "sexually transmitted diseases"). And, whenever possible, we replace the term "dysfunctional" with "sexual difficulties" or "sexual dissatisfaction," to emphasize that it is the individual himself or herself who finds the behavior a problem or not.

Changes   Even though it has been only three years since publication of the previous edition of *Human Sexuality,* a number of significant changes in the field have altered the content of some subjects. Consequently, we have gone line-by-line through the text to ensure that concepts and facts are current and representative of the most recent findings in the field. Because of the effectiveness reported by students and instructors, we have chosen to continue using the same pedagogy and organization as in the fourth edition. We have made a few changes, however, that we believe will enhance learning. These include

- Explanation of the background surrounding many studies
- Questions to ponder in most "Think About It" boxes
- Increased focus on language that is inclusive and nonjudgmental
- Expansion of the global perspective
- Updated media images and personalities
- Addition of a list of Web sites as well as books at the end of each chapter
- Increased focus on issues concerning gay, lesbian, bisexual, and transgendered individuals
- Topic-related links to video excerpts on the book's CD-ROM
- Inclusion of material from the previous edition's Resource Center in text chapters
- Additional figures, graphs, and charts to visually display data
- New boxes focused on current issues in the field of human sexuality
- Updated material related to STIs, HIV/AIDS, contraception, sexual difficulties and dissatisfaction, and laws related to sexuality

Additionally, we have addressed many new topics in this edition and expanded coverage of numerous others, including postmenopausal hormone therapy, *DSM-IV* diagnoses, sodomy laws, the surgeon general's report on sexual health and responsible sexual behavior, sexual education, and women's sexual problems. We hope that you find these and other changes helpful in expanding your understanding of and interest in the field of human sexuality.

INTEGRATED TEACHING PACKAGE

As noted previously, *Human Sexuality* includes a teaching package designed to increase the text's effectiveness as a teaching tool. At the heart of this package is the **Instructor's Resource Book.** Developed by Barbara Sayad and Bryan Strong, and updated by Jeff Perrotti of Harvard University, this book begins with general concepts and strategies for teaching human sexuality. We offer suggestions on issues such as setting the ground rules for creating a supportive classroom environment; guidelines for integrating ethnicity, popular culture, gay, lesbian, bisexual, and transgendered people into the course; and using the computer in research. We provide the following resources for each chapter: outline, learning objectives, discussion questions, activities, list of films and videos, bibliography, worksheets, handouts, transparency masters, and Internet activities. The Instructor's Resource Book can be found on the Instructor's Resource CD-ROM and the Online Learning Center.

A **Test Bank** of more than 2000 items was developed by Roy O. Darby III, University of South Carolina, Beaufort, and updated by Jeff Perrotti of Harvard University. They bring substantial experience in teaching and in testing and measurement to this revised test bank. Each chapter contains approximately 130 test items, including multiple-choice questions, true/false questions, fill-in questions tied to key terms, short-answer questions, and essay questions. The test bank can be used on all the major computer platforms and may be found on the Instructor's Resource CD-ROM in both text and computerized test bank format.

With this edition we now offer **PowerPoint** lecture outlines. Sarah Gibb at Harvard University has combined lecture notes with figures from the text for a complete set of chapter-by-chapter slides. The PowerPoints are available on the Instructor's Resource CD-ROM and on the Online Learning Center.

The **Online Learning Center** contains practice tests, key terms, and PowerWeb's news and in-depth articles for students, as well as free supplements for instructors. The PowerPoint lectures and Instructor's Resource Book are housed on the password-protected instructor's side of the OLC at http://www.mhhe.com/strong5.

PageOut is a tool designed to let you build your own Web site in less than an hour. PageOut requires no prior knowledge of HTML, no long hours of coding, and no design skills on your part. Even the most inexperienced computer user can quickly and easily create a professional-looking course Web site with PageOut by filling in templates with your information and with content provided by McGraw-Hill. Visit http://www.pageout.net for more information.

A new supplement to this book is the **Classroom Performance System** (CPS) by eInstruction. CPS is a revolutionary system that brings ultimate interactivity to the lecture hall or classroom. It is a wireless electronic response system that gives the instructor and students immediate feedback from the entire class. CPS is a great way to get students more involved in lectures, take attendance, and offer interactive quizzes.

McGraw-Hill publishes **Annual Edition: Human Sexuality,** a collection of articles on topics related to the latest research and thinking in human sexuality from over 300 public press sources. These editions are updated annually and contain helpful features, including a topic guide, an annotated table of contents, unit overviews, and a topical index. An Instructor's Guide containing testing materials is also available.

Sources: Notable Selections in Human Sexuality is a collection of articles, book excerpts, and research studies that have shaped the study of human sexuality and our contemporary understanding of it. The selections are organized topically around major areas of study within human sexuality. Each selection is preceded by a headnote that establishes the relevance of the article or study and provides biographical information on the author.

For a debate-style reader, try **Taking Sides: Clashing Views on Controversial Issues in Human Sexuality.** This reader introduces students to controversial viewpoints on the field's most crucial issues. Each topic is carefully framed for the students, and the pro and con essays represent the arguments of leading scholars and commentators in their fields. An Instructor's Guide containing testing materials is also available.

For information on any component of the teaching package, instructors should contact their McGraw-Hill representative.

STUDENT LEARNING RESOURCES

The **SexSource Student CD-ROM** has been especially developed to integrate key concepts in the book with key scientifically based educational videos. Icons appear throughout the text to indicate clips that correspond to specific topics. Each video is contextualized with pedagogy, including follow-up questions and web connections. Additionally, a short self-test section is available on the CD for each chapter, as a study aid.

A student **Study Guide** has been prepared by Bobbi Mitzenmacher, California State University, Long Beach, and Barbara Sayad, California State University, Monterey Bay, coauthor of the textbook. The study guide contains help to prepare students in meeting the course objectives by providing practice tests and reflection and observation activities.

Practice tests and key terms will also be available online, as part of our comprehensive **Online Learning Center.** PowerWeb, a password-protected portion of the Web site, is free with all new copies of the text. The password card is packaged at the front of your new textbook. These news articles and in-depth essays direct students to more than 6,000 high-quality academic sources. Online Learning Center with PowerWeb: http://www.mhhe.com/strong5.

ACKNOWLEDGMENTS

Many people contributed to the creation and development of this book. First and foremost, we wish to thank the many students whose voices appear in the introduction of each chapter. The majority of these excerpts come from Bobbi Mitzenmacher's and William L. Yarber's undergraduate human sexuality students (California State University, Long Beach, and Indiana University), who have courageously agreed to share their experiences. All of these students have given permission to use their experiences and quotations so that others might share and learn from their reflections.

A number of reviewers and adopters were instrumental in directing the authors to needed changes, updates, and resources, and we are most grateful for their insights and contributions. Whenever possible, we have taken their suggestions and integrated them into the text. Special thanks are due to

Heather Frasier Chabot, New England College
Betty Carter Dorr, Fort Lewis College
Jean Hoth, Rochester Community and Technical College
Catherine Kannenberg, Guilford College
Marilyn Myerson, University of South Florida
Blaise Parker, University of Georgia
Jacqueline Reza, DeAnza College
Yvonne Stephens, Ithaca College
Andrew S. Walters, Hobart and William Smith Colleges
Laurie M. Wagner, Kent State University
Clair Wiederholt, Madison Area Technical College

Since publication of the previous edition of this book, Mayfield Publishing Company has become part of McGraw-Hill. For those who transferred their time and talents, we thank you for the continuity and support you brought to this edition. Melissa Williams was especially instrumental in passing that torch. Our thanks go to publisher Steve Rutter for his vision and steady hand in guiding us to a new era of publishing while encouraging us to hold on to our original vision. We are particularly grateful to our new sponsoring editor, John Wannemacher, who, in trial by fire, energetically and enthusiastically threw himself into the production of this book. Jane Acheson oversaw the supplements package and was instrumental in the development of the SexSource CD. Becky Smith is to be thanked for overseeing the developmental editing process. Barbara Armentrout's conscientious eye in editing the book was vital in keeping us on course in many ways. A special thanks to our production editor, Christina Gimlin. Thanks also to our manuscript editor, Tom Briggs; designer, Kim Menning; art editor, Cristin Yancey; photo researcher, Brian Pecko; and permissions editor, Marty Granahan.

To the Reader

*B*EING SEXUAL IS AN ESSENTIAL PART of being human. Through our sexuality, we are able to connect with others on the most intimate levels, revealing ourselves and creating strong bonds. Sexuality is a source of great pleasure and profound satisfaction. It is the means by which we reproduce— bringing new life into the world and transforming ourselves into mothers and fathers. Paradoxically, sexuality can also be a source of guilt and confusion, a pathway to infection, and a means of exploitation and aggression. Examining the multiple aspects of human sexuality will help you understand your own sexuality and that of others. It will provide the basis for enriching your relationships.

Throughout our lives, we make sexual choices based on our experiences, attitudes, values, and knowledge. The decisions many of us may face include whether to become or remain sexually active; whether to establish, continue, or end an intimate relationship; whether to practice safer sex consistently; and how to resolve conflicts, if they exist, between our values and our sexual desires, feelings, and behaviors. The choices we make may vary at different times in our lives. Our sexuality changes and evolves as we ourselves change.

STUDYING HUMAN SEXUALITY

Students begin studying sexuality for many reasons: to gain insight into their sexuality and relationships, to become more comfortable with their sexuality, to explore personal sexual issues, to dispel anxieties and doubts, to resolve traumatic sexual experiences, to learn how to avoid STIs and unwanted pregnancy, to prepare for the helping professions, or to increase their general knowledge. Many students find the study of sexuality empowering. They develop the ability to make intelligent sexual choices based on their own needs, desires, and values rather than guilt, ignorance, pressure, fear, or conformity.

The study of human sexuality differs from the study of accounting, plant biology, and medieval history, for example, because human sexuality is surrounded by a vast array of taboos, fears, prejudices, and hypocrisy. For many Americans, sexuality creates ambivalent feelings. It is linked not only with intimacy and pleasure but also with shame, guilt, and discomfort. As a result, you may find yourself confronted with society's mixed feelings about sexuality as you study it. You may find, for example, that others perceive you as somehow "different" for taking a course in human sexuality. Some may feel threatened in a vague, undefined way. Parents, partners, or spouses (not to mention your own children, if you are a parent) may wonder why you want to take a "sex class"; they may want to know why you don't take something more "serious"—as if sexuality were not one of the most important issues we face as individuals and as a society. Sometimes this uneasiness manifests itself in humor, one of the ways in which we deal with ambivalent feelings: "You mean you have to take a *class* on sex?" "Are there labs?" "Why don't you let me show you?"

Ironically, despite societal ambivalence, you may quickly find that your human sexuality textbook becomes the most popular book in your dormitory or apartment. "I can never find my textbook when I need it," one of our students complained. "My roommates are always reading it. And they're not even taking the course!" Another student observed: "My friends used to kid me about taking the class, but now the first thing they ask when they see me is what we discussed in class." "People borrow my book so often without asking," wrote one student, "that I hide it now."

What these responses signify is simple: Despite their ambivalence, people *want* to learn about human sexuality. On some level, they understand that what they have learned may have been haphazard, unreliable, stereotypical, incomplete, unrealistic, irrelevant—or dishonest. As adults, they are ready to move beyond "sperm meets egg" stories.

As you study human sexuality, you will discover yourself exploring areas not ordinarily discussed in other classes. Sometimes they are rarely talked about even among friends. They may be prohibited by parental or religious teaching. The more an area is judged to be in some way "bad" or "immoral," the less likely it is to be discussed. Ordinary behaviors such as masturbation and sexual fantasies are often the source of considerable guilt and shame. But in your human sexuality course, they will be examined objectively. You may be surprised to discover, in fact, that part of your learning involves *unlearning* myths, half-truths, factual errors, and distortions you learned previously.

You may feel uncomfortable and nervous in your first class meetings. These feelings are not at all uncommon. Sexuality may be the most taboo subject you study as undergraduates. Your comfort level in class will probably increase as you recognize that you and your fellow students have a common purpose in learning about sexuality. Your sense of ease may also increase as you and your classmates get to know one another and discuss sexuality, both inside and outside of class.

You may find that, as you become accustomed to using the accepted sexual vocabulary, you are more comfortable discussing various topics. For example, your communication with a partner may improve, which will strengthen your relationship and increase sexual satisfaction for both of you. You may never before have used the words "masturbation," "sexual intercourse," "vulva," or "penis" in a class setting (or any kind of setting, for that matter). But after a while, they may become second nature to you. You may discover that discussing sexuality academically becomes as easy as discussing computer science, astronomy, or literature. You may even find yourself, as many students do, telling your friends what you learned in class while on a bus or in a restaurant, as other passengers or diners gasp in shock or lean toward you to hear better!

Studying sexuality requires respect for your fellow students. You'll discover that the experiences and values of your classmates vary greatly. Some students have little sexual experience, while others have substantial experience; some students hold progressive sexual values, while others hold restrictive ones. Some students are gay, lesbian, or bisexual individuals, while the majority are heterosexual people. Most students are young, others middle-aged, some old—each in a different stage of life and with different developmental tasks before them. Furthermore, the presence of students from any of the more than a hundred ethnic groups in the United States reminds us that there is no single behavioral, attitudinal, value, or belief system that encompasses sexuality in contemporary America. Finally, you will find that you become more accepting of yourself as a sexual being by studying human sexuality. Our culture conveys few positive messages affirming the naturalness of sexuality. Those studying sexuality often report that they become more appreciative of their sexuality and less apologetic, defensive, or shameful about their sexual feelings, attractions, and desires. Accepting one's sexuality also means viewing sexuality as normal and as an integral, beautiful, and joyful part of being human. Accepting one's own sexuality is an important component in owning one's own sexuality.

Because of America's diversity in terms of experience, values, orientation, class, ability, age, and ethnicity, the study of sexuality calls for us to be open-minded: to be receptive to new ideas and to differentness; to seek to understand what we have not understood before; to reexamine old assumptions, ideas, and beliefs; to encompass the humanness and uniqueness in each of us. In our quest for knowledge and understanding, we need to be intellectually curious. As writer Joan Nestle observes, "Curiosity builds bridges. . . . Curiosity is not trivial; it is the respect one life pays to another."

THE AUTHORS' PERSPECTIVE

We developed this textbook along several themes, which we believe will help you better understand your sexuality and that of others.

Sexuality as a Fundamental Component of Health

As one component of the human condition, sexuality can impact personal well-being. When balanced with other life needs, sexuality contributes positively to personal health and happiness. When expressed in destructive ways, it can impair health and well-being. We believe that studying about human sexuality is one way of increasing the healthy lifestyle of our students.

Biopsychosocial Orientation

Although we are creatures rooted in biology, hormones and the desire to reproduce are not the only important factors shaping our sexuality. We believe that the most significant factor is the interplay between biology, individual personalities, and social factors. As a result, we use a biopsychosocial perspective in explaining human sexuality. This perspective emphasizes the roles of biology (maleness or femaleness, the influence of genetics, the role of hormones), of psychological factors (such as motivation, emotions, and attitudes), and of social learning (the process of learning from others and from society). We look at how sexuality is shaped in our culture; we examine how it varies in different historical periods and between different ethnic groups in our culture. We also examine how sexuality takes different forms in other cultures throughout the world.

In addition, because we want students to apply the concepts presented in this book to their own lives, we present information and ideas in ways that encourage students to become proactive in their own sexual well-being. We highlight sexual-health-related topics in boxes called "Think About It"; we ask questions that prompt students to examine their own values and the ways they express their sexuality in boxes called "Practically Speaking"; and we encourage students to probe the subject beyond what the book presents in a feature called "Sex and the Internet."

Sex as Intimacy

We believe that sex in our culture is basically an expressive and intimate activity. It is a vehicle for expressing feelings, whether positive or negative. It is also a means for establishing and maintaining intimacy. Sex is important as a means of reproduction as well, but because of the widespread use of birth control, reproduction has increasingly become a matter of choice.

Gender Roles

Gender roles are societal expectations of how women and men should behave in a particular culture. Among other things, gender roles tell us how we are supposed to act sexually. Although women and men differ, we believe most differences are rooted more in social learning than in biology.

Traditionally, our gender roles have viewed men and women as "opposite" sexes. Men were active, women passive; men were sexually aggressive, women sexually receptive; men sought sex, women love. Research, however, suggests that we are more alike than different as men and women. To reflect our commonalities rather than our differences, we refer not to the "opposite" sex, but to the "other" sex.

Sexuality and Popular Culture

Much of what we learn about sexuality from popular culture and the media—from so-called sex experts, magazine articles, how-to books, the Internet, TV, and the movies—is wrong, half-true, or stereotypical. Prejudice may masquerade as fact. Scholarly research may also be flawed for various reasons. Throughout the textbook, we look at how we can evaluate what we read and see, both in popular culture and in scholarly research. We compare scholarly findings to sexual myths and beliefs, including research about gay men, lesbian women, bisexual individuals, and about ethnic groups.

Homosexuality as a Normal Sexual Variation

We recognize the normalcy of gay, lesbian, and bisexual sexual orientations. Gay, lesbian, bisexual, and transgendered individuals have been subjected to discrimination, prejudice, and injustice for centuries. But as society has become more enlightened, it has discovered that these individuals do not differ from heterosexual people in any significant aspect other than their sexual attractions. In 1972, the American Psychiatric Association removed homosexuality from its list of mental disorders, and in 2003, the U.S. Supreme Court struck down laws against sodomy. Today, the major

STUDENTS BEGIN THE STUDY of human sexuality for a multitude of reasons. When we asked our students to tell us what they wanted to learn in our class, their answers emphasized the personal dimension of learning. The student responses below are representative.

- My biggest issue is setting my own sexual guidelines, rather than accepting those of others, such as my friends, society, etc.

  —*a 20-year-old woman*

- I want to know the difference between sex and love. When I have sex with a woman, I think I'm in love with her, or at least want to be. Am I kidding myself?

  —*a 21-year-old man*

- I have a hard time telling my boyfriend what I want him to do. I get embarrassed and end up not getting what I need.

  —*a 19-year-old woman*

- I lost my virginity last week. What do you do when you sleep with someone for the first time?

  —*an 18-year-old man*

- I recently separated from my husband and am beginning to date again. I'd like to know what the proper sexual etiquette is today. Such as, do you kiss or have sex on the first date . . . or what?

  —*a 37-year-old woman*

- I'm gay, but my family would disown me if they found out. What can I do to make my parents understand that it's OK to be gay?

  —*a 20-year-old man*

- My parents continue to hassle me about sex. They want me to be a virgin when I marry (which is next to impossible, since I lost my virginity when I was sixteen). Any suggestions on how to raise parents?

  —*a 19-year-old woman*

- Is it wrong to masturbate if you have a regular partner?

  —*a 22-year-old man*

- Why do women get called "sluts" if they have more than one partner, and it doesn't matter for guys? In fact, the more women men "have," the more points they get.

  —*an 18-year-old woman*

- How do I know if I'm normal? What is normal? And why do I care?

  —*a 21-year-old man*

- I'm a sexy seventy-year-old. How come young people think sex stops when you're over forty? We don't spend all day just knitting, you know.

  —*a 70-year-old woman*

Some of these questions relate to facts, some concern attitudes or relationships, and still others concern values. But all of them are within the domain of human sexuality. As you study human sexuality, you may find answers to many of these questions, as well as those of your own. You will also find that your class will raise questions the textbook or instructor cannot answer. Part of the reason we cannot answer all your questions is that there is insufficient research available to give an adequate response. But part of the reason also may be that it is not the domain of social science to answer questions of value. As social scientists, it is our role to provide you with knowledge, analytical skills, and insights for making your own moral evaluations. It is you who are ultimately responsible for determining your sexual value system and sexual code of behavior.

professional psychological, sociological, and health associations in the United States regard homosexuality as a normal sexual variation. For this reason, we have integrated discussions of lesbian women, gay men, and bisexual people throughout the book.

The Significance of Ethnicity

Until recently, Americans have ignored ethnicity as a factor in studying human sexuality. We have acted as if being White, African American, Latino, Asian American, or Native American made no difference in terms of sexual attitudes, behaviors, and values. But there are important differences, and we discuss these throughout the textbook. It is important to examine these differences within their cultural context. Ethnic differences, therefore, should not be interpreted as "good" or "bad," "healthy" or "deficient," but as reflections of culture. Our understanding of the role of ethnicity, however, is limited because ethnic research is only now beginning to emerge.

* * *

Over the years, we have asked our students to briefly state what they learned or gained in our human sexuality class. Here are some of their answers:

> I learned to value the exploration of my sexuality much more. I learned that sexuality comes in many forms, and I'm one of them. The class gave me a forum or safe place to explore sexuality, especially since I have not yet had a fully sexual relationship.

> I found the psychological, historical, and anthropological elements of sexuality we discussed to be valuable. I see homosexuality in a totally new light.

> I learned that being sexual is OK, that basically we are all sexual beings and that it is normal to want to have sex. I am no longer afraid to talk about sex with my boyfriend.

> The information about AIDS cleared up many misconceptions and fears I had. I will always practice safer sex from now on.

> The class has helped me come to terms with things that have happened over the last few months that are disturbing to me.

> I have paid more attention to the erotic nature of things, not just the physical aspects of sex.

We believe that the knowledge you gain from studying human sexuality will be something you will carry with you the rest of your life. We hope that it will help you understand and appreciate not only yourself but those who differ from you, and that it will enrich, expand, and enliven your experiences and your relationships.

A Guided Tour Through the Fifth Edition

HUMAN SEXUALITY is written in an accessible style at a level appropriate for most undergraduates.

Chapter Outline.
To support both teaching and learning, we have incorporated many learning aids in the text. Each chapter begins with a chapter outline, designed to give the student an overview of topics discussed in the chapter.

Student Voices.
These quotations from former students begin each chapter, with stories to set the stage for the chapter's contents. These excerpts from student papers help showcase the variety of perspectives and experiences that students bring to the class.

SexSource CD-ROM.
New to this edition is the SexSource CD, with video clips about selected topics. You will find the video icon in the margins of your text, directing you to the CD for a short video of further perspective on aspects of the chapter.

Think About It.

Providing students with a greater understanding of timely, high-interest topics are boxes called "Think About It." Sample titles include "My Genes Made Me Do It: Sociobiology, Evolutionary Psychology, and the Mysteries of Love," "Bisexuality: The Nature of Dual Attraction," "How Common Are Condom Use Mistakes?," "A Couple Has Sex When They . . . ," and "Gay and Lesbian Parents."

Practically Speaking.

Also featured are boxes called "Practically Speaking," which give students the opportunity to reflect on their personal attitudes, beliefs, and behaviors, and to evaluate their own experiences in light of knowledge gained through reading the chapter. Sample titles include "Medical Care: What Do Women Need?," "Can an Erection Be Willed?," and "Assessing Your Attitude Toward Masturbation."

Important **key terms** are printed in boldface type and defined in context as well as in the glossary. Appearing at the ends of chapters are **chapter summaries,** designed to assist students in understanding main ideas and in reviewing chapter material. An annotated list of **suggested Web sites** and **suggested reading** is included at the end of every chapter as well, providing the student with sources of additional information and resources for research projects. To help students further probe each topic and their own sexuality, the **"Sex and the Internet"** feature links students to resources on the Internet and follows up with questions and reflections.

1

Perspectives on Human Sexuality

Student Voices

"The media, especially magazines and television, has had an influence on shaping my sexual identity. Ever since I was a little girl, I have watched the women on TV and hoped I would grow up to look sexy and beautiful like them. I feel that because of the constant barrage of images of beautiful women on TV and in magazines young girls like me grow up with unrealistic expectations of what beauty is and are doomed to feel they have not met this exaggerated standard."

—21-year-old White female

"The phone, television, and radio became my best friends. I never missed an episode of any of the latest shows, and I know all the words to every new song. And when they invented three-way calling, you would have thought the phone was glued to my ear. At school, we would talk about the shows: whom we thought was cute and how we wanted houses, cars, and husbands. All of the things we saw on TV were all of the things we fantasized about. Watching music videos and the sexual gestures were always [stereotyped as] male and female. These are the things we would talk about."

—23-year-old Black female

"Though I firmly believe that we are our own harshest critics, I also believe that the media has a large role in influencing how we think of ourselves. I felt like ripping my hair out every time I saw a skinny model whose stomach was as hard and flat as a board, with their flawless skin and perfectly coifed hair. I cringed when I realized that my legs seemed to have an extra "wiggle-jiggle" when I walked. All I could do was watch the television and feel abashed at the differences in their bodies compared to mine. When magazines and movies tell me that for my age I should weigh no more than a hundred pounds, I feel like saying, "Well, gee, it's no wonder I finally turned to laxatives with all these pressures to be thin surrounding me." I ached to be model-thin and pretty. This fixation to be as beautiful and coveted as these models so preoccupied me that I had no time to even think about anyone or anything else."

—18-year-old Filipina

"If there has been one recurring theme in my life, it's that I often look to the magic of Hollywood to inspire my quest for the perfect date. But because of my lack of experience in the field of dating, my primary source of advice has come from movies and TV. At the age of 19, it's quite a revelation for me to receive dating tips from movies like Fast Times at Ridgemont High, Can't Buy Me Love, and Swingers and TV shows such as Beverly Hills, 90210 and Friends. Other than these shows, I'm pretty much left on my own to fill in the blanks. After one date, I quickly realized no one should get their advice from TV and movies."

—20-year-old White male

SEXUALITY WAS ONCE HIDDEN from view in our culture: Fig leaves covered the "private parts" of nudes; poultry breasts were renamed "white meat"; censors prohibited the publication of the works of D. H. Lawrence, James Joyce, and Henry Miller; and homosexuality was called "the love that

dares not speak its name." But over the past few generations, sexuality has become more open. In recent years, popular culture and the media have transformed what we "know" about sexuality. Not only is sexuality *not* hidden from view; it often seems to surround us.

In this chapter, we examine popular culture and the media to see how they shape our ideas about sexuality. Then we look at how sexuality has been treated in different cultures and at different times in history. Finally, we examine how society defines various aspects of our sexuality as natural or normal.

SEXUALITY, POPULAR CULTURE, AND THE MEDIA

Much of sexuality is influenced and shaped by popular culture, especially the mass media. Popular culture presents us with myriad images of what it means to be sexual. But what kinds of sexuality do the media portray for our consumption? What messages do the media send about sex to children, adolescents, adults, and the aged? To men? To women? To Whites, African Americans, Latinos, Asian Americans, and other ethnic groups? To gay men and lesbian women? Perhaps as important as what the media portray sexually is what is not portrayed—masturbation, condom use, gay and lesbian sexuality, and erotic marital interactions, for example.

Media Portrayals of Sexuality

Media depictions of sexuality are increasingly frequent and explicit. In the United States, young people spend an average of 6–7 hours each day with some form of media (Brown, 2002) (Figure 1.1). Many of the televisions they have access to are hooked up to the cable and a DVD player. Television usually presents visual images that range from flirting to sexual intercourse. Movies depict sexual behaviors more frequently and depict a wider range.

FIGURE 1.1 Time U.S. Adolescents Spend Using Media per Week by Type of Media. (*Source:* American Academy of Pediatrics, 2001.)

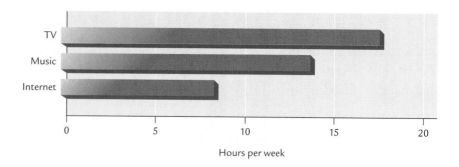

Hours per week

Steamy sex scenes and female nudity (often combined with violence) are part of the Hollywood formula for success. Movie producers apparently find it more acceptable to reduce females than males to their sexuality.

The music industry is awash with sexual images. Contemporary pop music, from rock 'n' roll to rap, is filled with lyrics about sexuality mixed with messages about love, rejection, violence, and loneliness. Popular music is transmitted through CDs and cassettes and through the Internet, television, and radio. MTV, VH1, BET, and music video programs broadcast videos filled with sexually suggestive lyrics, images, and dances. Because of censorship issues, the most overtly sexual music is not played on the radio, except for some college stations. Disk jockeys, "shock jocks" such as Howard Stern, and sportscasters make numerous sexual references.

Magazines, tabloids, and books contribute to the sexualization of our society. Popular novels, romances, and self-help books help disseminate ideas and values about sexuality. Supermarket tabloid headlines exploit the unusual ("Woman with Two Vaginas Has Multiple Lovers") or sensational ("Televangelist's Love Tryst Exposed").

Men's magazines have been singled out for their sexual orientation. *Playboy* and *Penthouse,* with their Playmates of the Month, Pets of the Month, and other nude pictorials, are among the most popular magazines in the world. *Sports Illustrated*'s annual swimsuit edition sells over 5 million copies, twice as many as its other issues. But it would be a mistake to think that only male-oriented magazines focus on sex.

Women's magazines such as *Cosmopolitan* and *Redbook* have their own sexual content. These magazines feature romantic photographs of lovers to illustrate stories with such titles as "Sizzling Sex Secrets of the World's Sexiest Women," "Making Love Last: If Your Partner Is a Premature Ejaculator," and "Turn on Your Man with Your Breasts (Even If They Are Small)." Preadolescents and young teens are not exempt from sexual images and articles in magazines such as *Seventeen* and *YM*. Some of the men's health magazines have followed the lead of women's magazines, featuring sexuality-related issues as a way to sell more copies.

For many, the World Wide Web has become an important part of the media. The Internet's contributions to the commercialization of sex include live videos and chats, news groups, and links to potential or virtual sex partners (complete with fetishes). The spread of the Web is making it easier to obtain information, social ties, and sexual gratification.

Telephone sex has become an increasingly popular means of attaining sexual arousal and pleasure. Each night between 9:00 P.M. and 1:00 A.M., approximately 250,000 Americans dial a commercial sex line and spend $5–30 per

Women's magazines such as Cosmopolitan, Redbook, YM, Seventeen, *and* Glamour *use sex to sell their publications. How do these magazines differ from men's magazines such as* Men's Health, Playboy, *and* Penthouse *in their treatment of sexuality?*

We know what makes you feel good.

Sexual images are used to sell products. What ideas are conveyed by this advertisement? How does its appeal differ according to whether one is male or female?

minute for phone sex. Because the FCC has banned obscene communication for commercial purposes in the United States, most calls made for this purpose are to overseas businesses.

Advertising in all media uses the sexual sell, promising sex, romance, popularity, and fulfillment if the consumer will only purchase the right soap, perfume, cigarettes, alcohol, toothpaste, jeans, or automobile. In reality, not only does one *not* become "sexy" or popular by consuming a certain product, but the product may actually be detrimental to one's sexual well-being, as in the case of cigarettes or alcohol.

Media images of sexuality permeate a variety of areas in people's lives (Figure 1.2). They can produce sexual arousal and emotional reactions, increase sexual behaviors, and be a source of sex information. Summarizing a handful of studies on the relationship between exposure to sexual media and our sexual behavior, professor and writer Jane D. Brown (2002) reports that the media (1) keep sexual behavior visible, (2) reinforce a consistent set of sexual and relationship norms, and (3) rarely include sexually responsible models. No doubt, this form of persuasive communication is altering patterns of social communication and interpersonal relationships.

Mass-media depictions of sexuality are meant to entertain and exploit, not to inform. As a result, the media do not present us with "real" depictions of sexuality. Sexual activities, for example, are usually not explicitly acted out or described in mainstream media, nor is interracial dating often portrayed. The social and cultural taboos that are still part of mainstream U.S. culture remain embedded in the media. Thus, the various media present the social *context* of sexuality; that is, the programs, plots, movies, stories, articles, newscasts, and vignettes tell us *what* behaviors are appropriate (e.g., kissing, sexual intercourse), *with whom* they are appropriate (e.g., girlfriend/boyfriend, partner, heterosexual), and *why* they are appropriate (e.g., attraction, love, loneliness, exploitation). Furthermore, regular

FIGURE 1.2   Percentage of Sexual Talk and Displays in the Media. (*Source:* Brown, 2002.)

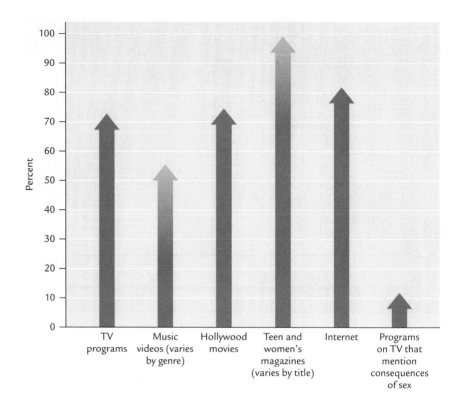

consumers of media sex are likely to believe that various sexual behaviors happen more frequently than they actually do—that there are, for example, more extrarelational sex, as well as more rape and prostitution (Greenberg, 1994).

Television

Television is one of the most pervasive and influential mediums affecting our views of sexuality. The networks are selling sex and selling it hard. However, the visual depiction of explicit sexual behavior on network television, though exciting and attractive, tends to be unrealistic. We see countless scenes of passionate kissing and fondling—but only between heterosexuals. Other sexual behaviors, such as coitus or oral sex, may be suggested through words ("Oh, it feels so good") or visual or sound cues (close-ups of faces tensing during orgasm, or Ravel's *Bolero* playing on the soundtrack). References to masturbation are rarely made; when they are, they are usually negative and consigned to an adolescent context, suggesting that such behavior is "immature." The popular sitcom *Seinfeld* was the first program to deal openly with masturbation, while *Sex and the City* and *Queer as Folk* have introduced themes related to sexual fantasies, domination, gay and lesbian relationships, and the sexually assertive woman. Though women represent just 36% of all prime-time characters ("Lack of TV Diversity Hit," 2002), suggestive breasts and low-cut jeans dominate the media. A 2000 study found that, although two-thirds of prime-time programs contained sexual content, only about 1 in 11 referred to the possible risks or responsibilities associated with sex (Brown & Keller, 2000).

> The vast wasteland of TV is not interested in producing a better mousetrap but in producing a worse mouse.
>
> —*Laurence Coughlin*

Television helps form our sexual perceptions through its depiction of stereotypes and its reinforcement of **norms,** which are cultural rules or standards. Television also provides us with a social template for discussions about and expectations of sexuality and relationships. Its countless verbal and visual references to dating and sexual activity are associated with adolescents' own sexual attitudes and expectations. In many respects, TV's sexual portrayals help to shape adolescents' sense of what is normal and expected (Ward, Gorvine, & Cytron, 2002). Our perceptions are shaped differently, however, depending on the TV genre, or type of program. There are six main genres in which sexual stereotyping and norms are especially influential: situation comedies, soap operas, crime/action-adventure programs, cable dramas, commercials, and music and game videos.

Up to 2000 hours of television programming are available in U.S. homes each day ("TV Parental Guidelines," 2000). To help parents sort through this volume of material and make decisions about the programs their children can watch, the TV industry, in response to the Telecommunications Act of 1996, developed a system of parental guidelines. Programs are categorized using age-related labels such as TV-Y7 (intended for children age 7 and older) and TV-PG (parental guidance suggested for younger children). They are also categorized using content descriptors: the symbols V (violence), S (sex), D (sexual dialogue), and L (adult language) for general programming, along with FV (fantasy violence) for children's shows. Parents can program an electronic filtering device called the V-chip to block shows according to specific classifications. One concern about ratings is the reliability of the coders who review the programs.

The Kaiser Family Foundation (Kunkel et al., 1998) investigated the rating system and found that the TV industry has limited its ratings of nearly all programs to just three categories: TV-G, TV-PG, or TV-14. Content descriptors have been virtually omitted. The researchers went on to say that parents cannot rely on content descriptors as currently employed to effectively block all shows containing violence, sexual content, or adult language. Naturally, it remains the parents' responsibility to monitor their children's TV-viewing habits.

Until recently, sexually explicit programming was allowed only during late-night hours as a way of minimizing the chance that children might view it. However, the courts have ruled that this restriction is an unconstitutional infringement of free speech, and cable companies are no longer limited to a handful of hours in which to air sexually oriented programs. Parents can keep such programming out of their home simply by calling their cable companies ("Steamy Cable TV," 2000).

Situation Comedies   Sex in sitcoms? When asked, most people think there is none. After all, sitcoms usually deal with families or familylike relationships, and children are often the main characters. Because they are family oriented, sitcoms do not explicitly depict sex. Instead, they deal with sexuality in the form of taboos centering around marital or family issues. The taboos are mild, such as the taboo against a married person flirting with another man or woman. If a sitcom were to deal with a major taboo, such as incest, the program would go beyond the genre's normal boundaries, and most viewers would not be amused.

In sitcoms, the formula is to put characters in situations in which they unknowingly violate conventional social rules, thereby creating chaos. The chaos, however, is resolved by the show's end, and everyone "lives happily ever after" until the next episode. Thus, a married man can be getting an eyelash out of his sister-in-law's eye when his wife comes home early and becomes jealous, thinking her husband and sister are kissing. While the laugh track plays, the husband tries to explain that she had something in her eye.

Sitcoms are sexually stereotypical and lack diversity. Their range of sexual standards and implied behaviors is limited, although the sexual references have increased considerably since the days of *I Love Lucy*. Despite the increase in sexual references, sitcoms barely touch on the variety of values and behaviors found in the real world. Will and Jack in *Will and Grace* and Ellen DeGeneres in *Ellen* (now off the air) are examples of openly gay characters in mainstream sitcoms, but they remain the exception. Conservative advocacy groups continue to oppose depictions of gay men and lesbian women as normal. Just 7% of prime-time sitcoms have racially mixed casts (Keintz-Knowles, 2002). Although sitcoms have a limited range, they nevertheless affirm human connectedness and family values. They usually provide a context of intimacy for sexuality. Whatever transgression occurs, it is forgotten by the next episode.

Soap Operas   Soap operas are one of the most popular TV genres. In 1999, the highest-rated soap opera, *The Young and the Restless*, reached 65 million households per episode ("Ratings," 1999). Although sexual transgressions are soon forgotten in sitcoms, they are never forgotten in soap operas. Rather, they are the lifeblood of soaps: jealousy and revenge are ever present. Most characters are now, or once were, involved with one another. The ghosts of past loves haunt the mansions and townhouses; each relationship carries a heavy history with it. Extrarelational sex, pregnancy alarms, betrayals, and jealousy punctuate every episode. Depictions of sexual behavior are fairly frequent.

Soap operas offer distinct visions of sexuality. Sexuality is portrayed as intense and as a cause of jealousy. Women are the primary audience. Why do you suppose this occurs?

In recent years, Spanish-language soaps (*telenovelas*) such as *Te Sigo Amando* (I Still Love You), *Me Destino Eres Tu* (You Are My Destiny), and *Tres Mujeres* (Three Women) have become increasingly popular among the Latino population. The content and messages of Latino soaps, however, do not differ significantly from those of soaps produced in the United States. They differ mainly in that they present fewer scenes suggestive of sexual activities, such as characters in bed together.

With regard to nudity on soaps: frontal shots of nude male torsos (genitals are not shown) and back shots of nude female torsos (to avoid the taboo naked female breast) are most common. Characters lounge in bed, wrapped in sheets; they are either about to engage in sex or are basking in its pleasurable aftermath. At the same time, no one seems to use contraception or take measures to prevent sexually transmitted infections (STIs). In 50 hours of daytime dramas, there were 156 scenes of intercourse, with only five references to contraception or safer sex (American Academy of Pediatrics, 2001). By the odds, one would expect many pregnancies and an epidemic of STIs.

Bradley Greenberg, a leading media researcher, and Mark Woods (1999) report that the most common sexual activity portrayed on soap operas is intercourse between two people not married to each other. Prostitution and intimate touching are depicted infrequently, and same-sex behaviors and references are virtually nonexistent. Despite American adults' willingness to have birth control information discussed and advertised on television, the networks continue to resist (American Academy of Pediatrics, 2001).

In one study, researchers found that TV viewing affects our perceptions of others' sexual attitudes and behaviors but not our perceptions of our own experiences (Ward & Rivadeneyra, 1999). Males were perceived as more sexually experienced by females who watch soap operas than by females who do not watch them. Soap watchers also believed that their male peers were quite sexually experienced. But TV viewing for males was only weakly associated with their sexual attitudes and expectations; the reasons for this finding are not clear. What is apparent, however, is that television—not just soaps but all genres—portrays sex in one-dimensional terms: Sex is only for the young, single, and beautiful, and sexual encounters are always spontaneous, romantic, and risk-free.

Although there is also intimacy in the world of soaps, it is intense, unstable, and desperate. Relationships are usually stormy and short-lived, setting the scene for jealousy and revenge in subsequent episodes. There is no satisfaction or fulfillment in most soap relationships. Despite the genre's focus on sex, TV soaps send a clear message that sex is guilt-ridden, unsatisfying, and exploitative.

Crime/Action-Adventure Programs   In crime and action-adventure programs, there are few intimate relationships. Instead, relationships are fundamentally sexual, based on attraction. They are the backdrop to crime and adventure, which form the basis of the plot. The basic theme of a crime program is disorder (a crime) that must be resolved so that order can be restored. Often, the disorder is caused by a sexual episode or a sexually related issue, such as prostitution, pornography, rape, cross-dressing, sexual blackmail, or seduction for criminal purposes. As such, we see the underside of sex. Plots involve police searching for female killers who turn out to be cross-dressers, prostitutes who are murdered by sociopaths, runaways lured into pornography, and so on. Detectives and police go undercover, leading the audience into the underworld of prostitutes, pimps, and johns.

The detectives live isolated lives lacking emotional ties. They are portrayed as loners, and their involvements are ephemeral, usually not lasting beyond a single episode. Often, their love interests are murdered; other times, the women themselves prove to be criminals. The only intimacy they may find is with their detective partners or with secretaries. Marital intercourse is virtually nonexistent. Most sexual intercourse takes place between unmarried people or between men and prostitutes (Greenberg, 1994).

Cable Dramas   Cable dramas, many of which are produced by HBO, focus on situational themes. In contrast to traditional network TV series, these dramas often revolve around a particular setting or issue, such as a singles household or mob family. Such programs as *Oz, Sex and the City,* and *The Sopranos* focus on sex as a social issue rather than in terms of intimacy. Pregnancy, extramarital liaisons, rape, sexual harassment, prostitution, and AIDS are addressed head-on and graphically. Because television often seeks to entertain and exploit rather than inform, most of the sexuality that appears in these programs lends itself to sensationalism, humor, or shock.

Commercials   Commercials are a unique genre in TV programming. Although they are not part of the TV program per se, because they are inserted before, after, and during it, they become a free-floating part of it. In these commercials, advertisers may manipulate sexual images to sell products. The most sexually explicit commercials generally advertise jeans, beer, and perfume.

These commercials tell a story visually through a series of brief scenes or images. They do not pretend to explain the practical benefits of their product, such as cost or effectiveness. Instead, they offer viewers an image or attitude. Directed especially toward adolescents and young adults, these commercials play upon fantasies of attractiveness, sexual success, and fun. They also work to shape our eating styles, appearance, body image, and sense of what is attractive and desirable in ourselves and others. We are led to believe that we can acquire these attributes by using a particular product.

Until recently, TV ads used gay themes only as the brunt of cheap jokes. However, today, rather than risk alienating this $425-billion market, dozens of companies are turning to more sensitive and honest portrayals of gay men and lesbian women to sell their products ("Sensitivity Training," 2002). For example, Subaru, aware of its lesbian following, has called upon openly gay tennis icon Martina Navratilova to pitch its autos.

Music and Game Videos   MTV, VH1, BET, and music video programs such as *Sex Appeal* are very popular among adolescents and young adults. Most viewers, however, do not watch music videos for longer than 15 minutes at a time because they are repetitive.

Unlike audio-recorded music, music videos play to the ear and the eye. Young female artists such as Jennifer Lopez, Britney Spears, Christina Aguilera, and the Dixie Chicks have brought energy, sexuality, and individualism to the young music audience. Male artists such as Justin Timberlake, Nellie, and Eminem provide young audiences with a steady dose of sexuality, power, and rhythm.

A few music groups and individuals have broken ground by expressing their views about alternative sexual orientations. Marilyn Manson is bisexual, and the members of the Pansey Division are gay and use a pink triangle as their symbol. Lesbian musicians k. d. lang and Melissa Etheridge have a strong following among gay men and lesbian women. All of this music is slowly finding its way to mainstream audiences.

Most music videos rely on flashy visual images to sustain audience interest. Because TV prohibits the explicit depiction of sexual behavior, music videos

Click on "Beautiful" to see an award-winning Nike commercial that challenges conventional notions of who is beautiful.

Confident female icons such as Pink reflect mainstream culture's acceptance of assertive women.

use sexual images to impart sexual meaning. Kissing, hugging, and suggestive sexual behavior occur at twice the rate of conventional TV shows.

Video games that promote sexist and violent attitudes toward women have filled the aisles of stores across the country. Pushing the line between obscenity and amusement, games such as *Panty Raider* and *BMX XXX* provide images of unrealistically shaped and submissive women mouthing sexy dialogues in degrading scenes. Men, in contrast are often revealed as studly, violent figures whose only purpose is to destroy and conquer. Though many of these video games are rated "M" (mature) by the Entertainment Software Ratings Board, they are both popular with and accessible to young people.

Other TV Genres Sex is present in other TV genres, too. Reality shows like *Mr. Personality, Elimidate,* and *The Bachelor* often play on the vulnerabilities of single people while rewarding others with sex and prestige. Popular daytime talk shows such as *Jerry Springer* and *Ricki Lake* feature unconventional guests and topics, such as women married to gay men or transsexual individuals, so-called sex addicts, and polygamists. Such talk shows use unconventional sexuality to provoke viewer interest. Although their prime purpose remains entertainment, these shows can provide illuminating, firsthand accounts of atypical sexual behavior. These shows reveal the diversity of human sexuality, as well as giving its participants a human face. As critic Walter Goodman (1992) observes: "They carry a gospel of tolerance, preaching openness for the unusual and encouraging greater acceptance of groups and behavior that have long been the objects of ignorance and fear."

News programs continually report rapes, child sexual abuse, pornography, sex therapies, and opinion polls on sexuality. TV newsmagazines examine various sexual issues "in depth"—that is, they devote more time than insight or thought. Both types of news programs usually deal with atypical or controversial aspects of sexuality.

Reality shows such as Joe Millionaire *frequently have sexual themes. What are some of the sexual themes or ideas of the most popular reality shows? Do they differ according to ethnicity?*

Like mainstream TV programs, religious TV networks and programs have wide appeal. Religious programming such as *The 700 Club* broadcasts fundamentalist Christian visions of sex, sin, and morality. These programs stress conservative themes such as adolescent sexual abstinence and opposition to comprehensive sexuality education, abortion, and homosexuality.

Hollywood Films Versus Independent Filmmakers

Hollywood motion pictures generally follow different rules from those of independent filmmakers regarding sexuality. Independents generally are permitted greater license in depicting sexual behavior, but they are still limited by audience acceptance. Hollywood films tend to depict sexual stereotypes and to adhere to mainstream sexual norms.

Mainstream Films   From their very inception, motion pictures have dealt with sexuality. In 1896, a film titled *The Kiss* outraged moral guardians when it showed a couple stealing a quick kiss. "Absolutely disgusting," complained one critic. "The performance comes near being indecent in its emphasized indecency. Such things call for police action" (quoted in Webb, 1983). Today, in contrast, film critics use "sexy," a word independent of artistic value, to praise a film. "Sexy" films are movies in which the requisite "sex scenes" are sufficiently titillating to overcome their lack of aesthetic merit.

In Hollywood films of the 1990s through today, there has been considerable female nudity, especially above the waist. But men are never filmed nude in the same manner as women. Men are generally clothed or partially covered; if they are fully nude, the scene takes place at night, the scene is blurred, or we see only their backsides. Only on rare occasions is the penis shown; if it is visible, it is flaccid (unaroused), not erect. Even when the central theme of the movie involves male genitals, as in *Goldmember* and *The Full Monty*, the erect penis is not shown. In *Basic Instinct*, the director reported that the motion picture ratings board permitted him to show the penis of a murdered man "because it was dead" (Andrews, 1992). (In the more liberal European version of the film, however, a scene reveals Michael Douglas's penis in a frontal nude shot; the image was cut for the American release.) A film psychologist notes: "People have gotten accustomed to wanting to see women nude. They don't think a nude woman looks vulnerable anymore. When a man is uncovered . . . the reaction is that he is extremely vulnerable" (Andrews, 1992).

Although movies today show more naked flesh, the old war-between-the-sexes theme continues with a significant variation. In today's film comedies and dramas, men pursue women and women resist, as they did before. What is new, however, is that the man's persistence awakens the woman's sexual desire. They fall in love, have sex (or vice versa), and have passionate sex happily ever after. In these films, sex takes place outside of marriage (usually before marriage), reflecting the widespread acceptance of nonmarital intercourse. Such scenarios reflect traditional male/female stereotypes of the active man and passive woman. At the same time, however, they validate nonmarital sexual intercourse as a social norm.

Shots suggesting sexual intercourse and oral sex are commonplace in today's films. But scenes of sexual intercourse are generally filmed from a

Of the delights of this world man cares most for sexual intercourse, yet he has left it out of his heaven.

—*Mark Twain (1835–1910)*

male perspective; the camera explores the woman's body and her reaction. Even family-centered films have scenes intimating sex. But other common forms of sexual behavior, such as masturbation, are virtually absent from serious contemporary films.

Dangerous men and dangerous women are depicted differently in movies. As film critic Jerome Weeks (1993) notes:

> Masculine menace on screen and stage is usually seen as a generalized threat: Anyone would fear this particular male because he's a master of violence or dangerously out of control. But if female performers are dangerous, they're dangerous only "to men." It's practically unheard of for a female character to be intimidating in any terms that are not sexual. If they're killers, they kill their husbands, lovers, or the patsies they need and therefore seduce.

Men seem to represent violence and untamed sexuality in nearly all film genres. The rape of the young drugged woman by the teen in *Kids* interweaves aggression with sex.

Gay Men, Lesbian Women, Bisexual and Transgendered People in Film

Gay men, lesbian women, and bisexual and transgendered individuals are generally absent from mainstream films. When gay men and lesbian women do appear, they are consistently defined in terms of their sexual orientation, as if there is nothing more to their lives than sexuality. Gay men are generally stereotyped as effeminate, flighty, or "arty," or they may be closeted, as Kevin Kline is in *In and Out*. Lesbian women are often stereotyped as humorless, mannish, or "butch" and excluded from the usual female norms of attractiveness in the media (Rothblum, 1994).

If gay men and lesbian women are not shown as effeminate or "butch," they are portrayed as sinister, with their sexual orientation symptomatic of a dangerous pathology. In *The Silence of the Lambs,* the killer is a gay cross-dresser. Violent women are often depicted as lesbians or as having "lesbian tendencies" (Hart, 1994). And one film critic (Weir, 1992) notes:

> In Hollywood movies, heterosexuals are never defined as evil or irrelevant simply *because* of their sexuality. Whether they act nobly or ignominiously,

In recent years, series such as Queer as Folk *have presented their lesbian, bisexual, and gay characters as fully realized human beings.*

other aspects of their personalities are brought to bear. Gay men and lesbians, on the other hand, are consistently characterized solely in terms of their homosexuality—when they are depicted at all. What's more, in American movies, homosexuality seems invariably to signal that a character is either sinister or irrelevant.

In recent years, gay, lesbian, bisexual, and transgendered films have increasingly integrated their characters' orientation into a wider focus. The poignant *If These Walls Could Talk 2*, stories of lesbian couples bonded by their passion and their politics, and *Boys Don't Cry*, a sensitive portrayal of an individual struggling with her gender identity, are not so much non-parallel about being gay, lesbian, bisexual, or transgendered as they are about being human. There is no more need to identify *Paragraph 175* as being about gay men and lesbian women than there is to identify *About Schmidt* as being about heterosexual persons. Compulsory heterosexuality prevails across all media.

Internet Sex and Dial-a-Porn

For millions, surfing the Web has become a major recreational activity and has altered the ways in which they communicate and carry on interpersonal relationships. Though social theorists have long been concerned with the alienating effects of technology, the Internet appears quite different from other communication technologies. Its efficacy, power, and influence, along with the anonymity and depersonalization that accompanies its use, have made it possible for consumers to more easily obtain and distribute sexual materials and information, as well as to interact sexually in different ways (Stern & Handel, 2001). The lack of empirical or scientific studies of sexuality and the media, however, prevents us from understanding the Internet's full impact on sexual attitudes and behaviors. Though the Internet has been found to encourage physical isolation (Putnam, 2000), non-normative sexual behaviors (Reid, 1998), and possible addiction in some individuals (Griffiths, 2001), many of these studies tend to take on an alarmist tone and fail to examine the issue in a larger scope (Stern & Handel, 2001). (For more information about sexual compulsion versus addiction, see Chapter 10.)

The accessibility and anonymity of the Internet also make it a source of health and sexuality information and therapeutic services. Although a number of excellent sexuality education sites exist, many more provide misleading and inaccurate information. Thus, it is the responsibility of the consumer to judge the reliability of sources of information and assistance.

In recent years, computer networks and telephone media have created new ways of conveying or creating sexual fantasies. As a result of technological developments, we now have cybersex and dial-a-porn.

Cybersex   **Cybersex** involves expressions of sexuality (e.g., fantasizing, talking about sex, and masturbating) while responding to images or words on a computer. It also includes online information about sexuality education and self-help groups. There is no question that the Internet is revolutionizing the way we think about sexuality. The popularity of cybersex is rooted in ease of access, affordability, and anonymity. For example, a person called "Hot Dog" can enter a "place" called "Hot Tub" and soak for a couple of

THE LURE OF A TWENTY-FIRST-CENTURY computerized sex toy is more than some individuals can resist. Just a few years ago, cybersex meant glancing at nude images on the computer screen. It now beckons users to join fantasy-filled chat rooms, observe images of another person, and watch live sex shows. What has made the Internet so popular is what is called the "triple-A engine": access, affordability, and anonymity. One no longer has to travel across town to a sleazy bar or movie theater and risk being caught by a co-worker or fellow student to access explicit, interactive sex or to share a fantasy with another person. Much of this interactive media is different from other sexually explicit material in that the user can manipulate the images and stimulation that he or she receives. Professor and writer Barrie Gunter (2002) suggests that this form of sexual stimulation, manufactured by the individual, reinforces his or her own preferences and provides more potent stimulation than does passive exposure to traditional forms of sexually explicit material.

Until recently, empirical data about excessive online sexual behavior has been lacking. What has surfaced is that men and women use cybersex differently (Cooper, Delmonico, & Burg, 2000; Schwartz & Southern, 2000; Young, Griffin-Shelley, Cooper, O'Mara, & Buchanan, 2000) and that only a relatively small percentage of people suffer from excessive use (Cooper et al., 2000).

"Compulsive use" of the Internet covers a wide variety of behaviors and impulsive control problems. Though the term "sexual addiction" has been used by a number of researchers, many in the field of psychology question whether the concept of addiction can be applied to nonchemical behaviors. Rather, many describe excessive or compulsive Internet sex in terms of behaviors or activities that take precedence over other parts of life and that dominate one's thinking and feelings. Until more empirical research occurs, the question of whether compulsive Internet sex is different from more traditional forms of sexual compulsion cannot be answered (Griffiths, 2001). There needs to be more research identifying both the risk factors and protective factors for those who might be susceptible to Internet sexual compulsion.

Psychologist Kimberly Young (1998) has created the Cybersexual Addiction Index to help people recognize potentially unhealthy uses of the Internet. Even though the term "addiction" in the questionnaire title might not be appropriate, completing this questionnaire may help you identify potentially excessive or compulsive cybersex use. Select the response that best fits the frequency of behavior described: 0 = not applicable; 1 = rarely; 2 = occasionally; 3 = frequently; 4 = often; 5 = always.

Cybersex—fantasy sex using computers—is a popular activity among many Internet users.

hours with "Bubbles," "Sexy Lady" (a transvestite), and others who pop in and out. "Hot Dog" flirts with everyone; he describes himself, tells his fantasies, and has kinky sex with "Sexy Lady" and a dozen others. "Hot Dog" is actually a woman, but she doesn't tell anyone. Every now and then, "Hot Dog" goes private and exchanges fantasies. But none of this happens in the physical world. "Hot Tub" is a chat room on a computer network. People at different locations, linked by the network, type their fantasies on their keyboards, and those fantasies almost immediately appear on the other people's computer screens.

As of 1999, there were over 12 million sex-related Web sites, accounting for a sizable chunk of the $4-billion U.S. adult entertainment industry ("More Buck," 1999). More than half of the requests on search engines are "adult oriented," and "sex" is the most popular search term on the Internet (Cyber Atlas, 2002). One such site is marketed by a stripper named Jenteal, who claims to earn $50,000 per month from the site. Not only can people conduct discussions or fantasies, they can transfer to their own computer text files describing endless sexual encounters. There are also personal ads and shopping places where users can order whips, chains, and other sex paraphernalia. Hundreds of animated X-rated computer software programs, such as "Danni's Hard Drive," are available.

1. How often do you neglect other responsibilities to spend more time having cybersex?

2. How often do you prefer cybersex to sexual intimacy with your partner?

3. How often do you spend significant amounts of time in chat rooms and private messaging with the sole purpose of finding cybersex?

4. How often do others in your life complain about the amount of time you spend online?

5. How often does your job performance or productivity suffer because of cybersex activities at work?

6. How often do you become defensive or secretive when anyone asks what you do online?

7. How often do you become anxious, nervous, or upset when you are unable to access sexually oriented Web sites?

8. How often do you fear that life without cybersex would be boring, empty, and joyless?

9. How often do you masturbate during cybersex?

10. How often do you snap, yell, or act annoyed if someone bothers you while you are online?

11. How often do you lose sleep because of late-night log-ins having cybersex?

12. How often do you feel preoccupied with cybersex when off-line and/or fantasize about having cybersex?

13. How often do you bookmark or subscribe to sexually oriented Web sites?

14. How often do you use cybersex as a reward for accomplishing something (eg., stressful day, end of a task)?

15. How often do you use anonymous communication to engage in sexual fantasies not typically carried out in real life?

16. How often do you anticipate your next online session with the expectation that you will find sexual arousal or gratification?

17. How often do you hide your online sexual interactions from your significant other?

18. How often do you move from cybersex to phone sex (or even real-life meetings)?

19. How often do you feel guilty or shameful after cybersex?

20. How often do you engage in deceptive or deviant online sexual behavior?

Scoring

Add the numbers for each response to obtain a final score. The higher the score, the greater the level of compulsion: 0–30 points = none; 31–49 = mild; 50–79 = moderate; 80–100 = severe.

Source: Reprinted with permission of Kimberly Young, Center for Online Addiction.

As Gerard Van der Leun (1995) writes of cybersex on the Internet:

A maze of steamy places that don't exist makes up the warp and woof of sex on the Net today. . . . [O]nline sex is as wild and far-ranging as the human imagination. . . . But remember that cybersex has been going on since humans received the gift of imagination. Cybersex is, at bottom, simply old sexual fantasies in a new electronic bottle.

Computers are also used to create virtual reality (VR) sex. Jaron Lanier, who coined the term "virtual reality," is working on VR technology that will allow cable TV subscribers to use goggles, gloves, and body sensors to create their own sexual virtual reality.

The ability to engage in open, frank, and explicit discussions about sex is one reason many people are turning to the Internet for sex therapy and sexual help. "Cybertherapy," as it is now called, is becoming an important venue for individuals striving to build a sense of connectedness, community, and empowerment. An example of this is the growing number of sites specifically directed at women. Without having to look at another person's face, individuals can use "sex coaches" or chat rooms to help reduce their feelings of isolation and guilt. Being accepted and heard are vital components to successful therapy. While searching for such sources, however, both consumers and professionals must be aware of the differences between therapy, consultation, and entertainment. Additionally, because entrepreneurs can make more money from hype and misinformation than from high-quality therapy and education, consumers must remain vigilant in assessing the background of the therapist and the source of the information.

Because of the high volume of sexual discussions and material available on the Internet, there is an increasing demand for government regulation. In 1996, Congress passed the Communications Decency Act, which made it illegal to use computer networks to transmit "obscene" materials or place "indecent" words or images where children might see or read them. Opponents have decried this legislation as a violation of freedom of speech. (For further discussion of this issue, see Chapter 18.)

Dial-a-Porn   Millions of individuals seek sexual gratification through telephone sex lines. Ads for phone sex services appear in most sexually oriented magazines; they depict nude or seminude women and men in sexually suggestive poses. For fees ranging from 5$ to 30$ a minute, a person can call a phone line and have a woman or man "talk dirty" with him or her. Fantasy phone sex often caters to "specialty" interests such as domination and submission, transvestism, and transsexualism.

Anonymous telephone sex provides the caller with pseudo-intimacy. Through the voice, the caller receives a sense of physical closeness. Because the phone worker is paid to respond to the caller's fantasies, the caller can move the conversation in the direction desired. The worker gives the caller the illusion that his or her fantasies are being fulfilled.

Although the ads depict the fantasy phone worker as highly erotic, the calls are often forwarded to the worker's home phone. At home, the worker is probably pursuing mundane tasks, such as washing dishes, changing a baby's diaper, or studying for an accounting exam. Sometimes, workers become involved in the fantasy, but more often, they only half-listen while doing other tasks.

SEXUALITY ACROSS CULTURES AND TIMES

What we see as "natural" in our culture may be viewed as unnatural in other cultures. Few Americans would disagree about the erotic potential of kissing. But other cultures perceive kissing as merely the exchange of saliva. To the Mehinaku of the Amazonian rain forest, for example, kissing is a disgusting sexual abnormality; no Mehinaku engages in it (Gregor, 1985). The fact that Whites press their lips against each other, salivate, *and* become sexually excited merely confirms their "strangeness" to the Mehinaku.

Culture takes our **sexual interests**—our incitements or inclinations to act sexually—and molds and shapes them, sometimes celebrating sexuality and other times condemning it. Sexuality can be viewed as a means of spiritual enlightenment, as in the Hindu tradition, in which the gods themselves engage in sexual activities; it can also be at war with the divine, as in the Judeo-Christian tradition, in which the flesh is the snare of the devil (Parrinder, 1980).

Among the variety of factors that shape how we feel and behave sexually, culture is possibly the most powerful. A brief exploration of sexual themes across cultures and times will give you a sense of the diverse shapes and meanings humans have given to sexuality.

The sensual movements of Latin American dancing have become popular in American culture.

Sexual Interests

All cultures assume that adults have the *potential* for becoming sexually aroused and for engaging in sexual intercourse for the purpose of reproduction (Davenport, 1987). But cultures differ considerably in terms of how strong they believe sexual interests are. These beliefs, in turn, affect the level of desire expressed in each culture.

The Mangaia Among the Mangaia of Polynesia, both sexes, beginning in early adolescence, experience high levels of sexual desire (Marshall, 1971). Around age 13 or 14, following a circumcision ritual, boys are given instruction in the ways of pleasing a girl: erotic kissing, cunnilingus, breast fondling and sucking, and techniques for bringing her to multiple orgasms. After 2 weeks, an older, sexually experienced woman has sexual intercourse with the boy to instruct him further on how to sexually satisfy a woman. Girls the same age are instructed by older women on how to be orgasmic: how to thrust their hips and rhythmically move their vulvas in order to have multiple orgasms. A girl finally learns to be orgasmic through the efforts of a "good man." If the woman's partner fails to satisfy her, she is likely to leave him; she may also ruin his reputation with other women by denouncing his lack of skill. Young men and women are expected to have many sexual experiences prior to marriage.

This adolescent paradise, however, does not last forever. The Mangaia believe that sexuality is strongest during adolescence. As a result, when the Mangaia leave young adulthood, they experience a rapid decline in sexual desire and activity, and they cease to be aroused as passionately as they once were. They attribute this swift decline to the workings of nature and settle into a sexually contented adulthood.

The Dani   In contrast to the Mangaia, the New Guinean Dani show little interest in sexuality. To them, sex is a relatively unimportant aspect of life. The Dani express no concern about improving sexual techniques or enhancing erotic pleasure. Extrarelational sex and jealousy are rare. As their only sexual concern is reproduction, sexual intercourse is performed quickly, ending with male orgasm. Female orgasm appears to be unknown to them. Following childbirth, both mothers and fathers go through 5 years of sexual abstinence. The Dani are an extreme example of a case in which culture, rather than biology, shapes sexual attractions.

Victorian Americans   In the nineteenth century, White middle-class Americans believed that women had little sexual desire. If they experienced desire at all, it was "reproductive desire," the wish to have children. Reproduction entailed the unfortunate "necessity" of engaging in sexual intercourse. A leading reformer wrote that in her "natural state" a woman never makes advances based on sexual desires, for the "very plain reason that she does not feel them" (Alcott, 1868). Those women who did feel desire were "a few exceptions amounting in all probability to diseased cases." Such women were classified by a prominent physician as suffering from "Nymphomania, or Furor Uterinus" (Bostwick, 1860).

Whereas women were viewed as asexual, men were believed to have raging sexual appetites. Men, driven by lust, sought to satisfy their desires by ravaging innocent women. Both men and women believed that male sexuality was dangerous, uncontrolled, and animal-like. It was part of a woman's duty to tame unruly male sexual impulses.

The polar beliefs about the nature of male and female sexuality created destructive antagonisms between "angelic" women and "demonic" men. These beliefs provided the rationale for a "war between the sexes." They also led to the separation of sex from love. Intimacy and love had nothing to do with male sexuality. In fact, male lust always lingered in the background of married life, threatening to destroy love by its overbearing demands.

Although a century has passed since the end of the Victorian era, many Victorian sexual beliefs and attitudes continue to influence us. These include the belief that men are "naturally" sexually aggressive and women sexually passive, the sexual double standard, and the value placed on women being sexually "inexperienced."

Sexual Orientation

Sexual orientation is the pattern of sexual and emotional attraction based on the gender of one's partner. **Heterosexuality** refers to emotional and sexual attraction between men and women; **homosexuality** refers to emotional and sexual attraction between persons of the same sex; **bisexuality** is an emotional and sexual attraction to both males and females. In contemporary

In ancient Greece, the highest form of love was that expressed between males.

American culture, heterosexuality is the only sexual orientation receiving full social and legal legitimacy. Although same-sex relationships are relatively common, they do not receive general social acceptance. Some other cultures, however, view same-sex relationships as normal, acceptable, and even preferable. Marriage between members of the same sex is recognized in 15–20 cultures throughout the world (Gregersen, 1986). In this country, same-sex marriages are still not recognized, although Vermont has legalized a "civil union" for same-sex couples. Same-sex marriage is legal in the Netherlands and Belgium, and a court in Canada has lifted a ban on same-sex marriages.

Ancient Greece   In ancient Greece, the birthplace of European culture, the Greeks accepted same-sex relationships as naturally as Americans today accept heterosexuality. For the Greeks, same-sex relationships between men represented the highest form of love.

The male-male relationship was based on love and reciprocity; sexuality was only one component of it. In this relationship, the code of conduct called for the older man to initiate the relationship. The youth initially resisted; only after the older man courted the young man with gifts and words of love would he reciprocate. The two men formed a close, emotional bond. The older man was the youth's mentor as well as his lover. He introduced the youth to men who would be useful for his advancement later; he assisted him in learning his duties as a citizen. As the youth entered adulthood, the erotic bond between the two evolved into a deep friendship. After the youth became an adult, he married a woman and later initiated a relationship with an adolescent boy.

Greek male-male relationships, however, were not substitutes for male-female marriage. The Greeks discouraged exclusive male-male relationships because marriage and children were required to continue the family and society. Men regarded their wives primarily as domestics and as bearers of children (Keuls, 1985). (The Greek word for woman, *gyne,* translates literally as "childbearer.") Husbands turned for sexual pleasure not to their wives but to *hetaerae* (hi-TIR-ee), highly regarded courtesans who were usually educated slaves.

The Sambians   Among Sambian males of New Guinea, sexual orientation is very malleable (Herdt, 1987). Young boys begin with sexual activities with older boys, move to sexual activities with both sexes during adolescence, and engage in exclusively male-female activities in adulthood. Sambians believe that a boy can grow into a man only by the ingestion of semen, which is, they say, like mother's milk. At age 7 or 8, boys begin their sexual activities with older boys; as they get older, they seek multiple partners to accelerate their growth into manhood. At adolescence, their role changes, and they must provide semen to boys to enable them to develop. At first, they worry about their own loss of semen, but they are taught to drink tree sap, which magically replenishes their supply. During adolescence, boys are betrothed to preadolescent girls, with whom they engage in sexual activities. When the girls mature, the boys give up their sexual involvement with other males. They become fully involved with adult women, losing their desire for men.

Gender

Although sexual interests and orientation may be influenced by culture, it may be difficult for some to imagine that culture has anything to do with **gender,** the characteristics associated with being male or female. Our sex appears solidly rooted in our biological nature. But is being male or female *really* biological? The answer is yes *and* no. Having male or female genitals is anatomical. But the possession of a penis does not *always* make a person a man, nor does the possession of a clitoris and vagina *always* make a person a woman. Men who consider themselves women, "women with penises," are accepted or honored in many cultures throughout the world (Bullough, 1991). Thus, culture and a host of other factors help to shape masculinity and femininity, while biology defines men and women.

Transsexual Persons   In the United States, there are approximately 15,000 **transsexuals,** people whose genitals and identities as men or women are discordant. In transsexuality, a person with a penis, for example, identifies as a woman, or a person with a vulva and vagina identifies as a man.

To make their genitals congruent with their gender identity, many transsexuals have their genitals surgically altered. If being male or female depends on genitals, then postsurgical transsexuals have changed their sex—men have become women, and women have become men. But defining sex in terms of genitals presents problems, as has been shown in the world of sports. In the 1970s, Renee Richards, whose genitals had been surgically transformed from male to female, began competing on the women's professional tennis circuit. Protests began immediately. Although Richards's genitals were female, her body and musculature were male. Despite the surgery, she remained genetically male because her sex chromosomes were male. Her critics insisted that genetics, not genitals, defines a person's sex; anatomy can be changed, but chromosomes cannot. Richards, however, maintained that she was a woman by any common definition of the word. (Issues of sex, gender, and biology are discussed in Chapter 5.)

Two-Spirits Most Americans consider transsexuality problematic at best. But this is not the case in all cultures. In some cultures, an anatomical man identifying as a woman might be considered a "man-woman" and be accorded high status and special privileges. He would be identified as a **two-spirit,** a man who assumes female dress, gender role, and status. Two-spirit emphasizes the spiritual aspect of one's life and downplays the homosexual persona (Jacobs, Thomas, & Lang, 1997). It is inclusive of transsexuality, transvestism (wearing the clothes of or passing as a member of the other sex), and a form of same-sex relationship (Roscoe, 1991). Two-spirits are found in numerous cultures throughout the world, including Native American, Filipino, Lapp, and Indian cultures. In Indian culture, the third gender is known as the *hijra.* Regarded as sacred, they perform as dancers or musicians at weddings and religious ceremonies, as well as providing blessings for health, prosperity, and fertility (Nanda, 1990). It is almost always men who become two-spirits although there are a few cases of women assuming male roles in a similar fashion (Blackwood, 1984). Two-spirits are often considered shamans, individuals who possess great spiritual power.

Among the Zuni of New Mexico, two-spirits are considered a third gender (Roscoe, 1991). Despite the existence of transsexual persons and pseudohermaphrodites (individuals with two testes or two ovaries but an ambiguous genital appearance), Westerners tend to view gender as biological, an incorrect assumption. The Zuni, in contrast, believe that gender is socially acquired.

Native American two-spirits were suppressed by missionaries and the U.S. government as "unnatural" or "perverted." Their ruthless repression led anthropologists to believe that two-spirits had been driven out of existence in Native American cultures, but there is evidence that two-spirits continue to fill ceremonial and social roles in tribes such as the Lakota Sioux. Understandably, two-spirit activities are kept secret from outsiders for fear of reprisals (Williams, 1985). Among gay and lesbian Native Americans, the two-spirit role provides historical continuity with their traditions (Roscoe, 1991).

In some cultures, men who dress or identify as women are considered shamans. We'wha was a Zuni man-woman who lived in the nineteenth century.

SOCIETAL NORMS AND SEXUALITY

The immense diversity of sexual behaviors across cultures and times immediately calls into question the appropriateness of labeling these behaviors as *inherently* natural or unnatural, normal or abnormal. Too often, we give such labels to sexual behaviors without thinking about the basis on which we make those judgments. Such categories discourage knowledge and understanding because they are value judgments, evaluations of right and wrong. As such, they are not objective descriptions about behaviors but statements of how we feel about those behaviors.

Natural Sexual Behavior

How do we decide if a sexual behavior is natural or unnatural? To make this decision, we must have some standard of nature against which to compare the behavior. But what is "nature"? On the abstract level, nature is the essence of all things in the universe. Or, personified as nature, it is the force regulating the universe. These definitions, however, do not help us much in trying to establish what is natural or unnatural.

THE QUESTION "AM I NORMAL?" seems to haunt many people. For some, it causes a great deal of unnecessary fear, guilt, and anxiety. For others, it provides the motivation to study the literature, consult with a trusted friend or therapist, or take a course in sexuality.

What is normal? We commonly use several criteria in deciding whether to label different sexual behaviors "normal" or "abnormal." According to professor and psychologist Leonore Tiefer (1995), these criteria are subjective, statistical, idealistic, cultural, and clinical. Regardless of what criteria we use, they ultimately reflect societal norms.

- *Subjectively "normal" behavior.* According to this definition, normalcy is any behavior that is similar to one's own. Though most of us use this definition, few of us will acknowledge it.

- *Statistically "normal" behavior.* According to this definition, whatever behaviors are more common are normal; less common ones are abnormal. However, the fact that a behavior is not widely practiced does not make it abnormal except in a statistical sense. **Fellatio** (fel-AY-she-o) (oral stimulation of the penis) and **cunnilingus** (cun-i-LIN-gus) (oral stimulation of the female genitals), for example, are widely practiced today because they have become "acceptable" behaviors. But a generation ago, oral sex was tabooed as something "dirty" or "shameful."

- *Idealistically "normal" behavior.* Taking an ideal for a norm, individuals who use this approach measure all deviations against perfection. They may try to model their behavior after Christ or Gandhi. Using idealized behavior as a norm can easily lead to feelings of guilt, shame, and anxiety.

- *Culturally "normal" behavior.* This is probably the standard most of us use most of the time: We accept as normal what our culture defines as normal. This measure explains why our notions of normalcy do not always agree with those of people from other countries, religions, cultures, and historical periods. Men who kiss in public may be normal in one place but abnormal in another. It is common for deviant behavior to be perceived as dangerous and frightening in a culture that rejects it.

- *Clinically "normal" behavior.* The clinical standard uses scientific data about health and illness to make judgments. For example, the presence of the syphilis bacterium in body tissues or blood is considered abnormal because it indicates that a person has a sexually transmitted infection. Regardless of time or place, clinical definitions should stand the test of time. The four criteria mentioned above are all somewhat arbitrary—that is, they depend on individual or group opinion—but the clinical criterion has more objectivity.

These five criteria form the basis of what we usually consider normal behavior. Often, the different definitions and interpretations of "normal" conflict with one another. How does a person determine whether he or she is normal if subjectively "normal" behavior—what that person actually does—is inconsistent with his or her ideals? Such dilemmas are commonplace and lead many people to question their normalcy. However, they should not question their normalcy so much as their *concept* of normalcy.

Source: Tiefer, L. (1995). *Sex Is Not a Natural Act and Other Essays.* Boulder, CO: Westview Press.

> If it makes you happy, it can't be that bad.
>
> — *Sheryl Crow*

When we asked our students to identify their criteria for determining which sexual behaviors they considered "natural" or "unnatural," we received a variety of responses, including the following:

- "If a person feels something instinctive, I believe it is a natural feeling."
- "Natural and unnatural have to do with the laws of nature. What these parts were intended for."
- "I decide by my gut instincts."
- "I think all sexual activity is natural as long as it doesn't hurt yourself or anyone else."
- "Everything possible is natural. Everything natural is normal. If it is natural and normal, it is moral."

When we label sexual behavior as "natural" or "unnatural," we are actually indicating whether the behavior conforms to our culture's sexual norms.

Declaration of Sexual Rights

As we emphasize in this book, organizations, groups, and entire cultures define "normal" or "natural" sexual expression in varied ways; many place narrow and restrictive codes on sexuality. These more restrictive standards, often a reflection of a particular view of morality, are ways of controlling sexual behavior. These messages are powerful and are most influential. Although some of these codes may help prevent some undesirable outcomes of sexual behavior, such as unwanted pregnancy and sexually transmitted infections, they often result in many people being denied expression of fundamental human sexual needs. In response, the World Association of Sexology (WAS) developed a "Declaration of Sexual Rights," which was adopted by the WAS General Assembly at the 14th World Congress of Sexology in Hong Kong, August 26, 1999.

Declaration of Sexual Rights

Sexuality is an integral part of the personality of every human being. Its full development depends upon the satisfaction of basic human needs such as the desire for contact, intimacy, emotional expression, pleasure, tenderness, and love. Sexuality is constructed through the interaction between the individual and social structures. Full development of sexuality is essential for individual, interpersonal, and social well being. Sexual rights are universal human rights based on the inherent freedom, dignity, and equality of all human beings. Since health is a fundamental human right, so must sexual health be a basic human right. In order to assure that human beings and societies develop healthy sexuality, the following sexual rights must be recognized, promoted, respected, and defended by all societies through all means. Sexual health is the result of an environment that recognizes, respects, and exercises these rights.

1. The right to sexual freedom. Sexual freedom encompasses the possibility for individuals to express their full sexual potential. However, this excludes all forms of sexual coercion, exploitation, and abuse at any time and situations in life.

2. The right to sexual autonomy, sexual integrity, and safety of the sexual body. This right involves the ability to make autonomous decisions about one's sexual life within a context of one's own personal and social ethics. It also encompasses control and enjoyment of our own bodies free from torture, mutilation, and violence of any sort.

3. The right to sexual privacy. This involves the right for individual decisions and behaviors about intimacy as long as they do not intrude on the sexual rights of others.

4. The right to sexual equity. This refers to freedom from all forms of discrimination regardless of sex, gender, sexual orientation, age, race, social class, religion, or physical and emotional disability.

5. The right to sexual pleasure. Sexual pleasure, including autoeroticism, is a source of physical, psychological, intellectual, and spiritual well being.

6. The right to emotional sexual expression. Sexual expression is more than erotic pleasure or sexual acts. Individuals have a right to express their sexuality through communication, touch, emotional expression, and love.

7. The right to sexually associate freely. This means the possibility to marry or not, to divorce, and to establish other types of responsible sexual associations.

8. The right to make free and responsible reproductive choices. This encompasses the right to decide whether or not to have children, the number and spacing of children, and the right to full access to the means of fertility regulation.

9. The right to sexual information based upon scientific inquiry. This right implies that sexual information should be generated through the process of unencumbered and yet scientifically ethical inquiry, and disseminated in appropriate ways at all societal levels.

10. The right to comprehensive sexuality education. This is a lifelong process from birth throughout the life cycle and should involve all social institutions.

11. The right to sexual health care. Sexual health care should be available for prevention and treatment of all sexual concerns, problems, and disorders.

Source: "Declaration of Sexual Rights" from World Association of Sexology. Reprinted by permission.

Our sexual norms appear natural because we have internalized them since infancy. These norms are part of the cultural air we breathe, and, like the air, they are invisible. We have learned our culture's rules so well that they have become a "natural" part of our personality, a "second nature" to us. They seem "instinctive."

Kissing is "natural" and "normal" in our culture. It is an expression of intimacy, love, and passion for young and old, heterosexual persons, gay men, and lesbian women.

The greatest pleasure in life is doing what people say you cannot do.

— *Walter Bagehot*
(1826–1877)

Normal Sexual Behavior

Closely related to the idea that sexual behavior is natural or unnatural is the belief that sexuality is either normal or abnormal. More often than not, describing behavior as "normal" or "abnormal" is merely another way of making value judgments. Although "normal" has often been used to imply "healthy" or "moral" behavior, social scientists use the word strictly as a statistical term. For them, **normal sexual behavior** is behavior that conforms to a group's average or median patterns of behavior. Normality has nothing to do with moral or psychological deviance.

Ironically, although we may feel pressure to behave like the average person (the statistical norm), most of us don't actually know how others behave sexually. People don't ordinarily reveal much about their sexual activities. If they do, they generally reveal only their most conformist sexual behaviors, such as sexual intercourse. They rarely disclose their masturbatory activities, sexual fantasies, or anxieties or feelings of guilt. All that most people present of themselves—unless we know them well—is the conventional self that masks their actual sexual feelings, attitudes, and behaviors.

The only guidelines most of us have for determining our normality are given to us by our friends, partners, and parents (who usually present conventional sexual images of themselves) through stereotypes, media images, religious teachings, customs, and cultural norms. None of these, however, tells us much about how people *actually* behave. Because we don't know how people really behave, it is easy for us to imagine that we are abnormal if we differ from our cultural norms and stereotypes. We wonder if our desires, fantasies, and activities are normal: Is it normal to fantasize? To masturbate? To enjoy erotica? To be attracted to someone of the same sex? Some of us believe that everyone else is "normal" and that only we are "sick" or "abnormal."

Because culture determines what is normal, there is a vast range of normal behaviors across different cultures. What is considered the normal sexual urge for the Dani would send most of us into therapy for treatment of low sexual desire. And the idea of teaching sexual skills to early adolescents, as the Mangaia do, would horrify most American parents.

> Morality is the custom of one's country and the current feelings of one's peers. Cannibalism is moral in a cannibal country.
>
> —*Samuel Butler (1612–1680)*

Sexual Behavior and Variations

Sex researchers have generally rejected the traditional sexual dichotomies of natural/unnatural, normal/abnormal, moral/immoral, and good/bad. Regarding the word "abnormal," Ira Reiss (1989) writes:

> We need to be aware that people will use those labels to put distance between themselves and others they dislike. In doing so, these people are not making a scientific diagnosis but are simply affirming their support of certain shared concepts of proper sexuality.

> Birds do it, bees do it. Even educated fleas do it.
>
> —*Cole Porter (1891–1964)*

Instead of classifying behavior into what are essentially moralistic normal/ abnormal and natural/unnatural categories, researchers view human sexuality as characterized by **sexual variation**—that is, sexual variety and diversity. As humans, we vary enormously in terms of our sexual orientation, our desires, our fantasies, our attitudes, and our behaviors. Alfred Kinsey and his colleagues (1948) succinctly stated the matter: "The world is not to be divided into sheep and goats."

Researchers believe that the best way to understand our sexual diversity is to view our activities as existing on a continuum. On this continuum, the frequency with which individuals engage in different sexual activities (e.g., sexual intercourse, masturbation, and oral sex) ranges from never to always. Significantly, there is no point on the continuum that marks normal or abnormal behavior. In fact, the difference between one individual and the next on the continuum is minimal (Kinsey, Pomeroy, & Martin, 1948; Kinsey, Pomeroy, Martin, & Gebhard, 1953). The most that can be said of a

My Genes Made Me Do It: Sociobiology, Evolutionary Psychology, and the Mysteries of Love

DO YOU EVER WONDER why you do what you do or feel as you feel—especially when it comes to matters like attraction, relationships, and sex? Do you wonder why the object of your affection behaves in such inexplicable ways—why he or she flies into a jealous rage for no reason? Or why your friend always seems to fall for the "wrong" person? Sometimes, the answers may be obvious, but other times, they are obscure. Our motivations come from a variety of sources, including personality traits, past experiences, peer pressure, and familial and cultural influences. Many of our feelings probably result from a complex yet subtle blending of these influences—combined with innate responses programmed into our genes. Our sexual urges and responses are largely governed by hormones, tiny chemical structures that perform a number of functions, including that of "messenger," triggering diverse actions and reactions in the brain and various parts of the body. Our genetic makeup has been passed down to us from our early primate ancestors—both human and nonhuman. We share 98–99% of our genetic material with our closest primate cousins, the chimpanzees and bonobos (Blum, 1997).

Our growing understanding of the biological bases of behavior comes largely from the field of **sociobiology** and its offshoot, evolutionary psychology. Sociobiologists base their study of human behavior on Charles Darwin's theory of evolution. According to Darwin's theory, evolution favors certain physical traits that enable a species to survive, such as, for early humans, the ability to walk upright. According to sociobiology, evolution also favors certain genetically based behaviors or "reproductive strategies" that enhance an individual's ability to pass along his or her genes and ensure their survival (Symons, 1979). Thus, sociobiology finds biological explanations for phenomena such as male dominance, the sexual double standard, and maternal behavior.

An example of a sociobiological explanation for behavior can be found when we look at the apparently different attitudes that men and women have about the roles of sex and love. From a sociobiological perspective, males, who are consistently fertile from early adolescence on, seek to impregnate as many females as possible to ensure genetic success. Females, however, ovulate only once a month. For them, a single episode of intercourse can result in pregnancy, childbirth, and years of child rearing. Thus, it is important to females to find partners on whom they can rely for protection and support over the long course of child rearing. In this way, they help ensure that the carriers of their genes (their children) will reach adulthood and pass along their parents' genetic legacy. The bonds of love are what keep the male around. Or, in other words, females trade sex for love, and males trade love for sex.

Evolutionary psychologists seek to explain the biological bases of love and other emotions such as hope, anger, jealousy, fear, and grief. We may wonder why Mother Nature made us so emotional when emotion so often leads to disaster. But, Mr. Spock notwithstanding, there are good reasons (evolutionarily speaking) for having emotions. Even though in the short term emotions can get us into trouble—if we act impulsively rather than rationally—over the long term our emotions have helped our genes survive and replicate (Pinker, 1999). Emotions exist to motivate us to do things that serve (or once served) the best interests of our genetic material—things like fleeing, fighting, or forming close relationships to protect our "genetic investment" (offspring).

Critics of sociobiology argue that inferences from animal behavior may not be applicable to human beings; they feel that sociobiologists base their assumptions about human behavior (such as men wanting sex versus women wanting love) more on cultural stereotypes than on actual behavior. Sociobiologists reply that they report what they observe in nature and suggest connections to human behavior (humans are part of nature, after all) but do not make judgments about the meaning or morality of their observations. In fact, we must take care not to assume that because something is "natural" it is appropriate or moral or the right thing to do. Thinking that confuses the "natural" with the "good" is called the "naturalistic fallacy." This fallacy can be used to justify all sorts of antisocial or just plain rude behavior. For example, a man could use this sort of reasoning to justify extrarelational sex ("My genes made me do it"). In reality, our genes don't "make" us do anything. As social beings, we are still expected to learn to think before we act and to take the feelings and needs of others into account. This process, in fact, has a name: It's called "growing up."

As you study human sexuality, we hope that the information you gain from this text will help you integrate your own feelings and experiences with the information and advice you get from family, friends, lovers, and society. In the text, we take what might be called a "bio-psycho-social" approach to our subject, recognizing that the sexual self is produced by the interconnections of body, mind, spirit, and culture. As you continue your study, remember that, although our culture, beliefs, and cognitive processes (what we might call the "software" of the mind) have been created by humans, our bodies and brains (the "hardware" of the mind) are the products of evolution. They've been developing over a long, long time.

person is that his or her behaviors are more or less typical or atypical of the group average. Furthermore, nothing can be inferred about an individual whose behavior differs significantly from the group average except that his or her behavior is atypical. The individual who differs is not sick, abnormal, or perverted; rather, he or she is a sexual nonconformist (Reiss, 1986, 1989). Except for engaging in sexually atypical behavior, one person may be indistinguishable from any other.

Many activities that are usually thought of as "deviant" or "dysfunctional" sexual behavior—activities diverging from the norm, such as exhibitionism, voyeurism, and fetishism—are engaged in by most of us to some degree. We may delight in displaying our bodies on the beach or in "dirty dancing" in crowded clubs (exhibitionism). We may like watching ourselves make love, viewing erotic videos, or seeing our partner undress (voyeurism). Or we may enjoy kissing our lover's photograph, keeping a lock of his or her hair, or sleeping with an article of his or her clothing (fetishism). Most of the time, these feelings or activities are only one aspect of our sexual selves; they are not especially significant in our overall sexuality. Such atypical behaviors represent nothing more than sexual nonconformity when they occur between mutually consenting adults and do not cause distress (Reiss, 1989).

The rejection of natural/unnatural, normal/abnormal, and moral/immoral categories by sex researchers does not mean that standards for evaluating sexual behavior do not exist. There are many sexual behaviors that are harmful to oneself (e.g., masturbatory asphyxia—suffocating or hanging oneself during masturbation to increase sexual arousal) and to others (e.g., rape, child molestation, exhibitionism, and obscene phone calls). Current psychological standards for determining the harmfulness of sexual behaviors center around the issues of coercion, potential harm to oneself or others, and personal distress. (These issues are discussed in greater detail in Chapter 10.)

We, the authors, believe that the basic standard for judging various sexual activities is whether they are between consenting adults and whether they cause harm. "Normality" and "naturalness" are not useful terms for evaluating sexual behavior, especially variations, because they are usually nothing more than moral judgments. What people consider "normal" is often statistically common sexual behavior, which is then defined as good or healthy. But for many forms of sexual behavior, a large percentage of people will not conform to the average. There is a great deal of variation, for example, in the extent to which people eroticize boxer shorts and lacy underwear. Who determines at what point on the continuum that interest in undergarments is no longer acceptable? The individual? Her or his peer group? Religious groups? Society? As Suzanna Rose and Victoria Sork (1984) note: "Because everyone's sexuality does not completely overlap with the norm, the only liberating approach to sexuality is to envision it from the perspective of variation."

As social scientists, sex researchers have a mandate to *describe* sexual behavior, not evaluate it as good or bad, moral or immoral. It is up to the individual to evaluate the ethical or moral aspects of sexual behavior in accordance with his or her ethical or religious values. At the same time, however, understanding diverse sexual attitudes, motives, behaviors, and values will help deepen the individual's own value system.

> Judge not, that ye be not judged.
> —*Matthew 7:1*

POPULAR CULTURE BOTH ENCOURAGES and discourages sexuality. It promotes stereotypical sexual interactions between men and women and fails to touch on the deeper significance sexuality holds for us. Love and sexuality in a committed relationship are infrequently depicted, in contrast to casual sex. (By ignoring sex between committed partners, popular culture implies that partnership is a sexual wasteland. Yet it is within couples that the overwhelming majority of sexual interactions take place.) The media ignore or disparage the wide array of sexual behaviors and choices—from masturbation to gay, lesbian, bisexual, and transgender relationships—that are significant in many people's lives. They discourage the linking of sex and intimacy, contraceptive responsibility, and the acknowledgment of STI risks.

What is clear from examining other cultures is that sexual behaviors and norms vary from culture to culture and, within our own society, from one time to another. The variety of sexual behaviors even within our own culture testifies to diversity not only between cultures but within cultures. Understanding diversity allows us to acknowledge that there is no such thing as inherently "normal" or "natural" sexual behavior. Rather, sexual behavior is strongly influenced by culture—including our own.

SUMMARY

Sexuality, Popular Culture, and the Media

- Popular culture, especially the media, strongly influences our sexuality through the depiction of sexual stereotypes and *norms*. Mainstream media do not depict explicit sexual behavior.

- Each television genre depicts sexuality according to its formula. Situation comedies focus on the violation of minor marital and family taboos. Soap operas deal with sexual transgressions, jealousy, and power linked to sex. Crime/action-adventure programs depict short-lived relationships based on attraction; detective heroes form close relationships primarily with their detective partners or secretaries. Cable dramas focus on "problem" themes such as rape, pregnancy, and AIDS. TV commercials may promote a product by suggesting that consuming it will lead to attractiveness or sexual success. Many popular music and game videos rely on suggestiveness and images to depict sexuality. Women are usually portrayed as sex objects.

- Although Hollywood films depict sexual behavior more graphically than television does, sex scenes are often gratuitous. Sexuality tends to be stereotypical. Gay men, lesbian women, bisexual and transgendered individuals have generally been absent from films except in stereotypical roles. More recently, a few nonstereotypical characters have been introduced.

- Computer networks and telephone media have created *cybersex*, providing new ways of establishing relationships and conveying sexual fantasies. The debate concerning the effects and transmittal of these materials continues.

Sexuality Across Cultures and Times

- One of the most powerful forces shaping human sexuality is culture. Culture molds and shapes our *sexual interests*.

- The Mangaia of Polynesia and the Dani of New Guinea represent cultures at the opposite ends of a continuum, with the Mangaia having an elaborate social and cultural framework for instructing adolescents in sexual technique and the Dani downplaying the importance of sex.

- Middle-class Americans in the nineteenth century believed that men had strong sexual drives but that women had little sexual desire. Because sexuality was considered animalistic, the Victorians separated sex and love.

- *Sexual orientation* is the pattern of sexual and emotional attraction based on the sex of one's partner. In contemporary America, *heterosexuality,* or attraction between men and women, is the only sexual orientation that receives full societal and legal legitimacy. *Homosexuality* refers to same-sex attractions, and *bisexuality* involves attraction to both males and females.

- In ancient Greece, same-sex relationships between men represented the highest form of love. Among the Sambians of New Guinea, boys have sexual contact with older boys, believing that the ingestion of semen is required for growth. When the girls to whom they are betrothed reach puberty, adolescent boys cease these same-sex sexual relations.

- A *transsexual person* has the genitals of one sex but identifies as a member of the other sex.

- A *two-spirit* is a person of one sex who identifies with the other sex; in some cultures, such as the Zuni, a two-spirit is considered a third gender and is believed to possess great spiritual power.

Societal Norms and Sexuality

- Sexuality tends to be evaluated according to categories of natural/unnatural, normal/abnormal, and moral/immoral. These terms are value judgments, reflecting social norms rather than any quality inherent in the behavior itself.

- There is no commonly accepted definition of natural sexual behavior. *Normal sexual behavior* is what a culture defines as normal. We commonly use five criteria to categorize sexual behavior as normal or abnormal: subjectively normal, statistically normal, idealistically normal, culturally normal, and clinically normal.

- Human sexuality is characterized by *sexual variation.* Researchers believe that the best way to examine sexual behavior is on a continuum. Many activities that are considered deviant sexual behavior exist in most of us to some degree. These include exhibitionism, voyeurism, and fetishism.

- Behaviors are not abnormal or unnatural; rather, they are more or less typical or atypical of the group average. Many of those whose behaviors are atypical may be regarded as sexual nonconformists rather than as abnormal or perverse.

Sex and the Internet

Sex and the Media

With over 12 million sex-related Web sites available, you might wonder about the issues and laws associated with access to cyberspace. Though the following sites each deal primarily with intellectual freedom, they also contain information and links to other sites that address issues of sex and the media. Select one of the following:

- American Library Association (ALA) Office for Intellectual Freedom: http://www.ala.org/alaorg/oif

- Electronic Frontier Foundation: http://www.eff.org

- Sex, Laws and Cyberspace: http://www.spectacle.org/freespch/

Go to the site and answer the following questions:

- What is the mission of the site—if any?

- Who are its supporters and advocates?

- Who is its target audience?

- What is its predominant message?

- What current issue is it highlighting?

Given what you have learned about this site, how do your feelings about sex and the Internet compare with those of the creators of this Web site?

SUGGESTED WEB SITES

Human Sexuality Web
http://www.umkc.edu/sites/hsw/index.html
Run by students at the University of Missouri–Kansas City; contains information on various sexual health topics, sexual counseling, and links.

National Gay and Lesbian Task Force
http://www.ngltf.org
Provides information and referrals on gay, lesbian, bisexual, and transsexual issues and rights.

National Sexuality Resource Center
http://nsrc.sfsu.edu/Index.cfm
Part of the Human Sexuality Studies program at San Francisco State University; provides accurate information on sexual health and other sexuality-related issues.

Variations in Sex Laws
http://www.geocities.com/CapitolHill/2269/
A fascinating collection of links to laws pertaining to sexuality in the United States and abroad.

SUGGESTED READING

Brown, Jane D., Steele, Jeanne R., & Walsh-Childers, Kim (Eds.). (2002). *Sexual Teens, Sexual Media: Investigating Media's Influence on Adolescent Sexuality.* Mahwah, NJ: Erlbaum. Explores the sexual content of mass media and its impact on adolescents.

Dines, Gail, & Humez, Jean (Eds.). (2002). *Gender, Race, and Class in the Media* (2nd ed.). Thousand Oaks, CA: Sage. An excellent introduction to popular culture and the media.

Gauntlett, David. (2002). *Media, Gender & Identity.* New York: Routledge. An introduction to the main themes of popular culture and the ways in which it influences lifestyles and concepts of gender and identity.

Middleton, Dwight R. (2001). *Exotics and Erotics: Human Culture and Sexual Diversity.* Prospect Heights, IL: Waveland Press. Explores universal human sexuality in conjunction with its local manifestations in specific cultural contexts; topics include the body, patterns of sexuality, sexual behavior, romantic passion, marriage, and kinship.

Reiss, Ira L., & Ellis, Albert. (2002). *At the Dawn of the Sexual Revolution.* Walnut Creek, CA: Rowman & Littlefield. Provides a chronicle of the controversial sexual issues of the 1950s and 1960s, and reveals how and why current views of sexuality in America have changed.

Stein, Edward. (2001). *The Mismeasure of Desire: The Science, Theory, and Ethics of Sexual Orientation* (2nd ed.). Oxford: Oxford University Press. A thorough and thoughtful investigation of homosexuality.

Suggs, David N., & Miracle, Andrew (Eds.). (1999). *Culture, Biology, and Sexuality.* Athens: University of Georgia Press. A collection of essays on sexuality in diverse cultures throughout the world.

For links, articles, and study material, go to the McGraw-Hill Web site, located at http://www.mhhe.com/strong5

2

Studying Human Sexuality

"I've heard about those sex surveys, and I wonder how truthful they are. I mean, don't you think that people who volunteer for those studies only admit to acts which they deem socially acceptable? I just don't think people who lose their virginity, for instance at age 12 or age 30, would actually report it. Besides, no sex study is going to tell me what I should do or whether I am normal."

—21-year-old Black male

"I feel that sexual research is a benefit to our society. The human sexuality class I took my sophomore year in college taught me a lot. Without research, many of the topics we learned about would not have been so thoroughly discussed due to lack of information. Sexual research and human sexuality classes help keep the topic of sex from being seen as such a faux pas by society."

—20-year-old White female

"I took a sex survey once, during my undergraduate years. I found that the survey was easy to take, and the process of answering the questions actually led me to ask myself more questions about my sexual self. The survey was detailed, and I was encouraged to answer truthfully. Ultimately, every answer I gave was accurate because I knew that the research would benefit science (and it was completely anonymous)."

—22-year-old White female

"I think sex research is great because it helps remove the taboo from the topic. Sex, in this country, is on TV all the time, but people do not want to seriously discuss it, especially adults with children. Sex research, when made public, can help ease the tension of discussing sex—especially when it reveals that something considered abnormal actually is normal and that many people practice the specific behavior."

—24-year-old White male

A NEW UNIVERSITY STUDY finds that many college students lie to a new sex partner about their sexual past . . . but first, a message from . . ." So begins a commercial lead-in on the evening news, reminding us that sex research is often part of both news and entertainment. In fact, most of us learn about the results of sex research from television, newspapers, the Internet, and magazines rather than from scholarly journals and books. After all, the mass media are more entertaining than most scholarly works. And unless we are studying human sexuality, few of us have the time to read the scholarly journals in which scientific research is regularly published.

But how accurate is what the mass media tell us about sex and sex research? In this chapter, we discuss the dissemination of sex information by the various media. Then we look at the critical-thinking skills that help us evaluate how we discuss and think about sexuality. When are we making objective statements? When are we reflecting biases or opinions? Next, we examine sex research methods because they are critical to the scientific study of human sexuality. Then we look at some of the leading sex researchers to see how they have influenced our understanding of sexuality. Next, we discuss six recent studies as examples of research being done in a variety of areas. Finally, we examine feminist, gay, lesbian, bisexual, transgender, and ethnic sex research to see how they enrich our knowledge of sexuality.

SEX, ADVICE COLUMNISTS, AND POP PSYCHOLOGY

As we saw in Chapter 1, the mass media convey seemingly endless sexual images. In addition to the various television, film, Internet, and advertising genres, there is another genre, which we might call the **sex information/ advice genre,** that transmits information and norms, rather than images, about sexuality to a mass audience to both inform and entertain in a simplified manner. For most college students, as well as many others, the sex information/advice genre is a major source of their knowledge about sex.

This genre is ostensibly concerned with transmitting information that is factual and accurate. For newspapers, it is represented by such popular national columns as "Annie's Mailbox," "Dear Prudence," and "Help Me Harlan." In addition, on an increasing number of college campuses, school newspaper sex columns have become popular and sometimes controversial.

Information and Advice as Entertainment

Newspaper columns, magazine articles, TV programs, and syndicated radio shows share several features. First, their primary purpose is to sell newspapers and magazines or to raise program ratings. This goal is in marked contrast to that of scholarly research, whose primary purpose is to increase knowledge. Even the inclusion of survey questionnaires in magazines asking readers about their sexual attitudes or behaviors is ultimately designed to promote sales. We fill out the questionnaires for fun, much as we would crossword puzzles or anagrams. Then we buy the subsequent issue or watch a later program to see how we compare to others.

Second, the success of media personalities rests not so much on their expertise as on their ability to present information as entertainment. Because the genre seeks to entertain, sex information and advice must be simplified. Complex explanations and analyses must be avoided because they would interfere with the entertainment purpose. Furthermore, the genre relies on high-interest or bizarre material to attract readers, viewers, and listeners. Consequently, we are more likely to read, hear, or view stories about unusual

LUANN reprinted by permission of United Feature Syndicate, Inc.

Campus Newspaper Sex Advice Columns: Education or Entertainment?

KISISS (THE KINSEY INSTITUTE Sexuality Information Service for Students) is a weekly sex advice column published in the Indiana University student-run newspaper, the *Indiana Daily Student*. A strength of this column is that graduate students at the Kinsey Institute at Indiana University manage it. These students have access to institute resources, which helps assure greater accuracy in the information they provide. Questions submitted by Indiana University students are personally answered via e-mail, and selected ones are printed in the newspaper and posted on the Web site (http://www.indiana.edu/~kisiss). Occasionally, KISISS answers questions submitted by the general public, but it cannot respond to all because of the large volume of questions submitted. Anyone can read past questions and answers online.

The number of college newspapers with sex advice columns has skyrocketed. These columns attempt to provide accurate information and sound advice on sex, dating, love, and relationships. Usually, an editor for the newspaper, typically an undergraduate student, is the "sex expert." The subject matter ranges from health-related topics such as contraception and safer sex to specific sexual issues such as orgasm, oral sex, masturbation, bondage, pleasure, and penis size. Although the columns have become popular on many campuses,

they are not universally liked. School administrators have worried that the columns lack taste and might tarnish the college's reputation. Some have even attempted to ban the columns. Some critics believe that the columns' main purpose is entertainment (thus increasing newspaper sales), not education. Moreover, the "sex expert" columnist may have little or no background in human sexuality or counseling and may provide misinformation or harmful advice. Defenders believe that the columns provide a valuable service—information about relevant issues—to their primary readers: college students.

Given the controversies about college sex advice columns, what are your thoughts about them? Should college newspapers have sex advice columns? If so, should the newspaper be required to get the school administration's approval for the column? Should all types of questions be answered, regardless of how explicit or "risqué"? Who should provide the responses to the questions? Should these "sex experts" be required to have a strong academic background in the field? Should the columns provide information only, or should they also give advice? Do you take the answers provided in the column seriously? Are these columns education or entertainment? Why?

sexual practices or ways to increase sexual attractiveness than stories about new research methods or the negative outcomes of sexual stereotyping.

Third, the genre focuses on how-to information or on morality. Some mix information and normative judgments. The how-to material tells us how to improve our sex lives. Advice columnists often give advice on issues of sexual morality: "Is it all right to have sex without commitment?" "Yes, if you love him/her" or "No, casual sex is empty," and so on. Advice columnists act as moral arbiters, much as ministers, priests, and rabbis do.

Fourth, the genre uses the trappings of social science and psychiatry without their substance. Writers and columnists interview social scientists and therapists to give an aura of scientific authority to their material. They rely especially heavily on therapists whose background is clinical rather than academic. Because clinicians tend to deal with people with problems, they often see sexuality as problematic.

The line between media sex experts and advice columnists is often blurred. This line is especially obscure on the Internet, where Web sites dealing with sex have proliferated. Most of these sites are purely for entertainment rather than education, and it can be difficult to determine a site's credibility. One way to assess the educational value of a Web site is to investigate its sponsor. Reputable national organizations like the American Psychological Association (http://www.apa.org) and the Sexuality Information and Education Council of the United States (http://www.siecus.org) provide reliable information and links to other, equally reputable, sites.

AFTER YOU HAVE READ several sex books and watched several sex experts on television, you will discover that they tend to be repetitive. There are two main reasons for this. First, the media repeatedly report more or less the same stories because sex research is a small discipline and fewer studies are conducted compared to other academic areas. Scientific research is painstakingly slow, and the results are tedious to produce. Research results rarely change the way we view a topic; often, they verify what we already know. Although research is seldom revolutionary, the media must nevertheless continually produce new stories to fill their pages and programs. Consequently, they report similar material in different guises—as interviews, survey results, and first-person stories, for example.

Second, the media are repetitive because their scope is narrow. There are only so many ways how-to books can tell you "how to do it." Similarly, the personal and moral dilemmas most of us face are remarkably similar: Am I normal? When should I be sexual with another person? Is sex without love moral?

With the media awash with sex information and advice, how can you evaluate what is presented to you? Here are some guidelines:

1. *Be skeptical.* Remember, much of what you read or see is meant to entertain you. If it seems superficial, it probably is.

2. *Search for biases, stereotypes, and lack of objectivity.* Information is often distorted by points of view. Is there any reason to suspect bias in the selection of subjects? What conflicting information may have been omitted? How are women and members of various ethnic groups portrayed?

3. *Look for moralizing.* Many times, what passes for fact is really disguised moral judgment. What are the underlying values of the article or program?

4. *Go to the original source or sources.* The media always simplify. Find out for yourself what the studies really reported. What were the backgrounds and credentials of the people or organizations who conducted the research? What organization, if any, funded the research study? How large were the samples? Did the story describe the parameters of the sample? How valid were the methodologies? What were their strengths and limitations?

5. *Seek additional information.* The whole story is probably not told. Look for additional information in scholarly books and journals, reference books, or textbooks.

Keeping these guidelines in mind will help you steer a course between blind acceptance and offhand dismissal of a study.

The Use and Abuse of Statistics

To reinforce their authority, the media also incorporate statistics, which are key features of social science research. However, as Susan Faludi (1991) notes:

> The statistics that the popular culture chooses to promote most heavily are the very statistics we should view with the most caution. They may well be in wide circulation not because they are true but because they support widely held media preconceptions.

For example, the media promoted the idea of a possible infertility "epidemic" occurring because of a decline in male sperm counts. Just 2 years later, a group of scientists discounted this theory, claiming "unaccounted-for regional differences" (Fisch et al., 1996). In the early 1990s, research showing a possible relationship between brain anatomy, genes, and sexual orientation was heavily covered by the media. But many reports exaggerated the certainty of the research findings, leading people to conclude that biology, and not social influences, causes males to be homosexual. The "nature versus nurture" influence on sexual orientation is still being debated and investigated by sexologists and remains controversial.

The media frequently quote or describe social science research, but they may do so in an oversimplified or distorted manner. Scholars tend to qualify their findings as tentative or limited to a certain group, and they are very cautious about making generalizations. In contrast, the media tend to make results sound more generalizable. The media may report, for example, a study finding that sexual problems are common among women, whereas a later study finds a lower prevalence of difficulties. On what basis do we decide which study to believe? Many of us think all studies are equal, that one is as good as another as long as they are conducted by experts who presumably know what they are doing. But all studies are not necessarily comparable or equally well done.

Many studies use the mean (average) when reporting findings. For example, they may report that college students have an average of three sex partners during their college years. Of course, some students may not have any partners, while others may have ten or more. Thus, the mean cannot represent the enormous variation of behavior within a group, nor does it represent "normal" behavior.

If researchers know or suspect that some scores are extreme, they often will report the median (middle) score. They may also report both the mean and the median; if these scores are similar, then there were probably not many outliers, or scores significantly higher or lower than the mean. Sometimes, researchers will discard extreme scores if there is reason to believe that they are not valid. Otherwise, relatively few outliers within a sample can lead to misleading conclusions.

Clearly, the media are not always the best place to learn about the latest sex research. As consumers of sex research, we need to determine whether the report mentions study limitations and whether the researchers are from a reputable university or institution. If the report overgeneralizes the results, beware.

THINKING CRITICALLY ABOUT SEXUALITY

Although each of us has our own perspective, values, and beliefs regarding sexuality, as students, instructors, and researchers, we are committed to the scientific study of sexuality. Basic to any scientific study is a fundamental commitment to **objectivity,** or the observation of things as they exist in reality as opposed to our feelings or beliefs about them. Objectivity calls for us to suspend the beliefs, biases, or prejudices we have about a subject in order to understand it.

Objectivity in the study of sexuality is not always easy to achieve, for sexuality can be the focal point of powerful emotions and moral ambivalence. We experience sex very subjectively. But whether we find it easy or difficult to be objective, objectivity is the foundation for studying sexuality.

Most of us think about sex, but thinking about it critically requires us to be logical and objective. It also requires that we avoid making value judgments; put aside our opinions, biases, and stereotypes; not confuse attitudes with behaviors; and not fall prey to common fallacies such as egocentric and ethnocentric thinking.

Value Judgments Versus Objectivity

For many of us, objectivity about sex is difficult because our culture has traditionally viewed sexuality in moral terms: Sex is moral or immoral, right or wrong, good or bad. When examining sexuality, we tend, therefore, to make **value judgments,** evaluations based on moral or ethical standards rather than objective ones. Unfortunately, value judgments are often blinders

He who knows nothing doubts nothing.

—*French proverb*

Morality is simply the attitude we adopt towards people we personally dislike.

—*Oscar Wilde (1854–1900)*

to understanding. They do not tell us about what motivates people, how frequently they behave in a given way, or how they feel. Value judgments do not tell us anything about sexuality except how we ourselves feel. In studying human sexuality, then, we need to put aside value judgments as incompatible with the pursuit of knowledge.

How can we tell the difference between a value judgment and an objective statement? Examine the following two statements. Which is a value judgment? Which is an objective statement?

- College students should be in a committed relationship before they have sex.
- The majority of students have sexual intercourse sometime during their college careers.

The first statement is a value judgment; the second is an objective statement. There is a simple rule of thumb for telling the difference between the two: Value judgments imply how a person *ought* to behave, whereas objective statements describe how people *actually* behave. The first statement is a value judgment because it makes a judgment about sexual behavior. The second statement is an objective one because it describes how people act.

There is a second difference between value judgments and objective statements: Value judgments cannot be empirically validated, whereas objective statements can be. That is, the truth or accuracy of an objective statement can be measured and tested. Despite claims of universality, however, standards of objectivity are generally regarded by social scientists as culturally relative. (**Cultural relativity** is an important anthropological concept involving the positive or negative appropriateness of any custom or activity that must be evaluated in terms of how it fits in with the culture as a whole.)

Opinions, Biases, and Stereotypes

Value judgments obscure our search for understanding. Opinions, biases, and stereotypes also interfere with the pursuit of knowledge.

Opinions An **opinion** is an unsubstantiated belief or conclusion about what seems to be true according to our thoughts. Opinions are not based on accurate knowledge or concrete evidence. Because opinions are unsubstantiated, they often reflect our personal values or biases.

Biases A **bias** is a personal leaning or inclination. Biases lead us to select information that supports our views or beliefs while ignoring information that does not. We need not be victims, however, of our biases. We can make a concerted effort to discover what they are and overcome them. To avoid personal bias, scholars apply the objective methods of social science research.

Stereotypes A **stereotype** is a set of simplistic, rigidly held, overgeneralized beliefs about an individual, a group of people, an idea, and so on. Stereotypical beliefs are resistant to change. Furthermore, stereotypes—especially sexual ones—are often negative.

Common sexual stereotypes include the following:

- Men are always ready for sex.
- "Nice" women are not interested in sex.

Ignorance is like a delicate exotic fruit; touch it and the bloom is gone.

—Oscar Wilde (1854–1900)

- Women need a reason for sex; men need a place.
- Virgins are uptight and asexual.
- The relationships of gay men never last.
- Lesbian women hate men.
- African American men lust after White women.
- Latino men are macho.

Psychologists believe that stereotypes structure knowledge. They affect the ways in which we process information: what we see, what we notice, what we remember, and how we explain things. Or, as humorist Ashleigh Brilliant said, "Seeing is believing. I wouldn't have seen it if I hadn't believed it." A stereotype is a type of **schema,** a way in which we organize knowledge in our thought processes. Schemas help us channel or filter the mass of information we receive so that we can make sense of it. They determine what we will regard as important. Although these mental plans are useful, they can also create blind spots. With stereotypes, we see what we expect to see and ignore what we don't expect or want to see.

Sociologists point out that sexual stereotyping is often used to justify discrimination. Targets of stereotypes are usually members of subordinate social groups (such as women and people of color) or individuals with limited economic resources. As we will see, sexual stereotyping is especially powerful in stigmatizing African Americans, Latinos, Asian Americans, gay men, lesbian women, and bisexual and transgendered individuals.

We all have opinions and biases, and most of us to varying degrees think stereotypically. But the commitment to objectivity requires us to become aware of our opinions, biases, and stereotypes and to put them aside in the pursuit of knowledge.

> No question is so difficult as that to which the answer is obvious.
>
> —*George Bernard Shaw (1856–1950)*

Confusing Attitudes and Behavior

An **attitude** is a predisposition a person has to act, think, or feel in certain ways. A **behavior** is the way a person acts. There are two problems we commonly experience when discussing sexual attitudes and behavior: (1) We fail to identify whether we are discussing attitudes or behavior, and (2) we assume attitudes reflect behavior, and vice versa.

Failure to identify whether we are discussing attitudes or behavior can lead to confusion and endless disagreement. Imagine, for example, two friends discussing nonmarital sex without either specifying whether he or she is talking about attitudes or behavior. One says, "Everyone I know accepts sex outside of marriage." The other disagrees: "That's not so. Almost all our friends are virgins." The fact is, both may be correct. But the first person is talking about *attitudes* toward nonmarital sex, while the second is talking about actual sexual *behavior.* The two may never come to an agreement because they are talking about different things.

There is often a discrepancy between attitudes and behavior. As a result, we cannot infer a person's behavior from his or her attitudes about sexuality, or vice versa. A person may disapprove of **casual sex,** for example, but nevertheless engage in it. A woman may oppose abortion but may terminate her own pregnancy.

Common Fallacies: Egocentric and Ethnocentric Thinking

A **fallacy** is an error in reasoning that affects our understanding of a subject. Fallacies distort our thinking, leading us to false or erroneous conclusions. In the field of sexuality, egocentric and ethnocentric fallacies are common.

The Egocentric Fallacy   The **egocentric fallacy** is the mistaken belief that our own personal experience and values generally are held by others. On the basis of our belief in this false consensus, we use our own beliefs and values to explain the attitudes, motivations, and behaviors of others. Of course, our own experiences and values are important; they are the source of personal strength and knowledge, and they can give us insight into the experiences and values of others. But we cannot necessarily generalize from our own experience to that of others. Our own personal experiences are limited and may be unrepresentative; sometimes, they are merely opinions or disguised value judgments.

The Ethnocentric Fallacy   The **ethnocentric fallacy,** also known as **ethnocentrism,** is the belief that our own ethnic group, nation, or culture is innately superior to others. Ethnocentrism is reinforced by opinions, biases, and stereotypes about other groups and cultures. As members of a group, we

Ethnocentrism is the belief that one's own culture or ethnic group is superior to others. Although child marriage is prohibited in our society, it is acceptable in many cultures throughout the world, including India. Such marriages generally do not include cohabitation or sexual contact until the couple are old enough in the eyes of their society.

tend to share similar values and attitudes with other group members. But the mere fact that we share these beliefs is not sufficient proof of their truth.

Ethnocentrism has been increasingly evident as a reaction to the increased awareness of **ethnicity,** or ethnic affiliation or identity. For many Americans, a significant part of their sense of self comes from identification with their ethnic group. An **ethnic group** is a group of people distinct from other groups because of cultural characteristics, such as language, religion, and customs, that are transmitted from one generation to the next. Contemporary American ethnic groups include African Americans, Latinos (Hispanics), Native Americans, Japanese Americans, Italian Americans, Irish Catholics, and Chinese Americans.

Although there has been little research on ethnicity and sexuality until recently, evidence suggests that there are significant ethnic variations in terms of sexual attitudes and behavior (Cortese, 1989; Holtzman, Bland, Lansky, & Mack, 2001; Okazaki, 2002; Staples, 1991; Staples & Johnson, 1993). When data are available, the variations by ethnicity will be presented throughout this book.

Ethnocentrism results when we stereotype other cultures as "primitive," "innocent," "inferior," or "not as advanced." We may view the behavior of other peoples as strange, exotic, unusual, or bizarre, but to them it is normal. Their attitudes, behaviors, values, and beliefs form a unified sexual system that makes sense within their culture. In fact, we engage in many activities that appear peculiar to those outside our culture.

> All universal judgments are weak, loose, and dangerous.
>
> *—Michel de Montaigne (1533–1595)*

SEX RESEARCH METHODS

One of the key factors that distinguishes the findings of social science from beliefs, prejudice, bias, and pop psychology is its commitment to the scientific method. The **scientific method** is the method by which a hypothesis is formed from impartially gathered data and tested empirically. The scientific method relies on **induction**—that is, drawing a general conclusion from specific facts. The scientific method seeks to describe the world rather than evaluate or judge it.

Although sex researchers use the same methodology as other social scientists, they are constrained by ethical concerns and taboos that those in other fields do not experience. Because of the taboos surrounding sexuality, some traditional research methods are inappropriate.

Sex research, like most social science research, uses different methodological approaches. These include clinical research, survey research (questionnaires and interviews), observational research, and experimental research. And as in many fields, no single paradigm has emerged in sexual science (Weis, 2002).

> The great tragedy of science—the slaying of a beautiful hypothesis by an ugly fact.
>
> *—Thomas Huxley (1894–1963)*

Research Concerns

Researchers face two general concerns in conducting their work: (1) ethical concerns centering on the use of human beings as subjects and (2) methodological concerns regarding sampling techniques and their accuracy. Without a representative sample, the conclusions that can be drawn using these methodologies are limited.

Ethical Issues   Ethics are important in any scientific endeavor. They are especially important in such an emotional and value-laden subject as sexuality. Among the most important ethical issues are informed consent, protection from harm, confidentiality, and the use of deception.

Informed consent is the full disclosure to an individual of the purpose, potential risks, and benefits of participating in a research project. Under informed consent, people are free to decide whether to participate in a project without coercion or deceit. Studies involving children and other minors typically require parental consent. Once a study begins, participants have the right to withdraw at any time without penalty.

Each research participant is entitled to **protection from harm.** Some sex research, such as the viewing of explicit films to measure physiological responses, may cause some people emotional distress. The identity of research subjects should be kept confidential. Because of the highly charged nature of sexuality, participants also need to be guaranteed anonymity.

Of all the ethical issues surrounding research, the use of **deception** is most problematic. Sometimes, it is necessary to deceive subjects in order for the experiment to work. For example, if participants in a study on the role of attractiveness at first meetings knew they were being studied in terms of their response to attractive people rather than, say, opening lines, their responses might be different. The issue of deception is generally resolved by requiring that the researcher **debrief** participants following the experiment. During the debriefing, the deception is revealed and its necessity explained. Participants are given the opportunity to ask questions. They may also request that their data be removed from the study and destroyed.

All colleges and universities have review boards or human subject committees to make sure that researchers follow ethical guidelines. Proposed research is submitted to the committee before the project begins. If the committee believes the research poses ethical problems, the project will not be approved until the problems are corrected.

> Anything more than truth would be too much.
>
> —*Robert Frost (1874–1963)*

Sampling   In each research approach, the choice of a sample—a portion of a larger group of people or population—is critical. To be useful, a sample should be a **random sample**—that is, a sample collected in an unbiased way, with the selection of each member of the sample based solely on chance. Furthermore, the sample should be a **representative sample,** with a small group representing the larger group in terms of age, sex, ethnicity, socioeconomic status, orientation, and so on. When a random sample is used, information gathered from a small group can be used to make inferences about the larger group. Samples that are not representative of the larger group are known as **biased samples.**

Using samples is important. It would be impossible, for example, to study the sexual behaviors of all college students in the United States. But we could select a representative sample of college students from various schools and infer from their behavior how other college students behave. Using the same sample to infer the sexual behavior of Americans in general, however, would mean using a biased sample. We cannot generalize the sexual activities of American college students to the larger population because the majority of college students sampled are biased in terms of age (young), education (college), socioeconomic status (middle class), and ethnicity (European American) (Dunne, 2002; Strassberg & Lowe, 1995).

Most samples in sex research are limited for several reasons:

▪ They depend on volunteers or clients. Because these samples are generally self-selected, we cannot assume that they are representative of the population as a whole. Volunteers for sex research are often more likely to be male, sexually experienced, liberal, and less religious and to have more positive attitudes toward sexuality and less sex guilt and anxiety than those who do not choose to participate (Strassberg & Lowe, 1995; Whitney, 2002; Wiederman, 1999).

▪ Most sex research takes place in a university or college setting with student volunteers. College students, however, are generally in late adolescence or early adulthood and are single; they are at the beginning of their sexual lives. Is the value they place on emotional intimacy during sex, for example, likely to be the same as the value older adults give it?

▪ Some ethnic groups are generally underrepresented. Representative samples of African Americans, Latinos, Native Americans, and some Asian Americans are not easily found because these groups are underrepresented at the colleges and universities where subjects are generally recruited.

▪ The study of gay men, lesbian women, and bisexuals and transgendered people presents unique sampling issues. Are gay men, lesbian women, and bisexual individuals who have **come out**—publicly identified themselves as gay, lesbian, or bisexual—different from those who have not? How do we find and recruit subjects who have not come out?

Because these factors limit most studies, we must be careful in making generalizations from studies.

Clinical Research

Clinical research is the in-depth examination of an individual or group that comes to a psychiatrist, psychologist, or social worker for assistance with psychological or medical problems or disorders. Clinical research is descriptive; inferences of cause and effect cannot be drawn from it. The individual is interviewed and treated for a specific problem. At the same time the person is being treated, he or she is being studied. In their evaluations, clinicians attempt to determine what caused the disorder and how it may be treated. They may also try to infer from dysfunctional people how healthy people develop. Clinical research often focuses on atypical, unhealthy behaviors, problems related to sexuality (e.g., feeling trapped in the body of the wrong gender), and sexual performance problems (e.g., lack of desire, early ejaculation, erectile difficulties, or lack of orgasm).

A major limitation of clinical research is its emphasis on **pathological behavior,** or unhealthy or diseased behavior. Such an emphasis makes clinical research dependent on cultural definitions of what is "unhealthy" or "pathological." These definitions, however, change over time and in the context of the culture being studied. In the nineteenth century, for example, masturbation was considered pathological. Physicians and clinicians went to great lengths to root it out. In the case of women, surgeons sometimes removed the clitoris. Today, masturbation is viewed more positively.

In evaluating clinical research, we should ask several questions (Gagnon, 1977; Whitney, 2002). First, on what basis is a condition defined as healthy or unhealthy? For example, are the bases for classifying homosexuality and masturbation as healthy or unhealthy behaviors scientific, cultural, or moral? Second, can inferences gathered from the behavior of patients be applied to others? For example, if we learn that male-to-female transsexuals tended to play with dolls when they were young, should we discourage male children from playing with dolls? Third, how do we know that the people we are studying are representative of the group with which we are identifying them? For example, most of what we know about the psychological makeup of rapists comes from the study of imprisoned rapists. But are imprisoned rapists representative of all rapists?

Survey Research

Survey research is a method that uses questionnaires or interviews to gather information. Questionnaires offer anonymity, can be completed fairly quickly, and are relatively inexpensive to administer; however, they usually do not allow an in-depth response. A person must respond with a short answer or select from a limited number of options. The limited-choices format provides a more objective assessment and results in a total score. Interview techniques avoid some of the shortcomings of questionnaires, as interviewers are able to probe in greater depth and follow paths suggested by the subject.

Although surveys are important sources of information, the method has several limitations. First, people tend to be poor reporters of their own sexual behavior. Men may exaggerate their number of sexual partners; women may minimize their casual encounters. Members of both sexes generally underreport experiences considered deviant or immoral, such as same-sex experiences and bondage. Second, interviewers may allow their own preconceptions to influence the way in which they frame questions and to bias their interpretations of responses. Third, some respondents may feel uncomfortable about revealing information—such as about masturbation or incestuous experiences—in a face-to-face interview. Fourth, the interviewer's sex may also influence how comfortable respondents are in disclosing information about themselves. Fifth, the accuracy of one's memory may fade as time passes. Sixth, providing an accurate estimation, such as how long sex lasted, may be difficult. Finally, some ethnic groups, because of their cultural values, may be reluctant to reveal sexual information about themselves.

Recently, some researchers have used computers to improve interviewing techniques for sensitive topics. With the audio computer-assisted self-interviewing (audio-CASI) method, the respondent hears the questions over headphones or reads them on a computer screen and then enters her or his responses into the computer. Audio-CASI apparently increases feelings of confidentiality and accuracy of responses. In studies comparing the face-to-face interview with audio-CASI, more respondents reported HIV risk behaviors and stigmatized activities in audio-CASI than in face-to-face interviews (Des Jarlais et al., 1999; Gribble, Miller, Rogers, & Turner, 1999).

Another new technique is the use of the Internet to administer questionnaires and conduct interviews. Respondents to such interviews tend to have a higher income and level of education than those without access to the Internet, making it difficult to generalize from their responses. However, geographically isolated persons can be reached more easily (Ross, 2000).

Answering a Sex Research Questionnaire: The Sexual Opinion Survey

MANY RESEARCHERS USE standardized (i.e., reliable and valid) questionnaires to measure variables related to sexuality. The Sexual Opinion Survey (SOS) (White et al., 1977) is a widely used questionnaire that measures tendencies toward erotophobia and erotophilia. (**Erotophobic** persons have a more negative affect toward sexually related situations; **erotophilic** persons respond more positively.) Research has shown, for example, that erotophobic (compared to erotophilic) persons engage in less masturbation and heterosexual behavior, are less likely to acquire and use contraception, are less likely to engage in certain sex-related health-care practices, report more negative attitudes toward sexuality, and are more homophobic (Fisher, 1998).

The SOS is provided below; take it to find out what it is like to complete a sex research questionnaire, as well as to get a general idea of whether you are more erotophobic or erotophilic.

Directions

Respond to each item as honestly as you can, using the key 1 = strongly agree to 4 = neutral to 7 = strongly disagree. Circle your response. There are no right or wrong answers.

| | Strongly agree | | | | | Strongly disagree |

1. I think it would be very entertaining to look at hard-core erotica (sexually explicit books, movies, etc.).   1 2 3 4 5 6 7

2. Erotica is obviously filthy and people should not try to describe it as anything else.   1 2 3 4 5 6 7

3. Swimming in the nude with a member of the opposite sex would be an exciting experience.   1 2 3 4 5 6 7

4. Masturbation can be an exciting experience.   1 2 3 4 5 6 7

5. If I found that a close friend of mine was homosexual, it would annoy me.   1 2 3 4 5 6 7

6. If people thought that I was interested in oral sex, I would be embarrassed.   1 2 3 4 5 6 7

7. Engaging in group sex is an entertaining idea.   1 2 3 4 5 6 7

8. I personally find that thinking about engaging in sexual intercourse is arousing.   1 2 3 4 5 6 7

9. Seeing an erotic movie would be sexually arousing to me.   1 2 3 4 5 6 7

10. Thoughts that I might have homosexual tendencies would not worry me at all.   1 2 3 4 5 6 7

11. The idea of my being physically attracted to members of the same sex is not depressing.   1 2 3 4 5 6 7

To address recall inaccuracy of past sexual behaviors, some researchers are beginning to use the written **sexual diary.** Although use of a diary has been common in other health areas, it has not been widely used to study sexual behavior. Often, research participants make daily diary entries about sexual variables such as interest, fantasies, and behavior. Or they may be requested to make entries only after a certain sexual activity has occurred, such as intercourse. Research suggests that event-specific behaviors such as condom use during sex will be more accurately recalled in diaries than by retrospective methods such as self-report questionnaires and interviews (Fortenberry, Cecil, Zimet, & Orr, 1997; Gilmore et al., 2001; Graham & Bancroft, 1997). The diary may also foster a richer, more conceptualized assessment of sexual behavior. Paul Okami (2002) states that the diary may also be a superior survey method for assessing sex-related variables because it may reduce problems of recall and because some people seem to prefer diaries to questionnaires. However, Okami notes that diaries require greater participant compliance (e.g., daily entries) and may produce underestimates or overestimates of sexual behavior in ways questionnaires do not.

12. Almost all erotic material is nauseating.   1 2 3 4 5 6 7

13. It would be emotionally upsetting to me to see someone exposing themselves publicly.   1 2 3 4 5 6 7

14. Watching a stripper of the opposite sex would not be very exciting.   1 2 3 4 5 6 7

15. I would not enjoy seeing an erotic movie.   1 2 3 4 5 6 7

16. When I think of seeing pictures showing someone of the same sex as myself masturbating, it nauseates me.   1 2 3 4 5 6 7

17. The thought of engaging in unusual sex practices is highly arousing.   1 2 3 4 5 6 7

18. Manipulating my genitals would be an arousing experience.   1 2 3 4 5 6 7

19. I do not enjoy daydreaming about sexual matters.   1 2 3 4 5 6 7

20. I am curious about explicit erotica.   1 2 3 4 5 6 7

21. The thought of having long-term sexual relations with more than one sex partner is not disgusting to me.   1 2 3 4 5 6 7

Scoring

Add your scores for items 2, 5, 6, 12, 13, 14, 15, 16, 19, and 20: _____ . Subtract from this total the sum of your scores for items 1, 3, 4, 7, 8, 9, 10, 11, 17, 18, and 21: _____ . Add 67 to this quantity: _____ . (For example, if your total for the first set of items is 79 and your total for the second set is 65, subtract 65 from 79, giving you 14. Add 67 to this for a final score of 81.) Scores range from 0 (most erotophobic) to 126 (most erotophilic).

Take some time to reflect on your experience in completing this survey:

- How honest were you in answering these questions?
- Would your responses have been the same if you had been asked these same questions on the telephone, in an interview, or via the Internet?
- How valid do you think the results from a questionnaire such as this are?
- Did you detect any assumptions about sexual orientation in this survey?
- Would your answers on the survey be affected by your status as a straight, gay or lesbian, or bisexual person?

Source: "The Sexual Opinion Survey" in Adolescents, Sex and Contraception by D. Byrne and W. A. Fisher, Lawrence, Erlbaum Associates, Inc. Copyright © 1983 Lawrence Erlbaum. Reprinted by permission of the publisher.

Observational Research

Observational research is a method by which a researcher unobtrusively observes and makes systematic notes about people's behavior without trying to manipulate it. The observer does not want his or her presence to affect the subject's behavior, although this is rarely possible. Because sexual behavior is regarded as significantly different from other behaviors, there are serious ethical issues involved in observing people's sexual behavior without their knowledge and consent. (Even with their knowledge and consent, such observation may be considered voyeuristic and subject to criminal prosecution.) Because researchers cannot observe sexual behavior as they might observe, say, flirting at a party, dance, or bar, such observations usually take place in a laboratory setting. In such instances, the setting is not a natural environment, and participants are aware that their behavior is under observation.

Participant observation, in which the researcher participates in the behaviors she or he is studying, is an important method of observational research. For example, a researcher may study prostitution by becoming a customer (Snyder, 1974) or anonymous sex between men in public restrooms by posing as a lookout (Humphreys, 1975). There are several questions

Discovery consists of seeing what everybody has seen and thinking what nobody has thought.

—*Albert Szent-Gyorgyi (1893–1986)*

Participant observation is an important means by which anthropologists gain information about other cultures.

raised by such participant observation. How does the observer's participation affect the interactions being studied? For example, does a prostitute respond differently to a researcher if she or he tries to obtain information? If the observer participates, how does this affect her or his objectivity? And what are the researcher's ethical responsibilities regarding informing those she or he is studying?

Participant observation is also the most important method used by anthropologists in studying other cultures (Frayser, 1994). Anthropologists may spend considerable time securing the trust of group members so that they reveal their group's beliefs and behaviors, including their sexual beliefs and behaviors. Because cultural differences can be great, researchers must avoid moral judgments. Anthropologists often find that their sex affects their ability to gather information. For example, male anthropologists rarely observe childbirth or menstrual rituals; female anthropologists are usually excluded from male initiation ceremonies. However, despite its limitations, anthropologists practicing participant observation may be able to gather information about sexuality that shows how it is integrated into a culture.

Experimental Research

Experimental research is the systematic manipulation of individuals or the environment to learn the effects of such manipulation on behavior. It enables researchers to isolate a single factor under controlled circumstances to determine its influence. Researchers are able to control their experiments by using **variables,** or aspects or factors that can be manipulated in experiments. There are two types of variables: independent and dependent.

Independent variables are factors that can be manipulated or changed by the experimenter; **dependent variables** are factors that are likely to be affected by changes in the independent variable.

Because it controls variables, experimental research differs from the previous methods we have examined. Clinical studies, surveys, and observational research are correlational in nature. **Correlational studies** measure two or more naturally occurring variables to determine their relationship to each other. Because these studies do not manipulate the variables, they cannot tell us which variable *causes* the other to change. But experimental studies manipulate the independent variables, so researchers *can* reasonably determine what variables cause the other variables to change.

Much experimental research on sexuality depends on measuring physiological responses. These responses are usually measured by **plethysmographs** (pluh-THIZ-muh-grafs)—devices attached to the genitals to measure physiological response. Researchers use either a penile plethysmograph, a **strain gauge** (a device resembling a rubber band), or a Rigiscan™ for men and a vaginal plethysmograph for women. Both the penile plethysmograph and the strain gauge are placed around the penis to measure changes in its circumference during sexual arousal. The Rigiscan™, probably the most widely used device to measure male genital response, consists of a recording unit strapped around the waist or the thigh and two loops, one placed around the base of the penis and the other around the shaft just behind the glans. The Rigiscan not only measures penile circumference but also assesses rigidity (Janssen, 2002). The vaginal plethysmograph is about the size of a menstrual tampon and is inserted into the vagina like a tampon. The device measures the amount of blood within the vaginal walls, which increases as a woman becomes sexually aroused.

Suppose researchers want to study the influence of alcohol on sexual response. They can use a plethysmograph to measure sexual response, the dependent variable. In this study, the independent variable is the level of alcohol consumption: no alcohol consumption, moderate alcohol consumption (1–3 drinks), and high alcohol consumption (3+ drinks). In addition, extraneous variables, such as body mass and tolerance for alcohol, need to be controlled. In such an experiment, subjects may view an erotic film. To get a baseline measurement, researchers measure the genitals' physiological patterns in an unaroused state, before participants view the film or take a drink. Then they measure sexual arousal (dependent variable) in response to erotica as they increase the level of alcohol consumption (independent variable).

Good experiments are difficult to design because the experimental situation must resemble the real world. There are four important concerns or limitations about experimental research. First, to what degree does the experiment replicate the complexities and settings of real-life sexuality? Does a laboratory setting radically alter responses? Second, do the devices used to measure sexual response affect the subjects' sexual responsiveness? Third, is it important that the measuring devices measure only genital response, given that overall sexual response includes increased heart rate and muscle tension, changed brain-wave patterns, and increased sexual fantasies and thoughts? Finally, can the results from the experiment be generalized to non-laboratory conditions? Because there are so many variables outside controlled laboratory conditions, many researchers believe that experimental findings are highly limited in their applicability to the real world.

Click on "The Plethysmograph" to see how a Rigiscan works.

THE SEX RESEARCHERS

It was not until the nineteenth century that Western sexuality began to be studied using a scientific framework. Prior to that time, sexuality was claimed by religion rather than science; sex was the subject of moral rather than scientific scrutiny. From the earliest Christian era, treatises, canon law, and papal bulls, as well as sermons and confessions, catalogued the sins of the flesh. Reflecting this Christian tradition, the early students of sexuality were concerned with the supposed excesses and deviances of sexuality rather than its healthy functioning. They were fascinated by what they considered the pathologies of sex, such as fetishism, sadism, masturbation, and homosexuality—the very behaviors that religion condemned as sinful. Alfred Kinsey ironically noted that nineteenth-century researchers created "scientific classifications . . . nearly identical with theological classifications and with moral pronouncements . . . of the fifteenth century" (Kinsey et al., 1948).

As we will see, however, there has been a liberalizing trend in our thinking about sexuality. Both Richard von Krafft-Ebing and Sigmund Freud viewed sexuality as inherently dangerous and needing repression. But Havelock Ellis, Alfred Kinsey, William Masters and Virginia Johnson, and many other more recent researchers have viewed sexuality more positively; in fact, historian Paul Robinson (1976) regards these later researchers as modernists, or "sexual enthusiasts." Three themes are evident in their work: (1) They believe that sexual expression is essential to an individual's well-being, (2) they seek to broaden the range of legitimate sexual activity, including homosexuality, and (3) they believe that female sexuality is the equal of male sexuality.

As much as possible, sex researchers attempt to examine sexuality objectively. But, as with all of us, many of their views are intertwined with the beliefs and values of their times. This is especially apparent among the early sex researchers, some of the most important of whom are described here.

Richard von Krafft-Ebing

Richard von Krafft-Ebing (1840–1902), a Viennese professor of psychiatry, was probably the most influential of the early researchers. In 1886, he published his most famous work, *Psychopathia Sexualis,* a collection of case histories of fetishists, sadists, masochists, and homosexuals. (He invented the words "sadomasochism" and "transvestite.")

Krafft-Ebing traced variations in Victorian sexuality to "hereditary taint," to "moral degeneracy," and, in particular, to masturbation. He intermingled descriptions of fetishists who became sexually excited by certain items of clothing with those of sadists who disemboweled their victims. For Krafft-Ebing, the origins of fetishism and murderous sadism, as well as most variations, lay in masturbation, the prime sexual sin of the nineteenth century. Despite his misguided focus on masturbation, Krafft-Ebing's *Psychopathia Sexualis* brought to public attention and discussion an immense range of sexual behaviors that had never before been documented in a dispassionate, if erroneous, manner. A darkened region of sexual behavior was brought into the open for public examination.

Richard von Krafft-Ebing (1840–1902) viewed most sexual behavior other than marital coitus as a sign of pathology.

Sigmund Freud

Few people have had as dramatic an impact on the way we think about the world as the Viennese physician Sigmund Freud (1856–1939). In his attempt to understand the **neuroses,** or psychological disorders characterized by anxiety or tension, plaguing his patients, Freud explored the unknown territory of the unconscious. If unconscious motives were brought to consciousness, Freud believed, a person could change his or her behavior. But, he suggested, **repression,** a psychological mechanism that kept people from becoming aware of hidden memories and motives because they aroused guilt, prevents such knowledge.

To explore the unconscious, Freud used various techniques; in particular, he analyzed dreams to discover their meaning. His journeys into the mind led to the development of **psychoanalysis,** a psychological system that ascribes behavior to unconscious desires. He fled Vienna when Hitler annexed Austria in 1938 and died a year later in England.

Freud believed that sexuality begins at birth, a belief that set him apart from other researchers. Freud described five stages in psychosexual development. The first stage is the **oral stage,** lasting from birth to age 1. During this time, the infant's eroticism is focused on the mouth; thumb sucking produces an erotic pleasure. Freud believed that the "most striking character of this sexual activity . . . is that the child gratifies himself on his own body; . . . he is autoerotic" (Freud, 1938). The second stage, between ages 1 and 3, is the **anal stage.** Children's sexual activities continue to be autoerotic, but the region of pleasure shifts to the anus. From age 3 through 5, children are in the **phallic stage,** in which they exhibit interest in the genitals. At age 6, children enter a **latency stage,** in which their sexual impulses are no longer active. At puberty, they enter the **genital stage,** at which point they become interested in genital sexual activities, especially sexual intercourse.

The phallic stage is the critical stage in both male and female development. The boy develops sexual desires for his mother, leading to an **Oedipal complex.** He simultaneously desires his mother and fears his father. This fear leads to **castration anxiety,** the belief that the father will cut off his penis because of jealousy. Girls follow a more complex developmental path, according to Freud. A girl develops an **Electra complex,** desiring her father while fearing her mother. Upon discovering that she does not have a penis, she feels deprived and develops **penis envy.** By age 6, boys and girls resolve their Oedipal and Electra complexes by relinquishing their desires for the parent of the other sex and identifying with their same-sex parent. In this manner, they develop their masculine and feminine identities. But because girls never acquire their "lost penis," Freud believed, they fail to develop an independent character like that of boys.

In many ways, such as in his commitment to science and his explorations of the unconscious, Freud seems the embodiment of twentieth-century thought. But over the past generation, his influence among American sex researchers has dwindled. Two of the most important reasons are his lack of empiricism and his inadequate description of female development.

Because of its limitations, Freud's work has become mostly of historical interest to mainstream sex researchers. It continues to exert influence in some fields of psychology but has been greatly modified by others.

Sigmund Freud (1856–1939) was the founder of psychoanalysis and one of the most influential European thinkers of the first half of the twentieth century. Freud viewed sexuality with suspicion.

The true science and study of man is man.

—*Pierre Charron (1541–1603)*

Even among contemporary psychoanalysts, Freud's work has been radically revised.

Havelock Ellis

Havelock Ellis (1859–1939), an English physician, argued that many behaviors previously labeled as abnormal were actually normal, including masturbation and female sexuality. For example, he found no evidence that masturbation leads to mental disorders, and he documented that women have sexual drives no less intense than those of men.

Havelock Ellis (1859–1939), who became one of the most influential sexual thinkers and reformers in the twentieth century, was a child of the Victorian era. His youth in his native England was marked by the sexual repression and fears of that time. He set himself against those sexual inhibitions to free humanity from ignorance. He was among the first modern affirmers of sexuality. "Sex lies at the root of life," he wrote, "and we can never learn to reverence life until we know how to understand sex" (Ellis, 1900). He believed that the negators of sexuality used morality and religion to twist and deform sex until it became little more than sin and degradation.

Ellis was the earliest important modern sexual thinker. His *Studies in the Psychology of Sex* (the first six volumes of which were published between 1897 and 1910) consisted of case studies, autobiographies, and personal letters. One of his most important contributions was pointing out the relativity of sexual values. In the nineteenth century, Americans and Europeans alike believed that their society's dominant sexual beliefs were the only morally and naturally correct standards. But Ellis demonstrated not only that Western sexual standards were hardly the only moral standards but also that they were not necessarily rooted in nature. In doing so, he was among the first researchers to appeal to studies in animal behavior, anthropology, and history.

Ellis also challenged the view that masturbation was abnormal. He argued that masturbation was widespread and that there was no evidence linking it with any serious mental or physical problems. He recorded countless men and women who masturbated without ill effect. In fact, he argued, masturbation had a positive function: It relieved tension.

In the nineteenth century, women were viewed as essentially "pure beings" who possessed reproductive rather than sexual desires. Men, in contrast, were driven by such strong sexual passions that their sexuality had to be severely controlled and repressed. In countless case studies, Ellis documented that women possessed sexual desires no less intense than those of men.

Ellis asserted that a wide range of behaviors was normal, including much behavior that the Victorians considered abnormal. He argued that both masturbation and female sexuality were normal behaviors and that even the so-called abnormal elements of sexual behavior were simply exaggerations of the normal.

He also reevaluated homosexuality. In the nineteenth century, homosexuality was viewed as the essence of sin and perversion. It was dangerous, lurid, and criminal. Ellis insisted that it was not a disease or a vice, but a congenital condition: A person was *born* homosexual; one did not *become* homosexual. By insisting that homosexuality was congenital, Ellis denied that it could be considered a vice or a form of moral degeneracy, because a person did not *choose* it. If homosexuality was both congenital and harmless, then, Ellis reasoned, it should not be considered immoral or criminal.

Alfred Kinsey

Alfred A. Kinsey (1894–1956), a biologist at Indiana University and America's leading authority on gall wasps, destroyed forever the belief in American sexual innocence and virtue. He accomplished this through two books, *Sexual Behavior in the Human Male* (Kinsey, Pomeroy, & Martin, 1948) and *Sexual Behavior in the Human Female* (Kinsey, Pomeroy, Martin, & Gebhard, 1953). These two volumes statistically documented the actual sexual behavior of Americans. In massive detail, they demonstrated the great discrepancy between *public* standards of sexual behavior and *actual* sexual behavior. In the firestorm that accompanied the publication of Kinsey's books (popularly known as the *Kinsey Reports*), many Americans protested the destruction of their cherished ideals and illusions.

Alfred Kinsey (1894–1956) shocked Americans by revealing how they actually behaved sexually. His scientific efforts led to the termination of his research funding because of political pressure.

Sexual Diversity and Variation What Kinsey discovered in his research was an extraordinary diversity in sexual behaviors. Among men, he found individuals who had orgasms daily and others who went months without orgasms. Among women, he found individuals who had never had orgasms and others who had them several times a day. He discovered one male who had ejaculated only once in 30 years and another who ejaculated 30 times a week on average. "This is the order of variation," he commented dryly, "which may occur between two individuals who live in the same town and who are neighbors, meeting in the same place of business and coming together in common social activities" (Kinsey et al., 1948).

A Reevaluation of Masturbation Kinsey's work aimed at a reevaluation of the role of masturbation in a person's sexual adjustment. Kinsey made three points about masturbation: (1) It is harmless, (2) it is not a substitute for sexual intercourse but a distinct form of sexual behavior that provides sexual pleasure, and (3) it plays an important role in women's sexuality because it is a more reliable source of orgasm than heterosexual intercourse and because its practice seems to facilitate women's ability to become orgasmic during intercourse. Indeed, Kinsey believed that masturbation is the best way to measure a woman's inherent sexual responsiveness because it does not rely on another person.

> You shall know the truth and the truth shall make you mad.
>
> —*Aldous Huxley (1894–1963)*

Sexual Orientation Prior to Kinsey's work, an individual was identified as homosexual if he or she had ever engaged in any sexual behavior with a member of the same sex. Kinsey found, however, that many people had sexual experiences with members of both sexes. He reported that 50% of the men and 28% of the women in his studies had had same-sex experiences and that 38% of the men and 13% of the women had had orgasms during these experiences (Kinsey et al., 1948, 1953). Furthermore, he discovered that sexual attractions could change over the course of a person's lifetime. Kinsey's research led him to conclude that it was erroneous to classify people as either heterosexual or homosexual. A person's sexuality was significantly more complex and fluid.

Kinsey wanted to eliminate the concept of heterosexual and homosexual *identities*. He did not believe that homosexuality, any more than heterosexuality, existed as a fixed psychological identity. Instead, he argued, there were only sexual behaviors, and behaviors alone did not make a person gay,

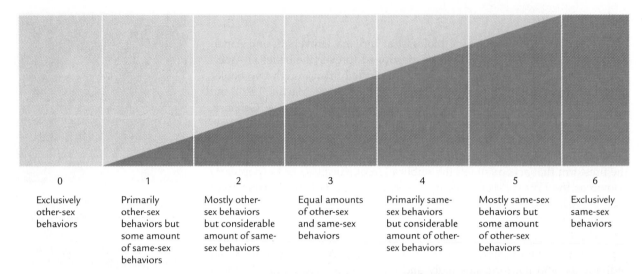

0	1	2	3	4	5	6
Exclusively other-sex behaviors	Primarily other-sex behaviors but some amount of same-sex behaviors	Mostly other-sex behaviors but considerable amount of same-sex behaviors	Equal amounts of other-sex and same-sex behaviors	Primarily same-sex behaviors but considerable amount of other-sex behaviors	Mostly same-sex behaviors but some amount of other-sex behaviors	Exclusively same-sex behaviors

FIGURE 2.1   The Kinsey Scale. This scale focuses on the degree to which a person engages in other-sex and same-sex sexual behaviors.

I don't see much of Alfred anymore since he got so interested in sex.

—*Mrs. Kinsey*

lesbian, bisexual, or heterosexual. It was more important to determine what proportion of behaviors were same-sex and other-sex than to label a person as gay, lesbian, or heterosexual.

He devised the Kinsey scale to represent the proportion of an individual's sexual behaviors with the same or other sex (Figure 2.1). This scale charted behaviors ranging from no behaviors with the same sex to behaviors exclusively with members of the same sex, with the behaviors existing on a continuum. His scale radicalized the categorization of human sexual behavior (McWhirter, 1990).

Rejection of Normal/Abnormal Dichotomy   As a result of his research, Kinsey insisted that the distinction between normal and abnormal was meaningless. Like Ellis, he argued that sexual differences were a matter of degree, not kind. Almost any sexual behavior could be placed alongside another that differed from it only slightly. His observations led him to be a leading advocate of the toleration of sexual differences.

Although Kinsey's statistical methodology has been criticized, the two most important criticisms of his work are (1) his emphasis on the quantification of sexual behavior and (2) his rejection of the psychological dimension. Because Kinsey wanted to quantify behaviors, he studied only those behaviors that could be objectively measured. Thus, he defined sexual behaviors as those that lead to orgasm. By defining sexuality in this way, Kinsey reduced sexual behavior to genital activity. He excluded from his research sexual activities, such as kissing and erotic fantasies, that do not ordinarily lead to orgasm.

He also neglected the psychological dimension of sexuality. Motivation and attitudes did not interest him because he did not believe they could be objectively measured. As a consequence, the role of emotions such as love did not enter into his discussion of sexuality.

Kinsey's lack of interest in the psychological dimension of human sexuality led him to reject homosexual/heterosexual *identities* as meaningless. Although a person's sexual behaviors may not correspond to his or her identity as homosexual or heterosexual, this identity is nevertheless a critical aspect of self-concept. By ignoring these elements, Kinsey seriously limited his understanding of human sexuality.

William Masters and Virginia Johnson

In the 1950s, William Masters (1915–2001), a St. Louis physician, became interested in treating sexual difficulties—such problems as early ejaculation and erection difficulties in men, and lack of orgasm in women. As a physician, he felt that a systematic study of the human sexual response was necessary, but none existed. To fill this void, he decided to conduct his own research. Masters was joined several years later by Virginia Johnson (1925–), a psychologist.

Masters and Johnson detailed the sexual response cycles of 382 men and 312 women during more than 10,000 episodes of sexual behavior, including masturbation and sexual intercourse. The researchers combined observation with direct measurement of changes in male and female genitals using electronic devices.

Human Sexual Response (1966), their first book, became an immediate success among both researchers and the public. What made their work significant was not only their detailed descriptions of physiological responses but the articulation of several key ideas. First, Masters and Johnson discovered that, physiologically, male and female sexual responses are very similar. Second, they demonstrated that women achieve orgasm primarily through clitoral stimulation. Penetration of the vagina is not needed for orgasm to occur. By demonstrating the primacy of the clitoris, Masters and Johnson destroyed once and for all the Freudian distinction between vaginal and clitoral orgasm. (Freud believed that an orgasm a woman experienced through masturbation was somehow physically and psychologically inferior to one experienced through sexual intercourse. He made no such distinction for men.) By destroying the myth of the vaginal orgasm, Masters and Johnson legitimized female masturbation.

In 1970, Masters and Johnson published *Human Sexual Inadequacy*, which revolutionized sex therapy by treating sexual problems simply as difficulties that could be treated using behavioral therapy. They argued that sexual problems were not the result of underlying neuroses or personality disorders. More often than not, problems resulted from a lack of information, poor communication between partners, or marital conflict. Their behavioral approach, which included "homework" exercises such as clitoral or penile stimulation, led to an astounding increase in the rate of successful treatment of sexual problems. Their work made them pioneers in modern sex therapy.

Clitoral or Vaginal Orgasms? Click on "Studying Female Sexual Response" to hear about various scientists' contributions to research on female sexual response.

William Masters (1915–2001) and Virginia Johnson (1925–) detailed the sexual response cycle in the 1960s and revolutionized sex therapy in the 1970s.

CONTEMPORARY RESEARCH STUDIES

Several large, national or multisite sexuality-related studies have recently been conducted. We briefly describe six survey studies here to illustrate research on various groups: the general population of men and women, adolescents, college students, and young men who have sex with men. Even though specific, no-risk sexual behaviors are addressed in some of the studies, the primary focus of most is sexual risk behaviors. Studies dealing with sexual risk behaviors are much more likely to receive federal and foundation funding than are studies on "nonrisky" sexual expression. The sources (Web site or journal article) of the studies are provided so that you can learn more about each study's purpose, methods, and results if you wish.

The National Health and Social Life Survey

In 1994, new figures were released showing us to be in a different place than when Kinsey did his research a half century earlier. Researchers from the University of Chicago published, according to their own description, the "only comprehensive and methodologically sound survey of America's sexual practices and beliefs." Their findings, which were released under two titles—the popular trade book *Sex in America: A Definitive Survey* (Michael, Gagnon, Laumann, & Kolata, 1994) and a more detailed and scholarly version, *The Social Organization of Sexuality* (Laumann, Gagnon, Michael, & Michaels, 1994)—not only raised questions about research methodology in human sexuality but also contradicted many previous findings and beliefs about sex in America.

The study, titled the National Health and Social Life Survey (NHSLS), was originally intended to be federally funded, but because of political opposition, it was completed with private funds. The authors set out to conduct a strong study by randomly sampling 3432 Americans, age 18–59, in 90-minute face-to-face interviews. Rigorous training of the interviewers, pretesting of the questionnaire, and built-in checkpoints to test the veracity of the responses were among the methods chosen to help ensure the accuracy and reliability of the test results. Even though this study had some sampling limitations, sexual scientists regard it as one of the most methodologically sound to date.

Researchers Robert T. Michael, John H. Gagnon, Stuart Michaels, and Edward O. Laumann conducted the National Health and Social Life Survey, a study of sexual behavior involving interviews with over 3000 adults. Their study is the most comprehensive investigation of sexual behavior in the United States since Kinsey's research.

Released as the first study to explore the social context of sexuality, the survey revealed the following:

- *Americans are largely exclusive.* The median number of sex partners since age 18 for men was six and for women, two.

- *On average, Americans have sex about once a week.* On frequency of sex, adults fell roughly into three groups: Nearly 30% had sex with a partner only a few times a year or not at all, 35% had sex once or several times a month, and about 35% had sex two or more times a week.

- *Extramarital sex is the exception, not the rule.* Among those who were married, 75% of men and 85% of women said they had been sexually exclusive with their spouse.

- *Most Americans are fairly traditional in the bedroom.* When respondents were asked to name their preferences from a long list of sexual practices, vaginal intercourse was considered "very appealing" by most of those interviewed. Ranking second, but far behind, was watching a partner undress. Oral sex ranked third.

- *Homosexuality is not as prevalent as originally believed.* Among men, 2.8% described themselves as homosexual or bisexual; among women, 1.4% did so.

- *Orgasms appear to be the rule for men and the exception for women.* Seventy-five percent of men claimed to have orgasms consistently with their partners, whereas only 29% of women did. Married women were most likely to report that they always or usually had orgasms.

- *Forced sex and the misperception of it remain critical problems.* Twenty-two percent of women said they had been forced to do sexual things they didn't want to do, usually by a loved one. Only 3% of men reported ever forcing themselves on women.

- *Three percent of adult Americans claim never to have had sex.*

Additional findings from this study are reported in subsequent chapters of this text. You can also obtain more information on the Web (http://www. norc.uchicago.edu/faqs/sex.htm).

The Youth Risk Behavior Survey

The Youth Risk Behavior Survey (YRBS), conducted biannually by the Centers for Disease Control and Prevention (CDC), measures the prevalence of six categories of health risk behaviors among youths through representative national, state, and local surveys using a self-report questionnaire. Sexual behaviors that contribute to unintended pregnancy and sexually transmitted infections, including HIV, are among those assessed. The 2001 YRBS, a national survey of 13,601 students (grades 9–12, from 150 school districts) revealed the following (CDC, 2002a):

- Forty-six percent of students (43% of females and 49% of males) reported having had sexual intercourse during their lifetime.

- Fourteen percent of students (11% of females and 17% of males) reported having had sexual intercourse with four or more partners during their lifetime.

- Seven percent of students (4% of females and 9% of males) reported having initiated sexual intercourse before age 13.

- Fifty-eight percent of students (51% of females and 65% of males) who reported being currently sexually active also reported using a condom during their most recent sexual intercourse.

- Eighteen percent of students (21% of females and 15% of males) who reported being currently sexually active also reported that either they or their partner had used oral contraceptives before their most recent sexual intercourse.

- Five percent of students reported that they had ever been pregnant or had ever gotten someone pregnant.

- Twenty-six percent of students (21% of females and 31% of males) who reported being currently sexually active also reported using alcohol or drugs prior to their most recent sexual intercourse.

- Eight percent of students (10% of females and 5% of males) reported ever being forced to have sexual intercourse.

See http://www.cdc.gov/mmwr/preview/mmwrhtml/ss510al.htm for more information on the 2001 YRBS.

Researchers often analyze YRBS data to determine the health risk behaviors of certain groups. For example, analysis of 1999 YRBS data of rural adolescents determined that there were relationships between several health and sexual risk behaviors. In general, the analysis found that rural adolescents who initiated sexual intercourse at an early age (prior to age 15) were at a markedly greater risk for engaging in subsequent sexual risk behaviors, such as having multiple sex partners and not using condoms during intercourse (Yarber, Milhausen, Crosby, & DiClemente, 2002).

The Behavioral Risk Factor Surveillance System

Initiated in 1984, the Behavioral Risk Factor Surveillance System is an annual state-based surveillance system sponsored by the Centers for Disease Control and Prevention. The system gathers information from the states on health behaviors such as physical injury, weight control, alcohol consumption, tobacco use, and, since 1990, HIV and AIDS. Data are collected monthly through random telephone interviews of individuals, age 18 or older. For the 1997 survey, 23 states, the District of Columbia, and Puerto Rico added HIV-related sexual behaviors to their surveys. The authors of a report on this survey of 35,484 adults, age 18–49, found that most of the respondents of this survey did engage in behaviors that placed them at risk for HIV infection. Major findings of the survey include the following:

- Over the past 12 months, 77% reported one sex partner, 18% reported no partners, and 2% reported four or more partners.

- Twenty-six percent reported using a condom during their most recent sexual intercourse. Slightly over half reported that the condom was used to prevent both disease and pregnancy. Less than 10% used a condom solely to prevent disease.

- Ninety percent said that a condom was very effective for preventing HIV.

- Less than 3% reported that they had been treated for an STI in the past 5 years.

- Less than 10% believed that their chances of acquiring HIV were medium to high.

- Males, younger persons, and Blacks were more likely to report two or more partners but were also more likely to report using a condom during their most recent sexual intercourse.

- Those who were single, separated, divorced, or widowed were more likely than those who were married to report two or more sexual partners in the previous year.

- Those reporting increased perceived risk for HIV were more likely to be tested for HIV voluntarily.

See D. Holtzman and his colleagues (2001) for more details.

The National Survey of Family Growth

Periodically, the National Center for Health Statistics (NCHS) conducts the National Survey of Family Growth (NSFG) to collect data related to marriage, divorce, contraception, infertility, and the health of women and infants in the United States. In their 2002–2003 survey, for the first time, the NSFG interviewed both men and women. More than 250 studies in academic journals and NCHS reports have been published using NSFG data. One journal report of 1995 NSFG data concerned marriage aspirations of cohabiting women (Manning & Smock, 2002). The report found that one in four unmarried women who were living with a man did not expect to marry him, a figure that has not changed much since the late 1980s. The most important factor in the women's expectation of marriage was the man's social and economic status; that is, those perceiving low status of the man did not expect to marry him. Further, older women and those who were divorced or who had previously cohabited were less likely to expect marriage. See the National Center for Health Statistics National Survey of Family Growth Web site (http://www.cdc.gov/nchs/nsfg.html) for information about the surveys and for copies of many of their reports.

The College Alcohol Study

The Harvard School of Public Health College Alcohol Study (CAS) is a multisite survey of a nationally representative sample of students at four-year colleges. Conducted several times during the past decade, the CAS examines college alcohol abuse and other high-risk behaviors, including tobacco and illegal drug use, violence, and unsafe sex. Study results have been published in more than 40 articles and reports. One recent report, using 1997 CAS data, examined the differences in the selected sexual health behaviors between college students with same-sex sexual experiences and those with only other-sex partners (Eisenberg, 2001). Questionnaires were mailed to a random sample of students at 130 colleges, and a total of 14,521 responded. Major findings include the following:

- Almost three-quarters (71%) of the respondents reported being sexually experienced.

- Ninety-five percent reported that their sexual experiences had been exclusively with other-sex partners, and 5% reported sexual experiences with their own sex (of those, 3% had partners of both sexes and 2% had only same-sex partners).

- Less than one-half (43%) reported always using a condom during sexual intercourse, and 24% reported never using condoms.

- About two-thirds (64%) reported a single sexual partner in the past 30 days; 30% reported no sexual partner in the same period.

- Female students reporting both-sex partners and males reporting both-sex and only same-sex partners were more likely to have had more than one sex partner than were students with only other-sex partners.

- Non-White students and older male students tended to report more sexual partners in the past 30 days, and younger students and those who lived on campus were more likely to report consistent condom use. Men reporting more sex partners tended to report less consistent condom use.

Source: "Difference in sexual risk behaviors between college students with same sex and opposite sex experience: Results from a national survey" by M. Eisenberg in Archives of Sexual Behavior, 30, pp. 575–89, 2001. Reprinted by permission of Kluwer Academic/Plenum Publishers and the author.

The Community Intervention Trial for Youth

The Community Intervention Trial for Youth (CITY) project, funded by the Centers for Disease Control and Prevention, is a multisite evaluation of a comprehensive community-level HIV prevention intervention being conducted in 13 urban areas of the United States. Men were eligible to participate if they, for example, were 15–25 years of age and reported sexual experiences with a male in the past year. During the summer of 2000, 3075 men completed a 20-minute interview dealing with their most recent sexual encounter with main and nonmain partners, including whether they were "high on drugs or alcohol." Nearly one-fifth (19%) with a main partner reported being high during their most recent sexual encounter. One-quarter with a main sex partner reported having anal intercourse without condom use. Among men with a nonmain partner, 29% reported being high, and 12% reported having anal intercourse without condom use. See Ann Stueve and her colleagues (2002) for more details.

EMERGING RESEARCH PERSPECTIVES

Although sex research continues to explore diverse aspects of human sexuality, some scholars feel that their particular interests have been given insufficient attention. Feminists and gay, lesbian, bisexual, and transgender scholars have focused their research on issues that mainstream scholars have largely ignored. And ethnic research, only now beginning to be undertaken, points to the lack of knowledge about the sexuality of some ethnic groups, such as African Americans, Latinos, Asian Americans, and Native Americans. These emerging research perspectives enrich our knowledge of sexuality.

Feminist Scholarship

The initial feminist research generated an immense amount of ground-breaking work on women in almost every field of the social sciences and humanities. Feminists made gender and gender-related issues significant research questions in a multitude of academic disciplines. In the field of sexuality, feminists expanded the scope of research to include the subjective experience and meaning of sexuality for women; sexual pleasure; sex and power; erotic material; and issues of female victimization, such as rape, the sexual abuse of children, and sexual harassment.

There is no single feminist perspective; instead, there are several. For our purposes, **feminism** is "a movement that involves women and men working together for equality" (McCormick, 1996); it cannot be construed more narrowly as only women working toward greater equality for women. Neither is feminism a license for political rigidity, division, or intolerance of diversity (McCormick, 1996). Feminism centers on understanding female experience in cultural and historical context—that is, the social construction of gender asymmetry (Pollis, 1988). **Social construction** is the development of social categories, such as masculinity, femininity, heterosexuality, and homosexuality, by society.

Feminists believe in these basic principles:

- *Gender is significant in all aspects of social life.* Like socioeconomic status and ethnicity, gender influences a person's position in society.

- *The female experience of sex has been devalued.* By emphasizing genital sex and such aspects of it as frequency of sexual intercourse and number of orgasms, both researchers and society ignore other important aspects of sexuality, such as kissing, caressing, love, commitment, and communication. Sexuality in lesbian relationships is even more devalued. Until the 1980s, most research on homosexuality centered on gay men, making lesbian women invisible.

- *Power is a critical element in male-female relationships.* Because women are subordinated to men as a result of our cultural beliefs about gender, women generally have less power than men. As a result, feminists believe that men have defined female sexuality to benefit themselves. Not only do men decide when to initiate sex, but the man's orgasm often takes precedence over the woman's. The most brutal form of the male expression of sexual power is rape.

- *Traditional empirical research needs to be combined with qualitative research and interpretive studies to provide a full understanding of human sexuality.* Because social science emphasizes objectivity and quantification, its methodology prevents us from fully exploring the complexity of what sex "means" and how it is personally experienced.

- *Ethnic diversity must be addressed.* Women of color, feminists point out, face a double stigma: being female *and* being from a minority group. Although very few studies exist on ethnicity and sexuality, feminists are committed to examining the role of ethnicity in female sexuality.

Despite its contributions, feminist research and the feminist approach have often been marginalized and considered subversive in many academic circles (McCormick 1996). However, the feminist perspective in sex research has expanded in recent years, and many more women are making important contributions to the advancement of sexual science. Women have increasingly assumed leadership roles in professional organizations and societies, and more are earning advanced degrees in sexuality-related fields. As one consequence, the literature, particularly that of a qualitative nature, will increase and will further our understanding of female as well as male sexuality.

Gay, Lesbian, Bisexual, and Transgender Research

During the nineteenth century, sexuality became increasingly perceived as the domain of science, especially medicine. Physicians competed with ministers, priests, and rabbis in defining what was "correct" sexual behavior. However, as noted previously, medicine's so-called scientific conclusions were not scientific; rather, they were morality disguised as science. "Scientific" definitions of healthy sex closely resembled religious definitions of moral sex. In studying sexual activities between men, medical researchers "invented" and popularized the distinction between heterosexuality and homosexuality (Gay, 1986; Weeks, 1986).

Early Researchers and Reformers   Although most physician-moralists condemned same-sex relationships as not only immoral but also pathological, a few individuals stand out in their attempt to understand same-sex sexuality.

KARL HEINRICH ULRICHS   Karl Ulrichs (1825–1895) was a German poet and political activist who in the 1860s developed the first scientific theory about homosexuality (Kennedy, 1988). As a rationalist, he believed reason was superior to religious belief and therefore rejected religion as superstition. He argued from logic and inference and collected case studies from numerous men to reinforce his beliefs. Ulrichs maintained that men who were attracted to other men represented a third sex, whom he called "Urnings." Urnings were born as Urnings; their sexuality was not the result of immorality or pathology. Ulrichs believed that Urnings had a distinctive feminine quality about them that distinguished them from men who desired women. He fought for Urning rights and the liberalization of sex laws.

KARL MARIA KERTBENY   Karl Kertbeny (1824–1882), a Hungarian physician, created the terms "heterosexuality" and "homosexuality" in his attempt to understand same-sex relationships (Feray & Herzer, 1990). Kertbeny believed that "homosexualists" were as "manly" as "heterosexualists." For this reason, he broke with Ulrichs's conceptualization of Urnings as inherently "feminine" (Herzer, 1985). Kertbeny argued that homosexuality was inborn and thus not immoral. He also maintained "the rights of man" (quoted in Herzer, 1985):

> The rights of man begin . . . with man himself. And that which is most immediate to man is his own body, with which he can undertake fully and freely, to his advantage or disadvantage, that which he pleases, insofar as in so doing he does not disturb the rights of others.

MAGNUS HIRSCHFELD   In the first few decades of the twentieth century, there was a great ferment of reform in England and other parts of Europe. While Havelock Ellis was the leading reformer in England, Magnus Hirschfeld (1868–1935) was the leading crusader in Germany, especially for homosexual rights.

Hirschfeld was a homosexual and possibly a transvestite (a person who wears clothing of the other sex). He eloquently presented the case for the humanity of transvestites (Hirschfeld, 1991). And in defense of homosexual rights, he argued that homosexuality was not a perversion but the result of the hormonal development of inborn traits. His defense of homosexuality led to the popularization of the word "homosexual." Hirschfeld's importance, however, lies not so much in his theory of homosexuality as in his sexual reform efforts. In Berlin in 1897, he helped found the first organization for homosexual rights. In addition, he founded the first journal devoted to the study of sexuality and the first Institute of Sexual Science, where he gathered a library of more than 20,000 volumes.

When Hitler took power in Germany, the Nazis attacked the sexual reform movement and destroyed Hirschfeld's institute. In fear for his life, Hirschfeld fled into exile and died several years later (Bullough, 1976; see Wolff, 1986, for Hirschfeld's biography).

Magnus Hirschfeld (1868–1935) was a leading European sex reformer who championed homosexual rights. He founded the first institute for the study of sexuality, which was burned when the Nazis took power in Germany. Hirschfeld fled for his life.

EVELYN HOOKER   As a result of Kinsey's research, Americans learned that same-sex sexual relationships were widespread among both men and women. A few years later, psychologist Evelyn Hooker (1907–1996) startled her colleagues by demonstrating that homosexuality in itself was not a psychological disorder. She found that "typical" gay men did not differ significantly in personality characteristics from "typical" heterosexual men (Hooker, 1957). The reverberations of her work continue to this day (McWhirter, 1990).

Earlier studies had erroneously reported psychopathology among gay men and lesbian women for two reasons. First, because most researchers were clinicians, their samples consisted mainly of gay men and lesbian women who were seeking treatment. The researchers failed to compare their results against a control group of similar heterosexual individuals. (A **control group** is a group that is not being treated or experimented on; it controls for any variables that are introduced from outside the experiment, such as a major media report related to the topic of the experiment.) Second, researchers were predisposed to believe that homosexuality was in itself a sickness, reflecting traditional beliefs about homosexuality. Consequently, emotional problems were automatically attributed to the client's homosexuality rather than to other sources.

Recent Contributions: Michel Foucault

One of the most influential social theorists in the twentieth-century was the French thinker Michel Foucault (1926–1984). A cultural historian and philosopher, Foucault explored how society creates social ideas and how these ideas operate to further the established order. His most important work on sexuality was *The History of Sexuality, Volume I* (1980), a book that gave fresh impetus to scholars interested in the social construction of sex, especially those involved in gender and gay and lesbian studies.

Foucault challenged the belief that our sexuality is rooted in nature. Instead, he argued, it is rooted in society. Society "constructs" sexuality,

Evelyn Hooker (1907–1996) conducted landmark research on homosexuals in the 1950s, finding that "typical" gay men had personalities similar to those of "typical" heterosexual men.

Michel Foucault (1926–1984) of France was one of the most important thinkers who influenced our understanding of how society "constructs" human sexuality.

including homosexuality and heterosexuality. Foucault's critics contend, however, that he underestimated the biological basis of sexual impulses and the role individuals play in creating their own sexuality.

Contemporary Gay, Lesbian, Bisexual, and Transgender Research   In 1973, the American Psychiatric Association (APA) removed homosexuality from its list of psychological disorders in its *Diagnostic and Statistical Manual of Mental Disorders (DSM-II)*. The APA decision was reinforced by similar resolutions by the American Psychological Association and the American Sociological Association. More recently, in 1997 at its annual meeting, the American Psychological Association overwhelmingly passed a resolution stating that there is no sound scientific evidence on the efficacy of reparative therapies for gay men and lesbian women. This statement reinforced the association's earlier stand that, because there is nothing "wrong" with homosexuality, there is no reason to try to change sexual orientation through therapy. In 1998, the APA issued a statement opposing reparative therapy, thus joining the American Psychological Association, the American Academy of Pediatrics, the American Medical Association, the American Counseling Association, and the National Association of Social Workers.

As a result of the rejection of the psychopathological model, social and behavioral research on gay men, lesbian women, and bisexual individuals has moved in a new direction. Research no longer focuses primarily on the causes and cures of homosexuality, and most of the new research approaches homosexuality in a neutral manner.

Directions for Future Research

Historically, sex research has focused on preventive health, which "prioritizes sexuality as a social problem and behavioral risk" (di Mauro, 1995). In light of the HIV/AIDS pandemic and other social problems, this emphasis is important, but it fails to examine the full spectrum of individuals' behaviors or the social and cultural factors that drive those behaviors.

According to Diane di Mauro (1995), three priorities of applied and basic research in sexuality need to be recognized: (1) research that integrates an expanded definition of sexuality, one that provides a thorough knowledge of human sexuality, (2) relevant intervention research that is attuned to communication needs and incorporates appropriate evaluative processes, and (3) a more accepting and positive depiction of sexuality.

Sex research, globally, faces several challenges. Few sex researchers and sex research centers exist worldwide, particularly in developing countries. Only a few Western countries have comprehensive statistics, and most of them are about fertility or STIs rather than sexual behaviors of various groups. There is no international depository for sex data. Few standardized terms exist in sex research. Lastly, quantitative data are especially difficult to obtain, and qualitative data are less suitable for international comparisons (MacKay, 2001).

Janet Hyde (2001), professor of psychology and women's studies at the University of Wisconsin–Madison, predicts that sexual science will advance the most in the next decade if researchers learn from their neighboring social and biological sciences, and the humanities as well.

ETHNICITY AND SEXUALITY

In recent years, researchers have begun to recognize the significance of ethnicity in various aspects of American life, including sexuality. Researchers are beginning to understand differences in sexual behavior among ethnic groups, as well as within specific ethnic groups. However, a review of ethnicity in 25 years of published sexuality research revealed a deficit in empirical investigation (Wiederman, Maynard, & Fretz, 1996). Though the results indicated modest increases in ethnic diversity of research samples, important questions must still be addressed. These include the differences that socioeconomic status and environment play in sexual behaviors, the way in which questions are posed in research studies, the research methods that are used, and researchers' preconceived notions regarding ethnic differences. Diversity-related bias can be so ingrained in the way research is conducted (Rogler, 1999) that is difficult to detect. Although limited research is available, we, the authors, attempt to provide some background to assist an understanding of sexuality and ethnicity.

African Americans

African Americans represent the second-largest ethnic group in America. Several factors must be considered when African American sexuality is studied, including sexual stereotypes, socioeconomic status, Black subculture, and the number of single adults.

Sexual stereotypes greatly distort our understanding of Black sexuality. One of the most common stereotypes is the depiction of Blacks as sexually driven. This stereotype, which dates back to the fifteenth century, continues to hold considerable strength among non-Blacks. Robert Staples (1991) writes: "Black men are saddled with a number of stereotypes that label them as irresponsible, criminalistic, hypersexual, and lacking in masculine traits."

Nearly half of all African Americans are middle class in lifestyle and income.

But the reality is, no one has attempted a comprehensive evaluation of the sexuality of Black males (Grimes, 1999).

Socioeconomic status is a person's ranking in society based on a combination of occupational, educational, and income levels. It is an important element in African American sexual values and behaviors (Staples & Johnson, 1993). Although stereotypes suggest that *all* Blacks have a low income, a well-educated and economically secure middle class has evolved (Giles, 1994).

Values and behaviors are shaped by culture and social class. The subculture of Blacks of low socioeconomic status is deeply influenced by poverty, discrimination, and structural subordination. In contrast to middle-class Whites and Blacks, low-income Blacks are more likely to engage in sexual intercourse at an earlier age and to have children outside of marriage. Because of the poverty, violence, and prejudice of inner-city life, many low-income Black children do not experience a prolonged or "innocent" childhood. They are forced to become adults at an early age.

For inner-city Blacks, nonmarital sexual activity is usually not considered immoral, nor is it stigmatized, as it is in middle-class communities. Because sexual activity is regarded as natural, sex outside of marriage is considered appropriate as relationships become more committed. Furthermore, as mere survival is hardly guaranteed, adolescents may see no reason to wait for a future they may never have. In the inner-city subculture, boys tend to use sex exploitatively and competitively. For them, sex is not so much a means of achieving intimacy with partners as it is a way of achieving status among their male peers. For girls, sex is a means of demonstrating their maturity; it is a sign of their womanhood.

For many inner-city Black adolescent females, one becomes a woman by becoming a mother (Zinn & Eitzen, 1990). In 2000, an estimated 44% of Black households were headed by a single mother (U.S. Department of Commerce, 2001). The Black community, which values children highly, generally does not stigmatize the unmarried mother. For Blacks of all classes, there is no such thing as an "illegitimate" or "illegally born" child. All children are considered valuable (Collins, 1991).

About 48% of African American women are single (U.S. Bureau of the Census, 2000). Among African Americans, there are many more "available" women than men. This gender imbalance is the result of high rates of death, incarceration, and drug use among Black men, often attributable to the effects of discrimination. If they wish to have children, many African American women are likely to be unmarried single parents. Furthermore, the single lifestyle, whether White or Black, is associated with more sexual partners, a lack of contraceptive responsibility, and a greater likelihood of contracting STIs.

Although there has been a significant increase in African American research, much still needs to be done. For example, researchers need to (1) explore the sexual attitudes and behaviors of the general African American population, not merely adolescents, (2) examine Black sexuality from an African American cultural viewpoint, and (3) utilize a cultural equivalency perspective that rejects differences between Blacks and Whites as signs of inherent deviance. (The **cultural equivalency perspective** is the view that the attitudes, values, and behaviors of one ethnic group are similar to those of another ethnic group.)

One example of a recent research project concerning African American sexuality was a study of the association of selected individual and family characteristics with age of sexual initiation and the lifetime number of sexual partners among African American men (Bakken & Winter, 2002). This study was conducted to further understand factors associated with sexual risk in Black men given that STI prevalence is higher among Black males than among males of other ethnic groups. Data from 1125 Black men participating in the 1991 National Survey of Men were analyzed. Men whose mothers worked were likely to initiate sexual intercourse at an earlier age than others. Those raised by both parents were likely to delay onset of sexual intercourse and to have fewer lifetime sexual partners. Men who were married or initiated sexual intercourse at an older age were likely to have fewer total number of partners than others. The study authors concluded that "school and community programs should provide culturally appropriate and accessible activities for black youth, and should reach black males early, while they are still in elementary school." They also recommended education programs to help parents communicate effectively with their children about sexuality-related issues.

Latinos

Latinos are the fastest-growing ethnic group in the United States. There is very little research, however, about Latino sexuality.

Two common stereotypes depict Latinos as sexually permissive and Latino males as pathologically macho. Like African Americans, Latino males are often stereotyped as being "promiscuous," engaging in excessive and indiscriminate sexual activities. No research, however, validates this stereotype.

The macho stereotype paints Latino males as hypermasculine—swaggering and domineering. But the stereotype of machismo distorts its cultural meaning among Latinos. (The Spanish word was originally incorporated into

In studying Latino sexuality, it is important to remember that Latinos come from diverse ethnic groups, including Mexican American, Cuban American, and Puerto Rican, each with its own unique background and set of cultural values.

English in the 1960s as a slang term to describe any male who was sexist.) Within its cultural context, however, **machismo** is a positive concept, celebrating the values of courage, strength, generosity, politeness, and respect for others. And in day-to-day functioning, relations between Latino men and women are significantly more egalitarian than the macho stereotype suggests. This is especially true among Latinos who are more acculturated (Sanchez, 1997). (**Acculturation** is the process of adaptation of an ethnic group to the values, attitudes, and behaviors of the dominant culture.)

Another trait of Latino life is **familismo,** a commitment to family and family members. Rafael Diaz (1998) notes that familismo can be a strong factor in helping heterosexual Latinos reduce rates of unprotected sex with casual partners outside of primary relationships. He warns, however, that for many Latino men who have sex with men familismo and homophobia can create conflict because families may perceive homosexuality as wrong.

Three important factors must be considered when Latino sexuality is studied: (1) diversity of ethnic groups, (2) significance of socioeconomic status, and (3) degree of acculturation. Latinos comprise numerous ethnic subgroups, the largest of which are Mexican Americans, Puerto Ricans, and Cubans (Vega, 1991). Each group has its own unique background and set of cultural traditions that affect sexual attitudes and behaviors. For example, because of issues related to economics, education, and access, many Latinas do not get timely prenatal care in the first three months of pregnancy. Specifically, 11% of Cuban Americans, 26% of Puerto Ricans, 27% of Central and South Americans, and 31% of Mexican Americans fail to do so. Yet Latinas have infant mortality rates comparable to those of White women (7%) and lower than those of African American women (17%) and Native American women (13%) ("Latina Women's Health," 2000).

Socioeconomic status is important, as middle-class Latino values appear to differ from those of low-income Latinos. The birth rate for single women, for example, is significantly higher among low-income Latinas than among middle-class Latinas (Bean & Tienda, 1987). Furthermore, Latino ethnic groups rank differently on the socioeconomic scale. The middle class is largest among Cuban Americans, followed by Puerto Ricans and then Mexican Americans.

Degree of acculturation may be the most important factor affecting sexual attitudes and behavior among Latinos. This can be viewed on a continuum, with traditional at one pole, bicultural in the middle, and acculturated at the other pole (Guerrero Pavich, 1986). (This same continuum may also be used with other ethnic groups, such as European Americans, Asian Americans, and Caribbean and Pacific Islanders.) *Traditional* Latinos were born and raised in Latin America; they adhere to the norms, customs, and values of their original homeland, speak mostly Spanish, and have strong religious ties. Foreign-born Latinos, who may number as many as 13 million, hold the most traditional values. *Bicultural* Latinos may have been born in either Latin America or the United States; they speak both Spanish and English, function well in both Latino and Anglo cultures, and have moderate religious ties. *Acculturated* Latinos do not identify with their Latino heritage; they speak only English and have (at most) moderate religious ties.

Rebellion against the native culture may be expressed through sexual behavior (Sanchez, 1997). Traditional Latinos tend to place a high value on female virginity while encouraging males, beginning in adolescence, to be sexually active (Guerrero Pavich, 1986). Females are viewed according to a virgin/whore dichotomy—"good" girls are virgins and "bad" girls are sexual (Espín, 1984). Females are taught to put the needs of others, especially males, before their own. Among traditional Latinos, fears about American "sexual immorality" produce their own stereotypes of Anglos. Adolescent boys learn about masturbation from peers; girls rarely learn about it because of its tabooed nature. There is little acceptance of gay men and lesbian women, whose relationships are often regarded as "unnatural" or sinful (Bonilla & Porter, 1990).

In traditional Latino culture, Catholicism plays an important role, especially in the realm of sexuality. The Church advocates premarital virginity and prohibits both contraception and abortion. For traditional Latinas, using contraception may lead to "considerable guilt and confusion on the part of the individual woman who feels she is alone in violating the cultural taboos against contraception" (Guerrero Pavich, 1986). Traditional Latinas are generally negative toward birth control; however, some evidence suggests that women are increasingly approving of and using available contraception (Baca-Zinn, 1994). Abortion is virtually out of the question; only the most acculturated Latinas view abortion as an option.

Among bicultural Latinos, there may be gender-role conflict (Salgado de Snyder, Cervantes, & Padilla, 1990). Emma Guerrero Pavich (1986) describes the conflicts some Latinas experience: "She observes the freedom and sexual expression 'Americanas' have. At first she may condemn them as 'bad women'; later she may envy their freedom. Still later she may begin to want those freedoms for herself" (Guerrero Pavich, 1986). For bicultural Latinos, sexual values and attitudes appear to lie at different points along the continuum, depending on the degree of acculturation.

There is significantly greater flux among Latinos as a result of continuing high rates of immigration and the acculturation process. Much current research on Latinos focuses on the acculturation of new immigrants. We know less, however, about bicultural Latinos and even less about acculturated Latinos.

Asian Americans and Pacific Islanders

Asian Americans and Pacific Islanders represent one of the fastest-growing and most diverse populations in the United States, accounting for about 4.1% of the total population in the United States today. Among the oldest and largest groups are Japanese Americans and Chinese Americans. Other groups include Vietnamese, Laotians, Cambodians, Koreans, Filipinos, Asian Indians, Native Hawaiians, and other Pacific Islanders. Numbering more than 9 million people, they speak more than 40 different languages and represent a similar number of distinct cultures.

Significant differences in attitudes, values, and practices make it difficult to generalize about these groups without stereotyping and oversimplifying. Given this caveat, we can say that many Asian Americans are less individualistic and more relationship oriented than members of other cultures. Individuals are seen as the products of their relationships to nature and other people (Shon & Ja, 1982). Asian Americans are less verbal and expressive in their interactions and often rely on indirection and nonverbal communication, such as silence and avoidance of eye contact as signs of respect (Del Carmen, 1990).

Access to health care can be limited among Asian Americans and Pacific Islanders due to cultural and language differences, as well as economic and other barriers. For example, breast and cervical cancer screening rates are much lower than the national average ("Asian American and Pacific Islander," 2000). Consequently, the cervical cancer incidence rate among Vietnamese women is nearly 5 times that of White women; Native Hawaiians have the highest breast cancer mortality rate of any ethnic group in the United States. Furthermore, hepatitis B is 25–75 times more common among Samoans and immigrants from Cambodia, Laos, Vietnam, and China than the U.S. average.

More than half of Chinese Americans are foreign born. In traditional Chinese culture, the in-laws of a married woman were responsible for safeguarding her chastity and keeping her under the ultimate control of her spouse. Where extended families worked and lived in close quarters for extended periods, many spouses found it difficult to experience intimacy with each other. Though not much is known about mate selection among the foreign-born U.S. Chinese population, of those born in the United States, love and compatibility are the basis for marriage partners (Ishii-Kuntz, 1997a). As in other Asian American populations, the rate of cross-cultural marriage among younger Chinese Americans is higher than in their parents' and grandparents' generations. Still, Confucian principles, which teach women to be obedient to their spouse's wishes and attentive to their needs and to be sexually loyal, play a part in maintaining exclusivity and holding down the divorce rate among traditional Chinese families (Ishii-Kuntz, 1997a). In contrast, men are expected to be sexually experienced, and their engagement in nonmarital sex is frequently accepted. Chinese American parents tend to teach their children to control their emotional expressions; thus, affection is not often displayed openly (Uba, 1994).

For more than a century, Japanese Americans have maintained a significant presence in the United States (Ishii-Kuntz, 1997b). Japanese cultural values of loyalty and harmony are strongly embedded in Confucianism and feudalism (loyalty to the ruler), yet Japanese lives are not strongly influenced by religion (Ishii-Kuntz, 1997b). Like Chinese Americans born in the United States, Japanese Americans born in the United States base partner selection more on love and individual compatibility than on family concerns (Nakano, 1990). Among the newest generation of Japanese Americans, the incidence of cross-cultural marriage has risen dramatically, to about 50–60% (Kitano, 1994).

Traditional Japanese values allowed sexual freedom for men but not for women. Traditionally, Japanese women were expected to remain pure; sexual permissiveness or nonexclusiveness on the part of women was considered socially disruptive and threatening (Ishii-Kuntz, 1997b). Over time, attitudes and conditions related to sexuality have changed, so that sexual activity is no longer considered solely procreational, and there is increased use of contraceptives. Japanese Americans have one of the lowest divorce rates of any group in the United States. A desire not to shame the family or the community may partially account for this low rate.

Within most Asian cultures, self-disclosure is viewed unfavorably. Quick self-disclosure of personal information may give the impression of emotional imbalance. Overall, educational achievement is highly valued, a strong sense of responsibility toward relatives exists, a failure to live up to

Among Asian Americans (as with other ethnic groups), attitudes toward relationships, family, and sexuality are related to the degree of acculturation.

elders' expectations results in self-blame, and respect for elders is equated with respect for authority. As with other groups, the degree of acculturation may be the most important factor affecting sexual attitudes and behaviors. Compared with those who were raised in the United States, those who were born and raised in their original homeland tend to adhere more closely to their culture's norms, customs, and values.

Sumie Okazaki (2002) reviewed the scientific literature concerning several aspects of Asian Americans' sexuality: sexual knowledge, attitudes, and norms; sexual behavior; sexual and reproductive health; sexual abuse and aggression; and sexual orientation. She found no literature on sexual dysfunction and treatment. Okazaki reports that she found notable differences in several sexuality-related areas between Asian Americans and other ethnic groups:

> For example, relative to other U.S. ethnic group cohorts, Asian American adolescents and young adults tend to show more sexually conservative attitudes and behavior and initiate intercourse at a later age. There are indications that as Asian Americans become more acculturated to the mainstream American culture, their attitudes and behavior become more consistent with the White American norm. Consistent with their more sexually conservative tendencies in normative sexual behavior, Asian American women also appear more reluctant to obtain sexual and reproductive health care, which in turn places them at greater risk for delay in treatment for breast and cervical cancer as well as other gynecological problems.

Available data suggest that the prevalence rate of sexual abuse in Asian American communities appears lower than those of other groups, although it is not clear to what extent the low rates are due to cultural reluctance to report shameful experiences.

As in other areas of social science research, there are gaps concerning the sexuality of Asian Americans and other racial and ethnic groups. Obviously, more empirical work is needed.

> Men do not seek truth. It is the truth that pursues men who run away and will not look around.
>
> —*Lincoln Steffens (1866–1936)*

POPULAR CULTURE SURROUNDS US with sexual images, disseminated through advertising, music, television, film, video games, and the Internet, that form a backdrop to our daily living. Much of what is conveyed is simplified, overgeneralized, stereotypical, shallow—and entertaining. But through sex research, we can evaluate the mass of sex information disseminated through the media. Studying sexuality enables us to understand how research is conducted and to be aware of its strengths and its limitations. Traditional sex research has been expanded in recent years by feminist, gay, lesbian, bisexual, and transgender research, which provides fresh insights and perspectives. Although the study of sexuality and ethnicity is only now beginning to emerge, it promises to enlarge our understanding of the diversity of attitudes, behaviors, and values in contemporary America.

SUMMARY

Sex, Advice Columnists, and Pop Psychology

- The *sex information/advice genre* transmits information to both entertain and inform; the information is generally oversimplified so that it does not interfere with the genre's primary purpose, entertainment. Much of the information or advice conveys dominant social norms. Although it uses the social science framework, it tends to overgeneralize and distort.

Thinking Critically About Sexuality

- *Objective statements* are based on observations of things as they exist in themselves. *Value judgments* are evaluations based on moral or ethical standards. *Opinions* are unsubstantiated beliefs based on an individual's personal thoughts. *Biases* are personal leanings or inclinations. *Stereotypes*—rigidly held beliefs about the personal characteris-

tics of a group of people—are a type of *schema*, which is the organization of knowledge in our thought processes.

- *Attitudes* are predispositions to acting, thinking, or feeling certain ways toward things. *Behaviors* are the ways people act. Behaviors cannot necessarily be inferred from attitudes, or vice versa.

- *Fallacies* are errors in reasoning. The *egocentric fallacy* is the belief that others necessarily share one's own values, beliefs, and attitudes. The *ethnocentric fallacy* is the belief that one's own ethnic group, nation, or culture is inherently superior to any other.

Sex Research Methods

- Ethical issues are important concerns in sex research. The most important issues are *informed consent, protection from harm,* confidentiality, the use of *deception,* and *debriefing.*

- In sex research, *sampling* is a particularly acute problem. To be meaningful, samples should be representative of the larger group from which they are drawn. But most samples are limited by volunteer bias, dependence on college students, underrepresentation of ethnic groups, and difficulties in sampling gay men and lesbian women.

- The most important methods in sex research are clinical, survey, observational, and experimental. *Clinical research* relies on in-depth examinations of individuals or groups who come to the clinician seeking treatment for psychological or medical problems. *Survey research* uses questionnaires, interviews, or diaries, for example, to gather information from a representative sample of people. *Observational research* requires the researcher to observe interactions carefully in as unobtrusive a manner as possible. *Experimental research* presents subjects with various stimuli under controlled conditions in which their responses can be measured.

- Experiments are controlled through the use of *independent variables* (which can be changed by the experimenter) and *dependent variables* (which change in relation to changes in the independent variable). Clinical, survey, and observational research efforts, in contrast, are *correlational studies* that reveal relationships between variables without manipulating them. In experimental research, physiological responses are often measured by *plethysmographs*, *strain gauges*, or *Rigiscans*™.

The Sex Researchers

- Richard von Krafft-Ebing was one of the earliest sex researchers. His work emphasized the pathological aspects of sexuality.

- Sigmund Freud was one of the most influential thinkers in Western civilization. Freud believed there were five stages in psychosexual development: the *oral stage, anal stage, phallic stage, latency stage*, and *genital stage*.

- Havelock Ellis was the first modern sexual thinker. His ideas included the relativity of sexual values, the normality of masturbation, a belief in the sexual equality of men and women, the redefinition of "normal," and a reevaluation of homosexuality.

- Alfred Kinsey's work documented enormous diversity in sexual behavior, emphasized the role of masturbation in sexual development, and argued that the distinction between normal and abnormal behavior was meaningless. The Kinsey scale charts sexual activities along a continuum ranging from exclusively other-sex behaviors to exclusively same-sex behaviors.

- William Masters and Virginia Johnson detailed the physiology of the human sexual response cycle. Their physiological studies revealed the similarity between male and female sexual responses and demonstrated that women achieve orgasm through clitoral stimulation. Their work on sexual inadequacy revolutionized sex therapy through the use of behavioral techniques.

Contemporary Research Studies

- The National Health and Social Life Survey is one of the largest and most comprehensive studies of sexual behavior to date. Though controversy surrounds it, the study reveals new and interesting findings related to the social context of sexuality in America.

- The Youth Risk Behavior Study is a large, national, school-based study of the health behaviors of adolescents. Behaviors related to sexuality and risk taking are assessed.

- The Behavioral Risk Factor Surveillance System, sponsored by the Centers for Disease Control and Prevention, is an annual, national, state-based surveillance system that gathers information on a number of health behaviors, including HIV-related sexual behavior. Data are collected monthly through random telephone interviews of individuals age 18 or older.

- The National Survey of Family Growth (NSFG) is a periodic survey that collects data related to marriage, divorce, contraception, infertility, and the health of women and infants in the United States. For the first time, the NSFG interviewed both men and women in its most recent survey.

- The Harvard School of Public Health College Alcohol Study (CAS) is a survey of a nationally representative sample of students at 4-year colleges. Conducted several times during the past decade, the CAS assesses college alcohol abuse and other high-risk behaviors, including unsafe sex, tobacco and illicit drug use, and violence.

- The Community Intervention Trial for Youth (CITY) project is an evaluation of a comprehensive community-level HIV prevention intervention conducted in 13 urban areas of the United States. The program is designed for young men, age 15–25, who have had sexual experiences with a male in the past year.

Emerging Research Perspectives

- There is no single feminist perspective in sex research.

- Most feminist researchers focus on gender issues, assume that the female experience of sex has been devalued, believe that power is a critical element in female-male relationships, argue that empirical research must be supplemented by qualitative research to capture the personal experience and meaning of sexuality, and explore ethnic diversity.

- Research on homosexuality has rejected the moralistic-pathological approach. Researchers in gay and lesbian issues include Karl Ulrichs, Karl Kertbeny, Magnus Hirschfeld, Evelyn Hooker, and Michel Foucault.

- Contemporary gay, lesbian, bisexual, and transgender research focuses on the psychological and social experience of being other than heterosexual.

Ethnicity and Sexuality

- The role of ethnicity in human sexuality has been largely overlooked until recently.

- *Socioeconomic status* is important in the study of African American sexuality. Other factors include the stereotype of Blacks as hypersexual and "promiscuous," the importance of the African American subculture, and the large number of single Black women.

- Two common stereotypes about Latinos are that they are sexually permissive and that males are pathologically macho. *Familismo* is a traditional Latino commitment to family support. Factors to consider in studying Latino sexuality include the diversity of national groups, such as Mexican American, Cuban American, and Puerto Rican; the role of socioeconomic status; and the degree of *acculturation*.

- Significant differences in attitudes, values, and practices make it difficult to generalize about Asian Americans and Pacific Islanders. Degree of acculturation may be the most important factor affecting sexual attitudes and behaviors. Religious and cultural values still play an important role in the lives of many Asian Americans and Pacific Islanders.

Sex and the Internet

The Kinsey Institute for Research in Sex, Gender, and Reproduction

Few centers that conduct research exclusively on sexuality exist in the world. One of the most respected and well known centers is The Kinsey Institute for Research in Sex, Gender, and Reproduction (KI) at Indiana University–Bloomington. The institute bears the name of its founder, Alfred C. Kinsey, whose research was described earlier in this chapter. Visit the institute's Web site (http://www.kinseyinstitute.org) and find out information about the following:

- The mission and history of KI
- A chronology of events and landmark publications
- The KI faculty and research staff
- KI's current research projects
- KI's clinics and exhibitions
- Graduate education in human sexuality at KI Indiana University
- Links to related sites in sexuality research

SUGGESTED WEB SITES

Advocates for Youth
http://www.advocatesforyouth.org
Focuses on teen sexual health; provides valuable data on issues related to teen sexual health.

Centers for Disease Control and Prevention
http://www.cdc.gov
A valuable source of research information about sexual behavior and related health issues in the United States.

Gallup Poll
http://www.gallup.com
Provides results of current surveys.

"Go Ask Alice"

http://www.goaskalice.com

A credible Internet question-and-answer service dealing with sexual and health issues, directed by the Columbia University Health Education Program.

Magnus Hirschfeld Archive for Sexology

http://www.rz.hu-berlin.de/sexology

Has an extensive history of early and contemporary sex researchers as well as other valuable sexology resources.

Society for the Scientific Study of Sexuality

http://www.sexcience.org

A nonprofit organization dedicated to the advancement of knowledge about sexuality; provides announcements of the SSSS conferences and other meetings.

U.S. Census Bureau

http://www.census.gov

The federal agency that collects and provides data about the people (e.g., family composition) and the economy of the United States.

SUGGESTED READING

Bancroft, John (Ed.). (1997). *Researching Sexual Behavior.* Bloomington: Indiana University Press. A discussion of the methodological issues of large-scale survey research in studying human sexuality.

Bullough, Vern L. (1994). *Science in the Bedroom: A History of Sex Research.* New York: Basic Books. A comprehensive history of sex research of the past century.

Wiederman, Michael, & Whitley, Bernard, Jr. (2002). *Handbook for Conducting Research on Human Sexuality.* Mahwah, NJ: Erlbaum. A reference tool for researchers and students interested in research in human sexuality from a variety of disciplines; examines the specific methodological issues inherent in conducting human sexuality research.

For links, articles, and study material, go to the McGraw-Hill Web site, located at http://www.mhhe.com/strong5

3

Female Sexual Anatomy, Physiology, and Response

"I identify with the passion [of women], the strength, the calmness, and the flexibility of being a woman. To me being a woman is like being the ocean. The ocean is a powerful thing, even at its calmest moments. It is a beauty that commands respect. It can challenge even the strongest men, and it gives birth to the smallest creatures. It is a provider, and an inspiration; this is a woman and this is what I am."

—20-year-old White female

"The more I think about things that annoy me about being a woman, the more I realize that those annoyances are what make it so special. When I get my period, it isn't just a "monthly curse"; it is a reminder that I can have children."

—19-year-old White female

"When I started my period, my father kept a bit of a distance. How could I forget [that day]? The entire family was at my aunt's house, and no one had pads. You would think among 67 or so people one female would have a pad. I remember crying and my grandmother asking me what was wrong. After I told her, she began to laugh and said it was a natural cycle. I knew this from sixth-grade sex education class, but I still didn't want it. I was finally a woman."

—19-year-old first-generation Indian female

ALTHOUGH WOMEN AND MEN are similar in many more ways than they are different, we tend to focus on the differences rather than the similarities. Various cultures hold diverse ideas about exactly what it means to be female or male, but virtually the only differences that are consistent are actual physical differences, most of which relate to sexual structure and function. In this chapter and the following one, we discuss both the similarities and the differences in the anatomy (body structures), physiology (body functions), and sexual response of females and males. This chapter introduces the sexual structures and functions of women's bodies, including hormones and the menstrual cycle. We also look at models of sexual arousal and response, the relationship of these to women's experiences of sex, and the role of orgasm. In Chapter 4, we discuss male anatomy and physiology, and in Chapter 5, we move beyond biology to look at gender and the meanings we ascribe to being female and male.

FEMALE SEX ORGANS: WHAT ARE THEY FOR?

Anatomically speaking, all embryos are female when their reproductive structures begin to develop (Figure 3.1). If it does not receive certain genetic and hormonal signals, the fetus will continue to develop as a female. In humans and most other mammals, the female, in addition to providing half the genetic instructions for the offspring, provides the environment in which it can develop until it becomes capable of surviving as a separate entity. She

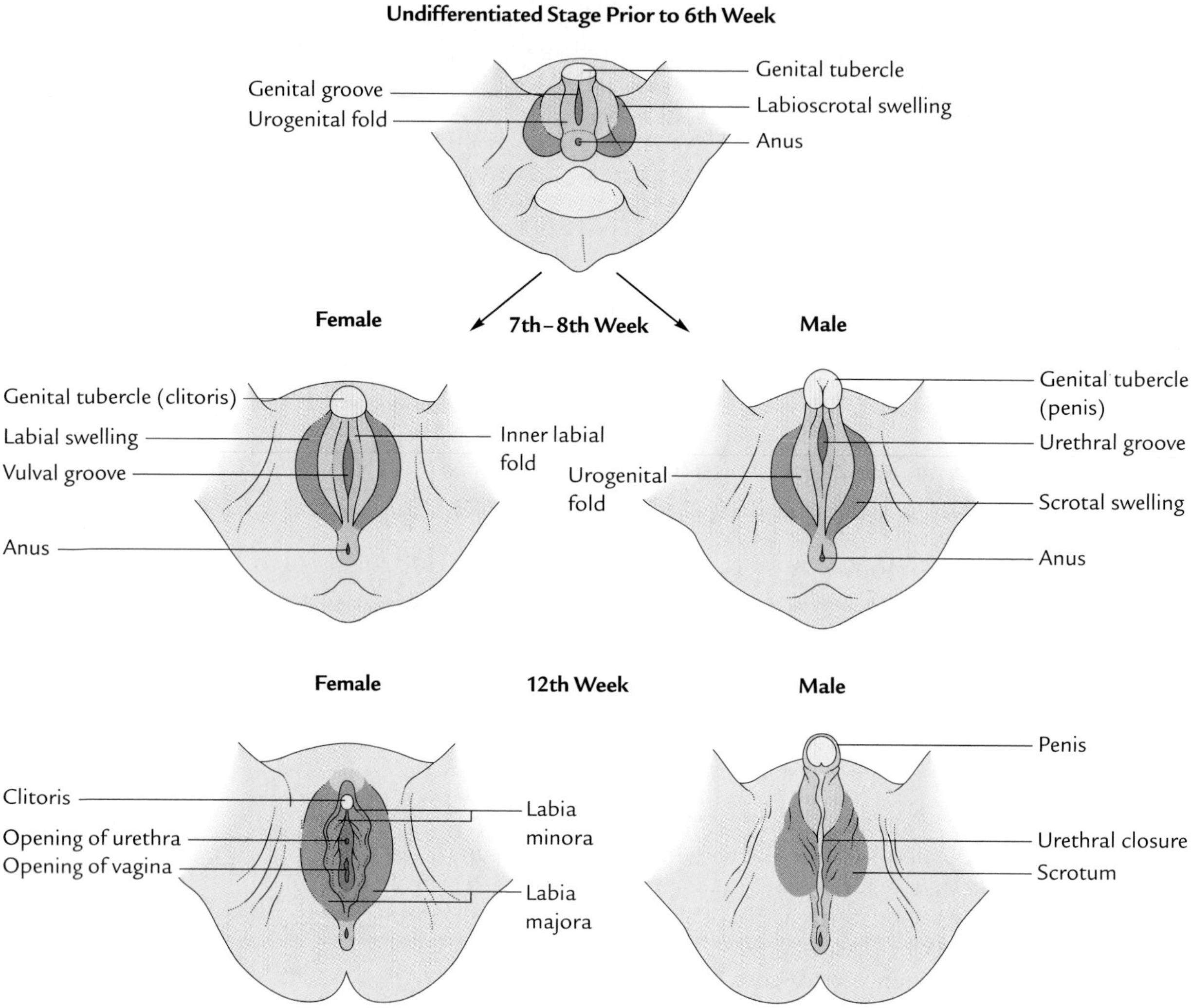

Undifferentiated Stage Prior to 6th Week

Genital groove — Genital tubercle
Urogenital fold — Labioscrotal swelling
— Anus

Female   **7th–8th Week**   **Male**

Genital tubercle (clitoris) —   — Genital tubercle (penis)
Labial swelling —   Inner labial fold   — Urethral groove
Vulval groove —   Urogenital fold   — Scrotal swelling
Anus —   — Anus

Female   **12th Week**   **Male**

Clitoris —   — Penis
Opening of urethra —   Labia minora
Opening of vagina —   Labia majora   — Urethral closure
          — Scrotum

FIGURE 3.1 Embryonic-Fetal Differentiation of the External Reproductive Organs. Female and male reproductive organs are formed from the same embryonic tissues. An embryo's external genitals are female in appearance until certain genetic and hormonal instructions signal the development of male organs. Without such instructions, the genitals continue to develop as female.

also nourishes the offspring, both during gestation (the period of carrying the young in the uterus) via the placenta and following birth via the breasts through lactation (milk production).

In spite of what we do know, researchers are finding that we haven't yet mapped all of the basic body parts of women, especially as they relate to the microprocesses of sexual response (Leland, 2000). Such issues as the range in average size of the clitoris, the existence and function of the G-spot, and the placement of the many nerves that spider through the pelvic cavity still loom large. Add to these puzzles the types, causes, and treatments of sexual problems and dysfunction and one can quickly see that the new science of sexual response is still emerging.

Clearly, the female sex organs serve a reproductive function. But they perform other functions as well. Some sexual parts serve to bring pleasure to their owners; they may also serve to attract potential sexual partners. Because of the mutual pleasure partners give each other, we can see that sexual structures also serve an important role in human relationships. People

Judy Chicago's The Dinner Party *comprises a triangular table consisting of 39 place settings. Each one forms a kind of abstract portrait of a woman of great historical significance. This one is a testimony to Margaret Sanger, the pioneering campaigner for birth control.*

demonstrate their affection for one another by sharing sexual pleasure and generally form enduring partnerships at least partially on the basis of mutual sexual sharing. Let's look at the features of human female anatomy and physiology that provide pleasure to women and their partners and that enable women to conceive and give birth.

External Structures (the Vulva)

The sexual and reproductive organs of both men and women are usually called **genitals,** or genitalia, from the Latin *genere,* "to beget." The external female genitals are the mons pubis, the clitoris, the labia majora, and the labia minora, collectively known as the **vulva** (Figure 3.2). (People often use the word "vagina" when they are actually referring to the vulva. The vagina is an internal structure.)

The Mons Pubis   The **mons pubis** (pubic mound), or **mons veneris** (mound of Venus), is a pad of fatty tissue that covers the area of the pubic bone about 6 inches below the navel. Beginning in puberty, the mons is covered with pubic hair. In many women, this area is sensitive to sexual stimulation.

FIGURE 3.2   External Female
Sexual Structures (Vulva)

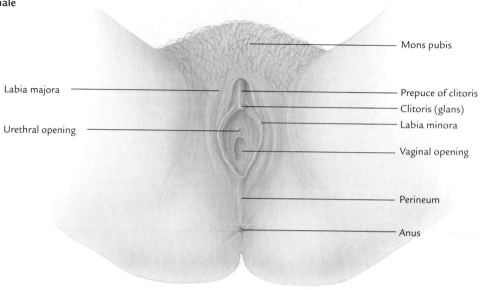

Mons pubis

Labia majora

Urethral opening

Prepuce of clitoris

Clitoris (glans)

Labia minora

Vaginal opening

Perineum

Anus

The Clitoris   The center of sexual arousal in the female is the **clitoris** (KLIH-tuh-rus). It contains a high concentration of nerve endings and is exquisitely sensitive to stimulation, especially at the tip of its shaft, the **glans clitoris.** A fold of skin called the **clitoral hood** covers the glans when the clitoris is not engorged. Although the clitoris is structurally analogous to the penis (it is formed from the same embryonic tissue), its sole function is sexual arousal. (The penis serves the additional functions of urine excretion and semen ejaculation.) The shaft of the clitoris is both an external and an internal structure. The external portion is about 0.25–1.0 inch long. Internally, the shaft is divided into two branches called **crura** (singular, *crus*), each of which is about 3.5 inches long. The crura contain two **corpora cavernosa,** hollow chambers that fill with blood and swell during arousal. The erectile tissue plus the surrounding muscle tissue all contribute to muscle spasms associated with orgasm. When stimulated, the clitoris enlarges initially and then retracts beneath the hood just before and during orgasm. With repeated orgasms, it follows the same pattern of engorgement and retraction, although its swellings may not be as pronounced after the initial orgasm.

The Labia Majora and Labia Minora   The **labia majora** (LAY-be-a ma-JOR-a) (major lips) are two folds of spongy flesh extending from the mons pubis and enclosing the labia minora, clitoris, urethral opening, and vaginal entrance. The **labia minora** (minor lips) are smaller folds within the labia majora that meet above the clitoris to form the clitoral hood. They are smooth and hairless and vary quite a bit in appearance from woman to woman. They are sensitive to the touch and swell during sexual arousal, doubling or tripling in size and changing in color from flesh-toned to a deeper hue. The area enclosed by the labia minora is referred to as the **vestibule.** During sexual arousal, the clitoris becomes erect, the labia minora widen, and the vestibule (vaginal opening) becomes visible. Within the vestibule, on either side of the vaginal opening, are two small ducts from

> Really that little dealybob is too far away from the hole. It should be built right in.
>
> —*Loretta Lynn*

IN A SPACE THAT IS comfortable for you, take time to look at your vulva, or outer genitals, using a mirror and a good light. The large, soft folds of skin with hair on them are the outer lips, or labia majora. The color, texture, and pattern of this hair vary widely among women. Inside the outer lips are the inner lips, or labia minora. These have no hair and vary in size from small to large and protruding. They extend from below the vagina up toward the pubic bone, where they form a hood over the clitoris. If you pull back the hood, you will be able to see your clitoris. The size and shape of the clitoris, as well as the hood, vary widely among women. These variations have nothing to do with a woman's ability to respond sexually. You may also find some cheesy white matter under the hood. This is called smegma and is normal.

Below the clitoris is a smooth area and then a small hole. This is the urinary opening, also called the meatus. Below the urinary opening is the vaginal opening, which is surrounded by rings of tissue. One of these, which you may or may not be able to see, is the hymen. Just inside the vagina, on both sides, are the Bartholin's glands. These may secrete a small amount of mucus during sexual excitement, but little else of their function is known. If they are infected, they will be swollen, but otherwise you won't notice them. The smooth area between your vagina and anus is called the perineum.

Once you're familiar with the normal appearance of your outer genitals, you can check for unusual rashes, soreness, warts, or parasites, such as crabs.

You can also examine your inner genitals, using a speculum, flashlight, and mirror. A speculum is an instrument used to hold the vaginal walls apart, allowing a clear view of the vagina and cervix. You should be able

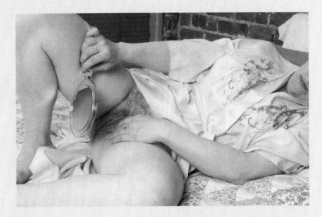

Examining your genitals can be an enlightening and useful practice that can provide you with information about the health of your body.

to obtain a speculum and information about doing an internal exam from a clinic that specializes in women's health or family planning.

It is a good idea to observe and become aware of what the normal vaginal discharges look and feel like. Colors vary from white to gray, and secretions change in consistency from thick to thin and clear (similar to egg white that is stretched between the fingers) over the course of the menstrual cycle. Distinct changes or odors, along with burning, bleeding between menstrual cycles, pain in the pelvic region, itching, or rashes, should be reported to a physician.

In doing a vaginal self-exam, you may initially experience some fear or uneasiness about touching your body. In the long run, however, your patience and persistence will pay off in increased body awareness and a heightened sense of personal health.

the **Bartholin's glands** (or vestibular glands), which secrete a small amount of moisture during sexual arousal.

Internal Structures

The internal female sexual structures and reproductive organs include the vagina; the uterus and its lower opening, the cervix; the ovaries; and the fallopian tubes (Figure 3.3).

The Vagina   The **vagina** (va-JI-na), from the Latin word for sheath, is a flexible, muscular structure that serves two reproductive functions: (1) It encompasses the penis during **coitus** (KOH-ee-tus) (sexual intercourse) so that sperm will be deposited near the entrance of the uterus, and (2) it is the **birth canal** through which an infant is born. Normally, the walls of the vagina are relaxed

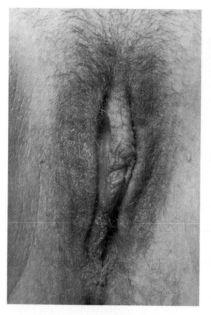
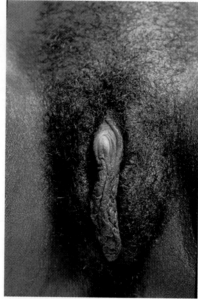

The external female genitalia (vulva) can assume many different colors, shapes, and structures.

and collapsed together, but during sexual arousal, the inner two-thirds of the vagina expands. Mucous membranes line the vagina, providing lubrication during arousal. The majority of sensory nerve endings are concentrated in the lower third of the vagina, or the **introitus** (in-TRO-tus). This part of the vagina is the most sensitive to erotic pressure and touch. In contrast, the inner two-thirds of the vagina have virtually no nerve endings. Although the vaginal walls are generally moist, sexual excitement causes lubrication to increase substantially. This lubrication serves two biological purposes. First, it increases the possibility of conception by alkalinizing the normally acidic chemical balance

FIGURE 3.3   Internal Female Sexual Structures

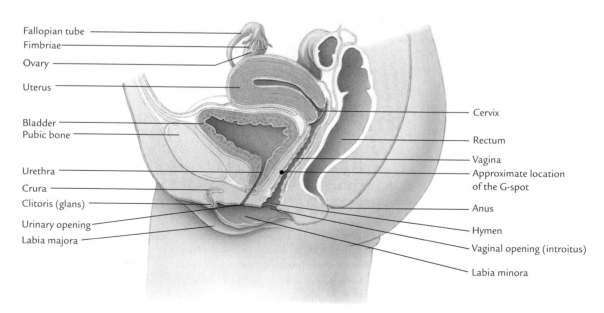

Fallopian tube
Fimbriae
Ovary
Uterus
Bladder
Pubic bone
Urethra
Crura
Clitoris (glans)
Urinary opening
Labia majora

Cervix
Rectum
Vagina
Approximate location of the G-spot
Anus
Hymen
Vaginal opening (introitus)
Labia minora

in the vagina, thus making it more hospitable to sperm, which die faster in acid environments. Second, it makes coitus easier and more pleasurable for both the woman and her partner by reducing friction between the vaginal wall and inserted object.

Prior to first intercourse or other intrusion, the introitus is partially covered by a thin membrane containing a relatively large number of blood vessels, the **hymen** (named for the Roman god of marriage). The hymen typically has one or several perforations, allowing menstrual blood and mucous secretions to flow out of the vagina (and generally allowing for tampon insertion). In many cultures, it is (or was) important for a woman's hymen to be intact on her wedding day. Blood on the nuptial sheets is taken as proof of her virginity. The stretching or tearing of the hymen may produce some pain or discomfort and possibly some bleeding. Usually, the man has little trouble inserting the penis through the hymen if he is gentle and there is adequate lubrication. Prior to first intercourse, the hymen may be stretched or ruptured by tampon insertion, by the woman's self-manipulation, by a partner during noncoital sexual activity, or by accident.

Controversial research has asserted that an erotically sensitive area, the **Grafenberg spot,** or **G-spot,** is located on the front wall of the vagina midway between the pubic bone and the cervix on the vaginal side of the urethra (Figure 3.4). This area varies in size from a small bean to a half dollar. It can be located by pressing one or two fingers into the front wall of a woman's vagina. Coital positions such as rear entry, in which the penis makes contact with the spot, may also produce intense erotic pleasure (Ladas, Whipple, & Perry, 1982; Whipple & Komisaruk, 1999). Initially, a woman may experience a slight feeling of discomfort or the need to urinate, but shortly thereafter, the tissue may swell and arousal may occur.

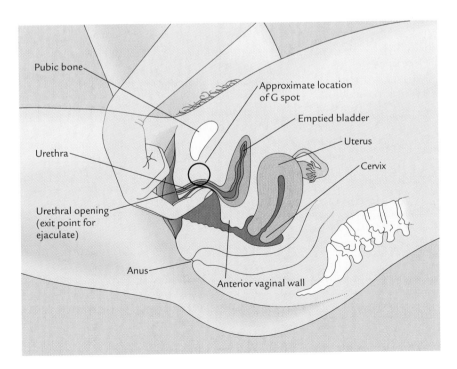

FIGURE 3.4 The Grafenberg Spot. To locate the Grafenberg spot, insert two fingers into the vagina and press deeply into its anterior wall.

THE MUCOUS MEMBRANES lining the walls of the vagina normally produce clear, white, or pale yellow secretions. These secretions pass from the cervix through the vagina and vary in color, consistency, odor, and quantity depending on the phase of the menstrual cycle, the woman's health, and her unique physical characteristics. It is important for you to observe your secretions periodically and note any changes, especially if symptoms accompany them. Call a health practitioner if you feel uncertain or suspicious and/or have been exposed to a sexually transmitted infection.

Here are some simple guidelines that may help a woman avoid getting vaginitis:

1. Do not use vaginal deodorants, especially deodorant suppositories or tampons. They upset the natural chemical balance of the vagina. Despite what pharmaceutical companies may advertise, a healthy vagina does not have a bad odor. If the vagina does have an unpleasant smell, then something is wrong, and you should check with your doctor or clinic.

2. For the same reason, do not use douches, except for medicated douches recommended by a clinician or vinegar solutions for yeast infections.

3. Maintain good genital hygiene by washing regularly (about once a day) with mild soap. Bubble baths and strongly perfumed soaps may irritate the vulva.

4. After a bowel movement, wipe the anus from front to back, away from the vagina, to prevent contamination with fecal bacteria.

5. Wear cotton underpants and pantyhose with a cotton crotch. Nylon does not "breathe," and it allows heat and moisture to build up, creating an ideal environment for infectious organisms to reproduce.

6. If you use a vaginal lubricant, be sure it is water-soluble. Oil-based lubricants such as Vaseline encourage bacterial growth.

7. If you have candidiasis (yeast infection), try douching every 2 or 3 days with a mild vinegar solution (2 tablespoons of vinegar to 1 quart of warm water). You can also try applying plain yogurt twice a day to the vulva and vagina. (It must be plain yogurt that contains live lactobacillus culture.) Adding yogurt to your diet and avoiding foods with a high sugar content may also help.

8. If you are diagnosed with a vaginal infection, particularly trichomoniasis, be sure to have your partner treated as well, to avoid being reinfected.

Vaginal Mucus and Secretions

Color	Consistency	Odor	Other Symptoms	Possible Causes	What to Do
Clear	Slightly rubbery, stretchy	Normal	—	Ovulation, sexual stimulation	Nothing
Milky	Creamy	Normal	—	Preovulation	Nothing
White	Sticky, curdlike	Normal	—	Postovulation, the pill	Nothing
Brownish	Watery and sticky	Normal or slightly different	—	Last day of period, spotting	Nothing
White	Thin, watery, creamy	Normal to foul or fishy	Itching	*Gardnerella* bacteria or nonspecific bacterial infection	See health practitioner
White	Curdlike or flecks, slight amount of discharge	Yeasty or foul	Itching or intense itching, inflammation of vaginal walls	Overgrowth of yeast cells, yeast infection	Apply yogurt, vinegar solution, or anti-fungal medication designed for this purpose
Yellow, yellow-green	Smooth or frothy	Usually foul	Itching, perhaps red dots on cervix	Possible *Trichomonas* infection	See health practitioner
Yellow, yellow-green	Thick, mucous	None to foul	Pelvic cramping or pelvic pain	Possible infection of fallopian tubes	See health practitioner right away

Source: From *Marriage and Family Experience: Intimate Relationships in a Changing Society,* 7th ed. by B. Strong, C. DeVault and B. Sayad. Copyright © 1998 Wadsworth. Reprinted with permission of Wadsworth, a division of Thomson Learning: www.thomsonrights.com. Fax 800/730-2215

Women who report orgasms as a result of stimulation of the G-spot describe them as intense and extremely pleasurable (Perry & Whipple, 1981). In some women, an emission of a clear fluid from the urethra also occurs (Ann, 1997; Belzer, 1984). (It has been suggested that the Skene's glands, which are located inside the urethra and function in a way similar to that of the prostate gland in males, may be responsible for the liquid that is sometimes expelled during intense orgasms.) Additional research is necessary before firm conclusions can be drawn about the placement and function of this spot. An exact gland or site has not been found in all women, nor do all women experience pleasure when the area is massaged.

The Uterus and Cervix   The **uterus** (YU-te-rus), or womb, is a hollow, thick-walled, muscular organ held in the pelvic cavity by a number of flexible ligaments and supported by several muscles. It is pear-shaped, with the tapered end, the **cervix,** extending down and opening into the vagina. If a woman has not given birth, the uterus is about 3 inches long and 3 inches wide at the top; it is somewhat larger in women who have given birth. The uterus expands during pregnancy to the size of a volleyball or larger, to accommodate the developing fetus. The inner lining of the uterine walls, the **endometrium** (en-doe-MEE-tree-um), is filled with tiny blood vessels. During the menstrual cycle, this tissue is built up and then shed and expelled through the cervical **os** (opening), unless fertilization has occurred. In the event of pregnancy, the pre-embryo is embedded in the nourishing endometrium.

In addition to the more or less monthly menstrual discharge, mucous secretions from the cervix also flow out through the vagina. These secretions tend to be somewhat white, thick, and sticky following menstruation, becoming thinner as ovulation approaches. At ovulation, the mucus flow tends to increase and to be clear, slippery, and stretchy, somewhat like egg white. (Birth control using cervical mucus to determine the time of ovulation is discussed in Chapter 11.)

The Ovaries   On each side of the uterus, held in place by several ligaments, is one of a pair of ovaries. The **ovary** is a **gonad,** an organ that produces **gametes** (GA-meets), the sex cells containing the genetic material necessary for reproduction. Female gametes are called **oocytes** (OH-uh-sites), from the Greek words for egg and cell. (Oocytes are commonly referred to as eggs or **ova** [singular, **ovum**]. Technically, however, the cell does not become an egg until it completes its final stages of division following fertilization.) The ovaries are the size and shape of large almonds. In addition to producing oocytes, they serve the important function of hormone production. (The basic female hormones, estrogen and progesterone, are discussed later in this chapter.)

At birth, the female's ovaries contain about half a million oocytes. During childhood, many of these degenerate; then, beginning in puberty and ending after menopause, a total of about 400 oocytes mature and are released on a more or less monthly basis. The release of an oocyte is called **ovulation.** The immature oocytes are embedded in saclike structures called **ovarian follicles.** The fully ripened follicle is called a vesicular or Graffian follicle. At maturation, the follicle ruptures, releasing the oocyte to begin its journey.

> Girls got balls. They're just a little higher up, that's all.
>
> —Joan Jett

After the oocyte emerges, the ruptured follicle becomes the **corpus luteum** (KOR-pus LOO-tee-um) (from the Latin for yellow body), a producer of important hormones; it eventually degenerates. The egg is viable for about 24 hours.

The Fallopian Tubes   At the top of the uterus, one on each side, are two tubes known as **fallopian tubes,** uterine tubes, or oviducts. The tubes are about 4 inches long. They extend toward the ovaries but are not attached to them. Instead, the funnel-shaped end of each tube (the **infundibulum**) fans out into fingerlike **fimbriae** (fim-BREE-ah), which drape over the ovary but may not actually touch it. Tiny, hairlike **cilia** on the fimbriae and ampulla become active during ovulation. Their waving motion, along with contractions of the walls of the tube, transports the oocyte that has been released from the ovary into the fallopian tube. Just within the infundibulum is the **ampulla,** the widened part of the tube in which fertilization normally occurs if sperm and oocyte are there at the same time. (The process of ovulation and the events leading to fertilization are discussed later in this chapter; fertilization is covered in Chapter 12.)

Other Structures

There are several other important anatomical structures in the genital areas of both men and women. Although they may not serve reproductive functions, they may be involved in sexual activities. Some of these areas may also be affected by sexually transmitted infections. In women, these structures include the urethra, anus, and perineum. The **urethra** (yu-REE-thra) is the tube through which urine passes; the **urethral opening,** or meatus, is located between the clitoris and the vaginal opening. Between the vagina and the **anus**—the opening of the rectum, through which excrement passes—is a diamond-shaped region called the **perineum** (per-e-NEE-um). This area of soft tissue covers the muscles and ligaments of the **pelvic floor,** the underside of the pelvic area extending from the top of the pubic bone (above the clitoris) to the anus. (To learn more about this muscle and Kegel exercises, see Chapter 14.) The anus consists of two sphincters, circular muscles that open and close like valves. The tissue that rings the opening is tender and is erotically sensitive for some people.

In sex play or intercourse involving the anus or rectum, care must be taken not to rupture the delicate tissues. Anal sex, which involves insertion of the penis into the rectum, is not considered safe, because abrasions of the tissue provide easy passage for pathogens, such as HIV (the virus that causes AIDS), to the bloodstream (see Chapter 16). To practice safer sex, partners who engage in anal intercourse should use a latex condom with a water-based lubricant.

The Breasts

Both women and men have breasts. At puberty, the female breasts begin to develop in response to hormonal stimuli (Figure 3.5). At maturity, the left breast is often slightly larger than the right (Rome, 1992).

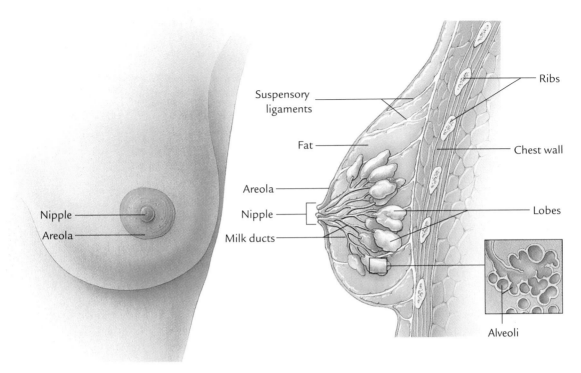

Suspensory ligaments

Fat

Areola

Nipple

Milk ducts

Ribs

Chest wall

Lobes

Alveoli

FIGURE 3.5   The Female Breast

The reproductive function of the breasts is to nourish offspring through **lactation,** or milk production. A mature female breast, also known as a **mammary gland,** is composed of fatty tissue and 15–25 lobes that radiate around a central protruding nipple. Around the nipple is a ring of darkened skin called the **areola** (a-REE-o-la). Tiny muscles at the base of the nipple cause it to become erect in response to touch, cold, or sexual arousal.

When a woman is pregnant, the structures within the breast undergo further development. Directly following childbirth, in response to hormonal signals, small glands within the lobes called **alveoli** (al-VEE-a-lee) begin producing milk. The milk passes into ducts, each of which has a dilated region for storage; the ducts open to the outside at the nipple. (Breast-feeding is discussed in detail in Chapter 12.) During lactation, a woman's breasts increase in size from enlarged glandular tissues and stored milk. Because there is little variation in the amount of glandular tissue among women, the amount of milk produced does not vary with breast size. In women who are not lactating, breast size depends mainly on fat content, often determined by hereditary factors.

In our culture, breasts also serve an erotic function. Many, but not all, women find breast stimulation intensely pleasurable, whether it occurs during breast-feeding or sexual contact. Partners tend to be aroused by both the sight and the touch of women's breasts. Although there is no basis in reality, some believe that large breasts denote greater sexual responsiveness than small breasts. (See Chapter 13 for a discussion of breast enhancement.)

Uncorsetted, her friendly bust gives promise of pneumatic bliss.

—*T. S. Eliot (1888–1965)*

What's the fascination with breasts? Click on "Breasts" to hear women discussing myths and pressures surrounding breast size and perkiness.

Western culture tends to be ambivalent about breasts and nudity. Many people are comfortable with artistic portrayals of the nude female body, as in this photograph by Imogen Cunningham titled Triangles.

FEMALE SEXUAL PHYSIOLOGY

The female reproductive cycle can be viewed as having two components (although, of course, multiple biological processes are involved): (1) the ovarian cycle, in which eggs develop, and (2) the menstrual, or uterine, cycle, in which the womb is prepared for pregnancy. These cycles repeat approximately every month for about 35 or 40 years. The task of directing these processes belongs to a class of chemicals called hormones.

Reproductive Hormones

Hormones are chemical substances that serve as messengers, traveling within the body through the bloodstream. Most hormones are composed of either amino acids (building blocks of proteins) or steroids (derived from cholesterol). They are produced by the ovaries and the endocrine glands—the adrenals, pituitary, and hypothalamus. Hormones assist in a variety of

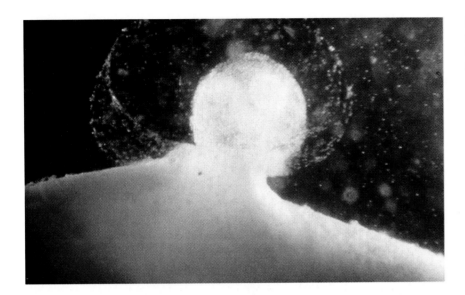

During ovulation, the ovarian follicle swells and ruptures, releasing the mature oocyte to begin its journey through the fallopian tube.

tasks, including development of the reproductive organs and secondary sex characteristics during puberty, regulation of the menstrual cycle, maintenance of pregnancy, initiation and regulation of childbirth, and initiation of lactation. Hormones that act directly on the gonads are known as **gonadotropins** (go-nad-a-TRO-pins). Among the most important of the female hormones are the **estrogens,** which affect the maturation of the reproductive organs, menstruation, and pregnancy, and **progesterone,** which helps to maintain the uterine lining. The principal hormones involved in a woman's reproductive and sexual life and their functions are described in Table 3.1. (Testosterone is discussed later in this chapter.)

The Ovarian Cycle

The development of female gametes is a complex process that begins even before a woman is born. In infancy and childhood, the cells that will develop into ova (eggs) undergo no further development. During puberty, hormones trigger the completion of the process of **oogenesis** (oh-uh-JEN-uh-sis), literally, "egg beginning" (Figure 3.6). This process, called the **ovarian cycle** (or menstrual cycle), continues until a woman reaches menopause.

The ovarian cycle averages 28 days in length, although there is considerable variation among women, ranging from 21 to 40 days. In their own particular cycle length after puberty, however, most women experience little variation. Generally, ovulation occurs in only one ovary each month, alternating between the right and left sides with each successive cycle. If a single ovary is removed, the remaining one begins to ovulate every month. The ovarian cycle has three phases: follicular (fo-LIK-u-lar), ovulatory (ov-UL-a-tor-ee), and luteal (LOO-tee-ul) (Figure 3.7). As an ovary undergoes its changes, corresponding changes occur in the uterus. Menstruation marks the end of this sequence of hormonal and physical changes in the ovaries and uterus.

The Follicular Phase   On the first day of the cycle, **gonadotropin-releasing hormone (GnRH)** is released from the hypothalamus. GnRH

TABLE 3.1 Female Reproductive Hormones		
Hormone	*Where Produced*	*Functions*
Estrogen (including estradiol, estrone, estriol)	Ovaries, adrenal glands, placenta (during pregnancy)	Promotes maturation of reproductive organs, development of secondary sex characteristics, and growth spurt at puberty; regulates menstrual cycle; sustains pregnancy
Progesterone	Ovaries, adrenal glands	Promotes breast development, maintains uterine lining, regulates menstrual cycle, sustains pregnancy
Gonadotropin-releasing hormone (GnRH)	Hypothalamus	Promotes maturation of gonads, regulates menstrual cycle
Follicle-stimulating hormone (FSH)	Pituitary	Regulates ovarian function and maturation of ovarian follicles
Luteinizing hormone (LH)	Pituitary	Assists in production of estrogen and progesterone, regulates maturation of ovarian follicles, triggers ovulation
Human chorionic gonadotropin (HCG)	Embryo and placenta	Helps sustain pregnancy
Testosterone	Adrenal glands and ovaries	Helps stimulate sexual desire
Oxytocin	Hypothalamus	Stimulates uterine contractions during childbirth and possibly during orgasm
Prolactin	Pituitary	Stimulates milk production
Prostaglandins	All body cells	Mediate hormone response, stimulate muscle contractions

FIGURE 3.6 **Oogenesis.** This diagram charts the development of an ovum, beginning with embryonic development of the oogonium and ending with fertilization of the secondary oocyte, which then becomes the diploid zygote. Primary oocytes are present in a female at birth; at puberty, hormones stimulate the oocyte to undergo meiosis.

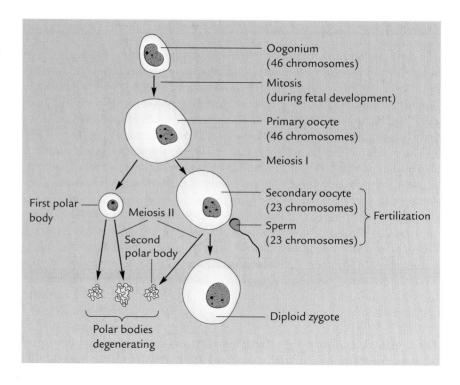

Menstrual Phase

(Menstruation)

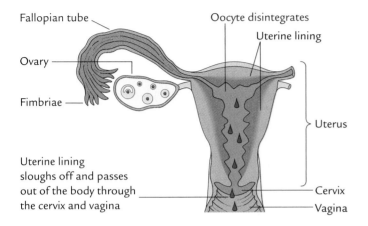

Fallopian tube

Oocyte disintegrates

Uterine lining

Ovary

Fimbriae

Uterus

Uterine lining
sloughs off and passes
out of the body through
the cervix and vagina

Cervix

Vagina

Follicular Phase
(also called the Proliferative Phase)

(Follicle development)

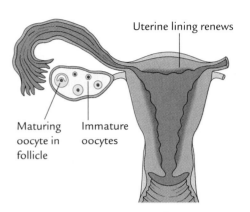

Uterine lining renews

Maturing
oocyte in
follicle

Immature
oocytes

Ovulatory Phase

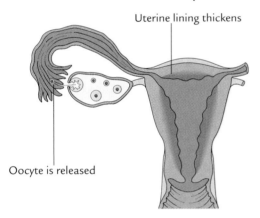

Uterine lining thickens

Oocyte is released

Luteal Phase

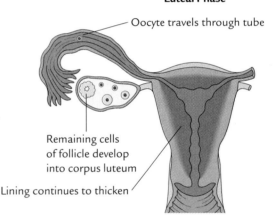

Oocyte travels through tube

Remaining cells
of follicle develop
into corpus luteum

Lining continues to thicken

begins to stimulate the pituitary to release **follicle-stimulating hormone (FSH)** and **luteinizing hormone (LH),** initiating the **follicular phase.** During the first 10 days, 10–20 ovarian follicles begin to grow, stimulated by FSH and LH. In 98–99% of cases, only one of the follicles will mature completely during this period. (The maturation of more than one oocyte is one factor in multiple births.) All the developing follicles begin secreting estrogen. Under the influence of FSH and estrogen, the oocyte matures, bulging from the surface of the ovary. This may also be referred to as the proliferative phase.

Ovulatory Phase   The **ovulatory phase** begins at about day 11 of the cycle and culminates with ovulation at about day 14. Stimulated by an increase of LH from the pituitary, the primary oocyte undergoes cell division and becomes ready for ovulation. The ballooning follicle wall thins and ruptures, and the oocyte enters the abdominal cavity near the beckoning fimbriae. Ovulation is now complete. Some women experience a sharp twinge on one side of the lower abdomen during ovulation. A very slight bloody discharge from the vagina may also occur.

FIGURE 3.7 **Ovarian and Menstrual Cycles.** The ovarian cycle consists of the activities within the ovaries and the development of oocytes; it includes the follicular, ovulatory, and luteal phases. The menstrual cycle consists of processes occurring in the uterus. Hormones regulate these cycles.

WOMEN HAVE UNIQUE SEXUAL and reproductive needs and may face difficulties in the health-care system. In part because of the medicalization of thinking about women's sexuality and the ways in which culture influences behavior and political agendas, power imbalances between physicians and patients are often ignored (Tiefer, 2001). The focus on getting the genitals to perform often results in neglect of the complexity of human sexuality and its impact on sexual behavior. Consequently, women should listen to themselves and seek a more active, self-determined role in the assessment of their reproductive and sexual well-being.

Whereas men are apt to receive medical care from one practitioner, women often receive either uncoordinated care from several physicians or care from a physician insensitive to or untrained in treating health problems peculiar to women. Gender bias is evident in the male- to-female ratio of physicians, the research decisions that are based on male subjects, and the observations by some that many male physicians are less focused on women's than on men's medical needs. Compared with women who see female practitioners, those who see male practitioners are less likely to have such diagnostic procedures as Pap smears and mammograms. They are also less likely to receive thorough diagnosis and treatment for coronary heart disease.

For these reasons, it is important for women to be aware and proactive in their medical care. That means learning as much as they can about their bodies and acknowledging their accompanying feelings and sensations. Much information can also be obtained by doing research on the Internet. Selecting a male or female physician who is knowledgeable and sensitive to their needs, knowing what services to expect, and making sure to get them are other important steps. The basic services unique to women are annual pelvic exams, Pap smears, and breast exams.

To avoid duplication and to maximize observations and opinions, the best option is for women to have both a gynecologist and a primary care physician and to be sure they communicate with each other. Either kind of physician alone can fulfill women's health-care needs; however, the combination is a better choice. Women should not be afraid to get a second (or third) opinion if they are confused, do not get a response to their symptoms, or are faced with differing diagnoses. It is important that women interview a new physician before seeking his or her care and be sure that the physician's attitude about women's health is similar to their own.

The Luteal Phase   Following ovulation, estrogen levels drop rapidly, and the ruptured follicle, still under the influence of increased LH, becomes a corpus luteum, which secretes progesterone and small amounts of estrogen. Increasing levels of these hormones serve to inhibit pituitary release of FSH and LH. Unless fertilization has occurred, the corpus luteum deteriorates. In the event of pregnancy, the corpus luteum maintains its hormonal output, helping to sustain the pregnancy. The hormone human chorionic gonadotropin (HCG)—similar to LH—is secreted by the embryo and signals the corpus luteum to continue until the placenta has developed sufficiently to take over hormone production.

The **luteal phase** typically lasts from day 14 (immediately after ovulation) through day 28 of the ovarian cycle. Even when cycles are more or less than 28 days, the duration of the luteal phase remains the same; the time between ovulation and the end of the cycle is always 14 days. At this point, the ovarian hormone levels are at their lowest, GnRH is released, and FSH and LH levels begin to rise.

The Menstrual Cycle

As hormone levels fall following the degeneration of the corpus luteum, the uterine lining (endometrium) is shed because it will not be needed to help sus-

And if a woman shall have an issue, and her issue in her flesh be blood, she shall be separated seven days; and whatsoever touches her shall be unclean.

—*Leviticus 15:19*

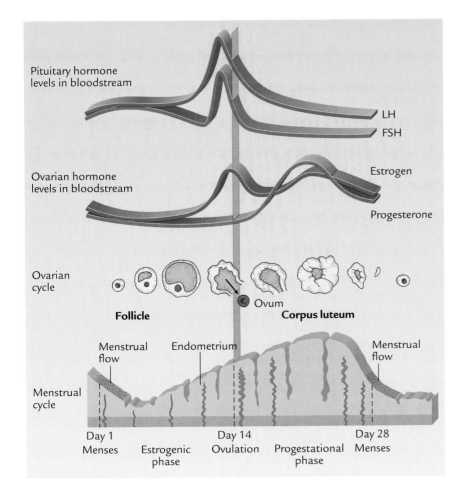

Pituitary hormone
levels in bloodstream

LH

FSH

Ovarian hormone
levels in bloodstream

Estrogen

Progesterone

Ovarian
cycle

Ovum

Follicle   **Corpus luteum**

Menstrual
flow   Endometrium   Menstrual
flow

Menstrual
cycle

Day 1   Day 14   Day 28
Menses   Ovulation   Menses
          Estrogenic   Progestational
          phase   phase

FIGURE 3.8 The Menstrual Cycle, Ovarian Cycle, and Hormone Levels. This chart compares the activities of the ovaries and uterus and shows the relationship of hormone levels to these activities.

tain the fertilized ovum. The shedding of endometrial tissue and the bleeding that accompanies it are, collectively, a monthly event in the lives of women from puberty through menopause. Cultural and religious attitudes, as well as personal experience, influence our feelings about this phenomenon. (The physical and emotional effects of menstruation are discussed later in this section. The onset of menstruation and its effect on a woman's psychosexual development is discussed in Chapter 6. Menopause is discussed in Chapter 13.)

The **menstrual cycle** (or uterine cycle), is divided into three phases. What occurs within the uterus is inextricably related to what is happening in the ovaries, but only in their final phases do the two cycles actually coincide (Figure 3.8).

The Menstrual Phase With hormone levels low because of the degeneration of the corpus luteum, the outer layer of the endometrium becomes detached from the uterine wall. The shedding of the endometrium marks the beginning of the **menstrual phase.** This endometrial tissue, along with mucus, other cervical and vaginal secretions, and a small amount of blood (2–5 ounces per cycle), is expelled through the vagina. The menstrual flow, or **menses** (MEN-seez), generally occurs over a period of 3–5 days. FSH and LH begin increasing around day 5, marking the end of this phase. A girl's first menstruation is known as **menarche** (MEH-nar-kee).

The Proliferative Phase   The **proliferative phase** lasts about 9 days. During this time, the endometrium thickens in response to increased estrogen. The mucous membranes of the cervix secrete a clear, thin mucus with a crystalline structure that facilitates the passage of sperm. The proliferative phase ends with ovulation.

The Secretory Phase   During the first part of the **secretory phase,** with the help of progesterone, the endometrium begins to prepare for the arrival of a fertilized ovum. Glands within the uterus enlarge and begin secreting glycogen, a cell nutrient. The cervical mucus thickens and starts forming a plug to seal off the uterus in the event of pregnancy. If fertilization does not occur, the corpus luteum begins to degenerate, as LH levels decline. Progesterone levels then fall, and the endometrial cells begin to die. The secretory phase lasts 14 days, corresponding with the luteal phase of the ovarian cycle. It ends with the shedding of the endometrium.

Menstrual Synchrony   Women who live or work together often report developing similarly timed menstrual cycles (Cutler, 1999). Termed **menstrual synchrony,** this phenomenon appears to be related to the sense of smell—more specifically, a response to pheromones. Though there is considerable controversy among researchers as to whether the phenomenon actually exists, if it does, there could be implications for birth control, sexual attraction, and other aspects of women's lives. (Pheromones are discussed later in the chapter.)

Menstrual Effects   For some women, menstruation is a problem; for others, it is simply a fact of life that creates little disruption. For individual women, the problems associated with their menstrual period may be physiological, emotional, or practical. The vast majority of menstruating women notice at least one emotional, physical, or behavioral change in the week or so prior to menstruation. Most women describe the changes negatively: breast tenderness and swelling, abdominal bloating, irritability, cramping, depression, or fatigue. Some women also report positive changes such as increased energy, heightened sexual arousal, or a general feeling of well-being. For most women, changes during the menstrual cycle are usually mild to moderate; they appear to have little impact on their lives. (Toxic shock syndrome, a blood infection associated with menstruation, is discussed in Chapter 13.) The most common problems associated with menstruation are discussed below.

Menstrual Period Slang
that time of the month
monthlies
the curse
female troubles
a visit from my friend
a visit from Aunt Sally
a visit from George
on the rag
on a losing streak
falling off the roof

PREMENSTRUAL SYNDROME   More severe menstrual problems have been attributed to what is called **premenstrual syndrome (PMS),** a term used to describe the most commonly reported cluster of physical and emotional symptoms. Eighty to 95% of women experience mild physical and behavioral changes premenstrually, while 5% report symptoms severe enough to impair normal functioning (O'Brien, Wyatt, & Dimmock, 2000). But because of the variety of symptoms and the difficulty involved in evaluating them, studies on PMS are contradictory and inconclusive. In 1994, the American Psychiatric Association included "premenstrual dysphoric disorder" (PMDD) in the fourth edition of its *Diagnostic and Statistical Manual of Mental Disorders (DSM-IV),* which is used for psychiatric diagnosis. To be diagnosed with PMDD, a woman must have at least five of the eleven specific symptoms listed, which are depression, nervousness, irritability, and anxiety (grouped under dysphoria); bloating, swelling, and weight gain (grouped under fluid retention); breast tenderness; headache; fatigue; and food cravings (especially for salt, sugar, or chocolate). Though the causes of PMS and PMDD are unknown, medications used for depression are often prescribed to alleviate the more severe symptoms (Saks, 2000).

The greatest difficulty in understanding PMS is knowing how to separate information that clearly indicates premenstrual symptoms from other aspects of a woman's physical and emotional health. Certain questions need to be answered before firm conclusions can be drawn.

DYSMENORRHEA   Approximately 7% of women experience pelvic cramping and pain during the menstrual cycle; this condition is called **dysmenorrhea** (dis-men-a-REE-a) (Leland, 2000). There are two basic types. Primary dysmenorrhea is characterized by pain that begins with uterine shedding (or just before) and by the absence of pain at other times in the cycle. It can be very severe and may be accompanied by nausea, weakness, or other physical symptoms. In secondary dysmenorrhea, the symptoms may be the same, but there is an underlying condition or disease causing them; pain may not be limited to the menstrual phase alone. Secondary dysmenorrhea may be caused by pelvic inflammatory disease (PID), endometriosis, endometrial cancer, or other conditions (see Chapters 13 and 15).

The effects of dysmenorrhea can totally incapacitate a woman for several hours or even days. Once believed to be a psychological condition, primary dysmenorrhea is now known to be caused by high levels of **prostaglandins** (pros-ta-GLAN-dins), a type of hormone with a fatty-acid base that is found throughout the body. Drugs like ibuprofen (Motrin and Advil) relieve symptoms by inhibiting the production of prostaglandins. Some doctors may prescribe birth control pills.

AMENORRHEA   When women do not menstruate for reasons other than aging, the condition is called **amenorrhea** (ay-meh-neh-REE-a). A principal cause of amenorrhea is pregnancy. Lack of menstruation, if not a result of pregnancy, is categorized as either primary or secondary amenorrhea. Women who have passed the age of 16 and never menstruated are diagnosed as having primary amenorrhea. It may be that they have not yet reached their critical weight (when an increased ratio of body fat triggers menstrual cycle–inducing hormones) or that they are hereditarily late maturers. But it can also signal hormonal deficiencies, abnormal body structure, or hermaphroditism. Most primary amenorrhea can be treated with hormone therapy.

Secondary amenorrhea exists when a previously menstruating woman stops menstruating for several months. If it is not due to pregnancy, breastfeeding, or the use of hormonal contraceptives, the source of secondary amenorrhea may be found in stress, lowered body fat, heavy physical training, or hormonal irregularities. Anorexia (discussed in Chapter 13) is a frequent cause of amenorrhea. If a woman is not pregnant, is not breastfeeding, and can rule out hormonal contraceptives as a cause, she should see her health practitioner if she has gone 3 months without menstruating.

Irregular menstrual periods in young women may be a sign of a hormonal shortage that could lead to **osteoporosis,** a loss of bone density that can make bones more likely to break (Alzubardi, Chapin, Vanderhoof, Calis, & Nelson, 2002). Estrogen and other reproductive hormones produced by the ovaries

THOUGH AS MANY as 200 premenstrual symptoms can occur before each menstrual cycle, their causes are unknown; there is no laboratory test that identifies PMS; and there are no universally effective ways to relieve its symptoms. Current research suggests that the most effective treatment for most women involves stress management; a reduction in caffeine, nicotine, and salt; a well-balanced diet; and exercise. For women, recognizing their menstrual patterns, learning about their bodies, and recognizing and dealing with existing difficulties can be useful in heading off or easing potential problems. Different remedies work for different women. We suggest that you try varying combinations of them and keep a record of your response to each. Following are suggestions for relieving the more common premenstrual and menstrual symptoms; both self-help and medical treatments are included.

For Premenstrual Symptoms

1. *Modify your diet.* Moderate amounts of protein and substantial amounts of carbohydrates (such as fresh fruits, some vegetables, whole-grain breads and cereals, beans, rice, and pasta) are recommended. Reduce or avoid salt, sugar, and caffeine products such as coffee and colas. Although you may crave chocolate, it can have a negative effect on you; try fruit or popcorn instead, and see how you feel. Frequent small meals may be better than two or three large meals.

2. *Avoid alcohol and tobacco.*

3. *Exercise.* Moderate exercise is suggested, but be sure to include a daily regimen of at least 30–45 minutes of movement. Aerobic exercise brings oxygen to body tissues and stimulates the production of endorphins, chemical substances that help promote feelings of well-being. Yoga may also be helpful, especially the "cobra" position.

4. *Seek medical treatments.* When symptoms are severe enough to impair work performance and relationships, you should seek medical attention. However, there is much controversy within the medical profession about treatment for PMS. Progesterone therapy, once advocated as a treatment, is now considered ineffective. Selective serotonin-reuptake inhibitors, such as Prozac and Zoloft, have been found to be effective in treating PMS in some women (Saks, 2000). These drugs substantially reduce tension and irritability in

help to maintain bone density. Premature ovarian failure occurs when the ovaries stop producing eggs and reproductive hormones prior to menopause. An estimated 1% of American women develop the condition by age 40.

Sexuality and the Menstrual Cycle   Although studies have tried to determine whether there is a biologically based cycle of sexual interest and activity in women that correlates with the menstrual cycle (such as higher interest around ovulation), the results have been conflicting. Researchers have found everything from no significant correlation (Bancroft, 1984; Meuwissen & Over, 1992) to significant correlations, particularly just prior to ovulation (Harvey, 1987; Matteo & Rissman, 1984). There is apparently a great deal of individual variation.

There is also variation in how people feel about sexual activity during different phases. If a woman believes she is ovulating, and if she and her partner do not want a pregnancy, they may feel negative or ambivalent about intercourse. If a woman is menstruating, she, her partner, or both of them may not wish to engage in intercourse or cunnilingus, for a number of reasons.

There is a general taboo in our culture, as in many others, against sexual intercourse during menstruation. This taboo may be based on religious beliefs. Among Orthodox Jews, for example, women are required to refrain from intercourse for 7 days following the end of menstruation. They may then resume sexual activity after a ritual bath, the *mikvah.* Contact with blood may make some people squeamish. A man may view menstrual blood as "somehow dangerous, magical, and apparently not something he wants to get on some women with severe symptoms. They are generally used throughout the month. Drawbacks of the drugs include their cost ($75–$150 per month) and the side effects of nausea, insomnia, fatigue, dizziness, decreased libido, and delayed orgasm for some women. No medication for PMS has yet received FDA approval.

5. *Join a support group*. Therapy or support groups may help you deal with the ways PMS affects your life. They may also help you deal with issues that may be exacerbated by the stress of coping with PMS.

For Cramps

1. *Relax*. Rest, sleep, and relaxation exercises can help reduce pain from uterine and abdominal cramping, especially in combination with one or more of the remedies listed below.

2. *Apply heat*. A heating pad or hot-water bottle (or, in a pinch, a cat) applied to the abdominal area may help relieve cramps; a warm bath may also help.

3. *Get a massage*. Lower back massage or other forms of massage, such as acupressure, Shiatsu, or polarity therapy, are quite helpful for many women. See *The New Our Bodies, Ourselves for a New Century* (Boston

Women's Health Book Collective, 1998) for guidelines for menstrual massage.

4. *Try herbal remedies*. Herbal teas, especially raspberry leaf, are helpful for some women. Health food stores carry a variety of teas, tablets, and other preparations. Use them as directed, but stop using them if you experience additional discomfort or problems.

5. *Take prostaglandin inhibitors*. Antiprostaglandins reduce cramping of the uterine and abdominal muscles. Aspirin is a mild prostaglandin inhibitor. Ibuprofen, a highly effective prostaglandin inhibitor, was often prescribed for menstrual cramps (as Motrin) before it became available over the counter. Aspirin increases menstrual flow slightly, whereas ibuprofen reduces it. Stronger antiprostaglandins may be prescribed. Taking medication at the first sign of cramping—as opposed to waiting until the pain is severe—increases its effectiveness greatly.

6. *Have an orgasm*. Some women report relief of menstrual congestion and cramping at orgasm (with or without a partner).

If pain cannot be controlled with these methods, further medical evaluation is needed. The symptoms may indicate an underlying problem, such as endometriosis or pelvic inflammatory disease (PID).

his penis" (Delaney, Lupton, & Toth, 1988). Many women, especially at the beginning of their period, feel bloated or uncomfortable; they may experience breast tenderness or a general feeling of not wanting to be touched. Others may find that lovemaking helps relieve menstrual discomfort.

For some couples, merely having to deal with the logistics of bloodstains, bathing, and laundry may be enough to discourage them from intercourse at this time. For many people, however, menstrual blood holds no special connotation. It is important to note that although it is unusual, conception *can* occur during menstruation, especially if the woman has short or irregular cycles. Some women find that a diaphragm or a new product called Instead can collect the menstrual flow. This latter product, however, is not a contraceptive. Although it is not recommended that women engage in intercourse while a tampon is inserted because of possible injury to the cervix, cunnilingus is a possibility. And inventive lovers can, of course, find many ways to give each other pleasure that do not require putting the penis into the vagina.

Sexual intercourse during menstruation may carry health risks for women who have multiple sex partners or whose partners may have been exposed to a sexually transmitted infection. Organisms, including HIV, have an easy pathway into a woman's bloodstream through uterine walls exposed by endometrial shedding. Moreover, a woman with a pathogen in her blood, such as the hepatitis virus or HIV, can pass it to a partner in her menstrual blood. Therefore, during menstruation, as well as at other times, safer sex practices, including condom and dental dam use, are strongly recommended. (See Chapter 15 for safer sex guidelines.)

FEMALE SEXUAL RESPONSE

Women's sexuality, though typically thought of as personal and individual, is significantly influenced by the social groups to which women belong. Sociocultural variables include gender, religious preference, class, educational attainment, age, marital status, race, and ethnicity (Laumann & Mahay, 2002). For many women, gender—the social and cultural characteristics associated with being male or female—is probably the most influential variable in shaping their sexual desires, behaviors, and partnerships. Because gender is largely defined by cultural expectations, women's sexual experiences must be understood in terms of cultural, political, and relational forces.

Though scientific research has contributed much to our understanding of sexual arousal and response, there is still much to be learned. One way in which researchers investigate and describe phenomena is through the creation of models, hypothetical descriptions used to study or explain something. However, although models are useful for promoting general understanding or for assisting in the treatment of specific clinical problems (e.g., lack of arousal), we should remember that they are only models. It may be helpful to think of sexual functioning as a circle linking desire, arousal, orgasm, and satisfaction. Turbulence or distraction at any one point affects the functioning of the others (Leland, 2000).

Sexual Response Models

Masters and Johnson's four-phase model of sexual response identifies the significant stages of response as excitement, plateau, orgasm, and resolution (Figure 3.9). Helen Singer Kaplan (1979) collapses the excitement and plateau phases into one, eliminates the resolution phase, and adds a phase to the beginning of the process. **Kaplan's tri-phasic model of sexual response** includes the desire, excitement, and orgasm phases. Though Masters and Johnson's and Kaplan's are the most widely cited models used to describe the phases of the sexual response cycle, they do little to acknowledge the affective parts of human response. A third but much less known pattern is **Loulan's sexual response model,** which incorporates both the biological and affective components into a six-stage cycle. These models are described and compared in Table 3.2.

Desire: Mind or Matter?

Desire is the psychological component of sexual arousal. Although we can experience desire without becoming aroused, and in some cases become aroused without feeling desire, some form of erotic thought or feeling is usually involved in our sexual behavior. The physical manifestations of sexual arousal involve a complex interaction of thoughts and feelings, sensory organs, neural responses, and hormonal reactions involving various parts of the body, including the cerebral cortex and limbic system of the brain, the nervous system, the circulatory system, and the endocrine glands—as well as the genitals. Approximately 22% of women report low sexual desire (Leland, 2000).

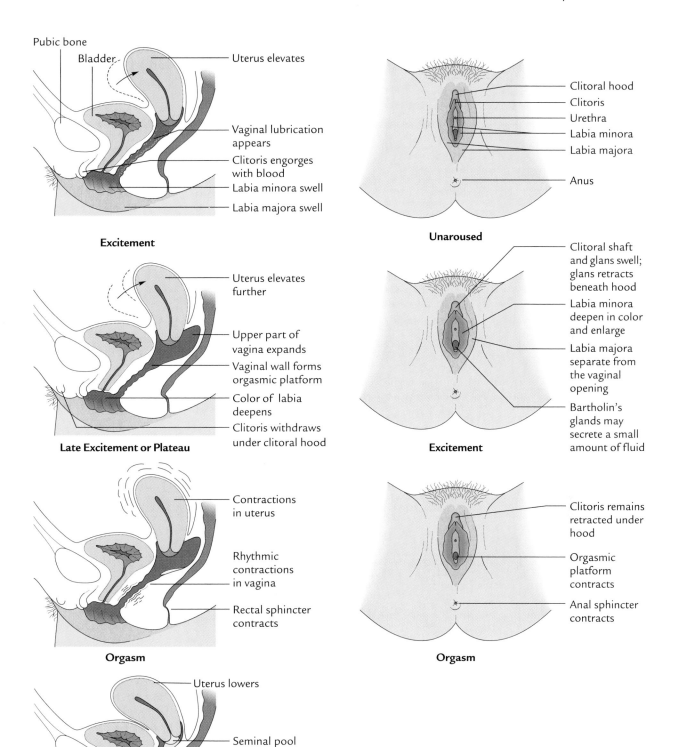

FIGURE 3.9 Masters and Johnson Stages of Female Sexual Response (internal, left; and external, right)

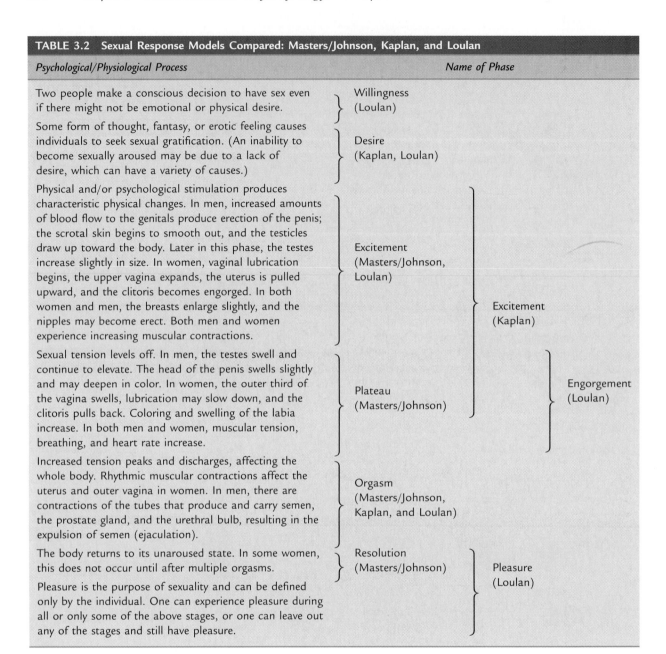

TABLE 3.2 Sexual Response Models Compared: Masters/Johnson, Kaplan, and Loulan	
Psychological/Physiological Process	*Name of Phase*
Two people make a conscious decision to have sex even if there might not be emotional or physical desire.	Willingness (Loulan)
Some form of thought, fantasy, or erotic feeling causes individuals to seek sexual gratification. (An inability to become sexually aroused may be due to a lack of desire, which can have a variety of causes.)	Desire (Kaplan, Loulan)
Physical and/or psychological stimulation produces characteristic physical changes. In men, increased amounts of blood flow to the genitals produce erection of the penis; the scrotal skin begins to smooth out, and the testicles draw up toward the body. Later in this phase, the testes increase slightly in size. In women, vaginal lubrication begins, the upper vagina expands, the uterus is pulled upward, and the clitoris becomes engorged. In both women and men, the breasts enlarge slightly, and the nipples may become erect. Both men and women experience increasing muscular contractions.	Excitement (Masters/Johnson, Loulan) — Excitement (Kaplan)
Sexual tension levels off. In men, the testes swell and continue to elevate. The head of the penis swells slightly and may deepen in color. In women, the outer third of the vagina swells, lubrication may slow down, and the clitoris pulls back. Coloring and swelling of the labia increase. In both men and women, muscular tension, breathing, and heart rate increase.	Plateau (Masters/Johnson) — Engorgement (Loulan)
Increased tension peaks and discharges, affecting the whole body. Rhythmic muscular contractions affect the uterus and outer vagina in women. In men, there are contractions of the tubes that produce and carry semen, the prostate gland, and the urethral bulb, resulting in the expulsion of semen (ejaculation).	Orgasm (Masters/Johnson, Kaplan, and Loulan)
The body returns to its unaroused state. In some women, this does not occur until after multiple orgasms.	Resolution (Masters/Johnson)
Pleasure is the purpose of sexuality and can be defined only by the individual. One can experience pleasure during all or only some of the above stages, or one can leave out any of the stages and still have pleasure.	Pleasure (Loulan)

> Passion, though a bad regulator, is a powerful spring.
>
> —*Ralph Waldo Emerson*
> *(1803–1882)*

The Neural System and Sexual Stimuli   The brain is crucial to sexual response, yet relatively little is known about how the brain functions to create these responses. Through the neural system, the brain receives stimuli from the five senses plus one: sight, smell, touch, hearing, taste, *and* the imagination.

THE BRAIN   The brain, of course, plays a major role in all of our body's functions. Nowhere is its role more apparent than in our sexual functioning. The relationship between our thoughts and feelings and our actual behavior is not well understood (and what is known would require a course in neurophysiology to satisfactorily explain it). Relational factors and cultural influences, as well as expectations, fantasies, hopes, and fears, combine with sensory inputs and hormonal messages to bring us to where we are ready, willing, and able to be sexual. Even then, potentially erotic messages may be short-circuited by the brain itself, which can inhibit as well as incite sexual responses. It is not known how the inhibitory mechanism works, but guilt, anxiety, fear, and negative conditioning will prevent the brain from sending messages to the genitals. In fact, the reason moderate amounts of alcohol and marijuana appear to enhance sexuality is that they reduce the control mechanisms of the brain that act as inhibitors.

Anatomically speaking, the areas of the brain that appear to be involved most in sexual behaviors of both men and women are the cerebral cortex and the limbic system. Using PET scans to map the brain, researchers have found increases in brain activity during sexual arousal (Rauch et al., 1999; Redoute et al., 2000). Interestingly, the sexual drive center, located in the nuclei of the hypothalamus, has been found to be twice as large in adult males as it is in adult females. Furthermore, the size of this area may decline with advancing age (Levine, 1997). The cerebral cortex is the convoluted covering of most of the brain area. It is the area that is associated with conscious behavior such as perception, memory, communication, understanding, and voluntary movement. Beneath the cortex, the **limbic system,** which consists of several separate parts, is involved with emotions and feelings. There are extensive connections between the limbic system and the cerebral cortex, explaining perhaps why "emotions sometimes override logic and, conversely, why reason can stop us from expressing our emotions in inappropriate situations" (Marieb, 1995).

THE SENSES   An attractive person (sight), a body fragrance or odor (smell), a lick or kiss (taste), a loving caress (touch), and erotic whispers (hearing) are all capable of sending sexual signals to the brain. Preferences for each of these are largely determined by culture and are very individualized. Many of the connections we experience between sensory data and emotional responses are probably products of the limbic system. Some sensory inputs may evoke sexual arousal without a lot of conscious thought or emotion. Certain areas of the skin, called **erogenous zones,** are highly sensitive to touch. These areas may include the genitals, breasts, mouth, ears, neck, inner thighs, and buttocks; erotic associations with these areas vary from culture to culture and from individual to individual. Our olfactory sense (smell) may bring us sexual messages below the level of our conscious awareness. Scientists have isolated chemical substances, called **pheromones,** that are secreted into the air by many kinds of animals, including ants, moths, pigs, dogs, and monkeys. One function of pheromones, in animals at least, appears to be to arouse the **libido** (li-BEE-doh), or sexual interest (Cutler, 1999; Small, 1999).

Fascinating work in this area, involving smell and the powerful role it plays in partnership selection, has been done by Swiss zoologist Claus Wedekind (cited in Blum, 1997). In a study involving 44 college women and 49 college men, Wedekind gave each man a clean cotton T-shirt and asked him to sleep in it over a weekend. He also instructed the men to avoid colognes, deodorants, spicy foods, and cigarettes. The sweaty T-shirts were collected at the end of the weekend, and each was stored in a clean plastic box. At the time of each woman's ovulation (during which time, studies

Sensory inputs, such as the sight, touch, or smell of someone we love or the sound of his or her voice, may evoke desire and sexual arousal.

show, the sense of smell becomes more acute), the woman was presented with a stack of plastic boxes containing both the sweaty T-shirts and some clean ones. The women were asked to rate every shirt for sexiness, pleasantness, and intensity of smell. The researchers found that the more different from her own was the man's MHC complex (genes that code for the body's own cells and send out an alert if unknown organisms are detected), the sexier the woman rated the shirt—and, presumably, the man. This research correlated with previous results obtained with mice. Wedekind's study implies that biology disposes an individual toward a mate who would provide a healthy mixture of genes. Obviously, this is not the only cue we use in partnership selection, but it does suggest a subtle yet powerful link among MHC genes, smell, and sex. Definitive research on human pheromones, however, has yet to be conducted.

Hormones   The libido in both men and women is biologically influenced by the hormone **testosterone.** In men, testosterone is produced mainly in the testes; in women, it is produced in the adrenal glands and the ovaries. Growing evidence suggests that testosterone may play an important role in the maintenance of women's bodies ("Women's Hormones," 2002). Although it does not play a large part in a woman's hormonal makeup, it is present in the blood vessels, brain, skin, bone, and vagina. Testosterone is believed to contribute to bone density, blood flow, hair growth, energy and strength, and libido.

Although women produce much less testosterone than men, this does not mean that they have less sexual interest; apparently, women are much more sensitive than men to testosterone's effects. Testosterone levels in women peak when they reach the age of 20; by their forties, they have about half as much. Though testosterone decreases in women as they age, the ovaries manufacture it throughout life. Symptoms produced by the decrease of testosterone can be similar to those related to estrogen loss, including fatigue, vaginal dryness, and bone loss. Signs specific to testosterone deficiency include thinning of body hair, depression, diminished motivation, fatigue, and lowered libido (Johnson, 2002; "Women's Hormones," 2002). (Testosterone replacement therapy is discussed in Chapter 13.)

Estrogen also plays a role in sexual functioning. In women, estrogen helps to maintain the vaginal lining; it is not clear how it specifically affects the libido. However, when a woman is given oral estrogen replacement, her serum levels of testosterone are decreased (Johnson, 2002). Men also produce small amounts of estrogen, but its particular function is not known. Too much estrogen, however, can cause erection difficulties.

The role of **oxytocin,** a hormone more commonly associated with contractions during labor, has been of considerable interest to those who are observing it in relation to sexual arousal. Oxytocin may work synergistically with other sex hormones to produce muscle contractions during orgasm (Mah & Binik, 2001).

Experiencing Sexual Arousal

For both males and females, physiological changes during sexual excitement depend on two processes: vasocongestion and myotonia. **Vasocongestion** is the concentration of blood in body tissues. For example, blood fills the genital regions of both males and females, causing the penis to become erect and the clitoris to swell. **Myotonia** is increased muscle tension accompanying the approach of orgasm; upon orgasm, the body undergoes involuntary muscle contractions and then relaxes. The sexual response pattern remains the same for all forms of sexual behavior, whether autoerotic or coital experiences, heterosexual or homosexual. Nevertheless, approximately 14% of women report problems related to arousal (Leland, 2000).

Sexual Excitement   Some women do not separate sexual desire from arousal (Tiefer, 2001). Additionally, many seem to care less about physical arousal but rather place more emphasis on the relational and emotional aspects of intimacy. In any case, for women, one of the first signs of sexual excitement is the moistening of the vaginal walls through a process called **sweating.** Some women also report "tingling" in the genital area. Caused by lymphatic fluids pushing through the vaginal walls during vasocongestion, these secretions lubricate the vagina, enabling it to encompass the penis easily. The inner two-thirds of the vagina expands in a process called **tenting;** the vagina expands about an inch in length and doubles its width. The labia minora begin to protrude outside the labia majora during sexual excitement, and breathing and heart rate increase. These signs do not occur on a specific timetable; each woman has her own pattern of arousal, which may vary under different conditions, with different partners, and so on.

> The reason so many women fake orgasms is that so many men fake foreplay.
>
> *—Graffito*

MANY OF US MEASURE both our sexuality and ourselves in terms of orgasm: Did we have one? Did our partner have one? Was it good? Did we have simultaneous orgasms? When we measure our sexuality by orgasm, however, we discount activities that do not necessarily lead to orgasm, such as touching, caressing, and kissing. We discount erotic pleasure as an end in itself. Our culture tends to identify sex with sexual intercourse, and the end of sexual intercourse is literally orgasm (especially male orgasm). As one female college student puts it: "The deification of intercourse belittles the other aspects of lovemaking that are equally valid and often more enjoyable" (Malcolm, 1994).

An Anthropological Perspective

A fundamental, biological fact about orgasm is that male orgasm and ejaculation are required for reproduction, whereas the female orgasm is not. The male orgasm is universal in both animal and human species, but sociobiologists and anthropologists have found immense variation in the experience of female orgasm. Anthropologists such as Margaret Mead (1975) found that some societies, such as the Mundugumor, emphasize the female orgasm but that it is virtually nonexistent in other societies, such as the Arapesh.

In our culture, women most consistently experience orgasm through clitoral stimulation; penile thrusting during intercourse is not always sufficient for orgasm. In cultures that cultivate female orgasm, according to sociobiologist Donald Symons (1979), there is, in addition to an absence of sexual repression, an emphasis on men's skill in arousing women. Among the Mangaians, for example, as boys enter adolescence, they are given expert advice on kissing and stimulating a woman's breasts, performing cunnilingus, and bringing their partners to multiple orgasms before they themselves ejaculate (Marshall, 1971). In our own culture, among men who consider themselves (and are considered) "good lovers," great emphasis is placed on their abilities to arouse their partners and bring them to orgasm. These skills include not only penile penetration but also, often more importantly, clitoral or G-spot stimulation. This, of course, is based on the sexual script that men are to "give orgasms to women," a message that places pressure on men and that tells women they are not responsible for their own sexual response. According to this script, the woman is "erotically dependent" on the man. The woman can, of course, also stimulate her own clitoris to experience orgasm.

The Tyranny of the Orgasm

Sociologist Philip Slater (1974) suggests that our preoccupation with orgasm is an extension of the Protestant work ethic, in which nothing is enjoyed for its own sake; everything is work, including sex. Thus, we "achieve" orgasm much as we achieve success. Those who achieve orgasm are the "successful workers" of sex; those who do not are the "failures."

Contractions raise the uterus, but the clitoris remains virtually unchanged during this early phase. Although the clitoris responds more slowly than the penis to vasocongestion, it is still affected. The initial changes, however, are minor. Clitoral tumescence (swelling) occurs simultaneously with engorgement of the labia minora. During masturbation and oral sex, the clitoris is generally stimulated directly. During intercourse, clitoral stimulation is mostly indirect, caused by the clitoral hood being pulled over the clitoris or by pressure in the general clitoral area. At the same time that these changes are occurring in the genitals, the breasts are also responding. The nipples become erect, and the breasts may enlarge somewhat because of the engorgement of blood vessels; the areolae may also enlarge. Many women (and men) experience a **sex flush,** a darkening of the skin or rash that temporarily appears as a result of blood rushing to the skin's surface during sexual excitement.

As excitement increases, the clitoris retracts beneath the clitoral hood and virtually disappears. The labia minora become progressively larger until they double or triple in size. They deepen in color, becoming pink, bright red, or a deep wine-red color, depending on the woman's skin color. This intense coloring is sometimes referred to as the "sex skin." When it appears,

As we look at our sexuality, we can see pressure to be successful lovers. Men talk of performance anxiety. We tend to evaluate a woman's sexual self-worth in terms of her being orgasmic (able to have orgasms). For men, the significant question about women's sexuality has shifted from "Is she a virgin?" to "Is she orgasmic?"

Faking Orgasm

Although during sexual intercourse women are not as consistently orgasmic as men, there is considerable pressure on them to be so. In one study, college students were asked whether they had faked orgasm; 60% of heterosexual women and 71% of lesbian or bisexual women said yes, while only 17% of heterosexual men and 27% of gay or bisexual men acknowledged doing so (Elliott & Brantley, 1997). The reason most women fake orgasm is not to protect their own feelings as much as to protect those of their partner. They want to please their partner and avoid hurting or disappointing him. Other reasons include fear of their own sexual inadequacy and a desire to prevent their partner from seeking another partner and to end boring or painful intercourse (Darling & Davidson, 1986; Ellison, 2000).

"Was It Good for You?"

A question often asked following intercourse is, "Was it good for you?" or its variation, "Did you come?"

Such questions are often asked by men rather than women, and women tend to resent them. Part of the pressure to pretend to have an orgasm is caused by these questions. What is really being asked? If the woman enjoyed intercourse? If she thinks the man is a good lover? Or is the question merely a signal that the lovemaking is over?

If a partner cares about the other's enjoyment and wants to improve the couple's erotic pleasures, the appropriate time to inquire about lovemaking is not during or immediately following intercourse. Researchers Carol Darling and Kenneth Davidson (1986) advise that such discussion be initiated at a neutral time and place. Moreover, each partner needs to be free to inquire about the other's satisfaction. The goal should be to increase a couple's fulfillment, rather than to complain about "performance" or soothe a ruffled ego. Even among lesbian women, who undoubtedly are more acquainted with female anatomy than most men are, partners need to be careful in making assumptions about what is sexually arousing. One woman comments (cited in Boston Women's Health Book Collective, 1996): "The more women I sleep with, the more I realize you can't assume what you like is what she likes. There are tremendous differences. All kinds of stuff needs to be talked about and often isn't."

S. J. Malcolm (1994), a writer for *Ms.* magazine, states:

It is ironic and distressing that something so universal as sex is a conversational taboo. . . . Many of us don't talk openly with our partners. My friends and I have found that, in the long run, it is worth the struggle and awkwardness. Once you have worked out with your partner what each of you specifically can do to make the other feel best, you'll find real sexual pleasure.

orgasm is imminent. Meanwhile, the vaginal opening and lower third of the vagina decrease in size as they become more congested with blood. This thickening of the walls, which occurs in the plateau stage of the sexual response cycle, is known as the **orgasmic platform.** The upper two-thirds of the vagina continues to expand, but lubrication decreases or may even stop. The uterus becomes fully elevated through muscular contractions.

Changes in the breasts continue. The areolae become larger even as the nipples decrease in relative size. If the woman has not breast-fed, her breasts may increase by up to 25% of their unaroused size; women who have breast-fed may have little change in size.

Orgasm Continued stimulation brings **orgasm,** a reflex that occurs when blood flow to the pelvis reaches a peak and is dispersed by rhythmic contractions of the vagina, uterus, and pelvic muscles, accompanied by intensely pleasurable sensations. The inner two-thirds of the vagina does not contract; instead, it continues its tenting effect. The labia do not change during orgasm, nor do the breasts. Heart and respiratory rates and blood pressure reach their peak during orgasm. (For a review of the literature related to the nature of orgasm, see Mah & Binik, 2001.)

What is the earth? What are the body and soul without satisfaction?

—*Walt Whitman (1819–1892)*

After orgasm, the orgasmic platform rapidly subsides. The clitoris reemerges from beneath the clitoral hood. (If a woman does not have an orgasm once she is sexually aroused, the clitoris may remain engorged for several hours, possibly creating a feeling of frustration.) The labia slowly return to their unaroused state, and the sex flush gradually disappears. About 30–40% of women perspire as the body begins to cool.

Interestingly, when women and men are asked to use adjectives to describe their experience of orgasm, data suggest that, beyond the awareness of ejaculation that men report, their sensations bear more similarities than differences (Mah & Binik, 2002).

Following orgasm, men experience a refractory period, in which they are unable to ejaculate. In contrast, women are often physiologically able to be orgasmic immediately following the previous orgasm. As a result, women can have multiple orgasms if they continue to be stimulated. Though findings vary on the percentage of women who experience multiple orgasms (estimates range from 14% to 40%), what is clear is that wide variability exists among women and within any one woman from one time to another.

IN THE NEXT CHAPTER, we discuss the anatomical features and physiological functions that characterize men's sexuality and sexual response. The information in these two chapters should serve as a comprehensive basis for understanding the material that follows.

SUMMARY

Female Sex Organs: What Are They For?

- All embryos appear as female at first. Genetic and hormonal signals trigger the development of male organs in those embryos destined to be male.

- Sex organs serve a reproductive purpose, but they perform other functions also: giving pleasure, attracting sex partners, and bonding in relationships.

- The external female *genitals* are known collectively as the *vulva*. The *mons pubis* is a pad of fatty tissue that covers the area of the pubic bone. The *clitoris* is the center of sexual arousal in the female. The *labia majora* are two folds of spongy flesh extending from the mons pubis and enclosing the other external genitals. The *labia minora* are smooth, hairless folds within the labia majora that meet above the clitoris.

- The internal female sexual structures and reproductive organs include the *vagina*, the *uterus*, the *cervix*, the *ovaries*, and the *fallopian tubes*. The vagina is a flexible muscular organ that encompasses the penis during sexual intercourse and is the *birth canal* through which an infant is born. The opening of the vagina, the *introitus*, is partially covered by a thin, perforated membrane, the *hymen*, prior to first intercourse or other intrusion.

- Controversial research has posited the existence of an erotically sensitive area, the *Grafenberg spot (G-spot)*, on the front wall of the vagina midway between the introitus and the cervix.

- The *uterus*, or womb, is a hollow, thick-walled, muscular organ; the tapered end, the *cervix*, extends downward and opens into the vagina. The lining of the uterine walls, the *endometrium*, is built up and then shed and expelled through the cervical *os* (opening) during menstruation. In the event of pregnancy, the pre-embryo is embedded in the nourishing endometrium. On each side of the uterus is one of a pair of ovaries, the female *gonads* (organs that produce *gametes*, sex cells containing the genetic material necessary for reproduction).

At the top of the uterus are the *fallopian tubes,* or uterine tubes. They extend toward the ovaries but are not attached to them. The funnel-shaped end of each tube (the *infundibulum*) fans out into fingerlike *fimbriae,* which drape over the ovary. Hairlike *cilia* on the fimbriae transport the ovulated *oocyte* (egg) into the fallopian tube. The *ampulla* is the widened part of the tube in which fertilization normally occurs. Other important structures in the area of the genitals include the *urethra, anus,* and *perineum.*

- The reproductive function of the female breasts, or *mammary glands,* is to nourish the offspring through *lactation,* or milk production. A breast is composed of fatty tissue and 15–25 lobes that radiate around a central protruding nipple. *Alveoli* within the lobes produce milk. Around the nipple is a ring of darkened skin called the *areola.*

Female Sexual Physiology

- *Hormones* are chemical substances that serve as messengers, traveling through the bloodstream. Important hormones that act directly on the gonads (*gonadotropins*) are *follicle-stimulating hormone (FSH)* and *luteinizing hormone (LH).* Hormones produced in the ovaries are *estrogen,* which helps regulate the menstrual cycle, and *progesterone,* which helps maintain the uterine lining.

- At birth, the human female's ovaries contain approximately half a million *oocytes,* or female gametes. During childhood, many of these degenerate. In a woman's lifetime, about 400 oocytes will mature and be released, beginning in puberty when hormones trigger the completion of *oogenesis,* the production of oocytes, commonly called eggs or ova.

- The activities of the ovaries and the development of oocytes for ovulation, the expulsion of the oocyte, are described as the three-phase *ovarian cycle,* which is usually about 28 days long. The phases are *follicular* (maturation of the oocyte), *ovulatory* (expulsion of the oocyte), and *luteal* (hormone production by the corpus luteum).

- The *menstrual cycle* (or uterine cycle), like the ovarian cycle, is divided into three phases. The shedding of the endometrium marks the beginning of the *menstrual phase.* The menstrual flow, or *menses,* generally occurs over a period of 2–5 days. Endometrial tissue builds up during the *proliferative phase;* it produces nutrients to sustain an embryo in the *secretory phase.*

- The most severe menstrual problems have been attributed to *premenstrual syndrome (PMS),* a cluster of physical and emotional symptoms, which are not agreed upon because of contradictory studies. Some women experience pelvic cramping and pain during the menstrual cycle (*dysmenorrhea*). When women do not menstruate for reasons other than aging, the condition is called *amenorrhea.* A principal cause of amenorrhea is pregnancy.

Female Sexual Response

- *Masters and Johnson's four-phase model of sexual response* identifies the significant stages of response as excitement, plateau, orgasm, and resolution. *Kaplan's tri-phasic model of sexual response* consists of three phases: desire, excitement, and orgasm. *Loulan's sexual response model* includes both biological and affective components in a six-stage cycle.

- The physical manifestations of sexual arousal involve a complex interaction of thoughts and feelings, sensory perceptions, neural responses, and hormonal reactions occurring in many parts of the body. For both males and females, physiological changes during sexual excitement depend on two processes: *vasocongestion,* the concentration of blood in body tissues, and *myotonia,* increased muscle tension with approaching orgasm.

- For women, a first sign of sexual excitement is the moistening of the vaginal walls, or *sweating.* The inner two-thirds of the vagina expands in a process called *tenting;* the labia may enlarge or flatten and separate; the clitoris swells. Breathing and heart rate increase. The nipples become erect, and the breasts may enlarge somewhat. The uterus elevates. As excitement increases, the clitoris retracts beneath the clitoral hood. The vaginal opening decreases by about one-third, and its outer third becomes more congested, forming the *orgasmic platform.*

- Continued stimulation brings *orgasm,* rhythmic contractions of the vagina, uterus, and pelvic muscles, accompanied by very pleasurable sensations. Women are often able to be orgasmic following a previous orgasm if they continue to be stimulated.

Sex and the Internet

Sexuality and Ethnicity

Of the 270 million people living in the United States, more than 36 million are women who are members of racial and ethnic minorities. Many of these women are in poor health, use fewer reproductive health services, and continue to suffer disproportionately from premature death, disease, and disabilities. In addition, there are tremendous economic, cultural, and social barriers to achieving optimal health. To find out more about the reproductive health risks of special concern to women of color, go to the National Women's Health Information Center Web site (http://www.4woman.gov/minority/index.cfm). From the menu, select one group of women and report on the following:

- One reproductive health concern
- Obstacles women may encounter that would prevent them from obtaining services
- Potential solutions to this problem

SUGGESTED WEB SITES

National Organization for Women (NOW)
http://www.now.org
An organization of women and men who support full equality for women in truly equal partnerships.

National Women's Health Network
http://www.womenshealthnetwork.org
Provides clear, well-researched, and unbiased information about a variety of women's health- and sexuality-related issues.

North American Menopause Society
http://www.menopause.org
Promotes women's health during midlife and beyond through an understanding of menopause.

PMS Access/Women's Health America Group
http://www.womenshealth.com
Provides information about PMS, as well as links to other sites dealing with PMS and women's health issues.

Vulvar Health
http://www.vulvarhealth.org
Describes various vulvar disorders and provides a list of resources and links.

A Woman's Guide to Sexuality/Planned Parenthood
http://www.plannedparenthood.org
Explores sexuality and relationships.

Women's Studies Resources
http://www.inform.umd.edu/EdRes/Topic/WomensStudies/
Maintained by the University of Maryland; provides a wealth of resources, including information on body image, comfort with sexuality, and sexually explicit material.

SUGGESTED READING

Angier, Natalie. (1999). *Women: An Intimate Geography.* Boston: Houghton Mifflin. A study that draws on science, medicine, mythology, history, and art to expand the definitions of female geography.

Boston Women's Health Book Collective. (1998). *Our Bodies, Ourselves: For the New Century.* New York: Simon & Schuster. A thorough, accurate, and proactive women's text covering a broad range of health issues.

Ellison, Carol. (2000). *Women's Sexualities.* Oakland, CA: New Harbinger. Interviews with women age 23–90 on the challenges and joys inherent in sexuality.

Wingood, Gina, & DiClemente, Ralph (Eds.). (2002). *Handbook of Women's Sexual and Reproductive Health.* New York: Kluwer Academic/Plenum. A sourcebook for women's sexuality.

For links, articles, and study material, go to the McGraw-Hill Web site, located at http://www.mhhe.com/strong5

4

Male Sexual Anatomy, Physiology, and Response

Student Voices

"Of course the media played a huge role in my sexual identity. It seemed everything in the media revolved around sex when I was young. Magazines such as Playboy and Penthouse offered pictures of nude female bodies, while more hard-core media such as Hustler offered a first look at penetration and a man's penis. Hustler magazine was a big step for me in my childhood; it gave me my first look at another man's erect penis and a first look at the actual act of intercourse. This was like the bible of sex to me; it showed what to do with the penis, how it fit into the vagina, and gave me a scale by which I could measure my own penis up to."

—23-year-old White male

"I noticed while talking among my friends about sex that exaggeration was common. Far-fetched stories were frequent and easily spotted based on the frequency and lack of details. At a certain point, I tried separating what I thought were the lies from the truth so that I could get a better understanding of what men did. Later, I found myself occasionally inserting their lies into the stories I shared with my friends."

—24-year-old Latino male

"In the meantime, I was going through some physical changes. That summer, I worked hard to try to make the varsity soccer team. I was growing, putting on weight, and I was "breaking out." When school resumed that fall, I returned a different person. Now, instead of being that cute little kid that no one could resist, I became this average-looking teenager with acne. The acne was one factor that affected my life more than anything."

—21-year-old White male

CLEARLY, MALE SEXUAL STRUCTURES and functions differ in many ways from those of females. What may not be as apparent, however, is that there are also a number of similarities in the functions of the sex organs and the sexual response patterns of men and women. In the previous chapter, we learned that the sexual structures of both females and males derive from the same embryonic tissue. But when this tissue receives the signals to begin differentiation into a male, the embryonic reproductive organs begin to change their appearance dramatically.

MALE SEX ORGANS: WHAT ARE THEY FOR?

Like female sex organs, male sex organs serve several functions. In their reproductive role, a man's sex organs manufacture and store gametes and deliver them to a woman's reproductive tract. Some of the organs, especially the penis, provide a source of physical pleasure for both the man and his partner.

External Structures

The external male sexual structures are the penis and the scrotum.

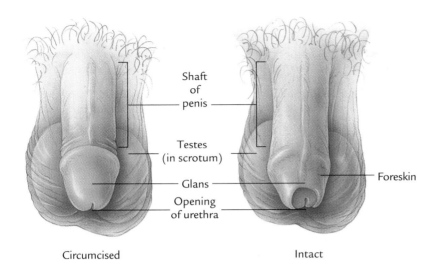

FIGURE 4.1 External Male Sexual Structures

Shaft
of
penis

Testes
(in scrotum)

Glans

Opening
of urethra

Foreskin

Circumcised

Intact

The Penis The **penis** (from the Latin word for tail) is the organ through which both sperm and urine pass. It is attached to the male perineum, the diamond-shaped region extending from the base of the scrotum to the anus.

The penis consists of three main sections: the root, the shaft, and the head (Figure 4.1). The **root** attaches the penis within the pelvic cavity; the body of the penis, the **shaft,** hangs free. At the end of the shaft is the enlarged head of the penis, the **glans penis,** and at its tip is the urethral opening. The rim at the base of the glans is known as the **corona** (Spanish for crown). On the underside of the penis is a triangular area of sensitive skin called the **frenulum** (FREN-you-lem), which attaches the glans to the foreskin. The glans penis is particularly important in sexual arousal because it contains a relatively high concentration of nerve endings, making it especially responsive to stimulation.

A loose skin covers the shaft of the penis and extends to cover the glans penis; the sleevelike covering of the glans is known as the **foreskin** or **prepuce** (PREE-pews). It can be pulled back easily to expose the glans. In the United States, the foreskins of male infants are often surgically removed by a procedure called **circumcision.** As a result of this procedure, the glans penis is left exposed. The reasons for circumcision seem to be rooted more in tradition and religious beliefs (it is an important ritual in Judaism and Islam) than in any firmly established health principles. Beneath the foreskin are several small glands that produce a cheesy substance called **smegma.** If smegma accumulates, it thickens, produces a foul odor, and can become granular and irritate the penis, causing discomfort and infection. It is important for uncircumcised adult men to observe good hygiene by periodically retracting the skin and washing the glans to remove the smegma. (For further discussion of circumcision, see Chapter 12.)

The shaft of the penis contains three parallel columns of erectile tissue. The two that extend along the front surface are known as the **corpora cavernosa** (KOR-por-a kav-er-NO-sa; cavernous bodies), and the third, which runs beneath them, is called the **corpus spongiosum** (KOR-pus spun-gee-OH-sum; spongy body), which also forms the glans (Figure 4.2). At the root of the penis, the corpora cavernosa form the **crura** (KROO-ra),

The sex organ has a poetic power, like a comet.

—*Joan Miró (1893–1983)*

Is size important? Click on "Male Anatomy" to hear men talking honestly about penis size.

There is nothing about which men lie so much as about their sexual powers. In this at least every man is, what in his heart he would like to be, a Casanova.

—*W. Somerset Maugham (1874–1965)*

MAN'S PREOCCUPATION WITH his "generative organ" extends far back into history and appears in diverse cultures all over the world. The penis is an almost universal symbol of power and fertility. It may also be a source of considerable pleasure and anxiety for the individuals who happen to possess one.

Power to the Penis

Earthenware figurines from ancient Peru, ink drawings from medieval Japan, painted walls in the villas of Pompeii—in the art and artifacts from every corner of the world, we find a common theme: penises! And not just any old penises, but organs of such length, girth, and weight that they can barely be supported by their possessors. Whether as an object of worship or an object of jest, the giant penis has been (and continues to be) a symbol that holds deep cultural significance, especially in societies in which men are dominant over women (Strage, 1980). Although it seems reasonable for the erect penis to be used as a symbol of love, or at least lust, many of its associations appear to be as an instrument of aggression and power. In New Guinea, Kiwai hunters pressed their penises against the trees from which they would make their harpoons, thereby assuring the strength and straightness of their weapons. Maori warriors in New Zealand crawled under the legs of their chief so that the power of his penis would descend onto them (Strage, 1980).

In our society, many people would argue that men are deeply attached to symbolic images of their potency—cars, motorcycles, missiles, and especially guns. Lest they become confused as to which is the symbol and which the reality, young grunts in Marine boot camp are instructed in the following drill (to be shouted with appropriate gestures):

> This is my rifle! This is my gun!
> This is for fighting! This is for fun!

To take away a man's gun is to threaten him with impotence. (The word "potent" is from the Latin *potens*, meaning ability or power; the word "impotent," in addition to meaning powerless, also implies the inability to get an erection. The term "erectile dysfunction" is now beginning to replace "impotence" as the appropriate term because it is descriptive, not demeaning.)

In many cultures, the penis has also represented fertility and prosperity. In India, large stone phalluses *(lingams)*, associated with the Hindu god Shiva, are adorned with flowers and propitiated with offerings. Ancient peoples as diverse as the Maya in Central America and the Egyptians in North Africa believed that the blood from the penises of their rulers was especially powerful. Mayan kings ceremonially pierced their penises with stingray spines, and the pharaohs and high priests of Egypt underwent ritual circumcision. In other places, men have ritually offered their semen to assure a plentiful harvest.

"Phallic Phallacies"

It is interesting (but perhaps not surprising) that the responsibility of owning an instrument of great power can carry with it an equally great burden of anxiety. In some ways, the choice of the penis as a symbol of domination seems rather unwise. Any man (and a good many women) can tell you that a penis can be disturbingly unreliable and appear to have a mind of its own. For men who are already insecure about their abilities on the job or in the bedroom, the penis can take on meanings quite beyond those of procreation, elimination, or sensual pleasure. How can a man be expected to control his employees or his children when he can't control the behavior of his own penis?

As discussed in Chapter 2, Sigmund Freud believed that women are unconsciously jealous of men's penises (penis envy). In reality, those who appear to suffer the most from penis envy are men, who indeed possess a penis but often seem to long for a bigger one. The idea that "the larger the penis, the more effective the male in coital connection" is referred to by Masters and Johnson as a "phallic phallacy" (Masters & Johnson, 1966).

Another manifestation of penile anxiety, also named by Freud, is castration anxiety (see Chapter 2). This term is misleading, for it does not describe what the actual fear is about. Castration is the removal of the testes, but castration anxiety is fear of losing the penis. In China and other parts of Asia and in Africa, there have been documented epidemics of *koro* (a Japanese term), the conviction that one's penis is shrinking and is going to disappear. A doctor in Singapore in 1968 reported 4500 cases of *koro*, which appears to have no physiological basis but to grow in the psyches of anxiety-prone men (Yap, 1993).

For his own psyche's sake, as well as the sake of his partner and that of society, a man would do well to consider how his feelings about his penis and his masculinity affect his well-being. At this point, we can only speculate, but perhaps there will come a time when men allow themselves to focus less on the size and performance of their equipment—both sexual and martial—and more on acceptance, communication, and the mutual sharing of pleasure.

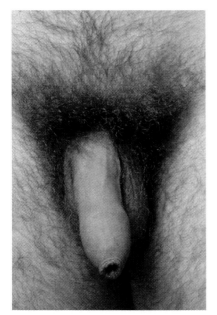 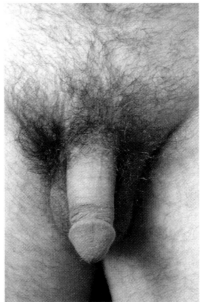 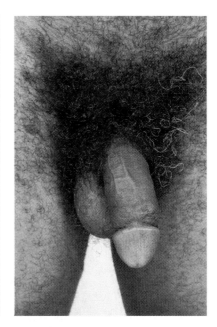

There is great variation in the appearance, size, and shape of the male genitalia. Note that the penis on the left is not circumcised.

which are anchored by muscle to the pubic bone. The **urethra,** a tube that transports both urine and semen, runs from the bladder (where it expands to form the **urethral bulb**), through the spongy body, to the tip of the penis, where it opens to the outside. Inside the three chambers are a large number of blood vessels through which blood freely circulates when the penis is flaccid (relaxed). During sexual arousal, these vessels fill with blood and expand, causing the penis to become erect. (Sexual arousal, including erection, is discussed in greater detail later in the chapter.)

In men, the urethra serves as the passageway for both urine and semen. Because the urinary opening is at the tip of the penis, it is vulnerable to injury and infection. The sensitive mucous membranes around the opening may be subject to abrasion and can provide an entrance into the body for infectious organisms. Condoms, properly used, provide an effective barrier between this vulnerable area and potentially infectious secretions or other substances.

In an unaroused state, the *average* penis is slightly under 4 inches long, although there is a great deal of individual variation. When erect, penises become more uniform in size, as the percentage of volume increase is greater with smaller penises than with larger ones. But in an unaroused state, an individual's penis size may vary. Cold air or water, fear, and anxiety, for example, often cause the penis to be pulled closer to the body and to decrease in size. When the penis is erect, the urinary duct is temporarily blocked, allowing for the ejaculation of semen. But erection does not necessarily mean sexual excitement. A man may have erections at night during REM sleep, the phase of the sleep cycle when dreaming occurs, or when he is anxious.

Myths and misconceptions about the penis abound, especially among men. Many people believe that the size of a man's penis is directly related to his masculinity, aggressiveness, sexual ability, or sexual attractiveness. Others believe that there is a relationship between the size of a man's penis

(top of penis)

Corpora cavernosa

Penile urethra

Corpus spongiosum

FIGURE 4.2   Cross Section of the Shaft of the Penis

It can safely be said that the adult male population suffers an almost universal anxiety in regard to penile size.

—*James F. Glenn, MD*

It is a Freudian thesis, with which I am inclined to agree, that the pistol, whether in the hands of an amateur or a professional gunman, has significance for the owner as a symbol of virility, an extension of the male organ, and that excessive interest in guns is a form of fetishism.

—*Ian Fleming (1908–1964)*

and the size of his hands, feet, thumbs, or nose. In fact, the size of the penis is not specifically related to body size or weight, muscular structure, race or ethnicity, or sexual orientation; it is determined by individual hereditary factors. Except in very rare and extreme cases, there is no relationship between penis size and a man's ability to have sexual intercourse or to satisfy his partner.

The Scrotum   Hanging loosely at the root of the penis is the **scrotum,** a pouch of skin that holds the two testicles. The skin of the scrotum is more heavily pigmented than the skin elsewhere on the body; it is sparsely covered with hair and divided in the middle by a ridge of skin. The skin of the scrotum varies in appearance under different conditions. When a man is sexually aroused, for example, or when he is cold, the testicles are pulled close to the body, causing the skin to wrinkle and become more compact. The changes in the surface of the scrotum help maintain a fairly constant temperature within the testicles (about 93°F). Two sets of muscles control these changes: (1) the dartos muscle, a smooth muscle under the skin that contracts and causes the surface to wrinkle, and (2) the fibrous cremaster muscle within the scrotal sac that causes the testes to elevate.

Internal Structures

Male internal reproductive organs and structures include the testes (testicles), seminiferous tubules, epididymis, vas deferens, ejaculatory ducts, seminal vesicles, prostate gland, and Cowper's (bulbourethral) glands (Figure 4.3).

The Testes   Inside the scrotum are the male reproductive glands or gonads, which are called **testicles** or **testes** (singular, *testis*). The testes have two major functions: sperm production and hormone production. Each olive-

FIGURE 4.3   Internal Side View of the Male Reproductive Organs

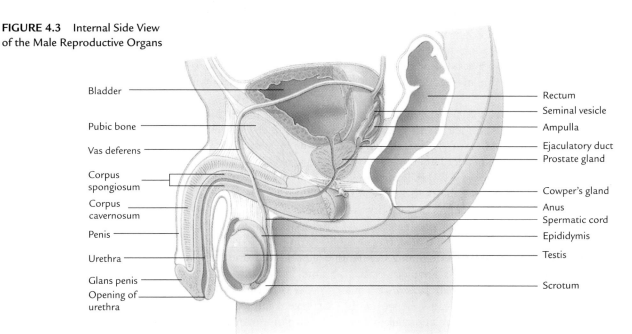

Bladder

Pubic bone

Vas deferens

Corpus spongiosum

Corpus cavernosum

Penis

Urethra

Glans penis

Opening of urethra

Rectum

Seminal vesicle

Ampulla

Ejaculatory duct

Prostate gland

Cowper's gland

Anus

Spermatic cord

Epididymis

Testis

Scrotum

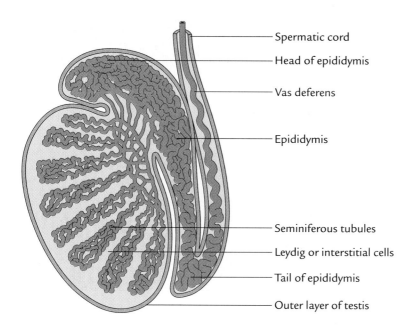

- Spermatic cord
- Head of epididymis
- Vas deferens
- Epididymis
- Seminiferous tubules
- Leydig or interstitial cells
- Tail of epididymis
- Outer layer of testis

FIGURE 4.4 Cross Section of a Testicle

shaped testis is about 1.5 inches long and 1 inch in diameter and weighs about 1 ounce; as a male ages, the testes decrease in size and weight. The testicles are usually not symmetrical; the left testicle generally hangs slightly lower than the right one. Within the scrotal sac, each testicle is suspended by a **spermatic cord** containing nerves, blood vessels, and a vas deferens (Figure 4.4). Within each testicle are around 1000 **seminiferous tubules,** tiny, tightly compressed tubes 1–3 feet long (they would extend several hundred yards if laid end to end). Within these tubes, spermatogenesis—the production of sperm—takes place.

As a male fetus grows, the testes develop within the pelvic cavity; toward the end of the gestation period, the testes usually descend into the scrotum. In about 2–5% of cases, however, one or both of the testes fail to descend, a condition that usually corrects itself within a year or two. If this condition is not corrected before puberty, usually by surgery or hormones, sperm will be less likely to mature because of the higher temperatures in the abdomen.

The Epididymis and Vas Deferens The epididymis and vas deferens (or ductus deferens) are the ducts that carry sperm from the testicles to the urethra for ejaculation. The seminiferous tubules merge to form the **epididymis** (ep-e-DID-i-mes), a comma-shaped structure consisting of a coiled tube about 20 feet long, where the sperm finally mature. Each epididymis merges into a **vas deferens,** a tube about 18 inches long, extending into the abdominal cavity, over the bladder, and then downward, widening into the flask-shaped **ampulla.** The vas deferens joins the **ejaculatory duct** within the prostate gland. The vas deferens can be felt easily in the scrotal sac. Because it is easily accessible and is crucial for sperm transport, it is usually the point of sterilization for men. The operation is called a vasectomy (it is discussed fully in Chapter 11). A vasectomy does not affect the libido or the ability to ejaculate because only the sperm are transported through the vas deferens. Most of the semen that is ejaculated comes from the prostate gland and the seminal vesicles.

Nowhere does one read of a penis that quietly moseyed out for a look at what was going on before springing and crashing into action.

—*Bernie Zilbergeld (1939–2002)*

Click on "Vasectomy" for a look at male genitals, and to see a vasectomy performed.

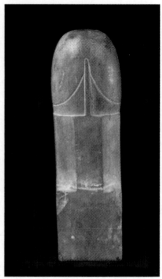

The penis is a prominent symbol in both ancient and modern art. Here we see a contemporary phallic sculpture in Frogner Park, Oslo, Norway, and a stone lingam *from Thailand.*

Men always want to be a woman's first love—women like to be a man's last romance.

—*Oscar Wilde (1854–1900)*

The Seminal Vesicles, Prostate Gland, and Cowper's Glands   At the back of the bladder lie two glands, each about the size and shape of a finger. These **seminal vesicles** secrete a fluid that makes up about 60% of the seminal fluid. Encircling the urethra just below the bladder is a small muscular gland about the size and shape of a chestnut. The **prostate gland** produces about 30–35% of the seminal fluid in the ejaculated semen. These secretions flow into the urethra through a system of tiny ducts. Some men who enjoy receiving anal sex experience erotic sensations when the prostate is gently stroked; others find that contact with the prostate is uncomfortable. Men, especially if they are older, may be troubled by a variety of prostate problems, ranging from relatively benign conditions to more serious inflammations and prostate cancer. (Problems and diseases of the prostate are covered in Chapter 13.)

Below the prostate gland are two pea-sized glands connected to the urethra by tiny ducts. These are **Cowper's,** or **bulbourethral** (bul-bo-you-REE-thrul), **glands,** which secrete a thick, clear mucus prior to ejaculation. This fluid may appear at the tip of the erect penis; its alkaline content may help buffer the acidity within the urethra and provide a more hospitable environment for sperm. Fluid from the Cowper's glands may contain sperm that have remained in the urethra since a previous ejaculation or that have leaked in from the ampullae. Consequently, it is possible for a pregnancy to occur from sperm left over even if the penis is withdrawn before ejaculation.

The Breasts and Anus

Male anatomical structures that do not serve a reproductive function but that may be involved in or affected by sexual activities include the breasts, urethra, buttocks, rectum, and anus.

Although the male breast contains the same basic structures as the female breast—nipple, areola, fat, and glandular tissue—the amounts of underlying fatty and glandular tissues are much smaller in men. Our culture appears to be ambivalent about the erotic function of men's breasts. We usually do not even call them breasts, but refer to the general area as the chest. Some men find stimulation of their breasts to be sexually arousing; others do not. **Gynecomastia** (gine-a-ko-MAS-tee-a), the swelling or enlargement of the male breast, can occur during adolescence or adulthood. In puberty, gynecomastia is a normal response to hormonal changes (see Chapter 6). In adulthood, its causes may include alcoholism, liver or thyroid disease, and cancer.

An organ used primarily for excretion, the anus can also be used by both men and women for sexual purposes. Because the anus is kept tightly closed by the external and internal anal sphincters, most of the erotic sensation that occurs during anal sex is derived from the penetration of the anal opening. Beyond the sphincters lies a larger space, the rectum. In men, the prostate gland is located in front of the rectum (in women, it's the vagina), and stimulation of this and nearby structures can be very pleasing. Because the anus and rectum do not provide significant amounts of lubrication, most people use some sort of water-based lubricant. Both men and women may enjoy oral stimulation of the anus ("rimming"); the insertion of fingers, a hand ("fisting"), a dildo, or a penis into the rectum may bring erotic pleasure to both the receiver and the giver. (Anal sex is discussed more fully in Chapter 9; safer sex guidelines appear in Chapter 15.)

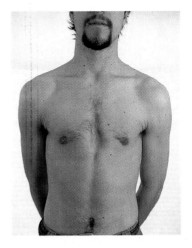

Male breasts, which are usually referred to euphemistically as "the chest," may or may not be considered erotic areas. Men are allowed to display their naked breasts in certain public settings. Whether the sight is sexually arousing depends on the viewer and the context.

MALE SEXUAL PHYSIOLOGY

The reproductive processes of the male body include the production of hormones and the production and delivery of sperm. Although men do not have a monthly reproductive cycle comparable to that of women, they do experience regular fluctuations of hormone levels; there is also some evidence that men's moods follow a cyclical pattern.

Sex Hormones

Within the connective tissues of a man's testes are **Leydig cells** (also called interstitial cells), which secrete **androgens** (male hormones). The most important of these is testosterone, which triggers sperm production and regulates the sex drive (Figure 4.5). Other important hormones in male reproductive physiology are GnRH, FSH, and LH. In addition, men produce the protein hormone inhibin, oxytocin, and small amounts of estrogen. Table 4.1 describes the principal hormones involved in sperm production and their function.

Testosterone   **Testosterone** is a steroid hormone synthesized from cholesterol. Testosterone is made by both sexes—by women mostly in the adrenal glands and ovaries and by men primarily in the testes (men produce 20–40 times more testosterone than women do [Rako, 1996]). Furthermore, the brain converts testosterone to estradiol (a female hormone). This flexibility of the hormone makes the link between testosterone and behavior precarious.

During puberty, besides acting on the seminiferous tubules to produce sperm, testosterone targets other areas of the body. It causes the penis, testicles, and other reproductive organs to grow and is responsible for the

BECAUSE MEN DO NOT get pregnant or bear children, and because condom use is possible without medical intervention, men's sexual and reproductive health needs are not as obvious as women's and often are ignored. In recent years, however, the high incidence of HIV and sexually transmitted infections and the critical role of condom use in their prevention, concerns regarding the role of males in teenage pregnancies and births, and the failure of many divorced and unmarried fathers to fulfill their parental responsibilities have begun to alter this trend. Clearly, a movement toward a more holistic and broad-based approach to sexual and reproductive health care for men is still needed.

From adolescence on, most men need information and referrals for their sexual and reproductive concerns. Unfortunately, health insurance often does not cover the services men need, and a high proportion of men, particularly low-income men, do not have health insurance. Thus, there are significant gaps between needs and services. Furthermore, few health professionals are specifically trained to provide men with sexual and reproductive health education and services. Men's reproductive health involves both their own well-being and their ability to engage in healthy, fulfilling relationships. To achieve this, all men need the following:

- Information and education about contraceptive use, pregnancy, and childbearing

- Education about and access to routine screening and treatment for sexually transmitted infections

- Information about where to obtain and how to use condoms correctly

- Counseling and support regarding how to talk about these issues with partners

- Surgical services for vasectomies, screening and treatment for reproductive cancers (particularly prostate and testicular cancer), sexual problems, and infertility treatment

Additionally, skills development related to self-advocacy, risk assessment and avoidance, resistance to peer pressure, communication with partners, fatherhood skills, and role expectations is both needed and desired.

The complex relationships between poverty, high-risk behaviors, and poor health outcomes are undeniable for both men and women. Helping men lead healthier sexual and reproductive lives is a goal that is garnering attention and legitimacy. What is increasingly seen as good for men in their own right should turn out to be just as good for women—to the ultimate benefit of society as a whole.

For more on men's health, see "In Their Own Right: Addressing the Sexual and Reproductive Health Needs of American Men" at the Alan Guttmacher Institute Web site (http://agi-usa.org/pubs/us_men.html).

TABLE 4.1	Male Reproductive Hormones	
Hormone	*Where Produced*	*Functions*
Testosterone	Testes, adrenal glands	Stimulates sperm production in testes, triggers development of secondary sex characteristics, regulates sex drive
GnRH	Hypothalamus	Stimulates pituitary during sperm production
FSH	Pituitary	Stimulates sperm production in testes
ICSH (LH)	Pituitary	Stimulates testosterone production in interstitial cells within testes
Inhibin	Testes	Regulates sperm production by inhibiting release of FSH
Oxytocin	Hypothalamus, testes	Stimulates contractions in the internal reproductive organs to move the contents of the tubules forward
Relaxin	Prostate	Increases sperm motility

development of **secondary sex characteristics,** those changes to parts of the body other than the genitals that indicate sexual maturity. In men, these changes include the growth of pubic, facial, underarm, and other body hair and the deepening of the voice. (In women, estrogen and progesterone combine to develop secondary sex characteristics such as breast development, growth of pubic and underarm hair, and the onset of vaginal mucous secre-

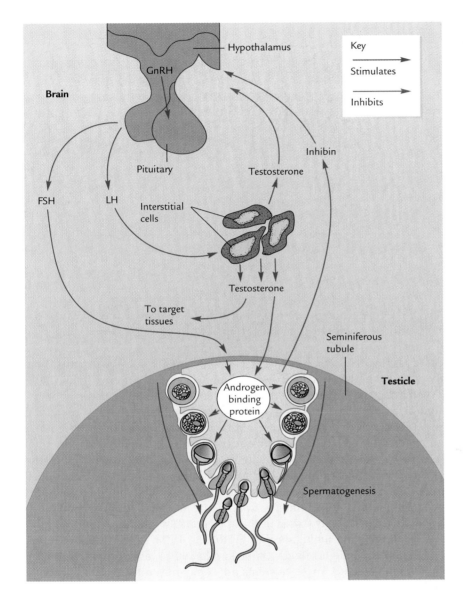

FIGURE 4.5 The Brain-Testicular Axis. The process of sperm production is regulated by this feedback system, which involves hormones produced by the hypothalamus, pituitary, and testes.

tions.) Testosterone also influences the growth of bones and increase of muscle mass and causes the skin to thicken and become oilier (leading to acne in many teenage boys).

Many researchers do see a correlation between testosterone and personality. It has been found to correspond with energy, confidence, and sexual drive (Sullivan, 2000). What complicates this equation, however, is the fact that testosterone levels are rarely stable; they appear to respond positively or negatively to almost every challenge, and not necessarily in a way we might predict.

Testosterone may also play a role in aggressiveness, according to some studies. Researcher Hilary Lips (1997) suggests, however, that these studies need to be carefully interpreted. Although there is some evidence that prenatal exposure to excess testosterone leads to increased rough-and-tumble play among children of both sexes (Reinisch, Ziemba-Davis, & Saunders,

FIGURE 4.6 Testosterone Cycles. Every 2–4 hours, testosterone levels in the blood peak. (*Source:* LaVay & Valente, 2002)

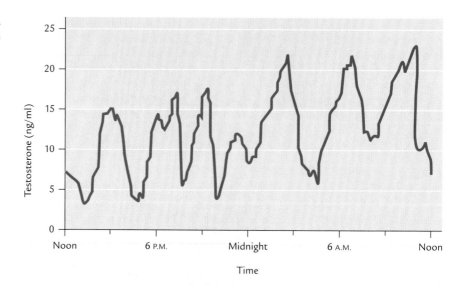

When people say women can't be trusted because they cycle every month, my response is that men cycle every day, so they should only be allowed to negotiate peace treaties in the evening.

—*June Reinisch*

1991), the connection between such play and actual aggressive behavior has not been adequately demonstrated (Lips, 2001).

Male Cycles   Studies comparing men and women have found that both sexes are subject to changes in mood and behavior patterns (Lips, 2001). Whereas such changes in women are often attributed (rightly or wrongly) to menstrual cycle fluctuations, it is not clear that male changes are related to levels of testosterone or other hormones, although there may well be a connection. Men do appear to undergo cyclic changes, although their testosterone levels do not fluctuate as dramatically as do women's estrogen and progesterone levels. On a daily basis, men's testosterone levels appear to be lowest in the evening and highest in the morning (midnight to noon) (Figure 4.6). (Winters et al., 2001). Moreover, their overall levels appear to be relatively lower in the spring and higher in the fall.

Throughout the night, specifically during REM sleep, men experience spontaneous penile erections. (Women experience labial, vaginal, and clitoral engorgement.) These erections are sometimes referred to as "battery-recharging mechanisms" for the penis, because they increase blood flow and bring fresh oxygen. Four or five times a night, both men and women experience this type of engorgement (Goldstein, 2000). If a man has erectile difficulties while he is awake, it is important to determine whether he has normal erections during sleep. If so, his problems may have to do with something other than the mechanics of erection. Approximately 90% of men and nearly 40% of women experience nocturnal orgasms; for men, these are often referred to as "wet dreams" (Kinsey, Pomeroy, & Martin, 1948; Wells, 1986).

Spermatogenesis

Within the testes, from puberty on, **spermatogenesis,** the production of **sperm,** is an ongoing process. Every day, a healthy, fertile man produces several hundred million sperm within the seminiferous tubules of his testicles (Figure 4.7). After they are formed in the seminiferous tubules, which takes 64–72 days, immature sperm are stored in the epididymis. It then takes

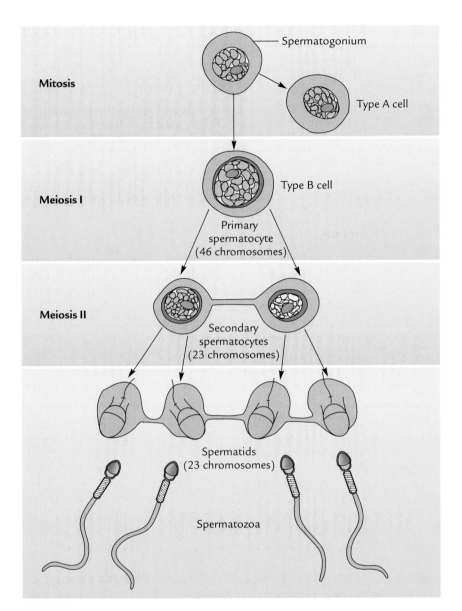

FIGURE 4.7 **Spermatogenesis.** This diagram shows the development of spermatozoa, beginning with a single spermatogonium and ending with four complete sperm cells. Spermatogenesis is an ongoing process that begins in puberty. Several hundred million sperm are produced every day within the seminiferous tubules of a healthy man.

about 20 days for the sperm to travel the length of the epididymis, during which time they become fertile and motile (able to move) (Figure 4.8). Upon ejaculation, sperm in the tail section of the epididymis are expelled by muscular contractions of its walls into the vas deferens; similar contractions within the vas deferens propel the sperm into the urethra, where they are mixed with semen and then expelled from the urethral opening.

The sex of the zygote produced by the union of egg and sperm is determined by the chromosomes of the sperm. The ovum always contributes a female sex chromosome (X), whereas the sperm may contribute either a female or a male sex chromosome (Y). The combination of two X chromosomes (XX) means that the zygote will develop as a female; with an X and a Y chromosome (XY), it will develop as a male. In some cases, combinations of sex chromosomes other than XX or XY occur, causing sexual development to proceed differently. (These variations are discussed in Chapter 5.)

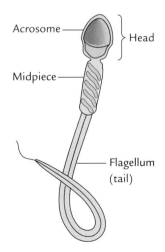

FIGURE 4.8 **The Human Spermatozoon (Sperm Cell).** The head contains the sperm's nucleus, including the chromosomes, and is encased in the helmetlike acrosome.

Between 100 million and 600 million sperm are present in the semen from a single ejaculation. Typically, following ejaculation during intercourse, fewer than 1000 will get as far as a fallopian tube, where an ovulated oocyte may be present. Though many sperm assist in helping to dissolve the egg cell membrane, typically only one sperm ultimately achieves fertilization.

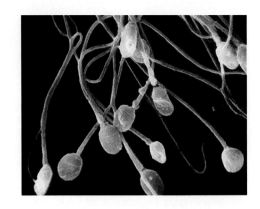

Semen Production

Semen, or **seminal fluid,** is the ejaculated liquid that contains sperm. The function of semen is to nourish sperm and provide them with a hospitable environment and means of transport when they are deposited within the vagina. Semen is mainly made up of secretions from the seminal vesicles and prostate gland, which mix together in the urethra during ejaculation. Immediately after ejaculation, the semen is somewhat thick and sticky from clotting factors in the fluid. This consistency keeps the sperm together initially; then the semen becomes liquefied, allowing the sperm to swim out. Semen ranges in color from opalescent or milky white to yellowish or grayish in tone upon ejaculation, but it becomes clearer as it liquefies. Normally, about 2–6 milliliters (about 1 teaspoonful) of semen is ejaculated at one time; this amount of semen generally contains between 100 million and 600 million sperm. In spite of their significance, sperm occupy only about 1% of the total volume of semen; the remainder comes primarily from the seminal vesicles (70%) and the prostate gland (30%). Fewer than 1000 sperm will reach the fallopian tubes. Though there is still much debate, a recent meta-analysis of studies that examined sperm-counting techniques found that average sperm counts in several Western countries dropped by approximately one-half between 1940 and 1996 (Swan, Elkin, & Fenster, 2000). Why this phenomenon has taken place remains a mystery.

MALE SEXUAL RESPONSE

At this point, it might be useful to review the material on sexual arousal and response in Chapter 3, including the models of Masters and Johnson, Kaplan, and Loulan. Even though their sexual anatomy is quite different, women and men follow roughly the same pattern of excitement and orgasm, with two exceptions: (1) Generally (but certainly not always), men become fully aroused and ready for penetration in a shorter amount of time than women do; and (2) once men experience ejaculation, they usually cannot do so again for some time, whereas women may experience multiple orgasms.

Probably one of the most controversial topics in the field of sexuality theory is whether sexual desire is shaped more by nature or culture. As suggested in Chapter 3, societal expectations, education, class, politics, and relational factors are thought to influence both men's and women's sexual desire and performance. Combined, these influence sexual desire and response in profound ways.

Male sexual response is far brisker and more automatic. It is triggered easily by things—like putting a quarter in a vending machine.

—*Dr. Alex Comfort (1920–2000)*

Bring me my bow of burning gold.
Bring me my arrows of desire.

—*William Blake (1757–1827)*

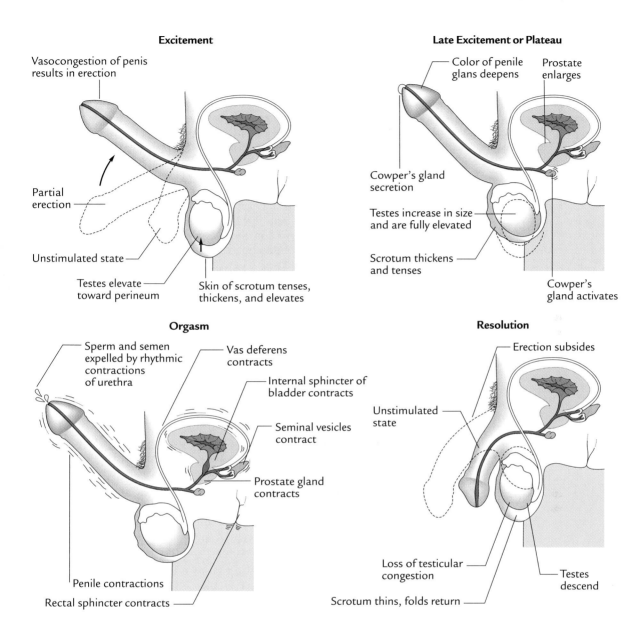

Excitement

Vasocongestion of penis results in erection

Partial erection

Unstimulated state

Testes elevate toward perineum

Skin of scrotum tenses, thickens, and elevates

Late Excitement or Plateau

Color of penile glans deepens

Prostate enlarges

Cowper's gland secretion

Testes increase in size and are fully elevated

Scrotum thickens and tenses

Cowper's gland activates

Orgasm

Sperm and semen expelled by rhythmic contractions of urethra

Vas deferens contracts

Internal sphincter of bladder contracts

Seminal vesicles contract

Prostate gland contracts

Penile contractions

Rectal sphincter contracts

Resolution

Erection subsides

Unstimulated state

Loss of testicular congestion

Testes descend

Scrotum thins, folds return

FIGURE 4.9   Masters and Johnson Stages in Male Sexual Response

Sexual arousal in men includes the processes of myotonia (increased muscle tension) and vasocongestion (engorgement of the tissues with blood). Vasocongestion in men is most apparent in the erection of the penis.

Erection

When a male becomes aroused, the blood circulation within the penis changes dramatically (Figure 4.9). During the process of **erection,** the blood vessels expand, increasing the volume of blood, especially within the corpora cavernosa. At the same time, expansion of the penis compresses the veins that normally carry blood out, so the penis becomes further engorged. (There are no muscles in the penis that make it erect, nor is there a bone in it.) Secretions from the Cowper's glands appear at the tip of the penis during erection.

An erection at will is the moral equivalent of a valid credit card.

—*Dr. Alex Comfort*

THE **ERECTION REFLEX** can be triggered by various sexual and nonsexual stimuli, including tactile stimulation (touching) of the penis or other erogenous areas; sights, smells, or sounds (usually words or sexual vocalizations); and emotions or thoughts. Even negative emotions such as fear can produce an erection. Conversely, emotions and thoughts can also inhibit erections, as can unpleasant or painful physical sensations. The erectile response is controlled by the parasympathetic nervous system and therefore cannot be consciously willed.

The length of time an erection lasts varies greatly from individual to individual and from situation to situation. With experience, most men are able to gauge the amount of stimulation that will either maintain the erection without causing orgasm or cause orgasm to occur too soon. Failure to attain an erection when one is desired is something most men experience at one time or another. (Erectile difficulties are discussed further in Chapter 14.)

There are, however, some things you can do to maximize your chances of producing viable erections. Because you need a steady flow of blood to your penis, you should get enough aerobic exercise and refrain from smoking to maintain your circulation. A diet low in fat and cholesterol and high in fiber and complex carbohydrates may also prevent hardening of the arteries, which restricts blood flow.

Some conditions, including diabetes, tension, depression, and abnormalities in blood pressure, and some medications that treat the abnormalities may have an adverse effect on blood flow and erectile capacity. If any of these conditions are present, or if the failure to attain an erection is persistent, see your physician.

What can you do about unwanted erections at inappropriate times? Distract yourself or stop your thoughts or images. Remember, the brain is the most erotic (and unerotic) organ of the body.

Ejaculation and Orgasm

Increasing stimulation of the penis generally leads to **ejaculation,** the process by which semen is forcefully expelled from a man's body. When the impulses that cause erection reach a critical point, a spinal reflex sets off a massive discharge of nerve impulses to the ducts, glands, and muscles of the reproductive system. Ejaculation then occurs in two stages.

Emission   In the first stage, **emission,** contractions of the walls of the tail portion of the epididymis send sperm into the vas deferens. Rhythmic contractions also occur in the vas deferentia, ampullae, seminal vesicles, and ejaculatory ducts, which spill their contents into the urethra. The bladder's sphincter muscle closes to prevent urine from mixing with the semen and semen from entering the bladder, and another sphincter below the prostate also closes, trapping the semen in the expanded urethral bulb. At this point, the man feels a distinct sensation of **ejaculatory inevitability,** the point at which ejaculation *must* occur even if stimulation ceases. These events are accompanied by increased heart rate and respiration, elevated blood pressure, and general muscular tension. About 25% of men experience a sex flush.

Expulsion   In the second stage of ejaculation, **expulsion,** there are rapid, rhythmic contractions of the urethra, the prostate, and the muscles at the base of the penis. The first few contractions are the most forceful, causing semen to spurt from the urethral opening. Gradually, the intensity of the contractions decreases and the interval between them lengthens. Breathing rate and heart rate may reach their peak at expulsion. When the sensations of orgasm were compared among college-age women and men, the only significant gender difference involved the "shooting" sensations reported by men. This variation most likely reflects ejaculation (Mah & Binik, 2002).

Some men experience **retrograde ejaculation,** the "backward" expulsion of semen into the bladder rather than out of the urethral opening. This unusual malfunctioning of the urethral sphincters may be temporary (e.g., induced by tranquilizers), but if it persists, the man should seek medical counsel to determine if there is an underlying problem. Retrograde ejaculation is not normally harmful; the semen is simply collected in the bladder and eliminated during urination.

Orgasm   The intensely pleasurable physical sensations and general release of tension that typically accompany ejaculation constitute the experience of orgasm. Orgasm is a series of muscular contractions of the pelvis that occurs at the height of sexual arousal. Orgasm does not always occur with ejaculation, however. It is possible to ejaculate without having an orgasm and to experience orgasm without ejaculating. Some men have reported having more than one orgasm without ejaculation ("dry orgasm") prior to a final, ejaculatory, orgasm (Dunn & Trost, 1989). Following ejaculation, men experience a **refractory period,** during which they are not capable of having an ejaculation again. This is the time in which nerves cannot respond to additional stimulation. Refractory periods vary greatly in length, ranging from a few minutes to many hours (or even days, in some older men). Other changes occur immediately following ejaculation. The erection diminishes as blood flow returns to normal, the sex flush (if there was one) disappears, and fairly heavy perspiration may occur. Men who experience intense sexual arousal without ejaculation may feel some heaviness or discomfort in the testicles; this is generally not as painful as the common term "blue balls" implies. If discomfort persists, however, it may be relieved by a period of rest or by ejaculation. There is no harm to a man's health if he does not ejaculate frequently or at all. When the seminal vesicles are full, feedback mechanisms diminish the quantity of sperm produced. Excess sperm die and are absorbed by the body.

> When the appetite arises in the liver, the heart generates a spirit which descends through the arteries, fills the hollow of the penis and makes it hard and stiff. The delightful movements of intercourse give warmth to all the members, and hence to the humor which is in the brain; this liquid is drawn through the veins which lead from behind the ears to the testicles and from them it is squirted by the penis into the vulva.
>
> —*Constantinus Africanus (c. 1070)*

IN THIS CHAPTER and the previous one, we have looked primarily at the *physical* characteristics that designate us as female or male. But, as we discover in the following chapter, there's more to gender than mere chromosomes or reproductive organs. How we feel about our physical selves (our male or female anatomy) and how we act (our gender roles) also determine our identities as men or women.

SUMMARY

Male Sex Organs: What Are They For?

- In their reproductive role, a man's sex organs produce and store gametes and deliver them to a woman's reproductive tract. The *penis* is the organ through which both sperm and urine pass. The *shaft* of the penis contains two *corpora cavernosa* and a *corpus spongiosum*, which fill with blood during arousal, causing an erection. The head is called the *glans penis;* in uncircumcised men, it is covered by the *foreskin.* Myths about the penis equate its size with masculinity and sexual prowess. The *scrotum* is a pouch of skin that hangs at the root of the penis. It holds the *testes*.

- The paired testes or testicles have two major functions: sperm production and hormone production. Within each testicle are about 1000 *seminiferous tubules*, where the production of sperm takes place. The seminiferous tubules merge to form the *epididymis*, a coiled tube where the sperm finally mature, and each epididymis merges into a *vas deferens*, which joins the *ejaculatory duct* within the *prostate gland*. The *seminal vesicles* and prostate gland produce semen, which nourishes and transports the sperm. Two tiny glands called *Cowper's* or *bulbourethral glands* secrete a thick, clear mucus prior to ejaculation.

- Male anatomical structures that do not serve a reproductive function but that may be involved in or affected by sexual activities include the breasts, *urethra*, buttocks, rectum, and anus.

Male Sexual Physiology

- The reproductive processes of the male body include the production of hormones and the production and delivery of sperm, the male gametes. Although men do not have a monthly reproductive cycle comparable to that of women, they do experience regular fluctuations of hormone levels; there is also some evidence that men's moods follow a cyclical pattern. The most important male hormone is *testosterone*, which triggers sperm production and regulates the sex drive. Other important hormones in male reproductive physiology are GnRH, FSH, LH, inhibin, and oxytocin.

- *Sperm* carry either an X chromosome, which will produce a female zygote, or Y chromosome, which will produce a male.

- *Semen*, or seminal fluid, is the ejaculated liquid that contains sperm. The function of semen is to nourish sperm and provide them with a hospitable environment and means of transport when they are deposited within the vagina. It is mainly made up of secretions from the seminal vesicles and prostate gland. The semen from a single ejaculation generally contains between 100 million and 600 million sperm, yet only about 1000 make it to the fallopian tubes.

Male Sexual Response

- Male sexual response, like that of females, involves the processes of vasocongestion and myotonia. *Erection* of the penis occurs when sexual or tactile stimuli cause its chambers to become engorged with blood. Continuing stimulation leads to *ejaculation*, which occurs in two stages. In the first stage, *emission*, semen mixes with sperm in the urethral bulb. In the second stage, *expulsion*, semen is forcibly expelled from the penis. Ejaculation and orgasm, a series of contractions of the pelvic muscles occurring at the height of sexual arousal, typically happen simultaneously. However, they can also occur separately. Following orgasm is a *refractory period*, during which ejaculation is not possible.

Sex and the Internet

Men's Sexuality

Try to locate Internet sites about men's sexuality. You'll find that, apart from those relating to erectile dysfunction, AIDS, and sexually explicit materials, few sites address this topic. What does this say about men? About the topic of men and sex? Because of this absence of content-specific sites, it is necessary to locate a broader topic: men's health. Go to the Men's Health Network (http://www.menshealthnetwork.org/index.htm) and, in the Library section, scroll down to one of the health links, "Health." If you don't find a topic there that interests you, go to "Links" and search for a relevant subject. When you find a topic that interests you, see if you can respond to the following:

- Background information about the topic

- The incidence or prevalence of the issue/problem

- Whom it impacts or affects

- The causes and potential solutions

- The recommendation you might make for someone who identified with this issue

- A related link that might broaden your understanding of this topic

SUGGESTED WEB SITES

Male Health Center
http://www.malehealthcenter.com/
Provides information on a wide variety of issues related to male genital health, birth control, and sexual functioning, from the male perspective.

Men's Health Resource Guide
http://www.menshealth.com/cda/home
A resource guide from *Men's Health* that offers links to many topics in men's health and to discussions of relationship and family issues.

Men's Issues Page
http://www.menweb.org/
Provides discussions on a wide variety of issues.

National Organization of Circumcision Information Resources
http://www.nocirc.org
Contains information and resources about male and female circumcision.

SUGGESTED READING

Bechtel, Stefan, & Roystains, Lawrence. (1997). *Sex: A Man's Guide.* Emmaus, PA: Rodale Press. Advice on more than 130 sex topics.

Bordo, Susan. (2000). *The Male Body: A New Look at Men in Public and Private.* New York: Farrar, Straus, & Giroux. An examination of the presentation of maleness in everyday life; rejects rigid categories in favor of an honest vision of men as flesh-and-blood human beings.

McCarthy, Barry, & McCarthy, Emily. (1998). *Male Sexual Awareness.* Berkeley, CA: Publishers Group West. A rich source of information on male sexuality and sexual functioning; designed to help men integrate their sexuality into their lives in a way that enhances awareness and satisfaction.

Zilbergeld, Bernie. (1999). *The New Male Sexuality.* (Rev. ed.). New York: Bantam Books. An explanation of both male and female anatomy and sexual response, plus communication, sexual problem solving, and much more; authoritative, interesting, and readable; written for men (but recommended for women as well).

For links, articles, and study material, go to the McGraw-Hill Web site, located at http://www.mhhe.com/strong5

5

Gender and Gender Roles

"*As* early as preschool I learned the difference between boy and girl toys, games, and colors. The boys played with trucks while the girls played with dolls. If a boy were to play with a doll, he would be laughed at and even teased. In the make-believe area, once again, you have limitations of your dreams. Girls could not be police, truck drivers, firemen, or construction workers. We had to be people that were cute, such as models, housewives, dancers, or nurses. We would sometimes model ourselves after our parents or family members."

— 23-year-old Black female

"*I* grew up with the question of "why?" dangling from the tip of my tongue. Why am I supposed to marry a certain person? Why do I have to learn how to cook meat for my husband when I am a vegetarian? Why can't I go out on dates or to school formals? The answer was the same every time: "Because you're a girl." Being that she is such a strong woman, I know it tore a bit of my grandmother's heart every time she had to say it."

— 19-year-old first-generation Indian female

"*My* stepfather and I did not get along. I viewed him as an outsider, and I did not want a replacement father. Looking back, I feel like I overcompensated for the lack of a male figure in my life. I enlisted in the Navy at 18, have a huge firearm collection, and play ice hockey on the weekends. All of these activities seem to be macho, even to me. I guess it's to prove that even though a woman raised me I'm still a man's man."

— 27-year-old White male

"*I* was in fifth grade, and my parents put me on restriction. My mom inquired where I got the [Playboy] magazine. I told her we found it on the way home from school. She wanted to know where. I lied and said it was just sitting in somebody's trashcan and I happened to see it. She wanted to know where. I said I forgot. My sexual identity was being founded on concealment, repression, and lies. Within my family, my sexual identity was repressed."

— 27-year-old White male

*H*OW CAN WE TELL the difference between a man and a woman? Everyone knows that women and men, at a basic level, are distinguished by their genitals. However, as accurate as this answer may be academically, it is not particularly useful in social situations. In most social situations—except in nudist colonies or while sunbathing au naturel—our genitals are not visible to the casual observer. We do not expose ourselves (or ask another person to do so) for gender verification. We are more likely to rely on secondary sex characteristics, such as breasts and body hair, or on bone structure, musculature, and height. But even these characteristics are not always reliable, given the great variety of shapes and sizes we come in as human beings. And from farther away than a few yards, we cannot always distinguish these characteristics. Instead of relying entirely on physical characteristics to identify individuals as male and female, we often look for other clues.

Culture provides us with an important clue for recognizing whether a person is female or male in most situations: dress. In almost all cultures, male and female clothing differs to varying degrees so that we can easily identify a person's gender. Some cultures, such as our own, may accentuate secondary sex characteristics, especially for females. Traditional feminine clothing, for example, emphasizes a woman's gender: dress or skirt, a form-fitting or low-cut top revealing the breasts, high heels, and so on. Most clothing, in fact, that emphasizes or exaggerates secondary sex characteristics is female. Makeup (lipstick, rouge, eyeliner) and hairstyles also serve to mark or exaggerate the differences between females and males. Even smells (perfume for women, cologne for men) and colors (blue for boys, pink for girls) help distinguish females and males.

Clothing and other aspects of appearance exaggerate the physical differences between women and men. And culture encourages us to accentuate (or invent) psychological, emotional, mental, and behavioral differences. But are men and women as different as we ordinarily think?

In this chapter, we examine some of the critical ways being male or female affects us both as human beings and as sexual beings. We look at the connection between our genitals, our identity as female or male, and our feelings of being feminine or masculine. We also examine the relationship between femininity, masculinity, and sexual orientation. Then we discuss how masculine and feminine traits result from both biological and social influences. Next, we focus on theories of socialization and how we learn to act masculine and feminine in our culture. Then we look at traditional, contemporary, and androgynous gender roles. Finally, we examine intersexuality, transsexuality, and transgenderism—phenomena that involve complex issues pertaining to gender and gender identity.

STUDYING GENDER AND GENDER ROLES

Let's start by defining some key terms, to establish a common terminology. Keeping these definitions in mind will make the discussion clearer.

Sex, Gender, and Gender Roles: What's the Difference?

The word **sex** refers to whether one is biologically female or male, based on genetic and anatomical sex. **Genetic sex** refers to one's chromosomal and hormonal sex characteristics, such as whether one's chromosomes are XY or XX and whether estrogen or testosterone dominates the hormonal system. **Anatomical sex** refers to physical sex: gonads, uterus, vulva, vagina, penis, and so on.

Although "sex" and "gender" are often used interchangeably, gender is not the same as biological sex. As noted in Chapter 3, gender relates to femininity or masculinity, the social and cultural characteristics associated with biological sex. Whereas sex is rooted in biology, gender is rooted in culture. **Assigned gender** is the gender given by others, usually at birth. When a baby is born, someone looks at the genitals and exclaims, "It's a boy!" or "It's a girl!" With that single utterance, the baby is transformed from an "it" into a "male" or a "female." **Gender identity** is the gender a person believes him- or herself to be.

The interaction of biological and psychological factors contributes to the development of gender. (Lisa Lyon, 1981. Copyright © 1981 The Estate of Robert Mapplethorpe.)

Gender roles are the attitudes, behaviors, rights, and responsibilities that society associates with each sex. Age, race, and a variety of other factors further define and influence these. The term "gender role" is gradually replacing the traditional term "sex role" because "sex role" continues to suggest a connection between biological sex and behavior. Biological males are expected to act out masculine gender roles; biological females are expected to act out feminine gender roles. A **gender-role stereotype** is a rigidly held, oversimplified, and overgeneralized belief that all males and all females possess distinct psychological and behavioral traits. Stereotypes tend to be false or misleading, not only for the group as a whole (e.g., women are more interested in relationships than sex) but for any individual in the group (e.g., Naoki may be more interested in sex than relationships). Even if a generalization is statistically valid in describing a group average (e.g., males are generally taller than females), such generalizations do not necessarily predict the facts (e.g. whether Roberto will be taller than Andrea). **Gender-role attitude** refers to the beliefs a person has about him- or herself and others regarding appropriate female and male personality traits and activities. **Gender-role behavior** refers to the actual activities or behaviors a person engages in as a female or a male.

> Whatever women do they must do twice as well as men to be thought half as good. Luckily, this is not difficult.
>
> —*Charlotte Whitton*

Sex and Gender Identity

We develop our gender through the interaction of its biological and psychosocial components. The biological component includes genetic and anatomical sex; the psychosocial component includes assigned gender and

Although strangers can't always readily tell the sex of a baby, once they learn the sex, they respond with gender stereotypes and expectations.

gender identity. Because these dimensions are learned together, they may seem to be natural. For example, if a person looks like a girl (biological), believes she should be feminine (cultural), feels as if she is a girl (psychological), and acts like a girl (social), then her gender identity and role are congruent with her anatomical sex. Our culture emphasizes that there are only two genders and that there should be coherence among the biological, social, cultural, and psychological dimensions (Frayser, 2002). Any deviation is labeled "abnormal."

Assigned Gender When we are born, we are assigned a gender based on anatomical appearance. Assigned gender is significant because it tells *others* how to respond to us. After all, one of the first questions people ask upon seeing an infant is whether it's a girl or a boy. As youngsters, we have no sense of ourselves as female or male. We *learn* that we are a girl or a boy from the verbal responses of others. "What a pretty *girl*" or "What a good *boy,*" our parents and others say. We are constantly given signals about our gender. Our birth certificate states our sex; our name, such as Jarrod or Felicia, is most likely gender-coded. Our clothes, even in infancy, reveal our gender.

By the time we are 2 years old, we are probably able to identify ourself as a girl or a boy based on what we have internalized from what others have told us. But we don't really know *why* we are a girl or a boy. We don't associate our gender with our genitals. In fact, until the age of 3 or so, most children identify girls or boys by hairstyles, clothing, or other nonanatomical signs. At around age 3, we begin to learn that the genitals are what make a person male or female. But it still takes us a while to understand that we are *permanently* a boy or a girl. We often believe that we can become the other sex later on.

Gender Identity By about age 2, we internalize and identify with our gender. We *think* we are a girl or a boy. This feeling of our femaleness or maleness is our gender identity. For most people, gender identity is permanent and is congruent with their sexual anatomy and assigned gender.

Some cultures, however, put off instilling gender identity in males until later. People in these cultures believe in a latent or dormant femaleness in males. As a consequence, such cultures institute rituals or ceremonies in childhood to ensure that males will identify themselves as males. In some East African societies, for example, male children are referred to as "woman-child"; there are few social differences between young boys and girls. Around age 7, the boy undergoes male initiation rites, such as circumcision, whose avowed purpose is to "make" him into a man. Such ceremonies may be a kind of benign "brainwashing," helping the young male make the transition to a new gender identity with new role expectations. Other cultures allow older males to act out a latent female identity with such practices as the couvade, in which husbands mimic their wives giving birth. And in our own society, into the early twentieth century, boys were dressed in gowns and wore their hair in long curls until age 2. At age 2 or 3, their dresses were replaced by pants and their hair was cut. From then on, masculine socialization was stressed (Garber, 1991).

Masculinity and Femininity: Opposites or Similar?

Each culture determines the content of gender roles in its own way. Among the Arapesh of New Guinea, for example, members of both sexes possess what we consider feminine traits. Both men and women tend to be passive, cooperative, peaceful, and nurturing. The father as well as the mother is said to "bear a child"; only the father's continual care can make the child grow healthily, both in the womb and in childhood. Eighty miles away, the Mundugumor live in remarkable contrast to the peaceful Arapesh. "Both men and women," Margaret Mead (1975) observed, "are expected to be violent, competitive, aggressively sexed, jealous, and ready to see and avenge insult, delighting in display, in action, in fighting." Biology creates males and females, but it is culture that creates our concepts of masculinity and femininity.

In the traditional Western view of masculinity and femininity, men and women are seen as polar opposites. Our popular terminology, in fact, reflects this view. Women and men refer to each other as the "opposite sex." But this implies that women and men are indeed opposites, that they have little in common. Our gender stereotypes fit this pattern of polar differences: Men are aggressive, whereas women are passive; men embody **instrumentality** and are task-oriented, whereas women embody **expressiveness** and are emotion-oriented; men are rational, whereas women are irrational; men want sex, whereas women want love; and so on.

It is important to recognize that gender stereotypes, despite their depiction of men and women as opposites, are usually not all-or-nothing notions. Most of us do not think that only men are assertive or only women are nurturing. Stereotypes merely reflect *probabilities* that a woman or man will have a certain characteristic based on her or his gender. When we say that men are more independent than women, we simply mean that there is a greater probability that a man will be more independent than a woman.

As technology becomes more advanced, we learn more about what contributes to making the sexes different. We are already getting hints that our identities as men and women are a combination of nature and nurture. It is through new technology that researchers can observe brains in the act of cogitating, feeling, or remembering. Other research has revealed that

One half the world cannot understand the pleasures of the other.

—*Jane Austen (1775–1817)*

The main difference between men and women is that men are lunatics and women are idiots.

—*Rebecca West (1892–1983)*

The perception of male/female psychological differences is far greater than they are in fact.

some differences between men and women may be due to differences in the part of the brain that controls emotional processing. In men, the part thought to control action-oriented responses appears to be more active; in women, the part thought to control more symbolic emotional responses is more active (Gur, Mozley, Mozley et al., 1995). Women's more active emotional processing may explain why it has been observed that males under stress tend to pull away from others, whereas stressed females tend to seek closeness (Gurian, 1999). In fact, many differences and similarities that we once attributed to learning or culture have been found to be biologically based. Add to this our individual choices, sense of identities, and life experiences, and we can begin to get a picture of what contributes to making each person unique.

Gender and Sexual Orientation

Gender, gender identity, and gender role are conceptually independent of sexual orientation (Lips, 2001). But, in many people's minds, these concepts are closely related to sexual orientation (discussed at greater length in Chapter 6). Our traditional notion of gender roles assumes that heterosexuality is a critical component of masculinity and femininity. That is, a "masculine" man is attracted to women and a "feminine" woman is attracted to men. From this assumption follow two beliefs about homosexuality: (1) If a man is gay, he cannot be masculine, and if a woman is lesbian, she cannot be feminine; and (2) if a man is gay, he must have some feminine characteristics, and if a woman is lesbian, she must have some masculine characteristics. What these beliefs imply is that homosexuality is somehow associated with a failure to fill traditional gender roles (De Cecco & Elia, 1993). A "real" man is not gay; therefore, gay men are not "real" men. Similarly, a "real" woman is not a lesbian; therefore, lesbian women are not "real" women.

Stereotypes of gay men often link them with "feminine" characteristics such as weakness, emotionality, and submissiveness. Such stereotypes can be traced back to the turn of the previous century, when both Havelock Ellis and Sigmund Freud (discussed in Chapter 2) suggested that homosexuality was the result of "inversion," or reversed gender roles. In general, lesbian women describe themselves as less feminine on a number of traits than do straight women, and gay men describe themselves as less masculine on a number of traits than do straight men (Lippa, 2000). In their choices of occupations, gay men and lesbian women often disregard gender norms (Lippa, 2002).

Studies on attitudes toward gay men and lesbian women indicate a relationship between negative attitudes and gender roles (Herek, 1998; Kite, 1984). Specifically, individuals holding negative attitudes were more likely to adhere to traditional gender roles, to stereotype men and women, and to support the sexual double standard, granting men greater sexual freedom than women. Men tended to be more negative than women toward gay men and lesbian women. And heterosexual men tended to be more negative toward gay men than toward lesbian women; heterosexual women were more negative toward lesbian women than toward gay men. It has recently been noted that this response can be moderated to some degree by the order in which questions are posed. In one survey, both White and Black men's attitudes toward gay men were less negative when they were asked about lesbian women first (Herek & Capitanio, 1999).

> Stereotypes fall in the face of humanity . . . this is how the world will change for gay men and lesbians.
>
> —*Anna Quindlen*

Gender Theory

What is the relationship between our biological sex as male or female and our gender role as masculine or feminine? Do we act the way we act because our gender role is inbred in us or because of socialization? As we discussed in Chapter 1, biological explanations of gender differences focusing on genes and hormones have found increasing support in recent years. Research in the fields of sociobiology and evolutionary psychology has demonstrated that nature is an important determinant of gender development. Nature alone, however, doesn't account for the variety of gender-related characteristics seen across cultures or for the ways in which gender roles are created. To really understand gender, we must look at social explanations as well as biological ones.

Traditionally, the social sciences have not paid much attention to *why* a culture develops its particular gender roles. They have been more interested in such topics as the process of socialization and male/female differences. In the 1980s, however, gender theory was developed to explore the role of gender in society. According to **gender theory,** a society may be best understood by how it is organized according to gender. Gender is viewed as a basic element in social relationships, based on the socially perceived differences between the sexes that justify unequal power relationships (Scott, 1986). Imagine, for example, an infant crying in the night. Which parent gets up to take care of the baby—the father or the mother? In most cases, the mother does because women are perceived to be nurturing, and it is the woman's "responsibility" as mother (even if she hasn't had a full night's sleep in a week and is employed full-time). Yet the father could just as easily care for the crying infant. He may not, because caregiving is socially perceived as "natural" to women.

In psychology, gender theory focuses on (1) how gender is created and what its purposes are and (2) how specific traits, behaviors, and roles are defined as male or female and how they create advantages for males and disadvantages for females. Gender theorists reject the idea that biology creates male/female differences. Rather, gender differences are largely, if not entirely, created by society.

The key to the creation of gender inequality lies in the belief that men and women are, indeed, "opposite" sexes—that they are opposite each other in personalities, abilities, skills, and traits. Furthermore, the differences between the sexes are unequally valued: Reason and aggressiveness (defined as male traits) are considered to be more valuable than emotion and passivity (defined as female traits). In reality, however, men and women are more like each other than they are different. Both are reasonable and emotional, aggressive and passive.

Gender is socially constructed. In other words, it is neither innate nor instinctive; it is the result of the exercise of cultural conditioning. Making the sexes appear to be opposite and of unequal value requires the suppression of natural similarities by the use of social power (Bem, 1995). The exercise of social power might take the form of greater societal value being placed on appearance than achievement for women, sexual harassment of women in the workplace or school, patronizing attitudes toward women, and so on.

> The war between the sexes is the only one in which both sides regularly sleep with the enemy.
>
> —*Quentin Crisp (1908–1999)*

GENDER-ROLE LEARNING

As we have seen, gender roles are socially constructed and rooted in culture. So how do individuals learn what their society expects of them as males or females?

Theories of Socialization

There are a number of ways of examining how we acquire our gender roles. Two of the most prominent are cognitive social learning theory and cognitive development theory.

Cognitive social learning theory is derived from behavioral psychology. In explaining our actions, behaviorists emphasize observable events and their consequences, rather than internal feelings and drives. According to behaviorists, we learn attitudes and behaviors as a result of social interactions with others—hence the term "social learning."

The cornerstone of cognitive social learning theory is the belief that consequences control behavior. Acts that are regularly followed by a reward are likely to occur again; acts that are regularly followed by a punishment are less likely to recur. Thus, girls are rewarded for playing with dolls ("What a nice mommy!"), but boys are not ("What a sissy!").

This behaviorist approach has been modified recently to include **cognition**—mental processes that intervene between stimulus and response, such as evaluation and reflection. The cognitive processes involved in social learning include our ability to (1) use language, (2) anticipate consequences, and (3) make observations. By using language, we can tell our daughter that we like it when she does well in school and that we don't like it when she hits someone. A person's ability to anticipate consequences affects behavior. A boy doesn't need to wear lace stockings in public to know that such dressing will lead to negative consequences. Finally, children observe what others do. A girl may learn that she "shouldn't" play video games by seeing that the players in video arcades are mostly boys.

We also learn gender roles by imitation, through a process called **modeling.** Most of us are not even aware of the many subtle behaviors that make up gender roles—the ways in which men and women use different mannerisms and gestures, speak differently, use different body language, and so on. We don't "teach" these behaviors by reinforcement. Children tend to model friendly, warm, and nurturing adults; they also tend to imitate adults who are powerful in their eyes—that is, adults who control access to food, toys, or privileges. Initially, the most powerful models that children have are their parents. As children grow older and their social world expands, so does the number of people who may act as their role models: siblings, friends, teachers, athletes, media figures, and so on. Children sift through the various demands and expectations associated with the different models to create their own unique selves.

In contrast to social learning theory, **cognitive development theory** focuses on children's active interpretation of the messages they receive from the environment. Whereas social learning assumes that children and adults learn in fundamentally the same way, cognitive development theory stresses that we learn differently depending on our age. At age 2, children can correctly identify themselves and others as boys or girls, but they tend to base this identification on superficial features such as hair and clothing. Girls have long hair and wear dresses; boys have short hair and wear pants. Some children even believe they can change their gender by changing their clothes or hair length.

Cognitive development theory recognizes gender as a characteristic people use to understand their social environment and interact with it (Cross & Markus, 1993). Thus, children compare themselves to others, including parents, and develop and attach to masculine or feminine values. When children are 6 or 7, they begin to understand that gender is permanent; it is not something they can alter in the same way they can change their clothes. They acquire this understanding because they are capable of grasping the idea that basic characteristics do not change. A woman can be a woman even if she has short hair and wears pants. Children not only understand the permanence of gender but tend to insist on rigid adherence to gender-role stereotypes.

According to cognitive social learning theory, boys and girls learn appropriate gender-role behavior through reinforcement and modeling. But, according to cognitive development theory, once children learn that gender is permanent, they independently strive to act like "proper" girls or boys. They do this on their own because of an internal need for congruence, or agreement between what they know and how they act. Also, children find performing the appropriate gender-role activities to be rewarding in itself. Models and reinforcement help show them how well they are doing, but the primary motivation is internal.

Gender-Role Learning in Childhood and Adolescence

It is difficult to analyze the relationship between biology and personality because learning begins at birth. Research has shown, for example, that infant girls are more sensitive than infant boys to pain and to sudden changes of environment. Such responses may be encouraged by learning that begins immediately after birth.

In our culture, infant girls are usually held more gently and treated more tenderly than boys, who are ordinarily subjected to rougher forms of play. The first day after birth, parents characterize their daughters as soft, fine-featured, and small and their sons as strong, large-featured, big, and bold. When boys do not measure up to this expectation, they may stop trying to express their feelings and emotions.

Parents as Socializing Agents   During infancy and early childhood, children's most important source of learning is the primary caregiver, whether the mother, father, grandmother, or someone else. Many parents are not aware that their words and actions contribute to their children's gender-role socialization. Nor are they aware that they treat their daughters and sons differently because of their gender. Although parents may recognize that they respond differently to sons than to daughters, they usually have a ready explanation: the "natural" differences in the temperament and behavior of girls and boys.

Children are socialized in gender roles through several very subtle processes (Oakley, 1985):

- *Manipulation.* Parents manipulate their children from infancy onward. They treat a daughter gently, tell her she is pretty, and advise her that nice girls do not fight. They treat a son roughly, tell him he is strong, and advise him that big boys do not cry. Eventually, children incorporate their parents' views in such matters as integral parts of their personalities.

- *Channeling.* Children are channeled by directing their attention to specific objects. Toys, for example, are differentiated by sex. Dolls are considered appropriate for girls, and cars for boys.

- *Verbal appellation.* Parents use different words with boys and girls to describe the same behavior. A boy who pushes others may be described as "active," whereas a girl who does the same is usually called "aggressive."

- *Activity exposure.* The activity exposure of girls and boys differs markedly. Although both are usually exposed to a variety of activities early in life, boys are discouraged from imitating their mothers, whereas girls are encouraged to be "mother's little helper."

It is generally accepted that parents socialize their children in outmoded and different ways according to gender. This occurs in spite of the fact that everything we've learned about the need for bonding and connecting for

What are little girls made of?
Sugar and spice
And everything nice.
That's what little girls are made of.
What are little boys made of?
Snips and snails
And puppy dogs' tails.
That's what little boys are made of.

—*Nursery rhyme*

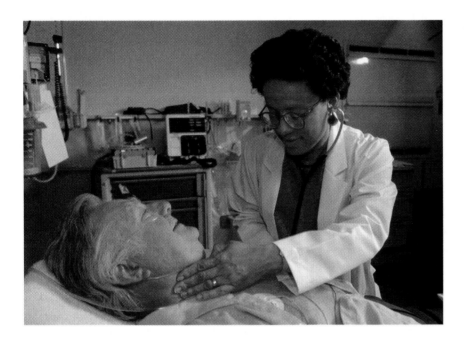

Among African Americans, the traditional female gender role includes strength and independence.

girls is also true for boys. In fact, noted researcher and author Michael Gurian (1999) recommends more connection between sons and mothers. His studies show that such closeness with a mother (as well as with a father) leads to a more successful and satisfying adulthood. Fathers, more than mothers, pressure their children to behave in "gender-appropriate" ways. Fathers set higher standards of achievement for their sons than for their daughters; with their daughters, fathers emphasize the interpersonal aspects of their relationship. But mothers also reinforce the interpersonal aspects of the parent-daughter relationship. Both parents tend to be more restrictive with their daughters and to allow their sons more freedom and to provide less intervention.

Although hundreds of studies have examined gender roles and their importance, few have compared ethnic groups to explore differences in gender roles (Konrad & Harris, 2002). The idea that women's roles should be centered around the home and family generally reflects the traditions of White, middle-class, heterosexual men in the United States (Blee & Tickamyer, 1995). African Americans have been found to have more fluid gender roles (McCollum, 1997), evidently to accommodate the stresses of racism and the relatively greater importance that race plays in African American identity (Shelton & Sellers, 2000). There is also evidence that African American families socialize their daughters to be more independent than White families do. Indeed, among African Americans, the "traditional" female role model may never have existed. The African American female role model in which the woman is both wage-earner and homemaker is more typical and more accurately reflects the African American experience (Blee & Tickamyer, 1995; Greene, 1994).

As children grow older, their social world expands, and so do their sources of learning. Around the time children enter day care or kindergarten, teachers and peers become important influences.

Teachers as Socializing Agents   Day-care centers, nursery schools, and kindergartens are often children's first experience in the world outside the family. Teachers become important role models for their students. Because most day-care workers and kindergarten and elementary school teachers are women, children tend to think of child-adult interactions as primarily the province of women. In this sense, schools reinforce the idea that women are concerned with children and men are not. Teachers may also tend to be conventional in the gender-role messages they convey to children. They may encourage different activities and abilities in boys and girls. Some research indicates that boys of all ages interrupt teachers in their activities much more than girls do and that teachers tend to interrupt girls more than they do boys (Henrick & Stange, 1991). Teachers often give children messages about appropriate activities, such as contact sports for boys and gymnastics or dance for girls. Academically, teachers tend to encourage boys more than girls in math and science and girls more than boys in language skills. Consequently, there is evidence of a downward spiral in test scores in math and science among girls who previously scored equal to or even higher than boys on nearly every standardized test (Sadker & Sadker, 1994). No such downward spiral is observed for boys. It has also been observed that teachers and parents may shame boys into conforming to the traditional image of masculinity. For example, boys are taught to hide their emotions, act brave, and demonstrate independence. Even though boys may get good grades and be considered normal, healthy, and well-adjusted by peers, parents, and teachers, they may also report feeling deeply troubled about the roles and goals of their gender.

Gender bias often follows students into the college arena. Though little research is available on the effects of a college education on women, there is evidence that undergraduate women tend to report more discrimination and sexual bias in their academic departments than do male students (Fischer & Good, 1994). There is also inequality in athletics, based on opportunities for participation and availability of scholarships, although this is gradually changing.

Peers as Socializing Agents   Children's age-mates, or **peers,** become especially important when they enter school. By granting or withholding approval, friends and playmates influence what games children play, what they wear, what music they listen to, what TV programs they watch, and even what cereal they eat. Peers provide standards for gender-role behavior in several ways (Absi-Simaan, Crombie, & Freeman, 1993; Moller, Hymel, & Rubin, 1992):

- Peers provide information about gender-role norms through play activities and toys. Girls play with dolls that cry and wet themselves or with glamorous dolls with well-developed figures and expensive tastes. Boys play with dolls known as "action figures," such as wrestling figures with bigger-than-life biceps.

- Peers influence the adoption of gender-role norms through verbal approval or disapproval. "That's for boys!" or "Only girls do that!" is a strong negative message to the girl playing with a football or the boy playing with dolls.

- Children's perceptions of their friends' gender-role attitudes, behaviors, and beliefs encourage them to adopt similar ones to be accepted. If a girl's friends play soccer, she is more likely to play soccer. If a boy's same-sex friends display feelings, he is more likely to display feelings.

When boys and girls participate in sports together, they develop comparable athletic skills. Segregation of boys and girls encourages the development of differences that otherwise might not occur.

Even though parents tend to fear the worst from peers, peers provide important positive influences. It is within their peer groups, for example, that adolescents learn to develop intimate relationships (Gecas & Seff, 1991).

Media Influences   Much of television programming promotes or condones negative stereotypes about gender, ethnicity, age, and ability, as well as gay men, lesbian women, and bisexual and transgendered individuals. Women are significantly underrepresented on television. One study conducted by the National Organization for Women examined who is doing the talking on Sunday morning political talk shows. To no one's surprise, the researchers discovered that it was mostly White men. In programs from January 2000 to June 2001, women were 11% of all guests. Regardless of the topic, women were underrepresented as experts and elected officials ("Viewpoint: News Hour," 2002). The study concluded that media and the public benefit when women's voices are included and that daughters benefit from female role models.

Female characters on television typically are under age 40, well groomed, attractive, and excessively concerned with their appearance. In contrast, male characters are more aggressive and constructive; they solve problems and rescue others from danger. Thus, boys must grapple daily with exaggerated images of men. Indeed, all forms of media glorify the enforcers and protectors, the ones who win by brute force, intimidation, and anger. Only in recent years on prime-time series have men been shown in emotional, nurturing roles.

Gay men and lesbian women are increasing in visibility in TV movies and in sitcoms such as *Will & Grace* and dramas such as *Queer as Folk*. However, such characters continue to come under scrutiny by show sponsors and are often portrayed stereotypically—as sinister or comical or as victims of AIDS—or solely in terms of their sexual orientation.

Gender Schemas: Exaggerating Differences

Actual differences between females and males are minimal or nonexistent, except in levels of aggressiveness and visual/spatial skills, yet culture exaggerates these differences or creates differences where none otherwise exist.

One way that culture does this is by creating a schema. Recall from Chapter 2 that a schema is a set of interrelated ideas that helps us process information by categorizing it in useful ways. We often categorize people by age, ethnicity, nationality, physical characteristics, and so on. Gender is one such way of categorizing.

Sandra Bem (1983) observes that, although gender is not inherent in inanimate objects or in behaviors, we treat many objects and behaviors as if they were masculine or feminine. These gender divisions form a complex structure of associations that affects our perceptions of reality. Bem refers to this cognitive organization of the world according to gender as a **gender schema.** We use gender schemas in many dimensions of life, including activities (nurturing, fighting), emotions (compassion, anger), behavior (playing with dolls or action figures), clothing (dresses or pants), and even colors (pink or blue), considering some appropriate for one gender and some appropriate for the other.

Children are taught the significance of gender differences. They learn that "the dichotomy between male and female has intensive and extensive relevance to virtually every domain of human experience" (Bem, 1983). Thus, children learn very early that it is important whether someone is female or male; they begin thinking in terms of gender schemas at a young age (Liben & Signorella, 1993). Knowledge about different aspects of gender is usually acquired between ages 2 and 4.

Adults who have strong gender schemas quickly assign people's behavior, personality characteristics, objects, and so on to masculine/feminine categories. They disregard information that does not fit their gender schema. Males with a high masculine schema tend to view women as stereotypically feminine, for example (Hudak, 1993).

Processing information by gender is important in cultures such as ours, for several reasons. First, gender-schema cultures make multiple associations between gender and other non-sex-linked qualities such as affection and strength. Our culture regards affection as a feminine trait and strength as a masculine one. Second, such cultures make gender distinctions important, using them as a basis for norms, status, taboos, and privileges. Men are assigned leadership positions, for example, whereas women are placed in the rank and file (if not at home). Men are sexually assertive; women are sexually passive.

CONTEMPORARY GENDER ROLES

In recent decades, there has been a significant shift toward more egalitarian gender roles. Although women's roles have changed more than men's, men's are also changing. These changes seem to affect all socioeconomic classes. Members of conservative religious groups, such as Mormons, Catholics, and fundamentalist and evangelical Protestants, adhere most strongly to traditional gender roles (Eitzen & Zinn, 1994). Despite the ongoing disagreement, it is likely that the egalitarian trend will continue.

Traditional Gender Roles

In social science research, those who are studied have defined the norms against which all other experience has been evaluated (Stevenson, 2002). Consequently, much of what we know about sexuality is confined to a limited sector of society: White and middle class. These represented groups along with researchers need to be especially careful not to project gender-role concepts based on their own values onto other groups. If, for example, research on sexual orientation is dominated by heterosexual, male researchers of European descent, to what extent are the results of that research relevant to African American lesbian women? Too often, such a limited view leads to a loss of the human experience and, even worse, to possible distortions and moral judgments. The important point here is to consider the relationships between the participants in sexuality research and the limitations regarding who this study actually describes.

The Traditional Male Gender Role   What does it mean to be a "real" man in America? Bruce Feirstein (1982) parodied him in his book *Real Men Don't Eat Quiche:*

> *Question:* How many Real Men does it take to change a light bulb?
> *Answer:* None. Real Men aren't afraid of the dark.

> *Question:* Why did the Real Man cross the road?
> *Answer:* It's none of your damn business.

Central personality traits associated with the traditional male role—whether White, African American, Latino, Native American, or Asian American—include aggressiveness, emotional toughness, independence, feelings of superiority, and decisiveness. Males are generally regarded as being more power-oriented than females, and they exhibit higher levels of aggression, especially violent aggression (such as assault, homicide, and rape), dominance, and competitiveness. Although these tough, aggressive traits may be useful in the corporate world, politics, and the military (or in hunting saber-toothed tigers), they are rarely helpful to a man in his intimate relationships, which require understanding, cooperation, communication, and nurturing.

Who perpetuates the image of the dominance of men, and what role does it serve in a society that no longer needs or respects such an image? In her book *Stiffed,* Susan Faludi (1999) explores the unseen battle over what it means to be masculine in our society and the pressures associated with what it means to be a man. Unlike previous social movements, in which an enemy could be identified, contested, and defeated, the new men's movement has no adversary. Faludi observes: "Men have no clearly defined enemy who is oppressing them. How can men be oppressed when the culture has already identified them as the oppressors and when even they see themselves that way?" It may be that a man's task is not to define masculinity but rather to redefine what it means to be human.

Men of color move between dominant and ethnic cultures with different role requirements. They are expected to conform not only to the gender-role norms of the dominant group but to those of their own group as well. Black males, for example, must conform to both stereotypical expectations related to success, competition, and aggression and expectations of the African American community—most notably, those regarding cooperation and the promotion of ethnic survival (Hunter & Davis, 1992). They must also confront negative stereotypes about Black masculinity, such as hypersexuality and violence.

Male Sexual Scripts   In sociology, a **script** refers to the acts, rules, and expectations associated with a particular role. It is like the script handed out to an actor. Unlike dramatic scripts, however, social scripts allow for considerable improvisation within their general boundaries. We are given many scripts in life according to the various roles we play. Among them are sexual scripts that outline how we are to behave sexually when acting out our gender roles. Sexual scripts and gender roles for heterosexuals may be different from those for gay, lesbian, bisexual, or transgendered people. Perceptions and patterns in sexual behavior are shaped by sexual scripts (Castillo & Leer, 1993). (See Chapter 9 for further discussion of sexual scripts.)

Bernie Zilbergeld (1992) suggested that the male sexual script includes the following elements:

- *Men should not have (or at least should not express) certain feelings.* Men should not express doubts; they should be assertive, confident, and aggressive. Tenderness and compassion are not masculine emotions.

- *Performance is the thing that counts.* Sex is something to be achieved, to win at. Feelings only get in the way of the job to be done. Sex is not for intimacy but for orgasm.

- *The man is in charge.* As in other realms, the man is the leader, the person who knows what is best. The man initiates sex and gives the woman her orgasm. A real man doesn't need a woman to tell him what women like; he already knows.

- *A man always wants sex and is ready for it.* No matter what else is going on, a man wants sex; he is always able to become erect. He is a machine.

- *All physical contact leads to sex.* Because men are basically sexual machines, any physical contact is a sign for sex. Touching is seen as the first step toward sexual intercourse, not an end in itself. There is no physical pleasure other than sexual pleasure.

- *Sex equals intercourse.* All erotic contact leads to sexual intercourse. Foreplay is just that: warming up, getting one's partner ready for penetration. Kissing, hugging, erotic touching, and oral sex are only preliminaries to intercourse.

- *Sexual intercourse leads to orgasm.* The orgasm is the "proof in the pudding." The more orgasms, the better the sex. If a woman does not have an orgasm, she is not sexual. The male feels that he is a failure because he was not good enough to give her an orgasm. If she requires clitoral stimulation to have an orgasm, she has a problem.

Common to all these myths is a separation of sex from love and attachment. Sex is seen as performance.

The Traditional Female Gender Role   Although many of the features of the traditional male gender role, such as being in control, are the same across ethnic lines, there are striking ethnic differences in the female gender role.

Among Whites, the traditional female gender role centers around women as wives and mothers. When this woman leaves adolescence, she is expected to get married and have children. Although the traditional woman may work prior to marriage, she is not expected to defer marriage for career goals.

In recent years, the traditional role has been modified to include work and marriage. Work roles, however, are clearly subordinated to marital and family roles. Upon the birth of the first child, the woman is expected to remain home, and if economically feasible, to become a full-time mother.

Husbands think we should know where everything is—like the uterus is a tracking device. He asks me, "Roseanne, do we have any Cheetos left?" Like he can't go over to the sofa cushion and lift it himself.

—*Roseanne Barr*

The traditional White female gender role does not extend to African American women. This may be attributed to a combination of the African heritage; slavery, which subjugated women to the same labor and hardships as men; and economic discrimination, which forced these women into the labor force (Hatchett, 1991). African American men are generally more supportive than White or Latino men of more egalitarian gender roles for both women and men.

Among traditional Latinas, stereotypical gender roles are characterized by *marianismo,* which involves being faithful and subordinate to husbands and maintaining family traditions and culture (McNeill et al., 2001). Though not all Latinas strive to maintain these gender-role stereotypes, those who do may experience conflict and stress as they try to balance these expectations with work-related and family demands.

Unlike in the Anglo culture, Latino gender roles are strongly affected by age roles, in which the young subordinate themselves to the old. In this dual arrangement, notes Rosina Becerra (1988), "females are viewed as submissive, naive, and somewhat childlike. Elders are viewed as wise, knowledgeable, and deserving of respect." As a result of this intersection of gender and age roles, older women are treated with greater deference than younger women.

According to available data, Asian Americans are relatively conservative in their attitudes about sexual behavior and norms. These attitudes, however, often change with increased exposure to the American culture (Okazaki, 2002). Asian Americans appear to share Asian cultural characteristics such as the central role of the family, the appropriateness of sexuality only within the context of marriage, and sexual restraint and modesty.

Female Sexual Scripts   Whereas the traditional male sexual script focuses on sex over feelings, the traditional female sexual script focuses on feelings over sex, on love over passion. The traditional female sexual script cited by Lonnie Barbach (1982) includes the following ideas:

> Women are made, not born.
> —*Simone de Beauvoir (1908–1986)*

- *Sex is good* and *bad*. Women are taught that sex is both good and bad. What makes sex good? Sex in marriage or a committed relationship. What makes sex bad? Sex in a casual or uncommitted relationship. Sex is "so good" that a woman needs to save it for her husband (or for someone with whom she is deeply in love). Sex is bad; if it is not sanctioned by love or marriage, a woman will get a bad reputation.

- *It's not okay to touch themselves "down there."* Girls are taught not to look at their genitals, not to touch them, and especially not to explore them. As a result, some women know very little about their genitals. They are often concerned about vaginal odors, making them uncomfortable about cunnilingus.

- *Sex is for men.* Men want sex; women want love. Women are sexually passive, waiting to be aroused. Sex is not a pleasurable activity as an end in itself; it is something performed *by* women *for* men.

- *Men should know what women want.* This script tells women that men know what they want even if women don't tell them. The woman is supposed to remain pure and sexually innocent. It is up to the man to arouse the woman even if he doesn't know what she finds arousing. To keep her image of sexual innocence, she does not tell him what she wants.

- *Women shouldn't talk about sex.* Many women are uncomfortable talking about sex because they are not expected to have strong sexual feelings. Some women may know their partners well enough to have sex with them but not well enough to communicate their needs to them.

- *Women should look like models.* The media present ideally attractive women as beautiful models with slender hips, supple breasts, and no fat or cellulite; they are always young, with never a pimple, wrinkle, or gray hair in sight. As a result of these cultural images, many women are self-conscious about their physical appearance. They worry that they are too fat, too plain, or too old. They often feel awkward without clothes on to hide their imagined flaws.

- *Women are nurturers.* Women give; men receive. Women give themselves, their bodies, their pleasures to men. Everyone else's needs come first: his desire over hers, his orgasm over hers. If a woman always puts her partner's enjoyment first, she may be depriving herself of her own enjoyment. As Barbach (1982) points out, "If our attention is so totally riveted on another person, or on external events rather than on ourselves, it is impossible to experience the full pleasure and sensation of the sexual event."

- *There is only one right way to have an orgasm.* Women often "learn" that there is only one "right" way to have an orgasm: during sexual intercourse as a result of penile stimulation. But there are many ways to have an orgasm: through oral sex; manual stimulation before, during, or after intercourse; masturbation; and so on.

Changing Gender Roles

Contemporary gender roles are evolving from traditional hierarchical gender roles (in which one sex is subordinate to the other) to more egalitarian roles (in which both sexes are treated equally) and to androgynous roles (in which both sexes display the instrumental and expressive traits previously associated with one sex). Thus, contemporary gender roles often display both traditional elements and egalitarian and androgynous ones.

Motherhood Reexamined   Changes in women's roles profoundly reinforce the contemporary trend to separate sex from reproduction. Record numbers of women are reexamining motherhood because of the conflicts child rearing creates with marriage and work. Parenthood may now be considered a choice because of the availability of birth control and the social acceptance of child-free lifestyles. Overall, 43% of women of childbearing age were childless in 2000 (Bachu & O'Connell, 2001).

Though there are differences in attitudes and customs in child rearing, mothers from all cultures share more similarities than they do differences. Hopes, aspirations, the desire to survive, the search for love, and the need for family are very much the same for all mothers, regardless of ethnicity or socioeconomic status (DeGenova, 1997). For African American mothers, however, the scope and character of family life are strongly related to socioeconomic status. African American families that are impoverished and female-headed have vastly different patterns and expectations than do those from the working, middle, and upper classes (Wilkinson, 1997). For Latinas,

> The beautiful bird gets caged.
>
> —*Chinese proverb*

Although attitudes toward motherhood are changing, especially among middle-class Whites, it continues to be highly valued in our culture.

lower socioeconomic status, lower levels of education, a strong affiliation with Catholicism, and a strong belief in consanguineal relationships contribute to higher birth rates (Sanchez, 1997).

Involvement in the church is central to many families in supporting and supplementing family and community life. Regardless of a family's circumstances or finances, the health and economic needs of the children are of primary concern. Child-centered homes, often supported by an extended family, are the constant for which most mothers strive.

Many people are also reexamining fatherhood and the male role in the family. Among those in the still-evolving men's movement, many share the beliefs of feminism: equal pay for equal work, more parental leave for mothers and fathers, and better child-care facilities. Others, such as those involved in Promise Keepers, embrace the expectations of traditional masculinity and seek the support of other men in defining themselves according to biblical models.

Contemporary Sexual Scripts   As gender roles change, so do sexual scripts. Traditional sexual scripts have been challenged by more liberal and egalitarian ones, and sexual attitudes and behaviors have become increasingly liberal for males and females. Many college-age women have made an explicit break with the more traditional scripts, especially the good girl/bad girl dichotomy and the belief that "nice" girls don't enjoy sex. Older professional women who are single also appear to reject the old images.

Contemporary sexual scripts include the following elements for both sexes:

- Sexual expression is positive.
- Sexual activities involve a mutual exchange of erotic pleasure.
- Sexuality is equally involving, and both partners are equally responsible.
- Legitimate sexual activities are not limited to sexual intercourse but also include masturbation and oral-genital sex.
- Sexual activities may be initiated by either partner.

I don't know why people are afraid of new ideas. I am terrified of the old ones.

—*John Cage (1912–1992)*

Changing traditional female sexual scripts: Click on "Women Talk Sex" to hear what women have to say about how they like to be sexually stimulated.

- Both partners have a right to experience orgasm, whether through intercourse, oral-genital sex, or manual stimulation.
- Nonmarital sex is acceptable within a relationship context.

These contemporary scripts give more recognition to female sexuality. They are increasingly relationship-centered rather than male-centered. Women, however, are still not granted full sexual equality with males. Only once men and women begin to recognize and free themselves from ineffectual and limiting stereotypes can they fully embrace their humanity.

Androgyny

Some scholars have challenged the traditional masculine/feminine gender-role dichotomy, arguing that such models are unhealthy and fail to reflect the real world. Instead of looking at gender roles in terms of polar opposites, they suggest examining them in terms of androgyny. **Androgyny** refers to flexibility in gender roles and the unique combination of instrumental and expressive traits as influenced by individual differences, situations, and stages in the life cycle (Bem, 1975; A. Kaplan, 1979). (The term "androgyny" is derived from the Greek *andros*, man, and *gyne*, woman.) An androgynous person combines both the instrumental traits traditionally associated with masculinity and the expressive traits traditionally associated with femininity. An androgynous lifestyle allows men and women to choose from the full range of emotions and behaviors, according to their temperament, situation, and common humanity, rather than their gender. Thus, men can cry and display tenderness; they can touch, feel, and nurture without being considered effeminate. Women can be aggressive or career-oriented; they can seek leadership and can be mechanical or physical.

Flexibility and adaptability are important aspects of androgyny (Vonk & Ashmore, 1993). Individuals who are rigidly instrumental or expressive, despite the situation, are not considered androgynous. A woman who is always aggressive at work and passive at home, for example, would not be considered androgynous, as work may call for compassion and home life for assertion.

Filling an androgynous gender role, however, may be just as stultifying to an individual as trying to be traditionally feminine or masculine. In advocating the expression of both feminine and masculine traits, perhaps we are imposing a new form of gender-role rigidity on ourselves. Bem, one of the leading proponents of androgyny, has become increasingly critical of the idea. She believes now that androgyny replaces "a prescription to be masculine or feminine with the doubly incarcerating prescription to be masculine *and* feminine. The individual now has not one but two potential sources of inadequacy to contend with" (Bem, 1983).

> Once made equal to man, woman becomes his superior.
>
> —*Socrates (c. 469–399 B.C.)*

> Throughout history the more complex activities have been defined and redefined, now as male, now as female—sometimes as drawing equally on the gifts of both sexes. When an activity to which each sex could have contributed is limited to one sex, a rich, differentiated quality is lost from the activity itself.
>
> —*Margaret Mead (1901–1978)*

WHEN GENDER IS AMBIGUOUS: INTERSEXUALITY, TRANSSEXUALITY, AND TRANSGENDERISM

For most of us, there is no question about our gender: We *know* we are female or male. We may question our femininity or masculinity, but rarely do we question being female or male. For intersexed and transgendered individuals, however, "What sex am I?" is a real and painful question. Their dilemma, however, reinforces the fact that gender identity as male or female is not "natural" but learned.

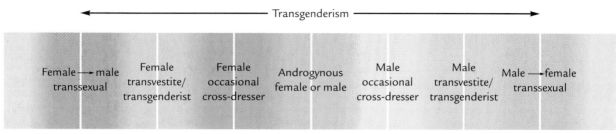

Masculine   Feminine

FIGURE 5.1 Nontraditional Gender Roles: The Gender Continuum. The concept of gender is viewed as a continuum, with a multitude of possible gender-variant behaviors.

Because our culture views sexual anatomy as a male/female dichotomy, it is difficult for many to accept the more recent view of anatomical sex differentiation as existing on a male/female continuum with several dimensions (Intersex Society of North America, 2003a) (Figure 5.1). Most people still think of genetic sex—XX or XY—as a person's "true sex." Because of the secrecy and deception that surround intersex, and depending on the conditions used to classify it, the prevalence ranges from 0.0128% to 1.7% of the population (Fausto-Sterling, 2000; Sax, 2002). According to the Intersex Society of North America (2003c), a voice for and educator about intersex:

> How people experience being born intersex is at least as diverse as how people experience being born non-intersex, and is impacted by various social factors such as race, class, ability, and sexual orientation, as well as actual medical conditions and personal factors. Do not assume that one intersex person you happen to meet represents all or even most intersex people.

Boy or Girl? Click on "First Do No Harm" to get a glimpse of the issues surrounding sex assignment of intersexed children.

Intersexuality: Atypical Chromosomal and Hormonal Conditions

Researchers have long recognized the existence of individuals who are **intersexed,** that is, whose biological sex is ambiguous or between male and female. This person is born with sex chromosomes, external genitalia, or an internal reproductive system that is not considered "standard" for either male or female, thereby making the person's sex unclear (Intersex Society of North America, 2003a). Such ambiguity is usually caused by chromosomal or hormonal variations during prenatal development. Sometimes, a child is born with an underdeveloped penis or an enlarged clitoris, making it uncertain whether the child is male or female. For example, such a child may look nearly male but have a small penis or hypospadias (discussed later in this section). The most common chromosomal and hormonal errors in prenatal development are discussed below and summarized in Table 5.1.

Intersexed Individuals   Until recently, the term given to individuals born with two sets of genitals, one male and one female, was **hermaphrodite.** Because those with this condition are in some sense "in between" the two sexes, they are now referred to as "intersex" (Sax, 2002). Because definitions and prevalence of this very rare condition continue to be debated in the literature, it is difficult to classify. What may occur is the appearance of one ovary and one testis, or one or both gonads containing both ovarian and testicular tissue. The internal and external genitalia are highly

TABLE 5.1   Atypical Patterns in Prenatal Development

	Chromosomal Sex[a]	*Gonads*	*Internal Reproductive Structures*	*External Reproductive Structures*	*Secondary Sex Characteristics*	*Fertility*	*Gender Identity*
Atypical Chromosomal Conditions							
Turner syndrome	Female (45, XO)	Nonfunctioning or absent ovaries	Normal female except for ovaries	Underdeveloped genitals	No breast development or menstruation at puberty	Sterile	Usually female
Klinefelter syndrome	Male (47, XXY)	Testes	Normal male	Small penis and testes, gynecomastia (breast development)	Female secondary sex characteristics develop at puberty	Sterile	Usually male, but there may be gender confusion at puberty
Atypical Hormonal Conditions							
Androgen-insensitivity syndrome	Male (46, XY)	Testes, but body unable to utilize androgen (testosterone)	Shallow vagina, lacks normal male structures	Labia	Female secondary sex characteristics develop at puberty; no menstruation	Sterile	Usually female
Congenital adrenal hyperplasia (pseudohermaphroditism)	Female (46, XX)	Ovaries	Normal female	Ambiguous tending toward male appearance; fused vagina and enlarged clitoris may be mistaken for empty scrotal sac and micropenis	Female secondary sex characteristics develop at puberty	Fertile	Usually male unless condition discovered at birth and altered by hormonal therapy
DHT deficiency	Male (46, XY)	Testes undescended until puberty	Partially formed internal structures but no prostate	Ambiguous; clitoral-appearing micropenis; phallus enlarges and testes descend at puberty	Male secondary sex characteristics develop at puberty	Viable sperm but unable to inseminate	Female identity until puberty; majority assume male identity later
Unknown Origin							
Hypospadias	Male (46, XY)	Normal	Normal	Opening of penis located on underside rather than tip of penis; penis may also be twisted and small	Male secondary sex characteristics develop at puberty	Fertile	Male

[a]Chromosomal sex refers to 46, XX (female) or 46, XY (male). Sometimes a chromosome will be missing, as in 45, XO, or there will be an extra chromosome, as in 47, XXY. In these notations, the number refers to the number of chromosomes (46, in 23 pairs, is normal); the letters *X* and *Y* refer to chromosomes and *O* refers to a missing chromosome.

variable, but female structures and gender identities usually predominate. In any case, intersexed people are multidimensional human beings with interests and concerns beyond intersex issues (Intersex Society of North America, 2003b,c).

The older term **pseudohermaphrodite,** or having two testes or two ovaries but an ambiguous genital appearance, now implies a lack of authenticity concerning gender. This term also has been replaced with the more neutral "intersex."

Chromosomal Conditions Chromosomal conditions are common. Chromosomal abnormalities occur when an individual has fewer or more X or Y chromosomes than normal. Two syndromes resulting from erroneous chromosomal patterns may result in gender confusion: Turner syndrome and Klinefelter syndrome. In both of these, the body develops with some marked physical characteristics of the other sex.

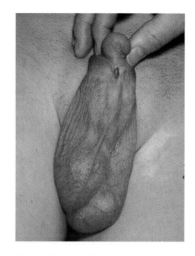

The genitals of a fetally androgenized female may resemble those of a male.

TURNER SYNDROME   Females with **Turner syndrome** are not XX and not XY (notated as 45, XO). It is one of the most common chromosomal disorders among females, occurring in 1 in 1666 live births (Blackless et al., 2000; Intersex Society of North America, 2003d). Infants and young girls with Turner syndrome appear normal externally, but they have no ovaries. At puberty, changes initiated by ovarian hormones cannot take place. The body does not gain a mature look or height, and menstruation cannot occur. The adolescent girl may question her femaleness because she does not menstruate or develop breasts or pubic hair like her peers. Girls with Turner syndrome may have academic problems and poor memory and attention (Ross et al., 2000). Hormonal therapy, including androgen therapy, estrogen therapy, and human growth hormone (HGH) therapy, replaces the hormones necessary to produce normal adolescent changes, such as growth and secondary sex characteristics. Even with ongoing hormonal therapy, women with Turner syndrome will likely remain infertile, although they may successfully give birth through embryo transfer following in vitro fertilization with donated ova.

KLINEFELTER SYNDROME   Males with **Klinefelter syndrome** have one or more extra X chromosomes (47, XXY; 48, XXXY; or 49, XXXXY). Klinefelter syndrome is quite common, occurring in 1 in 1000 male births (Blackless et al., 2000; Intersex Society of North America, 2003d). The effects of Klinefelter syndrome are variable, and many men with the syndrome are never diagnosed. The presence of the Y chromosome designates a person as male. It causes the formation of small, firm testes and ensures a masculine physical appearance. However, the presence of a double X chromosome pattern, which is a female trait, adds some female physical traits. At puberty, traits may vary: tallness, gynecomastia (breast development in men), sparse body hair, and/or small penis and testes. Long-term treatment with testosterone can alleviate some aspects of this syndrome. Because of low testosterone levels, there may be a low sex drive, inability to experience erections, and infertility. In vitro techniques can allow some men to become biological fathers.

Hormonal Disorders Hormonal imbalances may cause males or females to develop physical characteristics associated with the other sex.

DEPENDING ON THE CONDITIONS considered intersexual, each year an estimated 100–1000 babies are born in the United States whose bodies differ from standard male or female. These sexually ambiguous infants are typically given a gender assignment (usually female) along with treatment to support the assignment, including surgery and, later, hormones and psychotherapy. Physicians have defended the practice of "correcting" ambiguous genitals, citing the success of current technology. Recently, however, this practice has undergone scrutiny by researchers and patients who point to the lack of evidence supporting its long-term success.

The protocol of surgical correction was established largely by Dr. John Money, a medical psychologist at Johns Hopkins University Medical Center. Underlying Money's work are the beliefs that gender identity is determined not by biological traits but by the way a child is raised and that intersexed children are born psychosexually malleable. Since Money's research was first published, over 25,000 sex reassignment procedures have been performed on infants. According to the American Academy of Pediatrics (2000) guidelines for evaluation and management of intersexed infants, it is important to make a definitive diagnosis as quickly as possible and to establish an appropriate treatment plan to minimize medical, psychological, and social complications. The following beliefs are held strongly enough that they might be considered medical protocols: (1) Individuals are psychosexually neutral at birth, (2) healthy psychosexual development is dependent on the appearance of one's genitals, (3) doubt about sex assignment should not be allowed, and (4) sex should not be changed after 2 years of age.

Endocrinologists, physicians, ethicists, and intersex activists have challenged the traditional pediatric postulates for sex assignment/reassignment (Diamond, 1997; Intersex Society of North America, 2003b). This research suggests that one's sexual identity is not fixed by the gender one is reared in, that atypical as well as typical persons undergo psychosexual development, and that

sexual orientation develops independent of rearing. Consequently, the North American Task Force on Intersex, endorsed by the American Academy of Pediatrics, the American Urological Association, and others, has been formed in response to the growing debate over standards of practice for the medical treatment of intersexed children. The task force is expected to address a number of issues, including (1) the establishment of standards for informed consent, (2) a retrospective review of the long-term psychosexual status of patients treated for intersex, (3) the establishment of guidelines for the management of children born with ambiguous sex anatomy, (4) initiation of a prospective registry, and (5) a revision of medical nomenclature.

An emerging community of unhappy individuals willing to come out with their medical histories concurs with this response. They consider surgery to be a technology best delayed unless medically urgent (as when a genetic anomaly interferes with urination or creates a risk of infection) or requested by the individual. They believe that letting well enough alone is the better course and that the erotic and reproductive needs of the adult should take precedence over the cosmetic needs of the child. Pointing to their own dissatisfaction, as well as to the lack of research supporting the long-term success of surgical treatment, they recommend that the professional community offer support and information to parents and families and empower the intersexed individual to understand his or her status and choose (or reject) medical intervention (Intersex Society of North America, 2003b).

Because the etiology of gender identity disorder is not clear, resolution is not a simple matter. Many people feel it is time that both professionals and families begin to question the research and listen to the stories of those whose lives have been affected by the practice known as "gender correction." The following chart illustrates the two opposing models of treatment.

Source: Adapted from Dreger, A. (2003). Notes on the Treatment of Intersex. Intersex Society of North America. Available: http://www.isna.org. Reprinted with permission from the author.

Key Issues	Surgery-Centered Model	Patient-Centered Model
What is intersex?	A rare anatomical abnormality that is likely to lead to distress for the intersexed person and the family. Intersex is pathological and requires immediate medical attention.	A relatively common anatomical variation from the "standard" male and female types. Intersex is neither a medical nor a social pathology.
Is gender determined by nature or nurture?	Nurture. Virtually any child can be made into a boy or girl if you just make the genitals look convincing. It doesn't matter what the genes, brain, hormones, and/or prenatal life were like.	Both. People with intersex conditions ought to be treated with respect for their autonomy, truth about their bodies and lives, and freedom from discrimination.
Are intersexed genitals a medical problem?	Yes. Untreated intersex is highly likely to result in psychological problems. Intersexed genitals must be "normalized" to whatever extent possible if these problems are to be avoided.	No. They may signal an underlying metabolic concern, but they are not diseased. Metabolic concerns should be treated medically, but the genitals are not in need of medical treatment.
What should be the medical response?	The correct treatment for intersex is to "normalize" the abnormal genitals using surgical, hormonal, and other technologies. Doing so will eliminate the potential for parents' psychological distress.	The family should receive psychosocial support and as much information as they can handle. True medical problems should be treated medically, but all non-essential treatments should wait until the person can consent to them.
When should treatments to make the genitals look "normal" be done?	As soon as possible because intersex is a psychosocial emergency. The longer the wait, the greater the trauma.	ONLY if and when the intersexed person requests them, and then only after being fully informed of the risks and likely outcomes. These surgeries carry substantial risks to life, fertility, continence, and sensation.
What is motivating this treatment protocol?	The belief that our society can't handle genital ambiguity or non-standard sexual variation. If we don't fix the genitals, the child with an intersex condition will be ostracized, ridiculed, and rejected, even by his or her own parents.	The belief that the person with an intersex condition has the right to self determination. "Normalizing" surgeries without the individual's consent interfere with that right; many surgeries and hormone treatments are not reversible.
How do you decide what gender to assign a newborn with an intersex condition?	The doctors decide after genetic and other testing. If the child has a Y chromosome and an adequate (1 inch or longer) penis, the child will be assigned a male gender. If the child has a Y chromosome and an inadequate penis, the child will be assigned a female gender and be surgically reconstructed as such. If the child has no Y chromosomes, the child will be assigned a female gender and be surgically reconstructed as such.	The family and doctors decide after genetic and other testing. This does **not** advocate selecting an ambiguous gender. Intersex is not a discrete biological category. Gender assignment of infants as male or female is preliminary. Children with intersex conditions have significantly higher rates of gender transition than the general population, with or without treatment. That is a crucial reason why medically unnecessary surgeries should not be done without the patient's consent.
What should the intersexed person be told when he or she is old enough to understand?	Very little, because telling all we know will just lead to gender confusion that all these surgeries were meant to avoid. Withhold information and records if necessary.	The intersexed person and parents have the right to know as much about intersex conditions as their doctors do. Lack of information leads to shame, trauma, and medical procedures that may be dangerous to the patient. Conversely, some people harmed by secrecy and shame may avoid future health care.
What is the ideal future of intersex?	Elimination via improved scientific and medical technologies.	Social acceptance of human diversity and an end to the idea that difference equals disease.

ANDROGEN-INSENSITIVITY SYNDROME   **Androgen-insensitivity syndrome**, or **testicular feminization**, is a genetic, inherited condition passed through X chromosomes (except for occasional spontaneous mutations) (Williams, Patterson, & Hughes, 1993; see Kaplan & Owett, 1993, for female androgen-deficiency syndrome). It occurs in 1 in 13,000 individuals (Blackless et al., 2000; Intersex Society of North America, 2003d). A genetic male (XY) is born with testes, but because of the body's inability to absorb testosterone, the estrogen influence prevails. From the earliest stages, therefore, the body tends toward a female appearance while not developing male internal and external reproductive structures. Externally, the infant is female, with labia and vagina, but the internal female structures are not present. At puberty, the body develops breasts, hips, and other secondary female sex characteristics but does not grow pubic hair. The testes remain in the abdomen and are sterile. People with androgen insensitivity are usually assigned female gender status at birth (Gooren & Cohen-Kettenis, 1991; Shah, Woolley, & Costin, 1992).

Physically, individuals with androgen-insensitivity syndrome develop as females, except for their inability to menstruate. It is often not until puberty that the physical anomaly is discovered. Usually, the person is comfortable about her female gender identity and can enjoy sex and achieve orgasm. Medical treatment may involve removal of the undescended testes (to reduce the risk of cancer) and estrogen replacement therapy (to prevent osteoporosis).

CONGENITAL ADRENAL HYPERPLASIA   In **congenital adrenal hyperplasia** (also known as pseudohermaphroditism), a genetic female (XX) with ovaries and a vagina develops externally as a male, the result of a malfunctioning adrenal gland. This condition is the most prevalent cause of intersex among females, with a frequency of about 1 in 13,000 births (Blackless et al., 2000; Intersex Society of North America, 2003d). It occurs when the adrenal gland produces androgen instead of androgen-inhibiting cortisone.

At birth, the child appears to be a male with a penis and an empty scrotum. The appearance, however, may be ambiguous. Some have an enlarged clitoris, with or without a vaginal opening, some a micropenis, and some a complete penis and scrotum. When the condition is discovered at birth, the child is usually assigned female status, and treatment is given to promote female development. As the child matures, he or she can choose the gender and type of intervention that is congruent with his or her identity.

DHT DEFICIENCY   Because of a genetic disorder, some males are unable to convert testosterone to the hormone dihydrotestosterone (DHT). This disorder is known as **DHT deficiency** but sometimes is also referred to as 5-alpha reductase syndrome. There is no available estimate on how often this condition occurs. DHT is required for the normal development of external male genitals. At birth, children with DHT deficiency have internal male organs but a clitoris-like penis, undescended testes, a labia-like scrotum, and a closed vaginal cavity. They are usually identified as girls. At puberty, however, these "girls" seem to grow into men. Their testes descend and their phallus enlarges to resemble a penis. There is also an increase in muscle size, deepening of the voice, and no breast development.

A study of 18 children born with DHT deficiency in a small village in the Dominican Republic provides some evidence that hormones influence gender identity (Imperato-McGinley, 1974, 1979). Because of DHT deficiency, the children's penises were underdeveloped and resembled clitorides. The children led typical lives as girls, but when they reached adolescence, the DHT deficiency reversed, and their bodies developed normal male characteristics. Their testes descended and their "clitorides" matured into penises. In societies like these in which the condition is recognized, the children are treated as intersexed.

If socialization were the most important factor in developing gender identity and gender roles, we would expect the children to remain psychologically female. Of the 18 children, however, only one chose to remain female; the others adopted male gender roles. The child who remained female married a man and became transgendered. One child who adopted the male gender identity and gender role cross-dressed.

The research was provocative because it suggests that gender identity is biologically determined rather than learned and that gender identity can be changed without severe emotional trauma. The study has been criticized, however, on several counts. First, the children's genitals were ambiguous rather than completely female in appearance; it is unlikely that the children would have been treated as "normal" girls. Second, after the children developed penises, others may have encouraged them to act like males. Third, because DHT deficiency was relatively common for the village (the condition was known locally as *machihembra*—"male-female"), the transition from female to male may have been institutionalized. Finally, other studies conflict with the Dominican Republic studies. If there is a hormonal contribution to gender identity, it may be considerably weaker than the Dominican study suggests.

HYPOSPADIAS   Of unknown origin is a condition called **hypospadias** (hi-puh-SPAY-dee-as), in which the opening of the penis, rather than being at the tip, is located somewhere on the underside, glans, or shaft or at the junction of the scrotum. In addition, the foreskin may form a hood over the top of the glans, and there may be a twist in the shaft. In mild cases, the condition will form a slit in the underside of the glans. In more extreme cases, the urethra may be open from midshaft out to the glans, or the urethra may be entirely absent so that the urine exits the bladder behind the penis (Kappy, Blizzard, & Migeon, 1994). Between 1 and 770 baby boys are born with this condition (Aho, Koivisto, Tammela, & Auvinen, 2000; Blackless et al., 2000; Intersex Society of North America, 2003d). A variety of techniques are available to repair hypospadias when it is severe.

Gender Identity Disorder

According to the American Psychiatric Association, **gender identity disorder (GID)** consists of a strong and persistent cross-gender identification and persistent discomfort about one's assigned sex (American Psychiatric Association [APA], 2000). This diagnosis is not made if the individual has a concurrent physical intersex condition. Furthermore, there must be clinically significant distress or impairment in social, occupational, or other important areas of functioning.

Boys with GID might be preoccupied with traditionally feminine activities. For example, they may prefer to dress in girls' or women's clothes, be attracted to stereotypical games and pastimes of girls, and express a wish to be a girl. They may insist on sitting to urinate and, more rarely, find their penis or testes disgusting. Girls with GID might display intense negative reactions to parental expectations or attempts to have them dress in feminine attire. Their fantasy heroes are often powerful male figures. Furthermore, they prefer boys as playmates and show little interest in dolls or any form of feminine dress-up or role-play activity. They may claim that they will grow a penis and may not want to grow breasts or to menstruate. They may assert as well that they will grow up to be a man.

Adults with GID are preoccupied with their wish to live as a member of the other sex. This preoccupation may be manifested as an intense desire to adopt the social role of the other sex or to acquire the physical appearance of the other sex through hormonal or surgical correction. There is no diagnostic test specific for GID, nor are there data on its prevalence (APA, 2000).

Traditional medical treatment for GID has included three phases: (1) a real-life experience in the desired role, (2) hormones of the desired gender, and (3) surgery to change the genitalia and other sex characteristics. However, the diagnosis of GID invites the consideration of a broader spectrum of therapeutic options because the goal of treatment for people with GID is lasting comfort with the gendered self ("Standards of Care," 2001). The Harry Benjamin International Gender Dysphoria Association, a body of experts who study gender identity disorders and care for people with such problems, has articulated a variety of factors and issues in treating those with GID. Though there are limitations to the knowledge in this area, there is hope that some of the clinical uncertainties will be resolved in the future through scientific investigation ("Standards of Care," 2001).

Transsexuality

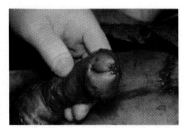

The genitals of a postoperative female-to-male transsexual, above, and the genitals of a postoperative male-to-female transsexual, below.

In transsexuality, a person's gender identity and sexual anatomy are not compatible. Transsexual individuals are convinced that by some strange quirk of fate they have been given the body of the wrong sex. They generally want to change their sex, not their personality. Many have little interest in sexual relationships. It is more important for them to acquire the anatomy of the desired gender than to have greater sexual satisfaction (Arndt, 1991).

Transsexuality revolves around issues of gender identity; it is a distinctly different phenomenon from homosexuality. Gay men and lesbian women are not transsexuals. Rather, lesbian women and gay men feel confident of their female or male identity. Being a lesbian or gay person reflects sexual orientation rather than gender questioning. Furthermore, following surgery, transsexual individuals may or may not change their sexual orientation, whether it is toward members of the same, the other, or both sexes.

As mentioned, transsexual people often seek surgery to bring their genitals in line with their gender identity. Male-to-female operations outnumber female-to-male by a ratio of 3 to 1. Some male-to-female transsexuals forgo the surgery but still identify themselves as women; they may choose to call themselves either transsexual or transgendered.

MANY TRANSSEXUAL PEOPLE VIEW their condition not as a psychological problem but as a medical one. As a result, they tend to seek surgeons to change their genitals rather than therapists to help them examine and then match their gender identity with their physical body. Gender reassignment is not about sex but about matching one's gender identity to one's physiological status.

For those diagnosed with gender identity disorder (GID), **sex reassignment** surgery, along with hormone therapy and real-life experience living as the other sex, has been proved effective in treating transsexualism. Such a therapeutic regimen, when recommended by qualified practitioners, is medically necessary—not experimental or cosmetic. The goal of the process is to reduce the suffering and psychological adjustment problems that occur when one's body does not conform to one's gender. In the early years of sex reassignment, people who came to a professional saying they were transsexual were forced to prove it. More recently, client-centered programs have been designed in which people can obtain whatever therapeutic services they need. The following treatment modalities are often followed.

Psychotherapy

Many individuals with GID find that psychotherapy can be helfpful in coming to an acceptance of themselves; however, not every adult gender patient requests therapy ("Standards of Care," 2001). Consequently, psychother-

apy is not an absolute requirement prior to hormone therapy, real-life experience, or surgery.

Hormone Therapy

Hormonal treatments play an important role in the anatomical and psychological gender transition process and are often medically necessary for successful living in the new gender. When physicians administer androgens to biological females and estrogens, progesterone, and testosterone-blocking agents to biological males, patients feel and appear more like members of their preferred gender. It is recommended that hormones be given to those who are 18 or older (though adolescents can receive puberty-delaying hormones as early as 11 or 12 and feminizing or masculinizing hormones as early as 16), who have demonstrable knowledge of what hormones can and cannot do, and who have either a documented real-life experience or psychotherapy for at least three months prior to the administration of hormones. These therapies induce the appropriate secondary sex characteristics, such as breasts for male-to-female transsexuals and facial and body hair and penises (enlarged clitorides) for female-to-male transsexuals. Dramatic changes are observable in the female-to-male therapies, such as male pattern baldness (if the gene is present), facial hair, and shifts in body weight. Hormone therapy can be provided to those who do not wish to cross-live or undergo surgery.

(continued)

The prevalence of transsexuality is unknown, though it is estimated that there may be 1 transsexual per 50,000 people over age 15. There are also no known statistics on the number of postoperative transsexuals, but it is estimated that at least 25,000 Americans have undergone sex reassignment surgery (Cloud, 1998). This number may be low, considering the cultural and religious biases, social stigmas, and financial constraints that many transsexual individuals experience. Some cultures, however, accept a gender identity that is not congruent with sexual anatomy and create an alternative third sex, as we saw in Chapter 1. "Men-women"—Native American two-spirits, Indian *hijas*, and Burmese *acaults*—are considered a third gender (Bullough, 1991; Coleman, Colgan, & Gooren, 1992; Roscoe, 1991). Members of this third gender are often believed to possess spiritual powers because of their "specialness."

Because primary transsexuals have lived much of their lives in their preferred gender (despite their genitals), they are often able to move into their "new" gender with relative ease. Secondary transsexuals, however, who have lived most of their lives in their assigned gender, have more difficulty in making the transition to the behaviors associated with their preferred gender (Leavitt & Berger, 1990).

The Real-Life Experience

Living as a member of the preferred gender is essential. This is not an easy task, for such subtle gender clues as mannerisms, voice inflections, and body movement, learned in childhood, must be altered. The decision to live as the preferred gender should be preceded by an awareness of what the familial, vocational, interpersonal, educational, economic, and legal consequences are likely to be.

Sex Reassignment Surgery (SRS)

Sex reassignment surgery, along with hormone therapy and real-life experience, is a treatment that has proved to be effective. Breast augmentation and removal are common operations. For the female-to-male patient, a mastectomy is usually the first surgery performed, sometimes when the individual begins hormones. For the male-to-female patient, augmentation may be performed if hormone treatment for 18 months is not sufficient.

Genital surgery for the male-to-female patient involves a penile inversion technique, in which doctors create a vaginal cavity with inverted penile skin, a rectosigmoid transplant, in which tissue is cut from the sigmoid section of the colon and used to create a vaginal cavity, or a free-skin graft to line the neovagina. A clitoris is formed from penile corpus spongiosum, and inner and outer lips are crafted from scrotal tissue. Other cosmetic procedures, such as nose surgery, tracheal shave, and electrolysis, may be performed. Though there may be some decline in orgasmic capacity, most male-to-female transsexuals report an enjoyment of sexual activities.

In female-to-male patients, the ovaries, uterus, and breasts are removed. The clitoris, which has been enlarged by testosterone therapy, is refashioned into a penis, and the labia are formed into a scrotum. Several techniques may be used to simulate penile erection, ranging from the insertion of a semierect rod to the surgical implantation of an inflatable device. Most female-to-male transsexuals report an increase in orgasmic capacity. Parenthood is a choice for many transsexuals, and reproductive options are discussed with them in detail.

Follow-Up and Prognosis

Long-term postoperative follow-up is encouraged, from both a physical and psychological perspective. Research suggests that the majority of people who have undergone gender reassignment procedures experience significant improvement in their adjustment to life (Carroll, 1999).

Source: Harry Benjamin International Gender Dysphoria Association. (2001). "Standards of Care for Gender Identity Disorders, Sixth Edition." Available http://www.hbigda.org. Reprinted by permission of Harry Benjamin International, Gender Dysphoria Association.

The Transgender Phenomenon

In recent years, there has been a major shift in the gender world. Upsetting old definitions and classification systems, a new **transgendered** community, one that embraces the possibility of numerous genders and multiple social identities, has emerged. This "complexity of gender offers serious challenges to scientific paradigms that conflate sex and gender" (Bolin, 1997).

Transgenderism is an inclusive category. The term "transgenderist" was first coined by Virginia Prince, the founding mother of the U.S. contemporary cross-dressing community, to describe someone who lives full-time in a gender role different from to the gender role presumed by society to match the person's genetic sex (Richards, 1997). The key difference between a transsexual person and a transgenderist is that the latter has no burning desire to alter his or her genitals to live in society in a role with which he or she feels comfortable. Thus, transgenderists do as little or as much as they wish to their bodies but stop short of genital surgery (Denny, 1997).

In past decades, those who were transgendered could escape from the traditional male and female categories only if they were "diagnosed" as transvestite or transsexual (Denny, 1997). This resulted in a larger number of "heterosexual" cross-dressers who were actually gay or bisexual or who had transsexual issues. It also involved diagnosis on the part of the psychiatric community and subsequent labeling and stigma. In recent years in North

America, a paradigm shift has occurred that challenges the male/female dichotomy of gender, thereby making it more acceptable to live in a permanent preoperative state without the threat of "cure." This acceptance has "opened the door for political and scientific activism and the realization that being preoperative is not inevitably a way-station on the road to surgery" (Denny, 1997).

According to Walter O. Bockting, a faculty member at the University of Minnesota School of Medicine's Human Sexuality Program, the paradigm shift in the transgendered experience includes changes in the following arenas (Bockting, 1997):

- *Sociocultural.* The prevailing gender schema of Western culture is challenged by transgendered identities that transcend two sexes. The number of transsexual men with vaginas, women with penises and breasts, and individuals who cross or transcend culturally defined gender lines is growing, and these people are becoming a more visible part of society.

- *Interpersonal.* In coming out to their families, friends, and co-workers, transgenderists are now affirming their unique transgendered sexual identity. No longer conforming to a conventional heterosexual or homosexual pattern, they are creating unique gender roles and new sexual scripts in intimate relationships.

- *Intrapersonal.* Self-affirmation of one's identity alleviates shame and is liberating. The pressure of trying to conform and the secrecy involved in hiding one's transgendered or transsexual status can be eliminated by coming out.

Transgenderist Sky Renfro describes his gender identity (quoted in Feinberg, 1996):

> My identity, like everything else in my life, is a journey. It is a process and an adventure that in some ways brings me back to myself, back into the grand circle of living. . . . My sense of who I am at any given time is somewhere on that wheel and the place that I occupy there can change depending on the season and life events as well as a number of other influences. Trying to envision masculine at one end of a line and feminine on the other, with the rest of us somewhere on that line, is a difficult concept for me to grasp. Male and female—they're so close to each other, they sit next to each other on that wheel. They are not at opposite ends as far as I can tell. In fact, they are so close that they're sometimes not distinguishable.

This paradigm shift in thinking regarding gender has implications for the clinical management of gender identity disorder. Treatment is no longer aimed at identifying the "true transsexual" but is open instead to the possibility of affirming a unique transgender identity and role (Bockting, 1997).

Recently, and with remarkable success, a political movement has emerged in support of gender nonconformists. Lawyers with the Transgender Law Conference have helped pass statutes in at least 17 states allowing transsexual persons to change the sex designation on their birth certificate so that their driver's license and passport reflect who they are (Cloud, 1998). In addition, some businesses and employers have added gender identity provisions to their equal opportunity policies.

> The fact that we are all human beings is infinitely more important than all the peculiarities that distinguish humans from one another.
> —*Simone de Beauvoir*

> Treat people as if they were what they ought to be and you help them become what they are capable of being.
> —*Johann Goethe (1749–1832)*

WE ORDINARILY TAKE our gender as female or male for granted. The making of gender, however, is a complex process involving both biological and psychological elements. Biologically, we are male or female in terms of genetic and anatomical makeup. Psychologically, we are male or female in terms of our assigned gender and our gender identity. Only in rare cases, as with chromosomal and hormonal disorders or gender dysphoria, is our gender identity problematic. For most of us, gender identity is rarely a source of concern. More often, what concerns us is related to our gender roles: Am I sufficiently masculine? Feminine? What it means to be feminine or masculine differs from culture to culture. Although femininity and masculinity are generally regarded as opposites in our culture, there are relatively few significant inherent differences between the sexes aside from males impregnating and females giving birth and lactating. The majority of social and psychological differences are exaggerated or culturally encouraged. All in all, women and men are more similar than different.

SUMMARY

Studying Gender and Gender Roles

- *Sex* is the biological aspect of being female or male. Gender is the social and cultural characteristics associated with biological sex. Normal gender development depends on both biological and psychological factors. Psychological factors include *assigned gender* and *gender identity*. *Gender roles* tell us how we are to act as men and women in a particular culture.

- Although our culture encourages us to think that men and women are "opposite" sexes, they are more similar than dissimilar. Innate gender differences are generally minimal; differences are encouraged by socialization.

- Masculine and feminine stereotypes assume heterosexuality. If men or women do not fit the stereotypes, they are likely to be considered gay or lesbian. Gay men and lesbian women, however, are as likely as heterosexuals to be masculine or feminine.

- *Gender theory* examines gender as a basic element in society and social arrangements. It focuses on how gender is created and how and why specific traits, behaviors, and roles benefit or cost women and men. In general, gender theorists believe gender differences are socially created to benefit men.

Gender-Role Learning

- *Cognitive social learning theory* emphasizes learning behaviors from others through *cognition* and *modeling*. *Cognitive development theory* asserts that once children learn gender is permanent they independently strive to act like "proper" girls and boys because of an internal need for congruence.

- Though the stereotypes are somewhat outmoded, children still learn their gender roles from parents through manipulation, channeling, verbal appellation, and activity exposure. Parents, teachers, *peers*, and the media are the most important agents of socialization during childhood and adolescence.

- A *gender schema* is a set of interrelated ideas used to organize information about the world on the basis of gender. We use our gender schemas to classify many non-gender-related objects, behaviors, and activities as male or female.

Contemporary Gender Roles

- The traditional male gender role is *instrumental*. It emphasizes aggression, independence, and sexual prowess. Traditional male sexual *scripts* include the denial of the expression of feelings, an emphasis on performance and being in charge, the belief that men always want sex and that all physical

PARENTAL INFLUENCE   Children learn a great deal about sexuality from their parents. For the most part, however, they learn, not because their parents set out to teach them, but because they are avid observers of their parents' behavior. Much of what they learn concerns the hidden nature of sexuality.

As they enter adolescence, young people are especially concerned about their own sexuality, but they are often too embarrassed to ask their parents directly about these "secret" matters. And most parents are ambivalent about their children's developing sexual nature. Parents often underestimate their children's involvement in sexual activities, even as their children progress through adolescence, and so perceive less need to discuss sexuality with them (Jaccard, Dittus, & Gordon, 1998). They are often fearful that their children (daughters especially) will become sexually active if they have "too much" information. They tend to indulge in wishful thinking: "I'm sure Jenny's not really interested in boys yet"; "I know Jose would never do anything like that." Parents may put off talking seriously with their children about sex, waiting for the "right time." Or they may bring up the subject once, make their points, breathe a sigh of relief, and never mention it again. Sociologist John Gagnon calls this the "inoculation" theory of sexuality education: "Once is enough" (Roberts, 1983). But children need frequent "boosters" of sexual knowledge. Not talking about sex-related issues can have serious consequences, leaving adolescents vulnerable to other sources of information and opinions, such as peers. When a parent does undertake to educate a child about sexuality, it is usually the mother (Raffaelli, Bogenschneider, & Flood, 1998). Thus, most children grow up believing that sexuality is an issue that men don't deal with unless they have a specific problem.

Research indicates that parental involvement and discussion about sexuality with sons and daughters is a key factor in preventing risky behaviors, including early sexual intercourse (Blake, Simkin, Ledsky, Perkins, & Calabrese, 2001). It has also been demonstrated that when these adolescents do become sexually active they are more likely to use contraceptives and to have fewer sexual partners than those who do not communicate about sexual matters with their parents (Beier, 2000; Whitaker & Miller, 2000). A strong bond with parents appears to lessen teenagers' dependence on the approval of their peers and their need for interpersonal bonding, which may lead to sexual relationships.

Though sexuality education begins at home, youths age 10–15 most often name the mass media as their prime source of information about sex and intimacy. Smaller percentages name parents, peers, sexuality education programs, and professionals as sources (Kaiser Family Foundation, 1997). "Given the high stakes involved, the kinds of messages teens receive about sex are vitally important" (Kaiser Family Foundation, 2003). School-based sexuality education complements and augments the sexuality education children receive from their families, the media, religious and community groups, and health-care professionals (SIECUS, 2001).

Parents can also contribute to their children's feelings of self-worth through ongoing demonstrations of acceptance and affection. Adolescents need to know that their sexuality is OK and that they are loved in spite of the changes they are going through. Whereas low self-esteem increases vulnerability to peer pressure, high self-esteem increases adolescents' confidence and can enhance their sense of responsibility regarding their sexual behavior.

> Most mothers think that to keep young people from love making it is enough not to speak of it in their presence.
>
> —*Marie Madeline de la Fayette (1678)*

In addition to biological factors, social forces strongly influence young teenagers. Peers are very important, especially for boys, whose self-esteem and social status may be linked to evaluations from their friends. Because certain types of violence and aggression are considered "manly" in our culture, the boy in this photograph (left) takes great pleasure in an arcade game featuring simulated violence. For adolescent girls, the physical and hormonal changes of puberty often result in a great deal of interest (some would say obsession) with personal appearance (right). Cultural norms and media influences emphasizing female beauty reinforce this interest.

PEER INFLUENCE   Adolescents garner a wealth of misinformation from each other about sex. They also put pressure on each other to carry out traditional gender roles. Boys encourage other boys to be sexually active even if they are unprepared or uninterested. They must camouflage their inexperience with bravado, which increases misinformation; they cannot reveal sexual ignorance. Bill Cosby (1968) recalled the pressure to have sexual intercourse as an adolescent: "But how do you find out how to do it without blowin' the fact that you don't know how to do it?" On his way to his first sexual encounter, he realized that he didn't have the faintest idea of how to proceed:

> So now I'm walkin', and I'm trying to figure out what to do. And when I get there, the most embarrassing thing is gonna be when I have to take my pants down. See, right away, then, I'm buck naked . . . buck naked in front of this girl. Now, what happens then? Do . . . do you just . . . I don't even know what to do . . . I'm gonna just stand there and she's gonna say, "You don't know how to do it." And I'm gonna say, "Yes, I do, but I forgot." I never thought of her showing me, because I'm a man and I don't want her to show me. I don't want nobody to show me, but I wish somebody would kinda slip me a note.

Even though many teenagers find their early sexual experiences less than satisfying, they still seem to feel a great deal of pressure to conform, which means continuing to be sexually active. One study of rural tenth-graders found that the students overestimated the percentage of their peers who had ever had sexual intercourse, who had had four or more coital partners, or who had used alcohol or drugs before their previous intercourse. The students underestimated the percentage of their sexually active peers who had used a condom during their previous intercourse. These findings may indicate that more students engage in risky sex-related behaviors because they believe that their peers are doing the same, and fewer may be using condoms because of their belief that their peers are not using them (Yarber, 1996).

For boys, especially those with working-class backgrounds, adolescence is characterized by relationships in which self-esteem and status are more closely linked to evaluations from people of the same sex than of the other sex. This characterization has important consequences in terms of relationships with girls. To a boy, his girlfriend's importance may lie in giving him status among other boys; his relationship with her may be secondary. The generalized role expectations of males—that they must be competitive, aggressive, and achievement-oriented—carry over into sexual activities. They receive recognition for "scoring" with a girl, much as they would for scoring a touchdown or hitting a home run. Girls, in contrast, run the risk of being labeled as "sluts" by both male and female peers if they have sex in any context other than a committed relationship.

Sexual encounters, as opposed to sexual relationships, function in large part to confer status among teenage boys. Those who have experienced rigidly boy-to-boy activities during adolescence are often limited in the range of their later heterosexual relationships. In adolescence, they may learn to relate to women in terms of their own status needs, rather than as people. As a result, some men find it difficult to develop friendships with members of the other sex or relationships in which sexual activities involve respect or love for a woman.

THE MEDIA   As discussed in Chapter 1, erotic portrayals—nudity, sexually provocative language, and displays of sexual passion—are of great interest to the American viewing public. This public includes many curious and malleable children and adolescents. In an era in which we are bombarded with sexual images, the challenge of making healthy choices about sex is substantial. Teens watch about 3 hours of television every day, and 3 out of 4 acknowledge that it influences the sexual behaviors of others their age. Given the pervasive and explicit sexual messages that the media provides, it quickly becomes apparent how important it is for parents to understand the nature and extent of the information being conveyed (Kaiser Family Foundation, 2003).

Although some people would protect young viewers by censoring what is shown on television or the Internet, or played on the radio, a more viable solution to sexual hype in the media is to balance it with information about real life. Parents can help their children understand that sexuality occurs in a context, that it is complex, and that it entails a great deal of personal responsibility. Themes from television can be used by parents to initiate discussions about sex, love, and desire (including the desire of advertisers to sell their products).

Most important of all, perhaps, parents can encourage their children to think for themselves. Because adolescents generally feel a strong need to conform to the ideals of their subculture, it can be especially hard for them to discriminate between what they think they should do and what they actually feel comfortable doing. Much of the process of becoming a mature adult involves the rejection of these images and the discovery and embracing of one's own unique identity.

Gay, Lesbian, and Questioning Adolescents   During adolescence and early adulthood, sexual orientation becomes a very salient issue. In fact, few adolescents experience this as a trouble- or anxiety-free time. Many young

Lesbian and gay teenagers often have an especially difficult time coming to terms with their sexuality because society generally disapproves of their orientation.

people experience sexual fantasies involving others of their own sex; some engage in same-sex play. For many, these feelings of sexual attraction are a normal stage of sexual development, but for 3–10% of the population, the realization of a romantic attraction to members of their own sex will begin to grow (Laumann, Gagnon, Michael, & Michaels, 1994; Remafedi, Resnick, Blum, & Harris, 1992). Some gay men and lesbian women report that they began to be aware of their "difference" in middle or late childhood. Thus, the term "questioning" is used to describe those individuals who are examining their sexual orientation during this time of life.

Gay and lesbian adolescents usually have heterosexual dating experiences, and some engage in intercourse during their teens, but they often report ambivalent feelings about them. Perhaps surprising is the fact that bisexual and lesbian women have reported a significantly higher prevalence of pregnancy and physical or sexual abuse than heterosexual adolescents (Saewyc, Bearinger, Blum, & Resnick, 1999). These same women also reported greater use of ineffective contraceptives and were the most likely to have frequent intercourse and to engage in prostitution.

Nowadays the polite form of homophobia is expressed in safeguarding the family, as if homosexuals somehow came into existence independent of families and without family ties.

—*Dennis Altman*

Society in general has difficulty dealing with the fact of adolescent sexuality. The fact of gay and lesbian (or bisexual) adolescent sexuality has been especially problematic. Although there is more understanding of homosexuality now than in decades past, and more counseling and support services are available in some areas, gay, lesbian, bisexual, and transgendered individuals are still subject to ridicule and rejection. The assumed heterosexuality of society has resulted in a collective homophobia such that the phrase "That's so gay" is part of mainstream and youth vernacular. Teachers, parents, and administrators also perpetuate homophobia by ignoring and/or contributing to the harassment of sexual minorities (Finz, 2000). One survey found that teens who identified themselves as gay, lesbian, or bisexual were more likely than heterosexual teens to have attempted suicide in the past year ("Gay Teens," 1998). They were also nearly 5 times as likely to have been absent from school because of fears for their safety and more than 4 times as likely to have been threatened with a weapon at school.

Very few gay and lesbian teens feel that they can talk to their parents about their sexual orientation. Many (especially boys) leave home or are kicked out because their parents cannot accept their sexuality. It is sobering to think that a significant number of our children are forced into lives of secrecy, suffering, and shame because of society's reluctance to openly acknowledge the existence of homosexual orientations.

Nevertheless, evidence suggests a positive association between coming out to oneself and feelings of self-worth. Those who are "out" to themselves and have integrated a sexual identity with their overall personal identity are usually more psychologically well-adjusted than individuals who have not moved through this process (Savin-Williams, 1995). Support groups such as the Gay/Straight Alliance are one means by which homosexual adolescents can deal with the discrimination and other difficulties they face.

Developing a mature identity is a more formidable task for gay, lesbian, bisexual, and transgendered individuals who also face issues of color. The racial or ethnic background of a youth may be both an impediment and an advantage in forming a sexual identity. Though racial, ethnic, and cultural communities can provide identification, support, and affirmation, all too often families and peer groups within the community present youths with biases and prejudices that undermine the process of self-acceptance as a lesbian, gay man, bisexual, or transgendered person. The individual may have to struggle with the question of whether sexual orientation or ethnic identification is more important; he or she may even have to choose one identity over the other.

Corey Johnson, co-captain of his highschool football team, made history when he came out to his teammates and they rallied around him. Click on "Corey Johnson" for more of his story.

Adolescent Sexual Behavior

Hormonal changes during puberty bring about a dramatic increase in sexual interest (Figure 6.1). Whether this results in sexual activity is individually determined.

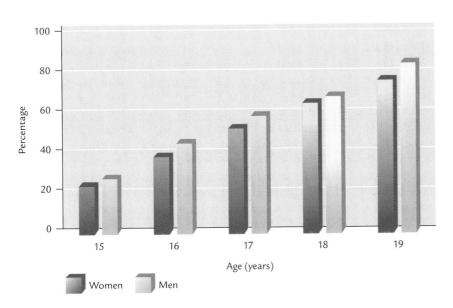

FIGURE 6.1   Proportion of U.S. Men and Women 15–19 Who Have Ever Had Sexual Intercourse, by Age, 1995. It is significant to note that sexual intercourse is only one indicator of teen sexuality. Focusing on it, apart from other sexual activity, reflects this culture's preoccupation with coitus. (*Source:* Abma et al., 2001.)

WHAT CAUSES HOMOSEXUALITY? What causes heterosexuality? Many have asked the first question, but few have asked the second. Although researchers don't understand the origins of sexual orientation in general, they have nevertheless focused almost exclusively on homosexuality. Their explanations generally fall into either biological or psychological categories.

Biological Theories

The earliest researchers, including Krafft-Ebing, Hirschfeld, and Ellis, believed that homosexuality was hereditary. But the biological perspective lost influence over the years; it was replaced by psychological theories, most notably psychoanalytic theories. Recently, however, there has been renewed interest in the biological perspective. Today, many researchers, as well as many gay men and lesbian women, believe that homosexuality is innate—people are "born" homosexual. Researchers point to possible genetic or hormonal factors.

In the first controlled genetic study of homosexuality in 40 years, researchers found a strong genetic link in male homosexuality (Bailey & Pillard, 1991). The researchers matched 157 identical and fraternal twin brothers and adopted brothers of the same age to determine if there was a genetic component in homosexuality. (Identical twins are genetic clones, having developed from a single egg that split after fertilization; fraternal twins develop simultaneously from two separate eggs and two sperm.) The study found that if one identical twin was gay, there was a 52% chance that his brother was also gay, compared with a 22% likelihood among fraternal twins and an 11% likelihood among genetically unrelated (adopted) brothers. The researchers estimated that the genetic contribution to male homosexuality could range from 30% to 70%. Next, they conducted a study of lesbian and heterosexual twins and came to similar conclusions. They found that if one identical twin was lesbian, there was about a 50% chance that her sister was also lesbian (Bailey, Pillard, Neale, & Agyei, 1993).

More recently, scientists studied genetic material from 40 pairs of gay brothers and discovered that 33 of the pairs had identical pieces of the end tip of the X chromosome (Hamer, Hu, Magnuson, Hu, & Pattatucci, 1993). Ordinarily, only half the pairs should have shared the same region. (The odds, in fact, of such an occurrence randomly happening were less than half of 1%.) This finding indicates that there may be one or more genes that play a role in predisposing some men to homosexuality. Researchers caution, however, that they have not identified a specific gene linked to homosexuality. Furthermore, because their findings have not been replicated, additional studies are necessary to validate their hypothesis. Finally, sexual orientation is an extremely complex biological and social phenomenon; a genetic link, if it exists, represents only part of the picture.

Other researchers have explored the possibility that homosexuality could have a hormonal basis. Because hormonal levels are sensitive to such factors as general health, diet, smoking, and stress, it is very difficult to control studies measuring sexual orientation. A review by researcher John Money (1988) of controlled studies comparing hormone levels of adult gay men, lesbian women, and heterosexuals found no difference in circulating hormones.

Masturbation If children have not begun masturbating before adolescence, they likely will begin once the hormonal and physical changes of puberty start. Masturbation is less common among African Americans and Latinos, however, than among Whites (Belcastro, 1985; Cortese, 1989). Many males begin masturbating between age 13 and 15, whereas the onset among females occurs more gradually (Bancroft et al., 2003). Data indicate that, of those adolescents who do masturbate, boys do so about 3 times more frequently than girls (Leitenber, Detzer, & Srebnik, 1993). One study of college students found that 78% of males and 43% of females masturbate at least once a month (Elliot & Brantly, 1997). Rates of masturbation appear to be affected by a wide range of social factors, though it is not clear whether they are also affected by sexual interaction with a partner (Laumann et al., 1994). In addition to providing release from sexual tension, masturbation gives us the opportunity to learn about our own sexual functioning, knowledge that can later be shared with a sex partner. Despite these positive aspects, adolescents, especially girls, often feel guilty about their autoerotic activities.

Because it is unethical to experiment with living fetuses, we cannot come to any meaningful conclusions about the effect of hormones on fetal brain development. There are some relevant studies, however. It has been found that women who took the synthetic estrogen DES when pregnant were more likely to have daughters with bisexual or same-sex attraction (Fagin, 1995). No such increase was found in males. The results suggest that, although exposure to estrogenic chemicals in the womb is not a dominant cause of homosexuality, it may be one of many causes—some inborn and some learned.

In a study on gay men and heterosexual men and women, Simon LeVay (1991) found that the brain's anterior hypothalamus, which influences sexual behavior, was smaller among gay men than among those he assumed were heterosexuals. But because the study was conducted on the cadavers of gay men who had died from AIDS, the smaller hypothalamic size may have resulted from the disease. It may also have resulted from their sexual behavior. A more recent replication study found a similar difference, but the statistical significance of this was borderline (Byne et al., 2001). Additional studies have examined other structural differences in the body, but no findings have been replicated.

Social Constructionism and Psychological Theories

A different school of thought, known as social constructionism, regards sexual orientation as a malleable concept that varies from one culture to another. Daryl Bem, a social psychologist from Cornell University, theorizes that children who infrequently view members of the other sex (and in a minority of the cases, members of the same sex) see them as exotic. Exotic peers elicit physio-logical tingles and jolts that seem offensive at first but that fire up sexual desire later in life (Bower, 1996).

Psychoanalysis provided the earliest psychological theory accounting for the development of homosexuality. Freud believed that human beings were initially bisexual but gradually developed heterosexual leanings. But if children did not successfully resolve their Oedipus or Electra complex, their development would be arrested. In the 1960s, psychoanalyst Irving Bieber (1962), reflecting popular stereotypes, proposed that men became homosexual because they were afraid of women. In a study of 200 heterosexual and gay men, Bieber found that, in contrast to heterosexual men, gay men tended to have overprotective, dominant mothers and passive or absent fathers. A review of Bieber's and similar studies uncovered some evidence to support the view that males from such families are slightly more likely to be gay (Marmor, 1980b). But one woman (Price, 1993) asks, tongue-in-cheek, "If having a dominant mother and a weak or absent father were truly a recipe for homosexuality, wouldn't most Americans be gay?"

Because research on the origins of sexual orientation focuses on homosexuality and not heterosexuality, there tends to be an underlying bias that homosexuality is not an acceptable or normal sexual variation. This bias has skewed research studies, especially psychoanalytic studies. Research should examine the origins of sexual orientation in general, not the origins of one type of orientation. As homosexuality has become increasingly accepted by researchers and psychologists as one type of sexual variation, scholars have shifted their research from determining the "causes" of homosexuality to understanding the nature of gay men and lesbian women in relationships.

First Intercourse With the advent of the "sexual revolution" in the 1960s, adolescent sexual behavior began to change. The average age for first intercourse dropped sharply, and almost as many girls as boys engaged in it. At the turn of the 21st century, however, a modification in this trend was observed. An analysis of three national surveys of adolescent health practices revealed that the percentage of sexually experienced teens declined from 54% in 1991 to 47% in 1997 (Lindberg, Boggs, Porter, & Williams, 2000). Most sexually active teens have partners who are close to their own age (Darroch, Landry, & Oslak, 1999). However, the minority of teens with much older male sex partners are at higher risk for HIV, other sexually transmitted infections (STIs), and unintended pregnancy (Darroch et al., 1999; Miller, Clark, & Moore, 1997). Approximately 22% of teenage girls report that their first intercourse was unwanted. Even with some important differences, men and women both experience similar sexual events. According to the Alan Guttmacher Institute (2002a), on average, men experience first intercourse at 16.9 years, and women at 17.4 years. By their late teenage years, at least

For most teens, increased commitment to the relationship is accompanied by increased likelihood of sexual intimacy.

three-quarters of all men and women have had intercourse, and more than two-thirds of all sexually experienced teens have had two or more partners.

Sex is rare among very young teens but common in the later teenage years (Figure 6.2). Among older teens and young adults who have experienced intercourse, many say they wish they had postponed first intercourse until they were more emotionally mature.

The most significant predictors of sexual intercourse among teenagers are alcohol use, the presence of a boyfriend or girlfriend, poor parental monitoring, and permissive parental sexual values (Small & Luster, 1994). Sexual activity is also closely associated with the socioeconomic status of the family and the neighborhood, with early activity more common when income is low (U.S. Department of Health and Human Services, 2000a). In the past, peer pressure among girls was an important factor in limiting their sexual behavior. Today, girls' peers seem to exert the opposite effect. However, teenagers may feel compelled to act more sexually sophisticated than they actually are; they may lie to protect themselves from being thought of as immature or inexperienced. The context in which they "give up" their virginity is still important for many girls; most feel that they are doing it

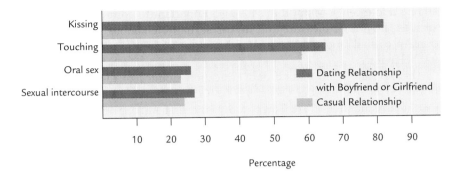

FIGURE 6.2 Percentage of Teens Who Say That Specific Activities Are Part of a Relationship "Almost Always" or "Most of the Time." (*Source:* From Kaiser Family Foundation and *Seventeen* magazine, October 2002. This information was reprinted with permission of the Henry J. Kaiser Family Foundation. The Kaiser Family Foundation, based in Menlo Park, California, is a nonprofit, independent national health care philanthropy and is not associated with Kaiser Permanente or Kaiser Industries.

for love. (For information on adolescents and contraception, see Chapter 11. For adolescent pregnancy, teen motherhood, and teen fatherhood, see Chapter 12.)

Sexuality Education

Sexuality education is a lifelong process. From the time that we are born, we learn about love, touch, affection, and our bodies. As we grow, the messages continue from both our families and the social environment, with school-based programs complementing and augmenting these primary sources of information.

It is the responsibility of schools and communities to develop their own curricula and pedagogy regarding sexuality education. Though programs vary widely, four types of sexuality education programs are currently offered in schools and communities (SIECUS, 2001):

- *Comprehensive.* These programs start in kindergarten and continue through twelfth grade. They include information on a broad range of topics and provide opportunities for students to develop relationship and interpersonal skills, as well as to exercise responsibility regarding sexual relationships.

- *Abstinence-based.* These programs emphasize the benefits of abstinence. They also include information about noncoital sexual behavior, contraception, and disease prevention methods.

- *Abstinence-only.* These programs emphasize abstinence from all sexual behaviors. They do not include any information about contraception or disease prevention methods.

- *Abstinence-only-until-marriage.* These programs emphasize abstinence from all sexual behaviors outside of marriage. They do not include any information about contraception or disease prevention methods. Marriage is presented as the only morally acceptable context for all sexual activity.

Different Values, Different Goals Among parents, teachers, and school administrators, there is substantial disagreement about what a "comprehensive" course in sexuality education should include. Some believe that only basic reproductive biology should be taught. Others see the prevention (or at least the reduction) of STIs as a legitimate goal of sexuality education. Still others would like the emphasis to be on the prevention of sexual activity among adolescents. Many think it's also important to address other issues, such as the role of pleasure and desire, sexual orientations, and the development of skills for making healthful, responsible decisions regarding sexual behavior.

The Sexuality Information and Education Council of the United States (SIECUS) developed the *Guidelines for Comprehensive Sexuality Education* (National Guidelines Task Force, 1996), the first national model for comprehensive sexuality education. The guidelines, the most widely recognized and implemented framework for comprehensive sexuality education in the United States, address four developmental levels—early childhood, preadolescence, early adolescence, and adolescence—and six main topics—human development, relationships, personal skills, sexual behavior, sexual health, and society and culture.

The majority of schools now have sexuality education programs. Approximately two-thirds describe them as comprehensive, and about one-third acknowledge having an abstinence-only-until-married focus (SIECUS, 2001). However, many of those programs described as comprehensive do not come close to meeting the six broad topics that the Sexuality Information and Education Council recommends. Currently, education on HIV/AIDS and other STIs is mandated in 38 states, but only 22 states require broader sexuality education (Alan Guttmacher Institute, 2002b). Even in those states that have mandates about the subject areas to be taught, local policymakers often dictate their own policies.

Although the opposition to comprehensive sexuality education may be small, it is very vocal. The coalition, led by the Bush administration and conservative parents, teachers, and religious groups, argues that to instruct children in birth control or abortion is to lead them down the path of self-destruction. In the absence of any national sexuality education consensus, the abstinence-only message has been adopted as the official curriculum in many of our schools across the United States.

HIV/AIDS Education The alarming spread of STIs, especially HIV, has added to the controversy over sexuality education. Though condom use has increased since the early 1990s, the data show that almost half of high school students had unprotected intercourse the last time they had sex (Contraception Report, 2001). In a survey of over 300 public school principals, researchers found a general consensus that a comprehensive program should encourage students to postpone sex, but if they do not, they should use birth control and practice safer sex ("School Sex Education," 2000). The quality of HIV/AIDS education is also crucial because misinformation can cause unnecessary anxiety and fear.

Abstinence-Only Programs One kind of sexuality education curriculum that is increasing in popularity, often with the help of federal funds, stresses abstinence for teenagers as the only form of birth control. There is little argument that children and adolescents should postpone sexual intercourse until they are mature. Not everyone, however, believes that schools should present sexuality in a negative light or attempt to scare young people into abstinence until they are married. The argument most often used against abstinence-only programs is that they are a thinly disguised effort to impose fundamentalist religious values on public school students, thus violating the constitutional separation of church and state. But abstinence education received a major boost when the federal Welfare Reform Act was passed in 1996. For 5 consecutive years starting in 1998, the federal government allocated $50 million for educational programs that had as their exclusive purpose teaching what are described as the "social, psychological, and health gains to be realized by abstaining from sexual activity." However, available research evidence does not support the benefit of abstinence-only approaches (Contraception Report, 2001).

Characteristics of Effective Sexuality Education Programs   Following the outbreak of AIDS in the 1980s, states were encouraged to reevaluate their sexuality education policies, programs, and requirements. The comprehensive sexuality education programs that resulted were those that integrated activities and personalized information, provided decision-making and assertiveness training, included information about avoiding undesirable consequences of sexual behavior, and promoted the use of techniques to do so.

Researcher Doug Kirby has investigated school-based sexuality education to determine the outcomes of such programs (Kirby, 2000). He studied evaluations of sexuality and HIV education programs that include both a comprehensive abstinence-and-contraception focus and an abstinence-only approach. He reported that the more comprehensive programs do not increase sexual intercourse or the number of sexual partners, that some reduced sexual behavior by either delaying the onset of intercourse or decreasing the frequency of intercourse, and that some increased the use of condoms and other contraceptives. Kirby found that few abstinence-only curricula have been evaluated and that many of these evaluations have been methodologically flawed. None of the abstinence-only programs had a consistent or significant impact on the delay of the onset of intercourse. He concluded that there is too little evidence to support the claim that different types of abstinence-only programs can delay the onset of intercourse. In his review of the most effective programs, Kirby identified some common characteristics:

- They focus on reducing one or more of the sexual behaviors that lead to unintended pregnancy or HIV/STI infection.
- They are based on theoretical approaches that have been shown to be effective in influencing other health-related risk behaviors.
- They send a clear message by continually taking a strong stance on these risky behaviors.
- They provide accurate information about the risks of unprotected intercourse and methods of avoiding unprotected intercourse.
- They include activities that address social pressures associated with sexual behaviors.
- They provide models of communication, negotiation, and refusal behaviors.
- They employ a variety of teaching methods designed to involve the participants and have them personalize the information.
- They incorporate behavioral goals, teaching methods, and materials that are appropriate to the age, sexual experience, and culture of the students.

- They last long enough that students can complete important activities adequately.
- They select teachers or peers who believe in the program they are implementing and then provide training for those instructors.

The most significant report to date in support of comprehensive sexuality education has come from the Office of the Surgeon General (2001). Dr. David Satcher, former surgeon general of the United States, examined science-based strategies to find a common ground for promoting sexual health and responsible sexual behavior. His report focused on increasing awareness, implementing and strengthening interventions, and expanding the research relating to sexual health throughout the life span. According to the report, sexuality education should do the following:

- Be thorough and wide-ranging.
- Begin early, continue throughout the life span, and recognize the special place that sexuality has in everyday life.
- Stress the value and benefits of remaining abstinent until involved in a committed, enduring, monogamous relationship.
- Assure awareness of optimal protection from STIs and unintended pregnancy.
- Stress that there are no infallible methods of contraception aside from abstinence and that condoms cannot protect against some forms of STIs.

Additionally, the report described intervention strategies to eliminate social and economic disparities in sexual health status and promoted basic research in human sexuality. It concluded that research-oriented strategies should encourage further scientific study of human sexual development and reproductive health over the life span, improve evaluation efforts, and assist in the development of educational materials. In response to the increased attention and funding that abstinence-only-until-marriage programs have been receiving in this administration, 35 organizations, including the American Psychological Association, American College of Obstetricians and Gynecologists, and Planned Parenthood Federation of America, have joined together to urge President Bush to reconsider funding abstinence-only education and to reexamine scientific evidence that demonstrates that responsible sexuality education works ("SSSS Signs Letter," 2002).

Although much more research needs to be done on sexuality education and its impact on young people, most professionals agree that it is one of the most important preventive means we have. Young people, guided by their parents and armed with knowledge and self-confidence, can make informed decisions and direct their own sexual destinies.

SEXUALITY IN EARLY ADULTHOOD

Like other life passages, the one from adolescence to early adulthood offers potential for growth if one is aware of and remains open to the opportunities this period brings (Figure 6.3).

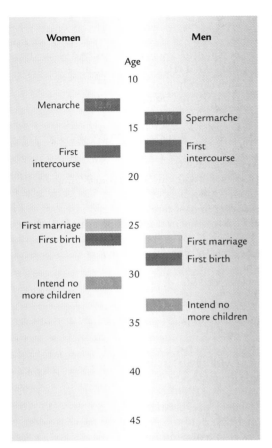

FIGURE 6.3 Sexual and Reproductive Time Line. (*Source:* The Alan Guttmacher Institute, Teenagers' sexual and reproductive health, *Facts in Brief,* New York: The Alan Guttmacher Institute, 2001. Reprinted with permission.)

Developmental Concerns

Several tasks challenge young adults as they develop their sexuality (Gagnon & Simon, 1973):

- *Establishing sexual orientation.* Children and adolescents may engage in sexual experimentation, such as playing doctor, kissing, and fondling, with members of both sexes, but they do not necessarily associate these activities with sexual orientation. Instead, their orientation as heterosexual, gay, lesbian, bisexual, or transgendered is in the process of emerging.

- *Integrating love and sex.* Traditional gender roles call for men to be sex-oriented and women to be love-oriented. In adulthood, this sex-versus-love conflict needs to be addressed. Instead of polarizing love and sex, people need to develop ways of uniting them.

- *Forging intimacy and making commitments.* Young adulthood is characterized by increasing sexual experience. Through dating, courtship, and cohabitation, individuals gain knowledge of themselves and others as potential partners. As relationships become more meaningful, the degree of intimacy and interdependence increases. Sexuality can be a means of enhancing intimacy and self-disclosure, as well as a source of physical pleasure. As adults become more intimate, most desire to develop their ability to make commitments.

IN 1996, THE Sexuality Information and Education Council of the United States (SIECUS) published the first national guidelines for comprehensive sexuality education in kindergarten through twelfth grade. These guidelines covered the life behaviors of a sexually healthy adult in six areas.

Behaviors of the Sexually Healthy Adult

1. Human development:

   a. Appreciate one's own body.
   b. Seek further information about reproduction as needed.
   c. Affirm that human development includes sexual development, which may or may not include reproduction or genital sexual experience.
   d. Interact with members of both sexes in respectful and appropriate ways.
   e. Affirm one's own sexual orientation and respect the sexual orientation of others.

2. Relationships:

   a. View family as a valuable source of support.
   b. Express love and intimacy in appropriate ways.
   c. Develop and maintain meaningful relationships.
   d. Avoid exploitative or manipulative relationships.
   e. Make informed choices about family options and relationships.
   f. Exhibit skills that enhance personal relationships.
   g. Understand how cultural heritage affects ideas about family, interpersonal relationships, and ethics.

3. Personal skills:

   a. Identify and live according to one's values.
   b. Take responsibility for one's own behavior.
   c. Practice effective decision making.
   d. Communicate effectively with family, peers, and partners.

4. Sexual behavior:

   a. Enjoy and express one's sexuality throughout life.
   b. Express one's sexuality in ways congruent with one's values.
   c. Enjoy sexual feelings without necessarily acting on them.
   d. Discriminate between life-enhancing sexual behaviors and those that are harmful to oneself and/or others.
   e. Express one's sexuality while respecting the rights of others.

   f. Seek new information to enhance one's sexuality.
   g. Engage in sexual relationships that are consensual, nonexploitative, honest, pleasurable, and protected against disease and unintended pregnancy.

5. Sexual health:

   a. Use contraception effectively to avoid unintended pregnancy.
   b. Prevent sexual abuse.
   c. Act consistent with one's values in dealing with an unintended pregnancy.
   d. Seek early prenatal care.
   e. Avoid contracting or transmitting an STD, including HIV.
   f. Practice health-promoting behaviors, such as regular checkups, breast and testicular self-exams, and early identification of potential problems.

6. Society and culture:

   a. Demonstrate respect for people with different sexual values.
   b. Exercise civic responsibility to influence legislation dealing with sexual issues.
   c. Assess the impact of family, cultural, religious, media, and societal messages on one's thoughts, feelings, values, and behaviors related to sexuality.
   d. Promote the rights of all people to have access to accurate sexuality information.
   e. Avoid behaviors that exhibit prejudice and bigotry.
   f. Reject stereotypes about the sexuality of diverse populations.
   g. Educate others about sexuality.

After examining these life behaviors, answer the following questions:

- Is it possible for an adult to enact all of the behaviors?
- Which of the behaviors would seem to be the most difficult to achieve?
- Would some of the behaviors change over the life span?
- Are there life behaviors related to sexuality that are missing from the list?
- Can adolescents enact and/or achieve these life behaviors?

Source: National Guidelines Task Force (1996). *Guidelines for Comprehensive Sexuality Education: Kindergarten–12th Grade.* New York: Sexuality Information and Education Council of the United States. 130 W. 42nd St., Suite 350 New York, NY 10036. Reprinted with permission.

- *Making fertility/childbearing decisions.* Childbearing is socially discouraged during adolescence, but it becomes increasingly legitimate when people reach their twenties, especially if they are married. Fertility issues are often critical but unacknowledged, especially for single young adults.

- *Practicing safer sex to protect against STIs.* An awareness of the various STIs and ways to best protect against them must be integrated into the communication, values, and behaviors of all young adults.

- *Evolving a sexual philosophy.* As individuals move from adolescence to adulthood, they reevaluate their moral standards, moving from moral decision making based on authority to standards based on their personal principles of right and wrong, caring, and responsibility. They become responsible for developing their own moral code, which includes sexual issues. In doing so, they need to evolve a personal philosophical perspective to give coherence to sexual attitudes, behaviors, beliefs, and values. They need to place sexuality within the larger framework of their lives and relationships. They need to integrate their personal, religious, spiritual, and humanistic values with their sexuality.

Establishing Sexual Orientation

A critical task of adulthood is establishing one's sexual orientation as heterosexual, gay, lesbian, bisexual, or transgendered. As mentioned previously, in childhood and early adolescence, there is considerable sex play or sexual experimentation with members of the other sex and same sex. These exploratory experiences are tentative in terms of sexual orientation. But in late adolescence and young adulthood, men and women are confronted with the important developmental task of establishing intimacy. And part of the task of establishing intimate relationships is solidifying one's sexual orientation.

Most people develop a heterosexual identity by adolescence or young adulthood. Their task is simplified because their development as heterosexuals is approved by society (Wilkinson & Kitzinger, 1993). But for those who are lesbian, gay, bisexual, or unsure, their development features more doubt and anxiety. Because those who are attracted to members of the same sex are aware that they are violating deep societal taboos, it can take them longer to confirm and accept their sexual orientation. It may also be difficult and dangerous for them to establish a relationship. In fact, fewer than 1 out of 5 gay and lesbian adolescents had their first sexual experience in the context of a relationship (Diamond, Savin-Williams, & Dube, 1999). This compares to one-half of male and three-fourths of female adolescent heterosexuals (Jessor & Jessor, 1997). Because adolescents who recognize themselves as homosexuals are often too young to go to places where other homosexuals meet, their only viable option is to seek out older, more overtly gay individuals.

Statistics on Sexual Orientation   We do not know the numbers of men and women who are heterosexual, gay, lesbian, bisexual, or transgendered. In large part, this is because homosexuality is stigmatized. Gay men and lesbian women are often reluctant to reveal their identities in random

"HETEROSEXUALITY" AND "HOMOSEXUALITY" are terms used to categorize people according to the sex of their sex partners. But, as noted in the discussion of Kinsey's work in Chapter 2, such categories do not always adequately reflect the complexity of sexual orientation or of human sexuality in general. Sex researcher Stephanie Sanders and her colleagues note that believing the labels "heterosexual" and "homosexual" reflect "actual sexual behavior patterns . . . leads to gross underestimates of the prevalence of behavioral bisexuality" (Sanders, Reinisch, & McWhirter, 1990).

Not everyone who has sexual experiences with members of both sexes identifies him- or herself as bisexual. Many more people who have had same-sex experiences identify themselves as heterosexuals than as bisexuals or homosexuals. The reason is simple: Most of these same-sex experiences took place during adolescent sexual experimentation and in situations in which males and females are segregated according to sex. This behavior is much closer to childhood sex play than to adult sexuality because it lacks the commitment to a heterosexual, homosexual, or bisexual orientation. In addition, some people seek occasional same-sex contacts to supplement their heterosexual activity.

Those people who do define themselves as bisexual have partners of both sexes. Sometimes, they have had only one or two same-sex experiences; nevertheless, they identify themselves as bisexual. They believe they can love and enjoy sex with both women and men. In other instances, those with predominantly same-sex experience and only limited other-sex experience consider themselves bisexual. In most cases, bisexual people do not have sex with men one night and women the next. Rather, their bisexuality is sequential. That is, they are involved in other-sex relationships for certain periods, ranging from a few weeks to years; later, they are involved in same-sex relations for another period.

Bisexual Identity Formation

In contrast to homosexuality, there is little research on bisexuality. The process of bisexual identity formation appears to be complex, requiring the rejection of the two recognized categories of sexual orientation. Bisexual people often find themselves stigmatized by gay men and lesbian women, as well as by heterosexuals. Among heterosexuals, bisexuals are likely to be viewed as "really" homosexual. In the lesbian/gay community, they may be viewed as "fence-sitters," not willing to admit their supposed homosexuality, or as simply "playing" with their orientation (Weinberg, Williams, & Pryor, 1994). Bisexuality is a legitimate sexual orientation that incorporates gayness and heterosexuality.

The first model of bisexual identity formation was developed by Martin Weinberg, Colin Williams, and D. W. Pryor (1994). According to this model, the process occurs in several stages. The first stage, often lasting years, is initial confusion. Many bisexual people are distressed to find that they are sexually attracted to members of both sexes; others feel that their attraction to members of the same sex means an end to their heterosexuality; still others are disturbed by their inability to categorize their feelings as either heterosexual or homosexual. The second stage is finding and applying the bisexual label. For many, discovering there is such a thing as bisexuality is a turning point; some find that their first heterosexual or same-sex experience permits them to view sex with *both* sexes as pleasurable; others learn of the term "bisexuality" from friends and are then able to apply it to themselves.

In the third stage, settling into the identity, the individual begins to feel at home with the label "bisexual." For many, self-acceptance is critical. A fourth stage is

surveys, and large-scale national surveys have been blocked until recently because of conservative opposition.

Some studies suggest that as many as 10% of Americans are lesbian or gay. Among women, about 13% have had orgasms with other women, but only 1–3% identify themselves as lesbian (Fay, Turner, Klassen, & Gagnon, 1989; Kinsey et al., 1948, 1953; Laumann et al., 1994; Marmor, 1980a). Among males, including adolescents, as many as 20–37% have had orgasms with other males, according to Kinsey's studies. Of these males, 10% were predominantly gay for at least 3 years, and 4% were exclusively gay throughout their entire lives (Kinsey et al., 1948). In a review of studies on male same-sex behavior between 1970 and 1990, researchers estimated that a minimum of 5–7% of adult men had had sexual contact with other men in adulthood.

continued uncertainty. Bisexual persons don't have a community or social environment that reaffirms their identity. Despite being settled in their sexual orientation, many feel persistent pressure from lesbian women or gay men to relabel themselves as homosexual and to engage exclusively in same-sex activities.

Types of Bisexual Persons

Researchers find that there is no single type of bisexual person (Weinberg et al., 1994). Instead, they have identified five types: pure, midrange, heterosexual leaning, homosexual leaning, and varied. The categories are based on the belief that sexual orientation consists of sexual feelings, sexual behaviors, and romantic feelings. Only 2% of the men and women studied were pure bisexuals—that is, were equally attracted to members of both sexes in terms of sexual feelings, behaviors, and romantic inclination. About one-third of the men and women were midrange—that is, were mostly bisexual in their various feelings and behaviors. About 45% of the men and 20% of the women ranked themselves as heterosexual leaning. About 15% each of the men and women called themselves homosexual leaning. (Men were almost three times as likely to identify themselves as heterosexual leaning; women were divided more or less evenly between heterosexual leaning and homosexual leaning.) About 10% could be identified as varied types. They were substantially more heterosexual on one dimension but much more homosexual on another.

The Nature of Bisexuality

As discussed in Chapter 5, sexuality runs along a continuum, with bisexuality falling midway between exclusive heterosexuality and exclusive homosexuality. Given this, one might ask whether bisexual people are merely in transition toward one or the other end of the continuum or whether bisexuality is a sexual orientation in its own right. The following list should help clarify some common myths and misconceptions about bisexuality (Stumper, 1997):

- *Myth 1: Bisexual persons are confused about their sexuality.* Confusion during the coming-out process is natural for both bisexual individuals and gay men. When people are oppressed and delegitimized, confusion is an appropriate reaction until they come out to themselves and find a supportive environment.

- *Myth 2: Bisexual people are denying their lesbianism or gayness.* Most bisexual individuals relate to the generic term "gay," and many are politically active in the gay community. Some identify themselves as "bisexual lesbian woman" or "bisexual gay man" to increase their visibility in both worlds.

- *Myth 3: Bisexual people are in transition.* Some individuals go through a transitional period of bisexuality on their way to adopting a lesbian, gay, or heterosexual identity. For many others, bisexuality remains a long-term orientation.

- *Myth 4: Being bisexual means having concurrent lovers of both sexes.* Being bisexual simply means having the potential for emotional and/or sexual involvement with members of either sex. Although some bisexual individuals may have male and female lovers at the same time, others may relate to members of different sexes at various times. Most bisexual people do not need to be involved with both men and women simultaneously in order to feel fulfilled.

- *Myth 5: Bisexual persons can hide in the heterosexual community when the "going gets tough."* Trying to pass for straight and denying one's bisexuality can be just as painful and damaging for a bisexual person as it is for a gay person to remain "in the closet." Bisexual individuals are not heterosexual and do not identify as such.

Ultimately, accepting bisexuality as a legitimate sexual orientation means acknowledging the value of our diversity.

Based on their review, the researchers suggest that about 4.5% of men are exclusively gay (Rogers & Turner, 1991). A more recent large-scale study of 3500 men and women, published by the University of Chicago, reported that 2.8% of men and 1.4% of women describe themselves as homosexual or bisexual (Laumann et al., 1994).

What are we to make of these different findings? In part, the variances may be explained by different methodologies, interviewing techniques, sampling procedures, or definitions of homosexuality. Furthermore, sexuality is more than simply sexual behaviors; it also includes attraction and desire. One can be a virgin or celibate and still be gay or heterosexual. Finally, because sexuality is varied and changes over time, its expression at any one time is not necessarily the same as at another time or for all time.

SEXUAL ORIENTATION IS an area of human sexuality that has been clouded by misunderstanding, myth, and confusion. To help explain the complex nature of sexual orientation, psychologists and researchers in sexuality have developed various models (Figure 6.4). Much as our views of gender, masculinity, and femininity have changed, so have conceptualizations of sexual orientation (although these are different phenomena).

Until the research of Alfred C. Kinsey and his colleagues, sexual orientation was dichotomized into "heterosexual" and "homosexual"— that is, a person could be one or the other. As shown in Model A, some considered a third category, bisexuality, although others believed that a bisexual was a homosexual person trying to be heterosexual. One of Kinsey's most significant contributions was his challenge to this traditional model. Research by Kinsey and others showed that homosexuality was not uncommon and that engaging in homosexual behaviors did not necessarily make a person homosexual. They also found that participation in both same- and other-sex behavior was not uncommon. This led them to conclude that sexual orientation is a continuum from exclusively heterosexual to exclusively homosexual, as depicted in model B, and that a person's sexual behavior pattern could change across a lifetime. This continuum has been widely utilized in

sexuality research, education, and therapy for the past 50 years.

Kinsey rejected the traditional explanation of sexual orientation and sexuality in general by saying:

> The world is not divided into sheep and goats. Not all things are black nor all things white . . . nature rarely deals with discrete categories. Only the human mind invents categories and tries to force facts into separated pigeonholes. The living world is a continuum in each and every one of its aspects. The sooner we learn this concerning human sexual behavior the sooner we shall reach a sound understanding of the realities of sex. (Kinsey et al., 1948)

The Kinsey continuum has been criticized for its implication that the more heterosexual a person is the less homosexual he or she must be, and vice versa. Sanders, Reinisch, and McWhirter (1990) note that some researchers have modified the Kinsey scale by using bipolar ratings of heterosexuality and homosexuality; that is, indicators such as sexual behavior, sexual fantasies, the person one loves, and feelings about which sex is more "attractive" can each be assessed independently. Storms (1980, 1981) suggested that homoeroticism and heteroeroticism are independent continua (model C). A bisexual individual is high on both homoeroticism and

The Gay/Lesbian/Bisexual Identity Process   Identifying oneself as lesbian, gay, or bisexual person takes considerable time and includes several phases, usually beginning in late childhood or early adolescence (Blumenfeld & Raymond, 1989; Troiden, 1988). The most intense phase in the development of one's sexual identity is during late adolescence and early adulthood. Researchers have found that college graduates are more likely to identify themselves as gay, lesbian, or bisexual while they are attending college because postsecondary education tends to engage students with issues of pluralism, diversity, and self-evaluation (Green, 1998). **Homoeroticism**— feelings of sexual attraction to members of the same sex—almost always precedes lesbian or gay activity by several years (Bell, Weinberg, & Hammersmith, 1981).

The first phase is marked by fear and suspicion that somehow one's desires are different. At first, the person may find it difficult to label these emotional and physical desires for members of the same sex. His or her initial reactions often include fear, confusion, or denial (Herdt & Boxer, 1992). In the second phase, the person actually labels these feelings of attraction, love, or desire as gay or lesbian feelings. The third phase includes the person's self-definition as gay. This may be difficult, for it entails accepting a status that society generally regards as deviant. Questions then arise about

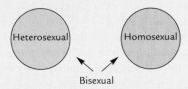

(a) Dichotomous-Psychoanalytic

(b) Unidimensional-Bipolar (Kinsey)

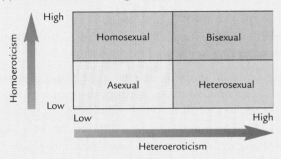

(c) Two-Dimensional—Orthogonal (Storms)

heteroeroticism dimensions, a heterosexual is high on heteroeroticism and low on homoeroticism, and a homosexual is high on homoeroticism and low on heteroeroticism. A person low on both dimensions would be considered asexual. Although the Storms model has been accepted by some in the sexuality field, it has not been as widely adopted as the original Kinsey scale or its variations.

Sanders, Reinisch, and McWhirter (1990) conclude by noting that:

> Sexual orientation cannot be understood in terms of simple dichotomies or unidimensional models. Sexual orientation is multidimensional in its essence, and its development is affected by many factors. Although nominal categories of heterosexual, homosexual, and bisexual exist, the application of such labels reflects a complex set of social, political, and developmental factors and does not always accurately reflect actual behavior patterns or erotic desire. (Sanders et al., 1990)

Which model do you think is most accurate? Can you find a place for yourself within each model? What are some of the social, political, and developmental factors that may have affected the adoption of these models?

FIGURE 6.4 **Three Models of Sexual Orientation.** (*Source:* Adapted from Sanders, S. A., Reinisch, J. M., & McWhirter, D. P. 1990.)

whether to tell parents or friends—whether to hide one's identity (stay in the closet) or make it known (come out of the closet).

Some, if not most, gay men and lesbian women may go through two additional phases. The next phase begins with a person's first gay or lesbian love affair (Troiden, 1988). This marks the commitment to unifying sexuality and affection. Most lesbian women and gay men have had such love affairs. The last phase a lesbian women or gay man may enter is becoming involved in the gay subculture. A gay man or lesbian woman may begin acquiring exclusively gay friends, going to gay bars and clubs, or joining gay activist groups. In the gay/lesbian world, individuals often incorporate a lifestyle in which sexual orientation is a major part of one's identity as a person.

For many, being a lesbian or gay person is associated with a total lifestyle and way of thinking. In making a gay or lesbian orientation a lifestyle, publicly acknowledging one's homosexuality (coming out) has become especially important. Coming out is a major decision because it may jeopardize many relationships, but it is also an important means of self-validation and self-affirmation. By publicly acknowledging a lesbian, gay, or bisexual orientation, a person begins to reject the stigma and condemnation associated with it. Generally, coming out to heterosexual people occurs in stages, first involving family members, especially the mother and siblings, and later the father.

Lesbian women, gay men, and bisexual individuals are often "out" to varying degrees. Some are out to no one, not even themselves. Some are out only to their lovers, and others to close friends and lovers but not to their families, employers, associates, or fellow students. Still others are out to everyone. Because of fear of reprisal, dismissal, or public reaction, gay, lesbian, and bisexual schoolteachers, police officers, military personnel, politicians, and members of other such professions are rarely out to their employers, co-workers, or the public.

Being Single

In recent decades, there has been a staggering increase in the numbers of unmarried adults (never married, divorced, or widowed). Most of this increase has been the result of men and women, especially young adults, marrying later.

The New Social Context of Singlehood   The consequences of this dramatic increase in unmarried young adults include the following:

▪ *Greater sexual experience.* Men and women who marry later are more likely to have more sexual experience and sex partners than earlier generations. Nonmarital sex is becoming the norm among adults.

▪ *Widespread acceptance of cohabitation.* As young adults are deferring marriage longer, cohabitation has become an integral part of young adult life. Because gay men and lesbian women are not legally permitted to marry, cohabitation has become for many of them a form of marriage.

▪ *Increased unintended pregnancies.* Because greater numbers of women are single and sexually active, they are more likely to become unintentionally pregnant as a result of unprotected sexual intercourse or contraceptive failure.

▪ *Increased numbers of abortions and births to single women.* The increased number of unintended pregnancies has led to more abortions and births to single mothers. (About 31% of childbirths are outside of marriage.) Birth to unmarried parents now rivals remarriage following divorce as a pathway by which children enter family structures. Sixty-two percent of African American children, 30% of Latino children, and 26% of White children are born to an unmarried parent (Bachu & O'Connell, 2001). About 83% of births to teenagers in 2000 occurred outside of a marriage.

▪ *Greater numbers of separated and divorced men and women.* Approximately 50–55% of all new marriages are likely to end in divorce (U.S. Bureau of the Census, 2000). Because of their previous marital experience, separated and divorced men and women tend to have different expectations about relationships than never-married young adults. Nearly half of all marriages are now remarriages for at least one partner.

▪ *A rise in the number of single-parent families.* Today, 31% of all family groups with children are single-parent situations, with the vast majority maintained by women (Bachu & O'Connell, 2001). Single parenthood is most prevalent in African American families, with 69% of the families headed by single parents, compared with 42% of Latino families and 22% of White families (Curtin & Martin, 2000).

The world that unmarried young adults enter is one in which greater opportunities than ever before exist for exploring intimate relationships.

The College Environment   The college environment is important not only for intellectual development but also for social development. The social aspects of the college setting—classes, dormitories, fraternities and sororities, parties, and athletic events—provide opportunities for meeting others. For many, college is a place to search for or find mates.

Dating in college is similar to high school dating in many ways. It may be formal or informal ("getting together"); it may be for recreation or for finding a mate. Features that distinguish college dating from high school dating, however, include the more independent setting (away from home, with diminished parental influence), the increased maturity of partners, more role flexibility, and the increased legitimacy of sexual interactions. There appears to be a general expectation among students that they will engage in sexual intercourse at some point during their college career (Sprecher & McKinney, 1993) and that sexual involvement will occur within a loving relationship (Sprecher, 2002).

Sociologist Ira Reiss (1967) describes four moral standards of nonmarital sexuality among college students. The first is the abstinence standard, which was the official sexual ideology in American culture until the early 1960s. According to this belief, it is wrong for either men or women to engage in sexual intercourse before marriage regardless of the circumstances or their feelings for each other. The second is the double standard, widely practiced but rarely approved publicly. This permits men to engage in nonmarital intercourse, but women are considered immoral if they do so. Permissiveness with affection represents a third standard. It describes sex between men and women who have a stable, loving relationship. This standard is widely held today. Permissiveness without affection, the fourth standard, holds that people may have sexual relationships with each other even if there is no affection or commitment.

Although acceptance of sex outside of marriage is widespread among college students, there are limits. If a woman has sexual intercourse, most people believe it should take place in the context of a committed relationship.

Women who "sleep around" are morally censured. Reflecting the continuing double standard, men are not usually condemned as harshly as women for having sex without commitment.

For gay men, lesbian women, and bisexual and transgendered individuals, the college environment is often liberating because campuses tend to be more accepting of sexual diversity than society at large is. College campuses often have lesbian, gay, bisexual, and transgendered organizations that sponsor social events, dances, and get-togethers. There, individuals can freely meet others in open circumstances that permit meaningful relationships to develop and mature. Although prejudice against those who are different continues to exist in colleges and universities, college life has been an important haven for many.

The Singles World   Men and women involved in the singles world tend to be older than college students, typically ranging in age from 25 to 40. They have never been married, or, if they are divorced, they usually do not have primary responsibility for children. Single adults are generally working rather than attending school. Of unmarried adults under 24 years of age, (56% of men and 43% of women live with someone else, usually their parents (Fields & Casper, 2001).

Although dating in the singles world is somewhat different from dating in high school and college, there are similarities. Singles, like their counterparts in school, emphasize recreation and entertainment, sociability, and physical attractiveness.

The problem of meeting other single people is very often central. In college, students meet each other in classes or dormitories, at school events, or through friends. There are many meeting places and large numbers of eligibles. Because they are working, singles have less opportunity to meet available people. For single adults, the most frequent means of meeting others are introductions by friends, common interests, parties, and work.

To fill the demand for meeting others, the singles world has spawned a multibillion-dollar industry—bars, resorts, clubs, housing, and the Internet. Singles increasingly rely on personal classified ads, Internet bulletin boards, or chat rooms, in which men advertise themselves as "success objects" and women advertise themselves as "sex objects." These ads, postings, and messages tend to reflect stereotypical gender roles. Men frequently advertise for women who are attractive, de-emphasizing intellectual, professional, and financial considerations. Women often advertise for men who hold jobs and who are financially secure, intelligent, emotionally expressive, and interested in commitment. Men are twice as likely as women to place ads. Additional forms of people meeting others include video dating services, introduction services, and 900 party-line phone services.

Single men and women often rely on their church and church activities to meet others. About 8% of married couples meet in church (Laumann et al., 1994). Churches are especially important for middle-class African Americans because they have less chance of meeting other African Americans in work and neighborhood settings. African Americans also attend Black-oriented concerts, plays, film festivals, and other social gatherings.

As a result of the growing acceptance of sexuality outside of marriage, single people are presented with various sexual options. Some choose celibacy for religious or moral reasons. Others choose celibacy over casual sex; when they are involved in a committed nonmarital relationship, they may become sexually intimate. Some are temporarily celibate; they are taking a "vacation from sex." They utilize their celibacy to clarify the meaning of sexuality in their relationships.

Sexual experimentation is important for many. Although individuals may derive personal satisfaction from sexual experimentation, they must also manage the stress of conflicting commitments, loneliness, and a lack of connectedness. Although the stereotype of singles as especially sexual is prevalent, their frequency of sexual intercourse is only about half that of married or cohabiting couples. In one study, 25% of nonpartnered singles reported having had sex only a few times a year, compared with only 10% of married people (Laumann et al., 1994).

Many single women reject the idea of casual sex. Instead, they believe that sex must take place within the context of a relationship. In relationship sex, intercourse becomes a symbol of the degree of caring between partners. Such relationships are expected to "lead somewhere," such as to fuller commitment, love, cohabitation, or marriage. As men and women get older, marriage becomes an increasingly important goal of a relationship.

In the late nineteenth century, as a result of the stigmatization of homosexuality, groups of gay men and lesbian women began congregating in their own secret clubs and bars. There, in relative safety, they could find acceptance and support, meet others, and socialize. Today, some neighborhoods in large cities are identified with gay, lesbian, bisexual, and transgendered people. These neighborhoods feature not only openly gay or lesbian bookstores, restaurants, coffeehouses, and bars but also churches, clothing stores, medical and legal offices, hair salons, and so on.

Gay, lesbian, bisexual, and transgendered businesses, institutions, and neighborhoods are important for affirming positive identities; they enable individuals to interact beyond a sexual context. They help make being a lesbian, gay, bisexual, or transgendered person a complex social identity consisting of many parts—student, parent, worker, professional, churchgoer—rather than simply a sexual role.

In these neighborhoods, men and women are free to express their affection as openly as heterosexual people. They experience little discrimination or intolerance and are involved in alternative social and political organizations. More recently, with increasing acceptance in some areas, many middle-class gay, lesbian, bisexual, and transgendered individuals have moved to suburban areas. In the suburbs, however, they remain more discreet than they are in large cities. In any case, various studies indicate that 45–80% of lesbian women and 40–60% of gay men are in steady romantic relationships (Kurdek, 1995).

The urban gay male subculture that emerged in the 1970s emphasized sexuality. Although relationships were important, sexual experiences and variety were even more important. Despite the emphasis on sex over relationships, however, two researchers found that most gay men in their study had at least one exclusive relationship (Weinberg & Williams, 1974). In fact, involvement in the gay subculture enhanced the likelihood of lasting relationships. The researchers speculated that closeted gay men were more likely than openly gay men to avoid attachments for fear of discovery.

As a result of the HIV/AIDS epidemic, beginning in the 1980s, the gay male community increasingly has emphasized the relationship context of sex

Many gay and lesbian couples choose to affirm their commitment in a marriage ceremony, although gay and lesbian marriages are not legally recognized in any state.

(Carl, 1986; Isensee, 1990). Relational sex has become the norm among large segments of the older gay male population (Levine, 1992). Most gay men have sex within dating or love relationships.

African American gay men often experience a conflict between their Black and gay identities (Peterson, 1992). African Americans are less likely to disclose their gay identity because the Black community is less accepting of homosexuality than is the White community. At the same time, African Americans may experience racial discrimination in the predominantly White gay male community. Gay African American men whose primary identity is racial tend to socialize in the Black community, where they are tolerated only as long as they are closeted. Few gay institutions are available to them. In most communities, they must rely on discreet friendship circles or clandestine bars to meet other gay Black men.

For gay Latino men in cities with large Latino populations, there is usually at least one gay bar. Such places specialize in dancing or female impersonation. The extent to which a gay Latino man participates in the Anglo or Latino gay world depends on the individual's degree of acculturation (Carrier, 1992).

JUST AS THERE ARE MYTHS about bisexuality, there are also numerous misconceptions about being a gay man or lesbian woman. These continue to circulate, fueling the fires of prejudice. The misconceptions include the following:

- *Misconception 1: Men and women are gay or lesbian because they can't get a heterosexual partner.* This belief is reflected in such remarks about lesbian women as "All she needs is a good lay" (implying a man). Similar remarks about men include "He just needs to meet the right woman." Research indicates that lesbian women and gay men have about as much heterosexual high school dating experience as their peers. Furthermore, the majority of lesbian women have had sexual experiences with men, and many of those experiences were pleasurable (Bell et al., 1981).

- *Misconception 2: Lesbian women and gay men "recruit" heterosexuals to become gay.* People are not recruited or seduced into being gay any more than they are recruited into being heterosexual. Most gay men and lesbian women have their first gay experience with a peer, either a friend or an acquaintance. They report having had same-sex feelings prior to their first experience (Bell et al., 1981).

- *Misconception 3: Gay men are child molesters.* This is a corollary to the recruitment misconception. The overwhelming majority of child molesters are heterosexual males who molest girls; these men include fathers, stepfathers, uncles, and brothers. A large percentage of men who molest boys identify themselves as heterosexual (Arndt, 1991).

- *Misconception 4: Homosexuality can be "caught."* Homosexuality is not the flu. Some parents express fear about having their children taught by homosexual teachers. They fear that their children will model themselves after the teacher or be seduced by him or her. But a child's sexual orientation is often established by the time he or she enters school, and a teacher would not have an impact on that child's orientation.

- *Misconception 5: Gay men and lesbian women could change if they wanted to.* Most gay men and lesbian women believe that they cannot change their sexual orientation. The belief that they should reflects assumptions that homosexuality is abnormal or sinful.

Most psychotherapy with gay men and lesbian women who are unhappy about their orientation aims at helping them adjust to it. So-called reparative therapy is based on the belief that orientation can be changed.

- *Misconception 6: Homosexuality is condemned in the Bible.* The Bible condemns same-sex sexual activities, not homosexuality. Some biblical scholars believe that the rejection of same-sex sexual activities is based on historical factors, including the lack of the concept of sexual orientation, the exploitative and abusive nature of much same-sex activity in ancient times, the belief that the purpose of sex was procreation, and concerns that such acts were impure (there were similar concerns about sexual intercourse with a menstruating woman). There is increasing debate among religious groups as to whether same-sex relationships are inherently sinful.

- *Misconception 7: All gay men are effeminate; all lesbian women are butch.* People often perceive the world selectively, paying attention to information that supports their stereotypes and ignoring information that contradicts them. Empirical research has demonstrated that perceptions of gay men as more theatrical, gentle, and liberated and of lesbian women as more dominant, direct, forceful, strong, and nonconforming have been shaped more by cultural ideologies about homosexuality than by individuals' own unbiased observations (cited in Herek, 1995).

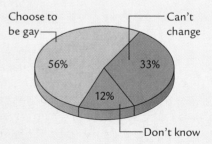

FIGURE 6.5 Percentage of Adults Who Believe Homosexuality Is Chosen or Can't Be Changed. (*Source:* "Can Gays Convert?" 2000.)

Beginning in the 1950s and 1960s, young and working-class lesbian women developed their own institutions, especially women's softball teams and exclusively lesbian bars, as places for socializing. During the late 1960s and 1970s, lesbian separatists, who wanted to create a separate "womyn's" culture distinct from those of heterosexual women *and* gay men, rose to prominence. They developed their own music, literature, and erotica; they had their own clubs and bars. But by the middle of the 1980s, the lesbian women's community had undergone a "shift to moderation" (Faderman, 1991). It became more diverse, welcoming Latinas, African American women, Asian American women, and older women. It also developed closer ties with the gay men's community. Lesbian women now view gay men as sharing much in common with them because of the prejudice directed against both groups.

Lesbian women tend to value the emotional quality of relationships more than the sexual component. Lesbian women usually form longer-lasting relationships than gay men (Tuller, 1988). Lesbian women's emphasis on emotions over sex and the more enduring quality of their relationships reflect their socialization as women. Being female influences a lesbian more than does being gay.

Cohabitation

In 2000, more than 3 million unmarried couples, or about 3.7% of the unmarried adult population, were living together in the United States (U.S. Bureau of the Census, 2001). Most of these individuals were in their mid-twenties. In contrast, only 400,000 heterosexual couples were cohabiting in 1960. Delaying marriage has increased the number of men and women cohabiting.

MONOGAMY, n. A common misspelling. See "Monotony."

— *Robert Tefton*

A New Norm   **Cohabitation** is increasingly accepted at almost every level of society. By age 30, half of all people will have cohabited. In fact, cohabitation perhaps is becoming institutionalized as part of the normal mate selection process. The concept of **domestic partnership** has led to laws granting some of the protections of marriage to men and women, including gay men and lesbian women, who cohabit in committed relationships.

Cohabitation has become more widespread and accepted in recent years for several reasons. First, the general climate regarding sexuality is more liberal than it was a generation ago. Sexuality is more widely considered to be an important part of people's lives, whether or not they are married. The moral criterion for judging sexual intercourse has shifted; love rather than marriage is now widely regarded as making a sexual act moral. Second, the meaning of marriage is changing. Because of the dramatic increase in divorce rates in recent decades, marriage is no longer thought of as necessarily a permanent commitment. Permanence is increasingly replaced by **serial monogamy,** a succession of marriages. Because the average marriage now lasts only 7 years, the distinction between marriage and cohabitation is losing its clarity. Third, young adults are continuing to defer marriage. At the same time, they want the companionship found in living intimately with another person.

For young adults, there are a number of advantages to cohabitation. First, because their lives are often in transition—as they finish school, establish careers, or become more secure financially—cohabitation represents a tentatively committed relationship. Second, in cohabiting relationships, partners tend to be more egalitarian. They do not have to deal with the more structured roles of husband and wife and are freer to develop their own individuality independent of marital roles. Third, the partners know they are together because they want to be, not because of the pressure of marital obligations. With the increased acceptance of cohabitation, more than half of the Fortune 500 companies have extended domestic partner benefits to both homosexual and heterosexual partners. This change has helped employers hire and keep qualified employees while at the same time providing employees with partners the same health benefits as married couples.

Although there are a number of advantages to cohabitation, there can also be disadvantages. Parents may refuse to provide support for education to a child who is cohabiting, and they may not welcome their child's partner into their home. Cohabiting couples also may find that they cannot easily buy a house together because some banks may not view their income as joint. If one partner has children, the other partner is usually not as involved as if the couple were married. Cohabiting couples may find themselves socially stigmatized if they have a child. Extrarelational sex is more likely to occur in cohabiting relationships than in married ones. Finally, cohabiting relationships generally don't last more than 5 years; couples either break up or get married (Tolson, 2000).

Although partners who are living together often argue that cohabitation helps prepare them for marriage, such couples are statistically more likely to divorce than those who do not live together before marriage (Tolson, 2000). People who live together before marriage tend to be more liberal, more sexually experienced, and more independent than people who do not live together before marriage.

In 1995, there were more than 1.5 million gay or lesbian couples living together. The relationships of gay men and lesbian women have been stereotyped as less committed than those of heterosexual couples because (1) lesbian women and gay men cannot legally marry, (2) they may not appear to emphasize sexual exclusiveness, and (3) heterosexuals misperceive love between lesbian and gay partners as somehow less "real" than love between heterosexuals. Numerous similarities, however, exist between gay and heterosexual couples, according to Letitia Peplau (1981, 1988). Regardless of their sexual orientation, most people want a close, loving relationship with another person. For gay men, lesbian women, and heterosexual persons, intimate relationships provide love, romance, satisfaction, and security. There is one important difference, however. Heterosexual couples tend to adopt a traditional marriage model, whereas gay couples tend to have a "best-friend" model.

Few lesbian and gay relationships are divided into the traditional heterosexual provider/homemaker roles. Among heterosexual couples, these divisions are gender-linked as male or female. In same-sex couples, however, tasks are often divided pragmatically, according to considerations such as who likes cooking more (or dislikes it less) and who works when. Most gay couples are dual-worker couples; neither partner supports or depends on the other economically. And because partners in gay and lesbian couples are the same sex, the economic discrepancies based on greater male earning power are absent. Although gay couples emphasize egalitarianism, if there are differences in power, they are attributed to personality; if there is an age difference, the older partner is usually more powerful.

Because they confront societal hostility, lesbian women and gay men fail to receive the general social support given heterosexual couples in maintaining relationships. One rarely finds parents, for example, urging their gay or lesbian children to make a commitment to a stable same-sex relationship or, if the relationship is rocky, to stick it out.

SEXUALITY IN MIDDLE ADULTHOOD

In the middle-adulthood years, family and work become especially important. Personal time is spent increasingly on marital and family matters, especially if a couple have children. Sexual expression often decreases in frequency, intensity, and significance, to be replaced by family and work concerns. Sometimes, the change reflects a higher value placed on family intimacy; other times, it may reflect habit, boredom, or conflict.

Developmental Concerns

In the middle adult years, some of the psychosexual developmental tasks begun in young adulthood may be continuing. These tasks, such as ones related to intimacy issues or childbearing decisions, may have been deferred or only partly completed in young adulthood. Because of separation or divorce, people may find themselves facing the same intimacy and commitment tasks at age 40 that they thought they had completed 15 years earlier (Cate & Lloyd, 1992). But life does not stand still; it moves steadily forward, and other developmental issues appear, including the following:

- *Redefining sex in marital or other long-term relationships.* In new relationships, sex is often passionate and intense; it may be the central focus. But in long-term marital or cohabiting relationships, habit, competing parental and work obligations, fatigue, and unresolved conflicts often erode the passionate intensity associated with sex. Sex may need to be redefined as an expression of intimacy and caring. Individuals may also need to decide how to deal with the possibility, reality, and meaning of extramarital or extrarelational sex.

- *Reevaluating one's sexuality.* Single women and men may need to weigh the costs and benefits of sex in casual or lightly committed relationships. In long-term relationships, sexuality often becomes less than central to relationship satisfaction, as nonsexual elements such as communication, intimacy, and shared interests and activities become increasingly important. Women who have deferred their childbearing begin to reappraise their decision: Should they remain child-free, race against their biological clock, or adopt a child? Some people may redefine their sexual orientation. One's sexual philosophy continues to evolve.

- *Accepting the biological aging process.* As people age, their skin wrinkles, their flesh sags, their hair turns gray (or falls out), their vision blurs—and they become, in the eyes of society, less attractive and less sexual. By their forties, their physiological responses have begun to slow noticeably. By their fifties, society begins to "neuter" them, especially women who have been

Seldom, or perhaps never, does a marriage develop into an individual relationship smoothly and without crisis; there is no coming to consciousness without pain.

—*Carl Jung (1875–1961)*

Marriage turns lovers into relatives.

—*John Rush*

through menopause. The challenge of aging is to come to terms with its biological changes.

Marital Sexuality

When people marry, they may discover that their sex lives are very different from what they were before marriage. Sex is now morally and socially sanctioned. It is in marriage that the great majority of heterosexual interactions take place, yet as a culture, we feel ambivalent about marital sex. On the one hand, marriage is the only relationship in which sexuality is legitimized. On the other, marital sex is an endless source of humor and ridicule.

Frequency of Sexual Interactions   Sexual intercourse tends to diminish in frequency the longer a couple are married. For newly married couples, the average rate of sexual intercourse is about 3 times a week. As couples get older, the frequency drops. In early middle age, married couples have sexual intercourse an average of 1½–2 times a week. After age 50, the rate is about once a week or less. Decreased frequency, however, does not necessarily mean that sex is no longer important or that the marriage is unsatisfactory. It may be the result of biological aging and declining sexual drive. It often means simply that one or both partners are too tired. For dual-worker families and families with children, fatigue and lack of private time may be the most significant factors in the decline of frequency. Philip Blumstein and Pepper Schwartz (1982) found that most people attributed the decline in frequency of sexual intercourse to lack of time or physical energy or to "being accustomed" to each other. In addition, other activities and interests engage them besides sex.

Most married couples don't seem to feel that declining frequency is a major problem if their overall relationship is good (Cupach & Comstock, 1990; Sprecher & McKinney, 1993). Sexual intercourse is only one erotic bond among many in marriage. There are also kisses, caresses, nibbles, massages, candlelight dinners, hand-in-hand walks, intimate words, and so on.

Sexual Satisfaction and Pleasure   In real life, higher levels of sexual satisfaction and pleasure seem to be found in marriage than in singlehood or extramarital relationships (Laumann et al., 1994). More than 50% of married men report that they are extremely satisfied physically and emotionally with their spouse; about 40% of married women report similar levels of satisfaction (Laumann et al., 1994). The lowest rates of satisfaction were among those who were neither married nor living with someone, a group thought to have the greatest sex.

If a person has more than one sex partner, physical and emotional satisfaction begin to decline. Although most American marriages are sexually exclusive, among those that are not, only 59% of spouses find sex with their spouse physically satisfying, and only 55% are emotionally satisfied. It is impossible to say, however, whether lower levels of satisfaction cause people to seek out an extramarital partner or whether having another partner lowers levels of sexual satisfaction in marriage (Laumann et al., 1994; Michael, Gagnon, Laumann, & Kolata, 1994).

About 75% of single, married, and cohabiting men always have an orgasm with their partner, but those who are married report the highest rates

Setting a good example for your children takes all the fun out of middle age.

—*William Feather*

The demands of parenting may diminish a couple's ability to be sexually spontaneous.

of physical and emotional satisfaction with their partner. Among women, the rate of always having an orgasm varies. The highest rate of orgasm—34%—is found among divorced women living alone, followed by married women, 30% of whom report always having an orgasm. Significantly, however, slightly more than 40% of the married women report being extremely sexually satisfied emotionally and physically with their partner (Laumann et al., 1994).

Edward Laumann and his colleagues (1994) observe that levels of sexual satisfaction in marriage are high because partners tend to have emotional and social involvement in the relationship. Marital partners have a commitment to pleasing each other, learning the other's likes, and being sensitive to the other's needs. The longer the partnership is likely to last, the greater the commitment to making it work in various aspects—including the sexual.

Lesbian Women, Gay Men, and Bisexual Persons in Heterosexual Marriages Although there are no reliable studies, it is estimated that about 20% of gay men and 33% of lesbian women have been married (Bell & Weinberg, 1978). Estimates run into the millions for married bisexual men and women (Gochoros, 1989; Hill, 1987). Relatively few men and women are consciously aware of their homosexuality or bisexuality at the time they marry. Those who are aware rarely disclose their feelings to their prospective partner (Gochoros, 1989). Like heterosexual people, lesbian women, gay men, and bisexual individuals marry because of pressure from family, friends, and girlfriend/boyfriend, genuine love for their heterosexual partner, the wish for companionship, and the desire to have children (Bozett, 1987a).

When spouses discover their partner's homosexuality or bisexuality, they initially experience shock, and then they feel deceived or stupid. Many feel shame (Hays & Samuels, 1989). "His coming out of the closet in some ways put the family in the closet," recalled one woman who felt ashamed to tell anyone of her situation (Hill, 1987). At the same time, homosexual or bisexual spouses often feel deeply saddened for hurting loved ones. If they have children, they fear losing them.

Divorce and After

Divorce has become a major force in American life. A quick observation of demographics in this country points to a new and growing way of life: post-divorce singlehood. In 2000, 10.1% of men and 12.6% of women 15 and over were either separated or divorced (Fields & Casper, 2001).

Scholars suggest that divorce represents, not a devaluation of marriage, but, oddly enough, an idealization of it. We would not divorce if we did not have such high expectations for marriage's ability to fulfill various needs (Furstenberg & Cherlin, 1991; Furstenberg & Spanier, 1987). Our high divorce rate further tells us that we may no longer believe in the permanence of marriage. Instead, we remain married only as long as we are in love or until a potentially better partner comes along.

Consequences of Divorce Because divorce is so prevalent, many studies have focused on its effects on partners and children. From these studies, a number of consequences have been identified (Amato, 2000; Thables, 1997):

- There is often stigmatization by family, friends, and co-workers.
- There is a change of income (usually a substantial decline for women).
- There is a higher incidence of physical and emotional problems among both men and women, including depression, injury, and illness.
- There are significantly more problems with children, including criminality, substance abuse, lower academic performance, earlier sexual activity, and a higher rate of divorce.
- Children are twice as likely as those in two-parent families to develop serious psychiatric problems and addictions later in life (Whitehead & Holland, 2003).

The long-term impact of divorce on children has recently been described in *The Unexpected Legacy of Divorce: A 25-Year Landmark Study* (2000). Here, authors Judith Wallerstein, Julia Lewis, and Sandra Blakeslee urge parents to consider staying together to spare their children a lifetime of failed relationships and emotional problems. In a longitudinal study of children in 100 divorced families from a predominantly upper-middle-class community, the authors found the following:

- Sixty percent of the adult children were married, as opposed to 80% of adults whose parents' marriages lasted.

- Thirty-eight percent of the adult children of divorce had their own children, 17% of them out of wedlock, as opposed to 61% in the comparison group, all in the context of marriage.

- Twenty-five percent of the children of divorce used drugs and alcohol before age 14, compared with 9% of the comparison group.

- Fifty percent of the children of divorce married before age 25, compared with 11% of the comparison group.

- Fifty-seven percent of these early marriages resulted in divorce, as opposed to 25% of early marriages in the comparison group.

Given the experiences that children of divorce have endured, it is not surprising that many suffer from relationship anxiety and ask themselves whether they can partner with another person. A question that researchers have been asking for years is, "What exactly is it about a single-parent home that puts children at higher risk for such problems?" Although there are several theories, it's unclear which factors are most significant. Experts cite the economic situation, the quality of the parenting, the timing of the divorce, the level of respect between the parents, and the quality of the social network, which includes teachers, parents, and other role models, as being significant in a child's ability to cope with the divorce.

At the same time, there are some positive outcomes from divorce that may offset or even provide relief from the negative ones. Divorce offers options for individuals in unhappy marriages. Divorce also may eliminate the stressful and frustrating experience of marriage and result in improved mental and emotional well-being. And divorce can provide both parents and children with a less idealized view of marriage, an opportunity for growth, and a more harmonious family situation. Obviously, most individuals would not opt for divorce if a viable alternative were available. However, when it is not, acknowledging that the process of divorce will involve change will help prepare those people for the transition that lies ahead.

Dating Again   A first date after years of marriage and subsequent months of singlehood evokes some of the same emotions felt by inexperienced adolescents. Separated or divorced men and women who are beginning to date again may be excited and nervous; worry about how they look; and wonder whether it's OK to hold hands, kiss, or make love. They may believe that dating is incongruous with their former selves, or they may be annoyed with themselves for feeling excited and awkward. Furthermore, they may know little about the norms of postmarital dating.

Dating serves several important purposes for separated and divorced people. Primarily, it is a statement to both the former spouse and the world at large that the person is available to become someone else's partner. Also, dating is an opportunity to enhance one's self-esteem (Spanier & Thompson, 1987). Free from the stress of an unhappy marriage, people may discover, for example, that they are more interesting and charming than either they or (especially) their former spouse had imagined. And dating initiates people into the singles subculture, where they can experiment with the freedom about which they may have fantasized when they were married.

Several features of dating following marital separation and divorce differ from premarital dating. For one thing, dating does not seem to be a leisurely matter. Divorced people usually feel too pressed for time to waste it on a first date that might not go well. And dating may be less spontaneous if the divorced woman or man has primary responsibility for children. The parent must make child-care arrangements; he or she may wish not to involve the children in the dates. In addition, finances may be strained. A divorced mother may have income only from a low-paying or part-time job or from welfare benefits while having many child-care expenses. In some cases, a father's finances may be strained by having to pay alimony or child support.

Sexual activity is an important component in the lives of separated and divorced men and women. Engaging in sexual behavior with someone for the first time following separation helps people accept their newly acquired single status. Because sexual exclusivity is usually an important element in marriage, becoming sexually active with someone other than one's spouse is a dramatic symbol that the old marriage vows are no longer valid. Little is known about the sexual behavior of divorced men and women. Using national data on 340 divorced people, researchers found that the level of sexual activity for the divorced was much lower than earlier studies and popular mythology had suggested (Stack & Gundlach, 1992). Over a year's time, the study revealed, 74% had either a single partner or none; 16% of the men and 34% of the women had no partner.

Single Parenting   Approximately 31% of all families are headed by single parents, 26% of which are headed by single mothers and 5% by single fathers (Fields & Casper, 2001). Several demographic trends have affected the shift from two-parent to one-parent families, including a larger proportion of births to unmarried women, the delay of marriage, and the increase in divorce among couples with children. White single mothers are more likely to be divorced than their African American or Latina counterparts, who are more likely to be unmarried at the time of birth or to be widowed.

Single parents are not often a part of the singles world, which involves more than simply not being married. It requires leisure and money, both of which single parents generally lack because of their family responsibilities. Because of stereotypes of single women as sexually "loose," single mothers are often cautious about developing new relationships (Kissman & Allen, 1993).

The presence of children affects a divorced woman's sexual activity. Single divorced parents are less likely than divorced women without children to be sexually active (Stack & Gundlach, 1992). Children enormously complicate a single parent's sexual decision making. A single mother must decide, for example, whether to permit a potential partner to spend the night with her when her children are present. This is often an important symbolic

Because of their child-rearing responsibilities, single parents are usually not part of the singles world.

act for a woman, for several reasons. First, it involves her children in her romantic relationships. Women are often hesitant to again expose their children to the distress associated with the initial parental separation and divorce, which is often seared into everyone's mind. Second, it reveals to her children that their mother is sexual, which may make her feel uncomfortable. Third, it opens her up to moral judgments from her children regarding her sexuality. Single parents are often fearful that their children will lose respect for them, which can happen when children reach middle childhood (approximately age 10–14). And finally, having someone sleep over may trigger the resentment and anger the children feel toward their parents for splitting up. They may feel deeply threatened and act out.

SEXUALITY IN LATE ADULTHOOD

Sexual feelings and desires continue throughout the life cycle. Though many of the standards of activity or attraction are constant, it may be necessary for each of us to overcome the taboos and stereotypes associated with sex and aging in order to create a place for its expression in our lives.

Developmental Concerns

Many of the psychosexual tasks older Americans must undertake are directly related to the aging process, including the following:

■ *Changing sexuality.* As older men's and women's physical abilities change with age, their sexual responses change as well. A 70-year-old, though still sexual, is not sexual in the same manner as an 18-year-old. As men and women continue to age, their sexuality tends to be more diffuse, less genitally oriented, and less insistent. Chronic illness and increasing frailty understandably result in diminished sexual activity. These considerations contribute to the ongoing evolution of the individual's sexual philosophy.

■ *Loss of a partner.* One of the most critical life events is the loss of a partner. After age 60, there is a significant increase in spousal deaths. Because having a partner is the single most important factor determining an older person's sexual interactions, the death of the partner signals a dramatic change in the survivor's sexual interactions.

Older adults accomplish these tasks within the context of continuing aging. Resolving these tasks as we age helps us to accept the eventuality of our death.

Stereotypes of Aging

Our society stereotypes aging as a lonely and depressing time, but most studies of older adults find that, relative to younger people, they express high levels of satisfaction and well-being. It is poverty, loneliness, and poor health that make old age difficult. But even so, the aged have lower levels of poverty than most Americans, including young adults, women, and children. More importantly, until their mid-seventies, most older people report few, if any, restrictions on their activities because of health.

One of the most famous twentieth-century sculptures is Auguste Rodin's The Kiss, *which depicts young lovers embracing. Here, the aging model Antoni Nordone sits before the statue that immortalized his youth.*

The sexuality of older Americans tends to be invisible, as society discounts their sexuality. In fact, according to one review of the literature on aging, the decline in sexual activity among aging men and women is more cultural than biological in origin (Kellett, 1991). Several factors account for this in our culture (Barrow & Smith, 1992). First, we associate sexuality with the young, assuming that sexual attraction exists only between those with youthful bodies. Interest in sex is considered normal in 25-year-old men, but in 75-year-old men, it is considered lecherous. Second, we associate the idea of romance and love with the young; many of us find it difficult to believe that the aged can fall in love or love intensely. Third, we continue to associate sex with procreation, measuring a woman's femininity by her childbearing and maternal role and a man's masculinity by the children he sires. Finally, the aged do not have sexual desires as strong as those of the young, and they do not express them as openly. Intimacy is especially valued and important for an older person's well-being (Mancini & Bliezner, 1992).

Aging gay men and lesbian women face a double stereotype: They are old *and* gay. But like other stereotypes of aging Americans, this one reflects myths rather than realities. Most gay men and lesbian women are satisfied with their sexual orientation; about half are worried about aging (Berger, 1982; Kehoe, 1988).

Stereotypes and myths about aging are not the only factors that affect the sexuality of the aged. The narrow definition of sexuality contributes to the problem. Sexual behavior is defined by researchers and the general population in terms of masturbation, sexual intercourse, and orgasm. But sexuality has emotional, sensual, and relationship aspects that are enjoyed by all people, regardless of age.

Sexuality and Aging

Men and women tend to view aging differently. As men approach their fifties, they generally fear the loss of their sexual capacity but not their attractiveness; in contrast, women generally fear the loss of their attractiveness but not their sexuality.

Sexual expression has historically been viewed in the United States as an activity reserved for the young and the newly married. Fortunately, this viewpoint is not universally accepted. Cross-cultural studies show that in many countries sexual activity is not only accepted but expected among the aging. Cultural attitudes toward sexuality and aging appear to influence whether sex among the aged is encouraged or discouraged.

Despite the conventional wisdom, recent studies in the United States have revealed that the aged continue to be sexual beings. An important study of sexuality and aging in the United States was sponsored by the American Association of Retired Persons (AARP) in 1999. Through a mail survey of a nationally representative sample of 1384 persons, age 45 or older, the AARP found that 45% were extremely or somewhat satisfied with their sex lives. Most felt that a satisfactory sexual relationship was an important factor to their quality of life, and a large majority found sexual activity to be pleasurable. Poor health and lack of an available partner contributed, in part, to a decreased frequency of sex as age increased (Figure 6.6) (Jacoby, 1999).

You only possess what will not be lost in a shipwreck.

—*Al Ghazali (1058–1111)*

Old age has its pleasures, which, though different, are not less than the pleasures of youth.

—*W. Somerset Maugham (1874–1965)*

How many have a partner? Decisively more men than women, and the gap widens with age. Half of women 60–74, and 4 out of 5 age 75-plus, are alone.

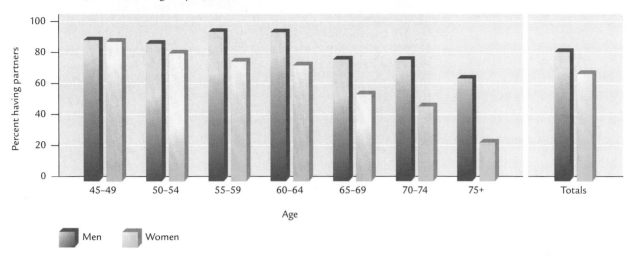

How often do they have sex? At least once a week, report more than 50% of men and women with partners. Those without partners are another story.

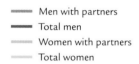

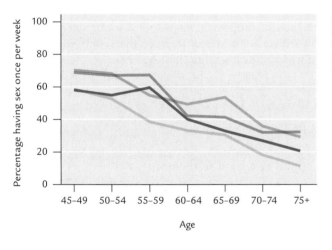

How satisfied are they? About two-thirds of those polled said they were "extremely" or "somewhat" satisfied with their physical relationships.

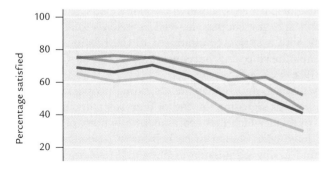

FIGURE 6.6 Older Americans' Likelihood of Having a Sexual Partner, Frequency of Sex, and Satisfaction with Sex Life. (*Source:* Copyright © 1999 AARP. Reprinted with permission.)

The greatest determinants of an aged person's sexual activity are the availability of a partner and health.

The AARP reported that for the female respondents a number of factors related to attitudes toward sex, attitudes of their partners, and self-concept affected their satisfaction with their sex life (Jacoby, 1999):

- Having a partner who is imaginative about sex
- Feeling that others like her
- Having an exciting partner
- Enjoying sex
- Feeling that sex is critical to a good relationship
- Feeling that sex is important to the overall quality of life
- Feeling that her partner understands her needs
- Feeling that sex is not just for younger people

For males, the main factors influencing their sexual satisfaction were related to their partners—specifically, feeling that their spouse or partner is romantic and that their spouse or partner is sensitive to their moods.

Among older lesbian and gay couples, as well as heterosexual couples, the happiest are those with a strong commitment to the relationship. The need for intimacy, companionship, and purpose transcends issues of sexual orientation (Lipman, 1986).

Because our society tends to desexualize the old, aging people may interpret their slower responses as signaling the end of their sexuality. Education programs for older people, in which they learn about anatomy, physiology, and sexual response, have been shown to be helpful in dispelling myths, building confidence, and giving permission to be sexual (Goldman & Carroll, 1990; Kellett, 1991).

Women's Issues Many women are relieved when they no longer have to worry about getting pregnant; not having to worry about birth control can

be very liberating. Most women are pleased as well when they no longer have to deal with a monthly menstrual flow. Some women may be bothered by the physical effects of menopause; for others, the positive psychological effects are greater. Even though most women close to their fifties no longer wish to bear children, the knowledge that she is no longer capable of reproduction may be painful for a woman. In addition to grieving for the loss of her fertility, she may also feel that she is losing her sexual attractiveness. Because women in our society are often judged on the basis of their appearance and youthfulness, those who have "used their glamour and sexiness to attract men and enhance their self-esteem" may find aging particularly painful (Greenwood, 1992). A young woman, for example, is "beautiful," but an older woman is "handsome," a term ordinarily used for men of any age. Much of how a woman's life is affected by menopause depends on how she views herself.

Many women do not consider menopause a medical condition and therefore do not feel that it requires any special treatment. Others may be bothered enough by attendant symptoms to seek medical advice or assistance. Some women may be concerned about the possibility of future problems such as osteoporosis. Others may be concerned about changes in their sexual feelings or patterns or about the implications of fertility loss, aging, and changing standards of attractiveness. Because physicians have a tendency to treat menopause as a medical "problem," women may find themselves subjected to treatments they don't understand or would not choose if they were better informed. It's important that women seek out practitioners who will work with them to meet their needs in the ways that are most appropriate for each individual.

What Physicians (and the Rest of Us) Need to Know About Sex and Aging

ENVISION YOURSELF NOW. How do you look? How do you feel about your sexuality? Move the clock ahead 45 years from now (or adjust it accordingly so that you are 70 years old). How do you feel about the way you look? Are you in a relationship? Are you sexual? If your image of yourself as a sexual person is dimmed by a different body image, lack of a partner, or poor health, you are not alone. Most of us (including physicians and other health professionals) have been conditioned to accept restrictive attitudes or an absence of images about older adults and their sexuality. A few facts about sex and aging are in order:

- *People remain sexual throughout their lives.* Though individuals may not be sexually active, they still have sexual histories, knowledge, and values that must not be denied. Though sexual activity declines over the decades and many older people choose abstinence as a lifestyle, physicians and health-care workers need to recognize that sexual feelings are healthy throughout life. With this understanding, they will be better able to alleviate feelings of guilt and remorse among older people about their sexuality.

- *Many older people have a need for a good sexual relationship.* Loss of health, friends, partner, children, and career may cause depression and a profound sense of loneliness. An excellent antidote to the loss is a loving, intimate, secure sexual relationship.

- *Sexual physiology changes with age.* Being aware of potential changes often helps older people accept and deal with them. Males may often have less turgid erections, less forceful ejaculations, and a longer refractory period. A longer refractory period may simply mean there may be sex without ejaculation. Men and their partners can learn that there can be gratifying sex without an erect penis. The slowing down of the sexual response cycle means that foreplay can be prolonged and intimacy and gratification increased.

Although some women celebrate the arrival of menopause, and the accompanying liberation from the concerns of pregnancy and menstruation, others find it disturbing, embarrassing, or painful. Vaginal dryness, the most common symptom and one that can make sexual intercourse quite painful, can be alleviated by an over-the-counter water-soluble lubricant or by saliva. An estrogen cream can also remedy this problem. Hot flashes and bone loss leading to osteoporosis are additional problems that women must contend with and should discuss with their physician.

- *Changes in body image may have a profound impact on sexuality.* This is particularly true in our society, in which image and youthfulness are valued over age and wisdom. Older people must try to reverse the influence of years of conditioning and consciously reevaluate their images of sex and aging.

- *People need to "use it or lose it."* This is not an empty phrase. Sexual activity is a physiological function that tends to deteriorate if not exercised; it is particularly fragile in the elderly. Sexual activity appears to keep the vagina more elastic, flexible, and lubricated. According to Masters, Johnson, and Kolodny (1992), intercourse and/or masturbation at least once a week over a period of years helps to keep the mucous secretions active, maintains muscle tone, and helps preserve the shape and size of the vagina.

- *Older people are better lovers.* Think about what experience and time bring to an individual. In the case of sexuality, experience brings awareness of self and (we hope) sensitivity to others. Given the quantity of leisure time and the slower-paced lifestyle of many older adults, relationships can often be nurtured and enjoyed. A more accepting attitude about oneself, others, and life in general can help to make people better sex partners later in life.

Source: Adapted from Cross, R. (1993, June–July). "What Doctors and Others Need to Know: Sex Facts on Human Sexuality and Aging." *SIECUS Report*, 7–9. Reprinted with permission from SIECUS.

Men's Issues Changes in male sexual responsiveness begin to become apparent when men are in their forties and fifties, a period of change sometimes referred to as the male climacteric. Some 15% of U.S. men have complete erectile dysfunction by age 70 (up from 5% at age 40), and one-third experience at least occasional erectile difficulties (Cowley, 1996a). The National Health and Social Life Survey (NHSLS) found that 18% of the men age 50–59 reported having trouble maintaining or achieving an erection

(Laumann, Paik, & Rosen, 1999). For about 5% of men, these physical changes of aging are accompanied by experiences such as fatigue, an inability to concentrate, depression, loss of appetite, and a decreased interest in sex (Kolodny, Masters, & Johnson, 1979). As a man ages, his frequency of sexual activity declines; achieving erection requires more stimulation and time, and the erection may not be as firm (Mulligan & Moss, 1991). Ejaculation takes longer and may not occur every time the penis is stimulated; also, the force of the ejaculation is less than before, as is the amount of ejaculate (Zilbergeld, 1992); and the refractory period is extended (up to 24 hours or longer in older men). However, sexual interest and enjoyment generally do not decrease (Schiavi et al., 1990). Although some of the changes are related directly to age and a normal decrease in testosterone production, others may be the result of diseases associated with aging (Mulligan, Retchin, Chinchilli, & Bettinger, 1988; Whitbourne, 1990). Poor general health, diabetes, atherosclerosis, urinary incontinence, and some medications can contribute to sexual dysfunction.

It is important for older men to understand that slower responses are a normal function of aging and are unrelated to the ability to give or receive sexual pleasure. "The senior penis," wrote Bernie Zilbergeld (1992), "can still give and take pleasure, even though it's not the same as it was decades ago." The prescription drugs Viagra and Levitra became available to aid men in achieving erections. Furthermore, nonprescription remedies are being advocated for erectile dysfunction. (For additional information on menopause, health issues and remedies, see Chapters 13 and 14.)

Click on "The Personals" to hear the challenges one older man faced in staying sexually active.

> You can take no credit for beauty at sixteen. But if you are beautiful at sixty, it will be your soul's own doing.
>
> —*Marie Stopes (1880–1958)*

As this chapter has shown, psychosexual development occurs on a continuum rather than as a series of discrete stages. Each person develops in his or her own way, according to personal and social circumstances and the dictates of biology. As adolescents grow toward sexual maturity, the gap between their physiological development and their psychological development begins to narrow; their emotional and intellectual capabilities begin to "grow into" their bodies. Nearing adulthood, young people become less dependent on their elders and more capable of developing intimacy on a new level. In young adulthood, tasks that define adult sexuality include establishing sexual orientation, making commitments, entering long-term intimate relationships, and making childbearing decisions. None of these tasks is accomplished overnight. Nor does a task necessarily end as a person moves into a new stage of life.

In middle adulthood, individuals face new tasks involving the nature of their long-term relationships. Often, these tasks involve reevaluating these relationships. As people enter late adulthood, they need to adjust to the aging process—to changed sexual responses and needs, declining physical health, the loss of a partner, and their own eventual death. Each stage is filled with its own unique meaning, which gives shape and significance to life and to sexuality.

SUMMARY

Sexuality in Infancy and Childhood

- *Psychosexual development* begins in infancy, when we begin to learn how we "should" feel about our bodies and our gender roles. Infants need stroking and cuddling to ensure healthy psychosexual development.

- Children learn about their bodies through various forms of sex play. Their sexual interest should not be labeled "bad" but may be deemed inappropriate for certain times, places, or persons. Children need to experience acts of physical affection and to be told nonthreateningly about "good" and "bad" touching by adults.

Sexuality in Adolescence

- *Puberty* is the biological stage when reproduction becomes possible. The psychological state of puberty is *adolescence,* a time of growth and often confusion as the body matures faster than the emotional and intellectual abilities. The traits of adolescence are culturally determined.

- Pubertal changes in girls begin between ages 7 and 14. They include a growth spurt, breast development, pubic and underarm hair, vaginal secretions, and menarche (first menstruation). Pubertal changes in boys generally begin about 2 years later than in girls. They include a growth spurt, a deepening voice, hair growth, development of external genitals, and ejaculation of semen. Preparing young people for these changes is helpful.

- Children and adolescents often learn from their parents that sex is secretive and "bad." A strong bond between parent and child reduces the risk of early sexual involvement and pregnancy.

- Peers are the strongest influence on the values, attitudes, and behavior of adolescents. They are also a source of much misinformation regarding sex.

- The media present highly charged images of sexuality that are often out of context. Parents can counteract media distortions by discussing the context of sexuality with their children and controlling access to television.

- Young gay and lesbian individuals are largely invisible because of society's assumption of heterosexuality. They may begin to come to terms with their homosexuality during their teenage years. Because of society's reluctance to acknowledge homosexuality openly, most gay, lesbian, and bisexual teens suffer a great deal of emotional pain.

- Most adolescents engage in masturbation. White adolescent heterosexual couples generally follow a normative sequence of adolescent behaviors, from hand-holding to intercourse. African American teens do not necessarily follow such a sequence. For most teenagers, increased emotional involvement leads to increased sexual activity.

- Most teenagers have pressing concerns about sexuality, and most parents favor sexuality education for their children. Yet the subject remains controversial in many school districts. This is mainly the result of opposition from a vocal minority. Areas of controversy include homosexuality, contraception (versus abstinence), and condom availability.

Sexuality in Early Adulthood

- Developmental tasks in young adulthood include establishing sexual orientation, integrating love and sex, forging intimacy and making commitments, making fertility/childbearing decisions, and evolving a sexual philosophy.

- Nonmarital sex among young adults (but not adolescents) in a relational context has become the norm. An important factor in this shift is the surge in the numbers of unmarried men and women.

- A critical task of adulthood is establishing one's sexual identity as heterosexual, gay, lesbian, bisexual, or transgendered person . Between 3% and 10% of Americans have had a significant amount of same-sex sexual contact. Identifying oneself as lesbian, gay, bisexual, or transgendered, however, is complex and includes several phases. *Coming out* is publicly acknowledging one's homosexuality or bisexuality. Though relatively few people identify themselves as bisexual, the existence of the term points to the fact that human sexual behavior cannot be easily categorized.

- The large increase in the number of unmarried adults has dramatically altered the nature of singlehood in our society.

- The two most widely held standards regarding nonmarital sexual intercourse are permissiveness with affection and the double standard. For gay men, lesbian women, bisexual, and transgendered individuals, the college environment is often liberating because of greater acceptance and tolerance.

- Among single men and women not or no longer attending college, meeting others can be a problem. Singles often meet at work, clubs, resorts, housing complexes, and churches.

- With the rise of the HIV/AIDS epidemic, the older gay subculture has placed an increased emphasis on the relationship context of sex.

- The contemporary lesbian community is currently more moderate and diverse than in prior years. Lesbian women's emphasis on emotions over sex and the more enduring quality of their relationships reflect their socialization as women.

- *Cohabitation* has become more widespread and accepted in recent years. By age 30, half of all people will have cohabited. *Domestic partnerships* provide some legal protection for cohabiting couples in committed relationships.

Sexuality in Middle Adulthood

- Developmental issues of sexuality in middle adulthood include redefining sex in long-term relationships, reevaluating one's sexuality, and accepting the biological aging process.

- In marriage, sex tends to diminish in frequency the longer a couple are married. Most married couples don't feel that declining frequency is a major problem if their overall relationship is good.

- Approximately 50–55% of all first marriages end in divorce. Sexual experiences following divorce are linked to well-being, especially for men. Single parents are usually not a part of the singles world because the presence of children constrains their freedom.

Sexuality in Late Adulthood

- Many of the psychosexual tasks older Americans must undertake are directly related to the aging process, including changing sexuality and the loss of a partner. Most studies of older adults find that they express relatively high levels of satisfaction and well-being. Older adults' sexuality tends to be invisible because we associate sexuality and romance with youthfulness and procreation.

- Sexual behavior in late adulthood often becomes more intimacy-based, involving touching and holding rather than genital activity. Physiologically, men are less responsive. Women's concerns are more social than physical.

- Although some physical functions may be slowed by aging, sexual interest, enjoyment, and satisfaction remain high for many older people. Women tend to be more concerned about the loss of attractiveness, whereas men tend to worry about their sexual capacity.

- In their forties, women's fertility begins to decline. Other physical changes occur, which may or may not present problems.

- Men need to understand that slower responses are a normal part of aging and are not related to the ability to give or receive sexual pleasure.

Sex and the Internet

Sexual Activity and Teens

Data on teen pregnancy have recently appeared in the headlines of our newspapers, not to remind us of the dismal figures, but to inform us that the rates have (surprisingly) decreased. One of the most helpful and thorough sites that report on this and other adolescent sexuality issues is the Alan Guttmacher Institute (http://www.agi-usa.org). Access this site and see if you can find each of the following:

- The age of first intercourse among teens
- The most common type of contraceptive used
- The risk of acquiring a specific STI with one act of intercourse
- The rate of teen pregnancy among 15- to 17-year-olds
- The percentage of all U.S. births that occur among teens
- The percentage of teen mothers who complete high school
- The number of pregnancies that are terminated by abortion

Now answer the following questions:

- Which fact was the most surprising to you?
- Which fact was the least surprising?
- If you had unlimited resources, how might you go about solving the problem of teen pregnancy?

SUGGESTED WEB SITES

American College Health Association
http://www.acha.org
A professional association that focuses on health promotion in the college community.

American Psychological Association
http://www.apa.org/pi/aging/sexuality.html
A source of information on sexuality and aging.

Kaiser Family Foundation
http://www.kff.org
An independent philanthropic group dedicated to providing information on and analysis of health issues.

Men's Issues Page
http://www.vix.com/pub/men
Provides discussions on a wide variety of issues for and about men.

National Federation of Parents and Friends of Lesbians and Gays (PFLAG)
http://www.pflag.org
Provides information and support for those who care about gay and lesbian individuals.

National Gay and Lesbian Task Force
http://www.ngltf.org
Provides information and referrals on gay and lesbian issues and rights.

National Institute of Child Health and Human Development
http://www.nichd.nih.gov
Conducts and supports research on the reproductive, neurobiological, behavioral, and developmental processes that influence the health of children and adults.

The National Women's Health Information Center
http://www.4women.gov/owh (for women) and www.4girls.gov (for girls)
Information and referrals for women and girls to support them in choosing healthy behaviors.

North American Menopause Society
http://www.menopause.org
Devoted to promoting women's health during midlife and beyond menopause.

SUGGESTED READING

The following journals contain articles on adolescent psychosexual development, sexuality education, and other issues concerning teenagers: *SIECUS Report; Perspectives on Sexual and Reproductive Health,* published by the Alan Guttmacher Institute; and *Journal of Adolescence.*

Bancroft, John (Ed.). (2003). *Sexual Development in Childhood.* Bloomington: Indiana University Press. Scholarly and well-researched edited text by one of the leaders in the field; also, one of the few books available on this subject.

Butler, Robert N., & Lewis, Myrna I. (2002). *The New Love and Sex After 60.* New York: Ballantine Books. A sex manual for older adults with thorough coverage of the physical issues of sex and aging and ways to overcome physical and emotional roadblocks.

D'Augelli, Anthony R., & Patterson, Charlotte (Eds.). (2001). *Lesbian, Gay, and Bisexual Identities in Youth: Psychological Perspectives.* New York: Oxford University Press. An overview of psychological research and theory on lesbian, gay, and bisexual identities by leading scholars.

Murray, Steven O. (2002). *Homosexualities.* Chicago: University of Chicago Press. Maps the varieties of homosexuality into categories; discusses age-structured, gender-stratified, and egalitarian roles.

Pipher, Mary. (2000). *Navigating the Emotional Terrain of Our Elders.* New York: Riverhead Books. A discussion of why our elders prefer to keep their feelings to themselves and why it is so difficult to discuss with them the issues that they face.

Steinberg, Laurence D. (2002). *Adolescence* (6th ed.). Boston: McGraw-Hill. A comprehensive, research-based examination of adolescent development within the context of environmental and social relationships.

Wallerstein, Judith S., Lewis, Julia, & Blakeslee, Sandra. (2000). *The Unexpected Legacy of Divorce.* New York: Hyperion. A long-term study assessing the effects of divorce on children as they grow into adulthood and pursue relationships of their own.

Weinberg, Martin; Williams, Colin; & Pryor, Douglas. (1995). *Dual Attraction: Understanding Bisexuality.* New York: Oxford University Press. The first major scientific study on the nature of bisexuality.

For links, articles, and study material, go to the McGraw-Hill Web sites, located at http://www.mhhe.com/strong5

7

Love, Intimacy, and Sexuality

"*Because my father was both a raving drug addict and a loving warm father, I grew up with a very dualistic look at men. I can be madly in love with them and bitterly hate them at the same time. This affects all of my relationships with men. I truly love them and can feel so connected to them one day, but other days I am so distant from them that I begin to wonder if I am there myself.*"

—22-year-old White female

"*My grandfather, being a Hindustani priest, talks to me a lot about love. It was not through a lecture but through stories he told from the Gita [somewhat like an Indian Bible]. Spending time with him, I learned to respect sex, even though he never plain-out meant it; he described how marriage is a love bond between two people who share mind, body, and soul with each other and no one else. These stories like Kama Sutra and Ramayan sound so beautiful. Because of his influence, I want to try my best to wait to have sex until I meet my soul mate.*"

—19-year-old first-generation Indian female

"*I have difficulty trusting women. Getting close to my girlfriend has been difficult. My first reaction in most instances is to wonder what her ulterior motive is. Being intimate is tough for me because those I have trusted most have betrayed me. Sometimes I feel like I am alone for the simple fact that I don't know how to act when I am with people.*"

—23-year-old White male

"*I am glad that my sexual outlet is guided by my religious upbringing. It has influenced my attitudes toward my sexuality. If it were not for my beliefs, I probably would not have thought twice and gone all the way with my girlfriend at that time. I knew she wanted more than petting, but because of my moral views, I controlled myself and did not give in. Up to this point, my morals and values always play a big role in my life. I choose to believe that lovemaking is a special and sacred act and should only be shared by a husband and a wife. I do not approve of premarital sex and never did practice it. Thus, I consider myself a virgin and would like to save it until my wedding night.*"

—25-year-old Filipino male

> Love doesn't make the world go round. Love is what makes the ride worthwhile.
>
> —*Franklin P. Jones*

LOVE IS ONE of the most profound human emotions, and it manifests itself in various forms across all cultures. In our culture, love binds us together as partners, parents, children, and friends. It is a powerful force in the intimate relationships of almost all individuals, regardless of their sexual orientation, and it crosses all ethnic boundaries. We make major life decisions, such as whom we marry, based on love. We make sacrifices for it, sometimes giving up even our lives for those we love. Sometimes, we are obsessed with love. Popular culture in America glorifies it in music, films, television, and print. Individuals equate romantic love with marriage and often assess the quality of their partnerships by what they consider love to be.

Love is both a feeling and an activity. We can feel love for someone and act in a loving manner. But we can also be angry with the person we love, or feel frustrated, bored, or indifferent. This is the paradox of love: It encompasses

At the start of a relationship, it is often impossible to tell whether one's feelings are infatuation or the beginning of love.

opposites. A loving relationship includes affection and anger, excitement and boredom, stability and change, bonds and freedom. Its paradoxical quality makes some ask whether they are really in love when they are not feeling "perfectly" in love or when their relationship is not going smoothly. Love does not give us perfection, however; it gives us meaning. In fact, as sociologist Ira Reiss (1980) suggests, a more important question to ask is not if one is feeling love, but, "Is the love I feel the kind of love on which I can build a lasting relationship or marriage?"

In this chapter, we examine the relationship between sex and love. We look at the always perplexing question of the nature of love. Next, we explore sex outside of committed relationships. We examine the ways that social scientists study love to gain new insights into it. We then turn to the darker side of love—jealousy—to understand its dynamics. Finally, we see how love transforms itself from passion to intimacy, providing the basis for long-lasting relationships.

FRIENDSHIP AND LOVE

Friendship and love breathe life into humanity. They bind us together, provide emotional sustenance, buffer us against stress, and help to preserve our physical and mental well-being.

What distinguishes love from friendship? Two researchers (Todd & Davis, 1985) set out to answer this question. In their study of 250 college students and community members, they found that, although love and friendship are alike in many ways, some crucial differences make love relationships both

A friend may well be reckoned a masterpiece of nature.

—*Ralph Waldo Emerson*
(1803–1882)

WHEN FRIENDS ARE ASKED, "Are you two attracted to each other?" the response by either person is likely to be more complex than the other may wish to hear. Research tells us that the transformation of a friendship into a romantic relationship depends on which person you are asking, at what point you are asking in the friendship, and what kind of attraction you are referring to (Reeder, 2000). The question remains: Can other-sexed (if one is heterosexual) or same-sex (if one is homosexual) friendships really exist, or are they merely the fertile ground for developing romantic attachments?

Friendships seem to occupy two places in the emotional landscape of people's lives: (1) They form a bond between two people, and (2) they create a space for a potential romantic relationship. Given this complex backdrop, it's not surprising that issues of intention, boundaries, sustainability, and outcome arise. Whether they are addressed, however, depends on the quality of the friendship and the willingness and maturity of the individuals involved. Although friendships can be maintained without experiencing sexual tension, especially in later life, many of these friendships are characterized by sexual attraction on the part of at least one of the friends (Kaplan & Keyes, 1997). Often, however, these desires stop short of finding expression in sexual activity, unless the relationship has shifted from one of friendship to a romantic one.

Most of the research on this topic is based on the responses and behaviors of college students. Adults older than 30 seem to have fewer opportunities to acquire and maintain friendships unless those friends are part of a couple. Researchers who have investigated friendships among college students have found that, though 64% of men and 44% of women acknowledged that friends could become sexual partners, 30% of the women and 20% of the men said they abstain from sex with friends because they fear it could ruin the friendship (Sapadin,

1988). In fact, 24% of terminated other-sex friendships were due to one or both friends' desire for romance or sexuality (Werking, 1997). A more recent study of college-age students found that 51% reported having "had sex" with an other-sex friend whom they had no intention of dating at the time of the sexual activity (Afifi & Faulkner, 2000). Moreover, 34% of participants reported engaging in sexual activity with a friend on multiple occasions (either with more than one friend or with the same friend).

The qualitative difference between being attracted to someone as a friend, as a dating partner, and as a sexual partner plays a significant role for those in the friendship. For example, we may find some friends to be good-looking but may not feel attracted to them. Or romantic attraction may occur when we believe that a friend would make a good partner. This type of attraction is found to be less common in other-sexed friendships (Reeder, 2000). Finding a friend handsome or attractive does not necessarily mean that we are attracted to him or her or that the attraction must be acted on.

Engaging in sexual activity in friendships may have important implications for relationship development. After all, friendship is the foundation for a strong love relationship. The question remains: How does a relationship based on friendship interface with a romantic one? Or should it? Although there is nothing inherent about sexual activity that should lead to a friendship's deterioration, many feel that safeguarding the relationship is a primary motivation for keeping their friendships platonic. Prior to engaging in sex within a friendship, we might consider the following questions: Can individuals be "just" friends? What are the meanings and implications for engaging in sex with a friend? How will the sexual relationship affect the friendship? What are the reasons underlying the decision to have sex? Does sexual activity imply sexual exclusiveness?

more rewarding and more vulnerable. Best-friend relationships are similar to spouse/lover relationships in several ways: levels of acceptance, trust, and respect; and levels of confiding, understanding, spontaneity, and mutual acceptance. Levels of satisfaction and happiness with the relationship were also found to be similar for both groups. What separates friends from lovers is that lovers have much more fascination and a greater sense of exclusiveness with their partners than do friends. Though love has a greater potential for distress, conflict, and mutual criticism, it runs deeper and stronger than friendship.

Friendship appears to be the foundation for a strong love relationship. Shared interests and values, acceptance, trust, understanding, and enjoyment are at the root of friendship and a basis for love. Adding the dimensions of passion and emotional intimacy alters the nature of the friendship and creates new expectations and possibilities.

Although some believe that marriage should satisfy all their needs, it is important to remember that when people marry they do not cease to be separate individuals. Friendships and patterns of social behavior continue, so the mix of friendship and love must be understood as it affects marital satisfaction.

With men and women marrying later than ever before and women being an integral part of the workforce, close friendships are more likely to be a part of the tapestry of relationships in people's lives. Partners need to communicate and seek understanding regarding the nature of activities and degree of emotional closeness they find acceptable in their partner's friendships. Boundaries should be clarified and opinions shared. Many couples find friendships acceptable and even desirable. Like other significant issues involving partnerships, success in balancing a love relationship and other friendships depends on the ability to communicate concerns and on the maturity of the people involved.

LOVE AND SEXUALITY

Love and sexuality are intimately intertwined (Aron & Aron, 1991). Although marriage was once the only acceptable context for sexual intercourse, for most people today, love legitimizes sex outside of marriage. With the "sex with affection" standard of sexual expression with others, we use individualistic rather than social norms to legitimize sexual relations. Our sexual standards may have become personal rather than institutional. This shift to personal responsibility makes love even more important in sexual relationships.

We can even see this connection between love and sex in our everyday use of words. Think of the words we use to describe sexual interactions. When we say that we "make love," are "lovers," or are "intimate" with someone, we generally mean that we are sexually involved. But this involvement has overtones of caring or love. Such potential meanings are absent in such technically correct words as "sexual intercourse," "fellatio," and "cunnilingus," as well as in such slang words as "fuck" and "screw."

What factors lead us to have sexual intercourse? Ultimately, for most couples, it is the desire to expand or enhance the relationship and its meaning (Cupach & Comstock, 1990; Henderson-King & Veroff, 1994). Once couples have sex, sexual satisfaction often improves relationship satisfaction, as well as feelings of love and commitment, for both genders (Sprecher, 2002). However, this satisfaction appears to be more significant for men than for women.

Two of the most important factors in sexual activity are the level of intimacy in the relationship and the length of time the couple has been together. Even those who are less permissive in their sexual attitudes accept sexual involvement if the relationship is emotionally intimate and longstanding. People who are less committed (or not committed) to a relationship are less likely to be sexually involved. Finally, people in relationships who share power equally are more likely to be sexually involved than those in inequitable relationships.

Environmental factors involving both the physical and the cultural setting play a role in the level of sexual activity. In the most basic sense, the physical

Among the most important factors associated with nonmarital sex for both men and women are their feelings for each other, willingness, level of pre-planning, and sexual arousal prior to their encounter.

environment affects the opportunity for sex. Because sex is a private activity, the opportunity for it may be precluded by the presence of parents, friends, roommates, or children. The cultural environment also affects the decision of whether to have sex. The values of one's parents or peers may encourage or discourage sexual involvement. A person's ethnic group also affects sexual involvement; generally, African Americans are more permissive than Whites, and Latinos are less permissive (Baldwin, Whitely, & Baldwin, 1992). Furthermore, a person's subculture—such as the university or religious environment, the singles world, or the gay and lesbian community—exerts an important influence on sexual decision making.

A factor that heterosexual men see as evidence of sexual interest and intensity in the context of an ongoing, romantic relationship is assertive, forceful, and even aggressive behavior on the part of the woman (Hill, 2002). Rather than viewing this behavior as inappropriate or threatening, men more often find it to be desirable. This contrasts with the perceptions of heterosexual women, who more often perceive forceful behavior by men as related to power; these overtures may seem threatening and dangerous rather than sexually arousing. Women see sexual activity as being more appropriate and desirable when their romantic partner engages in behavior that inspires trust and confidence (Hill, 2002).

Sex Outside of Committed Relationships

A little more than a generation ago, virginity was the norm until marriage. Sex outside of marriage was considered sinful and immoral. In 1969, according to a Gallup survey, only 32% of the American population believed that premarital sex was acceptable (Lord, 1985). Today, however, values have shifted. Nonmarital sex among young adults (but not adolescents) is a relational context has become the norm. However, older Americans and groups with conservative religious backgrounds, such as Catholics and fundamentalist Protestants, continue to view all nonmarital sex as morally wrong.

This shift from sin to acceptance is the result of several factors. Effective contraception, legal abortion, and changing gender roles legitimizing female sexuality have had major impacts. But one of the most significant factors may be traced to demography. Over the past 30 or so years, there has been a dramatic increase in the number of unmarried men and women over age 18. It is this group that has traditionally looked the most favorably on non-marital intercourse. In 2000, the median age for first marriage for men was 26.8 years, compared with 23.5 years in 1975. For women, the median age in 2000 was 25.1 years, compared with 21.1 years in 1975. Men spend a slightly longer time after first coitus being sexually active before getting married—nearly 10 years, compared with nearly 8 years for women (Alan Guttmacher Institute, 2002c).

Men, Sex, and Love

Men and women who are not in an established relationship often have different expectations for each other. Men are more likely than women to separate sex from affection. Studies consistently show that for the majority of men, sex and love can be easily separated (Blumstein & Schwartz, 1983; Carroll, Volk, & Hyde, 1985; Laumann, Gagnon, Michael, & Michaels, 1994).

Click on "Men Talk Sex" to see the role of sex and intimacy in men's lives.

Although men are more likely than women to separate sex and love, Linda Levine and Lonnie Barbach (1983) found that men indicated that their most erotic sexual experiences took place in a relational context. Most men in the study reported that it was primarily the emotional quality of the relationship that made their sexual experiences special.

Researchers suggest that heterosexual men are not as different from gay men in terms of their acceptance of casual sex as might be thought. Heterosexual men, they maintain, would be as likely as gay men to engage in casual sex if women were equally interested. Women, however, are not as interested in casual sex; as a result, heterosexual men do not have as many willing partners as gay men do (Blum, 1997; Foa, Anderson, Converse, & Urbansky, 1987).

Gay men are especially likely to separate love and sex. Although gay men value love, many also value sex as an end in itself. Furthermore, they place less emphasis on sexual exclusiveness in their relationships. Many gay men appear to successfully negotiate sexually open relationships. Keeping the sexual agreements they make seems to matter most to these men. Data from 560 self-selected gay couples indicate that the pursuit of outside sex should not be taken as evidence that sex between the partners is lacking (Demian, 1994).

Women, Sex, and Love

Women generally view sex from a relational perspective. They are more likely to report feelings of love if they are sexually involved with their partner than if they are not sexually involved (Peplau, Rubin, & Hill, 1977). For women, love is also more closely related to feelings of self-esteem (Chojnacki & Walsh, 1990).

See "What Women Want" out of a good sexual relationship.

Women generally seek emotional relationships; some men initially seek physical relationships. Whereas most men value independence and self-sufficiency (Buss & Schmidt, 1993), there is evidence that women derive their self-worth from the quality of their relationships (Cross & Madson, 1997). This difference in intentions and values can place women in a bind. Carole Cassell (1984) suggests that women face a "damned if you do, damned if you don't" dilemma in their sexual relationships. That is, if a woman has sexual intercourse with a man, he says good-bye; if she doesn't, he says he respects her and still says good-bye.

Traditionally, women were labeled "good" or "bad" based on their sexual experience and values. "Good" women were virginal, sexually naive, and passive, whereas "bad" women were sexually experienced, independent, and passionate. According to Lillian Rubin (1990), this attitude has not entirely changed. Rather, we are ambivalent about sexually active and experienced women. During an interview, one exasperated woman leaped out of her chair and began to pace the floor, exclaiming to Rubin, "I sometimes think what men really want is a sexually experienced virgin. They want you to know the tricks, but they don't like to think you did those things with anyone else."

Lesbian women share sex less often than gay male or heterosexual couples. They tend to postpone sexual involvement until they have developed emotional intimacy with a partner, to be more satisfied with their sexual lives, and to have a greater sense of intimacy with their partners (Schureurs, 1993). For many, caresses, nongenital stimulation, and affectionate foreplay are the preferred expressions of sexuality and love.

Comparing Relationships of Gay, Lesbian, and Heterosexual Couples

Love is equally important for heterosexuals, gay men, lesbian women, and bisexual individuals. Many heterosexual individuals, however, perceive lesbian and gay persons' love relationships as less satisfying and less loving than heterosexual ones. It is well documented that love is important for gay men and lesbian women; their relationships have multiple emotional dimensions and are not based solely on sex, as many people believe (Adler, Hendrick, & Hendrick, 1989; Zak & McDonald, 1997).

For lesbian women, gay men, and bisexual individuals, love has special significance in the formation and acceptance of their identities. Although significant numbers of men and women have had sexual experiences with members of the same sex or both sexes, relatively few identify themselves as gay or lesbian. As we saw in Chapter 6, same-sex sexual interactions are not in themselves sufficient to form a gay or lesbian identity. An important element in solidifying such an identity is loving someone of the same sex. Love signifies a commitment to being lesbian or gay by unifying the emotional and physical dimensions of a person's sexuality (Troiden, 1988). For the gay man or lesbian woman, it marks the beginning of sexual wholeness and acceptance of self. In fact, some researchers believe that being able to love someone of the same sex, rather than having sex with him or her, is the critical element that distinguishes homosexuality from heterosexuality (Money, 1980).

In a study involving 538 gay, lesbian, and heterosexual married couples over a 5-year period, a number of similarities and differences were identified. Gay partners reported more autonomy, fewer barriers to leaving, and more frequent dissolution of relationships. Relative to married couples,

> Familiar acts are beautiful through love.
>
> —*Percy Bysshe Shelley*
> *(1792–1822)*

lesbian partners reported more intimacy, more autonomy, more equality, fewer barriers to leaving, and more frequent relationship dissolution. But perhaps the most significant finding was that gay and lesbian couples did not assess the qualities of their relationship differently than married couples did. Regardless of the type of partnership, individuals' own relationship satisfaction was influenced by their partner's appraisal of the relationship, as well as their own appraisal. Not surprisingly, married couples (who are supported by social and cultural institutions) reported stronger barriers to leaving relationships than gay or lesbian couples did. Though this research sheds new light on relationship quality among gay, lesbian, and heterosexual couples, it is not necessarily representative of all couples, nor are the assessments exhaustive.

For lesbian women, gay men, and bisexual individuals, love is an important component in the formation and acceptance of their sexual orientation. The public declaration of love and commitment is a milestone in the lives of many couples.

Sex Without Love

Is love necessary for sex? We may assume that it is, but that assumption is based on intentions and values. The question cannot be answered by reference to empirical or statistical data. It becomes a more fundamental one: Is sexual activity legitimate in itself, or does it require justification? To believe that sex does not require love as a justification, argues researcher John Crosby (1985), does not deny the significance of love and affection in sexual relations. In fact, love and affection are important and desirable for enduring relationships. They are simply not necessary, Crosby believes, for encounters in which erotic pleasure is the central feature.

Ironically, although sex without love violates the beliefs of many about sexuality, it is the least threatening form of extrarelational sex. Even those who accept their partner's having sex outside the relationship find it especially difficult to accept their partner's having a meaningful relationship. "They believe that two intense romantic relationships cannot co-exist and that one would have to go" (Blumstein & Schwartz, 1983).

Love Without Sex: Celibacy as a Choice

In a society that often seems obsessed with sexuality, it may be surprising to find individuals who choose celibacy as a lifestyle. **Celibacy**—abstention from sexual activity—is not necessarily a symptom of a problem or disorder. It may be a choice for some, such as those who have taken religious vows or are in relationships in which nonsexual affection and respect provide adequate fulfillment. For others, it is a result of life circumstances, such as the absence of a partner or imprisonment. Still others report very low interest in sex or express concern over the spread of HIV or other sexually transmitted infections. According to the National Social Life Survey, 4% of men and 14% of women rarely or never think about sex (Laumann et al., 1994).

Individuals who choose celibacy may report a better appreciation of the nature of friendship and an increased respect for the bonds and boundaries of marriage. In giving up their sexual pursuits, celibate individuals may learn to relate to others without sexual tension. Although these traits may also be developed within a sexual relationship, those who choose celibacy as a lifestyle may feel that it frees up energy for personal growth or other kinds of relationships.

Love and you shall be loved. All love is mathematically just, as much as two sides of an algebraic equation.

—*Ralph Waldo Emerson*

HOW DO I LOVE THEE? APPROACHES AND ATTITUDES RELATED TO LOVE

For most people, love and sex are closely linked in the ideal intimate relationship. Love reflects the positive factors—such as caring—that draw people together and sustain them in a relationship. Sex reflects both emotional and physical elements in a relationship, such as closeness and sexual excitement, that differentiate romantic love from other forms of love, such as parental love or the love between friends. Although the two are related, they are not necessarily connected. One can exist without the other; that is, it is possible to love someone without being sexually involved, and it is possible to be sexually involved without love.

How do individuals know if they are good candidates for love? Sol Gordon, psychologist and author, suggests that, until they find equilibrium in their own lives, taking on a serious relationship may be ill-advised. Here's how to recognize whether you're a good candidate for love (Gordon, 2001):

- You're not tired; you have energy for the things you want to do.
- You're not searching for the meaning of life; you find meaning in everyday experiences.
- You don't need affirmation from others in order to feel valued.
- You're not troubled unduly by bad thoughts; you don't allow ghosts of the past to haunt you.
- You're kind to people.
- You appreciate your own worth and have the strength to be accountable for yourself.

Gordon's emphasis on kindness reflects elements of Buddhism, according to which the most important aspect of marriage is kindness. According to Gordon (2001), "In immature relationships, the opposite is true; kindness is not valued and meanness is supported."

Attitudes and Behaviors Associated with Love

LOVE, A temporary insanity, curable by marriage.

—*Ambrose Bierce (1842–1914)*

A review of the research reveals a number of attitudes, feelings, and behaviors associated with love (Kelley, 1983), as well as with sex. Zick Rubin (1973) suggested that four feelings identify love:

1. *Caring for the other:* wanting to help him or her
2. *Needing the other:* having a strong desire to be in his or her presence and to have him or her care for you
3. *Trusting the other:* mutually exchanging confidences
4. *Tolerating the other:* accepting his or her faults

It is only with the heart that one can see rightly; what is essential is invisible to the eye.

—*Antoine de Saint-Exupéry (1900–1944)*

Of these, caring appears to be the most important, followed by needing, trusting, and tolerating (Steck, Levitan, McLane, & Kelley, 1982). J. R. Davitz (1969) identified similar feelings associated with love but noted, in addition, that respondents reported feeling an inner glow and a sense of optimism and cheerfulness. They had a sense of harmony and unity with the person they loved. They were intensely aware of the other person, feeling that they were fully concentrated on him or her.

Love is also expressed in certain behaviors. One study found that romantic love is expressed in seven ways (Swensen, 1972):

1. *Verbally expressing affection,* such as saying "I love you"

2. *Self-disclosing,* such as revealing intimate facts about yourself

3. *Giving nonmaterial evidence,* such as offering emotional and moral support in times of need and respecting the other person's opinion

4. *Expressing nonverbal feelings,* such as feeling happier, more content, and
   more secure when the other person is present

5. *Offering material evidence,* such as giving gifts, flowers, or small favors,
   or doing more than your share of something

6. *Physically expressing love,* such as hugging, kissing, massaging, and
   being sexual

7. *Tolerating the other,* such as accepting her or his idiosyncrasies, habits,
   routines, and quirks

Research supports the belief that people "walk on air" when they are in love.
It has been found that those in love view the world more positively than
those who are not in love (Hendrick & Hendrick, 1988).

Styles of Love

Sociologist John Lee describes six basic styles of love (Borrello & Thompson,
1990; Lee, 1973, 1988). These styles of love, he cautions, reflect relationship
styles, not individual styles. The style of love may change as the relationship changes or when individuals enter different relationships.

Eros was the ancient Greek god of love, the son of Aphrodite, the goddess of love and fertility. (The Romans called him Cupid.) As a style of love,
eros is the love of beauty. Erotic lovers delight in the tactile, the sensual, the
immediate; they are attracted to beauty (though beauty is in the eye of the
beholder). They love the lines of the body, its feel and touch. They are fascinated by every physical detail of their beloved. Their love burns brightly
but soon flickers and dies.

Mania, from the Greek word for madness, is obsessive and possessive
love. For manic lovers, nights are marked by sleeplessness and days by pain
and anxiety. The slightest sign of affection brings ecstasy for a short while,
only to disappear. Satisfactions last for but a moment before they must be
renewed. Manic love is roller-coaster love.

Ludus, from the Latin word for play, is playful love. For ludic lovers, love
is a game, something to play at rather than to become deeply involved in.
Love is ultimately "*ludic*rous"; encounters are casual, carefree, and often
careless. "Nothing serious" is the motto of ludic lovers.

Storge (STOR-gay), from the Greek word for natural affection, is the love
between companions. It is, wrote Lee, "love without fever, tumult, or folly,
a peaceful and enchanting affection." It usually begins as friendship and
gradually deepens into love. If the love ends, that also occurs gradually, and
the people often become friends once again.

Agape (AH-ga-pay), from the Greek word for brotherly love, is the traditional Christian love that is chaste, patient, undemanding, and altruistic;
there is no expectation of reciprocation. It is the love of saints and martyrs.
Agape is more abstract and ideal than concrete and real. It is easier to love
all of humankind than an individual in this way.

> If you love somebody, let them go. If
> they return, they were always yours.
> If they don't, they never were.
>
> —*Anonymous*

> To love is to admire with the heart;
> to admire is to love with the mind.
>
> —*Théophile Gautier (1801–1872)*

According to sociologist John Lee, there are six styles of love: eros, mania, ludus, storge, agape, and pragma. What style do you believe this couple illustrates? Why?

Logic is like the sword—those who appeal to it shall perish by it.

—*Samuel Butler (1835–1902)*

When you are courting a nice girl an hour seems like a second. When you sit on a red-hot cinder a second seems like an hour. That's relativity.

—*Albert Einstein (1879–1955)*

Pragma, from the Greek word for business, is practical love. Pragmatic lovers are, first and foremost, businesslike in their approach to looking for someone who meets their needs. They use logic in their search for a partner, seeking background, education, personality, religion, and interests that are compatible with their own. If they meet a person who satisfies their criteria, erotic, manic, or other feelings may develop. In addition to these pure forms, there are mixtures of the basic types: storgic-eros, ludic-eros, and storgic-ludus.

Lee believes that, to have a mutually satisfying relationship, people have to find a partner who shares the same style and definition of love. The more different two people are in their styles of love, the less likely they are to understand each other's love.

Recent research reports the absence of significant gender differences in love attitudes across adulthood (Montgomery & Sorell, 1997). Individuals throughout the stages of marriage report love attitudes involving passion, romance, friendship, and selflessness. This finding contradicts the notion that romantic, passionate love is a privilege of young people and new relationships.

The Triangular Theory of Love

The **triangular theory of love,** developed by Robert Sternberg (1986), emphasizes the dynamic quality of love relationships. According to this theory, love is composed of three elements, as in the points of a triangle: intimacy, passion, and decision/commitment (Figure 7.1). Each can be

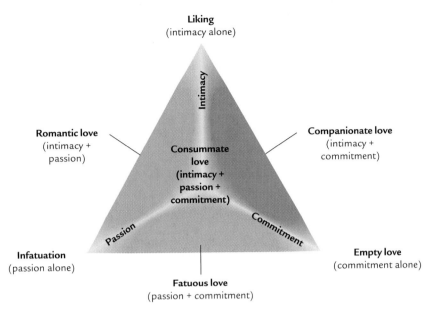

FIGURE 7.1 Sternberg's Triangular Theory of Love. The three elements of love are intimacy, passion, and decision/commitment.

enlarged or diminished in the course of a love relationship, which will affect the quality of the relationship. They can also be combined in different ways. Each combination produces a different type of love, such as romantic love, infatuation, empty love, and liking. Partners may combine the components differently at different times in the same love relationship.

The Components of Love   Intimacy refers to the warm, close, bonding feelings we get when we love someone. According to Sternberg and S. Grajek (1984), there are ten signs of intimacy:

1. Wanting to promote your partner's welfare
2. Feeling happiness with your partner
3. Holding your partner in high regard
4. Being able to count on your partner in times of need
5. Being able to understand your partner
6. Sharing yourself and your possessions with your partner
7. Receiving emotional support from your partner
8. Giving emotional support to your partner
9. Being able to communicate with your partner about intimate things
10. Valuing your partner's presence in your life

The passion component refers to the elements of romance, attraction, and sexuality in the relationship. These may be fueled by a desire to increase self-esteem, to be sexually active or fulfilled, to affiliate with others, to dominate, or to subordinate.

The decision/commitment component consists of two separate parts— a short-term part and a long-term part. The short-term part refers to an

> If love does not know how to give and take without restrictions, it is not love, but a transaction that never fails to lay stress on a plus and a minus.
>
> —*Emma Goldman (1869–1940)*

individual's decision that he or she loves someone. People may or may not make the decision consciously. But it usually occurs before they decide to make a commitment to the other person. The commitment represents the long-term part; it is the maintenance of love. But a decision to love someone does not necessarily entail a commitment to maintaining that love.

Kinds of Love   The intimacy, passion, and decision/commitment components can be combined in eight basic ways, according to Sternberg:

1. Liking (intimacy only)
2. Infatuation (passion only)
3. Romantic love (intimacy and passion)
4. Companionate love (intimacy and commitment)
5. Fatuous love (passion and commitment)
6. Consummate love (intimacy, passion, and commitment)
7. Empty love (decision/commitment only)
8. Nonlove (absence of intimacy, passion, and commitment)

These types represent extremes that few of us are likely to experience. Not many of us, for example, experience infatuation in its purest form, in which there is absolutely *no* intimacy. And empty love is not really love at all. These categories are nevertheless useful for examining the nature of love.

LIKING: INTIMACY ONLY   Liking represents the intimacy component alone. It forms the basis for close friendships but is neither passionate nor committed. As such, liking is often an enduring kind of love. Boyfriends and girlfriends may come and go, but good friends remain.

INFATUATION: PASSION ONLY   Infatuation is "love at first sight." It is the kind of love that idealizes its object; the infatuated individual rarely sees the other as a "real" person with normal human foibles. Infatuation is marked by sudden passion and a high degree of physical and emotional arousal. It tends to be obsessive and all-consuming; one has no time, energy, or desire for anything or anyone but the beloved (or thoughts of him or her). To the dismay of the infatuated individual, infatuations are usually asymmetrical: The passion (or obsession) is rarely returned equally. And the greater the asymmetry, the greater the distress in the relationship.

ROMANTIC LOVE: INTIMACY AND PASSION   Romantic love combines intimacy and passion. It is similar to liking except that it is more intense as a

Don't threaten me with love, baby.

—*Billie Holiday (1915–1959)*

Being deeply loved by someone gives you strength; loving someone deeply gives you courage.

—*Lao Tzu (sixth century* B.C.)

BEETLE BAILEY reprinted with special permission of King Features Syndicate.

result of physical or emotional attraction. It may begin with an immediate union of the two components, with friendship that intensifies into passion, or with passion that also develops intimacy. Although commitment is not an essential element of romantic love, it may develop.

COMPANIONATE LOVE: INTIMACY AND COMMITMENT   Companionate love is essential to a committed friendship. It often begins as romantic love, but as the passion diminishes and the intimacy increases, it is transformed into companionate love. Some couples are satisfied with such love; others are not. Those who are dissatisfied in companionate love relationships may seek extrarelational partners to maintain passion in their lives. They may also end the relationship to seek a new romantic relationship that they hope will remain romantic.

FATUOUS LOVE: PASSION AND COMMITMENT   Fatuous or deceptive love is whirlwind love; it begins the day two people meet and quickly results in cohabitation or engagement, and then marriage. It develops so quickly that they hardly know what happened. Often, nothing much really did happen that will permit the relationship to endure. As Sternberg (1988) observes, "It is fatuous in the sense that a commitment is made on the basis of passion without the stabilizing element of intimate involvement—which takes time to develop." Passion fades soon enough, and all that remains is commitment. But commitment that has had relatively little time to deepen is a poor foundation on which to build an enduring relationship. With neither passion nor intimacy, the commitment wanes.

CONSUMMATE LOVE: INTIMACY, PASSION, AND COMMITMENT   Consummate love results when intimacy, passion, and commitment combine to form their unique constellation. It is the kind of love we dream about but do not expect in all our love relationships. Many of us can achieve it, but it is difficult to sustain over time. To sustain it, we must nourish its different components, for each is subject to the stress of time.

EMPTY LOVE: DECISION/COMMITMENT ONLY   This is love that lacks intimacy or passion. Empty love involves staying together solely for the sake of appearances or the children, for example.

NONLOVE: ABSENCE OF INTIMACY, PASSION, AND COMMITMENT   Nonlove can take many forms, such as attachment for financial reasons, fear, or the fulfillment of neurotic needs.

The Geometry of Love

The shape of the love triangle depends on the intensity of the love and the balance of the parts. Intense love relationships lead to triangles with greater area; such triangles occupy more of one's life. Just as love relationships can be balanced or unbalanced, so can love triangles. The balance determines the shape of the triangle (Figure 7.2). A relationship in which the intimacy, passion, and commitment components are equal results in an equilateral triangle. But if the components are not equal, unbalanced triangles form. The size and shape of a person's triangle give a good pictorial sense of how that person feels about another. The greater the match between the triangles of the two partners in a relationship, the more likely each is to experience satisfaction in the relationship.

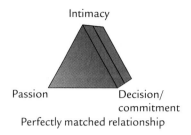

Intimacy

Passion   Decision/
                        commitment
Perfectly matched relationship

Closely matched relationship

Moderately mismatched
relationship

Severely mismatched relationship

 Self   Other

FIGURE 7.2 The Geometry of Love. According to the triangular theory of love, the shape and size of each person's triangle indicates how well each is matched to the other.

We are never so defenseless against suffering as when we love.
—*Sigmund Freud (1856–1939)*

FOR MANY, FORMING a new relationship appears to be a lot easier (and a lot more fun) than maintaining one. If this were not the case, then marital therapy and how-to articles and books on keeping love alive would not be so prevalent. One person who has spent a significant part of his career investigating the quandaries of partnerships is John M. Gottman, professor emeritus of psychology at the University of Washington–Seattle's Family Research Lab, better known as the "Love Lab". Over the past 24 years, Gottman and his colleagues have video-recorded thousands of conversations between couples, scoring words and sentences based on facial expressions such as disgust, affection, and contempt. Though most of his work has involved married couples, applications can be made to any couple interested in improving their relationship. Of the couples who have passed through the lab, Gottman and his colleagues have predicted which ones would divorce with what they claim is 90% accuracy.

According to Gottman, "It stands to reason that when a husband and wife respect each other and are open to each other's points of view, they have a good basis for resolving any differences that arise. And yet too often, couples lose their way when trying to persuade each other or settle disagreements." Gottman believes that in order to resolve difficulties in communication partners must learn new approaches to settling conflict. By studying what couples both overtly and covertly communicate, Gottman has arrived at what he considers to be a new model for resolving conflict in a loving relationship. His model entails the following steps:

1. *Soften up your startup.* Perhaps the most important aspect of this step is the avoidance of the "Four Horsemen of the Apocalypse"—criticism, contempt, defensiveness, and stonewalling. Only 40% of marriages end because of frequent, devastating fights. More often, partners end up distancing themselves so much that their friendship and sense of connection are lost. Softening the startup of a discussion is important because conversations usually end on the same note on which they begin. To get a sense of whether a harsh startup is a problem in your partnership, consider whether the following statements hold true for you:

- My partner is often very critical of me.
- Arguments often seem to come out of nowhere.
- My partner is negative out of all proportion.
- What is wrong is often not my responsibility.
- I feel I have to ward off personal attacks.

It's no surprise that the more true responses you have, the more inclined you or your partner is to trot out at least one of the four horsemen, which prevents the issue from being resolved. Some suggestions to ensure that your startup is soft include complaining but not blaming, making statements that start with "I" instead of "you," and describing what is happening rather than evaluating or judging it.

2. *Learn to make and receive repair attempts.* What seems to separate stable, emotionally intelligent partnerships from others is not that the partners' repair attempts are more skillful but that the attempts focus on getting through to each other. This is because the air between them hasn't been clouded by negativity. To assess the effectiveness of repair attempts in your own relationship, consider how you might resolve conflict:

Love as Attachment

Humans need to bond with other people. At the same time, many people fear bonding. Where do these contradictory impulses and emotions come from? Can they ever be resolved?

Attachment theory, the most prominent approach to the study of love, helps us understand how adult relationships develop, what can go wrong in them, and what to do when things do go wrong. In this theory, love is seen as a form of **attachment,** a close, enduring emotional bond that finds its roots in infancy (Hazan & Shaver, 1987; Shaver, 1984; Shaver, Hazan, & Bradshaw, 1988). Research suggests that romantic love and infant-caregiver attachment have similar emotional dynamics.

Infant-Caregiver Attachment

- The attachment bond's formation and quality depend on the attachment object's (AO) responsiveness and sensitivity.

- We are good at taking breaks when we need them.
- My partner usually accepts my apologies.
- I can say that I am wrong.
- We can maintain our sense of humor.
- We can be affectionate even when we are disagreeing.

Note that the more you agree with the statements, the stronger your partnership is. Thus, when discussions are at risk for getting out of hand, you are able to put on the brake and effectively calm each other down. Phrases such as "That hurts my feelings" and "I need things to be calmer right now" can repair damage done by harsh statements.

3. *Soothe yourself and each other.* Feeling overwhelmed, both emotionally and physically, often indicates that the body is in distress. To discover whether flooding is a problem in your relationship, consider the following statements:

- Our discussions get too heated.
- After a fight, I want to keep my distance.
- I can't think straight when my partner gets hostile.
- There's often no stopping my partner's temper.
- Small issues suddenly become big ones.

The more you agree with the statements, the greater the tendency to get flooded during arguments. When you are feeling too agitated to really hear what your partner is saying, you are less likely to resolve the problem. Calming the body through meditative techniques can help to prevent feelings of righteous indignation and innocent victimhood.

4. *Compromise.* Gottman puts it this way: "Like it or not, the only solution to marital problems is to find a compromise." Though that may seem rather obvious, earnest efforts to compromise on issues often fail because couples try to compromise in the wrong way. Negotiation begins with softening the startup, repairing the discussion, and keeping calm. The cornerstone of any compromise is accepting influence. This means that for a compromise to work each partner must be open to the other's opinions and desires. Deciding which solvable problem to tackle, looking for common bases of agreement, and sharing these with each other helps couples develop a common way of thinking about the issue. In this way, partners can work together to construct a real plan that both can live with. Asking yourself the following questions may be helpful:

- What do we agree about?
- What are our common feelings, or what is the most important feeling here?
- What common goals do we have?
- How can we understand this situation or issue?
- How do we think these goals should be accomplished?

If you are grappling with a solvable problem, finding the aspects of the problem that you can and cannot compromise on can help you develop a reasonable solution.

5. *Be tolerant of each other's faults.* As long as someone does not accept a partner's flaws and foibles, he or she will not be able to compromise successfully. Conflict resolution is not about one person changing; it's about negotiating, finding common ground, and identifying ways to accommodate each other.

Source: Adapted from Gottman, J., & Silver, N. (1999). *The Seven Principles for Making Marriage Work.* New York: Crown.

- When the AO is present, the infant is happier.
- The infant shares toys, discoveries, and objects with the AO.
- The infant coos, talks baby talk, and "sings."
- The infant shares feelings of oneness with the AO.

Romantic Love

- Feelings of love are related to lovers' interest and reciprocation.
- When the lover is present, the person feels happier.
- Lovers share experiences and goods and give gifts.
- Lovers coo, sing, and talk baby talk.
- Lovers share feelings of oneness.

The implications of attachment theory are far-reaching. Attachment affects the way we process information, interact with others, and view the world. Basically, it influences our ability to love and to see ourselves as lovable.

According to attachment theory, the holding and cuddling behaviors between parents and babies resemble those of adult lovers.

One study showed that we can carry an attachment style with us for life; this style predisposes us to behave in certain ways in love relationships (Shaver et al., 1988). In a later study, researchers found a significant association between attachment styles and relationship satisfaction (Brennan & Shaver, 1995).

The core elements of love appear to be the same for children as for adults: the need to feel emotionally safe and secure. When a partner responds to a need, for instance, adults view the world as a safe place. In this respect, we don't differ greatly from children.

The most basic concept of attachment theory is that to be whole adults we need to accept the fact that we are also vulnerable children. In a secure, intimate adult relationship, it is neither demeaning nor diminishing nor pathological to share honest emotions. It is the capacity to be vulnerable and open and accepting of others' giving that makes us lovable and human.

Based on observations made by Mary Ainsworth and colleagues (1978, cited in Shaver et al., 1988), Phillip Shaver and colleagues (1988) hypothesized that the styles of attachment developed in childhood—secure, anxious/ambivalent, and avoidant—continue through adulthood. Their surveys revealed similar styles in adult relationships.

Adults with secure attachments find it easy to get close to others.

Adults with **secure attachments,** for example, found it relatively easy to get close to other people. They felt comfortable depending on others and having others depend on them. They didn't frequently worry about being abandoned or having someone get too close to them. More than anxious/ambivalent and avoidant adults, they felt that others usually liked them; they believed that people were generally well intentioned and good-hearted. Their love experiences tended to be happy, friendly, and trusting. They accepted and supported their partners. On average, their relationships lasted 10 years. About 56% of the adults in the study were secure. One study reported that secure adults find greater satisfaction and commitment in their relationships than those with other attachment styles (Pistole, Clark, & Tubbs, 1995).

Adults with **anxious/ambivalent attachments** believed that other people did not get as close as they themselves wanted. They worried that their partners didn't really love them or would leave them. They also wanted to merge completely with another person, which sometimes scared others away. More than others, they felt that it is easy to fall in love. Their experiences in love were often obsessive and marked by desire for union, high degrees of sexual attraction, and jealousy. Their love relationships lasted an average of 5 years. Approximately 19–20% of the adults were identified as anxious/ambivalent.

Adults with **avoidant attachments** felt discomfort in being close to other people; they were distrustful and fearful of being dependent. More than others, they believed that romance seldom lasts but that at times it can be as intense as it was at the beginning. Their partners wanted more closeness than they did. Avoidant lovers feared intimacy and experienced emotional highs and lows and jealousy. Their relationships lasted an average of 6 years. Approximately 23–25% of the adults in the study were avoidant.

In adulthood, the attachment style developed in infancy combines with sexual desire and caring behaviors to give rise to romantic love. It is this combination that lays the groundwork for a relationship with another person.

IS MARRIAGE SYNONYMOUS with romantic love? In the United States, most people would agree that love is a prerequisite for marriage, a bond that can satisfy all of an individual's needs. Our culture's belief in the importance of love for marriage, however, is not universally accepted. In India, for example, romantic love and intense emotional attachment are typically seen as threats to the family structure. In collectivist societies, people identify with and conform to the expectations of extended groups—their family, clan, and others—which look after their needs in return for their loyalty. This contrasts with many Westernized cultures in which an individual's personal concerns and immediate family are primary.

Researchers recently asked over 1000 college students from 11 countries about the importance of love in marriage, with these results:

Question: *"If a man (woman) had all the other qualities you desired, would you marry this person if you were not in love with him (her)?"*

Response	India	Pakistan	Thailand	United States	England	Japan	Philippines	Mexico	Brazil	Hong Kong	Australia
Yes (%)	49.0	50.4	18.8	3.5	7.3	2.3	11.4	10.2	4.3	5.8	4.8
No (%)	24.0	39.1	33.8	85.9	83.6	62.0	63.6	80.5	85.7	77.6	80.0
Undecided (%)	26.9	10.4	47.5	10.6	9.1	35.7	25.0	9.3	10.0	16.7	15.2

Question: *"If love has completely disappeared from a marriage, I think it is probably best for the couple to make a clean break and start new lives."*

Response	India	Pakistan	Thailand	United States	England	Japan	Philippines	Mexico	Brazil	Hong Kong	Australia
Agree (%)	46.2	33.0	46.9	35.4	44.6	41.1	45.5	51.7	77.5	47.1	29.3
Disagree (%)	26.0	49.6	32.1	34.7	23.2	17.1	40.9	28.0	12.7	25.5	31.1
Neutral (%)	27.9	17.4	21.0	29.9	32.1	41.9	13.6	20.3	9.9	27.4	39.6

'Tis better to have loved and lost
Than never to have loved at all.

—*Alfred, Lord Tennyson (1809–1892)*

UNREQUITED LOVE

As most of us know from painful experience, love is not always returned. Several researchers (Baumeister, Wotman, & Stillwell, 1993) accurately captured some of the feelings associated with **unrequited love**—love that is not returned—in the title of their study: "Unrequited Love: On Heartbreak, Anger, Guilt, Scriptlessness, and Humiliation." They found that unrequited love is distressing for both the would-be lover and the rejecting person. Would-be lovers had both positive and intensely negative feelings about their failed relationship. The rejectors, however, felt uniformly negative about the experience. Unlike the rejectors, the would-be lovers felt that the attraction was mutual, that they had been led on, and that the rejection had never been clearly communicated. Rejectors, in contrast, felt that they had not led the other person on; moreover, they felt guilty about hurting him or her. Nevertheless, many found the other person's persistence intrusive and annoying; they wished he or she would have simply gotten the hint and gone away. Rejectors saw would-be lovers as

Question: "In my opinion, the disappearance of love is not a sufficient reason for ending a marriage and should not be viewed as such."

Response	India	Pakistan	Thailand	United States	England	Japan	Philippines	Mexico	Brazil	Hong Kong	Australia
Agree (%)	47.1	54.8	50.6	36.8	26.8	26.4	71.6	34.8	26.8	51.6	39.6
Disagree (%)	34.6	35.7	34.2	40.3	46.4	27.9	23.9	50.9	63.4	24.8	22.6
Neutral (%)	18.3	9.6	15.2	22.9	26.8	45.7	4.6	14.4	9.9	23.6	37.7

As the data show, cultures vary markedly in the importance they place on love as a prerequisite for establishing and maintaining a marriage. Love was perceived as more important in individualistic Westernized nations (the United States, Brazil, England, Australia) and less important in collectivist Eastern nations (India, Pakistan, Thailand, the Philippines). Furthermore, even though there were considerable differences in gender roles within many of the countries studied, men and women tended to hold the same opinions in each country, whether it was to place a high or a low value on romantic love. The survey also revealed that economic conditions were strongly related to beliefs about love, especially concerning the establishment of marriage. (One possible explanation for this is that industrial growth produces pressures toward individualism and away from collectivism.) Finally, beliefs about the importance of love seem to have behavioral consequences for marital decisions. Respondents assigning greater importance to love, particularly for making decisions about the formation of a marriage, tended to come from nations with higher marriage rates, lower fertility rates, and higher divorce rates.

Because college students are a biased sample of the overall population and do not necessarily represent the same subpopulations in each country, we must be very cautious when generalizing these beliefs to the general population. At the same time, we might expect these groups to be considerably less traditional than the people in their countries as a whole, and the fact that clear cross-cultural differences emerged demonstrates the perseverance and pervasiveness of cultural values.

What are the consequences of marrying for love in a culture that discourages individual choice or of marrying for pragmatic reasons in a culture that values marrying for love? Is there an inherent conflict between individualistic values and the interdependence demanded by romantic love? These are difficult questions that warrant further reflection and study.

Source: Adapted from Levine, R., Sato, S., Hashimoto, T., & Verma, J. (1995). "Love and Marriage in Eleven Cultures." Journal of Cross-Cultural Psychology, 26(5), 554–71. Reprinted by permission of Sage Publications, Inc.

self-deceiving and unreasonable; would-be lovers saw their rejectors as inconsistent and mysterious.

Styles of Unrequited Lovers

Unrequited love presents a paradox: If the goal of loving someone is an intimate relationship, why should we continue to love a person with whom we cannot have such a relationship? Arthur Aron and his colleagues addressed this question in a study of almost 500 college students (Aron, Dutton, & Aron, 1989). The researchers found several distinct styles underlying the experience of unrequited love:

- *The Cyrano style:* the desire to have a romantic relationship with a specific person regardless of how hopeless the love is. In this style, the benefits of loving someone are so great that it does not matter how likely it is that the love will be returned. Being in the same room with the beloved—because she or he is so wonderful—may be sufficient. This style is named after Cyrano de Bergerac, the seventeenth-century musketeer whose love for Roxane was so great that it was irrelevant that she loved someone else.

▪ *The Giselle style:* the misperception that a relationship is more likely to develop than it actually is. This might occur if someone misreads the other person's cues, such as in mistakenly believing that friendliness is a sign of love. This style is named after Giselle, the tragic ballet heroine who was misled by Count Albrecht to believe that her love was reciprocated.

▪ *The Don Quixote style:* the general desire to be in love, regardless of whom one loves. In this style, the benefits of being in love—such as being viewed as a romantic or enjoying the excitement of extreme emotions—are more important than actually being in a relationship. This style is named after Cervantes' Don Quixote, whose love for the commoner Dulcinea was motivated by his need to dedicate knightly deeds to a lady love. "It is as right and proper for a knight errant to be in love as for the sky to have stars," Don Quixote explained.

Attachment Theory and Unrequited Love

Applying attachment theory, the researchers found that some people were predisposed to be Cyranos, others Giselles, and still others Don Quixotes. For example, anxious/ambivalent adults tended to be Cyranos, avoidant adults Don Quixotes, and secure adults Giselles. Those who were anxious/ambivalent were most likely to experience unrequited love; those who were secure were least likely to experience such love. Avoidant adults experienced the greatest desire to be in love in general, yet they had the least probability of being in a specific relationship. Anxious/ambivalent adults showed the greatest desire for a specific relationship; they also had the least desire to be in love in general.

JEALOUSY

Beware, my lord, of jealousy. It is the green-eyed monster that mocks the meat it feeds on.

—*William Shakespeare (1564–1616)*

Many of us think that the existence of jealousy proves the existence of love. We may try to test someone's interest or affection by attempting to make him or her jealous by flirting with another person. If our date or partner becomes jealous, the jealousy is taken as a sign of love (Salovey & Rodin, 1991; White, 1980). But provoking jealousy proves only that the other person can be made jealous. Making jealousy a litmus test of love is dangerous, for jealousy and love are not necessarily companions. Jealousy may be a more accurate yardstick for measuring insecurity or immaturity than for measuring love (Pistole, 1995).

It's important to understand jealousy for several reasons. First, jealousy is a painful emotion associated with anger, hurt, and loss. If we can understand jealousy, especially when it is irrational, then we can eliminate some of its pain. Second, jealousy can help cement or destroy a relationship. Jealousy helps maintain a relationship by guarding its exclusiveness. But in its irrational or extreme forms, it can destroy a relationship by its insistent demands and attempts at control. We need to understand when and how jealousy is functional and when it is not. Third, jealousy is often linked to violence (Follingstad, Rutledge, Berg, & Hause, 1990; Laner, 1990; Riggs, 1993). It is a factor in precipitating violence in dating relationships among

ASSUMING THE FOLLOWING statements were true for you, which would you reveal to a partner or spouse?

- In order to become aroused and maintain arousal, you need to fantasize about another person or situation.
- You have had extrarelational sex.
- You no longer find your partner physically attractive.

If you would not reveal this information to your partner, are you being deceptive? Or are these private issues? How does deception differ from privacy?

Deception involves betrayal and delusion; it often takes the form of lies, omissions, fabrications, or secrets. Counselors and psychologists agree that, although deception is extremely common in intimate relationships, it has the power to destroy feelings of closeness and intimacy and ultimately to shatter trust. Whether or not a deception is revealed, it creates a sense of distance and disorientation in the relationship. It erodes bonds and blocks authentic communication and trust. Deception strips away spontaneity and often leaves a couple operating on a higher level of anxiety, states psychologist Harriet Lerner, author of *The Dance of Deception* (1993).

There are differences, some cultural and some personal, in what people consider acceptable and proper to reveal. Many people, for instance, do not reveal their sexual fantasies to their partners, considering it neither nec-essary nor important to do so. They consider this a matter of privacy rather than one of deceptiveness. Deception typically originates with betrayal or involves lies and secrets that drive couples apart.

Are you deceptive in your primary relationship? If so, in the process of identifying and confronting deception, it is helpful to understand your motivations. Are they the result of unfounded criticism by your partner? Anger toward your partner about an extrarelational relationship? Boredom in the bedroom? Dissatisfaction with the quality of communication? Perhaps you don't understand why your behavior exists. Our reasons and motivations are often complex, with their expression rooted in our early life experiences and the ways we have learned to behave. For some, therapy is a way to help unravel, understand, and communicate what often seems beyond comprehension.

If truth and intimacy are connected, then truth is usually the preferred choice. Given the high cost of deception, it is worthwhile to try to understand the reason for it, confront it with honesty, and communicate openly about it. This approach, though difficult and painful, will ultimately strengthen the relationship, whereas continued deception will only erode it further.

Source: Adapted from Adler, E. (1994, August 24). "How the Tangled Web of Deception Hurts Relationships." Reprinted by permission of Kansas City Star.

---

both high school and college students (Burcky, Reuterman, & Kopsky, 1988; Himelein, Vogel, & Wachowiak, 1994). Furthermore, marital violence and rape are often provoked by jealousy (Russell, 1990). Rather than being directed at a rival, jealous aggression is often used against the partner (Paul & Galloway, 1994).

Defining Jealousy

Jealousy is an aversive response that occurs because of a partner's real, imagined, or likely involvement with a third person. Jealousy sets boundaries for the behaviors that are acceptable in relationships; the boundaries cannot be crossed without evoking jealousy (Reiss, 1986). Though a certain amount of jealousy can be expected in any loving relationship, it is important that partners communicate openly about their fears and boundaries. Jealousy is a paradox; it doesn't necessarily signal difficulty between partners, nor does it have to threaten the relationship (Wiederman & Allgeier, 1993).

The Psychological Dimension   As most of us know, jealousy is a painful emotion. It is an agonizing compound of hurt, anger, depression, fear, and doubt. When we are jealous, we may feel less attractive and acceptable to our partner. Jealousy can also enrich relationships and spark passion by increasing the attention individuals pay to their partner. According to David Buss (2000), psychology professor at the University of Texas–Austin, the total absence of jealousy is a more ominous sign than its presence for romantic partners because it signifies emotional bankruptcy. Though both sexes may elicit jealousy intentionally as an assessment tool to gauge the strength of a partner's commitment, they seem to use it unequally. Buss (2000) found that 31% of women and 17% of men had intentionally elicited jealousy in their relationship.

Jealous responses are most intense in committed or marital relationships because both assume "specialness." This specialness occurs because our intimate partner is different from everyone else. With him or her, we are our most confiding, revealing, vulnerable, caring, and trusting. There is a sense of exclusiveness. Being intimate outside the relationship violates that sense of exclusiveness because intimacy (especially sexual intimacy) symbolizes specialness. Words such as "disloyalty," "cheating," and "infidelity" reflect the sense that an unspoken pledge has been broken. This unspoken pledge is the normative expectation that serious relationships will be sexually exclusive.

As our lives become more and more intertwined, we become less and less independent. For some, this loss of independence increases the fear of losing the partner. But it takes more than simple dependency to make us jealous. To be jealous, we must perceive that we have something to lose. Of the women who indicated that they had intentionally tried to make their partner jealous, 8% reported doing so to bolster their self-esteem, 10% to act out feelings of revenge, 38% to increase a partner's commitment, and fully 40% to test the strength of the bond (Buss, 2000). For both sexes, the key to understanding who experiences jealousy is determining who has the most to lose.

Love is like quicksilver in the hand. Leave the fingers open and it stays. Clutch it, and it darts away.

—Dorothy Parker (1893–1967)

Types of Jealousy   Social psychologists suggest that there are two types of jealousy: suspicious and reactive (Bringle & Buunk, 1991). **Suspicious jealousy** occurs when there is no reason to be suspicious or when only ambiguous evidence exists that a partner may be involved with a third person. Suspicious jealousy tends to occur most often when a relationship is in its early stages. The relationship is not firmly established, and the couple are unsure about their future. The smallest distraction, imagined slight, or inattention can be taken as evidence of interest in another person. Even without *any* evidence, a jealous partner may worry ("Is he or she seeing someone else but not telling me?"). He or she may engage in vigilance, watching the other person's every move ("I'd like to audit your human sexuality class"). He or she may snoop, unexpectedly appearing in the middle of the night to see if someone else is there ("I was just passing by and thought I'd say hello"). Or he or she may try to control the other person's behavior ("If you go to your friend's party without me, we're through").

Sometimes, however, suspicions are valid. Suspicious jealousy, in fact, may be a reasonable response to circumstantial evidence. Robert Bringle and Bram Buunk (1991) believe that a certain amount of suspicious jealousy may be functional. They observe that "emotional reactions to these [circumstantial] events may forewarn the partner of what will happen if there are serious transgressions and thereby serve the role of *preventing* extradyadic involvements" (Bringle & Buunk, 1991).

Reactive jealousy occurs when someone learns of a partner's present or past sexual involvement with another person. Not surprisingly, such involvement usually provokes the most intense jealousy. If the extrarelational sex occurred during the current relationship, the discovering partner may feel that the entire relationship has been based on a lie. Trust is questioned. Every word and event must be reevaluated: "If you slept with each other when you said you were going to the library, did you also sleep with him/her when you said you were going to the laundromat?" or "How could you say you loved me when you were seeing him/her?" The damage can be irreparable.

Boundary Markers   As noted previously, jealousy represents a boundary marker in a particular relationship. It determines to what extent and in what manner other people can interact with partners in the relationship. It also shows the limits to which the partners can interact with those outside the relationship. Culture prescribes the general boundaries of what evokes jealousy, but individuals adjust them to the dynamics of their own relationship.

Boundaries may vary depending on the type of relationship and the partners' gender, sexual orientation, and ethnicity. The majority of people believe sexual exclusiveness to be important in serious dating relationships and cohabitation; it is virtually mandatory in marriage (Blumstein & Schwartz, 1983; Buunk & van Driel, 1989). Fewer than 2% of adults believe that having sex with someone other than a spouse is "not wrong at all" (Laumann et al., 1994). Men are generally more restrictive than women, and heterosexual persons more restrictive than gay men and lesbian women. Although we know very little about jealousy and ethnicity, traditional Latinos and new Latino and Asian immigrants tend to be more restrictive than Anglos or African Americans (Mindel, Haberstein, & Wright, 1988). Despite variations in where the boundary lines are drawn, jealousy functions to guard those lines.

Managing Jealousy

Jealousy can be unreasonable, based on fears and fantasies, or realistic, in reaction to genuine threats or events. Unreasonable jealousy can become a problem when it interferes with an individual's well-being or that of the relationship. Dealing with irrational suspicions can often be very difficult, for such feelings touch deep recesses in ourselves. As noted previously, jealousy is often related to personal feelings of insecurity and inadequacy. The source of such jealousy lies within ourselves, not within the relationship.

If we can work on the underlying causes of our insecurity, then we can deal effectively with our irrational jealousy. Excessively jealous people may need considerable reassurance, but at some point, they must also confront their own irrationality and insecurity. If they do not, they emotionally imprison their partner. Their jealousy may destroy the very relationship they have been desperately trying to preserve.

But jealousy is not always irrational. Sometimes, there are valid reasons, such as the relationship boundaries being violated. In this case, the cause lies not within ourselves but within the relationship. If the jealousy is well founded, the partner may need to modify or end the relationship with the third party whose presence initiated the jealousy. Modifying the third-party relationship reduces the jealous response and, more importantly, symbolizes

> Jealousy is not a barometer by which the depth of love can be read. It merely records the depth of the lover's insecurity.
>
> —*Margaret Mead (1901–1978)*

Love withers under constraints: its very essence is liberty: it is not compatible either with obedience, jealousy, nor fear: it is there most pure, perfect, and unlimited where its votaries live in confidence, equality and unreserve.

—*Percy Bysshe Shelley*

What I have seen of the love affairs of other people has not led me to regret that deficiency in my experience.

—*George Bernard Shaw (1856–1950)*

the partner's commitment to the primary relationship. If the partner is unwilling to do this, because of a lack of commitment, unsatisfied personal needs, or problems in the primary relationship, the relationship is likely to reach a crisis point. In such cases, jealousy may be the agent for profound change.

There are no set rules for dealing with jealousy. Each person must deal with it using his or her own understanding and insights. As with many of life's problems, jealousy has no simple answers.

Extramarital Sex

A fundamental assumption in our culture is that marriages are sexually exclusive. Each person remains the other's exclusive intimate partner, in terms of both emotional and sexual intimacy. Extramarital sex alters that assumption.

A review of literature relating to the prevalence of extramarital sexuality found that 15–25% of ever-married Americans report having had extramarital sex but that this behavior occurs infrequently during any year (1.5–4% during the preceding 12 months) (Wiederman, 1997). Also, it appears that men are somewhat more likely than women to report it. Very little is known about extramarital sex in relation to ethnicity; however, Black men and women reported higher rates during the preceding year than White men and women. Similarly, Black women and Latinas reported higher rates than White women (Wiederman, 1997).

Although we tend to think of extrarelational involvements as being sexual, they actually assume several forms. They may be (1) sexual but not emotional, (2) sexual and emotional, or (3) emotional but not sexual. In a series of experiments in which participants were forced to choose between emotional nonexclusiveness and sexual nonexclusiveness as more distressing, women were found to choose emotional nonexclusiveness, whereas men were more likely to choose sexual nonexclusiveness (Buss, 1999; Buss, Larsen, & Westen, 1996; Cann, Mangum, & Wells, 2001). These results are consistent with findings reported across many cultures (Buss, 1999). This gender difference can partly be explained using an evolutionary model, which proposes that men, because they cannot be completely confident about the paternity of any offspring from a relationship, will be more upset by sexual nonexclusiveness. Women, in contrast, should be more upset by emotional nonexclusiveness which might signal the man's lack of commitment to the long-term success of the relationship and any offspring. Gender differences in how we respond to nonexclusiveness in romantic relationships reveal how social factors can and do shape the expression of betrayal (Cann, Mangum, & Wells, 2001).

Extrarelational Involvements in Dating and Cohabiting Relationships
Both cohabiting couples and those in committed relationships usually have expectations of sexual exclusiveness. But, like some married men and women who take vows of exclusivity, these couples do not always remain sexually and/or emotionally exclusive. Research has revealed that cohabitors are more likely to have relationships outside their primary one, suggesting that perhaps they have lower investments in their unions (Treas & Giesen, 2000). Gay men had more partners than cohabiting and married men, while lesbian women had fewer partners than any other group.

Large numbers of both women and men have sexual involvements outside dating relationships that are considered exclusive. Of those who knew of their partner's extrarelational involvement, a large majority felt that it had hurt their own relationship. When both partners had engaged in extrarelational sex, each believed that their partner's sex had harmed the relationship more than their own had.

Extramarital Sex in Exclusive Marriages   In marriages that assume emotional and sexual exclusivity, mutuality and sharing are emphasized. Extramarital sexual relationships are assumed to be destructive of the marriage; nonsexual heterosexual relationships may also be judged threatening. The possibility of infecting one's spouse with an STI must also be considered.

As a result of marital assumptions, both sexual and nonsexual extramarital relationships take place without the knowledge or permission of the other partner. If the extramarital sex is discovered, a marital crisis ensues. Many married people feel that the spouse who is not exclusive has violated a basic trust. Sexual accessibility implies emotional accessibility. When a person learns that his or her spouse is having another relationship, the emotional commitment of that spouse is brought into question. How can the person prove that he or she still has a commitment? He or she cannot—commitment is assumed; it can never be proved. Furthermore, the extramarital sex may imply to the partner (rightly or wrongly) that he or she is sexually inadequate or uninteresting.

Extramarital Sex in Nonexclusive Marriages   There are several types of nonexclusive marriage: (1) open marriage in which intimate but nonsexual friendships with others are encouraged, (2) open marriage in which outside sexual relationships are allowed, and (3) group marriage/multiple relationships. The marriage relationship is considered the primary relationship in both nonsexual extramarital relationships and open marriages. Only the group marriage/multiple relationships model rejects the primacy of the married relationship. Group marriage is the equal sharing

> There is one thing I would break up over, and that is if she caught me with another woman. I won't stand for that.
>
> —*Steve Martin*

> To be faithful to one is to be cruel to all the others.
>
> —*Wolfgang Amadeus Mozart (1756–1791)*

of partners, as in polygamy; it may consist of one man and two women, one woman and two men, or two couples. Open marriages are more common than group marriages.

In **open marriage,** partners may mutually agree to allow sexual contact with others. Little research has been done on open marriages. Philip Blumstein and Pepper Schwartz (1983) found that 15–26% of the couples in their sample had "an understanding" that permitted extramarital sex in certain circumstances, such as having a sexual liaison out of town, never seeing the same person twice, and never having sex with a mutual friend.

Motivations for Extramarital Sex   People who engage in extramarital relationships have a number of different motivations that satisfy a number of different needs (Moultrup, 1990). John Gagnon (1977) describes the attraction extrarelational sex has for the people involved:

> Most people find their extramarital relationships highly exciting, especially in the early stages. This is a result of psychological compression: the couple gets together; they are both very aroused (desire, guilt, expectation); they have only three hours to be together. . . . Another source of attraction is that the other person is always seen when he or she looks good and is on best behavior, never when feeling tired or grubby, or when taking care of children, or when cooking dinner. . . . Each time, all the minutes that the couple has together are special because they have been stolen from all these other relationships. The resulting combination of guilt and excitement has a heightening effect, which tends to explain why people may claim that extramarital sex and orgasms are more intense.

Research into why people have extramarital sex has been piecemeal and based on small samples that have limited generalizability. In spite of this, studies have shown that there is a higher likelihood of sexual activity outside the marriage among those with stronger sexual interests, more permissive sexual values, greater sexual opportunities, and weaker marital relationships (Treas & Giesen, 2000). This suggests that sexual behavior is positively correlated with social factors.

THE TRANSFORMATION OF LOVE: FROM PASSION TO INTIMACY

Ultimately, passionate or romantic love may be transformed or replaced by a quieter, more lasting love. Otherwise, the relationship will likely end, and each person will search for another who will once again ignite her or his passion.

Although love is one of the most important elements of our humanity, it seems to come and go. The kind of love that lasts is what we might call **intimate love.** In intimate love, each person knows he or she can count on the other. The excitement comes from the achievement of other goals—from creativity, from work, from child rearing, from friendships—as well as from the relationship. The key to making love endure seems to be, not maintaining love's passionate intensity, but transforming it into intimate love. Intimate love is based on commitment, caring, and self-disclosure.

Commitment is an important component of intimate love. It reflects a determination to continue a relationship or marriage in the face of bad times

---

Thou shalt not commit adultery . . . unless in the mood.

—W. C. Fields (1879–1946)

Love is patient and kind; love is not jealous or boastful; it is not arrogant or rude. Love does not insist on its own way; it is not irritable or resentful; it does not rejoice at wrong, but rejoices in the right. Love bears all things, believes all things, hopes all things, endures all things.

—1 Corinthians 13:4–7

ALTHOUGH WE GENERALLY make commitments because we love someone, love alone is not sufficient to make a commitment last. Our levels of commitment seem to be affected by several factors that can strengthen or weaken the relationship. Ira Reiss (1980) believes that there are three important factors: the balance of costs to benefits, normative inputs, and structural constraints.

The Balance of Costs to Benefits

Whether we like it or not, we tend to look at romantic, marital, and sexual relationships from a cost-benefit perspective. Most of the time, when we are satisfied, we are unaware that we may judge our relationships in this manner. But when there is stress or conflict, we often ask ourselves, "What am I getting out of this relationship?" Then we add up the pluses and minuses. If the result is on the plus side, we are encouraged to continue the relationship; if the result is negative, we are more likely to discontinue it, especially if the negativity continues over a long period. In this system, sexual interactions can have a positive or a negative value. But although sex is important, it is generally not the only factor or even necessarily the most important factor.

Normative Inputs

Normative inputs for relationships are the values that we, our partners, and society hold about love, relationships, marriage, and family. These values can either sustain or detract from a commitment. How do you feel about a love commitment? A marital commitment? Do you believe that marriage is for life? If you are a gay, lesbian, or bisexual person, what are the values you and your partner bring to your relationship in terms of commitment? How do you create your own positive norms in the face of negative societal norms?

Structural Constraints

The structure of a relationship will add to or detract from levels of commitment. Depending on the type of relationship—whether it is dating, cohabiting, or marriage, for example—there are different structural roles and expectations. In marital relationships, there are partner roles (husband/wife) and economic roles (employed worker/homemaker). There may also be parental roles (mother/father). There is usually the expectation of exclusivity. In gay and lesbian relationships, the marital relationship model is replaced by the best-friends model, in which sexual exclusiveness is generally negotiable.

These different factors interact to increase or decrease commitment in a relationship. Commitments are more likely to endure in marriage than in cohabiting or dating relationships, which may tend to be relatively short-lived. They are more likely to last in heterosexual relationships than in gay or lesbian relationships (Testa, Kinder, & Ironson, 1987). The reason commitments tend to endure in marriage may or may not have anything to do with the spouses' being happy. Marital commitments tend to last because of norms, and structural constraints may compensate for the lack of personal satisfaction.

For most people, love seems to include commitment, and commitment seems to include love. Though the two appear to overlap considerably, we can mistakenly assume that if someone loves us he or she is also committed to us. It is not uncommon for one partner to believe there is more commitment in a relationship than there actually is. Even if a person is committed, it is not always clear what the commitment means: Is it a commitment to the partner or to the relationship? For a short time or for a long time? For better and for worse?

as well as good (Reiss, 1986). It is based on conscious choices rather than on feelings, which, by their very nature, are transitory. Commitment involves a promise of a shared future, a promise to be together, come what may.

Commitment has become an important concept in recent years. We seem to be as much in search of commitment as we are in search of love or marriage. We speak of "making a commitment" to someone or to a relationship. A "committed" relationship has become almost a stage of courtship, somewhere between dating and being engaged or living together.

Caring involves the making of another person's needs as important as your own. It requires what the philosopher Martin Buber called an "I-Thou" relationship. Buber described two fundamental ways of relating to people: I-Thou and I-It. In an I-Thou relationship, each person is treated as a Thou—that is, as a person whose life is valued as an end in itself. In an I-It relationship, each

What determines whether a relationship will last? Click on "Staying in Love" to see a couple working to save their marriage.

243

person is treated as an It; the person has worth only as someone who can be used. When a person is treated as a Thou, his or her humanity and uniqueness are paramount.

Self-disclosure is the revelation of personal information that others would not ordinarily know because of its riskiness. When we self-disclose, we reveal ourselves—our hopes, our fears, our everyday thoughts—to others. Self-disclosure deepens others' understanding of us. It also deepens our own understanding, for we discover unknown aspects as we open up to others.

Without self-disclosure, we remain opaque and hidden. If others love us, such love makes us anxious: Are we loved for ourselves or for the image we present to the world?

Together, these elements help transform love. But in the final analysis, perhaps the most important means of sustaining love are our words and actions; caring words and deeds provide the setting for maintaining and expanding love.

> Everyone has experienced that truth: that love, like a running brook, is disregarded, taken for granted; but when the brook freezes over, then people begin to remember how it was when it ran, and they want it to run again.
>
> —*Khalil Gibran (1833–1931)*

THE STUDY OF LOVE is only beginning, but it is already helping us to understand the various components that make up this complex emotion. Although there is something to be said for the mystery of love, understanding how it works in the day-to-day world may help us keep our love vital and growing.

SUMMARY

Friendship and Love

- Close friend relationships are similar to spouse/lover relationships in many ways. But lovers/spouses have more fascination and a greater sense of exclusiveness with their partners.

Love and Sexuality

- Sexuality and love are intimately related in our culture. Sex is most highly valued in loving relationships. A loving relationship rivals marriage as an acceptable moral standard for intercourse. Love is valued by heterosexual men and women, gay men, lesbian women, and bisexual individuals.

- Nonmarital sex among young adults (but not adolescents) in a relational context has become the norm. An important factor in this shift is the surge in the numbers of unmarried men and women.

- Men are more likely than women to separate sex from love; women tend to view sex within a relational context. Gay men are more likely than heterosexual men to be involved in purely sexual relationships. The quality of relationships between gay men, lesbian women, and heterosexual married couples differs.

- For a variety of reasons, some people choose *celibacy* as a lifestyle. These individuals may have a better appreciation of the nature of friendship and an increased respect for the bonds of long-term partnerships.

How Do I Love Thee? Approaches and Attitudes Related to Love

- Attitudes and feelings associated with love include caring, needing, trusting, and tolerating. Behaviors associated with love include verbal, nonverbal, and physical expression of affection, self-disclosure, provision of nonmaterial and material evidence, and tolerance.

- According to John Lee, there are six basic styles of love: *eros, mania, ludus, storge, agape,* and *pragma.*

- The *triangular theory of love* views love as consisting of three components: intimacy, passion, and decision/commitment.

- The *attachment* theory of love views love as being similar in nature to the attachments we form as infants. The attachment (or love) styles of both infants and adults are *secure, anxious/ambivalent,* and *avoidant.*

Unrequited Love

- *Unrequited love*—love that is not returned—is distressing for both the would-be lover and the rejecting partner. A person's style of attachment affects the way in which she or he experiences unrequited love.

Jealousy

- *Jealousy* is an aversive response to a partner's real, imagined, or likely involvement with a third person. Jealous responses are most likely in committed or marital relationships because of the presumed "specialness" of the relationship, symbolized by sexual exclusiveness.

- As individuals become more interdependent, there is a greater fear of loss. There is some evidence that jealousy may serve to ignite the passion in a relationship.

- There are two types of jealousy: suspicious and reactive. *Suspicious jealousy* occurs when there is no reason to be suspicious or only ambiguous evidence. *Reactive jealousy* occurs when a partner reveals a current, past, or anticipated relationship with another person.

- Jealousy acts as a boundary marker for relationships. Boundaries vary according to the type of relationship and the partners' gender, sexual orientation, and ethnicity.

- Extrarelational sex exists in dating, cohabiting, and marital relationships. In exclusive marriages, extramarital sex is assumed to be destructive of the marriage and is kept secret. In nonexclusive marriages, extramarital sex is permitted. In *open*

marriage, partners mutually agree to allow sexual relationships with others.

- Extramarital sex appears to be related to three factors: values, opportunities, and the quality of the relationship.

The Transformation of Love: From Passion to Intimacy

- Time affects romantic relationships. *Intimate love* is based on *commitment, caring,* and *self-disclosure,* the revelation of information not normally known by others.

Sex and the Internet

Ask Me Anything

Sex therapist and licensed marriage and family counselor Marty Klein has established a Web site about love and sexuality (www.SexEd.org). This site contains numerous links and articles that provide information and resources intended to help people feel sexually adequate and powerful. Go to this site, locate the Article Archive, select and read an article that interests you, and then answer the following questions:

- Why did you select this article?
- What was the main point?
- How was your thinking influenced by the viewpoint of the author?
- What did you learn?

Now go to Hot Links and select a particular site. Once you have explored the options and links associated with this site, answer these questions:

- What did you learn about this organization or site?
- Would you recommend that other people visit this site? Why or why not?

SUGGESTED WEB SITES

Association for Couples in Marriage Enrichment
http://www.bettermarriages.org
Promotes better marriage by providing enrichment opportunities and exercises to strengthen couple relationships.

The Couples Place

http://www.couples-place.com/

Offers information on how to build and improve relationships.

DivorceSource

http://www.divorcesource.com

Provides information on various aspects of divorce, by state and by topic.

Healthy Sexuality

http://beWell.com/healthy/sexuality

Provides information related to sexual behaviors, sex therapy, midlife sex, and more.

SUGGESTED READING

Ackerman, Diane. (1995). *A Natural History of Love*. New York: Random House. A historical and cultural perspective on love.

Buss, David M. (2000). *The Dangerous Passion: Why Jealousy Is as Necessary as Love and Sex*. New York: Free Press. Discusses jealousy as evolutionary glue that can spark or rekindle sexual passion in a relationship.

Feeney, Judith, & Noller, Patricia. (1996). *Adult Attachment*. (Vol. 14). Thousand Oaks, CA: Sage. A coherent account of diverse strands of attachment research.

Gottman, John, & Silver, Nan. (1999). *The Seven Principles for Making Marriage Work*. New York: Crown. Uses research to help couples strengthen their partnerships and marriages.

Hendrick, Susan, & Hendrick, Clyde. (1992). *Romantic Love*. Newbury Park, CA: Sage. A concise review of social science research on romantic love.

Peck, M. Scott. (1995). *The Road Less Traveled: A New Psychology of Love, Traditional Values, and Spiritual Growth*. New York: Simon & Schuster. A psychological/spiritual approach to love that sees love's goal as spiritual growth.

Sternberg, Robert, & Barnes, Michael (Eds.). (1989). *The Psychology of Love*. New Haven, CT: Yale University Press. An excellent collection of essays by some of the leading researchers in the area of love.

For links, articles, and study material, go to the McGraw-Hill Web site, located at http://www.mhhe.com/strong5

Communicating About Sex

"When I turned sixteen years old, I got married to a wonderful man. I did not know much about sex because the only sex experience I had was when I was a child and it was a brutal experience. My first sex experience with my husband was terrible because I got depressed and had the feeling that sex acts were dirty, nasty, and immoral. I also used to think that sex was only for prostitutes, and I felt like one. Family and friends made me think that when a woman was sexually abused she then became a prostitute, and that's why I felt like one. My first month or two of having sex with my husband was a total nightmare; I would cry and feel dirty. My husband understood my feelings because he knew about my abuse, but he did not know what to do to help me overcome my depression."

—21-year-old Mexican female

"Through high school and college, my relationship with my father grew. . . . During the time I lived with my father, I noticed his inability to express his emotions and his closed relationships with others. Thankfully, I have not yet noticed this rubbing off on my relationships or me."

—20-year-old Italian male

"One night at a party on a farm in a small mountain town in Peru, I ended up kissing and playing around all night with a Peruvian girl. She did not speak any English, and I had only a moderate understanding of the Peruvian language, which contains a different dialect than Spanish. It was just incredible, considering the language barrier, how well our body language traveled from one to another through visual contact, sensual touching, and a tiny bit of verbal communication."

—24-year-old White male

*C*OMMUNICATION IS THE THREAD that connects sexuality and intimacy. The quality of the communication affects the quality of the relationship, and the quality of the relationship affects the quality of the sex (Byers & Demmons, 1999; Sprecher, 2002). Good relationships tend to feature good sex; bad relationships often feature bad sex. Sex, in fact, frequently serves as a barometer for the quality of the relationship. The ability to communicate about sex is important in developing and maintaining both sexual and relationship satisfaction. People who are satisfied with their sexual communication also tend to be satisfied with their relationships as a whole (Noller & Fitzpatrick, 1991). Effective communication skills do not necessarily appear when a person falls in love; they can, however, be learned with practice.

Most of the time, we don't think about our ability to communicate. Only when problems arise do we consciously think about it. Then we become aware of our limitations in communicating or, more often, our perceptions of the limitations of others: "You just don't get it, do you?" or "You're not listening to me." And as we know, communication failures are marked by frustration.

Communication problems in relationships usually arise from failure to self-disclose, poor communication skills, or negative intentions, motivations,

Words are given to man to enable him to conceal his true feelings.

—*Voltaire (1694–1778)*

or emotions (e.g., anger). Although much of what we discuss here refers to interpersonal communication, such knowledge will enrich your ability to communicate about sexual issues as well.

It's important to realize, however, that not all of a relationship's problems are communication problems. Often, we understand each other very clearly; the problem is that we are unable or unwilling to change or compromise. Good communication will not salvage a bad or a "wrong" relationship. But good communication will enable us to see our differences and the consequences of our actions or inactions, and it will enable us to make informed decisions.

In this chapter, we examine the characteristics of communication and the way different contexts affect it. We discuss forms of nonverbal communication, such as touch, which are especially important in sexual relationships. Then we examine the different ways we communicate about sex in intimate relationships. We also explore ways we can develop our communication skills in order to enhance our relationships. Finally, we look at the different types of conflicts in intimate relationships and at methods for resolving them.

THE NATURE OF COMMUNICATION

Communication is a transactional process by which we use symbols, such as words, gestures, and movements, to establish human contact, exchange information, and reinforce or change our own attitudes and behaviors and those of others. Communication takes place simultaneously within cultural, social, and psychological contexts. These contexts affect our ability to communicate clearly by prescribing rules (usually unwritten or unconscious) for communicating about various subjects, including sexuality.

The Cultural Context

The cultural context of communication refers to the language that is used and to the values, beliefs, and customs associated with it. Traditionally, reflecting our Judeo-Christian heritage, our culture has viewed sexuality negatively. Thus, sexual topics are often taboo. Children and adolescents are discouraged from obtaining sexual knowledge; they learn that they are not supposed to talk about sex. Censorship abounds in the media, with the ever-present "beep" on television or the "f—k" in newspapers and magazines to indicate a "forbidden" word. Our language has a variety of words for describing sex, including scientific or impersonal ones ("sexual intercourse," "coitus," "copulation"), moralistic ones ("fornication"), euphemistic ones ("doing it," "being intimate," "sleeping with"), and taboo ones ("fucking," "screwing," "banging"). A few terms place sexual interactions in a relational category, such as "making love." But love is not always involved, and the term does not capture the erotic quality of sex. Furthermore, the gay, lesbian, bisexual, and transgendered subcultures have developed their own sexual argot, or slang, because society suppresses the open discussion or expression of same-sex behavior.

Different ethnic groups within our culture also have different language patterns that affect the way they communicate about sex and sexuality.

African American culture, for example, creates distinct communication patterns (Hecht, Collier, & Ribeau, 1993). Among African Americans, language and expressive patterns are characterized by, among other things, emotional vitality, realness, confrontation, and a focus on direct experience (Mackey & O'Brien, 1999; White & Parham, 1990). Emotional vitality is communicated through the animated, expressive use of words. Realness refers to "telling it like it is," using concrete, nonabstract language. Direct experience is valued because "there is no substitute in the Black ethos for actual experience gained in the course of living" (White & Parham, 1990). In sexual (and other) matters, "mother wit"—practical or experiential knowledge—may be valued over knowledge gained from books or lectures. In the home and the marriage, confrontational conflict management is one way in which husbands, in particular, can assert themselves (Mackey & O'Brien, 1999).

Among Latinos, especially traditional Latinos, there may be power imbalances that are potentially more significant for women than men. This may be due to the cultural values of a traditionally *machista* society in which men are defined by their ability to maintain control and to assert dominance by being the active sexual partner (Melhuss, 1996). Among traditional Latinos, the type and frequency of sexual behaviors are most often determined by men (Amaro, 1988; Wood & Price, 1997). In gender-specific decision making, however, power varies across sexual domains (Harvey, Beckman, Browner, & Sherman, 2002). Although most Latinos agree that men tend to be the initiators of sexual activity and women are more likely to suggest condom use, they report that couples share responsibility for decisions regarding sexual activities and contraceptive use.

Asian Americans constitute a population group that defies simple characterizations; it includes a variety of demographic, historical, and cultural factors and traditions. At the same time, Asian Americans share many cultural characteristics, such as the primacy of the family and of collective goals over individual wishes, an emphasis on propriety and social roles, the appropriateness of sex only within the context of marriage, and sexual restraint and modesty (Okazaki, 2002). Because harmonious relationships are highly valued, Asian Americans have a greater tendency to avoid direct confrontation if possible. Japanese Americans, for example, "value implicit, nonverbal, intuitive communication over explicit, verbal, rational exchange of information" (Del Carmen, 1990). To avoid conflict, their verbal communication is often indirect or ambiguous; it skirts issues rather than confronting them. As a consequence, Asian Americans rely on each other to interpret the meaning of conversations or nonverbal cues.

The Social Context

The social context of communication refers to the roles we play in society as members of different groups. For instance, as men and women, we play out masculine and feminine roles. As members of marital units, we act out roles of husband and wife. As members of cohabiting units, we perform heterosexual, gay, or lesbian cohabiting roles.

Roles exist in relationship to other people. Without a female role, there would be no male role; without a wife role, there would be no husband role. Because roles exist in relationship to others, **status**—a person's position or ranking in a group—is important. In traditional gender roles, men are accorded higher status than women; in traditional marital roles, husbands are superior in status to wives. And in terms of sexual orientation, society awards higher status to heterosexual persons than to gay men, lesbian women, bisexual, or transgendered people. Because of this male/female disparity, heterosexual couples tend to have a greater power imbalance than do gay and lesbian couples (Lips, 1997).

The Psychological Context

Although the cultural and social contexts are important factors in communication, they do not *determine* how people communicate. The psychological context of communication does that. We are not prisoners of culture and society; we are unique individuals. We may accept some cultural or social aspects, such as language taboos, but reject, ignore, or modify others, such as traditional gender roles. Because we have distinct personalities, we express our uniqueness by the way we communicate: We may be assertive or submissive, rigid or flexible, and sensitive or insensitive; we may exhibit high or low self-esteem.

Our personality characteristics affect our ability to communicate, change, or manage conflict. Rigid people, for example, are less likely to change than are flexible ones, regardless of the quality of communication. People with high self-esteem may be more open to change because they do not necessarily interpret conflict as an attack on themselves. Personality characteristics such as negative or positive feelings about sexuality affect our sexual communication more directly.

Nonverbal Communication

There is no such thing as not communicating. Even when we are not talking, we are communicating by our silence (an awkward silence, a hostile silence, a tender silence). We are communicating by our body movements, our head positions, our facial expressions, our physical distance from another person, and so on. We can make sounds that aren't words to communicate nonverbally; screams, moans, grunts, sighs, and so on communicate a range of feelings and reactions. Look around you: How are the people in your presence communicating nonverbally?

Most of our communication of feeling is nonverbal (Guffey, 1999). We radiate our moods: A happy mood invites companionship; a solemn mood pushes people away. Joy infects; depression distances—all without a word being said. Nonverbal expressions of love are particularly effective—a gentle touch, a loving glance, or the gift of a flower.

One of the problems with nonverbal communication, however, is the imprecision of its messages. Is a person frowning or squinting? Does the smile indicate friendliness or nervousness? Is the silence reflective, or does it express disapproval or remoteness?

The ability to correctly interpret nonverbal communication is an important ingredient in successful relationships. The statement "I can tell when something is bothering him/her" reveals the ability to read nonverbal cues such as body language. This ability is especially important for members of ethnic groups and cultures that rely on nonverbal expression of

> The cruelest lies are often told in silence.
>
> —*Robert Louis Stevenson*
> *(1850–1894)*

Proximity, eye contact, and touching are important components of nonverbal communication. What do you think this man and woman are "saying" to each other?

feelings, such as Latino and Asian cultures. Although the value placed on nonverbal expression may vary among groups and across cultures, the ability to communicate and understand nonverbally remains important in all cultures.

Three of the most important forms of nonverbal communication are proximity, eye contact, and touching.

Proximity   Nearness in physical space and time is called **proximity.** Where we sit or stand in relation to another person signifies a level of intimacy. Many of our words that convey emotion relate to proximity, such as feeling "distant" or "close" or being "moved" by someone. We also "make the first move," "move in" on someone else's partner, or "move in together."

In a social gathering, the distances between individuals when they start a conversation are clues to how they wish to define the relationship. All cultures have an intermediate distance in face-to-face interactions that is neutral. In most cultures, decreasing the distance signifies either an invitation to greater intimacy or a threat. Moving away denotes the desire to terminate the interaction. When we stand at an intermediate distance from someone at a party, we send the message "Intimacy is not encouraged." If we move closer, however, we risk rejection.

Because of cultural differences, there can be misunderstandings. The neutral intermediate distance for Latinos, for example, is much closer than that for Anglos, who may misinterpret the same distance as "too close for comfort." In social settings, this can lead to problems. As Carlos Sluzki (1982) points out, "A person raised in a non-Latino culture will define as seductive behavior the same behavior that a person raised in a Latin culture defines as socially neutral." An Anglo may interpret the behavior as an invitation for intimacy; the Latino may interpret it as neutral. Because of the miscue, the Anglo may either withdraw or flirt, depending on his or her feelings. If the Anglo flirts, the Latino may respond to what he or she believes is the other's initiation. Additionally, among people whose culture features greater intermediate distances and less overt touching, such as Asian Americans, neutral responses may be misinterpreted negatively by those outside the culture.

Eye Contact   Much can be discovered about a relationship by watching how the two people look at each other. Making eye contact with another person, if only for a split second longer than usual, is a signal of interest. Brief and extended glances, in fact, play a significant role in women's expression of initial interest. When we can't take our eyes off another person, we probably have a strong attraction to him or her. In addition to eye contact, dilated pupils may be an indication of sexual interest. (They may also indicate fear, anger, and other strong emotions.)

The amount of eye contact between partners in conversation can reveal couples who have high levels of conflict and those who don't. Those with the greatest degree of agreement have the most eye contact with each other. Those in conflict tend to avoid eye contact (unless it is a daggerlike stare). As with proximity, however, the level of eye contact may differ by culture.

Touching   It is difficult to overestimate the significance of touch. A review of the research on touch shows it to be extremely important in human development, health, and sexuality (Hatfield, 1994). Touch is the most basic of all senses. The skin contains receptors for pleasure and pain, heat and cold, roughness and smoothness. "Touch is the mother sense and out of it, all the other senses have been derived," writes anthropologist Ashley Montagu (1986). Touch is a life-giving force for infants. If babies are not touched, they can fail to thrive and even die. We hold hands and cuddle with small children and with people we love.

But touch can also be a violation. Strangers or acquaintances may touch inappropriately, presuming a level of familiarity that does not actually exist. A date or partner may touch the other person in a manner she or he doesn't like or want. And sexual harassment includes unwelcome touching (see Chapter 17).

Like eye contact, touching is a form of communication. The amount of contact, from almost imperceptible touching to "hanging all over each other," helps differentiate lovers from strangers. How and where a person is touched can suggest friendship, intimacy, love, or sexual interest.

Levels of touching differ among cultures and ethnic groups. Although the value placed on nonverbal expression may vary across groups and cultures, the ability to communicate and understand nonverbally remains important in all cultures.

What about gender differences in touching? Despite stereotypes of women touching and men avoiding touch, studies suggest that there are no consistent differences between the sexes in the amount of overall touching (Andersen, Lustig, & Andersen, 1987). Men do not seem to initiate touch with women any more than women do so with men. Women are markedly unenthusiastic, however, about receiving touches from strangers and express greater concern in general about being touched. For women, there is more touch avoidance unless there is a relational context with the man. However, in situations with sexual overtones, men initiate more touching than women (Blumstein & Schwartz, 1983).

Touch: Overcoming Differences in Individuals' Preferences

CONSIDER THESE QUESTIONS:

- "How can I become more openly affectionate when expressing affection was discouraged by my family when I was growing up?"

- "My partner likes to touch and be touched, but I am uncomfortable with both. How can we overcome these differences?"

These are questions students ask over and over in human sexuality classes. These questioners are aware of the deep need for and value of human touch. So profound is this need that infants have been observed wasting away and becoming ill, in spite of good physical care, as a result of a lack of touching and cuddling. Among adults, professionals see a correlation between marital happiness and physical affection: The happiest couples tend to be the most physically demonstrative. The response to touch is indeed physical: Biochemical reactions produced by touch can cause an increase in heart rate, a drop in blood pressure, and an easing of pain.

A variety of factors appear to contribute to each individual's need for and ability to touch. Among these, culture is a strong determinant. Studies show that Americans tend to touch less than people from many Latin American countries, the Middle East, and Russia (Brenton, 1990). Families also play a key role in influencing how comfortable people are with touch. Both quantity and quality of touch among adults and between adults and children are observed by children and then translated into behavior that often repeats itself in adulthood. Inborn differences, gender, and individual preferences also influence touching.

Regardless of where the patterns and preferences originate, problems can occur in relationships if distinct discrepancies exist between partners in sending or receiving touch. Misunderstandings, discomfort, and a widening gap in the ability of each person to emotionally connect with the other often result.

The most obvious, and possibly the most difficult, solution to this problem is honest communication. Communication can replace assumptions (about why someone is not being touched), ignorance (about what does and does not feel good), misplaced anger and resentment (about the importance of touch), and misinterpretation (about the meaning of touch). Communication in a nonthreatening and relaxed environment can begin to help unravel and expose existing patterns and behaviors.

Discussing what touch means to each person is a beginning. For some, touch means intimacy; for others, it represents safety; for still others, it signals a readiness for sex. Often, the absence of touch is merely a response to previous learning. But the absence of touch can elicit feelings in another person ranging from abandonment to rage. Sharing the meaning of touch may expand its definition and allow partners to find a place for it in their patterns of expression.

If touching is an issue in your relationship, experiment with nonsexual touching. Learn to enjoy giving and receiving touch. Give and accept feedback nondefensively. Give feedback, especially verbal cues, about what does and does not feel good. Initiate touch when it is appropriate, even though it may be awkward at first. Don't be afraid to be adventurous in learning and utilizing methods that are pleasing to both you and your partner.

At the same time, be prepared to accept individual differences. In spite of forthright and ongoing communication, people still have unique comfort levels. Again, honest feedback will help you and your partner find a mutually acceptable level. If you are both able to understand and enjoy the rich and powerful messages that touch sends, then your relationship can be enriched by yet another dimension.

Married couples who love each other tell each other a thousand things without talking.

—*Chinese proverb*

Touch often signals intimacy, immediacy, and emotional closeness. In fact, touch may very well be the *closest* form of nonverbal communication. One researcher writes: "If intimacy is proximity, then nothing comes closer than touch, the most intimate knowledge of another" (Thayer, 1986). And touching seems to go hand in hand with self-disclosure. Those who touch appear to self-disclose more; in fact, touch seems to be an important factor in prompting others to talk more about themselves.

Sexual behavior relies above all else on touch: the touching of oneself and others. (Sex is a contact sport, some say, with more truth than they realize.) In sexual interactions, touch takes precedence over sight: We often close our eyes as we caress, kiss, and make love. In fact, we close our eyes to better focus on the sensations aroused by touch; we shut out visual distractions to intensify the tactile experience of sexuality. When touching leads to sexual arousal, the sensual aspects are all too often hurried along in order to initiate sexual activity.

SEXUAL COMMUNICATION

Communication is important in developing and maintaining sexual relationships. In childhood and adolescence, communication is critical for transmitting sexual knowledge and values and forming our sexual identities. As we establish our relationships, communication enables us to signal sexual interest and initiate sexual interactions. In developed relationships, communication allows us to explore and maintain our sexuality as couples.

Sexual Communication in Beginning Relationships

Our interpersonal sexual scripts provide us with "instructions" on how to behave sexually, including the initiation of potentially sexual relationships. Because as a culture we share our interpersonal sexual scripts, we know how we are supposed to act at the beginning of a relationship. The very process of acting out interpersonal scripts, in fact, communicates sexual meanings (Simon & Gagnon, 1987). But how do we begin relationships? What is it that attracts us to certain individuals?

The Halo Effect   Imagine yourself unattached at a party. You notice someone standing next to you as you reach for some chips. In a split second, you decide whether you are interested in her or him. On what basis do you make that decision? Is it looks, personality, style, sensitivity, intelligence, or what?

If you're like most people, you base this decision, consciously or unconsciously, on appearance. Physical attractiveness is particularly important during the initial meeting and early stages of a relationship. If you don't know anything else about a person, you tend to judge on appearance.

Most people would deny that they are attracted to others simply because of their looks. We like to think we are deeper than that. But looks are important, in part because we tend to infer qualities based on looks. This inference is based on what is known as the **halo effect,** the assumption that attractive or charismatic people also possess more desirable social characteristics. In one well-known experiment, students were shown pictures of attractive people and asked to describe what they thought these people were like (Dion, Berscheid, & Walster, 1972). Attractive men and women were assumed to be more sensitive, kinder, warmer, more sexually responsive, stronger, and more poised and outgoing than "ordinary" people; they were also assumed to be more exciting and to have better characters.

Interest and Opening Lines   After sizing someone up based on his or her appearance, what happens next in interactions between men and women? (Gaymen's and lesbian women's beginning relationships are discussed later.)

> Whereas a lot of men used to ask for conversation when they really wanted sex, nowadays they often feel obliged to ask for sex even when they really want conversation.
>
> —*Katherine Whitehorn*

Traditionally, when women and men are interested in meeting each other, the woman will often covertly initiate contact by sending nonverbal messages of interest. If the man believes the woman is interested, he will then initiate the conversation with an opening line.

Does the man initiate the encounter? On the surface, yes, but in reality, the woman often "covertly initiates . . . by sending nonverbal signals of availability and interest" (Metts & Cupach, 1989). The woman will "glance" at the man once or twice and "catch" his eye; she may smile or flip her hair. If the man moves into her physical space, the woman then communicates interest by nodding, leaning close, smiling, or laughing.

If the man believes the woman is interested, he then initiates a conversation with an opening line, which tests the woman's interest and availability. Men use an array of opening lines. According to women, the most effective ones are innocuous, such as "I feel a little embarrassed, but I'd like to meet you" or "Are you a student here?" The least effective lines are sexually blunt ones, such as "You really turn me on."

The First Move and Beyond   When we first meet someone, we weigh his or her attitudes, values, and philosophy to see if we are compatible. We evaluate his or her sense of humor, intelligence, "partner" potential, ability to function in a relationship, sex appeal, and so on. Based on our overall judgment, we may pursue the relationship. If the relationship continues in a romantic vein, we may decide to move into one that includes some kind of physical intimacy. To signal this transition from nonphysical to physical intimacy, one of us must "make the first move." Making the first move marks the transition from a potentially sexual relationship to one that is actually sexual.

If the relationship develops along traditional gender-role lines, one of the partners, usually the man, will make the first move to initiate sexual intimacy, whether it is kissing, fondling, or engaging in sexual intercourse. The point at which this occurs generally depends on two factors: the level of intimacy and the length of the relationship (Sprecher, 1989). The more emotionally involved the two people are, the more likely they will be sexually involved as well. Similarly, the longer the relationship, the more likely there is sexual involvement (Christopher & Sprecher, 2000).

Initial sexual involvement can occur as early as the first meeting or later, as part of a well-established relationship. Although some people become sexually involved immediately ("lust at first sight"), the majority begin their sexual involvements in the context of an ongoing relationship.

In new or developing relationships, communication is generally indirect and ambiguous about sexuality. There is considerable flirtation (Abrahams, 1994). As one communication scholar notes about developing relationships, "The typical relationship process is not dominated by open, direct communication, but rather involves the construction of a web of ambiguity by which parties signal their relationship indirectly" (Baxter, 1987). Direct strategies may be used to initiate sexual involvement, but these usually occur when the person is confident in the other's interest or is not concerned about being rejected.

In new relationships, we communicate *indirectly* about sex because, although we may want to become sexually involved with the other person, we also want to avoid rejection. By using indirect strategies, such as turning down the lights, moving closer, and touching the other person's face or hair, we can test his or her interest in sexual involvement. If he or she responds positively to our cues, we can initiate a sexual encounter.

Because so much of our sexual communication is indirect, ambiguous, or nonverbal, there is a high risk of misinterpretation. Both men and women may say "no" to sex while actually desiring it (Sprecher, Hatfield, Cortese, Potapova, & Levitskaya, 1994). Misunderstandings occur for several basic reasons (Cupach & Metts, 1991):

- *Men and women tend to disagree about* when *sexual activities should take place in a relationship.* Men more than women tend to seek sexual involvement earlier and with a lower level of emotional intimacy. Studies also show that emotionally valuing a partner is more of a motivation for women to engage in sexual intercourse than it is for men (Christopher & Sprecher, 2000).

- *Men may be skeptical about women's refusals.* Men often misinterpret women's cues, such as mistaking a woman's friendly touch as a sexual cue. Men also believe that women often say "no" when they actually mean "coax me." The "no" is seen as token resistance.

- *Because sexual communication is indirect, women may be unclear in signaling their disinterest.* A woman may turn her face aside, move a man's hand back to its proper place, say that it's getting late, or try to change the subject. Research indicates that women are most effective when they make strong, direct verbal refusals; men become more compliant if women are persistent in such refusals (Christopher & Frandsen, 1990; Murnen, Perot, & Byrne, 1989).

- *Men are more likely than women to interpret nonsexual behavior or cues as sexual.* As William Cupach and Sandra Metts (1991) write, "Men may wear sex-colored glasses." Although both men and women flirt for fun, men are more likely to flirt with a sexual purpose and to interpret a woman's flirtation as sexual.

Gay men and lesbian women, like heterosexual persons, rely on both nonverbal and verbal communication in expressing sexual interest in others. Unlike heterosexual people, however, they cannot necessarily assume that the person in whom they are interested is of the same sexual orientation. Instead, they must rely on specific identifying factors, such as meeting at a

Regardless of our sexual orientation, age, gender, or ethnicity, much of our sexual communication is nonverbal.

gay or lesbian bar, wearing a gay/lesbian pride button, participating in gay/lesbian events, or being introduced by friends to others identified as lesbian or gay. In situations in which sexual orientation is not clear, some gay men and lesbian women use "gaydar" (gay radar), in which they look for clues as to orientation. They give ambiguous cues regarding their own orientation while looking for cues from the other person. These cues can include mannerisms, speech patterns, slang, and lingering glances. They may also include the mention of specific places for entertainment or recreation that are frequented mainly by lesbian women or gay men, songs that can be interpreted as having "gay" meanings, or movies with gay or lesbian themes.

Once a like orientation is established, lesbian women and gay men use nonverbal communication to express interest. There are mutual glances, smiles, and subtle body movements. Someone initiates a conversation with an opening line. Like heterosexual persons, gay men and lesbian women prefer innocuous opening lines. To prevent awkwardness, the opening line usually does not overtly refer to sexual orientation unless the other person is clearly a lesbian or gay person. In these beginning interactions, physical appearance is important.

Because of their socialization as males, gay men are more likely than lesbian women to initiate sexual activity earlier in the relationship. In large part, this is because both partners are free to initiate and because men are not expected to refuse sex as women are. But this same sexual socialization makes it difficult for some gay men to refuse sexual activity. Lesbian women do not initiate sex as often as do gay or heterosexual men. In contrast to men, they often feel uncomfortable because women have not been socialized to initiate sexual activity. Philip Blumstein and Pepper Schwartz (1983) write that "many lesbians are not comfortable in the role of sexual aggressor and it is a major reason why they have sex less often than other kinds of couples."

Directing Sexual Activity   As we begin a sexual involvement, we have several tasks to accomplish. First and foremost, we must practice safer sex (see Chapters 15 and 16). We should gather information about our partner's sexual history, determine whether she or he knows how to practice safer sex, and use condoms. Unlike much of our sexual communication, which is

WE MAY CATCH THE FLU in a crowded bus or subway, but we won't be intimate enough (presumably) to give or get a sexually transmitted infection (STI). Acquiring an STI requires that we become physically intimate with another person. Just as getting STIs requires intimacy, so does preventing them. Avoiding an STI may even require more intimacy than getting one, because very often it means we have to talk. Learning to communicate isn't always easy. It can be embarrassing, especially if we are unaccustomed to sharing personal and sexual feelings. But it gets easier with practice. After all, embarrassment is not as bad as chlamydia, genital warts, or AIDS.

Important elements in communicating about STIs include initiation of the discussion, mutual disclosure of relevant information, and joint decision making.

Initiation of the Discussion

In some situations, we may be able to use nonverbal communication regarding STI prevention. Although it may lack the depth and intimacy that words can produce, nonverbal communication is certainly preferable to no communication at all. For example, if you think you are going to have sex with someone, you can be sure to have a condom with you, and, if you are a man, you can simply put it on at the appropriate time. If you are a woman, you can use or offer a condom to your partner when the moment is right. If your partner agrees, all will be well with this very minimal amount of communicating. But if your partner recoils in horror and says, "Why

are you using that? Do you think I've got a disease?" you will probably need to begin verbal communication if you are serious about protection.

It is preferable to initiate a discussion of safer sex before we become sexually aroused. In the heat of the moment, we may cease to think clearly and rationally. "Oh well, just this once won't matter," we may think. But it may matter very much indeed. When sexual intimacy looms on the horizon of a relationship, we need to be prepared with strategies for introducing the topics of contraception and STI prevention. Some people are able to state their concerns simply and directly: "Do you have condoms, or shall I get some?" Others broach the subject more indirectly: "What do you think about safer sex?" or "It's not easy for me to do this, but I think we should talk about protection." Once the ice has been broken, the other person will usually be receptive and responsive to the discussion. There's a good chance he or she has been trying to find the courage to say the same thing.

Mutual Disclosure

When we embark on a relationship that includes sexual activity, it is important to have some information about our partner's sexual health. It would be nice if our partner simply volunteered the relevant information, but that may not occur. We are most likely going to have to ask some very personal questions. One of the best ways to get someone to disclose personal information is to reveal important personal information about ourselves. There is

(continued)

nonverbal or ambiguous, practicing safer sex requires direct verbal communication. Second, heterosexual couples must discuss birth control (unless both partners have agreed to try for pregnancy). Contraceptive responsibility, like safer sex, requires verbal communication (see Chapter 11).

In addition to communicating about safer sex and contraception, we need to communicate about what we like and need sexually. What kind of touching do we like? For example, do we like to be orally or manually stimulated? If so, how? What stimulation does each partner need to be orgasmic? Many of our needs and desires can be communicated nonverbally by movements or physical cues. But if our partner does not pick up our nonverbal signals or cues, we need to discuss them directly and clearly to avoid ambiguity.

Sexual Communication in Established Relationships

In developing relationships, partners begin modifying their individual sexual scripts as they interact with each other. The scripts become less rigid and conventional as each partner adapts to the uniqueness of the other. Partners always some risk involved in self-disclosure. For example, you may say, "Before we go any further, you should know that I had an outbreak of herpes two years ago. It hasn't recurred, but I wanted you to know. We should still use a condom if we choose to have sex." If your partner does not know the facts about herpes, he or she may react negatively to your disclosure. But it is more likely that your honesty will be appreciated. (Besides, there's a 1 in 5 chance your partner has herpes, too.)

The information that potential sex partners should disclose to each other includes the following:

- The presence of an STI or symptoms that might indicate an STI
- A possible recent exposure to an STI
- A past history of STIs
- Current behaviors, including multiple sex partners and injecting drug use
- A past history of many sex partners, gay or bisexual male partners, or partners with a history of injecting drug use
- HIV status (positive or negative, as determined by an HIV blood test)

If both partners are sincerely concerned about the other's well-being, they will probably be able to overcome any feelings of embarrassment, guilt, or shame and share this important information. For this reason, relationships that develop over time and are founded on mutual caring and trust are likely to be safer sexually than one-night stands. Unfortunately, a person with no emotional investment in a relationship may not always be motivated to tell the truth. Taking some time to get to know our partners is a good way to help ensure our own sexual good health.

Joint Decision Making

If partners use a condom during intercourse, they probably are doing so by mutual consent. Either they have both agreed that it is important to use a condom or one of them has proposed condom use and the other has tacitly agreed. What may not be clear is that, if two people have sex without using a condom, they have mutually agreed that protection is unimportant or unnecessary. Perhaps they have not discussed their decision with each other, but it is a decision nonetheless. Perhaps one (or both) of the partners would prefer to use a condom but hasn't said anything because of embarrassment or fear of rejection. In choosing not to discuss the subject, the person has made the decision to risk getting an STI. In order to have safer sex, both partners need to agree on what practices they will engage in and under what circumstances they will or will not use condoms. Otherwise, "one partner who is not motivated to practice safer sex may not cooperate with the other partner, may undercut the other partner's resolve, or may refuse to use condoms properly" (Darrow & Siegel, 1990).

In negotiating safer sex with your partners, you need to ask yourself some questions: How honest are you or will you be in disclosing your sexual history to a potential partner? What do you want to know about a potential partner's sexual background? What might make this conversation difficult? Easy? When is the best time to have this conversation?

Click on "Sexual Techniques for Lovers" to see how one couple brought masturbation into their lovemaking.

Charm is a way of getting the answer without having asked any question.

—*Albert Camus (1913–1960)*

develop a shared sexual script. Through their sexual interactions, they learn what each other likes, dislikes, wants, and needs. Much of this learning takes place nonverbally: Partners in established relationships, like those in emerging relationships, tend to be indirect and ambiguous in their sexual communication. Like partners in new relationships, they want to avoid rejection. Indirection allows them to express sexual interest while at the same time protecting themselves from embarrassment or loss of face.

Initiating Sexual Activity   Within established heterosexual relationships, men continue to overtly initiate sexual encounters more frequently than women. But women continue to signal their willingness. They show their interest in intercourse with nonverbal cues, such as giving a "certain look" or lighting candles by the bed. (They may also overtly suggest "making love.") Their partners pick up on the cues and "initiate" sexual interactions. In established relationships, many women feel more comfortable with overtly

RESEARCHERS STUDYING relationship satisfaction have found a number of communication patterns that offer clues to enhancing our intimate relationships (Gottman & Carrere, 2000; Noller & Fitzpatrick, 1991; Schaap, Buunk, & Kerkstra, 1988). They found that men and women in satisfying heterosexual relationships tend to have the following common characteristics regarding communication:

- *The ability to disclose or reveal private thoughts and feelings, especially positive ones.* Dissatisfied partners tend to disclose mostly negative thoughts. Satisfied partners say such things as "I love you," "You're sexy," or "I feel vulnerable; please hold me." Unhappy partners may also say that they love each other, but more often they say things like "Don't touch me; I can't stand you," "You turn me off," or "This relationship makes me miserable and frustrated."

- *The expression of more or less equal levels of affective disclosures.* Both partners in satisfied couples are likely to say things like "You make me feel happy," "I love you more than I can ever say," or "I love the way you touch me."

- *More time spent talking, discussing personal topics, and expressing feelings in positive ways.* Satisfied couples talk about their sexual feelings and the fun they have in bed together.

- *A willingness to accept conflict but to engage in conflict in nondestructive ways.* Satisfied couples view conflict as a natural part of intimate relationships. When partners have sexual disagreements, they do not accuse or blame; instead, they exchange viewpoints, seek common ground, and compromise.

- *Less frequent conflict and less time spent in conflict.* Both satisfied and unsatisfied couples, however, experience perpetual problems surrounding the same issues, especially communication, sex, and personality characteristics.

- *The ability to accurately encode (send) verbal and nonverbal messages and accurately decode (understand) such messages.* This ability to send and understand nonverbal messages is especially important for men. In satisfied couples, for example, if a man wants his partner to initiate sex more often, he can say, "I'd like you to initiate sex more often," and she will understand the message correctly. In dissatisfied couples, the man may stop initiating sex, hoping his partner will be forced to initiate more often in order to have sex. Or he may ask her to initiate sex more often, but she may mistakenly interpret the request as a personal attack.

Many of these communication patterns appear to hold true for gay and lesbian relationships as well.

In developing communication patterns to enhance intimate relationships, you need to ask several questions: What characteristics regarding communication are important to you? What are your thoughts and feelings about the role of conflict in a relationship? What are some ways of developing good communication?

Obstacles to Sexual Discussions   The process of articulating our feelings about sex can be very difficult, for several reasons. First, we rarely have models for talking about sex. As children and adolescents, we probably never discussed sex with our parents, let alone heard them talking about sex. And if we talked about sex in their presence, they probably discouraged it or acted uncomfortable. We learned that sex is not an appropriate subject of conversation in "polite" company.

Second, talking about sexual matters defines us as being interested in sex, and interest in sex is often identified with being sexually obsessive, immoral, prurient, or "bad." If the topic of sex is tabooed, we further risk being labeled "bad."

Third, we may believe that talking about sex will threaten our relationships. We don't talk about tabooed sexual feelings, fantasies, or desires because we fear that our partners may be repelled or disgusted. We also are reluctant to discuss sexual difficulties or problems because doing so may bring attention to our own role in them.

Sexual vocabulary can also be a problem. We shift our sexual vocabulary depending on the context or the audience. Some words are inappropriate in

If you don't risk anything, you risk even more.

—*Erica Jong*

different contexts. To describe sexuality, we have medical terms that objectify and de-eroticize it: "penis," "vulva," "vagina," and "sexual intercourse." These are the words we use in formal situations, as in medical or academic settings or in conversation with our parents or our children; they are the acceptable terms for the printed page and for talk shows.

Slang words such as "cock," "cunt," and "screw" retain their sexual connotations; they are the "dirty" words of our language. They are most often used in informal settings, among friends or peers. Gay men and lesbian women have developed their own colloquial or slang terms as well.

Colloquial and slang words have powerful connotations. To modify their power, we have euphemisms—terms such as "making love" and "sleeping together"—whose emotional impact falls somewhere between the clinical and the colloquial. And, finally, we have our own private vocabulary of "pet names" for sexual body parts, such as "Miss Muff" or "Wilbur," that may develop within a relationship and be shared only with our partner.

Because men and women tend to have a different sexual vocabulary, it can be difficult for them to communicate with each other about sexual matters. A woman may be offended by the vocabulary her boyfriend uses among his friends; the man may think his girlfriend is unduly reticent because she uses euphemisms to describe sexuality. Partners often must negotiate the language they will use in order not to offend each other. Sometimes, they can settle on open, acceptable communication; other times, they may remain in silence.

Keys to Good Communication   Being aware of communication skills and actually using them are two separate matters. Furthermore, even though we may be comfortable sharing our feelings with another, we may find it more difficult to discuss our sexual preferences and needs. Self-disclosure, trust, and feedback are three keys to good communication.

> A little sincerity is a dangerous thing, and a great deal of it is absolutely fatal.
>
> —*Oscar Wilde (1854–1900)*

SELF-DISCLOSURE   Self-disclosure creates the environment for mutual understanding. Most people know us only through the conventional roles we play as female/male, wife/husband, parent/child, and so on. These roles, however, do not necessarily reflect our deepest selves. If we act as if we are nothing more than our roles, we may reach a point at which we no longer know who we are.

Through the process of **self-disclosure,** we not only reveal ourselves to others but also find out who we are. We discover feelings we have hidden, repressed, or ignored. We nurture forgotten aspects of ourselves by bringing them to the surface. Moreover, self-disclosure is reciprocal: In the process of our sharing, others share themselves with us. Men are less likely than women, however, to disclose intimate aspects of themselves (Lips, 1997). Because they have been taught to be "strong and silent," they are more reluctant to express feelings of tenderness or vulnerability. Women find it easier to disclose their feelings because they have been conditioned from childhood to express themselves (Tannen, 1990). These differences can drive wedges between men and women. Even when people cohabit or are married, they can feel lonely because there is no interpersonal contact. And the worst kind of loneliness is feeling alone when we are with someone to whom we want to feel close.

TRUST   When we talk about intimate relationships, the two words that most frequently pop up are "love" and "trust." Trust is the primary characteristic we associate with love. But what, exactly, is trust? **Trust** can be defined as a belief in the reliability and integrity of a person. When someone says, "Trust me," he or she is asking for something that does not easily occur. For trust to develop, several conditions must exist:

- *The relationship must have a strong likelihood of continuing.* We generally do not trust strangers or people we have just met with information that makes us vulnerable, such as our sexual anxieties. We trust people with whom we have a significant relationship.

- *Behavior must be predictable.* If we are married or in a committed relationship, we trust that our partner will not do something that will hurt us, such as become involved with another person. In fact, if we discover that our partner is involved with someone else, we often speak of our trust being violated or destroyed. If trust is destroyed, it is because the guarantee of sexual exclusiveness no longer exists.

- *Each person must have options.* If we were marooned on a desert island alone with our partner, she or he would have no choice but to be sexually monogamous. But if a third person, sexually attractive to our partner, swam ashore a year later, our partner would have an alternative. Our partner would then have a choice of being sexually exclusive or nonexclusive, and her or his behavior would be evidence of trustworthiness—or its absence.

Trust is critical in close relationships for two reasons. First, self-disclosure requires trust because it makes us vulnerable. A person will not self-disclose if he or she believes the information may be misused—by mocking or revealing a secret, for example. Second, the degree to which we trust a person influences how we interpret ambiguous or unexpected messages from him or her. If our partner says that he or she wants to study alone tonight, we are likely to take the statement at face value if we have a high level of trust. But if we have a low level of trust, we may believe that he or she actually will be meeting someone else.

Self-disclosure is reciprocal. If we self-disclose, we expect our partner to self-disclose as well. As we self-disclose, we build trust; as we withhold self-disclosure, we erode trust. To withhold ourselves is to imply that we don't trust the other person, and if we don't, she or he will not trust us.

FEEDBACK   A third critical element in communication is **feedback,** the ongoing process of restating, checking the accuracy of, questioning, and clarifying messages. If someone self-discloses to a partner, his or her response to that self-disclosure is feedback, and the partner's response is feedback to that feedback. It is a continuous process (Figure 8.1). The most important form of feedback for improving relationships is constructive feedback. Constructive feedback focuses on self-disclosing information that will help partners understand the consequences of their actions—for each other and for the relationship. For example, if your partner discloses her or his doubts about the relationship, you can respond in a number of ways. Among these are remaining silent, venting anger, expressing indifference, and giving constructive feedback. Of these responses, constructive feedback is the most likely to encourage positive change.

Ninety-nine lies may save you, but the hundredth will give you away.

—*West African proverb*

When in doubt, tell the truth.

—*Mark Twain (1835–1910)*

A half-truth is a whole lie.

—*Yiddish proverb*

GIVING CONSTRUCTIVE, effective feedback is an important skill in any intimate relationship. The following guidelines (developed by David Johnston for the Minnesota Peer Program) will help you engage in constructive dialogue and feedback with your partner:

1. *Focus on "I" statements.* An "I" statement is a statement about *your* feelings ("I feel unloved"). In contrast, "you" statements tell another person how *he* or *she* is, feels, or thinks ("You don't love me"). "You" statements are often blaming or accusatory. Because "I" messages don't carry blame, the recipient is less likely to be defensive or resentful.

2. *Focus on behavior rather than on the person.* If you focus on the behavior rather than on the person, you are more likely to secure change, because a person can change behaviors, but not him- or herself. If you want your partner to stimulate your clitoris, say, "I'd like you to touch my clitoris while we're making love because it would help me have an orgasm." This statement focuses on behavior that can be changed. If you say, "You're not a particularly hot lover," you are attacking the person, and he is likely to respond defensively: "Talk about crummy lovers—how come you need my help to have an orgasm? What's wrong with you?"

3. *Focus on observations rather than on inferences or judgments.* Focus your feedback on what you actually observe, not on what you think the behavior means. "I don't receive enough stimulation during intercourse to have an orgasm" is an observation about sexual activity. "You don't really care about how I feel because you never try to help me have an orgasm" is an inference about the partner's alleged lack of caring.

4. *Focus on observations based on a more-or-less continuum.* Behaviors fall on a continuum. Your partner doesn't *always* do or not do a particular thing. When you say your partner does something sometimes, or even most of the time, you are measuring behavior. "The last three times you wanted to make love I didn't want to because of the way you smelled" is a measuring statement; its accuracy can be tested. But if you say your partner *always* (or *never*) does something, you are probably distorting reality. "You *always* smell when you come to bed" or "You *never* take a shower before sex" is probably an exaggeration that may provoke a hostile response: "What do you mean? I showered last month. You got some kind of hang-up?"

5. *Focus on sharing ideas or offering alternatives rather than giving advice.* No one likes being told what to do. Un-

solicited advice often results in anger or resentment, because advice implies that you know more about what a person needs to do than she or he does. Advice implies a lack of respect. But by sharing ideas and offering alternatives, you give the other person the freedom to decide based on her or his own perceptions and goals. "What you need to do is pay attention to some of my needs" is advice. Compare that statement to this one: "I wish I could be more orgasmic in intercourse. Let's try some other things. If I had more clitoral stimulation, like your rubbing my clitoris when we are making love . . . something like that would be great. . . . Or I could stimulate myself. What do you think?" Such responses offer alternatives.

6. *Focus feedback according to its value for the recipient.* If your partner says something that upsets you, your initial response may be to lash back. A cathartic response may make you feel better at the time, but it may not be useful for your partner. For example, suppose your partner says that he or she has been faking orgasms. You can respond with anger or accusations, or you can express concern and try to find out why he or she felt it was necessary to do so.

7. *Focus feedback on the amount the recipient can process.* Don't overload your partner with your response. Your partner's disclosure may touch deep, pent-up feelings in you, but she or he may not be able to comprehend all that you say. If you respond to your partner's revelation of doubts about your relationship by listing all the doubts you have *ever* experienced about it, you may overwhelm her or him.

8. *Focus feedback at the appropriate time and place.* When you discuss anything of importance, choose an appropriate time and place so that nothing will distract you. Pick a time when you are not likely to be interrupted. Turn the television off, and put the answering machine on. Also, choose a time that is relatively stress-free. If you try to talk about something of great personal importance just before an exam or a business meeting, you are likely to sabotage the communication process. Finally, choose a place that will provide privacy; don't start an important conversation if you are worried about people overhearing or interrupting you. A crowded dormitory lounge, a kitchen filled with kids, a football stadium during a big game, a car full of people on the way to the beach—all are inappropriate places.

Incorporating these behaviors into your communication patterns will help you nurture your relationships in both the short and the long term.

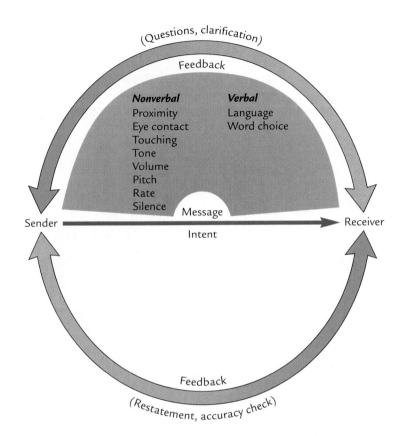

(Questions, clarification)

Feedback

Nonverbal   **Verbal**
Proximity   Language
Eye contact   Word choice
Touching
Tone
Volume
Pitch
Rate
Silence   Message

Sender   Intent   Receiver

Feedback

(Restatement, accuracy check)

FIGURE 8.1 Communication **Loop.** In successful communication, feedback between the sender and receiver ensures that both understand (or are trying to understand) what is being communicated. For communication to be clear, the message and the intent behind the message must be congruent. Nonverbal and verbal components must also support the intended message. Communication includes not just language and word choice but nonverbal characteristics such as tone, volume, pitch, rate, and silence.

CONFLICT AND INTIMACY

Conflict is the process in which people perceive incompatible goals and interference from others in achieving their goals. Conflict is a special type of communication.

We expect love to unify us, but sometimes it doesn't. Two people do not become one when they love each other, although at first they may have this feeling or expectation. Their love may not be an illusion, but their sense of ultimate oneness is. In reality, we retain our individual identities, needs, wants, and pasts—even while loving each other. It is a paradox that, the more intimate two people become, the more likely they are to experience conflict. In fact, a lack of arguing can signal trouble in a relationship because it may mean that issues are not being resolved or that there is indifference. Conflict itself is not dangerous to intimate relationships; it is the manner in which the conflict is handled. The presence of conflict does not necessarily indicate that love is waning or has disappeared. It may mean that love is *growing*.

Conflict in relationships is expressed differently by different ethnic groups. Whites tend to seek either dominance, which is confrontational and controlling, or integration, which is solution-oriented. They seem to believe that conflict is natural in a relationship, perhaps because of the high cultural value placed on individualism. Both African Americans and Mexican Americans view conflict less positively; they believe that conflict has both

Conflict is natural in intimate relationships because each person has her or his own unique identity, values, needs, and history.

short- and long-term negative effects. Whites tend to be more solution-oriented than African Americans, who tend to be more controlling. In interpersonal relationships, both groups tend to identify conflict in terms of issues and goals. In contrast, Mexican Americans view conflict more in relationship terms; conflict occurs when a relationship is out of balance or harmony (Collier, 1991).

These differing views of conflict and conflict resolution affect each group's willingness to deal with sexual conflicts. Understanding these differences will help in resolving sexual problems and issues.

Sexual Conflicts

Common practices such as using sex as a scapegoat for nonsexual problems and using arguments as a cover-up for other problems frequently lead to additional disagreements and misunderstandings. Clinging to these patterns can interfere with problem solving and inhibit conflict resolution.

Fighting About Sex   Fighting and sex can be intertwined in several ways. A couple may have a disagreement about sex that leads to a fight. For example, if one person wants to be sexual and the other does not, they may fight.

Sex can also be used as a scapegoat for nonsexual problems. If a man is angry because his partner has called him a lousy communicator, he may take it out on her sexually by calling her a lousy lover. They fight about their lovemaking rather than about the real issue, his communication role.

Finally, a fight can be a cover-up. If a man feels sexually inadequate and does not want to have sex as often as his partner, he may pick a fight and make her so angry that the last thing she would want to do is to be sexual with him.

It's difficult to tell during a fight if there are deeper causes than the one about which the partners are currently fighting. If two people repeatedly argue about sexual issues without ever resolving anything, the ostensible cause may not be the real one. If fighting does not clear the air and make intimacy possible again, the partners should look for other reasons for the fights. They need to discuss why the fights do not seem to accomplish anything. Specifically, they need to step back and look at what the circumstances of the fight are, what patterns occur, and how each of them feels before, during, and after a fight.

Men and women may differ in the ways that anger affects their sexual satisfaction. For example, it has been found that anxiety and anger reduce sexual desire in both sexes but that anger decreases women's sexual arousal more than it does men's (Beck & Bozman, 1995). A more recent study explored the linkages between the ways partners deal with angry feelings in their relationship and their level of sexual satisfaction (Belanger, Laughrea, & Lafontaine, 2001). A sample of 192 French-Canadian couples, age 25–65 and with an average length of marriage of 12 years, revealed that women's sexual satisfaction is affected by their own anger, but even more by their spouse's anger. In other words, the intensity of a husband's feelings toward his wife is the most significant predictor of her sexual dissatisfaction. The husband's sexual satisfaction is linked to his situational anger and his tendency to keep angry feelings toward his spouse to himself. These data suggest that women are more vulnerable to expressions of anger by their spouse and that they need to be in relationships with good communication and lower levels of conflict in order to have a satisfactory sexual response. In contrast, the link between anger and sexual satisfaction may be weaker for men, and their sexual response may be less influenced by their partner's expression of anger.

Relationships tend to follow a predictable pattern of satisfaction in the early years, a decrease in satisfaction during the childbearing years, and a return to a higher level after the children are grown. An awareness of this pattern can be helpful to couples whose levels of conflict are escalating. Acknowledging a relationship's changing nature and focusing on strengths that each person brings to the relationship are ways to adapt to the inevitable changes that occur over time.

Sexuality and Power Conflicts   In power struggles, sex can be used as a weapon, but this is generally a destructive tactic. A classic strategy for the weaker person in a relationship is to withhold something that the more powerful one wants. In male-female struggles, this is often sex. By withholding sex, a woman gains a certain degree of power. Men also use sex in its most violent form: They rape (including date rape and marital rape) to overpower and subordinate women (see Chapter 17).

IF YOU WANT to avoid intimacy, here are ten rules that have proved effective in nationwide testing with couples, lovers, husbands and wives, parents, and children. Follow these guidelines, and we guarantee you'll never have an intimate relationship.

1. *Don't talk.* This is the basic rule for avoiding intimacy. If you follow this one rule, you will never have to worry about being intimate again. Sometimes, however, you may be forced to talk. But don't talk about anything meaningful. Talk about the weather, sports, class, the stock market—anything but your feelings.

2. *Never show your feelings.* Showing your feelings is almost as bad as talking, because feelings are ways of communicating. If you cry or show anger, sadness, or joy, you are giving yourself away. You might as well talk, and if you talk, you could become intimate. So, the best thing to do is to remain expressionless (which, we acknowledge, is a form of communication, but at least it's sending the message that you don't want to be intimate).

3. *Always be pleasant.* Always smile and act friendly, especially if something's bothering you. You'll be surprised at how effective hiding negative feelings from your partner is in preventing intimacy. It may even fool your partner into believing that everything's OK in your relationship.

4. *Always win.* If you can't be pleasant, try this one. Never compromise; never admit that your partner's point of view may be as valid as yours. If you start compromising, it's an acknowledgment that you care about your partner's feelings, which is a dangerous step on the road to intimacy.

5. *Always keep busy.* Keeping busy at school or work will take you away from your partner, and you won't have to be intimate. Your partner may never figure out that you're using work to avoid intimacy. Because our culture values hard work, he or she will feel unjustified in complaining. Devoting yourself to your work will give your partner the message that he or she is not as important as your work. You can make your partner feel unimportant in your life without even talking!

6. *Always be right.* There is nothing worse than being wrong, because it is an indication that you are human. If you admit that you're wrong, you might have to acknowledge that your partner's right, and that will make her or him as good as you. If she or he is as

good as you, then you might have to view your partner as an equal, and before you know it, you will be intimate!

7. *Never argue.* If you can't always be right, don't argue at all. If you argue, you might discover that you and your partner are different. If you're different, you may have to talk about the differences in order to make adjustments. And if you begin making adjustments, you may have to tell your partner who you really are and what you really feel. Naturally, these revelations may lead to intimacy.

8. *Make your partner guess what you want.* Never tell your partner what you want. That way, when your partner tries to guess and is wrong (as he or she often will be), you can tell your partner that he or she doesn't really understand or love you. If your partner did love you, he or she would know what you want without asking. Not only will this prevent intimacy, but it will drive your partner crazy as well.

9. *Always look out for number one.* Remember, you are number one. All relationships exist to fulfill your needs and no one else's. Whatever you feel like doing is just fine. You're OK; your partner's not OK. If your partner can't satisfy your needs, she or he is narcissistic; after all, you are the one making all the sacrifices in the relationship.

10. *Keep the television or computer turned on at all times.* Do so while you're eating dinner, while you're reading, when you're in bed, and while you're talking (especially if you're talking about something important). This rule may seem petty compared with the others, but it is good preventive action. Watching television or using the computer keeps you and your partner from talking to each other. Best of all, it will keep you both from even noticing that you don't communicate. If you're cornered and have to talk, you can both be distracted by a commercial, a seduction scene, or a more interesting conversation in a chat room. And when you actually think about it, wouldn't you rather be watching *Seinfeld* reruns anyway?

This list is not complete. Everyone knows additional ways for avoiding intimacy. These may be your own inventions or techniques you have learned from your friends or parents. To round out this compilation, list additional rules for avoiding intimacy on a separate sheet of paper. The person with the best list wins—and never has to be intimate again.

In long-term gay relationships, refusing sex can take on symbolic meaning. Refusing sex is sometimes associated with power struggles between two sex initiators (Blumstein & Schwartz, 1983). Because initiating sex is associated with power and dominance, two male partners being sexually assertive can become a form of competition. The man who feels himself to be less powerful can try to reassert his power by refusing his partner's sexual advances. In many lesbian relationships, power issues are disguised because of the commitment of both partners to equality. In these cases, power struggles are often indirect and obscure. Sexual rejection or lack of interest may mask issues of power.

Genuine intimacy appears to require equality in power relationships. Decision making in the happiest relationships seems to be based, not on coercion or "tit for tat," but on a sense of caring, mutuality, and respect for the other person. Women who feel vulnerable to their mates may withhold feelings or pretend to feel what they do not. Unequal power may encourage power politics, as each partner struggles to keep or gain power.

It is not easy to change unequal power relationships after they become embedded in the overall structure of a relationship, yet they can be changed. Talking, trying to understand, and negotiating are the best approaches. Still, in attempting changes, a person may risk estrangement or the breakup of a relationship. He or she must weigh the possible gains against the possible losses in deciding whether change is worth the risk.

Conflict Resolution

The way in which couples deal with conflict reflects and perhaps contributes to their relationship happiness. Partners who communicate with affection and interest and who integrate humor when appropriate can use such positive affect to defuse conflict (Gottman & Carrere, 2000).

For a marriage to be peaceful, the husband should be deaf and the wife blind.

—*Spanish proverb*

Strategies for Resolving Conflicts   There are several ways to end conflicts. We can give in, but unless we believe that the conflict ended fairly, we are likely to feel resentful. We can try to impose our will through the use of power, force, or the threat of force. But using power to end conflict leaves the partner with the bitter taste of injustice. Or we can end the conflict through negotiation. In negotiations, the partners discuss their differences until they come to a mutually acceptable agreement.

Sometimes, even if we sincerely commit ourselves to working out our problems, it is difficult to see our own role in sustaining a pattern of interaction. If partners are unable to resolve their conflicts, they should consider entering relationship counseling. A therapist or other professional can often help identify underlying problems, as well as help couples develop negotiating skills.

Conflict Resolution and Relationship Satisfaction   Happy couples tend to act in positive ways to resolve conflicts, such as changing behaviors (putting the cap on the toothpaste rather than denying responsibility) and presenting reasonable alternatives (purchasing toothpaste in a pump dispenser). Unhappy or distressed couples, in contrast, use more negative strategies in attempting to resolve conflicts ("If the cap off the toothpaste bothers you, then put it on"). A study of happily and unhappily married couples found distinctive communication traits as these couples tried to resolve their conflicts (Ting-Toomey, 1983). The happily married couples displayed the following communication behaviors:

- *Summarizing.* Each person summarized what the other said ("Let me see if I can repeat the different points you were making").

- *Paraphrasing.* Each put what the other said into her or his own words ("What you are saying is that you feel bad when I don't acknowledge your feelings").

- *Validating.* Each affirmed the other's feelings ("If I were in the same situation, I would probably feel the same way").

- *Clarifying.* Each asked for further information to make sure that he or she understood what the other was saying ("Can you explain what you mean a little bit more to make sure that I understand you?").

In contrast, unhappily married couples displayed the following reciprocal patterns:

- *Confronting.* Each member of the couple confronted ("You're frigid!" "Not me, buddy. It's you who can't get it up").

- *Confronting and acting defensive.* One confronted while the other defended him- or herself ("You're a lousy lover!" "I did what you told me you wanted, and you still can't come").

- *Complaining and acting defensive.* One complained while the other was defensive ("I try to please you but it still does no good!" "I am too tired and distracted").

> Hatred does not cease by hatred at any time. Hatred ceases by love. This is an unalterable law.
>
> —*Siddhartha Gautama, the Buddha*
> (c. 563–483 B.C.)

Negotiating Conflicts   Conflicts can be solved through negotiation in three major ways: agreement as a gift, bargaining, and coexistence.

AGREEMENT AS A GIFT   If partners disagree on an issue, one can freely agree with the other as a gift. For example, if a woman wants her partner to stimulate her clitoris, and he doesn't want to because he feels it reflects badly on him, he can agree to try it because he cares about his partner. Similarly, a woman who does not want to perform oral sex can do so as a gift of caring. Neither, however, needs to continue if the activity remains objectionable.

Agreement as a gift is different from giving in. When we give in, we do something we don't want to do. But when we agree without coercion or threats, the agreement is a gift of love. It's acceptance in its best form—loving a partner not in spite of the differences but because of them. As in all exchanges of gifts, there will be reciprocation: Our partner will be more likely to give us a gift of agreement in return.

BARGAINING   Bargaining means making compromises. But bargaining in relationships is different from bargaining in the marketplace or in politics. In relationships, partners want not the best deal for themselves but the most equitable deal for *both* partners. At all points during the bargaining process, they need to keep in mind what is best for the relationship, as well as for themselves, and to trust each other to do the same. In a relationship, both partners need to win. The purpose of conflict resolution in a relationship is to solidify the relationship, not to make one partner the winner and the other the loser. Achieving our ends by exercising coercive power or withholding love, affection, or sex is a destructive form of bargaining. If we get what we want, how will that affect our partner and the relationship? Will he or she feel that we're being unfair and become resentful? A solution has to be fair to both partners, or it won't enhance the relationship.

COEXISTENCE   Sometimes, differences can't be resolved, but they can be lived with. If a relationship is sound, differences can be absorbed without undermining the basic ties. All too often, we regard differences as threatening rather than as the unique expression of two personalities. If one person likes to masturbate, the partner can accept it as an expression of her or his unique sexuality. Coexistence focuses on the person we have the most power over—ourself.

IF WE CAN'T TALK about what we like and what we want, there is a good chance we won't get either one. Communication is the basis for good sex and good relationships. Communication and intimacy are reciprocal: Communication creates intimacy, and intimacy, in turn, creates good communication. If we fail to communicate, we are likely to turn our relationships into empty facades. Each person acts according to a role rather than revealing his or her deepest self. But communication is learned behavior. If we have learned *not* to communicate, we can learn *how* to communicate. Communication allows us to expand ourselves and to feel more connected to and intimate with another person.

SUMMARY

The Nature of Communication

- The ability to communicate is important in developing and maintaining relationships. Partners satisfied with their sexual communication tend to be satisfied with their relationship as a whole.

- *Communication* is a transactional process by which we use symbols, such as words, gestures, and movements, to establish human contact, exchange information, and reinforce or change the attitudes and behaviors of ourselves and others.

- Communication takes place within cultural, social, and psychological contexts. The cultural context refers to the language that is used and to the values, beliefs, and customs associated with it. Ethnic groups communicate about sex differently, depending on their language patterns and values. The social context refers to the roles we play in society that influence our communication. The most

important roles affecting sexuality are those relating to gender and sexual orientation. The psychological context refers to our personality characteristics, such as having positive or negative feelings about sex.

- Communication is both verbal and nonverbal. The ability to correctly interpret nonverbal messages is important in successful relationships. *Proximity*, eye contact, and touching are especially important forms of nonverbal communication.

Sexual Communication

- In initial encounters, physical appearance is especially important. Because of the *halo effect*, we infer positive qualities about people based on their appearance. Women typically send nonverbal cues to men indicating interest; men often begin a conversation with an opening line.

- The "first move" marks the transition to physical intimacy. In initiating the first sexual interaction, people generally keep their communication non-verbal, ambiguous, and indirect. Sexual disinterest is usually communicated nonverbally. With sexual involvement, the couple must communicate verbally about contraception, STI prevention, and sexual likes and dislikes.

▪ Unless there are definite clues as to sexual orientation, gay men and lesbian women try to determine through nonverbal cues whether others are appropriate partners. Because of male gender roles, gay men initiate sex earlier than heterosexuals; for parallel reasons, lesbian women initiate sex later.

▪ In established heterosexual relationships, many women feel more comfortable in initiating sexual interactions than in newer relationships. Sexual initiations are more likely to be accepted in established relationships; sexual disinterest is communicated verbally. Women do not restrict sexual activities any more than do men.

▪ Research indicates that happy couples disclose private thoughts and feelings to partners, express equal levels of affective disclosure, spend more time together talking or expressing feelings in positive ways, are willing to engage in conflict in nondestructive ways, have less frequent conflict and spend less time in conflict, and accurately encode and decode messages.

▪ There are gender differences in partner communication. Women send clearer messages; men tend to send negative messages or withdraw; and women tend to set the emotional tone and escalate arguments more than men.

Developing Communication Skills

▪ Achieving self-awareness is an important first step in developing communication skills. Obstacles to talking about sex include a lack of role models, fear of being identified as "bad," cultural and personal taboos about unacceptable sexual subjects, and a lack of adequate vocabulary. Sexual vocabulary shifts according to the context.

▪ The keys to effective communication are self-disclosure, trust, and feedback. *Self-disclosure* is the revelation of intimate information about ourselves. *Trust* is the belief in the reliability and integrity of another person. *Feedback* is a constructive response to another's self-disclosure.

Conflict and Intimacy

▪ *Conflict* is natural in intimate relationships. Conflicts about sex can be specific disagreements about sex, arguments that are ostensibly about sex but that are really about nonsexual issues, or disagreements about the wrong sexual issue.

▪ In resolving conflicts, happy couples communicate by summarizing, paraphrasing, validating, and clarifying. Unhappy couples use confrontation, confrontation and defensiveness, and complaints and defensiveness. Conflict resolution may be achieved through negotiation in three ways: agreement as a freely given gift, bargaining, and coexistence.

Sex and the Internet

Family and Relationships

Recommendations on and insights into relationships are just a click away. The American Psychological Association (APA) has one such Web site that addresses a broad range of mental and emotional issues that individuals, couples, and families face (http://helping.apa.org/family/index.html). Access the site, click on "Family & Relationships," and, depending on your background and interests, select any one of the following:

▪ What Is Needed for a Good Marriage

▪ Interventions That Help Stepfamilies

▪ Single Parenting and Today's Families

Once you have read the article, answer the following questions:

▪ What situation in your life drew you to this topic?

▪ How do your observations and experiences related to this topic compare to the author's?

▪ What suggestions might you make to others regarding this issue?

▪ Can you make additional statements that might help others understand this topic?

You may also wish to explore some of the other topics that interest you.

SUGGESTED WEB SITES

American Association for Marriage and Family Therapy
http://aamft.org/index_nm.org
Provides referrals to therapists, books, and articles that address family and relationship problems and issues.

International Association for Relationship Research
http://www.sspr.org
An interdisciplinary organization of professionals interested in all aspects of personal relationships.

National Sexuality Resource Center
http://nsrc.sfsu.edu/Index
Seeks to create dialogues between the public, researchers, and community advocates, and provides links to sexuality-related organizations and research; is a sponsor of *American Sexuality* magazine.

Sex and Communication
http://www.health.arizona.edu/
Answers questions about sexuality and communication in the "Sexual Health" section of the Health Education On-Line Library.

Third Age: Love and Sex
http://www.thirdage.com/romance/
Explores ways of enhancing marriage, discusses the art of flirting, and introduces ways to reconnect with oneself.

SUGGESTED READING

Christensen, Andrew, & Jacobson, Neil. (2000). *Reconcilable Differences*. New York: Guilford Press. An argument that acceptance rather than change may be the key to a happier marriage.

Fletcher, Garth. (2002). *The New Science of Intimate Relationships*. Oxford, UK: Blackwell. By showcasing scientific work on intimate relationships, counters many of the stereotypes and misperceptions fostered by popular psychology books.

Gottman, John. (2002). *The Seven Principles for Making Marriage Work*. Waltham, MA: Adobe Systems. The results of a 10-year study of couples' patterns of communication.

Satir, Virginia. (1988). *The New Peoplemaking* (Rev. ed.). Palo Alto, CA: Science and Behavior Books. One of the most influential (and easy-to-read) books of the past 25 years on communication and family relationships.

Tannen, Deborah. (1998). *You Just Don't Understand: Women and Men in Conversation*. New York: HarperCollins. A best-selling, intelligent, and lively discussion of how women use communication to achieve intimacy and men use communication to achieve independence.

Ting-Toomey, Stella, & Korzenny, Felipe (Eds.). (1991). *Cross-Cultural Interpersonal Communication*. Newbury Park, CA: Sage. A ground-breaking collection of scholarly essays on communication and relationships among different ethnic and cultural groups, including African American, Latino, Korean, and Chinese ethnic groups and cultures.

For links, articles, and study material, go to the McGraw-Hill Web site, located at http://www.mhhe.com/strong5

9

Sexual
Expression

"*I remember the first time one of my girlfriends told me she went down on a guy. I was seventeen and she was eighteen. We were still in high school. I thought it was the grossest thing and couldn't imagine doing it. I'm embarrassed to admit that I kind of thought she was a slut. Then, a few months later, I tried it with my boyfriend. Then I began to feel like a slut.*"

—20-year-old White female

"*It's funny now how easy it is to talk about masturbation. When you get to college, some of the taboo is lifted from the subject, at least between the guys, I think. When someone brings up masturbating, we all kind of have that uncomfortable moment, but then we get into talking about when our last time was, how often, how we administer clean-up, techniques. It has become a normal subject with us. Considering how many males I have spoken to about masturbation, I think it is less taboo than thought.*"

—20-year-old White male

"*It bothers me as a woman that other women, or at least several I have come in contact with, feel that it is nasty for their partners to please them orally but have no problem pleasing their partners that way. That's crazy!*"

—21-year-old Black female

"*I grew up thinking that I would wait until I got married before having sex. It was not just a religious or moral issue—it was more about being a "good" girl. When I went away to college, some of my new friends were sexually active and had more open thoughts about having sex. I did have sex with someone during my first year in college, but afterwards I felt really embarrassed about it. When some of my friends at home found out, they were really shocked as well. Even though my first sexual relationship was one full of love and commitment, these feelings of shame and embarrassment and shock kept me from sleeping with my boyfriend for the next four months. I really struggled with the "good girl" versus "slut" extreme images I had grown up with.*"

—29-year-old White female

SEXUAL EXPRESSION is a complex process through which we reveal our sexual selves. Sexual expression involves more than simply sexual behaviors; it involves our feelings as well. "Behavior can never be unemotional," one scholar observes (Blechman, 1990). As human beings, we do not separate feelings from behavior, including sexual behavior. Our sexual behaviors are rich with emotions, ranging from love to anxiety and from desire to antipathy.

To fully understand our sexuality, we need to examine our sexual behaviors *and* the emotions we experience along with them. If we studied sexual activities apart from our emotions, we would distort the meaning of human sexuality. It would make our sexual behaviors appear mechanistic, nothing more than genitals rubbing against each other.

In this chapter, we discuss sexual attractiveness. Next, we turn to sexual scripts that give form to our sexual drives. Finally, we examine the most

Sex is one of the nine reasons for reincarnation. . . . The other eight are unimportant.

—*Henry Miller (1891–1980)*

277

common sexual behaviors, both autoerotic, such as fantasies and masturbation, and interpersonal, such as oral-genital sex, sexual intercourse, and anal eroticism. When we discuss sexual behaviors, we cite results from numerous studies to illustrate the prevalence of those behaviors in our society. These results most often represent self-reports of a certain group of people. As discussed in Chapter 2, self-reporting of sexual behavior is not always exact or unbiased. The research data provide only a general idea of what behaviors actually occur and do not indicate how people should express their sexuality or what "normal" behavior is. Sexuality is one of the most individualistic aspects of life; each of us has our own sexual values, needs, and preferences.

SEXUAL ATTRACTIVENESS

After people are clothed and fed, then they think about sex.

—*K'ung-Fu-tzu (Confucius)*
(551–479 B.C.)

Sexual attractiveness is an important component in sexual expression. As we shall see, however, there are few universals in what people from different cultures consider attractive.

A Cross-Cultural Analysis

In a landmark cross-cultural survey, Clelland Ford and Frank Beach (1951) discovered that there appear to be only two characteristics that women and men universally consider important in terms of sexual attractiveness: youthfulness and good health. All other aspects may vary significantly from culture to culture. Even though this large survey was conducted a half century ago, subsequent smaller and more local studies support the importance of youthfulness and good health in sexual attraction, as well as the significance of culture in determining sexual attractiveness. One might ask why youthfulness and health were the only universals identified by Ford and Beach. Why not other body traits, such as a certain facial feature or body type?

Although we may never find an answer, sociobiologists offer a possible (but untestable) explanation. They theorize, as we saw in Chapter 1, that all animals instinctively want to reproduce their own genes. Consequently, both humans and other animals adopt certain reproductive strategies. One of these strategies is choosing a mate capable of reproducing one's offspring. Men prefer women who are young because young women are the most likely to be fertile. Good health is also related to reproductive potential, because healthy women are more likely to be both fertile and capable of rearing their children. Evolutionary psychologist David Buss (1994) notes that our ancestors looked for certain physical characteristics that indicated a woman's health and youthfulness. Buss identifies certain physical features that are cross-culturally associated with beauty: good muscle tone; full lips; clear, smooth skin; lustrous hair; and clear eyes. Our ancestors also looked for behavioral cues such as animated facial expressions; a bouncy, youthful gait; and a high energy level. These observable physical cues to youthfulness and health (and hence to reproductive capacity) constitute the standards of beauty in many cultures.

Vitality and health are important to human females as well. Women prefer men who are slightly older than they are, because an older man is likely

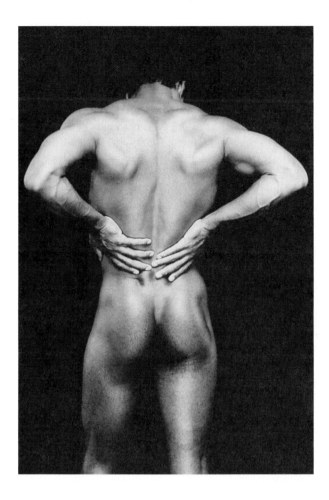

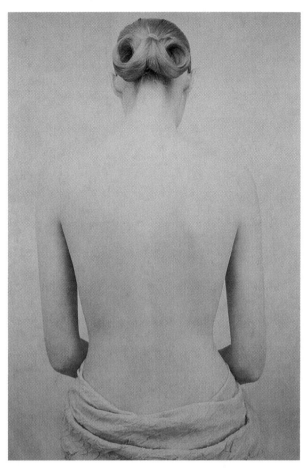

Cultures that agree on which body parts are erotic may still disagree on what constitutes attractiveness.

to be more stable and mature and to have greater resources to invest in children. Similarly, in the animal kingdom, females choose mates who provide resources, such as food and protection. Among American women, Buss (1994) points out, countless studies indicate that economic security and employment are much more important for women than for men. If you look in the personal ads in any newspaper, you'll find this gender difference readily confirmed. A woman's ad typically reads: "Lively, intelligent woman seeks professional, responsible gentleman for committed relationship." A man's ad typically reads: "Financially secure, fit man looking for attractive woman interested in having a good time. Send photo."

Women also prefer men who are in good health and physically fit so as to be a good provider. If a woman chooses someone with hereditary health problems, she risks passing on his poor genes to her children. Furthermore, an unhealthy partner is more likely to die sooner, cutting the woman and her children off from resources. Ford and Beach (1951) found that signs of ill health (including open sores, lesions, and excessive pallor) are universally considered unattractive.

Aside from youthfulness and good health, however, Ford and Beach found no universal standards of physical sexual attractiveness. In fact, they noted considerable variation from culture to culture in what parts of the body are considered erotic. In some cultures, the eyes are the key to sexual attractiveness; in others, it is height and weight; and in still others, the size and shape of the genitals matter most. In our culture, female breasts, for example, are considered erotic; in others, they are not.

Cultures that agree on which body parts are erotic may still disagree on what constitutes attractiveness. In terms of female beauty, American culture considers a slim body attractive. But worldwide, Americans are in the minority, for the type of female body most desired cross-culturally is plump. Similarly, we prefer slim hips, but in the majority of cultures in Ford and Beach's study, wide hips were most attractive. In our culture, large breasts are ideal, but others prefer small breasts or long and pendulous breasts. In recent years, well-defined pectoral, arm, and abdominal muscles have become part of the ideal male body.

Although attractiveness is important, looks certainly aren't everything. In a study spanning an amazing 57 years, undergraduate male and female college students rated the importance of 18 mate characteristics, including "good looks" (Buss, Shackelford, Kirkpatrick, & Larsen, 2001). Ratings were obtained using a questionnaire at one college in 1939 and 1956, four colleges in 1967 and 1977, and three colleges in 1996 in various locations across the United States. This longitudinal comparison allowed the researchers to determine which important characteristics in a mate had changed and if there were gender differences in ratings during the half century of dramatic cultural changes. One cultural change noted by the researchers was the proliferation of visual images of physically attractive models and actors via television, movies, and the Internet. The researchers explain: "From an evolutionary psychological perspective, such images may 'trick' our evolved mating mechanisms, deluding us into believing that we are surrounded by hundreds of attractive partners, as well as hundreds of potential intrasexual competitors." They ask whether this profusion of visual images in the twentieth century elevated the ranking of physical attractiveness relative to other traits.

Several patterns were identified across the 57-year span (Figure 9.1). Mutual attraction and love, dependable character, emotional maturity and stability, and pleasing disposition were rated highly at all times, suggesting that physical attractiveness is not the most important trait in mate selection. However, over the years, a large shift occurred in the importance of good looks for both genders. For men, it jumped from 14th in 1939 to 8th in 1996; for women, it increased from 17th in 1939 to 13th in 1996. The surge of media images of attractive people may have contributed to this shift. Certainly, the popularity of cosmetics, diet, cosmetic surgery, exercise programs, and drugs reflect this increasing value of physical attractiveness. Interestingly, the researchers note that the order of importance for both the male and female college students converged during the five decades, with the ordering showing maximum similarity in 1996. Also, domestic skills plummeted in importance for male students over the decades.

Adam Cohen and Hara Tannenbaum (2001) investigated physical attraction among nonheterosexual women by asking samples of lesbian and bisexual women to rate the figures of women according to weight (slender or heavy), waist-to-hip ratio (0.7 or 1.0), and breast size (small or large). The researchers found that the subjects preferred a heavy figure with the 0.7 waist-to-hip ratio and large breasts, rather than the low waist-to-hip ratio,

A pair of powerful spectacles has sometimes sufficed to cure a person in love.

—*Friedrich Nietzsche (1844–1900)*

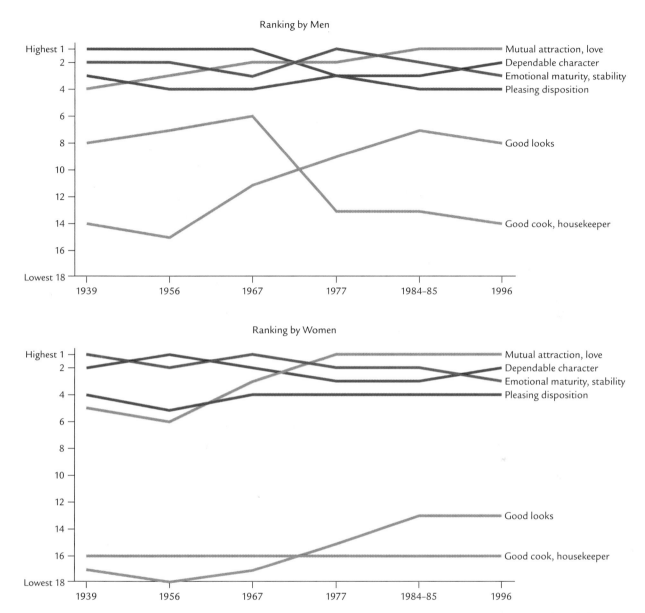

FIGURE 9.1 Rank Ordering of Mate Characteristics by College Undergraduates Across Six Decades, by Gender. (*Source:* Adapted from Buss, Shackelford, Kirkpatrick, & Larsen, 2001.)

large breasts, and slender figure preferred by most heterosexual females and males. In interpreting the results, the researchers note that lesbian women are heavier on average than heterosexual women and are more comfortable with their body weight, and that their preference for heavy body weight may be a rejection of an inappropriate societal fixation on thinness.

The Halo Effect Revisited

As discussed in Chapter 8, attractive people experience a halo effect—an effect that extends to assumptions about sexuality. A study of men from two universities revealed that, among the various traits attributed to attractive

HOW MUCH SEXUAL DESIRE is "normal," and what can couples do when one partner has more—or less—desire than the other? David Schnarch (2002) observes: "Couples frequently argue about low desire, but their real issue is *difference* in desires. Neither partner's desire need be particularly low or high. Disparity in sexual desire is couples' most common sexual complaint."

Although there is a great deal of variability in sexual desire, it is generally held that "healthy" individuals experience desire regularly and take advantage of appropriate opportunities for sexual expression when they arise. Individuals who are persistently uninterested in sexual expression and do not have sexual fantasies are said to be experiencing hypoactive sexual desire disorder (American Psychiatric Association [APA], 1994). For such individuals, therapy may be recommended.

Of course, terms like "regularly," "appropriate," and "persistent" are highly subjective. The *Diagnostic and Statistical Manual of Mental Disorders* (4th ed., text revision) of the APA uses these terms to avoid defining low desire in terms of frequency of sexual activity, because some people have sex out of feelings of obligation or coercion rather than interest or desire. Instead, the manual defines desire in terms of individuals' feelings and encourages clinical evaluation when a problem is experienced.

Regardless of measurements and clinical judgments, it is apparent to couples when one individual is more interested in sex than the other. Sometimes, differences arise because one or both partners may be fatigued, stressed, ill, under the influence of alcohol or other drugs, or consumed with the tasks of daily life. Or there may be problems with the couple or sexual relationship. Issues like these can often be resolved through honest discussion and feedback and changes in behavior. Elements contributing to a successful outcome in any discussion of sex include being aware, taking enough time to talk about it, using positive communication, and having a sense of humor.

Often, problems arise because individuals' expectations are based on unrealistic fantasy, media influences, or lack of information. A woman may, for instance, ask herself why she is unable to reach orgasm during intercourse, or a man may wonder why he does not get an erection even though he wants to have intercourse. In the case of the woman, is she aware of the effects of clitoral stimulation? Has she practiced stimulation techniques on herself and effectively demonstrated them to her partner? Does she position herself during intercourse so as to maximize the opportunities for stimulation? If she knows that most women require prolonged and effective amounts of stimulation up to and through orgasm, she may be able to enjoy intercourse more fully and may then feel more desire.

In the case of the man, does he know that erectile difficulties are a fairly common and often temporary

---

women, the trait most affected by their appearance was their sexual behavior (Tanke, 1982). Attractive women were viewed as more sexually receptive, exciting, and permissive than unattractive ones.

Although most studies on sexuality and attractiveness relate to beliefs about attractive people, an intriguing study of 100 college women found some evidence indicating a relationship between attractiveness and sexual behavior (Stelzer, Desmond, & Price, 1987). The so-called attractive women were significantly more likely to engage in sexual intercourse and oral sex and to be on top during intercourse than were the other women (Blumstein & Schwartz, 1983). This finding suggests that the halo effect may create a self-fulfilling expectation about sexual behavior: Because attractive women are *expected* to be more sexually active, they *become* more sexually active.

Sexual Desire

Desire can exist separately from overtly physical sexual expression. As discussed in Chapter 3, desire is the psychobiological component that motivates sexual behavior. But almost no scientific research exists on sexual desire. One of the most important reasons researchers have avoided studying it is that desire is difficult to define and quantify.

The degree and kind of a person's sexuality reaches up into the ultimate pinnacle of his spirit.

—*Friedrich Nietzsche*

problem? Does he know what kinds and amounts of stimulation are most effective for him? Does he feel comfortable fantasizing? Has he told his partner what he likes? Has he tried to discover noncoital means of pleasure with his partner? Once again, open and honest communication is the key to successful sexual interactions.

When the situation is partner-specific—that is, each person masturbates successfully and/or desires or fantasizes about others but does not desire or respond to a given partner—the problem is obviously more complex. The partners may be bored with each other or with the way they make love, or they may fear pregnancy or STIs. Other factors that interfere with desire and arousal are anger, depression, and relationship issues such as an imbalance of power between the partners. Some prescription drugs have been shown to reduce sexual desire and inhibit orgasm. When this is the case, individuals and couples may require the help of a physician or therapist.

If you and your partner are experiencing problems stemming from differences in desire, some simple techniques can increase interest and provide novelty in the bedroom. To set the stage, find a place where you are assured of no interruptions or distractions. Allow enough time to discover each other again. Approach lovemaking with an open mind, mutual respect, and a sense of humor and fun. And try some of these techniques:

1. Find a different location to be sexual—in the bathroom or shower, on the floor or in the pool, or in a hotel room.

2. Undress each other slowly, taking time to touch and to savor the removal of each article of clothing.

3. Use erotic films that appeal to each of you. If you don't have the same taste, alternate videos from time to time.

4. Prolong pleasuring and foreplay by using body oils and lotions; give each other erotic massages.

5. Bathe together, taking the time to wash and enjoy each other.

6. If you are comfortable doing so, use sex toys such as vibrators or feathers.

7. Share sexual fantasies, using graphic language if you are comfortable with it.

8. Tell each other what feels good.

Because fluctuations in individual sexual desire are a normal part of life, as are differences in desire between partners, individuals may choose masturbation as an acceptable and pleasurable outlet for sexual desire. Like all areas of sexual functioning, the important thing to remember, when sexual appetites differ, is that open and honest communication paves the way to resolution and fulfillment. Schnarch (2002) notes: "Long-term sexual desire in a committed relationship is more determined by self-respect and respect for your partner than it is by hormones and hardware. Fortunately, the process of resolving your sexual problem can increase your sexual desire, and mutual respect, in ways you've never dreamed."

Sexual desire is affected by erotophilia and erotophobia. Recall that erotophilia is a positive emotional response to sexuality, and erotophobia is a negative emotional response to sexuality. The Sexual Opinion Survey (SOS), which appears in Chapter 2, measures erotophilia and erotophobia. If you haven't done so already, take the SOS to get an idea of your own emotional response to sexuality.

In recent years, researchers have hypothesized that where someone falls on the erotophilic/erotophobic continuum strongly influences his or her overt sexual behavior (Fisher, 1986, 1998). In contrast to erotophobic individuals, for example, erotophilic men and women accept and enjoy their sexuality, experience less sex guilt, seek out sexual situations, engage in more autoerotic and interpersonal sexual activities, enjoy talking about sex, and are more likely to engage in certain sexual health practices, such as obtaining and using contraception. Furthermore, erotophilic people are more likely to have positive sexual attitudes, to engage in more involved sexual fantasies, to be less homophobic, and to have seen more erotica than erotophobic people. A person's emotional response to sex is also linked to how she or he evaluates other aspects of sex. Erotophilic individuals, for example, tend to evaluate sexually explicit material more positively.

Erotophilic and erotophobic traits are not fixed. Positive experiences can alter erotophobic responses over time. In fact, some therapy programs work on the assumption that consistent positive behaviors, such as loving, affirming, caring, touching, and communicating, can do much to diminish the fear of sex. Positive sexual experiences can help dissolve much of the anxiety that underlies erotophobia.

SEXUAL SCRIPTS

As you will recall from Chapter 5, gender roles have a huge impact on how we behave sexually, for sexual behaviors and feelings depend more on learning than on biological drives. Our sexual drives can be molded into almost any form. What is "natural" is what society says is natural; there is very little spontaneous, unlearned behavior. Sexual behavior, like all other forms of social behavior (such as courtship, classroom behavior, and sports), relies on scripts.

As you will also recall from Chapter 5, scripts are like plans that organize and give direction to our behavior. The **sexual scripts** we receive strongly influence our sexual activities as men and women in our culture. John Gagnon (1977) writes:

> A script is simpler than the activity we perform. . . . It is like a blueprint or roadmap or recipe, giving directions but not specifying everything that must be done. Regardless of its sketchiness, the script is often more important than the concrete acts. It is our script that we carry from action to action, modified by our concrete acts, but not replaced by them. Scripts do change, as new elements are added and old elements are reworked, but very few people have the desire, energy, or persistence to create highly innovative or novel scripts.

Our sexual scripts have several distinct components:

- *Cultural.* The cultural component provides the general pattern that sexual behaviors are expected to take. Our cultural script, for example, emphasizes heterosexuality, gives primacy to sexual intercourse, and discourages masturbation.

- *Intrapersonal.* The intrapersonal component deals with the internal and physiological states that lead to, accompany, or identify sexual arousal, such as a pounding heart and an erection or vaginal lubrication.

- *Interpersonal.* The interpersonal component involves the shared conventions and signals that enable two people to engage in sexual behaviors, such as body language, words, and erotic touching.

Cultural Scripting

Our culture sets the general contours of our sexual scripts. It tells us which behaviors are acceptable ("moral" or "normal") and which are unacceptable ("immoral" or "abnormal"). Among middle-class White Americans, the norm is a sequence of sexual events consisting of kissing, genital caressing, and sexual intercourse. If large numbers of people did not share these conventions, there would be sexual chaos. Imagine a scenario in which two people from different cultures try to initiate a sexual encounter. The person from our culture follows our culture's sexual sequence, while the one from a different

Many are saved from sin by being inept at it.

—*Mignon McLaughlin*

In our society, passionate kissing is part of the cultural script for sexual interactions.

culture follows a sequence beginning with sexual intercourse, moving to genital caressing, and ending with passionate kissing. At least initially, such a couple might experience frustration and confusion as one partner tried to initiate the sexual encounter with kissing and the other with sexual intercourse.

Yet this kind of confusion occurs fairly often because there is not necessarily a direct correlation between what our culture calls erotic and what any particular individual calls erotic. Culture sets the general pattern, but there is too much diversity in terms of individual personality, socioeconomic status, and ethnicity for everybody to have exactly the same erotic script. Thus, sexual scripts can be highly ambiguous.

We may believe that everyone shares our own particular script, projecting our experiences onto others and assuming that they share our erotic definitions of objects, gestures, and situations. But often, they initially do not. Our partner may have come from a different socioeconomic or ethnic group or religious background and may have had different learning experiences. Each of us has to learn the other's sexual script and be able to complement and adjust to it. If our scripts are to be integrated, we must make our needs known through open and honest communication involving words, gestures, and movements. This is the reason many people view their first intercourse as something of a comedy or tragedy—or perhaps a little bit of both.

Intrapersonal Scripting

On the intrapersonal level, sexual scripts enable people to give meaning to their physiological responses. The meaning depends largely on the situation. An erection, for example, does not always mean sexual excitement. Young boys sometimes have erections when they are frightened, anxious, or worried. Upon awakening in the morning, men may experience erections that are unaccompanied by arousal. Adolescent girls sometimes experience sexual arousal without knowing what these sensations mean. They report them as funny, weird kinds of feelings, or as anxiety, fear, or an upset stomach. The sensations are not linked to a sexual script until the girl becomes older and her physiological states acquire a definite erotic meaning.

The intrapersonal script also determines what physiological events our minds will become aware of. During masturbation or intercourse, for example, an enormous number of physiological events occur simultaneously, but we are aware of only a few of them. These are the events we associate with sexual arousal, such as increasing heartbeat and tensing muscles. Others, such as curling toes, may not filter through to our consciousness.

Finally, intrapersonal scripts provide a sequence of body movements by acting as mechanisms that activate biological events and release tension. We learn, for example, that we may create an orgasm by manipulating the penis or clitoris during masturbation.

Interpersonal Scripting

The interpersonal level is the area of shared conventions, which make sexual activities possible. Very little of our public life is sexual. Yet there are signs and gestures—verbal and nonverbal—that define encounters as sexual. We make our sexual motives clear by the looks we exchange, the tone of our voices, the movements of our bodies, and other culturally shared phenomena. A bedroom or a hotel room, for example, is a potentially erotic location; a classroom, office, or factory is not. The movements we use in arousing ourselves or others are erotic activators. Within a culture, there are normative scripts leading to intimate sexual behavior.

People with little sexual experience, especially young adolescents, are often unfamiliar with sexual scripts. What do they do after kissing? Do they embrace? Caress above the waist? Below? Eventually, they learn a comfortable sequence based on cultural inputs and personal and partner preferences. For gay men and lesbian women, learning the sexual script is more difficult because it is socially stigmatized. The sexual script is also related to age. Older children and young adolescents often limit their scripts to kissing, holding hands, and embracing, and they feel completely satisfied. Kissing for them may be as exciting as intercourse for more experienced people. When the range of their scripts increases, they lose some of the sexual intensity of the earlier stages.

AUTOEROTICISM

Autoeroticism consists of sexual activities that involve only the self. Autoeroticism is an *intrapersonal* activity rather than an *interpersonal* one. It includes sexual fantasies, erotic dreams, masturbation, and other self-stimulation. A universal phenomenon in one form or another (Ford & Beach, 1951), autoeroticism is one of our earliest expressions of sexual stirrings. It is also one that traditionally has been condemned in our society. By condemning it, however, our culture sets the stage for the development of deeply negative and inhibitory attitudes toward sexuality.

Many people purchase or seek out materials and activities for their auto-erotic behaviors. In the National Health and Social Life Survey (NHSLS), researchers found that 41% of men and 16% of women had engaged in an autoerotic activity in the past year. The most common activities for men were viewing X-rated movies or videos (23%) and visiting clubs with nude or seminude dancers (22%). The most common activity among women was also viewing videos (11%), followed by visiting clubs and viewing sexually explicit books or magazines (4% each). Sixteen percent of men reported purchasing explicit books or magazines. Other activities included using vibrators and other sex toys and calling sex phone lines (Laumann, Gagnon, Michael, & Michaels, 1994).

Do people participate in autoerotic activities because they do not have a sex partner? The same survey found the opposite to be true (Laumann et al., 1994):

> Those who engage in relatively little autoerotic activity are less likely to prefer a wider range of sexual techniques, are less likely to have a partner, and if they have a partner, are less likely to have sex frequently or engage in oral or anal sex. Similarly, individuals who engage in different kinds of autoerotic activity more often find a wider range of practices appealing and are more likely to have had at least one partner with whom they have sex frequently. Individuals who frequently think about sex, masturbate, and have used some type of pornography/erotica within the last year are much more likely to report enacting more elaborate interpersonal sexual scripts.

Sexual Fantasies and Dreams

Men and women, but especially men, think about sex often. According to the NHSLS, 54% of men and 19% of women think about sex at least once a day; 43% of men and 67% of women think about sex a few times per week or per month (Laumann et al., 1994). According to Harold Leitenberg and Kris Henning (1995), about 95% of men and women say that they have had sexual fantasies in one context or another. And a *Details* magazine study of over 1700 college students reported that 94% of men and 76% of women think about sex at least once a day (Elliott & Brantley, 1997).

"A fantasy is a map of desire, mastery, escape, and obscuration," writes Nancy Friday (1980), "the navigational path we invent to steer ourselves between the reefs and shoals of anxiety, guilt, and inhibition." Erotic fantasy is probably the most universal of all sexual behaviors. Nearly everyone has experienced such fantasies, but because they touch on feelings or desires considered personally or socially unacceptable, they are not widely discussed. Furthermore, many people have "forbidden" sexual fantasies that they never act on.

Whether occurring spontaneously or resulting from outside stimuli, fantasies are part of the body's regular healthy functioning. Research indicates that sexual fantasies are related to sexual drives: the higher the sexual drive, the higher the frequency of sexual fantasies and level of satisfaction in one's sex life (Leitenberg & Henning, 1995). Fantasies help create an equilibrium between our environment and our inner selves, as we seek a balance between the two. We use them to enhance our masturbatory experiences, as well as oral-genital sex, sexual intercourse, and other interpersonal experiences.

Our erotic fantasies develop with our experiences, although there are distinct gender differences. Sexual fantasies usually emerge between the ages of 11 and 13, with boys experiencing them earlier (Leitenberg & Henning, 1995) and feeling more positive about them than girls (Gold & Gold, 1991).

In their review of the research on sexual fantasies, Leitenberg and Henning (1995) found notable differences in the fantasies of men and women, reflecting the different gender-role stereotypes and sexual scripts taught to men and women:

- Men's fantasies are more active and focus more on women's bodies and on what they want to do with them, whereas women's fantasies are more passive and focus more on men's interest in their bodies.

- Men's sexual fantasies focus more on explicit sexual acts, nude bodies, and physical gratification, whereas women use more emotional content and romance in their sexual fantasies.

- Men are more likely to fantasize about multiple partners and group sex than are women.

- Men are more likely to have dominance fantasies, whereas women are more likely to have submission fantasies.

Thomas Hicks and Harold Leitenberg (2001) found gender differences in the proportion of sexual fantasies that involved someone other than a current partner (extradyadic fantasies). In a sample of 349 university students and employees in heterosexual relationships, 98% of men and 80% of women reported having extradyadic fantasies in the past two months.

Relative to types of fantasies based on sexual orientation, Leitenberg and Henning (1995) found that the content of sexual fantasies for gay men and lesbian women tends to be the same as for their heterosexual counterparts, except that homosexuals imagine same-sex partners and heterosexuals imagine other-sex partners.

The only way to get rid of temptation is to yield to it.

—*Oscar Wilde (1854–1900)*

The Function of Sexual Fantasies   Sexual fantasies have a number of important functions. First, they help direct and define our erotic goals. They take our generalized sexual drives and give them concrete images and specific content. We fantasize about certain types of men or women and reinforce our attraction through fantasy involvement. Unfortunately, our fantasy model may be unreasonable or unattainable, which is one of the pitfalls of fantasy; we can imagine perfection, but we rarely find it in real life.

Second, sexual fantasies allow us to plan for or anticipate situations that may arise. They provide a form of rehearsal, allowing us to practice in our minds how to act in various situations. Our fantasies of what *might* take place on a date, after a party, or in bed with our partner serve as a form of preparation.

Third, sexual fantasies provide escape from a dull or oppressive environment. Routine or repetitive labor often gives rise to fantasies as a way of coping with boredom.

Fourth, even if our sex lives are satisfactory, we may indulge in sexual fantasies to bring novelty and excitement into the relationship. Fantasy offers a safe outlet for sexual curiosity. One study found that some women are capable of experiencing orgasm solely through fantasy (Whipple, Ogden, & Komisaruk, 1992).

Fifth, sexual fantasies have an expressive function in somewhat the same manner that dreams do. Our sexual fantasies may offer a clue to our current interests, pleasures, anxieties, fears, or problems. Because fantasies use only a few details from the stream of reality, what we select is significant, expressing feelings that often lie beneath the surface of our consciousness (Sue, 1979). Fantasies of extramarital relationships, for example, may signify deep dissatisfaction with a marriage, whereas mental images centering around erectile dysfunction may represent fears about sexuality or a particular relationship.

Fantasies During Intercourse   A sizable number of people fantasize during sex. The fantasies are usually a continuation of daydreams or masturbatory fantasies, transforming one's partner into an Eminen or Halle Berry. According to various studies, 60–90% of the respondents fantasize during sex, depending on gender and ethnicity (Cado & Leitenberg, 1990; Knafo & Jaffe, 1984; Price & Miller, 1984). A study of midwestern college students revealed that about 60% of both female and male students fantasized during sexual intercourse (Figure 9.2). The two most frequent reasons for fantasizing during intercourse were to facilitate sexual arousal (46% for women, 38% for men) and to increase a partner's sexual attractiveness (32% for women, 30% for men) (Sue, 1979).

Women who fantasize about being forced into sexual activity or about being victimized do not necessarily want this to actually occur (Leitenberg & Henning, 1995). Rather, these women tend to be more interested in a variety of sexual activities and to be more sexually experienced (Gold, Balzano, & Stamey, 1991).

Erotic Dreams   Almost all of the men and two-thirds of the women in Alfred Kinsey's studies reported having had overtly erotic or sexual dreams (Kinsey, Pomeroy, & Martin, 1948; Kinsey, Pomeroy, Martin, & Gebhard, 1953). Sexual images in dreams are frequently very intense. Although people tend to feel responsible for their fantasies, which occur when they are awake, they are usually less troubled by sexual dreams.

Overtly sexual dreams are not necessarily exciting, although dreams that are apparently nonsexual may cause arousal. It is not unusual for individuals to awaken in the middle of the night and notice an erection or vaginal lubrication or find their bodies moving as if they were making love. They may also experience **nocturnal orgasm** (or **emission**). About 2–3% of women's total orgasms may be nocturnal, whereas for men the number may be around 8% (Kinsey et al., 1948, 1953). About 50% of the men interviewed by Kinsey had more than five nocturnal orgasms a year; less than 10% of the women experienced them that frequently.

Dreams almost always accompany nocturnal orgasm. The dreamer may awaken, and men usually ejaculate. Although the dream content may not be overtly sexual, it is always accompanied by sensual sensations. Erotic dreams run the gamut of sexual possibilities: other-sex, same-sex, or autoerotic behavior; incestuous, dominant and submissive, bestial, or fetishistic behavior. Women seem to feel less guilty or fearful about nocturnal orgasms than men do, accepting them more easily as pleasurable experiences.

> When two people make love, there are at least four people present—the two who are actually there and the two they are thinking about.
>
> —*Sigmund Freud (1856–1939)*

FIGURE 9.2 Percentages of Sexual Fantasies Occurring Frequently or Sometimes During Coitus Among a Sample of College Men and Women. (*Source:* Adapted from Sue, 1979.)

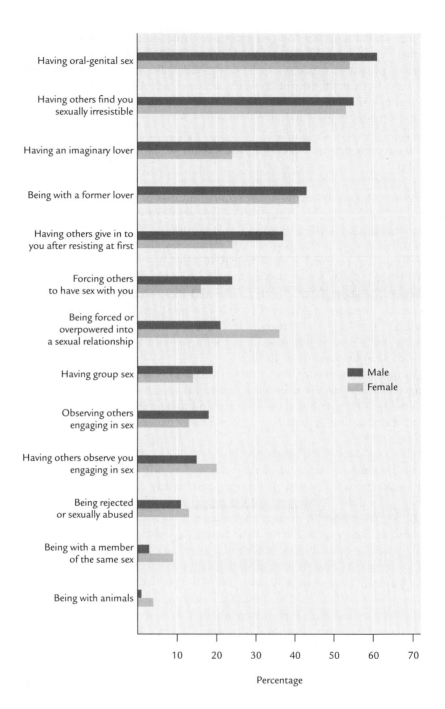

Masturbation

MASTURBATION, n. An extremely disgusting act performed on a regular basis by everyone *else.*

—*Robert Tefton*

People **masturbate** by rubbing, caressing, or otherwise stimulating their genitals. People report that they masturbate for several reasons: for relaxation, for relief of sexual tension, because a partner is not available or does not want sex, for physical pleasure, as an aid to falling asleep, and as a means to avoid STIs and HIV/AIDS (Laumann et al., 1994). They may masturbate during particular periods or throughout their entire lives.

Female Masturbation: Many people "discover" their sexual potential through masturbation. Sometimes, women learn to be orgasmic through masturbation and then bring this ability to their relationships.

Attitudes Toward Masturbation   Attitudes toward masturbation and masturbatory behaviors vary along ethnic lines (Figure 9.3). Whites are quite accepting of masturbation, for example, whereas African Americans are less so. The differences can be explained culturally. Because Whites tend to begin coital activities later than Blacks, Whites regard masturbation as an acceptable alternative to sexual intercourse. Black culture, in contrast, accepts sexual activity at an earlier age. In this context, Blacks may view masturbation as a sign of personal and sexual inadequacy. As a result, many Blacks tend to view sexual intercourse as normal and masturbation as deviant (Cortese, 1989; Kinsey et al., 1948; Wilson, 1986). However, masturbation is becoming more accepted within the African American community as a legitimate sexual activity.

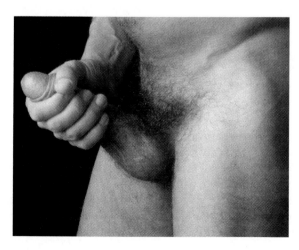

Male Masturbation: Masturbation is an important form of sexual behavior in which individuals explore their erotic capacities and bring pleasure to themselves.

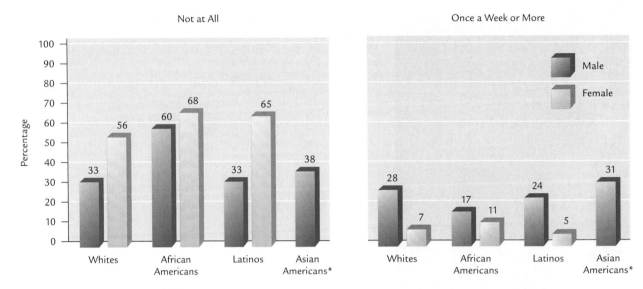

FIGURE 9.3 Frequency of Masturbation by Ethnicity in One Year.
(*Source:* Adapted from Laumann et al., 1994, p. 82.)

Latinos, like African Americans, are more conservative than Anglos in their attitudes toward masturbation (Cortese, 1989; Padilla & O'Grady, 1987). For many, masturbation is not considered an acceptable sexual option for either men or women (Guerrero Pavich, 1986). In part, this is because of the cultural emphasis on sexual intercourse and the influence of Catholicism, which regards masturbation as sinful. As with other forms of sexual behavior, however, acceptance becomes more likely as Latinos become more assimilated.

Even though masturbation is becoming more accepted in our culture, many people still have negative feelings about it. A large-scale survey (Laumann et al., 1994) reported that nearly an equal percentage—about 50%—of adult White and Latino males and females felt guilty after masturbating. For Blacks, about 50% of the males felt guilty afterward, but only about 36% of the females felt guilty. (To assess your attitude toward masturbation, take the questionnaire in the "Practically Speaking" box at the end of this section.)

Prevalence of Masturbation   Kinsey and his colleagues (1953) reported that 92% of the men and 58% of the women they interviewed said they had masturbated. Today, there appears to be a slight increase in both incidence and frequency. Nevertheless, gender differences continue to be significant (Atwood & Gagnon, 1987; Leitenberg, Detzer, & Srebnik, 1993). The *Details* magazine survey reported that 50% of college males and 31% of college females reported masturbating at least two or three times a week (Elliot & Brantley, 1997).

Masturbatory behavior is influenced by education, ethnicity, and religion, with education a particularly strong factor (Billy, Tanfer, Grady, & Klepinger, 1993; Laumann et al., 1994). Among men who have graduate degrees, 80% report having masturbated in the past year, with the prevalence declining with less education to 45% of those who have not completed high school. A similar pattern was found to occur among women, with 60% of those who have attended graduate school having masturbated in the past year, declining to

25% among women who have not finished high school. The better educated report masturbating more frequently as well.

Age is also significantly related to the frequency of masturbation (Laumann et al., 1994). Interestingly, young adults, often believed to have the highest levels of autoerotic activity, are less likely to have masturbated in the past year than those who are slightly older (age 24–35). The distribution rates seem to follow a U-shaped curve for both men and women, with the proportion not masturbating decreasing in the next two age groups and then stabilizing at about 33% of the men and 50% of the women until age 50. For people over 50, 50% of the men and 70% of the women report no masturbation. These figures may represent negative social attitudes, personal guilt, or unwillingness to report masturbating. Nevertheless, by the time married men and women reach their eighties, the most common overt genital activity is masturbation (Weizman & Hart, 1987).

Fewer women than men report achieving orgasm "usually" or "always," even with similar rates of masturbation. Researchers point out that their results suggest that "young women in our society simply do not find masturbation as pleasurable or acceptable as do young men." They point out that women, more than men, have been socialized to associate sex with romance, relationships, and emotional intimacy. Their results, they note, indicate that "the recent effort to encourage women to take more responsibility for their own sexuality and the explicit suggestion to masturbate more has not altered this socialization process" (Leitenberg et al., 1993).

Masturbation and Sexuality   Masturbation is an important means of learning about our bodies. Through masturbation, children and adolescents learn what is sexually pleasing, how to move their bodies, and what their natural rhythms are. The activity has no harmful physical effects. Although masturbation often decreases significantly when individuals are regularly sexual with another person, it is not necessarily a temporary substitute for sexual intercourse but rather is a legitimate form of sexual activity in its own right. Sex therapists may encourage clients to masturbate as a means of overcoming specific sexual problems and discovering their personal sexual potential. Masturbation, whether practiced alone or mutually with a partner (Figure 9.4), is also a form of safer sex, because ordinarily there is no exchange of semen, vaginal secretions, or blood, which could transmit HIV or other organisms that cause STIs (see Chapters 15 and 16). Regarding masturbation, former U.S. surgeon general M. Joycelyn Elders, M.D., states (Elders & Kilgore, 1997):

> Masturbation, practiced consciously or unconsciously, cultivates in us a humble elegance—an awareness that we are part of a larger natural system, the passions and rhythms of which live on in us. Sexuality is part of creation, part of our common inheritance, and it reminds us that we are neither inherently better nor worse than our sisters and brothers. Far from evil, masturbation just may render heavenly contentment in those who dare.

Elders went even further: She publicly encouraged schools to discuss masturbation as a healthy component of sexuality. For this, she was fired as surgeon general by President Clinton. She learned that there is little safe ground for speaking out in support of sexuality. Janice Irvine (2002) describes what happened to Elders as a cultural effort to regulate sexual morality through the control of sexual speech:

Masturbation is an intrinsically and seriously disordered act.

—*Vatican Declaration on Sexual Ethics*

Masturbation is the primary sexual activity of [human] kind. In the nineteenth century it was a disease; in the twentieth, it's a cure.

—*Thomas Szasz*

FIGURE 9.4 Mutual Masturbation. Many couples enjoy mutual masturbation, one form of safer sex.

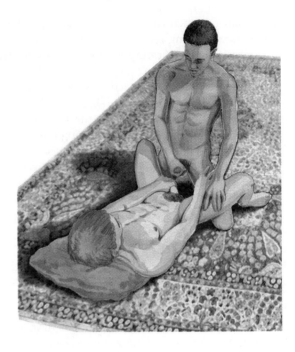

Talk about sex in the public realm is consistently met with ambivalence and outright efforts to contain and silence it. After all, Dr. Elders was fired for a speech act, not a sexual act. . . . Elders did not masturbate in public; she was fired for discussing how teachers might talk about masturbation. The fears that sexual language will trigger social chaos has historically fueled initiatives to regulate sexual speech.

We are capable of experiencing genital pleasure from birth through old age. Male infants have been observed with erect penises a few hours after birth. A baby boy may laugh in his crib while playing with his erect penis. Baby girls sometimes move their bodies rhythmically, almost violently, appearing to experience orgasm. And men as old as 102 have reported masturbating. In fact, for older adults, because of the loss of partners, masturbation regains much of the primacy it lost after adolescence as a means of sexual pleasure.

Masturbation in Childhood and Adolescence   Children often accidentally discover that playing with their genitals is pleasurable and continue this activity until reprimanded by an adult (see Chapter 6). By the time they are 4 or 5, children have usually learned that adults consider this form of behavior "nasty." Parents generally react negatively to masturbation, regardless of the age and sex of the child. Later, this negative attitude becomes generalized to include the sexual pleasure that accompanies the behavior. Children thus learn to conceal their masturbatory play.

When boys and girls reach adolescence, they no longer regard masturbation as ambiguous play; they know that it is sexual. As discussed in Chapter 6, this is a period of intense change, emotionally and biologically. Complex emotions are often involved in adolescent masturbation. Teenagers may feel guilt and shame for engaging in a practice that their parents and other adults indicate is wrong or bad, and they may be fearful of discovery. A girl who feels vaginal lubrication or finds stains on her underwear for the first time may be frightened, as may a boy who sees the semen of his first ejaculation. Although open discussion could alleviate fears, frank talk is not always possible in a setting that involves shame.

According to one survey of those adolescents who do masturbate, boys do so approximately 3 times more often than girls (Leitenberg et al., 1993). By the end of adolescence, virtually all males and about three-quarters of females have masturbated to orgasm. These gender differences may be the result of social conditioning and communication. Most boys discuss masturbatory experiences openly with one another, relating different methods and recalling "near misses" when they were almost caught by their parents. Among boys, masturbation is a source of camaraderie. In contrast, girls usually learn to masturbate through self-discovery. Because "nice girls" are not supposed to be sexual, they seldom talk about their own sexuality; instead, they hide it, repress it, or try to forget it.

Masturbation in Adulthood   Masturbation continues after adolescence, although the frequency often declines among men and increases among women.

WOMEN AND MASTURBATION   One way in which women become familiar with their own sexual responsiveness is through masturbation. According to the NHSLS, 42% of women surveyed had masturbated in the preceding year (Laumann et al., 1994). Women who masturbate appear to hold more positive sexual attitudes and are more likely to be orgasmic than those who don't (Kelly, Strassberg, & Kircher, 1990). Among women who experience multiple orgasms, 26% do so through masturbation (Darling, Davidson, & Jennings, 1991). Although the majority of women believe that orgasms experienced through masturbation differ from those experienced in sexual intercourse, they feel the same levels of sexual satisfaction (Davidson & Darling, 1986).

Though no two women masturbate in exactly the same manner, a number of common methods are used to achieve orgasm. Most involve some type of clitoral stimulation, by using the fingers, rubbing against an object, or using a vibrator. The rubbing or stimulation tends to increase just prior to orgasm and to continue during orgasm.

Because the glans clitoridis is often too sensitive for prolonged direct stimulation, women tend to stroke gently on the shaft of the clitoris. Another common method, which exerts less direct pressure on the clitoris, is to stroke the mons areas or the minor lips. Individual preferences play a key role in what method is chosen, how rigorous the stimulation is, how often masturbation occurs, and whether it is accompanied by erotic aids such as a vibrator or sensual oils. A number of women, for instance, may find that running a stream of warm water over the vulva or sitting near the jet stream in a hot tub is sexually arousing. Stimulation of the breasts and nipples is also very common, as is stroking the anal region. Some women enjoy inserting a finger or other object into their vagina; however, this is less common than clitoral stimulation. Some women apply deep pressure in the region of the G-spot to give themselves a different type of orgasm. Using common sense in relation to cleanliness, such as not inserting an object or finger from the anus into the vagina and keeping vibrators and other objects used for insertion clean, helps to prevent infection.

MASTURBATION HAS LONG been associated with sin or psychopathology. Our traditional aversion to it can be traced to antiquity. The Judeo-Christian grounding for the prohibition against masturbation is found in the story of Onan (Genesis 38:7–19):

> And Er, Judah's first born, was wicked in the sight of the Lord; and the Lord slew him. And Judah said unto Onan, Go in unto thy brother's wife, and marry her, and raise up the seed to thy brother. And Onan knew that the seed should not be his; and it came to pass, when he went in unto his brother's wife, that he spilled it on the ground, lest that he should give seed to his brother. And the thing which he did displeased the Lord; whereupon he slew him also.

Although God struck Onan down, it is not clear why he was slain: Was it because of withdrawal (coitus interruptus) or because he had disobeyed God's command? (The general consensus among biblical scholars is that he was slain for the sin of disobedience [Bullough, 1976].) But despite the message's reference to withdrawal, the "sin of Onan" has traditionally been interpreted as masturbation. "Onanism," in fact, has been used interchangeably with "masturbation."

In the Judeo-Christian tradition, masturbation was treated as a sin with a high price: damnation. The nineteenth century, however, exacted a new tribute from the sinner: physical debilitation, insanity, or death. Under the leadership of physicians, the consequences of masturbation shifted from moral to physical. Doctors believed that semen contained precious nutrients that were absorbed by the body to sustain life and growth. The Swiss physician Tissot had first warned of the physical dangers of masturbation in 1758, asserting that weakness was caused by the loss of semen and the draining of "nervous energy" from the brain. By the middle of the nineteenth century, physicians were warning of a masturbatory plague that was enveloping the civilized world (Figure 9.5) (Gay, 1986).

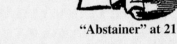

"Indulger" at 16   "Abstainer" at 21

FIGURE 9.5   A Victorian Warning Against Masturbation. In 1875, Emery Abbey illustrated what would happen if a person practiced "onanism" (masturbation) by contrasting abstainers to indulgers. Onanism was blamed for many mental and physical ailments, including blindness, epilepsy, and heart murmur. (*Source:* Laqueur, 2003.)

For nineteenth-century Americans, masturbation was *the* sexual evil against which individuals had to struggle. Children were especially susceptible to the practice. Victorians believed that children were not *naturally* sexual but learned to be sexual through exposure to vice and bad examples. By refusing to recognize spontaneous

MEN AND MASTURBATION   According to the NHSLS, 62% of men surveyed had masturbated in the preceding year (Laumann et al., 1994). Like women, men have individual preferences and patterns in masturbating. Nearly all methods involve some type of direct stimulation of the penis with the hand. Typically, the penis is grasped and stroked at the shaft, with up-and-down or circular movements of the hand, so that the edge of the corona around the glans and the frenulum on the underside are stimulated. How much childhood sexuality, Victorians were able to sustain the myth of childhood innocence.

Because children learned about masturbation by associating with "vile" playmates or being exposed to suggestive books, songs, or pictures, it became parents' duty to closely supervise their children's friends and activities. These fears virtually compelled parents to interfere with their children's developing sexuality (Foucault, 1980). Because masturbation was a "secret vice," parents were suspicious of everything. Responsible parents, despite their reticence about sex, warned their children against the dangers of "self-abuse." There were patented devices to be attached to a boy's penis so that if he touched it, an alarm sounded in his parents' bedroom, alerting them to the danger. Parents and masturbators alike purchased penile rings embedded with sharp prongs, which promised freedom from self-abuse. And in the early 1890s, a lockable metal genital device to prevent masturbation by mental hospital patients was patented (Figure 9.6).

Adding to these early efforts to control masturbation, the nineteenth-century health reformer Sylvester Graham, who gave us the names for Graham flour and Graham crackers, declared that people should follow the Graham diet and practice abstinence to be healthy. And

John Harvey Kellogg, a strong follower of Graham, invented cornflakes to help curb masturbation.

Dr. Homer Bostwick (1860) received patients who were suffering from the "damnable effects of masturbation," recording a case history that describes the treatment:

> I advised him to have 25 leeches applied to the perinaeum [base of the penis] immediately, and sit over a bucket of hot water as soon as they should drop off, so that the steam and warm bathing would keep up further bleeding. I ordered the leeches to be followed by a blister, and hot poultices, hot mustard, hip baths, etc., etc. I had his bowels opened with a dose of castor oil, and confined him to a light gruel, vegetable, and fruit diet, advising him to scrupulously avoid everything stimulating, to drink nothing but cold water and mucilaginous fluids.

The treatments continued for 5 weeks, until the man was pronounced "cured" and returned home. ("He was, of course, somewhat weakened and debilitated," Bostwick concluded.)

The almost hysterical attitude toward masturbation helped sustain the severe sexual restrictions that characterized the nineteenth century. Masturbatory hysteria instilled sexual fears and anxieties in the children of the nineteenth century. As these children matured, they were vulnerable to the myths of sexual danger that would regulate their adult lives.

Fears about masturbation continued in diminished form in the first half of the twentieth century. Masturbation now was associated, not with death and insanity, but with arrested psychological development in children and neuroses in adults. Today, it continues to be viewed as immoral and a sign of emotional immaturity by many conservative religious denominations, especially by the Roman Catholic Church, which declared masturbation "an intrinsically and seriously disturbed act" (Patton, 1986). Until the late 1970s, the *Boy Scout Handbook* warned against the moral and psychological dangers of masturbation (Rowan, 1989). Despite all of this historical, religious, and medical condemnation, there is no scientific evidence that masturbation is harmful.

FIGURE 9.6 Devices Designed to Curb Masturbation. Because of the widespread belief in the nineteenth century that masturbation was harmful, various devices were introduced to prevent the practice. (*Sources:* Crooks & Baur, 2002; Rathus, Nevid, & Fichner-Rathus, 2002.)

pressure is applied, how rapid the strokes are, how many fingers are used, where the fingers are placed, and how far up and down the hands move vary from one man to another. Whether the breasts, testicles, anus, or other parts of the body are stimulated also depends on the individual, but it appears to be the up-and-down stroking or rubbing of the penis that triggers orgasm. The stroking tends to increase just prior to orgasm and then to slow or stop during ejaculation.

PAUL ABRAMSON AND DONALD MOSHER (1975) developed a questionnaire, Attitudes Toward Masturbation (ATM), as a measure of negative attitudes toward masturbation or masturbation guilt. According to these researchers, masturbation guilt is a learned script in which the negative affects of guilt, disgust, shame, and fear are related to masturbation. As discussed in this chapter, feelings of shame and guilt have long been associated with masturbation, and a more positive attitude has emerged only recently. Still, many people continue to feel guilty about their own masturbatory activity. Take this inventory to determine how much you have been affected by negative messages about masturbation.

Directions

Indicate how true each of the following statements is for you, on a scale from "Not at all true" to "Very true," by circling the appropriate number.

	Not at all true			Very true	
1. People masturbate to escape feelings of tension and anxiety.	1	2	3	4	5
2. People who masturbate will not enjoy sexual intercourse as much as those who refrain from masturbation.	1	2	3	4	5
3. Masturbation is a private matter which neither harms nor concerns anyone else.	1	2	3	4	5
4. Masturbation is a sin against yourself.	1	2	3	4	5
5. Masturbation in childhood can help a person develop a natural, healthy attitude toward sex.	1	2	3	4	5
6. Masturbation in an adult is juvenile and immature.	1	2	3	4	5
7. Masturbation can lead to deviant sexual behavior.	1	2	3	4	5
8. Excessive masturbation is physically impossible, so it is needless to worry.	1	2	3	4	5
9. If you enjoy masturbating too much, you may never learn to relate to a sex partner.	1	2	3	4	5
10. After masturbating, a person feels degraded.	1	2	3	4	5
11. Experience with masturbation can potentially help a woman become orgasmic for sexual intercourse.	1	2	3	4	5
12. I feel guilt about masturbating.	1	2	3	4	5
13. Masturbation can be a "friend in need" when there is no "friend indeed."	1	2	3	4	5
14. Masturbation can provide an outlet for sex fantasies without harming anyone else or endangering oneself.	1	2	3	4	5

To add variety or stimulation, some men may elect to use lubricants, visual or written erotic materials, artificial vaginas, inflatable dolls, or rubber pouches in which to insert their penis. Regardless of the aid or technique, it is important to pay attention to cleanliness to prevent bacterial infections.

MASTURBATION IN SEXUAL RELATIONSHIPS Most people continue to masturbate after they marry, although the rate is significantly lower. Actually, the NHSLS found that married people are less likely to have masturbated during the preceding 12 months than those nevermarried or formerly married. About 57% and 37% of married men and women, respectively, reported having masturbated in the preceding year, as opposed to about 69% and 48% of never-married and formerly married men and women, respectively (Laumann et al., 1994).

There are many reasons for continuing the activity during marriage or other sexual relationships: Masturbation is pleasurable, a partner is away or unwilling, sexual intercourse is not satisfying, the partner(s) fear(s) sexual inadequacy, the individual acts out fantasies, or he or she seeks to release

15. Excessive masturbation can lead to problems with erections in men and women not being able to have an orgasm. Not at all true 1 2 3 4 5 Very true

16. Masturbation is an escape mechanism which prevents a person from developing a mature sexual outlook. 1 2 3 4 5

17. Masturbation can provide harmless relief from sexual tension. 1 2 3 4 5

18. Playing with your own genitals is disgusting. 1 2 3 4 5

19. Excessive masturbation is associated with neurosis, depression, and behavioral problems. 1 2 3 4 5

20. Any masturbation is too much. 1 2 3 4 5

21. Masturbation is a compulsive, addictive habit which once begun is almost impossible to stop. 1 2 3 4 5

22. Masturbation is fun. 1 2 3 4 5

23. When I masturbate, I am disgusted with myself. 1 2 3 4 5

24. A pattern of frequent masturbation is associated with introversion and withdrawal from social contacts. 1 2 3 4 5

25. I would be ashamed to admit publicly that I have masturbated. 1 2 3 4 5

26. Excessive masturbation leads to mental dullness and fatigue. 1 2 3 4 5

27. Masturbation is a normal sexual outlet. 1 2 3 4 5

28. Masturbation is caused by an excessive preoccupation with thoughts about sex. 1 2 3 4 5

29. Masturbation can teach you to enjoy the sensuousness of your own body. 1 2 3 4 5

30. After I masturbate, I am disgusted with myself for losing control of my body. 1 2 3 4 5

Scoring

To obtain an index of masturbation guilt, sum the circled numbers to yield a score from 30 to 150. Before summing, reverse the scoring for these ten items: 3, 5, 8, 11, 13, 14, 17, 22, 27. That is, a 1 would be converted to a 5, a 2 to a 4, a 4 to a 2, and 5 to a 1. The lower your score, the lower your guilt about and negative attitude toward masturbation.

Source: Adapted from Abramson, P. J., & Mosher, D. L. (1975). "The Development of a Measure of Negative Attitudes Toward Masturbation." *Journal of Consulting and Clinical Psychology, 43,* 485–490.

tension. During times of relationship conflict, masturbation may act as a distancing device, with the masturbating partner choosing masturbation over sexual interaction as a means of emotional protection.

SEXUAL BEHAVIOR WITH OTHERS

We often think that sex is sexual intercourse and that sexual interactions end with orgasm (usually the male's in heterosexual couples). But sex is not limited to sexual intercourse. Heterosexuals engage in a wide variety of sexual activities, which may include erotic touching, kissing, and oral and anal sex. Except for vaginal intercourse, gay and lesbian couples engage in basically the same sexual activities as do heterosexuals. Which of these "sexual" activities actually constitute sex? This topic has been publicly debated recently, largely fueled by former president Clinton's declaration that he did not have sex with Monica Lewinsky despite the fact that she performed fellatio on him. (To find out what a college sample believed constituted "having sex," see the "Think About It" box later in this section.)

FIGURE 9.7 Percentage of Females Ranking Selected Sexual Techniques/Practices Very Appealing, by Ethnicity. (*Source:* Adapted from Laumann et al., 1994, pp. 152–155.)

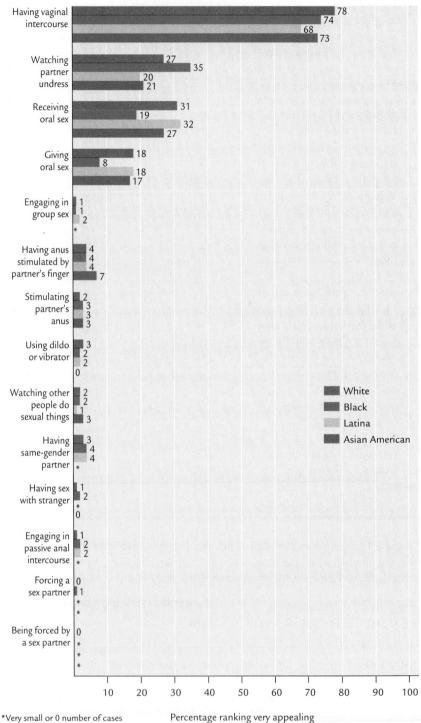

Love is the self-delusion we manufacture to justify the trouble we take to have sex.

—*Dan Greenberg*

In one study, American adults were asked to rank how appealing certain sexual activities are to them (Laumann et al., 1994) (Figures 9.7 and 9.8). For all the ethnic groups studied, overwhelmingly, vaginal intercourse was the most appealing activity, with watching the partner undress and giving

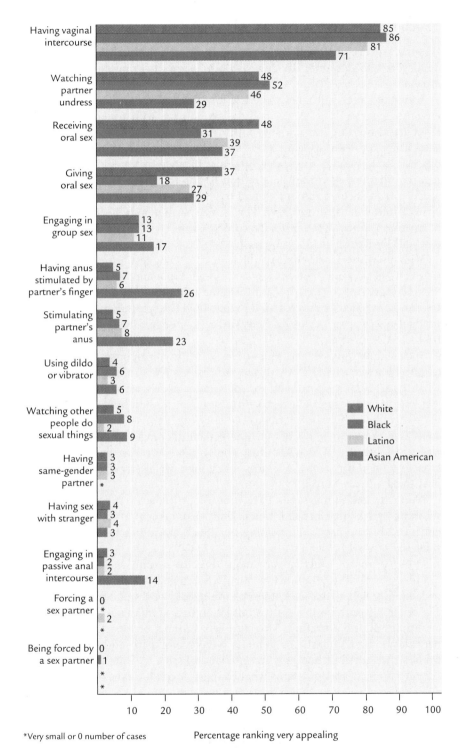

FIGURE 9.8 Percentage of Males Ranking Selected Sexual Techniques/Practices Very Appealing, by Ethnicity. (*Source:* Adapted from Laumann et al., 1994, pp. 152–155.)

*Very small or 0 number of cases   Percentage ranking very appealing

and receiving oral sex next. Only a small minority found other activities, such as anal sex or use of a vibrator or dildo, very appealing. Apparently, Americans are more traditional in their sexual behavior than previously believed.

Touching

Whether sex begins with the heart or the genitals, touch is the fire that melds the two into one. Touching is both a sign of caring and a signal for arousal.

Touching does not solely need to be directed toward the genitals or erogenous zones. The entire body is responsive to a touch or a caress. Even hand-holding can be sensual for two people sexually attracted to each other. Women appear to be especially responsive to touch, but traditional male gender roles give little significance to touching. Some men regard touching as simply a prelude to intercourse. When this occurs, touch is transformed into a demand for intercourse rather than an expression of intimacy or erotic play. The man's partner may become reluctant to touch or show affection for fear her gestures will be misinterpreted as a sexual invitation.

William Masters and Virginia Johnson (1970) suggest a form of touching they call "pleasuring." **Pleasuring** is nongenital touching and caressing. Neither partner tries to sexually stimulate the other; they simply explore, discovering how their bodies respond to touching. One partner guides the other partner's hand over her or his body, telling her or him what feels good; the roles are then reversed.

Such sharing gives each a sense of his or her own responses; it also allows each to discover what the other likes and dislikes. We can't assume we know what a particular person likes, for there is too much variation among people: Watching a partner masturbate can provide clues on how he or she likes to be stimulated. Pleasuring opens the door to communication; couples discover that the entire body, not just the genitals, is erogenous. Actually, Masters and Johnson (1979) noted that women tend to prefer genital touching after general body contact, whereas many men prefer stroking of their genitals early.

Nude or clothed massages, back rubs, foot rubs, scalp massages—all are soothing and loving forms of touch. The sensuousness of touching may be enhanced by the use of lubricating oils. Such erotic touching is a form of safer sex.

Other forms of touching are more directly sexual, such as caressing, fondling, or rubbing our own or our partner's genitals or breasts. Sucking or licking earlobes, the neck, toes, or the insides of thighs, palms, or arms can be highly stimulating. Oral stimulation of a woman's or man's breasts or nipples is often exciting. Moving one's genitals or breasts over a partner's face, chest, breasts, or genitals is very erotic for some people. The pressing together of bodies with genital thrusting is called **tribidism,** or "dry humping" among heterosexual couples. Many lesbians enjoy the overall body contact and eroticism of this form of genital stimulation; sometimes, the partners place their pelvic areas together to provide mutual clitoral stimulation (Figure 9.9). Rubbing the penis between the thighs of a partner is a type of touching calling **interfemoral intercourse.** Heterosexual couples who do not use contraception must be sure the man does not ejaculate near the vaginal opening so as to avoid conception, however unlikely it may be.

Stimulating a partner's clitoris or penis with the hand or fingers can increase excitement and lead to orgasm. A word of caution: Direct stimu-

Sex is the great amateur art.

—*David Cort*

FIGURE 9.9 Tribidism

lation of the clitoral glans may be painful for some women at specific stages of arousal, so stimulation of either side of the clitoris may work better. Certainly, the clitoris and surrounding areas should be moist before much touching is done. Inserting a finger or fingers into a partner's wet vagina and rhythmically moving it at the pace she likes can also be pleasing. Some women like to have their clitoris licked or stimulated with one hand while their vagina is being penetrated with the other. Men like having their penises lubricated so that their partner's hand glides smoothly over the shaft and glans penis. (Be sure to use a water-based lubricant if you plan to use a condom later, because oil-based lubricants may cause the condom to deteriorate.) Masturbating while one partner is holding the other can be highly erotic for both people. Mutual masturbation can also be intensely sexual. Some people use sex toys such as dildos, vibrators, or ben-wah balls to enhance sexual touching. (These are discussed in Chapter 14.)

As we enter old age, touching becomes increasingly significant as a primary form of erotic expression. Touching in all its myriad forms—from holding hands to caressing, from massaging to hugging, and from walking with arms around each other to fondling—becomes the touchstone of eroticism for the elderly.

The Advocate, a magazine focusing on gay and lesbian issues, conducted a survey of its readers concerning relationships and sexuality. A strong majority of the lesbian women said they loved many nongenital, touching activities: 91% loved hugging, caressing, and cuddling; 82% loved French kissing; 74% loved simply holding hands. Three-quarters loved both touching a woman's genitals and having their own touched. About 80% enjoyed caressing another woman's breasts or sucking her nipples; 68% enjoyed receiving such attention (Lever, 1995). For 85% of gay men, hugging, kissing, and snuggling were also the favorite activities (Lever, 1994).

WHEN PEOPLE SAY they "had sex" or did some things but did not have sex, what do they mean? It all depends on the behavioral criteria they use to define "having sex." Social and legal definitions of "sex," "sex act," and "sexual relations" and crimes related to "having sex" vary and are sometimes vague, depending on the source. For many people, sex is defined as having sexual intercourse, which may be referred to as "coitus" or "copulation." Actually, some definitions may be used by couples or individuals to justify a wide range of intimate behaviors other than penile-vaginal intercourse in order to preserve their virginity or not to "have cheated" on another person. Public discourse during the presidency of Bill Clinton about whether oral sex constitutes "having sex" further revealed cultural uncertainty about the definition of sex. Without a universal definition of "having sex," confusion or false assumptions can result (Sanders & Reinisch, 1999).

Percentages of undergraduate students answering "yes" to the question: "Would you say you 'had sex' with someone if the most intimate behavior you engaged in was . . ."

Behavior	Percentage of Women	Percentage of Men
Deep kissing	1.4	2.9
Oral contact on your breast/nipples	2.3	4.1
Person touches your breast/nipples	2.0	4.5
You touch other's breast/nipples	1.7	5.7
Oral contact on other's breast/nipples	1.4	6.1
You touch other's genitals	11.6	17.1
Person touches your genitals	12.2	17.1
Oral contact with other's genitals	37.3	43.7
Oral contact with your genitals	37.7	43.9
Penile-anal intercourse	82.3	79.1
Penile-vaginal intercourse	99.7	99.2

Kissing

Kissing is usually our earliest interpersonal sexual experience, and its primal intensity may be traced back to our suckling as infants. The kiss is magic: Fairy tales keep alive the ancient belief that a kiss can undo spells and bring a prince or princess back to life. Parental kisses show love and often remedy the small hurts and injuries of childhood.

Kissing is probably the most acceptable of all premarital sexual activities (Jurich & Polson, 1985). The tender lover's kiss symbolizes love, and the erotic lover's kiss, of course, simultaneously represents and *is* passion. Both men and women regard kissing as a romantic act, a symbol of affection as well as desire (Tucker, Marvin, & Vivian, 1991).

The lips and mouth are highly sensitive to touch and are exquisitely erotic parts of our bodies. Kisses discover, explore, and excite the body. They also involve the senses of taste and smell, which are especially important because they activate unconscious memories and associations. Often, we are aroused by familiar smells associated with particular sexual memories, such as a person's body scent or a perfume or fragrance. In some languages—among the Borneans, for example—the word "kiss" literally translates as "smell." In

The kiss originated when the first male reptile licked the first female reptile, implying in a subtle, complimentary way that she was as succulent as the small reptile he had for dinner the night before.

—*F. Scott Fitzgerald (1896–1940)*

I wasn't kissing her, I was whispering in her mouth.

—*Chico Marx (1886–1961)*

Researchers Stephanie A. Sanders and June Reinisch of the Kinsey Institute for Research in Sex, Gender, and Reproduction at Indiana University surveyed a stratified random sample of 599 undergraduate students at a midwestern university to determine which behavioral interactions the students considered as "having sex." Nearly 4 out of 5 classified themselves as politically moderate to conservative. However, the study revealed that students held widely divergent opinions about what behaviors constitute "having sex."

As can be seen in the preceding table, nearly all agreed that penile-vaginal intercourse qualifies as "having sex," with about 4 out of 5 considering penile-anal intercourse as sex. However, few considered deep kissing, breast contact, and manual stimulation of genitals as sex, and only about 4 out of 10 considered oral-genital contact as sex. For the behaviors less frequently included as "having sex," male students were slightly more likely to incorporate them into the "had sex" category.

"Hooking up" is a newer term used by some college students to describe being sexual with others. Hooking up has replaced traditional dating rituals—in fact, many have never gone out on a date—and is as ambiguous as "having sex." It may mean anything from kissing to engaging in sexual intercourse. After several weeks of intimacy with another person, some college students aren't sure if they are in a relationship or simply "hooking up." For many college-age students, marriage no longer comes on the heels of graduation. Hooking up for "casual sex" allows them to put off serious romance yet be sexual with another person and free to pursue personal and economic goals.

In light of the findings of Sanders and Reinisch and the recent college ritual of "hooking up," what are your thoughts on these questions: Do the results of the study surprise you? How would you respond to the questions? Would you respond differently based on the sexual orientation of the couple? Does having an orgasm make a difference in your responses? Does being the "giver" or "receiver" of a behavior, such as oral sex, make a difference in whether you had sex? What personal or social factors, such as age and religion, might make a difference in how you respond? Does "hooking up" occur on your campus? If you know someone who is hooking up, have they talked about it positively or negatively? What do you see as the advantages and disadvantages of "hooking up"?

Source: Sanders, S., & Reinisch, J. (1999). "Would You Say You 'Had Sex' If . . . ?" *Journal of the American Medical Association, 281,* 275–277.

fact, among the Eskimos and the Maoris of New Zealand, there is no mouth kissing, only the touching of noses to facilitate smelling.

Although kissing may appear innocent, it is in many ways the height of intimacy. The adolescent's first kiss is often regarded as a milestone, a rite of passage, the beginning of adult sexuality (Alapack, 1991). It is an important developmental step, marking the beginning of a young person's sexuality.

The amount of kissing differs according to sexual orientation. Lesbian couples tend to engage in more kissing than heterosexual couples, while gay couples kiss less than heterosexual couples (Blumstein & Schwartz, 1983).

Ordinary kissing is considered safer sex. French kissing is probably safe, unless the kiss is hard and draws blood or either partner has open sores or cuts in or around the mouth. (See Chapter 16 for further discussion of kissing and HIV.)

Oral-Genital Sex

In recent years, oral sex has become a part of many people's sexual scripts. The two types of **oral-genital sex** are cunnilingus and fellatio, which may be performed singly or simultaneously. Recall from Chapter 1 that cunnilingus

As for the topsy turvy tangle known as *soixante-neuf,* personally I have always felt it to be madly confusing, like trying to pat your head and rub your stomach at the same time.

—*Helen Lawrenson*

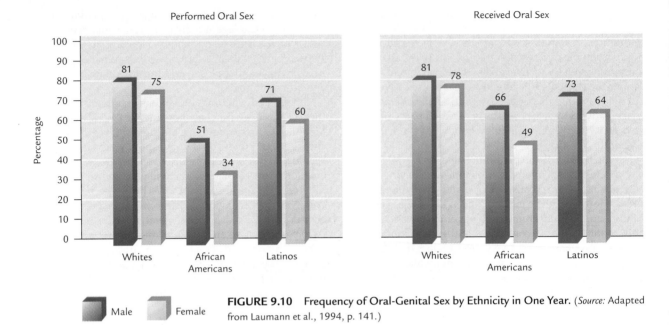

FIGURE 9.10   Frequency of Oral-Genital Sex by Ethnicity in One Year. (*Source:* Adapted from Laumann et al., 1994, p. 141.)

is the erotic stimulation of a woman's vulva and/or clitoris by her partner's mouth and tongue. Recall, too, that fellatio is the oral stimulation of a man's penis by his partner's sucking and licking. When two people orally stimulate each other simultaneously, their activity is sometimes called "sixty-nine." The term comes from the configuration "69," which visually suggests the activity.

For people of every orientation (especially among high school and college students), oral sex is an increasingly important and healthy aspect of their sexual selves (Wilson & Medora, 1990). Of the men and women in various studies, 70–90% report that they have engaged in oral sex (Billy et al., 1993; Janus & Janus, 1993; Laumann et al., 1994). Philip Blumstein and Pepper Schwartz (1983) found that 50% of gay couples, 39% of lesbian couples, and 30% of heterosexual couples usually or always had oral sex as part of their lovemaking routine.

Although oral-genital sex is increasingly accepted by White, middle-class Americans, it remains less permissible among some ethnic groups (Figure 9.10). African Americans, for example, have lower rates of oral-genital sex than Whites because many Blacks consider it immoral (Laumann et al., 1994; Wilson, 1986). A large-scale national study revealed that 81% of White men had performed oral sex, compared with 51% of African American men and 71% of Latinos. Eighty-one percent of White men had received oral sex, compared with 66% of African American men, and 73% of Latinos. Oral sex is increasingly accepted, however, among Black women, especially if they have a good relationship and communicate well with their partners (Wyatt & Lyons-Rowe, 1990). Among married Latinos, oral sex is relatively uncommon. When oral sex occurs, it is usually at the male's instigation, as women are not expected to be interested in erotic variety (Guerrero Pavich, 1986). Although little is known about older Asian Americans and Asian immigrants, college-age Asian Americans

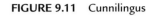

FIGURE 9.11   Cunnilingus

appear to accept oral-genital sex to the same degree as middle-class Whites (Cochran, Mays, & Leung, 1991).

A study of university students of both sexes revealed that a person's attitudes toward his or her genitals may be an important facet of sexual interaction (Reinholtz & Muehlenhard, 1995). Someone who believes his or her genitals are attractive and sexy may be more comfortable during sexual interaction than someone who feels self-conscious about them. Furthermore, this same study found that the vast majority of participants who had engaged in oral sex had both performed and received it. According to the *Details* magazine survey of college students, 80% of the women had performed oral sex, and 85% had received it; 82% of the men had performed oral sex, and 83% had received it (Elliot & Brantley, 1997). According to another survey of lesbian and gay sexuality, about 7 out of 10 lesbian women and gay men enjoy giving and receiving oral sex (Lever, 1994).

Cunnilingus   In cunnilingus, a woman's genitals are stimulated by her partner's tongue and mouth, which gently and rhythmically caress and lick her clitoris and the surrounding area (Figure 9.11). During arousal, the mouth and lips can nibble, lick, and kiss the inner thighs, stomach, and mons pubis and then move to the sensitive labia minora clitoral area. Orgasm may be brought on by rhythmically stimulating the clitoris. During cunnilingus, some women also enjoy insertion of a finger into the vagina or anus for extra stimulation. Many women find cunnilingus to be the easiest way to reach orgasm because it provides such intense stimulation.

Among lesbian women, cunnilingus is a common activity for achieving orgasm. In contrast to heterosexual couples, lesbian couples may be more inventive, less restrained, and more involved (Califia, 1979). This may be partly because, as women, each partner can identify with what the other enjoys. According to one study, however, as many as 25% of the lesbian women rarely or never engaged in cunnilingus (Blumstein & Schwartz, 1983). Instead, they relied on holding, kissing, manual stimulation, and pressing themselves erotically against each other. Nevertheless, the more often the women in the study had oral sex, the more likely they were to be satisfied with their sex lives and partners.

Some women, however, have concerns regarding cunnilingus. The most common worries revolve around whether the other person is enjoying it and, especially, whether the vulva has an unpleasant odor (Hite, 1976; Reinholtz & Muehlenhard, 1995). Concerns about vaginal odors may be eased by washing. Undeodorized white soap will wash away unpleasant smells without disturbing the vagina's natural erotic scent. If an unpleasant odor arises from the genitals, it may be because the woman has a vaginal infection.

A woman may also worry that her partner is not enjoying the experience because she or he is giving pleasure rather than receiving it. What she may not recognize is that such sexual excitement is often mutual. Because our mouths and tongues are erotically sensitive, the giver finds erotic excitement in arousing her or his partner.

Because of concerns about the spread of HIV through oral sex, experts have recommended the use of rubber dams over the vulva during cunnilingus. These devices may be the kind used in dental work, or they may be made by cutting a square sheet from a nonlubricated latex condom or rubber surgical glove. Though the risk of contracting HIV during oral-genital sex has not yet been established, experts suggest that any barrier that prevents the mixing of body fluids reduces the risks. These types of barriers, however, will not prevent the transmission of all sexually transmitted infections (STIs), such as transmission of organisms that cause urethral or vaginal infections from the mouth or transmission of throat infections from the genitals.

Fellatio   In fellatio, a man's penis is taken into his partner's mouth. The partner licks the glans penis and gently stimulates the shaft (Figure 9.12). Also, the scrotum may be gently licked. If the penis is not erect, it usually will become erect within a short time. The partner sucks more vigorously as excitement increases, down toward the base of the penis and then back up, in a rhythmical motion, being careful not to bite hard or scrape the penis with the teeth. While the man is being stimulated by mouth, his partner can also stroke the shaft of the penis by hand. Gently playing with the testicles is also arousing as long as they are not held too tightly. As in cunnilingus, the couple should experiment to discover what is most stimulating and exciting. The man should be careful not to thrust his penis too deeply into his partner's throat, for that may cause a gag reflex. He should let his partner control how deeply the penis goes into the mouth. The partner can do this by grasping the penis below his or her lips so that the depth of insertion can be controlled. Furthermore, gagging is less likely when the one performing fellatio is on top. The gag reflex can also be reconditioned by slowly inserting the penis into the mouth at increasing depth over time. Some women feel that fellatio is more intimate than sexual intercourse; others feel that it is less intimate. It is the most common form of sexual activity performed on

FIGURE 9.12   Fellatio

men by prostitutes (Freund, Lee, & Leonard, 1991; Monto, 2001). Most men find fellatio to be highly arousing.

For gay men, fellatio is an important component of their sexuality. As with sexual intercourse for heterosexual men, however, fellatio is only one activity in their sexual repertoire. Generally, the more often gay couples engage in giving and receiving oral sex, the more satisfied they are (Blumstein & Schwartz, 1983). Because oral sex often involves power symbolism, reciprocity is important. If one partner always performs oral sex, he may feel he is subordinate to the other. The most satisfied gay couples alternate between giving and receiving oral sex.

A common concern about fellatio centers around ejaculation. Should a man ejaculate into his partner's mouth? Some people find semen to be slightly bitter, but others like it. Some find it exciting to suck even harder on the penis during or following ejaculation; others do not like the idea of semen in the mouth. For many, a key issue is whether to swallow the semen. Some swallow it; others spit it out. It is simply a matter of personal preference, and the man who is receiving fellatio should accept his partner's feelings about it and avoid equating a dislike for swallowing semen with a personal rejection.

Some partners worry, as they should, about the transmission of HIV through fellatio (see Chapter 16). It is possible to contract HIV orally if there are sores or cuts within the mouth. Excessive toothbrushing and flossing and biting on the inside of the mouth, as well as orthodontia or dental work, can cause small cuts in the mouth that allow HIV, if present, to enter the bloodstream. A condom worn during fellatio will decrease the risk for STIs. Some men try to provide oral stimulation to their own penis, a praca practice called **autofellatio.** Kinsey and his colleagues (Kinsey, Pomeroy, & Martin, 1948) found that many males try this behavior, but less than 1% of their sample were actually able to achieve it.

Sexual Intercourse

In 1992, the World Health Organization reported that there are more than 100 million acts of **sexual intercourse** daily. Pregnancy and disease are only the most overt consequences of all this activity. Sexual intercourse has intense personal meaning; it is a source of pleasure, communication, and love. If forced, however, it becomes an instrument of aggression and pain. Its meaning changes depending on the context in which we engage in it (Sprecher & McKinney, 1993). How we feel about sexual intercourse may depend as much on the feelings and motives we bring to it as on the techniques we use or the orgasms we experience.

The Significance of Sexual Intercourse   Although sexual intercourse is important for most sexually involved couples, the significance of it differs between men and women (Blumstein & Schwartz, 1983; Sprecher & McKinney, 1993). For men, sexual intercourse is only one of several sexual activities that they enjoy. For many heterosexual women, however, intercourse is central to their sexual satisfaction. More than any other heterosexual sexual activity, sexual intercourse involves equal participation by both partners. Both partners equally and simultaneously give and receive. As a result, women feel a greater shared intimacy than they do in other sexual activities.

The Positions   There are two basic positions in sexual intercourse—face-to-face and rear entry—although the playfulness of the couple, their movement from one bodily configuration to another, and their ingenuity can provide an infinite variety. The same positions played out in different settings can cause an intensity that transforms the ordinary into the extraordinary.

The most common position is face-to-face with the man on top (Figure 9.13). Many people prefer this position, for several reasons. First, it is the

> The sexual act is in time what the tiger is in space.
>
> —*Georges Bataille*

> The sexual embrace can only be compared with music and prayer.
>
> —*Havelock Ellis (1859–1939)*

FIGURE 9.13   Face-to-Face, Man on Top

FIGURE 9.14   Face-to-Face, Woman on Top

traditional, correct, or "official" position in our culture, which many people find reassuring and validating in terms of their sexuality. (The man-on-top position is commonly known as the missionary position because it was the position missionaries traditionally encouraged people to use.) Second, it can allow the man maximum activity, movement, and control of coitus. Third, it allows the woman freedom to stimulate her clitoris to assist in her orgasm. The primary disadvantages are that it makes it difficult for the man to caress his partner or to stimulate her clitoris while supporting himself with his hands and for the woman to control the angle, rate, and depth of penetration. Furthermore, some men have difficulty controlling ejaculation in this position, because the penis is highly stimulated.

Another common position is face-to-face with the woman on top (Figure 9.14). The woman either lies on top of her partner or sits astride him. This position allows the woman maximum activity, movement, and control. She can control the depth to which the penis penetrates. Additionally, when the woman sits astride her partner, either of them can caress or stimulate her labia and clitoris, thus facilitating orgasm in the woman. As with the man-on-top position, kissing is easy. A disadvantage is that some men or women may feel uneasy about the woman assuming a position that signifies an active role in coitus. This position tends to be less stimulating for the man, thus making it easier for him to control ejaculation.

Intercourse can also be performed with the man positioned behind the woman. There are several variations on the rear-entry position. The woman may kneel supported on her arms and receive the penis in her vagina from behind. The couple may lie on their sides, with the woman's back to her partner (Figure 9.15). This position offers variety and may be particularly suitable during pregnancy. This position facilitates clitoral stimulation by the woman. Generally, it is also possible for the man to

FIGURE 9.15   Rear Entry

stimulate her during intercourse. Some people object to the rear-entry position as "animal-like," or they may feel it inhibits intimacy or resembles anal intercourse. Furthermore, it is sometimes difficult to keep the penis inside the vagina.

In the face-to-face side position, both partners lie on their sides facing each other (Figure 9.16). Each partner has greater freedom to caress and stimulate the other. As with the rear-entry position, a major drawback is that keeping the penis in the vagina may be difficult.

FIGURE 9.16   Face-to-Face on Side

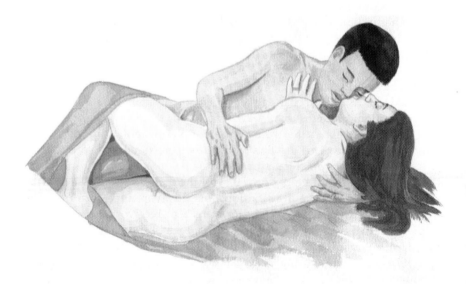

FIGURE 9.17   Tantric Sex

STIs, including HIV, can be passed on through heterosexual intercourse. Unless individuals are in a mutually exclusive relationship and have both tested negative for STIs, it is important to use a condom every time they have sex.

Tantric sex is a type of sexual intimacy based on Eastern religious beliefs beginning in India around 5000 B.C. The tantric sex technique of sexual intercourse involves the couple sharing their "energies" by initially thrusting minimally, generating energy via subtle, inner movements. They visualize the energy of the genitals moving upward in their bodies (Figure 9.17). The couple may harmonize their breathing and achieve intimacy (often looking into each other's eyes), ecstasy, and abandon (Crooks & Baur, 2002). Several books have been written on tantric sex, and numerous Web sites are devoted to it.

Anal Eroticism

Anal eroticism refers to sexual activities involving the anus, whose delicate membranes (as well as taboo nature) make it erotically arousing for many people. These activities include **analingus,** the licking of the anal region (colloquially known as "rimming" or "tossing salad"). Anal-manual contact consists of stimulating the anal region with the fingers; sometimes, an entire fist may be inserted (known as "fisting" among gay White males and "fingering" among gay African American males). Many couples engage in this activity along with fellatio or sexual intercourse. Though little is known about the prevalence of this activity, many report it to be highly arousing because of the sensitivity of the skin around the anus. Keeping this area clean is extremely important because the intestinal tract, which extends to the anus, carries a variety of microorganisms.

Anal intercourse refers to the male's inserting his erect penis into his partner's anus. Both heterosexual people and gay men participate in anal intercourse. According to the NHSLS, 26% of heterosexual men and 20% of heterosexual women have engaged in anal sex in their lifetime (Laumann et al., 1994). However, only 10% of sexually active heterosexual couples reported engaging in anal intercourse during the preceding year; it is not a common practice after it has been experienced once. For many heterosexuals, it is more of an experimental activity, but for others, it is a regular and pleasurable activity. Interestingly, the NHSLS found anal sex to be more common among the well educated (Laumann et al., 1994).

Anal intercourse is a major mode of sexual interaction for gay men. In fact, there are more colloquial terms for anal eroticism among gay men than for any other form of sexual activity (Mays, Cochran, Bellinger, & Smith, 1992). A national study of anal sex practices by American men (orientation not stated) found considerable variation by ethnicity (Billy et al., 1993). Among men age 20–39, about 21% of Whites, 13.6% of African Americans, and 24% of Latinos have experienced anal intercourse. The *Advocate* magazine survey found that 46% of gay men loved insertive anal intercourse and 43% loved receptive anal intercourse (Lever, 1994).

Among gay men, anal intercourse is less common than oral sex, but it is, nevertheless, an important ingredient to the sexual satisfaction of many gays (Berger, 1991; Blumstein & Schwartz, 1983). Although heterosexual imagery portrays the person who penetrates as "masculine" and the penetrated person as "feminine," this imagery does not generally reflect gay reality. For both partners, anal intercourse is regarded as masculine.

Although anal sex may heighten eroticism for those who engage in it, from a health perspective, it is riskier than most other forms of sexual interaction. The rectum is particularly susceptible to STIs. Because of HIV, anal intercourse is potentially the most dangerous form of sexual interaction. The delicate rectal tissues are easily lacerated, allowing the AIDS virus (carried within semen) to enter the bloodstream. If partners practice anal intercourse, they should engage in it *only* if both are certain that they are free from HIV *and* if they use a condom. When there is oral stimulation to the anal region, a rubber dam can be placed over the area to reduce the risk of transmission of HIV, other STIs, and bacteria.

If the penis or a foreign object is inserted into the anus, it must be washed before insertion into the vagina because it may cause a bacterial infection. Other health hazards associated with anal erotic practices include rupturing the rectum with foreign objects and lacerating the anus or rectal wall through the use of enemas. Licking the anus puts individuals at risk for acquiring HIV, hepatitis, and other STIs (see Chapters 15 and 16).

AS WE HAVE SEEN, sexual behaviors cannot be separated from attraction and desire. Our autoerotic activities are as important to our sexuality as are our interpersonal ones. Although the sexual behaviors we have examined in this chapter are the most common ones in our society, many people engage in other, less typical, activities. We discuss these atypical behaviors in Chapter 10.

SUMMARY

Sexual Attractiveness

- The characteristics that constitute sexual attractiveness vary across cultures. Youthfulness and good health appear to be the only universals. Our culture prefers slender women with large breasts and men with well-defined arm and pectoral muscles. Both men and women are attracted to the buttocks of the other sex. A study of college students over 5 decades found that "good looks" of a potential partner have increased in importance for both men and women.

- Because of the halo effect, attractive people are assumed to be more sexual and permissive than unattractive people. Attractive college women may be more likely to have engaged in sexual intercourse and oral sex than other women.

- Sexual desire is affected by *erotophilia,* a positive emotional response to sex, and by *erotophobia,* a negative response to sex.

Sexual Scripts

- Sexual scripts organize our sexual expression. They have three major components: cultural, intrapersonal, and interpersonal. The cultural script provides the general forms sexual behaviors are expected to take in a particular society. The intrapersonal script interprets our physiological responses as sexual or not. The interpersonal script is the shared conventions and signals that make sexual activities between two people possible.

Autoeroticism

- *Autoeroticism* refers to sexual activities that involve only oneself. These activities include sexual fantasies, erotic dreams and *nocturnal orgasm,* and *masturbation,* or stimulation of the genitals for pleasure. Persons practicing various types of autoerotic activity are also more likely to report enacting more elaborate interpersonal sexual scripts.

- Sexual fantasies and dreams are probably the most universal of all sexual behaviors; they are normal aspects of our sexuality. Erotic fantasies have several functions: They take our generalized sexual drives and help define and direct them, they allow us to

plan or anticipate erotic situations, they provide pleasurable escape from routine, they introduce novelty, and they offer clues to our unconscious.

- Most men and women masturbate. Masturbation may begin as early as infancy and continue throughout old age. Attitudes toward masturbation vary across ethnic groups.

Sexual Behavior with Others

- Sexual intercourse is the most appealing sexual activity for both female and male heterosexuals.

- The erotic potential of touching has been undervalued because our culture tends to be orgasm oriented, especially among males. *Pleasuring* is a means by which couples get to know each other erotically through touching and caressing.

- Lesbian women and gay men report that hugging, kissing, and cuddling are their favorite erotic activities.

- Erotic kissing is usually our earliest interpersonal sexual experience and is regarded as a rite of passage into adult sexuality.

- Oral-genital sex is becoming increasingly accepted, especially among young adults. Cunnilingus is the stimulation of the vulva with the tongue and mouth. It is engaged in by both heterosexuals and lesbian women. Fellatio is the stimulation of the penis with the mouth; it is engaged in by both heterosexuals and gay men.

- Sexual intercourse can be an intimate and rewarding interaction between two people. It is both a means of reproduction and a pleasurable form of communication.

- Anal eroticism refers to sexual activities involving the anus. It is engaged in by heterosexuals, gay men, and lesbian women.

Sex and the Internet

Sexual Health InfoCenter

A well-done and comprehensive Web site, the Sexual Health InfoCenter has many features, including "channels" on better sex, masturbation, sex health videos, STIs, birth control, safe sex, sexual problems, and "Sex Tip of the Week." The Web site also has featured programs and featured articles on a variety of sexuality topics. Visit this Web site (http://www.sexhealth.org) and find out the following:

- What are the options of the site?
- How did the site begin (see "Who Are We?")?
- What is the sex tip of the week?
- For one sexual expression topic, such as masturbation or oral sex, what information does the site provide?

SUGGESTED WEB SITES

JackinWorld
http://www.jackinworld.com
Provides honest, straightforward, nonexplicit information on masturbation.

The Kama Sutra of Tantra
http://www.tantramagic.com
Provides information about tantric sex as well as numerous commercial products for enhancing sexual expression.

Sex Coach at iVillage
http://www.ivillage.com/relationships
Provides information on a broad range of sexuality and relationship issues, including suggestions for enhancing sexual pleasure.

Sexual Health InfoCenter
http://www.sexhealth.org
One of the most poplar sources of sexual health information on the Internet; provides a forum for adults to discuss issues related to human sexuality.

World's Funniest Collection of Masturbation Synonyms
http://www.worldwidewank.com/funniest
A long list of synonyms for both female and male masturbation.

Yahoo! Directory on Masturbation
http://www.yahoo.com/society_and_culture/sexuality
Gives the names of and links to many Web sites concerning masturbation.

SUGGESTED READING

Caster, Wendy. (1993). *The Lesbian Sex Book*. Boston: Alyson Publications. A study of sexual function and technique, safer sex practices, relationships, and STIs.

Comfort, Alex. (2003). *The Joy of Sex*. New York: Crown. Fully revised and completely updated for the twenty-first century.

Cornog, Martha. (2003). The Big Book of Masturbation: From Angst to Zeal. San Francisco: Down There Press. An interdisciplinary examination of the history, evolution, psychology, literature, modern culture, and humor of masturbation.

Dodson, Betty. (1996). *Sex for One*. New York: Crown. Self-discovery techniques through masturbation for women and men; includes sensitive illustrations.

Klein, Marty. (2002). *Beyond Orgasm: Dare to Be Honest About the Sex You Really Want*. Berkeley, CA: Ten Speed Press. Designed to help readers accept their own sexuality, approach partners with confidence, and become involved in a wider range of erotic activities.

Millner, Denene, & Chiles, Nick. (1999). *What Brothers Think, What Sistahs Think: The Real Deal on Love and Relationships*. New York: Morrow. A study of sexuality-related issues written from a Black perspective and using the question-answer format.

Silverstein, Charles, & Picano, Felice. (2003). *The New Joy of Gay Sex* (3rd ed.). New York: HarperCollins. An illustrated guide to gay male sexuality.

For links, articles, and study material, go to the McGraw-Hill Web site, located at http://www.mhhe.com/strong5

10

Variations in Sexual Behavior

"I do like sex a lot, but I wouldn't call myself addicted. I think an addiction to sex would only be a bad thing in the event that it's interfering with other parts of a person's life."

—27-year-old Black male

"I really don't think that atypical sex exists. Everyone should find what feels good and natural for them; others' opinions and statistics shouldn't matter."

—20-year-old White male

"From my point of view, fetishism misses the main point of sex: physical pleasure and emotional closeness. This sort of "erotic communion" of sensation and emotion can be wholly fulfilling without the bells and whistles of whips, diapers, or anything else. To me, fetishism brings psychological incompleteness to the bedroom. It carries childhood problems, unresolved conflicts, and past trauma into an arena best suited for the psychologist's couch."

—23-year-old White female

"I think that some fetishes are good and healthy. I really don't think that someone who is turned on by feet or a pair of shoes is wrong. I do have a major problem with those who are into bondage because that is just sick."

—21-year-old biracial female

"My boyfriend always thought that having his feet licked would be weird and gross. I'd never tried it or had it done to me, but I'd heard a lot of people really love it, so on Valentine's day, I tried it. Now he likes it almost as much as oral sex. In fact, he gets excited when he hears me walking around barefoot!"

—20-year-old White female

SEXUALITY CAN BE EXPRESSED in a variety of ways, some more common than others. Many of the less common behaviors have been negatively labeled by the public, often implying that the behavior is unnatural or "perverted." In this chapter, we examine variations in sexual behavior, such as cross-dressing and domination and submission, which are not within the range of sexual behaviors in which people typically engage. Then we turn to sexual behaviors that are classified by the American Psychiatric Association as noncoercive paraphilias, including fetishism and transvestism. Finally, we examine the coercive paraphilias, which include zoophilia, pedophilia, sexual sadism, sexual masochism, and necrophilia.

SEXUAL VARIATIONS AND PARAPHILIC BEHAVIOR

The range of human sexual behavior is almost infinite. Yet most of our activities and fantasies, such as intercourse, oral-genital sex, and masturbation, and our orientation as heterosexual, gay, lesbian, or bisexual cluster within a general range of behaviors and desires. Those behaviors and fantasies that do not fall within this general range are considered variations. In this chapter, we use the term **sexual variations** to refer to those behaviors that are not *statistically* typical of American sexual behaviors.

What Are Sexual Variations?

"Sexual variation" is the most common term used, although **atypical sexual behavior** is sometimes used. It is important to remember, however, that atypical does not necessarily mean abnormal; it simply means that the majority of people do not engage in that particular behavior. Even though today's society is less judgmental about sex, resulting in people who engage in sexual variations feeling less guilt, some sexual variations are considered to be so extreme by the American Psychiatric Association (APA) that they are classified as mental disorders, or paraphilias. Paraphilic behaviors tend to be compulsive, long-standing, and distressing to the individual. Having a diagnostic category like paraphilic may indicate that our culture continues to find some sexual behaviors unacceptable.

What Is Paraphilia?

According to the fourth edition (text revision) of the APA's *Diagnostic and Statistical Manual of Mental Disorders (DSM-IV-TR)* (2000), a **paraphilia** is a mental disorder characterized by recurrent intense sexually arousing fantasies, sexual urges, or sexual behaviors lasting at least 6 months and involving (1) nonhuman objects, (2) the suffering or humiliation of oneself or one's partner, or (3) children or other nonconsenting people. The *DSM-IV-TR* lists eight paraphilias, along with a "not otherwise specified" category, of which six examples are given (Table 10.1). The "not specified" category actually contains many behaviors, which suggests that almost any behavior can take on erotic significance.

For people with a paraphilia, the paraphilic behavior is the predominant sexual behavior, although they may engage in other sexual activities as well. They may engage in the paraphilic behavior every day or several times a day, or they may participate in a variety of paraphilic behaviors. Even though the behavior may lead to legal or interpersonal difficulties, it may be so rewarding and irresistible that a person continues to practice it. Mild versions of paraphilias may manifest only in disturbing fantasies, often occurring during masturbation. Severe versions can include sexual victimization of children and the use of threats or force with others (Seligman & Hardenberg, 2000). The overwhelming majority of people with paraphilia are males (McConaghy, 1998); they are most likely to engage in paraphilic activities between the ages of 15 and 25. One of the most common paraphilias, sexual masochism, is diagnosed much less frequently in women; the ratio is estimated to be 20 males for each female (APA, 2000). Paraphilias are diagnosed in all ethnic and socioeconomic groups and among all sexual orientations. All people with paraphilia share one common trait: Their sexual behavior has been disconnected from a loving, consensual relationship with another adult (Schwartz, 2000). The prevalence of paraphilias is unknown because many people do not seek treatment due to the strong pleasure they derive and the social stigma associated with the fantasy or behavior (Seligman & Hardenberg, 2000). However, the prevalence of these behaviors is considered to be quite high (Kaplan, Sadock, & Grebb, 1994). To minimize the negative message of labeling and to recognize individuals' many components, it seems more appropriate to use the term "person with paraphilia" than "paraphiliacs."

TABLE 10.1 The *DSM-IV-TR* Paraphilias	
Specified Paraphilias	*Sexual Arousal Activity*
Exhibitionism	Exposing one's genitals to an unsuspecting person
Fetishism	Using a nonliving object
Frotteurism	Touching or rubbing one's genitals against a nonconsenting person
Pedophilia	Having sexual activity with a prepubescent child
Sexual masochism	Being humiliated, beaten, bound, or otherwise made to suffer
Sexual sadism	Inflicting psychological or physical suffering
Transvestic fetishism	Cross-dressing
Voyeurism	Observing an unsuspecting person who is disrobing or having sex
Paraphilias Not Otherwise Specified	*Sexual Arousal Activity*
Telephone scatologia	Making obscene phone calls
Necrophilia	Having sexual activity with corpses
Zoophilia	Having sexual activity with animals (bestiality)
Coprophilia	Being sexually aroused in response to feces
Klismaphilia	Being sexually aroused in response to enemas
Urophilia	Being sexually aroused in response to urine

Source: Adapted from American Psychiatric Association. (2000). *Diagnostic and Statistical Manual of Mental Disorders* (4th ed., text revision). Washington, DC: Author.

The distinction between sexual variations and behavior that might be classified as paraphilic behavior is sometimes more a difference of degree than kind. For example, many men find that certain objects, such as black lingerie, intensify their sexual arousal; for others, these objects are necessary for arousal. In the first case, there is nothing particularly unusual. But if a man is unable to become aroused without the lingerie and the purpose of sex is to bring him in contact with it, the behavior is considered paraphilic by the APA (2000).

It is also important to recognize that seemingly scientific or clinical terms may not be scientific at all. Instead, they may be pseudoscientific terms hiding moral judgments, as in the case of "nymphomania" and "satyriasis." **Nymphomania** is a pejorative term referring to "abnormal or excessive" sexual desire in a woman and is usually applied to sexually active single women. But what is "abnormal" or "excessive" is often defined moralistically rather than scientifically. Nymphomania is not recognized as a clinical condition by the APA (2000). Although the term "nymphomania" dates back to the seventeenth century, it was popularized in the nineteenth century by Richard von Krafft-Ebing and others. Physicians and psychiatrists used the term to pathologize women's sexual behavior if it deviated from nineteenth-century moral standards (see Chapter 2). Even today, "nymphomania," "nymphomaniac," and "nympho" retain pathological connotations.

"Sexual Interest Disorder": A Viable Alternative to Paraphilia or a Radical Departure?

SINCE THE APA BEGAN listing certain variant sexual behaviors as "paraphilia" in its 1980 edition of *Diagnostic and Statistical Manual of Mental Disorders (DSM)*, the paraphilia construct has been widely critiqued. Critics of the *DSM* paraphilias suggest that the types of sexual behaviors considered paraphilias should be expanded (Barth & Kinder, 1987; Carnes, 1983; Coleman, 1991; Freund, Seto, & Cuban, 1997; Schwartz & Brasted, 1985). They contend as well that the listing of behaviors as paraphilic is merely an attempt to pathologize sexual behaviors not approved of by society. Physician and sexologist Charles Moser (2001) has written about the limitations of the *DSM* paraphilia construct and suggested an alternative classification.

Moser notes that the term "paraphilia" was popularized by sexologist John Money (1980, 1984), as a way of describing nonstandard or unusual sexual behavior in a nonjudgmental manner. He indicates that paraphilias, unfortunately, were assimilated into the *DSM* as a classification of pathology. The *DSM* is the standard, worldwide resource for defining psychopathology (mental illness)—that is, for determining which behaviors and desires are healthy and unhealthy. These criteria for making specific psychiatric diagnosis are used not only by mental health practitioners but by the divorce courts and criminal justice system.

Moser notes that "neither sexology nor other disciplines have been able to explain how humans develop any or even particular sexual interests." He contends that different developmental processes can result in similar sexual interests and that the same process can end in different sexual interests, complicating the question further. In addition, each person has a unique sexual pattern, which has led to variations in sexual behaviors and to differences in acceptance by society. Moser explains:

> Simplistically, the general public finds some sexual interests acceptable (heterosexual coitus within marriage), some possibly acceptable (homosexual attraction), some odd (shoe fetishes), and some disgusting (pedophilia). Acceptable sexual interests vary cross-culturally and change transhistorically. Over the last century, we have seen a relative reversal in North American societal and scientific views of masturbation, oral-genital contact, and homosexuality. Each of these was thought to be the cause, sign, or result of mental illness and all were seen as particularly dangerous to children; these behaviors are now relatively accepted.

Nevertheless, society continues to classify certain sexual behaviors as unacceptable, resulting in imprisonment, executions, personal distress, and/or family dissolutions among persons expressing these behaviors. Medical and clinical sexological interventions have been applied, often with negative consequences (Moser, 2001).

Moser states that the creation of the diagnostic category of paraphilia represents a medicalization of nonstandard sexual behaviors and a pseudoscientific attempt to regularize sexuality. He further notes that the "diagnostic criteria have been written to pathologize those behaviors society deems sexually inappropriate." He questions why some behaviors are considered unlawful while others are considered as evidence of psychopathology. Moser believes, given the flaws of the *DSM* paraphilic construct and category, that "more radical solutions are required." He has proposed a new classification—"sexual interest disorder (SID)"—to replace the paraphilias. This new classification would emphasize the effect of the sexual interest on the individual rather than implying that participants in certain sexual behaviors are inherently "sick"; it would also avoid naming specific sexual behaviors. To quality as an SID, a behavior would have to meet two criteria:

- Specific fantasies, sexual urges, or behaviors that cause clinically significant distress or impairment in social, occupational, or other important areas of functioning

- The sexual interest not better accounted for in another Axis I disorder (e.g., schizophrenia disorder, mood disorder, or anxiety disorder), not due to the effects of a general medical disorder, and not the result of substance use, misuse, or abuse

This new classification does not suggest that all sexual interests are acceptable, nor that any interest should be afforded special rights or protections. As an example, Moser discusses pedophilia. He says, "To be perfectly clear, adult-child sexual contact should not be condoned under any circumstances." However, he says that the punishment of adults who have sexual contact with children "should not be mitigated by claims of mental illness." Moser further states that having sexual interest in prepubescent children is not a problem, but acting on it is and should be dealt with in the criminal justice system.

Consider these questions concerning the *DSM* paraphilias and Moser's suggested alternative classification: Do you think that the *DSM*'s classification of certain variant sexual behaviors as paraphilia is a "pseudoscientific attempt to regulate sexuality" or a necessary way to address sexual behaviors that indeed represent mental illness? Is Moser's alternative classification—SID—a viable alternative to or a radical departure from the *DSM* category of paraphilia?

Satyriasis, referring to "abnormal" or "uncontrollable" sexual desire in men, is less commonly used than "nymphomania" because men are expected to be more sexual than women. For this reason, definitions of satyriasis infrequently include the adjective "excessive." Instead, reflecting ideas of male sexuality as a powerful drive, "uncontrollable" becomes the significant adjective. Satyriasis is not recognized as a clinical condition by the APA (2000).

As you read this chapter, remember to distinguish clearly between the use of the various terms clinically, judgmentally, or casually. It can be tempting to define a behavior you don't like or approve of as paraphilic. But unless you are clinically trained, you cannot diagnose someone (including yourself) as having a mental disorder.

As touched on previously, the line between a sexual variation and a paraphilia is often not exact, and the "labeling" of specific behaviors as either may be open to debate and void of scientific justification. However, for the sake of discussion, several variations in sexual behaviors are presented in the context of the *DSM-IV-TR* classifications. Some mental health professionals believe that classifying some sexual behaviors as paraphilias is flawed and reflects a pseudoscientific attempt to control sexuality.

Sexual Variations Among College Students

We have no reliable estimates of the number of individuals with paraphilias, although various studies have produced some clues. For example, a *Details* magazine survey of college students reported the prevalence of some variant and paraphilic behaviors among the sample (Figure 10.1). Except for one behavior, "talked dirty," only a minority of the students reported having engaged in any of the behaviors listed. It is interesting to note that the percentages of female and male students who had participated in a behavior were often nearly equal; for example, 6% of both female and male students indicated that they had engaged in sadomasochism (Elliot & Brantley, 1997).

SEXUAL VARIATION: DOMINATION AND SUBMISSION

Variations in sexual behavior are not rare. Although the majority of people do not engage in these activities, they are not necessarily uncommon. One of the more widespread forms of sexual variation is domination and submission.

Sexual arousal derived from the *consensual* acting out of sexual scenes in which one person dominates and the other submits is called **domination and submission (D/S).** The term **sadomasochism (S&M)** is also used by the general public to describe domination and submission, but it is no longer used as a clinical term in psychiatry and psychology to describe consensual domination and submission (Breslow, 1989).

Domination and submission are forms of fantasy sex, and the D/S behaviors are carefully controlled by elaborate shared scripts. The critical element is not pain, but power. The dominant partner is all-powerful, and the sub-

Through me forbidden voices.
Voices of sexes and lusts . . .
Voices veiled, and I remove the veil,
Voices indecent by me clarified and
     transfigured.

—*Walt Whitman (1819–1892)*

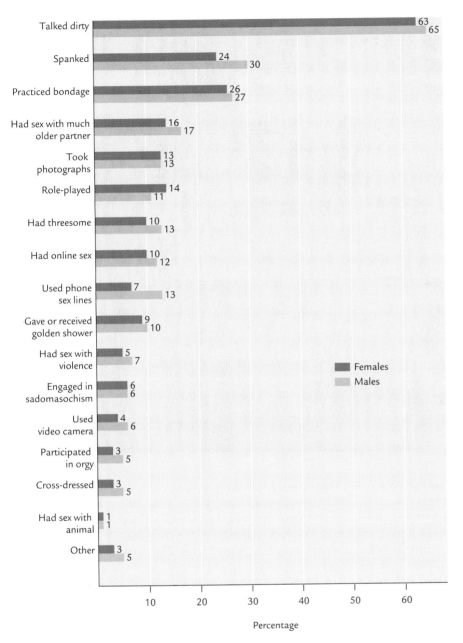

FIGURE 10.1 Percentage of College Students Reporting Engaging in Variations of Sexual Behavior. (*Source:* Adapted from Elliot & Brantley, 1997.)

missive partner is powerless. Significantly, the amount or degree of "pain," which is usually feigned or slight, is controlled by the submissive partner. As such, fantasy plays a central role, especially for the submissive person (Arndt, 1991). As two people enact the master-slave script, the control is not complete. Rather, it is the *illusion* of total control that is fundamental to D/S (Hyde & DeLameter, 2003).

A large-scale study of a nonclinical population revealed that the majority of people who engage in domination and submission do so as "a form of sexual enhancement which they voluntarily and mutually choose to explore" (Weinberg, Williams, & Moser, 1984). As such, domination and submission

Click on "Whipsmart: A Beginner's Guide to S/M to meet a couple experimenting with domination and submission.

Bondage and discipline, or B&D, often involves leather straps, handcuffs, and other restraints as part of its scripting.

are not paraphilic. To be considered paraphilic, such behavior requires that the suffering or humiliation of oneself or one's partner be real, not merely simulated (APA, 2000). (Sexual sadism and sexual masochism, which are considered paraphilias, are discussed later in the chapter.)

Domination and submission take many forms. The participants generally assume both dominant and submissive roles at different times; few are interested only in being on "top" or "bottom" (Moser, 1988). Probably the most widely known form is **bondage and discipline (B&D),** in which a person is bound with scarves, leather straps, underwear, handcuffs, chains, or other such devices while another simulates or engages in light-to-moderate discipline activities such as spanking or whipping. The bound person may be blindfolded or gagged. A woman specializing in disciplining a person is known as a **dominatrix,** and her submissive partner is called a slave.

Bondage and discipline may take place in specialized settings called "dungeons" furnished with restraints, body suspension devices, racks, whips, and chains (Stoller, 1991). Eleven percent of both men and women have had experience with bondage, according to one study (Janus & Janus, 1993).

Another common form of domination and submission is humiliation, in which the person is debased or degraded (Arndt, 1991). In the Janus study, 5% of the men and 7% of the women had engaged in verbal humiliation (Janus & Janus, 1993). One-third of the submission respondents in another study received enemas ("water treatment"), were urinated on ("golden

Ah beautiful, passionate body,
That never has ached with a heart!
On the mouth though the kisses are
    bloody,
Though they sting till it shudder and
    smart
More kind than the love we adore is
They hurt not the heart nor the brain
Oh bitter and tender Dolores
Our Lady of Pain.

—*Algernon Swinburne (1837–1909)*

Betty Page, who has become a cult figure among those interested in domination and submission, was one of the most photographed women in the 1950s.

showers"), or were defecated on ("scat") (Breslow, Evans, & Langley, 1985). In the Janus study, 6% of the men and 4% of the women had participated in golden showers (Janus & Janus, 1993). (According to the *DSM-IV-TR*, sexual pleasure derived from receiving enemas is known as **klismophilia** [klismo-FIL-ee-uh], that derived from contact with urine is called **urophilia** [yore-oh-FIL-ee-uh], and that derived from contact with feces is called **coprophilia** [cop-ro-FIL-ee-uh].) Humiliation activities may include servilism, infantilism (also known as babyism), kennelism, and tongue-lashing. In servilism, the person desires to be treated as a servant or slave. In infantilism, the person acts in a babyish manner—using baby talk, wearing diapers, and being pampered, scolded, or spanked by his or her "mommy" or "daddy." Kennelism refers to being treated like a dog (wearing a studded dog collar and being tied to a leash) or ridden like a horse while the dominant partner applies whips or spurs. Tongue-lashing is verbal abuse by a dominant partner who uses language that humiliates and degrades the other person.

People engage in domination and submission in private or as part of an organized subculture complete with clubs and businesses catering to the acting out of D/S fantasies (Stoller, 1991). This subculture is sometimes known as "the velvet underground." There are scores of noncommercial D/S clubs throughout the United States (Arndt, 1991). The clubs are often specialized: lesbian S&M, dominant men/submissive women, submissive men/dominant women, gay men's S&M, and transvestite S&M. Leather sex bars are meeting places for gay men who are interested in domination and submission. The D/S subculture includes D/S videos, Web sites, books, and magazines.

The world of domination and submission is secretive, but the degree of secrecy depends on the different groups involved and the types of activities undertaken. The world of heterosexual domination and submission is even more hidden, with contacts limited to small, private networks (Weinberg & Kamel, 1983).

> Don't do unto others as you would they should do unto you. Their taste may be different.
>
> —*George Bernard Shaw (1856–1950)*

NONCOERCIVE PARAPHILIAS

An important aspect of paraphilias is whether they involve coercion. Non-coercive paraphilias are regarded as relatively benign or harmless because they are victimless. Noncoercive paraphilias include fetishism and transvestism.

Fetishism

We attribute special or magical powers to many things: a lucky number, a saint's relic, an heirloom, a lock of hair, or an automobile. These objects possess a kind of symbolic magic (Belk, 1991). We will carry our boyfriend's or girlfriend's photograph (and sometimes talk to it or kiss it), ask for a keepsake if we part, and become nostalgic for a former love when we hear a par-

Inanimate objects or parts of the body, such as the foot, may be sexualized by some people.

ticular song. All these behaviors are common, but they point to the symbolic power of objects, or fetishes.

Fetishism is sexual attraction to objects, which become for the person with the fetish sexual symbols. The fetish is usually required or strongly preferred for sexual arousal, and its absence may cause erectile problems in males (APA, 2000). Instead of relating to another person, a fetishist gains sexual gratification from kissing a shoe, caressing a glove, drawing a lock of hair against his or her cheek, or masturbating with a piece of underwear. But the focus of a person with fetishism is not necessarily an inanimate object; he may be attracted to a woman's feet, ears, breasts, legs, or elbows or to any other part of her body (Cautela, 1986). (Exclusive attraction to body parts is known as **partialism.**) However, using objects for sexual stimulation, such as vibrators, or using articles of female clothing for cross-dressing is not a sign of fetishism (APA, 2000). According to the Janus study, 11% of the men and 6% of the women had engaged in fetishistic behaviors (Janus & Janus, 1993).

Fetishistic behavior may be viewed as existing on a continuum, or existing in degrees, moving from a slight preference for an object, to a strong preference for it, to the necessity of the object for arousal, and, finally, to the object as a substitute for a sexual partner (McConaghy, 1993). Most people have slight fetishistic traits. For example, men describe themselves as leg men or breast men; they prefer dark-haired or light-haired partners. Some women are attracted to muscular men, others to hairy chests, and still others to shapely buttocks. However, to meet the APA definition of fetishism, a person must not be able to have sex without that fetish (Schwartz, 2000).

Transvestism

Transvestism ("trans" means cross, "vest" means dress) is the wearing of clothing of the other sex, usually for sexual arousal. In one study, 6% of the men and 3% of the women reported cross-dressing (Janus & Janus, 1993). Although the literature indicates that cross-dressing occurs almost exclusively in males, there are studies of women who have erotic attachment to men's garments (Bullough & Bullough, 1993; Stoller, 1982).

Transvestism covers a broad range of behaviors. Some persons with transvestism prefer to wear only one article of clothing (usually a brassiere or panties) of the other sex in the privacy of their home; others choose to don an entire outfit in public. The distinction between fetishism and transvestism involves the wearing of the garment versus the viewing or fondling of it. The frequency of cross-dressing ranges from a momentary activity that produces sexual excitement, usually through masturbation, to more frequent and long-lasting behavior, depending on the individual, available opportunities, and mood or stressors.

Some who cross-dress are considered psychologically disordered, as in **transvestic fetishism.** According to the APA (2000), people with this disorder are heterosexual men who, over a period of at least 6 months, act upon intense, usually distressful, sexual urges and fantasies involving the wearing of women's clothes. Because many people with transvestism contend that they are not abnormal but are merely revealing a legitimate source of sexual expression and arousal, they resist and shun this diagnosis. Trans-

Of all the sexual aberrations, the most peculiar is chastity.

—*Remy de Gourmont (1858–1915)*

Girls will be boys and boys will be girls
It's a mixed up, muddled up, shook up world . . .

—*The Kinks*

Cross-dressing is not necessarily a paraphilia. It may be a source of humor and parody, as the traditional boundaries of gender are explored and challenged.

Those hot pants of hers were so damned tight, I could hardly breathe.

—*Benny Hill (1924–1992)*

I don't think painting my fingernails is a big deal. It's not like I'm sitting home by myself trying on lingerie. . . . When I cross-dress now, it's just another way I can show all the sides of Dennis Rodman.

—*Dennis Rodman*

I don't mind drag—women have been female impersonators for some time.

—*Gloria Steinem*

vestic fetishism usually begins prior to adulthood. Some men report childhood experiences of being humiliated or punished by women and forced to dress in female attire (Maxmen & Ward, 1995).

People with transvestism are usually quite conventional in their masculine dress and attitudes. Dressed as women or wearing only one women's garment, they may become sexually aroused and masturbate or have sex with a woman. As time passes, however, the erotic element of the female garment may decrease and the comfort level increase. The majority of people with transvestism have no desire to undergo a sex-change operation. If they do, there may be an accompanying diagnosis of gender dysphoria. Transvestism should not be confused with transsexualism. Most people with transvestism have no desire to change their anatomical sex, whereas transsexuals often do. People with transvestism are rarely attracted to other men (G. R. Brown, 1995; Wise & Meyer, 1980). They believe they have both masculine and feminine personalities within them. "TV" is the acronym for "transvestism" and often appears in personal ads in underground newspapers and in Internet dating services.

Many people with transvestism marry in hopes of "curing" their desire to cross-dress. Of those who marry, about two-thirds have children. Some voluntarily reveal their cross-dressing to their spouse after marriage, but the majority have it discovered. Invariably, the partners are distressed and blame themselves for somehow "emasculating" their partners. Some people with transvestism and their spouses and families are able to adjust to the cross-dressing. Data suggest, however, that women merely tolerate rather than support their partners' cross-dressing (Brown & Collier, 1989; Bullough & Weinberg, 1988). Often, however, the stress is too great, and separation follows soon after the transvestism is discovered.

As transvestism is neither dangerous nor reversible (Wise & Meyer, 1980), the preferred clinical treatment is to help the person and those close to her or him accept the cross-dressing. Though most individuals who engage in

EACH YEAR, VAST NUMBERS of ordinary men dress as women during Halloween, Mardi Gras, and Carnival. **Cross-dressing** is a staple of television shows such as *Saturday Night Live* and has been the focus of many movies, including *Tootsie* and *Mrs. Doubtfire*, in which Dustin Hoffman and Robin Williams, respectively, received wide acclaim for their impersonations of women. Rock culture includes cross-dressed performances by Marilyn Manson, Alice Cooper, Mick Jagger, David Bowie, and Madonna. In the gay subculture, cross-dressing (or **drag**) is a source of humor and parody. In all these cases, cross-dressing represents a loosening of traditional boundaries. Behind masks and costumes, men and women play out fantasies that are forbidden to them in their daily lives.

According to a study of 1032 cross-dressing men, excluding female impersonators and drag queens, 87% were heterosexual, 60% were married, 65% were college educated, and 76% reported being raised by both parents through age 18. For 65%, their first cross-dressing experience was before age 10. Sixty percent reported that sexual excitement and orgasm often or almost always occurred with cross-dressing. Ninety-three percent preferred complete cross-dressing, but only 14% reported frequently going out in public dressed as a woman (Docter & Prince, 1997). (**Female impersonators** are men who dress as women, often as part of their job in entertainment. Gay men who cross-dress to entertain are often referred to as **drag queens.** Because neither female impersonators nor drag queens typically cross-dress for sexual arousal, they are not considered transvestites.)

As can readily be seen, people cross-dress for a variety of reasons. Some cross-dress to relieve the pressure associated with traditional gender roles. Others are satirizing or parodying social conventions. Still others want to challenge what they see as narrow views of gender and sexuality.

Given the humor, playfulness, and sense of relaxation apparent in many cases of cross-dressing, how do we distinguish this phenomenon from fetishistic transvestism, which is considered a paraphilia? If those who cross-dress are labeled as having a paraphilia, what effect does it have on them? Does such labeling create mental distress in an otherwise relatively well adjusted person?

Questions like these lead us to consider the effect of labeling in general and to ask, "What's in a name?" Although clinical labels and definitions help professionals to diagnose illnesses and create treatment plans, labeling can also cause problems. Consider the difference between a 7-year-old boy who is called active and one who is labeled hyperactive. Or between a person described as compassionate and one labeled codependent. Or between someone said to have a strong libido and someone labeled a sex addict. In each case, the label adds a clinical dimension to the person's behavior. Labeling can have a profound effect both on an individual's self-concept and on the perceptions and behaviors of those involved with the person.

Among those who cross-dress, being labeled a person with a paraphilia can contribute to maladaptation by fostering unnecessary shame and guilt. It can even become a self-fulfilling prophecy if the person begins to experience significant distress and impairment as a result of being so labeled. Although cross-dressing is variant, the majority of people who cross-dress are not maladapted or mentally disordered, nor is their behavior pathological. To label all those who cross-dress as individuals with paraphilias is inaccurate and potentially harmful.

transvestism do not seek professional help (G. R. Brown, 1995), those who do often must deal with their feelings of guilt and shame (Peo, 1988).

Why does our culture seem disproportionately preoccupied with cross-dressing? Our interest, writes Marjorie Garber (1991), reflects a "crisis in categories." She asserts that the categories of male/female and heterosexual/homosexual are inadequate for describing the full range of human experience. Just as bisexuality challenges the heterosexuality/homosexuality dichotomy, cross-dressing challenges the traditional masculine/feminine dichotomy. Can a man wearing a dress really be a man? Can a heterosexual male wearing a dress really be heterosexual? Cross-dressing destroys our usual either/or ways of categorizing people (Garber, 1991).

Cross-dressing has been important in popular culture, including comedy and Hollywood. A scene from the movie Anger Management *shows Jack Nicholson with Woody Harrelson as Galaxia/Gary the Gaurd.*

COERCIVE PARAPHILIAS

Few noncoercive paraphilias are brought to public attention because of their private, victimless nature. But coercive paraphilias, which involve victimization, are a source of concern for society because of the harm they cause others. All of these paraphilias involve some kind of coercive or nonconsensual relationship with another person or with an animal.

Zoophilia

Zoophilia, sometimes referred to as "bestiality," involves deriving sexual pleasure from animals (APA, 2000). True zoophilia occurs only when animals are the preferred sexual contact regardless of what other sexual outlets are available. Zoophilia is classified as a coercive paraphilia based on the assumption that the animal is an unwilling participant. Alfred Kinsey and his colleagues reported that about 8% of the men and 3% of the women they surveyed had experienced at least one sexual contact with animals. Seventeen percent of the men who had been reared on farms had had such contact, but these activities accounted for less than 1% of their total sexual activity (Kinsey, Pomeroy, & Martin, 1948; Kinsey, Pomeroy, Martin, & Gebhard, 1953). Sexual contact with animals usually takes place among adolescents and is a transitory phenomenon. Males are likely to have intercourse with the animal or to have their genitals licked by the animal. Females are more likely to have contact with a household pet, such as having intercourse, having the animal lick their genitals, or masturbating the animal. Among adults, such contact usually occurs when human partners are not available (Money, 1981).

Voyeurism

Viewing sexual activities is a commonplace activity. Many individuals have used mirrors to view themselves during sexual behavior, watched their partners masturbate, or watched others having intercourse. Americans' interest in viewing sexual activities has spawned a multibillion-dollar sex industry devoted to fulfilling those desires. Sexually explicit magazines, books, and Web sites and x-rated videos are widely available. Topless bars, strip and peep shows, and erotic dancing attest to the attraction of visual erotica. These activities are not considered voyeurism because the observed person is *not* unwilling and these activities typically do not replace interpersonal sexuality.

Voyeurism involves recurring, intense sexual urges and fantasies related to secretly observing an unsuspecting person who is nude, disrobing, or engaging in sexual activity (APA, 2000). To be considered paraphilic behavior, voyeurism must be preferred over sexual expression with another person or entail some risk. In order to become aroused, people with voyeurism must hide and remain unseen, and the person or couple being watched must be unaware of their presence. The excitement is intensified by the possibility of being discovered. Sometimes, the person with voyeurism will masturbate or imagine having sex with the observed person while peering through a window or keyhole. People with voyeurism are sometimes called "peepers" or "peeping Toms." (Watching others who know they are being observed, such as a sex partner, stripper, or actor in a sexually explicit film, is not classified as voyeurism.)

Very little research has been done on people with voyeurism, the majority of whom are young men. They do not seek random females to watch undressing or engaging in sexual activities; instead, they seek out females they find sexually attractive. What people with voyeurism consider arousing differs from one individual to another. Some prefer to view nude bodies, breasts, or vulvas; others want to watch sexual intercourse or women having sex with women. Nancy Friday (1973, 1975) noted that some are "crotch watchers," while others are "breast watchers." Voyeurism appeals primarily to heterosexual men (Arndt, 1991), most of whom are content to keep their distance from their victim. Many lack social and sexual skills and may fear rejection.

Exhibitionism

Also known as "indecent exposure," **exhibitionism** is the recurring, intense urge or fantasy to display one's genitals to an unsuspecting stranger (APA, 2000). The individual, who is almost always male and is sometimes called a "flasher," has acted on these urges or is greatly disturbed by them. Although people with exhibitionism derive sexual gratification from the exposure of their genitals, the exposure is not a prelude or invitation to intercourse. Instead, it is an escape from intercourse, for the man never exposes himself to a willing woman—only to strangers or near-strangers. Typically, he obtains sexual gratification after exposing himself as he fantasizes about the shock and horror he caused his victim. Other people with exhibitionism experience orgasm as they expose themselves; still others may masturbate during the act of exhibitionism (APA, 2000). These men generally expose themselves to children, adolescents, and young women; they rarely expose themselves to older women. In those few instances in which a woman shows interest, the person with exhibitionism immediately flees. Usually, there is no physical contact. Exotic dancers and nude sun-

Some people like to exhibit their bodies within public settings that are "legit-imized," such as Mardi Gras. Such displays may be exhibitionistic, but they are not considered exhibitionism in the clinical sense.

bathers are not considered people with exhibitionism because they typi-cally do not derive sexual arousal from the behavior, nor do they expose themselves to unwilling people. Furthermore, stripping for a sex partner to arouse him or her involves willing participants.

Exhibitionism is a fairly common paraphilia; more than one-third of all males arrested for sexual offenses are arrested for exhibitionism. According to one study, 7% of college men expressed interest in exhibiting themselves; 2% actually had (Templeman & Stinnett, 1991). Because of the widespread incidence of exhibitionism, at least half of adult women may have witnessed indecent exposure at least once in their lives (Arndt, 1991).

The stereotype of the person with exhibitionism as a dirty old man, lurk-ing in parks or building entryways, dressed only in a raincoat and sneakers, is erroneous. Fewer than 10% of these individuals are more than 50 years old, although a few may be in their eighties when they first begin (Arndt, 1991; Kenyon, 1989).

People with exhibitionism are generally introverted, insecure, or sexually inadequate (Arndt, 1991; Marshall, Eccles, & Barabee, 1991). They feel pow-erless as men, and their sexual relations with their wives usually are poor. This sense of powerlessness gives rise to anger and hostility, which they direct toward other women by exhibiting themselves. However, they rarely are violent. If confronted with a person with exhibitionism, it is best to ignore and distance oneself from the person and then report the incident to the police. Reacting strongly only reinforces the behavior.

Telephone Scatologia

Telephone scatologia—the making of obscene phone calls to unsuspect-ing people—is considered a paraphilia because the acts are compulsive and repetitive or because the associated fantasies cause distress to the individual.

AN OBSCENE PHONE CALL can be shocking and even traumatizing. A person who receives such a call may feel attacked, singled out, or victimized. If you have had this experience, it may be helpful to know that the obscene phone caller often picks the victim at random and is merely trying to elicit a response. Obscene phone callers rarely follow up their verbal intrusions with physical attacks on their victims. Horror, anger, and shock are the reactions the caller anticipates and finds arousing; thus, your initial response is critical.

If you receive an obscene phone call, the best thing to do is to quietly hang up the telephone. Banging down the receiver or trying to retaliate by screaming or scolding gives the caller the desired response. The telephone company claims that tactics such as pretending to be hard of hearing, blowing a whistle into the telephone, pretending to go to another phone, and letting the phone remain off the hook simply are not necessary. If the phone immediately rings again, don't answer it. If obscene calls are repeated, the telephone company suggests changing your number (many companies will do this at no charge) or, in more serious cases, working with law enforcement officials to trace the calls. A service available through many telephone companies is "call trace." When the recipient of a call enters a designated code, the telephone company can trace the call. After a certain number of traces to the same telephone number, the offender will receive a warning that the unlawful behavior must stop. Ignoring this warning results in police or civil legal intervention. Other solutions include getting an unlisted phone number and obtaining caller ID. Furthermore, when listing a number in the telephone book, many women use initials for their first (and middle) names to help disguise their gender.

Those who engage in this behavior typically get sexually aroused when their victim reacts in a shocked or horrified manner. Obscene phone calls are generally made randomly, by chance dialing or phone book listings.

The overwhelming majority of callers are male, but there are female obscene callers as well (Saunders & Awad, 1991). Male callers frequently make their female victims feel annoyed, frightened, anxious, upset, or angry, while the callers themselves often suffer from feelings of inadequacy and insecurity (Matek, 1988). They may use obscenities, breathe heavily into the phone, or say they are conducting sex research. Also, they usually masturbate during the call or immediately afterward. The victims of male callers often feel violated, but female callers have a different effect on male recipients, who generally do not feel violated or who may find the call titillating (Matek, 1988).

Frotteurism

Frotteurism (also known as "mashing" or "frottage") involves recurrent, intense urges or fantasies—lasting over a period of at least 6 months—to touch or rub against a nonconsenting person for the purpose of sexual arousal and gratification (APA, 2000). It is not known how many people practice frotteurism, but 21% of college males in one study reported engaging in at least one frotteuristic act (Templeman & Stinnett, 1991).

The person with frotteurism, most often a male, usually carries out his touching or rubbing in crowded subways or buses or at large sporting events or rock concerts. When he enters a crowd, his initial rubbing can be disguised by the crush of people. He usually rubs against his victim's buttocks or thighs with his erect penis inside his pants. Other times, he may use his hands to rub a woman's buttocks, pubic region, thighs, or breasts. Generally, he rubs against the woman for 60–90 seconds. If he ejaculates, he stops; if he doesn't, he usually moves on to find another victim (Abel, 1989). He generally will run away if the female discovers what is happening. While

ARE YOU A SEX ADDICT? As you read descriptions of sexual addiction, you may begin to think that you are. But don't believe everything you read. Consider the following: "The moment comes for every addict," writes psychologist Patrick Carnes (1983, 1991), who developed and marketed the idea of sexual addiction, "when the consequences are so great or the pain so bad that the addict admits life is out of control because of his or her sexual behavior." Money is spent on pornography, affairs threaten a marriage, masturbation replaces jogging, and fantasies interrupt studying. Sex, sex, sex is on the addict's mind. And he or she has no choice but to engage in these activities.

Sex addicts' lives are filled with guilt or remorse, according to Carnes. They cannot make a commitment; instead, they move from one affair to another. They make promises to themselves, to their partners, and to a supreme being to stop, but they cannot. Like all addicts, they are powerless before their addiction (Butts, 1992; Carnes, 1983, 1991). Their addiction is rooted in deep-seated feelings of worthlessness, despair, anxiety, and loneliness. These feelings are temporarily allayed by the "high" obtained from sexual arousal and orgasm. Sex addicts, writes Carnes, go through a four-step cycle:

1. *Preoccupation with sex and an obsessive search for sexual stimulation.* Everything passes through a sexual filter. Sex becomes an intoxication, a high.

2. *Ritualization, or special routines that lead to sex.* The ritual may include using body oils and massage, cruising, watching others, placing candles next to the bed, and drinking champagne.

3. *Compulsive sexual behavior.* This includes masturbation, bondage, extramarital affairs, exhibitionism, and incest.

4. *Despair: the realization that he or she is incapable of changing.* Guilt, feelings of isolation, or suicidal tendencies may be present.

Carnes identifies several levels of sexual addiction, categorized according to behavior. The first level of behavior includes excessive masturbation, numerous heterosexual relationships, interest in pornography, relations with prostitutes, and homosexuality. The second level includes exhibitionism, voyeurism, and obscene phone calls. The third level includes child molestation, incest, and rape. The addict moves from one level of behavior to the next in search of excitement and satisfaction.

In this model, sexual addiction is viewed in the same light as alcoholism and drug addiction; it is an activity over which the addict has no control. And, as for alcoholism, a 12-step treatment program for sex addiction has been established by the National Council on Sexual Addiction/Compulsivity (Corley, 1994). The first step is for the addict to acknowledge that he or she is helpless to end the addiction. Subsequent steps include turning to a higher power for assistance, listing all moral shortcomings, asking for forgiveness from those who have been harmed and making amends to them, and finding a spiritual path to wholeness.

After reading this description of sexual addiction, do you feel a little uneasy? Do some of the signs of sexual addiction seem to apply directly to you? Are you wondering, "Am I a sex addict?" Don't worry; you're probably not. The reason you might think you're suffering from sexual addiction is that its definition taps into many of the underlying anxieties and uncertainties we feel about sexuality in our culture. The problem lies not in you but in the concept of sexual addiction.

Although the sexual addiction model has found some adherents among clinical psychologists, they are clearly a minority. Admittedly, some people are compulsive in their sexual behaviors, but compulsion is not addiction. The influence of the sexual addiction model is not the result of its impact on therapy, psychology, and social work. Its influence is due mainly to its popularity with the media, where talk-show hosts interview so-called sex addicts and advice columnists caution their readers about the signs of sexual addiction. The popularity of an idea is no guarantee of its validity, however.

Attempts to describe certain sexual behaviors or lifestyles by labeling them as sexual addictions continue

---

mashing, the male may fantasize about having consensual sex with the women, and he may recall the mashing episode during masturbation.

Frotteurism often occurs with other paraphilias, especially exhibitionism, voyeurism, pedophilia, and sadism. It is also associated with rape.

Necrophilia

Necrophilia is sexual activity with a corpse. It is regarded as nonconsensual because a corpse is obviously unable to give consent. There are relatively

The dead person who loves will love forever and will never be weary of giving and receiving caresses.

—*Ernest Jones*

to be problematic for the professional sexuality community. Different terms have been used in attempts to describe certain behavioral patterns. For example, Eli Coleman (1991, 1996), director of the human sexuality program at the University of Minnesota Medical School, favors "sexual compulsivity" over "sexual addiction" and goes further by distinguishing between compulsive and problematic sexual behavior:

> There has been a long tradition of pathologizing behavior which is not mainstream and which some might find distasteful. Behaviors which are in conflict with someone's value system may be problematic but not obsessive-compulsive. Having sexual problems is common. Problems are caused by a number of nonpathological factors. People make mistakes. They can at times act impulsively. Their behavior can cause problems in a relationship. Some people will use sex as a coping mechanism similar to the use of alcohol, drugs, or eating. This pattern of sexual behavior is problematic. Problematic sexual behavior is often remedied by time, experience, education, or brief counseling. Obsessive and compulsive behavior, by its nature, is much more resistant to change.

The sexual addiction model has been rejected by a number of sex researchers as nothing more than pop psychology. These researchers suggest that the idea of sexual addiction is really repressive morality in a new guise. It is a conservative reaction to sexual diversity, eroticism, and sex outside exclusive relationships. It makes masturbation a sign of addiction, just as in earlier times masturbation was viewed as a sign of moral degeneracy. According to the sexual addiction model, sex is healthy if it takes place within a relationship; outside a relationship, it is pathological (Levine & Troiden, 1988).

Critiques of the sexual addiction model by sex researchers have undermined its credibility (Kavich-Sharon, 1994; Satel, 1993). First, the researchers point out, addiction requires physiological dependence on a chemical substance arising from habitual use. Sex is not a substance. Nor are there symptoms of physiological distress, such as diarrhea, convulsions, or delirium, from withdrawal.

Second, research fails to convincingly document sexual addiction as a clinical condition. There is virtually no empirical evidence to support the sexual addiction model. What little evidence there is comes from small clinical samples in which there are no comparable control groups. Indeed, the case studies Carnes describes in his book are not even real. "The stories used in this book," Carnes (1983, 1991) writes, "are fictionalized composites." As a result, one researcher calls the sexual addiction model dangerously oversimplified (Klein, 1991).

Third, there is no sexual hierarchy. Suggesting that masturbation leads to pornography, pornography to exhibitionism, and exhibitionism to rape borders on the irresponsible, if not nonsensical.

Fourth, the sexual addiction model is highly moralistic. The committed, exclusive heterosexual relationship is the model against which all other behaviors are measured. Nonprocreative sex such as masturbation is viewed as symptomatic. Same-sex sexual expression is also considered symptomatic.

Fifth, the characteristics of the addictive process—"preoccupation, ritualization, compulsive sexual behavior"—are subjective and value laden. Sociologists Martin Levine and Richard Troiden (1988) note: "Each of these characteristics could just as well describe the intense passion of courtship or the sexual routines of conventional couples." Nor is there evidence to support the notion that a person goes through three levels of behavior in search of greater excitement. "Carnes' notion of levels of addiction is a classic instance of moral judgment parading as scientific fact" (Levine & Troiden, 1988).

The term "hypersexuality" has sometimes been used as a less prejorative term for sexual addiction. However, because of the limitations of the sexual addiction model, the APA chose not to include "hypersexuality" in its most recent edition of the *DSM*. Nevertheless, Carnes's work has challenged us to think about "out-of-control" behaviors and how to treat them (Hyde & DeLameter, 2003).

If your sexual fantasies and activities are distressing to you, or your behaviors are emotionally or physically harmful to yourself or others, you should consult a therapist. The chances are, however, that your sexuality and your unique expression of it are healthy.

---

few instances of necrophilia, yet it retains a fascination in horror literature, especially vampire stories and legends, and in gothic novels. It is also associated with ritual cannibalism in other cultures. Within our own culture, *Sleeping Beauty* features a necrophilic theme, as does the crypt scene in Shakespeare's *Romeo and Juliet.* Some heavy metal music deals with necrophilia.

In a review of 122 cases of supposed necrophilia or necrophilic fantasies, researchers found only 54 instances of true necrophilia (Rosman & Resnick,

1989). The study found that neither sadism, psychosis, nor mental impairment was inherent in necrophilia. Instead, the most common motive for necrophilia was the possession of a partner who neither resisted nor rejected. Clearly, many people with necrophilia are severely mentally disturbed.

Pedophilia

Pedophilia refers to "recurrent intense sexual urges and sexually arousing fantasies involving sexual activity with a prepubescent child or children" that the individual has acted upon or finds distressing or that results in interpersonal difficulty (APA, 2000). However, acting upon fantasies without personal distress is still considered a pedophilia by the APA. The children are age 13 or younger. A person with pedophilia must be at least 16 and at least 5 years older than the child. (A late adolescent is not considered to have pedophilia if he or she is involved in an ongoing sexual relationship with a 12-year-old or older child.) Almost all people with pedophilia are males. In this section, we discuss only pedophilia. Nonpedophilic child sexual abuse and incest, their impact on the victims, and prevention of child sexual abuse are discussed in Chapter 17. Child sexual abuse is illegal in every state.

Some individuals with pedophilia prefer only one sex, whereas others are aroused by both male and female children. Those attracted to females usually seek 8- to 10-year-olds, and those attracted to males usually seek slightly older children. Some people with pedophilia are sexually attracted to children only, and some are aroused by both children and adults (APA, 2000).

Other-Sex Pedophilia   Other-sex pedophilia is more common than same-sex pedophilia. About half of people with pedophilia report stressful events, such as marital or work conflict, personal loss, or rejection, preceding the act of molestation. Many are fearful that their sexual abilities are decreasing or that they are unable to perform sexually.

People with pedophilia often use seduction and enticement to manipulate children—either their own children, stepchildren, relatives, or children outside the family (APA, 2000). The emergence of the Internet has provided a new way for a person with pedophilia to make contact with unsuspecting children. A man sometimes cruises chat rooms designed for children, and he may convince a girl to agree to e-mail, postal, or telephone contact (Durkin, 1997; Crooks & Baur, 2002). He may befriend the girl, talking to her, giving her candy, taking her to the store, going for walks with her, and letting her watch TV at his house. Gradually, he initiates tactile contact with her, such as having her sit on his lap, rough-housing with her, or giving her a back rub. Eventually, he may attempt to fondle her (Lang & Frenzel, 1988). If she resists, he will stop and try again later. He will resort to added inducements or pressure but will rarely use force (Groth, Hobson, & Gary, 1982). The perpetrator is more likely to be a relative or someone else the victim knows (Table 10.2). Even though these latter cases are far more common, they are much less likely to be reported because of the pressures and consequences the molester threatens the child with.

Pedophilic acts rarely involve sexual intercourse. The person with pedophilia usually seeks to fondle or touch the child, usually on the genitals, legs, and buttocks. Sometimes, he exposes himself and has the child touch his penis. He may masturbate in the presence of the child. Occasionally, oral

TABLE 10.2   Relationship Between the Child Victim and the Perpetrator of Sexual Abuse

	Female Victims (%)	Male Victims (%)
Stranger	7	4
Teacher	3	4
Family friend	29	40
Mother's boyfriend	2	1
Older friend of victim	1	4
Older relative	29	13
Older brother	9	4
Stepfather	7	1
Father	7	1
Other	19	17
Number of cases	289	166

Source: Laumann, E.; Gagnon, J.; Michael, R.; & Michaels, S. (1994). *The Social Organization of Sexuality.* Chicago: University of Chicago Press.

Note: The columns add to more than 100% because some respondents were abused by more than one adult.

or anal stimulation is involved (Arndt, 1991; Laumann, Gagnon, Michael, & Michaels, 1994).

About half of people with pedophilia are or have been married. Most who are married claim that their marriages are happy although they describe their wives as controlling and sexually distant. Their frequency of marital intercourse does not differ from that of nonoffenders, but many report a low sex drive and erectile difficulties. Few have serious mental disorders, such as psychosis (Arndt, 1991).

Same-Sex Pedophilia   Same-sex pedophilia is a complicated phenomenon. It does not appear to be as closely linked to homosexuality as other-sex pedophilia is to heterosexuality. A different kind of psychosexual dynamic seems to be at work for a large number of same-sex pedophiles. Although most people with same-sex pedophilia have little interest in other-sex relationships, a significant number do not identify themselves as gay. In fact, many reject a gay identity or are homophobic. Although some people believe that pedophilia is the means by which the gay community "recruits" boys into homosexuality, pedophiles are strongly rejected by the gay subculture (Peters, 1992).

The mean age of the victim is between 10 and 12. A large number of men with same-sex pedophilia describe feelings of love, friendship, or caring for the boy. Others blatantly entice or exploit their victims. Force is rarely used. Voluntary interviews with 27 men with same-sex pedophilia reveal four themes to explain their involvement with children: (1) Their pedophilic desire feels "natural" to them, (2) children are appealing because they are gentle and truthful, (3) adult-child sexual involvement can be positive for the child, and (4) the relationship is characterized by romantic love, not casual sex (Li, 1990). Such views are generally regarded as cognitive distortions or rationalizations. Adult-child sexual relationships are by definition exploitive. The majority of children report feelings of victimization (Finkelhor, 1990).

The most common activities are fondling and masturbation, usually with the man masturbating the boy. Other acts include oral-genital sex, with the man fellating the boy, and anal sex, with the man assuming the active role.

Female Pedophilia   Although there are relatively few reports of females with pedophilia, they do exist (Arndt, 1991; Rowan, 1988). Female pedophilia appears to be underreported for two reasons (Rowan, 1988). First, women are viewed as maternal and nurturing. Because of these stereotypes, women are given greater freedom than men in touching children and expressing feelings for them. As a consequence, when a female with pedophilia embraces, kisses, or caresses a child, her behavior may be viewed as nurturing rather than sexual. But when a male not having pedophilia does the same thing, his behavior may be misinterpreted as sexual. Second, the majority of male children who have sexual contact with adult women generally view the experience positively rather than negatively. As a consequence, they do not report the contact (Condy, Templer, Brown, & Veaco, 1987).

Adult female sexual contact with young boys is fairly common. A study of almost 1600 male and female college students and prison inmates revealed that 16% of male college students and 46% of male prison inmates had sexual contacts with women when they were 12 years old or younger and the women were in their early twenties (Condy et al., 1987). More than half of the men in the study reported having sexual intercourse with the women. The majority of the women were friends, neighbors, or babysitters.

Female sexual abuse of male children differs from male sexual abuse of female children in several significant ways (Condy et al., 1987; Cooper, Swaminath, Baxter, & Poulin, 1990; Fritz, Stoll, & Wagner, 1981; Okami, 1991). First, half the female sexual abusers have sexual intercourse with the male children, whereas relatively few male abusers have sexual intercourse with the female children. Second, female abusers force male children to engage in sexual activities significantly less frequently than male abusers force female children to do so. Third, male children tend not to be as traumatized by female abusers as female children are by male abusers.

Sexual Sadism and Sexual Masochism

> I had to give up masochism—I was enjoying it too much.
>
> —*Mel Calman*

Sadism and masochism are separate but sometimes related phenomena. People with sadism do not necessarily practice masochism, and vice versa. In order to make this distinction clear, the APA (2000) has created separate categories: sexual sadism and sexual masochism.

Often, there is no clear dividing line between sexual sadism/sexual masochism and domination and submission. In the case of sadism, coercion separates sexual sadism from domination. But for consensual behaviors, there is no clear distinction. A rule of thumb for separating consensual sexual sadism and masochism from domination and submission may be that acts of sadism and masochism are extreme, compulsive, and dangerous. Sadomasochistic sex partners often make specific agreements ahead of time concerning the amount of pain and punishment that will occur during sexual activity. Nevertheless, the acting-out of fantasies involves risk, such as physical injury (e.g., a deep cut); thus, it is important that individuals communicate their preferences and limits before they engage in any new activity.

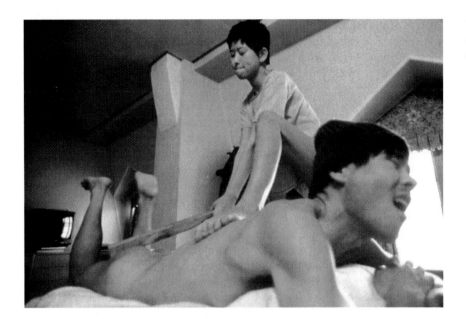

The movie Lies *(also called* Gojitmal*) explores the "Fantasy and Flesh" of sexual sadism.*

Sexual Sadism According to the *DSM-IV-TR*, a person may be diagnosed with **sexual sadism** if, over a period of at least 6 months, she or he experiences intense, recurring sexual urges or fantasies involving real (not simulated) acts in which physical or psychological harm (including humiliation) is inflicted upon a victim for purposes of sexual arousal. The individual either has acted on these urges with a nonconsenting person or finds them extremely distressful (APA, 2000). Characteristic symptoms include sexual thoughts and fantasies involving dominating acts centering on a victim's physical suffering, which is sexually arousing. The victim may be a consenting person with masochism or someone abducted by a person with sadism. The victim may be tortured, raped, mutilated, or killed; often, the victim is physically restrained and blindfolded or gagged (Money, 1990). However, most rapes are not committed by sexual sadists.

Sexual Masochism According to the *DSM-IV-TR*, for a diagnosis of **sexual masochism** to be made, a person must experience for a period of at least 6 months intense, recurring sexual urges or fantasies involving real (not simulated) acts of being "humiliated, beaten, bound, or otherwise made to suffer." These fantasies, sexual urges, or behaviors must result in significant distress or social impairment. Some individuals express the sexual urges by themselves (e.g., through self-mutilation or by binding themselves); others act with partners. Masochistic behaviors expressed with a partner may include restraining, blindfolding, paddling, spanking, whipping, beating, shocking, cutting, "pinning and piercing," and humiliating (e.g., being urinated or defecated on or forced to crawl and bark like a dog). The individual may desire to be treated as an infant and be forced to wear diapers ("infantilism"). The degree of pain one must experience to achieve sexual arousal varies from symbolic gestures to severe mutilations. As noted previously, sexual masochism is the only paraphilia that occurs with some frequency in women.

Autoerotic Asphyxia   A form of sexual masochism called **autoerotic asphyxia** (also called hypoxphilia or asphyxiphilia) links strangulation with masturbation. Those who participate in this activity seek to heighten their masturbatory arousal and orgasm by cutting off the oxygen supply to the brain. A person may engage in this practice either alone or with a partner. If death occurs, it is usually accidental. According to data from the United States, England, Australia, and Canada, one to two autoerotic asphyxia deaths per 1 million people are reported each year (APA, 2000).

Because of the secrecy and shame that accompany this and other masturbatory activities, it is difficult to estimate the number of individuals who find this practice arousing. Reports by survivors are extremely rare. Although the majority of those who die accidentally are adolescent heterosexual males, men in their twenties and thirties have also been victims of this practice (Hazelwood, Burgess, & Dietz, 1983).

The practice involves a variety of techniques, all of which cut off oxygen to the brain and can cause death. It is suggested that the interference with the blood supply to the brain causes cerebral anoxia (lack of oxygen), which is experienced as giddiness, light-headedness, and exhilaration, thereby heightening and reinforcing the masturbatory sensation (Resnick, 1972).

Individuals often use ropes, cords, or chains along with padding around the neck to prevent telltale signs. Others may place bags or blankets over their heads. Still others inhale asphyxiating gases such as aerosol sprays or amyl nitrate ("poppers"), a drug used to treat heart pain. The corpses are usually found either naked or partially clothed, often in women's clothing. Various forms of bondage have also been observed (Blanchard & Hucker, 1991). The characteristic clues that the death was not a suicide are the presence of sexually explicit materials, the use of a mirror or video camera, evidence of penile engorgement and/or ejaculation, and the absence of a suicide note (Sheehan & Garfinkel, 1988).

Although researchers have some understanding of why people participate in this practice, it is more important that medical personnel, parents, and other adults recognize signs of it and respond with strategies commensurate with its seriousness. Those who engage in such sexual practices rarely realize the potential consequences of their behavior; therefore, parents and others must be alert to physical and other telltale signs. An unusual neck bruise; bloodshot eyes; disoriented behavior, especially after the person has been alone for a while; and unexplained possession of or fascination with ropes or chains are the key signs (Saunders, 1989). Until we as a society can educate about, recognize, and respond to autoerotic asphyxia assertively and compassionately, we can expect to see more deaths as a result of this practice.

ORIGINS AND TREATMENT OF PARAPHILIAS

How do people develop paraphilias? As with many other behaviors, paraphilias probably result from some type of interaction among biology, sociocultural norms, and life experiences. Because most people with paraphilia are male, biological factors may be particularly significant. Some researchers have postulated that males with paraphilia may have higher testosterone levels than those without paraphilias, that they have had brain damage, or that the paraphilia may be inherited. Because the data are inconclusive, however, it has not been possible to identify a specific biological cause of paraphilia. People with paraphilia seem to have grown up in dysfunctional environments and to have had early experiences that limited their ability to be sexually stimulated by consensual sexual activity; as a result, they obtain arousal through varied means. They may have low self-esteem, poor social skills, and feelings of anger and loneliness; be self-critical; and lack a clear sense of self (Fisher & Howells, 1993; Goodman, 1993; Marshall, 1993). Another factor may be a limited ability to empathize with the victims of their behavior. The psychological outcomes of these behaviors serve to direct sexual attraction and response away from intimate relationships in later life (Schwartz, 2000).

Therapists have found paraphilias to be difficult to treat (McConaghy, 1998). Most people who are treated are convicted sex offenders, who have the most severe paraphilias, while those with milder paraphilias go untreated. Multifaceted treatments, such as psychodynamic therapy, aversive conditioning, cognitive-behavioral programs, relapse prevention, and medical intervention, have been tried to reduce or eliminate the symptoms of the paraphilia. Enhancing social and sexual skills and providing sexuality and relationship education may help people engage in more appropriate behavior (Seligman & Hardenberg, 2000). However, even when the client desires to change, treatments may not be effective, and relapses often occur. Hence, some experts believe that prevention is the best approach, although prevention programs are currently very limited.

STUDYING VARIATIONS IN SEXUAL BEHAVIORS reveals the variety and complexity of sexual behavior. It also underlines the limits of tolerance. Some unconventional sexual behaviors, undertaken in private between consenting adults as the source of erotic pleasure, should be of concern only to the people involved. As long as physical or psychological harm is not done to oneself or others, it is no one's place to judge. Coercive paraphilic behavior, however, may be injurious and should be treated.

SUMMARY

Sexual Variations and Paraphilic Behavior

- *Sexual variation* is behavior in which less than the majority of individuals engage. Variant sexual behavior is not abnormal behavior, the definition of which varies from culture to culture and from one historical period to another.

- Recurring, intense, sexually arousing fantasies, urges, or behaviors involving nonhuman objects, suffering or humiliation, or children or other nonconsenting persons or animals are known as *paraphilias*. Paraphilias tend to be injurious, compulsive, and long-standing. They may be noncoercive or coercive.

Sexual Variation: Domination and Submission

- *Domination and submission (D/S)*, also known as *sadomasochism (S&M)*, is a form of fantasy sex with power as the central element.

Noncoercive Paraphilias

- Although there are no reliable data on the number of individuals involved, paraphilic activities are widespread in the nonoffender population.

- *Fetishism* is sexual attraction to objects. The fetishism is usually required or strongly preferred for sexual arousal.

- *Transvestism* is the wearing of clothes of a member of the other sex, usually for sexual arousal.

Coercive Paraphilias

- *Zoophilia* involves animals as the preferred sexual outlet even when other outlets are available.

- *Voyeurism* is the nonconsensual and secret observation of others for the purpose of sexual arousal.

- *Exhibitionism* is the exposure of the genitals to a nonconsenting stranger.

- *Telephone scatologia* is the nonconsensual telephoning of strangers and often involves the use of obscene language.

- *Frotteurism* involves touching or rubbing against a nonconsenting person for the purpose of sexual arousal.

- *Necrophilia* is sexual activity with a corpse.

- *Pedophilia* refers to sexual arousal and contact with children age 13 or younger by adults, or with children age 11 or younger by adolescents older than age 16. Child sexual abuse is illegal in every state. For most people with pedophilia, the fact that a child is a child is more important than gender. Heterosexuals and gay men may both be pedophilically attracted to boys; gay men with pedophilia are less attracted to girls.

- The Internet has recently become a place for people with pedophilia to contact unsuspecting children.

- The majority of people with pedophilia know their victim. About half of pedophiles have been married. The most common activities are fondling and masturbation.

- There are relatively few reported cases of females with pedophilia, but it may be underreported for two reasons. Because of stereotypes of female nurturance, pedophilic activities may not be recognized; and the majority of male children apparently view the event positively or neutrally.

- *Sexual sadism* refers to sexual urges or fantasies of intentionally inflicting real physical or psychological pain or suffering on a person.

- *Sexual masochism* is the recurring sexual urge or fantasy of being humiliated or caused to suffer through real acts, not simulated ones.

- *Autoerotic asphyxia* is a form of sexual masochism linking strangulation with masturbatory activities.

Origins and Treatment of Paraphilias

- Paraphilias are likely the result of social/environmental, psychological, and biological factors.
- Paraphilias are difficult to treat, and relapses often occur.
- Prevention programs may be the most effective way to address paraphilias.

Sex and the Internet

Paraphilias

The Web is one resource for locating information about paraphilias. Go to the Google Web site (www.google.com) and type "paraphilias" in the Google Search box. As you can see, there are a wide range of different sites posted. Look over the posted sites and answer the following questions:

- What types of Web sites are listed?

- Are the sites from medical and academic organizations, individuals, or commercial groups?

- Are there sites for specific paraphilias?

- Which sites provide the most valuable information to you? Why?

- Did you learn anything new about paraphilias from the Web sites? If so, what?

- Do you believe that any of the sites contain inaccurate or harmful information? Explain.

SUGGESTED WEB SITES

AllPsych Online
http://allpsych.com/disorders/paraphilias
Offers information on numerous psychiatric disorders, including symptoms, etiology, treatment, and prognosis for sexual dysfunctions.

Discovery Health Channel, Sexual Health Center
http://health.discovery.com/centers/sex
Provides comprehensive information about sexuality, including an "Ask the Experts" section.

Mental-Health-Matters.com
http://www.mental-health-matters.com/disorders
Provides information, help sources, and advocacy suggestions concerning mental health issues, including sexual dysfunctions.

National Council on Sexual Addiction and Compulsivity
http://www.ncsac.corg
Offers resources for those seeking information about sexual addiction.

SUGGESTED READING

Arndt, William B., Jr. (1991). *Gender Disorders and the Paraphilias*. Madison, CT: International Universities Press. A comprehensive look at transvestism, transsexuality, and the paraphilias.

Laws, D. Richard, & O'Donohue, William (Eds.). (1997). *Sexual Deviance: Theory, Assessment and Treatment*. New York: Guilford Press. A collection of papers that examine the theories, assessment procedures, and treatment techniques for a spectrum of sexually variant behaviors.

Money, John. (1989). *Lovemaps*. Buffalo: Prometheus Books. A description of variant and paraphilic behavior.

Moser, Charles, & Madeson, J. J. (1996). *Bound to Be Free: The SM Experience*. New York: Continuum. A collaborative personal view of S&M by a sexologist and a practitioner of S&M.

For links, articles, and study material, go to the McGraw-Hill Web site, located at http://www.mhhe.com/strong5

11

Contraception and Birth Control

"*My* parents and I never talked about sex until I had to ask them questions for one of my high school classes. They got so excited about the topic. I guess they were just waiting for me to ask. I remember my mom throwing a pack of condoms on the bed. She said, 'Just in case!' We just all laughed."

—20-year-old Filipino male

"*During* the summer before my sophomore year, things started to change. My father came into my room much as he had done the first time. It was 'The Talk, Part Two.' He asked me if I knew what a condom was and told me about abstinence. I told him I wasn't planning on having sex for a while, but I was lying; it was all I thought about. I felt awkward and embarrassed. Nevertheless, he made his point, and before he left he said, 'I love you.'"

—20-year-old White male

"*Mom* gave me an important sense that my body was mine, that it was my responsibility and under my control. Birth control was always discussed whenever sex was mentioned, but when it was, it was treated like a joke. The message was that sex can be a magical thing as long as you are being responsible—responsible for not getting yourself or anyone else pregnant. Back then, sexually transmitted diseases were not discussed, so it was the pill or a diaphragm for me and condoms for my brothers."

—26-year-old White female

*T*ODAY, MORE THAN EVER BEFORE, we are aware of the impact of fertility on our own lives, as well as on the world. Reproduction, once considered strictly a personal matter, is now a subject of open debate and political action. Yet, regardless of our public views, we must each confront fertility on a personal level. In taking charge of our reproductive destinies, we must be informed about the available methods of birth control, as well as ways to protect ourselves against sexually transmitted infections (STIs). But information is only part of the picture. We also need to understand our own personal needs, values, and habits so that we can choose methods we will use consistently, thereby minimizing our risks.

In this chapter, we begin by examining the psychology of risk taking and the role of individual responsibility in contraception. We then describe in detail the numerous contraceptive devices and techniques that are used today: methods of use, effectiveness rates, advantages, and possible problems. Finally, we look at abortion and its effect on individuals and society.

The command "be fruitful and multiply" was promulgated according to our authorities, when the population of the world consisted of two people.

—*Dean Inge (1860–1954)*

RISK AND RESPONSIBILITY

In the United States, half of all pregnancies each year are unintended, resulting in 1.3 million abortions and 1.1 million births that women either did not plan until later in life or did not want at all (Alan Guttmacher Institute, 2003). Although on average a woman has only about a 2–4% chance of becoming

MOST PEOPLE KNOW they are taking a chance when they don't use contraception. But the more frequently a person takes chances with unprotected intercourse without resultant pregnancy, the more likely he or she is to do so again. A subtle psychology develops: Somehow, apparently by willpower, "good vibes," or divine intervention, the woman does not get pregnant. Eventually, the woman or couple will feel almost magically invulnerable to pregnancy. Each time they are lucky, their risk taking is reinforced.

The consequences of an unintended pregnancy—economic hardships, adoption, or abortion—may be overwhelming. So why do people take chances in the first place? Part of the reason is faulty knowledge. People often underestimate how easy it is to get pregnant, or they may not know how to use a contraceptive method correctly.

Let's examine some of the perceived costs of contraceptive planning versus the anticipated benefits of pregnancy.

Perceived Costs of Contraceptive Planning

One reason people avoid taking steps to prevent pregnancy is that they don't want to acknowledge their own sexuality. On the surface, it may seem fairly simple to acknowledge that we are sexual beings, especially if we have conscious sexual desires and engage in sexual intercourse. Yet acknowledging our sexuality is not necessarily easy, for it may be accompanied by feelings of guilt, conflict, and shame. The younger or less experienced we are, the more difficult it is for us to acknowledge our sexuality.

Planning contraception requires us to acknowledge not only that we are sexual but also that we plan to be sexually active. Without such planning, men and women can pretend that their sexual intercourse "just happens"—when a moment of passion occurs, when they have been drinking, or when the moon is full—even though it may happen frequently.

Another reason people don't use contraception is difficulty in obtaining it. It is often embarrassing for sexually inexperienced people to be seen in contexts that identify them as sexual beings. The person who sits behind you in your chemistry class may be sitting next to you in the waiting room of the family planning clinic. If you go to a store to buy condoms, your mother, teacher, minister, or rabbi might be down the aisle buying toothpaste (or contraceptives, for that matter) and might see you. The cost of contraceptives is also a problem for some. Although free or low-cost contraceptives may be obtained through family planning clinics or other agencies, people may have transportation or work considerations that keep them away.

Many people also have trouble planning and continuing contraception. Contraceptive developments in the past few decades (especially the pill) shifted responsibility from the man to the woman. Required to more consciously define themselves as sexual, women have had to abandon traditional, passive sexual roles. Some women, however, are reluctant to plan contraceptive use because they fear they will be regarded as sexually aggressive or "loose."

Because it is women who get pregnant, men tend to be unaware of their responsibility or to downplay their role in conception, although with the popularity of the condom, responsibility may become more balanced (especially if women insist on it). Nevertheless, males, especially adolescents, often lack the awareness that supports contraceptive planning. Yet males are more fertile than

FIGURE 11.1 Pregnancy Outcomes in the United States. Each year, 6 million of the 60 million American women of childbearing age (15–44) become pregnant. (*Source:* Alan Guttmacher Institute, 2002d.)

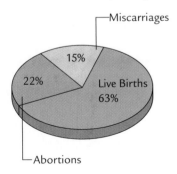

pregnant during intercourse without contraception, timing affects the odds. For example, if intercourse occurs the day before ovulation, the chance of conception is about 30%; and if intercourse occurs on the day of ovulation, the chance of conception is about 15%. Over a period of a year, couples who do not use contraception have a 90% chance of conception (Figure 11.1).

Because the potential for getting pregnant is so high for a sexually active, childbearing-age couple, it would seem reasonable that sexually active couples would use contraception to avoid unintended pregnancy. Unfortunately, all too often, this is not the case. One major study revealed that during their first intercourse only about 59% of couples used contraception (Abma, Chandra, Mosher, Peterson, & Piccinino, 1997). As men and women age, they become more consistent contraception users. Of the 60 million women in the United States of childbearing age (15–44), one-third do not need contraceptives because they are either sterile, pregnant, postpartum, trying to become pregnant, or abstinent (Foster-Rosales & Stewart, 2002). Approximately 90% of the remaining women at risk for unintended pregnancy use some method females. The average male is fertile 24 hours a day for 50 years or more. Females, in contrast, are fertile only a day or two out of the month for 35 or so years.

Many people, especially women using the pill, practice birth control consistently and effectively within an ongoing relationship but give up their contraceptive practices if the relationship breaks up. They define themselves as sexual only within the context of a relationship. When men or women begin a new relationship, they may not use contraception because the relationship has not yet become established. They do not expect to have sexual intercourse or to have it often, so they are willing to take chances.

Using contraception such as a condom or diaphragm may destroy the feeling of "spontaneity" in sex. For those who justify their sexual behavior by romantic impulsiveness, using these devices seems cold and mechanical. Others do not use them because they feel doing so would interrupt the passion of the moment.

Anticipated Benefits of Pregnancy

Many men and women fantasize that even an "accidental" pregnancy might be beneficial. Ambivalence about pregnancy is a powerful incentive *not* to use contraception. What are some of the perceived benefits of pregnancy?

First, for many people, being pregnant proves that a woman is indeed feminine on the most fundamental biological level. Getting a woman pregnant provides similar proof of masculinity for a man. Being a mother is one of the most basic definitions of traditional womanhood. In an era in which there is considerable confusion about women's roles, pregnancy helps, and even forces, a woman to define herself in a traditional manner. Young men may also find the idea of fatherhood compelling. They may feel that fathering a child will give them a sense of accomplishment and an aura of maturity.

Pregnancy also proves beyond any doubt that a person is fertile. Many men and women have lingering doubts about whether they can have children. This is especially true for partners who have used contraception for a long time, but it is also true for those who constantly take chances. If they have taken chances many times without pregnancy resulting, they may begin to have doubts about their fertility.

Another anticipated benefit of pregnancy is that it requires the partners to define their relationship and level of commitment to each other. It is a form of testing, albeit often an unconscious one. It raises many questions that must be answered: How will the partner react? Will it lead to marriage or a breakup? Will it solidify a marriage or a relationship? Will the partner be loving and understanding, or will he or she be angry and rejecting? What is the real nature of the commitment? Many men and women unconsciously expect their partners to be pleased, but this is not always the reaction they get.

Finally, pregnancy involves not only two partners but their parents as well (especially the woman's). Pregnancy may force a young person's parents to pay attention to and deal with him or her as an adult. Being pregnant puts a female on the very verge of adulthood, for in most cultures, motherhood is a major rite of passage. Similarly, fatherhood is an adult status for a male, transforming him from a boy into a man. Pregnancy may mean many things with regard to the parent-child relationship: a sign of rebellion, a form of punishment for a parental lack of caring, a plea for help and understanding, or an insistence on autonomy, independence, or adulthood.

Do you take risks in your sexual activities? What kinds? Why? When do you believe a person is more inclined to take risks? What are some ways of overcoming or addressing the various reasons individuals do not use contraception?

of contraception (Figure 11.2). Not surprisingly, the nonusers of contraception account for about half of unintended pregnancies; those who used contraception report that the method either failed or was not used correctly or consistently (Hatcher, Nelson, Zieman, et al., 2002).

Numerous studies have indicated that the most consistent users of contraception are men and women who explicitly communicate about the subject. People at greatest risk for not using contraceptives are those in casual dating relationships and those who infrequently discuss contraception with their partners or others.

Women, Men, and Birth Control: Who Is Responsible?

Because women bear children and have most of the responsibility for raising them, they may have a greater interest than their partners in controlling

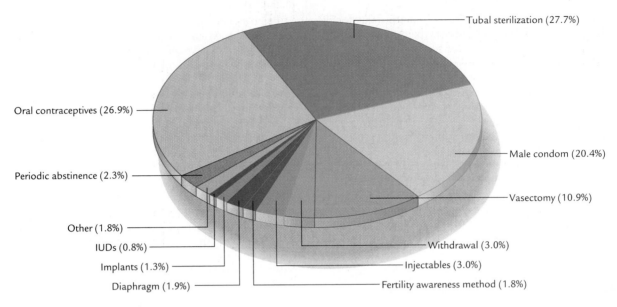

FIGURE 11.2 Contraceptive Methods Used by American Women Age 15–44. (*Source:* Alan Guttmacher Institute, 1999d.)

their fertility. Also, it is generally easier to keep one egg from being fertilized once a month than to stop millions of sperm during each act of intercourse. For these and other reasons, responsibility for birth control has traditionally been seen as the woman's job, but attitudes and practices are changing. Heightened efforts to enforce men's financial obligations toward any children they have fathered have increased the impact of unintended pregnancy on men (Darroch, 2000). Regardless of the motive, society no longer views the responsibility for birth control to lie solely with women. Rather, the majority of men (as well as women) perceive that there is gender equality in sexual decision making and equal responsibility for decisions

Planning contraception requires us to acknowledge our sexuality. One way a responsible couple can reduce the risk of unintended pregnancy is by visiting a family planning clinic—together.

about contraception. Male methods now account for 38% of all reversible contraceptive use, and 28% of reproductive-age women who use surgical contraception rely on their partner's vasectomy (Alan Guttmacher Institute, 2000a). This attitude shift is taking place in such countries as Italy and Japan as well, where male methods of contraception (such as withdrawal or condoms) are used more than female methods. Although withdrawal is not considered a reliable method of birth control, the condom is quite effective when used properly, especially in combination with a spermicide. (The role of nonoxynol-9 is discussed later in the chapter.)

In addition to using a condom, a man can take contraceptive responsibility by (1) exploring ways of being sexual without intercourse; (2) helping to pay doctor or clinic bills and sharing the cost of pills, injections, or other birth control supplies; (3) checking on supplies, helping to keep track of his partner's menstrual cycle, and helping her with her part in the birth control routine; and (4) in a long-term relationship, if no (or no more) children are planned, having a vasectomy.

Adolescents and Contraception   We know that approximately 76% of young people have intercourse during their teenage years ("National Survey of Adolescents," 2003). We also know that many young people aren't protecting themselves against unintended pregnancy and STIs as well as they could.

Condoms are the method of choice among sexually active teens. In their first experience with intercourse, more than two-thirds rely on the condom (Alan Guttmacher Institute, 2002b). After that, about two-thirds of sexually active females age 15–19 use contraceptives, but not every time they have intercourse (Kaiser Family Foundation, 2003a). Teens appear to have conflicting views when it comes to condoms and the implications of carrying one. On the one hand, 8 in 10 say that a girl carrying a condom looks "prepared," and almost 7 in 10 say that she is being responsible. On the other hand, 7 in 10 also say that she seems easy, and 6 in 10 say that it implies she is expecting sex. This ambivalence related to condom use seems to apply to boys as well (Kaiser Family Foundation, 2002d).

Preventing Sexually Transmitted Infections

Most sexually transmitted infections (STIs), if treated in their early stages, are not particularly dangerous. HIV infection is the notable exception. Because of AIDS, people are much more aware of their vulnerability to STIs. (STIs are discussed in Chapter 15; HIV and AIDS are discussed in Chapter 16.)

Fortunately, some contraceptive methods do excellent double duty as prophylactics (disease preventers). Latex rubber and polyurethane condoms provide a barrier against most STIs, including HIV infection. They work both ways, protecting the wearer of the condom from a disease carried by his partner, and vice versa. (Animal membrane condoms, however, do *not* protect against all disease-carrying organisms—notably the viruses, which include HIV—and should only be used for contraception by partners in exclusive relationships who know they are free of STIs.)

It is vital to note that condoms (or any other methods) do *not* guarantee absolute protection from STIs, just as they do not guarantee absolute

What is the message of these posters? What myths or stereotypes do they challenge? There is no such thing as safe sex, only safer sex.

protection from pregnancy. They have been known to leak, break, or slip off. Furthermore, disease may be spread by intimate contact with infected body areas not covered by the condom.

METHODS OF CONTRACEPTION AND BIRTH CONTROL

The methods we use to prevent pregnancy or to keep it from progressing vary widely according to our personal and religious beliefs, tastes, health, accessibility to contraception, and other life circumstances. For many people, especially women, the search for an "ideal" method of birth control involves ongoing frustration. Some methods pose health risks to certain women, others run counter to religious or moral beliefs, and still others are inconvenient, aesthetically displeasing, or too expensive. There are several methods and techniques to choose from, however, and scientific research is slowly increasing our options for safe and effective contraception. Most individuals and couples can find a method that they can use comfortably, and, most importantly, regularly and safely.

Birth Control and Contraception: What's the Difference?

Although the terms "birth control" and "contraception" are often used interchangeably, there is actually a subtle difference in meaning. **Birth control** is any means of preventing a birth from taking place. Thus, methods that prevent a fertilized egg from implanting in the uterine wall (such as the IUD in some instances and emergency contraceptive pills) and methods that remove the **conceptus**—the fertilized egg, embryo, or fetus—from the uterus (such as RU-486 and surgical abortions) are forms of birth control. These are not, however, true contraceptive methods. **Contraception**—the prevention of conception altogether—is the category of birth control in which the sperm and egg are prevented from uniting. This is done in a variety of ways, including (1) barrier methods, such as condoms and diaphragms, which place a physical barrier between sperm and egg, (2) spermicides, which kill the sperm before they can get to the egg, and (3) hormonal methods, such as the pill, the shot, and the patch, which inhibit the release of the oocyte from the ovary.

Barrier methods for women—the diaphragm, cervical cap, and female condom—help protect against diseases of the cervix and uterus. The prophylactic function of these barriers is increased when they are used with spermicide.

No matter what method is used, there is no absolute guarantee against contracting an STI (or becoming pregnant). Therefore, the value of caution and sound judgment for sexually active people cannot be overstated.

Choosing a Method

To be fully responsible in using birth control, individuals must know what options they have, how reliable these methods are, and what advantages and disadvantages (including possible side effects) each has. Thus, it is important to be aware of both personal health issues and the specifics of the methods themselves.

Most women who are not currently using contraception go to a clinic or doctor's office knowing exactly what method they want (Hatcher, Nelson, Zieman, et al., 2002). However, many of these women are not aware of other options available to them. In some instances, the method they think they want may not be medically appropriate or may not be one they will use correctly and consistently. Knowing the facts about the methods gives you a solid basis from which to make decisions, as well as more security once a decision is reached. If you need to choose a birth control method for yourself, remember that *the best method is the one you will use consistently and correctly.* When you are having intercourse, a condom left in a purse or wallet, a diaphragm in the bedside drawer, or a forgotten pill in its packet on the other side of town is *not* an effective means of birth control.

To help make an informed decision about which method of birth control is medically appropriate and will be used every time, consider the following questions (Hatcher, Nelson, Zieman, et al., 2002):

- Do you have any particular preferences or biases related to birth control?
- Do you know the advantages and disadvantages of each of the contraceptive methods?
- How convenient and easy is it to use this method?
- If you or your partner is at risk, does this method provide protection against STIs, including HIV?
- What are the effects of this method on menses?
- Is it important that you negotiate with your partner to help determine the method?
- What other influences (e.g., religion, privacy, past experience, friend's advice, and frequency of intercourse) might affect your decision?
- Have you discussed potential methods with your health practitioner?

FIGURE 11.3 Failure Rates of Contraceptives During the First Year of Use. (*Source:* Hatcher, R.A., Nelson, A.L., Zieman, M. et al. (2002). A Pocket Guide to Managing Contraception. Tiger, Georgia: Bridging the Gap Foundation.

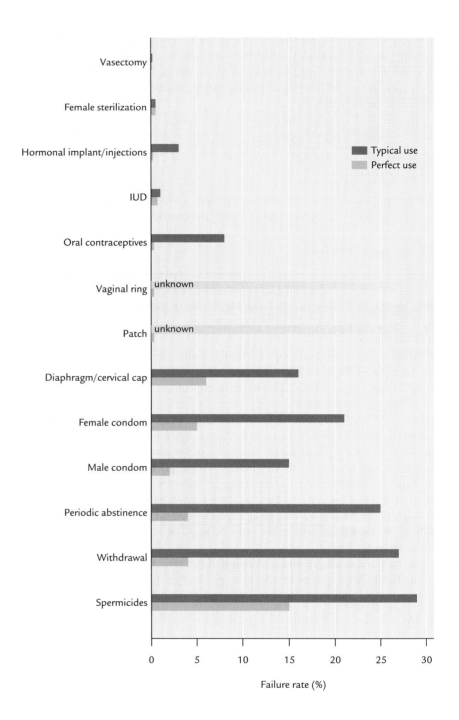

In the following discussion of method effectiveness, "correct and consistent use" (or "perfect use") refers to the percentage of women who become pregnant during their first year of use when they use the method *correctly and consistently.* "Typical use" refers to the percentage of women who become pregnant during their first year of use; this number includes both couples who use the method correctly and consistently and those who do not (Figure 11.3). Thus, typical use is the more significant number to use when considering a method of contraception. In spite of very effective contraceptive options, the rate of unintended pregnancy in this country is still approximately 50%.

Sexual Abstinence

Before we begin our discussion of devices and techniques for preventing conception, we must acknowledge the oldest and most reliable birth control method of all: abstinence. There is a wide variety of opinion about what constitutes sexual activity. However, from a family planning perspective, **abstinence** is the absence of genital contact that could lead to a pregnancy (i.e., penile penetration of the vagina). The term "celibacy" is sometimes used interchangeably with "abstinence." We prefer "abstinence" because "celibacy" often implies the avoidance of *all* forms of sexual activity and, often, the religious commitment to not marry or to maintain a nonsexual lifestyle.

Individuals who choose not to have intercourse are still free to express affection (and to give and receive sexual pleasure if they so desire) in a variety of ways. Ways to express intimacy include talking, hugging, massaging, kissing, petting, and manually and orally stimulating the genitals. Those who choose sexual abstinence as their method of birth control need to communicate this clearly to their dates or partners. They should also be informed about other forms of contraception. And, in the event that either partner experiences a change of mind, it can't hurt to have a condom handy. An advantage of abstinence is that refraining from sexual intercourse may allow two people to get to know and trust each other gradually before experiencing greater intimacy.

Hormonal Methods

In addition to the tried-and-true birth control pill, several new forms of hormonal contraception have recently become available. These include a pill that causes temporary menstrual suppression, injectable hormones, a vaginal ring, and a patch.

The Pill   **Oral contraceptives,** popularly called "the pill," are the most popular form of reversible contraception in the United States. The pill is actually a series of pills (20, 21, or 28 to a package) containing synthetic estrogen and/or progesterone that regulates egg production and the menstrual cycle. When taken for birth control, oral contraceptives accomplish some or all of the following:

- Suppress ovulation (90–95% of the time).
- Thicken cervical mucus (preventing sperm entry).
- Thin the lining of the uterus to inhibit implantation of the fertilized ovum.
- Slow the rate of ovum transport.

The pill produces basically the same chemical conditions that would exist in a woman's body if she were pregnant.

TYPES AND USAGE   Oral contraceptives must be prescribed by a physician or family planning clinic. Over 30 combinations are available, containing various amounts of hormones. Most commonly prescribed are the combination pills, which contain a fairly standard amount of estrogen (usually about 35 micrograms) and different doses of progestin according to the pill type. In the triphasic pill, the amount of progestin is altered during the cycle, purportedly to approximate the normal hormonal pattern. There is also a "minipill" containing progestin only, but it is generally prescribed only for women who should not take estrogen. It is considered slightly less effective than the combined pill, and it must be taken with precise, unfailing regularity to be effective.

With the 20- and 21-day pills, one pill is taken each day until they are all used; 2–5 days later, the menstrual flow will begin, which typically is quite light. (If the flow does not begin, the woman should start the next series of pills 7 days after the end of the previous series. If she repeatedly has no flow, she should talk to her health-care practitioner.) On the fifth day of her menstrual flow, the woman starts the next series of pills.

The 28-day pills are taken continuously. Seven of the pills have no hormones. They are there simply to avoid breaks in the routine; some women prefer them because they find them easier to remember.

The pill is considered the most effective birth control method available (except for sterilization) when used correctly. But the pill is not effective when used carelessly. It must be taken every day, as close as possible to the same time each day. If one pill is missed, it should be taken as soon as the woman remembers, and the next one taken on schedule. If two are missed, the method cannot be relied on, and an additional form of contraception should be used for the rest of the cycle. A year's supply of birth control pills costs from a few dollars a month to more than $500. Though the share of employees with company coverage for oral contraceptives has risen significantly in recent years, they are still less likely to have coverage for oral contraceptives than for other prescription drugs. Recent legislative action, court rulings, and grassroots efforts suggest that this disparity will remain an issue until parity is obtained (Kaiser Family Foundation, 2002d).

In 2003, the Food and Drug Administration (FDA) approved the first birth control pill designed to reduce the frequency of menstruation from once a month to four times a year. Called *Seasonale,* these pills contain the same ingredients as conventional birth control pills, except that they are packaged and prescribed differently: 12 straight weeks of active pills, followed by one week of placebos. The idea of menstrual suppression is not new. For decades, doctors have told women how they could skip a period by continually taking birth control pills. Seasonale simply helps to make this option more convenient. One of the most noticeable side effects, however, is the risk of unexpected or breakthrough bleeding, especially in the first few months of use (Kalb, 2003). The most significant safety question is whether four periods a year are enough to allow the uterus to shed any tissue that builds up.

None of the hormonal methods of birth control offer protection against STIs. Women on the pill should consider the additional use of a condom to reduce the risk of STIs.

EFFECTIVENESS   The combined pill is more than 99.7% effective if used correctly. The typical-use rate is 92%. Progestin-only pills are somewhat less effective and may contribute to irregular bleeding. However, they have fewer side effects and health risks than the combined pill.

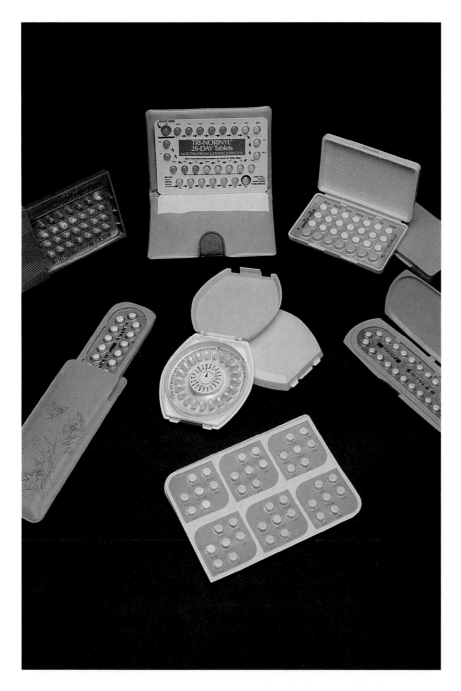

Although oral contraceptives are effective in preventing pregnancy, they do not provide protection against STIs, including HIV infection.

ADVANTAGES   Pills are easy to take. They are dependable. No applications or interruptions are necessary before or during intercourse. Some women experience side effects that please them, such as more regular or reduced menstrual flow, fewer menstrual cramps, enlarged breasts, or less acne. The pill may offer some protection against osteoporosis and rheumatoid arthritis. There is also a reduced risk (which can last up to 15 years after discontinuing the pill) for ovarian and endometrial cancers and benign breast disease.

POSSIBLE PROBLEMS   There are many possible side effects, which may or may not prevent the user from taking the pill. Those most often reported are spotting, changes (usually a decrease) in menstrual flow, breast tenderness, nausea or vomiting, and weight gain or loss. Other side effects include spotty darkening of the skin, nervousness and dizziness, loss of scalp hair, headaches, changes in appetite, sex drive, and moods.

These side effects can sometimes be eliminated by changing the prescription, but not always. Certain women react unfavorably to the pill because of existing health factors or extra sensitivity to female hormones. Women with heart or kidney diseases, asthma, high blood pressure, diabetes, epilepsy, gall bladder disease, or sickle-cell disease and those prone to migraine headaches or depression are usually considered poor candidates for the pill. Certain medications may react differently or unfavorably with the pill, either diminishing in their therapeutic effect or interfering with oral contraceptive effectiveness. Thus, it is important to check with your doctor before starting any new prescriptions if you are taking the pill.

The pill also creates certain health risks, but to what extent is a matter of controversy. Though the pill has been studied extensively and is very safe, in rare instances hormonal methods can lead to serious problems. Some of the warning signs to look for spell out the word **"ACHES."** If you experience any of these, you need to check with your clinician as soon as possible:

- Abdominal pain (severe)

- Chest pain

- Headaches (severe)

- Eye problems (including blurred vision, spots, or a change in shape of the cornea)

- Severe leg pain

You should also consult your clinician if you develop severe mood swings or depression, become jaundiced (yellow-colored skin), miss two periods, or have signs of pregnancy.

Though a number of studies have linked oral contraceptive (OC) use with certain types of cancer, none have proved to be conclusive. Most researched has been the connection between the pill and breast cancer. Recently published data from the National Institute of Child Health and Human Development (2002) provide reassurance that OC use is not associated with an increased risk of breast cancer. A large, population-based, case-control investigation, including interviews with nearly 10,000 women age 35–64 (when the risk of breast cancer is highest), found that past or current OC use, even for many years, did not increase the risk of breast cancer. Additionally, no association between OCs and breast cancer was found for women who used high-dose OCs, women who used OCs for a long time, either White or Black women, women who used OCs before their first full-term pregnancy, and women with a family history of the disease.

The health risks are low for the young (about half the number of risks encountered at childbirth), but they increase with age. The risk for smokers, women over 35, and those with certain other health disorders is considered high. Current literature on the pill especially emphasizes the risks for women who smoke. Definite risks of cardiovascular complications and various forms of cancer exist because of the synergistic action of the ingredients in cigarettes and oral contraceptives.

Certain other factors may need to be taken into account in determining if oral contraceptives are appropriate. Nursing mothers cannot use pills containing estrogen because the hormone inhibits milk production, although some lactating women use the minipill successfully once lactation has been established.

Once a woman stops taking the pill, her menstrual cycle will usually resume the next month, though it may take several months before it becomes regular. Approximately 2–4% of pill users experience prolonged delays. If a woman does become pregnant during her first or second cycle after discontinuing pill use, she may be at greater risk for miscarriage. She is also more likely to conceive twins. If a woman wants to become pregnant, it is recommended that she change to another method of contraception for 2–3 months after she stops taking the pill and then start efforts to conceive.

Millions of women use the pill with moderate to high degrees of satisfaction. For many women, if personal health or family history do not contraindicate it, the pill is both effective and safe. Each of the hormonal methods of contraception cost between $30 and $35 a month.

Injectable Contraceptives   The injectable contraceptive medroxyprogesterone acetate, or **Depo-Provera (DMPA),** provides protection from pregnancy for 3 months. Generally, DMPA has been considered to have few serious side effects and complications. In approximately half the women taking DMPA, menstruation stops completely after a year of use. Menstrual spotting, weight gain, headaches, breast tenderness, dizziness, loss of libido, and depression have also been reported, though less frequently. Research has shown that women who use DMPA are likely to experience a reduction in bone density, thereby increasing their risk of suffering a bone fracture ("Bone Loss in Depo-Provera Users," 2002). There is also evidence that Depo-Provera's effects on bone density appear to be largely reversible. DMPA may also contribute to delayed fertility (up to a year in some cases) until its effects wear off. However, because the drug does not accumulate in the body, the return to fertility is independent of the number of injections received, though it may be affected by a woman's height and weight. The perfect-use effectiveness rate is 99.7%; the typical-use rate is less at 97%. A woman should get her first injection of DMPA within 5 days of the start of her menstrual period. The drug is effective immediately. A year's worth of protection with DMPA (given in four injections at 3-month intervals) costs about $400.

Lunelle, which contains both estrogen and progestin, is another option available to women in the United States. Lunelle injections are given every month instead of every 3 months as with Depo-Provera. Because it contains estrogen and progestin, Lunelle has many of the same benefits and side effects as oral contraceptives. It may be preferred by women who do not want to either take a pill every day or be exposed to the relatively long-term consequences of injections. Fertility usually returns within about 2–3 months after the last injection. The perfect-use effectiveness rate is 99.5%; the typical-use rate is 97%.

The Patch   In 2001, the FDA approved a transdermal contraceptive **patch.** Called Ortho Evra, this reversible method of birth control releases synthetic estrogen and progestin to protect against pregnancy for 1 month. Consisting of three layers, the 4.5-centimeter beige patch may be applied to the lower abdomen, buttocks, upper outer arm, or upper torso (but never the breasts). After 7 days, the woman removes the patch and applies a new one to another site. Three consecutive 7-day patches are typically followed by a patch-free week to allow for menstruation to occur. The combination of hormones works the same way that oral contraceptives do. The patch is most effective when it is changed on the same day of the week for 3 weeks in a row. Pregnancy can happen if an error is made in using the patch, especially if it becomes loose for longer than 24 hours or falls off or if the same patch is left on for more than one week.

EFFECTIVENESS   Overall, contraceptive efficacy of the patch is similar to that of oral contraceptives; if used perfectly, the patch is more than 99% effective. Typical use results in a success rate of 92%. Recent data have raised concerns about the patch's efficacy in women with a body weight over 200 pounds; however, additional information is needed to evaluate this association.

ADVANTAGES   The patch is simple, safe, and convenient. Like those who take OCs, many women who use the patch report more regular, lighter, and shorter periods. Furthermore, a woman's ability to become pregnant returns quickly when the patch is discontinued. The patch does not interfere with sex. And though results of long-term studies will not be available for some time, researchers assume that the noncontraceptive benefits associated with the patch are similar to those associated with the pill.

DISADVANTAGES   As with all medications, there may be some undesirable side effects. However, the patch is much safer than pregnancy and childbirth for healthy women—except among smokers age 35 and older ("Is Ortho Evra Right for You?" 2003). The most common side effects reported by users of the patch include headaches, nausea, application site reactions, breast discomfort, upper respiratory tract infections, dysmenorrhea, and abdominal pain (Audet, Moreau, Koltun, et al., 2001). Additionally, there may be problems with contact lens use, including blurred vision or difficulty with fitting the lenses. Serious problems are rare and usually have warning signs.

The Vaginal Ring   In 2001, the FDA approved a **vaginal ring,** commonly referred to as NuvaRing, the vaginal form of a reversible, hormonal method of birth control. It is a small, flexible ring inserted into the vagina once a month, left in place for 3 weeks, and taken out of the vagina for the remaining week. The ring releases synthetic estrogen and progestin, preventing ovulation in a manner similar to that of other combined hormonal contraceptives. The ring may be removed during the 3-week period, but it must be returned within 3 hours to ensure the prevention of ovulation. If a woman takes the ring out for more than 3 hours, she should use an alternative contraceptive methods for the next 7 days. During the 1-week break, a woman will usually have her period. Nevertheless, the ring must be inserted on the same day of the week as it was inserted in the previous cycle, or pregnancy may occur. Pregnancy can happen if an error is made in using the ring, especially if the unopened package is exposed to very high temperatures or direct sunlight, if it slips out of the vagina and is not replaced within 3 hours, if it does not

Easy to insert, NuvaRing provides contraception for 3 weeks at a time.

stay in the vagina for 3 weeks in a row, or if it is left in the vagina for more than 3 weeks ("Is NuvaRing Right for You?" 2003). The ring costs between $30 and $35 a month.

EFFECTIVENESS   Like the other methods of hormonal contraception, if used perfectly, the vaginal ring is more than 99% effective. Typical use results in a success rate of 92%.

ADVANTAGES   The ring protects against pregnancy for 1 month and does not involve taking a daily pill, applying a patch, using a spermicide, or being fit by a clinician. Many women who use the ring have a more regular, lighter, and shorter period. A woman can stop using NuvaRing at any time, offering her more control over contraception than with other hormonal methods of birth control.

DISADVANTAGES   The side effects of the ring are similar to those associated with oral contraceptives. Additionally, there may be increased vaginal discharge and vaginal irritation or infection. Some women may not be able to use the ring if they have weak pelvic floor muscles, have chronic constipation, or are unable to use a diaphragm or cervical cap for a backup method of birth control. Serious problems are rare and usually have warning signs.

Implants   In 2000, after receiving reports that the **implant** Norplant was releasing lower-than-expected amounts of the hormone levonorgestrel,

Wyeth, the company that produced it, urged its users to adopt a second method of birth control as a backup. Although subsequent studies found the implants to be more than 99% effective, Wyeth eventually called it quits. In July 2002, the company permanently withdrew the device from the market. Norplant consisted of a set of matchstick-sized silicone capsules containing levonorgestrel (a progestin) implanted under the skin of the upper arm in a simple office procedure, with a local anesthetic. Over a period of up to 5 years, the hormone was slowly released. When the implants were removed, which could be done at any time, fertility was restored. Once in place, the capsules were not visible (or were barely visible) but could be felt under the skin.

Norplant was an extremely effective long-term contraceptive. Unlike with other forms of birth control, user error was almost nonexistent with Norplant, and so its theoretical and actual effectiveness rates were virtually the same. Effectiveness rates were slightly lower for women who weighed more than 155 pounds.

Side effects of contraceptive implants were similar to those of oral contraceptives. In addition to the difficult removal of the device in some women, the chief negative side effect, experienced by about half of users, was a change in the pattern of menstrual bleeding, such as lengthened periods, spotting between periods, or no bleeding at all. The menstrual cycle usually became more regular after 1 year of use. Other possible complications included headaches, weight gain, acne, breast tenderness, hair growth, and ovarian cysts. Progestin implants should not have been used by women with acute liver disease, breast cancer, cardiovascular conditions, or unexplained vaginal bleeding or by those who might have been pregnant. Implant users were also advised not to smoke.

Barrier Methods

Barrier methods are designed to keep sperm and egg from uniting. The barrier device used by men is the condom. Barrier methods available to women include the diaphragm, the cervical cap, the female condom, and the contraceptive sponge. These methods of birth control have become increasingly popular because, in addition to preventing conception, they can reduce the risk of STIs. The effectiveness of all barrier methods is increased by use with spermicides, which are discussed later in this chapter.

The Condom   A **condom** (or **male condom**) is a thin, soft, flexible sheath of latex rubber, polyurethane, or processed animal tissue that fits over the erect penis to prevent semen from being transmitted. Condoms are available in a variety of sizes, shapes, and colors. Some are lubricated. Condoms are easily obtainable from drugstores and family planning clinics, and most kinds are relatively inexpensive. Condoms are the third most widely used form of birth control in the United States (after sterilization and the pill). Their use has increased significantly since the late 1980s, due in large part to their effectiveness in helping prevent the spread of STIs, including HIV when they are used properly. (For a further discussion on the use of condoms, see chapter 15.) A condom costs anywhere from about 50¢ (for "plain") to $2.50 (for textured). Condoms should be checked for their expiration date.

Until recently, scientists believed that **nonoxynol-9 (N-9),** the spermicide used on condoms, offered limited protection against STIs and HIV. However, in 2002, under pressure from public health officials, several makers and vendors of condoms and sexual lubricants stopped selling products treated with N-9 after studies indicated that the substance actually can increase the risk of transmitting HIV and other infections contracted sexually. Researchers say that N-9, working like a detergent, can break up or irritate the cell lining, or epithelium, of the rectum and the vagina, the first lines of defense against HIV and other STIs. The danger in anal sex is especially significant because the rectum has only a single-cell wall; the vagina has a wall that is about 40 cells thick (Zimmerman, 2002). The World Health Organization and the Centers for Disease Control have reported that, because N-9 can cause small lesions that increase the risk of STIs, condoms with this ingredient should be avoided. At the same time, they acknowledge that latex (but not those made with animal tissue) condoms lubricated *without* N-9 are extremely effective in both reducing the risk of infection and preventing pregnancy.

A condom made of polyurethane (soft plastic) is now available. Polyurethane has been demonstrated to be at least as effective as latex as a barrier against sperm- and virus-sized particles. It is thinner than latex, allowing for excellent transmission of heat and receptivity to sensation, and it is 40% stronger than latex. This condom presents a welcome alternative for those allergic to latex. However, the cost is considerably higher than that for latex.

WOMEN AND CONDOM USE   Today, nearly half of male condoms are purchased by women, and condom advertising and packaging increasingly reflect this trend. Several key points are relevant to the issue of women and condom use:

- Women have more health problems than men from STIs; they can suffer permanent infertility, for example.

- Women are far more likely to contract an STI from intercourse with a male partner than vice versa.

- Condoms help protect women against unplanned pregnancy, ectopic pregnancy, bacterial infections such as vaginitis and pelvic inflammatory disease (PID), viral infections such as herpes and HIV, cervical cancer, and infections that may harm a fetus or an infant during delivery.

- A woman can protect herself by insisting on condom use. Even if a woman regularly uses another form of birth control, such as the pill or an IUD, she may want to have the added protection provided by a condom.

EFFECTIVENESS   Condoms are 98% effective in preventing conception—perfect use—but user effectiveness is about 85%. Failures sometimes occur from mishandling the condom, but they are usually the result of not putting it on until after some semen has leaked into the vagina or simply not putting it on at all. When used in anal sex, a male condom is more likely to break and slip than when used for vaginal sex, although these problems occur infrequently.

> It is now vitally important that we find a way of making the condom a cult object of youth.
>
> —*Germaine Greer*

ADVANTAGES   Condoms are easy to obtain and do not cause harmful side effects. They are easy to carry and are inexpensive or even free. Latex rubber and polyurethane condoms help protect against STIs, including HIV infection. Some men appreciate the slightly reduced sensitivity they experience when using a condom because it helps prolong intercourse.

POSSIBLE PROBLEMS   Condoms can reduce but cannot eliminate the risks of STIs, nor are they 100% effective in preventing pregnancy. The chief drawback of a condom is that it should be put on after the penis has become erect but before penetration. This interruption is the major reason for users to neglect to put them on. Some men and women complain that sensation is dulled, and (very rarely) cases of allergy to rubber are reported. Couples who experience significant loss of feeling with a condom are advised to try other kinds. Many of the newer condoms are very thin (but also strong); they conduct heat well and allow quite a bit of sensation to be experienced. Latex condoms that are flavored, glow in the dark, or are brightly colored should not be used for vaginal or anal intercourse. The condom user (or his partner) must take care to hold the sheath at the base of his penis when he withdraws, in order to avoid leakage. Latex condoms should be used with water-based lubricants (like K-Y Jelly) or glycerine only because oil-based lubricants such as Vaseline can weaken the rubber. If a condom breaks, slips, or leaks, there are some things a person can do (see the section "Emergency Contraception" later in the chapter).

The Female Condom   Currently, there is one **female condom** available for women. Called Reality, it is a disposable, soft, loose-fitting polyurethane sheath with a diaphragm-like ring at each end. It is designed to line the inner walls of the vagina and to protect women against sperm. Although not as thoroughly tested as latex condoms, polyurethane condoms, if used consistently and correctly, may provide protection against STIs, including HIV infection. One ring, which is sealed shut, is inside the sheath and is used to insert and anchor the condom against the cervix. The larger outer ring remains outside the vagina and acts as a barrier, protecting the vulva and the base of the penis (Figure 11.4).

FIGURE 11.4   The Female Condom in Position (right). The female condom, a sheath of soft polyurethane, is anchored around the cervix with a flexible ring (much like a diaphragm). A larger ring secures the sheath outside the vagina and also helps protect the vulva.

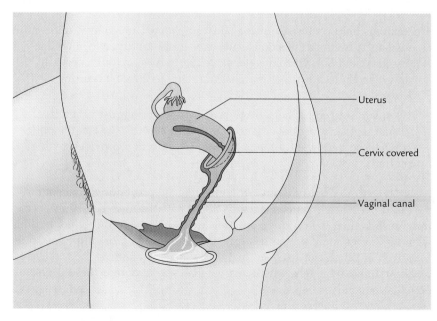

Uterus

Cervix covered

Vaginal canal

CONDOMS CAN BE very effective contraceptive devices when used properly. They also can protect against STIs. Here are some tips for their use:

1. Use condoms every time you have sexual intercourse; this is the key to successful contraception and disease prevention.

2. Carefully open the condom package—teeth or fingernails can tear the condom.

3. If the penis is uncircumcised, pull back the foreskin before putting on the condom.

4. Do not use a condom lubricated with nonoxynol-9 (N-9) for vaginal or anal intercourse; N-9 can damage the cells lining the vagina and rectum and can provide a portal of entry for HIV and other STIs.

5. Put on the condom before it touches any part of a partner's body.

6. If you accidentally put the condom on wrong-side up, discard the condom and use another.

7. Leave about a half inch of space at the condom tip, and roll the condom all the way down to the base of the penis. Push out any air bubbles.

8. Withdraw the penis soon after ejaculation. Make sure someone holds the base of the condom firmly against the penis as it is withdrawn.

9. After use, check the condom for possible tears. If you find a tear or hole, consider the use of emergency contraception (see the section "Emergency Contraception" later in the chapter). If torn condoms are a persistent problem, use a water-based lubricant such as K-Y jelly.

10. Do not reuse a condom.

11. Keep condoms in a cool, dry, and convenient place.

12. To help protect against HIV and other STIs, always use a latex rubber or polyurethane condom, *not* one made of animal tissue.

If you or your partner is uncomfortable with condom use, consider the following:

1. *Stand your ground.* Unless you want to be pregnant and are sure your partner is free of STIs, you need protection during sex. If your partner says no to condoms, you can also say no. If your partner cares about

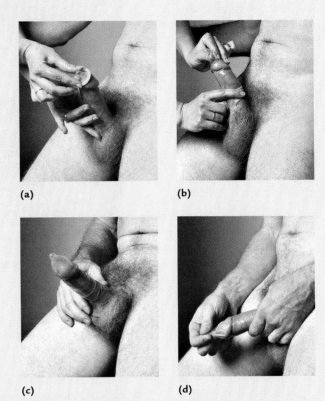

(a)   **(b)**

(c)   **(d)**

(a) Place the rolled condom on the erect penis, leaving about a half inch of space at the tip (first, squeeze any air out of the condom tip). (b) Roll the condom down, smoothing out any air bubbles. (c) Roll the condom to the base of the penis. (d) After ejaculation, hold the condom base while withdrawing the penis.

you, he or she will work with you to find birth control and safer sex methods that suit you both.

2. *Remember that communication is crucial.* It may seem "unromantic," but planning your contraception and STI prevention strategy before you are sexually entangled is essential. Consider visiting a family planning or another health clinic for counseling—together. The issue of protection must be dealt with by both of you.

3. *Keep your sense of humor and playfulness.* Condoms can provide lots of laughs, and laughter and sex go well together.

This condom can also be inserted into the rectum to provide protection during anal intercourse. The pouch is lubricated both inside and out and is meant for one-time use. It can be inserted up to 8 hours before intercourse and can be used without additional spermicide. Female and male condoms should not be used together because they can adhere to each other and cause one or both to slip out of position. The cost of female condoms is approximately $2.50 each.

Male condoms come in a variety of sizes, colors, and textures; some are lubricated, and many have a reservoir tip designed to collect semen.

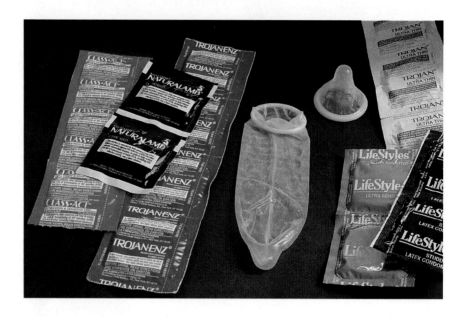

EFFECTIVENESS   The perfect-use contraceptive effectiveness rate for female condoms is 95%, similar to that for other barrier methods in protecting against pregnancy. The typical-use effectiveness rate is 79%.

ADVANTAGES   One advantage of the female condom over the male condom is that it not only protects the vagina and cervix from sperm and microbes but also is designed so that the open end covers the woman's external genitals and the base of her partner's penis, thus offering both people excellent protection against disease. Because polyurethane is stronger than latex, the device is less likely than the male latex condom to break. Female condoms may prove advantageous for women whose partners are reluctant to use a male condom, in part because they do not constrict the penis as do male latex condoms. They also give women an additional way to control their fertility and do not require a prescription.

POSSIBLE PROBLEMS   The female condom is relatively problem-free. The major complaint is aesthetic: Some women dislike the complete coverage of the female genitals provided by the condom (one of its chief health advantages) and don't want to use it for this reason. Noise made during intercourse may be distracting; however, additional lubricant can quiet this.

"Hear me, and hear me good, kid. Unroll the condom all the way to the base of the erect penis, taking care to expel the air from the reservoir at the tip by squeezing between the forefinger and thumb . . . " (Reproduced by Special Permission of Playboy *Magazine. Copyright © 1989 by* Playboy.)

The Diaphragm   A **diaphragm** is a rubber cup with a flexible rim that is placed deep inside the vagina, blocking the cervix, to prevent sperm from entering the uterus and fallopian tubes. Different women require different sizes, and a woman's size may change, especially after a pregnancy; the size must be determined by an experienced practitioner. Diaphragms are available by prescription from doctors and family planning clinics. Somewhat effective by itself, the diaphragm is highly effective when used with a spermicidal cream or jelly. (Creams and jellies are considered more effective than foam for use with a diaphragm.) Diaphragm users should be sure to use an adequate amount of spermicide and to follow their practitioner's instructions carefully. Diaphragms are relatively inexpensive—about $25, plus the cost of spermicide and the initial exam and fitting.

The diaphragm can be put in place up to 2 hours before intercourse. It should be left in place for 6–8 hours afterward. A woman should not dislodge it or douche before it is time to remove it. If intercourse is repeated within 6 hours, the diaphragm should be left in place and more spermicide inserted with an applicator. However, a diaphragm should not be left in place for more than 24 hours. To remove a diaphragm, the woman inserts a finger into her vagina and under the front of the diaphragm rim and then gently pulls it out. The diaphragm should be washed in mild soap and water and patted dry before being put away in its storage case.

A diaphragm should be replaced about once a year; the rubber may deteriorate and lose elasticity, thus increasing the chance of its splitting. Any change in the way the diaphragm feels means that a visit to a doctor or clinic to check the fit is in order. A woman who gains or loses a lot of weight should also have the fit of her diaphragm checked.

In 2002, the US Food and Drug Administration (FDA) approved a female barrier contraceptive, Lea's Shield® ("FDA Approves Lea's Shield," 2002). A reusable, vaginal contraceptive made of medical-grade silicone rubber, Lea's Shield contains a centrally-located valve which allows the passage of cervical secretions and air. The shape and size also help to create a snug fit over the cervix. The device comes in one size only, can be worn for up to 48 hours, and should be used with a spermicidal gel. It may be inserted at any time prior to intercourse, but should be left in place for 8 hours after last penetration. Additional spermicidal jelly is not required for each repeated act of intercourse. Failure rates are reportedly similar to other female barrier mathods—9% to 14% annually—and vary by parity.

When used correctly and consistently and with a spermicide, the diaphragm can be an effective method of contraception.

EFFECTIVENESS   Studies of diaphragm effectiveness have yielded varying results. Though the perfect-use effectiveness rate is quite high at 94%, the typical-use rate falls considerably, to 84%. Consistent, correct use is essential to achieve maximum effectiveness.

ADVANTAGES   The diaphragm can be put in place up to 2 hours before the time of intercourse. For most women, there are few health problems associated with its use. It helps protect against STIs of the cervix and PID (see Chapter 15) but should not be assumed to protect against HIV.

POSSIBLE PROBLEMS   Some women dislike the process of inserting a diaphragm, or the mess or smell of the chemical contraceptives used with them. Some men complain of rubbing or other discomfort caused by the diaphragm. Occasionally, a woman will be allergic to rubber. Some women have a slightly increased risk of repeated urinary tract infections (see Chapter 15). Because there is a small risk of toxic shock syndrome (TSS) associated with its use, a woman should not leave a diaphragm in her vagina for more than 24 hours.

The Cervical Cap

The **cervical cap** is a small rubber barrier device that fits snugly over the cervix; it is held in place by suction and can be filled with a small amount of spermicidal cream or jelly. Following intercourse, it

The cervical cap is smaller than a diaphragm and covers only the cervix.

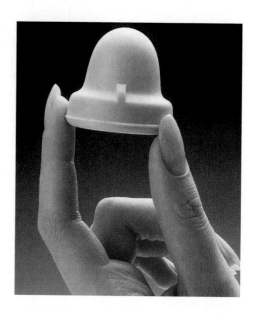

must remain in place for at least 6 hours. Cervical caps are available in four sizes and shapes, so proper fit is extremely important. Fitting must be done by a physician or health-care practitioner.

EFFECTIVENESS   Reported user effectiveness differs, depending on whether a woman has had a baby. Perfect-use effectiveness for women who have not had a vaginal delivery of a child is 91%; for those who have, it's 74%. Typical-use effectiveness for women who haven't delivered vaginally is 84%; for women who have, it's 68%.

ADVANTAGES   The cervical cap may be more comfortable and convenient than the diaphragm for some women. Much less spermicide is used than with the diaphragm, and spermicide need not be reapplied if intercourse is repeated. The cap can be inserted many hours before intercourse and can be worn for as long as 48 hours. It does not interfere with the body physically or hormonally. It may also protect against some STIs, but not HIV.

POSSIBLE PROBLEMS   Some users are bothered by an odor that develops from the interaction of the cap's rubber with either vaginal secretions or the spermicide. There is some concern that the cap may contribute to erosion of the cervix. If a partner's penis touches the rim of the cap, it can become displaced during intercourse. Theoretically, the same risk of TSS exists for the cervical cap as for the diaphragm. (See also possible problems associated with the diaphragm.)

The Sponge   After being taken off the market in 1994, the Today **sponge** is back. Now available over the Internet and expected to be on U.S. shelves by 2004, the sponge is expected to have an increase in sales in no time. Prior to its being removed from the market, neither the safety nor the effectiveness of the sponge itself was ever in question, and FDA approval of the product was never rescinded; rather, the company that produced it simply stopped selling it rather than paying to upgrade its plant. This round polyurethane shield measures about 2 inches in diameter and has a pouch in the center that fits over the cervix. The sponge is filled with the spermicide nonoxynol-9 (N-9). Because N-9 does not reduce the risk of STIs, including HIV infection, women who want to reduce the risk of infection should always use a latex condom—just as they should with all other contraceptive methods. An advantage of the sponge is that it can be left in place for up to 24 hours without reinsertion or the application of more spermicide. The perfect-use effectiveness rate is similar to that of a diaphragm—94%; for typical use, and for those who have had a child, the rate drops to 84%. This lowered effectiveness rate for women who have delivered a child vaginally may be because the one size in which the sponge is available may not adequately cover the cervix after childbirth. Shelf life of the sponge is limited. The cost is approximately $3 per sponge.

The FemCap Similar in shape to the sponge and diaphragm, a new female contraceptive device called the *FemCap* is now on the market. Made from silicon rubber, the device can be worn for up to 48 hours, double the time recommended for similar birth control devices. A single FemCap can be reused for 2 years and comes in three sizes. The device, which prevents pregnancy by covering the cervix to stop sperm from reaching the uterus, is also equipped with a delivery system for microbicides and spermicides ("New Non-Hormonal Contraceptive," 2003). The device costs approximately $50.

Spermicides

A **spermicide** is a substance that is toxic to sperm. The most commonly used spermicide in products sold in the United States is the chemical nonoxynol-9 (N-9). Originally developed as a detergent, N-9 has been used for nearly 50 years as a vaginal cream that rapidly kills sperm cells. Though cautions on N-9 have been leaking out for several years, the World Health Organization (2002) and the U.S. Centers for Disease Control and Prevention (2002b) reinforced concern by issuing warnings that the additive may promote STIs, including HIV infection. Spermicidal preparations are available in a variety of forms: foam, film, cream, jelly, and suppository. Some condoms are also treated with spermicides. Spermicidal preparations are considered most effective when used in combination with a barrier method of contraception. Spermicidal preparations are sold in tubes, packets, or other containers that hold 12–20 applications. The cost per use ranges from about 50¢ to $2.50. The overall effectiveness rate of spermicides is approximately 75%, with variation depending on the motivation of the user and, to a lesser degree, the type of spermicide used.

Contraceptive Foam **Contraceptive foam** is a chemical spermicide sold in aerosol containers. It is a practical form of spermicide for use with a condom. Methods of application vary with each brand, but foam is usually released deep in the vagina either directly from the container or with an applicator. The foam forms a physical barrier to the uterus, and its chemicals inactivate sperm in the vagina. It is most effective if inserted no more than half an hour before intercourse. Shaking the container before applying the foam increases

> Since if the parts be smooth conception is prevented, some anoint that part of the womb on which the seed falls with oil of cedar, or with ointment of lead or with frankincense, commingled with olive oil.
>
> —*Aristotle (384–322 B.C.)*

its foaminess so that it spreads further. The foam begins to go flat after about half an hour. It must be reapplied when intercourse is repeated.

Some women dislike applying foam, complaining of messiness, leakage, odor, or stinging sensations. Occasionally, a woman or man may have an allergic reaction to the foam. Because it is impossible to know how much remains in a container of foam, it is wise to keep a backup can available at all times.

Contraceptive Film   **Contraceptive film** (also called vaginal contraceptive film [VCF]) is a relatively new spermicidal preparation. It is sold in packets of small (2-inch-square), translucent tissues. This paper-thin tissue contains nonoxynol-9, which dissolves into a sticky gel when inserted into the vagina. It is placed directly over the cervix 15–60 minutes before intercourse and remains effective for 2 hours after insertion. Like other spermicides, contraceptive film works effectively in conjunction with the male condom.

Many women find film easy to use. It can be obtained from a drugstore and carried in a purse, wallet, or pocket. However, some women may not like inserting the film into the vagina, and others may be allergic to it. Increased vaginal discharge and temporary pain while urinating after using contraceptive film have been reported.

Creams, Jellies, and Vaginal Suppositories   Spermicidal creams and jellies come in tubes and are inserted with applicators or placed inside diaphragms or cervical caps. These chemical spermicides can be bought without a prescription at most drugstores. They work in a manner similar to that of foams but are considered less effective when used alone.

Contraceptive film is among the types of spermicides that are available without a prescription.

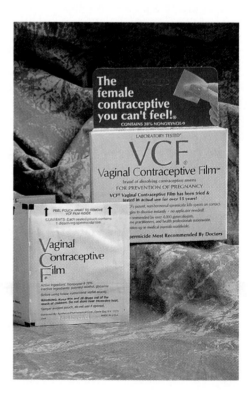

Suppositories are chemical spermicides inserted into the vagina before intercourse. Body heat and fluids dissolve the ingredients, which will inactivate sperm in the vagina. They must be inserted early enough to dissolve completely before intercourse.

Spermicidal creams, jellies, and suppositories are simple to use and easy to obtain. They may reduce the danger of acquiring pelvic inflammatory disease. The use of spermicides does not affect any pregnancy that may follow.

Some people have allergic reactions to spermicides. Some women dislike the messiness or odor involved or the necessity of touching their own genitals. Others experience irritation or inflammation, especially if they use any of the methods frequently. A few women lack the vaginal lubrication to dissolve the suppositories in a reasonable amount of time. And a few women complain of being anxious about the effectiveness of these methods during intercourse.

The IUD (Intrauterine Device)

The **intrauterine device,** or **IUD,** is a tiny plastic or copper device that is inserted into the uterus through the cervical os (opening) to prevent conception (Figure 11.5). The type of device inserted determines how long it may be left in place; the range is 1–12 years.

Although a number of IUDs have been withdrawn from the U.S. market because of the proliferation of lawsuits against their manufacturers, they are still considered a major birth control method. Approximately 1% of American women who use contraceptives rely on the IUD. The two IUDs currently available in the United States are the Copper T 380A, marketed as the ParaGard®, and a hormone-releasing intrauterine system, marketed as Mirena®. The Copper T 380A is made of polyethylene; the stem of the T is wrapped with fine copper wire. It can be left in place for 10–12 years. The Mirena is also in the form of a T. It is made of a polymer plastic with a hollow stem containing levonorgestrel, a progestin, which is continually released. The Mirena is effective for at least 5 years. At the time an IUD is removed, a new one may be inserted. The cost of an IUD, including

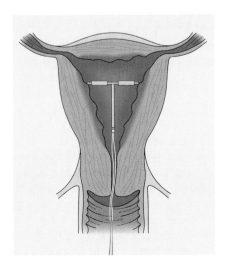 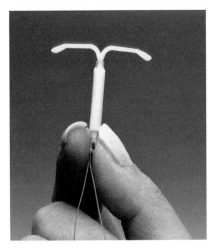

FIGURE 11.5   An IUD (Copper T 380A) in Position (left) and the Progestin-Releasing IUD (Mirena), (right). Once the IUD is inserted, the threads attached to the IUD will be clipped to extend into the vagina through the cervical opening.

insertion, ranges from $300 to $500. IUDs must be inserted and removed by a trained practitioner.

Current evidence does not support the common belief that the IUD is an **abortifacient,** a device or substance that causes an abortion. Rather, it primarily prevents pregnancy by preventing fertilization (Hatcher, Nelson, Zieman, et al., 2002). IUDs apparently work in a number of ways, some of which are not clearly understood. Both IUD types produce a reaction in the uterus that causes production of white blood cells and prostaglandins. Their presence in the uterus and fallopian tubes interferes with the movement of sperm and egg. If the IUD also contains copper, the effect on sperm is enhanced by the copper's ability to activate an enzyme so that sperm rarely reach the tube to be fertilized.

IUDs are 99% effective with perfect use; the typical user effectiveness rate is 98%. The Mirena has the lowest failure rate of any IUD developed to date.

Once inserted, IUDs require little care and don't interfere with spontaneity during intercourse. If used over a period of years, they are also relatively inexpensive. However, insertion may be painful. Also, heavy cramping typically follows and sometimes persists. Menstrual flow usually increases, often significantly, with the use of the Copper T 380A but decreases after 3–6 months of using Mirena. This device may actually cause a woman to stop having periods. An estimated 2–10% of IUD users, especially women who have never borne children, expel the device within the first year. This usually happens during the first 3 months after insertion. Another IUD can be inserted, however, and many women retain it the second time.

The IUD has been associated with increased risk of PID (see Chapter 15). Studies suggest, however, that most cases of pelvic infection that occur with an IUD in place are attributable to STIs and that women at low risk for STIs are also at low risk for pelvic infection while they are using an IUD. Recent evidence suggests that the hormone-releasing IUD, Mirena, may help to prevent PID (Grimes, 2002). However, because of the risk of sterility induced by PID, many physicians recommend that women planning to have children use alternative methods of birth control. Women who have had PID or who have multiple sex partners should be aware that an IUD will place them at greater risk for PID.

If a woman becomes pregnant with an IUD in place, the device should be removed immediately. When the IUD is removed early in pregnancy, the rate of spontaneous abortion is about 25%. About 5% of women pregnant with an IUD in place will have an ectopic pregnancy (implantation within the fallopian tube). Still, the overall mortality rate associated with the use of IUDs appears to be low compared with the rates associated with pregnancy.

Fertility Awareness Methods

Fertility awareness methods of contraception require substantial education, training, and diligence. They are based on a woman's knowledge of her body's reproductive cycle. Requiring a high degree of motivation and self-control, these methods are not for everyone. Fertility awareness is also referred to as "natural family planning." Some people make the following distinction between the two: With fertility awareness, the couple may use an alternative method (such as a diaphragm with jelly or a male condom with

It is now quite lawful for a Catholic woman to avoid pregnancy by resort to mathematics, though she is still forbidden to resort to physics and chemistry.

—*H. L. Mencken (1880–1956)*

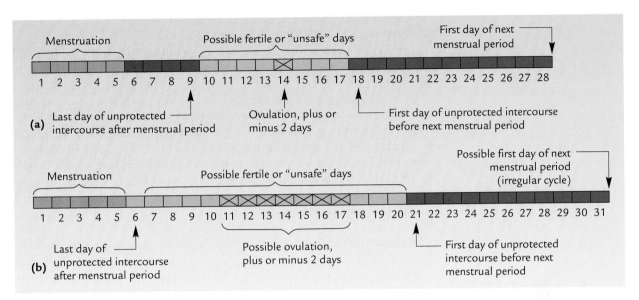

FIGURE 11.6 Fertility Awareness Calendar. To use the calendar method or other fertility awareness methods, a woman must keep track of her menstrual cycles. (a) The top chart shows probable safe and unsafe days for a woman with a regular 28-day cycle. (b) The bottom chart shows safe and unsafe days for a woman whose cycles range from 25 to 31 days. Note that the woman with an irregular cycle has significantly more unsafe days. The calendar method is most effective when combined with the basal body temperature (BBT) and cervical mucus methods.

foam) during the fertile part of the woman's cycle. Natural family planning does not include the use of any contraceptive device and is thus considered to be more natural; it is approved by the Catholic Church.

Fertility awareness methods include the calendar (rhythm) method, the basal body temperature (BBT) method, the cervical mucus method, and the symptothermal method, which combines the latter two (Figure 11.6). These methods are not recommended for women who have irregular menstrual cycles, including postpartum and lactating mothers.

All women can benefit from learning to recognize their fertility signs. It is useful to know when the time of greatest likelihood of pregnancy occurs, both for women who wish to avoid pregnancy and for those who want to become pregnant.

The Calendar (Rhythm) Method   The **calendar (rhythm) method** is based on calculating "safe" days, which depends on the range of a woman's longest and shortest menstrual cycles. It may not be practical or safe for women with irregular cycles. For women with regular cycles, the calendar method is reasonably effective because the period of time when an oocyte is receptive to fertilization is only about 24 hours. Because sperm generally live 2–4 days, the maximum period of time in which fertilization could be expected to occur may be calculated with the assistance of a calendar.

Ovulation generally occurs 14 (plus or minus 2) days before a woman's menstrual period. (However, ovulation can occur anytime during the cycle, including the menstrual period.) Taking this into account, and charting her menstrual cycles for a minimum of 8 months to determine the longest and shortest cycles, a woman can determine her expected fertile period. (Figure 11.6 shows the interval of fertility calculated in this way.) During the fertile period, a woman must abstain from sexual intercourse or use an alternative method of contraception. A woman using this method must be meticulous in her calculations, keep her calendar up to date, and remain aware of what day it is. Among typical users of fertility awareness, about 25% of women

Women who miscalculate are called mothers.

—*Abigail Van Buren*

experience unintended pregnancy during the first year of use because it is difficult to predict when ovulation will occur.

Fertility awareness (or natural family planning) methods are free and pose no health risks. If a woman wishes to become pregnant, awareness of her own fertility cycles is useful. But these methods are not suitable for women with irregular menstrual cycles or for couples not highly motivated to use them. Certain conditions or circumstances, such as recent menarche, approaching menopause, recent childbirth, breast-feeding, and recent discontinuation of hormonal contraceptives, make fertility awareness methods more difficult to use and require more extensive monitoring. Couples practicing abstinence during fertile periods may begin to take risks out of frustration. These couples can benefit from exploring other forms of sexual expression, and counseling can help.

The Basal Body Temperature (BBT) Method   A woman's temperature tends to be slightly lower during menstruation and for about a week afterward. Just before ovulation, it dips a few tenths of a degree; it then rises sharply (one-half to nearly one whole degree) following ovulation. It stays high until just before the next menstrual period.

A woman practicing the **basal body temperature (BBT) method** must record her temperature every morning upon waking for 6–12 months to gain an accurate idea of her temperature pattern. This change can best be noted using a BBT thermometer, before getting out of bed. When she can recognize the rise in her temperature and predict when in her cycle it will occur, she can begin using the method. She should abstain from intercourse or use an alternative contraceptive method for 3–4 days before the expected rise and for 4 days after it has taken place.

The Cervical Mucus Method   Women who use the **cervical mucus method** determine their stage in the menstrual cycle by examining the mucus secretions of the cervix. In many women, there is a noticeable change in the appearance and character of cervical mucus prior to ovulation. After menstruation, most women experience a moderate discharge of cloudy, yellowish or white mucus. Then, for a day or two, a clear, stretchy mucus is secreted. Ovulation occurs immediately after the clear, stretchy mucus secretions appear. The preovulatory mucus is elastic in consistency, rather like raw egg white, and a drop can be stretched into a thin strand. Following ovulation, the amount of discharge decreases markedly. The 4 days before and 4 days after these secretions are considered the unsafe days.

The Symptothermal Method   When the BBT and cervical mucus methods are used together, the approach is called the **symptothermal method.** Additional signs that may be useful in determining ovulation are midcycle pain in the lower abdomen on either side, a slight discharge of blood from the cervix ("spotting"), breast tenderness, feelings of heaviness, and/or abdominal swelling.

Sterilization

Sterilization is the most widely used method of contraception in the world, in both developing and developed countries (Landry, 2003). Among married

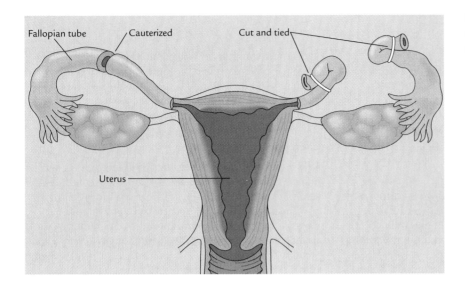

FIGURE 11.7   Tubal Ligation. A variety of techniques are used to render a woman sterile.

Fallopian tube

Cauterized

Cut and tied

Uterus

couples in the United States, sterilization is the most common form of birth control. Couples and individuals choose sterilization because they want to limit or end childbearing. About 40% of all users of contraception rely on sterilization as their preferred technique. **Sterilization** involves surgical intervention that makes the reproductive organs incapable of producing or delivering viable gametes (sperm and eggs). Though the sterilization procedure is simpler, safer, and cheaper when performed on men, nearly three-fourths of all sterilizations done in the United States are performed on women.

Sterilization for Women   Female sterilization is now a relatively safe, simple, and common procedure for many women, most of whom are over 30. Most female sterilizations are **tubal ligations,** familiarly known as "tying the tubes" (Figure 11.7). The two most common operations are laparoscopy and minilaparotomy. Less commonly performed types of sterilization for women are laparotomy and culpotomy or culdoscopy. Generally, this surgery is not reversible; only women who are completely certain that they want no (or no more) children should choose this method.

Sterilization for women is quite expensive. Surgeon, anesthesiologist, and hospital fees are substantial. Costs may range from $2000 to $3000, depending on whether it is performed in the public or the private sector. Most health insurance policies will cover all or part of the cost of sterilization for both men and women. In some states, Medicaid pays for certain patients.

LAPAROSCOPY AND MINILAPAROTOMY   Sterilization by **laparoscopy** is the most frequently used method. This procedure is performed on an outpatient basis and takes 15–30 minutes. General anesthesia is usually recommended. The woman's abdomen is inflated with gas to make the organs more visible. The surgeon inserts a rodlike instrument with a viewing lens (the laparoscope) through a small incision at the edge of the navel and locates the fallopian tubes. Through this incision or a second one, the surgeon inserts another instrument that closes the tubes, usually by electrocauterization (burning). Special small forceps that carry an electric current clamp the tubes

HUMANS ARE A very inventive species. In the area of birth control, however, some of our inventions do not deserve to be patented. "Traditional" birth control techniques such as withdrawal and lactation have some merit in that they work some of the time for some people. Other methods, such as douches and plastic bag condoms, are worse than useless; they may be harmful.

Coitus Interruptus (Withdrawal)

The oldest contraceptive technique known is **coitus interruptus** (also known as withdrawal, or "pulling out"), which involves removing the penis from the vagina before ejaculation. This method is widely used throughout the world and can be considered somewhat successful for some people. Success may depend on technique, on use in conjunction with calendar methods, or on the physical characteristics of the partners (such as the tendency toward infertility in one or both partners).

A problem with this method is its riskiness. Secretions from the man's Cowper's glands, urethra, or prostate, which sometimes seep into the vagina before ejaculation, can carry thousands of healthy sperm. Also, the first few drops of ejaculate carry most of the sperm. If the man is slow to withdraw or allows any ejaculate to spill into (or near the opening of) the vagina, the woman may get pregnant. A man using this method should wipe off any fluid at the tip of the penis before insertion into the vagina. If he has difficulty determining when he is about to ejaculate, he should *not* rely on withdrawal for contraception. The typical-use effectiveness rate is 73%. Although it is generally considered an unreliable method of birth control, coitus interruptus is certainly better than no method.

Douching

Douching involves flushing the vagina with water or a medicated liquid. As a contraceptive method, it is faulty because once ejaculation occurs douching is too late. By the time a woman can douche, the sperm may already be swimming through the cervix into the uterus. The douche liquid may even push the sperm into the cervix. Douching with any liquid, especially if done often, also tends to upset the normal chemical balance in the vagina and may cause irritation or infection.

Lactation

When a woman breast-feeds her child after giving birth, she may not begin to ovulate as long as she continues to nourish her child exclusively by breast-feeding. When used as a method of birth control, nursing should be done at least every 4 hours, and little or no other foods or liquids should be given to the baby. Some women do not ovulate while lactating, but others do. Cycles may begin immediately after delivery or in a few months. The woman never knows when she will begin to be fertile. Lactation is considered a contraceptive method in some countries, but the success rate is low, especially if used for more than 6 months.

Mythical Methods

There are many myths about contraception. Widely known methods that are *totally* useless include these:

- Standing up during or after intercourse (sperm have no problem swimming "upstream").

- Taking a friend's pill the day of, or the day after, intercourse (this doesn't work and may even be dangerous).

- Having intercourse only occasionally (it is when, not how often, that makes a difference; once is enough if the woman is fertile at that time).

- Using plastic wrap or plastic bags as condoms (these are too loose, undependable, and unsanitary).

What mythical methods have you heard about or tried? Why do you suppose someone would use these techniques? What is it about these methods that might hold appeal? What are some ways to educate the public about their ineffectiveness?

Click on "Tubal Ligation" to see what's involved in an actual laparoscopy.

and cauterize them. The tubes may also be closed off or blocked with tiny rings, clips, or plugs; no stitches are required. There is a recovery period of up to a week. During this time, the woman will experience some tenderness, cramping, and vaginal bleeding. Rest is important.

Local or general anesthesia is used with **minilaparotomy.** A small incision is made in the lower abdomen, through which the fallopian tubes are brought into view. They are then tied off or sealed with electric current, clips, or rings. The incision is then sewn up. Recovery is the same as with laparoscopy.

CULPOTOMY AND CULDOSCOPY   In these procedures, the fallopian tubes are reached through the vagina and cervix. In **culpotomy,** the tubes are viewed through the incision, tied or otherwise blocked, and then cut. **Culdoscopy** involves the same procedure, but a viewing instrument called a "culdoscope" is used. The advantage of these procedures is that they leave no visible scars. They require more expertise on the part of the surgeon, however, and have higher complication rates than laparoscopy and minilaparotomy.

ESSURE   In 2003, a new permanent method of birth control, called Essure®, was released (U.S. Food and Drug Administration, 2003). This micro-insert is placed into each fallopian tube in a 35-minute procedure that does not require general anesthesia. For three months following insertion the body and the device work together to form a tissue barrier that prevents sperm from reaching the egg. During that time, it is recommended that a woman use another method of birth control. The device is considered 99.8% effective.

Evaluating the Sterilization Methods for Women   Once sterilization has been done, no other method of birth control will ever be necessary. (A woman who risks exposure to STIs, however, should protect herself with a condom.)

Sterilization does not reduce or change a woman's hormone levels. It is not the same as menopause, nor does it hasten the onset of menopause, as some people believe. A woman still has her menstrual periods until whatever age menopause naturally occurs for her. The regularity of menstrual cycles is also not affected. A woman's ovaries, uterus (except in the case of hysterectomy), and hormonal system have not been changed. The only difference is that sperm cannot now reach her eggs. (The eggs, which are released every month as before, are reabsorbed by the body.) Sexual enjoyment is not diminished. In fact, a high percentage of women report that they feel more relaxed during intercourse because anxiety about pregnancy has been eliminated. There seem to be no harmful side effects associated with female sterilization. Sterilization should be considered irreversible.

The tubal ligation itself is a relatively safe procedure. With electrocauterization, there is a chance that other tissues in the abdomen will be damaged or that infection will occur, especially if the surgeon is not highly skilled. There may also be complications from the anesthesia.

Sterilization for Men   A **vasectomy** is a minor surgical procedure that can be performed in a doctor's office under a local anesthetic. It takes approximately half an hour. In this procedure, the physician makes a small incision (or two incisions) in the skin of the scrotum. Through the incision, each vas deferens (sperm-carrying tube) is lifted, cut, tied, and often cauterized with

BECAUSE STERILIZATION IS CONSIDERED permanent, the decision to have this procedure done is a serious one. If you are considering sterilization, ask yourself these questions:

- *Are there any circumstances in which I might later want children?* Should a child die or a new relationship develop, would a child enhance or enrich your life? If, however, you have a health problem that can make pregnancy unsafe, if you do not wish to pass on a hereditary disease or disability, or if you have all the children you want, sterilization may be a good choice.

- *What are the circumstances in which sterilization makes sense?* Sterilization may be a good choice if you and your partner cannot or do not want to use the reversible contraceptive methods currently available.

- *Which partner should get sterilized?* Medically speaking, a vasectomy is simpler, safer, and less expensive than female sterilization. However, because a number of other issues are often tied to this decision, a couple should discuss their feelings about both options.

- *How does my partner feel about the decision?* Although the permission of a spouse is not legally required for sterilization, the decision should certainly be discussed beforehand.

- *Am I eligible for sterilization?* Individuals who wish to be sterilized must be legally competent to make this decision, which usually means being over age 21 and mentally sound. If the sterilization is being paid for with federal funds, the person must sign a consent form for voluntary surgical contraception and then wait 30 days before having the surgery. Federally funded sterilizations include those paid for by Medicaid or performed in U.S. public health, military, or Indian Health Services facilities.

- *How might I feel as a result of this procedure?* If your sense of masculinity or femininity is tied to your fertility, this procedure may not be best for you. Also, if you are young, if you are not sure about having children, or if you are considering sterilization because of pressure from a partner or the hope that it will solve conflict within the relationship, then this is probably not a good decision for you.

Source: Adapted from Winikoff, B., & Wymelenberg, S. (1997). *The Whole Truth About Contraception.* Washington, DC: National Academy of Sciences.

electricity (Figure 11.8). After a brief rest, the man is able to walk out of the office; complete recuperation takes only a few days.

A man may retain some viable sperm in his system for days or weeks following a vasectomy. Because it takes about 15–20 ejaculations to get rid of these sperm, a couple should use other birth control until his semen has been checked.

Vasectomies are 99.9% effective. In very rare cases, the ends of a vas deferens may rejoin. But this is virtually impossible if the operation is correctly performed. Thus, following a vasectomy, no birth control method will ever be needed again. But the man may still wish to use a condom to prevent acquiring or transmitting STIs. Sexual enjoyment will not be diminished; the man will still have erections and orgasms and ejaculate semen. A vasectomy is relatively inexpensive compared with female sterilization. Depending on where the surgery is performed, it costs from $250 to $1000.

Compared with other birth control methods, the complication rates for vasectomy are very low. Most problems occur when proper antiseptic measures are not taken during the operation or when the man exercises too strenuously in the few days after. Hematomas (bleeding under the skin) and granulomas (clumps of sperm) can be treated with ice packs and rest. Epididymitis (inflammation of the tiny tubes that connect the testicle and vas deferens) can be treated with heat and scrotal support.

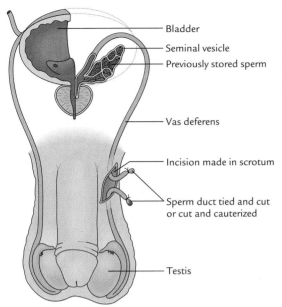

Bladder

Seminal vesicle

Previously stored sperm

Vas deferens

Incision made in scrotum

Sperm duct tied and cut
or cut and cauterized

Testis

FIGURE 11.8 Male Sterilization, or Vasectomy. This is a relatively simple procedure that involves local anesthesia and results in permanent sterilization.

Men who equate fertility with virility and potency may experience psychological problems following a vasectomy. However, most men experience no adverse psychological reactions if they understand what to expect and have the opportunity to express their concerns and ask questions. Vasectomy should be considered permanent.

Emergency Contraception (EC)

No birth control device is 100% effective: Condoms can tear, spermicides can expire, and devices can be used incorrectly. Furthermore, intercourse sometimes occurs unexpectedly, and rape is, unfortunately, always a possibility. **Emergency contraception (EC)** involves taking, within 72 hours after unprotected intercourse, a large dose of the same hormones found in birth control pills. When used in concentrated doses, these hormones can prevent a pregnancy from occurring. A second, less common, method involves the insertion of a copper IUD within 7 days after unprotected intercourse. EC is not the "abortion pill" (RU-486), and it will not terminate an established pregnancy, in which the fertilized egg has already attached itself to the wall of the uterus, nor will it cause any harm to the developing fetus. Rather, EC inhibits ovulation, fertilization, or implantation. In fact, EC is so safe that a growing number of medical and public health organizations have publicly supported efforts to make it available over the counter (Moore & Smith, 2003).

Two hormonal products available are Preven and Plan B, both of which contain the progestin levonorgestrel. Preven also contains estrogen and causes more nausea, which makes Plan B the preferred choice (Long, 2003). Actually, any oral contraceptive containing these hormones can be used for EC. The dosage varies depending on which birth control pill a woman uses. A second dose of each of these drugs is repeated after 12 hours. Treatment initiated within 72 hours after unprotected intercourse reduces the risk of

Preven, emergency contraception that can prevent a pregnancy from occurring, should be taken within 72 hours after unprotected intercourse.

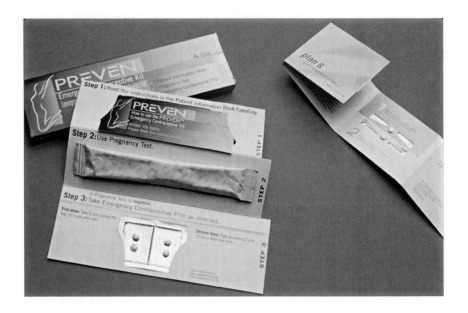

pregnancy by 75–85%. Effectiveness rates may be higher if EC is initiated in the first 12 hours after intercourse.

ParaGard, a copper-containing IUD, can be used as EC when inserted within 5 days after unprotected sexual intercourse. The mechanism interferes with implantation and may act as a contraceptive if inserted prior to ovulation. Because this method is most appropriate for women who plan to continue using an IUD as their contraceptive method, it is not widely utilized.

EC is both cost-effective, usually costing about $25, and relatively safe compared with the alternatives of abortion or childbirth. Potential side effects of EC are nausea and vomiting, breast tenderness, and irregular bleeding.

ABORTION

When most people hear the word "abortion," they think of a medical procedure. But **abortion,** or expulsion of the conceptus, can happen naturally or can be made to happen in one of several ways. Many abortions occur spontaneously—because a woman suffers a physical trauma, because the conceptus is not properly developed, or, more commonly, because physical conditions within the uterus break down and end the development of the conceptus. Approximately one-third of all abortions reported annually in the United States are **spontaneous abortions;** these are commonly referred to as miscarriages (see Chapter 12). In this section, however, we examine *induced* abortions, or intentionally terminated pregnancies, of which there are about 1.3 million reported annually in the United States (Alan Guttmacher Institute, 2003). Unless otherwise noted, when we refer to abortion, we mean induced abortion.

Under safe, clean, and legal conditions, abortion is a very safe medical procedure. Self-administered or illegal, clandestine abortions, however, can be very dangerous. The continued availability of legal abortion is considered by most physicians, psychologists, and public health professionals to be critical to the public's physical and mental well-being.

Abortions cannot be viewed as if they are all the same. Distinctions must be made, for example, among wanted, unintended, and unwanted pregnancies. It is also important to know at what stage of pregnancy an abortion occurs. Abortions occurring during the first trimester, for example, use simpler procedures, involve an embryo or less-developed fetus, and are psychologically easier than abortions occurring later. Finally, it is important to know the woman's age and motivation because these vary considerably and are associated with different emotional responses to abortion.

Methods of Abortion

An abortion can be induced in several ways. Surgical methods are most common in this country, but the use of medications is also possible, as is suction. Methods for early abortions (those performed in the first 3 months of pregnancy) differ from those for late abortions (those performed after the third month). Nearly 90% of all abortions occur in the first 3 months of pregnancy (Alan Guttmacher Institute, 2003).

Medical Abortion (RU-486)   After a decade of controversy, **medical abortion** (long known as **RU-486** and marketed as Mifeprex) is available in the United States. Doctors can now prescribe the two-drug regimen (mifepristone with misoprostol) to terminate early pregnancy, provided they have some surgical backup arrangement should the treatment fail or side effects result. Mifepristone prevents the cells of the uterine lining from getting the progesterone they need to support a blastocyst (fertilized ovum); the embryo therefore cannot survive and is expelled from the uterus. This method is most effective when used up to 49 days after the last period begins.

Medical abortion is a three-step process (Figure 11.9):

FIGURE 11.9   Medical Abortion with Mifepristone and Misoprostol. *Source: Human Sexuality* by Simon LeVay and Sharon Valente. Reprinted by permission of Sinauer Associates, Inc.

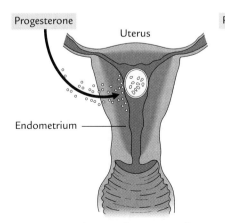

a. In normal pregnancy, the endometrium is sustained by progesterone.

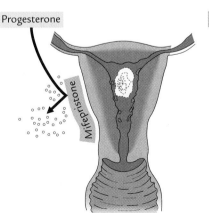

b. Mifepristone blocks the action of progesterone, leading to breakdown of the endometrium and blastocyst.

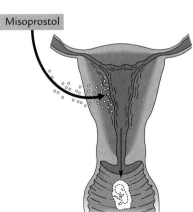

c. Misoprostol, given a few days later, causes myometrial contractions and expulsion of the blastocyst.

- Step 1: The clinician injects methotrexate or gives mifepristone in tablet form. Methotrexate stops the pregnancy in the uterus. It can also stop one that develops in the fallopian tubes. Mifepristone blocks the hormone progesterone. Without progesterone, the lining of the uterus breaks down, ending the pregnancy. Because each of these drugs affects the body differently, a clinician can help the woman decide which is best for her. About 10% of women abort before they take the second drug.

- Step 2: After a few days, the woman takes a second medication in tablet form: misoprostol. This drug causes the uterus to contract and empty, a process that can take a week. Most women abort within 4 hours of taking it. For others, bleeding begins within 24 hours, with the whole process taking about a week.

- Step 3: A follow-up visit allows the clinician to make sure that the abortion is complete.

Because a single small dose of each medication is used and most of the drug is eliminated from the body in a few days, the risk of long-term adverse health effects is low. The cost of the pills is similar to that of a surgical abortion—about $350–$575.

Surgical Methods   Surgical methods include vacuum aspiration, dilation and evacuation (D&E), and hysterotomy. To facilitate the dilation of the cervix prior to abortion, the health-care practitioner may use a metal or other type of dilator or insert a **laminaria,** a small stick of sterilized, compressed seaweed, into the cervical opening. The laminaria expands gradually, dilating the cervix gently in the process. It must be in place at least 6 hours prior to the abortion.

VACUUM ASPIRATION (FIRST-TRIMESTER METHOD)   **Vacuum aspiration,** sometimes called vacuum curettage or suction curettage, is performed under local anesthesia. The first step involves the rinsing of the vagina with an antiseptic solution. Next, the cervix is dilated with a series of graduated rods (a laminaria may have been used to begin dilation). Then a small tube attached to a vacuum is inserted through the cervix. The uterus is gently vacuumed, removing the conceptus, placenta, and endometrial tissue (Figure 11.10). If the pregnancy is less than 9 weeks along, a large syringe may be used. The entire process takes 10–15 minutes.

FIGURE 11.10   Vacuum Aspiration. (a) The vagina is opened with a speculum, and a thin vacuum tube is inserted through the cervix into the uterus. (b) The uterus is gently vacuumed. (c) The curette end of the vacuum tube may be used to gently scrape the uterine wall; the conceptus and other contents of the uterus are suctioned out.

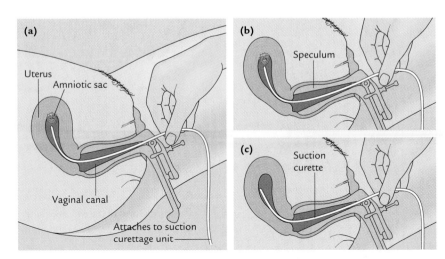

Curettage (scraping with a curette, a small, spoon-shaped instrument) may follow. The patient returns home the same day. She will experience cramping, bleeding, and, possibly, emotional reactions over the following days. Serious complications are unusual for a properly performed abortion. If a pregnancy progresses past 12 weeks, vacuum aspiration is not used because the uterine walls have become thinner, making perforation and bleeding more likely. This method is sometimes referred to as dilation and curettage (D&C).

DILATION AND EVACUATION (D&E) (SECOND-TRIMESTER METHOD) **Dilation and evacuation (D&E)** is usually performed during the second trimester of pregnancy, but it can be done up to week 20 or beyond. Only about 1.5% of abortions in the United States are carried out in the second trimester, and most of them are done in the early weeks of this trimester. Local or general anesthesia is used. The cervix is slowly dilated, and the fetus is removed by alternating curettage and other procedures. Because it is a second-trimester procedure, a D&E is somewhat riskier and often more traumatic than a first-trimester abortion.

Late Term Abortion   A rarely performed and extremely controversial technique used after 20 weeks of gestation is called late term abortion, sometimes also referred to as partial birth abortion. Since about 1% of abortions occur between weeks 20 and 24, this rarely-used procedure has been reserved for cases involving severe fetal abnormalities or dangerous health risks for the woman. It involves dilation of the cervix, emerging of the fetus feet first out of the uterus, and collapse of the fetal skull to allow passage of the head through the cervix and vagina.

As of the writing of this book, President Bush has signed a bill to restrict this method of abortion. The measure, however, has been blocked. Abortion rights groups say that the ban chips away at the rights of women to seek an abortion and that the measure is so vaguely worded that it may be expanded to include any abortion performed after the first trimester. Anti-abortion activists hail Bush's decision.

A Decline in the Prevalence of Abortion

Abortion is a common experience among women in the United States; an estimated 1.3 million procedures were performed in 2000 (Alan Guttmacher Institute, 2003). Approximately half of unintended pregnancies end in abortion. Women who are age 18–29, unmarried, Black or Hispanic, or economically disadvantaged have higher abortion rates (Jones, Darroch, & Henshaw, 2002a). However, because abortion is a sensitive topic for many people, its incidence is most likely underrepresented in national surveys. There were 110,000 fewer abortions in 2000 than in 1994, a decrease of 11% (Jones, Darroch, & Henshaw, 2002a). An estimated 47,000 of these abortions were prevented by increased use of emergency contraception ("Emergency Contraception," 2002).

Women and Abortion

There are many stereotypes about women who have an abortion: They are selfish, "loose" or "promiscuous," single, unwilling to accept family responsibilities, childless, nonmaternal, depressed, sinful, and immoral. Many

Click on "The Secret Club" to hear women who have had abortions discuss what was most helpful to them.

women are reluctant to talk openly about their abortion experiences, but accurate information about women who have abortions may help dispel these labels. In a representative sample of more than 10,000 women obtaining abortions in 2000–2001, the typical woman was age 20–30, had never married, lived in a metropolitan area, was economically disadvantaged, and was Christian (Table 11.1) (Jones, Darroch, & Henshaw, 2002a). However, it is important to remember that women who have abortions are as diverse as their reasons for doing so. The high levels of unintended pregnancy and subsequent abortion can be attributed to three factors: (1) the failure of couples to practice contraception, (2) incorrect or inconsistent use of contraceptive methods, and (3) method failure among those practicing contraception correctly and consistently (Jones, Darroch, & Henshaw, 2002b).

Although the national abortion rate has decreased in the past decade, it remains high among economically disadvantaged women. The high cost of child care, changes in welfare policy (e.g., rules requiring welfare recipients to seek employment), and economic stagnation have made it less feasible for low-income women to have children (Jones, Darroch, & Henshaw, 2002a). Additionally, accessing family planning services (about one-third of women live in a county with no abortion provider) may have contributed to this higher rate.

Making an abortion decision, regardless of the ultimate outcome, raises many emotional issues for women. There are few painless ways of dealing with an unintended pregnancy. For many women, such a decision requires a reevaluation of their relationships, an examination of their childbearing plans, a search to understand the role of sexuality in their lives, and an attempt to clarify their life goals. Clearly, women *and* men need accurate information about fertility cycles and the risk of pregnancy when a contraceptive is not used consistently or correctly, as well as access to contraceptive and abortion services.

Men and Abortion

In the abortion decision-making process, the man is often forgotten. Attention is usually focused on the woman, who is making an agonizing decision. If the man is thought of, it is often with hostility. And yet the man, like the woman, may be experiencing his own private guilt and anxiety, feeling ambivalent about the possibility of parenthood.

A common feeling men experience is powerlessness. They may try to remain cool and rational, believing that if they reveal their feelings they will be unable to give their partners emotional support. Because the drama is within the woman and her body, a man may feel he must not influence her decision.

There is the lure of fatherhood, all the same. A pregnancy forces a man to confront his own feelings about parenting. Parenthood for males, as for females, is a profound rite of passage into adulthood. For young men, there is a mixture of pride and fear about potential fatherhood and adulthood.

After an abortion, many men feel residual guilt, sadness, and remorse. It is not uncommon for men to temporarily experience erectile or ejaculatory difficulties. It is also fairly common for couples to split up after an abortion; the stress, conflict, and guilt can be overwhelming. Many clinics now provide counseling for men, as well as women, involved in an abortion.

TABLE 11.1 Characteristics of Women Obtaining Abortions, 1994 and 2000

Characteristics	Year 1994	2000
Age		
<15	1.2%	0.7%
15–19	20.6	18.6
15–17	8.8	6.5
18–19	11.5	12.0
20–24	32.8	33.0
25–29	21.4	23.1
30–34	14.4	13.5
35–39	7.5	8.1
≥40[a]	2.3	3.1
Marital Status		
Married	18.4	17.0
Previously married[b]	17.1	15.6
Never married	64.4	67.3
Residence		
Metropolitan	88.5	88.0
Nonmetropolitan	11.5	12.0
Poverty Status[c]		
<100%	25.4	26.6
100–199%	24.4	30.8
200–299%	18.9	18.0
≥300%	31.3	24.6
Race/Ethnicity		
Non-Hispanic		
White	48.0	40.9
Black	30.0	31.7
Asian/Pacific Islander	4.4	6.4
Native American	1.2	0.9
Hispanic	16.5[d]	20.1
Education[e]		
Not H.S. graduate	12.0	12.7
H.S. graduate/GED	30.4	30.3
Some college	40.3	40.6
College graduate	17.3	16.4
Religion[f]		
Protestant	37.4	42.8
Catholic	31.3	27.4
Other	7.6	7.6
None	23.7	22.2

[a]Denominator is women age 40–44.
[b]Includes separated women.
[c]Percentage of federal poverty level.
[d]Previously published figures for Hispanics have been adjusted according to state abortion reports.
[e]Limited to women older than 19.
[f]Limited to women older than 17.

Source: From Jones, R. K., J. E. Darroch, & S. K. Henshaw, "Patterns in socioeconomic characteristics of women obtaining abortions in 2000–2001." *Perspectives on Sexual and Reproductive Health,* 2002, *34*(5), 225–235. Reprinted with the permission of the Alan Guttmacher Institute.

The Abortion Debate

The majority of Americans—between 55% and 65%—believe that women should have legal access to abortion (Cooper, 2000). In the abortion debate, those who believe abortion should be prohibited generally identify themselves as "pro-life." Those who support a woman's right to choose for herself whether to have an abortion generally identify themselves as "pro-choice."

> I have noticed that all the people who favor abortion have already been born.
>
> —Ronald Reagan

The Pro-Life Argument For those who oppose abortion, there is a basic principle from which their arguments follow: The moment an egg is fertilized, it becomes a human being, with the full rights and dignity afforded other humans. An embryo is no less human than a fetus, and a fetus is no less human than a baby. Morally, aborting an embryo is the equivalent of murder.

Even though the majority of those opposing abortion would consider rape and incest (and sometimes a defective embryo or fetus) to be exceptions, the pro-life leadership generally opposes any justification for an abortion other than to save the life of the pregnant woman. To abort the embryo of a rape or incest survivor, they reason, is still to take an innocent human life.

In addition, pro-life advocates argue that abortion is the first step toward a society that eliminates undesirable human beings. If we allow the elimination of embryos, they argue, what is to stop the killing of the disabled, the elderly, or the merely inconvenient? Finally, pro-life advocates argue that there are thousands of couples who want to adopt children but are unable to do so because so many pregnant women choose to abort rather than to give birth.

> There are few absolutes left in the age after Einstein, and the case of abortion like almost everything else is a case of relative goods and ills to be evaluated one against the other.
>
> —Germaine Greer

The Pro-Choice Argument Those who believe that abortion should continue to be legal present a number of arguments. First, for pro-choice men and women, the fundamental issue is who decides whether a woman will bear children: the woman or the government. Because women continue to bear the primary responsibility for rearing children, pro-choice advocates believe that women should not be forced to give birth to unwanted children. Becoming a mother alters a woman's role more profoundly than almost any other event in her life. When women have the *choice* of becoming mothers, they are able to decide the timing and direction of their lives.

Second, although pro-choice advocates support comprehensive sexuality education and contraception to eliminate much of the need for abortion, they believe that abortion should continue to be available as birth control backup. Because no contraceptive method is 100% effective, unintended pregnancies occur even among the most conscientious contraceptive users.

Third, if abortion is made illegal, large numbers of women nevertheless will have illegal abortions, substantially increasing the likelihood of procedural complications, infections, and death. Those who are unable to have an abortion may be forced to give birth to and raise a child they did not want or cannot afford to raise.

> If men could get pregnant, abortion would be a sacrament.
>
> —Florynce Kennedy (attributed)

Abortion and Religion Although the morality of abortion is often hotly debated among Christians and Jews, there are no direct statements in the Old or New Testaments regarding abortion. Neither Moses nor Jesus nor

Paul addressed the question. Any scriptural basis for or against abortion is inferred or based on interpretation.

A key element in both pro-choice and pro-life arguments turns on when *human* life begins. Both pro-life and pro-choice supporters believe that the fetus *is* life. They disagree as to whether it is *human* life in the same sense as the life of those of us who have been born. The debate, however, is theological rather than scientific. The answer to the question of *when* embryonic or fetal life becomes *human* life depends on one's moral or religious beliefs, not on scientific evidence. And even among religious groups, there is no unanimity. During the Middle Ages, for example, it was believed that the soul entered a male conceptus 40 days after conception but waited 80 days before entering a female. Because the conceptus did not become human until it was ensouled, aborting an "unensouled" conceptus was not considered grounds for excommunication. It was not until 1869 that Pope Pius IX promulgated the doctrine that the soul enters the ovum at the time of fertilization. From this doctrine follows the belief that to abort an embryo or fetus is to kill a human being. Many Protestants hold similar beliefs about the soul and conception. As a result of such beliefs, Catholics and Christian fundamentalists are the most likely to oppose abortion as immoral.

Other religious groups, such as Methodists, Unitarians, and more mainstream Protestants, tend to support abortion choice. Although they generally believe that an embryo or a fetus is life, they also believe that other human issues must be considered. And some Catholics support abortion rights based on the primacy of conscience, which asserts that every Catholic has the right to follow his or her conscience in matters of morality.

Constitutional Issues   In 1969 in Texas, 21-year-old Norma McCorvey, a single mother, discovered she was pregnant. In the hope of obtaining a legal abortion, she lied to her doctor, saying that she had been raped. Her physician informed her, however, that Texas prohibited all abortions except those to save the life of the mother. He suggested that she travel to California, where she could obtain a legal abortion, but she had no money. Two lawyers heard of her situation and took her case in order to challenge abortion restrictions as an unconstitutional invasion of the individual's right to privacy. For the case, McCorvey was given "Roe" as a pseudonym. In 1970, a court in Texas declared the law unconstitutional, but the state appealed the decision. Meanwhile, McCorvey had her baby and gave it up for adoption. Ultimately, the case reached the Supreme Court, which issued its famous *Roe v. Wade* decision in 1973.

Under the 1973 *Roe* decision, a woman's right to abortion is guaranteed as a fundamental right, part of the constitutional right to privacy (Tribe, 1992). In delivering the Court's opinion in *Roe*, Justice William Brennan stated:

> The right to privacy . . . is broad enough to encompass a woman's decision whether or not to terminate a pregnancy. The detriment that the State would impose upon the pregnant woman by denying this choice altogether is apparent. Specific and direct harm medically diagnosable even in early pregnancy may be involved. Maternity, or additional offspring, may force upon the woman a distressful life and future. Psychological harm may also be imminent. Mental and physical health may be taxed by childcare. There

is also the distress, for all concerned, associated with the unwanted child, and there is the problem of bringing a child into a family already unable, psychologically or otherwise, to care for it. In other cases, as in this one, the . . . stigma of unwed motherhood may be involved. All these are factors the woman and her responsible physician necessarily will consider in consultation.

At the time, only four states permitted abortion at the woman's discretion.

The *Roe* decision created a firestorm of opposition among political and religious conservatives and fueled a right-wing political resurgence. But because abortion was determined a fundamental right by the *Roe* decision, efforts by the states to curtail it failed.

The 1989 *Webster v. Reproductive Rights* case was a turning point. For the first time, the Supreme Court rejected the definition of abortion as a fundamental right. Instead, abortion became a "limited constitutional right." Under the new standard, the Court gave states the right to limit abortion access, provided the limitations did not place an "undue burden" on the pregnant woman. States were allowed to impose extensive restrictions, as long as they did not actually prohibit abortion.

In 1992, the landmark decision in *Planned Parenthood v. Casey* replaced *Webster* as the reigning constitutional doctrine on abortion and government regulation. Under the *Casey* ruling, states can require a 24-hour waiting period before a woman can obtain an abortion, as well as parental notification for women younger than 18. Since that time, 37 states have passed laws that require a minor to obtain at least one parent's consent ("Restrictions on Minors," 2001). Though many adolescents may discuss contraception and pregnancy-related options with their parents, for a variety of reasons, some feel they cannot. Thus, many leading medical groups, including the American Medical Association, the American Academy of Pediatrics, and the American Academy of Family Physicians, oppose mandatory parental consent requirements for abortion.

More recently, the Clinton administration changed a number of laws to provide access, information, and support for women seeking abortion. Some of these laws were quickly rescinded by President Bush, who has also sought legislation to further restrict access to abortion. Because so many abortion-related decisions have been made by the U.S. Supreme Court, the appointment of new justices will be critical in influencing access to abortion in this country.

RESEARCH ISSUES

A lily pond, so the French riddle goes, contains a single leaf. Each day the number of leaves doubles—two leaves the second day, four the third, eight the fourth, and so on. Question: If the pond is completely full on the thirtieth day, when is it half full? Answer: On the twenty-ninth day. The global lily pond in which [six] billion of us live may already be half full.

—*Lester Brown*

Most users of contraception find some drawback to whatever method they choose. Hormonal methods may be costly or have undesirable side effects. Putting on a condom or inserting a diaphragm may seem to interrupt love-making too much. The inconveniences, the side effects, the lack of 100% effectiveness—all point to the need for more effective and more diverse forms of contraception than we have now.

High developmental costs, government regulations, social issues, political constraints, and marketing priorities all play a role in restricting contraceptive research. The biggest barrier to developing new contraceptive techniques may be the fear of lawsuits. Pharmaceutical manufacturers will not

WITH A VARIETY OF OPTIONS on the horizon for men and women, the future of contraception appears promising. In what the media called the second contraceptive revolution, between 2000 and 2003 the FDA approved seven new birth control products. Most of these purported new methods rely on hormones to prevent pregnancy—technology that has been available since the advent of the pill (Tone, 2003). Though nearly one-third of contraception in the United States is now accomplished by male techniques (15% by vasectomy and 15% by condoms), it is significant that, since the invention of the condom hundreds of years ago, no new male methods have been marketed ("New $9.5 Million NIH Grant," 2003).

Researchers are currently testing new designs and developing improvements for both male and female contraception. These include the following (Foster-Rosales & Stewart, 2001; Hatcher, Nelson, Zieman, et al., 2002; Kennedy & Insel, 2000):

- Several lower-dose oral contraceptives are currently available in Europe and appear to show promise for use in the United States.

- The Gynefix copper IUD consists of six sleeves of copper on a string with one end embedded in the upper part of the uterus and the other end protruding through the cervix. So far, this IUD has demonstrated a low expulsion rate and a 3-year life.

- Microbicides, which are also spermicidal, may not be available for 5–10 years. These have the potential to combine pregnancy prevention and STI/HIV prevention in the same product.

- Progestin-only implants for women include Norplant II and Jadelle, which work like the original Norplant; however, instead of the six levonorgestrel-containing rods, there are just two. The reduction in the number of rods allows for faster, easier, and less painful insertion and removal. Though not yet marketed in the United States, this device has been approved as a 3-year contraceptive by the FDA. In addition, there is the Implanon rod, a single rod that uses a self-contained, disposable insertion device. Like Norplant, it is highly effective and can be kept in place for 3 years.

- Weekly injections of the hormone testosterone enanthate have proved to prevent pregnancy. Researchers hope to develop a pill or implant for men.

- Contraceptive vaccines can sensitize men and women to their own sperm or egg cells. This causes the body to produce antibodies that inactivate the sperm or egg cells as if they were a disease.

- New methods of sterilization for men include a temporary polymer injection in the vas deferens to block sperm.

Ultimately, the best devices will be the ones that are safe and that people use consistently and correctly.

easily forget that the IUD market was virtually destroyed in the 1970s and 1980s by numerous costly lawsuits.

Another reason for limited contraceptive research is extensive government regulation, which requires exhaustive product testing. Although no one wants to be poisoned by medicines, perhaps it wouldn't hurt to take a closer look at the process by which new drugs become available to the public. Approval by the FDA takes an average of 7.5 years. Drug patents are in effect for only 17 years, so the pharmaceutical companies have less than 10 years to recover their developmental costs once a medication is approved for sale. Furthermore, pharmaceutical companies are not willing to expend millions in research only to have the FDA refuse to approve the marketing of new products. According to Carl Djerrasi (1979), the "father" of the birth control pill, safety is a relative, not an absolute, concept. We may need to reexamine the question "How safe is safe?" and weigh potential benefits along with possible problems.

Though research has investigated a number of contraceptives for men, none have been found to adequately eliminate sperm production while maintaining the libido.

CONTROL OVER OUR FERTILITY helps us control our lives. It also allows the human race to survive and, at least in parts of the world, to prosper. The topic of birth control provokes much emotional controversy. Individuals and institutions alike are inclined to believe in the moral rightness of their particular stance on the subject, whatever that stance may be. As each of us tries to find his or her own path through the quagmire of controversy, we can be guided by what we learn. We need to arm ourselves with knowledge—not only about the methods and mechanics of contraception and birth control but also about our own motivations, needs, weaknesses, and strengths.

SUMMARY

Risk and Responsibility

- Over the period of 1 year, sexually active couples who do not use contraception have a 90% chance of pregnancy. Most couples do not use contraception during their first intercourse. As people become older, they tend to become more consistent users of contraceptive methods.

- Many people knowingly risk pregnancy by having unprotected intercourse. The more "successful" they are at risk taking, the more likely they are to take chances again. People also take risks because of faulty knowledge, denial of their sexuality, or a subconscious desire for a child.

- Because women are the ones who get pregnant, they may have a greater interest than men in controlling their fertility. More men are now sharing the responsibility.

Methods of Contraception and Birth Control

- *Birth control* is any means of preventing a birth from taking place. *Contraception* is birth control that works specifically by preventing the union of sperm and egg.

- The most reliable method of birth control is *abstinence*—refraining from sexual intercourse.

- *Oral contraceptives* are the most widely used form of reversible birth control in the United States. Birth control pills contain synthetic hormones: progestin and (usually) estrogen. The pill is highly effective if taken regularly. There are side effects and possible problems for some users. The greatest risks are to smokers, women over 35, and women with certain health disorders, such as cardiovascular problems. Newer methods of hormonal contraception include the *patch* and the *vaginal ring*. The patch is applied to specific parts of the body and worn for 3 weeks at a time; the ring is inserted into the vagina and left in place for 3 weeks. The costs, actions, effectiveness, and side effects of both devices are similar to those of the pill.

- Implants, previously marketed as Norplant, are no longer available. Thin capsules containing progestin were implanted under the skin of a woman's arm and protected against pregnancy for 5 years. When they were removed, fertility was restored. Injectable hormones *Depo-Provera (DMPA)* and *Lunelle* are now available in the United States.

- A *condom* (or *male condom*) is a thin sheath of latex, rubber, polyurethane, or processed animal tissue that fits over the erect penis and prevents semen from being transmitted. It is the third most widely used birth control method in the United States. Condoms are very effective for contraception when used correctly. Latex and polyurethane condoms also help provide protection against STIs.

- The *female condom, diaphragm, cervical cap* and *FemCap* are barrier methods used by women. The diaphragm and cervical cap cover the cervical opening. They are used with spermicidal jelly or cream. The diaphragm and cervical cap are effective if used properly. Female condoms, in addition to lining the vagina, cover much of the vulva, providing more protection against disease organisms.

- *Spermicides* are chemicals that are toxic to sperm. Though *nonoxynol-9* is the most common ingredient in spermicides, it is no longer recommended for use on condoms for anal sex or as a method of contraception. *Contraceptive foam* provides fairly good protection when used alone, but other chemicals are more effective if combined with a barrier method. Other spermicidal products are *film,* cream, jelly, and vaginal suppositories.

- An *intrauterine device (IUD)* is a tiny plastic or metal device that is inserted through the cervical os into the uterus. It disrupts the fertilization and implantation processes.

- *Fertility awareness methods* (or natural family planning) involve a woman's awareness of her body's reproductive cycles. These include the *calendar (rhythm), basal body temperature (BBT), cervical mucus,* and *symptothermal methods.* These methods are suitable only for women with regular menstrual cycles and for couples with high motivation.

- *Sterilization* is the most widely used method of contraception in the world. The most common form for women is *tubal ligation,* closing off the fallopian tubes. A new female sterilization device, called *Essure,* that does not require surgical incision is now available. The surgical procedure that sterilizes men is a *vasectomy,* in which each vas deferens (sperm-carrying tube) is closed off. These methods of birth control are very effective.

- The use of *emergency contraception* prevents pregnancy by keeping a fertilized egg from implanting into the uterus. When used within 72 hours of unprotected intercourse, it can be quite effective. The copper IUD can also be used as a postcoital form of birth control.

Abortion

- *Abortion,* the expulsion of the conceptus from the uterus, can be spontaneous or induced. *Medical abortion* (also known as *RU-486*) is now available in the United States to terminate early pregnancy. Surgical methods of abortion are *vacuum aspiration, dilation and evacuation (D&E),* and *hysterotomy.* Nonsurgical methods utilize injections of prostaglandins or saline solution. Abortion is generally safe if done in the first trimester. Second-trimester abortions are significantly riskier.

- In the United States, there are about 1.3 million abortions annually. The abortion rate has declined slightly in recent years, due in part to the increased use of emergency contraception.

- For women, the abortion decision is complex and raises many emotional issues. Men often feel powerless and ambivalent when their partner has an abortion, and many feel residual guilt and sadness following the abortion.

- In the abortion controversy, pro-life advocates argue that life begins at conception, that abortion leads to euthanasia, and that many who want to adopt are unable to because fewer babies are born as a result of abortion. Pro-choice advocates argue that women have the right to decide whether to continue a pregnancy, that abortion is needed as a birth control alternative because contraceptives are not 100% effective, and that if abortion is not legal women will have unsafe illegal abortions. A key issue in the debate is when the embryo or fetus becomes human life.

- The current constitutional doctrine on abortion was established by *Planned Parenthood v. Casey* in 1992, in which the Supreme Court ruled that states can require a 24-hour waiting period before a woman obtains an abortion and parental notification for women younger than 18.

Research Issues

- High developmental costs, government regulations, political agendas, and marketing priorities all play a part in restricting contraceptive research. The biggest barrier, however, is the fear of lawsuits.

Sex and the Internet

Planned Parenthood

Most of us have heard about Planned Parenthood and the services it offers related to family planning. What we might not be aware of is the scope of the organization and the information it provides to aid us in our decisions. To learn more about Planned Parenthood or a specific topic related to their work, go to the group's Web site (http://www.plannedparenthood.org). Either select a content area ("Sexual Health," "Take Action,"

"Research," etc.) or use a key term from this chapter and enter it as a keyword search. After reading more about this topic, answer the following:

- What area or word did you choose? Why?
- What are five key points related to this topic?
- As a result of what you have learned, what opinions do you have or action would you take concerning this issue?
- Would you recommend this site to a person interested in learning more about family planning? Why or why not?

SUGGESTED WEB SITES

Association of Reproductive Health Professionals (ARHP)
http://www.arhp.org
A site for health-care providers, as well as those interested in reproductive health news.

Centers for Disease Control and Prevention Reproductive Health Information Source
http://www.cdc.gov/nccdphp/drh/
Provides information, research, and scientific reports on men's and women's reproductive health.

The Contraception Report
http://www.contraceptiononline.org
Aimed primarily at physicians and sponsored by Baylor College of Medicine; a peer-reviewed journal that provides up-to-date findings concerning all forms of contraception.

Global Campaign for Microbicides
info@global-campaign.org
An effort to build support for investment into microbicides and other user-controlled preventive methods.

Managing Contraception
http://www.managingcontraception.com
Provides a pocket guide for contraception, as well as an up-to-date Web site with reliable links and a question-and-answer section.

National Abortion and Reproductive Rights Action League
http://www.naral.org
Advocates for comprehensive reproductive health policies to secure reproductive *choice* for all Americans.

Population Connection Now (previously known as Zero Population Growth)
http://www.populationconnection.org
A nonprofit membership organization that works to achieve a sustainable balance between the earth's population and its environment and resources.

SUGGESTED READING

Chesler, Ellen. (1993). *A Woman of Valor: Margaret Sanger and the Birth Control Movement in America*. New York: Simon & Schuster. The biography of Margaret Sanger, who, in the early decades of the twentieth century, fought for women's contraceptive rights, an idea as divisive then as abortion rights are today.

Hatcher, Robert; Nelson, Anita; Zieman, Miriam; et al. (2002). *A Pocket Guide to Managing Contraception*. Tiger, GA: Bridging the Gap Communications. A comprehensive and technically reliable book on contraceptive technology.

Tone, A. (2001). *Devices and Desires: Men, Women, and the Commercialization of Contraception in the United States*. New York: Hill & Wang. A history of contraception in the United States.

For links, articles, and study material, go to the McGraw-Hill Web site, located at http://www.mhhe.com/strong5

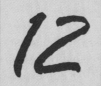

12

Conception, Pregnancy, and Childbirth

"When I was in my teens, I moved from my home [Guatemala] to the states and found things turned upside [down] from my traditional background. Take, for example, breast-feeding. In my country, it is a normal thing to breast-feed; you would not think twice about seeing a nurturing mother breast-feeding her child in public. Here, it seems to upset people's sensibilities when a nursing mother feeds her child in public. I wonder, that which is so natural and necessary, how can we debate whether a woman has a right to feed her child in public?"

—20-year-old Black/Latino female

"Pregnancy and childbirth have changed my life. As the mother of three young children, I look back at my pregnancies as probably three of the best periods of my life. Oh, sure, there were the days of exhaustion and nausea, pelvic heaviness, the large cumbersome breasts, and lost sleep, but in retrospect, they were overshadowed by the life growing inside of me. In giving life, I celebrate my womanhood."

—43-year-old White female

*T*HE BIRTH OF A CHILD is considered by many parents to be the happiest event of their lives. Today, however, pain and controversy surround many aspects of this completely natural process. As we struggle to balance the rights of the mother, the father, the fetus, and society itself in these matters, we find ourselves considering the quality of life, as well as life's mere existence.

For most American women, pregnancy is relatively comfortable and the outcome predictably joyful. Yet for increasing numbers of others, especially among the poor, the prospect of having children raises the specters of drugs, disease, malnutrition, and familial chaos. And there are those couples who have dreamed of and planned for families for years, only to find that they are unable to conceive.

In this chapter, we view pregnancy and childbirth from biological, social, and psychological perspectives. We consider pregnancy loss, infertility, and reproductive technology. And we look at the challenges of the transition to parenthood.

FERTILIZATION AND FETAL DEVELOPMENT

If your parents didn't have any children, there's a good chance that you won't have any.

—*Clarence Day (1874–1935)*

As you will recall from Chapter 3, once the ovum has been released from the ovary, it drifts into the fallopian tube, where it may be fertilized if live sperm are present (Figure 12.1). If the pregnancy proceeds without interruption, the birth will occur in approximately 266 days. (Traditionally, physicians count the first day of the pregnancy as the day on which the woman began her last menstrual period; they calculate the due date to be 280 days, which is also 10 lunar months, from that day.)

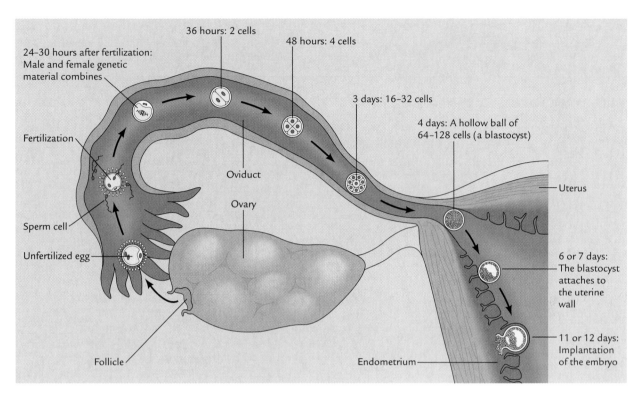

FIGURE 12.1 Ovulation, Fertilization, and Development of the Blastocyst. This drawing charts the progress of the ovulated oocyte (unfertilized egg) through fertilization and pre-embryonic development.

The Fertilization Process

The oocyte remains viable for 12–24 hours after ovulation; most sperm are viable in the female reproductive tract for 12–48 hours, although some may be viable for up to 5 days. Therefore, for fertilization to occur, intercourse must take place within 5 days before and 1 day after ovulation (Wilcox, Weinberg, & Baird, 1996).

Of the millions of sperm ejaculated into the vagina, only a few thousand (or even a few hundred) actually reach the fallopian tubes. The others leak from the vagina or are destroyed within its acidic environment. Those that make it into the cervix (which is easier during ovulation, when the cervical mucus becomes more fluid) may still be destroyed by white blood cells within the uterus. Furthermore, the sperm that actually reach the oocyte within a few minutes of ejaculation are not yet capable of getting through its outer layers. They must first undergo **capacitation,** the process by which their membranes become fragile enough to release the enzymes from their acrosomes (the helmetlike coverings of the sperm's nuclei). It takes 6–8 hours for this acrosomal reaction to occur. It has recently been observed that sperm have receptor molecules that are attracted to a chemical released by the egg. Furthermore, the membrane of the sperm cell contains a chemical that helps the sperm adhere to, and eventually penetrate, the outer layer of the egg (Cho et al., 1998).

Once a single sperm is inside the oocyte cytoplasm, an electrical reaction occurs that prevents any other sperm from entering the oocyte. Immediately, the oocyte begins to swell, detaching the sperm that still cling to its outer layer. Next, it completes the final stage of cell division and becomes a mature ovum by forming the ovum nucleus. The nuclei of sperm and ovum then

> Expectant parents who want a boy will get a girl, and vice versa; those who practice birth control will get twins.
>
> —*John Rush*

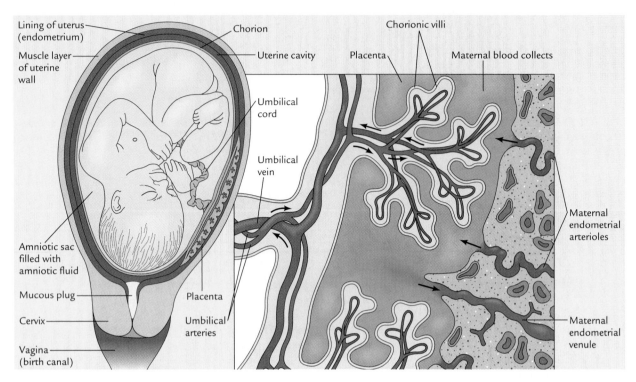

FIGURE 12.2 The Fetus in the Uterus and a Cross Section of the Placenta. The placenta is the organ of exchange between mother and fetus. Nutrients and oxygen pass from the mother to the fetus, and waste products pass from the fetus to the mother via blood vessels within the umbilical cord.

release their chromosomes, which combine to form the diploid zygote, containing 23 pairs of chromosomes. (Each parent contributes one chromosome to each of the pairs.) Fertilization is now complete, and pre-embryonic development begins. Within 9 months, this single cell, the zygote, may become the 600 trillion cells that constitute a human being.

Development of the Conceptus

Following fertilization, the zygote undergoes a series of divisions, during which the cells replicate themselves. After 4 or 5 days, there are about 100 cells, now called a **blastocyst.** On about the fifth day, the blastocyst arrives in the uterine cavity, where it floats for a day or two before implanting in the soft, blood-rich uterine lining (endometrium), which has spent the past 3 weeks preparing for its arrival. The process of **implantation** takes about 1 week. Human chorionic gonadotropin (HCG) secreted by the blastocyst maintains the uterine environment in an "embryo-friendly" condition and prevents the shedding of the endometrium, which would normally occur during menstruation.

The blastocyst, or pre-embryo, rapidly grows into an **embryo,** which will, in turn, be referred to as a **fetus** after the eighth week of **gestation** (pregnancy). During the first 2 or 3 weeks of development, the **embryonic membranes** are formed. These include the **amnion** (amniotic sac), a membranous sac that will contain the embryo and **amniotic fluid;** the **yolk sac,** producer of the embryo's first blood cells and the germ cells that will develop into gonads; and the **chorion,** the embryo's outermost membrane (Figure 12.2).

During the 3rd week, extensive cell migration occurs, and the stage is set for the development of the organs. The first body segments and the brain

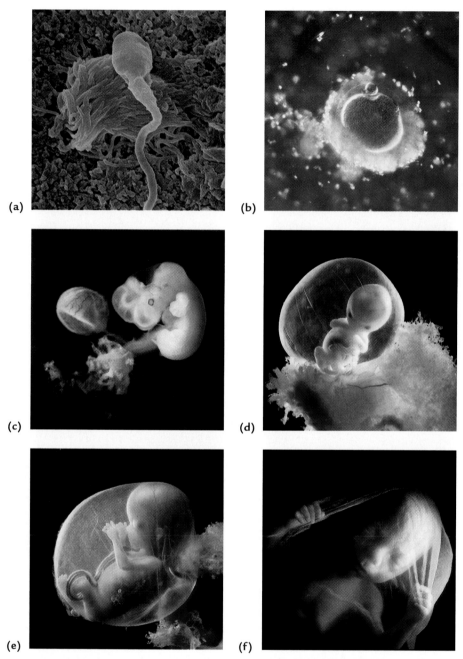

(a)   (b)   (c)   (d)   (e)   (f)

(a) After ejaculation, several million sperm move through the cervical mucus toward the fallopian tubes; an ovum has moved into one of the tubes. On their way to the ovum, millions of sperm are destroyed in the vagina, uterus, or fallopian tubes. Some go the wrong direction in the vagina, and others swim into the wrong tube. (b) The mother's and father's chromosomes have united, and the fertilized ovum has divided for the first time. After about 1 week, the blastocyst will implant itself in the uterine lining. (c) The embryo is 5 weeks old and is ⅖ of an inch long. It floats in the embryonic sac. The major divisions of the brain can be seen, as well as an eye, hands, arms, and a long tail. (d) The embryo is now 7 weeks old and is almost 1 inch long. Its external and internal organs are developing. It has eyes, nose, mouth, lips, and tongue. (e) At 12 weeks, the fetus is over 3 inches long and weighs almost 1 ounce. (f) At 16 weeks, the fetus is more than 6 inches long and weighs about 7 ounces. All its organs have been formed. The time that follows is now one of simple growth.

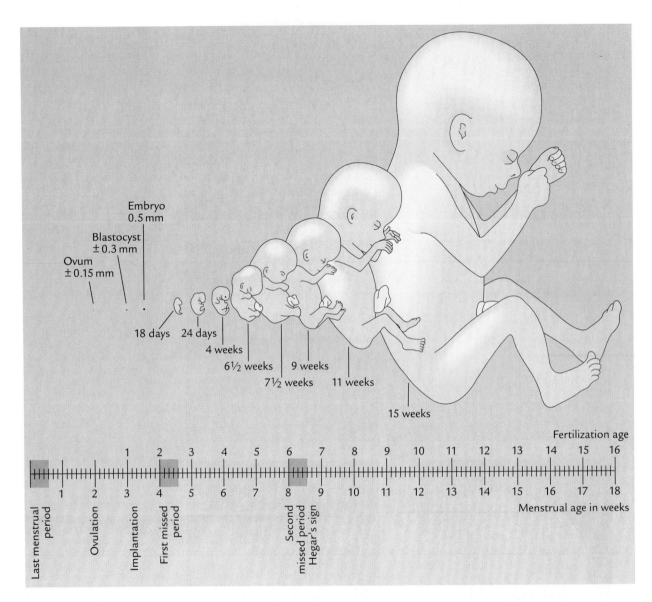

FIGURE 12.3 Growth of the Embryo and Fetus. In this drawing, the actual sizes of the developing embryo and fetus are shown, from conception through the first 15 weeks.

What was your original face before you were born?

—*Zen koan (riddle)*

begin to form. The digestive and circulatory systems begin to develop in the 4th week, and the heart begins to pump blood. By the end of the 4th week, the spinal cord and nervous system have also begun to develop. The 5th week sees the formation of arms and legs. In the 6th week, the eyes and ears form. At 7 weeks, the reproductive organs begin to differentiate in males; female reproductive organs continue to develop. At 8 weeks, the fetus is about the size of a thumb, although the head is nearly as large as the body. The brain begins to function to coordinate the development of the internal organs. Facial features begin to form, and bones begin to develop. Arms, hands, fingers, legs, feet, toes, and eyes are almost fully developed at 12 weeks. At 15 weeks, the fetus has a strong heartbeat, some digestive functioning, and active muscles. Most bones are developed by then, and the eyebrows appear. At this stage, the fetus is covered with a fine, downy hair called **lanugo** (Figure 12.3).

PARENTHOOD IS NOW A MATTER of choice, thanks to the widespread use of contraception. For the most part, women and men who want to have children can decide not only how many children they want but when to have them. Approximately 9% of American women age 15–44 do not plan to have children (Lauer & Lauer, 2000). In the past, couples without children were referred to as "childless," conveying the sense that they were missing something they wanted or were supposed to have. But this term has been replaced with **child-free,** as we have experienced a cultural shift and demographic trend in the direction of increasing numbers of women who expect and intend to remain nonparents. The term "child-free" suggests that couples who do not choose to have children need no longer be seen as sympathetic figures, lacking something considered essential for personal and relationship fulfillment.

Even with less familial and social pressure to reproduce, the decision not to have children can be a difficult one. Factors include timing, divorce, ambivalence on the part of one partner, lack of desire to conceive or adopt a child when single, and career ambitions and promotions (Peterson, 2002). Couples usually have some idea that they will or will not have children before they marry. If the intent isn't clear from the start or if one partner's mind changes, the couple may have serious problems ahead.

Do you want to have children? Why or why not? What are your feelings about those who choose to remain child-free? Do you believe that the government should provide tax incentives to couples who are child-free?

Throughout its development, the fetus is nourished through the **placenta.** The placenta begins to develop from part of the blastocyst following implantation. It grows larger as the fetus does, passing nutrients from the mother's bloodstream to the fetus, to which it is attached by the **umbilical cord.** The placenta serves as a biochemical barrier, allowing dissolved substances to pass to the fetus but blocking blood cells and large molecules.

By 5 months, the fetus is 10–12 inches long and weighs between ½ and 1 pound. The internal organs are well developed, although the lungs cannot function well outside the uterus. At 6 months, the fetus is 11–14 inches long and weighs more than 1 pound. At 7 months, it is 13–17 inches long and weighs about 3 pounds. At this point, most healthy fetuses are viable—that is, capable of surviving outside the womb. (Although some fetuses are viable at 5 or 6 months, they require specialized care to survive.) The fetus spends the final 2 months of gestation growing rapidly. At term (9 months), it will be about 20 inches long and will weigh about 7 pounds.

BEING PREGNANT

From the moment it is discovered, a pregnancy affects people's feelings about themselves, their relationships with their partners, and the interrelationships of other family members as well. Women in the United States are now having more children than at any time in almost 30 years (Centers for Disease Control and Prevention [CDC], 2002c). In 2000, the average number of children born to a woman was 2.1, up from fewer than 2 children in the 1970s and 1980s. The average number of children was fairly consistent along racial lines, with White, Asian/Pacific Islander, and American Indian women having a fertility rate of 2.1, and Black women a rate of 2.2. Among Hispanic women, the fertility rate was 3.1, higher than the national rate, with the highest rates for Mexican women (3.3) and Puerto Rican women (2.6) and the lowest rate for Cuban women (1.9). This increased fertility was reported for all age groups except teenagers.

Pregnancy Tests

Chemical tests designed to detect the presence of **human chorionic gonadotropin (HCG),** secreted by the developing placenta, can usually determine pregnancy approximately 2 weeks following a missed (or spotty) menstrual period. Pregnancy testing may be done in a doctor's office or family planning clinic, or home pregnancy tests may be purchased in most drugstores. The directions must be followed closely. Blood analysis can also be done to determine if a pregnancy exists. Although such tests diagnose pregnancy within 7 days after conception and with better than 95% accuracy, no absolute certainty exists until fetal heartbeat and movements can be detected or ultrasound is performed.

The first reliable physical sign of pregnancy can be observed about 4 weeks after a woman misses her period. By this point, changes in her cervix and pelvis are apparent during a pelvic examination. At this stage, the woman is considered to be 8 weeks pregnant, according to medical terminology; physicians calculate pregnancy as beginning at the time of the woman's last menstrual period rather than at the time of actual fertilization (because that date is often difficult to determine). Another signal of pregnancy, called **Hegar's sign,** is a softening of the uterus just above the cervix, which can be felt during a vaginal examination. In addition, a slight purple hue colors the labia minora; the vagina and cervix also take on a purplish color rather than the usual pink.

Changes in Women During Pregnancy

A woman's feelings during pregnancy will vary dramatically according to who she is, how she feels about pregnancy and motherhood, whether the pregnancy was planned, whether she has a secure home situation, and many other factors. Her feelings may be ambivalent, and they will probably change over the course of the pregnancy.

A woman's first pregnancy is especially important because it has traditionally symbolized her transition to maturity. Even as social norms change and it becomes more common and "acceptable" for women to defer childbirth until they've established a career or to choose not to have children, the significance of a first pregnancy should not be underestimated. It is a major developmental milestone in the lives of mothers—and of fathers as well.

A couple's relationship is likely to undergo changes during pregnancy. It can be a stressful time, especially if the pregnancy was unanticipated. Women with supportive partners have fewer health problems in pregnancy and more positive feelings about their changing bodies ("Especially for Fathers," D.U.). Communication is especially important during this period, because each partner may have preconceived ideas about what the other is feeling. Both partners may have fears about the baby's well-being, the approaching birth, their ability to parent, and the ways in which the baby will interfere with their own relationship. All of these concerns are normal. Sharing them, perhaps in the setting of a prenatal group, can strengthen the relationship. If the pregnant woman's partner is not supportive or if she does not have a partner, it is important that she find other sources of support—family, friends, women's groups—and that she not be reluctant to ask for help.

A pregnant woman's relationship with her own mother may also undergo changes. In a certain sense, becoming a mother makes a woman the equal of her own mother. She can now lay claim to co-equal status as an adult. Women who have depended on their mother tend to become more independent and assertive as their pregnancy progresses. Women who have been distant from, hostile to, or alienated from their mother may begin to identify with their mother's experience of pregnancy. Even women who have delayed childbearing until their thirties may be surprised to find their relationships with their mother changing and becoming more "adult." Working through these changing relationships is a kind of "psychological gestation" that accompanies the physiological gestation of the fetus.

The first trimester (3 months) of pregnancy may be difficult physically for the expectant mother. Approximately two-thirds of women may experience nausea, vomiting, fatigue, and painful swelling of the breasts. New data reveal that the nausea and vomiting that often occur during the first trimester of pregnancy may serve an adaptive, prophylactic function. A pregnant woman's aversion to such foods as meat, fish, poultry, and eggs may actually protect her from infection and miscarriage (Flaxman & Sherman, 2000). She may also have fears that she will miscarry or that the child will not be normal. Her sexuality may undergo changes, resulting in unfamiliar needs (for more, less, or differently expressed sexual expression), which may, in turn, cause anxiety. (Sexuality during pregnancy is discussed further in the accompanying box.) Education about the birth process and her own body's functioning and support from partner, friends, relatives, and health-care professionals are the best antidotes to fear.

During the second trimester, most of the nausea and fatigue disappear, and the pregnant woman can feel the fetus move within her. Worries about miscarriage will probably begin to diminish, too, for the riskiest part of fetal development has passed. The pregnant woman may look and feel radiant. She will very likely be proud of her accomplishment and be delighted as her pregnancy begins to show. She may feel in harmony with life's natural rhythms. Some women, however, may be concerned about their increasing size, fearing that they are becoming unattractive. A partner's attention and reassurance will ease these fears.

The third trimester may be the time of the greatest difficulties in daily living. The uterus, originally about the size of the woman's fist, enlarges to fill the pelvic cavity and push up into the abdominal cavity, exerting increasing pressure on the other internal organs (Figure 12.4). Water retention (edema) is a fairly common problem during late pregnancy. Edema may cause swelling in the face, hands, ankles, and feet, but it can often be controlled by cutting down on the intake of salt and carbohydrates. If dietary changes do not help this condition, the woman should consult her physician. Her physical abilities also are limited by her size, and she may need to cut back or stop her work. A family dependent on the pregnant woman's income may suffer a severe financial crunch.

The woman and her partner may become increasingly concerned about the upcoming birth. Some women experience periods of depression in the weeks preceding delivery; they may feel physically awkward and sexually unattractive. Many feel a sense of exhilaration and anticipation marked by bursts of industriousness. They feel that the fetus already is a member of the

IT IS NOT UNUSUAL for a woman's sexual feelings and actions to change during pregnancy, although there is great variation among women in these expressions of sexuality. Some women feel beautiful, energetic, and sensual and are very much interested in sex; others feel awkward and decidedly unsexy. More often, there may be a lessening of women's sexual interest during pregnancy, a corresponding decline in coital frequency, and/or a shift in the type of activities preferred (De Judicibus & McCabe, 2002). It is also quite possible for a woman's sexual feelings to fluctuate during this time. Men may also feel confusion or conflicts about sexual activity. Like many women, they may have been conditioned to find the pregnant body unerotic. Or they may feel deep sexual attraction to their pregnant partners yet fear that their feelings are "strange" or unusual. They may also worry about hurting their partner or the baby.

Although there are no "rules" governing sexual behavior during pregnancy, a few basic precautions should be observed:

- If the woman has had a prior miscarriage, she should check with her health practitioner before having intercourse, masturbating, or engaging in other activities that might lead to orgasm. Powerful uterine contractions could induce a spontaneous abortion in some women, especially during the first trimester.

- If the woman has vaginal bleeding, she should refrain from sexual activity and consult her physician or midwife at once.

- If the insertion of the penis or other object into the vagina causes pain that is not easily remedied by a change of position, the couple should refrain from penetration.

- Pressure on the woman's abdomen should be avoided, especially during the final months of pregnancy.

- Late in pregnancy, an orgasm is likely to induce uterine contractions. Generally, this is not considered harmful, but the pregnant woman may want to discuss it with her practitioner. (Occasionally, labor begins when the waters break as the result of orgasmic contractions.)

A couple may be uncertain as to how to express their sexual feelings, especially if it is their first pregnancy. The following guidelines may be helpful:

- Even during a normal pregnancy, sexual intercourse may be uncomfortable. The couple may want to try such positions as side by side or rear entry to avoid pressure on the woman's abdomen and to facilitate more shallow penetration. (See the illustrations of different sexual positions in Chapter 9.)

- Even if intercourse is not comfortable for the woman, orgasm may still be intensely pleasurable. She may wish to consider masturbating (alone or with her partner) or engaging in cunnilingus. It is important to note that air should *not* be blown into the vagina during cunnilingus.

- Both partners should remember that there are no "rules" about sexuality during pregnancy. This is a time for relaxing, enjoying the woman's changing body, talking a lot, touching each other, and experimenting with new ways—both sexual and nonsexual—of expressing affection.

Once the baby has been born, a couple can resume intercourse after the bleeding has stopped and the vaginal walls have healed. This may take anywhere from 4 to 8 weeks.

Have you ever thought about sex during pregnancy? If so, what are your views? What new information did you learn as a result of reading this box?

family. Both parents may begin talking to the fetus and "playing" with it by patting and rubbing the mother's belly.

The principal developmental tasks for the expectant mother and father are summarized in Table 12.1

Teen Pregnancy

Births to teenagers have fallen to their lowest rate in the 60 years that statistics have been kept, from an all-time high of 96 births per 1000 women age 15–19 in 1957 to an all-time low of 49 per 1000 in 2000 (Alan Guttmacher Institute, 2002b). In recent years, this downward trend has occurred among teens of all ages and races. Even with this progress, however, the U.S. teen

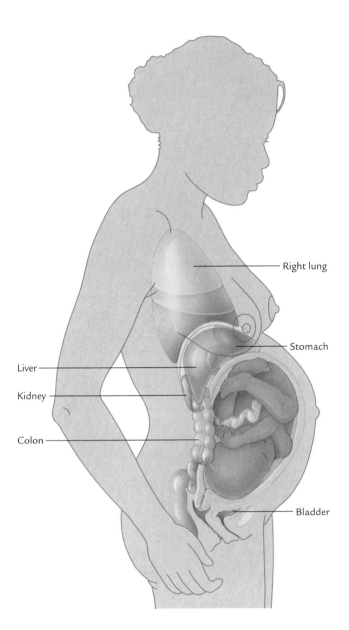

FIGURE 12.4 Mother and Fetus in Third Trimester of Pregnancy. The expanding uterus affects the mother's internal organs, causing feelings of pressure and possible discomfort.

birth rate is one of the highest in the developed world. More than three-fourths of pregnancies to teens are unplanned, and half of those pregnancies end in births (Figure 12.5).

Although the rate of births to teenagers has declined over the past 30 years, the rate of teen pregnancy is still high (Figure 12.6). Teen pregnancies trap most of the young mothers and fathers and their children in a downward spiral of lowered expectations, economic hardship, and poverty. Because of poor nutrition and inadequate medical care during pregnancy, babies born to teenagers have twice the normal risk of low birth weight, which is responsible for numerous physical and developmental problems. Also, many of these children will have disrupted family lives, absent fathers, and the attendant problems of poverty, such as

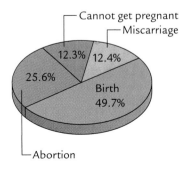

FIGURE 12.5 Pregnancy Outcomes for Women Under Age 20. (*Source:* Henshaw, 2003.)

TABLE 12.1 Principal Tasks of Expectant Parents	
Mothers	*Fathers*
Development of an emotional attachment to the fetus	Acceptance of the pregnancy and attachment to the fetus
Differentiation of the self from the fetus	Acceptance and resolution of the relationship with his own father
Acceptance and resolution of the relationship with her own mother	Resolution of dependency issues (involving wife/partner)
Resolution of dependency issues (generally involving parents or husband/partner)	Evaluation of practical and financial responsibilities
Evaluation of practical and financial responsibilities	

poor diet, violent neighborhoods, limited health care, and limited access to education. They are also at higher risk for being abused than children born to older parents.

Contraception can fail or not be available or used. But not all teen pregnancies are unintended; about 22% of them are planned (Alan Guttmacher Institute, 1999b). The idea of having someone to love them exclusively and

FIGURE 12.6 Birth Rates for Teenagers by Age, 1970–2000. (*Source:* Ventura, Mathews, & Hamilton, 2001.)

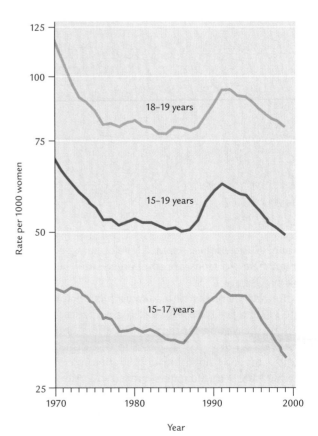

unconditionally is a strong incentive for some teenage girls. Others see having a baby as a way to escape from an oppressive home environment. Both teen males and females may see parenthood as a way to enhance their status, to give them an aura of maturity, or to enhance their masculinity or femininity. Some believe a baby will cement a shaky relationship. (Many adult women and men choose to have babies for these same less-than-sensible reasons). Unfortunately, for many expectant teens, parenthood may turn out to be as much a disaster as a blessing.

Teenage Mothers   Twelve percent of all births in the United States are to teens. Most teenage mothers feel that they are "good" girls and that they became pregnant in a moment of unguarded passion. The reality of the *boy + girl = baby* equation often doesn't sink in until pregnancy is well advanced. This lack of awareness makes it difficult (emotionally and physically), if not impossible, for those who might otherwise choose to do so to have an abortion. Teenage mothers are far more likely than other mothers to live below the poverty level and to receive welfare. In part because most teen mothers come from disadvantaged backgrounds, 28% of them remain poor in their twenties and early thirties, compared with 7% of mothers who first gave birth after adolescence (Alan Guttmacher Institute, 1999b). Teenage mothers also are significantly less likely to go on to college compared with women who delay childbearing.

A relatively new trend is the dramatic increase in the proportion of teen births that are nonmarital, from 13% in 1950 to 79% in 2000 (Alan Guttmacher Institute, 2002b). Two factors seem to be at play: (1) Marriage in the teen years has become quite rare, and (2) few teens who become pregnant marry before their baby is born. The implications of these factors on the outcomes of pregnancy are still uncertain.

Not only are African American teens twice as likely to be sexually active as Whites, but their birth rates are also higher (Figure 12.7). This is partly explained by the way in which the forces of racism and poverty combine to limit the options of young people of color. (Poor Whites also have disproportionately high teenage birth rates.) But additional factors contribute to pregnancy and childbirth among Black and Latino teens. For one thing,

Click on "Baby Love" to hear teenage mothers talk about when they became sexually active.

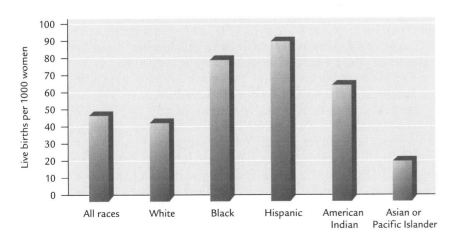

FIGURE 12.7   U.S. Birth Rates by Race, 15- to 19-Year-Olds, 1999 (*Source:* Ventura, Matthews, & Hamilton, 2001, p. 10.)

African American communities are far more accepting of births to unmarried women than their White counterparts; among Latinos and African Americans, three-generation families are much more common, with the result that grandparents often play an active role in child rearing. For another, there is often a great deal of pressure among young men of color (especially in communities with lower socioeconomic status) to prove their masculinity by engaging in sexual activity (Staples & Johnson, 1993; Yawn & Yawn, 1997).

Teenage mothers have special needs. The most pressing that can be provided for within the community are health care and education. Regular prenatal care is essential to monitor fetal growth and the mother's health, including diet, possible sexually transmitted infections (STIs), and possible alcohol or drug use. Nevertheless, one-third of pregnant teens receive inadequate prenatal care. Babies born to young mothers are more likely to have childhood health problems and to be hospitalized than those born to older mothers (Alan Guttmacher Institute, 1999b). After the birth, both mother and child need continuing care. The mother may need contraceptive counseling and services, and the child needs regular physical checkups and immunizations. Graduation from high school is an important goal of education programs for teenage mothers because it directly influences their employability and ability to support (or help support) themselves and their children. Some teenage mothers need financial assistance, at least until they complete their education. Government programs such as food stamps, Medicaid, and WIC (Women, Infants, and Children, which provides coupons for essential foods) are often crucial to the survival of young mothers and their children. Such programs are often underfunded and are periodically threatened with termination. Even with programs such as these in place, most families need additional income to survive.

Coordination of health, educational, and social services is important because it reduces costs and provides the most comprehensive support. School-based health clinics, which offer prenatal and postnatal care, contraception, and counseling, and teenage mother education programs, which provide general education and teach job and life skills, are examples of coordinated care. Such programs may be costly, but the costs of *not* providing them are far greater.

Teenage Fathers   The incidence of teenage fatherhood is lower than that of teenage motherhood. Teen fatherhood is not a function of any single risk factor (Thornberry, Smith, & Howard, 1997). Living in an inner city, having certain expectations and values about early childbearing, having poor school achievement, and engaging in delinquent behavior seem to be pathways leading to adolescent fatherhood. Other risk factors include a minority ethnic background and socioeconomic disadvantages.

Adolescent fathers typically remain physically or psychologically involved throughout the pregnancy and for at least some time after the birth. It is usually difficult for teenage fathers to contribute much to the support of their children, although most express the intention of doing so during the pregnancy. Most have a lower income, less education, and more children than men who postpone having children until age 20 or older. They may feel overwhelmed by the responsibility and may doubt their ability to be good providers. Though many teenage fathers are the sons of absent fathers, most

COMPARED WITH OTHER developed countries, the United States has the highest rates of teen pregnancy and childbirth (Alan Guttmacher Institute, 2002b). In addition, teenagers in the United States are more likely to have intercourse before age 15 and appear, on average, to have shorter and more sporadic sexual relationships than teenagers in other developed countries (Figure 12.8). The United States also leads developed countries in abortion rates by a wide margin. Given that these countries have similar levels of sexual activity among teenagers, what is the reason for this huge discrepancy? There are no easy answers to this question.

A multifaceted approach to reducing teen pregnancy is suggested by family planning experts, sociologists, demographers, and others who have studied the problems (Alan Guttmacher Institute, 2000b; Kirby, 2002):

- The underlying issues of poverty and the racism that often reinforces it must be dealt with. There must be a more equitable distribution of income so that all children have a true variety of educational, occupational, social, and personal options in their future.

- Contraception must be integrated into regular medical care and made available, along with practical information and a climate of openness about sexuality. This is one of the lessons to be learned from developed countries that have low teenage birth rates. Both sexuality education and tolerance of teenage sexual activity prevail in western Europe. The United States appears prudish and hypocritical by comparison.

- At the same time, schools, health-care agencies, and welfare agencies need to work cooperatively to educate young people and to help them combat feelings of worthlessness and despair.

- Because parental attitudes play an important role in the sexual development of children, parents must

also be educated so they become more knowledgeable and effective in communicating about sexuality with their children. An emphasis on wise and healthy expression of sexuality must prevail. At the same time, an appreciation of preexisting attitudes, as well as a respect for cultural and ethnic differences, must be built into any program that educates parents and children.

- Reliable, specific information about sex and responsibility needs to be present on television and radio; in books, magazines, music, and advertisements; and on the Web. This requires a major overhaul in the way society presents sex to its children and adolescents and may demand that adults reexamine their purchasing habits.

- Comprehensive sexuality education, and not exclusively abstinence promotion, should be emphasized. This includes balanced and thorough information about sexuality and clear expectations about the role of sexuality, and the prevention of pregnancy and STIs within these relationships.

- Strong public support and expectations for the transition to adult economic roles and parenthood would provide incentives to delay childbearing.

- Countries with low levels of adolescent pregnancy, childbearing, and STIs have high levels of social acceptance of adolescent sexual relationships and comprehensive sexuality education.

What factors do you believe contribute to the high rates of teen pregnancy in this country? Should comprehensive sexuality education be promoted in all schools across the country? Why or why not?

(continued)

do want to learn to be fathers. Teen fathers are a seriously neglected group who face many hardships. Policies and interventions directed at reducing teen fatherhood will have to take into consideration the many factors that influence it and focus efforts throughout the life cycle (Thornberry et al., 1997).

Complications of Pregnancy and Dangers to the Fetus

Usually, pregnancy proceeds without major complications. Good nutrition, a moderate amount of exercise, and manageable levels of stress are among

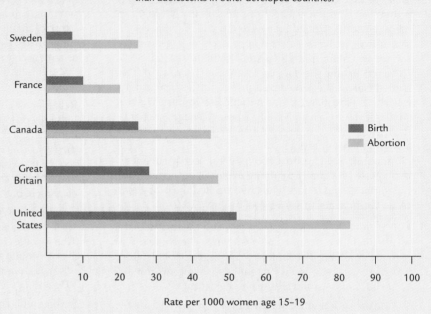

U.S. teenagers have higher pregnancy rates, birthrates and abortion rates than adolescents in other developed countries.

Rate per 1000 women age 15–19

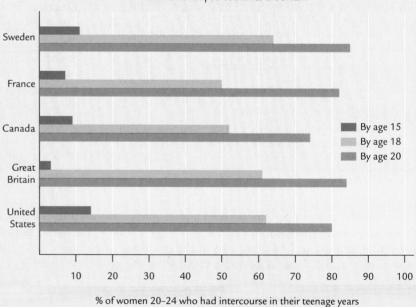

Differences in levels of teenage intercourse across developed countries are small.

% of women 20–24 who had intercourse in their teenage years

FIGURE 12.8 Teen Pregnancy and Sexual Activity Across Developed Countries, mid-1990s. (*Source:* Alan Guttmacher Institute, 2000b.)

the most significant factors in a complication-free pregnancy. In addition, early and ongoing prenatal care is important. Over an 18-year period, the percentage of pregnant African American women who received adequate prenatal care—as measured by the month care began and the number of prenatal visits in the first trimester—rose from 26.9% to 44%; the percentage of White women receiving adequate prenatal care rose from 33.6% to 50.2% (HRSA News, 2002). Overall, the ethnic gap in adequate care has narrowed steadily since the 1980s, but the gap is widening between White and African American mothers age 17 and younger. In any case, some women still experience minor to serious complications.

Effects of Teratogens   Substances other than nutrients may reach the developing embryo or fetus through the placenta. Although few extensive studies have been done on the subject, toxic substances in the environment can also affect the health of the fetus. Whatever a woman breathes, eats, or drinks is eventually received by the conceptus in some proportion. A fetus's blood-alcohol level, for example, is equal to that of the mother (Rosenthal, 1990). **Teratogens** are substances that cause defects (e.g., brain damage or physical deformities) in developing embryos or fetuses.

Chemicals and environmental pollutants are also potentially threatening. Continuous exposure to lead, most commonly in paint products or water from lead pipes, has been implicated in a variety of learning disorders. Mercury, from fish contaminated by industrial wastes, is a known cause of physical deformities. Solvents, pesticides, and certain chemical fertilizers should be avoided or used with extreme caution both at home and in the workplace. X-rays should also be avoided if possible during pregnancy.

Infectious Diseases   Infectious diseases can also damage the fetus. If a woman contracts German measles (rubella) during the first 3 months of pregnancy, her child may be born with physical or mental disabilities. Immunization against rubella is available, but it must be done before the woman is pregnant; otherwise, the injection will be as harmful to the fetus as the disease itself. Group B streptococcus, a bacterium carried by 15–40% of pregnant women, is harmless to adults but can be fatal to newborns. Each year, about 12,000 infants are infected; 1600–2000 of them die. The American Academy of Pediatrics recommends that all pregnant women be screened for strep B. Antibiotics administered to the newborn during labor can greatly reduce the danger.

Sexually Transmitted Infections   STIs can be transmitted from a pregnant woman to the fetus, newborn, or infant before, during, or after birth. The CDC recommends that all pregnant women be screened for chlamydia, gonorrhea, hepatitis B, HIV, and syphilis. Pregnant women should request these tests specifically because some doctors don't routinely perform them. A woman with gonorrhea may expose her child to blindness from contact with the infected vagina; the baby will need immediate antibiotic treatment. HIV may be transmitted to the fetus through the mother's blood system or during delivery. Cesarean section delivery, and ZDV (AZT) therapy can dramatically decrease the risk of transmission of HIV infection to the infant (see Chapter 16). HIV-infected mothers should not breast-feed their babies.

Pregnancy and Drugs: A Bad Mix

AMONG THE LESSONS most of us learn from our parents is to be good to our children. This lesson is crucial during pregnancy, when the unborn child is most vulnerable to substances ingested by the mother.

Because the placenta does not block all substances from entering the fetus's bloodstream, it is prudent to assume that there is no safe drug during pregnancy. Sometimes, the effect of a drug depends on when in the pregnancy it is used. With the exception of a handful of prescription and over-the-counter medications, all drugs—including alcohol, tobacco, street drugs, and many legal drugs—have the potential to cause physical damage, malformation, and miscarriage. The most devastating outcomes occur for pregnant women who lack information about drugs and whose judgment is impaired because they are under the influence of uncontrolled street drugs or alcohol.

The following is a partial list of drugs and their effects on the fetus. Not well understood or studied are the effects of the father's drug use on the health of the fetus. Regardless, it is prudent for both partners to assume healthy lifestyles before considering pregnancy.

Alcohol

When it comes to alcohol and pregnancy, how much is too much? The short answer is that we really don't know. Moderate drinking—that is, as little as one drink a day—has been shown to retard the growth of the infant (Mills & England, 2001), and a single drinking binge can permanently damage the brain of the fetus. Studies have linked chronic ingestion of alcohol during pregnancy to **fetal alcohol syndrome (FAS),** which can include unusual facial characteristics, small head and body size, congenital heart defects, defective joints, and intellectual and behavioral impairment. About half of all FAS children are mentally retarded (Jacobson & Jacobson, 1999). Lower levels of alcohol consumption (7–14 drinks per week) may result in **fetal alcohol effect (FAE).** Children affected by FAE often experience moderate intellectual and behavioral deficits that resemble those of FAS children but at a less severe level. These deficits are subtler but far more prevalent among children than FAS. FAS and FAE are often difficult to diagnose right away, but the incidence of FAS is probably in the range of 4000–12,000 cases per year. There are thousands more cases of FAE. Because alcohol can also be transmitted to the infant through breast milk, most experts counsel pregnant and nursing women to abstain entirely from alcohol because there is no safe quantity known at this time.

Opiates and Cocaine

Mothers who regularly use opiates (heroin, morphine, codeine, and opium) are likely to have infants who are addicted to opiates at birth. A study in New York of drug-exposed infants revealed that the opiate-exposed babies showed more neurological damage than the cocaine-exposed babies and that those infants exposed to multidrug abuse (both opiates and cocaine) were worse off than those exposed to any single drug in terms of

The increasingly widespread incidence of genital herpes may present some hazards for newborns. Although the spread of herpes to newborns occurs only rarely, newborns can contract herpes simplex virus if they come into contact with active lesions during birth. This may result in infections of the skin, eyes, mucous membranes, and central nervous system, and in death. Once the baby is born, a mother who is experiencing an outbreak of either oral or genital herpes should wash her hands often and carefully and not permit contact between her hands, contaminated objects, and the baby's mucous membranes (inside of eyes, mouth, nose, penis, vagina, vulva, and rectum). If the father is infected, he should do likewise until the lesions have subsided.

Women who are pregnant can acquire an STI from their own risky behavior or from an infected partner. Because avoidance of STIs is critical throughout a woman's pregnancy, she may want to consider consistent and correct use of latex condoms for each act of sexual intercourse.

Older Mothers   Women who give birth at age 40 or older are highly likely to require an operative delivery and, especially if they have never had a baby gestational age at birth, birth weight, and length of hospital stay (Kaye, Elkind, Goldberg, & Tytan, 1989). It has also been found that children exposed to cocaine before birth had IQ scores about 3.26 points lower than children born to mothers who did not use cocaine while pregnant ("Mom's Cocaine Hurts," 1998). It should be noted that many drug-exposed infants have been exposed to alcohol as well.

Tobacco

Cigarette smoking is associated with spontaneous abortion, persistent breathing problems, and a variety of complications during pregnancy and birth. Babies born to women who smoke during pregnancy are an average of ¼ to ½ pound lighter at birth than babies born to nonsmokers. Secondhand smoke breathed by the mother is also considered dangerous to the developing fetus. Maternal smoking during pregnancy may also create a serious risk for smoking dependence in offspring (Gilliland et al., 2000).

Prescription and Over-the-Counter Drugs

Prescription drugs should be used only under careful medical supervision because some may cause serious harm to the fetus. The most dramatic illustration of the teratogenic effects of a prescription drug occurred in the 1950s, when the drug thalidomide, given to alleviate morning sickness, caused severe birth defects in more than 10,000 babies. Thalidomide has been off the market for more than 40 years, but the FDA has approved its rerelease for treatment of such conditions as

leprosy, some cancers, and autoimmune diseases such as lupus. Isotretinoin (Acutane), a popular antiacne drug, can cause spontaneous abortion of the fetus or severe birth defects. Vitamins, aspirin, and other over-the-counter drugs, as well as large quantities of caffeine-containing food and drink (coffee, tea, cola, chocolate), should be avoided or used only under medical supervision. Vitamin A in large doses can cause serious birth defects. Tranquilizers such as Librium and Valium can cause fetal malformations, and anticonvulsants such as those used to control epilepsy can cause birth defects.

Harmful Work Agents

Women may be exposed at work to agents that could disable them and harm the fetus. Your employer can tell you about health-care benefits, disability benefits, and maternity leave. The federal Pregnancy Discrimination Act (PDA) requires employers that have at least 15 employees to treat workers disabled by pregnancy or childbirth the same as workers disabled by illness or accident. The Occupational Safety and Health Administration (OSHA) requires employers to provide a workplace free from known hazards that cause, or are likely to cause, serious physical harm or death.

How might you assess whether a drug is safe during pregnancy? If you were in a situation with a pregnant woman who wished to consume a drug, what (if anything) might you do or say? Do you feel that pregnant women who use drugs should be charged with child endangerment? Why or why not?

before, to have an elevated risk of pregnancy complications. The most common problems are abnormal fetal position, prolonged labor, and pre-eclampsia (Hollander, 1999). In addition, infants born to older women have a lower gestational age, lower birth weight, and higher risk of birth asphyxia and fetal growth restriction than those whose mothers are in their twenties.

Though twin and triplet pregnancies are riskier than singleton pregnancies at any age, twins born to older mothers do not appear to have a greater risk of birth complications than do twins born to younger mothers (National Institutes of Health, 2002a). This may be due in part to older mothers' use of assisted reproductive technology (ART). Multiples conceived through ART are less likely than those conceived naturally to be identical. Nonidentical multiples have a lower risk of poor birth outcomes than do identical multiples.

Ectopic Pregnancy   In **ectopic pregnancy** (tubal pregnancy), the incidence of which has more than quadrupled in recent decades, the fertilized egg grows outside the uterus, usually in the fallopian tube. Any sexually active woman of childbearing age is at risk for ectopic pregnancy. Women who have abnormal fallopian tubes are at higher risk for ectopic pregnancy. Generally, this occurs because the tube is obstructed, most often as a result of pelvic inflammatory disease (Tenore, 2000). Factors such as a previous ectopic pregnancy and **endometriosis** (growth of tissue outside the uterus) can also increase the risk. The pregnancy will never come to term. The embryo may spontaneously abort, or the embryo and placenta will continue to expand until they rupture the fallopian tube. If the pregnancy is early and has not ruptured, drugs may be used instead of surgery to treat ectopic pregnancy. A ruptured ectopic pregnancy, however, is a true medical emergency. It is the leading cause of maternal mortality in the first trimester and accounts for 10–15% of all maternal deaths (Tenore, 2000). Salpingectomy (removal of the tube) and abortion of the conceptus may be necessary to save the mother's life.

Pregnancy-Induced Hypertension   Previously referred to as toxemia or eclampsia, **pregnancy-induced hypertension** is characterized by high blood pressure and edema along with protein in the urine. It occurs in less than 10% of pregnancies and can usually be treated by diet, bed rest, and medication. If untreated, it can progress to maternal convulsions that pose a threat to mother and child. It is important for a pregnant woman to have her blood pressure checked regularly.

Premature Births   Births that take place prior to 37 weeks of gestation are considered to be **premature births.** About 10% of all pregnancies in the United States result in premature births. A consequence of this is low-birth-weight infants (those who weigh less than 5.5 pounds at birth). About three-quarters of infant deaths in the United States are associated with prematurity. The fundamental problem of prematurity is that many of the infant's vital organs are insufficiently developed. Most premature infants will grow normally, but many will experience disabilities and health problems, including cranial abnormalities, various respiratory problems, and infections. Feeding, too, is a problem because the infants may be too small to suck a breast or bottle, and their swallowing mechanisms may be too underdeveloped to permit

Low birth weight affects about 7% of newborns in the United States. Adequate prenatal care significantly reduces the risk of low birth weight.

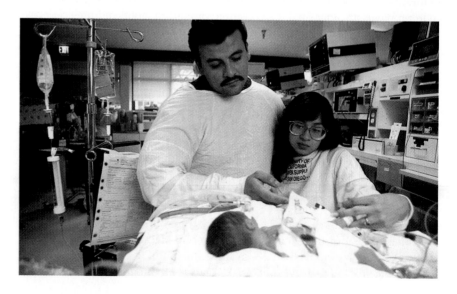

TABLE 12.2   The Demographic Facts of Life

	United States	*World*
Population, mid-2001	284.5 million	6.1 billion
Population per square mile	77	118
Births per 1000 people	15	22
Deaths per 1000 people	9	9
Doubling time in years at current growth rate	115	53
Projected population, 2025	346.0 million	7.8 billion
Total fertility rate	2.1	2.8
Percentage of population under age 15	21	30
Percentage of population over age 65	13	7
Life expectancy in years	74 (male), 80 (female)	65 (male), 69 (female)
Infant deaths per 1000 live births	7.1	56
Percentage of children under 5 who are underweight	1	29
Percentage of married women using contraception	76	60
Births per 1000 women age 15–19	49	50

Source: The Demographic Facts of Life. Copyright © 2001 Population Connection. Reprinted by permission.

them to drink. As premature infants get older, problems such as low intelligence, learning difficulties, poor hearing and vision, and physical awkwardness may become apparent. Nevertheless, the majority of preterm babies eventually catch up with their peers and thrive.

Premature delivery is one of the greatest problems confronting obstetrics today; most of the cases are related to teenage pregnancy, smoking, poor nutrition, and poor health in the mother. In addition, women who conceive again less than 18 months after giving birth are about 10–50% more likely to have a premature infant than are women whose interpregnancy intervals are between 18 and 59 months (Gerstein, 2000).

Prenatal care is extremely important as a means of preventing prematurity. We need to understand that if children's needs are not met today we will all face the consequences of their deprivation tomorrow. The social and economic costs are bound to be very high. (Table 12.2 lists various demographic "facts of life" for the United States and the rest of the world.)

Delayed Labor   About 10% of women have **delayed labor,** or pregnancies that go longer than 2 weeks after the expected delivery date. The primary risks associated with this are the fetus growing too large to pass through the birth canal and the placenta ceasing to nourish the child. Because postterm

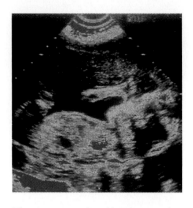

The pictures produced by ultrasound are called sonograms. They are used to determine fetal age, position of the fetus and placenta, and possible developmental problems.

babies are about 3 times more likely to die neonatally than babies born at term, labor is often induced with drugs such as prostaglandins and oxytocin.

Diagnosing Abnormalities of the Fetus

Both the desire to bear children and the wish to ensure that those children are healthy have encouraged the development of new diagnostic technologies. In cases in which serious problems are suspected, these technologies may be quite helpful, but sometimes they seem to be used simply "because they're there."

Ultrasound examinations use high-frequency sound waves to create a computer-generated picture of the internal structure of the fetus in the uterus. The results are interpreted on a television-like screen; the picture is called a **sonogram.** Sonograms are used to determine fetal age and the location of the placenta; when used with amniocentesis (see below), they help determine the fetus's position so that the needle may be inserted safely. Often, it is possible to determine the fetus's sex during ultrasound. More extensive ultrasound techniques can be used to gain further information if there is the possibility of a problem with fetal development. Ultrasound may also be used to check for ectopic pregnancy or for other causes of bleeding.

In **amniocentesis** (am-nee-oh-sen-TEE-sis), amniotic fluid is withdrawn from the uterus using a long, thin needle inserted through the abdominal wall (Figure 12.9). The fluid, which contains chromosomal information from the developing fetus, is then examined for evidence of possible birth defects, such as Down syndrome, cystic fibrosis, Tay-Sachs disease, spina bifida, and conditions caused by chromosomal abnormalities. The sex of the fetus can also be determined. The vast majority of amniocentesis tests are performed on women over age 35 and around week 15 of gestation. Amniocentesis carries a risk (1 in 300) of causing a miscarriage.

An alternative to amniocentesis more recently introduced in the United States is **chorionic villus sampling (CVS)** (Figure 12.9). This procedure involves removal through the abdomen (by needle) or through the cervix (by catheter) of tiny pieces of the membrane that encases the embryo; it can be performed between 9 and 12 weeks of gestation. CVS is less useful than amniocentesis because it does not detect neural tube defects or anterior abdominal wall defects. There may be a somewhat greater-than-normal chance of miscarriage with CVS.

Alpha-fetoprotein (AFP) screening is a test (or series of tests) performed on the mother's blood at around 16–18 weeks of pregnancy. It reveals defects of the spine, spinal cord, skull, and brain, such as anencephaly and spina bifida. It is much simpler than amniocentesis but sometimes yields false positive results (Samuels & Samuels, 1996). If the results are positive, other tests, such as amniocentesis and ultrasound, will be performed to confirm or negate the AFP screening findings.

For approximately 95% of women who undergo prenatal testing, the results are negative. The results of amniocentesis and AFP screening can't be determined, however, until approximately 20 weeks of pregnancy; consequently, if the pregnancy is terminated through abortion at this stage, the process is likely to be physically and emotionally difficult. If a fetus is found to be defective, it may be carried to term, aborted, or, in rare but an increasing number of instances, surgically treated while still in the womb.

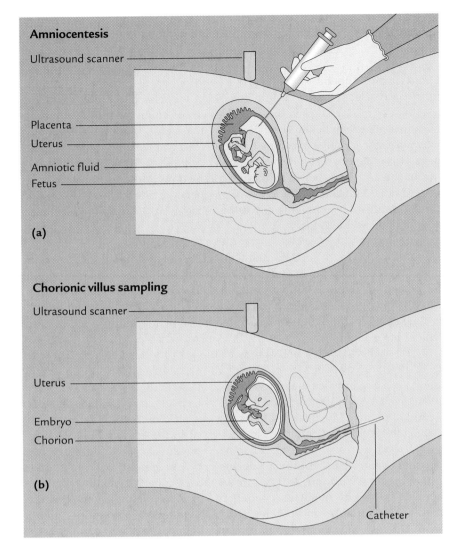

Amniocentesis

Ultrasound scanner

Placenta
Uterus
Amniotic fluid
Fetus

(a)

Chorionic villus sampling

Ultrasound scanner

Uterus

Embryo
Chorion

(b)

Catheter

FIGURE 12.9 Diagnosing Fetal Abnormalities is done via (a) Amniocentesis and (b) Chorionic Villus Sampling.

Visual examinations of the fetus are now possible through the use of an endoscope, an instrument that penetrates the uterus and amnion. The technology is used to assess possible developmental abnormalities and may be used to plan surgery or treatment during the first trimester of pregnancy. A new and expanding field in prenatal care involves surgical procedures on a fetus when it is still in the uterus. This has been used primarily to address urinary tract problems and has also been used to repair diaphragmatic hernias and fetal heart defects.

Pregnancy Loss

A normal pregnancy lasts about 40 weeks. The loss of a fetus before 20 weeks is called **early pregnancy loss.** Often, the loss is a **miscarriage** (spontaneous loss of a fetus before it can survive on its own), stillbirth, or death during early infancy—a devastating experience that has been largely ignored in our society. The statement "You can always have another one" may be meant as consolation, but it can be particularly chilling to a grieving mother or father. In the past few years, however, the medical community has begun to respond to the emotional needs of parents who have lost a fetus or an infant.

Spontaneous Abortion   Spontaneous abortion, or miscarriage, is a powerful natural selective force in bringing healthy babies into the world. More than half of miscarriages in the first 13 weeks of pregnancy are due to chromosomal abnormalities in the fetus. The first sign that a pregnant woman may miscarry is vaginal bleeding (spotting). If a woman's symptoms of pregnancy disappear and she develops pelvic cramps, she may be miscarrying; the fetus is usually expelled by uterine contractions. Most miscarriages occur between the sixth and eighth weeks of pregnancy. Evidence is increasing that certain occupations involving exposure to chemicals increase the likelihood of spontaneous abortions.

Infant Mortality   The U.S. infant mortality rate, although at its lowest point ever, remains far higher than that of most of the developed world: 7.6 deaths for every 1000 live births in 1995 (Centers for Disease Control, 2003a). Among developed nations, our country ranks 20th in infant mortality, meaning that 19 countries have *lower* infant mortality rates than the United States. Of the more than 35,000 American babies less than 1 year old who die each year, most are victims of the poverty that often results from racial or ethnic discrimination. The infant mortality rate for African Americans is more than twice that for Whites or Hispanics (6.3 versus 14.7). Many infant deaths could be prevented if mothers were given adequate health care.

Although many infants die of poverty-related conditions, others die from congenital problems (conditions appearing at birth) or from infectious diseases, accidents, or other causes. Sometimes, the causes of death are not apparent; more than 3000 infant deaths per year are attributed to **sudden infant death syndrome (SIDS),** a perplexing phenomenon wherein an apparently healthy infant dies suddenly while sleeping. Sleeping position may be one variable contributing to SIDS in vulnerable infants. The American Academy of Pediatrics recommends that infants be placed on their backs while sleeping. Maternal smoking during pregnancy and exposure of the baby to secondhand smoke are also implicated in spontaneous abortion, stillbirth, preterm birth, and SIDS (Action on Smoking and Health, 1999). No one knows what all the factors are that contribute to this unpredictable event. Recently, closer investigation of a number of alleged SIDS deaths has led to the appalling discovery that perhaps 5–10% were actually cases of infanticide in which the infants were smothered (Firstman & Talan, 1997; Southall, 1997). Physicians are now urged to consider all factors and to report any suspicions when presented with SIDS cases or repeated "near-SIDS" cases, especially if there has already been a SIDS death in the family (Begley, 1997b).

Dear Auntie will come with presents and will ask, "Where is our baby, sister?" And, Mother, you will tell her softly, "He is in the pupils of my eyes. He is in my bones and in my soul."

—*Rabindranath Tagore (1864–1941)*

Coping with Loss   The feelings of shock and grief felt by individuals whose child dies before or during birth can be difficult to understand for those who have not had a similar experience. What they may not realize is that most women form a deep attachment to their children even before birth. At first, the attachment may be to a fantasy image of the unborn child. During the course of the pregnancy, the mother forms an acquaintance with her infant through the physical sensations she feels within her. Thus, the death of the fetus can also represent the loss of a dream and of a hope for the future. This loss must be acknowledged and felt before psychological healing can take place (Vredeveldt, 1994).

The healing process takes time—months, a year, perhaps more for some. Support groups and counseling often are helpful, especially if healing does not seem to be progressing—if, for example, depression and physical symptoms don't appear to be diminishing (DeSpelder & Strickland, 1999).

INFERTILITY

Some couples experience the pain of loss when they plan to have a child and then discover that they cannot get pregnant. **Infertility** is defined as the inability to conceive a child after a year of unprotected intercourse or the inability to carry a fetus to term. Infertility affects over 4.9 million couples, or 1 in 7, in the United States each year (Planned Parenthood, 2003). Infertility is a medical problem in the man, the woman, or both. Approximately 40% of infertility problems are attributed to men, and 40% to women; 20% are attributed to both or are unexplained. The most common risk factors for infertility are body weight, age, STIs, tubal disease, endometriosis, diethylstilbestrol (DES, a potent estrogen) exposure, smoking, and alcohol ("Frequently Asked Questions," 2002).

Female Infertility

Most cases of infertility among women are due to physical factors. Hormones, stress, immunological factors, and environmental factors may also be involved.

Physical Causes   One of the leading causes of female infertility is blocked fallopian tubes, generally the result of **pelvic inflammatory disease (PID)**, an infection of the fallopian tubes or uterus that is usually the result of an STI such as chlamydia (see Chapter 15). About 1 million cases of PID are treated each year; doctors estimate that about half of the cases go untreated because PID is often symptomless, especially in the early stages. Other causes include endometriosis, fibroids, a tilted uterus, diabetes, and hypertension. Smoking may also influence a woman's ability to conceive. The greatest increase in infertility is found among women age 35–44.

A below-normal percentage of body fat, due to excessive dieting or exercise, may inhibit ovulation and delay pregnancy. In addition, benign growths such as fibroids and polyps on the uterus, ovaries, or fallopian tubes may affect a woman's fertility. Surgery can restore fertility in many of these cases.

Hormonal and Psychological Causes   In addition to physical causes, there may be hormonal reasons for infertility. The pituitary gland may fail to produce sufficient hormones (follicle-stimulating hormone, or FSH, and luteinizing hormone, or LH) to stimulate ovulation, or it may release them at the wrong time. Stress, which may be increased by the anxiety associated with trying to become pregnant, may also contribute to lowered fertility.

Occasionally, immunological causes may be present, the most important of which is the production of sperm antibodies by the woman. For some unknown reason, a woman may be allergic to her partner's sperm, and her immune system will produce antibodies to destroy them. Nature also plays a part. On average, female fertility begins its meaningful slide at age 27 ("Study Tracks Decline," 2002). By age 35, about one-quarter of women are infertile.

Environmental Factors   Toxic chemicals, such as those found in paint, solvents, and insecticides, or exposure to radiation therapy can threaten a woman's reproductive capacity. Excessive drug and alcohol use can also affect fertility. Evidence indicates that the daughters of mothers who took DES, a drug once thought to increase fertility and reduce the risk of miscarriage, have a significantly higher infertility rate.

Male Infertility

The primary causes of male infertility are low sperm count, decrease of sperm motility, and poor sperm morphology (misshapen sperm). Sperm ducts may become blocked, or for some reason, the male may not ejaculate.

As with women, environmental factors may contribute to men's infertility. Increasing evidence suggests that toxic substances, such as lead or chemicals found in some solvents and herbicides, are responsible for decreased sperm counts. Alcohol and tobacco use may produce reduced sperm counts or abnormal sperm. Prescription drugs such as cimetidine (Tagamet, for ulcers), prednisone (a corticosteroid that reduces tissue inflammation), and some medications for urinary tract infections have also been shown to affect the number of sperm a man produces. Men's fertility starts dwindling after age 27 ("Study Tracks Decline," 2002).

Large doses of marijuana cause decreased sperm counts and suppression of certain reproductive hormones. These effects are apparently reversed when marijuana smoking stops. Men are more at risk than women from environmental factors because they are constantly producing new sperm cells; for the same reason, men may also recover faster once the affecting factor has been removed.

Sons of mothers who took DES may have increased sperm abnormalities and fertility problems. Also, too much heat may temporarily reduce a man's sperm count (the male half of a couple trying to conceive may want to stay out of the hot tub for a while). A fairly common problem is the presence of a varicose vein called a **varicocele** above the testicle. Because it impairs circulation to the testicle, the varicocele causes an elevated scrotal temperature and thus interferes with sperm development. The varicocele may be surgically removed, but unless the man has a fairly good sperm count to begin with, his fertility may not improve.

Emotional Responses to Infertility

By the time partners seek medical advice about their fertility problems, they may have already experienced a crisis in confronting the possibility of not being able to become biological parents. Many such couples feel they have lost control over a major area of their lives.

Infertility Treatment

Almost without exception, fertility problems are physical, not emotional, despite myths to the contrary. The two most popular myths are that anxiety over becoming pregnant leads to infertility and that if an infertile couple adopt a child the couple will then be able to conceive on their own. Neither has any basis in medical fact, although some presumably infertile couples have conceived following an adoption. (This does not mean, however, that one should adopt a child to remedy infertility.) In some cases, fertility is restored for no discernible reason; in others, the infertility remains a mystery.

Enhancing Fertility   In some cases, fertility can be enhanced with simple techniques. For example, if a man wears tight underwear, he might switch to boxer-type shorts to allow his testicles to descend from his body. Having the woman lie on her back for an hour after coitus can aid sperm in traveling up the vagina, and more frequent intercourse near the time of ovulation can increase the chances of conception. Following intercourse, a pillow can be placed under the woman's buttocks to help sperm swim into the uterus. In addition, the man-on-top position can increase the chances of conception by allowing the cervix to drop into the seminal pool. However, for many couples, these techniques are not enough; they may seek medical intervention to diagnose and treat infertility.

Medical Intervention   Medical technology now offers more treatment options to men and to women trying to conceive a child. At least 50% of those who undergo infertility treatment will have a successful pregnancy (Resolve, 2002). Those who do not seek help have a "spontaneous cure rate" of about 5% after a year of infertility. The techniques and technologies developed to promote conception include the following ("Understanding Your Treatment Options," 2002):

- *Fertility medications.* A variety of medications can be used to treat infertility, so it is important to understand each one and its purpose.

- *Surgery.* This is a treatment option for both male and female infertility. Used to correct a structural problem, surgery can often return normal fertility.

- **Intrauterine insemination (IUI).** In this procedure, commonly referred to as **artificial insemination,** the woman is injected with sperm from her partner or a donor. Used to treat unexplained infertility, minimal male factor infertility, or women with cervical mucus problems, IUI is often performed in conjunction with ovulation-stimulating medications.

- **Assisted reproductive technology (ART).** In this procedure, the woman's ovaries are stimulated and her eggs are surgically removed, combined with sperm, and returned to her body (Figure 12.10). **In vitro fertilization,** the procedure whereby a sperm and oocyte are combined in a laboratory dish and subsequently implanted into the uterus, is the most widely used ART procedure.

- **Micromanipulation.** This technique is used to achieve or improve fertilization and implantation rates. This method uses tiny glass tools connected to robot arms that are linked to a specialized microscope.

> Rarely is moral queasiness a match for the onslaught of science.
> —*Sharon Begley*

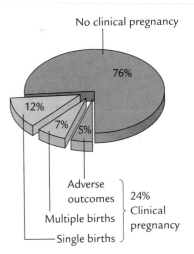

FIGURE 12.10 Results of Assisted Reproductive Technology Cycles, 1995. Most ART cycles (76%) performed in 1995 did not produce a pregnancy. However, 12% produced a single birth and 7% produced a multiple birth, for a combined "take-home baby" rate of 19%. (*Sources:* CDC, ASRM, & Resolve, 1997.)

When in vitro procedures are used to combat infertility, there is about a 1 in 3 chance of a multiple birth.

In one method, called CSI (for intra-cytoplasmic sperm injection), a single sperm is placed inside the egg using micromanipulation. The resulting embryo is observed for normal cell division and, when appropriate, transferred into the woman's uterus. These techniques may also be used to remove a cell from a developing embryo for assessment of the DNA.

- *Third party: donor egg, donor sperm, surrogacy, embryo donation.* These are all options for couples who are unable to conceive a genetically related child. **Surrogate motherhood,** in which one woman bears a child for another, results in several hundred births in the United States each year. Women's motivations for becoming surrogates include money (surrogates are usually paid $10,000–$25,000 or more), enjoyment of pregnancy, and unresolved birth traumas such as abortion or relinquishing a child for adoption.

Click on "The Surrogate Motherhood Debate" to hear women discuss their experiences as surrogate mothers.

- *Sperm banks.* These are used to collect, freeze, and store sperm so that it is available for conception when the individual or couple decides.

These procedures are all quite costly. For example, a single cycle of in vitro fertilization typically costs $8000, and the procedure usually needs to be repeated a number of times before a viable pregnancy results. Regardless of the method chosen, it is important to periodically reassess treatment and parenting goals. Though continuity is important, a break can sometimes provide needed rest for the next steps.

Cloning is the reproduction of an individual from a single cell taken from a donor or parent. Specifically, this technique involves replacing the nucleus from a donor to produce an embryo that is genetically identical to it. The success of reproductive cloning depends on the species (Soules, 2001). For example, plant cloning occurs every day, as when an apple grows from a cloned fruit tree. Cloning in small animal species has been somewhat successful, though the spontaneous abortion rate is high, as are the rates of fetal mortality and genetic anomalies. What has caught the attention of the public is the potential for human reproductive cloning and the questions that accompany this procedure: When does human life begin, and what is the moral and legal status of the human embryo? Human embryonic stem cells, which are extracted from embryos when they are still tiny clusters of no more than 300 cells, are generating great excitement in science because they can, in theory, grow into any of the body's cell types. Scientists hope someday to use them for replacement tissue and organs for patients with a variety of diseases, including diabetes and Parkinson's (Stolberg, 2001). Cloning has huge potential as a source of organs for implantation or as an alternative in cases of infertility. Although some people speculate that human reproductive cloning has already been attempted, no documentation supports that contention (Soules, 2001).

Sex selection, a technique that would allow couples to choose whether to have a boy or a girl, is another emerging technology. Controversy arises, however, over potential sex imbalances in our population and cases in which the sex selection results do not match the parents' expectations.

Each of these techniques raises questions. For example, some lesbian women, especially those in committed relationships, are choosing to create families through artificial insemination. To date, there are no reliable data on the number of such births, but anecdotal information indicates that it is in the thousands. Many questions are raised when a lesbian couple contemplate having a baby in this way: Who will be the birth mother? What will the role status of the other mother be? Will the donor be known or unknown? If known, will the child have a relationship with him? Will the child have a relationship with the donor's parents? Which, if any, of the child's grandparents will have a relationship with him or her? Will there be a legal contract between the parenting parties? There are few precedents to learn from or role models to follow in these cases. Another issue that such couples face is that the nonbiological parent may have no legal tie to the child (in some states, the nonbiological parent may adopt the child as a "second parent"). Furthermore, society may not recognize a nonbiological parent as a "real" parent, because children are expected to have only one real mother and one real father.

GIVING BIRTH

Throughout pregnancy, numerous physiological changes occur to prepare the woman's body for childbirth. Hormones secreted by the placenta regulate the growth of the fetus, stimulate maturation of the breasts for lactation, and ready the uterus and other parts of the body for labor. During the later months of pregnancy, the placenta produces the hormone **relaxin,** which increases flexibility in the ligaments and joints of the pelvic area. In the last trimester, most women occasionally feel uterine contractions that are strong but generally not painful. These **Braxton Hicks contractions** exercise the uterus, preparing it for labor.

Labor and Delivery

During labor, contractions begin the **effacement** (thinning) and **dilation** (gradual opening) of the cervix. It is difficult to say exactly when labor starts, which helps explain the great differences reported in lengths of labor for different women. True labor begins when the uterine contractions are regularly spaced, thinning and dilation of the cervix occurs, and the fetus presents a part of itself into the vagina. During the contractions, the lengthwise muscles of the uterus involuntarily pull open the circular muscles around the cervix. This process generally takes 2–36 hours. Its duration depends on the size of the baby, the baby's position in the uterus, the size of the mother's pelvis, and the condition of the uterus. The length of labor tends to shorten after the first birth experience.

> If men had to have babies, they would only ever have one each.
>
> —*Princess Diana (1961–1997)*

Labor can generally be divided into three stages. The first stage is usually the longest, lasting 4–16 hours or longer. An early sign of first-stage labor is the expulsion of a plug of slightly bloody mucus that has blocked the opening of the cervix during pregnancy. At the same time or later on, there is a second fluid discharge from the vagina. This discharge, often referred to as the "breaking of the waters," is the amniotic fluid, which comes from the ruptured amnion. (Because the baby is subject to infection after the protective membrane breaks, the woman should receive medical attention soon thereafter, if she has not already.)

The hormone oxytocin produced by the fetus, along with prostaglandins from the placenta, stimulates strong uterine contractions. At the end of the first stage of labor, which is called the **transition,** the contractions come more quickly and are much more intense than at the beginning of labor. Most women report that transition is the most difficult part of labor. During the last part of first-stage labor, the baby's head enters the birth canal. This marks the shift from dilation of the cervix to expulsion of the infant. The cervical opening is now almost fully dilated (about 10 centimeters [4 inches] in diameter), but the baby is not yet completely in position to be pushed out. Some women feel despair, isolation, and anger at this point, and many appear to lose faith in those assisting in the birth. A woman may believe that management of the contractions is beyond her control; she may be afraid that something is wrong. At this time, she needs the full support and understanding of her helpers. The transition is usually, though not always, brief (½–1 hour).

Second-stage labor begins when the baby's head moves into the birth canal and ends when the baby is born. During this time, many women experience a great force in their bodies. Some women find this the most difficult part of labor; others find that the contractions and bearing down bring a sense of euphoria.

The baby is usually born gradually. With each of the final few contractions, a new part of the infant emerges (Figure 12.11). The baby may even cry before he or she is completely born, especially if the mother did not have medication.

The baby will still be attached to the umbilical cord connected to the mother, which is not cut until it stops pulsating. He or she will appear wet and often be covered by a waxy substance called **vernix.** The head may look oddly shaped at first, from the molding of the soft plates of bone during birth. This shape is temporary; the baby's head usually achieves a normal appearance within 24 hours.

After the baby has been delivered, the uterus continues to contract, expelling the placenta, the remaining section of the umbilical cord, and the

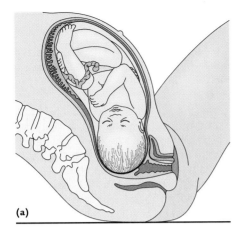

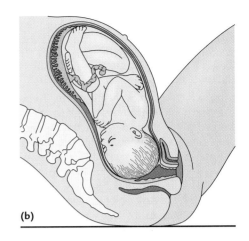

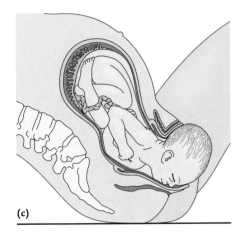

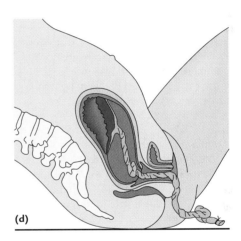

FIGURE 12.11   The Birth Process: Labor and Delivery. (a) In the first stage, the cervix begins to dilate. (b) In the transition stage, the cervix dilates. (c) In the second stage, the infant is delivered. (d) In the third stage, the placenta (afterbirth) is delivered.

fetal membranes. Completing the third and final stage of labor, these tissues are collectively referred to as the **afterbirth.** The doctor or midwife examines the placenta to make sure it is whole. If the practitioner has any doubt that the entire placenta has been expelled, he or she may examine the uterus to make sure no parts of the placenta remain to cause adhesions or hemorrhaging. Immediately following birth, the attendants assess the physical condition of the **neonate,** or newborn. Heart rate, respiration, skin color, reflexes, and muscle tone are individually rated with a score of 0 to 2. The total, called an **Apgar score,** will be at least 8 if the baby is healthy. For a few days following labor (especially if it is a second or subsequent birth), the mother will probably feel strong contractions as the uterus begins to return to its prebirth size and shape. This process takes about 6 weeks. She will also have a bloody discharge called **lochia,** which continues for several weeks.

Following birth, if the mother did not receive pain medication, the baby will probably be alert and ready to nurse. Breast-feeding (discussed later)

In 1975, WHEN ABOUT 93% of newborn boys were circumcised, the American Academy of Pediatrics and the American College of Obstetricians and Gynecologists issued a statement declaring that there is "no absolute medical indication" for routine circumcision. This procedure, which involves slicing and removing the sleeve of skin (foreskin) that covers the glans penis, has been performed routinely on newborn boys in the United States since the 1930s. Parents should discuss with their pediatrician the use of an anesthetic cream or medication. Circumcision carries medical risks, including excessive bleeding, infection, and faulty surgery.

In 1989, the American Academy of Pediatrics modified its stance on circumcision, stating that "newborn circumcision has potential medical benefits and advantages as well as disadvantages and risks." It recommended that "the benefits and risks should be explained to the parents and informed consent obtained."

The most recent position of the American Academy of Pediatrics is that the benefits of circumcision are "not sufficient" to recommend that baby boys undergo the procedure ("Just the Facts," 2003). If the baby is circumcised, the academy strongly advises that he be given a local anesthetic—something that currently is done less than half the time.

Uncircumcised infant boys are more likely to acquire a urinary tract infection in the first year of life than circumcised boys. However, the absolute risk is small. In the first year of life, there is about a 1 in 100 chance an uncircumcised boy will develop a urinary tract infection; a circumcised boy has about a 1 in 1000 chance. In nearly all cases, the infections can be easily treated with antibiotics.

Most, although not all, studies have shown that circumcision reduces the risk of contracting an STI and that penile cancer, while extremely rare among the uncircumcised, is virtually unknown in circumcised males. (For more information, see Chapter 15.) More research in this area needs to be conducted before conclusive statements can be made. The effects of circumcision on sexual functioning also need to be assessed because the removal of the foreskin destroys numerous nerve endings, although a national study found that being circumcised did not increase the odds of having sexual functioning difficulties (Laumann, Gagnon, Michael, & Michaels, 1994). Noncircumcised boys can avoid potential problems by being taught to clean under their foreskin and, if they become sexually active, to use a condom.

Today, about two-thirds of American boys are circumcised. Although this represents a substantial drop from about four-fifths in the 1960s, it still places the United States far ahead of other Western countries, which circumcise less than 1% of their newborn boys. The exception is Israel. In Judaism, the ritual circumcising, the *brit milah* or *bris,* is an important religious event. Within the Jewish community, some parents are developing alternative *brit milah* ceremonies (Rothenberg, 1991). Circumcision has religious significance for Muslims as well.

Aside from religious considerations, the other common reasons given by parents for circumcising their infants are "cleanliness" and "so he'll look like his dad." A circumcised penis is not necessarily any cleaner than an uncircumcised one. Infants do not require cleaning under their foreskins; adults do. If reasonable cleanliness is observed, an intact penis poses no more threat of disease to a man's sex partner than a circumcised one would. As for "looking like dad," there is no evidence to suggest that little boys are seriously traumatized if dad's penis doesn't look exactly like theirs.

A growing movement of parents and medical practitioners is seeking to educate prospective parents so that they can make informed choices about circumcising their infant sons.

Given the information we have about circumcision, would you have your son circumcised? Why or why not? (See Chapter 13 for a discussion of female genital mutilation.)

And you shall circumcise the flesh of your foreskin: and it shall be a token of the covenant between Me and you.
    —*Genesis 17:11*

provides benefits for both mother and child. If the infant is a boy, the parents will need to decide about circumcision, the surgical removal of the foreskin of the penis.

Choices in Childbirth

Women and couples planning the birth of a child have decisions to make in a variety of areas: place of birth, birth attendant(s), medications, preparedness classes, circumcision, breast-feeding—to name just a few. The "childbirth

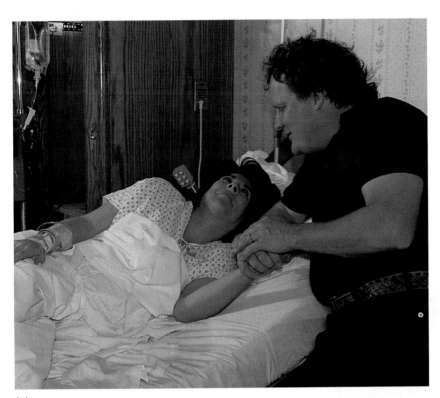

(a)

During labor, uterine contractions cause the opening and thinning of the cervix. The length of labor varies from woman to woman and birth to birth; it is usually between 4 and 16 hours. During the transition, the end of first-stage labor, contractions are the most intense. *(a)* Encouragement from her partner can help the mother relax. *(b)* The second stage of labor is the delivery of the infant. The mother is coached to push as the baby's head begins to crown. *(c)* The baby may be ready to nurse following delivery. Medical staff can give advice for getting started.

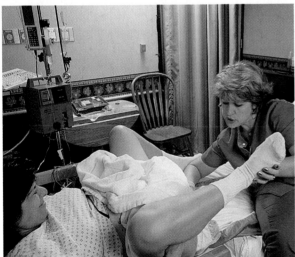

(b)

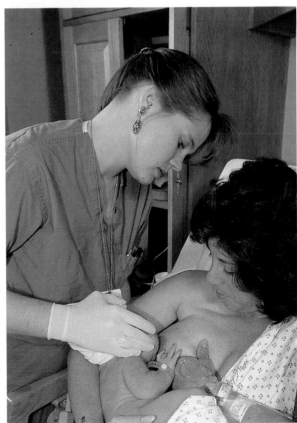

(c)

market" has responded to consumer concerns, so it's important for prospective consumers to fully understand their options.

Hospital Birth   Because of the traditional impersonal care provided in some hospitals, in recent decades, many people have recognized the need for family-centered childbirth. Fathers and other relatives or close friends often participate today. Most hospitals permit rooming-in, in which the baby stays with the mother rather than in the nursery, or a modified form of rooming-in. Regulations vary as to when the father and other family members and friends are allowed to visit.

Some form of anesthetic is administered during most hospital deliveries, as are various hormones to intensify the contractions and to shrink the uterus after delivery. The most common form of anesthetic administration is the **epidural,** in which a pain-killing drug is continuously administered through a tiny catheter placed in the woman's lower back. When administered properly, an epidural eliminates the sensations of labor and numbs the body from the lower belly to the knees. Drugs have been used successfully and safely during labor. However, the mother isn't the only recipient of the drug; it goes directly through the placenta to the baby, in whom it may reduce heart and respiration rates. Epidural anesthesia may be accompanied by artificial rupture of the amniotic membranes, fetal monitoring, and the placement of a urinary catheter. It entails a higher risk of vacuum or forceps delivery and cesarean section than does a drug-free birth.

During delivery, the mother will probably be given an **episiotomy,** a surgical procedure that enlarges the vaginal opening by cutting through the perineum toward the anus. Approximately 39% of women having vaginal deliveries in the United States are given an episiotomy ("Trends in the Use of Episiotomy," 2001). The incision is sutured following birth, and healing usually occurs without problems. Sometimes, the area becomes infected or causes discomfort or pain. Although an episiotomy may be helpful if the infant is in distress, it is usually performed in order to prevent possible tearing of the perineum.

The baby is usually delivered on a table. If such factors as medication or exhaustion slow labor, he or she may be pulled from the womb with a vacuum extractor (which has a small suction cup that fits onto the baby's head) or a forceps. (In some cases of acute fetal distress, these instruments may be crucial in order to save the infant's life, but they are sometimes used by physicians as a substitute for patience and skill.)

Cesarean Section   **Cesarean section,** or **C-section,** involves the delivery of a baby through an incision in the mother's abdominal wall and uterus. In 1970, 5.5% of American births were done by C-section. Today, 23% of all births are cesareans, approximately 37% of which are repeated cesareans ("Vaginal Births," 2002).

There are many reasons to deliver a baby by C-section, such as the abdominal position of the baby, abnormalities of the placenta and umbilical cord, and/or prolonged or ineffective labor. Although there is a lower mortality rate for infants born by C-sections, the mother's mortality rate is higher. As with all major surgeries, there are possible complications, and recovery can be slow and difficult.

> Wash, don't amputate.
>
> —*Alex Comfort, MD*

> Minor surgery is one that is performed on someone else.
>
> —*Eugene Robin, MD*

PROSPECTIVE PARENTS MUST MAKE many important decisions. The more informed they are, the better able they will be to decide what is right for them. If you were planning a birth, how would you answer the following questions?

- Who will be the birth attendant—a physician or a nurse-midwife? Do you already have someone in mind? If not, what criteria are important to you in choosing a birth attendant? Have you considered hiring a labor assistant (sometimes called a *doula*, a professional childbirth companion employed to guide the mother during labor)?

- Who will be present at the birth—your spouse or partner? Other relatives or friends? Children? How will these people participate? Will they provide emotional support and encouragement? Will they provide practical help, such as "coaching" the mother, giving massages, fetching supplies, and taking photographs or videos? Will these people be sensitive to the needs of the mother?

- Where will the birth take place—in a hospital, in a birthing center, or at home? If in a hospital, is there a choice of rooms?

- What kind of environment will you create in terms of lighting, room furnishings, and sounds? Is there special music you would like to hear?

- What kinds of medication, if any, do you feel comfortable with? Do you know what the options are for pain-reducing drugs? What about hormones to speed up or slow down labor? How do you feel about having an IV inserted as a precaution, even if medication is not planned? If you should change your mind about medication partway through labor, how will you communicate this to your attendants?

- What about fetal monitoring? Will there be machines attached to the mother or the baby? What types and degree of monitoring do you feel comfortable with?

- What is your attendant's policy regarding food and drink during labor? What kinds of foods or drinks, such as ice cream, fruit, juices, or ice chips, do you think you (or your partner) might want to have?

- What about freedom of movement during labor? Will you (or your partner) want the option of walking around during labor? Will there be a shower or bath available? Will the baby be delivered with the mother lying on her back with her feet in stirrups, or will she be free to choose her position, such as squatting or lying on her side?

- Do you want a routine episiotomy? Under what conditions would it be acceptable?

- What do you wish the role of instruments or other interventions, such as forceps or vacuum extraction, to be? Who will determine if and when they are necessary?

- Under what conditions is a cesarean section acceptable? Who will decide?

- Who will "catch" the baby as she or he is born? Who will cut the umbilical cord, and at what point will it be cut?

- What will be done with the baby immediately after birth? Will he or she be with the mother or the father? Who will bathe and dress the baby? What kinds of tests will be done on the baby, and when? What other kinds of procedures, such as shots and medicated eyedrops, will be given, and when?

- Will the baby stay in the nursery, or is rooming-in available? Is there a visiting schedule?

- How will the baby be fed—by breast or by bottle? Will feeding be on a schedule or "on demand"? Is there someone with breast-feeding experience available to answer questions if necessary? Will the baby have a pacifier between feedings?

- If the baby is boy, will he be circumcised? When? Will anesthesia be used during the procedure to decrease pain?

The fact that a woman has had a previous cesarean delivery does not mean that subsequent deliveries must be C-sections. However, a study of over 31,200 births in Scotland found that for women with previous cesareans the delivery-related death rate for subsequent babies was about 11 times higher in vaginal births than in planned repeat cesareans ("Second Cesarean," 2002).

Prepared Childbirth   Increasingly, Americans are choosing among such childbirth alternatives as prepared childbirth, rooming-in birthing centers, home birth, and midwifery.

Childbirth classes enable both partners to understand and share the birth process.

Prepared childbirth (or natural childbirth) was popularized by Grantly Dick-Read (1972), who observed that fear causes muscles to tense, which, in turn, increases pain and stress during childbirth. He taught both partners about childbirth and gave them physical exercises to ease muscle tension. Encouraged by Dick-Read's ideas, women began to reject anesthetics during labor and delivery and were consequently able to take a more active role in childbirth, as well as be more aware of the whole process.

In the 1950s, Fernand Lamaze (1970) developed a method of prepared childbirth based on knowledge of conditioned reflexes. Women learn to mentally separate the physical stimulus of uterine contractions from the conditioned response of pain. With the help of a partner, women perform breathing and other exercises throughout labor and delivery. Prepared childbirth, then, is not so much a matter of controlling the birth process as of understanding it and having confidence in nature's plan. Clinical studies consistently show better birth outcomes for mothers who have had prepared childbirth classes. Prepared mothers (who usually attend classes with the father or another partner) handle pain better, use less medication and anesthetics, express greater satisfaction with the childbirth process, and experience less postpartum depression than women who undergo routine hospital births (Hetherington, 1990).

Birthing Rooms and Centers   Birthing (or maternity) centers, institutions of long standing in England and other European countries, have now been developed in the United States. Although they vary in size, organization, and orientation, birthing centers share the view that childbirth is a normal, healthy process that can be assisted by skilled practitioners (midwives or physicians) in a homelike setting. The mother (or couple) has considerable autonomy in deciding the conditions of birth: lighting, sounds, visitors, delivery position, and so on. Some centers provide emergency care; all have procedures for transfer to a hospital if necessary.

Home Birth Home births have increased during the past two decades, although they still constitute a small fraction of total births, amounting to not quite 2%, according to available data. Careful medical screening and planning that eliminate all but the lowest-risk pregnancies can make this a viable alternative for some couples. A couple can create their own birth environment at home, and home births cost considerably less, usually at least one-third less, than hospital delivery. Home births can be as safe as hospital delivery if the woman's pregnancy is low-risk (Stewart, 1998).

Midwifery and **Doulas** The United States has an increasing number of certified nurse-midwives who are registered nurses trained in obstetrical techniques. They are qualified for routine deliveries and minor medical emergencies. They also often operate as part of a medical team that includes a backup physician. Their fees are generally considerably less than a doctor's. Nurse-midwives usually participate in both hospital and home births, although this may vary according to hospital policy, state law, and the midwife's preference.

Unlike midwives, who are medical professionals, *doulas* do not make clinical decisions. Rather, they offer emotional support and manage pain using massage, acupressure, and birthing positions.

If a woman decides she wants to give birth with the aid of a midwife outside a hospital setting, she should have a thorough medical screening to make sure she and her infant will not be at risk during delivery. She should investigate the midwife's or doula's training and experience, the backup services available in the event of complications or emergencies, and the procedures for a transfer to a hospital if necessary.

Breast-Feeding

About 3 days after childbirth, lactation—the production of milk—begins. Before lactation, sometimes as early as the second trimester, a yellowish liquid called **colostrum** is secreted by the nipples. It is what nourishes the newborn infant before the mother's milk comes in. Colostrum is high in protein and contains antibodies that help protect the baby from infectious diseases. Hormonal changes during labor trigger the changeover from colostrum to milk, but unless a mother nurses her child, her breasts will soon stop producing milk. If she chooses not to breast-feed, she is usually given an injection of estrogen soon after delivery to stop lactation. It is not certain, however, whether estrogen is actually effective; furthermore, it may increase the risk of blood clotting.

The most recent statistics indicate that only 21% of infants are still being exclusively breast-fed for 4 months, and this percentage drops to 16% by 6 months of age ("Undersize Infants Score Higher," 2002). Children who were breast-fed are less likely to develop certain diseases such as diabetes, and they score higher on intelligence tests. However, because HIV infection can be transmitted through breast milk, HIV-positive women should not breast-feed their babies.

The Huichol people of Mexico traditionally practiced couvade. The father squatted in the rafters above the laboring mother. When the mother experienced a contraction, she would pull the ropes that had been attached to his scrotum, so that he could "share" the experience of childbirth.

All is beautiful
All is beautiful
All is beautiful, yes!
Now Mother Earth
And Father Sky
Join one another and meet
forever helpmates
All is beautiful
All is beautiful
All is beautiful, yes!
Now the night of darkness
And the dawn of light
Join one another and meet
forever helpmates
All is beautiful
All is beautiful
All is beautiful, yes!
Now the white corn
And the yellow corn
Join one another and meet
forever helpmates
All is beautiful
All is beautiful
All is beautiful, yes!
Life that never ends
Happiness of all things
Join one another and meet
forever helpmates
All is beautiful
All is beautiful
All is beautiful, yes!

—*Navajo night chant*

Breast-feeding provides the best nutrition for infants. It also helps protect against many infectious diseases and gives both mother and child a sense of well-being.

Before I got married, I had six theories about bringing up children. Now I have six children and no theories.

—*John Wilmot, Earl of Rochester (1647–1680)*

We learn from experience. A man never wakes up his second baby just to see it smile.

—*Grace Williams*

BECOMING A PARENT

Men and women who become parents enter a new phase of their lives. Even more than marriage, parenthood signifies adulthood—the final, irreversible end of childhood. A person can become an ex-spouse but never an ex-parent. The irrevocable nature of parenthood may make the first-time parent doubtful and apprehensive, especially during the pregnancy. Yet, for the most part, parenthood has to be learned experientially, although ideas can modify practices. A person may receive assistance from more experienced parents, but ultimately, each new parent has to learn on his or her own.

Many of the stresses felt by new parents closely reflect gender roles. Overall, mothers seem to experience greater stress than fathers. When we speak of "mothering" a child, everyone knows what we mean: nurturing, caring for, diapering, soothing, loving. Mothers generally "mother" their children almost every day of the year for at least 18 years. The meaning of "fathering" is quite different. Nurturant behavior by a father toward his child has not typically been referred to as "fathering." However, because the lines between roles are becoming increasingly blurred as fathers play a more active part in raising their children, the verb "to parent" has been used to describe the caregiving behaviors of both mothers and fathers.

IF YOU ARE A WOMAN who plans to have children, you will have to decide whether to breast- or bottle-feed. Perhaps you already have an idea that breast-feeding is healthier for the baby but are not sure why.

The following list of benefits and advantages should help you understand why breast-feeding is recommended (assuming that the mother is healthy and has a good diet). The American Academy of Pediatrics now recommends breast-feeding for an infant's first year.

Physical Benefits of Breast-Feeding

- Breast milk contains antibodies that protect the baby from many infectious diseases, ear infections, diarrhea, and other maladies for at least 6 months.
- Breast milk forms softer curds in the infant's stomach, making digestion and elimination easier.
- Breast milk puts less stress on the infant's immature liver and kidneys because its total protein is lower than that of other mammalian milk.
- Breast milk is high in cholesterol, which is needed for proper development of the nervous tissue.
- Breast milk causes fewer allergic reactions because of its concentration and type of protein.
- Breast milk is a better source of nutrition for low-birth-weight babies because nature adapts the content of the mother's milk to meet the infant's needs.
- Babies who have been breast-fed have fewer problems with tooth decay.
- Breast-feeding is thought to encourage the development of the dental arch, helping prevent the need for orthodontia later on.
- Breast-fed babies have a 30% reduction in obesity rates (Severson, 2003).
- Full-term babies who are born small score an average of 11 points higher on IQ tests if they are exclusively breast-fed for the first 6 months of life (National Institutes of Health, 2002b).

- For mothers, hormonal changes stimulated by breast-feeding cause the uterus to contract and return to its normal size.
- Breast-feeding mothers reduce their risk of ovarian cancer, early breast cancer, and postmenopausal hip fractures due to osteoporosis.

Psychological Benefits of Breast-Feeding

- The close physical contact of breast-feeding provides a sense of emotional well-being for mother and baby.
- Sustaining the life of another through her milk may affirm a woman's sense of self and ability to give.
- Breast-feeding is natural and pleasurable.

Health and Logistical Advantages of Breast-Feeding

- Breast-feeding requires no buying, mixing, or preparing of formulas.
- Breast milk is not subject to incorrect mixing or spoilage.
- Breast milk is clean and is not easily contaminated.
- Breast-feeding provides some protection against pregnancy (if the woman is breast-feeding exclusively).
- The breast is always available.

Bottle-Feeding

For those women whose work schedules, health problems, or other demands prohibit them from breast-feeding, holding and cuddling the baby while bottle-feeding can contribute to the sense of emotional well-being that comes from a close parent-baby relationship. Bottle-feeding affords a greater opportunity for fathers to become involved in the feeding of the baby. Working women and mothers whose lifestyles or choices do not include breast-feeding often find bottles more convenient.

Regardless of the choices that parents make regarding their infants' feeding, it may well be the care and love with which it is done that are most important to the growth and development of a healthy child.

The time immediately following birth is a critical period for family adjustment. No amount of reading, classes, and expert advice can prepare expectant parents for the "real thing." The 3 months or so following childbirth (the "fourth trimester") constitute the **postpartum period.** This time is one of physical stabilization and emotional adjustment. The abrupt transition from being a nonparent to being a parent may create considerable stress. Parents take on parental roles literally overnight, and the job goes on without relief around the clock.

ALTHOUGH STATISTICS are difficult to obtain, researchers believe that there are as many as 9 million children in the United States with at least one gay or lesbian parent (Tanner, 2002). Most of these parents are or have been married; consequently, many children of lesbian women and gay men begin their lives in "traditional" families, even though separation or divorce may occur later on. Adoption, insemination, surrogacy, and foster parenting are also options being used increasingly by both singles and couples who are lesbian or gay. Because of the non-traditional nature of these families, it is difficult to determine the number of gay men and lesbian women who choose these alternatives.

In 2002, the American Academy of Pediatrics endorsed homosexual adoptions, saying gay couples can provide the loving, stable, and emotionally healthy family life that children need (American Academy of Pediatrics, 2002). Joseph Hagan, Jr., M.D., chair of the committee that wrote the policy based on related research, stated: "There's no existing data to support the widely held belief that there are negative outcomes for children raised by gay parents." The policy went on to say: "Denying legal parent status through adoption prevents these children from enjoying the psychological and legal security that comes from having two willing, capable and loving parents." This policy is important for several reasons. First, gay parents are often the primary caregivers, but if they do not have parental rights, they have no legal say in matters. Second, children in gay households may lack health insurance if the family's only breadwinner is a gay parent without parental rights.

In addition, gay parents lacking parental rights may lose visitation or custody battles if the couple separate or if one partner dies (Tanner, 2002).

Heterosexual fears about gay men and lesbian women as parents center around concerns about parenting abilities, fears of sexual abuse, and worries that the children will "catch" the homosexual orientation. All of these fears are unwarranted. A review of the literature on children of gay men and lesbian women found virtually no documented cases of sexual abuse by gay parents or their partners; such exploitation appears to be disproportionately committed by heterosexual people (Barret & Robinson, 1990).

Fears that gay and lesbian parents may reject children of the other sex also appear unfounded. Such fears reflect two common misconceptions: that being gay or lesbian is a rejection of members of the other sex and that people are able to choose their sexual orientation. A number of studies of children of lesbian women and gay men have shown that the parents' orientation has no impact on the children's sexual orientation or their feelings about their gender (Flaks, Ficher, Masterpasqua, & Joseph, 1995; Patterson, 1992). According to Dr. Michael Lamb, chief of the Section on Social and Emotional Development at the National Institute of Child Health and Human Development, "What evidence there is suggests there are no particular developmental or emotional deficits for children raised by gay or lesbian parents. . . . These kids look OK." In fact, studies have confirmed that gay and lesbian families provide as healthy an environment as heterosexual families (Buxton, 1999).

A loud noise at one end and no sense of responsibility at the other.

—*Father Ronald Knox (1888–1957)*

Many parents express concern about their ability to meet all the responsibilities of child rearing.

Sexual desire in the majority of women generally decreases during pregnancy and following delivery (De Judicibus & McCabe, 2002). Though 84% of couples in one study reported reduced frequency of sexual intercourse at 4 months postpartum, enjoyment of sexual intercourse tends to return gradually after childbirth (Hyde, DeLamater, Plant, & Byrd, 1996). By 12 weeks postpartum, the majority of women have resumed sexual intercourse; however, many experience sexual difficulties, particularly dyspareunia and lowered sexual desire. A more recent study of 138 pregnant and postpartum women found that, at 12 weeks postpartum, depression, dyspareunia, fatigue, and breast-feeding negatively influenced women's level of sexual desire, frequency of intercourse, and sexual satisfaction (De Judicibus & McCabe, 2002). The researchers speculated that this was a stage of adjustment for many mothers. Depending on a woman's ability to adjust to the physical and psychological changes that occur during this time, she may or may not experience a fulfilling sexual relationship.

Despite the abundance of research and millions of case scenarios to support the above conclusion, gay men and lesbian women still fight for the legal rights and protections they deserve. Nationwide, as of 2002, about half the states allowed second-parent gay adoptions when one partner is already a legal parent. Additionally, a handful of states have prohibitive statutes. Because they cannot legally marry and because of pervasive anti-gay prejudices, such issues as custody, visitation, and adoption remain legal dilemmas or obstacles for many contemplating becoming or trying to become parents.

A number of services and programs have been established to assist prospective gay and lesbian parents in sorting through the myriad questions and issues they face. In the end, it is the welfare of the child that society should support. This can best be achieved with loving, caring, responsible parents, regardless of sexual orientation.

What are your thoughts and feelings about this issue? Why does society perpetuate fears about gay men and lesbian women as parents?

At 6 months, when the baby's presence and the demands of parenting intrude on the sex lives of the parents, the women continued to report significantly decreased sexuality. Information about what changes to expect may help new parents avoid making unfounded and harmful assumptions about their relationship.

The postpartum period may be a time of significant emotional upheaval. Even women who had easy and uneventful pregnancies may experience the "baby blues." On the third or fourth day postpartum, 80% of women notice a brief period of mild weepiness, irritability, and depressed mood (Tam, 2001). New mothers often have irregular sleep patterns because of the needs of their newborn, the discomfort of childbirth, or the strangeness of the hospital environment. Some mothers may feel isolated from their familiar world. These are considered normal, self-limiting postpartum symptoms and generally go away within a week or two.

Postpartum depression occurs in 10–15% of new mothers and can have its onset at any time in the first year postpartum. Like the blues, postpartum depression is thought to be related to hormonal changes brought on by

Click on "That's a Family" to hear children of gay and lesbian parents talk about their families.

sleep deprivation, weaning, and the resumption of the menstrual cycle. A prior history of depression also increases a woman's risk. It is common as well for anxiety disorders to arise or recur in the postpartum period, when some women may feel hyper-vigilant about possible harm to their baby. The most serious and rarest postpartum mental illness is **postpartum psychosis.** Unlike the other disorders, postpartum psychosis is thought to be exclusively biologically based and related to hormonal changes. Affected women tend to have difficulty sleeping, be prone to agitation or hyperactivity, and intermittently experience delusions, hallucinations, and paranoia. This behavior represents a medical emergency and usually requires hospitalization. Interestingly, the incidence of postpartum psychosis is the same the world over, suggesting little cultural difference (Tam, 2001). Depression rates, in comparison, vary from industrialized cultures (more) to nonindustrialized ones (less), suggesting that psychological, cultural, and social factors have a more significant effect on whether a woman experiences postpartum depression.

Biological, psychological, and social factors are all involved in postpartum depression. Biologically, during the first several days following delivery, there is an abrupt drop in certain hormone levels. The physiological stress accompanying labor, as well as dehydration, blood loss, and other physical factors, contribute to lowering the woman's stamina. Psychologically, conflicts about her ability to mother and communication problems with her baby or partner may contribute to the new mother's feelings of depression and helplessness. Finally, the social setting into which the child is born is important, especially if the infant represents a financial or emotional burden for the family. Postpartum counseling prior to discharge from the hospital can help new parents gain perspective on their situation so that they know what to expect and can evaluate their resources. Although the postpartum blues are felt by many mothers (and even some fathers), they usually don't last more than a couple of weeks.

> Cleaning and scrubbing can wait till tomorrow.
> For babies grow up we've learned to our sorrow.
> So quiet down cobwebs, dust go to sleep.
> I'm rocking my baby and babies don't keep.
>
> —*Anonymous*

FOR MANY PEOPLE, the arrival of a child is one of life's most significant events. It signifies adulthood and conveys social status for those who are now parents. It creates the lifelong bonds of family. And it can fill the new parents with a deep sense of accomplishment and well-being.

SUMMARY

Fertilization and Fetal Development

- Fertilization of the oocyte by a sperm usually takes place in the fallopian tube. The chromosomes of the ovum combine with those of the sperm to form the diploid zygote; it divides many times to form a *blastocyst*, which *implants* itself in the uterine wall.

- The blastocyst becomes an *embryo* and then a *fetus*, which is nourished through the *placenta* via the *umbilical cord*.

- Parenthood is now a matter of choice. Increasing numbers of individuals and couples are choosing to remain *child-free*.

Being Pregnant

- The most commonly used chemical pregnancy test can be taken 2–4 weeks after a woman misses her menstrual period. *Hegar's sign* can be detected by a trained examiner. Pregnancy is confirmed by the detection of the fetal heartbeat and movements or through examination by *ultrasound.*

- A woman's feelings vary greatly during pregnancy. It is important for her to share her fears and to have support from her partner, friends, relatives, and health-care workers. Her feelings about sexuality are likely to change during pregnancy. Men may also have conflicting feelings. Sexual activity is generally safe unless there is pain, bleeding, or a history of miscarriage.

- Harmful substances may be passed to the embryo or fetus through the placenta. Substances that cause birth defects are called *teratogens;* these include alcohol, tobacco, certain drugs, and environmental pollutants. Infectious diseases such as rubella may damage the fetus. Sexually transmitted infections may be passed to the infant through the placenta or the birth canal during childbirth.

- Births to teenagers have fallen to their lowest rate in 60 years. Nevertheless, the United States leads the world's developed nations in teen pregnancies, births, and abortions. Adolescents get pregnant mainly because they do not use contraception or use it improperly; some get pregnant intentionally.

- *Ectopic pregnancy, pregnancy-induced hypertension,* and *premature birth* are the most common complications of pregnancy.

- Abnormalities of the fetus may be diagnosed using *ultrasound, amniocentesis, chorionic villus sampling (CVS),* or *alpha-fetoprotein (AFP) screening.*

- Some pregnancies end in *spontaneous abortion (miscarriage).* Infant mortality rates in the United States are extremely high compared with those in other industrialized nations. Loss of a pregnancy or death of a young infant is a serious life event.

Infertility

- *Infertility* is the inability to conceive a child after a year of unprotected intercourse or the inability to carry a child to term. The most common risk factors for infertility are body weight, age, sexually transmitted infections, tubal disease, endometrio-sis, DES exposure, smoking, and alcohol. Couples with fertility problems often feel they have lost control over an important area of their lives.

- Techniques for combating infertility include fertility medications, surgery, *intrauterine insemination, assisted reproductive technology,* and *micromanipulation. Surrogate motherhood* is also an option for childless couples, but it raises many legal and ethical issues. *Cloning,* the most controversial of reproductive technologies, is still in its infancy.

Giving Birth

- In the last trimester of pregnancy, a woman feels *Braxton Hicks contractions.* These contractions also begin the *effacement* and *dilation* of the cervix to permit delivery.

- Labor can be divided into three stages. First-stage labor begins when uterine contractions become regular. When the cervix has dilated approximately 10 centimeters, the baby's head enters the birth canal; this is called *transition.* In second-stage labor, the baby emerges from the birth canal. In third-stage labor, the *afterbirth* is expelled.

- *Cesarean section,* or *C-section,* is the delivery of a baby through an incision in the mother's abdominal wall and uterus. C-sections account for 23% of all births.

- *Prepared childbirth* encompasses a variety of methods that stress the importance of understanding the birth process, teaching the mother to relax, and giving her emotional support during childbirth.

- Birthing centers and birthing rooms in hospitals provide attractive alternatives to traditional hospital birth settings for normal births. Instead of medical doctors, many women now choose trained nurse-midwives or *doulas.*

- *Male Circumcision* has been performed routinely in this country for many years, but controversy in the medical community exists regarding its usefulness. Circumcision holds religious meaning for Jews and Muslims.

- About 21% of infants are still being breast-fed at 4 months of age. Mother's milk is more nutritious than formula or cow's milk and provides immunity to many diseases. Nursing also offers emotional rewards to mother and infant.

Becoming a Parent

- Because the roles involving "mothering" and "fathering" are becoming blurred, the term "to parent" has been used to describe caregiving behaviors.

- A critical adjustment period—the *postpartum period*—follows the birth of a child. The mother may experience feelings of depression (sometimes called "baby blues") that are a result of biological, psychological, and social factors. The majority of women also experience a decrease in sexual desire.

Sex and the Internet

Pregnancy and Childbirth

Even though pregnancy is a natural and normal process, there are still myriad issues, questions, and concerns surrounding it. This is especially true when couples are considering pregnancy, are trying to become pregnant, or find out that the woman is pregnant. Fortunately, there is help and support on the Internet. One Web site was established specifically to educate men and women about pregnancy (http://www.childbirth.org). Go to this site and select two topics you wish to learn more about. You might choose "Signs of Pregnancy," "Cesareans," "Episiotomy," "Birth Plans," or "Fertility." After you have investigated the topics and perhaps linked them to another resource, answer the following questions for each:

- What topics did you choose? Why?

- What three new facts did you learn about each?

- How might you integrate this information into your own choices and decisions around pregnancy or parenthood?

- What additional link did you follow, and what did you learn as a result?

SUGGESTED WEB SITES

American College of Nurse-Midwives
http://www.midwife.org
Provides a directory of certified nurse-midwives in your area.

American College of Obstetricians and Gynecologists
http://www.acog.org
A professional association with information for the lay public about pregnancy and childbirth.

Father's Rights and Equity Exchange
http://www.dadsrights.org
Dedicated to the premise that parenting is a 50-50 proposition; it works to ensure that both parents are allowed to be involved with their children.

La Leche League International
http://www.lalecheleague.org
Provides advice and support for nursing mothers.

National Campaign to Prevent Teen Pregnancy
http://www.teenpregnancy.org
A nonprofit, nonpartisan organization whose mission is to improve the well-being of children, youths, and families by decreasing by a third the pregnancy rate of teens.

Resolve: The National Infertility Association
http://www.resolve.org
Dedicated to providing education, advocacy, and support for men and women facing the crisis of infertility.

Society for Assisted Reproductive Technology
http://www.sart.org
Promotes and advances the standards for the practice of assisted reproductive technology.

Sudden Infant Death Syndrome (SIDS) Alliance
http://www.sidsalliance.org
Promotes infant health and survival during the prenatal period through 2 years of age.

SUGGESTED READING

For the most current research findings in obstetrics, see *Obstetrics and Gynecology, The New England Journal of Medicine,* and *JAMA: Journal of the American Medical Association.*

American College of Obstetricians and Gynecologists. (2002). *Planning Your Pregnancy and Birth.* (3rd ed.). Washington, DC: Author. A comprehensive and scientifically accurate guide to pregnancy and birth.

Brott, Armin A., & Ash, Jennifer. (2001). *The Expectant Father.* (2nd ed.). New York: Abbeville Press. A guide to the emotional, physical, and financial changes the father-to-be may experience during the course of his partner's pregnancy.

Carson, Sandra A.; Casson, Peter R.; & Shuman, Deborah J. (1999). *The Complete Guide to Fertility.* Lincolnwood, IL: Contemporary Books. An up-to-date guide to the myriad choices faced by infertile couples.

Gotsch, Gwen; Fazal, Anwar; & Torgas, Judy. (1997). *The Womanly Art of Breastfeeding.* (6th ed.). Schaumburg, IL: La Leche League International. A comprehensive and supportive guide to breast-feeding.

Ilse, Sherokee (Ed.). (2000). *Empty Arms: Coping After Miscarriage, Stillbirth, and Infant Death.* Itasca, IL:

Wintergreen Press. A focus on the range of conflicting emotions parents have during this life-altering time.

Leach, Penelope. (1997). *Your Baby and Child: From Birth to Age Five* (Rev. ed.). New York: Knopf. Complete, concise, sympathetic advice for parents and parents-to-be.

Marsiglio, William. (1998). *Procreative Man.* New York: New York University Press. A discussion of how men are affected by a partner's pregnancy and by fatherhood.

Nilsson, Lennart, & Hamberger, Lars. (1990). *A Child Is Born.* New York: Delacourt/Seymour Lawrence. The story of birth, beginning with fertilization, told in stunning photographs with text.

For links, articles, and study material, go to the McGraw-Hill Web site, located at http://www.mhhe.com/strong5

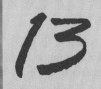

13

The Sexual Body in Health and Illness

Student Voices

"I have learned not to take the media or anyone else's opinion as the gospel. Now when I look in the mirror, I see the strong, beautiful, Black woman that I am. I no longer see the woman who wanted breast implants and other superficial aspects of beauty. My beauty now flows from within, and all I had to acquire was love for myself and knowledge of myself, and it did not cost me anything."

—21-year-old Black female

"It was never about food; it was always about the way I felt inside. The day that changed my life forever was January 29, 1998. It was the mortifying reflection of myself off the porcelain toilet I hovered over that made me see the truth. At that moment, I knew I could no longer go on living or dying like a parched skeleton. I had to hit rock bottom before I realized that what I was doing was wrong. I feel that, even if twenty people had sat me down at that time and told me I had an eating disorder, I would have laughed. I was blind."

—20-year-old White female

"Interestingly, I am writing this paper with a bald head. I used to have long, beautiful blonde hair. Chemotherapy took care of that little social/sexual status symbol. I was not at all prepared for losing my looks along with that much of my sexual identity. It has taken me by surprise to realize how much the way you look influences how people react to you, especially the opposite sex. The real lesson comes from the betrayal I feel from my body. I was healthy before, and now that I am sick, I feel as if my identity has changed. I always saw my body as sexual. Now after surgery, which left a large scar where my cleavage used to be, and with chemotherapy, which left me bald, I feel like my body is a medical experiment. My sexual desire has been very low, and I think it is all related to not feeling good about the way I look. Amazing how much of our identities are wrapped around the way we feel about the way we look. The good news for me is that my foundation is strong: I am not just what is on the outside."

—26-year-old White female

"On the weekend, I like to go out with my friend. When I drink alcohol in excessive amounts, I never have any problems performing sexually. But when I smoke marijuana, I have a major problem performing up to my standards."

—19-year-old Black male

THE INTERRELATEDNESS OF OUR PHYSICAL HEALTH, our psychological well-being, and our sexuality is complex. It's not something that most of us even think about, especially as long as we remain in good health. But as we age, we are more and more likely to encounter physical and emotional problems and limitations, many of which may profoundly influence our sexual lives. Our bodies may appear to betray us in a variety of ways: They grow too much or not enough or in the wrong places, they develop aches and pains and strange symptoms, and they are subject to devastating injuries and diseases. We need to inform ourselves about these problems so that we can deal with them effectively.

437

Contrary to popular stereotypes, people of all shapes, sizes, and ages can lead healthy and happy lives.

In this chapter, we examine our attitudes and feelings about our bodies, in addition to looking at specific health issues. We begin with a discussion of body image and eating disorders. Then we look at the effects of alcohol and other drugs on our sexuality. Next, we discuss aging and its effects on the sexual lives of both women and men. Then we turn to issues of sexuality and disability. We also discuss the physical and emotional effects of specific diseases such as diabetes, heart disease, arthritis, and cancer as they influence our sexual functioning. Finally, other issues specific to women or men are addressed.

As we grow emotionally and physically, we may also develop new perceptions of what it means to be healthy. We may discover new dimensions in ourselves to lead us to a more fulfilled and healthier sex life.

LIVING IN OUR BODIES: THE QUEST FOR PHYSICAL PERFECTION

Health is more than the absence of disease, and sexual health is more than the presence of healthy sexual parts. According to the World Health Organization (2002),

> **Sexual health** is a state of physical, emotional, mental and social well-being related to sexuality; it is not merely the absence of disease, dysfunction or infirmity. Sexual health requires a positive and respectful approach to sexuality and sexual relationships, as well as the possibility of having pleasurable and safe sexual experiences, free of coercion, discrimination and violence. For sexual health to be attained and maintained, the sexual rights of all persons must be respected, protected and fulfilled.

IN THEIR SEARCH for the "perfect" body, many people try to achieve what they consider to be the cultural ideal for breast and penis size. Our culture, more than most, places emphasis on size: Bigger is better. In our preoccupation with size, many of us have come to believe that a larger penis or breasts will make us more alluring, a better lover, and more self-confident. Amazingly, some women have had surgery (usually augmentation) on their labia to make them the supposedly "ideal" size.

Both men and women inaccurately rate the importance of size to other people, as well as inaccurately judge their own size in comparison to the average. Hence, they often underestimate their own breast or penis size in comparison to that of others. In addition, women overestimate men's preferences for breast size; both men and women believe that their peers prefer larger breasts than their own ideal smaller size. And research has shown that women are no more sexually aroused by videos featuring men with large penises than by those depicting men with medium-sized or small penises.

The desire to be bigger has led to ads in newspapers and magazines and to Web sites that try to make people feel inadequate or embarrassed if they are not "large." The ads promote methods such as special pills or drugs to increase size and promise quick and easy results. What they may not address, however, are questions of safety, functioning, erotic pleasure, and necessity. Rarely, if ever, have the products been approved by the Food and Drug Administration (FDA) or been shown to be effective in clinical tests. Some of these products are "herbal supplements," which are not regulated by the FDA. Dr. Adriane Fugh-Berman of the George Washington University School of Medicine (2003) evaluated the scientific literature about the ingredients often found in "bust-enhancing" dietary supplements, including hops, black cohosh, dong quai, fennel, kava, saw palmetto, and chaste-tree berry. She found no scientific evidence that these products increase breast size; no clinical trial of a bust-enhancing herbal product has been published. Fugh-Berman worries that there may be long-term health concerns because some of the herbal ingredients may mimic estrogen and could increase risk of breast cancer. Some women have surgery for reasons other than wanting an increase in size. For example, breast reconstruction may follow a mastectomy to treat breast cancer. In 2002, according to the American Society of Plastic Surgeons (2003), 236,888 breast augmentation surgical procedures (less than half occurred following a mastectomy) were performed, including 56,822 breast lifts and 43,507 breast implant removals. The number of breast augmentations done annually has increased 413% since 1992 (National Women's Health Information Center, 2000). Furthermore, the average size of implants has increased 40% since the 1980s. Even though saline implants are much safer than the previously used silicone gel, implants can cause serious and costly complications, including the need eventually to be replaced.

Only rarely is a man's penis actually too small; a more common problem is a partner's complaint that it is too large. Nevertheless, a variety of products and techniques promise penis enlargement, including vacuum pumps, exercises, pills, and surgical procedures such as suctioning fat from the abdomen and injecting it into the penis. The short- and long-term effectiveness and safety of these methods has not been well established, and the degree of patient satisfaction varies. Also, surgical procedures often result in loss of sensation in the penis, as well as in the breasts.

If you are unhappy with your breast or penis size, talk to a professional health-care provider such as a physician or mental health counselor. Meet with friends and talk about how society attempts to make women and men feel inadequate about their bodies and how to increase self-esteem. Support each other's refusal to buy enhancement products or to have augmentation surgery. And if you are in a relationship, talk to your partner; in most cases, you will learn that size is not an important issue. Intimacy, communication skills, and acceptance of your own body and sexuality are the most important aspects of a rewarding sexual relationship. Each person's body is special and capable of giving and receiving erotic pleasure in its unique way.

Sexual health has to do with how we function biologically, but it is also a function of our behavior and our awareness and acceptance of our bodies. In terms of sexuality, good health requires us to know and understand our bodies, to feel comfortable with them. It requires a woman to feel at ease with the sight, feel, and smell of her vulva, and to be comfortable with and aware of her breasts—their shape, size, and contours. Sexual health requires a man to accept his body, including his genitals, and to be aware of physical sensations such as lower back pain or a feeling of congestion in his bladder.

We have to have faith in ourselves. I have never met a woman who, deep down in her core, really believes she has great legs. And if she suspects she might have great legs, then she's convinced that she has a shrill voice and no neck.

—*Cynthia Heimel*

A sexually healthy man abandons the idea that masculinity means he should ignore his body's pains, endure stress, and suffer in silence.

Our general health affects our sexual functioning. Fatigue, stress, and minor ailments all affect our sexual interactions. If we ignore these aspects of our health, we are likely to experience a decline in our sexual drive, as well as suffer physical and psychological distress. A person who always feels tired or stressed or who is constantly ill or debilitated is likely to feel less sexual than a healthy, rested person. Health and sexuality are gifts we must care for and respect, not use and abuse.

Eating Disorders

Many of us are willing to pay high costs—physical, emotional, and financial—to meet the expectations of our culture and to feel worthy, lovable, and sexually attractive. Although having these desires is clearly a normal human characteristic, the means by which we try to fulfill them can be extreme and even self-destructive. Many American women and some men try to control their weight by dieting, but some people's fear and loathing of fat (often combined with fear or disgust regarding sexual functions) impels them to extreme eating behaviors. Compulsive overeating (binge eating) and compulsive overdieting (which may include self-starvation and binge eating and purging)—and combinations thereof—are the behaviors classified as **eating disorders.** The eating disorders we will discuss are known as anorexia nervosa, bulimia, and binge eating. The American Psychiatric Association (2000) characterizes anorexia nervosa as a refusal to maintain a minimally normal body weight and bulimia nervosa as repeated episodes of binge eating followed by inappropriate compensatory methods such as self-induced vomiting. A study of college female athletes revealed that 15% of swimmers, 62% of gymnasts, and 32% of all varsity athletes exhibited disordered eating patterns (Wardlow, 1997).

Click on *"The Inner Voice"* to hear the experiences of young people who have struggled with food issues.

Most people with eating disorders have certain traits, such as low self-esteem, perfectionism, difficulty dealing with emotions, unreasonable demands for self-control, negative perceptions of self in relation to others, and, of course, a fear of becoming fat. Often, the person lacks adequate skills for dealing with stress.

Although most studies of eating disorders have singled out White middle-class and upper-class women, these problems transcend ethnic and socio-economic boundaries. Research suggests that eating disorders are equally common among White females and Latinas, more frequent among Native American females, and not as common among African American and Asian American females. Among minority groups, the females who are younger, have more body weight, are better educated, and identify with middle-class values are at higher risk for eating disorders than their peers (Insel & Roth, 2000).

Muscles I don't care about—my husband likes me to be squishy when he hugs me.

—*Dixie Carter*

Anorexia Nervosa   "Anorexia" is the medical term for loss of appetite. The term "anorexia nervosa" is a misnomer for the condition it purports to describe. Those with anorexia are, in fact, obsessively preoccupied with food; they live in a perpetual struggle with the pangs of hunger. Loss of appetite is rare (American Psychiatric Association [APA], 2000). Dr. Hilde Bruch (1978), a pioneer in the study of eating disorders, defined **anorexia nervosa** as the "relentless pursuit of excessive thinness." More than 90% of people with anorexia nervosa are female (APA, 2000). Anorexia usually develops between the ages of 10 and 18.

Most people with anorexia share a number of characteristics. They are ruled by a desire for thinness, the conviction that their bodies are too large (even in the face of evidence to the contrary), and the "grim determination" to sustain weight loss (Levine, 1987). The individual refuses to maintain a minimally normal body weight and has a significant disturbance in perception of body shape or size (American Psychiatric Association, 2000). Typically, a person with anorexia has a body weight at least 15% below normal. Often, the illness begins with a significant amount of weight loss; later, the person becomes debilitated and ill as a result but refuses help and so continues in a potentially life-threatening downward spiral. Like other eating disorders, anorexia is often the "tip of the iceberg," a symptom of an underlying psychological disturbance or set of disturbances (Zerbe, 1992).

Physiologically, anorexics suffer from amenorrhea, delay of menarche or cessation of menstrual periods for at least three menstrual cycles (see Chapter 3); they may also suffer from hypothermia, the body's inability to maintain heat. Hormone levels decline in both men and women. Adolescents with this disorder may not achieve the secondary sex characteristics that are normal for this stage, such as breast development and a growth spurt. Other symptoms include the growth of lanugo (fine body hair), insomnia, constipation, dry skin and hair, problems with teeth and gums, and weakening and thinning of the bones.

The American Psychiatric Association (2000) identifies two types of anorexia nervosa: restricting and binge eating/purging. The restricting type involves weight loss that occurs as a result of dieting, fasting, or excessive exercise but no regular binge eating or purging. The binge eating/purging type occurs as a result of binge eating or purging (or both) at least weekly. A person may purge by self-induced vomiting or misuse of laxatives, diuretics, or enemas. Some do not binge eat but regularly purge after consuming small amounts of food.

Bulimia   The word "bulimia" is derived from Greek roots meaning "ox hunger." **Bulimia** is characterized by episodes of uncontrolled, often secret, overeating (binge eating), which the person then tries to counteract by purging—vomiting, excessive exercising or dieting, or using laxatives or diuretics. Differentiating between anorexia nervosa, binge eating/purging, and bulimia is often a matter of clinical judgment; however, the "sense of lack of control" is more characteristic of bulimia (APA, 2000).

Many people with bulimia viewed themselves with extreme disdain during childhood, grappled with obesity at a young age, and have a history of conflict with their parents ("Community Study," 1997). Other traits that may distinguish the individual with bulimia from others include childhood physical and sexual abuse, severe physical health problems, perfectionism, and parental depression. Bulimia has also been shown to develop more frequently in women who began to menstruate by age 12 than in those who began later. Early changes in body shape associated with puberty may be seen as another incentive to diet. Other characteristics associated with bulimia are dramatic weight fluctuations, major life changes, emotional instability, and a high need for approval. Lifetime prevalence of bulimia among women is about 1–3%, with the rate among males being one-tenth that of females (APA, 2000).

> When I go to the beauty parlor, I always use the emergency entrance. Sometimes I just go for an estimate.
>
> —*Phyllis Diller*

Binge Eating Disorder   Another recognized eating disorder, **binge eating disorder,** more commonly known as compulsive overeating, is similar to bulimia except that there is no purging behavior. Loss of control may be accompanied by a variety of symptoms, including rapid eating, eating to the point of discomfort or beyond, continual eating throughout the day, eating alone to hide the binge eating, and eating large amounts when not hungry. Compulsive overeaters rarely eat because of hunger; rather, they use food to cope with stress, conflict, and other difficult emotions (Insel & Roth, 2000). Obsessive thinking, embarrassment, depression, and feelings of guilt and disgust often accompany the overeating. Those with binge eating disorder are often overweight; many are dieters. Evidence indicates that 25–45% of obese dieters, most of whom are women, may have binge eating disorder. The prevalence rate is 0.7–4%, with females being about 1.5 times more likely to have this disorder than males (American Psychiatric Association, 2000).

Retreating from Sexuality

Clinicians who work with people with eating disorders often find that they have histories of abuse, including incest or other sexual abuse (Simpson & Ramberg, 1992). They may also have been raised to be fearful of sex and to view the body as dirty or sinful. According to a review of studies dealing with eating disorders and sexuality, women with anorexia are relatively less likely to have sexually intimate relationships, are relatively self-critical of their sexual attractiveness to others, report lower interest in sex, and have more sexual dysfunctions than women with normal eating patterns. Women with bulimia, however, are as likely as, and sometimes more likely than, women without an eating disorder to engage in sexual relationships and a variety of sexual activities (Wiederman, 1996).

Eating disorders, especially anorexia, often develop during adolescence. It is not unusual for adolescents to experience feelings of fear and powerlessness as their bodies and roles change. For some women, eating is a strategy for coping with a variety of abusive situations. Control over the size of their bodies is one of the few forms of control that women have been allowed to exercise. The refusal of food, in spite of the intense demands of hunger, may be equated with strength.

Many people with eating disorders are ambivalent toward their bodies and their sexual natures in general. An adolescent girl may feel (possibly on a subconscious level) that accepting a "curvy" woman's body means accepting a traditional gender role. Becoming asexual by becoming excessively fat or thin can be seen as a rebellion against models of feminine subservience and ineffectiveness. Acquiring an asexual body is also a means of retreating from the powerful forces of sexuality. For adolescents especially, sexuality may appear dangerous and evil on the one hand and desirable and beautiful on the other. The conflict generated by these opposing views can result in sexuality's becoming "curiously disembodied from the person" (Orbach, 1982).

Sexual abuse may also be involved in rejection of the body. Through self-starvation, a young woman may demonstrate her wish to simply disappear. Others may express their rejection of sexuality by insulating themselves in a protective layer of fat.

The body type that is idealized by ultra thin fashion models is impossible for most women to obtain without imperiling their health.

Anabolic Steroids: A Dangerous Means to an End

Athletes and body-builders often embrace the goal of great success at their activity and optimal body composition. However, in their quest for enhanced performance, many of them reach the limits of their genetic endowment and training and turn to substances known as ergogenic aids. Among these is a synthetic version of the hormone testosterone, otherwise referred to as **anabolic steroids.** These drugs are used by body-builders and other athletes to enhance their strength and add bulk to their bodies. In addition, they may produce a state of euphoria, diminished fatigue, and increased sense of power in both sexes, which gives them an addictive quality. But anabolic steroids can also have serious adverse effects, some of which are irreversible. These include sterility, heart attacks, strokes, liver damage, and personality changes, the most common being pathological aggressiveness (Ahrendt, 2001). When taken by healthy men, anabolic steroids can cause the body to shut down its production of testosterone, causing their breasts to grow and testicles to atrophy. In women, the drugs can cause hirsutism (excessive hair growth), acne, reproductive problems, and voice change. Anabolic steroids such as testosterone and its derivatives are prescription medications with clearly defined uses. Procuring and using them without a prescription is both illegal and dangerous.

ALCOHOL, DRUGS, AND SEXUALITY

Alcohol and other drugs can significantly affect our sexual health and well-being. In the minds of many Americans, sex and alcohol (or sex and "recreational" drugs) go together like a burger and fries. Although experience shows us that sexual performance and enjoyment generally decrease as alcohol or drug consumption levels increase, many people cling to the age-old myths.

Alcohol Use and Sexuality

The belief that alcohol and sex go together, although not new, is certainly reinforced by popular culture. Alcohol advertising often features beautiful, scantily clad women. Beer drinkers are portrayed as young, healthy, and fun-loving. Wine drinkers are romantics, surrounded by candlelight and roses. Those who choose Scotch are the epitome of sophistication. These images reinforce long-held cultural myths associating alcohol with social prestige and sexual enhancement.

Research has shown that nearly all college students drink alcohol, with 85–95% reporting alcohol consumption within the past month. Of these, 20–44% report binge drinking, defined as having five drinks in a row for men and four in a row for women (Edmundson, Clifford, Serines, & Wiley, 1994; Wechsler, Davenport, Dowdell, Moeykens, & Castillo, 1994; Wechsler, Mulnar, Davenport, & Baer, 1999). Numerous studies among college students have also been conducted concerning the prevalence of alcohol use during sex. As reported in *Details* magazine, 68% of college males and 69% of college females reported that they had consumed alcohol before having sex (Elliot & Brantley, 1997). Drinking also increases sexual risks. Of college-age frequent binge drinkers, 52% reported engaging in unprotected sex, and nearly 50% in unplanned sex. The majority also experienced problems related to safety, class attendence, and friends (Wechsler et al., 1999).

Because of the ambivalence we often have about sex ("It's good but it's bad"), many people feel more comfortable about initiating or participating in sexual activities if they have had a drink or two. This phenomenon of activating behaviors that would normally be suppressed is known as **disinhibition.** Although a small amount of alcohol may have a small disinhibiting, or relaxing, effect, greater quantities can result in aggression, loss of judgment, poor coordination, and loss of consciousness. Studies have shown that there may be an indirect relationship between substance abuse and behavioral disinhibition ("Risky Sex," 1998). This means that some people who are under the influence of alcohol are less able to process the negative consequences of an action (e.g., not using a condom) or the cues that normally inhibit them (e.g., having sex with someone they might not otherwise choose to have sex with). Alcohol is also generally detrimental to sexual performance and enjoyment. Furthermore, ingestion of large amounts of alcohol by both men and women can contribute to infertility and birth defects.

Alcohol affects the ability of both men and women to become sexually aroused. Men may have difficulty achieving or maintaining an erection, and women may not experience vaginal lubrication. Physical sensations are likely to be dulled. Chronic users of alcohol typically experience desire and arousal difficulties (Schiavi, Schreiner-Engle, Mandeli, Schanzer, & Cohen, 1990). Researchers have determined that drinking a six-pack of beer in less than 2 hours can affect testosterone and sperm production for up to 12 hours.

Among college students, the use of alcohol is associated with increased risk of unwanted intercourse, sexual violence, unintended pregnancy, and sexually transmitted infections.

This does not mean, however, that no sperm are present; production is slowed, but most men will remain fertile.

Alcohol use also puts people at high risk for numerous unwanted or dangerous consequences, including unwanted intercourse, sexual violence, unintended pregnancy, and sexually transmitted infections (STIs). Other researchers have found that college males who reported alcohol use during their last sexual encounter were more likely not to discuss HIV/STIs, birth control, or emotional commitment with their female partners before having sex with them than men who reported little or no alcohol use (Koch, Palmer, Vicary, & Wood, 1999). Furthermore, a study of college men found that the more they drank, the more they expected alcohol to impair their condom use skills, predicting lower intention to use condoms in sexual episodes involving alcohol (LaBrie, Schiffman, & Earleywine, 2002). The disinhibiting effect of alcohol allows some men to justify acts of sexual violence they would not otherwise commit (Abbey, 1991; Roenrich & Kinder, 1991). Men may expect that alcohol will make them sexually aggressive and act accordingly. In drinking situations, women are viewed as more sexually available and impaired. Thus, males may participate in drinking situations expecting to find a sex partner. Additionally, a woman who has been drinking may have difficulty in sending and receiving cues about expected behavior and in resisting assault (Abbey, 1991). Alcohol use is often a significant factor in sexual violence of all types. The American College Health Association estimates that drinking contributes to approximately two-thirds of all violence on campus and one-third of all emotional and academic problems. Furthermore, it may play a role in 90% of rapes and sexual assaults (Rivinus & Larimer, 1993).

Other Drug Use and Sexuality

Human beings have always been interested in the effects of drugs and other concoctions on sexual interest and performance. Substances that supposedly increase sexual desire or improve sexual performance are called **aphrodisiacs.** In addition to drugs, aphrodisiacs can include perfumes and certain foods, particularly those that resemble genitals, such as bananas and oysters. Ground rhinoceros horn has been considered an aphrodisiac in Asia, possibly giving rise to the term "horny" (Taberner, 1985). Painstaking research, both personal and professional, inevitably leads to the same conclusion: One's inner fantasy life and a positive image of the sexual self, coupled with an interested and responsive partner, are the most powerful aphrodisiacs. Nevertheless, the search continues for this elusive magic potion, and many people take a variety of drugs in an attempt to enhance their sexual experiences. For example, in one survey, over 1700 college students were asked if they had used any recreational drugs during sex and then to indicate how the drug affected their sexual experience (Figure 13.1). As other studies have shown, alcohol and marijuana are the most widely used and abused drugs among those desiring to increase libido and enhance performance. In this study, alcohol was by far the most frequently used drug, with about two-thirds of students indicating use; marijuana was a distant second. The students indicated that some of the drugs enhanced their sexual experience but that others had no effect or made the experience worse. Often, when someone does something to enhance an experience, the "halo effect" occurs, meaning that merely the thought of doing something seems to improve the experience even though there may not be an actual improvement. Also called the "placebo effect," the halo effect of aphrodisiacs has been estimated at 50% (Yates & Wolman, 1991).

Most recreational drugs, although perceived as increasing sexual enjoyment, actually have the opposite effect. (Many prescribed medications have negative effects on sexual desire and functioning as well, and users should read the information accompanying the prescription or ask the pharmacist about any sexual side effects.) Although drugs may reduce inhibitions and appear to enhance the sexual experience, many also have the capacity to interfere with the libido and sexual functioning. They also have the potential to interfere with fertility and have a serious impact on overall health and well-being.

The effects of marijuana are in large part determined by the expectations of its users ("Marijuana and Sex," 1996); therefore, no definitive statement can be made about how marijuana affects sexual encounters. Specific information about its effects in a relationship can be found by looking at the role it plays in a couple's life. In some cases, marijuana (or any drug) can become a crutch to help people deal with situations or behaviors they find uncomfortable. Some evidence suggests that marijuana stimulates the body to convert testosterone to estrogen, resulting in delayed puberty for young teenage boys ("Effects of Marijuana," 1995). Long-term marijuana use can also cause or contribute to low motivation to achieve and to low sex drive.

The substance amyl nitrate, also known as "poppers," is a fast-acting muscle relaxant and coronary vasodilator, meaning it expands the blood vessels around the heart. Medically, it is used to relieve attacks of angina. Some people attempt to intensify their orgasms by "popping" an amyl nitrate vial and inhaling the vapor. The drug causes engorgement of the blood vessels in the penis. It also causes a drop in blood pressure, which may result in feelings of dizziness and giddiness. The most common side effects are severe headaches, fainting, and, because it is flammable, burns.

Another drug widely considered to be an aphrodisiac is cantharides, or "Spanish fly." This substance is produced by drying and heating certain

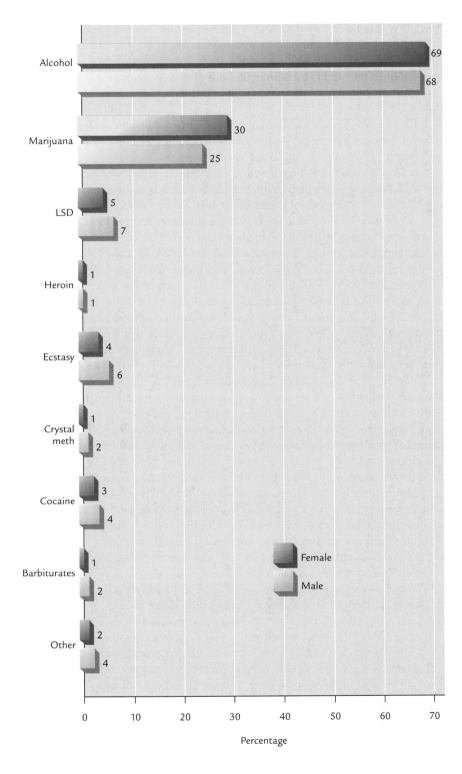

FIGURE 13.1 Percentage of Female and Male College Students Indicating They Had Used the Drug During Sex. (*Source:* Adapted from Elliot & Brantley, 1997, pp. 19–20.)

beetles' bodies until they disintegrate into a powder. There have not yet been controlled studies to confirm its aphrodisiac effect ("Aphrodisiacs," 1996). Taken internally, the substance causes acute irritation and inflammation of the genitourinary tract, including the kidneys, bladder, and urethra, and it can result in permanent tissue damage and death. This substance is banned in the United States.

LSD and other psychedelic drugs (including mescaline and psilocybin) have no positive effects on sexual ability. They may actually cause constant and painful erections, a condition called **priapism.**

Cocaine, a central nervous system stimulant, reduces inhibitions and enhances feelings of well-being. But regular use nearly always leads to sexual dysfunction in both men and women, as well as an inability to achieve erection or orgasm. Male cocaine users also have a lower sperm count, less active sperm, and more abnormal sperm than nonusers. The same levels of sexual impairment occur among those who snort the drug and those who smoke or "freebase" it. Those who inject cocaine experience the greatest dysfunction.

Ecstasy (MDMA) is a hallucinogenic amphetamine that produces heightened arousal, a mellowing effect, and an enhanced sense of self ("Ecstasy Effects," 1996). The use of Ecstasy has increased dramatically on college campuses, with almost one out of four students reporting using it (Hales, 2000). The drug is illegal and has no legitimate use. It has been associated with dehydration due to physical exertion without breaks for water; heavy use has been linked to paranoia, liver damage, and heart attacks. Because users feel increased empathy, Ecstasy can lower sexual inhibitions. However, men generally cannot get erections when they are high but are often very sexual when the effects of the drug begin to fade. Men who use Ecstasy are 2.8 times more likely to have unprotected sex than nonusers ("Ecstasy: Happiness Is," 2000).

Some young men, in seeking the enhanced sexual experience, are mixing recreational drugs such as cocaine, poppers, and Ecstasy with Viagra, a prescription medication for erectile dysfunction (see Chapter 14). The combination of Ecstasy and Viagra, often called "Sextasy," "Trail Mix," and "Hammerheading," has gotten the attention of public health officials worldwide, resulting in increased efforts to warn about the dangers of drug use and the combining of drugs. This mixing is very dangerous; lower blood pressure, heart attacks, or death may occur.

The use of methamphetamine, often referred to as "crystal," "Christina," or "Tina," is increasingly becoming part of the club scene in several major cities. In New York, for instance, methamphetamine has gained popularity among gay club-hoppers. Prized as an aphrodisiac and a long-lasting stimulant, methamphetamine can be snorted, inhaled, swallowed, or injected. The sharp increase in sexual interest caused by crystal use can lead to dangerous behavior. For example, some HIV-positive men often begin skipping some of their medications (Jacobs, 2002).

Aside from the adverse physical effects of drugs themselves, a major negative consequence of substance abuse is that it puts many people at significant risk for acquiring STIs, including HIV infection. Addiction to cocaine, especially crack cocaine, has led to the widespread practice of bartering sex for cocaine. This practice, as well as the practice of injecting cocaine or heroin, combined with the low rate of condom use, has led to epidemics of STIs, including AIDS, in many urban areas. (For additional information on drugs and HIV, see Chapter 16.)

IT'S NEARLY IMPOSSIBLE to watch MTV, televised sports, or fashion events these days without seeing someone with a small tattoo or ring discreetly (or not so discreetly) displayed on his or her body. As the latest expression of individuality, piercing and tattooing have attracted a diverse set of enthusiasts and have moved into mainstream culture.

Every culture and time has had its own standards of beauty and sexual attractiveness, and piercing and tattooing have been used to enhance both. A pierced navel was considered a sign of royalty among the ancient Egyptians, and the Crusaders of the Middle Ages were tattooed with crosses to ensure a Christian burial.

A study of 454 students at one college found that body art (body piercing and tattooing) was common. Half said that they had nontraditional body piercings (other than for women's earrings) and just under a quarter reported having tattoos. Females were more likely to be pierced than males, but there was no significant difference in the prevalence of tattooing by sex. No significant relationships were found between piercing/tattooing and age or measures of body types. The most common "nontraditional" piercing sites among women were the navel (29%), upper ear (27%), tongue (12%), nipple (5%), and genitals (2%). Piercing other than in the ears was rare among the male students: 2% had pierced tongues, and 1% reported pierced eyebrows, nipples, or genitals. Male athletes were more likely to be tattooed than male nonathletes, with the hand/arm (12%), back (7%), and shoulder (6%) the most common sites. The most common tattoo body sites for the female students were the back (14%), foot/leg (5%), and shoulder and abdomen (4% each) (Mayers, Judelson, Moriarty, & Rundell, 2002).

Tattooing in our culture has become widespread and nearly routine, with tattoo "studios" presenting their services as art. The tattooing procedure involves injecting dye into the skin, resulting in a permanent marking. Potential problems associated with the painful procedure include the risk of infection, including hepatitis and HIV. Studies indicate that nearly half of those who have a tattoo want it removed, most often because of psychological discomfort and/or job discrimination (Marin, Hannah, Colin, Annin, & Gegax, 1995). Although the removal procedure is also painful, new technology and lower costs have allowed many individuals to have their tattoos removed. Using the flickering beam of a laser, physicians can explode the indelible ink into minute particles, which are absorbed into and discarded by the body.

"The last taboo is the body," states Fakir Musafar, considered by many to be the father of the "modern primitive movement" (cited in Ryan, 1997). Musafar believes that the popularity of body modification is the final stage of evolution that began in the 1960s, when young people challenged social institutions such as the church, family, and government. Like tattooing, body piercing has become increasingly popular as a dramatic way to help define oneself. What keeps piercing exotic is not only the look but the pain factor that accompanies it. "Pain is relative," says Musafar (cited in Ryan, 1997). "People in other cultures can transmit the strong physical sensation of pain into ecstasy, healing and many other states. It's a way of using the body to explore inner space and spiritual dimensions." For some, the pain is viewed as a drug, a way of releasing anxiety or aggression, and/or a means of erotic stimulation. Psychologists report that cutting and other self-injury provide relief by releasing endorphins, which can actually boost one's mood (Ryan, 1997).

Piercing capitalizes on a fascination with the look of deviance and its sadomasochistic undertones. If placed strategically, rings and studs provide both physical stimulation and psychological titillation. Each type of piercing involves a specific method of puncturing and a prescribed course of healing. Some plastic surgeons report a doubling of business involving stitching together body parts damaged by piercing.

A third practice is branding, now becoming more common in the mainstream, with some clubs offering branding as a stage show. Hot-iron branding leaves a scar that may be treated with steroid injections but that can never be totally removed.

An analysis of the 1997 Centers for Disease Control and Prevention Youth Risk Behavior Survey found that adolescents with tattoos and/or body piercings were more likely to have engaged in risk behaviors such as sexual risk taking and drug use, and at greater degrees of involvement, than those without either. The researchers concluded that tattoos and/or body piercings among adolescents can alert health-care providers to possible risk-taking behaviors (Carroll, Riffenburgh, Roberts, & Myhre, 2002).

Because all these markings are considered permanent and potentially dangerous, the procedures should be performed only by professionals. The study of 454 undergraduates cited earlier found medical complications (bleeding, tissue trauma, and infection) in 17% of those having had body piercings. Pierced navels were particularly prone to infection. No medical complications were reported for tattoos (Mayers et al., 2002). Keys to safety and satisfaction include basic aftercare, which involves keeping the site clean and avoiding contact with dirty hands, saliva, or other body fluids; an awareness of anatomy and knowledge of proper healing procedures on the part of the person providing the services; proper placement of the marks or piercings; and the use of sterile tools ("Piercing Exquisite," 1998).

SEXUALITY AND AGING

As men and women reach middle and older ages, body changes often impact their sexuality. In this section, we focus on changes associated with decline in the level of the hormones estrogen and testosterone and on health problems associated with the prostate. Information about physical changes in the body and sexual expression is presented in Chapter 6.

Women's Issues

Beginning sometime in their forties, most women begin to experience a normal biological process resulting in a decline in fertility. The ovaries produce less and less estrogen and progesterone, and ovulation becomes less regular. This period of gradual change and adjustment is referred to as **perimenopause.** Over a few years' time, menstrual periods become irregular and eventually stop, usually between the ages of 45 and 55. The average age of **natural menopause,** the complete cessation of menstruation for at least one year, is 52, although about 10% of women complete it before age 40 (Beck, 1992). A woman can also undergo menopause as a result of a hysterectomy, the surgical removal of the uterus, if both ovaries are also removed. In postmenopausal women, estrogen levels are about one-tenth those in premenopausal women, and progesterone is nearly absent (National Cancer Institute, 2002a). Most women experience some physiological or psychological symptoms during menopause, but for only about 5–15% of women are the effects severe enough to cause them to seek medical assistance (Brody, 1992).

Physical Effects of Menopause   Whether a woman goes through menopause naturally or surgically, symptoms can appear as the woman's body attempts to adjust to the drop in estrogen levels. The symptoms vary from one woman to the next: Some may breeze through menopause with few symptoms, while other may experience many discomforting symptoms for several months or even years. The most common symptoms of menopause are hot flashes or flushes, sweating, and sleeping disturbances (National Institutes of Health, 2002c). Another symptom, thinning of the vaginal walls, can result in the length and width of the vagina decreasing and the vagina not being able to expand during penile-vaginal intercourse as it once could. Intercourse can be painful, bleeding can occur, and the vagina can be more susceptible to infection. These effects may begin while a woman is still menstruating and may continue after menstruation has ceased. As many as 75% of women experience some degree of hot flashes, which usually diminish within 2 years following the end of menopause. A **hot flash** is a period of intense warmth, flushing, and (often) perspiration, typically lasting for a minute or two, but ranging anywhere from 15 seconds to 1 hour in length. A hot flash occurs when falling estrogen levels cause the body's "thermostat" in the brain to trigger dilation (expansion) of blood vessels near the skin's surface, producing a sensation of heat. Hot flashes that occur with severe sweating during sleep are called night sweats. Some women who are going through menopause experience insomnia (which can be related to hot flashes), changes in sexual interest (more commonly a decrease), urinary incontinence, weakening of pelvic floor muscles, headaches, or weight gain. Some women also report depression, irritability, and other emotional problems ("Menopause—Another Change in Life," 2001).

Long-term effects related to lowered estrogen levels may be experienced by some women. Osteoporosis, the loss of bone mass, leads to problems such as wrist and hip fractures in about 25% of mainly postmenopausal White and Asian American women and Latinas; African American women are less susceptible to osteoporosis (Greenwood, 1992). Lowered estrogen can also contribute to diseases of the heart and arteries related to rising levels of LDL (low-density lipoprotein, or "bad" cholesterol) and falling levels of HDL (high-density lipoprotein, or "good" cholesterol). Hereditary factors also play a part in cardiovascular disease.

Newly developed treatments can control osteoporosis indefinitely. Because the disease stems mainly from the loss of estrogen at menopause, replacing estrogen, along with progesterone, is a common treatment. Other approaches include prescription drugs such as Evista, exercise, and calcium and vitamin D supplements to reduce bone loss.

Other changes that may reduce the physical effects of menopause include low-cholesterol diets, exercise and nutritional supplements to lower cholesterol, maintenance of a healthy weight, topical lubricants to counteract vaginal dryness, and Kegel exercises to strengthen pelvic floor muscles. Frequent sexual stimulation (by self or partner) may help maintain vaginal moistness. For women who smoke, quitting provides benefits in many areas, including reducing the risk of osteoporosis, diminishing the intensity of hot flashes, and establishing an improved sense of well-being (Greenwood, 1992).

Postmenopause Hormone Therapy   To relieve the symptoms of menopause, a physician may prescribe **postmenopause hormone therapy (PHT),** a new name for **hormone replacement therapy (HRT).** This therapy involves the use of the hormone estrogen or a combination of estrogen with another hormone, progesterone, or progestin in its synthetic form. Until the release of a study on menopause and hormone therapy sponsored by the National Institutes of Health (NIH) and conducted by the Women's Health Initiative (WHI) in 2002 that reported some significant risks for some types of menopause hormone therapy (Hulley et al., 2002), "HRT" was the commonly used term. However, since the report, the NIH has been using "PHT," believing the new terminology to be more accurate. HRT never replaced a woman's natural hormones, nor did it restore the physiology of youth. The new belief is that the processes of aging and menopause should be separated, and taking "replacement" hormones may give a false sense that there are no serious side effects of such treatment. It remains to be seen whether "PHT" becomes the preferred term in medical circles or the popular press, but we have chosen to follow the NIH change for this discussion on menopause and hormone therapy.

Estrogen and progestin normally help regulate a woman's menstrual cycle. In PHT, progestin is added to estrogen to prevent the overgrowth of cells in the lining of the uterus, which can lead to uterine cancer. If a woman is going through natural menopause and is experiencing symptoms that are interfering with her quality of life, she might be prescribed estrogen-plus-progestin therapy; a woman who has had a hysterectomy would receive estrogen-only therapy. The hormones can be taken daily or only on certain days of the month. Depending on their purpose, the hormones can be taken orally, applied as a patch on the skin, used as a cream or gel, or absorbed via an intrauterine device (IUD) or vaginal ring. A vaginal estrogen ring or cream can minimize vaginal dryness, urinary leakage, and vaginal or urinary infection, but it does not ease hot flashes. PHT may cause side effects such as bloating, breast tenderness or enlargement, bleeding, headaches, mood changes, and nausea.

The natural reduction of estrogen can lead to an increased risk of developing heart disease and osteoporosis. Both of these conditions can be relieved with supplemental doses of estrogen. For the more than 40 million American women over age 50, the prospect of estrogen hormone "replacement" was enticing. The early studies seemed to show that hormone therapy protected women against the maladies that tend to appear after menopause, such as heart disease. For example, some studies supported the idea that treatment prevents osteoporosis, but other studies failed to provide evidence or were inconclusive. And no large clinical studies proved that hormone therapy prevented heart disease or bone fractures. Research on the possible effects of long-term use of hormones to treat breast and colorectal cancers was needed. Furthermore, most prior research on the effect of PHT on heart disease had mainly been observational, not clinical, studies. Observational studies follow a test group's medical and lifestyle practices, indicating possible relationships between behaviors or treatments and disease. Because they do not have an intervention component, observational studies are not able to establish cause and effect. In contrast, in clinical trials, considered the "gold standard" in establishing cause and effect, researchers administer specific medical interventions, such as PHT, using both treatment and control groups. Thus, women who receive PHT are compared with women who do not receive PHT, making it possible to tie any difference between the two groups to the medical intervention.

The NIH has sponsored several major clinical trials of menopause and hormone therapy. In 1991, the NIH launched the WHI, a clinical trial study focusing on the major causes of death, disability, and frailty in more than 161,000 postmenopausal women. The WHI is an ongoing 15-year study including clinical trials and observational study and community prevention components. One clinical trial involved 16,608 postmenopausal women with a uterus, age 50–79, who took either estrogen-plus-progestin therapy or a placebo. (A separate study in which women who had a hysterectomy received estrogen only was also begun.) The women were enrolled in the study between 1993 and 1998, and their health was carefully monitored by an independent panel, the Data and Safety Monitoring Board (DSMB). The estrogen/progestin combination was chosen because it was the most commonly prescribed PHT in the United States (used each day by more than 6 million women who have a uterus), and it had appeared to benefit women's health, as shown in several observational studies. The main goal of the study was to determine if therapy would help prevent heart disease and hip fractures and to see if those possible benefits were greater than the possible risks of breast cancer, uterine cancer, and blood clots. The study was initiated because many prior studies had presented a complicated picture of the risks and benefits of hormone therapy in preventing disease (National Institutes of Health, 2002c).

The estrogen-plus-progestin study was to have continued until 2006, but it was stopped in July 2002 by the DSMB because it found an increased risk of breast cancer and no significant reduction in the risk of heart attacks, strokes, or blood clots in the lungs and legs. The main benefits were fewer hip and other fractures and fewer cases of colorectal cancer. The study was discontinued because the results showed that the risks clearly outweighed and outnumbered the benefits. ("Outnumbered" means that more women had adverse effects from the therapy than benefited from it.)

In an article in the *Journal of the American Medical Association* (Hulley et al., 2002) WHI researchers reported the findings:

- *Breast cancer.* An increased risk of breast cancer appeared after 4 years of estrogen-plus-progestin use. After 5.2 years, the hormones resulted in a 26% increase in the risk of breast cancer, or 8 more breast cancers (38 versus 30) each year for every 10,000 women. The hormones may have had a cumulative effect, as those women who had used estrogen plus progestin before the study were more likely to develop breast cancer.

- *Heart attack.* The risk of heart attack began to increase in the first year and became more pronounced in the second year. After 5.2 years, there were 29% more heart attacks in the estrogen-plus-progestin group, or 7 more heart attacks (37 versus 30) each year for every 10,000 women.

- *Stroke.* For the first time, estrogen plus progestin was shown to cause more strokes in healthy women. By the end of the study, the hormone group had 41% more strokes than the placebo group, or 8 more strokes (29 versus 21) each year for every 10,000 women.

- *Blood clots.* The risk of blood clots was greatest during the first 2 years and was 4 times higher for the estrogen-plus-progestin group than for the placebo users. By the end of the study, the rate had decreased to 2 times greater, or 18 more women with blood clots (34 versus 16) each year for every 10,000 women.

- *Fractures.* Estrogen plus progestin reduced hip fractures by 34%, or 5 fewer hip fractures (10 versus 15) each year for every 10,000 women. This is the first solid evidence from a clinical trial that hormone therapy protects women against bone loss and osteoporosis.

- *Colorectal cancer.* The hormone therapy lowered the risk of colorectal cancer by 37%, or 6 fewer colorectal cancers (10 versus 16) each year for every 10,000 women. The reduction appeared after 3 years of estrogen-plus-progestin use and became significant thereafter.

The study found no differences in risk based on prior health status, age, or ethnicity. The findings did not apply to postmenopausal use of estrogen alone. That part of the WHI study did not find the same increased cancer risk, so it will continue until 2005.

The WHI findings on estrogen-plus-progestin use sent a shock wave to the millions of postmenopausal women using PHT and their health-care providers. Prior to the report, estrogen-plus-progestin therapy was one of the most universally accepted treatments in medicine. Even though there have been some critics of the study, its findings have been widely accepted and are important in establishing a causal link between use of the particular hormone therapy studied and its effects on diseases. In any case, the findings have left many postmenopausal women wondering whether PHT will prolong their youth or hasten their death. Some have stopped PHT, but others have continued because they feel better on hormones. Certainly, the findings

Making the Best Decision About Postmenopausal Hormone Therapy

IN 2002, A MASSIVE National Institutes of Health (NIH) study on the benefits of treating menopausal women with estrogen plus progestin was halted because of disturbing findings. The study, part of the Women's Health Initiative (WHI), a long-term investigation of menopause and hormone therapy, debunks many of the widely acclaimed benefits of hormone therapy, traditionally called "hormone replacement therapy" (HRT) but now referred to by the NIH as "postmenopausal hormone therapy" (PHT). The study, which showed an increased risk for breast cancer, as well as the previously identified risk for heart attacks, strokes, and blood clots, received widespread attention in the media. Many postmenopausal women said that they were confused by the findings and felt that their health-care provider had not adequately explained the risks ("Questions About HRT," 2002). A subsequent study indicating that hormone therapy doubled the risk of Alzheimer's disease and other types of dementia in women age 65 and older only heightened concerns about estrogen-plus-progestin therapy (Shumaker et al., 2003).

The NIH notes that factors such as lifestyle, environmental influences, heredity, and personal medical history affect health. The NIH also points out that most treatments have both risks and benefits, so a postmenopausal woman and her health-care provider must decide what is best for her. The information and advice from the study should be of particular interest to women considering undergoing PHT for longer than 3 or 4 years. Here is the specific advice on PHT given by the NIH (National Institutes of Health, 2002c):

- *Short-term hormone use.* Short-term hormone use (estrogen alone or estrogen plus progestin) can relieve menopausal symptoms. "Short term" means the shortest time needed to manage menopausal symptoms, generally 2 to 3 years. The benefits of short-term PHT outweigh any risks. Women should talk with their health-care providers about personal risks and needs.

- *Long-term estrogen-plus-progestin therapy.* Estrogen-plus-progestin therapy should not be used to prevent heart disease, because it actually *increases* the chance of a heart attack or stroke, as well the risk of breast cancer and blood clots. Women should talk with their health-care providers about other ways to prevent heart disease, such as a healthier lifestyle and improved diet. Also, women should not use long-term postmenopausal hormone therapy if they already have heart disease.

- *Long-term estrogen-only therapy.* The WHI has not yet issued findings about the risks and benefits of long-term use of estrogen-only therapy.

- *Prevention of osteoporosis.* Women and their health-care providers need to weigh the risks of heart disease, stroke, and breast cancer against the benefits of PHT and consider alternate approaches to preventing osteoporosis and fractures.

- *Other hormone alternatives.* The NIH makes specific recommendations about other hormone medications, such as micronized progesterone or natural hormones, or about hormones women take in lower dosages or in different ways, such as lower-dose estrogen or patches instead of pills.

Questions that women can ask their health-care providers include the following:

- Why am I taking hormone therapy? Or why should I take hormone therapy?

- Which hormone therapy am I on?

- What are my risks for heart disease, breast cancer, and osteoporosis?

- Should I stop taking the hormone therapy?

- What's the best way for me to stop? What side effects will I experience?

- Is there an alternative therapy that I can use long-term?

- What alternatives can help prevent heart disease?

- What alternatives can help prevent osteoporosis?

- What can I do to keep menopausal symptoms from returning?

The NIH warns that health-care providers may not be able to answer all of these questions, given that many questions about postmenopausal hormone therapy remain unanswered. The NIH is conducting further clinical trials and observational studies on menopause and hormones and within a few years may have answers for questions about other medical postmenopausal hormone therapy and alternatives to hormone therapy. More information about hormone therapy–related topics can be found on the WHI Web site (http://www.whi.org) or at the National Heart, Lung, and Blood Institute Health Information Center Web site (http://www.nhlbi.nih.gov).

Subsequent to the WHI report, the U.S. Preventive Services Task Force (2002a), a group of health experts that reviews published research and makes recommendations about preventive health, recommended against women taking PHT for the sole purpose of preventing chronic conditions. The decision about whether to take PHT to reduce the symptoms of menopause depends on each woman's preferences and risk of osteoporosis, heart disease, dementia, blood clots, stroke, and cancer.

have spurred people to take a second look at estrogen-plus-progestin therapy (National Institutes of Health, 2002c).

A recent study of WHI data, published in 2003 in the *Journal of the American Medical Association (JAMA),* struck another blow against hormone therapy for postmenopausal women (Shumaker et al., 2003). For a group of 4532 women, researchers reported that estrogen-plus-progestin therapy doubled the risk of Alzheimer's disease and other dementia in postmenopausal women age 65 or older. This means that in a given year there will be 23 more cases of dementia for every 10,000 women taking the estrogen-plus-progestin therapy. Furthermore, this type of hormone therapy did not prevent mild cognitive impairment in the women. The researchers concluded that "the findings, coupled with previously reported WHI data, support the conclusion that the risks of estrogen plus progestin outweigh the benefits." In the same issue of *JAMA,* two other studies reported additional bad news about estrogen-plus-progestin hormone therapy. One study found that women on the hormone therapy did not perform as well as a placebo group on cognitive tests (Rapp et al., 2003); the second study confirmed prior research that estrogen-plus-progestin therapy increased the risk of stroke (Wassertheil-Smoller et al., 2003).

Click on "Menopause" to hear how the health issues associated with menopause differ in various parts of the world.

Men's Issues

About half of men over age 50 are affected to some degree by **benign prostatic hypertrophy,** an enlargement of the prostate gland. The enlarged prostate may put pressure on the urethra, resulting in the frequent and urgent need to urinate. It does not affect sexual functioning. If the blockage of the urethra is too severe, surgery can correct the problem. The surgery may lead to retrograde ejaculation, in which the ejaculate is released into the bladder instead of the urethra upon orgasm (see Chapter 4). Retrograde ejaculation is not dangerous, and the sensations of orgasm are generally unchanged (Thompson, 1990).

Testosterone Supplement   Testosterone plays an important role in puberty and throughout a man's life. Although it is the main sex hormone of men, women produce small amounts of it as well. Testosterone production is the highest in adolescence and early adulthood and declines as a man ages. Most older men, however, maintain a sufficient amount for normal functioning.

As men age, changes such as less energy and strength, decreased bone density, and erectile difficulties occur; these changes are often erroneously blamed on decreasing testosterone levels. Because of changes like these—particularly sexual declines—a rapidly growing number of older men are taking supplemental testosterone, typically called **testosterone replacement therapy (TRT).** (It will be interesting to see if the term "testosterone replacement therapy," like "hormone replacement therapy," is changed as further research is conducted. Currently, the NIH uses both "TRT" and "**testosterone supplement,**" a term we have chosen to use here.) Testosterone is currently available in deep muscle injections, patches, and topical gels. Over $200 million was spent on testosterone supplements in 2002, and over 1 million prescriptions for testosterone products were written in 2001 (Rubin, 2003a; Uhlenhuth, 2003). However, despite the fact that some older men who have tried these supplements report feeling more energetic, testosterone supplements are controversial. The NIH states that it remains a scientifically unproven method for preventing or relieving any physical or psychological changes that men with normal testosterone levels may experience as they age (National Institutes of Health, 2002d). Furthermore, not much is known about the potential health risks associated with testosterone supplements.

Many questions need to be answered about the use of testosterone supplements in later life. For example, do men at the lower end of the normal range of testosterone production benefit from supplements? Might supplemental testosterone have long-term effects on the aging body? Do testosterone supplements increase the risk of prostate cancer, the second leading cause of cancer death among men? In addition, some studies suggest that supplemental testosterone might trigger excessive red blood cell production, increasing a man's risk of stroke. Preliminary studies are inconclusive as to whether this hormone can sharpen memory or help men maintain strong muscles, sturdy bones, or robust sexual functioning.

A small percentage of men may be helped by prescription testosterone supplements. These supplements are often prescribed for men whose bodies do not produce enough of the hormone, such as men whose pituitary glands have been destroyed by infections or tumors or whose testes have been damaged. For the few men with extreme testosterone deficiencies, supplements may help maintain strong muscles and bones and increase sex drive. However, the effects of testosterone replacement in healthy older men without extreme deficiencies require more study (National Institutes of Health, 2002d).

SEXUALITY AND DISABILITY

A wide range of disabilities and physically limiting conditions affect human sexuality, yet the sexual needs and desires of those with disabilities have generally been overlooked and ignored. In 1987, Ellen Stohl, a young woman who uses a wheelchair, created a controversy by posing seminude in an eight-page layout in *Playboy*. Some people (including some editors at *Playboy*) felt that the feature could be construed as exploitive of disabled people. Others, Stohl among them, believed that it would help normalize society's perception of people with disabilities. She said, "I realized I was still a woman. But the world didn't accept me as that. Here I am a senior in college [with] a 3.5 average, and people treat me like I'm a 3-year-old" (quoted in Cummings, 1987).

One study found that women with a physical disability had as much sexual desire as women in general (Nosek, Howland, Rintala, Young, & Chanpong, 1997). Nearly one-half were sexually active at the time of the study. However, women with disabilities reported significantly lower levels of sexual activity, sexual responses, and satisfaction with their sex lives. They also had fewer partners, and those with a partner reported less satisfaction in their sexuality than the women without a disability. Interestingly, the severity of the disability was not related to the level of sexual functioning or satisfaction with sex life. Women with disabilities who had a more positive sexual self-concept and who judged themselves as approachable by potential romantic partners also had higher levels of sexual activity. Four out of 10 women with disabilities believed that they did not have adequate information about how their disability affects their sexual functioning. A study of lesbian women and gay men with disabilities revealed that they were dealing with several issues affecting their sexuality (Lew-Starowicz, 1994). Their main problems were difficulty in finding a partner and a lack of acceptance of their sexual orientation.

Physical Limitations

Many people are subject to sexually limiting conditions for some or all of their lives. These conditions may be congenital, appearing at birth, such as cerebral palsy (a neuromuscular disorder) and Down syndrome (a developmentally disabling condition). They may be caused by a disease such as diabetes, arthritis, or cancer or be the result of an accident, as in the case of spinal cord injuries.

Changing Expectations   Educating people with physical limitations about their sexuality and providing a holistic approach that includes counseling to build self-esteem and combat negative stereotypes are increasingly being recognized as crucial issues by the medical community.

To establish sexual health, people with disabilities must overcome previous sexual performance expectations and realign them with their actual sexual capacities. In cases in which the spinal cord is completely severed, for example, there is no feeling in the genitals, but that does not eliminate sexual desires or exclude other possible sexual behaviors. Many men with spinal cord damage are able to have full or partial erections; some may ejaculate, although the orgasmic feelings accompanying ejaculation are generally absent. Nearly 40% of quadriplegic men are able to experience orgasm and ejaculation (Ducharme & Gill, 1997). Those who are not capable of ejaculation may be able to father a child through electroejaculation sperm retrieval and intrauterine insemination of the man's partner. In this procedure, the prostate gland is electrically stimulated through the rectum, causing erection and ejaculation.

Women with spinal cord injuries generally do not experience orgasm, although they are able to experience sensuous feelings in other parts of their bodies. People with spinal cord injuries (and anyone else, for that matter) may engage in oral or manual sex—anything, in fact, they and their partners find pleasurable and acceptable. They may discover new erogenous areas of their bodies, such as their thighs, necks, ears, or underarms. A study by The Kinsey Institute for Research in Sex, Gender, and Reproduction at Indiana University of 186 people (140 men and 46 women) with spinal cord injuries revealed that the injury affected masturbation, coitus, noncoital sex, sexual response during sleep, and fertility (Donohue & Gebhard, 1995). Within 3 years of the injury, however, 95% of the women (excluding three who were virgins) and 90% of the men had resumed coitus.

Spinal cord injuries do not usually affect fertility. Many women with such injuries are able to have painless childbirth, although forceps delivery, vacuum extraction, or cesarean section may be necessary.

Overcoming Guilt   A major problem for many people with disabilities is overcoming the guilt they feel because their bodies don't meet the cultural "ideal." They often live in dread of rejection, which may or may not be realistic, depending on whom they seek as partners. Many people with disabilities have rich fantasy lives. This is fortuitous, because imagination is a key ingredient to developing a full sex life. Robert Lenz, a consultant in the field of sexuality and disability, received a quadriplegic (paralyzed from the neck down) spinal cord injury when he was 16 (Lenz & Chaves, 1981). In the film *Active Partners,* he says:

> One thing I do know is that I'm a much better lover now than I ever was before. There are a lot of reasons for that, but one of the biggest is that I'm more relaxed. I don't have a list of do's and don'ts, a timetable or a proper sequence of moves to follow, or the need to "give" my partner an orgasm every time we make love. Sex isn't just orgasm for me; it's pleasuring, playing, laughing, and sharing.

Important tasks of therapists working with people with disabilities are to give their clients "permission" to engage in sexual activities that are appropriate to their capacities and to suggest new activities or techniques (Kolodny, Masters, & Johnson, 1979). Clients should also be advised about the use of vibrators, artificial penises and vaginas, and other aids to sexual excitement. Certainly, with proper information and sexual self-esteem, people with disabilities can have rich and rewarding sex lives.

Vision and Hearing Impairment

Loss of sight or hearing, especially if it is total and has existed from infancy, presents many difficulties in both the theoretical and the practical understanding of sexuality. A young person who has been blind from birth is unlikely to know what a person of the other sex actually "looks" (or feels) like. Children who are deaf often do not have parents who communicate well in sign language; as a result, they may not receive much instruction about sexuality at home, nor are they likely to understand abstract concepts such as "intimacy." Older individuals who experience significant losses of sight or hearing may become depressed, develop low self-esteem, and withdraw from contact with others. Because they don't receive the visual or auditory cues that most of us take for granted, the hearing-impaired or sight-impaired may have communication difficulties within their sexual relationships. These difficulties often can be overcome with education or counseling, depending on the circumstances. Schools and programs for visually and hearing-impaired children offer specially designed curricula for teaching about sexuality.

Chronic Illness

Diabetes, cardiovascular disease, and arthritis are three of the most prevalent diseases in America. Although these conditions are not always described as disabilities, they may require considerable adjustments in a person's sexuality because they (or the medications or treatments given to control them) may affect libido, sexual capability or responsiveness, and body image. Many older partners find themselves dealing with issues of disease and disability in addition to those of aging.

There may be other disabling conditions, too numerous to discuss here, that affect our lives or those of people we know. Some of the information presented here may be applicable to conditions not specifically dealt with, such as multiple sclerosis or postpolio syndrome. We encourage readers with specific questions regarding sexuality and chronic diseases to seek out networks, organizations, and self-help groups that specialize in those issues.

Diabetes   **Diabetes mellitus,** commonly referred to simply as diabetes, is a chronic disease characterized by an excess of sugar in the blood and urine, due to a deficiency of insulin, a protein hormone. About 17 million people in the United States, or 6.2% of the population, have diabetes (American Diabetes Association, n.d.). Nerve damage or circulatory problems caused by diabetes can cause sexual problems. Men with diabetes are often more affected sexually by the disease than are women. Almost half of men with diabetes experience erectile dysfunctions, although there is apparently little or no relationship between the severity of the diabetes and the dysfunction. Heavy alcohol use and poor blood-sugar control also increase the risk of erectile problems.

Diabetes can affect a woman's sexuality. Some women with diabetes may have less interest in being sexual because of frequent yeast infections. High blood-sugar levels can make some women feel tired, resulting in reduced sexual interest. Also, intercourse may be painful because of vaginal dryness (American Diabetes Association, 2001).

Cardiovascular Disease   Obviously, a heart attack or stroke is a major event in a person's life, affecting important aspects of daily living. Following an attack, a person often enters a period of depression in which the appetite declines, sleep habits change, and there is fatigue and a loss of libido. There is often an overwhelming fear of sex based on the belief that sexual activity might provoke another heart attack or stroke. The partners of male heart attack patients also express great concern about sexuality. They are fearful of the risks, concerned over sexual difficulties, and apprehensive during intercourse about the possibility of another attack. Usually, sexual activity is safe 2–3 weeks after the heart attack patient returns home from the hospital, but it depends on the individual's physical and psychological well-being. In general, the chance of a person with a prior heart attack having another one during sex is no greater than that of anyone else; however, the patient should consult with a physician.

LAMENT OF A CORONARY

My doctor has made a prognosis
That intercourse fosters thrombosis,
But I'd rather expire fulfilling desire
Than abstain, and suffer neurosis.

—*Anonymous*

Arthritis   Whereas more men suffer from cardiovascular disease, the majority of people with arthritis (about 70%) are women. About 1 in 7 Americans have some type of arthritis, most of them older women, but the disease may afflict and disable children and adolescents as well. Arthritis is a painful inflammation and swelling of the joints, usually of the knees, hips, and lower back, which may lead to deformity of the limbs. Sometimes, the joints can be moved only with great difficulty and pain; sometimes, they cannot be moved at all. Arthritis is a leading cause of disability in Americans, resulting in activity limitations in about 7 million Americans (National Institutes of Health, 1997). The cause of arthritis is not known.

Sexual intimacy may be difficult for people with arthritis because of the pain. Oral sex, general pleasuring of the body, and creative sexual positioning have definite advantages for those with arthritis. Applying moist heat to the joints prior to sexual activity with a partner can help.

Children with physical or developmental disabilities may have special needs when it comes to sexuality education. Here, students with visual impairments take a hands-on approach to learning about pregnancy and childbirth with the help of lifelike models.

Developmental Disabilities

Over 6 million Americans have varying degrees of developmental disabilities (sometimes referred to as "mental retardation"). The sexuality of those who are developmentally disabled has only recently been widely acknowledged by those who work with them. Their sexual rights are now recognized, although there is a great deal of debate about this issue. The capabilities of the developmentally disabled vary widely. Mildly or moderately disabled people may be able to learn to behave appropriately, protect themselves from abuse, and understand the basics of reproduction. Some may manage to marry, work, and raise families with little assistance (Yohalem, 1995).

Sexuality education is extremely important for adolescents who have developmental disabilities. Some parents may fear that this will "put ideas into their heads," but it is more likely, given the combination of explicit media and Internet images and the effects of increased hormonal output, that the ideas are already there. It may be difficult or impossible to teach more severely affected people how to engage in safe sexual behaviors. There is ongoing debate about the ethics of mandatory birth control or sterilization for those who are developmentally disabled. These issues are especially salient in cases in which there is the chance of passing the disability genetically to a child.

The Sexual Rights of People with Disabilities

Although many of the concerns of people with disabilities are becoming more visible through the courageous efforts of certain groups and individuals, much of their lives still remains hidden. By refusing to recognize the existence and concerns of those with physical and developmental limitations, the rest of us do a profound disservice to our fellow human beings—and, ultimately, to ourselves.

The sexual rights of those with disabilities include the following:

- The right to sexual expression
- The right to privacy
- The right to be informed about and have access to needed services, such as contraceptive counseling, medical care, genetic counseling, and sex counseling
- The right to choose one's marital status
- The right to have or not have children
- The right to make one's own decisions and develop to one's fullest potential

SEXUALITY AND CANCER

In ancient Greece, physicians examining the invasive tissues extending from malignant breast tumors thought these tissues looked like the jutting claws of a crab. From the Greek word for crab, *karkinos,* we have derived our word, "cancer." Cancer, however, is not a single disease; it is more than 300 distinct illnesses that can affect any organ of the body. These various cancers grow at different speeds and have different treatment success and failure rates. Most cancers, but not all (e.g., leukemia), form solid tumors.

All cancers have one thing in common: They are the result of the aberrant behavior of cells. Cancer-causing agents (carcinogens) are believed to jumble up the messages of the DNA within cells, causing the cell to abandon its normal functions. Tumors are either benign or malignant. **Benign tumors** usually are slow growing and remain localized. **Malignant tumors,** however, are cancerous. Instead of remaining localized, they invade nearby tissues and disrupt the normal functioning of vital organs. The process by which the disease spreads from one part of the body to another, unrelated, part is called **metastasis.** This metastatic process, not the original tumor, accounts for 80% of cancer deaths.

Women and Cancer

Because of their fear of breast cancer and cancer of the reproductive organs, some women avoid having regular breast examinations or Pap tests. If a woman feels a breast lump or her doctor tells her she has a growth in her uterus, she may plunge into despair or panic. These reactions are understandable, but they are also counterproductive. Most lumps and bumps are benign conditions, such as uterine fibroids, ovarian cysts, and fibroadenomas of the breast.

Breast Cancer   Excluding cancers of the skin, breast cancer is the most common cancer among women, accounting for nearly 1 out of every 3 cancers diagnosed in American women. Over 210,000 women were found to have invasive breast cancer in 2003, with nearly 40,000 dying from the disease (American Cancer Society, 2003a). The National Cancer Institute (2002b) estimates that 1 in 8 women in the United States will develop breast cancer. Even though the incidence of breast cancer has increased over the past decade, breast cancer deaths have declined, largely because of greater use of mammography screening and improved therapy. Nearly 90% of women diagnosed with breast cancer survive at least 5 years after diagnosis, and 53% survive 20 years (American Cancer Society, 2001).

Several factors increase a woman's risk for developing breast cancer. Some of these factors cannot be altered, while others can be affected by changes in lifestyle. Simply being a woman who is aging increases the risk. Breast cancer is about 140 times more common in women than in men, most breast cancers (75%) occur in women over the age of 50, and the risk is especially high for women over age 60. The risk of breast cancer in women gradually increases with age: Women age 30–40 have a 1 in 252 chance of developing breast cancer; women age 60–70 have a 1 in 27 chance (National Cancer Institute, 2002b). Women who have had breast cancer have an increased risk of getting breast cancer again.

After controlling for age, the biggest risk factor is a family history of breast and/or ovarian cancer, with the risk being higher when the biological relationship of the affected relative is closer—that is, the cancer occurs in a first-degree relative (e.g., a mother or sister) rather than a second-degree relative (e.g., a grandmother or aunt). Within the group of women with a family history of breast and/or ovarian cancer, a relatively small subset have inherited two genetic mutations. Women who are known carriers of mutations of these two genes have a particularly high risk of breast and ovarian cancer (Smith et al., 2003). Non-Hispanic White, Hawaiian, and Black women have the highest levels of breast cancer risk; other Asian/Pacific Islander, Hispanic, and Native American women have the lowest levels (National Cancer Institute, 2002b).

Having had certain types of abnormal biopsy results may increase a woman's risk of developing breast cancer. Women who have had no children, had fewer children, or had their first child after the age of 30 have a greater chance of developing breast cancer than women who had children at a younger age. Higher risk also is associated with an increased amount of time a woman's body is exposed to estrogen, such as for women who started menstruating at an early age (before age 12) or experienced menopause late (after age 55). Other factors implicated in increased risk for breast cancer include estrogen-plus-progestin hormone replacement therapy for more than 5 years (see the prior discussion on postmenopause hormone therapy), not breast-feeding, alcohol use, obesity and high-fat diets, physical inactivity, and environmental pollution. The relationship between oral

BY REGULARLY EXAMINING your own breasts, you are likely to notice any changes that occur. The best time for breast self-examination (BSE) is about a week after your period ends, when your breasts are not tender or swollen. If you are not having regular periods, do BSE on the same day every month.

1. Stand in front of a mirror that is large enough for you to see your breasts clearly. Check each breast for anything unusual. Check the skin for puckering, dimpling, or scaliness. Look for a discharge from the nipples.

2. Watching closely in the mirror, clasp your hands behind your head and press your hands forward.

3. Next, press your hands firmly on your hips and bend slightly toward the mirror as you pull your shoulders and elbows forward. As you do these motions, check for any change in the shape or contour of your breasts. You should feel your chest muscles tighten as you do this.

4. Gently squeeze each nipple and look for a discharge.

5. Raise one arm. Use the pads of the fingers of your other hand to check the breast and the surrounding area firmly, carefully, and thoroughly. Some women like to use lotion or powder to help their fingers glide easily over the skin. Feel for any unusual lump or mass under the skin. Feel the tissue by pressing your fingers in small overlapping areas the size of a dime. Be sure to cover your whole breast, taking your time, and follow one of the definite patterns shown to the right.

6. Repeat step 5 while you are lying down. Lie flat on your back, with one arm over your head, and a pillow or folded towel under the shoulder. This position flattens the breast and makes it easier to check. Check each breast and the area around it very carefully using one of the patterns described below.

Some women repeat step 5 in the shower. Your fingers will glide easily over soapy skin, so you can concentrate on feeling for changes underneath.

Source: Reprinted with permission from Planned Parenthood ® Federation of America Inc. Copyright © 1987 PPFA. All rights reserved.

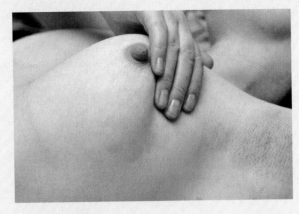

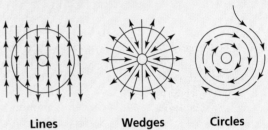

Lines   **Wedges**   **Circles**

Using any one of these patterns, be sure to check the entire breast, underarm area, and upper chest.

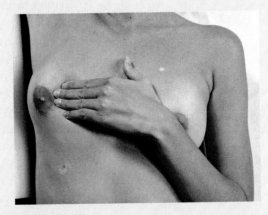

Breast examination is more effective when specific steps are followed. Any new symptoms should be promptly reported to a health-care provider.

FIGURE 13.2 Types of Surgical Treatment for Breast Cancer. (*Source:* American Cancer Society website, www.cancer.org. Reprinted with permission.)

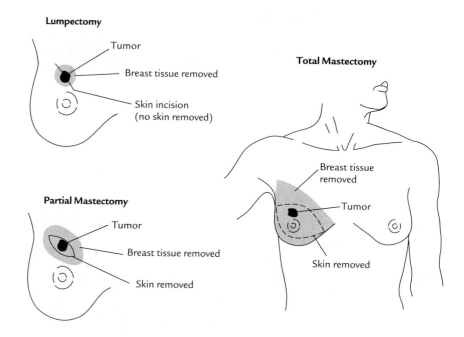

cancer. Common breast cancer surgeries described by the American Cancer Society (2003a) include the following (Figure 13.2):

- *Lumpectomy.* This procedure involves the removal of only the breast lump and some normal tissue around it and is followed by 6 weeks of radiation treatment.
- *Partial **mastectomy**.* This surgery involves the removal of more of the breast tissue than with a lumpectomy and is followed by 6 or 7 weeks of chemotherapy.
- *Simple or total mastectomy.* This operation involves the removal of the entire breast, but not the lymph nodes from under the arm or muscle tissue from beneath the breast.
- *Modified radical mastectomy.* This surgery involves the removal of the entire breast and some of the lymph nodes under the arm.
- *Radical mastectomy.* This operation involves the removal of the entire breast, lymph nodes, and chest wall muscles under the breast. Because the modified radical mastectomy has proved to be just as effective, with less disfigurement and fewer side effects, radical mastectomy is rarely done now.

Surgery may also be combined with other treatments such as chemotherapy, hormone therapy, or radiation therapy.

Sometimes, women must choose between lumpectomy and mastectomy. The American Cancer Society (2003a) suggests that, for most women with stage I or stage II breast cancer (stages are I–IV, from least to most serious), lumpectomy or partial mastectomy is as effective as mastectomy; the survival rates of women treated with these two approaches are no different. Research reported in the *New England Journal of Medicine* in 2002 confirmed that women do just as well with breast-conserving therapy as with more radical surgery if the tumor is not more than about 2 inches in diameter (Fisher

Surviving cancer can deepen one's appreciation of life. Notice the tattoo along this woman's mastectomy scar.

et al., 2002; Veronesi et al., 2002). However, lumpectomy is not an option for all women. A woman's physician can provide information on which surgery is best. Possible side effects of mastectomy and lumpectomy include infection and blood or fluid collecting at the incision location (American Cancer Society, 2003a).

Other treatments for cancer are radiation and chemotherapy (treatment with powerful drugs or hormones). When combined with conventional chemotherapy, radiation has been found to dramatically reduce the incidence of death among young women who have undergone a mastectomy ("Breast Cancer Studies," 1997).

Some individuals who have considered surgically removing a healthy breast to avoid future breast cancer can now contemplate taking a daily pill to prevent the disease. One such drug, tamoxifen, works by keeping estrogen from stimulating the cancer cells. A large-scale, 4-year study revealed that women at high risk for breast cancer reduced their chances of getting the disease 45% by taking tamoxifen (Mishra, 1998). However, the drug brings with it increased risk of uterine cancer, especially if it is taken for more than 5 years. But uterine cancer is usually diagnosed at a very early stage and almost always cured by surgery (American Cancer Society, 2003a). Despite the difficult choices associated with its use, the benefits of taking tamoxifen far outweigh the risks for most women (American Cancer Society, 2000).

A woman who undergoes a mastectomy is confronted with the loss of one or several visible parts of her body. First, she has lost her breast. Second (in the case of radical surgery), the removal of chest muscles and auxiliary lymph tissues not only leaves visible scars but also may restrict the movement and strength of her arm. Psychologically, the loss of her breast may symbolize for her the loss of sexuality; she may feel scarred and be fearful of rejection, because breasts in American culture are such primary sexual symbols. She also may experience a decrease in her sexual excitability. Because the breasts play an important role in sexual arousal and foreplay for many women, their loss may prevent some women from becoming fully aroused sexually. However, physiologically, breast surgery or radiation does not decrease a woman's ability to become sexually aroused or to reach orgasm (American Cancer Society, 2000).

Sexuality is one aspect of life that may be profoundly altered by cancer. Changes in appearance, stress associated with treatment, emotional vulnerability, and a sense of mortality can often cause a woman to reexamine her feelings about herself, her desire for intimacy, and the way she perceives her relationship. It is important for a woman to realize that there is no "right" way to express her sexuality. It is useful for her and her partner to decide what is pleasurable and satisfying. Being comfortable with her sexuality can enhance self-esteem, improve personal comfort, and make coping with cancer easier.

In the course of diagnosing and treating people with cancer, health-care providers may be inclined to ignore or forget the issue of sexual adjustment following surgery and treatment (Smith & Reilly, 1994). Unfortunately, many women face the potential effects of cancer on their sexuality alone because it is the rare doctor, nurse, or social worker who will bring up the subject of sex during postsurgical care. At the same time, women are often reluctant to voice their concerns because they experience embarrassment and guilt in thinking about sex when they feel they should simply be grateful to be alive. Psychosocial interventions focused on reducing stress, increasing knowledge, and improving coping skills are beneficial to breast cancer patients (Smith & Saslow, 2002). Therefore, even apart from any humanitarian motives, the doctor's recognition of the sexual side effects of cancer treatments, his or her sensitivity to the devastating impact that these problems can have on highly vulnerable patients, and his or her skills in the psychological and medical management of these problems are crucial ingredients in the holistic medical care of these women.

To address symptoms that may interfere with their enjoyment of sex, women can do the following ("Sexuality and Cancer," 2002; Smith & Saslow, 2002):

1. Address the possible emotional stresses that the cancer may be causing. It's important to inform a doctor or nurse of feelings of anxiety, worry, or depression. Joining a support group focused on stress has been shown to help improve immune function.

2. Rest before sexual activities, or engage in sexual activity in the morning to counter the problem of fatigue that often occurs with treatment. Others have found it helpful to maintain a healthy diet. Positions that require minimal effort, such as side-by-side positions, may be helpful.

3. Relieve pain with relaxation, warm baths, and massages.

4. Reduce nausea by eating light meals or crackers. Antinausea medications may be helpful before engaging in sexual activity.

BREAST RECONSTRUCTION OR BREAST IMPLANT SURGERY   Because most breast cancer is treated by surgical removal of the breast, the subject of breast reconstruction—literally, building a new breast—is one of paramount interest to many women (and those who care about them).

In 1978, the total number of American women who had undergone breast reconstruction was 15,000. Today, due to sophisticated plastic surgery and the fact that most insurance companies are willing to provide coverage for it, breast reconstruction is undertaken by more than 100,000 women annually, typically after mastectomies. An estimated 1% of American women have had breast implants (Janowsky, Kupper, & Hulka, 2000).

Although many women do not feel the need to restore a missing breast or at least do not feel it strongly enough to go through additional surgery, many others welcome the opportunity to restore their sense of physical integrity and balance. For these women, reconstruction is an important step in recovering from breast cancer.

Depending on a woman's age, general health, type of tumor, and individual preference, breast reconstruction may be performed at the same time as mastectomy or several months (or longer) afterward. Hence, a woman having a mastectomy and thinking about having breast reconstruction at the same time should consult a plastic surgeon before the operation. The reconstructive surgery itself varies according to the extent of the mastectomy and the amount of remaining muscle, skin, and underlying tissue with which to work. For women who have undergone modified radical or total mastectomy, the operation involves inserting a breast-shaped implant under the remaining chest muscle. In cases of radical mastectomy, extra muscle and skin must be taken from another part of the body to cover the implant. This may be done by rotating a flap of the latissimus dorsi muscle and a covering piece of skin from the back to the chest. Or it may involve using skin and fatty tissue from the abdominal area, a procedure known as a "transflap."

The implants are usually pouches filled with saline solution; silicone is no longer used. During reconstructive surgery or in a subsequent operation, the surgeon may also attach a nipple fashioned out of skin from the labia, inner thigh, inside of the mouth, or other tissue. If there are no cancerous cells in it, the woman's own nipple sometimes can be saved ("banked") by temporarily attaching it to another part of the body, such as the inner thigh, and moving it to the new breast after reconstruction. Other times, a tattoo can be used to create the illusion of a nipple. Common problems in surgery involve scarring, impaired arm movement, and swelling of the upper arm. Physical therapy can help restore mobility in the arm and upper body. Implants occasionally "migrate" or leak, especially with time. Pain or swelling in conjunction with silicone implants should be reported to a physician at once. Additional surgeries may be required to make adjustments and repairs.

Deciding about breast reconstruction involves many issues. For example, the feeling of pleasure from fondling the breast and nipple is typically decreased, but the reconstruction may provide the woman with increased feelings of wholeness and attractiveness (National Cancer Institute, 2000). It is not a decision contemplated lightly by women who have already undergone the pain and trauma of cancer and surgery. But it provides a significant option to many by filling an important need.

Cervical Cancer and Cervical Dysplasia   **Cervical dysplasia,** also called **cervical intraepithelial neoplasia (CIN),** is a condition of the cervical epithelium (covering membrane) that *may* lead to cancer if not treated. If cancer develops, it usually takes several years, but sometimes it happens in less than a year. For most women, CIN will remain unchanged and will go away without treatment (American Cancer Society, 2003b). Because cervical dysplasia is confined to the cervix, it is nearly 100% treatable. Approximately 15% of sexually active teenage girls show evidence of CIN (Strider, 1997).

The more advanced and dangerous malignancy is invasive cancer of the cervix (ICC), also called **cervical cancer.** Each year, about 15,000 women are diagnosed with cancer of the cervix (National Cancer Institute, 2002c). The most important risk factor for cervical cancer is infection by the sexually transmitted human papillomavirus (HPV). Additional risk factors include age (the average age for cervical cancer diagnosis is 50–55), HIV infection (which makes women more vulnerable to HPV), chlamydia infection, poor diet, multiple sex partners, a mother who was given diethylstilbestrol (DES) during pregnancy, sexual intercourse before age 18, cigarette smoking, and low socioeconomic status. Some lesbian women are at risk for cervical cancer, as many report a history of having had heterosexual intercourse (Institute of Medicine, 1999). When detected in its early stages, the disease is both preventable and curable. Unusual bleeding from the vagina may be a sign of cervical cancer (American Cancer Society, 2000).

DETECTION: THE PAP TEST   The most reliable means of early detection of cervical cancer is the **Pap test** (or Pap smear). This is a simple procedure that can not only detect cancer but also reveal changes in cells that make them precancerous. A Pap test can warn against cancer even before it begins, and the use of the Pap test has resulted in dramatic decreases in cervical cancer deaths in the United States. The importance of the Pap test is shown by the fact that 60–80% of American women with newly diagnosed invasive cervical cancer have not had a Pap test in the past 5 years, and many have never had a Pap test (National Cancer Institute, 2000). Analysis of cervical screening records of 348,419 British women found that, for every 100,000 women, 10 deaths could be avoided by regular screening (Raffle, Alden, Quinn, Babb, & Brett, 2003).

The Pap test is usually done during a pelvic exam and takes about a minute. Cell samples are gently and usually painlessly scraped from the cervix and examined under a microscope. If any are suspicious, the physician will do further tests. Women should have a Pap test annually unless their physician recommends otherwise. Unfortunately, the test is not as effective in detecting cancer in the body of the uterus, which occurs in women most frequently during or after menopause.

The American Cancer Society (2003b) offers the following guidelines for early detection of precancerous changes of the cervix:

▪ All women should begin screening for cervical cancer about 3 years after they begin having penile-vaginal intercourse, but no later than age 21. Screening should be done every year using the regular Pap test and every 2 years using the newer liquid-based Pap test.

▪ Starting at age 30, women having 3 normal Pap test results in a row may get screened every 2–3 years with either the conventional or liquid-based test. Women having certain risk factors, such as DES exposure before birth, HIV infection, or a weakened immune system, should continue to be screened each year.

■ Another reasonable option for women over age 30 is to get screened every 3 years (but not more often) with a Pap test (conventional or liquid-based) and the HPV DNA test. Health-care professionals can now test for certain types of HPV that are most likely to cause cervical cancer by searching for pieces of their DNA in cervical cells. The sample is collected in a way similar to the one used with the Pap test.

■ Women age 70 or older who have had 3 or more normal Pap tests in a row and no abnormal Pap test results in the previous 10 years may choose to stop having cervical cancer screening. Women with a history of cervical cancer, DES exposure before birth, HIV infection, or weakened immune system should continue screening.

■ Women who have had their uterus and cervix removed (total hysterectomy) may also choose to stop having cervical cancer screening unless the surgery was done as a treatment for cervical cancer or precancer. Women who have had a hysterectomy without the cervix being removed should continue to follow the preceding guidelines.

To make the Pap test more accurate, women should not schedule the appointment for a time during their menstrual period, and for 48 hours prior to the test, they should not douche, have intercourse, or use tampons, birth control foams, jellies, or other vaginal creams or vaginal medications.

TREATMENT   Cervical dysplasia is very responsive to treatment in its early stages. With an irregular Pap smear, a **biopsy**—surgical removal of tissue for diagnosis—may be performed. Some abnormalities clear up on their own, so the physician may wait several months and do a follow-up smear. The British study cited previously also concluded that there is only a 1-in-80 chance that a woman will develop cervical cancer following an abnormal cervical screening (Raffle et al., 2003). There may be some risk in delaying treatment, however. If the cervix shows visible signs of abnormality, a biopsy should be performed at once. Cervical biopsies are done with the aid of a colposcope, an instrument that contains a magnifying lens. Sometimes, conization, the removal of a cone of tissue from the center of the cervix, is performed. This procedure is time-consuming and requires hospitalization. Depending on the extent and severity of the dysplasia and whether it has progressed to cancer, other treatment options range from electrocauterization (or cryosurgery) to laser surgery, radiotherapy, or hysterectomy. The 5-year survival rate for the earliest stage of cervical cancer is 91%; for all stages combined, it's 70% (American Cancer Society, 2000).

Ovarian Cancer   Ovarian cancer is the sixth most common cancer in women and is the fifth-ranked cause of cancer death in women. The American Cancer Society (2003c) estimates that there were about 25,000 new cases of ovarian cancer in the United States in 2003, and about 14,300 women will die from the disease. The number of new cases of ovarian cancer has been slowly decreasing since 1991. Evidence links pregnancy, breast-feeding, tubal ligation or hysterectomy, and use of oral contraceptives with a lower risk of ovarian cancer, perhaps because each gives the woman a rest from ovulation and eases wear and tear on the ovaries. Factors that increase risk include age (half of all ovarian cancers are found in women over 65), use of the fertility drug clomiphene citrate, more monthly periods, a family history of ovarian cancer, breast cancer, and poor diet. Ovarian cancer is hard to diagnose because there are no symptoms in the early stages; it is not usually detectable by a Pap test. Diagnosis is done by pelvic examination and needle aspiration (removal of fluid) or biopsy. Treatment involves surgical removal of the tumor and ovary, often followed by radiation or chemotherapy. Follow-up care is especially important. If ovarian cancer is found early, the chances of survival are much greater. Ninety-five percent of women will survive at least 5 years if the cancer is found and treated before it has spread outside the ovary. However, only one-quarter of ovarian cancers are found at this stage. About 78% of all women with ovarian cancer survive at least 1 year after the cancer is found, and over 50% survive longer than 5 years (American Cancer Society, 2003c). Because lesbian women are not likely to use oral contraceptives or have children, they may be at increased risk for ovarian cancer (Institute of Medicine, 1999).

Uterine Cancer   Slightly more than 40,000 new cases of cancers of the uterus occurred in 2003, with about 7000 women in the United States dying from uterine cancer (American Cancer Society, 2003d). More than 95% of cancers of the uterus involve the endometrium, the lining of the uterus. Certain women appear more at risk for developing endometrial cancer than others. Obesity, certain types of estrogen replacement therapy, treatment with tamoxifen, infertility, diabetes, menstruation before age 12, and menopause after age 52 are risk factors for endometrial cancer (American Cancer Society, 2000).

Hysterectomy   The surgical removal of the uterus is known as a **hysterectomy.** Hysterectomy is the second most frequent major surgical procedure among reproductive-age women, with about 600,000 performed each year. More than one-fourth of U.S. women will have a hysterectomy by the time they are 60 years of age (Keshavarz, Hillis, Kieke, & Marchbanks, 2003). A simple hysterectomy removes the uterus and a portion of the vagina, and a radical hysterectomy involves the removal of the upper part of the vagina and the ovaries, fallopian tubes, cervix, and adjacent tissues. Certain conditions make a hysterectomy necessary: (1) when a cancerous or precancerous growth cannot be treated otherwise, (2) when noncancerous growths on the uterus become so large that they interfere with other organs (such as when they hinder bladder or bowel functions) or cause pain or pressure, (3) when bleeding is so heavy that it cannot be controlled or when it leads to anemia, and/or (4) when severe infection cannot be controlled in any other way. If a woman's physician recommends a hysterectomy, she should have the opinion confirmed by a second physician. A radical hysterectomy does not alter a woman's ability to feel sexual pleasure. A woman does not need a uterus or cervix to have an orgasm. Actually, in a study of more than 1100 Maryland women age 35–49 who had a hysterectomy, the women reported increased libido; sexual activity, enjoyment, and orgasm; and relief from painful intercourse (Rhodes, Kjerulff, Langenberg, & Guzinski, 1999).

A hysterectomy is performed by removing the uterus surgically through the vagina or through an abdominal incision. At the same time, there may be an **oophorectomy,** removal of one or both ovaries, because of endometriosis, cysts, or tumors. If both ovaries are removed from a premenopausal woman, she may begin hormone supplement therapy to control the symptoms caused by the lack of estrogen. But because estrogen therapy may be linked to increased breast cancer risk, such therapy should be undertaken with caution, in consultation with a physician.

Removal of the ovaries can result in lowered libido because testosterone (the sex-drive hormone) is mainly produced there. Furthermore, the absence of ovarian estrogen can cause menopausal symptoms such as vaginal dryness and thinning of the vaginal walls. Therapy and self-help groups for posthysterectomy patients can be very useful for women who wish to increase sexual desire and pleasure. Most women who have had a hysterectomy are satisfied with the results. Researchers at the University of Maryland interviewed 1300 women before and 3, 6, 12, and 24 months after surgery. At 1 and 2 years after the hysterectomy, 96% of the women said it had completely or mostly resolved the problems or symptoms they experienced before the surgery; 93% and 94%, respectively, said the results were better than or about what they expected. Over 80% said their health was better than before the procedure (Kjerulff, Rhodes, Langenberg, & Harvey, 2000).

Vaginal Cancer   Vaginal cancer is rare, accounting for only about 3% of the cancers of the female reproductive system, although some cancers start in other organs (such as the uterus or bladder) and spread to the vagina. In 2003, there were about 2000 new cases of vaginal cancer and about 800 deaths attributed to it (American Cancer Society, 2003e). Although the exact cause of most vaginal cancers is not known, established risk factors include age (most cases are diagnosed in women age 50–70), mother's use of DES when pregnant, HPV infection, previous cervical cancer, and smoking. Symptoms include abnormal vaginal bleeding, vaginal discharge, a mass that can be felt, and pain during intercourse. Treatment options, based on the type of cancer and the stage of the disease when diagnosed, are radiation therapy and surgery. New surgical operations for repairing the vagina after radical surgery are being developed (American Cancer Society, 2000).

Men and Cancer

Generally, men are less likely than women to get regular checkups and to seek help at the onset of symptoms. This tendency can have unfortunate consequences where reproductive cancers are concerned, because early detection can often mean the difference between life and death. Men should pay attention to what goes on in their genital and urinary organs.

Prostate Cancer   Prostate cancer is the most common form of cancer (excluding skin cancer) among men; it causes the second highest number of deaths among men diagnosed with cancer (lung cancer is first). Of all men diagnosed with cancer each year, more than one-fourth have prostate cancer. According to the American Cancer Society (2003f), over 200,000 new cases of prostate cancer are diagnosed each year in the United States, and nearly 30,000 men will die from this disease. One man in 6 will get prostate cancer during his lifetime, and only 1 man in 32 will die from this disease. The mortality rate from prostate cancer is decreasing. For reasons still unknown, African American men are more likely to have prostate cancer and to die of it than White or Asian men.

Risk factors for prostate cancer include increasing age, a family history, being African American, a high-fat diet, obesity, and physical inactivity. Some research suggests that high levels of testosterone may increase a man's chance of having prostate cancer. An inherited predisposition to prostate cancer may account for 5–10% of cases ("Links Between Genetic," 1999). Some early studies suggested that men who had a vasectomy were at a slightly greater risk for prostate cancer. However, more recent studies have not shown any increased risk among men who have had this surgery.

DETECTION   Various signs may point to prostate cancer, a slow-growing disease, but often there are no symptoms. Although these signs are more likely to indicate prostatic enlargement or benign tumors than cancer, they should never be ignored. They include the following:

- Weak or interrupted flow of urine
- Inability to urinate or difficulty in beginning to urinate
- Difficulty holding back urine
- Frequent need to urinate, especially at night; bed-wetting
- Urine flow that is not easily stopped
- Painful or burning urination
- Difficulty in having an erection
- Painful ejaculation
- Blood in urine or semen
- Continuing pain in lower back, pelvis, or upper thighs

All of these symptoms may be caused by cancer or less serious health problems.

The first step in diagnosing prostate cancer is to have a physician conduct a digital rectal exam (DRE). By inserting a finger into the rectum, the physician can usually feel an irregular or unusually firm area on the prostate that may indicate a tumor. If the physician discovers a suspicious area, he or she will then run a battery of tests, including X-rays, urine and blood analyses, and biopsy.

A blood test, called the **prostate-specific antigen (PSA) test,** can be used to help diagnose prostate cancer with 90% accuracy. This test is more accurate than previous methods in detecting prostate cancer, but levels of PSA can be elevated in men with a benign condition called prostatic hyperplasia. Ultrasound is often used as a follow-up to the PSA test to detect lumps too small to be felt. A needle biopsy of suspicious lumps can be performed to determine if the cells are benign or malignant.

Since the use of early-detection tests became more common beginning in about 1990, the prostate cancer death rate has decreased. But it has not been proved that this drop was the direct result of screening; the findings have been conflicting. Some research has shown that many, and probably most, tumors discovered during the screenings are so small and slow growing that they are unlikely to do any harm to patients. Prostate cancer develops slowly over many years, and most cases are not life threatening. Other research has shown that when dangerous tumors are found the mortality rates are usually the same among men who had regular screenings and those who did not see a physician until they developed symptoms. Still other studies have shown that those who get the screenings have a higher survival rate. The American Cancer Society recommends that, until more definitive research findings are established, whether a man has the screening is something that he and his physician can decide (American Cancer Society, 2003f; "Prostate Screenings Gain Acceptance," 2002; U.S. Preventive Services Task Force, 2002c).

TREATMENT   Eighty-five percent of all prostate cancers are detected while they are still in the prostate or nearby area, and the 5-year survival rate for these cancers is nearly 100%. Overall, 97% of men diagnosed with prostate cancer survive at least 5 years, and 79% survive at least 10 years. For the 6% of men whose cancer has already spread to other parts of the body, the 5-year survival rate is 34% (American Cancer Society, 2003f).

Depending on the stage of the cancer, treatment may include surgery, hormone therapy, radiation therapy, and chemotherapy. If the cancer has not spread beyond the prostate gland, all or part of the gland is removed by surgery. Radical surgery has a high cure rate, but it often results in incontinence and erectile dysfunction. An alternative to removal of the prostate is "watchful waiting," in which men do not have surgery immediately after cancer diagnosis but are closely followed by their physicians to see if their tumors begin to grow and advance. A recent study of Scandinavian men with early prostate cancer compared surgical removal with watchful waiting; it found that those who had surgery were less likely to die of prostate cancer itself than those treated with watchful waiting. But after 6 years of follow-up, the overall survival rate was about the same for the two groups. The study also found that sexual problems and urinary incontinence were more common in men who had surgery and that difficulty passing urine was a more common problem for men who were treated via watchful waiting (Holmberg et al., 2002; Steineck et al., 2002). A less invasive and equally effective treatment involves radiation (via radioactive seeds) surgically implanted in the prostate. Although the 5-year survival rate for this procedure is nearly 90%, it can also cause erectile dysfunction, rectal problems, and damage to the urinary tract.

Some men are using Viagra following prostate treatment. A study revealed that over half of men who had erectile dysfunction after radical treatment responded to Viagra (American Cancer Society, 2000). In any event, sensitive sex counseling should be an integral part of treatment. Some men who retain the ability to become erect experience retrograde ejaculation and are infertile because semen does not pass out of the urethra.

Testicular Cancer   According to the American Cancer Society (2003g), about 7600 new cases of testicular cancer were diagnosed in 2003, with an estimated 400 deaths. The exact cause of most cases of testicular cancer is unknown, but risk factors include age (most occur between the ages of 15 and 40), undescended testicle(s), a family history of testicular cancer, occupations that might involve greater exposure to certain chemicals, HIV

Practically Speaking   Testicular Self-Examination

SOME DOCTORS BELIEVE that a man increases the chances of early cancer detection by performing a monthly testicle self-exam. It is important that you know what your own testicles feel like normally so that you'll recognize any changes. The best time to perform the examination is after a warm shower or bath, when the scrotum is relaxed.

1. Stand in front of a mirror and look for any swelling on the scrotum.

2. Examine each testicle. With your thumb on top of the testicle and two fingers underneath, gently roll the testicle to check for lumps or areas of particular firmness. A normal testicle is smooth, oval, and uniformly firm to the touch. Don't worry if your testicles differ slightly in size; this is common. And don't mistake the epididymis, the sperm-carrying tube at the rear of the testicle, for an abnormality.

3. If you find any hard lumps or nodules, or if there has been any change in shape, size, or texture of the testicles, consult a physician. These signs may not indicate a malignancy, but only your physician can make a diagnosis.

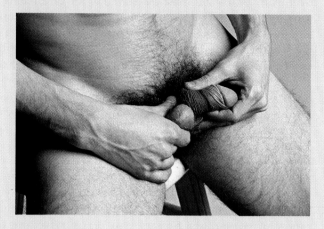

Testicular self-examination can enhance a man's familiarity with his genitals.

Source: From Fahey, T., Insel, P., & Roth, W. (2000). *Fit and Well: Core Concepts and Labs in Physical Fitness and Wellness.* Reprinted by permission of The McGraw-Hill Companies.

infection, cancer of the other testicle, and ethnicity. The risk of testicular cancer in the United States is 5 times greater for White men than for African American men and more than double that for Asian American men. The risk for Hispanics is between that of Asians and non-Hispanic Whites. The reasons for these differences are not known. In the past 40 years, rates of testicular cancer have more than doubled among White men but have remained the same for African Americans. Although some earlier studies raised the possibility of increased risk for testicular cancer following a vasectomy, recent studies have not found any such increased risk (American Cancer Society, 2003g).

DETECTION   Most cases of testicular cancer can be found at an early stage. The first sign of testicular cancer is usually a painless lump or slight enlargement and a change in the consistency of the testicle; the right testicle is more often involved than the left. Although the tumors that grow on the testes are generally painless, there is often a dull ache in the lower abdomen and groin, accompanied by a sensation of dragging and heaviness. If the tumor is growing rapidly, there may be severe pain in the testicles. Because of the lack of symptoms and pain in the early stage, men often do not go to a doctor for several months after discovering a slightly enlarged testicle.

The examination of a man's testicles is a valuable part of a general physical examination, and the American Cancer Society includes testicular examination in its recommendations for routine cancer-related checkups. Whether a man should perform a regular testicular self-examination is

476

debated. The American Cancer Society believes that it is important to make men aware of testicular cancer and to remind them that any testicular mass should be immediately evaluated by a physician. Some doctors recommend monthly testicular self-examination by all men after puberty. The American Cancer Society believes that for men with average testicular cancer risk there is no medical evidence to suggest that monthly examination is any more effective than simple awareness and prompt medical attention. However, whether to perform this examination is a decision best made by each man. Men with certain risk factors, such as previous testicular cancer or a family history, have an increased risk of developing testicular cancer, and they should consider monthly self-examinations and discuss the issue with their doctor (American Cancer Society, 2003g). Sometimes, ultrasound and blood tests are diagnostic tools for testicular cancer.

TREATMENT Testicular cancer is a highly treatable form of cancer. The three main methods of treatment are surgery, radiation therapy, and chemotherapy. After the affected testicle is removed, an artificial one may be inserted in the scrotal sac. Radiation treatment or chemotherapy may follow. Although the cure rate for all testicular cancer is over 90% (provided the disease has not widely metastasized), the treatment can result in the man becoming infertile. Sperm banks and support groups may be helpful resources for some men and their partners. The success of treatment for testicular cancer was recently highlighted by the athletic achievements of Lance Armstrong. Following treatment for testicular cancer, he won yet another Tour de France bicycle race.

Penile Cancer Cancer of the penis affects only 1 out of every 100,000 men in the United States. Although it is very rare in North America and Europe, it is more common in Africa and South America. Risk factors include HPV infection, smoking, smegma (the material that accumulates underneath the foreskin), and phimosis (difficulty in retracting the foreskin, resulting in more smegma). Many cases of penile cancer can be detected early on. Men should be alert to any unusual growths on or other abnormalities of the penis. If such changes occur, men should promptly consult a physician. Treatment options include surgery, radiation, and chemotherapy. Most early-stage penile cancers can be completely cured by fairly minor surgery; removal of all or part of the penis is rare. The overall survival rate for men with penile cancer is about 72%. The consensus among medical experts is that circumcision should not be done as a strategy for preventing penile cancer (American Cancer Society, 2003h).

Male Breast Cancer Breast cancer affects more than 1300 men in this country a year, which means it is 100 times more common among women. As is the case for women, most breast disorders in men are benign. Known risk factors include aging (the average age is about 65 at diagnosis), family history of breast cancer for both male and female blood relatives, Klinefelter's syndrome, radiation exposure, liver disease, physical inactivity and obesity, and estrogen treatment. Symptoms of possible breast cancer include a lump or swelling of the breast, skin dimpling or puckering, nipple retraction (turning inward), redness or scaling of the nipple or breast skin, and discharge from the nipple. Diagnosis involves clinical breast examination, mammography, ultrasound, nipple discharge examination, and biopsy. Male breast cancer is treated with surgery, radiation therapy, and chemotherapy. The survival rate is over 90% following early-stage detection (American Cancer Society, 2003i).

OTHER SEXUAL HEALTH ISSUES

In this section, we discuss two disorders of the female reproductive system, toxic shock syndrome and endometriosis, as well as some other sexual health issues. Sexually transmitted infections and related problems are discussed in Chapters 15 and 16.

Toxic Shock Syndrome

Toxic shock syndrome (TSS) is caused by the *Staphylococcus aureus* bacterium, a common agent of infection. This organism is normally present in the body and usually does not pose a threat. Tampons, especially the superabsorbent type, or other devices that block the vagina or cervix during menstruation apparently lead to the creation of an ideal culture medium for the overgrowth of staph bacteria. The annual incidence in women age 15–44 is 1–2 cases per 100,000, but 5% of the cases are fatal. TSS can occur in men, but it is uncommon.

The risk of developing TSS is quite low; after the initial epidemic in the late 1970s and early 1980s, the number of reported cases decreased significantly. The federal Food and Drug Administration (2000) advises all women who use tampons to reduce the already low risk by carefully following the directions for insertion, choosing the lowest-absorbing one for their flow, changing the tampon at least every 4 hours, alternating pads with tampons, and not using tampons between periods.

TSS can be treated effectively if it is detected. The warning signs are fever (101°F or higher), diarrhea, vomiting, muscle aches, and/or a sunburnlike rash. Early detection is critical; otherwise, TSS can do significant damage. Women should talk with their health-care provider about any new information regarding prevention.

Endometriosis

Endometriosis is one of the most common gynecological diseases; it affects at least 5.5 million women in the United States. Endometriosis involves the growth of endometrial tissue (uterine lining) outward into the organs surrounding the uterus. Between 2% and 10% of women of reproductive age are estimated to have endometriosis. Endometriosis can affect any menstruating woman from the time of her first period to menopause, regardless of whether she has had children, her race or ethnicity, and her socioeconomic status. The exact cause of endometriosis has not been identified. About 30–40% of women with endometriosis are infertile, making it among the top three causes of infertility in women (National Institute of Child Health and Human Development, 2002).

IN NEARLY 30 AFRICAN countries, some parts of Asia, and the Middle East, and immigrant communities elsewhere, female infants, girls, or young women may undergo **female genital mutilation (FGM)**. (Interestingly, some people have begun calling male circumcision male genital mutilation.) An estimated 135 million girls and women have undergone FGM. About 2 million girls a year are at risk for FGM. One type of FGM is **clitoridectomy,** or **female circumcision:** having their clitoris slit or cut out entirely and all or part of their labia sliced off. The sides of their vulvas or their vaginal openings may be stitched together—a process called **infibulation**—leaving only a tiny opening for the passage of urine and menstrual blood. These surgeries are generally performed with a knife, a razor, or even a tin can lid or piece of broken glass, without medical anesthesia; antiseptic powder or concocted pastes may be applied. Conditions are often unsanitary. The effects of these devastatingly painful operations include bleeding, infections, infertility, scarring, the inability to enjoy sex, and, not uncommonly, death. Upon marriage, a young woman may undergo considerable pain and bleeding as the entry to the vagina is reopened by tearing her flesh. In childbirth, the old wounds must be reopened surgically, or tearing will result.

This ancient custom, practiced mainly by Muslims but also by Christians and animists, is difficult for outsiders to understand. Why would loving parents allow this to be done to their defenseless daughter, and even hold her down during the procedure? As with many other practices (including male circumcision in our own culture), the answer is "tradition." Although the surgery undoubtedly began as a way of controlling women's sexuality (for many women, FMG does impair sexual enjoyment), many Muslims believe (erroneously) that it is required by the Koran, the Islamic holy book (Simons, 1993). A recent study of 1836 Nigerian women found no difference in the frequency of sex and coital orgasm in women having undergone female genital cutting and those not having done so (Okonofua, Larsen, Oronsage, Snow, & Slanger, 2002). Clitoridectomy was practiced by physicians in the nineteenth century in both England and the United States, mainly as a cure for masturbation, which was thought to awaken women's insatiable sexual appetites (Barker-Benfield, 1976). It continued in this country until at least 1937. "Female castration" (oophorectomy) and hysterectomy were practiced as cures for a variety of psychological disorders, especially between 1880 and 1900 but continuing well into the twentieth century.

Amnesty International (1998), a worldwide organization that promotes human rights, calls for the end of FGM, stating, "The World Health Organization condemns the practice of genital mutilation including cir-

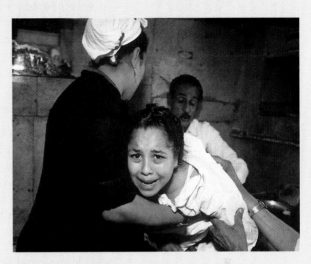

Female genital mutilation is common in many African, Asian, and Middle Eastern countries.

cumcision where women and girls are concerned and condemns the participation of physicians in the execution of such practices." In 1997, three United Nations organizations—the World Health Organization, the UN Children's Health Fund, and the UN Population Fund—released a joint plan for a major reduction in FGM within 10 years and complete eradication within three generations (Amnesty International, 1998). African medical workers stress the health dangers and feel that education has helped curb the practice to some degree. But there is still strong social pressure for it, and the operation often is carried out in secret. A law passed in 2001 prohibits FGM in Kenya but allows girls over age 16 to decide for themselves. Despite this law, forced female circumcision still occurs in rural Kenya (Lacey, 2002). The practice has been outlawed in Egypt, where a poll of nearly 15,000 women revealed that 97% of them had been circumcised ("Ban on Female Circumcision," 1997). Custom and gender identity are frequently cited reasons for FGM, as illustrated by these two quotes from Egyptian women (Amnesty International, 1998):

> "Of course I shall have them [my daughters] circumcised exactly as their parents, grandparents and sisters were circumcised. This is our custom."

> "We are circumcised and insist on circumcising our daughters so that there is no mixing between male and female. . . . An uncircumcised woman is put to shame by her husband, who calls her 'you with the clitoris.' Her organ would prick the man."

Symptoms of endometriosis include pain (usually pelvic pain, which can be very intense), very painful cramps or periods, and heavy periods. It is usually diagnosed by imaging tests (e.g., ultrasound) to produce a picture of the inside of the body or by laparoscopic examination. Prompt treatment is crucial if endometriosis is suspected. Hormone therapy, pain therapy, and/or surgery are used to treat it.

Lesbian Women's Health Issues

Research specifically focused on lesbian women did not begin until the 1950s. The origins of sexual orientation and the psychological functioning of lesbian women were major topics of study. During the 1970s, studies on lesbian women as psychologically healthy individuals emerged, and some of the research of the 1980s examined issues related to the development of lesbian women across their life span (Tully, 1995). The federal Insititute of Medicine Committee on Lesbian Health Research Priorities (1999) recommends three areas of additional health-related research priorities, one of which is specific to sexual orientation issues. The committee states that "research is needed to better understand how to define sexual orientation in general and lesbian sexual orientation in particular and to better understand the diversity of the lesbian population" (Institute of Medicine, 1999).

In addition to many of the medical concerns shared by all women, lesbian women face additional challenges. Several studies have shown that lesbian women encounter prejudice and discrimination when seeking health care (Rankow, 1997; Robertson, 1992; Stevens, 1992). First, it may be assumed that they are heterosexual, leading to the inclusion of inappropriate questions, comments, or procedures and the exclusion of appropriate measures. Second, if they do disclose their orientation, they are likely to be treated with hostility. As a result of these experiences, lesbian women are less likely than heterosexuals to seek health care. Thus, they may put themselves at higher risk for diseases that could be detected early on. Older lesbian women are especially vulnerable because they are not generally as willing to disclose their sexual orientation; they often feel "invisible." Surveys of lesbian women regarding health-care choices have found preferences for female practitioners, holistic approaches, preventive care and education, and woman-managed clinics (Lucas, 1992; Trippet & Bain, 1992).

Prostatitis

Many of men's sexual health problems are related to STIs. One condition affecting men that is not sexually transmitted is **prostatitis,** the inflammation of the prostate gland. Prostatitis may account for up to 25% of all office visits by young and middle-aged men for complaints involving the genital and urinary systems (National Institute of Diabetes and Digestive and Kidney Diseases, 2000). There are two types: infectious prostatitis and congestive prostatitis. Infectious prostatitis is generally caused by the *E. coli* bacterium. Congestive prostatitis usually results from abstention from ejaculation or infrequent ejaculation.

If a man does not ejaculate, this fluid begins to decompose, and the prostate becomes congested, causing congestive prostatitis. Congestive prostatitis can also be caused by dramatic changes in a man's sexual behavior

EACH TIME WORD of a new medical risk reaches us, we are thrown into confusion and possibly even despair. What do we do if we've just had a type of surgery that supposedly has no negative side effects, and now we read that it does? Or if we've been taking a medication that is suddenly purported to cause a life-threatening disease? Do we stop taking it? Health writer Jane Brody advises: Don't panic (Brody, 1993).

In assessing newly discovered medical "risks," we need to proceed calmly and carefully. Brody offers these questions for consideration:

- *What is the source of the report?* The most reliable studies appear in professional journals and on Web sites that are subject to peer review, such as *The New England Journal of Medicine, Journal of the American Medical Association, Lancet*, and *Med Pulse.* For example, unpublished studies done at private, nongovernment-funded institutions are probably not as reliable. Also potentially less reliable are the many Web sites that do not publish the credentials of an author or source of publication or that are not supported by a governmental or other reputable agency.

- *Are there other studies on the same subject?* Even in scientific studies, results can occur by chance alone. It is therefore important that findings be replicated by independent researchers before they are used as the basis for making radical changes.

- *What is the degree of risk compared with the benefits?* Even when doubled or tripled, a risk that was initially small does not become great (e.g., a 2% risk increases to a 4–6% risk). A 50% risk that increases by half (to 75%), however, is much more alarming. Also, a procedure or medication may increase some risks but greatly reduce others, so it is important not to generalize, but to consider risks versus benefits case by case.

- *Are there comparable but safer alternatives?* It may take some investigation, but there may be alternatives or variations to a procedure that are less risky.

- *Is the research biologically explainable or supported by animal studies?* If the study results are only theoretical and not based on actual biological findings, Brody suggests that researchers should be sent "scurrying to the laboratory." A risk that may be serious should be scientifically demonstrated as soon as possible.

patterns. The prostate develops its own production pattern based on the man's sexual activity; therefore, if a highly active man cuts back his sexual routine, his prostate will continue its high production levels and eventually become congested with fluid. Similarly, if the man goes from no ejaculations a day to several, he may develop congestive prostatitis. A man may need to adjust his frequency of ejaculations: Too few may result in prostate congestion, and too many may irritate the gland. However, a new study may dampen beliefs about ejaculating to avoid an enlarged prostate, at least when it comes to frequency of ejaculations. Researchers at the Mayo Clinic evaluated 2115 men age 40–79 to determine if any relationship exists between frequency of ejaculation and enlarged prostate. After adjusting for age, they found no relationship. However, men who ejaculated more often were in better health and reported more sexual satisfaction (Jacobson et al., 2003).

Symptoms of prostatitis include swelling in the genital area, a feeling of heat, difficult or painful urination that is often accompanied by a burning sensation, a frequent urge to urinate that often results in only a small amount of urine, and pain. Frequently, there is pain in the lower back. When there is infection, there may be a thin mucous discharge from the penis that may be visible in the morning before urination. Acute prostatitis often results in a loss of libido and painful ejaculations; chronic prostatitis is often associated with sexual dysfunction.

Infectious prostatitis resulting from a bacterial infection is treated with antibiotics. But treatment may be problematic, because antibiotics are unable to pass into the prostatic fluid, which acts as a reservoir for the infection.

Congestive prostatitis may be treated with warm baths and prostatic massage, which is done by inserting a finger in the anus and gently massaging the prostate. If the prostatitis is especially painful, any form of sexual excitement should be avoided. Neither prostatitis nor prostate enlargement is known to cause cancer. However, it is possible for men who have one or both of these conditions to develop prostate cancer as well.

DES Daughters and Sons

Between 1941 and 1971, an estimated 6 million women used **diethylstilbestrol (DES)**, a synthetic estrogen, to prevent miscarriages, particularly if they had a previous history of miscarriage or bleeding during pregnancy or were diabetic. About 3 million women whose mothers took DES were born during these years. They now range in age from early adulthood to middle age. Some grown children of women who were given DES while pregnant have developed genital tract abnormalities, including cancer. DES sons and daughters need to be aware of their special health needs and seek treatment accordingly.

IN THIS CHAPTER, WE'VE explored issues of self-image and body image as they interact with our society's ideas about beauty and sexuality. We've considered the effects of alcohol and certain drugs on our sexuality. We've looked at aging, physical limitations and disabilities, and cancer and other health issues. Our intent is to give you information to assist you in personal health issues and to stimulate thinking about how society deals with certain aspects of sexual health. We encourage you to learn more about your own body and your own sexual functioning. If things don't seem to work right, if you don't feel well, or if you have questions, consult your physician or other health-care practitioner. If you're not satisfied, get a second opinion. Read about health issues that apply to you and the people you're close to. Because we live in our bodies, we need to appreciate and respect them. By taking care of ourselves physically and mentally, we can maximize our pleasures in sexuality and in life.

SUMMARY

Living in Our Bodies: The Quest for Physical Perfection

- Our society is preoccupied with bodily perfection. As a result, *eating disorders* have become common, especially among young women. Eating disorders reduce a person's health and vigor; are carried out in secrecy; are accompanied by obsessions, depression, anxiety, and guilt; lead to self-absorption and emotional instability; and are characterized by a lack of control. Those with eating disorders may have a history of psychological or sexual abuse in childhood.

- *Anorexia nervosa* is characterized by an all-controlling desire for thinness. Those with anorexia, usually female teenagers, are convinced that their bodies are too large, no matter how thin they actually are.

Sexual difficulties often accompany anorexia. Those with anorexia diet (and often exercise) obsessively. Anorexia is potentially fatal.

- *Bulimia* is characterized by episodes of uncontrolled overeating (binge eating), counteracted by purging—vomiting, dieting, exercising excessively, or taking laxatives or diuretics.

- *Binge eating* is similar to bulimia except that the purging does not occur.

- *Anabolic steroids,* used to enhance body size and athletic performance, can cause serious and permanent body damage.

Alcohol, Drugs, and Sexuality

- Drugs and alcohol are commonly perceived as enhancers of sexuality, although in reality this is rarely the case. These substances have the effect of *disinhibition,* activating behaviors that would otherwise be suppressed.

- Some people use alcohol to give themselves permission to be sexual. Some men may use alcohol to justify sexual violence. People under the influence of alcohol or drugs tend to place themselves in risky sexual situations, such as exposing themselves to sexually transmitted infections.

Sexuality and Aging

- In their forties, women's fertility begins to decline. Generally, between ages 45 and 55, *menopause,* the cessation of menstrual periods, occurs. Other physical changes occur, which may or may not present problems. The most common are hot flashes, changes in the vagina, and a gradual loss of bone mass. *Postmenopausal hormone therapy (PHT)* is sometimes used to treat these symptoms. Women need to weigh the risks and benefits of PHT with their health-care provider.

- Men need to understand that slower sexual responses are a normal part of aging and are not related to the ability to give or receive sexual pleasure. About half of men experience some degree of prostate enlargement after age 50. If it is severe, surgery can be performed.

Sexuality and Disability

- A wide range of disabilities and physical limitations can affect sexuality. People with these limitations need support and education so they can enjoy their full sexual potential. Society as a whole needs to be aware of the concerns of the disabled and to allow them the same sexual rights as others.

- Chronic illnesses such as diabetes, cardiovascular disease, and arthritis pose special problems with regard to sexuality. People with these diseases (and their partners) can learn what to expect of themselves sexually and how to best cope with their particular conditions.

Sexuality and Cancer

- Cancer (in its many forms) occurs when cells begin to grow aberrantly. Most cancers form tumors. *Benign tumors* grow slowly and remain localized. *Malignant tumors* can spread throughout the body. When malignant cells are released into the blood or lymph system, they begin to grow away from the original tumor; this process is called *metastasis.*

- Breast cancer is the most common cancer among women. Although the survival rate is improving, those who survive it may still suffer psychologically. *Mammograms* (low-dose X-ray screenings) are the principal methods of detection. Surgical removal of the breast is called *mastectomy;* surgery that removes only the tumor and surrounding lymph nodes is called *lumpectomy.* Radiation and chemotherapy are also used to fight breast cancer. The decision to undertake breast reconstruction involves many issues.

- *Cervical dysplasia,* or *cervical intraepithelial neoplasia (CIN),* the appearance of certain abnormal cells on the cervix, can be diagnosed by a *Pap test.* It may then be treated by *biopsy,* cauterization, cryosurgery, or other surgery. If untreated, it may lead to cervical cancer.

- The most common gynecological cancer that poses a serious threat is uterine cancer; more than 99% of these cancers affect the endometrium, the uterine lining. Uterine cancer is treated with surgery (hysterectomy), radiation, or both.

- *Hysterectomy* is the surgical removal of the uterus. A hysterectomy is required when cancerous or precancerous growths cannot be treated otherwise, when noncancerous growths interfere with other organs, when heavy bleeding cannot be otherwise controlled, and when severe infection cannot be otherwise controlled. Other problems may sometimes require a hysterectomy. The removal of the ovaries *(oophorectomy)* will precipitate menopausal symptoms because the estrogen supply stops.

- Vaginal cancer represents only 3% of the cancers of the female reproductive system.

- Prostate cancer is the most common form of cancer among men. If detected early, it has a high cure rate. One useful test is the *prostate-specific antigen (PSA) test*. Surgery, radiation, hormone therapy, and chemotherapy are possible treatments. If the entire prostate is removed, sterility results, and erectile difficulties may occur.

- Testicular cancer primarily affects young men age 18–35. If caught early, it is curable; if not, it may be deadly. Self-examination is the key to detection; even slight symptoms should be reported at once.

- Penile cancer affects only 1 in 10,000 men in the United States, with most early-stage cancers being completely cured. Men can suffer from breast cancer, but this cancer is 140 times more common among women.

Other Sexual Health Issues

- *Toxic shock syndrome (TSS)* is a potentially fatal disease caused by the *Staphylococcus aureus* bacterium. The disease is easily cured with antibiotics if caught early.

- *Endometriosis* is the growth of endometrial tissue outside the uterus. It is a major cause of infertility. Symptoms include intense pelvic pain and abnormal menstrual bleeding. Treatment depends on a number of factors. Various hormone treatments and types of surgery are employed.

- Lesbian women tend to have poorer health care than heterosexual women, partly because they face hostility from health-care practitioners. Fear of discrimination may keep them from getting early diagnosis of serious diseases, such as breast cancer.

- *Prostatitis* is the inflammation of the prostate gland. Congestive prostatitis may be the result of a major change in frequency of ejaculation, although research has not shown a link between frequency of ejaculation and enlarged prostate. Infectious prostatitis is difficult to treat, although antibiotics are prescribed for it; chronic prostatitis is painful and can lead to sexual dysfunction.

- *DES (diethylstilbestrol)* is a synthetic estrogen that was widely prescribed between 1941 and 1971 to prevent miscarriages. Women who took DES, and their children, are subject to genital tract abnormalities, including cancer. DES sons and daughters need to be aware of their special health risks and seek treatment accordingly.

Sex and the Internet

Cancer and Sexuality

The American Cancer Society (ACS) has an extensive Web site that provides detailed information on prevention of and risk factors for, detection and symptoms of, and treatment for the various cancers, including those of the reproductive system. The impact of cancer of the reproductive structures on sexuality also is discussed. Go to the ACS Web site (http://www.cancer.org) to research this issue. After getting on the Web site, answer the following questions concerning a specific cancer:

- What are the risk factors for the cancer?

- How can the cancer be prevented?

- What are some of the methods used to treat this form of cancer?

- What are the sexuality-related outcomes of the cancer and its treatment?

SUGGESTED WEB SITES

American Prostate Society
http://www.ameripros.org
Provides information on the latest treatments for prostatitis, prostate cancer, prostate growth, and erectile dysfunction.

Harvard Center for Cancer Prevention
http://www.yourcancerrisk.harvard.edu
Provides information on many types of cancer, as well as questions to help individuals estimate the risk for 12 different cancers.

National Cancer Institute
http://bcra.nci.nih.gov/brc
Provides information on many types of cancer, as well as the Breast Cancer Risk assessment tool.

National Institutes of Health
http://www.nih.gov
Offers information on an array of health topics, including cancer.

National Prostate Cancer Coalition
http://www.4npcc.org
Contains information on prostate cancer, as well as outreach and advocacy information.

National Women's Health Network
http://www.womenshealthnetwork.org
Offers evidence-based, independent information about women's health issues online, by mail, and through an information clearinghouse.

North American Menopause Society
http://www.menopause.org
Contains information on perimenopause, early menopause, menopause symptoms and long-term effects of estrogen loss, and a wide variety of therapies to enhance health.

SUGGESTED READING

Journals with articles relevant to sexual health include *JAMA: Journal of the American Medical Association, The New England Journal of Medicine, Harvard Women's Health Watch,* and the British journal *Lancet.*

Blackburn, Maddie. (2000). *Sexuality and Disability.* Woburn, MA: Butterworth-Heinemann. A compassionate and comprehensive look at sexuality and disability.

Institute of Medicine. (1999). *Lesbian Health: Current Assessment and Directions for the Future.* Washington, DC: National Academy Press. A federal report on health issues and problems of lesbians and areas needing research.

Link, John; Forsthoff, Cynthia; & Waisman, James. (2003). *The Breast Cancer Survival Manual* (3rd ed.). New York: Owl Books. Updated information on the nature and biology of breast cancer, treatment options, side effects, and medications.

Love, Susan, & Lindsey, Karen. (2000). *Dr. Susan Love's Breast Book* (3rd ed.). Reading, MA: Perseus Book Group. Breast-care advice and information on breast cancer from a leading authority.

Peterson, K. Jean. (1996). *Health Care for Lesbians and Gay Men.* New York: Haworth Press. A discussion of the special needs of gay and lesbian individuals and how homophobia and heterosexism affect them.

Wingood, Fina, & DiClemente, Ralph. (2002). *Handbook of Women's Sexual and Reproductive Health.* New York: Kluwer Academic/Plenum Publishers. Examines social structures including historical, familial, developmental, the media, cultural factors, and gender issues that influence women's sexual and reproductive health.

For links, articles, and study material, go to the McGraw-Hill Web site, located at http://www.mhhe.com/strong5

14

Sexual Difficulties, Dissatisfaction, Enhancement, and Therapy

"*Sometimes my sexual desire gets so low that I will not be intimate with my girlfriend for a few weeks. And then there are times when sexual desire is so high that I can't control myself. Why is this?*"

— 19-year-old Latino male

"*My friend has a problem that seems to occur once every few months. He suddenly becomes not able to get erect. It seems like it happens very suddenly.*"

— 18-year-old Black male

"*When having a sexual experience with a new partner, I sometimes have a sense of guilt about past relationships. This can make performing in the new situation really difficult.*"

— 21-year-old White male

"*I have not experienced any sexual dysfunctions. On the other hand, I have been with my boyfriend for three years and I only had two orgasms. I enjoy having sex with him even though I don't have an orgasm every time. Sometimes I'm really into it, but sometimes I'm not. I do sometimes feel like something is wrong, but I do feel it is normal and okay as long as I enjoy it. I guess I may be thinking about it too hard, but like I said, I enjoy it either way.*"

— 21-year-old Black female

"*I always had a really low sex drive with past boyfriends. I never understood why until I started dating my current boyfriend. The key is communication! We're open with each other and honest about what we like and dislike. Now my sex drive is through the roof!*"

— 20-year-old White female

*T*HE QUALITY OF OUR SEXUALITY is intimately connected to the quality of our lives and relationships. Because our sexuality is an integral part of ourselves, it reflects our excitement and boredom, intimacy and distance, emotional well-being and distress, and health and illness. As a consequence, our sexual desires and activities ebb and flow. Sometimes, they are highly erotic; other times, they may be boring. Furthermore, many of us who are sexually active may sometimes experience sexual difficulties or problems, often resulting in disappointment in ourselves, our partners, or both. Studies indicate that many men and women report occasional or frequent lack of desire, problems in arousal or orgasm, and pain during intercourse or noncoital sex. (Later in this chapter, we discuss the prevalence and predictions of sexual difficulties found in two nationally representative studies to illustrate the commonality of sexual problems.) The widespread variability in our sexual functioning suggests how "normal" at least occasional sexual difficulties are. Sex therapist Bernie Zilbergeld (1999) wrote:

> Sex problems are normal and typical. I know, I know, all of your buddies are functioning perfectly and never have a problem. If you really believe that, I have a nice piece of oceanfront property in Kansas I'd like to talk to you about.

In this chapter, we look at several common sexual difficulties, their causes, and ways to enhance your sexuality to bring greater pleasure and intimacy.

SEXUAL DIFFICULTIES: DEFINITIONS, TYPES, AND PREVALENCE

Nearly all of the literature concerning sexual difficulties or problems with sexual functioning deals with heterosexual couples; thus, most of the discussion in this chapter reflects that bias. Unfortunately, too little research has been done on the sexual difficulties of gay, lesbian, bisexual, or transgendered individuals and couples. One study a number of years ago did find that heterosexual individuals, gay men, and lesbian women experience similar kinds of sexual problems (Margolies, Becher, & Jackson-Brewer, 1988). However, further research is needed on sexual difficulties among varied populations.

Defining Sexual Difficulties: Different Perspectives

The line between "normal" sexual functioning and a sexual difficulty or problem is not always clear. Enormous variation exists in levels of sexual desire and forms of expression, and these differences do not necessarily indicate any sexual difficulty. It can be difficult to determine exactly when something is a sexual problem, and so we must be careful in defining a particular sexual functioning difficulty as a problem. Some people have rigid and possibly unrealistic expectations for their own or their partner's sexual performance and may perceive something wrong with their behavior that need not be considered a "sexual problem." Still, people sometimes experience difficulties in sexual functioning that are so persistent that they would benefit from sex therapy.

Health-care providers, including sex therapists, need to be aware of different types of sexual functioning difficulties that can interfere with sexual satisfaction and intimacy. Therefore, a structure to diagnose and address difficulties can be valuable. However, there has been some debate among sexuality and mental health professionals about which terms accurately describe sexual difficulties and how to classify sexual difficulties. Though categories such as "dysfunction," "disorder," "difficulty," and "problem" have been used, this chapter presents alternate classification models.

The standard medical diagnostic classification of sexual difficulties is found in the American Psychiatric Association's *Diagnostic and Statistical Manual of Mental Disorders* (2000), which uses the terms "dysfunction" and "disorders." Because the *DSM*'s is the most widely used classification system, the discussion of various sexual difficulties in the professional literature is largely based on the *DSM* and uses the terms "sexual dysfunction" and "sexual disorders." Thus, the *DSM* terminology is quoted often in this chapter, particularly in the context of the *DSM* categories of sexual dysfunction.

An alternative term to "sexual dysfunction" is **sexual dissatisfaction.** Sexual dissatisfaction is a common outcome of a difficulty in sexual functioning.

In contrast to the broad medical focus of the *DSM* term, this term reflects an individual perception. That is, a person or couple could experience some of the *DSM* dysfunctions yet be satisfied with their sex lives. The difficulty might be considered a "dysfunction" only when the two people are dissatisfied and decide they may have a problem. The "dissatisfaction" concept is a fundamental tenet of the new classification system for women's sexual problems of the Working Group for a New View of Women's Sexual Problems (2001). The system begins with a woman-centered definition of sexual problems as "discontent or dissatisfaction with any emotional, physical, or relational aspects of sexual experience"—a definition that could also be applied to men. Furthermore, according to the World Health Organization's International Classification of Diseases (ICD-10) (1992), "sexual dysfunction" includes "the various ways in which an individual is unable to participate in a sexual relationship as he or she would wish."

An advantage of the term "sexual dissatisfaction" is that it acknowledges sexual scripts as individual and avoids an overarching definition of what is "normal" versus what is dysfunctional (i.e., pathological). Adopting this subjective and personal view might help people be more comfortable with their own sexuality and less likely to feel "sexually flawed." We favor the terms "sexual difficulties" and "sexual dissatisfaction" and use them in this chapter whenever possible. However, in citing reports or research related to sexual difficulties, we often utilize the terms used therein.

Three alternate classifications of sexual difficulties and dissatisfaction, based on medical and feminist models, illustrate different perspectives on the origins and causes of sexual problems: the *DSM*, the Consensus Development Panel on Female Sexual Dysfunction, and the Working Group for a New View of Women's Sexual Problems.

***The* Diagnostic and Statistical Manual of Mental Disorders**   The fourth edition (text revision) of the American Psychiatric Association's *Diagnostic and Statistical Manual of Mental Disorders (DSM-IV-TR)* (2000) labels sexual difficulties as disorders and characterizes them according to the four phases of Masters and Johnson's sexual response cycle. The *DSM-IV-TR* defines **sexual dysfunctions** as "disturbance in sexual desire and in the psychophysiological changes that characterize the sexual response cycle and cause marked distress and interpersonal difficulty" (Table 14.1). For any clinical diagnosis of sexual disorders, the term "persistent or recurrent" must also apply. The disorders could occur at one or more of the response cycle stages, meaning that a person could have more than one disorder, as often occurs. The *DSM-IV-TR* notes that other factors—such as age, psychological problems, sexual desires and expectations, ethnic and sociocultural background, the adequacy of sexual stimulation during sexual encounters, and drug use—should be considered in making any diagnosis of sexual disorders. The *DSM-IV-TR* contains disorders associated with sexual pain and includes a category called "sexual dysfunction due to general medical concern." The essential feature of the later category is the presence of a clinically significant sexual dysfunction that is judged to be due exclusively to the direct physiological effects of a general medical condition.

For each sexual dysfunction, the *DSM-IV-TR* has subtypes based on the onset of the dysfunction and the context in which it occurs. Lifelong dysfunctions are those present since the beginning of sexual functioning;

Is it not strange that desire should so many years outlive performance?

—*William Shakespeare*
(1564–1616)

TABLE 14.1 *DSM-IV-TR* Categories of Sexual Dysfunctions	
Disorder	*Symptoms or Characteristics*
Sexual Desire Disorders	
Hypoactive sexual desire disorder	Persistent or recurrent absence or deficiency of sexual fantasies and desire for sexual activity, causing marked or interpersonal difficulty
Sexual aversion disorder	Aversion to and active avoidance of genital sexual contact with a sex partner, causing marked or interpersonal difficulty
Sexual Arousal Disorders	
Female sexual arousal disorder	Inability to attain and maintain an adequate lubrication-swelling response to sexual excitement until completion of sexual activity, causing marked or interpersonal difficulty
Male erectile disorder	Inability to attain or maintain an adequate erection until completion of sexual activity, causing marked or interpersonal difficulty
Orgasmic Disorders	
Female orgasmic disorder	Delay or absence of orgasm following normal sexual excitement, causing marked or interpersonal difficulty
Male orgasmic disorder	Delay or absence of orgasm following normal sexual excitement, causing marked or interpersonal difficulty
Premature ejaculation	Ejaculation with minimal sexual stimulation, before the person or partner desires it, causing marked or interpersonal difficulty
Sexual Pain Disorders	
Dyspareunia	Persistent or recurrent pain associated with intercourse in either the female or male, causing marked or interpersonal difficulty
Vaginismus	Involuntary spasms of the vaginal muscles that interfere with penetration, causing marked or interpersonal difficulty

acquired patterns develop only after a period of normal functioning. A generalized pattern of dysfunction is one that occurs in practically all sexual situations; a situational type of dysfunction is limited to certain types of situations, stimulation, or partners. In most instances, the dysfunction whether generalized or situational, occurs during sexual activity with a partner. The acquired and situational dysfunctions typically are more successfully addressed in sex therapy.

Although the *DSM-IV-TR* is the most widely used categorization of sexual disorders, it largely reflects a psychiatric medical model and has been criticized. Further, it generally presents problems only in the heterosexual context.

Consensus Development Panel on Female Sexual Dysfunction   The goal of a panel of sexuality clinicians and research experts (the first Consensus Development Panel on Female Dysfunction) was to develop a consensus-based definition and classification system for female sexual difficulties (Basson et al., 2001). The panel noted that, "in contrast to the widespread interest in research and treatment of male sexual dysfunction, less attention has been paid to the sexual problems of women" and asserted the need for new definitions and classifications of female sexual dysfunction, as well as a new set of diagnostic criteria.

The "new" classification system developed by the panel is very similar to the four basic sexual dysfunction categories of the *DSM* (1994) and the ICD-10: desire, arousal, orgasmic, and sexual pain (from intercourse or noncoital stimulation) disorders. The consensus panel divided female sexual dysfunction into specific disorders that cause personal distress:

- *Desire disorder:* persistent hypoactive sexual desire disorder and sexual aversion disorder
- *Sexual arousal disorder:* persistent inability to attain or maintain sufficient sexual excitement
- *Orgasmic disorder:* persistent difficulty or delay in or absence of orgasm following sufficient stimulation
- *Sexual pain disorder:* persistent genital pain associated with sexual intercourse or noncoital stimulation

According to the panel report, these four categories were maintained for continuity in research and clinical practice.

This new classification has been criticized for, among other things, following the traditional Masters and Johnson model of sexual response (arousal followed by orgasm), which may reflect males' experiences with sex more than that of females. And some critics questioned the independence of the panel, which was sponsored by several pharmaceutical companies.

A New View of Women's Sexual Problems   An alternative perspective on female sexual problems has been proposed by a group of sexuality-related clinicians and social scientists, one that is more useful in understanding and treating women's sexual problems (Working Group for a New View of Women's Sexual Problems, 2001). Being a rather drastic departure from the other two classification systems described in this chapter, we highlight the report in the box "A New View of Women's Sexual Problems."

Prevalence and Cofactors

Local and national studies have been conducted concerning the prevalence of sexual difficulties. Two national studies are featured here: The National Health and Social Life Survey and The Kinsey Institute's survey of women in heterosexual relationships.

The National Health and Social Life Survey: Sexual Dysfunction Findings   The National Health and Social Life Survey (NHSLS) (1999), according to the authors, "provides the first population-based assessment of sexual dysfunction in the half-century since Kinsey et al." Using a national

THE WORKING GROUP for a New View of Women's Sexual Problems, a group of clinicians and social scientists, offers a new classification system called "A New View of Women's Sexual Problems" (Working Group for a New View of Women's Sexual Problems, 2001). According to their report, "Women's sexual problems differ from men's in basic ways which are not being examined or addressed." The goal of the group was to propose a new and more useful system of classifying women's sexual difficulties based on women's own needs and sexual realities.

The Working Group believes that a fundamental barrier to understanding women's sexuality is the *DSM* medical classification system. It contends that the *DSM* framework has shortcomings as applied to women, in that it "reduces sexual problems to disorders of physiological function compared to breathing or digestive disorders." The distortions of female sexuality mentioned by the group include the following:

- *A false notion of sexual equivalency between men and women.* Early researchers emphasized similarities in men's and women's physiological responses during sexual activities and concluded that their sexual problems must also be similar. The few studies that asked women to describe their own experiences found significant differences. For example, women's accounts vary from Masters and Johnson's four-phase model; many women do not separate "arousal" from "desire," and many care more about subjective feelings than physical arousal. Furthermore, the focus on genital and physiological response similarities between men and women "ignores the implications of inequalities related to gender, social class, ethnicity, sexual orientation, etc."

- *The unacknowledged role of relationships in sexuality.* The group states that the *DSM* does not address the relational aspects of women's sexuality, which are often fundamental to sexual satisfaction and problems. The *DSM* describes sexual problems from a broad-based, nonindividual perspective and "assumes that if the sexual parts work, there is no problem; and if the parts don't work, there is a problem." However, many women do not define their sexual difficulties in these terms. The group contends that the *DSM* reduction of "normal sexual functioning" to physiology implies, incorrectly, that sexual dissatisfaction can be treated without considering the relationship in which sex occurs.

- *The leveling of differences among women.* The group contends that women are dissimilar, and the varied components of their sexuality do not fit neatly into the categories of desire, arousal, orgasm, or pain. Rather, "women differ in their values, approaches to sexuality, social and cultural backgrounds, and current situations, and these differences cannot be smoothed over into an identical notion of 'dysfunction'—or an identical one-size-fits-all treatment."

A New Classification

The Working Group suggests a women-centered definition of sexual problems "as discontent or dissatisfaction with any emotional, physical, or relational aspect of sexual experience," which may arise in one or more of four categories underlying the dissatisfaction. These causes are usually attributed, not to medical problems, but to individual sexual distress and inhibition arising from cultural and relational factors such as the following:

- *Sociocultural, political, or economic factors.* These include inadequate sexuality education, lack of access to health services, a perceived inability to meet cultural norms regarding correct or ideal sexuality, inhibitions due to conflict between the sexual norms of the subculture or culture of origin and those of the dominant culture, and a lack of interest, time, or energy due to family and work obligations.

- *Partner and relationship problems.* These include discrepancies in desire for sexual activity or in preferences for various sexual activities, inhibitions about communicating preferences, loss of interest due to conflicts over commonplace issues, and inhibitions due to a partner's health status or sexual problems.

- *Psychological problems.* These include past abuse; problems with attachment, rejection, cooperation, or entitlement; fear of pregnancy and sexually transmitted infections (STIs); and loss of partner or reputation.

- *Medical factors.* These include numerous local or systemic medical conditions, pregnancy, STIs, and side effects of drugs, medications, and medical treatments, including surgery.

If you are a woman, does the new classification system make sense to you? If you are a man, consider asking a woman for her views of the classification. Are there other factors that should be added to this classification? Would the factors of the new classification also be applicable to men's sexual problems? If not, what factors should be added or deleted?

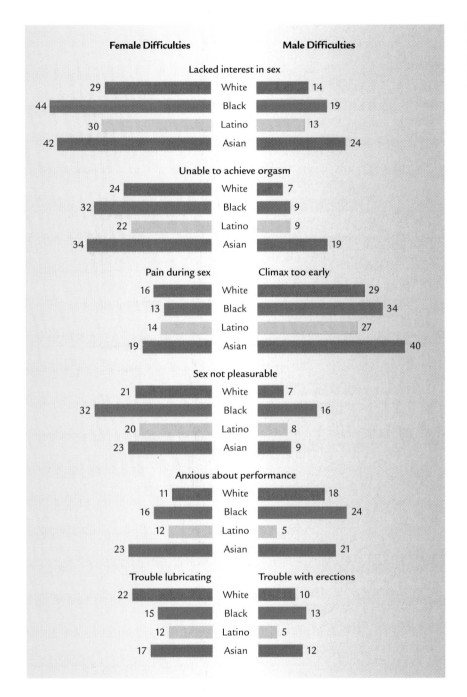

FIGURE 14.1 Percentage of Sexual Difficulties in the Past 12 Months by Gender and Ethnicity. (*Source:* Adapted from Laumann et al., 1999.)

sample of 1749 women and 1410 men age 18–59, the researchers found that self-reported sexual difficulties are widespread and are influenced by both health-related and psychosocial factors. According to the NHSLS, sexual difficulties were more prevalent among women (43%) than men (31%) (Figure 14.1) and were generally most common among young women and older men (Figure 14.2). For both genders, African Americans are more likely to have sexual problems, and Latinos are less likely to. Sexual difficulties are associated with poor quality of life, although females appear to

FIGURE 14.2 Percentage of Sexual Difficulties in the Past 12 Months by Gender and Age.
(*Source:* Adapted from Laumann et al., 1994.)

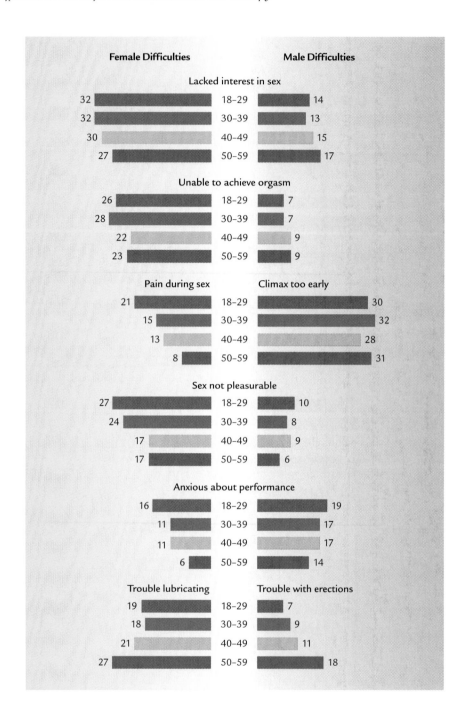

be impacted by this factor more than males. Those who experienced emotional or stress-related problems had more difficulties. Those having had an STI, reporting moderate to high consumption of alcohol, or (for men) having been circumcised generally were not any more likely to have had a sexual difficulty. Having had more than five lifetime partners or regularly masturbating did not generally increase the relative risk for sexual difficulty for either women or men. Other important findings by gender include the following:

Females

- The prevalence of sexual problems for women tends to decrease with increasing age except for those who report trouble lubricating.

- Nonmarried women are about 1.5 times as likely to have orgasm problems and sexual anxiety as married women.

- Women who have graduated from college are about half as likely to experience low sexual desire, problems achieving orgasm, sexual pain, and sexual anxiety as women who have not graduated from high school. Overall, women with lower educational attainment report less pleasure with sex and greater levels of sexual anxiety.

- African American women have higher rates of low sexual desire and derive less sexual pleasure than White women, and Whites are more likely to have sexual pain. Overall, Latinas experience lower rates of sexual problems than other women, and African American women appear more likely to have sexual problems.

- Poor health is associated with sexual pain for women.

- Deterioration in economic status is associated with a moderate increase in sexual difficulties for women.

- Women with low sexual activity or interests are at higher risk for low sexual desire and arousal problems.

- Rates of difficulties are the same for women who report any same-sex activity and those who do not.

- Sexual arousal problems appear to be more common among women who have experienced sexual victimization through adult-child or forced sexual contact.

- All types of sexual difficulties are correlated with levels of physical and emotional satisfaction and happiness.

Males

- The prevalence of erectile problems and lack of sexual desire increases with age for men.

- Nonmarried men report higher rates for most sexual difficulties than married men.

- Male college graduates are only two-thirds as likely to report early orgasm and half as likely to report nonpleasurable sex and sexual anxiety as men who have not graduated from high school.

- Men with poor health have an elevated risk for all types of sexual difficulties.

- Deterioration in economic position is generally related to erectile difficulties in men.

- Low sexual activity or interest is not related to low sexual desire and arousal problems in men.

- Men reporting any same-sex activity are more than 2 times as likely to experience early ejaculation and low sexual desire.

- Male victims of adult-child sexual contact are 3 times as likely to experience erectile difficulties and 2 times as likely to experience early ejaculation and low sexual desire than those who have not been victims of adult-child sexual contact.

- Men who have sexually assaulted women are 3½ times as likely to report erectile difficulty.
- Men reporting erectile dysfunction and low sexual desire experience diminished quality of life, but those with early ejaculation are not affected.

Distress About Sex: A National Survey of Women in Heterosexual Relationships   The Kinsey Institute studied the prevalence of distress about sexuality and predictors of such distress among a national sample of women in a random telephone survey (Bancroft, Loftus, & Long, 2003). The sample included 835 White and African American women age 20–65 who had been in a heterosexual relationship for at least 6 months. In the study, 24.4% of the women reported "marked distress" about their sexual relationship, their own sexuality, or both, within the previous month. This figure is much lower than the NHSLS finding that 43% of women have one or more sexual dysfunctions.

The best predictors of sexual distress in the Kinsey study were markers of general emotional well-being and the emotional relationship with the partner during sexual activity. That is, women with good mental health who felt close to their partner during sex were most likely to be sexually satisfied. Physical aspects of sexual response in women, including arousal, vaginal lubrication, and orgasm, were poor predictors. The Kinsey report also stated, "In general, the predictors of distress about sex did not fit well with the *DSM-IV-TR* criteria for the diagnosis of sexual dysfunction in women." Dr. John Bancroft, director of The Kinsey Institute and lead author of the study, notes that a woman who is distressed or has children and a job might put sex aside for a while as an adaptive behavior, not because there is anything wrong with her or she is dysfunctional (Elias, 2003). The report also cautioned that treatment for "sexual dysfunction" should consider whether the difficulty is the primary problem or a "reaction to circumstances."

Disorders of Sexual Desire

Hypoactive Sexual Desire Disorder   The persistent or recurrent deficiency or lack of sexual fantasies and desire for sexual activity that causes marked distress or interpersonal difficulty is called **hypoactive sexual desire (HSD)** in the *DSM-IV-TR* (2000). It is sometimes called "inhibited sexual desire" or "low sexual desire." This disorder may encompass all types of sexual behavior or may be limited to one partner or to a specific problem such as arousal or orgasm difficulties. In the NHSLS, about 3 out of 10 women report a lack of interest in sex, although the number decreases slightly with age; fewer men report HSD disorder, with a very slight increase with age (see Figure 14.2).

Defining low desire is tricky and often subjective as there is no norm level for sexual desire. Certainly, sexually "normal" people vary considerably in their sexual fantasies and desires. People with HSD disorder reluctantly participate in sex when it is initiated by a partner. Most often, the disorder develops in adulthood in association with psychological distress resulting from depression, stressful life events, or interpersonal difficulties. The loss of desire, whether ongoing or situational, can negatively affect a relationship (American Psychiatric Association, 2000). Anger within a relationship can also diminish sexual desire. Over time, if the anger is not resolved, it may develop into resentment or hatred that colors every aspect of the relationship. Most people cannot experience sexual desire for someone with whom they are angry or whom they deeply resent. Drugs, hormone deficiency, and illness can also decrease desire.

Gay men and lesbian women may experience HSD disorder if they are having difficulty with their sexual orientation (Margolies et al., 1988; Reece, 1988).

Sexual Aversion Disorder According to the *DSM-IV-TR*, persistent and recurrent aversion to and avoidance of genital contact with a partner that causes marked distress is called **sexual aversion disorder.** The possibility of sexual contact may cause anxiety, disgust, or fear in a person with this disorder, and some sufferers create covert strategies (e.g., traveling, sleeping, or being heavily involved with work) to avoid sex (American Psychiatric Association, 2000). A mere kiss, touch, or caress may cause a phobic response out of fear that it might lead to something sexual. Sometimes, these responses are internalized; other times, they can lead to panic attacks and physiological responses such as sweating, nausea, vomiting, and diarrhea. For people with this disorder, the frequency of sexual contact with a partner is rare and can lead to severe relationship stress. Sexual aversion often results from severely negative parental attitudes during childhood; sexual trauma, such as rape or sexual abuse, especially in women; consistent sexual pressure from a long-term partner; a history of erectile difficulties in men; and/or gender identity confusion (Masters, Johnson, & Kolodny, 1992).

As with heterosexuals, gay men and lesbian women may enjoy certain activities, such as kissing or mutual masturbation, but feel aversion to other activities. For gay men, sexual aversion often focuses on issues of anal eroticism (Reece, 1988). For lesbian women, it may focus on cunnilingus (Nichols, 1987), which is often their preferred activity for reaching orgasm.

Interestingly, the *DSM-IV-TR* does not include a "hyperactive sexual desire disorder," implying that its authors, mental health professionals, do not believe that high sexual desire is a mental disorder. This is contrary to the view of the general public and some professionals who espouse the concept of sexual addiction (see Chapter 10). Sexual desire exists on a continuum, with some people having very low desire and others having very high desire. Most people seem to be somewhere in the middle, however.

Sexual Arousal Disorders

Female Sexual Arousal Disorder The persistent or recurring inability to attain or maintain the level of vaginal lubrication and swelling associated with sexual excitement, causing marked distress or interpersonal difficulty, is called **female sexual arousal disorder** by the *DSM-IV-TR*. This disorder may be accompanied by sexual desire disorder and female orgasmic disorder. The term "frigid" was once used to describe this problem, but this pejorative and value-laden term is no longer used by professionals. This difficulty can occur when a woman desires sex but has difficulty maintaining arousal, resulting in vaginal dryness and tightness and subsequent discomfort if sex is attempted. About one-fifth to one-quarter of women in the NHSLS report trouble lubricating, with increasing difficulty as they age (see Figure 14.2). Female sexual arousal disorder is often accompanied by sexual desire and orgasm disorders, as well as sexual avoidance and stress in sexual relationships. If there are no physiological or substance use reasons for poor lubrication, this disorder is diagnosed as psychological in origin (American Psychiatric Association, 2000). However, the lack of vaginal lubrication may be misleading, as some women reporting dryness indicate the presence of sexual excitement and arousal. These women often use artificial lubricants.

Male Erectile Disorder   The persistent or recurring inability to attain or maintain an adequate erection until completion of sexual activity, causing marked distress or interpersonal difficulty, is called **male erectile disorder,** or **erectile dysfunction,** by the *DSM-IV-TR*. At one time, this disorder was called "impotence," but like "frigid," this value-laden and pejorative term is no longer used. This was a very common male sexual difficulty treated by therapists, before the introduction of Viagra. Sexual anxiety, fear of failure, high performance standards, concerns about sexual performance, and low sexual excitement, as well as specific medical conditions and medications, are often associated with male erectile disorder (American Psychiatric Association, 2000).

The prevalence of male erectile disorder increases with age, with more than twice as many men age 50–59 reporting problems with erections as men age 18–29 in the NHSLS (see Figure 14.2). A study sponsored by Viagra maker Pfizer of 2400 men (600 each in four countries) found male erectile disorder to be a problem worldwide. In response to a standardized questionnaire, 34% of men in Japan, 22% in Malaysia, 17% in Italy, and 15% in Brazil were either never or only sometimes able to maintain an erection. Erectile difficulties increased with age, affecting 9% of men age 40–44 years and 54% of those age 65–70 years (Nicolosi et al., 2003).

It is important to note that, like female arousal disorders, male erectile disorders are not an inevitable consequence of aging. However, the health problems that often accompany aging increase the disorder's prevalence. The prevalence of erectile difficulty has been directly correlated with certain diseases, such as hypertension, diabetes mellitus, and heart disease; certain medications, such as cardiac drugs and antihypertensives; cigarette smoking in association with treated heart disease and treated hypertension; excessive alcohol consumption; suppression and expression of anger; and depression (Feldman, Goldstein, Hatzichristou, Krane, & McKinlay, 1994).

The diagnosis of male erectile disorder is usually psychologically based. Men who have erections while sleeping or masturbating obviously are physically able to have erections, meaning that an erectile disorder during two-person sexual activity has a psychological origin. As with the other *DSM-IV-TR* sexual dysfunctions, male erectile disorder is typically diagnosed only when the man or his partner is dissatisfied and distressed by the occurrence (Schwartz, 2000).

Persistent Sexual Arousal Syndrome   A sexual problem not included in the *DSM-IV-TR* and only recently described in the professional literature is **persistent sexual arousal syndrome (PSAS).** Sex therapists Sandra Leiblum

> Thou treacherous, base deserter of
>   my flame,
> False to my passion, fatal to my
>   fame,
> Through what mistaken magic dost
>   thou prove
> So true to lewdness, so untrue to
>   love?
>
> —*John Wilmot, Earl of Rochester*
> *(1647–1680)*

and Sharon Nathan note several cases of women reporting that their sexual arousal does not resolve in ordinary ways and continues for hours, days, or even weeks (Leiblum & Nathan, 2001). The therapists state that the women came to them for therapy because of distress about their symptoms, but they point out that other women may not find the symptoms to be upsetting. To date, no obvious hormonal, vascular, neurological, or psychological causative factors have been linked to PSAS. The number of women experiencing PSAS is unknown, because some women may be embarrassed to report it to their health-care provider or not be distressed by it. Leiblum and Nathan hope that their report will stimulate further efforts to investigate PSAS. The recent identification of PSAS highlights the fact that female sexuality is underinvestigated and not adequately understood.

Orgasmic Disorders

Female Orgasmic Disorder   According to the *DSM-IV-TR,* the persistent and recurrent absence of or delay in orgasm for women following normal sexual excitement is called **female orgasmic disorder.** It is one of the most common sexual difficulties treated by therapists. This disorder has also been called anorgasmia, inorgasmia, pre-orgasmia, and the pejorative "frigidity." Some women who enjoy sexual activity with a partner have difficulty achieving orgasm with them, thereby sometimes causing dissatisfaction or distress within the relationship. Many women with female orgasmic disorder have negative or guilty attitudes about their sexuality, as well as relationship difficulties. Inadequate sexual stimulation is also a factor in this disorder (American Psychiatric Association, 2000).

In the NHSLS, about one-quarter of women report they were unable to achieve orgasm with a partner in the past 12 months, although the percentage decreases slightly with age (see Figure 14.2). No relationship between certain personality traits or psychopathology has been found, nor is vaginal size or pelvic muscle strength associated with orgasm. Most female orgasmic disorders are lifelong rather than acquired problems; once a woman learns how to have an orgasm, it is uncommon for her to lose that capacity (American Psychiatric Association, 2000).

Women have a wide variation in the type or intensity of stimulation that results in orgasm. Some women can achieve orgasm during intercourse only; others can achieve orgasm only through manual or oral simulation, illustrating a possible problem in defining this sexual difficulty. Should the context of this difficulty be considered? The *DSM-IV-TR* does not specify the context of orgasm difficulties. For example, should a woman be considered to have female orgasmic disorder if she is able to have an orgasm by masturbation but not during intercourse even though she desires to? This woman may seek therapy to address her disappointment at not having an orgasm during coitus. Many factors can inhibit female orgasm during intercourse (Table 14.2). Female orgasm is not universal; 10–15% of women never have orgasms, and another 10–15% have them rarely. Do women need to have orgasms to feel sexually satisfied with their partners? As described in the box "Sex and the Big 'O'," many women surveyed for the NHSLS report that they do not need to have an orgasm to be physically and emotionally satisfied with sex.

TABLE 14.2 Factors Inhibiting Women's Orgasm During Coitus	
Factors	Percentage Affected
Lack of foreplay	63.8
Fatigue	53.6
Preoccupation with nonsexual thoughts	45.5
Ejaculation too soon after intromission[a]	43.1
Conflicts between partners unrelated to intromission	34.6
Lack of interest or foreplay by partner	24.3
Lack of adequate vaginal lubrication	23.7
Lack of tenderness by partner	22.7
Lack of privacy for intromission	20.3
Overindulgence in alcohol	16.3
Desire to perform well after intromission	14.9
Difficulty with sexual arousal with partner	14.3
Painful sexual intercourse	12.0
Overeating	10.3

[a]Insertion of the penis into the vagina.

Source: Darling, C. A., Davidson, J. K., & Cox, R. P. (1991). "Female Sexual Response and the Timing of Partner Orgasm." *Journal of Sex and Marital Therapy, 17*(1), 11.

Male Orgasmic Disorder   The *DSM-IV-TR* defines **male orgasmic disorder** as the persistent or recurrent delay in or absence of orgasm following a normal sexual excitement phase of Masters and Johnson's sexual response cycle that causes marked distress or interpersonal difficulty. Because ejaculation and orgasm are two separate events (see Chapter 4), the delay or absence of ejaculation is a more accurate description of the disorder. A component of this disorder is **inhibited ejaculation,** in which the man is unable to ejaculate no matter how long stimulation is maintained. In **delayed ejaculation,** the man is not able to ejaculate easily; it may take 40 minutes or more of concentrated thrusting before ejaculation occurs. In the NHSLS, only a small percentage of men were unable to achieve orgasm (i.e., unable to ejaculate) (see Figure 14.2).

In the most common form of male orgasm disorder, the man cannot ejaculate during intercourse but can ejaculate from a partner's manual or oral stimulation. To be considered a disorder, the lack of ejaculation cannot be caused by substance abuse or illness (American Psychiatric Association, 2000). Anxiety-provoking sexual situations can interfere with a man's ejaculatory reflex, or he may not be able to have an orgasm in situations in which he feels guilty or conflicted. Often, the man can overcome this disorder when the situation or partner changes or when he engages in a fantasy or receives additional stimulation.

Premature Ejaculation   The persistent and recurrent ejaculation with minimal sexual stimulation, before or shortly after penetration, that causes marked distress or interpersonal difficulty is called **premature ejaculation** by the *DSM-IV-TR*. This disorder is fairly common, with about 3 out of every 10 men in the NHSLS reporting it (see Figure 14.2). Some professionals use

IS ORGASM—THE BIG "O"—the goal of sexual activity? Is it possible to have an intimate sexual relationship, and even be sexually satisfied, without having an orgasm? Some answers to these questions may be found in the results of the National Health and Social Life Survey, which questioned people about their sexual activities and satisfaction. In that survey, only 29% of females reported always having an orgasm with their partner during the preceding year. Yet 41% of women said that they were "extremely physically satisfied" by sex, and 39% reported "extreme emotional satisfaction." In other words, females did not need to have an orgasm to be physically and emotionally satisfied with sex. Tenderness, intimacy, and affection may be more important determinants of gratification than having an orgasm.

The results for males were intriguing as well. Seventy-five percent claimed to always have had an orgasm while having sex with their partner during the preceding year. This is more than twice the percentage of females. On the other hand, 47% of males reported being extremely physically satisfied by sex, and 42% reported extreme emotional satisfaction. It seems that males are more likely to have orgasms than females, but their physical and emotional satisfaction with sex is not much different from the levels reported by females. In other words, for males as

well as females, satisfaction is not directly tied to having an orgasm. Fulfillment, in a loving relationship, seems more a matter of expressing tender feelings than achieving an orgasm.

Despite these findings, many of the *DSM-IV* sexual dysfunctions involve absent, delayed, or too-rapid orgasms. Clearly, many people are troubled enough by their orgasmic performance to seek clinical assistance. What these survey results suggest is that their worries may be misplaced. People are able to have a satisfying sex life despite infrequent orgasms.

As an aside, when people were asked about their partners rather than themselves, 44% of men reported that their female partners always had an orgasm during sex. This figure is 14% higher than the one reported by the females themselves. There are two possible explanations for this discrepancy: Men may not recognize the signs of orgasm in their partners, or their partners may have misled them into believing that they had had an orgasm in order to bolster their partner's self-esteem.

Source: Reprinted by permission from Schwartz, S. (2000). *Abnormal Psychology: A Discovery Approach,* p. 577. Reprinted by permission of The McGraw-Hill Companies.

---

the term **early ejaculation** or "rapid ejaculation," believing it is less pejorative than "premature ejaculation."

Couples often are confused, bewildered, and unhappy when the man consistently ejaculates too early, although the woman often seems to be more disturbed by the disorder than the man is. The woman may be sexually dissatisfied, while her partner may feel that she is too demanding. He may also feel considerable guilt and anxiety. They may begin to avoid sexual contact with each other. The man may experience erectile problems because of his anxieties over early ejaculation, and he may withdraw from sexual activity completely.

Most men with this disorder can delay ejaculation during self-masturbation for a longer period of time than during coitus. With sexual experience and aging, many males learn to delay ejaculation, but others continue to ejaculate early and may seek professional help (American Psychiatric Association, 2000). This disorder often occurs in young and sexually inexperienced males, especially those who have primarily been in situations in which speed of ejaculation was important so as to avoid, for example, being discovered.

As with many sexual difficulties, there is a problem with definitions: What is "too early" ejaculation? Some have defined it according to how long intercourse lasts, how many pelvic thrusts there are, and how often the woman achieves orgasm. Therapist Helen Singer Kaplan (1974) suggested that the absence of voluntary control at orgasm is the key to defining premature ejaculation. Early ejaculation is a problem when the man or his partner is dissatisfied by the amount of time it takes him to ejaculate. Some couples want intercourse to last a long time, but others are not concerned about that.

Interestingly, the *DSM-IV-TR* does not have a premature or rapid orgasm category for women. Some women do have orgasms very quickly and may not be interested in continuing sexual activity; others, however, are open to continued stimulation and may have multiple orgasms.

Sexual Pain Disorders

Dyspareunia   Persistent or recurrent genital pain, ranging from mild to severe, that is associated with intercourse and that causes marked distress or interpersonal difficulty is called **dyspareunia** by the *DSM-IV-TR*. This disorder can occur in both men and women, although it most often is considered to occur in women. The NHSLS, for example, only reported pain during sex for women. In that study, about one-fifth of the women age 18–29 reported pain during sex, decreasing to 8% for women age 50–59 (Laumann, Paik, & Rosen, 1999). Many women experience occasional pain during intercourse, but persistent dyspareunia may indicate difficulties that need to be addressed. The diagnosis of dyspareunia usually has a strong psychological component. When the pain occurs exclusively as a result of a medical or physiological condition, the person has, not dyspareunia, but "sexual dysfunction due to a general medical condition" or "substance-induced sexual dysfunction" (American Psychiatric Association, 2000). This disturbance is not caused exclusively by vaginismus or lack of lubrication.

Sexual inhibitions, a poor relationship with her partner, and hormonal imbalances may contribute to a woman's pain associated with intercourse. If longer stimulation or the use of lubricants does not relieve the dyspareunia, a woman should consult her physician or health-care practitioner to determine the cause.

A type of pain associated with sex that is not included in the *DSM-IV-TR* is **anodyspareunia,** pain occurring during anal intercourse. Gay men sometimes experience this, often due to lack of adequate lubrication. The depth of penile penetration into the anus, the rate of thrusting, and anxiety or embarrassment about the situation often are associated with anodyspareunia (Rosser, Short, Thurmes, & Coleman, 1998).

Vaginismus   According to the *DSM-IV-TR*, the persistent or recurrent involuntary spasm of the muscles of the outer third of the vagina that interferes with sexual intercourse and causes marked distress or interpersonal difficulties is called **vaginismus.** In vaginismus, the muscles around the vaginal opening go into involuntary spasmodic contractions, preventing the insertion of the penis, finger, tampon, or speculum. Vaginismus occurs in some women during sexual activity or during a pelvic examination; it is found more often in younger than older women (American Psychiatric Association, 2000). In rare cases, the vaginal entrance becomes so tight that the penis or another object cannot penetrate it (Leiblum & Nathan, 2001). Vaginismus may occur in conjunction with other sexual difficulties, such as hyposexual disorder or dyspareunia.

During the nineteenth century, vaginismus was one of the most common complaints among women, who were taught to dread intercourse or to perform it perfunctorily. An estimated 2% of women experience vaginismus (Renshaw, 1988a). Vaginismus is essentially a conditioned response that reflects fear, anxiety, or pain. It may result from negative attitudes about sexuality, harsh early sexual experiences, sexual abuse or rape, or painful pelvic examinations (Vandeweil, Jaspers, Schultz, & Gal, 1990).

Other Disorders

Two other disorders not mentioned in the *DSM-IV-TR* because they are based on physical conditions are Peyronie's disease and priapism. These conditions can also cause other difficulties in sexual functioning.

Peyronie's Disease   A condition in which calcium deposits and tough fibrous tissue develop in the corpora cavernosa within the penis is known as **Peyronie's disease.** This problem occurs primarily in older men and can be quite painful. The disease results in a curvature of the penis that, in severe cases, interferes with erection and intercourse (Wilson & Delk, 1994). Medical treatments can alleviate the source of discomfort.

Priapism   Prolonged and painful erection, occurring when blood is unable to drain from the penis, is called **priapism** (see Chapter 13). Lasting from several hours to a few days, this problem is not associated with sexual thoughts or activities. Rather, it results from certain medications, including some antidepressants and excessive doses of penile injections. Medical conditions such as sickle-cell disease and leukemia may also cause priapism ("What Is Priapism?" 1997).

PHYSICAL CAUSES OF SEXUAL DIFFICULTIES AND DISSATISFACTION

Until recently, researchers believed that most sexual problems were almost exclusively psychological in origin. Current research challenges this view as more is learned about the intricacies of sexual physiology, such as the subtle influences of hormones. Our vascular, neurological, and endocrine systems are sensitive to changes and disruptions. As a result, various illnesses may have an adverse effect on our sexuality. Some prescription drugs, such as medication for hypertension or for depression, may affect sexual responsiveness. Chemotherapy and radiation treatment for cancer affect sexual desire and responsiveness.

Physical Causes in Men

Diabetes and alcoholism are the two leading causes of male erectile difficulties; together, they account for several million cases. Alcoholism, smoking, and drug use are widely associated with sexual difficulties (Vine, Margolin, Morrison, & Hulka, 1994). Diabetes, which causes male erectile disorder in as many as 1 million men, damages blood vessels and nerves, including those within the penis. Other causes of sexual difficulties include lumbar disc disease and multiple sclerosis, which interfere with the nerve impulses regulating erection (Weiss, 1992). In addition, atherosclerosis causes blockage of the arteries, including the blood flow necessary for erection. Spinal cord injuries may affect erectile abilities as well (Stein, Chamberlin, Lerner, & Gladshteyn, 1993). Smoking may also contribute to sexual difficulties. One study found that men who are heavy smokers are 50% more likely to experience erectile dysfunction than nonsmokers (National Center for Environmental Health, 1995). Bicycle-induced sexual difficulties can occur as a result of a flattening of the main penile artery, thereby temporarily blocking the blood flow required for erections ("A Very Sore Spot," 1997). Diseases of the heart and circulatory system may be associated with erectile difficulty (Jackson, 1999). The four-country study of 2400 men cited earlier found that "erectile dysfunction was associated with diabetes, heart disease, lower urinary tract symptoms, heavy smoking and depression and increased by 10 percent per year of age" (Nicolosi et al., 2003). Interestingly, erectile difficulties were inversely associated with education and physical activity (Nicolosi et al., 2003).

Although sexual dissatisfaction often reflects conflict and discord within a relationship or disrupt a relationship, if the problem is due to cancer, paraplegia, or diabetes, there may be less relationship strain. If the relationship was stable before the onset of the illness, a couple may have a satisfactory relationship without sexual intercourse. Other forms of sexual interaction may also provide sexual intimacy and pleasure. "When the bond between the mates is love and intimacy," observes Peter Martin (1981), "the loss of sex due to physical illness does not make the marriage an unhappy one."

Physical Causes in Women

Organic causes of female orgasmic disorder in women include medical conditions such as diabetes and heart disease, hormone deficiencies, and neurological disorders, as well as general poor health, extreme fatigue, drug use, and alcoholism. Spinal cord injuries may affect sexual responsiveness (Stein et al., 1993). Multiple sclerosis can decrease vaginal lubrication and sexual response (Weiss, 1992).

Dyspareunia may result from an obstructed or thickened hymen, clitoral adhesions, infections, painful scars, a constrictive clitoral hood, or a weak **pubococcygeus,** the pelvic floor muscle surrounding the urethra and the vagina. Antihistamines used to treat colds and allergies can reduce vaginal lubrication, as can marijuana. Endometriosis and ovarian and uterine tumors and cysts may affect a woman's sexual response.

The skin covering the clitoris can become infected. Women who masturbate too vigorously can irritate their clitoris, making intercourse painful. A partner can also stimulate a woman too roughly, causing soreness in the vagina, urethra, or clitoral area. And dirty hands may cause a vaginal or urinary tract infection.

PSYCHOLOGICAL CAUSES OF SEXUAL DIFFICULTIES AND DISSATISFACTION

Sexual difficulties may have their origin in any number of psychological causes. Some difficulties originate from immediate causes, others from conflict within the self, and still others from a particular sexual relationship. Gay men and lesbian women often have unique issues affecting their sexual functioning.

Immediate Causes

The immediate causes of sexual difficulties include fatigue, stress, ineffective sexual behavior, and sexual anxieties.

Fatigue and Stress   Many difficulties have fairly simple causes. Men and women may find themselves physically exhausted from the demands of daily life. They may bring their fatigue into the bedroom in the form of sexual apathy or disinterest. "I'm too tired to make love tonight" can be a truthful description of a person's feelings. What these couples may need is not therapy or counseling but temporary relief from their daily routines.

Long-term stress can also contribute to lowered sexual drive and reduced responsiveness. A man or woman preoccupied with making financial ends meet, raising an unruly child, or coping with prolonged illness can temporarily lose sexual desire.

Ineffective Sexual Behavior   Ignorance, ineffective sexual communication, and misinformation prevent partners from being effectively sexual with each other. Ineffective sexual behavior is especially relevant in explaining why some women do not experience orgasm in sexual interactions. The couple may not be aware of the significance of the clitoris in sexual arousal or the necessity for direct stimulation.

Some gay men and lesbian women have not learned effective sexual behaviors because they are inexperienced. They have grown up without easily accessible sexual information or positive role models (Reece, 1988).

Sexual Anxieties   A number of anxieties, such as performance anxiety, can lead to sexual dissatisfaction. If a man fails to experience an erection or a

The demands of work and child rearing may create fatigue and stress, which can create sexual apathy for one or both partners.

woman is not orgasmic, he or she may feel anxious and fearful. And the anxiety may block the very response the man or woman desires.

Performance anxieties may give rise to **spectatoring,** in which a person becomes a spectator of her or his own sexual performance (Masters & Johnson, 1970). When people become spectators of their sexual activities, they critically evaluate and judge whether they are "performing" well or whether they are doing everything "right." Kaplan (1983) suggests that spectatoring is involved in most orgasmic dysfunctions.

Performance anxiety may be even more widespread among gay men. Rex Reece (1988) writes: "Many gay men move in a social, sexual milieu where sexual arousal is expected immediately or soon after meeting someone. If response is not rapidly forthcoming, rejection is very likely."

Excessive Need to Please a Partner   Another source of anxiety is an excessive need to please a partner (Kaplan, 1974). A man who experiences this anxiety may want a speedy erection to please (or impress) his partner. He may feel that he must always delay his orgasm until after his partner's. A woman who experiences this anxiety may want to have an orgasm quickly to please her partner. She may worry that she is not sufficiently attractive to her partner.

One result of the need to please is that men and women may pretend to have orgasms. (Meg Ryan famously demonstrated faking an orgasm in a deli in the film *When Harry Met Sally.*) One study found that two-thirds of the women and one-third of the men reported faking orgasm (Darling & Davidson, 1986). Women fake orgasm most often to avoid disappointing their partner or hurting his feelings. Both also fake orgasm to present a false image of their sexual performance. Unfortunately, faking orgasm miscommunicates to the partner that each is equally satisfied. Because the orgasmic problem is not addressed, negative emotions may simmer.

Conflict Within the Self

Negative parental attitudes toward sex are frequently associated with subsequent sexual problems (McCabe, 1994). Much of the process of growing up is a casting off of the sexual guilt and negativity instilled in childhood. Some people fear becoming emotionally intimate with another person. They may enjoy the sex but fear the accompanying feelings of vulnerability and so withdraw from the sexual relationship before they become emotionally close to their partner (Hyde & DeLamater, 2003). And among gay men and lesbian women, **internalized homophobia**—self-hatred because of one's homosexuality—is a major source of conflict that can be traced to a conservative religious upbringing (Nichols, 1988; Reece, 1988).

Sources of severe sexual difficulties include childhood sexual abuse, adult sexual assault, and rape. Guilt and conflict do not usually eliminate a person's sex drive; rather, they inhibit the drive and alienate the individual from his or her sexuality. He or she may come to see sexuality as something bad or "dirty," rather than something to happily affirm. Sexual expression is forced "to assume an infinite variety of distorted, inhibited, diverted, sublimated, alienated and variable forms to accommodate the conflict" (Kaplan, 1974).

Relationship Causes

Sexual difficulties do not exist in a vacuum, but usually within the context of a relationship (Crowe, 1995). All couples at some point experience difficulties in their sexual relationship. Sex therapist David Schnarch (2002) writes that "sexual problems are common among healthy couples who are normal in every other way—so common, in fact, that they are arguably a sign of normality." Most frequently, married couples go into therapy because they have a greater investment in the relationship than couples who are dating or cohabiting. Sexual difficulties in a dating or cohabiting relationship often do not surface; it is sometimes easier for couples to break up than to change the behaviors that contribute to their sexual problems.

If left unresolved, disappointment, rage, anger, resentment, power conflicts, and hostility often become a permanent part of couple interaction. Desire discrepancies become sources of conflict rather than of acceptance, and underlying fears of rejection or abandonment help form the relationship structure. These factors all influence the nature and quality of the relationship between partners. Ideas for enhancing sex within a couple relationship are given in the next section.

SEXUAL ENHANCEMENT

Improving the quality of a sexual relationship is referred to as **sexual enhancement.** There are several sexual-enhancement programs for people who function well sexually but who nevertheless want to improve the quality of their sexual interactions and relationships. The programs generally seek to provide accurate information about sexuality, develop communication skills, foster positive attitudes, and increase self-awareness (Cooper, 1985). In some ways, the study of human sexuality involves many of the same cognitive, attitudinal, and communication themes explored in sexual-enhancement programs.

Bernie Zilbergeld (1999) suggested that there are specific requirements for what he calls "great sex." They form the basis of many sexual-enhancement programs:

- Having accurate information about sexuality, especially your own and your partner's
- Having an orientation toward sex based on pleasure, such as arousal, fun, love, and lust, rather than performance and orgasm
- Being involved in a relationship that allows each partner's sexuality to flourish
- Developing an ability to communicate verbally and nonverbally about sex, feelings, and relationships
- Being equally assertive and sensitive about your own sexual needs and those of your partner
- Accepting, understanding, and appreciating differences between you and your partner

Good sex involves the ability to communicate nonverbally—through laughter and good times—as well as verbally.

Developing Self-Awareness

Being aware of our own sexual needs is often critical to enhancing our sexuality. Because of gender-role stereotypes and negative learning about sexuality, we often lose sight of our own sexual needs.

What Is Good Sex?   Sexual stereotypes present us with images of how we are supposed to behave sexually. Images of the "sexually in charge" man and the "sexual but not too sexual" woman may interfere with our ability to express our own sexual feelings, needs, and desires. We follow the scripts and stereotypes we have been socialized to accept, rather than our own unique responses. Following these cultural images may impede our ability to have what therapist Carol Ellison calls "good sex." In an essay about intimacy-based sex therapy, Ellison (1985) writes that we will know we are having good sex if we feel good about ourself, our partner, our relationship, and our sexual behavior. Good sex does not necessarily include orgasm or intercourse. It can be kissing, cuddling, masturbating, performing oral or anal sex, and so on; it can be other-sex or same-sex sexual expression.

Zilbergeld (1999) suggested that to fully enjoy our sexuality we need to explore our "conditions for good sex." There is nothing unusual about requiring conditions for any activity. For a good night's sleep, for example, each of us has certain conditions. Some of us may need absolute quiet, total darkness, a soft pillow, and an open window. Others, however, can sleep during a loud dormitory party, curled up in a corner of a stuffy room. Of conditions for good sex, Zilbergeld writes:

> In a sexual situation, a condition is anything that makes you more relaxed, more comfortable, more confident, more excited, more open to your experience. Put differently, a condition is something that clears your nervous system of unnecessary clutter, leaving it open to receive and transmit sexual messages in ways that will result in a good time for you.

Discovering Your Conditions for Good Sex   Different individuals report different conditions for good sex. Some common conditions, according to Zilbergeld (1999), include the following:

- *Feeling intimate with your partner.* Intimacy is often important for both men and women. Partners who are feeling distant from each other may need to talk about their feelings before becoming sexual. Emotional distance can take the heart out of sex.

- *Feeling sexually capable.* Generally, feeling sexually capable relates to an absence of anxieties about sexual performance. For men, these include anxiety about becoming erect or ejaculating too soon. For women, these include anxiety about painful intercourse or lack of orgasm. For both men and women, they include worry about whether one is a good lover.

- *Feeling trust.* Both men and women may need to know that they are emotionally safe with their partner. They need to feel confident that they will not be judged, ridiculed, or talked about.

- *Feeling aroused.* A partner does not need to be sexual unless he or she is sexually aroused or excited. Just because one partner wants to be sexual does not mean that the other has to be.

- *Feeling physically and mentally alert.* This condition requires that partners not feel particularly tired, ill, stressed, or preoccupied, as well as not be excessively under the influence of alcohol or drugs.

- *Feeling positive about the environment and situation.* A partner may need privacy, to be in a place where he or she feels protected from intrusion. Each needs to feel that the other is sexually interested and wants to be sexually involved.

Each individual has his or her own unique conditions for good sex. If you are or have been sexually active, to discover your conditions for good sex, think about the last few times you were sexual and were highly aroused. Then compare those times with other times when you were much less aroused (Zilbergeld, 1999). Make a list of the factors that differed between the two. Consider the following areas: your feelings about your partner at the time (e.g., intimate, distant, indifferent, or angry); your degree of interest in being sexual; any anxieties about sexual performance; the surroundings; your preoccupation with or worries about nonsexual matters; your health; and the influence of alcohol or other drugs.

Put the list away for a few days, and then see if there is anything you want to add or change. Reword the list so that each of the conditions is specific. For example, if you wrote, "Felt pressured to have sex," rewrite it as "Need to feel unpressured." When you rewrite these conditions, you can get a clearer sense of what your conditions for good sex are. Communicate your needs to your partner.

Doing Homework Exercises   We are often unaware of our body and our erotic responses. Sexual-enhancement programs often specify exercises for couples to undertake in private. Such "homework" exercises require individuals to make a time commitment to themselves or their partner. Typical assignments include the following exercises. If you feel comfortable with any of the assignments, you might want to try one or more. (For additional exercises for men, see Zilbergeld, 1999; for exercises for women, see Barbach, 1982.)

Click on "Self-Awareness" to see a woman doing a mirror examination and other "homework" exercises.

- *Mirror examination.* Use a full-length mirror to examine your nude body. Use a hand mirror to view your genitals. Look at all your features in an uncritical manner; view yourself with acceptance.

- *Body relaxation and exploration.* Take 30–60 minutes to fully relax. Begin with a leisurely shower or bath; then, remaining nude, find a comfortable place to touch and explore your body and genitals.

- *Masturbation.* In a relaxed situation, with body oils or lotions to enhance your sensations, explore ways of touching your body and genitals that bring you pleasure. Do this exercise for several sessions without having an orgasm; experiencing erotic pleasure without orgasm is the goal. If you are about to have an orgasm, decrease stimulation. After several sessions without having an orgasm, continue pleasuring yourself until you have an orgasm.

- *Erotic aids.* Products designed to enhance erotic responsiveness, such as vibrators, dildos, explicit videos, oils, and lotions, are referred to as **erotic aids.** They are also called **sex toys,** emphasizing their playful quality. A major study found that 2.9% of men and 3.3% of women bought sex toys during the previous year (Laumann, Gagnon, Michael, & Michaels, 1994). You may wish to try using a sex toy or shower massage as you masturbate, with your partner or by yourself. You may also want to view videos at home

Some individuals and couples use erotic aids like vibrators, dildos, videos, oils, and lotions to enhance their sexual responsiveness.

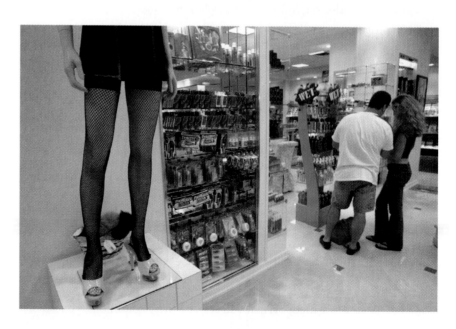

PREYING ON PEOPLE'S INSECURITIES and distorted images of perfect sex, "natural sexual enhancers" promise to "spice up your sex life," "rekindle desire," "improve sexual performance," and "enhance the body's own natural sexual health." The number of homeopathic products sold in grocery stores, convenience stores, health food stores, and drugstores surged following the Food and Drug Administration's approval of Viagra in 1998. Supported by unsubstantiated claims and personal testimonials, these "magic bullet" capsules, herbal Viagra pills, creams, sprays, lubricants, gels, and tonics promise greater sexual arousal and rock-hard erections. These products are promoted via the Internet, radio, TV, magazines, and newspapers. Apparently, a lot of people have been persuaded by the advertising campaigns, as sales have increased dramatically (Riscol, 2003). A Tufts University *Health and Nutrition Letter* (2002) titled "Better Sex Life Not Found over the Counter" states: "Unfortunately, when the desire for a product to work is emotional and strong, as with sex or weight loss, the market gets flooded with merchandise making unfounded claims. It's also why companies can charge $ 100 or more for a month's supply."

Not surprisingly, very few, if any, of these products have demonstrated effectiveness in their claims. The Tufts newsletter observes that "there are no well established over-the-counter treatments for male impotence [erectile dysfunction] or female sexual dysfunction." The newsletter continues by noting that the products fall into the largely unregulated category of dietary supplements, and as a result, what you buy may not contain all or any of the ingredients listed on the label. Many people believe that because the products are "natural" they are also safe (Riscol, 2003). The newsletter reports the findings of one study: "In fact, an independent testing agency found that out of 22 over-the-counter sexual enhancement products, only nine actually contained the ingredients listed and were properly labeled." The labels of these "natural" herbal products include these disclaimers as required by law: "These statements have not been evaluated by the Food and Drug Administration" and "This product is not intended to diagnose, treat, cure or prevent any disease." The newsletter continues:

> Granted, there is some weak, preliminary evidence of a few substances. But that's all. For instance, yohimbe, an herb derived from the bark of a West African evergreen tree, contains the chemical yohimbine, a drug used for such things as pupil dilation. However, there is no support for yohimbe as an effective treatment for impotence. The amino acid L-Arginine, or arginine, is another popular sexual aid supplement. It is typically combined with other ingredients (including yohimbe), but again clinical proof for the efficacy of the substance is lacking. These findings don't mean there's no evidence, but it is much too fragile for consumers to invest money and hopes in any of these products, which have names like VasoRect, Crescendo for Men, X-treme, and Ultimate Libido.

Other herbs, such as Asian ginseng and Ginkgo biloba, and antioxidants such as vitamins E and C have been touted as improving sexual performance, but the research is not conclusive. In short, there aren't any natural "magic bullets" that will "transform you into an instant lovemaking machine" (Riscol, 2003). As suggested throughout this book, enhancing your emotional and physical health, as well as your relationship with your partner, is usually the best path to sexual pleasure.

or read erotic poetry or stories to yourself or your partner. Recently, there has been a dramatic increase in natural herbal sexual enhancers that promise terrific sex. Do they work? See the accompanying box to find out.

Intensifying Erotic Pleasure

One of the most significant elements in enhancing our physical experience of sex is intensifying arousal. In intensifying arousal, the focus is on erotic pleasure rather than on sexual performance. This can be done in a number of ways.

Sexual Arousal Sexual arousal refers to the physiological responses, fantasies, and desires associated with sexual anticipation and activity. We have different levels of arousal, and they are not necessarily associated with particular types of sexual activities. Sometimes, we feel more sexually aroused when we kiss or masturbate than when we have sexual intercourse or oral sex.

The first element in increasing sexual arousal is having your conditions for good sex met. If you need privacy, find a place to be alone; if you need a romantic setting, go for a walk on the beach by moonlight or listen to music by candlelight; if you want limits on your sexual activities, tell your partner; if you need a certain kind of physical stimulation, show or tell your partner what you like.

A second element in increasing arousal is focusing on the sensations you are experiencing. Once you begin an erotic activity such as massaging or kissing, do not let yourself be distracted. When you're kissing, don't think about what you're going to do next or about an upcoming test. Instead, focus on the sensual experience of your lips and heart. Zilbergeld (1999) wrote:

> Focusing on sensations means exactly that. You put your attention in your body where the action is. When you're kissing, keep your mind on your lips. This is *not* the same as thinking about your lips or the kiss; just put your attention in your lips. As you focus on your sensations, you may want to convey your pleasure to your partner. Let him or her know through your sounds and movements that you are excited.

Alternatives to Intercourse   Waiting, delaying, and facing obstacles may intensify arousal. This is one of the pleasures of sexual abstinence that may get lost soon after you begin intercourse. Lonnie Barbach (1982) suggests that sexually active people may intensify arousal by placing a ban on sexual intercourse for a period of time. If you are a gay or lesbian person, you may place a comparable ban on your preferred activity. During this time, explore other ways of being erotic or sexual. Barbach (1982), JoAnn Loulan (1984), and Zilbergeld (1992) suggest the following activities, among others:

1. Sit or lie down close to each other. Gaze into each other's eyes to establish an intimate connection. Gently caress each other's face and hair as you continue gazing. Tell each other what fantasies you have about the other.

2. Bathe or shower with your partner, soaping his or her body slowly and sensually but not touching the genitals. Another time, you may want to include genital stimulation.

3. Give and receive a sensual, erotic massage. Do not touch the genitals, but massage around them teasingly. Use body oils and lotions to increase tactile sensitivity. Later, you may want to include genital stimulation.

4. Use your lips, tongue, and mouth to explore your partner's body, especially the neck, ears, nipples, inner thighs, palms, fingers, feet, and toes. Take your time.

5. "Dirty dance" together, feeling the curves and textures of your partner's body; put your hands under your partner's clothes, and caress him or her. Kiss and caress each other as you slowly remove each other's clothing. Then hold each other close, kiss and massage each other, and explore each other's body with your mouth, tongue, and lips.

License my roving hands, and let them go,
Behind, before, above, between, below.

—*John Donne (1572–1631)*

Changing a Sexual Relationship

In his book *Resurrecting Sex,* David Schnarch (2002) discusses common sexual difficulties of couples and provides practical suggestions for addressing them. Schnarch says that every couple has sexual problems at some point, although most couples do not anticipate that they will end up being bedeviled by sexual dissatisfaction. In a statement that might seem surprising, Schnarch notes, "If your sexual relationship stays the same, you are more likely to have sexual dysfunctions (and be bored to death)." He suggests that we "think of medical-related sexual problems as 'problems given the way we usually have sex,' as opposed to 'intractable problems you'll have no matter what you do.'"

Schnarch declares that changing the sexual relationship is necessary for couples having sex problems:

> Expect to shake up your sexual relationship every once in a while. I know that's exactly opposite what couples want to do. People usually like stability in their sexual relationships. Just incorporate episodic shake-ups into your notion of long-term stability. You have a dormant sexual potential that's ready and waiting to be developed.

Schnarch suggests 22 ways to "resurrect sex." His concepts and strategies for resolving sexual difficulties include the following:

1. Put some effort into the nonsexual aspects of the relationship. Focus on the daily things.

2. Expand your repertoire of sexual behaviors, "tones," styles, and meanings. Push yourself to try sexual behaviors that might seem to be a stretch. To increase sexual desire, try mixing carnality and communion. Resurrecting sex means doing things differently.

3. Address any issues you and your partner have swept under the carpet. Trying to be intimate and sexual when you are angry, frustrated, or resentful often does not work.

4. Deal with unresolved personal issues. They can hinder your arousal and make you vulnerable to sexual difficulties.

5. Do not become overly concerned with possible unconscious meanings of your sexual problems, and don't get sidetracked playing amateur psychoanalyst. No personality traits or life experiences invariably result in sexual difficulties. Pay attention to your specific situation, and focus on what is actually happening to you.

6. Recognize that changing sexual relationships typically involves embracing a deeper connection. Given that many couples do not achieve much emotional connection through sex, this can be a challenge. Intimate, deep connection during sex requires a sensory and emotional bond with your partner.

Schnarch guarantees one thing: To resurrect or improve an intimate relationship, you have to change the current relationship. He notes that this is no small task. Rather, it involves raising your level of stimulation, growing up, accepting new truths, becoming closer, and changing yourself in the process. Resurrecting sex requires becoming unstuck without taking out frustrations on your partner, even if she or he deserves it. Schnarch observes:

You can simply try to make your sexual problems go away, or you can approach them in ways that bring out the best in you and your relationship. When sex is at its best, it is full of generosity. When you're having sexual problems, generosity is what your partner desperately needs. Helping your partner increase his or her total stimulation is generosity in action. This is more readily accomplished if your intent includes generosity toward your mate. So whether you lend your partner a helping hand—or improve how you use yours—compassion, friendship, and operating from the best in you are generally required.

TREATING SEXUAL DIFFICULTIES

VIDEO

Click on "Taking a Sexual History" to see a urologist taking a sexual history from a man with erectile dysfunction.

There are several psychologically based approaches to sex therapy, the most important ones being behavior modification and psychosexual therapy. William Masters and Virginia Johnson were the pioneers in the cognitive-behavioral approach; the most influential psychosexual therapist is Helen Singer Kaplan. The cognitive-behavioral approach works well with sexual difficulties such as erectile and orgasmic problems. Psychosexual therapy is more effective in treating other sexual difficulties, such as hypoactive sexual desire disorder and sexual aversion disorder (Atwood & Dershowitz, 1992). Medical approaches may be effective with some sexual problems.

Masters and Johnson: A Cognitive-Behavioral Approach

The program developed by Masters and Johnson for the treatment of sexual difficulties was the starting point for contemporary sex therapy. Not only did they reject the Freudian approach of tracing sexual problems to childhood; they relabeled sexual problems as sexual dysfunctions rather than aspects of neuroses. Masters and Johnson (1970) argued that the majority of sexual problems are the result of sexual ignorance, faulty techniques, or relationship problems. They treated difficulties using a combination of cognitive and behavioral techniques, and they treated couples rather than individuals. In cases in which a partner was unavailable, Masters and Johnson used, as part of their therapeutic team, **sex surrogates,** whose role was to have sexual interactions with a client.

Couples with Difficulties   Cognitive-behavioral therapists approach the problems of erectile and orgasmic difficulties by dealing with the couple rather than the individual. They regard sexuality as an interpersonal phenomenon rather than an individual one. In fact, they tell their clients that there are no individuals with sexual difficulties, only couples with sexual difficulties, and that faulty sexual interaction is at the root of sexual problems. Neither individual is to blame; rather, it is their mutual interaction that sustains a difficulty or resolves a problem. Masters and Johnson called this principle "neutrality and mutuality" (Masters & Johnson, 1974).

Therapists using this approach prefer to treat only those couples who are genuinely committed to their relationship. Treatment lasts 12 days on average. During this time, couples are seen daily by the therapists. The partners

FIGURE 14.3 Sensate Focus

are told not to attempt sexual intercourse until they are given permission by their therapist team, a man and a woman. In this way, each partner is immediately relieved of any pressure to perform, thus easing anxieties and allowing the development of a more relaxed attitude toward sex.

Case Histories   During the first session, each individual is interviewed separately by the therapist of the same sex; in the afternoon, the interview is repeated by the therapist of the other sex. The therapists are careful not to assign blame to either partner, for it is the couple, rather than the individuals, who are being treated.

After the interviews and the case histories have been completed, the couple meet with both therapists to discuss what has been learned so far. The therapists explain what they have learned about the couple's personal and sexual interaction, encouraging the man and woman to expand on or correct what they are saying. Then the therapists discuss any sexual myths and fallacies the partners hold that may interfere with their sexual interaction.

Sensate Focus   At the end of the third session, the therapists introduce **sensate focus,** focusing on touch and the giving and receiving of pleasure (Figure 14.3). The other senses—smell, sight, hearing, and taste—are worked on indirectly as a means of reinforcing the touch experience. To increase their sensate focus, the couple are given "homework" assignments. In the privacy of their own room, the partners are to take off their clothes so that nothing will restrict their sensations. One partner must give pleasure and the other receive it. The giver touches, caresses, massages, and strokes his or her partner's body everywhere except the genitals and breasts. The purpose is not sexual arousal but simply sense awareness.

Through the fourth day, therapy is basically the same for any type of sexual problem. Thereafter, the therapists begin to focus on the particular problem affecting the couple.

Treating Male Difficulties   The therapists use different techniques for treating the specific problem.

ERECTILE DIFFICULTIES   When the problem is erectile difficulties, the couple are taught that fears and anxieties are largely responsible and that the

> Full nakedness! All joys are due to
>   thee,
> As souls unbodied, bodies unclothed
>   must be,
> To taste whole joys.
>
> *—John Donne*

FIGURE 14.4   Manual Stimulation of the Penis

removal of these fears is the first step in therapy. Once the fear is removed, the man is less likely to be an observer of his sexuality; he can become an actor rather than a spectator or judge.

After the sensate focus exercises have been integrated into the couple's behavior, the partners are told to play with each other's genitals, but not to attempt an erection. Often, erections may occur because there is no demand on the man; but he is encouraged to let his penis become flaccid again, then erect, then flaccid, as reassurance that he can successfully have erections. This builds his confidence, as well as his partner's, by letting her know that she can excite him.

During this time, the partners are counseled on other aspects of their relationship that contribute to their sexual difficulties. Then, on about the tenth day, they attempt their first intercourse, if the man has had erections with some success. Eventually, in the final session, the man will have an orgasm.

EARLY EJACULATION   Cognitive-behavioral therapists treat early or rapid ejaculation by using initially the same pattern as in treating erectile difficulties. They concentrate especially on reducing fears and anxieties and increasing sensate focus and communication. Then they use a simple exercise called the **squeeze technique** (Figures 14.4 and 14.5). (This technique was developed in the 1950s and remains the most effective treatment to date [St. Lawrence & Madakasira, 1992].) The man is brought manually to a full erection. Just before he is about to ejaculate, his partner squeezes his penis with thumb and forefinger just below the corona. After 30 seconds of inactivity, the partner arouses him again and, just prior to ejaculation, squeezes again. Using this technique, the couple can continue for 15–20 minutes before the man ejaculates.

MALE ORGASMIC DISORDER   This condition is treated by having the man's partner manipulate his penis. The partner asks for verbal and physical directions to bring him the most pleasure possible. It may take a few sessions before the man has his first ejaculation. The idea is to identify his partner with sexual pleasure and desire. He is encouraged to feel stimulated, not

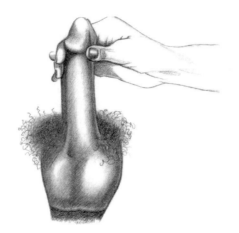

FIGURE 14.5 The Squeeze Technique: (a) Base of Penis and (b) Head of Penis

only by his partner but also by her erotic responses to him. After the man has reached orgasm through manual stimulation, he then proceeds to vaginal intercourse. With further instruction and feedback, the man should be able to function sexually without fear of delayed ejaculation.

Treating Female Difficulties   Each female difficulty is treated differently in behavior modification therapy.

FEMALE ORGASMIC DISORDER   After the sensate focus sessions, the woman's partner begins to touch and caress her vulva; she guides his hand to show him what she likes. The partner is told, however, not to stimulate the clitoris directly because it may be extremely sensitive and stimulation may cause pain rather than pleasure. Instead, the partner caresses and stimulates the area around the clitoris, the labia, and the upper thighs. During this time, the partners are told not to attempt to achieve orgasm because it would place undue performance pressure on the woman. They are simply to explore the woman's erotic potential and discover what brings her the greatest pleasure.

VAGINISMUS   Vaginismus is one of the easiest sexual problems to overcome. The woman uses a set of vaginal dilators (plastic, penile-shaped rods) graduated in diameter. She inserts one before going to bed at night and takes it out in the morning. As soon as the woman is able to receive a dilator of one size without having vaginal spasms, a larger one is used. In most cases, the vaginismus disappears.

Kaplan: Psychosexual Therapy

Helen Singer Kaplan (1974, 1979, 1983) modified Masters and Johnson's behavioral treatment program to include psychosexual therapy. The cognitive-behavioral approach works well for arousal and orgasmic difficulties resulting from mild to midlevel sexual anxieties. But if the individual experiences severe anxieties resulting from intense relationship or psychic conflicts or from childhood sexual abuse or rape, a behavioral approach alone frequently does not work. Such severe anxieties usually manifest themselves in sexual aversion disorder or hypoactive sexual desire.

The role of the therapist in such instances is to provide clients with insight into the origins of the problem. Individuals with desire disorders, for example, often resist behavioral exercises such as sensate focus and pleasuring. They may respond to these exercises with boredom, anxiety, or discomfort; they resist experiencing pleasure. The therapist can intervene by pointing out that they are actively (consciously or unconsciously) creating inhibitions by focusing on negative feelings ("She makes strange sounds"; "His arms are too hairy"), by distracting themselves with thoughts of work or household matters, or by calling up performance fears ("I won't be able to come").

The therapist creates a crisis by confronting individuals with their resistances and then pointing out that they are in control of their resistances and that they can change if they want to. Some individuals will improve as a result of the crisis. Others, however, feel powerless to change. They require additional psychosexual therapy to gain insight into their problem. They need to discover and resolve the unconscious roots of their problem to permit themselves to experience desire once again for their partners.

Other Nonmedical Approaches

Both cognitive-behavioral and psychosexual therapy are expensive and take a considerable amount of time. In response to these limitations, "brief" sex therapy and self-help and group therapy have developed.

PLISSIT Model of Therapy   One of the most common approaches used by sex therapists is based on the **PLISSIT model** (Annon, 1974, 1976). "PLISSIT" is an acronym for the four progressive levels of sex therapy: **p**ermission, **li**mited information, **s**pecific **s**uggestions, and **i**ntensive **t**herapy. About 90% of sexual difficulties can be successfully addressed in the first three levels; only about 10% of patients require extensive therapy.

The first level in the PLISSIT model involves giving permission. At one time or another, most sexual behaviors were prohibited by important figures in our lives. Because desires and activities such as fantasies or masturbation were not validated, we often question their "normality" or "morality." We shroud them in secrecy or drape them with shame. Without permission to be sexual, we may experience sexual disorders and dysfunctions.

Sex therapists act as "permission givers" for us to be sexual. They become authority figures who validate our sexuality by helping us accept our sexual feelings and behaviors. They reassure us and help us clarify our sexual values. They also validate our ability to say no to activities with which we are uncomfortable.

The second level involves giving limited information. This information is restricted to the specific area of difficulties. If a woman has an orgasmic disorder, for example, the therapist might explain that not all women are orgasmic in coitus without additional manual stimulation before, during, or after penetration. The therapist might discuss the effects of drugs such as alcohol, marijuana, and cocaine on sexual responsiveness.

The third level involves making specific suggestions. If permission giving and limited information are not sufficient, the therapist next suggests specific "homework" exercises. For example, if a man experiences early or rapid ejaculation, the therapist may suggest that he and his partner try the squeeze technique. A woman with female orgasmic disorder might be instructed to masturbate with or without her partner to discover the best way for her partner to assist her in experiencing orgasm.

The fourth level involves undergoing intensive therapy. If the individual continues to experience a sexual problem, he or she will need to enter intensive therapy, such as psychosexual therapy.

Self-Help and Group Therapy   The PLISSIT model provides a sound basis for understanding how partners, friends, books, self-help exercises, and group therapy can be useful in helping us deal with the first three levels of therapy: permission, limited information, and specific suggestions. Partners, friends, books, and group therapy sessions under a therapist's guidance, for example, may provide "permission" for us to engage in sexual exploration and discovery. From these sources, we may learn that many of our sexual fantasies and behaviors are very common. Such methods are most effective when dysfunctions arise from a lack of knowledge or mild sexual anxieties. They also are considerably less expensive than most other types of sex therapy.

The first step in dealing with a sexual difficulty can be to tap your own immediate resources. Begin by discussing the problem with your partner; find out what she or he thinks. Discuss specific strategies that might be useful. Sometimes, simply communicating your feelings and thoughts will resolve the dissatisfaction. Seek out friends with whom you can share your feelings and anxieties. Find out what they think; ask them whether they have had similar experiences and how they handled them. Try to keep your perspective—and your sense of humor.

Group therapy may be particularly valuable in providing an open, safe forum in which people can discuss their sexual feelings. It is an opportunity to experience and discover that many of their sexual behaviors, fantasies, and problems are very common. The therapist leading these sessions can also provide valuable insight and direction. Another benefit of group therapy is that it is often less expensive than most other types of therapy.

Medical Approaches

Sexual difficulties are often a combination of physical and psychological problems (LoPiccolo, 1991). Even people whose difficulties are physical may develop psychological or relationship problems as they try to cope with their difficulties. Thus, treatment for organically based problems may need to include psychological counseling.

Vaginal pain caused by inadequate lubrication and thinning vaginal walls often occurs as a result of the decreased estrogen associated with menopause. A lubricating jelly or estrogen therapy may help. Vaginitis, endometriosis, and pelvic inflammatory disease may also make intercourse painful. Lubricants or postmenopausal hormone therapy (discussed in Chapter 13) often resolves difficulties. The sex lives of people with significant testosterone deficiencies may be helped by testosterone supplements.

The FDA has approved an apparatus called EROS-CTD, a clitoral stimulation device the size of a computer mouse. This device creates a gentle suction over the clitoris, increasing blood flow and sensation (Leland, 2000). The device is quite expensive and available only by prescription.

KEGEL EXERCISES WERE originally developed by Dr. Arnold Kegel (KAY-gul) to help women with problems controlling urination. They were designed to strengthen and give women voluntary control of a muscle called the pubococcygeus (pew-bo-kawk-SEE-gee-us), or P.C. for short. The P.C. muscle is part of the sling of muscle stretching from the pubic bone in front to the tailbone in back. Because the muscle encircles not only the urinary opening but also the outside of the vagina, some of Kegel's patients discovered a pleasant side effect—increased sexual awareness. Many report that the sensations are similar for men and women.

Why Do Kegel Exercises?

- They can help you be more aware of feelings in your genital area.
- They can increase circulation in the genital area.
- They may help increase sexual arousal started by other kinds of stimulation.
- They can be useful during childbirth to help control the strength and duration of pushing.
- They can be helpful after childbirth to restore muscle tone in the vagina.
- They can help men control the timing of ejaculation.
- If urinary incontinence is a problem, strengthing these muscles may improve urinary control.

Identifying Your P.C. Muscle

Sit on the toilet. Spread your legs apart. See if you can stop and start the flow of urine without moving your legs. That's your P.C. muscle, the one that turns the flow on and off. If you don't find it the first time, don't give up; try again the next time you have to urinate.

How to Do the Exercises

- *Slow Kegels:* Tighten the P.C. muscle as you did to stop the urine. Hold it for a slow count of three. Relax it.

- *Quick Kegels:* Tighten and relax the P.C. muscle as rapidly as you can.
- *Pull in—push out:* Pull up the entire pelvic floor as though trying to suck water into your vagina. Then push or bear down as if trying to push the imaginary water out. (This exercise will use a number of stomach or abdominal muscles as well as the P.C. muscle.)

At first, do 10 of each of these three exercises (one set) five times every day. Each week, increase the number of times you do each exercise by five (15, 20, 25, etc.). Keep doing five "sets" each day.

Exercise Guidelines

- You can do these exercises any time during daily activities that don't require a lot of moving around—for example, while driving your car, watching television, sitting in school or at your desk, or lying in bed.
- When you start, you will probably notice that the muscle doesn't want to stay "contracted" during "slow Kegels" and that you can't do "quick Kegels" very rapidly or evenly. Keep at it. In a week or two, you will probably notice that you can control the muscle quite well.
- Sometimes, the muscle will start to feel a little tired. This is not surprising—you probably haven't used it very much before. Take a few seconds' rest and start again.
- A good way to check on how you are doing is to insert one or two lubricated fingers into your vagina. Because it may be a month or so before you notice results, be patient.

Finally, always remember to keep breathing naturally and evenly while doing your Kegels!

Most medical and surgical treatment for men has centered on erectile difficulties. Such approaches include microsurgery to improve a blood flow problem, suction devices to induce and maintain an erection, a prosthesis implanted in the penis and abdomen, and drugs injected into the penis. Even though these methods have been used with many men, they are not very practical or pleasant, and they became virtually obsolete with the introduction of **Viagra** in 1998. Viagra, the trade name for sildenafil, is the first effective and safe oral drug for the treatment of male erectile difficulty, whether caused by psychological or medical conditions. It is also one of the most

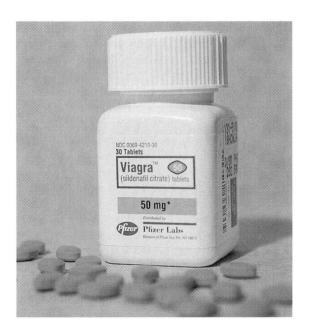

Sildenafil (Viagra), approved by the FDA in 1998, has revolutionized the treatment of male erectile disorder.

popular drugs in the history of the pharmaceutical industry, with millions of prescriptions already written in the United States and abroad. Viagra has revolutionized the treatment of erectile problems. It is effective for most men with erectile problems, although about one-quarter or so of men are not helped (Derry et al., 1998; Goldstein et al., 1998; Pallas, Levine, Althof, & Risen, 2000; Rendell, Rajfer, Wicker, & Smith, 1999; Steers, 1999). The primary psychological role of Viagra is to eliminate the anticipatory and performance anxiety surrounding intercourse (McCarthy, 1998).

Viagra allows the muscles in the penis to relax and the penile arteries to dilate, thus expanding the erectile tissues that squeeze shut the veins in the penis. This shuts down the blood flow out of the penis, creating firmness in the penis. The manufacturer recommends that the drug be taken an hour before sexual activity, with its effects lasting up to 4–5 hours. Viagra does not increase sexual desire, nor does it produce an erection by itself; the man still must be sexually excited. After sex is over, the erection goes away. Viagra has minimal side effects (e.g., headache, flushing, blurred vision), and very few men discontinue use because of adverse reactions (Hartmann et al., 1999). However, blood pressure may drop suddenly to life-threatening levels for individuals who are also taking medications containing nitrates, such as nitroglycerin for circulatory disease (Kloner & Jarow, 1999). However, for men not taking nitroglycerin or other nitrate-based drugs, the drug is apparently safe as prescribed. The long-term safety of Viagra among 1008 men with erectile dysfunction was assessed. The occurrence of treatment-related cardiovascular adverse effects, such as hypertension, tachycardia, and palpitation, was less than 1 percent (Steers et al., 2001).

A review of the literature 4 years after the introduction of Viagra concluded that the drug is an effective and well-tolerated treatment for erectile difficulties, even in men who have taken the drug since its introduction (Padma-Nathan, Eardley, Kloner, Laties, & Montorsi, 2002). Some men have had to increase the dosage to maintain the benefits, but the side effects seem to diminish as well (Harvard's Men's Health Watch, 2003). Studies have shown that Viagra's efficacy and safety is maintained across ethnic groups (Young, Bennett, Gilhooly, Wessells, & Ramos, 2002). A recent report identified a greater risk of HIV and sexually transmitted infections among gay and bisexual Viagra users than among nonusers (Kim, Kent, & Klausner, 2002). And the mixing of Ecstasy and Viagra can cause heart problems and erections lasting more than 4 hours, which might lead to anatomical damage (Leinwand, 2002).

Although Viagra facilitates penile vascular function, it does not treat any of the psychological difficulties, such as depression, anger, or resentment, associated with erectile difficulties. The best use of Viagra is in the context of a comprehensive assessment and intervention by a sex therapist (McCarthy, 1998). People should never use others' Viagra; they should always get their own prescription from a doctor.

Because Viagra increases pelvic blood flow, many women have used it to increase sensation and orgasm. These experiences, and the results of medical research, have yielded mixed results. More research is being conducted.

Viagra represents the beginning of the pharmacological approach to treating sexual difficulties. Other drugs designed to assist both men and women in becoming sexually aroused currently are being tested, and more will undoubtedly come on the market. Pharmaceutical companies continue to produce new drugs for treating erectile difficulties. Two such drugs are GlaxoSmithKline and Bayer's Levitra (vardenafil) and Lilly's Cialis (tadalafil). Both of these drugs, which went on the market in Europe in 2003, supposedly act more quickly and last longer than Viagra (Swiatek, 2002). Levitra received FDA approval for sale in the United States in August 2003 and Cialis received FDA approval in November 2003. However, some experts caution people to not overrely on medical approaches to solve sexual difficulties (Black, 1999; Melman & Tiefer, 1992; Segraves & Segraves, 1998; Tiefer, 1986). Most sexual difficulties can be resolved through individual and couple therapy. As stated previously, the optimal approach in the use of drugs is in concert with psychotherapy.

Gay, Lesbian, and Bisexual Sex Therapy

Until recently, sex therapists treated sexual difficulties as implicitly heterosexual. The model for sexual functioning, in fact, was generally orgasmic heterosexual intercourse. There was virtually no mention of gay, lesbian, bisexual, or transgender sexual concerns.

For gay men, lesbian women, and bisexual individuals, sexual issues differ from those of heterosexuals in several ways. First, although gay men and lesbian women may have arousal, desire, erectile, or orgasmic difficulties, the context in which they occur may differ significantly from that of heterosexual persons. Problems among heterosexual individuals most often focus on sexual intercourse, whereas the sexual dissatisfaction of gay men, lesbian women, and bisexual persons focuses on other behaviors. Gay men in sex therapy, for example, most often experience aversion toward anal eroticism (Reece, 1988). Lesbian women in sex therapy frequently complain about aversive feelings toward cunnilingus. Female orgasmic difficulty, however, is not frequently viewed as a problem (Margolies et al., 1988). Heterosexual women, in contrast, frequently complain about lack of orgasm.

Second, lesbian women, gay men, and bisexual individuals must deal with both societal homophobia and internalized homophobia (Friedman,

FEMALE SEXUALITY AND SEXUAL difficulties experienced by women have not received as much research attention as the male sexual response. This disparity may be due to the greater complexity of female sexuality, the lack of accepted models of sexual response in women, deficiencies in measuring female sexual response, and lack of funding (Goldstein & Rosen, 2002).

The "Viagra phenomenon," the most recent event in a long history of the medicalization of male sexuality, has had both positive and negative consequences. Certainly, millions of men now are having reliable erections. Thus, calls for a similar drug to increase female sexual response are being heard, and female sexual problems and possible medical solutions are receiving attention (Bancroft, 2002). After all, the prevailing medical model promotes a norm of sexuality: correct genital performance (Tiefer, 2001). However, this impoverished "sex equals intercourse" equation is overly focused on the genitals.

An article by Ray Moynihan (2002) in the *British Medical Journal*, titled "The Making of a Disease: Female Sexual Dysfunction," is strongly critical of current work on female sexual difficulties. Moynihan argues that drug companies have exaggerated and "medicalized" female sexual difficulties to support future sales of Viagra-like drugs to women. He is skeptical about the close partnerships between some sexuality researchers and drug companies:

> The corporate sponsored creation of disease is not a new phenomenon, but the making of female sexual dysfunction is the freshest, clearest example we have. A cohort of researchers with close ties to drug companies are working with colleagues in the pharmaceutical industry to develop and define a new category of human illness at meetings heavily sponsored by companies racing to develop new drugs.

Moynihan adds that, to build drug markets for women similar to those of Viagra, "companies first require clearly defined medical diagnosis with measurable characteristics to facilitate credible clinical trials." In the Moynihan article, Dr. John Bancroft, director of the Kinsey Institute, is quoted as saying that the term "sexual dysfunction" is misleading and dangerous: Portraying sexual difficulties as dysfunctions "encourages physicians to prescribe drugs to change sexual function when the attention should be paid to other aspects of the woman's life." That may cause women to think they have a dysfunction when they do not. He asserts that the inhibition of sexual desire is healthy and functional in women facing fatigue, stress, or threatening behavior from their partners.

Drug companies and many sex therapists and researchers think that new drugs can play a valuable role in the treatment of female sexuality difficulties, as Viagra has done for many men. Bancroft (2002) states that "the possibility that Viagra-type drugs might influence female sexual response and enjoyment should be taken seriously." He further notes that caution must be taken and that methods of treatment should not separate sexual expression from other factors that accompany the human experience.

Moynihan summarizes:

> The potential benefits of this current medicalisation campaign are a more humanised doctor-patient relationship, effective and safe new drugs, and increased public and research attention to the complexity of female sexual problems. The potential risk in a process so heavily sponsored by drug companies, is that the complex, social, personal, and physical causes of sexual difficulties—and the range of solutions to them—will be swept away in the rush to diagnose, label, and prescribe. Perhaps the greatest concern comes from the flip side of inflated estimates of disease prevalence—the ever-narrowing definitions of "normal" which help turn the complaints of the healthy into the conditions of the sick.

With Moynihan's and Bancroft's observations in mind, consider these questions. Are you concerned about the close relationship between some sexuality researchers and drug companies? Do you think female sexual difficulties are being medicalized? Is a drug similar to Viagra for treatment of female sexual difficulties needed? Would it be very popular? Do you concur with Bancroft that personal factors like stress and fatigue account for a large portion of female sexual difficulties? How does this model address women's self-determination?

1991; Margolies et al., 1988). Fear of violence makes it difficult for gay men, bisexual individuals, and lesbian women to openly express their affection in the same manner as heterosexuals. As a consequence, lesbian women, bisexual individuals, and gay men learn to repress their expressions of feelings in public; this repression may carry over into the private realm as well. Internalized homophobia may result in diminished sexual desire, creating sexual aversion and fostering guilt and negative feelings about sexual activity.

It is important for gay, lesbian, and bisexual people with sexual difficulties to choose a therapist who affirms their orientation and understands the special issues confronting them.

Third, gay men must deal with the association between sex and HIV infection that has cut a deadly swath through the gay community. The death of friends, lovers, and partners has left many depressed, which, in turn, affects sexual desire and creates high levels of sexual anxiety. Many gay men are fearful of contracting HIV even if they practice safer sex. And HIV-positive men, even if they are practicing safer sex, are often afraid of transmitting the infection to their loved ones.

These unique lesbian, bisexual, and gay concerns require that sex therapists expand their understanding and treatment of sexual problems. If the therapist is not a gay man or lesbian woman, he or she needs to have a thorough knowledge of homosexuality and the gay and lesbian world. Therapists further need to be aware of their own assumptions and feelings about homosexuality (Coleman, Rosser, & Strapko, 1992). Therapists working with gay, bisexual, or lesbian clients need to develop inclusive models of sexual treatment that are "gay-positive."

Seeking Professional Assistance

Because something is not "functioning" according to a therapist's model does not necessarily mean that something is wrong. You need to evaluate your sexuality in terms of your own and your partner's satisfaction and the meanings you give to your sexuality. If, after doing this, you are unable to resolve your sexual difficulties yourself, seek professional assistance. It is important to realize that seeking such assistance is not a sign of personal weakness or failure. Rather, it is a sign of strength, for it demonstrates an ability to reach out and a willingness to change. It is a sign that you care for your partner, your relationship, and yourself. As you think about therapy, consider the following:

▪ What are your goals in therapy? Are you willing to make changes in your relationship to achieve your goals?

- Do you want individual, couple, or group therapy? If you are in a relationship, is your partner willing to participate in therapy?

- What characteristics are important for you in a therapist? Do you prefer a female or a male therapist? Is the therapist's age, religion, or ethnic background important to you?

- What are the therapist's professional qualifications? There are few certified sex therapy programs; most therapists who treat sexual difficulties come from various professional backgrounds, such as psychiatry, clinical psychology, psychoanalysis, marriage and family counseling, and social work. Because there is no licensing in the field of sex therapy, it is important to seek out those trained therapists who have licenses in their generalized field. This way, you have recourse if questionable practices arise. It is worth noting that professionals view sexual contact between themselves and their clients as unethical and unlawful.

- What is the therapist's approach? Is it behavioral, psychosexual, psychoanalytic, medical, religious, spiritual, feminist, or something else? What is the therapist's attitude toward gender roles? Do you feel comfortable with the approach?

- If necessary, does the therapist offer a sliding-scale fee, based on your level of income?

- If you are a lesbian, gay, or bisexual person, does the therapist affirm your sexual orientation? Does the therapist understand the special problems gay men, bisexual individuals, and lesbian women face?

- After a session or two with the therapist, do you have confidence in him or her? If not, discuss your feelings with the therapist. If you believe your dissatisfaction is not a defense mechanism, change therapists.

Just how successful is sex therapy? Nobody really knows. Though Masters and Johnson have reported higher success rates than other therapists, some of their methods of evaluating patients have been questioned. What constitutes success or failure is subjective and open to interpretation. Much of therapy's success depends on a person's willingness to confront painful feelings and to change. This entails time, effort, and often considerable amounts of money. But, ultimately, the difficult work may reward partners with greater satisfaction and a deeper relationship.

AS WE CONSIDER OUR SEXUALITY, it is important to realize that sexual difficulties and dissatisfaction are commonplace. But sex is more than orgasms or certain kinds of activities. Even if we have difficulties in some areas, there are other areas in which we may be fully sexual. If we have erectile or orgasmic problems, we can use our imagination to expand our repertoire of erotic activities. We can touch each other sensually, masturbate alone or with our partner, and caress, kiss, eroticize, and explore our bodies with fingers and tongues. We can enhance our sexuality if we look at sex as the mutual giving and receiving of erotic pleasure, rather than a command performance. By paying attention to our conditions for good sex, maintaining intimacy, and focusing on our own erotic sensations and those of our partner, we can transform our sexual relationships.

Impulse arrested spills over, and the flood is feeling, the flood is passion, the flood is even madness: It depends on the force of the current, the height and strength of the barrier. . . . Feeling lurks in that interval of time between desire and its consummation.

—*Aldous Huxley (1894–1963)*

SUMMARY

Sexual Difficulties: Definitions, Types, and Prevalence

- The line between "normal" sexual functioning and a sexual difficulty is often not definitive.

- Difficulties in sexual functioning are often called sexual problems, sexual disorders, or *sexual dysfunctions.*

- *The Diagnostic and Statistical Manual of Mental Disorders* classifies four types of sexual dysfunction: disorders of desire, sexual arousal disorders, orgasmic disorders, and sexual pain disorders. According to a newer, woman-centered classification system, sexual difficulties arise from cultural and relational factors, and not medical problems.

- A sexual difficulty can be defined as a disappointment on the part of one or both partners.

- The NHSLS found that sexual difficulties are more common in women (43%) than men (31%) and are associated with health-related and psychosocial factors. A Kinsey Institute study of women found that 24% reported marked distress in their sexual relationship.

- *Hypoactive sexual desire (HSD)* is low sexual desire. This disorder usually develops in adulthood and is associated with psychologically stressful life situations. *DSM sexual aversion* is a consistently phobic response to sexual activities or the idea of such activities.

- *Female sexual arousal disorder* is an inability to attain or maintain the normal vaginal lubrication and swelling that accompany sexual excitement. It is usually accompanied by desire and orgasmic disorders.

- Male sexual problems typically focus on the excitement stage. *Male erectile disorder* is the inability to have or maintain an erection until completion of sexual activity. Erectile difficulties may occur because of fatigue, too much alcohol, smoking, depression, conflict, certain medical conditions, or a host of other transitory reasons.

- *Persistent sexual arousal syndrome,* a newly reported difficulty in women, is the persistent arousal that does not resolve itself in ordinary ways and continues for hours, days, and even weeks.

- *Female orgasmic disorder* refers to the condition of not being orgasmic. Negative or guilty sexual attitudes, inadequate sexual stimulation, and relationship difficulties contribute to this disorder.

- *Male orgasmic disorder* is the delay or absence of ejaculation following normal sexual excitement. Psychosocial factors contribute to this condition. In *inhibited ejaculation,* the penis is erect, but the man is unable to ejaculate. In *delayed ejaculation,* the man is not able to ejaculate easily during intercourse.

- *Early or rapid ejaculation* is the inability to control or delay ejaculation as long as desired, causing personal or interpersonal distress.

- *Dyspareunia,* painful intercourse, often occurs because a woman is not entirely aroused before her partner attempts intercourse. Sexual inhibitions, a poor relationship with her partner, or hormonal imbalances may contribute to dyspareunia. In *vaginismus,* the muscles around the vaginal entrance go into spasmodic contractions. Vaginismus is essentially a conditioned response that reflects fear, anxiety, or pain.

Physical Causes of Sexual Difficulties and Dissatisfaction

- Health problems such as diabetes and alcoholism can cause erectile difficulties. Some prescription drugs affect sexual responsiveness.

- Coital pain caused by inadequate lubrication and thinning vaginal walls often occurs as a result of decreased estrogen associated with menopause. Lubricants can resolve the difficulties.

Psychological Causes of Sexual Difficulties and Dissatisfaction

- Sexual difficulties may have their origin in any number of psychological causes. The immediate causes of sexual difficulties lie in the current situation, including fatigue and stress, ineffective sexual behavior, sexual anxieties, and an excessive need to please a partner. Internal conflict, caused by religious teachings, guilt, negative learning, and internalized homophobia, can contribute to dissatisfaction, as can relationship conflicts.

Sexual Enhancement

- Many people and all couples experience sexual difficulties and dissatisfaction at one time or another. The widespread variability of sexual functioning suggests the "normality" of at least occasional sexual difficulties.

- *Sexual enhancement* refers to improving the quality of one's sexual relationship. Sexual-enhancement programs generally provide accurate information about sexuality, develop communication skills, foster positive attitudes, and increase self-awareness. Awareness of your own sexual needs is often critical to enhancing your sexuality. Enhancement of sex includes the intensification of arousal.

- There has been a dramatic increase in over-the-counter, natural sexual enhancers, but none have been shown to be effective.

Treating Sexual Problems

- Masters and Johnson developed a cognitive-behavioral approach to sexual difficulties. They relabeled sexual problems as dysfunctions rather than neuroses or diseases, used direct behavior modification practices, and treated couples rather than individuals. Treatment includes *sensate focus* exercises without intercourse, "homework" exercises, and, finally, "permission" to engage in sexual intercourse. Kaplan's psychosexual therapy program combines behavioral exercises with insight therapy.

- The *PLISSIT model* of sex therapy refers to four progressive levels: permission, limited information, specific suggestions, and intensive therapy. Individuals and couples can often resolve their difficulties by talking over their problems with their partners or friends, reading self-help books, and attending sex therapy groups. If they are unable to resolve their difficulties in these ways, they should consider intensive sex therapy.

- Viagra was introduced in the United States in 1998 and is the first effective and safe oral drug for treatment of male erectile difficulty. Viagra does not increase sexual excitement but rather facilitates blood engorgement in the penis.

- Some sexuality professionals claim that drug companies have exaggerated and "medicalized" female sexual difficulties to promote future sales of Viagra-like drugs for women.

- There are three significant concerns for gay men, bisexual individuals, and lesbian women in sex therapy. First, the context in which problems occur may differ significantly from that of a heterosexual person; there may be issues revolving around anal eroticism and cunnilingus. Second, they must deal with both societal homophobia and internalized homophobia. Third, gay men must deal with the association between sex and HIV/AIDS.

- In seeking professional assistance for a sexual problem, it is important to realize that seeking help is not a sign of personal weakness or failure, but rather a sign of strength.

Sex and the Internet

Sexual Difficulties

The Web site WebMD provides information on various health issues, including sexual difficulties. Go to this site (http://www.webmd.com/) and find the "Search" box. Type in various sexual difficulty terms, such as "sexual dysfunction," "erectile dysfunction," "premature ejaculation," "female orgasmic disorder," and "dyspareunia." Review the information for each topic.

- Is the information given appropriate for non-medical people?

- For which topics is the most information provided?

- What new information is provided?

- Are there links to other sites that provide sexuality information?

SUGGESTED WEB SITES

American Family Physician
http://www.aafp.org
Focuses on both female and male sexual difficulties.

FSD Alert
http://www.fsd-alert.org
Promotes an alternative view of female sexual difficulties, challenges the pharmaceutical industry, and calls for further research on women's sexual difficulties.

Masters and Johnson
http://www.mastersandjohnson.com
Provides information about various sexual difficulties, a frequently-asked-questions section, and ways to get help for relationships.

Sexual Health On-line
http://www.sexualhealth.org
Gives information on most sexuality-related topics, including sexual functioning problems.

Women's Sexual Health
http://www.womenssexualhealth.org
Addresses the questions and concerns of women and their partners concerning female sexual difficulties and includes a "Physician Locator" to help them find local physicians who treat female sexual difficulties.

SUGGESTED READING

Berman, Jennifer; Berman, Laura; & Bumiller, Elizabeth. (2001). *For Women Only: A Revolutionary Guide to Overcoming Sexual Dysfunction and Reclaiming Your Sex Life.* New York: Henry Holt. A woman-centered approach to understanding and addressing sexual difficulties.

Heiman, Julia, & LoPiccolo, Joseph. (1988). *Becoming Orgasmic: A Sexual Growth Program for Women.* Englewood Cliffs, NJ: Prentice-Hall. Suggestions on how to develop one's orgasmic responsiveness.

Metz, Michael, & McCarthy, Barry. (2004). *Coping with Premature Ejaculation.* Oakland, CA: New Harbinger Publications. Presents simple, effective techniques to help couples work together to improve ejaculatory control.

Schnarch, David. (2002). *Resurrecting Sex.* New York: HarperCollins. Deals with the sexual problems of couples and offers straight talk about sex, intimacy, and relationships.

Zilbergeld, Bernie. (1999). *The New Male Sexuality* (Rev. ed.). New York: Bantam Books. The book most widely recommended by therapists for men on enhancing sexual relationships. Women can profit equally from it, not only for themselves but also as insight into male sexuality.

For links, articles, and study material, go to the McGraw-Hill Web site, located at http://www.mhhe.com/strong5

15

Sexually Transmitted Infections

"Up to this date, I have slept with about thirteen men. My most recent "wake-up call" was from a threat from a prospective partner and from a human sexuality course. I took a test for HIV; the result was negative. However, I did get infected and passed on genital warts to my ex-boyfriend. I simply pretended that I had never slept with anyone else and that if anyone had cheated it was him. It never fazed me that I was at such a risk for contracting HIV. My new resolutions are to educate my family, friends, and peers about sex, take a proactive approach toward sex with prospective partners, and discuss sex openly and honestly with my mother."

— 23-year-old Latina

"My partner and I want to use a condom to protect ourselves from STIs. But I feel inadequate when we are intimate and he cannot keep an erection to put a condom on. I feel too embarrassed for him to discuss the situation. So, we both walk away a bit disappointed—him because he could not stay erect and me because I did not take the time or have the courage to help him. I think if he masturbated with a condom on it would help him with his performance anxiety problem."

— 22-year-old White female

"STIs and HIV are precisely the reason I exercise caution when engaging in sexual activity. I don't want to ever get an STI, and I'd rather never have sex again than have HIV."

— 24-year-old White male

"Why do males often convince women to have sex without proper protection? I don't understand this because there is always a risk of getting an STI. I know that women think about this just as often as men do, but why is it that men do not seem to care?"

— 21-year-old biracial female

"I am usually very careful when it comes to my sexual relations and protecting myself from STIs, but there have been a couple of times when I've been intoxicated and have not practiced safe sex. It scares me that I have done things like that and have tried to make sure it doesn't happen again. STIs are just a very uncomfortable subject."

— 27-year-old White female

THE TERM "SEXUALLY TRANSMITTED INFECTIONS" (STIs) refers to more than 25 infectious organisms passed from person to person primarily through sexual contact. STIs were once called venereal diseases (VDs), a term derived from Venus, the Roman goddess of love. More recently, the term "sexually transmitted diseases" (STDs) replaced "venereal diseases." Actually, many health professionals continue to use "STD." However, some believe that "STI" is a more accurate and less judgmental term. That is, a person can be infected with an STI organism but not have developed the illness or disease associated with the organism. So, in this book, we use "STI", although "STD" may appear when other sources are cited.

There are two general types of STIs: (1) those that are bacterial and curable, such as chlamydia and gonorrhea, and (2) those that are viral and incurable—but treatable—such as HIV infection and genital warts. STIs are a serious health problem in our country, resulting in considerable human suffering.

In this chapter and the next, we discuss the incidence and prevalence of STIs in our country, the disparate impact of STIs on certain population groups, the factors that contribute to the STI epidemic, and the consequences of STIs. We also discuss the incidence, transmission, symptoms, and treatment of the principal STIs that affect Americans, with the exception of HIV/AIDS, which is the subject of Chapter 16. The prevention of STIs, including protective health behaviors, safer sex practices, and communication skills, are also addressed in this chapter.

> O rose, thou art sick!
> The invisible worm
> That flies in the night,
> In the howling storm,
> Has found thy bed
> Of crimson joy,
> And his dark secret love
> Does thy life destroy.
>
> —*William Blake (1757–1827)*

THE STI EPIDEMIC

The federal Institute of Medicine (IOM) characterizes STIs as "hidden epidemics of tremendous health and economic consequences in the United States," adding that "STDs represent a growing threat to the nation's health and national action is urgently needed." The IOM notes that STIs are a challenging public health problem because of their "hidden" nature. The IOM adds that "the sociocultural taboos related to sexuality are a barrier to STD prevention" (Eng & Butler, 1997). The "silent" infections of STIs make them a serious public threat requiring greater personal attention and increased health-care resources.

STIs: The Most Common Reportable Infectious Diseases

STIs are common in the United States, but identifying exactly how many cases there are is impossible, and even estimating the total number is difficult. Often, an STI is "silent"—that is, it goes undiagnosed because it has no early symptoms or the symptoms go ignored and untreated, especially among people with limited access to health care. Asymptomatic infections can be diagnosed through testing, but routine screening programs are not widespread, and social stigmas and the lack of public awareness about STIs may result in no testing during visits to health-care professionals. And even when STIs are diagnosed, reporting regulations vary. Four STIs—gonorrhea, syphilis, chlamydia, and AIDS—must be reported by health-care providers to health departments in *each* state and to the federal Centers for Disease Control and Prevention (CDC). But no such reporting requirement exists for the other five major STIs: genital herpes, human papillomavirus (HPV), hepatitis B, HIV, and trichomoniasis. In addition, the reporting of STI diagnoses is inconsistent. For example, some private physicians do not report STI cases to their state health departments (American Social Health Association [ASHA], 1998a; CDC, 2002b). In spite of the underreporting and undiagnosed cases, several significant indicators illustrate the **incidence** (number of new cases) and **prevalence** (total number of cases) of STIs in the United States:

FIGURE 15.1 Estimated Annual New Cases of STIs, 1996. (*Source:* "Sexually Transmitted Diseases in America: How Many Cases and at What Cost?" The Henry J. Kaiser Family Foundation, December 1998. This information was reprinted with permission of the Henry J. Kaiser Family Foundation. The Kaiser Family Foundation, based in Menlo Park, California, is a nonprofit, independent national health care philanthropy and is not associated with Kaiser Permanente or Kaiser Industries.)

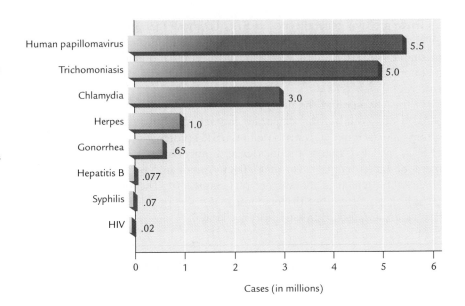

- STIs are the most common reported infectious diseases in the United States. In 1995, according to the CDC, STIs represented 87% of all cases of the most frequently reported infectious diseases in the United States. Of the top ten infections, five were STIs: chlamydia, gonorrhea, AIDS, syphilis, and hepatitis B (CDC, 1996a).

- There were an estimated 15.3 million new cases of STIs in the United States in 1996, up from the CDC estimate of 12 million cases (Figure 15.1). This increase most likely reflects a more accurate count, not an actual increase in cases. More than two-thirds of the total cases were attributable to sharp increases in two infections—HPV and trichomoniasis—that reflect better detection and estimation methodologies. The incidences of three STIs—chlamydia, gonorrhea, and syphilis—were found to have decreased, largely due to national control programs. The number of cases of genital herpes, hepatitis B, and HIV/AIDS held steady over the past decade (ASHA, 1998b) (Figure 15.2). These diseases cannot be cured, so cases accrue year after year.

- STI rates in the United States far exceed those of every other industrialized nation, including Canada, Japan, and Australia and the countries of

FIGURE 15.2 Total Cases of Viral STIs, 1996. (*Source:* "Sexually Transmitted Diseases in America: How Many Cases and at What Cost?" The Henry J. Kaiser Family Foundation, December 1998. This information was reprinted with permission of the Henry J. Kaiser Family Foundation. The Kaiser Family Foundation, based in Menlo Park, California, is a nonprofit, independent national health care philanthropy and is not associated with Kaiser Permanente or Kaiser Industries.)

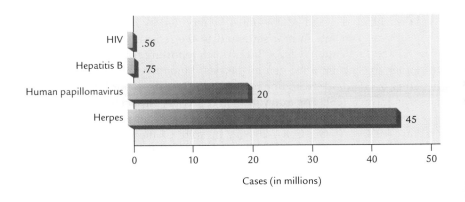

western and northern Europe. A more pragmatic approach to sexuality issues, more comprehensive school and public sexuality education, and easier access to health care in these countries contribute to their lower STI rates (Eng & Butler, 1997).

- By age 24, at least 1 in 3 sexually active people are estimated to have contracted an STI (ASHA, 1998a).

Who Is Affected: Disparities Among Groups

Anyone, regardless of gender, race/ethnicity, social status, or sexual orientation, can get an STI. What people do—not who they are—exposes them to the organisms that cause STIs. Nevertheless, some population groups are disproportionately affected by STIs; this disparity reflects gender, age, and racial and ethnic differences (U.S. Department of Health and Human Services, 2000b), with women, teens and young adults, and minorities at highest risk (ASHA, 1998a).

Click on "STDs: The Silent Epidemic" to hear about a peer education program designed to reach those at highest risk for contracting sexually transmitted infections.

Gender Disparities   Overall, the consequences of STIs for women often are more serious than those for men. Generally, women contract STIs more easily than men and suffer greater damage to their health and reproductive functioning. STIs often are transmitted more easily from a man to a woman than vice versa. Women's increased likelihood of having an asymptomatic infection results in a delay in diagnosis and treatment. Furthermore, women in general have less say than men about whether to have sex and whether to use condoms (ASHA, 1998a).

A kind of "biological sexism" means that women are biologically more susceptible to infection when exposed to an STI organism than men are. According to Robert Hatcher and his colleagues (1998), this is partly a result of the "fluid dynamics of intercourse [wherein] women are apparently more likely than men to acquire an STD infection from any single sexual encounter." For example, a woman's chances of acquiring gonorrhea from a single sexual intercourse episode with a man may be as high as 90%, but the man's chances of acquiring gonorrhea in the same episode are about 20–30% (Donovan, 1993). A woman's anatomy may increase her susceptibility to STIs. The warm, moist interior of the vagina and uterus is an ideal environment for many organisms. The thin, sensitive skin inside the labia and the mucous membranes lining the vagina may also be more receptive to infectious organisms than the skin covering a man's genitals. The complications of STIs in women are often very mild or absent, and STIs are more difficult to diagnose in women due to the physiology of the female reproductive system (U.S. Department of Health and Human Services, 2000b). For example, 75% of women diagnosed with chlamydia do not have any symptoms, compared to 50% of men (CDC, 2001a). The long-term effects of STIs for women may include pelvic inflammatory disease (PID), ectopic pregnancy, infertility, cervical cancer, and chronic pelvic pain, as well as possible severe damage to a fetus or newborn, including spontaneous abortion, stillbirth, low birth weight, neurological damage, and death.

Lesbian women may be at similar risk for STIs as heterosexual women. According to a study conducted in Sydney, Australia, women who had sex with other women had a higher rate than heterosexual women of bacterial vaginosis, with herpes and genital warts being common and the incidence of gonorrhea and chlamydia being low in both groups. The self-identified lesbian women were more than 3 times as likely to report having had sex with a homosexual or bisexual male as the heterosexual women. Among the women who had sex with other women, 93% reported previous sexual contact with men; they had a median of 12 lifetime male sex partners, compared with 6 lifetime partners for the heterosexual women. Thus, lesbian women may not be free of STI risk because many women who have sex with other women and self-identify as lesbian also have sex with men (Fetters, Marks, Mindel, & Estcourt, 2000). Two studies found that women who had sex with both men and women had more HIV/STI behavioral risk factors, such as having multiple male sex partners, having sex with men who have sex with men, and having sex with an injecting drug user, than women who had sex only with men (Gonzales et al., 1999; Scheer et al., 2002). A case report study found that female-to-female transmission of syphilis occurred through oral sex (Campos-Outcalt & Hurwitz, 2002).

Age Disparities   About two-thirds of all new cases of STIs occur in people age 15–24, with one-fourth of those cases occurring in people under age 20 (Eng & Butler, 1997). Young people are at greater risk because they are more likely to have multiple sex partners as opposed to one long-term partner, to engage in risky behavior, and to select higher-risk partners (Division of STD Prevention, 2000). STIs are also a serious problem among adolescents and young adults because of factors such as a lack of health insurance or ability to pay, lack of transportation to health-care providers, uneasiness with medical facilities and services, and concerns about confidentiality (Division of STD Prevention, 2000).

Racial and Ethnic Disparities   STIs are reported at higher rates among certain minority groups, mainly African Americans, Native Americans, and Latinos. For example, in 2001, the reported gonorrhea rates for African Americans, Latinos (Hispanics), and American Indian/Alaska Natives were 27.0, 2.5, and 3.9 times higher, respectively, than the rate reported for non-Hispanic Whites (CDC, 2002b). Race and ethnicity in the United States are STI risk markers that correlate with other basic determinants of health status, such as poverty, access to quality health care, health-care-seeking behavior, illegal drug use, and communities with high prevalence of STIs.

Factors Contributing to the Spread of STIs

According to the Institute of Medicine, "STDs are behavioral-linked diseases that result from unprotected sex," and behavioral, social, and biological factors contribute to their spread (Eng & Butler, 1997). These factors are obstacles to the control of STIs in the United States.

Behavioral Factors

EARLY INITIATION OF INTIMATE SEXUAL ACTIVITY   People who are sexually active at an early age are at greater risk for STIs because this early initiation increases the total time they are sexually active and because they are more likely to have nonvoluntary intercourse, to have a greater number of sex partners, and to use condoms less consistently (Aral, 1994). For example, analysis of data from the 1995 National Survey of Family Growth revealed that women who had sexual intercourse before age 15 were nearly 4 times as likely to report a bacterial STI and more than 2 times as likely to report PID as were women who first had sex after age 18 (Miller, Cain, Rogers, Gribble, & Turner, 1999).

MULTIPLE SEX PARTNERS   The more sex partners an individual has, the greater the chance of acquiring an STI. For example, according to one national study, 1% of respondents with 1 sex partner within the past year, 4.5% of those with 2–4 partners, and 5.9% of those with 5 or more partners became infected with an STI (Laumann, Gagnon, Michael, & Michaels, 1994). In addition, the more sex partners respondents had, the more likely it was that each of those partners was unfamiliar and nonexclusive. Being unfamiliar with partners, especially knowing the person for less than 1 month before first having sex, and having nonexclusive partners were both strongly associated with higher STI incidence. The National Survey of Men (NSM) and the National Survey of Women (NSW) found that, compared with respondents who had only 1 partner, those reporting having 2–3 partners were 5 times as likely to have had an STI; those reporting having 16 or more partners were 31 times as likely (Tanfer, Cubbins, & Billy, 1995). Other studies have shown that 34% of sexually active women, age 15–44, were at risk for STIs because they either had more than 1 sex partner (21%) or their partners had 2 or more sex partners (23%). Interestingly, 20% of the women who had partners who had multiple sex partners thought that they were in mutually exclusive sexual relationships. Among men age 18–24, 24% were at risk for STIs because of having 2 or more sex partners (Finer, Darroch, & Singh, 1999). A national study involving a random sample of 34,000 males in 25 states found that 2.1% reported having four or more sex partners in the past 12 months (Holtzman, Bland, Lansky, & Mack, 2001).

HIGH-RISK SEX PARTNERS   Having sex with a person who has had many partners increases the risk of acquiring an STI. One example of this is a female who has a bisexual male partner. Often, the female does not know that her male partner also has sex with men. One study of 415 men who reported having sex with men revealed that 87% also reported having sex with women. These men were more than 2 times as likely as heterosexuals to be HIV-positive, and 29% were married or had been married (Lehner & Chiasson, 1998). A study of 303 sexually experienced, racially diverse adolescents revealed that those with an older, regular sex partner were more likely to have a history of STIs. Other factors associated with having had an STI included being African American, having more sex partners, and using marijuana (Boyer et al., 2000).

HIGH-RISK SEXUAL BEHAVIOR   Certain sexual behaviors with a partner put individuals at higher risk for acquiring an STI than other behaviors. For example, studies have shown that men and women who have engaged in anal intercourse, have paid for sex, or have had one-night stands are more likely to report an STI than those who did not participate in those behaviors (Foxman, Aral, & Holmes, 1998; Tanfer et al., 1995). A study of southern rural women found that those who reported engaging in more high-risk behaviors in the past 12 months were more likely to report having an STI during that same time (Yarber, Crosby, & Sanders, 2000).

Preventing STIs: Male Condoms, Female Condoms, and Nonoxynol-9

FOR DECADES, THE MALE CONDOM has been promoted by public health officials as an important STI prevention device for sexually active individuals. However, there has been much discussion recently about how effective condoms really are in preventing HIV and other STIs. Some skeptics argue that condoms fail too often and that claims of condom effectiveness are misleading and exaggerated. Many of these skeptics thus strongly denounce efforts to promote condoms as a reliable way of avoiding STIs. STI prevention specialists, however, continue to promote condoms as a valuable component of STI control, believing that condoms are indeed very effective when used properly. This battle over condom effectiveness is often highlighted in the media, leaving many sexually active people confused about whether condoms help to prevent the various STIs, including HIV. Some even hesitate to use condoms.

This controversy has prompted several federal agencies to examine the literature on condom effectiveness in an attempt to clarify the value of condoms for STI prevention. The Centers for Disease Control and Prevention (CDC) has issued statements and recommendations on male condoms, **female condoms, nonoxynol-9,** and STI prevention for public health personnel. These recommendations are presented here to help you in making better decisions about protecting yourself from HIV and other STIs.

Male Condoms

The CDC's (2002d) recommendations about the male latex condom and the prevention of STIs, including HIV,

are based on information about the ways the various STIs are transmitted, the physical nature of condoms, the coverage or protection that condoms provide, and epidemiological studies of condom use and STIs. The CDC also notes that laboratory studies have shown that latex condoms provide an essentially impermeable barrier to particles the size of STI pathogens, including HIV. The CDC reports that most of the epidemiological studies comparing rates of STI transmission for condom users and nonusers focus only on penile-vaginal intercourse and have several other methodological limitations. For example, because sexuality is a private behavior, it is difficult to determine whether an individual is a condom user or uses condoms consistently and correctly. In addition, it is nearly impossible to determine the level of exposure to STIs among research participants. However, many epidemiological studies for HIV infection employed more rigorous methods and measures and have shown that consistent condom use is a highly effective means of preventing HIV transmission. Overall, the CDC concludes, the epidemiological data are inconclusive for most STIs, indicating that more research is needed. The inconclusive epidemiological data do not necessarily mean that latex condoms do not work.

According to the CDC, the surest way to avoid STIs is to abstain from sexual intercourse or to be in a long-term, sexually exclusive relationship with a partner who has been tested and is known to be uninfected. About STI prevention and condoms, the CDC has this to say:

INCONSISTENT AND INCORRECT CONDOM USE Correctly using a latex **male condom** during each sexual encounter and at any time the penis comes into contact with the partner significantly reduces the risk of STIs. For example, one national study revealed that those who always used condoms reported far lower STI rates than those who did not (Laumann et al., 1998). Although considerable research has been conducted on whether persons at risk use condoms, very little research has investigated whether people use condoms correctly. A study of sexually active college men from a large midwestern university showed a considerable number of errors that could expose the men and/or their partner to STIs (Crosby, Sanders, Yarber, Graham, & Dodge, 2002; Yarber, Sanders, Crosby, Graham, & Dodge, 2001).

SUBSTANCE ABUSE The abuse of alcohol and drugs is associated with high-risk sexual behavior. Substances may affect cognitive and negotiating skills before and during sex, lowering the likelihood that partners will protect themselves from STIs and pregnancy (U.S. Department of Health

For persons whose sexual behaviors place them at risk for STDs, correct and consistent use of the male latex condom can reduce the risk of STD transmission. However, no protective method is 100 percent effective, and condom use cannot guarantee absolute protection against any STD. In order to achieve the protective effect of condoms, they must be used correctly and consistently. While condom use has been associated with a lower risk of cervical cancer, the use of condoms should not be a substitute for routine screening with Pap smears to detect and prevent cancer.

The CDC notes that there are two primary ways STIs are transmitted: (1) the discharge diseases—HIV, gonorrhea, chlamydia, and trichomoniasis—in which the organisms are transmitted when infected semen or vaginal fluids contact mucosal surfaces such as the male urethra, the vagina or cervix, and anus, and (2) the genital ulcer diseases—genital herpes, syphilis, and chancroid—and human papillomavirus (HPV), which are primarily transmitted through contact with infected skin or mucosal surfaces. Relative to delineation and the research literature, the CDC states:

- Latex condoms, when used consistently and correctly, are highly effective in preventing the transmission of HIV, the virus that causes AIDS.

- Latex condoms, when used consistently and correctly, can reduce the risk of transmission of gonorrhea, chlamydia, and trichomoniasis.

- Genital ulcer diseases and HPV infections can occur in both male and female genital areas that are covered or protected by a latex condom, as well as in areas that are not covered. Correct and consistent use of latex condoms can reduce the risk of genital herpes, syphilis, and chancroid only when the infected area or site of potential exposure is protected. While the effect of condoms in preventing human papillomavirus is unknown, condom use has been associated with a lower rate of cervical cancer, and HPV-associated disease.

Female Condoms

The CDC (2000d) indicates that the female condom (Reality™) is an effective mechanical barrier to viruses, including HIV. However, the efficacy of the female condom in providing protection against STIs, including HIV, has not been shown clinically. The CDC states that, used consistently and correctly, the female condom may substantially reduce the risk of STIs. The CDC recommends that when a male condom cannot be used properly sex partners should consider using a female condom.

Nonoxynol-9

The CDC (2000e) states that vaginal spermicides containing nonoxynol-9 (N-9) are not effective in preventing cervical gonorrhea, chlamydia, or HIV infection. Researchers say that N-9, working like a detergent, can break up or irritate the cell lining, or epithelium, of the rectum and the vagina, the first lines of defense against HIV and other STIs. The danger in anal sex is especially significant because the rectum has only a single-cell wall; the vagina has a wall that is about 40 cells thick (Zimmerman, 2002). The World Health Organization and the CDC have reported that, because N-9 can cause small legions that increase the risk of STI/HIV, condoms with this ingredient should be avoided. At the same time, they acknowledge that condoms lubricated *without* N-9 are extremely effective in both reducing the risk of infection and preventing pregnancy.

Sources: CDC, 2002d; CDC, 2002e; Roddy, 2002; Zimmerman, 2002.

and Human Services, 2000b). One study of persons in a program for those convicted of driving under the influence showed that those with a substance abuse problem were more likely to have sex without condoms while high on alcohol or drugs (Siegal et al., 1999).

SEXUAL COERCION Not all people enter sexual relationships as willing partners, particularly women. The 2001 Youth Risk Behavior Survey (CDC, 2002a) revealed that 7.7% of the adolescents surveyed had experienced forced sexual intercourse, with a greater percentage of females (10.3%) being coerced than males (5.1%). Persons experiencing violence are less able to protect themselves from STIs.

LACK OF KNOWLEDGE OF AND CONCERN ABOUT STIS Studies sponsored by the Kaiser Family Foundation revealed that many Americans are uninformed about STIs. When asked to name STIs they had heard of, only 2% named HPV, the most common STI, and only 11% named genital warts (Kaiser Family

Foundation/Harvard School of Public Health, 2000). About one-third (36%) were not aware that having an STI increases one's risk of becoming infected with HIV, and almost 70% thought that only 1 in 10 Americans would get an STI in their lifetime (the actual figure is 3 in 10) (Kaiser Family Foundation/*Glamour*, 1998). Analysis of the National Longitudinal Study of Adolescent Health data of over 16,000 adolescents in grades 7–12 showed that about one-third erroneously believed that no space is needed at the end of the condom when it is used and that Vaseline can be safely used with condoms. About one-fifth held the false belief that lambskin condoms protect against HIV better than do latex condoms (Crosby & Yarber, 2001). People also often do not have an adequate perception of their partners' risk. In one study of STI clinic patients in Southern California, participants indicated that they did not use condoms when they perceived new sex partners to be STI-free. Instead of directly discussing their partners' sexual history, they relied on both visual and verbal cues to judge whether their partners were disease-free. This assessment reflected serious error in judgment because most of the study participants had, in fact, contracted an STI (Hoffman & Cohen, 1999). Another study found that HIV-infected people had poor knowledge regarding their sex partner's HIV infection status. Sixty-four percent of partners thought to be infected were actually uninfected, and 42% of partners thought to be uninfected were actually infected (Niccolai, Farley, Ayoub, Magnus, & Kissinger, 2002). This kind of information underscores the need for communication and honesty as part of STI prevention.

Social Factors

POVERTY AND MARGINALIZATION   Disenfranchised individuals and those in social networks in which high-risk behavior is common and access to health care is limited are disproportionately affected by STIs. These groups include sex workers (people who exchange sex for money, drugs, or other goods), adolescents, migrant workers, and incarcerated persons. STIs, substance abuse, and sex work are closely connected (Eng & Butler, 1997; U.S. Department of Health and Human Services, 2000b).

ACCESS TO HEALTH CARE   Access to high-quality and culturally sensitive health care is imperative for early detection, treatment, and prevention counseling for STIs. Unfortunately, health services for STIs are limited in many low-income areas where STIs are common, and funds for public health programs are scarce. Without such programs, many people in high-risk social networks have no access to STI care.

SECRECY AND MORAL CONFLICT ABOUT SEXUALITY   One factor that separates the United States from other countries with lower rates of STIs is the cultural stigma associated with STIs and our general discomfort with sexuality issues. Historically, a moralistic, judgmental stance on STIs has hindered public health efforts to control STIs. For example, significant funding for AIDS research did not begin until it was clear that heterosexual individuals as well as gay men were threatened (Altman, 1985; Shilts, 1987). Also, the federal government has funded school and community adolescent abstinence-only educational programs in which the use of condoms for HIV/STI prevention cannot be mentioned. Educational efforts related to

Social factors contributing to the spread of STIs include situations that support risky sexual behavior.

STIs in particular and to sexuality in general often are hampered by vocal minorities who feel that knowledge about sex is what causes people to engage in it.

Biological Factors

ASYMPTOMATIC NATURE OF STIS   Most STIs either do not produce any symptoms or cause symptoms so mild that they go unnoticed or disregarded. A long time lag—sometimes years—often exists between the contracting of an STI and the onset of significant health problems. During the time in which the STI is asymptomatic, a person can unknowingly infect others. The individual may not seek treatment, allowing the STI to do damage to the reproductive system. Furthermore, people often do not attribute long-term consequences of STIs, such as STI-related cancers, to this kind of infection (Eng & Butler, 1997).

RESISTANCE TO TREATMENT OR LACK OF A CURE   Because resistant strains of viruses, bacteria, and other pathogens are continually developing, antibiotics that have worked in the past may no longer be effective in treating STIs. Infected people may continue to transmit the STI, either because they believe they have been cured or because they currently show no symptoms. The clinician or the patient may underrate the value of a follow-up examination to ensure that the initial treatment has worked or to try an alternative medication if necessary. And some STIs, such as herpes, genital warts, and HIV, cannot be cured. The individual who has any of these viruses is always theoretically able to transmit them to others.

OTHER BIOLOGICAL FACTORS   Adolescent women are highly susceptible to acquiring chlamydia and gonorrhea because of an immature cervix (ASHA, 1998c). Women who practice vaginal douching are also at greater risk for STIs (Scholes et al., 1993; Wolner-Hanssen, Eschenbach, & Pasvonen, 1990). For males, an uncircumcised penis has been linked to an increased risk for STIs

THIS SCALE WAS DEVELOPED by William L. Yarber, Mohammad Torabi, and C. Harold Veenker to measure the attitudes of young adults to determine whether they may be predisposed to high or low risk for contracting a sexually transmitted infection. Follow the directions, and mark your responses to the statements below. Then calculate your risk as indicated.

Directions

Read each statement carefully. Indicate your first reaction by writing the letter that corresponds to your answer.

Key

SA = Strongly agree
A = Agree
U = Undecided
D = Disagree
SD = Strongly disagree

1. How I express my sexuality has nothing to do with STIs.
2. It is easy to use the prevention methods that reduce my chances of getting an STI.
3. Responsible sex is one of the best ways of reducing the risk of STIs.
4. Getting early medical care is the main key to preventing the harmful effects of STIs.
5. Choosing the right sex partner is important in reducing my risk of getting an STI.
6. A high prevalence of STIs should be a concern for all people.
7. If I have an STI, I have a duty to get my sex partners to seek medical treatment.
8. The best way to get my sex partner to STI treatment is to take him or her to the doctor with me.
9. Changing my sexual behaviors is necessary once the presence of an STI is known.
10. I would dislike having to follow the medical steps for treating an STI.
11. If I were sexually active, I would feel uneasy doing things before and after sex to prevent getting an STI.
12. If I were sexually active, it would be insulting if a sex partner suggested we use a condom to avoid getting an STI.
13. I dislike talking about STIs with my peers.
14. I would be uncertain about going to the doctor unless I was sure I really had an STI.

15. I would feel that I should take my sex partner with me to a clinic if I thought I had an STI.
16. It would be embarrassing to discuss STIs with my sex partner if I were sexually active.
17. If I were to have sex, the chance of getting an STI makes me uneasy about having sex with more than one partner.
18. I like the idea of sexual abstinence (not having sex) as the best way of avoiding STIs.
19. If I had an STI, I would cooperate with public health people to find the source of my infection.
20. If I had an STI, I would avoid exposing others while I was being treated.
21. I would have regular STI checkups if I were having sex with more than one partner.
22. I intend to look for STI signs before deciding to have sex with anyone.
23. I will limit my sexual activity to just one partner because of the chances of getting an STI.
24. I will avoid sexual contact any time I think there is even a slight chance of getting an STI.
25. The chance of getting an STI will not stop me from having sex.
26. If I had a chance, I would support community efforts to control STIs.
27. I would be willing to work with others to make people aware of STI problems in my town.

Scoring

Calculate points as follows:

Items 1, 10–14, 16, and 25: Strongly agree = 5, Agree = 4, Undecided = 3, Disagree = 2, Strongly disagree = 1

Items 2–9, 15, 17–24, 26, and 27: Strongly agree = 1, Agree = 2, Undecided = 3, Disagree = 4, Strongly disagree = 5

The higher the score, the stronger the attitude that predisposes a person toward risky sexual behaviors. You may also calculate your points within three subscales: items 1–9 represent the "belief subscale," items 10–18 the "feeling subscale," and items 19–27 the "intention to act" subscale.

Source: Adapted from Yarber, W. L., Torabi, M. R., & Veenker, C. H. (1989). "Development of a Three-Component Sexually Transmitted Diseases Attitude Scale." *Journal of Sex Education and Therapy, 15,* 36–49. With permission from the authors.

such as HPV, gonorrhea, HIV, and syphilis (Bolan, Ehrhardt, & Wasserheit, 1999; Xavier et al., 2002). Whether male circumcision should be carried out routinely as an STI/HIV prevention strategy is being debated. In speaking about male circumcision as an HIV intervention, Dr. K. Bonner (2001) of St. George's Hospital Medical School in London notes:

> Proponents of male circumcision as an HIV prevention strategy are convinced and convincing, but circumcision is a surgical procedure with associated risks and has strong religious and cultural significance for many groups. Hence, there are ethical and practical barriers to implementing it as a public health intervention. The evidence suggests that circumcision may reduce the risk of infection, but circumcision does not appear to have any impact on transmission rates from HIV-positive men to their partners. Until we know why and how circumcision is protective, exactly what the relationship is between circumcision status and other STIs, and whether the effect seen in high-risk populations is generalizable to other groups, the wisest choice is to recommend risk reduction strategies of proven efficacy, such as condom use.

Consequences of STIs

The list of problems caused by STIs seems almost endless. Women and infants suffer more serious health damage than men from all STIs. Without medical attention, some STIs can lead to blindness, cancer, heart disease, sterility, ectopic pregnancy, miscarriage, and even death (Eng & Butler, 1997; Yarber, 2003). About 15% of women who become infertile do so because of tubal damage caused by PID resulting from an untreated STI (Donovan, 1993).

A serious outcome of STI infection is that the presence of other STIs increases the likelihood of both transmitting and acquiring HIV (St. Louis, Wasserheit, & Gayle, 1997). When someone is infected with another STI, the likelihood of HIV transmission is at least 2–5 times higher than when he or she is not infected with an STI. Research has also shown that when other STIs are present an individual's susceptibility to HIV is increased; the likelihood of a dually infected person (one with both HIV and another STI) infecting other people with HIV also is increased (U.S. Department of Health and Human Services, 2000b).

Besides having human costs, the direct cost of STI treatment within the health-care system is at least $8.4 billion annually. This amount does not include indirect, nonmedical costs such as lost wages and productivity due to illness, out-of-pocket expenses, and costs related to STI transmission to infants (ASHA, 2000). Only $1 is invested in STI prevention efforts for every $43 spent on the STI-associated costs every year (Eng & Butler, 1997).

PRINCIPAL STIs

In this section, we discuss the principal STIs by their mode of transmission and infection, starting with chlamydia and progressing through the bacterial STIs (gonorrhea, urinary tract infections, and syphilis) and then the viral STIs (genital warts, genital herpes, and hepatitis). (Table 15.1 at the end of the chapter summarizes information about the principal STIs.)

Chlamydia

The most common bacterial STI in the United States, affecting more than 3 million people each year, is caused by an organism called *Chlamydia trachomatis,* commonly known as **chlamydia,** which has properties of both a bacterium and a virus. It affects the urinary tract and reproductive organs of both women and men. The CDC reports that 15- to 19-year-old girls account for 46% of chlamydia infections, and 20- to 24-year-old women for another 33% (CDC, 2000a). Chlamydia is so common in young women that, by age 30, 50% of sexually experienced women show evidence that they had chlamydia sometime during their lives (CDC, 2001a). Chlamydia is responsible for as many as 80% of all cases of tubal infertility (National Women's Health Resources Center [NWHRC], 1998). Women who develop the infection 3 or more times have as great as a 75% chance of becoming infertile. Also, recent research shows that women infected with chlamydia have a 3- to 5-times greater chance of acquiring HIV if exposed (CDC, 2000a). Untreated chlamydia can be quite painful and can lead to conditions requiring hospitalization, including acute arthritis. Infants of mothers infected with chlamydia may develop dangerous eye, ear, and lung infections.

Although *C. trachomatis* has undoubtedly been around for centuries, it is only within the past few decades that large-scale screening has been possible. As mentioned earlier, symptoms of chlamydia often do not appear early in the infection, especially among women. Hence, chlamydia is often called a "silent" disease.

When early symptoms do occur in women, they are likely to include the following:

- Unusual vaginal discharge
- A burning sensation when urinating and frequent urination
- Unexplained vaginal bleeding between menstrual periods

Later symptoms, occurring up to several months after exposure, are these:

- Low abdominal pain
- Lower back pain
- Bleeding between menstrual periods
- A low-grade fever
- Pain during intercourse

One-third to one-half of men are asymptomatic when first infected. Men's symptoms may include these:

- Unusual discharge from the penis
- A burning sensation when urinating
- Itching and burning around the urethral opening (urethritis)
- Pain and swelling of the testicles
- A low-grade fever

The last two symptoms may indicate the presence of chlamydia-related **epididymitis,** inflammation of the epididymis. Untreated epididymitis can lead to infertility. For both women and men, early symptoms appear 7–21 days after exposure, if they appear at all. Chlamydia responds well to antibiotic therapy.

All sex partners must be treated. Furthermore, women with chlamydial infections should be tested again 3 or 4 months after they finish treatment.

In many instances, chlamydia is not detected unless the affected person is tested for it in the process of being treated for something else or unless she or he has been named as a partner, or "contact," of someone diagnosed with chlamydial infection (CDC, 1997a). Because so many people with chlamydial infections are asymptomatic, it is a sound health practice for those who are sexually active—especially if they have numerous partners—to be checked for it regularly (every 3–6 months). Two types of laboratory tests can be used to detect chlamydia. One kind tests a urine sample; another tests fluid from a man's penis or a woman's cervix. A Pap smear does not test for chlamydia (ASHA, 1998b).

Gonorrhea

Gonorrhea, the second most common bacterial STI, affects an estimated 650,000 Americans yearly (CDC, 2002b). Following a 72% decline in the reported rate of gonorrhea from 1975 to 1999, in 1999 the gonorrhea rate increased for a second year in a row but remained essentially unchanged through 2001 (CDC, 2002b). Popularly referred to as "the clap" or "the drip," gonorrhea is caused by the *Neisseria gonorrhoeae* bacterium. The organism thrives in the warm, moist environment provided by the mucous membranes lining the mouth, throat, vagina, cervix, urethra, and rectum. Gonorrhea is transmitted during vaginal intercourse, anal intercourse, or oral sex with an infected person. Symptoms of gonorrhea, if they occur, generally appear within 2–26 days of exposure but possibly after 30 days or more. Men tend to experience the symptoms of gonorrhea more readily than women, notably as a watery discharge ("drip") from the penis, the first sign of urethritis. ("Gonorrhea" is from the Greek, meaning "flow of seed.") Five percent to 20% have no symptoms. Other symptoms in men may include the following:

- Itching or burning at the urethral opening
- Pain when urinating

If untreated, the disease soon produces these other symptoms:

- Thick yellow or greenish discharge
- Increasing discomfort or pain with urination
- Painful or swollen testicles

Although most men seek treatment by this stage, some do not. Even if the symptoms diminish, the bacteria are still present. Those who do not get treatment can still infect their partners and may develop serious complications such as abscesses of the prostate gland and epididymitis.

Up to 80% of women with gonorrhea show no symptoms or very mild symptoms, which they tend to ignore. Because untreated gonorrhea, like untreated chlamydia, can lead to PID, it is important for women to be on guard for symptoms and to be treated if they think they may have been exposed to gonorrhea (e.g., if they have had multiple sex partners). Symptoms a woman may experience include the following:

- Thick yellow or white vaginal discharge, which might be bloody
- A burning sensation when urinating

I had the honor
To receive, worse luck!
From a certain empress
A boiling hot piss.

—*Frederick the Great (1712–1786)*

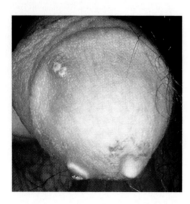

Gonorrhea infection in men is often characterized by a discharge from the penis.

- Unusual pain during menstruation
- Severe lower abdominal pain

Both females and males may have mucous discharge from the anus, blood and pus in feces, irritation of the anus, and mild sore throat.

Gonorrhea may be passed to an infant during childbirth, causing conjunctivitis (an eye infection) and even blindness if not treated. (Most states require that all newborn infants have their eyes treated with antibiotics in the event that they may have been exposed to gonorrhea in the birth canal.) Gonorrhea is curable with antibiotics.

Untreated gonorrhea can cause sterility in both sexes, ectopic pregnancy, prostate damage, scarring of the urethra in men, and testicular pain. People with gonorrhea can more easily contract HIV. People with HIV infection and gonorrhea are more likely than people with HIV infection alone to transmit HIV to others. Avoiding risky sexual behavior and using male latex or polyurethane condoms correctly and consistently can help protect against infection.

Urinary Tract Infections (NGU/NSU)

Both women and men are subject to STIs of the urinary tract. Among the several organisms that cause these infections, the most common and most serious is *Chlamydia* (ASHA 1998c). Urinary tract infections are sometimes referred to as **nongonococcal urethritis (NGU)** or **nonspecific urethritis (NSU).** In men, **urethritis,** inflammation of the urethra, may produce these symptoms:

- A burning sensation when urinating
- Burning or itching around the opening of the penis
- White or yellowish discharge from the penis

Women are likely to be asymptomatic. They may not realize they are infected until a male partner is diagnosed. If a woman does have symptoms, they are likely to include these:

- Itching or burning while urinating
- Unusual vaginal discharge

It is important to have a laboratory test for an unusual discharge from the penis or vagina so that the appropriate antibiotic can be prescribed. Antibiotics are usually effective against NGU. Untreated NGU may result in permanent damage to the reproductive organs of both men and women, resulting in infertility; problems in pregnancy, resulting in premature delivery or low birth weight; and/or eye, ear, and lung infections in newborns. The most common urinary tract infection among women, cystitis, is discussed later in this chapter.

Syphilis

When **syphilis** first appeared in Europe in the late 1490s, its manifestations were considerably more horrible than they are today. Whether syphilis was introduced to Europe from the New World by Spanish explorers or from Africa by those who plied the slave trade is debated by historians. Its legacy of suffering, however, is debated by no one.

And he died in the year fourteen-
   twenty.
Of the syphilis, which he had
   a-plenty.
   —*François Rabelais (1490–1553)*

In the 1940s, researchers discovered that penicillin very effectively kills *Treponema pallidum*, the bacterium that causes syphilis. At last, the disease that had caused widespread pain, anguish, and death for centuries began to fade from view in most parts of the developed world. In the United States, strict control measures were instituted, requiring the testing of many citizens for syphilis, including those in the armed services and couples seeking marriage licenses. Health departments and medical laboratories were (and still are) required to report all cases of syphilis to the government. Despite these efforts, however, beginning in the 1980s, the number of cases in the United States began increasing dramatically, especially within inner cities. In 1990, the syphilis rate was the highest it had been since the 1940s and more than 10 times as high as rates in other developed countries (Kilmarx et al., 1997). Since then, the rate has declined to an estimated 70,000 cases annually (ASHA, 1998b). The rate of primary and secondary syphilis reported in the United States was at its lowest level since reporting began in 1941, and the rate declined by 88% from 1990 through 1999 (Division of STD Prevention, 2000). However, the number of reported cases of syphilis increased slightly in 2001 (CDC, 2002f). The epidemic appeared to be concentrated mainly in urban areas and the South and among young, heterosexual minority populations. Recently, outbreaks of syphilis among men who have sex with men have been reported, which largely contributed to the 2001 increase (CDC, 2002f; Miller et al., 1999). In some instances, the increase seems to be correlated with crack cocaine use, possibly related to the practice of exchanging sex (principally fellatio) for the drug (Kilmarx et al., 1997). Individuals who have syphilis have a 2- to 5-times greater chance of contracting HIV (Division of STD Prevention, 2000).

T. pallidum is a spiral-shaped bacterium (a **spirochete**) that requires a warm, moist environment such as the genitals or the mucous membranes inside the mouth to survive. It is spread through vaginal, anal, and oral sexual contact. A mother infected with syphilis can pass it to the fetus through the placenta. Because neonatal syphilis can lead to brain damage and death, it is imperative for pregnant women to be screened for it within the first trimester. If they are treated during this period, the newborn will not be affected. Untreated syphilis in adults may lead to brain damage, heart disease, blindness, and death. As it appears today, syphilis progresses through four discrete stages, although it is most often treated during the first two:

- *Stage 1: Primary syphilis.* The first symptom of syphilis appears 1 week to 4 months after contact with an infected partner. It is a small, red, pea-sized bump that soon develops into a round, painless sore called a **chancre**

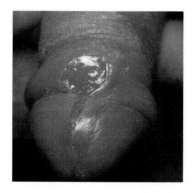
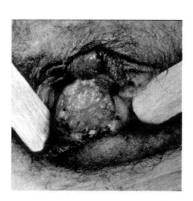

The first symptom of syphilis is a red, pea-sized bump called a chancre at the site where the bacterium originally entered the body.

The Tuskegee Syphilis Study: "A Tragedy of Race and Medicine"

IN 1932 IN MACON COUNTY, Alabama, the U.S. Public Health Service, with the assistance of the Tuskegee Institute, a prestigious Black college, recruited 600 African American men to participate in an experiment involving the effects of untreated syphilis on Blacks. Of this group, 399 men had been diagnosed with syphilis, and 201 were controls. The study was originally meant to last 6–9 months, but "the drive to satisfy scientific curiosity resulted in a 40-year experiment that followed the men to 'end point' (autopsy)" (Thomas & Quinn, 1991). The history of this experiment—the racial biases that created it, the cynicism that fueled it, and the callousness that allowed it to continue—is chillingly chronicled by James Jones (1993) in *Bad Blood: The Tuskegee Experiment—a Tragedy of Race and Medicine.*

The purpose of the study was to determine if there were racial differences in the developmental course of syphilis. There was speculation in the (White) medical community that tertiary syphilis affected the cardiovascular systems of Blacks, whereas it affected Whites neurologically. The racial prejudice behind this motivation may seem hard to fathom today, yet, as we shall see, the repercussions still reverberate strongly through African American communities.

Much of the original funding for the study came from the Julius Rosenwald Foundation (a philanthropic organization dedicated to improving conditions within African American communities), with the understanding that treatment was to be a part of the study. Although Alabama law required prompt treatment of diagnosed venereal diseases, the state Public Health Service managed to ensure that treatment was withheld from the participants. In the 1940s, the Public Health Service kept draft boards from ordering treatment for 250 A-1 registrants who were part of the experiment. It involved health departments across the country in a conspiracy to withhold treatment from subjects who had moved from Macon County. Even after 1951, when penicillin became the standard treatment for syphilis, the Public Health Service refused to treat the Tuskegee "subjects" on the grounds that the experiment was a "never-again-to-be-repeated opportunity" (Jones, 1993).

The Tuskegee participants were never informed that they had syphilis. The Public Health Service, assuming they would not understand medical terminology, referred to it as "bad blood," a term used to describe a variety of ailments in the rural South. The participants were not told their disease was sexually transmitted, nor were they told it could be passed from mother to fetus. We can only speculate on the extent to which this wanton disregard for human life allowed the disease to spread and wreak its misery and death in the Black South and beyond.

It was not until 1966 that anyone within the public health system expressed any moral concern over the study. Peter Buxtun, an investigator for the Public Health Service, wrote a concerned letter to the director of the Division of Venereal Diseases, William Brown. Nothing changed. In 1968, Buxtun wrote a second letter, questioning the study's ramifications in light of the current climate of racial unrest in the nation. Dr. Brown showed the letter to the Centers for Disease Control (CDC), which convened a panel to discuss the issue. Having reviewed the study, the panel decided to allow it to continue until "end point." In 1972, Peter Buxtun told his story to Edith Lederer, a friend who was an international reporter for the Associated Press. Ultimately the story was assigned to Jean Heller, who broke it in the *Washington Post* on July 25, 1972, whereupon it became front-page news across the country. A congressional subcommittee headed by Senator Edward Kennedy began hearings in 1973. The results included the rewriting of the Department of Health, Education, and Welfare's regulations on the use of human subjects in scientific experiments. A $1.8-billion class-action suit was filed on behalf of the Tuskegee participants and their heirs. A settlement of $10 million was reached out of court.

Since the original disclosure and outcry, there has been little discussion of the Tuskegee experiment within the public health system or in the public media. (David Feldman's powerful 1989 play, *Miss Evers' Boys*, and an hour-long 1992 PBS documentary are the exceptions.) Stephen Thomas and Sandra Crouse Quinn (1991) of the Minority Health Research Laboratory at the University of Maryland's Department of Health cite the "failure of

(SHANK-er). The person's lymph nodes may also be swollen. The chancre may be covered by a crusty scab; it may be hard around the edges and ringed by a pink border. It appears at the site where the bacterium initially entered the body, usually within the vagina or on the cervix in women or on the glans of the penis in men. The chancre may also appear on the labia, the shaft of the penis, the testicles, or the rectum; within the mouth; or on the lips. Unless it is in a visible area, it may not be noticed. Without treatment, it will disappear in 3–6 weeks, but the bacterium remains in the body, and the person is still highly contagious.

public health professionals to comprehensively discuss the Tuskegee experiment" as an ongoing "source of misinformation [that] helps to maintain a barrier between the Black community and health care service providers." Current public health efforts to control the spread of HIV infection, AIDS, and other STIs raise the specter of genocide among many members of the African American community. For example, in 1990, as part of an HIV education program conducted by the Southern Christian Leadership Conference with CDC funding, a survey of 1056 Black church members found that 35% of them believed AIDS to be a form of genocide and another 30% were unsure. Thirty-four percent thought the virus was man-made, and an additional 44% were unsure. Even today, some African Americans, particularly in the South, remain suspicious of the federal government's health programs and associate AIDS with genocidal beliefs.

A tremendous gap exists in this country between the health-care needs of minority-status families and the beliefs within those communities. To begin closing the gap, we must, as stated by Stephen Thomas and Janet Quinn (1991), "recognize that Blacks' belief in AIDS as a form of genocide is a legitimate attitudinal barrier rooted in the history of the Tuskegee syphilis study." On both physiological and psychological levels, there is much healing to be done. Even though it is unthinkable that such a study would be done today, efforts must still be made to ensure that all people are protected against such tragedies.

For reflections on the legacy of the Tuskegee study, see Caplan, 1992; Jones, 1992; and King, 1992. Two Internet sites provide further descriptions of this terrible experiment (http://www.aabhs.org/tusk.html and http://www.infoplease.com/ipa/A0762136.html).

'NOW can we give him penicillin?'

Editorial cartoon by Tony Auth, *Philadelphia Inquirer*, July 1972. (Courtesy Tony Auth).

■ *Stage 2: Secondary syphilis.* Untreated primary syphilis develops into secondary syphilis about 6 weeks after the chancre has disappeared. The principal symptom at this stage is a skin rash that neither itches nor hurts. The rash is likely to occur on the palms of the hands and the soles of the feet, as well as on other areas of the body. The individual may also experience fever, swollen lymph nodes, patchy hair loss, headaches, weight loss, muscle aches, and fatigue. The rash or other symptoms may be very mild or may pass unnoticed. The person is still contagious.

▪ *Stage 3: Latency.* If secondary syphilis is not treated, the symptoms disappear within 2–6 weeks, and the latent stage begins. The infected person may experience no further symptoms for years or perhaps never. Or he or she may have symptoms that are vague or difficult to diagnose without a blood test to screen for *T. pallidum.* After about a year, the bacterium can no longer be spread to sex partners, although a pregnant woman can still transmit the disease to her fetus.

▪ *Stage 4: Tertiary syphilis.* In the United States, syphilis is rarely seen in its tertiary stage because treatment usually prevents the disease from progressing that far. The symptoms of tertiary syphilis may appear years after the initial infection. Possible effects include gummas (large ulcers) within the muscles, liver, lungs, eyes, or endocrine glands; heart disease; and neurosyphilis (leading to "general paralysis" or "paresis"), involving the brain and spinal cord and leading to muscular paralysis, psychosis, and death.

In the primary, secondary, and early latent stages, syphilis can be successfully treated with antibiotics. Later stages may require additional injections. Other antibiotics can be used if the infected person is allergic to penicillin.

Human Papillomavirus (HPV)/Genital Warts

Human papillomavirus (HPV), or genital HPV infection, is a group of viruses that includes more than 100 different strains; over 30 infect the genital area. The number of new cases of HPV has increased dramatically in the past two decades. Currently, at least 20 million people are infected with HPV, with 5.5 million new infections each year. HPV is the most common STI among young, sexually active people, particularly women. An estimated 75% of the reproductive-age population has been infected with sexually transmitted HPV.

The type of HPV that infects the genital area is spread primarily through sexual contact with an infected person. In rare instances, a pregnant woman can pass HPV to her baby during vaginal delivery. The incubation period (the period between the time a person is first exposed to a disease and the time the symptoms appear) is usually 6 weeks to 8 months. Most people who have a genital HPV infection do not know they are infected, and most infections are temporary. The virus lives in the skin or mucous membranes and usually causes no symptoms, although some people get visible **genital warts.** Most women are diagnosed with HPV following abnormal Pap smears. All types of HPV can cause mild Pap smear abnormalities that do not have serious outcomes. About 10 of the 30 identified genital HPV types can lead, in rare cases, to the development of cervical cancer. Persistent cervical HPV infection is a key risk factor for cervical cancer. Sexually active women should have regular Pap smears to screen for cervical cancer or precancerous conditions. Research has shown that for most (90%) women cervical HPV infection becomes undetectable within 2 years. Being a virus, HPV has no "cure," but the infection usually goes away on its own. Cancer-related types are more likely to persist (CDC, 2001c).

Genital warts may appear within several weeks after sexual contact with an infected person, may take months to appear, or may never appear. When they do appear, they generally range in size from a pencil point to ¼ inch in

Click on "HPV" to hear about the experience of a woman with human papillomavirus.

diameter. They may be flat, bumpy, round, or smooth; and white, gray, pink, or brown. Some look like miniature cauliflowers; others, like tiny fingers. In men, genital warts usually develop on the shaft or glans of the penis or around the anus. In women, they are found on the cervix, vaginal wall, vulva, and anus. Warts inside the cervix, vagina, and rectum are difficult to detect without examination. If the warts cause discomfort or problems (such as interfering with urination), they can be removed by cryosurgery (freezing) or laser surgery. Removal of the warts does not eliminate HPV from the person's system. Because the virus can lie dormant in the cells, in some cases warts can return months or even years after treatment. The extent to which a person can still transmit HPV after the visible warts have been removed is unknown.

Avoiding risky sexual behavior and using male latex or polyurethane condoms consistently and correctly can help protect against infection. Condoms can reduce, but not eliminate, risk, as the genital warts may appear in areas not covered by the condom. Certainly, individuals should not have sex with anyone who has genital sores or unusual growths in the genital or anal area.

ASHA has developed a support service for people with HPV called the National HPV and Cervical Cancer Prevention Resource Center (http://www.asha.org). It provides information about HPV and its link to cancer, support for emotional issues surrounding HPV, and an Internet chat room (http://www.ashastd.org/hpvccprc/chat).

Genital Herpes

An estimated 45 million Americans have **genital herpes,** caused by the **herpes simplex virus (HSV).** The greatest increase in the incidence of genital herpes is among White teens and young adults. The incidence is increasing by approximately 1 million each year (ASHA, 1998a). HSV exists in two strains: HSV type 1 (V-1), which is usually responsible for cold sores and fever blisters around the mouth, and HSV type 2, which is usually associated with genital lesions. Both types of HSV, however, can and do develop equally well on the mouth or genitals. Serious complications from HSV are rare in adults but may result if the individual's general health is not good or his or her immune system is depressed. Having genital herpes can put people at greater risk for HIV because the presence of the herpes lesions can facilitate its transmission (CDC, 2002d). Although the spread of herpes to newborns is rare, and most mothers with a history of herpes have normal vaginal deliveries, newborns can contract HSV if they come into contact with active lesions during birth. This may result in infections of the eyes, skin, or mucous membranes; infections of the central nervous system; and even death.

For many people with HSV, the initial infection is the most severe. Sometimes, it is the only outbreak a person experiences. Within 3–20 days after exposure, small bumps called vesicles or papules appear on the penis, anus, perineum, vulva, or vagina. The papules may itch at first; they then form blisters or pustules that rupture, resulting in small, often painful, ulcers. These sores may be further irritated by tight clothing, moisture, or urine. These ulcers or sores crust over in 2–4 weeks. Over time, the sores heal faster and occur less often. In addition, an affected person may experience the following:

- Swollen lymph nodes in the groin
- Flulike symptoms

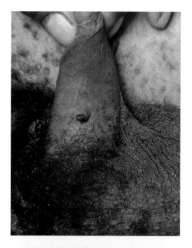

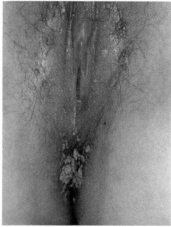

Genital warts appear in a variety of forms.

Click on "Herpes" to meet a man with genital herpes.

The first outbreak lasts an average of 12 days, and subsequent outbreaks may last 5 days each. Individuals with HSV experience an average of 4–5 subsequent outbreaks a year. These may begin with feelings of itchiness or tingling at the site where the lesions will appear. Just prior to the outbreak is a period of a few days known as the **prodrome.** During this time, and while there are actual lesions, the virus is active; live viruses are shed from the affected areas and are spread upon contact. Some people with HSV may shed the virus without experiencing symptoms; men and women are equally infectious when no symptoms are noticeable (Johnson, 2000).

Managing HSV   There is no cure for herpes, but there are medications that can help to keep the virus in check. Medications can relieve pain, shorten the duration of sores, prevent bacterial infections at the open sores, and prevent outbreaks while the person is taking the medications. For example, the antiviral drug acyclovir (trade name Zovirax) is often helpful in reducing or suppressing HSV symptoms. It can be administered either orally (as a pill) or topically (as an ointment). Valacyclovir (trade name Valtrex) uses acyclovir as its active ingredient, but it is better absorbed by the body and can be taken less often. Famcyclovir (trade name Famvir) works similarly to acyclovir, but it is also better absorbed and can be taken less often. All three drugs, which appear to be equally effective, work by disrupting the virus's ability to reproduce. All are safe and have virtually no side effects. Genital herpes appears to respond better to the oral than to the topical medications. Patients can choose either episodic therapy, which involves taking medication during an outbreak to speed healing, or suppressive therapy, which involves taking antiviral medication every day to hold HSV in check.

Other treatments that may be useful in preventing, shortening the duration of, or lessening the severity of recurrent outbreaks include these:

1. *Get plenty of rest.* For the immune system to work at its highest capacity, the body needs rest.

2. *Maintain a balanced diet.* Healthful eating also fosters a healthy immune system. Avoiding foods that appear to trigger outbreaks may be helpful.

3. *Avoid tight clothes.* Tight jeans, tight or nylon underwear, and nylon panty hose create an ideal warm, moist environment for HSV. Loose-fitting cotton clothing is recommended.

Herpes legions may develop on the penis, perineum, anus, vulva, or within the vagina.

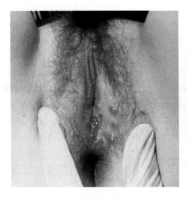
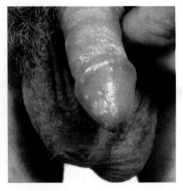

4. *Keep the area cool and dry.* If lesions do appear, an icepack may provide temporary relief. Baby powder or cornstarch may be used to absorb moisture.

5. *Take aspirin or other pain relievers.* Medications may be helpful in relieving the discomfort that is associated with an outbreak.

6. *Reduce stress.* Stress may trigger a recurrence of sores in some people.

Taking Reasonable Precautions   HSV can be spread by hand to another person or even to a different location on one's own body. Anyone experiencing an outbreak should wash his or her hands frequently with soap. Caution should also be taken not to touch one's eyes (or another's) if one has touched a lesion, because serious eye infection can result. Individuals with HSV should inform their partners and together decide what precautions are right for them. Because having sex during a recognized outbreak puts an uninfected partner at risk, people should abstain from sex when signs and symptoms of either oral or genital herpes are present. The male latex or polyurethane condom can help prevent infections, but only when the condom covers the ulcer. Condoms should be used between outbreaks of the ulcers. Pregnant women or their partners who have HSV should be sure to discuss precautionary procedures with their medical practitioners.

ASHA has developed a support service for people with herpes infections called the National Herpes Resource Center. It provides self-help support for groups, a quarterly newsletter, and an Internet chat room (http://www.ashastd.org/hrc/chat).

Hepatitis

Hepatitis is a viral disease affecting the liver. The most common types of the virus that can be sexually transmitted are hepatitis A and hepatitis B. A third type, hepatitis C, is a common virus passed on primarily through contact with infected blood; risk of transmittal from sex partners or from mothers to newborns during birth is low. Hepatitis A is transmitted primarily through oral contact with contaminated food or water or through sexual contact, especially oral-anal sex. A highly effective vaccine can prevent hepatitis A, and immune serum globulin injections provide some immunity. Although the symptoms of hepatitis A are similar to those of hepatitis B, the disease is not considered as dangerous. Affected individuals usually recover within 6 weeks and develop immunity against reinfection.

Hepatitis B is 100 times more infectious than HIV (ASHA, 1996a). It is commonly spread through sexual contact, in blood, semen, saliva, vaginal secretions, and urine. It can also be contracted by using contaminated needles and syringes, including those used in ear piercing, acupuncture, and tattooing, and by sharing the toothbrush or razor of an infected person. There are an estimated 77,000 new cases in the United States annually, for a total of 750,000 cases; those who contract it are mainly adolescents and young adults (ASHA, 1998b). The incidence of hepatitis B is declining among gay men (probably due to safer sex practices) but is increasing among heterosexual individuals. Anyone can get hepatitis B, but individuals in their teens and twenties are at greater risk. Because hepatitis B spreads "silently"—that is, without easily noticeable symptoms—many people are not aware it is in their communities.

Hepatitis B can be prevented by a simple, widely available vaccination. The CDC recommends routine vaccination for those most at risk, including people with more than one sexual partner, teenagers, gay men, injecting drug users, and health-care workers who come into contact with blood. Screening for hepatitis B is also recommended for pregnant women so that their newborns can be immediately vaccinated if necessary. The vaccine is safe and effective and provides lasting protection. Tattoos and body piercings should be done at parlors that thoroughly sterilize the instruments used to penetrate the skin.

Hepatitis C now infects 30,000 Americans annually, 85% of whom develop chronic infections. Currently, 4 million people nationwide carry this blood-borne virus, but only 1 million are aware of it ("HIV–Hepatitis C," 1999). Although several studies indicate an association, the role of sexual activity in the transmission of hepatitis C is controversial (CDC, 2002d). Risk of infection from sexual activity is low unless it involves blood contact; multiple sex partners, failure to use condoms, a history of STIs, and sexual activities involving trauma (e.g., "rough" sex) increase the risk. Most cases of hepatitis C can be traced to blood transfusions before 1992, the sharing of needles during injection drug use, and accidental needle-sticks. Known as the "silent epidemic," the disease damages the liver over the course of many years, and even decades, before symptoms appear. To date, there is no vaccine.

The symptoms of hepatitis include the following:

- Fatigue
- Diarrhea
- Nausea
- Abdominal pain
- Jaundice (caused by accumulating blood pigments not destroyed by the liver)
- Darkened urine
- An enlarged liver, which can lead to cirrhosis or liver cancer (Your chances of getting liver cancer are 200 times higher if you are a hepatitis B carrier.)

There is no medical treatment for hepatitis. Rest and fluids are recommended until the disease runs its course, generally in a few weeks. Occasionally, serious liver damage or death results.

Dual infection with both hepatitis C and HIV is increasingly common. As many as 40% of individuals with HIV are also infected with hepatitis C ("HIV–Hepatitis C," 1999). Having both viruses complicates an already-complex treatment regimen, making daily life difficult because of multiple side effects of treatment. Although the hepatitis C virus does not accelerate the course of HIV and AIDS, the AIDS virus does speed up the liver damage caused by hepatitis C.

Vaginal Infections

Vaginal infections, or **vaginitis,** affect 3 out of 4 women at least once in their lives. These infections are often, though not always, sexually transmitted. They may also be induced by an upset in the normal balance of vaginal organisms by such things as stress, birth control pills, antibiotics, nylon panty hose, and douching. The three principal types of vaginitis are bacterial vaginosis, candidiasis, and trichomonal infection.

Bacterial Vaginosis   Bacterial vaginal infections, referred to as **bacterial vaginosis,** may be caused by a number of different organisms, most commonly *Gardnerella vaginalis,* often a normal inhabitant of the healthy vagina. An overabundance of *Gardnerella,* however, produces these symptoms:

- Vaginal itching
- Whitish discharge, with a fishy odor that is more pronounced when the discharge is combined with semen

Bacterial vaginosis is the most common vaginal infection in women of childbearing age, and as many as 16% of pregnant women have the infection. Little is known about how women are infected. Women who have never had sexual intercourse are rarely affected, but what role sexual activity plays in the development of bacterial vaginosis is unclear (CDC, 2000a).

Most men who carry *Gardnerella* are asymptomatic; some may experience inflammation of the urethra or glans. Bacterial vaginosis in women is commonly treated with metronidazole (Flagyl) or clindamycin. Either can be used for nonpregnant or pregnant women, but dosages differ. There is disagreement about the usefulness of treating men unless they actually have symptoms. However, if a man has symptoms, then treating him is necessary to prevent infection or reinfection of his partner. The risk of bacterial vaginosis can be reduced by limiting the number of sex partners, using condoms, and not douching.

Candidiasis   The fungus *Candida albicans* is normally present in the healthy vagina of many women. Various conditions may cause *C. albicans* to multiply rapidly, producing the condition known as **candidiasis** (can-di-DYE-a-sis), moniliasis, or, more commonly, yeast infection. Symptoms include these:

- Intense itching of the vagina and vulva
- A lumpy, cottage cheese–like discharge

C. albicans may be transmitted sexually, although this does not necessarily lead to symptoms. Conditions that may induce candidiasis include dietary imbalances (eating large amounts of dairy products, sugars, and artificial sweeteners), antibiotics or birth control pills, and pregnancy. The yeast organism, if not already present in the woman's vagina, can be transmitted from the anus via wiping back-to-front or on the surface of a menstrual pad; it can also be transmitted through sexual contact, because the foreskin of an uncircumcised male partner can harbor the organism. Vaginal creams or suppositories such as clotrimazole (Gyne-Lotrimin) and miconazole (Monistat) are available over the counter. A woman who is uncertain about the symptoms or whose symptoms persist should see a physician.

> Sex is a pleasurable exercise in plumbing, but be careful or you'll get yeast in your drainpipe.
>
> —*Rita Mae Brown*

Trichomoniasis   *Trichomonas vaginalis* is a single-cell protozoan responsible for about 25% of all cases of vaginitis. **Trichomoniasis,** commonly referred to simply as "trich" (pronounced TRICK), is a hardy parasite that may survive for several hours on damp items such as towels and toilet seats. About 5 million new cases of trichomoniasis occur in the United States annually, and it is among the most common conditions found in women seeking reproductive health services (ASHA, 1998b).

Trichomoniasis is usually transmitted during vaginal intercourse or vulva-to-vulva contact with an infected person. Women can acquire the disease from infected men and women, whereas men usually acquire it only from infected women. Most women and few men have symptoms of infection. For women, symptoms may include these:

- Frothy, yellow-green vaginal discharge with a strong odor
- Discomfort during vaginal intercourse and urination
- Irritation and itching of the genital area
- In rare cases, low abdominal pain

Men may experience the following:

- Irritation inside the penis
- Mild penile discharge
- A slight burning after urination or ejaculation

Trichomoniasis can cause preterm delivery in pregnant women. Women having the genital inflammation caused by trichomoniasis may have an increased risk of acquiring HIV if exposed to it. Women who have both trichomoniasis infection and HIV infection also have an increased chance of transmitting HIV to a sex partner.

Avoiding risky sexual behavior and using male latex or polyurethane condoms consistently and correctly can help protect against infection. Metronidazole (Flagyl) is effective in treating trichomoniasis. To prevent reinfection, both partners must be treated, even if the man is asymptomatic.

Other STIs

A number of other STIs appear in the United States, but with less frequency than they do in some developing countries. Among these other STIs are the following:

- Chancroid is a painful sore or group of sores on the penis, caused by the bacterium *Hemophilus ducreyi*. Women may carry the bacterium but are generally asymptomatic for chancroid.
- Cytomegalovirus (CMV) is a virus of the herpes group that affects people with depressed immune systems. A fetus may be infected with CMV in the uterus.
- Enteric infections are intestinal infections caused by bacteria, viruses, protozoans, or other organisms that are normally carried in the intestinal tract. Amebiasis, giardiasis, and shigellosis are typical enteric infections. They often result from anal sex or oral-anal contact.
- Granuloma inguinale appears as single or multiple nodules, usually on the genitals, that become lumpy but painless ulcers that bleed on contact.
- Lymphogranuloma venereum (LGV) begins as a small, painless lesion at the site of infection and then develops into a painful abscess, accompanied by pain and swelling in the groin.
- Molluscum contagiosum, caused by a relatively large virus, is characterized by smooth, round, shiny lesions that appear on the trunk, on the genitals, or around the anus.

Parasites

Although they are not infections per se, parasites such as scabies and pubic lice can be spread by sexual contact.

Scabies The red, intensely itchy rash caused by the barely visible mite *Sarcoptes scabiei* is called **scabies.** It usually appears on the genitals, buttocks, feet, wrists, knuckles, abdomen, armpits, or scalp as a result of the mites' tunneling beneath the skin to lay their eggs and the baby mites' making their way back to the surface. It is highly contagious and spreads quickly among people who have close contact, both sexual and nonsexual. The mites can also be transferred on clothes, towels, and bedding. Scabies is usually treated with a prescribed ivermectin lotion containing lindane, applied at bedtime and washed off in the morning. Infants, young children, and pregnant or nursing women should be treated, not with ivermectin, but with permethrin. Clothing, towels, and bedding of people who have scabies should be disinfected by washing in hot water and drying in high heat or by dry cleaning.

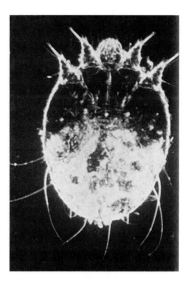

Pubic lice, or "crabs," are easily spread during intimate contact; they may also be transmitted via bedclothes, towels, or underwear.

Pubic Lice The tiny *Phthirus pubis,* commonly known as a "crab," moves easily from the pubic hair of one person to that of another (probably along with several of its relatives). When **pubic lice** mate, the male and female grasp adjacent hairs; the female soon begins producing eggs (nits), which she attaches to the hairs at the rate of about three eggs a day for 7–10 days. The nits hatch within 5–10 days and begin reproducing in about 2 weeks, creating a very ticklish (or itchy) situation. Pubic lice can be transmitted nonsexually. They may fall into underwear, sheets, or towels, where they can survive up to a day *and* lay eggs that hatch in about a week. Thus, it is possible to get crabs simply by sleeping in someone else's bed, wearing his or her clothes, or sharing a towel.

People can usually tell when they have pubic lice. There is intense itching, and upon inspection, they discover a tiny, pale, crablike louse or its minuscule, pearly nits attached near the base of a pubic hair. There are both prescription and over-the-counter treatments for pubic lice. In addition to killing all the lice and nits on the body, infected individuals must wash all infected linen and clothing in hot water and dry it in high heat, or the crabs may survive.

STIs AND WOMEN

In addition to the direct effects that STIs have on the body, women are vulnerable to complications from STIs that threaten their fertility. These are related to the biological factors, discussed earlier, that make women more susceptible to STIs and make STIs more difficult to detect in women than in men.

Pelvic Inflammatory Disease (PID)

As discussed in Chapter 12, pelvic inflammatory disease (PID), also known as salpingitis, is one of the leading causes of female infertility. Approximately 1 million cases of PID occur annually, resulting in about 165,000

TABLE 15.1   Principal Sexually Transmitted Infections

STI and Infecting Organism	Symptoms	Time from Exposure to Occurrence	Medical Treatment	Comments
Chlamydia (*Chlamydia trachomatis*)	*Women:* 75% asymptomatic; others may have vaginal discharge or pain with urination. *Men:* 50% asymptomatic; others may have discharge from penis, burning urination, pain and swelling in testicles, or persistent low fever.	7–21 days.	Antibiotics.	If untreated, may lead to pelvic inflammatory disease (PID) and subsequent infertility in women. By age 30, one-half of sexually active women have evidence of previous chlamydial infection.
Genital herpes (herpes simplex virus)	Small sore or itchy bumps on genitals, becoming blisters that may rupture, forming painful sores; possibly swollen lymph nodes; flulike symptoms with first outbreak.	A few days to about 3 weeks.	No cure, although acyclovir and related antiviral medications may relieve symptoms.	Virus remains in body, and outbreaks of contagious sores may recur. Most people diagnosed with first episode have four to five symptomatic recurrences a year, although recurrences are most noticeable in first year.
Human papillomavirus/ genital warts	Most people who have genital warts do not know they are infected. Often, people get warts on the vulva, in or around the vagina or anus, or on the penis, scrotum, groin, or thigh.	6 weeks to 8 months.	Surgical removal by freezing or laser therapy if warts are large or cause problems.	Virus remains in body after warts are removed. There is no "cure" for HPV, but infection usually goes away on its own.
Gonorrhea (*Neisseria gonorrhoeae*)	*Women:* Up to 80% asymptomatic; others may have symptoms similar to chlamydia. *Men:* 5–20% asymptomatic; others may have itching, burning or pain with urination, discharge from penis ("drip").	*Women:* Often no noticeable symptoms. *Men:* Usually 2–6 days, but possible 30 days or more.	Antibiotics.	If untreated, may lead to pelvic inflammatory disease (PID) and subsequent infertility in women. People with gonorrhea can more easily contract HIV.
Hepatitis (hepatitis A or B virus)	Fatigue, diarrhea, nausea, abdominal pain, jaundice, darkened urine due to impaired liver function.	1–4 months.	No medical treatment available; rest and fluids are prescribed until disease runs its course.	Hepatitis B more commonly spread through sexual contact. Both A and B can be prevented by vaccinations.

TABLE 15.1   continued

STI and Infecting Organism	Symptoms	Time from Exposure to Occurrence	Medical Treatment	Comments
HIV infection and AIDS (human immunodeficiency virus)	Possible flulike symptoms but often no symptoms during early phase. Variety of later symptoms, including weight loss, persistent fever, night sweats, diarrhea, swollen lymph nodes, bruiselike rash, persistent cough.	Several months to several years (most commonly within 6 months).	No cure available, although new treatment drugs have improved the health and lengthened the lives of many HIV-infected persons. Good general health practices can delay or reduce severity of symptoms.	Cannot be self-diagnosed; HIV infection is usually diagnosed by tests for antibodies against HIV.
Pubic lice, crabs (*Pediculosis pubis*)	Itching, blue and gray spots, and insects or nits (eggs) in pubic area; some people may have no symptoms.	Hatching of eggs in 5–10 days.	Creams, lotions, or shampoos—both over-the-counter and prescription.	Avoid sexual contact with people having unusual spots or insects or nits in the genital area. Also avoid contaminated clothing, sheets, and towels.
Syphilis (*Treponema pallidum*)	*Stage 1:* Red, painless sore (chancre) at bacteria's point of entry. *Stage 2:* Skin rash over body, including palms of hands and soles of feet.	*Stage 1:* 1–12 weeks. *Stage 2:* 6 weeks to 6 months after chancre appears.	Penicillin or other antibiotics.	Easily cured, but untreated syphilis can lead to ulcers of internal organs and eyes, heart disease, neurological disorders, and insanity.
Urethritis (various organisms)	Painful and/or frequent urination; discharge from penis; women may be asymptomatic. Can have discharge from vagina and painful urination.	1–3 weeks.	Antibiotics.	Laboratory testing is important to determine appropriate treatment.
Vaginitis (*Gardnerella vaginalis*, *Trichomonas vaginalis*, or *Candida albicans*)	Intense itching of vagina and/or vulva, unusual discharge with foul or fishy odor, painful intercourse. Men who carry organisms may be asymptomatic.	2–21 days.	Depends on organism; oral medications include metronidazole and clindamycin. Vaginal medications include clotrimazole and miconazole.	Not always acquired sexually. Other causes include contact with contaminated toilet seat, stress, oral contraceptives, pregnancy, tight pants or underwear, antibiotics, douching, and diet.

hospitalizations of women age 15–44 (ASHA, 1998a). PID begins with an initial infection of the fallopian tube (or tubes) by an organism such as *C. trachomatis* or *N. gonorrhoeae*, which makes it possible for bacteria to invade and develop (Ault & Faro, 1993). As the infection spreads, the tubes swell and fester, often causing acute pain. Scar tissue begins to form within the tubes; it may block the passage of eggs en route to the uterus or cause a fertilized egg to implant within the tube itself—an ectopic pregnancy. PID occurs more commonly in women who have had a number of sex partners, women with a previous history of PID, and very young women. A woman may be more susceptible to PID during the first few days of her period or if she uses an IUD. Symptoms of PID include the following:

- Lower abdominal pain
- Cervical discharge
- Cervical tenderness
- Fever

Because definitive diagnosis of PID usually requires laparoscopy (an expensive examination involving minor surgery to insert the viewing instrument), physicians may simply prescribe antibiotics once such conditions as appendicitis and ectopic pregnancy have been ruled out. Untreated PID can lead to life-threatening conditions such as pelvic abscesses and ectopic pregnancy. Once the infection is under control, further examination and treatment may be necessary to prevent infertility, ectopic pregnancy, or chronic abdominal pain, all of which may result from scar tissue buildup. To prevent reinfection, women with PID should have their partners examined and treated for STIs. Prevention of chlamydial infection by screening and treating high-risk women reduces the incidence of PID.

Cystitis

A bladder infection that affects mainly women, **cystitis** is often related to sexual activity, although it is not transmitted from one partner to another. Cystitis is characterized by these symptoms:

- Painful, burning urination
- A nearly constant need to urinate

Cystitis occurs when a bacterium such as *Escherichia coli*, normally present in the lower intestine and in fecal material, is introduced into the urinary tract. This can occur when continuous friction (from intercourse or manual stimulation) in the area of the urethra traumatizes the tissue and allows nearby bacteria to enter the urinary tract. It often occurs at the beginning of a sexual relationship, when sexual activity is high (hence the nickname "honeymoon cystitis"). If cystitis is not treated promptly, more serious symptoms such as these will occur:

- Lower abdominal pain
- Fever
- Kidney pain

Damage to the kidneys may occur.

PREVENTING STIs

It seems that STIs should be easy to prevent, at least in theory. But in reality, STI prevention involves a subtle interplay of knowledge, psychological factors, and behaviors. In other words, STI prevention is easy *if* you know the facts, *if* you believe in prevention, and *if* you act in accordance with your knowledge and beliefs. Earlier in the chapter, you read the facts. Now let's think about the psychological and behavioral components of preventing STIs and some important individual health behaviors you can adapt to prevent STIs.

Avoiding STIs

STIs can be transmitted by sexual contact, by infected blood in injecting drug equipment, and from an infected mother to her child. Because we know that STIs are transmitted by certain behaviors, we know exactly how to keep from getting them. Those behaviors are particularly important because many young people underestimate their risk of becoming infected with an STI and the risk behavior of potential sex partners (Kaiser Family Foundation, 2001).

1. *Practice abstinence.* The closest thing to a foolproof method of STI prevention is abstaining from intimate sexual contact, especially penile-vaginal intercourse, anal intercourse, and oral sex. Hugging, kissing, caressing, and mutual masturbation are all ways of sharing intimacy that are extremely unlikely to transmit STIs. Abstinence is the only

An important part of controlling the spread of STIs is having free access to condoms and relevant information.

FOR THOSE WANTING TO PREVENT STIs and pregnancy, condom use is necessary for *all* sexual episodes. But consistent use is only part of the answer—the condom must be used correctly if it is to be effective. Most education concerning condoms has been designed to encourage use, not to provide detailed instruction on how to use the condom correctly. Given this educational void, those using condoms may not be using them properly.

Very little research has been conducted on correct condom use, but the first comprehensive study of college male students produced some startling and alarming results. Researchers William L. Yarber, Stephanie Sanders, Cynthia Graham, and Brian Dodge at Indiana University and Richard Crosby at Emory University determined the prevalence of condom use errors and problems among a sample of 158 undergraduate, single, heterosexual male students at a large midwestern university who reported condom use for sex at least once during the past 3 months and who put the condom on themselves. For this study, sex was defined as when the male put his penis in a partner's mouth, vagina, or rectum. Participants completed a self-report questionnaire listing 35 possible errors and problems with condom use before, during, and after sex. Major findings included:

- For before sex, 75% reported that they did not check the condom for visible damage; 61% did not check the expiration date on the condom; 60% did not discuss condom use before sex; and 42% wanted to use a condom but did not have one available.

- For during sex, 81% of those switching between various sexual behaviors reported that they did not change condoms between oral, vaginal, and anal sex; 43% put the condom on after starting sex; 40% did not leave space at the tip of the condom; 30% had the condom the wrong side up when trying to put it on; 29%

reported that the condom broke during sex; 22% lost their erection before the condom could be put on; 20% lost their erection after the condom was put on and sex had begun; 19% used a condom without a lubricant; 15% took the condom off before sex was over; and 13% reported that the condom slipped off during sex.

- For after sex, 67% for whom the condom broke, slipped off, or leaked reported that they did not discuss the possibility of infection or pregnancy with the partner and did not contact a health-care provider; 41% flushed the condom down the toilet; and 39% did not wrap the condom before discarding it.

The researchers concluded that the condom use errors reported in this study indicate a possible high risk of exposure of the participants to HIV/STIs and unintended pregnancy. They also stated that the effectiveness of condom use against HIV/STIs and unintended pregnancy is contingent upon correct condom use, and that condom promotion programs must discuss and enhance skills for correct condom use prior, during, and after sex, including health protection strategies in the event of errors.

With the findings of this study in mind, consider some questions: Do the types and frequency of errors surprise you? Why were so many errors and problems reported? Is it really that difficult to use condoms correctly? What can be done to promote correct condom use?

Sources: Crosby, R. A.; Sanders, S. A.; Yarber, W. L.; Graham, C. A.; & Dodge, B. (2002). "Condom Use Errors and Problems Among College Men." *Sexually Transmitted Diseases, 29*, 552–557; Yarber, W. L.; Sanders, S. A.; Graham, C.; & Dodge, B. (2001). "A Comprehensive Assessment of Male Condom Use Errors Among a Midwestern University Sample of Single Heterosexual Men." Paper presented at the meeting of the Rural Center for AIDS/STD Prevention, Indianapolis, IN.

reliable course of action for a person who has an STI or whose partner has an STI (or a suspected STI). Freely adopted, abstinence is a legitimate personal choice regarding sexuality. If you wish to remain abstinent, you need to communicate your preferences clearly and unambiguously to your dates or partners. You also need to learn to avoid high-pressure situations and to stay away from alcohol and drugs, which can impair your judgment. Interestingly, research on the success rate of persons practicing abstinence has revealed failure rates between 26% and 86% (Haignere, Gold, & McDaniel, 1999). Apparently, people find it very difficult to maintain abstinence.

2. *Practice sexual exclusivity.* Uninfected persons who practice sexual exclusivity in a long-term relationship or marriage will not contract an STI through sexual contact unless one partner had an STI when they started

having sexual contact. Certainly, it is not always possible to know if someone is infected or if she or he is exclusive. This is one reason it is wise to refrain from sexual activity until you can form a trusting relationship with an uninfected partner.

3. *Reduce risk during sexual intimacy.* Unless you are certain that your partner is not infected, you should not allow blood, semen, or vaginal fluids to touch your genitals, mouth, or anus. One of the best ways to prevent these fluids from entering your body is to properly use the male latex or polyurethane condom. (Guidelines on proper use of the condom are provided in Chapter 11.) Douching, washing, and urinating after sex have been suggested as possible ways of reducing STI risk, but their effectiveness has not been proved.

4. *Select partners carefully.* Knowing whether a partner might be infected with an STI can be tricky. Thus, this strategy is not always reliable. Certainly, you should avoid sexual contact with someone at high risk for having an STI, such as an individual who has had multiple partners and/or who injects drugs. A person may not be honest about their sexual partners or drug use. It is usually impossible to determine who is infected by merely looking at the person or by his or her reputation. Actually, according to one study, the participants had used visual and verbal cues to judge if their partners were disease-free. But in this case, their judgment was wrong, as most of their partners had contracted an STI (Hoffman & Cohen, 1999). If you do not know each other well, you would be wise to exchange phone numbers in the event of an STI infection or other problem or, better yet, wait until you know each other better before initiating sexual activity. Interestingly, one national study found that unfamiliarity with the partner, especially knowing the partner for less than 1 month, was associated with a higher incidence of being infected with an STI (Laumann et al., 1994).

5. *Avoid multiple partners.* As noted in this chapter, having multiple sex partners increases the risk for STIs.

6. *Avoid injecting and other drugs.* Another way to avoid HIV and hepatitis B is to not inject drugs and to not share needles and syringes if drugs are injected. Certainly, the drug equipment should be cleaned if sharing occurs. Not only can drugs harm your health, but they can also alter your judgment. A person drinking alcohol, smoking marijuana, or using other drugs may not be able to think clearly or make wise health decisions, and so may engage in risky sexual behaviors such as having sex without using a condom. The mixing of alcohol, drugs, and sex is a serious problem among young people. Alcohol and/or drugs are often involved in date rapes; people who drink beverages laced with "date-rape drugs" become vulnerable to having sex against their will.

7. *Get vaccinated.* Unfortunately, only one STI, hepatitis B, has a vaccine.

8. *Protect babies.* Most STIs can be transmitted from mother to child during pregnancy or childbirth. Most often, proper medical treatment can protect the baby from permanent damage. HIV-infected mothers should not breast-feed their babies. A woman who has an STI and becomes

SAFER SEX PRACTICES are an integral part of good health practices. (Many people prefer the term "safer sex" to "safe sex" because all sexual contact carries at least a slight risk—a condom slipping off, perhaps—no matter how careful we try to be.)

Safer Practices

- Hugging
- Kissing (but possibly not deep, French kissing)
- Massaging
- Petting
- Masturbation (solo or mutual, unless there are sores or abrasions on the genitals or hands)
- Erotic videos, books, and so on

Possibly Safe Practices

- Deep, French kissing, unless there are sores in the mouth
- Vaginal intercourse with a latex or polyurethane condom
- Fellatio with a latex or polyurethane condom
- Cunnilingus, if the woman is not menstruating or does not have a vaginal infection (a latex dental dam provides extra protection)
- Anal intercourse with a latex or polyurethane condom (experts disagree about whether this should be considered "possibly safe" even with a condom because it is the riskiest sexual behavior without one)

Unsafe Practices

- Vaginal or anal intercourse without a latex or polyurethane condom
- Fellatio without a latex or polyurethane condom
- Cunnilingus, if the woman is menstruating or has a vaginal infection and a dental dam is not used
- Oral-anal contact without a dental dam
- Contact with blood, including menstrual blood
- Semen in the mouth
- Use of vibrators, dildos, and other "toys" without washing them between uses

pregnant should inform her doctor, and any pregnant woman should be checked for STIs.

9. *Be a good communicator.* Acquiring an STI requires that you have been sexually intimate with another person. Avoiding an STI demands even more intimacy because it frequently means having to talk. Putting aside embarrassment and learning to communicate isn't always easy—but it is much simpler than dealing with herpes, gonorrhea, or AIDS. You need to learn how best to discuss prevention with potential sex partners and to communicate your thoughts, feelings, values, needs, and standards of behavior. Good communicators are less likely to do things against their values or beliefs. You should be clear about your beliefs and values and should stand by them. And you should never have sex with someone who will not talk about STI prevention.

Treating STIs

If you contract an STI, you can infect others. Acting responsibly will prevent others from acquiring an STI.

1. *Recognize STI symptoms.* People practicing risky sexual behaviors or injecting drugs should be alert to possible STI symptoms, especially if they have sex with partners at risk for STIs. To help avoid STIs, you should know what symptoms to look for, in yourself and others. Changes in the genitals may indicate an infection, although symptoms

of some STIs can appear anywhere, and some changes may indicate a health problem other than an STI. If you suspect an infection, you should not try to diagnose the condition yourself, but should consult a physician or health-care provider. In general, the symptoms of STIs are genital or rectal discharge, abdominal pain, painful urination, skin changes, genital itching, and flulike conditions. However, some STIs do not have any symptoms until the disease is well advanced, symptoms often disappear and then come back, and most STIs can still be passed on to someone even when the symptoms are not visible, are absent, or disappear. Actually, most people who are infected with an STI have no noticeable symptoms. Males are likely to notice symptoms earlier and more frequently than females. If you suspect an infection, you should stop having sex, stop injecting drugs, promptly see a health-care provider, and have sex partners go to a doctor or clinic.

2. *Seek treatment.* If you suspect that you might have an STI, you should seek medical care immediately. Public STI and HIV/AIDS clinics, private doctors, family planning clinics, and hospitals are all places to get treatment. Put aside any feelings of guilt or shame. The important concern is to get treatment promptly. Do not use home remedies, products bought in the mail or through the Internet, or drugs obtained from friends. Only qualified professionals can give proper care. People suspecting an STI shouldn't gamble that it might be something else or that it will go away.

3. *Get partners to treatment.* People who get treatment for an STI are doing the right thing, but they also need to encourage sex and injecting-drug-use partners to seek professional care quickly. This helps prevent serious illness in the partner, prevents reinfection, and helps control the STI epidemic. Because the first sign that a woman has an STI is often when her male partner shows symptoms, female partners especially should be advised. And even if a partner has no symptoms of an STI, he or she should still see a health-care provider.

AS INDIVIDUALS, WE HAVE the knowledge and means to protect ourselves from STIs. As a society, we should have a larger goal. ASHA (1998b), in its report *Sexually Transmitted Diseases in America: How Many Cases and at What Cost?*, writes:

> The American public remains generally unaware of the risk for STDs and the importance of prevention and screening. The secrecy and shame surrounding STDs interfere with communication between parents and children, sexual partners, teachers and students, and even patients and health care providers. There is a clear need for public and private sector organizations, medical professions, educational systems, the media, and religious and community groups to break the silence on the topic of sexual health. Public education programs are essential to alert consumers, health care providers, and policy makers to the reality of the STD epidemic.

We kill our selves, to propagate our kinde.

—*John Donne (1572–1631)*

SUMMARY

The STI Epidemic

- STIs are a "hidden" epidemic in the United States, accounting for 87% of all cases of the most frequently reported infectious diseases. Women, teens and young adults, and minorities are disproportionately affected by STIs. The scope and impact of STIs has been underestimated by public health officials. The STI rates in the United States exceed those of other industrialized countries.

- STIs are behavior-linked diseases resulting largely from unprotected sexual contact. Behavioral, social, and biological factors contribute to the spread of STIs. The behavioral risk factors include early initiation of intimate sexual activity, multiple and high-risk sex partners, high-risk sexual behavior, inconsistent and incorrect condom use, substance abuse, sexual coercion, and lack of personal knowledge and concern about STIs. Social risk factors include poverty and marginalization, lack of access to health care, and secrecy and moral conflict about sexuality. Biological factors include the asymptomatic nature of STIs, resistance to treatment, and lack of cures.

- Without medical attention, STIs can lead to serious health problems, including sterility, cancer, heart disease, blindness, ectopic pregnancy, miscarriage, and death. The presence of an STI increases the risk of acquiring an HIV infection if exposed. The direct cost of STIs is at least $8.4 billion annually.

Principal STIs

- The principal STIs affecting Americans are *chlamydia, gonorrhea, urinary tract infections, syphilis, genital warts, genital herpes, hepatitis, vaginitis,* and HIV/AIDS. Parasites that may be sexually transmitted include *scabies* and *pubic lice.*

STIs and Women

- Women tend to be more susceptible than men to STIs and to experience graver consequences, such as *pelvic inflammatory disease (PID),* an infection of the fallopian tubes that can lead to infertility, and ectopic pregnancy. Intense stimulation of the vulva can irritate the urethra, leading to *cystitis* (bladder infection).

Preventing STIs

- STI prevention involves the interaction of knowledge, psychological factors, and risk-avoiding behaviors. Ways to avoid STIs include abstinence, sexual exclusivity, careful partner selection, male condom use, and avoidance of multiple partners and injecting drugs. Persons practicing risky behavior should be alert to possible STI symptoms, seek treatment promptly if an STI is suspected, and inform partners.

Sex and the Internet

The American Social Health Association

The American Social Health Association (ASHA), founded in 1914, is a nonprofit organization focusing on STI prevention. ASHA publishes a variety of educational materials, provides direct patient support through national telephone hotlines, and advocates increased federal funding for STI programs and sound public policies on STI control. ASHA also operates a Web site (http://www.ashastd.org). Go to it and then answer the following questions:

- What programs does ASHA offer?
- What services are provided on its Web site?
- What are the current ASHA headlines?
- What is the STI Action Plan?

If you were diagnosed with an STI, would you seek more information from this site? Why or why not?

SUGGESTED WEB SITES

CDC National Prevention Information Network
http://www.cdcdnpin.org
Claims to house the nation's largest collection of information resources on HIV/AIDS, STI, and TB prevention.

Centers for Disease Control and Prevention
http://www.cdc.gov/hiv/adhap
Provides information on HIV/AIDS.
http://www.cdc.gov/nchstp/dstd
Provides information on STIs.

Joint United Nations Programme on HIV/AIDS
http://www.unaids.org
Contains epidemiological information on HIV/AIDS worldwide, as well as perspectives on HIV/AIDS-related issues.

Kaiser Family Foundation
http://www.kff.org
Offers fact sheets and new releases on STI and HIV/AIDS.

Rural Center for AIDS/STD Prevention
http://www.indiana.edu/~aids
Provides information about issues related to HIV/STI prevention in rural communities.

SUGGESTED READING

American Social Health Association. (2003). *HPV in Perspective: A Patient Guide* (2nd ed.). Research Triangle Park, NC: *Author*. Summarizes the latest information about HPV and genital warts in clear, easy-to-understand terms.

Brandt, Allan M. (1987). *No Magic Bullet: A Social History of Venereal Disease in the United States Since 1880*. New York: Oxford University Press. An informative and highly readable history of the social and political aspects of STIs.

Ebel, C., & Wald, A. (2002). *Managing Herpes: How to Live and Love with an STD*. Research Triangle Park, NC: American Social Health Association. Takes a patient-oriented approach to the impact of herpes, the basic facts, and the latest findings.

Eng, T. R., & Butler, W. T. (Eds.). (1997). *The Hidden Epidemic: Confronting Sexually Transmitted Diseases*. Washington, DC: National Academy Press. A discussion of why STDs have not been controlled and what the nation should do about the problem.

Holmes, King K.; Sparling, P. F.; Mardh, R. A.; Stanley, M.; Stammo, W. E.; Piot, P.; & Wasserheit, J. (Eds.). (1999). *Sexually Transmitted Diseases* (3rd ed.). New York: McGraw-Hill. The definitive collection of recent research by leading authorities on STDs in the United States and Europe.

Jones, James. (1993). *Bad Blood: The Tuskegee Syphilis Experiment—a Tragedy of Race and Medicine* (Rev. ed.). New York: Free Press. A fascinating—and chilling—account of a 40-year experiment by the Public Health Service, using African Americans in the rural South as human guinea pigs; discusses the experiment's impact on current HIV/AIDS prevention efforts in the Black community.

For links, articles, and study material, go to the McGraw-Hill Web site, located at http://www.mhhe.com/strong5

16

HIV and AIDS

"My father had AIDS. When he found out, I was only four years old. My parents chose to keep it a secret from me and my brothers. I lived with my dad then. Though he felt sick sometimes, we did the normal things that a family would do throughout the rest of my childhood. When I turned twelve Dad became very sick and was hospitalized. I went to live with my mother. When Dad came out of the hospital, he went to live with my grandparents. Still, no one told me what was wrong with him. Two years later, my mom finally told me that Dad had AIDS and was going to die soon. I was shocked and mad at both of my parents for not telling me earlier. My mom wouldn't let me go see Dad because he looked really bad and was in a lot of pain. I didn't get to see him or talk to him before he died. If I had known he was going to die so soon, I would have found a way to see him."

— 19-year-old White female

"I no longer hate you or feel angry with you [AIDS]. I realize now that you have become a positive force in my life. You are a messenger who has brought me a new understanding of my life and myself. So for that I thank you, forgive you, and release you. Because of you I have learned to love myself."

— 21-year-old White male

"I am aware of HIV and STDs, and they are not something I take lightly. In my relationship, trust and honesty are key points, and we discussed our histories ahead of time. We then made educated decisions."

— 20-year-old Black female

"You have to deal not only with the illness [AIDS] but with the prejudices that you encounter every day."

— 19-year-old White male

"I think HIV and STDs are the biggest reasons why I'm not promiscuous. I'd love to have sex with multiple partners and experiment, but even if I used a condom every time, I would still feel very much at risk. That is why I am monogamous in my relationship."

— 20-year-old White female

OVER THE PAST TWO DECADES, no single phenomenon has changed the face of sexuality as much as the appearance of the microscopic virus known as **HIV,** or **human immunodeficiency virus.** In the early 1980s, physicians in San Francisco, New York, and Los Angeles began noticing repeated occurrences of formerly rare diseases among young and relatively healthy men. Kaposi's sarcoma, a cancer of the blood vessels, and pneumocystis carinii pneumonia, a lung infection that is usually not dangerous, had become killer diseases because of the breakdown of the immune system of the men in whom these diseases were being seen (Centers for Disease Control [CDC], 1982). Even before the virus responsible for the immune system breakdown was discovered, the disease was given a name: acquired immunodeficiency syndrome, or AIDS. In the mid-1980s, the causative agent of

Ring around the rosy,
Pocket full of posies.
Ashes! Ashes!
We all fall down.

—*Nursery rhyme*

AIDS, HIV, was discovered. At first, AIDS within the United States seemed to be confined principally to three groups: gay men, Haitians, and people with hemophilia. Soon, however, it became apparent that AIDS was not confined to just a few groups; the disease spread into communities with high rates of injecting drug use and into the general population, including heterosexual men and women (and their children) at all socioeconomic levels. The far-reaching consequences of the AIDS epidemic, in addition to the pain and loss directly caused by the illness, have included widespread fear, superstition, stigmatization, prejudice, and hatred. Ignorance of its modes of transmission has fueled the flames of homophobia among some people. Among others, it has kindled a general fear of sexual expression. In many communities, however, it has engendered compassion and solidarity as people have come together to care for those who are living with HIV or AIDS and to educate themselves and others. Although the crisis is not over, the availability of new drugs has allowed many individuals with HIV or AIDS to live longer, healthier, and more productive lives.

By now, most of us know how HIV is spread. And yet, for a variety of reasons, people continue to engage in behaviors that put them at risk. Our goal in this chapter is to present a basic description of the biological, psychological, and sociological aspects of the disease. Because it is not likely that a cure for AIDS will be found in the near future, we must develop the attitudes and behaviors that will stop its deadly progression. AIDS *is* preventable. We hope that the material in this chapter will help you make healthy, informed choices for yourself and become a force for education and positive change in the community. Because of the tremendous amount of AIDS research being conducted, some of the information presented here, particularly HIV/AIDS incidence and prevalence, could be outdated by the time this book appears in print. For updates on HIV/AIDS research findings and news, contact the U.S. Centers for Disease Control and Prevention (the Web address is given in the "Sex and the Internet" section) or one of the agencies or Web sites listed at the end of this chapter.

We begin the chapter by describing the biology of the disease and the immune system. We next discuss modes of transmission, the effects of HIV and AIDS on certain groups of people, means of prevention, HIV testing, and current treatments. Then we deal with the demographic aspects of the epidemic—its effect on various communities and groups. Finally, we discuss living with HIV or AIDS, offering practical advice for those who have the virus or whose friends or loved ones do.

WHAT IS AIDS?

AIDS is an acronym for **acquired immunodeficiency syndrome.** This condition is so named for the following reasons:

A   Acquired, because it is not inherited

I   Immuno, because it affects the immune system, which protects the body against disease-causing organisms

D   Deficiency, because the body lacks immunity

S   Syndrome, because the symptoms occur as a group

OUR CULTURE EXTOLS the attractions of uninhibited sexual activity (during which no one ever uses a condom or contracts an STI) in movies, music, TV programs, and advertising. But people who follow this lead and end up with HIV or another STI may feel ashamed and guilty. What is going on here?

The deep ambivalence our society feels about sexuality is clearly brought to light by the way in which we deal with HIV and other STIs. If we think we have strep throat, we waste no time getting ourselves to a health center or doctor to obtain the appropriate medication. We probably take precautions not to spread the germs to those around us, and we do not hesitate to call a friend or our boss and croak, "Guess what? I've got strep throat!"

But let's say we're experiencing some discomfort when we urinate, and there's an unusual discharge. We may disregard the symptoms at first. We may hope they'll go away if we simply ignore them. But they don't. Soon, we're feeling some pain, and we know something is definitely not right. With fear and trepidation, we slink into the clinic or doctor's office, hoping we don't see anyone we know so we won't have to explain why we're there. The doctor or clinician examines our "private parts," which makes us very uncomfortable, and asks a lot of embarrassing questions. When we pick up our prescription, we can't look the pharmacist in the eye. And then there's the whole problem of telling our partner—or, worse yet, partners—about our predicament. Sound familiar? We hope not! But for many young adults, at least part of this scenario will ring true.

Why all this emotion over an STI but not over strep throat? Where does all the fear, denial, embarrassment, guilt, shame, and humiliation come from? Why are STIs the only class of illnesses we categorize by their *mode of transmission* rather than by the type of organism that causes them? All these questions stem from a common source: Many people have confused and conflicting feelings about issues surrounding sexuality. And because we, as a society, are so ambivalent and anxious, we don't deal with STIs rationally. We pretend that we won't get them and ignore them when we do. We lie to ourselves and our partners. And even if we feel *we* wouldn't put someone down or think badly of him or her for having an STI, if we get one ourselves, we feel embarrassed, ashamed, and guilty. We may even feel (or others may tell us) that we are being punished for being bad. This attitude, indicative of our national ambivalence about sexuality, does little to help us deal rationally with STIs, especially those that cannot be cured.

Fear of stigmatization and feelings of shame are among the principal factors contributing to the spread of HIV and other STIs. For example, in a sample of clinic patients and others at high risk for gonorrhea and HIV in seven cities, both shame and stigma were related to seeking STI-related care, but stigma may have been a more powerful barrier to obtaining such care (Fortenberry et al., 2002). People with HIV/AIDS and the groups to which they belong have been stigmatized since the AIDS epidemic began. This stigma slowed societal response to AIDS and has posed numerous difficulties for people with HIV/AIDS, their families, and health-care givers. In comparing HIV stigma in 1991 and 1999, researchers found that, although support for extremely punitive policies for people with AIDS declined somewhat, AIDS remained a stigmatized condition in the United States. In 1999, about one-third of a national probability sample expressed discomfort with and negative feelings toward people with AIDS (Herek, Capitanio, & Widaman, 2002).

In your view, what can be done to eliminate the cultural stigma of HIV/STI? If you became infected with HIV or another STI, would shame and stigma be an issue for you? If so, how would you deal with it? From what resources would you seek help and support?

To monitor the spread of AIDS through a national surveillance system, the CDC has established a definition of AIDS. To receive an AIDS diagnosis under the CDC's classification system (and thus be eligible for treatments, programs, and insurance funds that would not otherwise be available), a person must, in most cases, have a positive blood test indicating the presence of HIV antibodies and a T-cell count (discussed later) below 200 (CDC, 1992). If the T-cell count is higher, he or she must have one or more of the diseases or conditions associated with AIDS (discussed shortly). If a person has HIV antibodies, as measured by a blood test, but does not meet the other criteria, he or she is said to "have HIV," "be HIV-positive," "be HIV-infected," or "be living with HIV." Infection with HIV produces a spectrum of diseases that progress from a latent or asymptomatic state to AIDS as a late manifestation. The rate of this progression varies (CDC, 1998a).

In 1993, T-cell count, along with cervical cancer/cervical intraepithelial neoplasia (CIN), pulmonary tuberculosis, and recurrent bacterial pneumonia, was added to the CDC definition of AIDS (CDC, 1992). These additions led to a dramatic increase in the number of people who "officially" have AIDS.

Conditions Associated with AIDS

The CDC currently lists 27 clinical conditions to be used in diagnosing AIDS along with HIV-positive status (CDC, 1996b). These conditions fall into several categories: opportunistic infections, cancers, conditions associated specifically with AIDS, and conditions that *may* be diagnosed as AIDS under certain circumstances. The most commonly occurring diseases and conditions within these categories are listed here.

Opportunistic Infections   Diseases that take advantage of a weakened immune system are known as **opportunistic infections (OIs).** Normally, these infections do not develop in healthy people or are not life-threatening. Common OIs associated with HIV include the following:

- **Pneumocystis carinii pneumonia (PCP).** The most common opportunistic infection of people with AIDS, PCP is a lung disease caused by a common organism (probably a protozoan or fungus) that is not usually harmful. The organisms multiply, resulting in the accumulation of fluid in the lungs (pneumonia).

- *Mycobacterium avium intracellulare (MAI).* This atypical tuberculosis usually affects the lungs, but it may also affect the liver, spleen, lymphatic system, bone marrow, gastrointestinal tract, skin, or brain. MAI is the most common form of TB among people with AIDS. It is resistant to most antibiotics.

- *Mycobacterium tuberculosis (TB).* This infection generally occurs in the lungs and may appear at other sites, such as the lymph nodes. This "old-fashioned" form of TB is infectious but treatable with common antibiotics.

- *Bacterial pneumonia.* This condition is characterized by accumulation of fluid in the lungs due to the presence of any of several common bacteria. Multiple episodes of bacterial pneumonia may occur in people with AIDS.

- *Toxoplasmosis.* This disease of the brain and central nervous system is caused by a parasite frequently present in cat feces.

Cancers   Certain types of cancer are commonly associated with AIDS, including the following:

- **Kaposi's sarcoma.** This cancer of the blood vessels, which causes red or purple blotches to appear under the skin, is rare in healthy people, except older men of central African or Mediterranean descent. Among people with AIDS, it is more common in gay or bisexual men than in women or heterosexual men.

- *Lymphomas.* These cancers of the lymphatic system may also affect the brain.

- *Invasive cervical cancer.* Dysplasia of the cervix can lead to cancer. Cervical cancer and CIN are more common in women who are HIV-positive than in other women. Cervical cancer can lead to uterine cancer if untreated.

Clinical Conditions Conditions that are specifically linked to AIDS include the following:

- *Wasting syndrome.* Symptoms include severe weight loss, usually accompanied by weakness and persistent diarrhea.

- *HIV encephalopathy (AIDS dementia).* This condition is characterized by impairment of mental functioning, changes in mood or behavior, and impaired movement caused by direct infection of the brain with HIV.

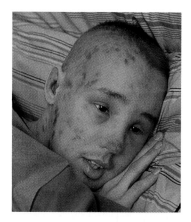

Kaposi's sarcoma is a cancer of the blood vessels commonly associated with AIDS. It causes red or purple blotches to appear under the skin's surface.

Other Infections Infections listed by the CDC that may lead to an AIDS diagnosis under certain circumstances include the following:

- *Candidiasis (thrush).* This fungal (yeast) infection affects the mouth, throat, esophagus, trachea, lungs, and vagina. Recurring candidiasis is especially common in women with AIDS.

- *Herpes simplex.* This common viral STI causes persistent lesions (lasting a month or more) or lesions on the lungs or esophagus.

- *Cytomegalovirus (CMV).* This virus of the herpes family is often sexually transmitted. In people with AIDS, it can lead to encephalitis (a brain infection), retinitis (infection of the retina that can lead to blindness), pneumonia, and hepatitis.

Because the immune systems of people with HIV may not be functioning well (and those of people with advanced AIDS certainly are not), they may be subject to numerous other infections that would not normally be much of a problem, such as colds, flus, and intestinal infections. Health precautions for people living with HIV are discussed later in the chapter.

Symptoms of HIV Infection and AIDS

A person with HIV may feel fine; many people with HIV do not have symptoms for many years. Or a person may experience one or more of the symptoms listed here. Someone who has received an AIDS diagnosis is more likely to experience at least some of these symptoms. It is important to remember, however, that all of these are also common symptoms of conditions that are not related to HIV or AIDS. No one should assume they are infected if they have any of these symptoms. *AIDS cannot be self-diagnosed.* A person who is experiencing persistent discomfort or illness should be checked out by a medical practitioner. Remember, AIDS is a medical diagnosis made by a physician using the specific CDC criteria. Symptoms that *may* be associated with HIV or AIDS include the following:

- Unexplained persistent fatigue

- Unexplained fever, chills, or night sweats for a period of several weeks or more

- Unexplained weight loss greater than 10 pounds or 10% of body weight in less than 2 months
- Swollen lymph nodes in the neck, armpits, or groin that are unexplained and last more than 2 months—a condition known as lymphadenopathy
- Pink, red, purple, or brown blotches on or under the skin or inside the mouth, nose, eyelids, or rectum that do not disappear
- Persistent fuzzy white spots or other sores in the mouth on the tongue or in the throat (indicative of either hairy leukoplakia or candidiasis)
- Persistent dry cough and shortness of breath
- Persistent diarrhea that lasts more than a week
- Pneumonia
- Memory loss, depression, and other neurological disorders

In addition, women may experience the following:

- Abnormal Pap smears
- Persistent vaginal candidiasis
- Abdominal cramping (due to pelvic inflammatory disease)

Understanding AIDS: The Immune System and HIV

The principal components of blood are plasma (the fluid base), red blood cells, white blood cells, and platelets.

Leukocytes   There are several kinds of **leukocytes,** or white blood cells, all of which play major roles in defending the body against invading organisms or mutant (cancerous) cells. Because HIV invades and eventually kills some kinds of leukocytes, it impairs the body's ability to ward off infections and other harmful conditions that ordinarily would not be threatening. The principal type of leukocyte we discuss is the lymphocyte.

Macrophages, Antigens, and Antibodies   White blood cells called **macrophages** engulf foreign particles and display the invader's antigen (*anti*body *gen*erator) like a signal flag on their own surfaces. **Antigens** are large molecules that are capable of stimulating the immune system and then reacting with the antibodies that are released to fight them. **Antibodies** bind to antigens, inactivate them, and mark them for destruction by killer cells. If the body has been previously exposed to the organism (by fighting it off or being vaccinated), the response is much quicker because memory cells are already biochemically programmed to respond.

B Cells and T Cells   The **lymphocytes** (a type of leukocyte) crucial to the immune system's functioning are **B cells** and several types of **T cells.** Like macrophages, **helper T cells** are programmed to "read" the antigens and then begin directing the immune system's response. They send chemical signals to B cells, which begin making antibodies specific to the presented antigen. Helper T cells also stimulate the proliferation of B cells and T cells (which are genetically programmed to replicate, or make copies of themselves) and activate both macrophages and **killer T cells,** transforming them

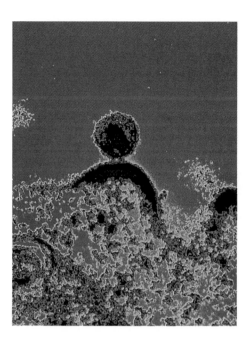

A T cell infected with HIV begins to replicate the virus, which buds from the cell wall, eventually killing the host cell.

into agents of destruction whose only purpose is to attack and obliterate the enemy. Helper T cells display a type of protein receptor called CD4. The number of helper T cells in an individual's body is an important indicator of how well the immune system is functioning, as we discuss later.

The Virus

A **virus** is a protein-coated package of genes that invades a cell and alters the way in which the cell reproduces itself. Viruses can't propel themselves independently, and they can't reproduce unless they are inside a host cell. It would take 16,000 human immunodeficiency viruses to cover the head of a pin in a single layer. Under strong magnification, HIV resembles a spherical pincushion, bristling with tiny pinheadlike knobs (Figure 16.1). These knobs are the antigens, which contain a protein called GP 120; the CD4 receptors on a helper T cell are attracted (fatally, as it turns out) to GP 120. Within the virus's protein core is the genetic material (RNA) that carries the information the virus needs to replicate itself. Also in the core is an enzyme called **reverse transcriptase,** which enables the virus to "write" its RNA (the genetic software or program) into a cell's DNA. Viruses with the ability to reverse the normal genetic writing process are known as **retroviruses.** There are numerous variant strains of HIV as a result of mutations. The virus begins undergoing genetic variation as soon as it has infected a person, even before antibodies develop. This tendency to mutate is one factor that makes HIV difficult to destroy.

Effect on T Cells   When HIV enters the bloodstream, helper T cells rush to the invading viruses, as if they were specifically designed for them. Normally at this stage, a T cell reads the antigen, stimulating antibody production in the B cells and beginning the process of eliminating the invading

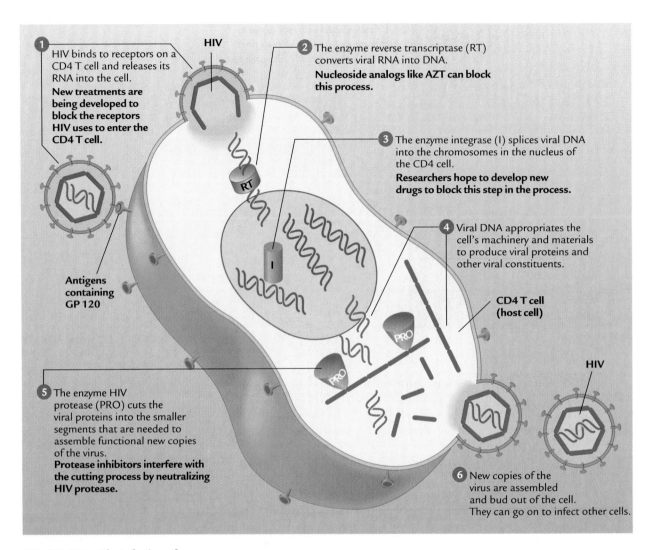

FIGURE 16.1 The Infection of a CD4 T Cell by HIV. Different classes of drugs block the replication of HIV at different points in the virus's life cycle.

organism. In the case of HIV, however, although antibody production does begin, the immune process starts to break down almost at once. HIV injects its contents into the host T cell and copies its own genetic code into the cell's genetic material (DNA). As a result, when the immune system is activated, the T cell begins producing HIV instead of replicating itself. The T cell is killed in the process. HIV also targets other types of cells, including macrophages, dendritic cells (leukocytes found in the skin, lymph nodes, and intestinal mucous membranes), and brain cells.

HIV-1 and HIV-2   Almost all cases of HIV in the United States involve the type of the virus known as HIV-1. Of the subtypes of HIV-1 that have been identified, subtype B is by far the most common in North America. Scientists note that different strains may differ in their effects on the body—which cells they prefer to attack, for example—indicating the need for further research. Another type, HIV-2, has been found to exist mainly in West Africa.

AIDS Pathogenesis: How the Disease Progresses

As discussed earlier, when viruses are introduced into the body, they are immediately snatched up by helper T cells and whisked off to the lymph nodes. Although HIV begins replication right away within the host cells, the virus itself may not be detectable in the blood for some time. HIV antibodies, however, are generally detectable in the blood within 2–6 months (the testing process is discussed later). The process by which a person develops antibodies is called **seroconversion.** A person's **serostatus** is HIV-negative if antibodies to HIV are not detected and HIV-positive if antibodies are detected.

T-Cell (CD4) Count   T-cell count—also called CD4 count—refers to the number of helper T cells that are present in a cubic milliliter of blood. A healthy person's T-cell count averages about 1000, but it can range from 500 to 1600, depending on a person's general health and whether she or he is fighting off an illness.

Phases of Infection   The pace of disease progression is variable, with the time between infection with HIV and development of AIDS ranging from a few months to as long as 17 years (the average is 10 years) (CDC, 1998b) (Figure 16.2). When a person is first infected with HIV, he or she may experience severe flulike symptoms as the immune system goes into high gear to fight off the invader. His or her T-cell count may temporarily plunge as

FIGURE 16.2   The General Pattern of HIV Infection. The blue line represents the number of CD4 cells in the blood, a marker for the status of the immune system. The red line shows the amount of HIV RNA in the blood. (*Source:* From Fauci, et al. "Immuno-pathogenic Mechanisms of HIV Infection." *Annals of Internal Medicine 1996; 124:* 654–63. Reprinted by permission of American College of Physicians.)

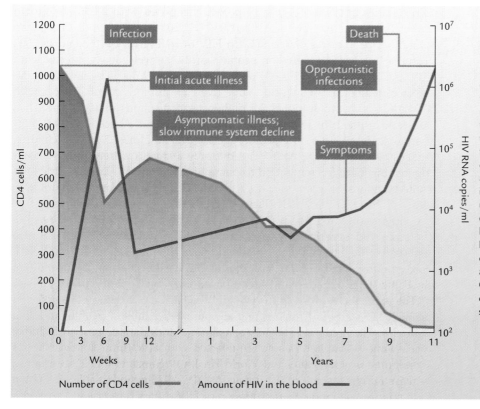

During the initial acute illness, CD4 levels fall sharply and HIV RNA levels increase; more than 50% of infected people experience flulike symptoms during this period. Antibodies to HIV usually appear 2–12 weeks after the initial infection. During the asymptomatic phase that follows, CD4 levels gradually decline, and HIV RNA levels again increase. Due to declines in immunity, infected individuals eventually begin to experience symptoms; when CD4 levels drop very low, people become vulnerable to serious opportunistic infections characteristic of full-blown AIDS. Chronic or recurrent illnesses continue until the immune system fails and death results.

the virus begins rapid replication. During this period, the virus is dispersed throughout the lymph nodes, where it replicates, a process called "seeding" (Kolata, 1992). The virus may stay localized for years, but it continues to replicate and destroy T cells. One study has shown that viral load is the chief predictor of heterosexual transmission of HIV; the HIV-infected person is most infectious when the viral load is the highest (Quinn et al., 2000). Detecting infection early and beginning treatment can reduce viral load and possibly an individual's infectiousness (Cates, Chesney, & Cohen, 1997).

As time goes by, the T cells gradually diminish in number, destroyed by newly created HIV. During this phase, as the number of infected cells goes up, the number of T cells goes down, generally to between 200 and 500 per milliliter of blood.

When AIDS is in the advanced phase the T cells and other fighter cells of the immune system are no longer able to trap foreign invaders. Infected cells continue to increase, and the T-cell count drops to under 200. The virus is detectable in the blood. At this point, the person is fairly ill to very ill. The T-cell count may continue to plummet to zero. The person with AIDS dies from one or more of the opportunistic diseases.

THE EPIDEMIOLOGY AND TRANSMISSION OF HIV

Epidemiology is the study of the incidence, process, distribution, and control of diseases. An epidemic is the wide and rapid spread of a contagious disease. In this country, since the diagnosis of the first AIDS case more than two decades ago, the number of people diagnosed with AIDS has grown from a few dozen to more than 800,000 (CDC, 2001d). Worldwide, more than 42 million people were infected with HIV or had AIDS by the end of 2002 (Figure 16.3). In 2002, 5 million people worldwide were newly infected with HIV, and 3.1 million died from AIDS. Sub-Saharan Africa is by far the worst-affected region of the world, with over 29 million people living with HIV/AIDS and an additional 3.5 million new infections in 2002. The AIDS epidemic claimed the lives of an estimated 2.4 million Africans in 2002. Furthermore, 10 million young people, age 15–24, and almost 3 million children under age 15 are living with HIV. And only a small fraction of those needing treatment are receiving it. In response to this desperate situation, the Joint United Nations Program on HIV/AIDS (UNAIDS) and World Health Organization (2002) has declared, "These figures reflect the world's continuing failure, despite the progress in recent years, to mount a response that matches the scale and severity of the global HIV/AIDS epidemic." UNAIDS also reports that the number of people living with HIV in 2002 was 1.2 million in Eastern Europe and Central Asia and that HIV/AIDS is expanding rapidly in the Baltic states, the Russian Federation, and several Central Asian republics.

The epidemic is growing in Asia and the Pacific (7.2 million HIV-infected people), especially in China, where an estimated 1 million people are living with HIV. The epidemic also has potential for considerable growth in India, where almost 4 million people are infected with HIV (Joint United Nations Programme on HIV/AIDS and World Health Organization, 2002). Certainly, as these numbers suggest, the impact of HIV/AIDS is undeniable. As shown in the figure, the mode of transmission of HIV differs throughout the world,

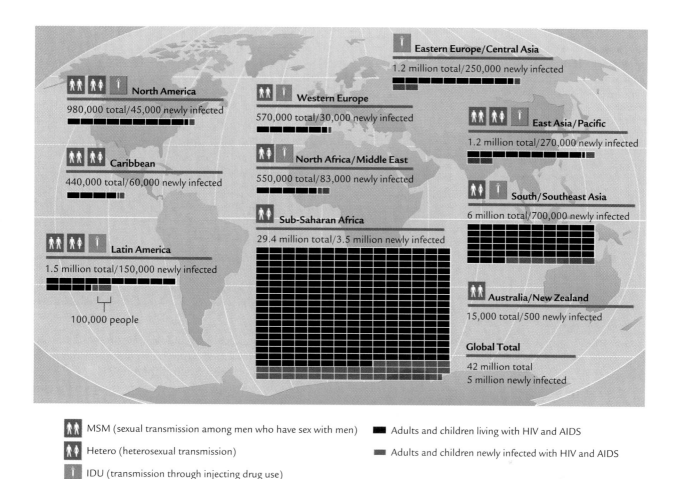

MSM (sexual transmission among men who have sex with men)

Hetero (heterosexual transmission)

IDU (transmission through injecting drug use)

Adults and children living with HIV and AIDS

Adults and children newly infected with HIV and AIDS

FIGURE 16.3 Adults and Children Newly Infected with HIV or Living with HIV/AIDS, and Main Modes of Transmission. (*Sources:* Joint United Nations Programme on HIV/AIDS [UNAIDS] and World Health Organization, 2002.)

although heterosexual contact is the most prominent mode. Worldwide, adult HIV cases are split almost evenly between men and women.

A great deal has been discovered about AIDS since it first perplexed physicians and scientists in 1981. Much of what we now know regarding HIV transmission is due to the work of epidemiologists who track the progress of the disease in the United States and throughout the world.

The Epidemiology of HIV/AIDS

As of this book's publication, data from the CDC indicate that, since 1981, 816,149 people—807,075 adults and adolescents and 9074 children—have been diagnosed with AIDS in the United States. AIDS prevalence (total cases) has increased steadily over time, and at the end of 2001, an estimated 362,827 people in the United States were living with AIDS. An estimated 900,000 people may be living with HIV, although about one-third do not know that they are infected. The HIV infection rates seem to have stabilized since the early 1990s, with about 40,000 new infections a year (CDC, 2001d; National Institute of Allergy and Infectious Diseases, 2002). However, in early 2003, the CDC reported that HIV infection rates appear to be rising, possibly because of improved treatment and increased risky behavior due to the

Sharing needles and other injecting drug paraphernalia is a common mode of HIV transmission via infected blood. Groups such as the AIDS Brigade provide clean needles for injecting drug users.

belief of some that AIDS is more medically treatable (Sternberg, 2003). By the end of 2001, 467,910 Americans had died from AIDS, although the number of deaths is decreasing because of antiretroviral treatments.

HIV/AIDS has been reported in virtually all population groups. Ongoing studies since the early 1980s indicate that four distinct populations are most affected by HIV/AIDS, as described below. Within these populations, the HIV/AIDS epidemic has disproportionately impacted various groups, which we discuss later.

- *Men who have sex with men* (this terminology is commonly used by AIDS prevention specialists because some men who have sex with other men do not label themselves as homosexual or bisexual). Their infection rate is facilitated by frequent changes in sex partners in highly infected sex networks and high-risk sexual practices.

- *Injecting drug users.* Sharing needles and syringes contaminated with HIV-infected blood increases the risk of contracting HIV.

- *Heterosexual people.* Higher rates are seen among drug-using populations, those with high rates of other STIs, and those who engage in high-risk sexual practices associated with sex in exchange for drugs.

- *Infants.* Perinatal transmission is caused by undetected or untreated HIV infection in pregnant women (U.S. Department of Health and Human Services, 2000a).

At the end of 2001, 46% of the total reported U.S. AIDS cases involved men who had sex with men; 25%, injecting drug users; 11%, persons infected heterosexually; and 1%, persons infected through blood or blood products. The modes of transmission of HIV differ by gender (Figure 16.4), and the proportion of AIDS cases associated with different risk behaviors and in various populations has changed over time (Figures 16.5 and 16.6). The AIDS epidemic has shifted steadily toward a growing proportion of cases in minority populations and women and a decreasing proportion of cases in men who have sex with men. Since the beginning of the epidemic, Blacks

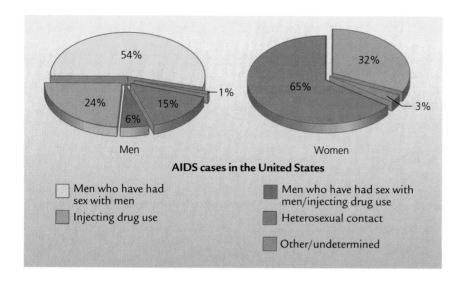

FIGURE 16.4 Estimated AIDS Incidence Among U.S. Adults and Adolescents by Gender and Exposure Category, 2001. (*Source:* CDC, 2003b.)

and Hispanics have been disproportionately affected by HIV/AIDS (Figure 16.7). In 2001, 67% of AIDS cases reported among adolescents and adults were Blacks and Hispanics. The proportion of women with AIDS has also increased, from about 7% of the total cases in 1983 to about 26% in 2001. The number of new perinatally acquired AIDS cases has decreased sharply because of the use of the drug zidovudine (ZDV) (CDC, 2001d).

Myths and Modes of Transmission

Before we discuss further the ways in which HIV has been shown to be transmitted, we should mention some of the ways in which it is *not* transmitted. Myths about how HIV is transmitted have caused some people to have an unreasonable fear of AIDS. For example, they may be afraid of HIV-infected persons and refuse to be near them. You *cannot* get HIV from any of the following:

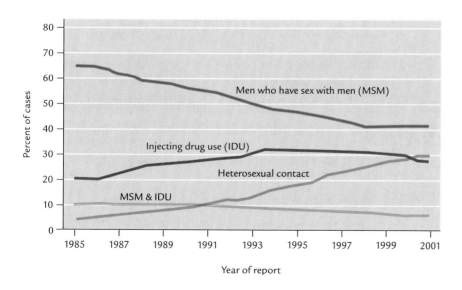

FIGURE 16.5 Change in U.S. Adult and Adolescent AIDS Cases by Exposure Category and Year of Diagnosis, 1985–2001. (*Source:* CDC, 2003b.)

FIGURE 16.6 Change in U.S. AIDS Cases by Race/Ethnicity and Year of Report, 1985–2001. (*Source:* CDC, 2003c.)

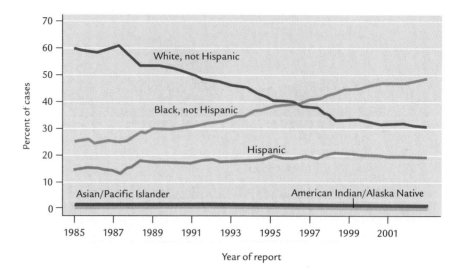

▪ *Casual contact.* Normal household or social contact does not transmit HIV. Shaking hands, hugging, kissing, playing, and providing personal care such as bathing, feeding, and dressing are extremely unlikely to transmit HIV. Extensive studies of households with an HIV-infected member have shown no evidence of transmission through casual contact.

▪ *Contact sports.* Some young people worry about acquiring HIV while playing sports. However, the CDC reports no documented cases of HIV being transmitted during athletic events. The risk of HIV transmission is very low in contact sports, and there is minimal risk of HIV transmission when bleeding does occur. If someone is bleeding, she or he should stop participating until the wound is cleaned and bandaged.

▪ *Inanimate objects.* HIV cannot live outside the body fluids in which it is normally found. It cannot survive on countertops, toilet seats, drinking fountains, telephones, eating utensils, door knobs, and so on. If a surface or object is contaminated by infected blood or semen, it can be disinfected with bleach, alcohol, hydrogen peroxide, Lysol, or other household cleaners.

FIGURE 16.7 U.S. AIDS Cases by Race/Ethnicity, 2001. (*Source:* CDC, 2003c.)

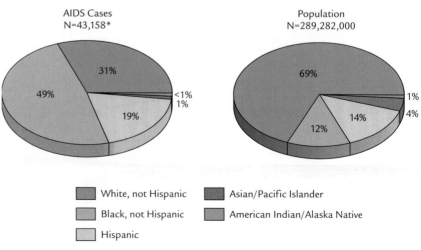

*Includes 57 persons with unknown race/ethnicity

- *Blood donation.* In the United States, it is not possible to get HIV from donating blood. Sterilized needles are used to draw the blood, and they are disposed of afterward; they are never reused.

- *Animals.* Household pets and farm animals can neither get HIV nor pass it on. Laboratory chimpanzees may be intentionally infected with HIV, but there are no known cases of transmission from chimps to humans.

- *Insect bites.* Extensive research has shown that HIV is not transmitted by biting insects such as mosquitoes. The virus has been demonstrated not to replicate in flies, ticks, or mosquitoes.

- *Saliva.* Only a small fraction of people with HIV have detectable virus in their saliva. The amounts are very small, and enzymes in the saliva are hostile to the virus. There are no known cases of transmission from saliva, although theoretically there could be a slight risk if the saliva from a person with advanced AIDS were to enter another's bloodstream or if a person with HIV had blood in the mouth.

- *Tears or sweat.* HIV exists in minute quantities in the tears of some infected people, but researchers have found no evidence of transmission via tears. Researchers also have been unable to find the virus in the sweat of HIV-infected people.

- *Vaccines.* The processes by which vaccines are manufactured effectively remove or inactivate HIV. In the United States, sterile, fresh needles are used to give vaccinations, and they are destroyed after use.

- *Water.* HIV cannot live or replicate in water. It is not transmitted in drinking water, or in hot tubs, whirlpool baths, or swimming pools.

For HIV to replicate in the body, it must have a path of entry into the bloodstream. The most common modes of transmission involve HIV-infected semen, blood, or vaginal secretions. Activities or situations in which HIV may be transmitted include the following:

- Vaginal or anal intercourse without a latex or polyurethane condom, fellatio without a latex or polyurethane condom, and cunnilingus without a latex or other barrier

- The sharing of needles contaminated with HIV-infected blood during injecting drug use, tattoos, body piercings, home injections of medications, or self-administered steroid injections

- Passage of the virus from mother to fetus in the uterus (20–50% chance) or in blood during delivery

- Breast-feeding, if the mother is HIV-positive

- The sharing of sex toys, such as dildos or vibrators, without disinfecting them

- Accidental contamination when infected blood enters the body through the mucous membranes of the eyes or mouth or through cuts, abrasions, or punctures in the skin

- Before 1985, from contaminated blood (transfusions) or organs (transplants)

The first three modes of transmission are the most common. We discuss each of these in greater detail in the following sections.

Sexual Transmission

Semen and vaginal secretions of people with HIV may contain infected cells, especially in the later phases of AIDS. Latex barriers, condoms, dental dams, and surgical gloves, if used properly, can provide good protection against the transmission of HIV.

Anal Intercourse   The riskiest form of sexual interaction for both men and women is receiving anal sex. The membrane lining the rectum is delicate and ruptures easily, exposing tiny blood vessels to infection from virus-carrying semen. Infected blood from the rectum may also enter the penis through the mucous membrane at the urethral opening or through small cuts, abrasions, or open sores. Heterosexual anal intercourse is more common than many people realize; studies show that 9% of heterosexual couples practice it (Laumann, Gagnon, Michael, & Michaels, 1994).

Vaginal Intercourse   Vaginal sex is also quite risky as an HIV transmission route, especially for women, and is the most common way HIV is transmitted in much of the world. Several factors contribute to this phenomenon. First, semen contains a high concentration of HIV. Second, the large area of exposed mucosal tissue in the vagina puts women at an additional disadvantage compared to men in terms of exposure. Third, a large number of couples regularly engage in unprotected vaginal intercourse. Finally, adolescent females are biologically more susceptible to HIV than older women because their immature cervixes may be more easily infected (Braverman & Strasburger, 1994). Males are at less risk than females for contracting HIV through vaginal intercourse. However, the virus can enter the bloodstream through the urethra or through small cuts or open sores on the penis. Menstrual blood containing HIV can facilitate transmission of the virus to a sex partner.

Oral Sex   HIV may be transmitted during fellatio, cunnilingus, or anilingus (oral-anal contact), although the risk is less than that from unprotected anal or vaginal sex. Individuals performing oral sex can contract HIV from the semen or vaginal secretions of people with HIV via sores or cuts in or around the mouth. Individuals receiving oral sex can become infected if their partner has HIV and blood from his or her mouth enters the urethra, vagina, or anus. The person performing oral sex is generally at greater risk.

Measuring the precise risk of HIV transmission as a result of oral sex is very difficult. Because most sexually active people participate in other sexual behaviors besides oral sex, it is difficult to determine whether transmission occurred during oral sex or other, riskier, sexual activities. Though findings have been conflicting, a few studies have documented HIV transmission through oral sex between men and women and between men and men. For example, in one study, 8% of HIV-infected men who had sex with men reported oral sex as their only risk factor (CDC, 2000b). But another study involving over 19,000 exposures of heterosexual HIV-serodiscordant couples (i.e., one person HIV-positive and one HIV-negative) whose only risk exposure to HIV was unprotected oral sex with their HIV-infected partner found not a single HIV transmission (del Romero et al., 2002). Nevertheless, the CDC states that oral sex with someone who is infected with HIV is certainly not risk-free (CDC, 2001e). The CDC also notes that several STIs, such as genital herpes, genital warts, gonorrhea, and syphilis, can be transmitted through oral sex.

Sex Toys   HIV can be transmitted in vaginal secretions on such objects as dildos and vibrators; therefore, it is very important that these objects not be shared or that they be washed thoroughly before use.

Drug Use

Sharing needles or other paraphernalia (including cotton pieces) used to inject drugs provides an ideal pathway for HIV. Infection via the blood-stream is called **parenteral transmission.** An injecting drug user (IDU) may have an immune system that has already been weakened by poor health, poor nutrition, or an STI. IDUs who become infected often pass the virus sexually to their partners.

Sobering data from the CDC indicate that injecting drug use accounts for 32%, 24%, and 26% of the 2001 U.S. AIDS cases for women, men, and men who have sex with men and inject drugs, respectively. Noninjecting drugs such as "crack" cocaine also contribute to the growth of the epidemic when users trade sex for drugs or money or when they engage in risky sexual behaviors, which they might not do when sober. One CDC study of more than 2000 young adults in three inner-city neighborhoods found that crack smokers were 3 times more likely to be HIV-infected than nonsmokers (CDC, 2002g).

When we think of injecting drug use, we usually think in terms of psychotropic (mind-affecting) drugs such as heroin or cocaine. We may conjure up images of run-down tenement rooms or "shooting galleries," where needles are passed around. But these are not the only settings for sharing drugs. HIV transmission in connection with the recreational use of injecting drugs also occurs among people from the middle or upper class. Moreover, injecting drug use exists among athletes and body-builders, who may share needles to inject steroids. HIV can be transmitted just as easily in a brightly lit locker room or upscale living room as in a dark alley.

Mother-to-Child Transmission

The passing of a disease from mother to child in the womb is known as **perinatal transmission.** Infants whose mothers are HIV-positive will have HIV antibodies at birth. This does not necessarily mean they will become infected with the virus, however. Treatment during pregnancy can help an HIV-infected woman protect her baby from becoming infected. Since 1994, there has been a dramatic reduction in the risk for perinatal HIV transmission with ZDV (AZT) therapy. (Drugs used in HIV treatment are discussed later in the chapter.) The rate of mother-to-infant transmission has plummeted to 2%, and in some cases less than 1%, when C-section is used with AZT therapy (Irvine, 1998). Without such treatment, 15–25% of all infants born to HIV-infected mothers will have the virus and will eventually develop symptoms (CDC, 1998a).

It is not known exactly how HIV is passed from mother to fetus, although it is generally accepted that HIV manages to cross the placental barrier. The likelihood of the offspring's becoming infected rises with the amount of the virus in a pregnant woman's blood ("AIDS Test," 1995). The CDC (1998a) now recommends that all pregnant women be tested for HIV as early in the pregnancy as possible and, if infected, be given ZDV (AZT) at 14–34 weeks' gestation and during labor. The drug should also be given to infants of infected mothers for the first 6 weeks of life. Furthermore, HIV-infected women are advised not to breast-feed their infants (CDC, 1998a).

Uncommon Modes of Transmission

Although the great majority of HIV infections are acquired in the ways just discussed, many people still worry about getting the virus through casual (nonsexual) contact or accidents. There is also concern about transmission through blood transfusions, although this mode is very unlikely today in countries that routinely test donated blood for HIV.

Nonsexual Contact As mentioned previously, nonsexual, casual contact that typically occurs with health-care workers and family members and in school and day-care settings is highly unlikely to result in transmission of HIV under ordinary circumstances. Much media attention has focused on the possibility of transmission in health-care contexts, either from infected providers (doctors, dentists, nurses, and so on) to their patients or from infected patients to their providers. All studies of these situations show that the risk of transmission is very low, especially if providers take standard infection control precautions (CDC, 1998b).

Accidents People sometimes express concern about the possibility of accidental blood exchange—during children's play or contact sports, for example. Although it is theoretically possible for blood to be passed in this way, it is highly unlikely that the blood of one person could spill into another person's open wound and then enter the bloodstream. It was this kind of fear, expressed by professional basketball players, that led HIV-positive basketball superstar Magic Johnson to retire. However, as noted previously, there are no documented cases of HIV transmission during sports. As a precaution, if a participant is bleeding, he or she should be kept out of competition until the wound stops bleeding and can be cleaned and bandaged.

Medical and dental accidents are also a concern, although the chance of transmission in these situations is slight. Greater awareness among both patients and health-care providers of the risk factors associated with HIV transmission has led to increased testing for HIV and early diagnosis of the infection (CDC, 1998b).

Blood Transfusions and Organ Donations Theoretically, donated blood, plasma, body organs, and semen are all capable of sustaining HIV. Because of this, medical procedures involving these materials now include either screening for HIV or destroying it. Since 1985, blood has been screened for HIV. Plasma is treated to inactivate any virus that may be present. An estimated 1 in 450,000 to 660,000 donations per year are infected with HIV but not detected by current screening tests (CDC, 1998c). Even though the U.S. blood supply is among the safest in the world, to be absolutely safe, some people who know they will have surgery donate their own blood a few weeks before the operation. This blood is stored in a blood bank and then given to the donor during surgery if needed. Donated organs are screened for HIV, and there are guidelines regarding semen donation for artificial insemination (discussed in Chapter 12).

Factors Contributing to Infection

Although most researchers agree that HIV is responsible for AIDS, many believe that there may be additional factors that need to come into play before the immune system is seriously impaired. Certain actions or conditions appear to put some people at higher risk than others for infection. And other conditions may make individuals with HIV more prone to developing AIDS.

Researchers have found that certain physiological or behavioral factors increase one's risk of contracting HIV. For people of both sexes, these include behaviors already discussed, such as anal intercourse, multiple sex partners, and injecting drug use. The spread of HIV in the United States has paralleled that of other STIs. For example, some areas of the South have high concentrations of syphilis, gonorrhea, and HIV. There is considerable biological evidence that the presence of other STIs increases the likelihood of both transmitting and acquiring HIV (Fleming & Wasserheit, 1999). This is true whether or not the STI causes open sores or breaks in the skin. People are 2–5 times more likely to become infected with HIV when other STIs are present. In addition, an HIV-infected person also infected with an STI is 3–5 times more likely than other HIV-infected people to transmit HIV through sexual contact. Multiple exposures to HIV also increase the risk of contracting it, although it can be transmitted in a single encounter. Moreover, the probability of HIV transmission is greater when the viral load is the highest, particularly in the early stage of the infection (Cates et al., 1997; Gray et al., 2001). Noninjecting "recreational" drug use is also considered a risk factor for HIV. In part, this is because drug use is associated with risk taking in general.

Cofactors—conditions that *may* make a person who is HIV-positive more likely to develop AIDS—include a history of STIs, drug use, alcohol use, poor nutrition, stress, smoking, pregnancy, and repeated exposure to HIV. Individual genetic conditions that predispose some people to developing AIDS may exist, as may genetic elements that provide resistance to HIV or the development of AIDS (Johnson, 1993). There is a need for more research concerning possible cofactors for AIDS development.

AIDS DEMOGRAPHICS

The statistical characteristics of populations are called **demographics.** Public health researchers often look at groups of people in terms of age, socioeconomic status, living area, ethnicity, sex, and so on in order to understand the dynamics of disease transmission and prevention. When STIs are involved, they naturally look at sexual behaviors as well. This may entail studying groups based on sexual orientation and other characteristics that may be considered risk markers. No one is exempt from HIV exposure by virtue of belonging or not belonging to a specific group. But certain groups appear *as a whole* to be at greater risk than others or to face special difficulties where HIV is concerned. Many individuals within these groups may not be at risk, however, because they do not engage in risky behaviors.

Ethnicity and HIV

In the early 1980s in the United States, HIV/AIDS was primarily considered a gay White disease. Today, however, the epidemic has expanded, and the proportional distribution of AIDS cases among racial and ethnic groups has shifted. Surveillance data also show higher reported rates of many STIs among some minority groups when compared with rates among Whites (CDC, 2002b). Since 1996, the proportion of AIDS cases has decreased among Whites and increased among African Americans and Hispanics; the proportion of cases among Asian/Pacific Islanders and American Indians/Alaska Natives has remained relatively constant, representing about 1% of all cases. In 2001, 49% of people with AIDS were Black, 31% White, 10% Hispanic, 1% Asian/Pacific Islander, and less than 1% American Indian/Alaska Native. In 2001, an estimated 29,723 new AIDS cases were diagnosed among minority group members, accounting for more than 68% of all AIDS cases diagnosed in that year in the United States. Of the 816,149 AIDS cases reported to the CDC through 2001, Blacks and Hispanics accounted for 57% of the total (CDC, 2001d, 2003b).

Ethnicity is not, in itself, a risk factor for HIV infection and other STIs. However, ethnicity in the United States is a risk marker that correlates with other, more fundamental, determinants of health status, such as poverty, homelessness, lack of access to quality health care, avoiding seeking health care, substance abuse, and residence in communities with a high prevalence of HIV and other STIs. Although poverty itself is not a risk factor, studies have found a direct relationship between higher AIDS incidence and lower income (CDC, 2000b). A study of a diverse sample of women from urban health clinics found that socioeconomic status, not race/ethnicity, had both direct and indirect associations with HIV risk behaviors; the women with lower income had riskier sexual behaviors (Ickovics et al., 2002). Several socioeconomic problems associated with poverty directly or indirectly raise HIV risk, including limited access to health care. Some minority communities

The HIV epidemic has dramatically affected African Americans. The disease poses a serious threat to the future health and well-being of many African American communities.

are reluctant to acknowledge sensitive issues such as homosexuality and drug use. And some men in minority groups who have sex with men identify themselves as heterosexual, meaning they may not relate to prevention messages designed for gay men.

African Americans   AIDS remains a major health crisis in the African American community. Though Blacks make up about 12% of the U.S. population, they accounted for about half of the AIDS cases reported in 2001, and nearly 10 times the rate reported for Whites. Among Black men, of the AIDS cases reported through 2001, 42% resulted from men who had sex with men (MSM), 37% from injecting drug use, and 12% from heterosexual contact. Among Black women, of the AIDS cases reported through 2001, 52% resulted from heterosexual contact and 44% from injecting drug use (CDC, 2001d, 2003b). Indicators of the severity of HIV/AIDS among Blacks include the following:

- AIDS is the leading cause of death among African American women age 25–34 and African American men age 35–44. AIDS is among the top three causes of death among African American women age 35–44 and African American men age 25–54 (National Center for Health Statistics, 2002).

- A CDC study of Job Corps entrants age 16–21 found that, compared with their White counterparts, African American women were 7 times more likely to be infected with HIV, and African American men were 4 times more likely to be infected (Valleroy, MacKellar, Karon, Janssen, & Hayman, 1998).

- From 1994 to 1998, the rate of HIV infection among African American women age 20–44 in 25 states with long-standing HIV, was 80.1 per 100,000 population—4 times the rate among Latinas of the same age and more than 16 times the rate among White women (Lee & Fleming, 2001).

- In a recent six-city study of men age 23–29, 32% of African American MSM were found to be HIV-infected, compared with 14% of Latinos and 7% of Whites (CDC, 2001d).

- From 1994 to 1998, 14% of young African American MSM were infected with HIV, nearly 4 times the rate of their White counterparts, according to a 5-year study of almost 3500 gay and bisexual men age 15–22 in seven U.S. cities (Valleroy et al., 1998).

- A recent CDC study of 9113 patients in 11 U.S. cities found that HIV-infected African Americans were less likely than infected Whites to receive the powerful new combination treatments for HIV. (CDC, 2002b).

African Americans view AIDS as the number one health problem facing the nation and the world, with youths, women, parents, and those with less education and lower incomes particularly concerned. Given the disproportionate impact of HIV/AIDS on African Americans, the ability to curtail the epidemic will depend significantly on the extent to which prevention, care, and support programs reach African Americans (CDC, 2002b).

Hispanics   The United States has a large and growing Hispanic population that is heavily affected by the HIV/AIDS epidemic. Hispanics in the United

States include a diverse mixture of ethnic groups and cultures, and HIV exposure risks vary among the groups. In 2001, Hispanics represented 14% of the U.S. population but accounted for 19% of the total number of new AIDS cases reported that year. The AIDS incidence rate per 100,000 population among Hispanics in 2001 was 28.0, about 4 times the rate for Whites (7.9) but lower than the rate for African Americans (76.3). Among Hispanic men, of the estimated AIDS cases through 2001, 48% resulted from MSM, 29% from injecting drug use, and 16% from heterosexual contact. Among Hispanic women, of the AIDS cases reported through 2001, 55% resulted from heterosexual contact and 42% from injecting drug use (CDC, 2001d, 2003b). Like Blacks, Latinos rank AIDS as the number one health problem facing the nation, and Latino parents express high levels of concern about their children's risk. Given that the Hispanic population is the largest and fastest-growing ethnic minority group in the United States, the prevalence of HIV/AIDS among Latinos will increasingly affect the health status of the nation. Prevention programs must give special attention to the cultural diversity that exists within this community (National Association of People with AIDS, 2002).

Members of ethnic communities are often suspicious of outsiders, whom they may perceive as interfering or threatening. In Chapter 15, we discussed the infamous Tuskegee syphilis study and its effects on African Americans' perceptions of the health-care establishment. In 1988, the CDC began to respond to the need for ethnically sensitive programs by establishing grants for ongoing HIV prevention programs targeting specific ethnic groups, including African Americans, Latinos, Native Americans, Asian Americans and Pacific Islanders, and Alaskan natives.

The Gay Community

The poor homosexuals—they have declared war upon nature and now nature is exacting an awful retribution.

—*Pat Buchanan*

"AIDS has given a human face to an invisible minority," says Robert Bray of the National Gay and Lesbian Task Force. From the beginning of the HIV/AIDS epidemic in the United States, the most disproportionate impact has been among the MSM group. Men who have sex with men is a behavioral description of a diverse population, many of whom identify themselves either privately or publicly as a gay man or bisexual person. Others may engage in sex with men but not think of themselves as a gay men or bisexual person. Even though the AIDS rate among MSM declined sharply and then leveled between 1996 and 2001, this still represents the largest exposure category among men, accounting for 42% of AIDS cases in 2001 and 55% through 2001. By the end of 2001, 368,971 men in this group had been diagnosed with AIDS. For White men, MSM accounted for 60% of the total 2001 AIDS cases reported; for Black and Hispanic men, 29% and 35% of cases, respectively, were attributed to MSM (CDC, 2000b, 2003a). Young African American and Latino MSM account for at least three-quarters of the new infections among young men.

Although epidemiologists do not know for certain how HIV first arrived in the gay community, they do know that it spread like wildfire, mainly because anal sex is such an efficient mode of transmission. Furthermore, initial research, education, and prevention efforts were severely hampered by a lack of government and public interest in what was perceived to be a "gay disease" (Shilts, 1987). Now, nearly 25 years after the virus first appeared, the gay community continues to reel from the repeated blows dealt by AIDS.

Overall, sexual practices have become much safer, and the rate of new infection has fallen dramatically. But men who were infected years ago continue to grow sick and die.

Many members of the gay community have lost dozens of friends. They may be coping with multiple-loss syndrome, a psychological condition characterized by depression, hypochondria, feelings of guilt, sexual difficulties, and/or self-destructive behavior.

In spite of the initial lack of public support for the fight against AIDS, or perhaps at least partly because of it, the gay and lesbian communities rallied together in a variety of ways to support each other, educate themselves and the public, and influence government policies. Clinics, self-help groups, and information clearinghouses were created by people from both the gay and the straight communities whose lives were affected by HIV. The role of volunteers remains a crucial component of many AIDS organizations. Many people have devoted themselves to supporting the HIV/AIDS community or educating the public. Finding appropriate primary medical care and social support linkages for the MSM who are HIV-positive is extremely important.

Members of the gay community not only motivate themselves to face the AIDS epidemic but also inspire and empower many people outside the community to lend their voices and support to the cause of AIDS prevention. Nonetheless, the perception of AIDS as a gay disease rather than a viral disease lingers, and some who have moral objections to same-sex behavior still blame gay men for AIDS.

In recent years, some gay men seem to have abandoned safer sex practices. Although the number of AIDS cases is decreasing among groups such as older gay adults, a "second wave" of HIV infection may be occurring among specific parts of the gay community, especially young men (Kalichman, 1998). The reasons for this second wave are varied. Despair may have led some men to intentionally put themselves at risk; others may have feelings of invulnerability or be less concerned about HIV because of the new treatment regimes. In a study involving 547 gay men, HIV-negative men who most agreed that treatment reduces concerns about HIV infection were 3 times more likely than

> I think God did send AIDS for a reason. It was to show how mean and sinful a healthy man can be toward a sick man.
>
> —*Joe Bob Briggs*

Members of ACT UP focus public attention on issues affecting people with HIV and AIDS.

other HIV-negative gay men to report unprotected receptive anal sex. HIV-positive gay men with the greatest reduced concern due to treatment options were 6 times more likely than the other HIV-positive men to report unprotected insertive anal sex (Ostrow et al., 2002).

The Internet has become a popular "meeting place" for gay men and is associated with higher-risk sexual behavior. A study of 609 gay men found that 75% used the Internet to access gay-oriented Web sites and 34% reported having met a partner via the Internet. Men meeting partners online, compared with those not meeting partners in this manner, reported higher methamphetamine use, sex with more partners in the previous 6 months, and higher rates of sexual risk behaviors, including unprotected receptive and insertive anal intercourse (Benotsch, Kalichman, Lawrence, & Nordling, 2002).

Women and HIV

Although women as a group are not at special risk for HIV, the activities that put them at risk include using injecting drugs, being a sex partner of an injecting drug user or a gay or bisexual man, and having multiple sex partners. Many women may be unaware of their partners' risk factors. In 2001, there were an estimated 48,360 women and adolescent girls age 15–44 living with AIDS in the United States. The proportion of AIDS cases among this group increased from 8% in 1986 to 26% in 2001. The incidence of AIDS in this group began to decline in 1996 because of the success of antiretroviral therapies. From 1996 through 2001, an average of 10,500 cases of AIDS were diagnosed in women and adolescent girls. In 2001, 63% of this group were Black; the rate was 47.8 cases per 100,000 females. Although the proportion of cases reported among Latinas (17%) and Whites (18%) was nearly equal, the rate among Latinas (12.9) was nearly 5 times that of Whites (2.4). The CDC estimates that 66% of the 11,082 AIDS cases diagnosed among women and adolescent girls in 2001 can be attributed to heterosexual transmission; 16% were from heterosexual contact with an injecting drug user, and 50% were from sexual contact with high-risk partners such as bisexual or HIV-infected men. In addition, 32% were attributed to injecting drug use and 3% to other risks (CDC, 2003b).

HIV transmission between females appears to be a rare occurrence. However, vaginal secretions and menstrual blood are potentially infectious, and oral and vaginal exposure to these secretions can result in HIV infection. Less than 2% of women with AIDS reported having sex with other women, and many of these women also reported other risk factors such as injecting drug use and sex with high-risk men. Of the few women with AIDS who reported having sex only with women, 98% also had another high-risk behavior, with injecting drug use being the most common. CDC reports indicated that no cases of female-to-female HIV transmission had been confirmed, and a study of more than 1 million female blood donors found no HIV-infected women whose only high-risk behavior was sex with women. However, some women who have sex with other women have relatively high rates of high-risk behaviors, such as having unprotected vaginal sex with gay or bisexual men and injecting drug users or injecting drugs themselves (CDC, 1999a). One study found that the risk for HIV infection may be underestimated in some subgroups of women who have sex with women. The sexual and drug behaviors associated with HIV and STIs among women age 18–29 were studied. Eighty-eight percent reported having sex exclusively with men, 7% reported having sex with both men and women, and 1% reported having sex only with women. Compared with women who had sex exclusively with men, women who had sex with both women and men were more likely to report having sex with an HIV-positive man, sex with a man who had sex with a man, and sex with an injecting drug user, as well as multiple sex partners. They were also more likely to report trading sex for drugs or money, having anal sex, and injecting drugs (Scheer et al., 2002).

Children and HIV

Through 2001, a total of 9074 children (those less than 13 years of age) were reported as having AIDS; of these, 5257 (58%) had died. During 2001, 175 new cases of AIDS in children were reported, with 150 of these attributed to perinatal exposure. The impact of HIV is greatest among African American and Latino children. Of the pediatric AIDS cases reported through 2001, 5337 involved Black children, and 2060 involved Hispanic children. White children accounted for 1579 cases (CDC, 2001d).

The incidence of AIDS among children has been dramatically reduced by recommendations by the CDC, which suggests routine counseling and voluntary prenatal HIV testing for women and the use of AZT to prevent perinatal transmission (CDC, 1999b).

Teens and College Students and HIV

HIV/AIDS significantly impacts adolescents and young adults in the United States. In 2001, 1461 young people age 13–24 were reported to have AIDS, bringing the total to 28,665 cases (20,337 males and 8328 females). Among young men age 13–24, 47% of all AIDS cases reported in 2001 were among men who had sex with men, 6% were from injecting drug use, and 6% were from heterosexual contact. In 2001, among young women the same age, 40% of all cases were acquired heterosexually, and 4% were acquired through injecting drug use. The CDC notes that, even though the overall number of AIDS cases among all ages has recently declined and then leveled, there has not been a comparable decline in the number of newly diagnosed HIV cases among youths. The CDC believes that the cases of HIV infection diagnosed among 13- to 24-year-olds are indicative of overall trends in HIV incidence because this group is increasingly engaging in high-risk sexual behaviors (CDC, 2001d, 2002a).

The White House Office of National AIDS Policy released these figures in fall 2000:

- Half of the estimated 40,000 new HIV infections in the United States every year occur among young people age 13–24.

- Young Americans age 13–25 are contracting HIV at the rate of two per hour.

- An estimated 250,000 young Americans are unaware that they are infected with HIV.

- More than 123,000 young adults in the United States have developed AIDS in their twenties; the majority were infected with HIV as teenagers.

> I have never shared needles. And obviously I'm not a gay man. The only thing I did was something every single one of you has already done or will do.
>
> —*Krista Blake, infected with HIV as a teenager*

Click on "Just Like Me" to hear young people with AIDS talk about risk factors for becoming infected with HIV.

- African Americans and Latinos make up about 15% of U.S. teenagers, yet African Americans account for 49% of AIDS cases ever reported among those age 13–19, and Latinos account for 20%. Of the AIDS cases reported so far among those age 12–24, people from minority groups account for about 65% of the cases.

The office calls for increased youth-focused HIV prevention programs and promotion of routine, voluntary HIV testing and counseling for at-risk youths (Office of National AIDS Policy, 2000).

Older Adults and HIV

By the end of 2001, 76,402 AIDS cases had been diagnosed among men age 50 and older, representing 14% of the total cases for all ages. For women age 50 and older, 14,117 cases had been diagnosed by the end of 2001, representing 10% of the total cases (CDC, 2001d). Compared with the early days of the epidemic, when most cases among older adults were contracted through a blood transfusion, more cases are now the result of unprotected sex and injecting drug use. Contributing to the higher rates among both men and women are the similarity of diseases that signal AIDS to the illnesses associated with aging, a lack of awareness on the part of physicians, and a sense among older people that they are not vulnerable to AIDS. Little data are available on STIs in older people. However, according to Washington State's STI surveillance data from 1992 to 1998, 1535 episodes of STIs were reported for people age 50–80, accounting for 1.3% of all reported STIs. This rate was considerably lower than that among younger people (Fujie, Shillinger, Aubin, St. Louis, & Markowitz, 2001).

Geographic Region and HIV

HIV/AIDS and other STIs have had a disparate impact in the United States, with the South (16 states and the District of Columbia) being harder hit than the Northeast, West, and Midwest. The South represents about 36% of the total population, but it accounts for 39% of people estimated to be living with AIDS and 46% of the estimated number of new AIDS cases. In 2001, about 140,000 (39%) people living with AIDS resided in the South, 106,600 (29%) in the Northeast, 70,050 (19%) in the West, and 36,730 (13%) in the Midwest. The South has accounted for an increasing share of the estimated number of new AIDS cases diagnosed each year, rising from 40% in 1996 to 46% in 2001. AIDS incidence declined and then leveled off in the other three regions during the same period. The majority of people estimated to be living with AIDS in the South are African American (53% at the end of 1999), even though African Americans represent only 19% of the overall population in the South. Latinos represent 10% of people estimated to be living with AIDS in the South and 12% of the South's overall population. (The South also has the highest case rates for chlamydia, gonorrhea, and primary and secondary syphilis.) Several factors may contribute to this disparity: lack of availability of and access to health-care services, poverty, and stigma. These barriers are particularly difficult to overcome in the rural areas, which are common in the South (CDC, 2001d, 2002b; Kaiser Family Foundation, 2002c).

MOHAMMAD TORABI AND WILLIAM L. YARBER developed a scale to measure attitudes toward HIV and its prevention. Completing this scale can help you determine which behaviors you might need to improve your HIV prevention attitude.

Directions

Read each statement carefully. Record your immediate reaction to each statement by writing the letter that corresponds to your answer. There is no right or wrong answer for each statement.

Key

A = Strongly agree
B = Agree
C = Undecided
D = Disagree
E = Strongly disagree

1. I am certain that I could be supportive of a friend infected with HIV.
2. I feel that people infected with HIV got what they deserve.
3. I am comfortable with the idea of using condoms for sex.
4. I would dislike the idea of limiting sex to just one partner to avoid HIV infection.
5. It would be embarrassing to get the HIV antibody test.
6. It is meant for some people to get HIV.
7. Using condoms to avoid HIV is too much trouble.
8. I believe that AIDS is a preventable disease.
9. The chance of getting HIV makes using injecting drugs stupid.
10. People can influence their friends to practice safe behavior.
11. I would shake hands with a person infected with HIV.
12. I will avoid sex if there is a slight chance that my partner might have HIV.
13. If I were to have sex, I would insist that a condom be used.
14. If I used injecting drugs, I would not share the needles.
15. I intend to share HIV facts with my friends.

Scoring

Calculate the total points for each statement using the following point values:

Items 1, 3, 8–15: Strongly agree = 5, Agree = 4, Undecided = 3, Disagree = 2, Strongly disagree = 1.

Items 2, 4–7: Strongly agree = 1, Agree = 2, Undecided = 3, Disagree = 4, Strongly disagree = 5

The higher the score, the more positive the prevention attitude.

Source: Adapted from Torabi, Mohammad R., & Yarber, William L. (1992). "Alternate Forms of the HIV Prevention Attitude Scale for Teenagers." *AIDS Education and Therapy, 4,* 172–182. With permission from the authors.

PREVENTION AND TREATMENT

As a whole, our society remains ambivalent about the realities of HIV risk. Many people assume that their partners are not HIV-infected because they look healthy, "clean," and/or attractive. In addition, some believe that the federal government has failed to provide enough resources to combat the HIV/AIDS epidemic. With tens of thousands of Americans—more than half of them teenagers or young adults—becoming infected with HIV each year, inactivity and apathy become enemies in the fight against this disease. To assess your own attitudes toward HIV prevention, see "Practically Speaking: HIV Prevention Attitude Scale."

Protecting Ourselves

To protect ourselves and those we care about from HIV infection, there are some things we should know in addition to the basic facts about transmission and prevention. First, we should be aware that the use of alcohol and

THE HEALTH PROTECTIVE SEXUAL COMMUNICATION SCALE (HPSCS) assesses how often people discuss health protection, safer sex, sexual histories, and condom/contraception use with a first-time partner. High scores on the HPSCS are strongly linked to high-risk sexual behaviors, including multiple partners, incorrect or inconsistent condom use, and alcohol use before sex. An adapted form of the HPSCS follows.

The HPSCS is designed for persons who have had a new sex partner in the past 12 months. If this is not the case for you, it might be in the future. The scale can alert you to health protection issues that are important to discuss, so go ahead and look at the questions.

Directions

Read each question carefully, and record your immediate reaction by writing the number that best applies.

Key

1 = Always
2 = Almost always
3 = Sometimes
4 = Never
5 = Don't know
6 = Decline to answer

Note: Questions 9 and 10 are excluded for gay men and lesbian women.

How often in the past 12 months have you:

1. Asked a new sex partner how he/she felt about using condoms before you had intercourse?

2. Asked a new sex partner about the number of past sex partners he/she had?

3. Told a new sex partner about the number of sex partners you have had?

4. Told a new sex partner that you won't have sex unless a condom is used?

5. Discussed with a new sex partner the need for both of you to get tested for HIV before having sex?

6. Talked with a new sex partner about not having sex until you have known each other longer?

7. Asked a new sex partner if he/she has ever had some type of STD, like genital herpes, genital warts, syphilis, chlamydia, or gonorrhea?

8. Asked a new sex partner if he/she has ever shot drugs like heroin, cocaine, or speed?

9. Talked about whether you or a new sex partner has ever had homosexual experiences?

10. Talked with a new sex partner about birth control before having sex for the first time?

Scoring

To obtain your score, add up the points for all items. The lower your score, the more health protective sexual communication occurred with a new partner.

Source: Catania, Joseph A. (1998). "Health Protective Sexual Communication Scale." In Clive M. Davis, William L. Yarber, Robert Bauserman, George Schreer, & Sandra L. Davis (Eds.), *Handbook of Sexuality Related Measures.* Thousand Oaks, CA: Sage, pp. 544–557. Reprinted by permission of Sage Publications, Inc.

drugs significantly increases risky behaviors. If we are serious about protecting ourselves, we need to assess our risks when we are clearheaded and act to protect ourselves. Second, we need to develop our communication skills so that we can discuss risks and prevention with our partner or potential partner. (To assess how often you discuss health protective concerns related to safer sex, sexual histories, and condom or contraception use with a new partner, see "Practically Speaking: Health Protective Sexual Communication Scale.") If we want our partner to disclose information about past high-risk behavior, we have to be willing to do the same. One study of 203 HIV-positive hospital patients found that 40% did not tell their sex partners about their HIV status (Stein et al., 1998). However, another study of 322 HIV-infected women found that the majority disclosed their HIV-positive status to some sex partners: 75% disclosed to their current sex partner, and 67% disclosed to all of their partners (Sowell, Seals, Phillips, & Julious, 2003). Disclosure of HIV-positive status is critical, as research has shown that people poorly judge their sex partner's HIV status (Niccolai, Farley, Ayoub, & Magnus, 2002). Third, we may need to have information on HIV testing. If we have engaged in high-risk behavior, we may want to be tested for our own peace of mind and that of our partner. If we test positive for HIV, we need to make important decisions regarding our health, sexual behavior, and lifestyle. Finally, if we are sexually active with more than one long-term, exclusive partner, we need to become very familiar with condoms.

Although Americans have responded to the threat of AIDS by purchasing more condoms, rates of condom use remain low among many segments of the population. Many people remain unconvinced regarding either their own vulnerability to HIV or the usefulness of condoms in preventing its spread. Male latex and polyurethane condoms, when used consistently and correctly, can greatly reduce the risk of HIV and other STIs. But the effectiveness of condoms has been disputed lately, leaving some people confused. (To help clarify the current beliefs about condoms among the leading federal health authorities, the position of the CDC is presented in the box "Practically Speaking: Preventing STIs: Male Condoms, Female Condoms, and Nonoxynol-9" in Chapter 15.) Female condoms and nonoxynol-9 are discussed relative to HIV/STI prevention.

Saving Lives Through Education

Education is the key to HIV prevention, and education can work. According to the CDC (2000b), "overwhelming evidence proves that HIV prevention efforts have saved countless lives, both in the U.S. and worldwide." As an example, the CDC indicates that prevention efforts have slowed the rate of new infections in the United States from over 150,000 per year in the late 1980s to about 40,000 per year. The CDC notes that many interventions have proved effective in preventing HIV transmissions in a variety of populations, including clinic patients, heterosexual men and women, high-risk youths, incarcerated individuals, injecting drug users, and men who have sex with men. These interventions have been delivered to individuals, groups, and

President of AMFAR (American Foundation for AIDS Research), Dr. Mathilde Krim, and actor Adrien Brody smile as they arrive at the Moulin de Mougins restaurant to attend an annual AIDS benefit for AMFAR during the 56th annual Cannes Film Festival in 2003.

communities in settings such as storefronts, gay bars, health centers, housing developments, and schools (CDC, 2001f). Nevertheless, many people remain uninformed about and unsympathetic to people with AIDS and HIV—at least until it strikes someone they care about.

AIDS has changed us forever. It has brought out the best in us, and the worst.

—*Michael Gottlieb, MD*

Obstacles to Education: Blame and Denial   HIV/AIDS is still seen by many people as a disease of "marginalized" groups, those who are outside the mainstream of American life. People who are not White, not middle class, and not heterosexual are often viewed with suspicion by people who are. People who are gay or lesbian are often ignored or reviled even within their own ethnic communities. People who use drugs are written off as useless, worthless, and criminal. Prostitutes are frequently blamed for spreading STIs, even though they undoubtedly contract these diseases from their clients, who more than likely have or will spread them to their partner or partners.

One effect of AIDS has been to make gay men more vulnerable to hate-motivated violence. Men who have been victims of vicious incidents of gay bashing report that their attackers accuse them of causing AIDS. Assigning blame for AIDS to certain groups not only stigmatizes people in those groups but also keeps the blamers from scrutinizing their own behavior. This denial is one of the biggest obstacles AIDS educators face. And it affects not only adults but their children as well.

HIV and AIDS Education in Schools   Information about HIV/AIDS is offered in many upper elementary schools (Landry, Singh, & Darroch, 2000) and in nearly all secondary schools (Darroch, Landry, Singh, 2000; Kaiser Family Foundation, 2000; Yarber, Torabi, & Haffner, 1997), but such teaching remains controversial. As we discussed in Chapter 6, controversy exists concerning whether young people should be directed toward abstinence only or be taught prevention behaviors such as condom use. Fear abounds among adults: fear that sexuality education will lead to sex, that teaching about homosexuality will lead to people becoming gay, and that discussion of sexuality is immoral. Some conservative groups feel that sexuality education should be provided only by parents (who are the least informed) or that abstinence should be taught as the only way to avoid HIV.

Most parents want AIDS education for their children, especially those of high school age. According to a national survey, approximately 75% of parents support teaching about HIV/AIDS and STIs in grades 7 and 8, over 90% in grades 9 and 10, and 96% in grades 11 and 12 (Sexuality Information and Education Council of the United States/Advocates for Youth, 1999). According to a report by the Kaiser Family Foundation, 98% of parents of students in grades 7–12 believed that school sexuality education should cover HIV/STI, 97% said that abstinence should be covered, and 85% indicated that "how to use a condom" should also be discussed (Kaiser Family Foundation, 2000). In another study by the Kaiser Family Foundation, 57% of teens indicated that they wanted to know more about "how to protect themselves from HIV," and 36% of 15- to 17-year-olds wanted to know more about "the proper way to use condoms" (Kaiser Family Foundation, 2001).

Outreach Programs   Outreach programs for groups at particularly high risk for HIV can be very effective if they are sensitive to the unique cultural, ethnic, and social issues relevant to these groups. The CDC has

Community outreach programs provide information about prevention and assistance available to those at high risk for HIV.

begun identifying community-based outreach programs nationwide that have proved to reduce high-risk sexual behavior and drug use among people who are at greatest risk (CDC, 2001f). It evaluated HIV prevention programs targeted at four specific groups: heterosexual adults, men who have sex with men, youths, and drug users. Examples of four programs scientifically shown to have positive outcomes for each of the following groups include:

- *Heterosexual adults.* Enhanced (four sessions of 200 minutes) and brief (two sessions of 40 minutes) counseling interventions designed to facilitate condom use were administered to a diverse sample of 5758 men and women in five large U.S. cities. Participants in both counseling interventions reported significantly higher condom use and 30% fewer new STIs than participants in the comparison group. In the counseling interventions, benefits accrued equally to men and women (Kamb et al., 1998).

- *Men who have sex with men.* The Mpowerment Project was an intervention designed and conducted by young gay men over 8 months in Eugene, Oregon. This multicomponent intervention included outreach, peer-led small groups, and an ongoing publicity campaign. Three hundred young gay men of diverse ethnicities participated. Men who participated in the project reduced their frequency of unprotected anal intercourse significantly more than did men in the comparison community (Kegeles, Hays, & Coates, 1996).

▪ *Youths.* This intervention, consisting of eight sessions, was delivered to peer groups consisting of three to ten same-gender African American friends to determine the effects of a peer network intervention to increase condom use among sexually active youths. Of the 383 youths who participated in the study, 56% were male and 44% were female, with an average age of 11. The sexually active youths who participated in the intervention reported significantly greater condom use than the sexually active youths in the comparison group (Stanton et al., 1996).

▪ *Drug users.* At an inpatient drug detoxification and rehabilitation center, adult drug users participated in group sessions focused on reducing drug use and high-risk behavior. After the intervention, participants reported significantly lower rates of cocaine use and a reduction in drug injection frequency (McCusker, Stoddard, Zapka, & Lewis, 1993).

Needle exchange programs, especially those that provide information about risks and HIV prevention, also play an important role. However, these programs are controversial because some people believe that they endorse or encourage drug use. Others feel that because the drug use already exists, saving lives should be the first priority. Although needle exchange programs are illegal in some areas, they are often allowed to continue as long as the workers keep a low profile. Needle exchange activists believe that high priority should be given to legalizing and expanding these programs, which are cost-effective and have the potential of saving thousands of lives.

HIV Testing

Free or low-cost and anonymous or confidential HIV testing is available in many areas, including local health departments, offices of private physicians, hospitals, and sites specifically set up for that purpose.

Types of Tests   Almost everyone infected with HIV develops antibodies within 2–6 months after exposure. Most people will develop detectable antibodies within 3 months, with the average being 25 days. In rare cases, antibodies do not appear until 6 months after infection. Hence, the test should be taken at least 12 weeks after high-risk behavior (CDC, 1998b). The most common tests look for these antibodies.

The most common test for HIV is called the **ELISA,** an acronym for enzyme-linked immunosorbent assay (the CDC uses the acronym EIA). This simple blood test screens for the antibodies to HIV that are usually present after infection with the virus. A negative test result—meaning no antibodies are found—is considered highly (99.7%) accurate if received 6 months after the date of the last possible exposure. In the event of a positive or inconclusive test result, a person should be retested. The test used to recheck positive ELISA results is called the **Western blot.** In this procedure, the antibodies are tested to determine whether they are specific to HIV. Usually, Western blot results are clearly either positive or negative. If there is an inconclusive result, the person should be tested again in 6 months; a few people who are HIV-negative repeatedly get inconclusive results. If necessary, more complex tests can be performed. Because it takes up to several weeks to process the ELISA test, a rapid test for detecting HIV antibodies was approved and licensed by the FDA in 2002.

The OraQuick Rapid HIV-1 Antibody Test provides results in as little as 20 minutes and is 99.6% accurate. Each year, 8000 HIV-infected people who come to public clinics for HIV testing do not return a week later to receive their results, but with this new test, results are available on the spot. As with other screening tests for HIV, positive test results must be confirmed with an additional test. Widespread availability of the rapid test is likely to increase overall HIV testing and decrease the number of people—an estimated 225,000 Americans—who are unaware that they are infected with HIV. The rapid test enables infected individuals to obtain medical care earlier in the course of their infection, potentially saving lives and limiting the spread of HIV (U.S. Department of Health and Human Services, 2003).

For those who choose not to be tested at a clinic or doctor's office, the Home Access Express HIV-1 Test System is an option. The kit costs about $60 and is more than 99% sensitive for detecting HIV infection ("Home-Use HIV Test Kits," 1998). Unlike many common home tests, Home Access does not provide users with a result at home. Instead, the user collects a blood sample, mails it anonymously with the kit's code number, and calls 3 days later for the test results. Those who test negative get their results via a recorded message or speak to a counselor; all of those who test positive speak to a counselor. Inadequate counseling, a false sense of security if the test turns out negative, and insufficient information about the increased risk for other STIs are issues that concern many health-care providers (Kisabeth, Pontius, Statland, & Galper, 1997). People using the Internet to locate and purchase tests must be cautious about the many kits that are marketed but not yet approved for sale by the FDA ("Home Access Health," 1997). In spite of the many concerns and caveats, home testing is a viable option for those who might otherwise not get tested.

Getting Tested   Most people who go for an HIV test are anxious. Even though the vast majority of test results are negative, there is still the understandable fear that one has "drawn the short straw." For many people, there are probably also feelings of ambivalence or guilt about the risky behaviors that led them to this situation. Because of these kinds of responses, which are normal, counseling is a key part of the testing process. It is important for people being tested to understand what their risks for HIV actually are and to know what the results mean. It is also important for everyone, no matter what the results of their tests are, to understand the facts of transmission and prevention. For the majority who test negative, practicing abstinence or safer sex, remaining sexually exclusive, avoiding injecting drug use, and taking other preventive measures can eliminate much of the anxiety associated with HIV. (These measures reduce the risk of other STIs as well.)

Counseling is vital for individuals who are HIV-positive. Early treatment and positive health behaviors are essential to maintaining good health and prolonging life. Pregnancy counseling should be made available for women. It is also essential that people know they can pass the virus on to others.

Partner Notification   Both current and past partners should be notified so that they can be tested and receive counseling. AIDS counselors and health-care practitioners currently encourage those with HIV to make all possible efforts to contact past and current partners. In some cases, counselors try to make such contacts, with their clients' permission.

Treatments

Viral load tests and T-cell counts are used together to help make decisions about starting or changing a treatment. **Viral load tests** measure the amount of HIV in the bloodstream and serve as an indicator for determining the risk of progressing to AIDS.

When AIDS first surfaced in the United States, there were no medicines to combat the immune deficiency, and few treatments existed for the opportunistic diseases that resulted. However, during the past 10 years, researchers have developed drugs to fight both HIV infection and its associated infections and cancers. The FDA has approved a number of drugs for treating HIV infection. The first group of drugs used to treat HIV infection, called nucleoside reverse transcriptase (RT) inhibitors, interrupts an early stage of the virus making copies of itself. These drugs include AZT (azidothymidine), ddC (zalcitabine), ddl (dideoxyinosine), d4T (stavudine), 3TC (lamivudine), abacavir (ziagen), and tenofovir (viread). These drugs may slow the spread of HIV in the body and delay the onset of opportunistic diseases. More recently, the FDA has approved a second class of drugs for treating HIV infection. These drugs, called protease inhibitors, interrupt virus replication at a later stage in its cycle. They include Ritonavir (Norvir), Saquinivir (Invirase), Indinavir (Crixivan), Amprenivir (Agenerase), Nelfinavir (Viracept), and Lopinavir (Kaletra) (National Institute of Allergy and Infectious Diseases, 2002). And in 2003, the FDA approved a new anti-HIV drug called a fusion inhibitor. The drug, Fuzen, unlike existing AIDS drugs, blocks HIV before it enters the cell, thereby reducing viral load (CNN, 2003)

Click on "Undetectable: The New Face of AIDS" to hear an AIDS activist speak about the side effects of highly active antiretroviral therapy (HAART).

Because HIV can become resistant to any of these drugs, health-care providers must use a combination of treatments, sometimes referred to as a "cocktail," to effectively suppress the virus. When RT inhibitors and protease inhibitors are used in combination, it is referred to as **highly active antiretroviral therapy, or HAART.** This can be used by people who are newly infected with HIV, as well as people who have AIDS. Researchers have credited HAART with being a major factor in significantly reducing the number of deaths from AIDS in this country. Although HAART is not a cure for AIDS, it has greatly improved the health of many people with AIDS, and it reduces the amount of virus circulating in the blood to nearly undetectable levels. But researchers have shown that HIV remains present in hiding places, such as the lymph nodes, brain, testes, and retinas, even in patients who have been treated. Despite the beneficial effects of HAART, severe side effects can be associated with the use of antiviral drugs. Therefore, experts recommend that people using antiretroviral therapy be routinely seen by their health-care providers. Also, a number of drugs are available to help treat opportunistic infections to which people with HIV are especially prone (National Institute of Allergy and Infectious Diseases, 2002).

As new drug combinations change the course of HIV infection, questions arise about how best to use the drugs, who will pay for them, when to discontinue use of the most powerful drugs because of their unbearable side effects, and how the delay of symptoms and death will affect patients. Because antiretroviral drugs are very expensive, they are not an option for everyone. The annual cost of a HAART regimen, for example,

The Names Project has created a giant quilt, each square of which has been lovingly created by friends and families of people who have died of AIDS. The quilt now contains over 44,000 panels.

is approximately $20,000. Furthermore, physicians may judge that some patients will be less able or likely to follow the complicated drug regimen accurately. Another issue is that many people diagnosed with HIV infection have already faced their own mortality; now they must adopt a new attitude. For some, this may mean learning to live with a manageable chronic disease rather than a death sentence—a course that will require a different kind of courage and perseverance.

The search for a cure for AIDS continues. Learning more about the genetics of the small number of HIV-infected individuals who remain healthy may lead to new therapies that can help others. Gene therapy, in which the immune system is reconstructed with genetically altered resistant cells, is one potentially promising approach. For HIV/STI prevention, researchers are working on topical microbicides, chemical or biological substances that can kill or neutralize viruses and bacteria that may be present in semen or cervical or vaginal secretions. The goal is to develop a microbicidal gel, cream, film, or suppository that individuals can apply to either the vagina or the rectum prior to intercourse. A major value of microbicides is that women can have much more control of HIV/STI prevention, particularly when they have limited ability to get their male partners to use condoms. Development of an effective and safe vaccine for HIV is the ultimate goal, but many biological and social challenges have to be overcome. Microbicides and a vaccine would provide another barrier to HIV transmission, although individual practice of safe sex would remain paramount.

LIVING WITH HIV OR AIDS

People with AIDS, sometimes referred to as PWAs, and people with HIV have the same needs as everyone else—and a few more. If you are HIV-positive, in addition to dealing with the issues of loss and grief, you need to pay special attention to maintaining good health. If you are caring for someone with HIV or AIDS, you also have special needs.

If You Are HIV-Positive

A positive antibody test is scary to just about anyone. Many people view it as a death sentence, while others try to pretend it isn't true. Whatever else it may be, a positive test result is valuable news: It is news that may make it possible to actually save your life. If you don't learn about your status in this way, you probably will not know until a serious opportunistic infection announces the presence of HIV. At that point, many of your best medical options have been lost, and you might have spread the virus to others who would not otherwise have been exposed.

Taking Care of Your Health   It is important to find a physician who has experience working with HIV and AIDS, and—even more importantly, perhaps—who is sensitive to the issues confronted by PWAs and persons infected with HIV. In addition to appropriate medical treatment, factors that can help promote your continuing good health include good nutrition, plenty of rest, appropriate exercise, limited (or no) alcohol use, and stress reduction. People with HIV or AIDS should stop smoking tobacco because it increases susceptibility to pneumonia. Also, you need to reduce your chances of exposure to infectious organisms. This doesn't mean shutting yourself up in a room and never coming out. It simply means that you need to take more than ordinary care not to expose yourself to infectious organisms—for example, from spoiled or improperly cooked foods, or unwashed glasses or utensils used by sick household members, or certain kinds of pets. Your doctor or nearest HIV/AIDS resource group should have more information on these measures.

In addition, if you decide to have sexual contact with another person, it means practicing safer sex, even if your partner is also HIV-positive. Researchers caution that one can become reinfected with different HIV strains. Moreover, STIs of all kinds can be much worse for people with an impaired immune system. HIV doesn't mean an end to being sexual, but it does suggest that different ways of expressing love and sexual desire may need to be explored.

It is recommended that women who are HIV-positive have Pap tests every 6–12 months. Cervical biopsies may also be necessary to determine whether CIN or cancer is present.

Addressing Your Other Needs   Besides taking care of your physical health, you need to address psychological and emotional needs. The stigma and fear surrounding HIV and AIDS often make it difficult to get on with the business of living. Suicide is the leading cause of non-HIV-related death among people who are HIV-positive. Among gay and bisexual men, social support is generally better for Whites than for Blacks; in Black communities, there tends to be less affirmation from primary social support networks and less openness about sexual orientation. Women, who usually concern themselves with caring for others, may not be inclined to seek out support groups and networks. But people who live with HIV and AIDS say that it's important not to feel isolated. If you are HIV-positive, we encourage you to seek support from AIDS organizations in your area.

If You Are Caring for Someone with HIV or AIDS

When someone you know is diagnosed with HIV or AIDS, you, as a support person, should be aware of the uncharted territory ahead in terms of societal discrimination, experimental drug treatments, the unpredictable course of the disease, new and strong emotions, and the hope that always accompanies each treatment. Added to all this are a changing sense of time and increasing feelings of urgency, which intensify all of the preceding.

Caring for someone with HIV or AIDS also means dealing with your own profound emotions. This includes confronting your fears about death and dying; accepting your changing relationship with your friend, partner, or family member; and addressing your anger, depression, loneliness, guilt, and/or sense of abandonment.

To help your friend, partner, or family member, you may need to actively seek information and support from legal, medical, and psychological sources. National and local hotlines, referral agencies, books, professionals with experience and compassion, and support groups can be found by searching through telephone directories and/or libraries in your region. Reaching out and sharing empower you to meet the challenges you face today and will continue to face in the future.

PETER PIOT, EXECUTIVE DIRECTOR of the Joint United Nations Programme on HIV/AIDS, says, "The evidence demonstrates that we are not powerless against this epidemic, but our response is still a fraction of what it needs to be. The real task now is to increase, massively, the political will, resources, systems, and social commitment needed to turn the tide" (UNAIDS, 2000). As we have seen, there are many public misperceptions concerning HIV and AIDS, and the denial of risk appears to be epidemic in many areas. But AIDS can be prevented. We hope that this chapter has provided you with information that will serve as your vaccine.

What we learn in times of pestilence [is] that there are more things to admire in men than to despise.

—*Albert Camus (1913–1960)*

SUMMARY

What Is AIDS?

- *AIDS* is an acronym for *acquired immunodeficiency syndrome*. For a person to receive an AIDS diagnosis, he or she must have a positive blood test indicating the presence of *HIV (human immunodeficiency virus)* antibodies and have a T-cell count below 200; if the T-cell count is higher, the person must have 1 or more of the 27 diseases or conditions associated with AIDS to be diagnosed with the disease. These include *opportunistic infections* such as *Pneumocystis carinii pneumonia* and tuberculosis; cancers such as *Kaposi's sarcoma*, lymphomas, and cervical cancer or CIN; and conditions associated with AIDS such as *wasting syndrome* and AIDS dementia. Other conditions may lead to an AIDS diagnosis, including persistent candidiasis and outbreaks of herpes.

- A host of symptoms are associated with HIV/AIDS. Because these symptoms may be indicative of many other diseases and conditions, HIV and AIDS cannot be self-diagnosed; testing by a clinician or physician is necessary.

- *Leukocytes,* or white blood cells, play a major role in defending the body against invading organisms and cancerous cells. One type, the *macrophage,* engulfs foreign particles and displays the invader's *antigen* on its own surface. *Antibodies* bind to antigens, inactivate them, and mark them for destruction by *killer T cells.* Other white blood cells called *lymphocytes* include *helper T cells,* which are programmed to "read" the antigens and then begin directing the immune system's response. The number of helper T cells in an individual's body is an important indicator of how well the immune system is functioning.

- *Viruses* are primitive entities; they can't propel themselves independently, and they can't reproduce unless they are inside a host cell. Within the HIV's protein core is the genetic material (RNA) that carries the information the virus needs to replicate itself. A *retrovirus* can "write" its RNA (the genetic program) into a host cell's DNA.

- Although HIV begins replication right away within the host cells, it is not detectable in the blood for some time—often years. HIV antibodies, however, are generally detectable in the blood within 2–6 months. A person's *serostatus* is HIV-negative if antibodies are not present and HIV-positive if antibodies are detected. "T-cell count" or "CD4 count" refers to the number of helper T cells that are present in a cubic milliliter of blood. A healthy person has a T-cell count in the range of 500–1600.

- When a person is first infected with HIV, he or she may experience severe flulike symptoms. During this period, the virus is dispersed throughout the lymph nodes and other tissues. The virus may stay localized in these areas for years, but it continues to replicate and to destroy T cells. As the number of infected cells goes up, the number of T cells goes down. In advanced AIDS, the T-cell count drops to under 200, and the virus itself is detectable in the blood.

The Epidemiology and Transmission of HIV

- More than 816,000 people are currently diagnosed with AIDS in the United States; 900,000 are estimated to be infected with HIV. Worldwide, more than 42 million people are infected with HIV or have developed AIDS. Rates of new infections are rising most dramatically in sub-Saharan Africa. Heterosexual transmission is the prominent mode of transmission worldwide.

- HIV is not transmitted by casual contact.

- Activities or situations that may promote HIV transmission include sexual transmission through vaginal or anal intercourse without a condom; fellatio without a condom; cunnilingus without a latex or other barrier; the sharing of needles contaminated with infected blood; in utero infection from mother to fetus, from blood during delivery, or in breast milk; the sharing of sex toys without disinfecting them; accidental contamination when infected blood enters the body through mucous membranes (eyes or mouth) or cuts, abrasions, or punctures in the skin (relatively rare); or blood transfusions administered prior to 1985.

- Certain physiological or behavioral factors increase the risk of contracting HIV. In addition to anal intercourse, multiple sex partners, and injecting drug use, these factors include having an STI (especially if genital lesions are present), multiple exposures to HIV, and drug and alcohol use.

AIDS Demographics

- HIV/AIDS is often linked with poverty, which has roots in racism and discrimination. In the United States, African Americans and Latinos have been disproportionately affected by HIV and STIs in comparison to other ethnic groups.

- Certain groups appear as a whole to be at greater risk than others or to face special difficulties where HIV is concerned, including gay men, women, teenagers, and young, inner-city African Americans.

- The gay and lesbian communities, along with other concerned individuals, have rallied together in a variety of ways to support people with HIV and AIDS, to educate themselves and the public, and to influence government policies.

- Women face unique issues where HIV is concerned. As the number of infected women rises, the number of infected children is also expected to rise. Because teenagers often have a sense of invulnerability, they may put themselves at great risk without really understanding the consequences that may result from their sexual behavior.

- HIV/AIDS, as well as most STIs, have disproportionately affected the southern region of the United States.

Prevention and Treatment

- To protect ourselves and those we care about from HIV, we need to be aware that alcohol and drug use significantly increases risky behaviors, develop communication skills so that we can talk with our partner, and get information on HIV testing. If we are sexually active with more than one long-term, exclusive partner, we need to use condoms correctly and consistently.

- Free or low-cost and anonymous or confidential HIV testing is available in many areas. The most common test, *ELISA,* looks for antibodies to the virus. A new HIV test in which the results are available in about 20 minutes is now used at many testing sites.

- There are three basic types of medical treatments for HIV and AIDS: therapies to treat the symptoms and infections, such as antibiotics and pain medications; drugs that affect the virus in some way; and therapies that boost the immune system.

Living with HIV or AIDS

- An HIV or AIDS diagnosis may be a cause for sadness and grief, but it also can be a time for reevaluation and growth. Those whose friends or family members are living with HIV, or who are themselves HIV-positive, need information and practical and emotional support.

- Early detection of HIV can greatly enhance both the quality and quantity of life. Appropriate medical treatment and a healthy lifestyle are important. People with HIV or AIDS also need to practice safer sex and consider seeking support from AIDS organizations. AIDS caregivers need support, too.

Sex and the Internet

Frequently Asked Questions on HIV/AIDS

The U.S. Centers for Disease Control and Prevention (CDC) provides information about HIV infection and AIDS on its Web site. One section is titled "Frequently Asked Questions on HIV/AIDS." Go there (http://www.cdc.gov/hiv/pubs/faqs.htm) and answer these questions:

- What are the categories of questions?

- Are there questions that address issues you are curious about?

- Choose a few questions and look at the responses. Do they seem adequate?

- Are there questions you have that are not included?

- Is there information here that was not covered in this chapter?

- What did you learn about HIV/AIDS from looking at this site?

Also, go to the home page of the CDC's Division of HIV/AIDS Prevention and find out what other information it provides.

SUGGESTED WEB SITES

CDC National Prevention Information Network
http://www.cdcdnpin.org
Claims to house the nation's largest collection of information resources on HIV/AIDS, STI, and TB prevention

Centers for Disease Control and Prevention
http://www.cdc.gov/hiv/adhap
Provides information on HIV/AIDS.
http://www.cdc.gov/nchstp/dstd
Provides information on STIs.

Joint United Nations Programme on HIV/AIDS
http://www.unaids.org
Contains epidemiological information on HIV/AIDS worldwide, as well as perspectives on HIV/AIDS-related issues.

Kaiser Family Foundation
http://www.kff.org
Offers fact sheets and new releases on STI and HIV/AIDS.

National Institutes of Health
http://www.nih.gov
Provides current information about HIV/AIDS.

Rural Center for AIDS/STD Prevention
http://www.indiana.edu/~aids
Provides information about issues related to HIV/STI prevention in rural communities in the United States.

SUGGESTED READING

Ciambrone, D. (2003). *Women's Experiences with HIV/AIDS.* New York: Haworth Press. Based on interviews with 37 HIV-infected women, details their ongoing efforts to come to grips with the disease and rebuild their lives.

Levine, Martin P.; Nardi, Peter M.; & Gagnon, John H. (Eds.). (1997). *In Changing Times: Gay Men and Lesbians Encounter HIV/AIDS.* Chicago: University of Chicago Press. Essays on the ways in which HIV/AIDS has changed the lives of gay men and lesbian women.

Shilts, Randy. (1987). *And the Band Played On: People, Politics, and the AIDS Epidemic.* New York: St. Martin's Press. The fascinating story behind the "discovery" of AIDS, complete with real heroes and, unfortunately, real villains.

Smith, P. A. (Ed.). (2002). *Encyclopedia of AIDS: A Social, Cultural, and Scientific Study.* Cambridge, MA: Perseus. Discusses AIDS and its effect on culture, politics, law, and the individual.

For links, articles, and study material, go to the McGraw-Hill Web site, located at http://www.mhhe.com/strong5

17

Sexual Coercion: Harassment, Aggression, and Abuse

"I was sexually harassed at work, but I stood my ground. I told the guy to knock it off or I'd sue him. It worked—he quit two weeks later."

—20-year-old Latina

"At a very young age, I remember being sexually molested by two neighbors who were a couple years older than I. They did not insert anything in me. I was not physically hurt, but I remember losing my voice and the will to defend myself. I remember my father calling my name from the back porch and I could not answer him. I felt I had lost all power to speak or move. The regret of allowing this to happen to me still lingers in my feelings toward others and myself. I believe this event has contributed to shaping some deep paranoia and mistrust toward my peers, and I have carried this for a long time."

—22-year-old White female

"I was sexually abused when I was about eight years old. My cousin and uncle molested me several times. They abused me for as long as three years. After this time, I decided to run away because I did not have a father, and I knew that my mother would not believe what happened to me. I tried to tell people what had happened to me, but everyone would call me a liar or crazy. In my town, people believed that if a woman was sexually abused it was her fault because she provoked the men. This includes child abuse. In my home, my family never talked about sex or sexuality, and I think that is one of the reasons I did not know that what happened to me wasn't my fault."

—21-year-old Mexican female

"When I reached the first grade, my mother's boyfriend moved in with us. Living with him was the biggest nightmare of my life. One night I was asleep and was awakened by something. It was my mother's boyfriend, and what woke me up was his hand. He was touching me in my sleep while he watched television. He did not touch me under my clothes and he did not caress me, but he would place his hand on my private parts and that made me feel very uncomfortable. I used to move and roll around a lot so he would move his hand. I became afraid to sleep at night because I thought he would be there. These events affected me emotionally and psychologically."

—20-year-old Japanese female

Being forced is poison for the soul.
—*Ludwig Borne (1786–1837)*

ALTHOUGH SEXUALITY PERMITS US to form and sustain deep bonds and intimate relationships, it may also have a darker side. For some people, sex is linked with coercion, degradation, aggression, and abuse. In these cases, sex becomes a weapon—a means to exploit, humiliate, or harm others. In this chapter, we first examine the various aspects of sexual harassment, including the distinction between flirting and harassment and the sexual harassment that occurs in schools, colleges, and the workplace. Next, we look at harassment, prejudice, and discrimination directed against gay men and lesbian women. Then we examine sexual aggression, including date rape and stranger rape, the motivations for rape, and the consequences of rape. Finally, we discuss child sexual abuse, examining the factors contributing to abuse, the types of abuse and their consequences, and programs for preventing it.

SEXUAL HARASSMENT

Sexual harassment has become a public issue in recent years, with several episodes receiving major media attention. In 1992, Anita Hill accused Clarence Thomas of sexual harassment during his confirmation hearings for the U.S. Supreme Court. The proceedings were aired on national television and captured widespread interest among the American public. The 1991 Tailhook scandal involving the harassment of women by U.S. Navy personnel also received national attention. Later in the decade, allegations of sexual harassment emerged concerning President Clinton's involvement with Paula Jones, Kathleen Willey, and Monica Lewinsky. The 1994 Hollywood movie *Disclosure*, starring Michael Douglas and Demi Moore, illustrated sexual harassment, although it was unusual in depicting a female work supervisor using the power of her position to attempt to persuade a male subordinate to have sex. These episodes not only brought sexual harassment to the public's attention but also raised questions about what does and does not constitute harassment.

Sexual harassment refers to two distinct types of behavior: (1) the abuse of power for sexual ends and (2) the creation of a hostile environment. In terms of abuse of power, sexual harassment consists of unwelcomed sexual advances, requests for sexual favors, or other verbal or physical conduct of a sexual nature as a condition of instruction or employment (Frazier, Cochran, & Olson, 1995). Refusal to comply may result in reprisals (Charney & Russell, 1994). Only a person with power over another can commit the first kind of harassment (Pierce, 1994). In a **hostile environment,** someone acts in sexual ways that interfere with a person's performance at school or in the workplace. Such harassment is illegal.

What Is Sexual Harassment?

The Civil Rights Act of 1964 first made various kinds of discrimination, including sexual harassment, illegal in the workplace. In 1980, the U.S. Office of Equal Employment Opportunity Commission (EEOC) issued guidelines regarding both verbal and physical harassment in the work and education environments. The EEOC defined sexual harassment as unwelcome sexual advances, requests for sexual favors, and other verbal or physical conduct of a sexual nature when (1) submission to such conduct is made either explicitly or implicitly a term or condition of an individual's employment, (2) employment decisions are based on submission to or rejection of such conduct by an individual, or (3) such conduct has the purpose or effect of unreasonably interfering with an individual's work performance or creating an intimidating, hostile, or offensive working environment. A major component of the EEOC guidelines is that the behavior is unwanted and unwelcome and might affect employment conditions. Also note that the sexual aggression does not have to be explicit and that even the creation of a hostile work environment that can affect work performance constitutes

Sexual harassment, particularly in the workplace, creates a stressful and hostile environment for the victim.

sexual harassment (U.S. Merit Systems Protection Board, 1995). In 2002, 14,376 sexual harassment charges were filed, up from 10,532 in 1992 (U.S. Equal Employment Opportunity Commission, 2003).

Sexual harassment is a mixture of sex and power; power may often be the dominant element. In school and the workplace, men and women are devalued by calling attention to their sexuality. For women especially, sexual harassment may be a way to keep them "in their place" and make them feel vulnerable.

There are other forms of behavior that, although not illegal, are considered by many to be sexual harassment. These include unwanted sexual jokes and innuendos and unwelcome whistles, taunts, and obscenities directed from a man or group of men to a woman walking past them. As with all harassment, these apply to male-female, male-male, and female-female interactions. They also include a man "talking to" a woman's breasts or body during conversation or persistently giving her the "once-over" as she walks past him, sits down, or enters or leaves a room. Elizabeth Powell (1996) lists the following as examples of sexual harassment:

- Verbally harassing or abusing someone
- Exerting subtle pressure for sexual activity
- Making remarks about a person's clothing, body, or sexual activities
- Leering at or ogling a person's body
- Engaging in unwelcome touching, patting, or pinching
- Brushing against a person's body
- Making demands for sexual favors accompanied by implied or overt threats concerning one's job or student status
- Physically assaulting someone

Such incidents may make women feel uncomfortable and vulnerable. (They have been described, in fact, as "little rapes.") The cumulative effect of these behaviors is to lead women to limit their activities, to avoid walking past groups of men, and to stay away from beaches, concerts, parties, and sports events unless they are accompanied by others (Bowman, 1993). Sometimes, charges of sexual harassment are ignored or trivialized, and blame often falls on the victim (Powell, 1996). Sexual harassment more commonly occurs in school or the workplace, as well as in other settings, such as between patients and doctors or mental health and sex therapists.

Flirtation Versus Harassment

There is nothing wrong with flirtation per se. A smile, look, or compliment can give pleasure to both people. But persistent and unwelcome flirtation can be sexual harassment if the flirtatious person holds power over the other or if the flirtation creates a hostile school or work environment. Whether flirtation is sexual harassment depends on three factors.

- *Whether you have equal power.* A person's having power over you limits your ability to refuse, for fear of reprisal. For example, if a professor or teaching assistant in your class asks you for a date, you are placed in an awkward position. If you say no, will your grade suffer? Will you be ignored in class? What other consequences might occur? Or if your boss asks for a date, you may be similarly concerned about losing your job, being demoted, or having your work environment become hostile if you refuse.

- *Whether you are approached appropriately.* "Hi babe, nice tits, wanna get it on?" and "Hey stud, love your buns, wanna do it?" are obviously offensive. But approaches that are complimentary ("You look really nice today"), indirect ("What do you think of the course?"), or direct ("Would you like to have some coffee?") are acceptable because they do not pressure you. You have the opportunity to let the overture pass, respond positively, or politely decline. Sometimes, it is difficult to distinguish the intent of the person doing the approaching. One way to ascertain the intent is to give a direct "I" message and ask that the behavior cease. If the person stops the behavior, and especially if an apology follows, the intent was friendly; if the behavior continues, it is the beginning of sexual harassment. If he or she does not stop, you should contact a trusted supervisor, an academic advisor/counselor, or a resident assistant.

- *Whether you wish to continue contact.* If you find the other person appealing, you may want to continue the flirtation. You can express interest or flirt back. But if you don't, you may want to stop the interaction by not responding or by responding in a neutral or discouraging manner.

The issue is complicated by several factors related to culture and gender. Differing cultural expectations may lead to misinterpretation. For example, when a Latino, whose culture encourages mutual flirting, says "muy guapa" (good looking) to a Latina walking by, the words may be meant *and* received as a compliment. But when a Latino says the same thing to a non-Latina, he may be dismayed at her negative reaction. He perceives her as uptight, and she perceives him as rude, but each is misinterpreting the other because of cultural differences.

Three significant gender differences may contribute to sexual harassment. First, men are generally less likely to perceive activities as harassing than are women (Jones & Remland, 1992; Popovich, Gehlauf, Jolton, & Somers, 1992;

U.S. Merit Systems Protection Board, 1995). The difference in perception often is for the more subtle forms of harassment, as both men and women believe that overt activities such as deliberate touching constitute sexual harassment. Second, men tend to misperceive women's friendliness as sexual interest (Johnson, Stockdale, & Saal, 1991; Stockdale, 1993). Third, men are more likely than women to perceive male-female relationships as adversarial (Reilly, Lott, Caldwell, & DeLuca, 1992). Given all this, not surprisingly, 86% of the harassment claims filed in 2002 were by women. (Interestingly, the percentage of males filing sexual harassment claims increased from 9.1% in 1992 to 14.8% in 2002 (U.S. Equal Employment Opportunity Commission, 2003).

Power differences also affect perception. Personal questions asked by an instructor or supervisor, for example, are more likely to be perceived as sexual harassment than they would be if a student or co-worker asked them. What needs to be clarified is the basis of the relationship: Is it educational, business, or professional? Is it romantic or sexual? Flirtatious or sexual ways of relating are inappropriate in the first three contexts.

Harassment in School and College

Sexual harassment in various forms is widespread. It does not necessarily begin in adulthood; it may begin as early as middle childhood.

Harassment in Elementary and High School   It's a "time-honored" practice for boys to "tease" girls: flipping up their skirts, calling them names, touching their breasts, spreading sexual gossip, and so on. If such behavior is defined as teasing, its impact is discounted; it is just "fun." But if the behavior is thought of as sexual harassment, then the acts may be viewed in a new light. Such behavior, researcher Carrie Herbert (1989) found, leads girls to "become more subordinated, less autonomous, and less capable of resisting. This behavior controls the girls through intimidation, embarrassment, or humiliation."

According to a national study of sexual harassment among 2064 8th- through 11th-graders, 83% of girls and 79% of boys reported experiencing some type of sexual harassment in school, the vast majority being peer-to-peer harassment (American Association of University Women Educational Foundation, 2001). Over 1 in 4 students experienced sexual harassment often, no matter whether the school was urban, suburban, or rural. Most of the harassment occurred within the classroom or hallways. Being subjected to sexual comments, jokes, gestures, or looks; being touched, grabbed, or pinched in a sexual way; and being intentionally brushed up against in a sexual way were the most common types of harassment (Figure 17.1). Thirty-three percent of the girls and 12% of the boys no longer wished to attend school because of the harassment. Other outcomes of the harassment included not wanting to talk as much in class, finding it hard to pay attention in school, staying home from school or cutting a class, and getting lower grades on tests. Feeling embarrassed and self-conscious, being less self-confident, and feeling afraid were the most common emotional consequences of the harassment. Both girls and boys experienced the consequences of harassment, although the impact was greater for the girls. Almost all students (96%) said they knew what sexual harassment is; the definitions of boys and girls did not differ substantially.

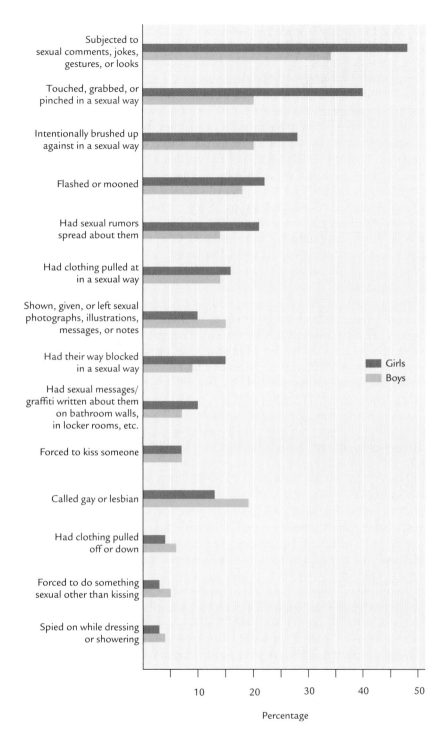

FIGURE 17.1   Types of Sexual Harassment Experienced Often or Occasionally Among a National Sample of 8th- and 11th-Graders.
(*Source:* Adapted from *Hostile Hallways: The AAUW Survey on Sexual Harassment in America's Schools* (1993) with permission from the AAUW Educational Foundation.)

Among students, sexual harassment occurs most often when boys are in groups. Their motives may be homosocial—heightening their group status by denigrating girls—rather than based on any specific animosity toward a particular girl (Carr, 1992). Harassment is usually either ignored by adults or regarded as normal or typical behavior among boys—"boys will be boys."

Girls are frequently blamed for the harassment because they do not "stand up for themselves" or they take the incidents "too seriously" (Herbert, 1989).

Harassment in College   Sexual harassment on college and university campuses has become a major concern in recent years. Various studies suggest that about one-quarter to one-half of college students (female and male) have experienced some form of harassment from other students, faculty members, or administrators. In one study of female university students, 20% of the undergraduate students and 19% of the graduate students reported having been sexually harassed while in school (interestingly, 30% of female staff, 22% of female faculty, and 43% of female administrators also reported being sexually harassed) (Kelly & Parsons, 2000). In another study of both male and female university students, 20–55% of the women and 15–44% of the men reported being subjected to harassment (Shepela & Levesque, 1998). Fifteen percent of the men and 12% of the women reported significant sexual advances from university faculty. Most of the sexual harassment was from fellow students.

Two major problems in dealing with issues of sexual harassment in college are gender differences in levels of tolerance and attribution of blame. Women are often blamed for not taking a "compliment" and for provoking unwanted sexual attention by what they wear or how they look. These attitudes are widely held, especially among men.

Because of sexual harassment, many students find it difficult to study; others worry about their grades. If the harasser is an instructor controlling grades, students fear reporting the harassment. They may use strategies such as avoiding courses taught by the harasser or choosing another advisor. In extreme cases, the emotional consequences may be as severe as for rape victims (Paludi, 1990). However, many students view the dating of students by professors as unethical behavior rather than harassment (Quatrella & Wentworth, 1995).

Most universities and colleges have developed sexual harassment policies, most of which prohibit sexual relationships between students and professors. A fundamental principle of these policies is that the student-professor relationship cannot be truly consensual given the professor's considerable power over the student's academic standing and career plans. Although such policies help make students aware of harassment issues, their effectiveness depends on educating students about what constitutes harassment (Gressman et al., 1992; Williams, Lam, & Shively, 1992). With the exception of coercive or highly intrusive behaviors, many students are uncertain about what behaviors constitute sexual harassment (Fitzgerald & Ormerod, 1991).

Harassment in the Workplace

Issues of sexual harassment are complicated in the workplace because the work setting, like college, is one of the most important places where adults meet potential partners. As a consequence, sexual undercurrents or interactions often take place. Flirtations, romances, and affairs are common in the work environment. The line between flirtation and harassment can be problematic—especially for men. Many women do not realize they were being harassed until much later. When they identify the behavior, they report

TABLE 17.1 Percentage of Federal Employees Experiencing Sexual Harassment, 1992–1994		
Behavior	*Men*	*Women*
Sexual remarks, jokes, teasing	14	37
Sexual looks, gestures	9	29
Deliberate touching, cornering	8	24
Pressure for dates	4	13
Suggestive letters, calls, materials	4	10
Stalking	2	7
Pressure for sexual favors	2	7
Actual/attempted rape, assault	2	4

Source: Adapted from U.S. Merit Systems Protection Board. (1995). *Sexual Harassment in the Federal Workplace: Trends, Progress, Continuing Challenges.* Washington, DC: Author.

feeling naive or gullible, as well as guilty and ashamed. As they learn more about sexual harassment, they are able to identify their experiences for what they were—harassment (Kidder, Lafleur, & Wells, 1995).

A study of sexual harassment in federal offices found that 44% of women and 19% of men had experienced some form of unwanted sexual attention during the preceding 2 years (U.S. Merit Systems Protection Board, 1995). Sexual remarks, jokes and teasing, sexual looks and gestures, and deliberate touching and cornering were the most common forms of sexual harassment experienced (Table 17.1). For many of the survey respondents, the unwanted attention they experienced lasted a month or more. Among those reporting unwanted sexual attention, most males (65%) had been harassed by women, and the overwhelming majority of females (93%) had been harassed by men. About 1% of the women and 21% of the men reported being harassed by a person of the same sex. Almost 80% of the victims were subjected to unwanted sexual behaviors by people they identified as co-workers or other employees without supervisory authority over them. The victims of sexual harassment experienced mental and emotional stress and even loss of income resulting from taking leave from their jobs. The productivity loss to the federal government involving sick leave, job turnover, and decreases in individual and group productivity was estimated to be $327 million in the 2 years studied. Sexual harassment may be decreasing in the workplace as more companies promote prevention and self-police. According to an Employment Law Alliance survey of 1000 American workers in 2000, 21% of the women had been sexually harassed at work, in contrast to 7% of the men (Hirschfeld, 2002).

Sexual harassment tends to be most pervasive in formerly all-male occupations, in which sexual harassment is a means of exerting control over women and asserting male dominance. Such male bastions as the building trades, the trucking industry, law enforcement, and the military have been especially resistant to the presence of women (Niebuhr & Boyles, 1991; Schmitt, 1990). For example, female African American firefighters report high levels of harassment (Yoder & Aniakudo, 1995). Sexual harassment can be perpetrated by both fellow employees and supervisors. Recognizing this, the U.S. Supreme Court recently ruled that employers are liable for their supervisors' behavior even if the companies were unaware of their actions (Sward, 1998). Although most sexual harassment situations involve men harassing women, men can be the victims of harassment, from either a woman or another man. The U.S. Supreme Court has ruled that a man can file legal action against another man for sexual harassment (Solomon, 1998).

Sexual harassment can have a variety of consequences for the victim, including depression, anxiety, shame, humiliation, and anger (Charney & Russell, 1994; Paludi, 1990).

HARASSMENT AND DISCRIMINATION AGAINST GAY, LESBIAN, BISEXUAL, AND TRANSGENDERED PEOPLE

Researchers have identified two forms of discrimination or bias based on sexual orientation: heterosexual bias and anti-gay prejudice.

Heterosexual Bias

Heterosexual bias, also known as **heterosexism,** involves the tendency to see the world in heterosexual terms and to ignore or devalue homosexuality (Herek, Kimmel, Amaro, & Melton, 1991; Rich, 1983). Heterosexual bias may take many forms. Examples of this type of bias include the following:

Click on "Learning to Be Straight" to hear students discussing heterosexual bias and privilege.

- *Ignoring the existence of lesbian, gay, bisexual, and transgendered people.* Discussions of various aspects of human sexuality may ignore gay, lesbian, bisexual, and transgendered people, assuming that such individuals do not exist, are not significant, or are not worthy of inclusion. Without such inclusion, discussions of human sexuality are really discussions of *heterosexual* sexuality.

- *Segregating gay, lesbian, bisexual, and transgendered people from heterosexuals.* When sexual orientation is irrelevant, separating certain groups from others is a form of segregation, as in proposals to separate HIV-positive gay men (but not other HIV-positive individuals) from the general population.

- *Subsuming gay, lesbian, bisexual, and transgendered people into a larger category.* Sometimes, it is appropriate to make sexual orientation a category in data analysis, as in studies of adolescent suicide rates. If orientation is not included, findings may be distorted (Herek et al., 1991).

Prejudice, Discrimination, and Violence

Anti-gay prejudice is a strong dislike, fear, or hatred of gay, lesbian, bisexual, and transgendered people because of their sexual orientation. **Homophobia** is an irrational or phobic fear of gay, lesbian, bisexual, and transgendered people. Not all anti-gay feelings are phobic in the clinical sense of being excessive and irrational, but they may be unreasonable or biased. (The feelings may, however, be within the norms of a biased culture.)

As a belief system, anti-gay prejudice justifies discrimination based on sexual orientation. Gay, lesbian, bisexual, and transgendered people are discriminated against in terms of housing, employment opportunities, adoption, parental rights, family acceptance, and so on. And they are the victims of violence, known as **gay-bashing** or **queer-bashing.**

Several colleges have reported a form of discrimination called "biophobia," in which some bisexual students, feeling shunned by support groups for gay and lesbian students, are forming their own organizations (Morgan, 2002). Bisexual students have said that many of the student groups set up as havens for gay, lesbian, bisexual, and transgendered students have "succumbed to the very kinds of intolerance and discrimination that they were chartered to fight" in their antipathy toward those who identify as bisexual. Typical criticisms of bisexual students are that they are confused about their sexual identity, that they are "riding the fence," and that by being bisexual they have access to "heterosexual privilege." Apparently, many bisexual students have been disappointed at not getting the support from the gay-student groups that they anticipated.

Effects on Heterosexuals   Anti-gay prejudice adversely affects both heterosexuals and gay, lesbian, bisexual, and transgendered people. First, it creates fear and hatred, negative emotions that cause distress and anxiety. Second, it alienates heterosexuals from their gay family members, friends, neighbors, and co-workers. Third, it limits their range of behaviors and feelings, such as hugging or being emotionally intimate with same-sex friends, for fear that such intimacy may be "homosexual." Fourth, among men, it may lead to exaggerated displays of masculinity to prove that one is not gay, that is, effeminate.

Discrimination and Antidiscrimination Laws   As mentioned, gay, lesbian, bisexual, and transgendered people are discriminated against in many areas and experience high levels of stress as a result (Meyer, 1995). For example, the efforts of medical and public health personnel to combat HIV/AIDS were inhibited initially because AIDS was perceived as the "gay plague" and was considered by some to be justified "punishment" of gay men for their "unnatural" sexual practices (Altman, 1985). The fear of HIV/AIDS has contributed to increased anti-gay prejudice among some heterosexuals (Lewes, 1992). Anti-gay prejudice influences parental reactions to their gay and lesbian children, often leading to estrangement.

Gay men and lesbian women have been seeking legislation to protect themselves from discrimination based on their sexual orientation. For example, a federal law was passed protecting employees from being sexually harassed in the workplace by people of the same sex ("Same-Sex Harassment," 1998). Such legislation guarantees lesbian women and gay men equal protection under the law. Public opinion overwhelmingly supports equal employment opportunities for gay men and lesbian women.

Violence Against Gay Men and Lesbian Women   Violence against gay men and lesbian women has a long history. At times, such violence has been sanctioned by religious institutions. During the Middle Ages, the Inquisition burned "sodomites," and in the sixteenth century, England's King Henry VIII made sodomy punishable by death. In our own times, homosexuals were among the first victims of the Nazis, who killed 50,000 in concentration camps. Because of worldwide violence and persecution against lesbian

women and gay men, the Netherlands, Germany, and Canada in 1992 granted asylum to men and women based on their homosexuality (Farnsworth, 1992).

Today, gay men and lesbian women continue to be targets of violence. In 2002, 1968 violent incidents involving 2257 gay, lesbian, transgendered, or bisexual people were reported, including 21 murders (National Coalition of

During the Middle Ages, gay men (called sodomites) were burned at the stake as heretics (previous page). In Germany in 1933, the Nazis burned Magnus Hirschfeld's library and forced him to flee the country (above). Gay men and lesbian women were among the first Germans the Nazis forced into concentration camps, where over 50,000 of them were killed. Today, violence against gay men and lesbian women, known as gay-bashing, continues (right). The pink triangle recalls the symbol the Nazis required lesbian women and gay men to wear, just as they required Jews to wear the Star of David.

Anti-Violence Programs, 2002). Besides murder, the incidents included sexual assault/rape, robbery, vandalism, assault/attempted assault, intimidation, and verbal harassment. The brutal murder of Matthew Shepard, a gay University of Wyoming student, in 1998 was one of several cases receiving national media attention.

Personal Sources of Anti-Gay Prejudice Anti-gay prejudice in people may come from several sources (Marmor, 1980a): (1) a deeply rooted insecurity concerning a person's own sexuality and gender identity, (2) a strong fundamentalist religious orientation, and (3) simple ignorance concerning homosexuality. The literature also indicates fairly consistent gender differences in attitudes toward lesbian women and gay men (Herek, 1984). Heterosexuals tend to have more negative attitudes toward gays of their own sex than toward those of the other sex. Heterosexual men tend to be less tolerant than heterosexual women (Whitley & Kite, 1995).

MANY AMERICANS HAVE AMBIVALENT FEELINGS about most issues concerning gay, lesbian, and bisexual people. The public has shown greater acceptance in some areas, although recent polls have revealed less tolerance about others, showing the volatility of public opinion on this controversial issue. Two recent polls are highlighted here. Subsequent polls may reveal even greater changes in public opinion as issues related to gay rights, such as legalizing gay marriage, become even more important on the political agenda.

USA Today/CNN/Gallup Poll

According to a public opinion poll of 1006 adults conducted in July 2003, 48% of Americans felt that "homosexual relations" between consenting adults should be legal. This acceptance level represents a sharp drop from the 60% support in early May 2003, which was the highest level of acceptance of the legality of homosexuality over the 26 years Gallup has been asking that question. Backlash after the U.S. Supreme Court decision striking down a Texas law banning sodomy in same-sex couples (see Chapter 18) is considered the major factor contributing to the dramatic drop in acceptance. On this issue, younger respondents and those residing in the western states and big cities were more accepting. Residents of southern states and small towns or rural communities were least accepting.

Nearly 9 out of 10 believed that homosexuals should have equal rights in terms of job opportunities, nearly 1 out of 2 believed that homosexual couples should have the legal right to adopt a child, and slightly more than 6 out of 10 felt that homosexuals should have the same legal rights as married heterosexual couples regarding health-care benefits and Social Security survivor benefits. Slightly more than one-half indicated that they have had friends, relatives, or co-workers who have told them they are gay or lesbian. One-half said they favored a constitutional amendment that would define marriage as between a man and a woman (Page, 2003).

Kaiser Family Foundation Poll on Issues and Policies Related to Sexual Orientation

In the fall of 2000, the Kaiser Family Foundation conducted two national public opinion surveys: the general public's attitudes toward lesbian, gay, and bisexual people, and their own views on key policy issues related to sexual orientation; and the experiences of self-identified lesbian, gay, and bisexual people. Although the Gallup poll provides more current public opinion, the key findings of the Kaiser survey are given here.

The experiences and opinions of self-identified gay, lesbian, and bisexual people were obtained through 405 telephone interviews among randomly selected adults, age 18 or older, in 15 major U.S. metropolitan areas. The respondents reported varied personal experiences with acceptance, prejudice and discrimination, verbal abuse and physical violence, and views about gay rights. Specific findings of the survey include the following:

- Thirty-four percent said that their family or a family member had refused to accept them because of their sexual orientation, with lesbian women (50%) being accepted less than gay men (32%) and bisexual people (26%).

- Seventy-four percent reported experiencing prejudice and discrimination based on their sexual orientation, with lesbian women (85%) having experienced more discrimination than gay men (76%) and bisexual people (60%).

- Seventy-four percent reported having been the target of verbal abuse such as slurs or name-calling because of their sexual orientation.

- Thirty-two percent said that they had been the target of physical violence, against either them or their property, because someone believed they were a gay, lesbian, or bisexual person.

- Twenty-eight percent reported living with a partner as if they were married, and 74% said they would like to marry legally someday.

- Among those who were not parents of children under 18, 49% reported wanting to adopt children of their own someday.

To find out more about the Kaiser Family Foundation poll, visit their Web site (http://www.kff.org) and locate the publication *Inside-OUT: A Report on the Experiences of Lesbians, Gays and Bisexuals in America and the Public's Views on Issues and Policies Related to Sexual Orientation.*

What is your opinion about the issues addressed in the two polls? Does your opinion seem to be similar to that of most of your friends or family? Has your opinion on these issues changed over time? Do you think conducting opinion polls on these issues is important? Should the results of opinion polls be used in shaping public policy toward gay, lesbian, bisexual, and transgendered people?

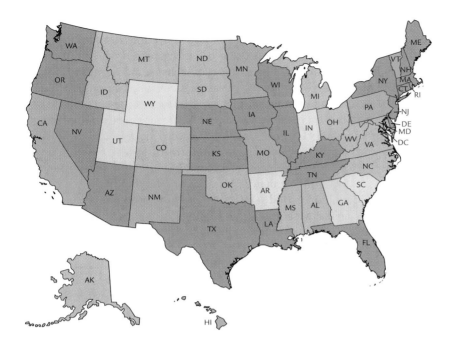

FIGURE 17.2 States with Hate Crime Laws Protecting People Based on Sexual Orientation and Gender Identity. (*Source:* Human Rights Campaign Foundation, 2003.)

■ States having hate crime law protecting sexual orientation and gender identity

■ States having hate crime law protecting sexual orientation

■ States having have crime law but do not include either sexual orientation or gender identity

□ States having hate crime law but do not list any categories at all

□ States having no hate crime law

Ending Anti-Gay Prejudice

As of November 2003, 22 states have a law that addresses hate crimes based on sexual orientation, and 7 states and the District of Columbia have a law that addresses hate crimes motivated by sexual orientation or gender identity (Figure 17.2). Although legislation to prohibit discrimination is important for ending prejudice, education and positive social interactions are also important vehicles for change. Negative attitudes about homosexuality may be reduced by arranging positive interactions between heterosexuals and gay, lesbian, transgendered, and bisexual people.

SEXUAL AGGRESSION

In recent years, we have increasingly expanded our knowledge about sexually aggressive behavior and its consequences. We have expanded our focus beyond stranger rape and examined the consequences of sexually aggressive behavior on survivors. Earlier, researchers had focused primarily on **rape,** usually defined as penile-vaginal penetration performed against a *woman's* will through the use or threat of force. They assumed that rape was committed by strangers for the purpose of sexual gratification. In their work, researchers generally examined the sexual psychopathology of male offenders

Undismayed, he plucks the rose
In the hedgerow blooming.
Vainly she laments her woes,
Vainly doth her thorns oppose,
Gone her sweet perfuming.

—German art song

and the characteristics of women that "precipitated" rapes, such as acting docile, living alone, and dressing in a certain way (White & Farmer, 1992).

In the 1970s, feminists challenged the belief that rape is an act of sexual deviance. Instead, they argued, rape is an act of violence and aggression against women, and the principal motive is power, not sexual gratification (Brownmiller, 1975). As a result of feminist influence, the focus of research shifted.

Contemporary research now views rape as a category of sexual aggression. **Sexual aggression** refers to sexual activity, including petting, oral-genital sex, anal intercourse, and sexual intercourse, performed against a person's will through the use of force, argument, pressure, alcohol or drugs, or authority (Cate & Lloyd, 1992; Muehlenhard, Ponch, Phelps, & Giusti, 1992). Unlike rape, which by definition excludes men as victims, sexual aggression includes both women *and* men as victims. It also includes gay men and lesbian women, who traditionally had been excluded from such research because of rape's heterosexual definition (Muehlenhard et al., 1992). **Sexual coercion** is a broader term than "rape" or "sexual aggression." It includes arguing, pleading, and cajoling, as well as force and the threat of force. **Sexual assault** is a term used by the criminal justice system to describe forced sexual contact that does not necessarily include penile-vaginal intercourse, and so does not meet the legal definition of rape. Thus, for example, individuals could be prosecuted for engaging in forced anal intercourse or for forcing an object into the anus.

The Nature and Incidence of Rape

Rape is a means of achieving power or expressing anger and hatred. Rape *forces* its victim into an intimate physical relationship with the rapist against her or his will. The victim does not experience pleasure; she or he experiences terror. In most cases, the victim is a woman; sometimes, the victim is a man. In almost every case, however, the assailant is a man. The weapon in rape is the penis (which may be supplemented by a knife or a gun); the penis is used to attack, subordinate, and humiliate the victim.

Rape is not only an act but also a threat. As small girls, women are warned against taking candy from strangers, walking alone down dark streets, and leaving doors and windows unlocked. Men may fear assault, but women fear assault *and* rape. As a result, many women live with the possibility of being raped as a part of their consciousness. Rape and the fear of rape are facts of life for women; this is not true for men.

The actual prevalence rates of rape in the United States are unknown, because many victims do not report the crime. According to the U.S. Justice Department's National Crime Victimization Survey (NCVS) the total number of rapes, attempted rapes, and sexual assaults in 2001 was 248,000, down by 13,000 (13%) from 2000 (U.S. Department of Justice, 2002). This decrease reflects an overall downward trend in criminal victimization that began in 1994. The NCVS found that 91% of the sexual crime victims were female; for every 1000 women age 12 and older, 1.9 were raped or sexually assaulted, as opposed to 0.2 per 1000 men. Blacks and Whites were nearly equally likely to be raped (1.1 per 1000 versus 1.0 per 1000, respectively), and 70% of the female victims and 67% of the male victims knew their assailant (Figures 17.3 and 17.4).

A large-scale survey reported that 1.3% of the male respondents and nearly 22% of the females had been forced to have sex by a man. At the same time, only 2.8% of the men in the survey reported forcing a woman to have

The fear of sexual assault is a special fear: its intensity in women can best be likened to the male fear of castration.

—*Germaine Greer*

Click on "Behind Closed Doors" to hear campus activists talk about factors that lead to rape.

THERE ARE NO GUARANTEED WAYS to prevent sexual assault or coercion. Each situation, assailant, and targeted woman or man is different. But rape education courses may be effective in reducing the rape myths that provide support for sexual aggression (Fonow, Richardson, & Wemmerus, 1992).

To reduce the risk of date rape, consider these guidelines:

1. When dating someone for the first time, go to a public place such as a restaurant, movie, or sports event.

2. Share expenses. A common scenario is a date expecting you to exchange sex for his or her paying for dinner, the movie, drinks, and so on.

3. Avoid using drugs or alcohol if you do not want to be sexual with your date. Such use is associated with date rape.

4. Avoid ambiguous verbal or nonverbal behavior, particularly any behavior that might be interpreted as "teasing." Make sure your verbal and nonverbal messages are identical. If you only want to cuddle or kiss, for example, tell your partner that those are your limits. Tell him or her that if you say no you mean no. If necessary, reinforce your statement emphatically, both verbally and physically (by pushing him or her away).

5. If your date becomes sexually coercive despite your direct communication, consider physical denials such as pushing, slapping, and kicking.

To reduce the risk of stranger rape, consider the following guidelines. But try to avoid becoming overly vigilant; use reasonable judgment. Do not let fear control your life.

1. Do not identify yourself as a person living alone, especially if you are a woman. Use initials on the mailbox and in the telephone directory.

2. Don't open your door to strangers; keep your house and car doors locked. Have your keys ready when you approach your car or house. Look in the back seat before getting into your car.

3. Avoid dark and isolated areas. Carry a whistle or airhorn, and take a cell phone when you are out by yourself. Let people know where you are going.

4. If someone approaches you threateningly, turn and run. If you can't run, resist. Studies indicate that resisting an attack by shouting, causing a scene, or fighting back can deter the assailant. Fighting and screaming may reduce the level of the abuse without increasing the level of physical injury. Most women who are injured during a rape appear to have been injured *before* resisting (Ullman & Knight, 1991). Trust your intuitions, whatever approach you take.

5. Be alert to possible ways to escape. Talking with an assailant may give you time to find an escape route.

6. Take self-defense training. It will raise your level of confidence and your fighting abilities. You may be able to scare off the assailant, or you may create an opportunity to escape. Many women take self-defense training following an incidence of sexual aggression to reaffirm their sense of control.

If you are sexually assaulted (or the victim of an attempted assault), report the assault as soon as possible. You are probably not the assailant's first victim. As much as you might want to, do not change clothes or shower. Semen and hair or other materials on your body or clothing may be very important in arresting and convicting a rapist. You may also want to contact a rape crisis center; its staff members are knowledgeable about dealing with the police and the traumatic aftermath of rape. But most importantly, remember that you are not at fault. The rapist is the only one to blame.

---

sex (Laumann, Gagnon, Michael, & Michaels, 1994). A study of first sexual intercourse of undergraduate women revealed that 6% had sex against their will (Bajracharya, Sarvela, & Isberner, 1995). A look at first sexual intercourse among younger women (grades 8–12) found sexual assault to occur up to 26% of the time, though it is seldom reported (Rhynard, Krebs, & Glover, 1997). A *Details* magazine study of college students found that 29% of the females and 11% of the males had ever had a date, sexual partner, or friend physically force them into unwanted sexual behavior (Elliot & Brantley, 1997). The Centers for Disease Control and Prevention (CDC) found that nationwide 10.3% of female students and 5.1% of male students in grades 9–12 had ever been forced to have sexual intercourse when they did not want to (CDC, 2002a). A nationally representative telephone survey of 8000

FIGURE 17.3   Type of Relationship with Offender of Female Victims of Rape and Sexual Assault.
(*Source:* Data from Bureau of Justice Statistics, 2002.)

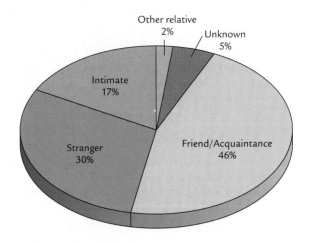

women and 8000 men about their experiences with rape and other violence was cosponsored by the National Institute of Justice and the CDC (Tjaden & Thoennes, 1998). Using a definition of rape that included forced vaginal, oral, and anal intercourse, the survey found that 1 out of 6 women and 1 out of 33 men had experienced an attempted or completed rape as a child and/or as an adult. The study found that rape is primarily a crime against youths: More than half (54%) of the surveyed female rape victims were under 18 years old when they experienced their first rape (22% were under 12 years old when they experienced their first rape).

An analysis of 1076 sexual assault victims (96% female, 4% male) found that force was used in 80% of the assaults, and in 27% a weapon was used. Vaginal intercourse was involved in 83% of female victimizations, oral assault in 25%, and anal penetration in 17%. General body trauma was seen in 67% of the cases, and genital trauma occurred in 53% of victims. Evidence of semen was found in 48% of all cases (Riggs, Houry, Long, Markovchick, & Feldhaus, 2000).

A community study comparing Latino and Anglo rape rates found a significantly lower incidence among Latinos. The researchers speculate that the lower rate may be attributed to machismo, which requires Latino men to be protective of women (Sorenson & Siegel, 1992). The lower rate, however, may also be attributed to Latinas' greater reluctance to report rape because of the strong emphasis on female virginity and purity in Latino culture.

FIGURE 17.4   Type of Relationship with Offender of Male Victims of Rape and Sexual Assault.
(*Source:* Data from Bureau of Justice Statistics, 2002.)

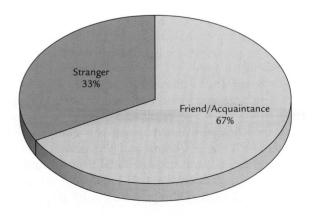

Myths About Rape

Our society has a number of myths about rape, which serve to encourage rather than discourage it. According to one myth, women are to blame for their own rapes, as if they somehow "deserved" them or were responsible for them. In fact, in a large national sample, two-thirds of the women who were raped worried that they might be blamed for their assaults (National Victim Center and Crime Victims Research and Treatment Center [NVC], 1992).

Belief in rape myths is part of a larger belief structure that includes gender-role stereotypes, sexual conservatism, acceptance of interpersonal violence, and the belief that men are different from women. Men are more likely than women to believe rape myths (Brady, Chrisler, Hosdale, & Osowiecki, 1991; Kalof & Wade, 1995; Quackenbush, 1991; Reilly et al., 1992). Sandra Byers and Raymond Eno (1991) found that acceptance of rape-supportive myths among college men is associated with the use of physical force, verbal coercion, and belief in "uncontrollable physical arousal." It is unclear what relationship, if any, exists between exposure to sexually explicit material and acceptance of rape myths; results from studies are contradictory (Allen, Emmers, Gebhardt, & Giery, 1995; Davies, 1997).

Ethnicity and gender appear to influence the acceptance of rape myths. One study found that White and African American women are less likely than men of either group to accept rape myths, interpersonal violence, gender-role stereotyping, and adversarial relationships. Furthermore, African American women's attitudes toward these behaviors and beliefs are significantly less traditional than those of White women (Kalof & Wade, 1995). Another study showed that Latino and White women were less accepting of rape myths and showed more empathy toward persons raped than their male counterparts (Jimenez & Abreu, 2003).

The following list of rape myths can clarify misunderstandings about rape:

- *Myth 1: Women want to be raped.* It is popularly believed that women have an unconscious wish to be raped. The fact that many women have rape fantasies is cited as proof. Also, some believe that many women mean "yes" when they say "no." This myth supports the misconception that a woman enjoys being raped because she sexually "surrenders," and it perpetuates the belief that rape is a sexual act rather than a violent one.

- *Myth 2: Women ask for it.* Many people believe that women "ask for it" by their behavior. According to one study, 25% of male students believed this myth (Holcomb, Holcomb, Sondag, & Williams, 1991). Another study found that provocative dress on the part of the victim of a date rape resulted in a greater perception that the victim was responsible and that the rape was justified (Cassidy & Hurrell, 1995). Despite some attempts to reform rape laws, women continue to bear the burden of proof in these cases (Goldberg-Ambrose, 1992).

- *Myth 3: Women are raped only by strangers.* Women are warned to avoid or distrust strangers as a way to avoid rape; such advice, however, isolates them from normal social interactions. Furthermore, studies indicate that about 70% of all rapes are committed by nonstrangers such as acquaintances, friends, dates, partners, husbands, or relatives (U.S. Department of Justice, 2002).

- *Myth 4: Women could avoid rape if they really wanted to.* This myth reinforces the stereotype that women "really" want to be raped or that they

THE RAPE OF WOMEN by the enemy during war has been common throughout history. Forced sex with the enemy women traditionally was considered "spoils" for soldiers, particularly the victors. Rarely were the rapists held accountable for their behavior. However, that has changed with a recent ruling by the Yugoslav war crimes tribunal. The tribunal was formed in 1993 by the United Nations Security Council to prosecute the alleged creators of the Bosnian Serbs' "ethnic cleansing" campaign.

In early 2001, the Yugoslav war crimes tribunal established "sexual enslavement" as a war crime. The tribunal convicted three Bosnian Serbs of crimes against humanity for the repeated rape and torture of Muslim women in so-called rape camps. The judges held that the rapes by members of the Bosnian Serb armed forces were devised as a terror strategy to force Muslims in Foca to leave after the Serbs overran the Bosnian town in 1992.

The defendants were convicted of 19 counts of war crimes and crimes against humanity, and they received sentences ranging from 12 to 28 years.

The ruling set a legal precedent by outlining the criteria necessary for conviction in future sexual enslavement cases, including the following:

- Women being detained under conditions in which they have no choice but to do what they are told
- Women being reserved for specific men who repeatedly rape them and then pass them on to other soldiers
- Women being denied any control over their lives

Source: Adapted from Comiteau, W. (2001, February 21). "Sexual Enslavement Established as a War Crime." *USA Today,* p. A10.

should curtail their activities. In one study, 25% of male students believed this myth (Holcomb et al., 1991). Women are often warned not to be out after dark alone. Approximately two-thirds of rapes/sexual assaults occur between 6 P.M. and 6 A.M., but nearly 6 out of 10 occur at the victim's home or the home of a friend, relative, or neighbor (Greenfeld, 1997). Women are also approached at work, on their way to or from work, or at their place of worship, or they are kidnapped from shopping centers or parking lots at midday. Restricting women's activities does not seem to have an appreciable impact on rape. Men are often physically larger and stronger than women, making it difficult for women to resist. And assailants catch their victims "off guard" because they choose the time and place of attack.

- *Myth 5: Women cry rape for revenge.* This myth suggests that women who are "dumped" by men accuse them of rape as a means of revenge. About 25% of the men in one study believed this (Holcomb et al., 1991). FBI crime statistics show that only about 2% of rape reports are false; this rate is lower than the rate for most other crimes. False reporting is unlikely because of the many obstacles women face before an assailant is brought to trial and convicted.

- *Myth 6: Rapists are crazy or psychotic.* Very few men who rape are clinically psychotic. The vast majority are psychologically indistinguishable from other men, except that rapists appear to have more difficulty handling feelings of hostility. Studies on date rape find that rapists differ from nonrapists primarily in a greater hostility toward women, acceptance of traditional gender roles, and greater willingness to use force (Cate & Lloyd, 1992).

- *Myth 7: Most rapists are a different race than their victims.* Most rapists and their victims are members of the same ethnic group.

- *Myth 8: Men cannot control their sexual urges.* This myth is based on the belief that men, when subjected to sexual stimuli, cannot control their sexual feelings. This also implies that women have some responsibility for rape by provoking this "uncontrollable" sexuality of men through their attire or appearance (Cowan, 2000). Men, like women, can learn to appropriately and responsibly express their sexuality.

- *Myth 9: Men cannot be raped.* Men can be victims of sexual violence from either men or women. This issue is discussed in more detail later in this section.

Forms of Rape

Rapists may be acquaintances, dates, partners, husbands, fathers, or other family members, as well as strangers.

Date Rape   The most common form of rape is sexual intercourse with a dating partner that occurs against the victim's will, with force or the threat of force. It is known as **date rape** or **acquaintance rape.** One study found that women are more likely than men to define date rape as a crime. Men are less likely than women to agree that the assailant should have stopped when the woman asked him to. Disturbingly, respondents considered date rape less serious when the woman was African American (Foley, Evancic, Karnik, & King, 1995).

Date rapes are usually not planned. Two researchers (Bechhofer & Parrot, 1991) describe a typical date rape:

> He plans the evening with the intent of sex, but if the date does not progress as planned and his date does not comply, he becomes angry and takes what he feels is his right—sex. Afterward, the victim feels raped while the assailant believes that he has done nothing wrong. He may even ask the woman out on another date.

Alcohol and/or drugs are often involved in date rapes. According to one study, 70% of women who had been date-raped had been drinking or taking drugs prior to the rape, and 71% said their assailant had been drinking or taking drugs (Copenhaver & Gauerholz, 1991). Male and female drunkenness is believed by students to be an important cause of date rape (Gillen & Muncher, 1995). There are often high levels of alcohol and drug use among middle school and high school students who have unwanted sex. When both individuals are drinking, they are viewed as more sexual. Men who believe in rape myths are more likely to see alcohol consumption as a sign that females are sexually available (Abbey & Harnish, 1995).

To draw attention to the date rape problem and other sexual coercions by men, many college campuses have held "Take Back the Night" rallies, at which survivors of school assault share their stories and offer support for other victims. Also, many colleges provide extensive prevention education on rape, as well as escort services for participants in late-night activities on campus.

INCIDENCE   Lifetime experience of date rape ranges from 15% to 28% for women, according to various studies. If the definition is expanded to include attempted intercourse as a result of verbal pressure or the misuse of authority, then women's lifetime incidence increases significantly. Among college students, the most likely victimizer is a peer (Bridgeland, Duane, &

Sexual assault peer educators at Brown University dramatize date rape to make students aware of its dynamics.

Stewart, 1995). There is also considerable sexual coercion in gay and lesbian relationships. One study found that 57% of gay men and 45% of lesbian women had experienced some form of sexual coercion. Thirty-three percent of the gay men and 32% of the lesbian women reported unwanted fondling, with 55% of the gay men and 50% of the lesbian women having experienced unwanted penetration. The coercive tactics used against both groups, such as threats of force, physical restraint, and use of alcohol, were similar (Waldner-Haugrud & Gratch, 1997).

CONFUSION OVER CONSENT   There is confusion about what constitutes consent. As we saw in Chapter 8, much sexual communication is nonverbal and ambiguous. The fact that we don't usually give verbal consent for sex indicates the significance of nonverbal clues. Nonverbal communication is imprecise, however, and can be misinterpreted easily if not reinforced verbally. For example, men frequently mistake a woman's friendliness for sexual interest (Johnson et al., 1991; Stockdale, 1993). They often misinterpret a woman's cuddling, kissing, and fondling as a desire to engage in sexual intercourse (Gillen & Muncher, 1995). A woman must make her boundaries clear verbally, and men need to avoid misinterpreting clues. In 2003, Illinois became the first state to pass a law explicitly stating that people have a right to withdraw their consent to sexual activity at any time. The new law specifies that, no matter how far the sexual interaction has progressed, a "no" means no when someone wants to stop (Parsons, 2003). The high-profile

A CHEAP AND POWERFUL SEDATIVE called Rohypnol has found its way into the hands of sexual predators and street gangs across the country. Sometimes referred to as "Roofie," "Rope," "Roche," "Forget-Me Pill," "Mexican Valium," or "R-2," the white, dime-sized drug can be slipped into alcoholic or other beverages and cause severe mental incapacitation and amnesia in its victims. Those committing sexual assault rely on the drug's effects to make it difficult, if not impossible, for the rape victim to recall the circumstances surrounding the assault (Woodworth, 1996).

The effects of Rohypnol are similar to those of alcohol intoxication. Taken alone and in low doses, Rohypnol can produce drowsiness, dizziness, motor uncoordination, memory loss, dry mouth, and visual disturbances. Higher doses can cause coma and death. More commonly, the drug is combined with alcohol, marijuana, or amphetamines. Heroin addicts use Rohypnol to enhance the effects of heroin; cocaine addicts use it to modulate the effect of cocaine binges. Within 10–20 minutes after the drug is taken, the victim will feel dizzy, disoriented, and either hot or cold; she or he will sometimes have trouble speaking or moving. Most victims pass out and have no memory of what happened to them while they were under the drug's influence. The effects may persist for 8 hours or more (Monroe, 1997).

Rohypnol ranks as the most widely prescribed sedative/sleeping pill in Europe, but it is not approved for sale in the United States. Most Rohypnol that is obtained in this country is smuggled from Mexico and South America, where it is sold legally. In 1996, the Drug-Induced Rape Prevention and Punishment Act was passed, making it a felony to distribute Rohypnol or similar substances to someone without that person's knowledge and with the intent to commit violence, including rape, against that person. In response to the threat the drug poses to communities and individuals, the Drug Enforcement Administration has taken specific actions to eliminate Rohypnol abuse and trafficking (Woodworth, 1996).

Three other date-rape drugs are GHB (gamma hydroxybutyric acid), Ketamine, and MDMA (4-methylenedioxymethamphetamine). When GHB, whose street names include "Liquid Ecstasy," "Scope," "Easy Lay," and "Liquid X," is mixed with alcohol, memory loss, unconsciousness, and even death can result. Ketamine, whose street names include "Special K" and "Cat Valium," can also cause such effects in 5–10 minutes, and these can last up to an hour. MDMA, whose street names include "Ecstasy," "XTC," and "E," is the most popular of the club drugs; it reduces inhibitions and eliminates anxiety (Ellis, 2002; Layman, Hughes-McLain, & Thompson, 1998). The Drug Awareness Warning Network (U.S. Department of Health and Human Services, 2002) notes that the use of these four drugs has skyrocketed since the early 1990s. Hospital emergency room reports involving Rohypnol, GHB, Ketamine, or MDMA in 21 of the nation's largest cities increased from 337 in 1994 to more than 6700 in 1999.

To protect yourself from date-rape drugs, it is essential that you watch what you drink at parties or on dates. Do not take any drinks (soda, coffee, or alcohol) from someone you do not know well and trust, and refuse open-container beverages. Never leave your drink unattended, and go to parties with a friend and leave with a friend. If you think you've been drugged, call 911 or get to an emergency room. If possible, try to keep a sample of the beverage (Ellis, 2002; Monroe, 1997).

---

sexual assault case against National Basketball Association star Kobe Bryant has drawn attention to a person's right to change his or her mind at any point during sex, as both parties in the case admit that the encounter began consensually (Karmen, 2003).

Our sexual scripts often assume "yes" unless a "no" is directly stated (Muehlenhard et al., 1992). This makes individuals "fair game" unless they explicitly say "no." But the assumption of consent puts women at a disadvantage. Because men traditionally initiate sex, a man can initiate sex whenever he desires without the woman explicitly consenting. A woman's withdrawal can be considered "insincere" because consent is always assumed. Such thinking reinforces a common sexual script in which men initiate and women refuse so as not to appear "promiscuous." In this script, the man continues, believing that the woman's refusal is "token." Some common reasons for offering "token" refusals include a desire not to appear "loose," unsureness of how the partner feels, inappropriate surroundings, and game playing, which few women (and men) actually engage in (Muehlenhard & McCoy, 1991; Muehlenhard & Rodgers, 1998). Token resistance often occurs after perhaps the tenth date, whereas resistant behavior generally occurs earlier (Shotland & Hunter, 1995). Because some women sometimes say "no" when they mean "coax me," male-female communication may be especially unclear regarding consent.

POSTREFUSAL SEXUAL PERSISTENCE   Men are more likely than women to think of male-female relationships as a "battle of the sexes" (Reilly et al., 1992). Because relationships are conflictual, they believe, refusals are to be expected as part of the battle. A man may feel he should persist because his role is to conquer, even if he's not interested in sex (Muehlenhard & McCoy, 1991; Muehlenhard & Schrag, 1991). Cindy Struckman-Johnson and her colleagues (2003) investigated college students' pursuit of sexual contact with a person after he or she has refused an initial advance, a behavior they call **postrefusal sexual persistence.** They believe that all postrefusal behaviors are sexually coercive in that the other person has already communicated that he or she does not consent to the sexual behavior. The researchers examined tactics in four areas: (1) sexual arousal (e.g., kissing and touching, taking off clothes), (2) emotional manipulation and deception (e.g., repeatedly asking, telling lies), (3) exploitation of the intoxicated (e.g., taking advantage of and purposely getting a target drunk), and (4) physical force (e.g., blocking a target's retreat, using physical restraint) (Figure 17.5). The researchers found that postrefusal sexual persistence was fairly common: Nearly 70% of the students had been subjected to at least one tactic of postrefusal sexual persistence since the age of 16, and one-third indicated that they had used a tactic. More women (78%) than men (58%) reported having been subjected to such tactics since age 16, and more men (40%) than women (26%) reported having used such tactics.

A DATE-RAPER PROFILE   A review of research (Cate & Lloyd, 1992; Koss & Dinero, 1989; Malamuth, 1998; Malamuth, Sockloskie, Koss, & Tanaka, 1991; Muehlenhard & Linton, 1987) found that sexually coercive men, in contrast to noncoercive ones, tend to share several characteristics:

- They hold traditional beliefs about women and women's roles.
- They grew up in a violent home environment.
- They had been involved in delinquency.
- They display hostility toward women.
- They believe in rape-supportive myths.
- They accept general physical violence.
- They express anger and dominance sexually.
- They report high levels of sexual activity.
- They use exploitative techniques.
- They report alcohol and drug use.
- They report early sexual experiences.

Women involved in sexually coercive dating relationships do not differ significantly from those in noncoercive relationships (Cate & Lloyd, 1992).

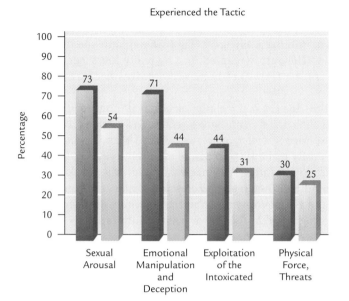

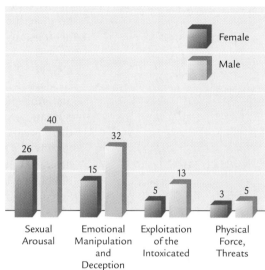

FIGURE 17.5 Percentage of College Men and Women Experiencing Postrefusal Sexual Persistence Tactics. (*Source:* Adapted from Struckman-Johnson, Struckman-Johnson, & Anderson, 2003.)

They have more or less the same levels of self-esteem, assertiveness, feminist ideology, and belief in rape-supportive myths.

Stranger Rape As mentioned previously, the Bureau of Justice Statistics reports that, of the individuals involved, in 30% of cases involving women and 33% of cases involving men who were raped or sexually assaulted, it was done so by a stranger (U.S. Department of Justice, 2002). A typical stranger-rape scenario does not necessarily involve an unknown assailant hiding in the bushes or a stairwell on a dark night. Rather, it is likely to involve a chance meeting with a man who seems friendly and congenial. The woman relaxes her guard because the man seems nice and even protective. He casually maneuvers her to an isolated place—an alley, park, apartment, or house—where the rape occurs.

A study of women age 57–82 who were raped revealed that they were more likely to have been raped by strangers and to have been raped in their homes than younger rape victims (Muram, Miller, & Cutler, 1992). Stranger rapes are more likely to involve guns or knives than date rapes. Almost one-third of stranger rapes involve weapons (Harlow, 1991). A stranger rape is more likely to be taken seriously by the police because it reflects the rape stereotype better than does date or marital rape (Russell, 1990).

Marital Rape By 1993, marital rape had become a crime in all 50 states, although the majority still have exceptions, usually with regard to the use of force. Laws against marital rape, however, have not traditionally been widely enforced.

Many people discount rape in marriage as a "marital tiff" that has little relation to "real" rape (Finkelhor & Yllo, 1985). Women are more likely than men to believe that a husband would use force to have sexual intercourse with his wife. White women are more likely than African American women

The husband cannot be guilty of rape committed by himself upon his lawful wife, for by their mutual matrimonial consent and contract, the wife gives herself in kind unto the husband which she cannot retract.

—Sir Matthew Hale (1609–1676)

to identify sexual coercion in marriage as rape (Cahoon, Edmonds, Spaulding, & Dickens, 1995). When college students were asked to describe marital rape, they created "sanitized" images: "He wants to and she doesn't, so he does anyway," or "They are separated, but he really loves her, so when he comes back to visit, he forces her because he misses her." The realities are very different.

Marital rape victims experience feelings of betrayal, anger, humiliation, and guilt. Following their rape, many wives feel intense anger toward their husbands; others experience constant terror because they are living with their assailant. A minority feel guilt and blame themselves for not being better wives. Others develop negative self-images and view their lack of sexual desire as a reflection of their own inadequacies rather than as a consequence of abuse. Many do not report rape, thinking that no one will believe them. Some do not even recognize that they have been legally raped.

Gang Rape   Gang rape may be perpetrated by strangers or acquaintances. It may be motivated not only by the desire to wield power but also by male-bonding factors (Sanday, 1990). It is a common form of adolescent rape, most often occurring with strangers (Holmes, 1991). Among adults, gang rape disproportionately occurs in tightly knit groups such as fraternities, athletic teams, street gangs, and military units. When gang rape takes place on campus, the attackers may know the woman, who may have been invited to a party or apartment, and alcohol is often involved (O'Sullivan, 1991). The assailants demonstrate their masculinity and "share" a sexual experience with their friends.

One study compared 44 college women who experienced gang sexual assault to 44 who were individually assaulted (Gidyez & Koss, 1990). In general, gang sexual assaults were more violent. The victims of gang assaults offered greater resistance and were more likely to report the attack to the police. Gang assault victims were also more traumatized. As a result, they were more likely to contemplate suicide and seek psychotherapy.

People who would not rape alone may rape in groups for several reasons (O'Sullivan, 1991). Responsibility is diffused in a group; no single individual is to blame. A person may lose his sense of individuality and merge with the group's standards, modeling his behavior on the sexual aggressiveness of the others.

Statutory Rape   Consensual sexual intercourse with a person beneath a state's **age of consent**—the age at which a person is legally deemed capable of giving informed consent—is termed **statutory rape.** Today, the laws are applied to both female and male victims. It may not matter whether the offender is the same age as, older than, or younger than the victim. If a victim is younger than a certain age—varying from age 14 in Hawaii to age 18 in 16 states—the court ignores the consent. The enforcement of statutory rape laws, however, is generally sporadic or arbitrary.

Male Rape   Sexual assaults against males may be perpetrated by other men or by women. Most rapes of men are by other men. (In some states, the word "rape" is used only to define a forced act of vaginal sexual intercourse, whereas an act of forced anal intercourse is termed "sodomy." More recently, states have started using gender-neutral terms such as "sexual assault" or "criminal sexual conduct," regardless of whether the victim is a man or a woman. To be specific, we have chosen the term "male rape.")

According to the Bureau of Justice Statistics (U.S. Department of Justice, 2002), in 2001, 22,930 men age 12 or older in the United States were raped or sexually assaulted. Experts, however, believe that the statistics vastly underrepresent the actual number of males who are raped (National Victim Center, 1997a). Though society is becoming increasingly aware of male rape, the lack of tracking of sexual crimes against men and the lack of research about their effects on victims are indicative of the attitude held by society at large—that although male rape occurs it is not an appropriate topic for discussion.

There are also many reasons male victims do not come forward and report being raped. Perhaps the main reason is the fear of many that they will be perceived as homosexual. Male sexual assault has nothing to do with the sexual orientation of the attacker or the victim, just as a sexual assault does not make the victim gay, bisexual, or heterosexual. Male rape is a violent crime that affects heterosexual men as often as gay men (National Victim Center, 1997a). Furthermore, the sexual orientation of the victim does not appear to be of significance to half of the offenders, and most assailants in male rape are heterosexual (Groth & Birnbaum, 1979; Groth & Burgess, 1980).

Although many people believe that the majority of male rape incidents occur in prison, research suggests that the conditions for male rape are not unique to prison. Rather, all men, regardless of who or where they are, should be regarded as potential victims (Lipscomb et al., 1992). It is believed that 10–20% of all men will be sexually violated at some point in their lifetime ("Men Can Stop Rape," 2000a).

In the aftermath of an assault, many men blame themselves, believing that they in some way granted permission to the rapist (Brochman, 1991). One study of 358 men who had been sexually assaulted by another male found that those exposed to nonconsensual sex were about 3 times more likely to abuse alcohol and have attempted suicide than those free of victimization (Ratner et al., 2003). Male rape victims suffer from fears similar to those felt by female rape victims, including the belief that they actually enjoyed or somehow contributed or consented to the rape. Some men may suffer additional guilt because they became sexually aroused and even ejaculated during the rape. However, these are normal, involuntary physiological reactions connected to the parasympathetic fear response and do not imply consent or enjoyment. Another concern for male rape victims is society's belief that men should be able to protect themselves and that the rape was somehow their own fault.

Research indicates differences in how gay men and heterosexual men react in the aftermath of rape. Gay men may have difficulties in their sexual and emotional relationships with other men and think that the assault occurred because they are gay. Heterosexual men often begin to question their sexual identity and are more disturbed by the sexual aspect of the assault than by the violence involved (Brochman, 1991).

Although they are uncommon, there are some instances of women sexually assaulting men. Despite being threatened with knives and guns, the men were able to have erections (Sarrell & Masters, 1982). After the assault, the men suffered rape trauma syndrome similar to that experienced by women (discussed later). They experienced sexual difficulties, depression, and anxiety. Most felt abnormal because they did respond sexually during the assault. And because they were sexually assaulted by women, they doubted their masculinity. Rape of a man by a woman may not be categorized as rape in states that define rape as forced vaginal penetration by a man. In these cases, the assailant or assailants may be charged under laws governing physical or sexual assaults (Rathus, Nevid, & Fichner-Rathus, 2002).

Motivations for Rape

Most stranger rapes and some acquaintance or marital rapes can be characterized as anger rapes, power rapes, or sadistic rapes (Groth, Burgess, & Holmstrom, 1977). This typology has been very influential, but it is based on interviews with incarcerated stranger rapists. As a result, it may not reflect the motivations of the majority of rapists, who are acquaintances, boyfriends, partners, and husbands.

Anger Rape   Anger rapists are physically violent, and their victims often require hospitalization. Victims are often forced to perform certain sexual acts, such as fellatio, on the assailant. Nicholas Groth (1979) describes anger rape in this way:

> The assault is characterized by physical brutality. Far more actual force is used . . . than would be necessary if the intent were simply to overpower the victim and achieve sexual penetration. . . . His aim is to hurt and debase his victim, and he expresses contempt for her through abusive and profane language. . . .

Power Rape   Power rapes are acts of dominance and control. Typically, the rapist wishes, not to hurt the woman, but to dominate her sexually. The rape may be triggered by what the rapist regards as a slight to his masculinity. He attempts to restore his sense of power, control, and identity by raping. He uses sex to compensate for his sense of inadequacy, applying only as much force as is necessary to rape his victim.

Sadistic Rape   A violent fusion of sex and aggression, sadistic rapes are by far the most brutal. A sadistic rapist finds "intentional maltreatment of his victim intensely gratifying and takes pleasure in her torment, anguish, distress, helplessness and suffering" (Groth & Birnbaum, 1978). Bondage is often involved, and the rape may have a ritualistic quality. The victim is often severely injured and may not survive the attack. Although sadistic rapes are overwhelmingly the most brutal, they are also by far the least frequent.

The Aftermath of Rape

Most rape victims report being roughed up by the rapist, and about 90% report some physical injury (Rape Network, 2000), although the vast majority do not sustain serious injury.

It is important that rape victims gain a sense of control over their lives to counteract the feelings of helplessness they experienced during their rape. They need to cope with the depression and other symptoms resulting from their trauma.

If a man seizes a betrothed virgin in the city and lies with her, then you shall bring them both out to the gate of the city, and you shall stone them to death, the young woman because she did not cry for help, though others could have heard her, and the man because he violated his neighbor's wife.

—*Deuteronomy 22:23–24*

Although White and African American women experience rape at more or less the same rate, the African American woman's experience may be somewhat different. As Gail Wyatt (1992) writes, "In American culture, rape and sexual vulnerability have a unique history because of the sexual exploitation of slaves for over 250 years." Historically, there were no penalties for the rape of Black women by Whites. Because Whites believed that African American women were "promiscuous" by nature, they believed as well that Black women could not actually be raped. According to contemporary White stereotypes, Black women still are promiscuous. There are three important consequences of this stereotype. First, African American women who are raped assume that they are less likely to be believed than White women, especially if the rapist is White. Second, African American women are less likely to report the rape to the police, whom they view as unsympathetic to Blacks in general and to raped Black women in particular. Third, African American women are less likely to seek treatment and support to help the healing process.

Rape Trauma Syndrome   Rape is a traumatic event, to which a woman may have a number of responses. The emotional changes she undergoes as a result of rape are collectively known as **rape trauma syndrome.** Rape survivors are likely to experience depression, anxiety, restlessness, and guilt. These responses are consistent with **posttraumatic stress disorder (PTSD),** a group of characteristic symptoms that follow an intensely distressing event outside a person's normal life experience. PTSD is an official diagnostic category of the American Psychiatric Association (2000). Both Whites and African Americans experience similar symptoms (Wyatt, 1992). A large-scale study found that nearly 31% of all those who had been a victim of forcible rape had developed PTSD (National Victim Center, 1992).

Rape trauma syndrome consists of two phases: an acute phase and a long-term reorganization phase. The acute phase begins immediately following the rape and may last for several weeks or more. In the first few hours after

> If a man seizes a virgin who is not betrothed and lies with her and they are discovered, then the man shall give the young woman's father 50 silver shekels and he shall have her as his wife because he has violated her.
>
> —*Deuteronomy 22:28–29*

Rape crisis centers help sexual assault survivors cope with the effects of rape trauma.

THE ORGANIZATION MEN CAN STOP RAPE empowers men to work with women as allies in preventing rape and other forms of male violence. The organization's Web site (http://www.mencanstoprape.org) includes a listing of its programs, fact sheets, a monthly newsletter, and other important information about males and rape. One valuable fact sheet provides suggestions on helping people who say they were raped:

Supporting survivors: When someone says, "I was raped":

1. *Believe the person.* It is not your role to question whether a rape occurred, but to be there to ease the pain.

2. *Help the person explore the options.* Don't take charge of the situation and pressure rape survivors to do what you think they should do. That's what the rapist did. Give them the freedom to choose a path of recovery that is comfortable for them, even if you'd do it differently. Remember, there is no one right way for a survivor to respond after being assaulted.

3. *Listen to the person.* It is critical that you let survivors in your lives know that they can talk to you about their experience when they are ready. Some may not wish to speak with you immediately, but at some point during the healing process, it is likely that they will come to you for support. When that happens, don't interrupt, or yell, or inject your feelings. Just open your ears to the pain of being raped. Your caring but silent attention will be invaluable.

4. *Ask before you touch.* Don't assume that physical contact, even in a form of a gentle hug, will be comforting to survivors. Many survivors, especially within the first 5 weeks after assault, prefer to avoid sex or simple touching even with those they love and trust. Be patient and give them the space they need, and try your best to not take it personally. One way to signal to survivors that you are ready to offer physical comfort is to sit with an open posture and a hand palm up nearby.

5. *Recognize that you have been assaulted, too.* We can't help but be hurt when someone we love is made to suffer. Don't blame yourself for the many feelings you will likely have in response to learning that someone close to you has been raped. Sadness, confusion, anger, helplessness, fear, guilt, disappointment, shock, anxiety, desperation, compassion—all are common reactions for survivors and their significant others. Awareness of these emotions may ultimately help you to better understand survivors' experiences and support them more effectively.

6. *Never blame them for being assaulted.* No one ever deserves to be raped—no matter what they wore, how many times they had sex before, if they were walking alone at night, if they got drunk, if they were married, or if they went to the perpetrator's room. Even if survivors feel responsible, say clearly and caringly that being raped wasn't their fault.

7. *Get help for yourself.* Whether you reach out to a friend, family member, counselor, religious official, or whomever, make sure you don't go through the experience alone. Most rape crisis centers offer counseling for significant others and family members because they realize that the impact of rape extends far beyond the survivors. Keeping your feelings inside will only make you less able to be there for the survivors. Remember, getting help when needed is a sign of strength, not weakness.

Source: Reprinted by permission of Men Can Stop Rape.

a rape, the woman's responses are characterized by feelings of self-blame and fear. She may believe that she was somehow responsible for the rape: She was wearing something provocative, she should have kept her doors locked, she should have been suspicious of her attacker, and so on. Self-blame, however, only leads to deeper depression (Frazier, 1991).

The woman may be wracked by fears: that the attacker will return, that she may be killed, that others will react negatively. She may act out these feelings through expressive, controlled, or combined reactions. With an expressive response, the woman experiences feelings of fear, anger, rage, anxiety, and tension. If she controls her responses, she hides her feelings and tries to appear calm. Nevertheless, there are often signs of tension, such as difficulty concentrating, hyper-vigilance, nausea, gastrointestinal problems, headaches, irritability, sleeplessness, restlessness, and jumpiness (Krakow et al., 2000). The woman may also feel humiliated, angry, embarrassed, and vengeful. In general, women are more likely than men to display these varied symptoms following rape (Fergusson, Swain-Campbell, & Horwood, 2002; Sorenson & Siegel, 1992).

Following the acute phase, the rape survivor enters the long-term reorganization phase. The rape is a crisis in a woman's life and relationships. If the rape took place at home, the woman may move, fearing that the rapist will return. Some women develop fears of being indoors if the rape occurred indoors, while those raped outside sometimes fear being outdoors. About 3 months after their rapes, 60% of the women in one study reported depression, and 40% rated their depression as severe (Mackey et al., 1992). In a national sample of women, those with histories of sexual assault in both childhood and adulthood had significantly greater odds of lifetime suicide attempts (Ullman & Brecklin, 2002).

Long-term stress reactions are often exacerbated by the very social support systems and staff designed to assist people. These systems and individuals have sometimes proved to be more psychologically damaging to survivors than the rape itself (National Organization for Victim Assistance, 1992), a phenomenon known as secondary victimization. Examples of these support systems and individuals include the criminal justice system, the media, emergency and hospital room personnel, social workers, family and friends, employers, and clergy. Nevertheless, the most important thing you can do to help someone you care about who suffers from symptoms of PTSD is to help her (or him) get professional help (National Victim Center, 1995).

Effects on Sexuality   Typically, women find that their sexuality is severely affected for a short time or longer after a rape (Meana, Binik, Khalife, & Cohen, 1999; Nadelson, 1990). Some begin avoiding sexual interactions, because sex reminds them of the rape. Those who are less depressed, however, have fewer sexual difficulties (Mackey et al., 1992). Two common sexual problems are fear of sex and a lack of sexual desire. Both White and African American women report similar sexual problems (Wyatt, 1992).

Singer Tori Amos, herself a rape survivor, founded the Rape, Abuse, and Incest National Network (RAINN), an organization that operates a national toll-free hotline for victims of sexual assault (see the section "Sex and the Internet").

CHILD SEXUAL ABUSE

Child sexual abuse, by both relatives and nonrelatives, occurs widely. **Child sexual abuse** is *any* sexual interaction (including fondling, sexual kissing, and oral sex, as well as vaginal or anal penetration) between an adult and a prepubescent child. A broad definition also includes nonphysical contact, such as people exposing their genitals to children or having children pose nude or stimulate themselves while being filmed or photographed. It does not matter whether the child is perceived by the adult to be engaging in the sexual activity voluntarily. Because of the child's age, he or she cannot give informed consent; the activity can only be considered as self-serving to the adult. The topic of child sexual abuse has recently received increased national attention due to the problems in the Catholic Church and the allegations of child molestation by pop star Michael Jackson. The revelation of widespread child sexual abuse by priests, bishops, and cardinals has rocked the nation, resulting in resignations, lawsuits, imprisonments, and even deaths.

There are no reliable annual surveys of sexual assaults on children. The U.S. Justice Department's annual National Crime Victimization Survey does not include victims age 12 or younger. According to the latest report of child sexual assault from the Bureau of Justice Statistics, from 1991 through 1996, in one-third of all sexual assaults reported to law enforcement officials the victim was younger than age 12. About 25% of the sexual assault victims under 12 were male, and 84% of the sexual assaults on children under age 12 occurred in a residence or home. The offender was a family member in 47% of incidents, an acquaintance in 49%, and a stranger in only 4% (U.S. Department of Justice, 2000). And these are the *reported* cases. Many cases of child sexual abuse are not reported. Twelve percent of men and 17% of women who participated in the National Health and Social Life Survey (Laumann et al., 1994) reported that they had been sexually touched when they were children. At least 90% of child sexual abuse is committed by men (Finkelhor, 1994). There has been a dramatic decline in reported child sexual abuse in recent years. Possible reasons for the decline include fear among professionals and the public about the legal consequences of false reporting and abatement of the problem resulting from prevention programs (Jones & Finkelhor, 2003).

According to the congressionally mandated Third National Incidence Study of Child Abuse and Neglect (Sedlak & Broadhurst, 1996), girls are sexually abused 3 times as often as boys; however, boys are more likely to be seriously injured or killed during such assaults. The risk of being sexually abused does not vary among races, but children from lower-income groups and from single-parent families are more frequently victimized, as are children who have experienced parental inadequacy or unavailability, conflict, harsh punishment, and emotional deprivation (Finkelhor, 1994). Every incident of child sexual abuse causes the victim a loss of trust and sense of self.

Child sexual abuse is generally categorized in terms of kin relationships. **Extrafamilial abuse** is sexual abuse by unrelated people. **Intrafamilial abuse** is sexual abuse by biologically related people and step-relatives. The abuse may be pedophilic or nonpedophilic. (As explained in Chapter 10, pedophilia refers to an adult's sexual attraction to children.) **Nonpedophilic sexual abuse** refers to an adult's sexual interaction with a child that is not sexually motivated; the most important nonsexual motives are the desire for power and affection.

The victimization may involve force or the threat of force, pressure, manipulation, and loss of trust or innocence. Genital fondling and touching are the most common forms of child sexual abuse (Haugaard & Rappucee, 1998). The most serious or harmful forms of child sexual abuse include actual or attempted penile-vaginal penetration, fellatio, cunnilingus, and anilingus, with or without the use of force. Other serious forms of abuse range from forced digital penetration of the vagina to fondling of the breasts (unclothed) or simulated intercourse without force. Less serious forms range from kissing to intentional sexual touching of the clothed genitals or breasts or other body parts, with or without the use of force (Russell, 1984).

Most victimized children are between 8 and 12 years of age. Although boys and girls are equally likely to be abused (Kilpatrick, Edmunds, & Seymour, 1992), we have more recently recognized the sexual abuse of boys. This neglect has been part of the more general lack of attention to sexual victimization of males. The most likely abusers of girls are stepfathers; boys are most often abused by unrelated males (Levesque, 1994). Regardless of whether the perpetrators were intrafamilial or extrafamilial, child sexual abuse victims are equally traumatized (Whitcomb et al., 1994).

General Preconditions for Child Sexual Abuse

Researchers have found that intrafamilial and extrafamilial sexual abuse share many common elements. Because there are so many variables—such as the age and sex of the victims and perpetrators, their relationship, the type of acts involved, and possible force—we cannot automatically say that abuse within the family is more harmful than extrafamilial abuse.

David Finkelhor (1984) suggests that certain preconditions need to be met by the offender for sexual abuse to occur. These preconditions, which apply to pedophilic, nonpedophilic, incestuous, and nonincestuous abuse, include the following:

- *Being motivated to sexually abuse a child.* This consists of three components: (1) emotional congruence, in which relating sexually to a child fulfills some important emotional need, (2) sexual attraction toward the child, and (3) blockage, in which alternative sources of sexual gratification are not available or are less satisfying.

- *Overcoming internal inhibitions against acting on the motivation.* Inhibitions may be overcome by the use of alcohol or poor impulse control.

- *Overcoming external obstacles to committing sexual abuse.* The most important obstacle appears to be the supervision and protection a child receives from others, such as family members, neighbors, and peers. The mother is especially significant in protecting children. Growing evidence suggests that children are more vulnerable to abuse when the mother is absent, neglectful, or incapacitated in some way, such as through illness, marital abuse, or emotional problems.

- *Undermining or overcoming a child's potential resistance.* The abuser may use outright force or select psychologically vulnerable targets. Certain children may be more vulnerable because they feel insecure, needy, or unsupported and will respond to the abuser's offers of attention, affection, or bribes. Children's ability to resist may be undercut because they are young or naive or have a special relationship to the abuser as friend, neighbor, or family member.

According to Finkelhor (1984), *all* these preconditions or factors must come into play for sexual abuse to occur. Each factor acts as a filter for the previous one. Some people have strong motivation to sexually abuse a child. Of these, however, only some are able to overcome their internal inhibitions, fewer can overcome the external obstacles, and still fewer can overcome the child's resistance.

Forms of Intrafamilial Sexual Abuse

The incest taboo is nearly universal in human societies. **Incest** is generally defined as sexual intercourse between people too closely related to legally marry (usually interpreted to mean father-daughter, mother-son, or brother-sister combinations). (The few documented exceptions to the incest taboo involve brother-sister marriages in the royal families of ancient Egypt, China, Peru, and Hawaii.) Sexual abuse in families can involve blood relatives, most commonly uncles and grandfathers, and step-relatives, most often stepfathers and stepbrothers. In grandfather-granddaughter abuse, the grandfathers frequently have sexually abused their children as well.

It is not clear what type of familial sexual abuse occurs most frequently (Peters et al., 1986; Russell, 1986). Some researchers believe that father-daughter (including stepfather-daughter) abuse is the most common; others think that brother-sister abuse is most common. Still other researchers believe that incest committed by uncles is the most common (Russell, 1986). Mother-son sexual relations are considered to be rare (or are underreported).

Father-Daughter Sexual Abuse   There is general agreement that the most traumatic form of sexual victimization is father-daughter abuse, including that committed by stepfathers. One study indicated that 54% of the girls sexually abused by their fathers were extremely upset (Russell, 1986). In contrast, 25% who were abused by other family members reported the same degree of emotional upset. Over twice as many abused daughters reported serious long-term consequences.

In the past, many people have discounted the seriousness of sexual abuse by a stepfather because there is no *biological* relationship. The emotional consequences are just as serious, however. Sexual abuse by a stepfather still represents a violation of the basic parent-child relationship.

Brother-Sister Sexual Abuse   There are contrasting views concerning the consequences of brother-sister incest. Researchers generally have expressed little interest in it. Most have tended to view it as harmless sex play or sexual exploration between mutually consenting siblings. The research, however, has generally failed to distinguish between exploitative and nonexploitative brother-sister sexual activity. One study found that brother-sister incest can represent a devastating violation of individual boundaries (Canavan, Myers, & Higgs, 1992). Sibling incest needs to be taken seriously (Adler & Schultz, 1995). Diane Russell (1986) suggests that the idea that brother-sister incest is usually harmless and consensual may be a myth. In her study, the average age difference between the brother (age 17.9 years) and sister (10.7 years) is so great that the siblings can hardly be considered peers. The age difference represents a significant power difference. Furthermore, not all brother-sister sexual activity is "consenting"; considerable physical force may be involved. In most instances, the brother initiates the sexual contact and is the dominant person during the sexual contact.

Uncle-Niece Sexual Abuse   Alfred Kinsey (Kinsey, Pomeroy, Martin, & Gebhard, 1953) and Russell (1986) found that the most common form of intrafamilial sexual abuse involves uncles and nieces. Russell reported that almost 5% of the women in her study had been molested by their uncles, slightly more than the percentage abused by their fathers. The level of severity of the abuse was generally less in terms of the type of sexual behavior and the amount of force. Although such abuse did not take place within the nuclear family, many victims found it quite upsetting. One-quarter of the respondents reported long-term emotional effects (Russell, 1986).

Children at Risk

Incest does not discriminate. It occurs in families that are financially privileged and in those of low socioeconomic status. All racial and ethnic groups are vulnerable, as are members of all religious traditions. Boys and girls and infants and adolescents are all victims of incest. Incest occurs between fathers and daughters, fathers and sons, mothers and daughters, and mothers and sons. Perpetrators can be family members or people without a direct blood or legal relationship to the victim, such as a parent's lover or a live-in nanny (National Victim Center, 1997a).

Nevertheless, not all children are equally at risk for sexual abuse. Although any child can be sexually abused, some groups of children are more likely to be victimized than others. A review (Finkelhor & Baron, 1986) of the literature indicated that children at higher risk for sexual abuse include females, preadolescents (particularly those age 10–12), children with absent or unavailable parents, children whose relationships with their parents are poor, children whose parents are in conflict, and children who live with a stepfather. Finkelhor (1994) notes that the most significant risk factors are children separated from their parents and children whose parents have such serious problems that they cannot attend to or supervise their children. The result is emotionally deprived children who are vulnerable to the ploys of sexually abusive individuals.

Effects of Child Sexual Abuse

Until recently, much of the literature on child sexual abuse was anecdotal, case studies, or small-scale surveys of nonrepresentative groups. Nevertheless, numerous well-documented consequences of child sexual abuse hold true for both intrafamilial and extrafamilial abuse. These include both initial and long-term consequences. Many child sexual abuse survivors experience symptoms of posttraumatic stress disorder (McLeer, Deblinger, Henry, & Ovraschel, 1992).

In recent years, some adults have claimed that they repressed their childhood memories of abuse and only later, as adults, recalled them. These accusations have given rise to a fierce controversy about the nature of memories of abuse, as described in the box "The Memory Wars."

Initial Effects   The initial consequences of sexual abuse occur within the first 2 years. The proportion of victimized children who experience these effects ranges from one-quarter to almost two-thirds, depending on the study. Typical effects include the following:

- *Emotional disturbances,* including fear, anger, hostility, guilt, and shame
- *Physical consequences,* including difficulty in sleeping, changes in eating patterns, pregnancy, and STIs (Anderson, 1995)
- *Sexual disturbances,* including significantly higher rates of open masturbation, sexual preoccupation, exposure of the genitals, and indiscriminate and frequent sexual behaviors (Briere & Elliott, 1994; Hibbard & Hartman, 1992)
- *Social disturbances,* including difficulties at school, truancy, running away from home, and early marriages by abused adolescents (a large proportion of homeless youths are fleeing parental sexual abuse [Athey, 1991]).

Ethnicity appears to influence how a child responds to sexual abuse. One study compared sexually abused Asian American children with a random sample of abused White, African American, and Latino children (Rao, Diclemente, & Poulton, 1992). The researchers found that Asian American children suffered less sexually invasive forms of abuse, but they tended to be more suicidal and to receive less support from their parents than non-Asians, and they were less likely to express anger or to act out sexually. These different responses point to the importance of understanding cultural and ethnic context when treating victims.

Long-Term Effects   Although there can be some healing of the initial effects, child sexual abuse may leave lasting scars on the adult survivor (Beitchman et al., 1992; Jumper, 1995). These adults often have significantly higher incidences of psychological, physical, and sexual problems than the general population. Abuse may predispose some women to sexually abusive dating relationships (Cate & Lloyd, 1992).

Long-term effects of child sexual abuse include the following (Beitchman et al., 1992; Briere & Elliott, 1994; Browne & Finkelhor, 1986; Elliott & Briere, 1992; Wyatt, Guthrie, & Notgass, 1992):

- *Depression,* the symptom most frequently reported by adults sexually abused as children
- *Self-destructive tendencies,* including suicide attempts and thoughts of suicide (Jeffrey & Jeffrey, 1991; "Risk of Suicide," 1996)
- *Somatic disturbances and dissociation,* including anxiety and nervousness, eating disorders (anorexia and bulimia), feelings of "spaciness," out-of-body experiences, and feelings that things are "unreal" (De Groot, Kennedy, Rodin, & McVey, 1992; Walker, Katon, Hansom, & Harrop-Griffiths, 1992; Young, 1992)
- *Negative self-concept,* including feelings of low self-esteem, isolation, and alienation
- *Interpersonal relationship difficulties,* including problems in relating to both sexes and to parents, in responding to their own children, and in trusting others
- *Revictimization,* in which women abused as children are more vulnerable to rape and marital violence
- *Sexual problems,* in which survivors find it difficult to relax and enjoy sexual activities or in which they avoid sex and experience hypoactive (inhibited) sexual desire and lack of orgasm (Noll, Trickett, & Putnam, 2003)

One study of revictimization found that among rape survivors about 66% had a history of child sexual abuse (Urquiza & Goodlin-Jones, 1994). Another study found that the women most likely to be harassed at work and in social settings had also been sexually abused as children (Wyatt & Riederle, 1994). There is serious concern that a woman's continued revictimization could lead to a decline in her sense of well-being and make her more vulnerable sexually.

Gay men and lesbian women who were sexually abused as children or adolescents may have additional issues to deal with. This is especially true if they were in the process of becoming aware of their sexual orientation at the time of the abuse. They may have avoided telling anyone about the abuse because of their orientation and their fear of being blamed if their homosexuality were suspected by a family member or caseworker. The community may be unsupportive. The survivor's age and stage in the coming-out process are particularly significant (Arey, 1995; Burke, 1995). The abuse may create or intensify self-directed homophobia.

Sexual Abuse Trauma   The consequences of child sexual abuse may involve a traumatic dynamic that affects the child's ability to deal with the world. Angela Browne and David Finkelhor (1986) suggest a model of **sexual abuse trauma** that contains four components: traumatic sexualization, betrayal, powerlessness, and stigmatization. When these factors converge as a result of sexual abuse, they affect the child's cognitive and emotional orientation to the world. They create trauma by distorting the child's self-concept, worldview, and emotional development. These consequences affect abuse survivors not only as children but also as adults.

TRAUMATIC SEXUALIZATION   Traumatic sexualization refers to the process by which the sexually abused child's sexuality develops inappropriately and he or she becomes interpersonally dysfunctional. Sexually traumatized children learn inappropriate sexual behaviors (e.g., manipulating an adult's genitals for affection), are confused about their sexuality, and inappropriately associate certain emotions (e.g., loving and caring) with sexual activities. Childhood sexual abuse may be associated with the reasons some women later become prostitutes (Simons & Whitbeck, 1991).

Sexual issues may become especially important when abused children become adults. Survivors may experience flashbacks, suffer from sexual difficulties, and develop negative feelings about their bodies. They may also be confused about sexual norms and standards. A fairly common confusion is the belief that sex may be traded for affection. Some women label themselves as "promiscuous," but this label may be more a result of their negative self-image than their actual behavior.

BETRAYAL   Children feel betrayed when they discover that someone on whom they have been dependent has manipulated, used, or harmed them. They may also feel betrayed by other family members, for not protecting them from abuse.

As adults, survivors may experience depression as a manifestation, in part, of extended grief over the betrayal of trusted figures. Some may find it difficult to trust others; others may feel a deep need to regain a sense of trust and become extremely dependent. Distrust may manifest itself in hostility and anger. For adolescents, antisocial or delinquent behavior may be a means of protecting themselves from further betrayal. Anger may express a need for revenge or retaliation, while distrust may manifest itself in social isolation and avoidance of intimate relationships.

POWERLESSNESS   Children experience a basic sense of powerlessness when their bodies and personal space are invaded against their will. This powerlessness is reinforced as the abuse is repeated.

UNTIL THE LATE 1960s, child sexual abuse was believed to be virtually nonexistent. Before the rise of the feminist movement in the 1970s, women's reports of such abuse were generally downplayed or dismissed as neurotic fantasies.

Over the past few decades, however, we have become painfully aware of the extent of child sexual abuse. Most recently, some women and men have stated that they had been sexually abused during childhood but had repressed their memories of it. They later recovered the memory of it, often with the help of therapists. When these recovered memories surface, those accused of the abuse often profess shock and deny that the abuse ever took place. Instead, they insist that these memories are figments of the imagination. Who is to be believed—the person making the accusation or the accused?

The question of whom to believe has given rise to a vitriolic "memory war": recovered memories versus false memories. Each side has its proponents, emotions run high, and debates often deteriorate into shouting matches. A **repressed memory** is a memory of a powerfully traumatic event that is buried in the unconscious and generates symptoms, such as anxiety or nervousness. The individual is unaware of the existence of her or his repressed memories. According to Freud, who developed the concept of repression, the content of the memory could be an actual event or a fantasized one. More recently, research suggests that some victims of incest may suffer from biochemically induced amnesia. Triggered by a severe trauma, the amnesia occurs as a result of a number of complex endocrine and neurological changes. Any immediate and/or latent memory of the

incident is repressed (Matsakis, 1991). A **recovered memory** is a repressed memory brought to consciousness so that the individual is aware of it. It is assumed that the recovered memory describes an actual event that has been repressed. A **false memory** is a fictitious memory of an event that never occurred (Bass & Davis, 1988; Terr, 1994; Yapko, 1994).

According to advocates of recovered memory, repressed memories are brought to consciousness by various therapeutic techniques through which clients are encouraged to reimagine their childhood. Their recovered memories may be very vivid, detailed, and concise (Terr, 1994). If a person has certain symptoms, including anxiety, low sexual desire, or an inability to maintain relationships, some therapists may infer that these are symptoms of repressed memories and that their client was sexually abused. Ellen Bass and Laura Davis wrote in *The Courage to Heal* (1988): "If you are unable to remember any specific instances . . . but still have a feeling that something abusive happened, it probably did." The researchers note that they have not encountered a single woman who "suspected she might have been abused, explored it, and determined that she was not." If the client does not remember the abuse, the therapist may use techniques such as hypnosis, dream interpretation, relaxation, or free association to help in the recovery of memories.

One study of women who were sexually abused as children suggests that abuse memories might be forgotten (Williams, 1994). Researchers reinterviewed 129 adult women in the 1990s who, according to documentation from the 1970s, were confirmed as sexually abused children. In those follow-up interviews seventeen years later,

In adulthood, powerlessness may be experienced as fear or anxiety, with the person feeling unable to control events. Adult survivors often believe that they have impaired coping abilities. This feeling of ineffectiveness may be related to the high incidence of depression and despair among survivors. Powerlessness may also be related to increased vulnerability or revictimization through rape or marital violence; survivors feel incapable of preventing subsequent victimization. Other survivors may attempt to cope with their earlier powerlessness by attempting to control or dominate others.

STIGMATIZATION   Stigmatization—the guilt and shame associated with sexual abuse that are transmitted to abused children and then internalized by them—is communicated in numerous ways. The abuser blames the child or, through his secrecy, communicates a sense of shame. If the abuser pressures the child to keep the abuse a secret, the child may also internalize feelings the researchers found that 38% of them did not remember the abuse that had been confirmed earlier. The study did not indicate whether these women suffered symptoms consistent with repression of abuse.

In the past several years, there has been a response to the recovered memory movement by parents who assert that they have been falsely accused. One group of accused parents began the False Memory Foundation (Yapko, 1994). They developed the term **false memory syndrome,** which they define as a collection of fictitious memories elicited by a therapist and believed by the client to be authentic and accurate. ("False memory syndrome" is not recognized by any scientific or psychiatric organization.)

Critics of recovered memories make several points:

- *There is a lack of evidence of memory repression* There are no controlled laboratory experiments supporting the theory that people repress memories of traumatic events. Studies indicate that concentration camp and crime victims over age 6, for example, have not repressed their traumatic experiences (Crews, 1995).

- *Memories are unreliable and impermanent.* Events are forgotten, reconstructed, combined with other events, and remembered. We use our memories to create a narrative or story about our self; they help us to explain who we are and to form and validate our self-image. Sometimes, we combine and confuse memories or even invent them to validate ourselves. Early memories, for example, are often distorted through a normal "retrospective bias" (Boakes, 1995; Loftus & Ketcham, 1994).

- *People have the ability to "create" false memories.* Laboratory experiments demonstrate that false memories can be created by repeatedly questioning subjects until they "remember" events that never actually happened. Some young children were tricked, for example, into falsely believing that they had once been hospitalized (Ceci, Loftus, Leichtman, & Bruck, 1994).

- *People are susceptible to therapeutic suggestion.* Some therapists may unwittingly plant the suggestion in the minds of their clients that they were abused (Yapko, 1994).

What are we to make of the recovered- versus false-memory debate? In a review of the research, the American Psychological Association (1994) came to several conclusions:

- Most people who were sexually abused as children at least partially remember the abuse.

- Memories of sexual abuse that have been forgotten may later be remembered.

- False memories of events that never happened may occur.

- The process by which accurate or inaccurate recollections of childhood abuse are made is not well understood.

Children can be highly suggestible, so the interviewing style of therapists is important in obtaining accurate information. Interviewers, for example, must be careful in phrasing questions so as not to be leading and suggestive. Specific guidelines have been proposed for avoiding suggesting abuse (Goldberg, 1998), and we can hope that therapists who use techniques that result in false memories will be identified and avoided. Because firm scientific conclusions cannot be drawn at this time, the debate is likely to continue.

of shame and guilt. Children's prior knowledge that their family or community considers such activities deviant may contribute to their feelings of stigmatization.

As adults, survivors may feel extreme guilt or shame about having been sexually abused. They may have low self-esteem because they feel that the abuse made them "damaged merchandise." They also feel different from others because they mistakenly believe that they alone have been abused.

Treatment Programs

It is common now to deal with child sexual abuse, especially father-daughter sexual abuse, by offering therapy programs that function in conjunction with the judicial system, rather than by breaking up the family by removing the child or the offender (Nadelson & Sauzier, 1986). Because the offender is often also the breadwinner, incarcerating him may greatly increase the family's

One objective of child abuse prevention programs is to teach children the difference between "good" touching and "bad" touching.

emotional distress. The district attorney's office may work with clinicians in evaluating the existing threat to the child and deciding whether to prosecute or to refer the offender for therapy—or both. The goal is not simply to punish the offender but to try to help the victim and the family come to terms with the abuse.

Many of these clinical programs work on several levels simultaneously; that is, they treat the individual, the father-daughter relationship, the mother-daughter relationship, and the family as a whole. They work on developing self-esteem and improving the family and marital relationships. If appropriate, they refer individuals to alcohol- or drug-abuse treatment programs.

A crucial component of many treatment programs is individual and family attendance at self-help group meetings. Self-help groups are composed of incest survivors, offenders, mothers, and other family members.

Preventing Sexual Abuse

The idea of working to prevent sexual abuse is relatively new (Berrick & Barth, 1992). Prevention programs began over a decade ago, a few years after programs were started to identify and help child and adult survivors of sexual abuse. Such prevention programs have been hindered, however, by several factors. In confronting these problems, child abuse prevention (CAP) programs have been very creative. Most programs include group instruction in schools, either as a component of regular classroom instruction or as an after-school program (Daro, 1994). These programs typically address three audiences: children, parents, and professionals. CAP programs aimed at children use plays, puppet shows, films, videotapes, books, and comic books to teach children that they have rights: to control their own bodies (including their genitals), to feel "safe," and to not be touched in ways that feel confusing or wrong. The CAP programs stress that children are not at fault when such abuse does occur. These programs generally teach children three strategies (Gelles & Conte, 1991): (1) to say "no," (2) to get away from the assailant or situation, and (3) to tell a trusted adult about what happened (and to keep telling until they are believed). It is not known how well these strategies work, however, because assessment studies cannot ethically duplicate the various situations.

Other programs focus on educating parents, who, it is hoped, will in turn educate their children. These programs seek to help parents discover abuse or abusers by identifying warning signs. Such programs, however, need to be culturally sensitive, as Latinos and Asians may be reluctant to discuss these matters with their children (Ahn & Gilbert, 1992). Parents seem reluctant in general to deal with sexual abuse issues with their children, according to Finkelhor (1986). Many do not feel that their children are at risk, are fearful of unnecessarily frightening their children, and may also feel uncomfortable about talking with their children about sex in general, much less about such taboo subjects as incest. In addition, parents may not believe their own children's reports of abuse or may feel uncomfortable confronting a suspected abuser, who may be a partner, uncle, friend, or neighbor.

CAP programs also seek to educate professionals, especially teachers, physicians, mental health workers, and police officers. Because of their close contact with children and their role in teaching children about the world, teachers are especially important. Professionals are encouraged to watch for signs of sexual abuse and to investigate children's reports of such abuse.

Overall, CAP programs have beneficial outcomes and appear to be most valuable for children age 7–12. Research on any negative outcomes is limited (Daro, 1994).

In 1997, the U.S. Supreme Court ruled in favor of what is now referred to as Megan's Law. Enacted in 1995, the law calls for schools, day-care centers, and youth groups to be notified about moderate-risk sex offenders in the community. For high-risk offenders, the law requires that the police go door-to-door notifying neighborhood residents. It also requires sex offenders who have been paroled or recently released from prison to register with local authorities when moving to a community. The law is named for Megan Kanka, a 7-year-old who was raped and murdered by a twice-convicted sex offender who lived across the street from her. Although parts of the law have been challenged, the Supreme Court has rejected objections (Carelli, 1998). Actually, the Court ruled in 2003 that photos of convicted offenders may be posted on the Internet (CNN.com/Law Center, 2003). Most communities see the law as a welcome victory for their children.

SEXUAL HARASSMENT, anti-gay harassment and discrimination, sexual aggression, and sexual abuse of children represent the darker side of human sexuality. Their common thread is the humiliation, subordination, or victimization of others. But we need not be victims. We can educate ourselves and others about these activities; we can work toward changing attitudes and institutions that support these destructive and dehumanizing behaviors.

SUMMARY

Sexual Harassment

- *Sexual harassment* includes two distinct types of illegal harassment: the abuse of power for sexual ends and the creation of a *hostile environment*. Sexual harassment may begin as early as middle childhood. In college, about one-fifth to one-half of female students and male students have experienced some form of sexual harassment from other students, faculty members, or administrators.

- In the workplace, both fellow employees and supervisors may engage in sexual harassment. In many instances, harassment may not represent sexual attraction as much as an exercise of power.

Harassment and Discrimination Against Gay, Lesbian, Bisexual, and Transgendered People

- Researchers have identified two forms of discrimination or bias against gay, lesbian, bisexual, and transgendered people: heterosexual bias and anti-gay prejudice. *Heterosexual bias* includes ignoring, segregating, and submerging gay, lesbian, bisexual, and transgendered people into larger categories that make them invisible.

- *Anti-gay prejudice* is a strong dislike, fear, or hatred of gay, lesbian, bisexual, and transgendered people. It is acted out through offensive language, discrimination, and violence. Anti-gay prejudice is derived from a deeply rooted insecurity concerning a person's own sexuality and gender identity, a strong fundamentalist religious orientation, or simple ignorance.

Sexual Aggression

- *Rape* is penile-vaginal penetration performed against a woman's will. *Sexual aggression* refers to any sexual activity against a person's will through the use of force, argument, pressure, alcohol/ drugs, or authority. *Sexual coercion,* a broader term than "rape" or "sexual aggression," includes arguing, pleading, and cajoling, as well as force or the threat of force. *Sexual assault* is the term used by the legal system for criminal sexual contact that does not meet the legal definition of rape.

- Myths about rape encourage rape by blaming women. Men are more likely than women to believe rape myths.

- *Date rape* is the most common form of rape. Date rapes are usually not planned, and alcohol or drugs are often involved. There is also considerable sexual coercion in gay relationships; there is less coercion in lesbian relationships. There is extensive confusion over and argument about consent issues, especially because much sexual communication is nonverbal and ambiguous.

- The majority of reported rapes are by strangers. Stranger rapes are more likely to involve guns or knives than date rapes.

- In every state, a husband can be prosecuted for raping his wife. Marital rape victims experience feelings of betrayal, anger, humiliation, and guilt.

- Gang rape may be perpetrated by strangers or acquaintances. It may be motivated by a desire for power and by male-bonding factors.

- Most male rape victims have been raped by other men. Because the motive in sexual assaults is power and domination, sexual orientation is often irrelevant.

- Most stranger rapes (and some acquaintance or marital rapes) can be characterized as anger rapes, power rapes, or sadistic rapes. This typology, however, may not reflect the motivations of the majority of rapists, who are acquaintances, boyfriends, partners, or husbands.

- The emotional changes women undergo as a result of rape are collectively known as *rape trauma syndrome.* These women may experience depression, anxiety, restlessness, and guilt. The symptoms following rape are consistent with *posttraumatic stress disorder (PTSD).* Rape trauma syndrome consists of an acute phase and a long-term reorganization phase. Women find their sexuality severely affected for a short time or for a longer period after rape.

Child Sexual Abuse

- *Child sexual abuse* is any sexual interaction between an adult and a prepubescent child. *Incest* is sexual intercourse between individuals too closely related to legally marry.

- The preconditions for sexual abuse include having the motivation to sexually abuse a child, overcoming internal inhibitions against acting on the motivation, overcoming external obstacles, and undermining or overcoming the child's potential resistance.

- The initial effects of abuse include physical consequences and emotional, social, and sexual disturbances. Child sexual abuse may leave lasting scars on the adult survivor.

- *Sexual abuse trauma* includes traumatic sexualization, betrayal, powerlessness, and stigmatization. Treatment programs simultaneously treat the individual, the father-child relationship, the mother-child relationship, and the family as a whole.

- Child abuse prevention (CAP) programs have been hindered by different concepts of appropriate sexual behavior, adult fear of discussion, and controversy over sex education. CAP programs generally teach children to say "no," to get away from the assailant or situation, and to tell a trusted adult about what happened.

Sex and the Internet

The Rape, Abuse, and Incest National Network

The Rape, Abuse, and Incest National Network (RAINN) is a nonprofit organization based in Washington, DC, that operates a national toll-free hotline for survivors of sexual assault (1-800-656-HOPE). RAINN offers free, confidential counseling and support 24 hours a day. Founded by singer Tori Amos, RAINN also has an information-filled Web site (http://www.rainn.org). Go to the RAINN site and answer the following questions:

- What type of information is provided?
- What are some of the RAINN highlights?
- Who are the celebrity supporters and corporate sponsors?
- What is in the "What's New" section?
- What types of stories are published in the RAINN monthly newsletter?
- How can one support RAINN?

SUGGESTED WEB SITES

Feminist Majority Foundation
http://www.feminist.org
Discusses their latest projects and gives information about feminist issues.

Human Rights Campaign
http://www.hrc.org
Offers the latest information on political issues affecting lesbian, gay, bisexual, and transgendered Americans.

National Clearinghouse on Child Abuse and Neglect Information
http://www.calib.com/nccanch
Serves as a resource for professionals and others seeking information on child abuse and neglect and child welfare.

National Coalition Against Domestic Violence
http://www.ncadv.org
Provides information about domestic violence and suggestions for getting help.

National Sexual Violence Resource Center
http://www.nsvrc.org
A project of the Pennsylvania Coalition Against Rape; is a resource for information about rape and links to other sites.

U.S. Department of Justice, Bureau of Justice Statistics
http://www.ojp.usdoj.gov
Gives statistics and information on legal and enforcement issues related to victimization crime, as well as press releases.

U.S. Equal Employment Opportunity Commission
http://www.eeoc.gov
Provides information on federal laws prohibiting job discrimination, and gives directions for filing a charge.

SUGGESTED READING

Maltz, Wendy. (2001). *The Sexual Healing Journey.* New York: HarperCollins. A comprehensive guide designed to help survivors of sexual abuse improve their relationships and discover the joys of sexual intimacy.

Raine, Nancy Venable. (1999). *After Silence: Rape and My Journey Back.* New York: Three Rivers Press/Crown. An award-winning book that describes the long-term aftereffects of rape through an account of the author's own experience as a rape victim.

Scarce, Michael. (1997). *Male on Male Rape.* New York: Plenum. One of few resources for survivors of male rape, written from the perspective of a rape survivor.

Schewe, P. A. (2002). *Preventing Violence in Relationships: Interventions Across the Lifespan.* Washington, DC: American Psychological Association. Focuses on building healthy relationships and preventing family violence.

Wiehe, Vernon R. (1997). *Sibling Abuse: Hidden Physical, Emotional, and Sexual Trauma.* Thousand Oaks, CA: Sage. Defines terminology, describes various forms of abuse, cites incidence, and offers firsthand accounts to help us better understand sibling violence.

For links, articles, and study material, go to the McGraw-Hill Web site, located at http://www.mhhe.com/strong5

18

Sexually Explicit Materials, Prostitution, and Sex Laws

"*I was only sixteen when I traveled to Peru with Carlos, who was twenty-nine. We were in Lima for two days, and while we were there, Carlos took me to a hotel so we could both have sex with prostitutes. At the time, I did not really understand what was happening until after it occurred. Carlos knew that I was a virgin and thought this would be a fantastic way for me to become a 'man.' I felt embarrassed, dirty, and ashamed of myself.*"

—24-year-old Latino male

"*She (my aunt) actually started molesting me when I was six. She would come home late at night, drunk, and carry me into her bed so that she could perform oral sex on me. She molested me until I was twelve years old. She was a prostitute, so later in my molestation she tried to include her tricks, but I cried my way out of it every time.*"

—26-year-old African-Mexican–Native American female

"*My boyfriend and I sometimes use X-rated movies while we have sex. We have learned some new techniques from them, and they really help us get turned on. Some of our friends had recommended that we get them. At first, we were a little hesitant to use them, but now watching the movies has become a regular part of our sex. But I wonder if something is wrong with us having to use the movies. And, at times, I still feel uncomfortable using them. I sure haven't told any of my friends about them.*"

—21-year old White female

*M*ONEY AND SEX are bound together in the production and sale of sexually explicit material and in prostitution. Money is exchanged for sexual images or descriptions contained in videos, films, electronic media, magazines, books, music, and photographs that depict people in explicit or suggestive sexual activities. Money is also exchanged for sexual services provided by streetwalkers, call girls, massage parlor workers, and other sex workers. The sex industry is a multibillion-dollar enterprise with countless millions of consumers and customers. As a nation, however, we feel profoundly ambivalent about sexually explicit material and prostitution. Many people condemn it as harmful, immoral, and exploitative and wish to censor or eliminate it. Others see it as a harmless and even beneficial activity, an erotic diversion, or an aspect of society that cannot (or should not) be regulated; they believe censorship and police action do greater harm than good.

In this chapter, we examine sexually explicit material, including depictions of sex in popular culture, the role of technology in developing new forms of sexually explicit material, the effects of sexually explicit material, and censorship issues. We also examine prostitution, focusing on females and males working in the sex industry, the legal issues involved, and the impact of HIV/AIDS.

SEXUALLY EXPLICIT MATERIAL IN CONTEMPORARY AMERICA

Studying sexually explicit material objectively is difficult because such material touches deep and often conflicting feelings we have about sexuality. Many people enjoy it, others find it degrading, and still others believe it may lead to violence or moral chaos.

Pornography or Erotica: Which Is It?

Much of the discussion about sexually explicit material concerns the question of whether such material is, in fact, erotic or pornographic—that is, whether viewing it causes positive or harmful outcomes. Unfortunately, there is a lack of agreement about what constitutes erotica or pornography. Part of the problem is that "erotica" and "pornography" are subjective terms, and the line separating them can be blurred. **Erotica** describes sexually explicit material that can be evaluated positively. (The word "erotica" is derived from the Greek *erotikos*, meaning a love poem.) It often involves mutuality, respect, affection, and a balance of power (Stock, 1985) and may even be considered to have artistic value. **Pornography** represents sexually explicit material that is generally evaluated negatively. ("Pornography" is a nineteenth-century word derived from the Greek *porne*, meaning prostitute, and *graphos*, meaning depicting.) Although the U.S. judicial system has not been able to agree on a consistent definition of "pornography," such material might include anything that depicts sexuality and causes sexual arousal in the viewer. Webster's *New World Collegiate Dictionary* defines pornography as "writing, pictures, etc. intended to arouse sexual desire." Sexually explicit materials are legal in the United States; however, materials that are considered to be obscene are not. Although the legal definition of **obscenity** varies, the term generally implies a personal or societal judgment that something is offensive; it comes from the Latin word for "filth" (Bullough & Bullough, 1995). Often, material depicting the use of violence and aggression or degrading and dehumanizing situations is deemed obscene. Because such a determination involves a judgment, critics often point to the subjective nature of this definition. (Obscenity and the law are discussed in detail later in the section.)

The same sexually explicit material may evoke a variety of responses in different people. Some people may enjoy the material, others may be repulsed, and still others may simultaneously feel aroused and guilty. "What I like is erotica, but what you like is pornography" may be a facetious statement, but it's not entirely untrue. It has been found that people view others as more adversely affected than themselves by sexually explicit material (Gunther, 1995). Judgments about sexually explicit material tend to be relative.

Because of the tendency to use "erotica" as a positive term and "pornography" as a negative term, we will use the neutral term "sexually explicit material" whenever possible. **Sexually explicit material** is material such as photographs, videos, films, magazines, and books whose primary themes, topics, or depictions involve sexuality or cause sexual arousal; the genitals or intimate sexual behaviors typically are shown. Sometimes, however, the context of studies we are citing may require us to use either "erotica" or

How can you accuse me of liking pornography when I don't even have a pornograph?

—*Groucho Marx (1895–1977)*

Obscenity is whatever happens to shock some elderly and ignorant magistrate.

—*Bertrand Russell (1872–1970)*

"pornography" rather than "sexually explicit material." This is especially true if the studies use those terms or are clearly making a positive or negative evaluation.

Sexually Explicit Material and Popular Culture

In the nineteenth century, technology transformed the production of sexually explicit material. Cheap paper and large-scale printing, combined with mass literacy, created an enormous market for books and drawings, including sexually explicit material. Today, technology is once again extending the forms in which this material is conveyed.

In recent decades, sexually explicit material, especially softcore, has become an integral part of popular culture. *Playboy, Penthouse,* and *Hustler* are among the most widely circulated magazines in America, selling about 5 million copies a month (Marvel, 2002). The depiction of sexual activities is not restricted to books and magazines, however. Various establishments offer live entertainment. Bars, for example, feature topless dancers. Some clubs or adult entertainment establishments employ erotic dancers who expose themselves and simulate sexual acts before their audience. The Internet and video/VCR/DVD revolutions have been so great that homes have largely supplanted adult theaters or "porno" movie houses as sites for viewing "X-rated" movies.

> Perversity is the muse of modern literature.
>
> —*Susan Sontag*

The sexually explicit material industry is big business in the United States: Millions of people are spending billions of dollars each year. Frank Rich (2001), in his article "Naked Capitalists" in *The New York Times Magazine,* describes the magnitude of the "porno" industry:

> The $4 billion that Americans spend on video pornography is larger than the annual revenue accrued by either the N.F.L., the N.B.A. or Major League Baseball. But that's literally half of it: the porn business is estimated to total between $10 billion to $14 billion annually in the United States when you toss in porn networks and pay-for-view movies on cable and satellite, Internet Web sites, in-room hotel movies, phone sex, sex toys and that archaic medium of my own occasionally misspent youth, magazines.

An estimated 700 million X-rated videos and DVDs are rented or bought annually in the United States. In 2001, an estimated 11,000 hardcore videos were released in Los Angeles, far exceeding the 400 Hollywood studio releases. As noted in Chapter 1, the word "sex" is the most frequent search term used on the Internet today (Cooper, Scherer, Boies, & Gordon, 1999; Freeman-Longo & Blanchard, 1998; Marvel, 2002; Rich, 2001; Webb, 2001).

Videos and DVDs have had a profound effect on *who* views erotic films. Adult movie houses were the domain of men; relatively few women entered them. Most explicit videos, as well as books and magazines, have been marketed to heterosexual men. But with erotic videos available for viewing in the privacy of the home, women have become consumers of sexually explicit material. The inclusion of women in the audience has led to the proliferation of **femme porn**, sexually explicit material catering to women and heterosexual couples. Femme porn avoids violence, depicts emotional intimacy, is less male centered, and is more sensitive to women's erotic fantasies. (For more about other types of sexually oriented forms of mass media, see Chapter 1.)

The video/VCR/DVD and Internet revolution drove "porno" movie houses out of business as individuals became able to view X-rated videos, DVDs, and Web sites in the privacy of their own homes.

A Blurring of Boundaries   As sexual themes, ideas, images, and music increasingly appear in art, literature, and popular culture, the boundaries blur between what is socially acceptable and what is considered obscene. Thus, we are confronted with questions like these: Is Eminem's crotch grabbing obscene or expressive? Is the explicit talk show of Jerry Springer prurient or informative? Is the titillating radio show of Howard Stern vulgar or entertaining?

Looking at beauty pageants, we can see how essentially sexual portrayals of women may be defined as either legitimate or illegitimate. Women walking down a runway in bathing suits while their beauty and grace are judged is an all-American tradition. To some people, however, such pageants exploit women as sex objects.

The older one grows, the more one likes indecency.

— *Virginia Woolf (1882–1941)*

Content and Themes   Many of the themes found in sexually explicit material are also found in the mainstream media. Music videos, TV shows, and movies, for example, contain sexual scenes and innuendoes, images of the subordination of women, and acts of violence. They differ primarily in their levels of explicitness. When researchers analyzed the contents of sexually explicit media, they found four common themes: diverse sexual activity, high levels of sexual desire, pleasure as the purpose of sexual activity, and many readily available sexual partners (Schlosser, 1997).

Many "mainstream" sexually explicit videos target a male, heterosexual audience and portray stereotypes of male sexuality: dominant men with huge, erect penises, able to "last long" and satisfy acquiescent women who are driven mad by their sexual prowess. The major theme of the videos is sexual behavior; they show fellatio, cunnilingus, and vaginal and anal sex and climax with the man ejaculating on the woman's body. Very little focus is on relationships, emotional intimacy, or nonsexual aspects of life. Some criticize these films as reinforcing an unhealthy and unrealistic image of sexuality: that men are all-powerful and that women are submissive and objects, deriving all sexual satisfaction from male domination.

As touched on previously, however, there is evidence that some sexually explicit videos are moving away from impersonal sex to more romantic views of sexual encounters (Quackenbush, Strassberg, & Turner, 1995). This trend may be the result of women's becoming an increasingly large segment of the market. Women traditionally place sexual relationships within a romantic or relational context. One study found that women who viewed

The performances of pop music artists are often highly sexual; Beyonce Knowles uses sexuality as an integral theme in her videos and concerts, as do many pop artists.

videos targeted at a female audience were more aroused, absorbed, and positive about such videos than they were toward impersonal videos (Mosher & MacIan, 1994).

With few exceptions, most studies are of material featuring White heterosexuals. As a result, we know very little about sexually explicit material directed toward ethnic groups such as African Americans and Latinos, or toward gay men and lesbian women. Such research is limited or nonexistent.

Gay male sex is rarely shown in heterosexual videos, presumably because it would make heterosexual men uncomfortable. But heterosexual videos may sometimes portray lesbian sex because many heterosexual men find such depictions sexually arousing.

The Effects of Sexually Explicit Material

There are a number of concerns about the effects of sexually explicit material: Does it cause people to engage in "deviant" acts? Is it a form of sex discrimination against women? And, finally, does it cause violence against women?

Sexual Expression   People who read or view sexually explicit material usually recognize it as fantasy; they use it as a release from their everyday lives. Exposure to such material temporarily encourages sexual expression and may activate a person's *typical* sexual behavior pattern.

Sexually explicit material deals with fantasy sex, not sex as we know it in the context of human relationships. This sex usually takes place in a world in which people and situations are defined in exclusively sexual terms. People are stripped of their nonsexual connections.

> Western man, especially the Western critic, still finds it very hard to go into print and say: "I recommend you go and see this because it gave me an erection."
>
> —*Kenneth Tynan (1927–1980)*

> The worst that can be said about pornography is that it leads not to anti-social acts but to the reading of more pornography.
>
> —*Gore Vidal*

People are interested in sexually explicit material for a number of reasons. First, they enjoy the sexual sensations erotica arouses; it can be a source of intense pleasure. Masturbation or other sexual activities, pleasurable in themselves, may accompany the use of sexually explicit material or follow it. Second, since the nineteenth century, sexually explicit material has been a source of sexual information and knowledge. Eroticism generally is hidden from view and discussion. When sexuality is discussed in the family, in schools, or in public, it is typically discussed moralistically, rationally, or objectively. And most discussions are in the context of sexual intercourse; other activities are avoided. Because the erotic aspects of sexuality are rarely talked about, sexually explicit material can fill the void. Third, sexually explicit material, like fantasy, may provide an opportunity for people to rehearse sexual activities. Fourth, reading or viewing sexually explicit material to obtain pleasure or to enhance one's fantasies or masturbatory experiences may be regarded as safer sex.

Sexually explicit material may perform an additional function for those who are HIV-positive or have AIDS. Because having this disease creates anxieties about HIV transmissions to others, sexually explicit material permits those with HIV or AIDS to explore their own sexuality with masturbatory images and scenes while refraining from potentially risky sexual encounters with a partner.

Variation in Personal Response　Men are by far the largest consumers of sexually explicit material and tend to react more positively to it than women (Thompson, Chaffee, & Oshagan, 1990). Men more than women believe that sexually explicit material has positive effects, such as sexual release and a lowering of inhibitions. Both men and women believe, however, that sexually explicit material may also have negative effects, such as dehumanizing women and causing a loss of respect between men and women.

> Obscenity is best left to the minds of man. What's obscene to one may not offend another.
>
> —*William O. Douglas (1898–1980)*

Why does one person evaluate sexually explicit material negatively and another positively? The answer seems to lie in the individual's emotional response to the material. A person's erotophobic/erotophilic attitudes affect his or her response to sexually explicit material (see Chapter 9). Erotophilic people tend to respond positively to such material; erotophobic people do not. Ira Reiss (1990) writes:

> Our reactions to sexually arousing films or books provide insight into our personal sexual attitudes. What we really are reacting to is not the objective material but rather a projection of our own innermost feelings concerning the type of sexuality presented. We may feel that sexuality being portrayed is too revealing, too embarrassing, too suggestive, or too private.

> Pornography is the theory and rape is the practice.
>
> —*Robin Morgan*

Sexual Aggression　In 1970, the President's Commission on Pornography and Obscenity concluded that pornography did not cause harm or violence. It recommended that all legislation restricting adult access to it be repealed as inconsistent with the First Amendment.

In the 1980s, President Ronald Reagan established a new pornography commission under Attorney General Edwin Meese. In 1986, the Attorney General's Commission on Pornography stated that "the most prevalent forms of pornography" were violent; it offered no evidence, however, to substantiate its assertion (U.S. Attorney General's Commission on Pornography [AGCOP], 1986). There is, in fact, no evidence that the majority of sexually explicit material is violent; actually, very little contains aggression, physical violence, or rape.

In the 1970s, feminists and others working to increase rape awareness began to call attention to the violence against women portrayed in the media. They found rape themes in sexually explicit material especially disturbing, arguing that those images reinforced rape myths. Again, however, there is no evidence that nonviolent sexually explicit material is associated with actual sexual aggression against women. Even the conservative commission on pornography agreed that nonviolent sexually explicit material had no such effect (AGCOP, 1986). It did assert that "some forms of sexually explicit materials bear a causal relationship . . . to sexual violence," but it presented no scientific proof.

Researchers have studied the relationship between violent sexually explicit material and aggression toward women. Most studies have been experimental; that is, male college students were exposed to various media, and factors related to their attitudes about, for example, the rape of women were measured. In studying male responses to depictions of rape, researchers have found that realistic portrayals of rape tend not to be arousing to men and may actually produce negative emotional responses (Bauserman, 1998). This is in contrast to the responses that are elicited to "rape myths," or unrealistic portrayals in films in which women become aroused and participate willingly. In a national sample of men enrolled in postsecondary education, researchers reported that men having the highest levels of hostility, sexual "promiscuity," and pornography use were the most likely to report a history of sexual aggression against women. But the researchers noted that we cannot conclude from this analysis that pornography use causes or is an outcome of aggressive sexual tendencies (Malamuth, Addison, & Koss, 2001). In another study, researchers found no association between university men's social desirability, sensation seeking, attitudes toward women, rape myth acceptance, hypermasculinity, or erotophobia-erotophilia and time spent surfing sexually explicit Internet sites. The only factor related to the time the men spent surfing the sexually explicit sites was their history of viewing sexually explicit media (Barak, Fisher, Belfry, & Lashambe, 1999).

In yet another study, undergraduate men were given a choice of 14 sexually explicit videos to view, including ones depicting common sexual acts, novel sexual acts, sexually insatiable females, sexual violence, and child pornography. Although half of the men declined to view any sexually explicit videos, the men who decided to view a video chose a broad range. "Female insatiability" films were the most common choice (15%), and the violence (4%) and child sexuality (3%) films were the least frequently chosen. Interestingly, men with lower intelligence and higher aggressive/antisocial tendencies had a higher preference for violent sexual stimuli (Bogaert, 1993, 2001).

Contact with sexually explicit material is a self-regulated choice, and research on factors related to such self-directed behavior is very limited: "Existing findings by and large fail to confirm fears of strong antisocial effects of self-directed exposure to sexually explicit media" (Fisher & Barak, 2001). Furthermore, findings from experimental studies—the paradigm for most prior studies—cannot be readily generalized to the effects of self-directed exposure to sexually explicit Internet materials. Despite some of these more recent findings, whether violent sexually explicit material causes sexual aggression toward women remains a fractious issue.

Sex Discrimination   Since the 1980s, feminists have been divided over the issue of sexually explicit material. One segment of the feminist movement, which identifies itself as antipornography, views sexually explicit material as inherently degrading and dehumanizing to women. Many in this group believe that sexually explicit material provides the basis for women's subordination by turning them into sex objects. They argue that sexually explicit material inhibits women's attainment of equal rights by encouraging the exploitation and subordination of women.

Feminist and other critics of this approach point out that it has an antisexual bias that associates sex with exploitation. Sexually explicit images, rather than specifically sexist images, are singled out. Furthermore, discrimination against and the subordination of women in Western culture have existed since ancient times, long before the rise of sexually explicit material. The roots of subordination lie far deeper. One researcher even suggests that differences in response to sexually explicit mass media are the result of inherited differences (Malamuth, 1996). The elimination of sexual depictions of women would not alter discrimination against women significantly, if at all. Finally, some feminists believe that the approach represents a double standard. One study suggests that exposure to pornography and its effects are related to broad and fundamental ways of understanding men, women, and gender relations (Frable, Johnson, & Kellman, 1997).

Child Pornography   Child pornography is a form of child sexual exploitation. Children used for the production of sexually explicit materials, who are usually between the ages of 6 and 16, are motivated by friendship, interest in sexuality, offers of money, or threats. Younger children may be unaware that their photographs are being used sexually. A number of these children are related to the photographer. Many children who have been exploited in this way exhibit distress and poor adjustment; they may suffer from depression, anxiety, and guilt. Others engage in destructive and antisocial behavior.

Digital cameras and the ability to download photographs onto computers have made this into what some call the "golden age of child pornography." The fact that the possession of such images is a crime does not deter people from placing or viewing them on the Internet. Laws governing obscenity and child pornography already exist and, for the most part, can be applied to cases involving the Internet to adequately protect minors. Unlike some sexually explicit material, child pornography has been found to be patently offensive and therefore not within the zone of protected free speech.

Censorship, Sexually Explicit Material, and the Law

To censor means to examine in order to suppress or delete anything considered objectionable. **Censorship** occurs when the government, private groups, or individuals impose their moral or political values on others by suppressing words, ideas, or images they deem offensive. Obscenity, as noted previously, is the state of being contrary to generally accepted standards of decency or morality. During the first half of the twentieth century, under American obscenity laws, James Joyce's *Ulysses* and the works of D. H. Lawrence were prohibited, Havelock Ellis's *Studies in the Psychology of Sex* was banned, nude paintings were removed from gallery and museum walls, and everything but chaste kisses was banned from the movies for years.

Congress shall make no law . . . abridging the freedom of speech, or of the press . . .

—*First Amendment to the Constitution of the United States*

Two of the most heavily censored books in America are Leslea Newman's Heather Has Two Mommies, *about a lesbian family, and Michael Willhoite's* Daddy's Roommate *(shown here), about a child who visits his gay father and his father's partner. These books are opposed because they depict gay and lesbian families.*

U.S. Supreme Court decisions in the 1950s and 1960s eliminated much of the legal framework supporting literary censorship on the national level. But censorship continues to flourish on the state and local levels, especially among schools and libraries. The women's health book *The New Our Bodies, Ourselves* has been a frequent object of attack because of its feminist perspective and descriptions of lesbian sexuality. More recently, two children's books have been added to the list of most censored books: Leslea Newman's *Heather Has Two Mommies* and Michael Willhoite's *Daddy's Roommate*. Both books have come under attack because they describe children in healthy lesbian and gay families. Judy Blume's books for teenagers, J. D. Salinger's *The Catcher in the Rye*, and the *Sports Illustrated* swimsuit issue are regular items on banned-publications lists. Exhibits of the photographs taken by the late Robert Mapplethorpe have been strenuously attacked for "promoting" homoeroticism.

Obscenity Laws   Sexually explicit material itself is not illegal, but materials defined as legally obscene are. It is difficult to arrive at a legal definition of obscenity for determining whether a specific illustration, photograph, novel, or movie is obscene. Traditionally, U.S. courts have considered material obscene if it tended to corrupt or deprave its user. Over the years, the law has been debated in a number of court cases. This process has resulted in a set of criteria for determining what is obscene:

- The dominant theme of the work must appeal to prurient sexual interests and portray sexual conduct in a patently offensive way.

- Taken as a whole, the work must be without serious literary, artistic, political, or scientific value.

- A "reasonable" person must find the work, when taken as a whole, to possess no social value.

The problem with these criteria, as well as the earlier standards, is that they are highly subjective. For example, who is a reasonable person? There

> If a man is pictured chopping off a woman's breast, it only gets an "R" rating; but if, God forbid, a man is pictured kissing a woman's breast, it gets an "X" rating. Why is violence more acceptable than tenderness?
>
> —*Sally Struthers*

> If America persists in the way it's going, and the Lord doesn't strike us down, He ought to apologize to Sodom and Gomorrah.
>
> —*Jesse Helms*

VISUAL DEPICTIONS OF SEXUAL BEHAVIOR and genitals have always been a part of society. Recently, because of the Internet, there has been an explosion in the number of sexually explicit images. These materials add to already existing books and magazines such as *Playboy, Penthouse, Hustler,* and *Playgirl,* as well as explicit videos available via mail and at video rental stores and "adult" bookstores. Some videos, such as *The Better Sex Video Series,* are touted as sex education tools designed to increase sexual skills and enhance sexual pleasure for couples. The widespread availability of sexually explicit materials has heightened concerns about the impact of such materials. The fundamental question remains: Are sexually explicit materials helpful or harmful?

Some people believe that sexually explicit materials are useful or, at the least, harmless. They contend that the materials provide information about sexual expression, enhance a couple's sexual behavior, provide an outlet for sexual expression, and offer entertainment; thus, they should be readily available to adults. Others feel that sexually explicit materials cause sexual crimi-

nality, lead to moral decay and societal breakdown, demean and objectify women, and damage children; therefore, access should be restricted. The debate over sexually explicit materials has forced us to confront core issues related to freedom of speech, definitions of "erotica" versus "pornography," protection of children, the impact of sexual information, the rights of citizens, censorship, and the role of government in "protecting" its citizens. Various efforts have been made by the federal government to restrict access to sexually explicit materials, and some statutes have received Supreme Court support.

Do you think sexually explicit materials are helpful or harmful? Does your answer vary based on the content of such materials or the audience exposed to the materials? Should the federal government regulate access to such materials? If so, what types of materials, and what audiences? Should any attempts to limit or deny access to sexually explicit materials on the Internet be made, given that national laws cannot extend to other countries?

> I would like to see an end to all obscenity laws in my lifetime. I don't know that it will happen, but it's my goal. If I can leave any kind of legacy at all, it will be that I helped expand the parameters of free speech.
>
> —*Larry Flynt*

are also many instances in which reasonable people disagree about whether material has social value. Most of us, however, would probably find that a reasonable person has opinions regarding obscenity that closely resemble our own. (Otherwise, we would think that he or she was unreasonable.) In 1969, the U.S. Supreme Court ruled, in *Stanley v. Georgia,* that private possession of obscene material in one's home is not illegal (Sears, 1989). This does not, however, apply to child pornography.

As we saw earlier, our evaluation of sexually explicit material is closely related to how we feel about such material. Our judgments are based not on reason but on emotion. Justice Potter Stewart's exasperation in *Jacobelis v. Ohio* (1965) reveals a reasonable person's frustration in trying to define pornography: "But I know it when I see it."

The Issue of Child Protection   In 1988, the United States passed the Child Protection and Obscenity Enforcement Act, which supports stiff penalties for individuals involved in the production, distribution, and possession of child pornography. Since then, the development and distribution of child pornography of all types have been targeted by the U.S. Department of Justice (Dickerson, 1994), resulting in an increase in both new legislation and prosecutions (Servi, 1995). More recently, the Communications and Decency Act of 1996 tried to address the problem of sexual exploitation of children and teens over the Internet. However, in 1997, the U.S. Supreme Court ruled that the statute was not constitutional because it violated the First Amendment's guarantee of free speech. In two subsequent rulings, the Court rejected the law that made it a crime to send an indecent message online to a person under age 18 and the ban on computer-generated "virtual" child pornography and other fake images of sex (Biskupic, 2002, 2003a). One side of this argument is represented by those who agree with Deputy Solicitor General Waxman that "the Internet threatens to give every child with access to a connected computer a free pass into the equivalent of every adult bookstore and video store in the country" (cited in Levy, 1997). The other side is represented by those who feel their rights to free speech, including information about sexually transmitted infections, gay rights, and free speech debates, may be blocked as a result of censorship.

The most recent law intended to keep adult material away from Net-surfing children is the Child Online Protection Act (COPA). Passed in 1998, it sought to require Internet users to give an adult ID before accessing a commercial site containing "adult" materials (Miller, 2000). The law was blocked, however, on constitutional grounds. However, in 2003, the U.S. Supreme Court upheld a provision of the Children's Internet Protection Act that requires public libraries receiving federal funding to put antipornography Internet filters on their computers or lose funding. More than 95% of the nation's libraries offer Internet access. The Court rejected arguments that filters violate library patrons' First Amendment free speech rights and said that adults should be able to ask librarians to disable the filters. Opponents of Internet filters contend that filtering software is so imprecise that it blocks constitutionally protected sexual material and medical information (Locy & Biskupic, 2003). They note that for some young people the Internet is their only source of valuable information about sexual health, sexually transmitted infections, birth control, and pregnancy. This contention was confirmed in a report in the *Journal of the American Medical Association* (Richardson, Resnick, Hansen, Derry, & Rideout, 2002); it concluded that an unintended outcome of Internet filtering software is the blocking of "legitimate" information. In a simulation of adolescent Internet searching, the researchers compiled search results from 24 health information searches and 6 pornography searches and tested several blocking filters commonly used in schools, libraries, and homes. At the least restrictive blocking setting, an average of 10% of health sites were blocked using search terms related to sexuality, such as "safe sex," "condoms," and "gay," whereas the average blocking rate for the pornography sites was 87%. For moderate settings, the average blocking rate was 5% for health information and 90% for pornography. At the most restrictive filter setting, health information blocking increased substantially (24%), but the pornography blocking rate was only slightly higher (91%).

With an estimated 10 million children accessing the Internet from home, serious questions must be asked about their access to certain kinds of information, pictures, graphics, videos, animation, and interactive experiences. Government censorship, academic freedom, constitutionally protected speech, child safety concerns, public health dilemmas—these and other troublesome issues are at the core of the Internet–free speech debate (Portelli & Meade, 1998).

Our inability to find criteria for objectively defining obscenity makes it potentially dangerous to censor such material. We may end up using our own personal standards to restrict speech otherwise guaranteed by the First Amendment. By enforcing our own biases, we endanger the freedom of others.

> To slurp or not to slurp at the fountain of filth is a decision to which each of us is entitled.
>
> —*Stephen Kessler*

> I may disagree with what you say but I will defend to the death your right to say it.
>
> —*Voltaire (1694–1778)*

PROSTITUTION

The exchange of sexual behaviors such as intercourse, fellatio, anal intercourse, discipline and bondage, and obscene insults, for money and/or goods, is called **prostitution.** Both men and women, including transvestites and transsexuals, work as prostitutes. By far the most common form of prostitution is women selling sex to men. The second most common is male prostitutes making themselves available to men. Less common is males selling sex to females. Prostitution between two women is rare. Estimates of the number of persons who currently work or have ever worked as prostitutes are difficult to obtain for many reasons, including the various definitions of prostitution.

Male customers of female prostitutes, called "johns," represent a wide range of occupations, ethnicities, ages, and marital statuses. Men go to prostitutes for many reasons. Some want to experience a certain sexual behavior that their partner is unwilling to try, or they may not have a regular partner. Some like the anonymity of being sexual with a prostitute: No courting is required, there are no postsex expectations, and it is less entangling than having an affair. Sometimes, young men go to a prostitute as their first sexual experience. Curiously, in a recent study of 140 men from large cities in the Midwest and on the West Coast who have used prostitutes, only one-third reported that they enjoyed sex with a female prostitute, and 57% reported that they had tried to stop use. The study also found that the common impression that men seek prostitutes when sexually dissatisfied with marital sex was only mildly supported, and the data did not support the notion that men seek "unusual" sexual behaviors such as bondage with a female prostitute. Nearly 30% indicated that they used alcohol prior to visiting a prostitute (Sawyer, Metz, Hinds, & Brucker, 2001–2002).

Females Working in Prostitution

> Prostitution gives her an opportunity to meet people. It provides fresh air and wholesome exercise, and keeps her out of trouble.
>
> —*Joseph Heller (1923–1999)*

Many women who accept money or drugs for sexual activities do not consider themselves prostitutes. According to Samuel and Cynthia Janus (1993), 5% of the women and 20% of the men in their representative study reported exchanging sex for money. Edward Laumann and his colleagues (1994) report that 16% of the men surveyed ever paid for sex.

Sex as Work   Prostitutes often identify themselves as "working girls" or "sex workers," probably an accurate description of how they perceive themselves in relation to sex. Common, but more pejorative, terms are "whore" and "hooker." They are usually prostitutes, not because they like anonymous sex and different partners per se, but because they perceive it as good-paying work. They generally do not expect to enjoy sex with their customers and avoid emotional intimacy. They separate sex as a physical act for which they are paid from sex as an expression of intimacy and pleasure. One prostitute (quoted in Zausner, 1986) describes her feelings about sex:

> I don't think about sex when I'm working. You have to be a good actress to make men think that you like it when you don't. I only enjoy sex if I'm with someone I care about.

Forced Against Their Will: International Child Prostitution

IT IS ESTIMATED that 4 million people worldwide are bought and sold each year—into marriage, prostitution, or slavery. An estimated 1 million children (mostly girls) are forced into the sex trade each year, but the actual total may be as high as 10 million (Chelala, 2000; Willis & Levy, 2002). As part of this trafficking in human beings, as many as 50,000 women and children from Latin America, Southeast Asia, and eastern Europe are brought to the United States and forced to work as prostitutes or servants. With prosecutions lacking and profits soaring, this pathological phenomenon shows no signs of abating.

"Trafficking often originates in countries with poverty, few opportunities for women, and few laws to prosecute traffickers," said Laura Lederer, a Harvard professor, in congressional testimony. Families may sometimes feel they have little choice but to send their children into deplorable situations. In some cases, girls who are abducted from their families or parents are misled about where they are going. But in other cases, families are simply too poor to feed their children (McCormick & Zamora, 2000). Increased trade across borders, lack of education (including sexuality education) of children and their parents, inadequate legislation, lack of or poor law enforcement, the eroticization of children by the media—all have contributed to commercial sexual exploitation of children (Chelala, 2000).

Individual cultural and social forces are also at work in certain countries. In eastern and southern Africa, children who are orphaned as a result of AIDS may lack the support they need from other family members. Children from industrialized countries may be fleeing abusive homes. In Southeast Asia, attitudes and practices perpetuate the low status of girls.

Children who enter sexual servitude at an early age suffer profound physical and psychological consequences. They can become malnourished, be at an increased risk for STIs and HIV/AIDS, and suffer feelings of guilt and inadequacy, to name just a few of the effects.

The United Nations in 1997 raised the issue of state participation and complicity in the trafficking of women and children across borders. Children are particularly vulnerable to smugglers or corrupt government officials and businesspeople because of their language deficiencies, lack of legal protection, undocumented status, and age. Government and nonprofit agencies worldwide have been active in calling attention to the problem of sexual exploitation and trying to address its root causes. Education, social mobilization and awareness building, legal support, social services, psychosocial counseling, and prosecution of perpetrators are but a few of the strategies that have been used to address this problem. Much more must be done to protect the endangered lives and well-being of the world's children.

Although prostitutes may be willing to perform various sexual behaviors, many will not kiss; they regard kissing as a particular form of intimacy that they reserve for partners whom they care about.

Entrance into Prostitution   According to one study, the majority of prostitutes began working as prostitutes at an average age of 21.8 (Albert, Warner, Hatcher, Trussell, & Bennett, 1995). But many prostitutes are under age 16 when they begin (Weisberg, 1990).

Childhood sexual abuse is often a factor in both adolescent girls' and boys' entrance into prostitution, for two reasons (Simons & Whitbeck, 1991; Widom & Kuhns, 1996). First, sexual abuse increases the likelihood that a preadolescent or adolescent will become involved in deviant street culture and activities. Physically and sexually abused youths are more likely to be rejected by their conventional peers and to become involved in delinquent activities. Second, one major reason young people flee home is parental abuse—generally sexual abuse for girls and physical abuse for boys.

Girls usually are introduced into prostitution by pimps, men upon whom prostitutes are emotionally and financially dependent. Prostitutes give their pimps the money they earn; in turn, pimps provide housing, buy them clothes and jewelry, and offer them protection on the streets. Although girls meet their pimps in various ways, pimps most frequently initiate the contact, using both psychological and physical coercion. Many girls and young women are "sweet-talked" into prostitution by promises of money, protection, and companionship. Adolescent prostitutes are more likely than adults to have pimps.

Once involved with pimps, women are frequently abused by them. The women also run the risk of abuse and violence from their customers. Streetwalkers are especially vulnerable.

Personal Background and Motivation   Adult prostitutes are often women who were targets of early male sexual aggression, had extensive sexual experience in adolescence, were rejected by peers because of sexual activities, and were not given adequate emotional support by their parents. There are high rates of physical and sexual abuse (including intrafamilial abuse) and neglect in their childhoods (Widom & Kuhns, 1996; Zausner, 1986). Their parents failed to provide them with a model of affectionate interaction. As a result, as the girls grew up, they tended to be anxious, to feel lonely and isolated, and to be unsure of their own identity. Another common thread running through the lives of most prostitutes is an economically disadvantaged background. However, there is a wide range of motivations and backgrounds among those who enter this "oldest profession." As one ex-prostitute notes (quoted in Queen, 2000):

> When I began sex work, I did not expect the range of education and life experience I found in my colleagues. Like many people, I believed prostitution was mainly engaged in by women who have no options. But I ended up working with women who were saving to buy houses, put kids through school, put themselves through school, start businesses.

Adolescent prostitutes describe their general psychological state of mind as very negative, depressed, unhappy, or insecure at the time they first entered prostitution. There were high levels of drug use, including alcohol, marijuana, cocaine, and heroin, and many of those who became drug addicts later turned to prostitution to support their drug habit (Miller, 1995; Potterat, Rothenberg, Muth, Darrow, & Phillips-Plummer, 1998). Their emotional state made them particularly vulnerable to pimps.

No single motive seems to explain why someone becomes a prostitute. It is probably a combination of environmental, social, financial, and personal factors that leads a woman to this profession. When women describe the most attractive things about life in the prostitution subculture, they describe them in monetary and material terms. One prostitute notes, "I said to myself how can I do these horrible things and I said money, money, money" (quoted in Weisberg, 1990). Compared with a minimum-wage job, which may be the only alternative, prostitution appears to be an economically rational decision. But prostitutes also are aware of the psychological and physical costs. They fear physical and sexual abuse, AIDS and other STIs, harassment, jail, and legal expenses. They are aware as well of the damage done to their self-esteem from stigmatization and rejection by family and society, negative feelings toward men and sex, bad working conditions, lack of a future, and control by pimps (Weisberg, 1990).

In many countries, the availability of prostitutes has become part of the tourist economy, with the money paid to prostitutes an important part of the national income ("Asia," 1996; Baker, 1995). In developing countries such as Thailand and the Philippines, for example, where social and economic conditions combine with a dominant male hierarchy and acceptance of a sexual double standard, prostitution is seen by many as a necessary and accepted occupation.

Prostitutes exhibit a range of feelings toward their customers. Some may project onto others their feelings of being deviant. If customers regard prostitutes as bad, the women feel that the so-called respectable people who come to them are worse—hypocrites, freaks, weirdos, and perverts who ask them to perform sexual acts that the women often consider degrading. Prostitutes encounter such people frequently and may generalize from these experiences. Other prostitutes, however, are accepting of and nonjudgmental toward their customers. "My customers are people like everyone else," reports one prostitute (quoted in Zausner, 1986). "If they're nice to me and don't try to fuck with me, then I like them."

Forms of Female Prostitution Female prostitutes work as streetwalkers, in brothels, in massage parlors, and as call girls. Some academics believe that the great majority of prostitutes in the United States live indoor and, for the most part, unnoticed lives (Queen, 2000).

STREETWALKERS Estimates vary, but approximately 10% of American prostitutes are streetwalkers (Queen, 2000). Streetwalking is usually the first type of prostitution in which adolescents become involved; it is also the type they prefer, despite its being at the bottom of the hierarchy of prostitution. Many advertise by dressing provocatively and hang out at locales noted for prostitution. Women working as streetwalkers are often high school dropouts or runaways who fled abusive homes and went into prostitution simply to survive. Not all streetwalkers come out of desperate situations; some are married and have satisfactory sexual relationships in their private lives. Because streetwalkers make their contacts through public solicitation, they are more

Because of their inability to screen clients, streetwalkers are the most likely of prostitutes to be victimized.

visible and more likely to be arrested. Without the ability to easily screen their customers, streetwalkers are more likely to be beaten, robbed, or raped. One study found that more than 90% of street prostitutes had been sexually assaulted (Miller & Schwartz, 1995). The study also found that people often consider prostitutes to be "unrapable" or even deserving of being raped. Streetwalkers are also susceptible to severe mental health problems. A qualitative study of 29 street youths engaged in the sex trade found that they had a high suicide attempt rate (Kidd & Kral, 2002).

Streetwalkers in one study worked an average of 5 days a week and had four or five clients a day, half of whom were repeats (Freund, Leonard, & Lee, 1989). Fellatio was their most common activity; less than one-quarter of their contacts involved sexual intercourse. In a study of men arrested for soliciting female prostitutes in three western U.S. cities, fellatio was the most common behavior experienced in prior contact with a prostitute (Monto, 2001). Clearly, fellatio is an important reason men seek female prostitutes.

BROTHELS   Brothels, also called "houses of prostitution," "cathouses," "whorehouses," and "houses of ill repute," can be found in most large cities and are legal in some counties in Nevada. Prostitution in brothels has higher status than streetwalking, and it is usually safer. A major attraction of brothels is their comfortable and friendly atmosphere. In brothels, men can have a cup of coffee or a drink, watch television, or casually converse with the women. Many customers are regulars. Sometimes, they go to the brothel simply to talk or relax rather than to engage in sex.

MASSEUSES   There are relatively few brothels today; most have been replaced by massage parlors. The major difference between brothels and massage parlors is that brothels present themselves as places of prostitution, whereas massage parlors try to disguise their intent. Most massage parlors provide only massages. However, some massage parlors offer customers any

Prostitution is legal and subject to government regulation in some parts of Nevada.

type of sexual service they wish for a fee, which is negotiated with the masseuses. But most are "massage and masturbation only" parlors. These so-called M-and-M parlors are probably the most widespread; their primary service is the "local" or "relief" massage in which there is only masturbation. By limiting sex to masturbation, these parlors are able to avoid legal difficulties, because most criminal sex statutes require genital penetration, oral sex, discussion of fees, and explicit solicitation for criminal prosecution. Women who work M-and-M parlors are frequently referred to as "hand whores"; these women, however, often do not consider themselves prostitutes, although they may drift into prostitution later. Many masseuses run newspaper ads for their services and work on an out-call basis, meeting customers at their hotel rooms or homes.

CALL GIRLS　Call girls have the highest status among prostitutes. They are usually better educated than other prostitutes, often come from a middle-class background, dress fashionably, and live on "the right side of the tracks." A call girl is expensive; her fees may be $100–$250 an hour or $500–$2500 a night. She operates through contacts and referrals; instead of the street, she takes to the telephone and arranges to meet her customers. Call girls often work for escort services that advertise through newspapers.

Males Working in Prostitution

Although there is extensive research into prostitution, most of it concerns female prostitution. Most research on male prostitution focuses on street hustlers, the male equivalent of streetwalkers. There are other kinds of male prostitutes, such as call boys, masseurs, and prostitutes who work out of gay bars, who have not been extensively investigated. Males tend to enter into the life of prostitution early, usually by the age of 16 (Cates & Markley, 1992). Few males who work as prostitutes are gigolos—heterosexual men

Street hustlers, like female prostitutes, are often young adults from broken homes.

providing sexual services for women in exchange for money. The customers are usually wealthy, middle-aged women who seek sex, a social "companion," or a young man. The gigolo phenomenon illustrates that women, like men, will pay for sex. Gigolos are probably more the products of male fantasies—being paid for "having fun"—than reality. Another type of male prostitute is kept boys—young men financially supported for sexual services by an older "sugar daddy." The overwhelming majority of male prostitutes sell their sexual services to other males. The most common types of sexual behaviors male prostitutes engage in are fellatio, either alone or with other activities (99%); anal sex (80%); and oral stimulation of the anus, also called rimming (63%) (Morse, Simon, Balson, & Osofsky, 1992).

Male prostitution is shaped by three subcultures: the peer delinquent subculture, the gay subculture, and the transvestite subculture. Young male prostitutes are called "chickens," and the customers who are attracted to them are known as "chickenhawks."

In female adolescent prostitution, the pimp plays a major role: He takes the girl's money and maintains her in the life. In contrast, there is usually no pimp role in male prostitution. Most males are introduced to prostitution through the influence of their peers. A typical male begins when a friend suggests that he can make "easy money" on the streets. Hustlers usually live alone or with roommates, whereas female streetwalkers usually live with their pimps. Many of the psychological symptoms associated with hustling are as attributable to the delinquent environment as to the hustler's innate psychological condition (Simon et al., 1992).

The **peer delinquent subculture,** an antisocial street subculture, is characterized by male and female prostitution, drug dealing, panhandling, theft, and violence. Young people in this culture sell sex for the same reason they sell drugs or stolen goods—to make money. Teenage hustlers may not consider themselves gay, because they are selling sex rather than seeking erotic gratification. Instead, they may identify themselves as a bisexual or heterosexual person. They may find their customers in urban "sex zones"—adult bookstores, topless bars, and adult movie houses—which cater to the sexual interests of people of all sexual orientations. They are more likely to work the street than bars.

In contrast to male delinquent prostitutes, gay male prostitutes engage in prostitution as a means of expressing their sexuality *and* making money (Weisberg, 1990). They identify themselves as gay and work primarily in gay neighborhoods or gay bars. Many are "pushed-away" children who fled their homes when their parents and peers rejected them because of their sexual orientation (Kruks, 1991). The three most important reasons they give for engaging in prostitution are money, sex, and fun/adventure.

Very little is known about male transvestite prostitutes (Boles & Elifson, 1994). They are a diverse group and are distinct from other male and female prostitutes (Elifson, Boles, Posey, & Sweat, 1993). Their clients are both heterosexual and gay men. Many of their heterosexual clients believe that the transvestites are women, but others are aware that the prostitutes are transvestites. Transvestite prostitutes can be found in most major cities.

Another type of male prostitute is the **she-male,** a male who has undergone breast augmentation. The she-male's client may mistakenly believe that the he is a she. Often, the client is another she-male or a male who knows that the prostitute is genitally a male (Blanchard, 1993).

Prostitution and the Law

Arrests for prostitution and calls for cleanups seem to be a communal ritual practiced by influential segments of the population to reassert their moral, political, and economic dominance. The arrests are symbolic of community disapproval, but they are not effective in ending prostitution.

Female prostitution is the only sexual offense for which women are extensively prosecuted; the male patron is seldom arrested. Prostitutes are subject to arrest for various activities, including vagrancy and loitering, but the most common charge is for solicitation. **Solicitation**—a word, gesture, or action that implies an offer of sex for sale—is defined vaguely enough that women who are not prostitutes occasionally are arrested on the charge because they act "suspiciously." It is usually difficult to witness a direct transaction in which money passes hands, and such arrests are also complicated by involving the patron. Laws may also include actions not ordinarily associated with prostitution; for example, some states define prostitution as offering oneself for promiscuous and indiscriminate intercourse without payment.

There are periodic attempts to repeal laws criminalizing prostitution because it is perceived as a victimless crime: Both the woman and her customer engage in it voluntarily. Others, especially feminists, want to repeal such laws because they view prostitutes as being victimized by their pimps, their customers, and the law enforcement system (Barry, 1995; Bullough & Bullough, 1996). Studies of prostitutes and their clients, as well as psychological and sociological studies, provide significant support for decriminalization (Rio, 1991).

Reformers propose that prostitution be either legalized or decriminalized. Those who support legalizing prostitution want to subject it to licensing and registration by police and health departments, as in Nevada and parts of Europe. Those who propose decriminalization want to remove criminal penalties for engaging in prostitution; prostitutes would be neither licensed nor registered. Some prostitutes have organized in a group called COYOTE (Call Off Your Old Tired Ethics) to push for decriminalization and support. COYOTE also advocates the unionization of prostitutes and recognition of their work as satisfying a widespread public demand.

Whatever one's opinion about decriminalizing adult prostitution, the criminalization of adolescent prostitution needs to be reevaluated. Treating juvenile prostitutes as delinquents overlooks the fact that in many ways adolescent prostitutes are more victims than criminals. As researchers examine such social problems as the sexual and physical abuse of children, running away, and adolescent prostitution, they are discovering a disturbing interrelationship. The law, nevertheless, does not view adolescent prostitution as a response to victimization and an attempt to survive on the streets. Instead, it treats it as a criminal behavior and applies legal sanctions. A more appropriate response might be to offer counseling, halfway houses, alternative schooling, or job training.

The Impact of HIV/AIDS

Prostitution has received increased attention as a result of the HIV/AIDS epidemic. There are several reasons female and male prostitutes are at higher risk than the general population. First, many prostitutes are injecting drug users, and injecting drug use is one of the primary ways of transmitting HIV infection. Women exchanging sex for crack in crack houses are also at high risk for

I regret to say that we of the FBI are powerless to act in case of oral-genital intimacy, unless it has in some way obstructed interstate commerce.

—*J. Edgar Hoover (1895–1972)*

HIV infection (Inciardi, 1995). Second, prostitutes are at higher risk for HIV infection because they have multiple partners. Third, prostitutes do not always require their customers to use condoms. Male prostitutes are at even greater risk than female prostitutes because of their high-risk sexual practices, especially anal intercourse, and their high-risk gay/bisexual clientele.

The question of who acts as the bridge population in the spread of AIDS generates controversy. Although some people point to the male clients of prostitutes (Dingman, 1996), others claim that the prostitutes themselves, both male and female, are responsible for much of the heterosexual transmission of HIV. Many male prostitutes reported having girlfriends or wives, some of whom were also prostitutes. The male prostitutes indicated that they believed the majority of their clients were heterosexual or bisexual.

Supporters of continued criminalization of prostitution point to the prevalence of HIV/AIDS as an additional reason for arresting prostitutes. Prostitutes, they argue, are likely to contribute to the AIDS epidemic. Some suggest additional penalties for prostitutes who have AIDS or who test positive for HIV. Those who wish to decriminalize prostitution point out that the current laws have not reduced the incidence of prostitution. Furthermore, they argue, if prostitution were regulated and prostitutes were made subject to routine STI/HIV testing, there would be a greater likelihood of preventing HIV transmission. In Nevada, for example, where brothel prostitution is legal in some counties, health officials require monthly HIV tests and the use of condoms.

What can we learn from all of the above? That clients of prostitutes are putting themselves, *as well as their partners,* at high risk for HIV and other STIs if they do not use condoms.

SEXUALITY AND THE LAW

A basic tenet of our society is that all Americans are equal under the law. But state laws relating to sexuality vary from one state to another, with people having widely differing rights and privileges ("SIECUS Looks," 1999). Though most Americans don't give much thought to the government's decision making concerning their sexual lives, they generally agree that sexual behavior is private and that what occurs in their bedrooms is their own business. They may even think that sexuality-related laws are for other people, not themselves. As a result, most Americans don't think about how their lives can be impacted by the law depending on where they live or visit.

Historically, the United States has enacted laws that criminalize certain sexual behaviors, such as rape, incest, child-adult sex, and prostitution. For the most part, there has been a strong consensus among Americans as to the need for and value of such laws. However, one area of sexual behavior, referred to as **sodomy,** has provoked considerable debate. Sodomy has had several definitions, including any sexual behaviors between members of the other or the same sex that cannot result in procreation (some of which were considered "crimes against nature") and sexual behaviors considered to be "homosexual acts." Today, oral and anal sex are the behaviors typically considered to be sodomy. Rooted in sixteenth-century English laws prohibiting nonprocreative sex, the first American antisodomy law was passed in 1610 in colonial Virginia; the penalty was death. In 1873, South Carolina became the last state to repeal capital punishment for sodomy. More recently, sodomy laws have been used to target individuals participating in same-sex behaviors (Greenberg, 2003; "Social Evolution Changed," 2003).

Every state had laws banning sodomy until 1961, when Illinois repealed its sodomy ban. By mid-2003, only 13 states had sodomy laws. Nine states—Alabama, Florida, Idaho, Louisiana, Mississippi, North Carolina, South Carolina, Utah, and Virginia—had laws prohibiting sodomy between both same-sex and other-sex partners. Four states—Kansas, Missouri, Oklahoma, and Texas—outlawed sodomy between same-sex partners only. Civil rights activists and the gay community protested that the laws violated individual rights, were rarely enforced, and provided grounds for other types of discrimination based on sexual orientation. Other groups, particularly those that believe homosexuality is immoral, fought to retain the laws.

In 2003, in *Lawrence et al. v. Texas*, the U.S. Supreme Court struck down, by a decisive 6–3 vote, the Texas law that banned sex between people of the same gender. Considered by many as a "watershed moment" in American culture, the verdict reversed the Supreme Court's 1986 ruling in *Bowers v. Harwick* that upheld a state's right (Georgia) to criminalize sodomy. The Court said that the *Bowers* ruling was incorrect then and is incorrect today. This landmark ruling also invalidated the antisodomy laws in the 13 remaining states that have them.

The Texas case originated in 1998 when John Geddes Lawrence and Tyron Garner were discovered having sex by a Harris County sheriff's officer who had entered Lawrence's residence while responding to a false report about an armed intruder. They were fined $200 each (Biskupic, 2003b) for violating state law prohibiting oral and anal sex between same-sex partners. In writing for the majority, Justice Anthony Kennedy (Supreme Court of the United States, 2003a) stated that

> the case does involve two adults who, with full and mutual consent from each other, engaged in sexual practices common to a homosexual lifestyle. The petitioners [Lawrence and Garner] are entitled to respect for their private lives. The State cannot demean their existence or control their destiny by making their private sexual conduct a crime. The right to liberty under the Due Process Clause gives them the full right to engage in their conduct without intervention of the government.

Kennedy also noted that the Council of Europe (45 nations) and other nations recognize the rights of gay adults to engage in consensual sexual behavior. He further declared that the criminalization of homosexual conduct is an invitation in and of itself for discrimination against homosexuals in the public and private spheres (Supreme Court of the United States, 2003a). In a dissenting opinion, Justice Antonin Scalia stated that the Court "has largely signed on the so-called homosexual agenda" (Supreme Court of the United States, 2003b). Scalia also stated that the Court was taking sides in a cultural war that could result in the government legalizing gay marriages.

Policymakers and advocates of free speech continue to scrutinize states' sexuality laws and enforcement practices and to monitor and report on them. One such advocacy group is the Sexuality Information and Education Council of the United States (SIECUS), which states (1999):

> SIECUS advocates for the right of individuals to make responsible sexual choices. The right is composed of a variety of specific rights—the right to information, the right to sexual health services, the right to engage in sexual behaviors in private with another consenting adult, the right to live

I would rather be exposed to the inconveniences attending too much liberty than to those attending too small a degree of it.

—*Thomas Jefferson (1743–1826)*

Whether and to whom to marry, how to express sexual intimacy, and whether and how to establish a family—these are among the most basic of every individual's liberty and due process rights.

—*Margaret Marshall, Massachusetts chief justice*

The Invalidation of State Antisodomy Laws: A Triumph for Equality and a Path to Gay Marriage?

THE HISTORIC RULING in June 2003 by the U.S. Supreme Court that overturned state antisodomy laws directed toward both same-sex and other-sex partners has been hailed as one of the most significant advances in terms of individual rights in America and the Court's most far-reaching decision for gay men and lesbian women. In reversing a 1986 ruling that upheld antisodomy laws, the Court said that the Constitution's guarantee of individual liberty extends to consensual sex between same-sex people in the confines of their homes. The Court's ruling invalidated antisodomy laws in the 13 states that still have them.

For gay men in particular, not only did the decriminalization of same-sex behavior bring relief, but it helped validate them as human beings and reduce some of the stigmas they face. The ruling came at a time of increased visibility and power of the gay community, in the United States and other countries. And many people think the ruling changes the legal landscape by opening the door for legal attacks on other laws that discriminate against gay men and lesbian women. Individuals can, for example, be fired from their jobs, denied the opportunity to adopt children, denied custody of their own children, and denied housing because of their sexual orientation. Fourteen states still have laws prohibiting discrimination in employment, housing, or public accommodations based on a person's sexual orientation (Biskupic, 2003c).

Some criticized the Court's ruling, claiming that it hurts the "natural family," validates immoral behavior, and will lead to sexual chaos and more cases of AIDS. In the dissenting opinion, Justice Antonin Scalia said that the ruling would lead to government-sanctioned gay marriages. However, the majority of justices noted that the case involved consenting adults in the privacy of their own homes, not government recognition of gay marriages (Biskupic, 2003a, 2003b). In any case, the ruling renewed the commitment of gay rights activists to overturn laws prohibiting same-sex marriage. And the ruling came on the heels of a Canadian court lifting of a ban on same-sex marriage. Currently, the Netherlands and Belgium recognize gay marriages.

The right of gay men and lesbian women to legally marry has become a major source of controversy. No state licenses same-sex marriage, although Vermont recognizes civil unions of same-sex couples. In September 2003, California enacted a law granting state-registered domestic partners all the same rights, protections, benefits, obligations, and duties as married spouses, but it stopped short of recognizing gay and lesbian marriage ("California Governor Signs," 2003).

In November 2003, the Massachusetts Supreme Court ruled that same- and other-sex couples must be given equal civil marriage rights under the state constitution. The ruling detailed the benefits that would be extended to same-sex couples who marry, such as public and private pensions, health care benefits through private insurance, and the state's Medicaid program, life insurance, and bereavement benefits (Bayles, 2003).

In fear that some states might legalize gay marriages, Congress in 1996 passed the Defense of Marriage Act, which defined marriage as a union between one man and one woman. Most states subsequently adopted their own version. If the U.S. Supreme Court rules that these laws violate the constitutionally protected right to privacy, they will become invalid (Biskupic, 2003c). The battle over gay marriage in the United States will continue.

Do you agree with the Supreme Court ruling overturning state antisodomy laws? Why or why not? In what way was the ruling helpful to gay men and lesbian women? Do you think the ruling will lead to the legalization of same-sex marriages? Do you support or oppose same-sex marriage? Why? What are your thoughts about other areas in which gay men and lesbian women are discriminated against? For example, should they be able to adopt children, have custody of their own children, and be protected from being fired at work?

according to one's sexual orientation, and the right to obtain and use materials that have a sexual theme or content.

In many ways, sexuality-related laws reflect an ambivalence about sexuality in America's culture. For some sexuality-related issues, there is not a consensus, although laws have been enacted. This is particularly evident with issues relating to sexuality education and abortion. Although some laws seem to be based on sexuality as something from which we must be protected, in other cases, the absence of laws speaks loudly. Many states have yet to protect against sexual harassment and discrimination based on sexual orientation, and every state has work to do in developing laws that support sexual rights and sexual health.

Click on "It's Elementary" to hear children discussing gay marriage.

THE WORLD OF COMMERCIAL SEX is one our society approaches with confusion. Society simultaneously condemns sexually explicit material and prostitution and provides the customers. Because of conflicting attitudes and behaviors, our society rarely approaches the issues surrounding sexually explicit material and prostitution with disinterested logic. Now, in every state, adults can legally participate in sexual behavior with other adults, no matter what their sexual orientation is.

SUMMARY

Sexually Explicit Material in Contemporary America

- There is a lack of agreement about what constitutes *erotica, pornography,* and *obscenity* because they are subjective terms. The term *sexually explicit material* is a more neutral term.

- Millions of people spend billions of dollars on sexually explicit material each year in the United States.

- The increasing availability of erotic videos in the privacy of the home has led to an increase in women viewers. The inclusion of women in the audience has led to *femme porn.*

- People who read or view sexually explicit material usually recognize it as fantasy. They use it as a release from their everyday lives. Sexually explicit material temporarily encourages sexual expression, activating a person's typical sexual behavior pattern. People are interested in sexually explicit material because they enjoy sexual sensations, it is a source of sexual information and knowledge, it enables people to rehearse sexual activities, and it is safer sex.

- In 1970, the President's Commission on Pornography and Obscenity concluded that pornography does not cause harm or violence. Over the years, there has been a heated debate over the effects of sexually explicit material. There is no definitive evidence, however, that nonviolent sexually explicit material is associated with sexual aggression against women, nor is there evidence that sexually violent material produces lasting changes in attitudes or behaviors.

- Some feminists believe that sexually explicit material represents a form of sex discrimination against women because it places them in what they believe to be a degrading and dehumanizing context. Others believe that opponents of sexually explicit material have an antisex bias.

- Child pornography is a form of sexual exploitation that appeals to a very limited audience. Courts have prohibited its production, sale, and possession.

- The legal guidelines for determining whether a work is obscene are that the dominant theme of the work must appeal to prurient sexual interests and portray sexual conduct in a patently offensive way; taken as a whole, the work must be without serious literary, artistic, political, or scientific value; and a reasonable person must find the work, when taken as a whole, to possess no social value. Obscene material is not protected by law.

Prostitution

- *Prostitution* is the exchange of sexual behaviors for money and/or goods. Both men and women work as prostitutes. Women are generally introduced into prostitution by pimps. Adolescent prostitutes describe their psychological state as negative when they first entered prostitution. Streetwalkers run the risk of abuse and violence from their customers. Prostitutes report various motives for entering prostitution, including quick and easy money, the prostitution subculture, and the excitement of "the life."

- Prostitutes solicit on streets and work in brothels and massage parlors. Some masseuses have intercourse with clients, but most provide only masturbation. Call girls have the highest status among prostitutes.

- Most research on male prostitution focuses on street hustlers. Male prostitution is shaped by the peer delinquent, gay male, and transvestite subcultures. The three most important reasons given for engaging in prostitution are money, sex, and fun/adventure.

- Arrests for prostitution are symbols of community disapproval; they are not effective in curbing prostitution. Female prostitution is the only sexual offense for which women are extensively prosecuted; the male patron is seldom arrested. Decriminalization of prostitution is often urged because it is a victimless crime or because prostitutes are victimized by their pimps, customers, police, and the legal system. Some people advocate regulation by police and health departments.

- Prostitutes are at higher risk for HIV/AIDS than the general population because many are injecting drug users, have multiple partners, and do not always require their customers to use condoms. Female and male prostitutes and their customers may provide a pathway for HIV and other STIs into the general heterosexual community.

Sexuality and the Law

- In 2003, the U.S. Supreme Court overturned state anti*sodomy* laws in the 13 remaining states that had them, making it legal for consenting adult gay men and lesbian women to have sex in private.

Sex and the Internet

American Civil Liberties Union

Protection of our First Amendment rights is part of the mission of the American Civil Liberties Union (ACLU). But what exactly is this organization, what does it do, and how can it help you? To find out, click to the ACLU's home page (http://www.aclu.org) and find one topic related to this chapter or text that interests you. This could include cyber liberties, free speech, HIV/AIDS, lesbian and gay rights, privacy, reproductive rights, or women's rights. After reading information related to this topic, answer the following:

- What new information or news release did you find related to this topic?

- What is the history or background of laws related to it?

- What is the ACLU's stance?

- What is your position, and why?

SUGGESTED WEB SITES

National Coalition Against Censorship
http://www.ncasc.org
Provides action alerts, censorship news, and frequently asked questions about censorship.

Prostitutes' Education Network
http://www.bayswan.org
Provides information and resources related to prostitution.

U.S. Supreme Court
http://www.findlaw.com
Lists U.S. Supreme Court decisions by year and volume.

SUGGESTED READING

Delacoste, Frédérique, & Alexander, Priscilla (Eds.). (1998). *Sex Work: Writing by Women in the Sex Industry.* (2nd ed.). Pittsburgh: Cleis Press. A collection of short, personal stories by women who work as prostitutes, masseuses, topless dancers, models, and actresses, many of whom regard themselves as feminists.

Jeffreys, Sheila. (1998). *The Idea of Prostitution.* North Melbourne, Australia: Spinifex Press. Argues that the involvement of women in prostitution is a variety of male sexual violence and a violation of women's human rights.

Kempadoo, Kamala, & Doezema, Jo (Eds.). (1998). *Global Sex Workers: Rights, Resistance, and Redefinition.* New York: Routledge. A collection of essays on the sex workers' rights movement around the world.

Strosser, Natalie. (2000). *Defending Pornography.* New York: New York University Press. A lucid, broad exploration of the long debate over pornography.

Weitzer, Ronald (Ed.). (2000). *Sex for Sale: Prostitution, Pornography, and the Sex Industry.* New York: Routledge. Examines sex work and the sex industry.

For links, articles, and study material, go to the McGraw-Hill Web site, located at http://www.mhhe.com/strong5

Glossary

abortifacient   A device or substance that causes an abortion.

abortion   The expulsion of the conceptus, either spontaneously or by induction.

abstinence   Refraining from sexual intercourse.

acculturation   The process of adaptation by an ethnic group to the attitudes, behaviors, and values of the dominant culture.

acquired immunodeficiency syndrome (AIDS)   A chronic disease caused by the human immunodeficiency virus (HIV), in which the immune system is weakened and unable to fight opportunistic infections such as pneumocystis carinii pneumonia (PCP) and Kaposi's sarcoma.

adolescence   The social and psychological state that occurs between the beginning of puberty and full adulthood.

afterbirth   The placenta, the remaining section of the umbilical cord, and the fetal membranes.

agape   In John Lee's typology of love, altruistic love.

age of consent   The age at which a person is legally deemed capable of giving consent.

alpha-fetoprotein (AFP) screening   A blood test of a pregnant woman's blood to determine the existence of neural tube defects.

alveoli (singular, *alveolus*)   Small glands within the female breast that begin producing milk following childbirth.

amenorrhea   The absence of menstruation, unrelated to aging.

amniocentesis   A process in which amniotic fluid is withdrawn by needle from the uterus and then examined for evidence of possible birth defects.

amnion   An embryonic membranous sac containing the embryo and amniotic fluid.

amniotic fluid   The fluid within the amniotic sac that surrounds the embryo or fetus.

ampulla   The widened part of the fallopian tube or the vas deferens.

anal intercourse   The insertion of the erect penis into the partner's anus.

anal stage   In Freudian theory, the period from age 1 to 3, during which the child's erotic activities center on the anus.

analingus   The licking of the anal region.

anatomical sex   Identification as male or female based on physical sex characteristics such as gonads, uterus, vulva, vagina, and penis.

androgen   Any of the male hormones, including testosterone.

androgen-insensitivity syndrome or **testicular feminization**   A genetic, hereditary condition passed through X chromosomes in which a genetic male is born with testes but is unable to absorb testosterone; as a result, the estrogen influence prevails, and his body tends toward a female appearance, failing to develop male internal and external sex organs.

androgen replacement therapy   The administration of testosterone to increase sex drive, especially after oophorectomy.

androgyny   The unique and flexible combination of instrumental and expressive traits in accordance with individual differences, situations, and stages in the life cycle.

anodyspareunia   Pain occurring during anal intercourse.

anorexia nervosa   An eating disorder characterized by the pursuit of excessive thinness.

antibody   A cell that binds to the antigen of an invading cell, inactivating it and marking it for destruction by killer cells.

anti-gay prejudice   A strong dislike, fear, or hatred of gay men and lesbian women because of their same-sex behavior.

antigen   A molecular structure on the wall of a cell capable of stimulating the immune system and then reacting with the antibodies that are released to fight it.

anus   The opening of the rectum, consisting of two sphincters, circular muscles that open and close like valves.

anxious/ambivalent attachment   A style of infant attachment characterized by separation anxiety and insecurity in relation to the primary caregiver.

Apgar score   The cumulative rating of the newborn's heart rate, respiration, color, reflexes, and muscle tone.

aphrodisiac   A substance that supposedly increases sexual desire or improves sexual performance.

areola   A ring of darkened skin around the nipple of the breast.

artificial insemination (AI)   *See* assisted reproductive technology.

assigned gender   The gender ascribed by others, usually at birth.

assisted reproductive technology (ART)   A procedure in which a woman's ovaries are stimulated and her eggs surgically removed, combined with sperm, and returned to her body. Commonly referred to as artificial insemination.

attachment The emotional tie between an infant and his or her primary caregiver.

attitude The predisposition to act, think, or feel in certain ways toward particular things.

atypical sexual behavior Sexual activity that is not statistically typical of American sexual behavior.

autoerotic asphyxia A form of sexual masochism linking strangulation with masturbation.

autoeroticism Sexual self-stimulation or behavior involving only the self; includes masturbation, sexual fantasies, and erotic dreams.

autofellatio Oral stimulation of the penis by oneself.

aversion therapy Treatment in which an aversion stimulus such as an electric shock is paired with the behavior that the person wishes to change.

avoidant attachment A style of infant attachment characterized by avoidance of the primary caregiver as a defense against rejection.

bacterial vaginosis A vaginal infection commonly caused by the bacterium *Gardnerella vaginalis*.

Bartholin's gland One of two small ducts on either side of the vaginal opening that secretes a small amount of moisture during sexual arousal. Also known as vestibular gland.

basal body temperature (BBT) method A contraceptive method based on a woman's temperature in the morning upon waking; when her temperature rises, she is fertile.

B cell A type of lymphocyte involved in antibody production.

behavior The way a person acts.

benign prostatic hypertrophy Enlargement of the prostate gland, affecting many men over age 50.

benign tumor A nonmalignant (noncancerous) tumor that grows slowly and remains localized.

bias A personal leaning or inclination.

biased sample A nonrepresentative sample.

binge eating disorder An eating disorder characterized by rapid eating, eating to the point of discomfort or beyond, continual eating, and eating when not hungry. Also called compulsive overeating.

biopsy The surgical removal of tissue for diagnosis.

birth canal The passageway through which an infant is born; the vagina.

birth control Any means of preventing a birth from taking place, including contraception and abortion.

bisexuality An emotional and sexual attraction in which one is attracted to members of both sexes.

blastocyst A collection of about 100 human cells that develops from the zygote.

bondage and discipline (B&D) Sexual activities in which one person is bound while another simulates or engages in light or moderate "disciplinary" activities such as spanking and whipping.

Braxton-Hicks contractions Uterine contractions during the last trimester of pregnancy that exercise the uterus, preparing it for labor.

bulimia An eating disorder characterized by episodes of uncontrolled overeating followed by purging (vomiting).

calendar (rhythm) method A contraceptive method based on calculating "safe" days depending on the range of a woman's longest and shortest menstrual cycles.

candidiasis A yeast infection caused by the fungus *Candida albicans*. Also known as moniliasis.

capacitation The process by which a sperm's membranes become fragile enough to release the enzymes from its acrosomes.

caring Making another's needs as important as one's own.

castration anxiety In Freudian theory, the belief that the father will cut off the child's penis because of competition for the mother/wife.

casual sex Typically, sex outside of a relationship or sex happening by chance with someone not known well.

celibacy Not engaging in any kind of sexual activity.

censorship The suppression of words, ideas, or images by governments, private groups, or individuals based on their political or moral values.

cervical cancer Invasive cancer of the cervix (ICC).

cervical cap A small rubber contraceptive barrier device that fits snugly over the cervix.

cervical dysplasia or **cervical intraepithelial neoplasia (CIN)** A condition of the cervical epithelium (covering membrane) that may lead to cancer if not treated.

cervical mucus method A contraceptive method using a woman's cervical mucus to determine ovulation.

cervix The end of the uterus, opening toward the vagina.

cesarean section (C-section) The delivery of a baby through an incision in the mother's abdominal and uterine walls.

chancre A round, pea-sized, painless sore symptomatic of the first stage of syphilis.

child-free Individuals or couples who choose not to have children.

child sexual abuse Any sexual interaction (including fondling, erotic kissing, oral sex, and genital penetration) between an adult and a prepubertal child.

chlamydia An STD caused by the *Chlamydia trachomatis* organism. Also known as chlamydial infection.

chorion The embryo's outermost membrane.

chorionic villus sampling (CVS) A procedure in which tiny pieces of the membrane that encases the embryo are removed and examined for evidence of possible birth defects.

cilia Tiny, hairlike tissues on the fimbriae and ampulla that become active during ovulation, conducting the oocyte into the fallopian tube.

CIN *See* cervical dysplasia.

circumcision The surgical removal of the foreskin, which covers the glans penis. *See also* clitoridectomy.

clinical research The in-depth examination of an individual or group by a clinician who assists with psychological or medical problems.

clitoral hood A fold of skin covering the glans of the clitoris.

clitoridectomy The surgical removal of the clitoris and all or part of the labia. Also known as female genital mutilation and female circumcision.

clitoris (plural, *clitorides*) An external sexual structure that is the center of arousal in the female; located above the vagina at the meeting of the labia minora.

cloning Reproduction of an individual from a single cell taken from a donor or parent.

coercive paraphilia Sexual behavior involving victimization and causing harm to others.

cofactor A condition that may make a person who is HIV-positive more likely to develop AIDS.

cognition Mental processes that intervene between stimulus and response, such as evaluation and reflection.

cognitive development theory A child development theory that views growth as the mastery of specific ways of perceiving, thinking, and doing that occurs at discrete stages.

cognitive social learning theory A child development theory that emphasizes the learning of behavior from others, based on the belief that consequences control behavior.

cohabitation The practice of two people sharing living space and having a sexual relationship.

coitus Sexual intercourse.

coitus interruptus The removal of the penis from the vagina prior to ejaculation. Also called withdrawal.

colostrum A yellowish substance containing nutrients and antibodies that is secreted by the breasts 2–3 days prior to actual milk production.

coming out The public acknowledgment of one's gay, lesbian, or bisexual orientation.

commitment A determination, based on conscious choice, to continue a relationship or a marriage.

communication A transactional process in which symbols such as words, gestures, and movements are used to establish human contact, exchange information, and reinforce or change attitudes and behaviors.

conceptus In medical terminology, the developing human offspring from fertilization through birth.

condom or **male condom** A thin, soft, flexible sheath of latex rubber or polyurethane (or processed animal tissue) that fits over the erect penis to prevent semen from being transmitted and to help protect against STIs. *See also* female condom.

conflict A communication process in which people perceive incompatible goals and interference from others in achieving their goals.

congenital adrenal hyperplasia A condition in which a genetic female with ovaries and a vagina develops externally as a male as a result of a malfunctioning adrenal gland. Previously known as adrenogenital syndrome.

contraception The prevention of conception.

contraceptive film A small, translucent tissue that contains spermicide and dissolves into a sticky gel when inserted into the vagina.

contraceptive foam A chemical spermicide dispensed in an aerosol container.

contraceptive patch A transdermal, reversible method of birth control that releases synthetic estrogen and progestin to protect against pregnancy for 1 month. Commonly known as Ortho Evra®.

control group A group that is not being treated in an experiment.

coprophilia A paraphilia in which a person gets sexual pleasure from contact with feces.

corona The rim of tissue between the glans and the penile shaft.

corpora cavernosa The hollow chambers in the shaft of the clitoris or penis that fill with blood and swell during arousal.

corpus luteum The tissue formed from a ruptured ovarian follicle that produces important hormones after the oocyte emerges.

corpus spongiosum A column of erectile tissue within the penis enclosing the urethra.

correlational study The measurement of two or more naturally occurring variables to determine their relationship to each other.

Cowper's gland or **bulbourethral gland** One of two small structures below the prostate gland that secrete a clear mucus into the urethra prior to ejaculation.

cross-dressing Wearing the clothing of a member of the other sex.

crura (singular, *crus*) The internal branches of the clitoral or penile shaft.

culposcopy A form of tubal ligation in which an incision is made at the back of the vagina and the tubes are viewed with a culdoscope.

culpotomy A form of tubal ligation in which a small incision is made at the back of the vagina.

cultural equivalency perspective The view that attitudes, behaviors, and values of diverse ethnic groups are basically similar, with differences resulting from adaptation to historical and social forces such as slavery, discrimination, or poverty.

cultural relativity The perspective that any custom must be evaluated in terms of how it fits within the culture as a whole.

cunnilingus Oral stimulation of the female genitals.

curettage Scraping of the inside of the uterus with a small, spoon-shaped instrument called a curette.

cybersex Expressions of sexuality while responding to words or images on a computer.

cystitis A bladder infection affecting mainly women that is often related to sexual activity, although it is not transmitted from one partner to another.

date rape or **acquaintance rape** Sexual penetration with a dating partner that occurs against the victim's will, with force or the threat of force.

debrief The process of explaining to research participants the nature of and reasons for the study following its completion.

deception Actions aimed at betraying, misleading, or deluding another person, including lies, omissions, fabrications, and secrets.

delayed ejaculation A sexual problem characterized by the male's inability to ejaculate easily during intercourse.

delayed labor Pregnancy that has gone beyond 2 weeks of full term.

demographics The statistical characteristics of human populations.

dependent variable In an experiment, a factor that is likely to be affected by changes in the independent variable.

Depo-Provera (DMPA) An injectable contraceptive containing medroxyprogesterone acetate.

DHT deficiency A genetic disorder in which some males are unable to convert testosterone to the hormone dihydrotestosterone (DHT), required for the normal development of external male genitals; usually identified as girls at birth, the children begin to develop male genitals in adolescence.

diabetes mellitus A chronic disease characterized by excess sugar in the blood and urine due to a deficiency of insulin.

diaphragm A rubber cup with a flexible rim that is placed deep inside the vagina, blocking the cervix, to prevent sperm from entering the uterus.

diethylstilbestrol (DES) A synthetic estrogen once used to prevent miscarriages; associated with a possible increased cancer risk among the women who took it and their children.

dilation Gradual opening of the cervix.

dilation and evacuation (D&E) A second-trimester abortion method in which the cervix is slowly dilated and the fetus removed by alternating curettage with other instruments and suction.

disinhibition The phenomenon of activating behaviors that would normally be suppressed.

domestic partnership A legal category granting some rights ordinarily reserved to married couples to committed, cohabiting heterosexual, gay, and lesbian couples.

domination and submission (D/S) Sexual activities involving the consensual acting out of fantasy scenes in which one person dominates and the other submits.

dominatrix In bondage and discipline, a woman who specializes in "disciplining" a submissive partner.

doulas Specially trained individuals who offer birthing mothers emotional support and help in managing pain during the birth process.

drag Cross-dressing, often with comic intent.

drag queens Gay men who cross-dress to entertain.

dysmenorrhea Pelvic cramping and pain experienced by some women during menstruation.

dyspareunia A female sexual difficulty characterized by painful intercourse.

early pregnancy loss Loss of a pregnancy before 20 weeks.

eating disorder Eating and weight management practices that endanger a person's physical and emotional health.

ectopic pregnancy A pregnancy in which the fertilized egg implants in a fallopian tube instead of in the uterus. Also known as tubal pregnancy.

effacement Thinning of the cervix during labor.

egocentric fallacy An erroneous belief that one's own personal experiences and values are held by others in general.

ejaculation The process by which semen is forcefully expelled from the penis.

ejaculatory duct One of two structures within the prostate gland connecting with the vasa deferentia.

ejaculatory inevitability The point at which ejaculation *must* occur.

Electra complex In Freudian theory, the female child's erotic desire for the father and simultaneous fear of the mother.

ELISA A simple blood test that screens for HIV antibodies.

embryo The early form of life in the uterus between the stages of blastocyst and fetus.

embryonic membranes The embryo's membranes include the amnion, amniotic fluid, yolk sac, chorion, and allantois.

emergency contraception (EC) The use of hormones or a copper IUD to prevent a pregnancy from occurring.

emission The first stage of ejaculation, in which sperm and semen are propelled into the urethral bulb.

endometriosis A disease caused by endometrial tissue (uterine lining) spreading and growing in other parts of the body; a major cause of infertility.

endometrium The inner lining of the uterine walls.

epidemiology The study of the causes and control of disease epidemics.

epididymis The coiled tube, formed by the merging of the seminiferous tubules, where sperm mature.

epididymitis Inflammation of the epididymis.

epidural A method of anesthetic delivery during childbirth in which a pain-killing drug is continuously administered through a catheter in the woman's lower back.

episiotomy A surgical procedure during childbirth that enlarges the vaginal opening by cutting through the perineum toward the anus.

erectile dysfunction A sexual difficulty characterized by the inability to have or maintain an erection during intercourse. Previously referred to as impotence.

erection The process of the penis becoming rigid through vasocongestion; an erect penis.

erogenous zone Any area of the body that is highly sensitive to touch and associated with sexual arousal.

eros In John Lee's typology of love, the love of beauty.

erotica Sexually explicit material that can be evaluated positively.

erotic aid or **sex toy** A device, such as a vibrator or dildo, or a product, such as oils or lotions, designed to enhance erotic responsiveness.

erotophilia A positive emotional response to sexuality.

erotophobia A negative emotional response to sexuality.

Essure A permanent method of birth control that relies on a micro insert placed into each fallopian tube.

estrogen The principal female hormone, regulating reproductive functions and the development of secondary sex characteristics.

ethnic group A group of people distinct from other groups because of cultural characteristics transmitted from one generation to the next.

ethnicity Ethnic affiliation or identity.

ethnocentric fallacy or **ethnocentrism** The belief that one's own ethnic group, nation, or culture is innately superior to others.

exhibitionism A paraphilia involving recurrent, intense urges to expose one's genitals to nonconsenting person.

experimental research The systematic manipulation of an individual or the environment to learn the effect of such manipulation on behavior.

expressiveness Revealing or demonstrating one's emotions.

expulsion The second stage of ejaculation, characterized by rapid, rhythmic contraction of the urethra, prostate, and muscles at the base of the penis, causing semen to spurt from the urethral opening.

extrafamilial abuse Child sexual abuse by someone unrelated to the child.

fallacy An error in reasoning that affects one's understanding of a subject.

fallopian tube One of two uterine tubes extending toward an ovary.

false memory A fictitious memory of an event that never occurred.

false memory syndrome A collection of fictitious memories elicited by a therapist and believed by the individual to be authentic and accurate; whether such a syndrome exists is a matter of debate.

familismo Emphasis on family among Hispanics/Latinos.

feedback The ongoing process in which participants and their messages create a given result and are subsequently modified by that result.

fellatio Oral stimulation of the penis.

female condom A soft, loose-fitting, disposable polyurethane sheath with a diaphragm-like ring at each end that covers the cervix, vaginal walls, and part of the external genitals to prevent conception and to help protect against sexually transmitted infections.

female genital mutilation The surgical removal of the clitoris and all or part of the labia. Also known as clitoridectomy or female circumcision.

female impersonators Men who dress as women.

female orgasmic disorder The absence of or delay in orgasm for women following normal sexual excitement.

female sexual arousal disorder The persistent or recurring inability of women to attain or maintain the level of vaginal lubrication and swelling associated with sexual excitement.

feminism Efforts by both men and women to achieve greater equality for women.

femme porn Sexually explicit material catering to women and heterosexual couples.

fertility awareness method One of several contraceptive methods based on a woman's knowledge of her body's reproductive cycle, including calendar (rhythm), basal body temperature (BBT), cervical mucus, and symptothermal methods.

fetal alcohol effect (FAE) Lower-level alcohol consumption by pregnant women resulting in moderate behavioral and intellectual deficits in children.

fetal alcohol syndrome (FAS) Chronic ingestion of alcohol by pregnant women resulting in unusual facial features, congenital heart defects, defective joints, and behavioral and intellectual impairment in children.

fetishism A paraphilia in which a person is sexually attracted to certain objects.

fetus The stage of life from 8 weeks of gestation to birth.

fibrocystic disease A common and generally harmless breast condition in which fibrous tissue and benign cysts develop in the breast.

fimbriae Fingerlike tissues that drape over the ovaries, but without necessarily touching them.

follicle-stimulating hormone (FSH) A hormone that regulates ovulation.

follicular phase The phase of the ovarian cycle during which a follicle matures.

foreskin The portion of the sleevelike skin covering the shaft of the penis that extends over the glans penis. Also known as prepuce.

frenulum The triangular area of sensitive skin on the underside of the penis, attaching the glans to the foreskin.

frotteurism A paraphilia involving recurrent, intense urges to touch or rub against a nonconsenting person for the purpose of sexual arousal.

gamete A sex cell containing the genetic material necessary for reproduction; an oocyte (ovum) or sperm.

gay-bashing or **queer-bashing** Violence directed against gay men or lesbian women because of their sexual orientation.

gender The social and cultural characteristics associated with being male or female.

gender dysphoria Dissatisfaction with one's gender.

gender identity The gender one feels him- or herself to be.

gender identity disorder A strong and persistent cross-gender identification and persistent discomfort about one's assigned sex.

gender role The attitudes, behaviors, rights, and responsibilities that society associates with each sex.

gender-role attitude Beliefs about appropriate male and female personality traits and activities.

gender-role behavior The activities in which individuals engage in accordance with their gender.

gender-role stereotype A rigidly held, oversimplified, and overgeneralized belief that all males and all females possess distinct psychological and behavioral traits.

gender schema A set of interrelated ideas used to organize information about the world on the basis of gender.

gender selection A technique that allows couples to choose whether to have a boy or a girl.

gender theory A theory that a society is best understood by how it is organized according to gender.

genetic sex Identification as male or female based on chromosomal and hormonal sex characteristics.

genital herpes An STI caused by the herpes simplex virus (HSV).

genitals The reproductive and sexual organs of males and females. Also known as genitalia.

genital stage In Freudian theory, the period in which adolescents become interested in genital sexual activities, especially sexual intercourse.

genital warts An STI caused by the human papillomavirus (HPV).

gestation Pregnancy.

glans clitoris The erotically sensitive tip of the clitoris.

glans penis The head of the penile shaft.

gonad An organ (ovary or testis) that produces gametes.

gonadotropin A hormone that acts directly on the gonads.

gonadotropin-releasing hormone (GnRH) A hormone that stimulates the pituitary gland to release follicle-stimulating hormone (FSH) and luteinizing hormone (LH), initiating the follicular phase of the ovarian cycle.

gonorrhea An STI caused by the *Neisseria gonorrhoeae* bacterium.

Grafenberg spot (G-spot) According to some researchers, an erotically sensitive area on the front wall of the vagina midway between the introitus and the cervix.

gynecomastia Swelling or enlargement of the male breast.

halo effect The assumption that attractive or charismatic people possess more desirable social characteristics than others.

Hegar's sign The softening of the uterus above the cervix, indicating pregnancy.

helper T cell A lymphocyte that "reads" antigens and directs the immune system's response.

hepatitis A viral disease affecting the liver; several types of the virus can be sexually transmitted.

hermaphrodite A person with both male and female gonads: either one of each, two of each, or two ovotestes (gonads that have both ovarian and testicular tissue in the same gland). Also known as true hermaphrodite.

herpes simplex virus (HSV) The virus that causes genital herpes.

heterosexual bias or **heterosexism** The tendency to see the world in heterosexual terms and to ignore or devalue homosexuality.

heterosexuality Emotional and sexual attraction between members of the other sex.

highly active antiretroviral therapy (HAART) An aggressive anti-HIV treatment usually including a combination of protease inhibitors and reverse transcriptase inhibitors whose purpose is to bring viral load infection down to undetectable levels.

homoeroticism Sexual attraction, desire, or impulses directed toward members of the same sex; homosexuality.

homophobia An irrational or phobic fear of gay men and lesbian women. *See also* anti-gay prejudice, heterosexual bias.

homosexuality Emotional and sexual attraction between members of the same sex.

hormone A chemical substance that acts as a messenger within the body, regulating various functions.

hormone replacement therapy (HRT) The administration of estrogen, often with progestin, in the form of pills, vaginal cream, or a small adhesive patch. Also known as postmenopause hormone therapy (PHT).

hostile environment As related to sexuality, a work or educational setting that interferes with a person's performance because of sexual harassment.

hot flash An effect of menopause consisting of a period of intense warmth, flushing, and perspiration, typically lasting 1–2 minutes.

human chorionic gonadotropin (HCG) A hormone secreted by the developing placenta and needed to support a pregnancy.

human immunodeficiency virus (HIV) The virus that causes AIDS.

human papillomavirus (HPV) The virus that causes genital warts.

hymen A thin membrane partially covering the introitus prior to first intercourse or other breakage.

hypoactive sexual desire (HSD) or **inhibited sexual desire** A sexual problem characterized by low or absent sexual desire.

hypospadias A hormonal condition in which the opening of the penis, rather than being at the tip, is located somewhere on the underside, glans, or shaft or at the junction of the scrotum and penis.

hysterectomy The surgical removal of the uterus.

hysterotomy A late-pregnancy abortion method in which the fetus is removed through an incision in the woman's abdomen; an extremely rare procedure.

implantation The process by which a blastocyst becomes embedded in the uterine wall.

incest Sexual intercourse between individuals too closely related to legally marry, usually interpreted to mean father-daughter, mother-son, or brother-sister activity.

incidence The number of new cases of a disease within a specified time, usually 1 year.

independent variable In an experiment, a factor that can be manipulated or changed.

induction A type of reasoning in which arguments are formed from a premise to provide support for its conclusion.

infertility The inability to conceive a child after a year of unprotected intercourse, or the inability to carry a child to term.

infibulation The stitching together of the sides of the vulva or vaginal opening; part of the process of female circumcision.

informed consent Assent given by a mentally competent individual at least 18 years old with full knowledge of the purpose and potential risks and benefits of participation.

infundibulum The tube-shaped ends of the fallopian tubes.

inhibited ejaculation A sexual problem characterized by the male's inability to ejaculate despite an erection and stimulation.

instrumentality Being oriented toward tasks and problem solving.

interfemoral intercourse Movement of the penis between the partner's thighs.

internalized homophobia Self-hatred because of one's homosexuality.

intersex Having an ambiguous or unclear biological sex.

intimate love Love based on commitment, caring, and self-disclosure.

intrafamilial abuse Child sexual abuse by biologically and step-related individuals.

intrauterine device (IUD) A T-shaped device inserted into the uterus through the cervical os to prevent conception or implantation of the fertilized egg.

intrauterine insemination (IUI) or **artificial insemination (AI)** A means of achieving pregnancy by depositing semen by syringe near the cervical opening during ovulation.

introitus The opening of the vagina.

in vitro fertilization (IVF) An ART procedure that combines sperm and oocyte in a laboratory dish and transfers the blastocyst to the mother's uterus.

jealousy An aversive response that occurs because of a partner's real, imagined, or likely involvement with a third person.

Kaplan's tri-phasic model of sexual response A model that divides sexual response into three phases: desire, excitement, and orgasm.

Kaposi's sarcoma A rare cancer of the blood vessels that is common among people with AIDS.

Kegel exercises A set of exercises designed to strengthen and give voluntary control over the pubococcygeus and to increase sexual pleasure and awareness.

killer T cell A lymphocyte that attacks foreign cells.

Klinefelter syndrome A condition in which a male has one or more extra X chromosomes, causing the development of female secondary sex characteristics.

klismophilia A paraphilia in which a person gets sexual pleasure from receiving enemas.

labia majora (singular, *labium majus*) Two folds of spongy flesh extending from the mons pubis and enclosing the labia minora, clitoris, urethral opening, and vaginal entrance. Also known as major lips.

labia minora (singular, *labium minus*) Two small folds of skin within the labia majora that meet above the clitoris to form the clitoral hood. Also known as minor lips.

lactation The production of milk in the breasts (mammary glands).

laminaria A small stick of seaweed placed into the cervical opening about 6 hours prior to an abortion to dilate the cervix.

lanugo The fine, downy hair covering the fetus.

laparoscopy A form of tubal ligation using a viewing lens (the laparoscope) to locate the fallopian tubes and another instrument to cut or block and close them.

latency stage In Freudian theory, the period from age 6 to puberty in which sexual impulses are no longer active.

leukocyte White blood cell.

Leydig cell Cell within the testes that secretes androgens. Also known as an interstitial cell.

libido The sex drive.

limbic system A group of structures in the brain associated with emotions and feelings; involved with producing sexual arousal.

lochia A bloody vaginal discharge following childbirth.

Loulan's sexual response model A model that incorporates both the biological and the affective components into a six-stage cycle.

ludus In John Lee's typology of love, playful love.

lumpectomy   Breast surgery that removes only the malignant tumor and surrounding lymph nodes.

Lunelle   An injectable contraceptive given once per month that contains both estrogen and progestin and offers many of the same benefits as oral contraceptives.

luteal phase   The phase of the ovarian cycle during which a follicle becomes a corpus luteum and then degenerates.

luteinizing hormone (LH)   A hormone involved in ovulation.

lymphocyte   A type of leukocyte active in the immune response.

machismo   In Latino culture, highly prized masculine traits.

macrophage   A type of white blood cell that destroys foreign cells.

male climacteric   Changes in male sexual responsiveness that may begin to become apparent when men are in their forties or fifties.

male condom   *See* condom.

male erectile disorder   The persistent or recurring inability of men to attain or maintain an adequate erection until completion of sexual activity.

male orgasmic disorder   The persistent delay in or absence of orgasm for men following normal sexual excitement.

malignant tumor   A cancerous tumor that invades nearby tissues and disrupts the normal functioning of vital organs.

mammary gland   A mature female breast.

mammogram   A low-dose X-ray of the breast.

mammography   The use of X-rays to detect breast tumors before they can be seen or felt.

mania   In John Lee's typology of love, obsessive love.

mastectomy   The surgical removal of part or all of the breast.

Masters and Johnson's four-phase model of sexual response   A model that divides sexual response into four phases: excitement, plateau, orgasm, and resolution.

masturbation   Stimulation of the genitals for pleasure.

medical abortion   A two-drug regimen used to terminate early pregnancy. Previously known as RU-486.

menarche   The onset of menstruation.

menopause   The complete cessation of menstruation.

menses   The menstrual flow, in which the endometrium is discharged.

menstrual cycle   The more-or-less monthly process during which the uterus is readied for implantation of a fertilized ovum. Also known as uterine cycle.

menstrual phase   The shedding of the endometrium during the menstrual cycle.

menstrual synchrony   Simultaneous menstrual cycles that occur among women who work or live together.

metastasis   The process by which cancer spreads from one part of the body to an unrelated part via the bloodstream or lymphatic system.

micromanipulation technique   Tools and techniques used to achieve or improve fertilization and implantation.

minilaparotomy   A form of tubal ligation in which a small incision is made in the lower abdomen.

miscarriage   The spontaneous expulsion of the fetus from the uterus. Also called spontaneous abortion.

modeling   The process of learning through imitation of others.

mons pubis   In the female, the mound of fatty tissue covering the pubic bone; the pubic mound. Also known as mons veneris.

mons veneris   The pubic mound; literally, mountain of Venus. Also known as mons pubis.

myotonia   Increased muscle tension.

necrophilia   A paraphilia involving recurrent, intense urges to engage in sexual activities with a corpse.

neonate   A newborn.

neurosis   A psychological disorder characterized by anxiety or tension.

nocturnal orgasm or **emission**   Male orgasm and ejaculation while sleeping; usually accompanied by erotic dreams. Also known as wet dream.

noncoercive paraphilia   Harmless and victimless sexual behavior.

nongonococcal urethritis (NGU)   Urethral inflammation caused by something other than the gonococcus bacterium.

nonoxynol-9   The sperm-killing chemical in spermicide.

nonpedophilic sexual abuse   An adult's sexual interaction with a child that is motivated not by sexual desire but by nonsexual motives such as for power or affection.

nonspecific urethritis (NSU)   Inflammation of the urethra with an unspecified, nongonococcal cause.

norm   A cultural rule or standard of behavior.

normal sexual behavior   Behavior that conforms to a group's average or median patterns of behavior.

Norplant   The trade name of a contraceptive implant that is inserted under the skin of a woman's arm.

nymphomania   A pseudoscientific term referring to "abnormal" or "excessive" sexual desire in a woman.

objectivity   The observation of things as they exist in reality as opposed to one's feelings or beliefs about them.

obscenity   That which is deemed offensive to "accepted" standards of decency or morality.

observational research   Studies in which the researcher unobtrusively observes people's behavior and records the findings.

Oedipal complex   In Freudian theory, the male child's erotic desire for his mother and simultaneous fear of his father.

oocyte   The female gamete, referred to as an egg or ovum.

oogenesis   The production of oocytes; the ovarian cycle.

oophorectomy   The removal of one or both ovaries.

open marriage A marriage in which both partners agree to allow each other to have openly acknowledged and independent relationships with others, including sexual ones.

opinion An unsubstantiated belief in or conclusion about what seems to be true according to an individual's personal thoughts.

opportunistic infection (OI) An infection that normally does not occur or is not life threatening, but that takes advantage of a weakened immune system.

oral contraceptive A series of pills containing synthetic estrogen and/or progesterone that regulate egg production and the menstrual cycle. Commonly known as "the pill."

oral-genital sex The touching of a partner's genitals with the mouth or tongue.

oral stage In Freudian theory, the period lasting from birth to age 1 in which infant eroticism is focused on the mouth.

orgasm The climax of sexual excitement, including rhythmic contractions of muscles in the genital area and intensely pleasurable sensations; usually accompanied by ejaculation in males beginning in puberty.

orgasmic platform A portion of the vagina that undergoes vasocongestion during sexual arousal.

os The cervical opening.

osteoporosis The loss of bone density that can lead to weaker bones.

ovarian cycle The more-or-less monthly process during which oocytes are produced.

ovarian follicle A saclike structure in which an oocyte develops.

ovary One of a pair of organs that produces oocytes.

ovulation The release of an oocyte from the ovary during the ovarian cycle.

ovulatory phase The phase of the ovarian cycle during which ovulation occurs.

ovum (plural, *ova*) An egg; an oocyte; the female gamete.

oxytocin A hormone that stimulates uterine contractions during birth, and possibly orgasm.

Pap test A method of testing for cervical cancer by scraping cell samples from the cervix and examining them under a microscope.

paraphilia A mental disorder characterized by the American Psychiatric Association as recurrent, intense, sexually arousing fantasies, sexual urges, or behaviors generally lasting at least 6 months and involving nonhuman objects, the suffering or humiliation of oneself or one's partner, or children or other nonconsenting persons.

parenteral transmission Infection via the bloodstream.

partialism A paraphilia in which a person is sexually attracted to a specific body part.

participant observation A method of observational research in which the researcher participates in the behaviors being studied.

pathological behavior Behavior deemed unhealthy or diseased by current medical standards.

pedophile A person who is sexually attracted to children.

pedophilia A paraphilia characterized by recurrent, intense urges to engage in sexual activities with a prepubescent child.

peer An age-mate.

peer delinquent subculture An antisocial youth subculture.

pelvic floor The underside of the pelvic area, extending from the top of the pubic bone to the anus.

pelvic inflammatory disease (PID) An infection of the fallopian tube (or tubes), caused by an organism such as *C. trachomatis* or *N. gonorroehae*, in which scar tissue may form within the tubes and block the passage of eggs or cause an ectopic pregnancy; a leading cause of female infertility. Also called salpingitis.

penis The male organ through which semen and urine pass.

penis envy In Freudian theory, female desire to have a penis.

perimenopause A period of gradual changes and adjustments a woman's body goes through prior to menopause, before menstruation stops completely.

perinatal transmission The passing of a disease from mother to fetus.

perineum An area of soft tissue between the genitals and the anus that covers the muscles and ligaments of the pelvic floor.

persistent sexual arousal disorder Sexual arousal in women that does not resolve in ordinary ways but continues for hours, days, or weeks.

Peyronie's disease A painful male sexual disorder, resulting in curvature of the penis, that is caused by fibrous tissue and calcium deposits developing in the corpora cavernosa of the penis.

phallic stage In Freudian theory, the period from age 3 through 5 during which both male and female children exhibit interest in the genitals.

pheromone A sexually arousing chemical substance secreted into the air by many kinds of animals.

placenta The organ of exchange between mother and fetus.

pleasuring Erotic, nongenital touching.

plethysmograph A device attached to the genitals to measure physiological response.

PLISSIT model A model for sex therapy consisting of four progressive levels: Permission, Limited Information, Specific Suggestions, and Intensive Therapy.

pneumocystis carinii pneumonia (PCP) An opportunistic lung infection caused by a common, usually harmless organism; the most common opportunistic infection among people with AIDS.

pornography Sexually explicit material that is generally evaluated negatively.

postmenopause hormone therapy (PHT) The administration of estrogen (often along with progestin) to relieve the symptoms of menopause. Also known as hormone replacement therapy (HRT).

postpartum depression A form of depression thought to be related to hormonal changes following the delivery of a child.

postpartum period The period (about 3 months) following childbirth, characterized by physical stabilization and emotional adjustment.

postpartum psychosis A serious and rare postpartum mental illness thought to be biologically based and related to hormonal changes.

postrefusal sexual persistence Continued requests for sexual contact after being refused.

posttraumatic stress disorder (PTSD) A group of characteristic symptoms, such as depression, that follow an intensely distressing event outside a person's normal life experience.

pragma In John Lee's typology of love, practical love.

pregnancy-induced hypertension Condition characterized by high blood pressure, edema, and protein in the urine.

premature birth Birth that takes place prior to 27 weeks of gestation.

premature ejaculation or **rigid ejaculation** A sexual difficulty characterized by the inability to control or delay ejaculation as long as desired, causing distress.

premenstrual syndrome (PMS) A set of severe symptoms associated with menstruation.

prepared childbirth An approach to childbirth that encourages the mother's understanding of the process and teaches exercises to reduce tension. Also known as natural childbirth.

prepuce The foreskin of the penis.

prevalence Overall occurrence; the total number of cases of a disease, for example.

priapism Prolonged and painful erection due to the inability of blood to drain from the penis.

prodrome A period prior to a viral outbreak when live viruses are shed from the affected areas.

progesterone A female hormone that helps regulate the menstrual cycle and sustain pregnancy.

proliferative phase The buildup of the endometrium in response to increased estrogen during the menstrual cycle.

prophylaxis Protection from disease.

prostaglandins A type of hormone with a fatty-acid base that stimulates muscle contractions.

prostate gland A muscular gland encircling the urethra that produces about one-third of the seminal fluid.

prostate-specific antigen (PSA) test A blood test used to help diagnose prostate cancer.

prostatitis Inflammation of the prostate gland.

prostitution The exchange of sex for money and/or goods.

protection from harm A basic entitlement of all participants in research studies, including the right to confidentiality and anonymity.

proximity Nearness in physical space and time.

pseudohermaphrodite A person with two testes or two ovaries but an ambiguous genital appearance.

psychoanalysis A psychological system developed by Sigmund Freud that traces behavior to unconscious motivations.

psychodynamic therapy Treatment in which an individual is guided toward insight into and interpretation of a problem behavior.

psychosexual development Development of the psychological components of sexuality.

puberty The stage of human development when the body becomes capable of reproduction.

pubic lice *Phthirus pubis*, colloquially known as crabs; tiny lice that infest the pubic hair.

pubococcygeus A part of the muscular sling stretching from the pubic bone in front to the tailbone in back.

random sample A portion of a larger group collected in an unbiased way.

rape Sexual penetration against a person's will through the use or threat of force.

rape trauma syndrome The emotional changes an individual undergoes as a result of rape.

reactive jealousy A type of jealousy that occurs because of a partner's current, past, or anticipated relationship with another person.

recovered memory A repressed memory brought to consciousness so that the individual is aware of it.

refractory period For men, a period following orgasm during which they are not capable of having an orgasm again.

relapse prevention Therapy designed to assist an individual in recognizing and avoiding repetition of a problem behavior.

relaxin A hormone produced by the placenta in the later months of pregnancy that increases flexibility in the ligaments and joints of the pelvic area. In men, relaxin is contained in semen, where it assists in sperm motility.

representative sample A small group representing a larger group in terms of age, sex, ethnicity, socioeconomic status, orientation, and so on.

repressed memory A memory of a powerfully traumatic event that is buried in the unconscious and that produces symptoms such as anxiety or nervousness.

repression A psychological mechanism that keeps people from becoming aware of hidden memories and motives because they arouse guilt or pain.

retrograde ejaculation The backward expulsion of semen into the bladder rather than out of the urethral opening.

retrovirus A virus capable of reversing the normal genetic writing process, causing the host cell to replicate the virus instead of itself.

reverse transcriptase An enzyme in the core of a retrovirus enabling it to write its own genetic program into a host cell's DNA.

Rigiscan A device used in a laboratory or medical clinic to measure arousal of the penis.

root The portion of the penis attached to the pelvic cavity.

RU-486 *See* surgical abortion.

sadomasochism (S&M) A popular, nonclinical term for domination and submission.

salpingitis *See* pelvic inflammatory disease.

satyriasis A pseudoscientific term referring to "abnormal" or "uncontrollable" sexual desire in a man.

scabies A red, intensely itchy rash appearing on the genitals, buttocks, feet, wrists, knuckles, abdomen, armpits, or scalp, caused by the barely visible mite *Sarcoptes scabiei*.

schema A set of interrelated ideas that helps individuals process information by organizing it in useful ways.

scientific method A systematic approach to acquiring knowledge by collecting data, forming a hypothesis, testing it empirically, and observing the results.

script In sociology, the acts, rules, and expectations associated with a particular role.

scrotum A pouch of skin that holds the two testicles.

Seasonale A birth control pill designed to reduce the frequency of a woman's period from once a month to four times a year.

secondary sex characteristics The physical changes that occur as a result of increased amounts of hormones targeting other areas of the body.

secretory phase The phase of the menstrual cycle during which the endometrium begins to prepare for the arrival of a fertilized ovum; without fertilization, the corpus luteum begins to degenerate.

secure attachment A style of infant attachment characterized by feelings of security and confidence in relation to the primary caregiver.

self-disclosure The revelation of personal information that others would not ordinarily know because of its riskiness.

semen The ejaculated fluid containing sperm. Also known as seminal fluid.

seminal vesicle One of two glands at the back of the bladder that secrete about 60% of the seminal fluid.

seminiferous tubule Tiny, tightly compressed tubes in which spermatogenesis takes place.

sensate focus The focusing on touch and the giving and receiving of pleasure as part of the treatment of sexual difficulties.

serial monogamy A succession of monogamous marriages.

seroconversion The process by which a person develops antibodies.

serostatus The absence or presence of antibodies for a particular antigen.

sex Identification as male or female based on genetic and anatomical sex characteristics.

sex flush A darkening of the skin or a rash that temporarily appears as a result of blood rushing to the skin's surface during sexual excitation.

sex information/advice genre A media genre that transmits information and norms about sexuality to a mass audience.

sex reassignment A process that combines surgery with hormone treatment and real-life experience to treat transsexuality.

sex surrogates Sex partners who assist clients having sexual difficulties without spouses or other partners in sex therapy.

sexual abuse trauma A dynamic marked by traumatic sexualization and feelings of betrayal, powerlessness, and stigmatization exhibited by children and adults who have been sexually abused.

sexual aggression Any kind of sexual activity performed against a person's will through the use of force, argument, pressure, alcohol or drugs, or authority.

sexual assault Legal term for forced sexual contact that does not necessarily include penile-vaginal intercourse.

sexual aversion disorder A sexual disorder characterized by a consistently phobic response to sexual activities or the idea of such activities.

sexual coercion A broad term referring to any kind of sexual activity initiated with another person through the use of argument, pressure, pleading, or cajoling, as well as force, pressure, alcohol or drugs, or authority.

sexual disorder An impairment of an individual's sexual responsiveness caused by interference with the brain's arousal capacity.

sexual dissatisfaction A condition in which an individual or couple, not based on a medical diagnosis, decide they are unhappy with their sexual relationship and that they have a problem. Also known as sexual difficulties or sexual dysfunction.

sexual dysfunction An impaired physiological response that prevents an individual from functioning sexually, such as erectile difficulties or absence of orgasm. Also called sexual dissatisfaction, sexual problems, or sexual disorder.

sexual enhancement Improvement in the quality of one's sexual relationship.

sexual harassment The abuse of power for sexual ends; the creation of a hostile work or educational environment because of unwelcomed conduct or conditions of a sexual nature.

sexual health Physical, mental, and social well-being related to sexuality.

sexual intercourse The movement of bodies while the penis is in the vagina. Sometimes also called vaginal intercourse or penile-vaginal intercourse.

sexual interest An inclination to act sexually.

sexuality The emotional, intellectual, and physical aspects of sexual attraction and expression.

sexually explicit material Material such as photographs, videos, films, magazines, or books whose primary themes, topics, or depictions involve sexuality or cause sexual arousal.

sexually transmitted infections (STIs) Infections most often passed from person to person through sexual contact.

sexual masochism A paraphilia characterized by recurrent, intense urges to engage in real (not fantasy) sexual acts in which the person is humiliated, harmed, or otherwise made to suffer.

sexual orientation The pattern of sexual and emotional attraction based on the gender of one's partner.

sexual sadism A paraphilia characterized by recurrent, intense urges to engage in real (not fantasy) sexual acts in which the person inflicts physical or psychological harm on a victim.

sexual script A "blueprint" for sexual behaviors.

sexual variation Sexual variety and diversity in terms of sexual orientation, attitudes, behaviors, desires, fantasies, and so on; sexual activity not statistically typical of American sexual behavior.

shaft The body of the penis.

she-male A male who has undergone breast augmentation.

smegma A cheesy substance produced by several small glands beneath the foreskin of the penis and hood of the clitoris.

social construction The development by society of social categories such as masculinity, femininity, heterosexuality, and homosexuality.

socioeconomic status Ranking in society based on a combination of occupational, educational, and income levels.

sodomy Term used in the law to define sexual behaviors other than penile-vaginal intercourse, such as anal sex and oral sex.

solicitation In terms of prostitution, a word, gesture, or action that implies an offer of sex for sale.

sonogram A visual image created by ultrasound.

spectatoring The process in which a person becomes a spectator of his or her sexual activities, thereby causing sexual difficulties.

sperm The male gamete. Also known as a spermatozoon.

spermatic cord A tube suspending the testicle within the scrotal sac, containing nerves, blood vessels, and a vas deferens.

spermatogenesis The process by which a sperm develops from a spermatid.

spermicide A substance that is toxic to sperm.

spirochete A spiral-shaped bacterium.

sponge A contraceptive device consisting of a round polyurethane shield with a pouch in the center that covers the cervix.

spontaneous abortion The natural expulsion of the conceptus, commonly referred to as miscarriage.

squeeze technique A technique for the treatment of early or premature ejaculation in which the partner squeezes the erect penis below the glans immediately prior to ejaculation.

status An individual's position or ranking in a group.

statutory rape Consensual sexual intercourse with a female under the age of consent.

stereotype A set of simplistic, rigidly held, overgeneralized beliefs about a person or group of people.

sterilization or **voluntary surgical contraception** A surgical procedure that makes the reproductive organs incapable of producing or "delivering" viable gametes (sperm and eggs).

storge In John Lee's typology of love, companionate love.

strain gauge A device resembling a rubber band that is placed over the penis to measure physiological response.

sudden infant death syndrome (SIDS) A phenomenon in which an apparently healthy infant dies suddenly while sleeping.

surrogate motherhood An approach to infertility in which one woman bears a child for another.

survey research A method of gathering information from a small group to make inferences about a larger group.

suspicious jealousy A type of jealousy that is groundless or that arises from ambiguous evidence.

sweating The moistening of the vagina by secretions from its walls.

symptothermal method A fertility awareness method combining the basal body temperature and cervical mucus methods.

syphilis An STI caused by the *Treponema pallidum* bacterium.

Tantric sex A sexual technique based on Eastern religions in which a couple shares "energy" during sexual intercourse.

T cell Any of several types of lymphocytes involved in the immune response.

telephone scatologia A paraphilia involving recurrent, intense urges to make obscene telephone calls.

tenting The expansion of the inner two-thirds of the vagina during sexual arousal.

teratogen A toxic substance that causes birth defects.

testicle or **testis** (plural, *testes*) One of the paired male gonads inside the scrotum.

testosterone A steroid hormone associated with sperm production, the development of secondary sex characteristics in males, and the sex drive in both males and females.

testosterone supplement or **testosterone replacement therapy** The administration of testosterone through an injection or ointment to increase sexual interest and potency and reduce depression.

toxic shock syndrome (TSS)   A potentially life-threatening condition caused by the *Staphylococcus aureus* bacterium and linked to the use of superabsorbent tampons.

transgender   An inclusive gender category; a transgenderist is someone who lives full-time in a gender role opposite to the gender role presumed by society to match the person's genetic sex.

transition   The end of the first stage of labor, when the infant's head enters the birth canal.

transsexual   A person whose genitals and gender identity as male or female are discordant; postsurgical transsexuals have surgically altered their genitals to fit their gender identity.

transvestic fetishism   A paraphilia in which a heterosexual male cross-dresses for sexual arousal.

transvestism   A clinical term referring to the wearing of clothing of the other sex, usually for sexual arousal.

triangular theory of love   A theory developed by Robert Sternberg emphasizing the dynamic quality of love as expressed by the interrelationship of three elements: intimacy, passion, and decision/commitment.

tribidism   An act in which one partner lies on top of the other and moves rhythmically for genital stimulation.

trichomoniasis   A vaginal infection caused by *Trichomonas vaginalis*. Also known as trich.

trust   Belief in the reliability and integrity of another person, process, thing, or institution.

tubal ligation   The cutting and tying off (or other method of closure) of the fallopian tubes so that ova cannot be fertilized.

Turner syndrome   A chromosomal disorder affecting females born lacking an X chromosome, resulting in the failure to develop ovaries.

two-spirit   In many cultures, a male who assumes female dress, gender role, and status.

ultrasound   The use of high-frequency sound waves to create a visual image, as of the fetus in the uterus.

umbilical cord   The cord connecting the placenta and fetus, through which nutrients pass.

unrequited love   Love that is not returned.

urethra   The tube through which urine (and in men, semen) passes.

urethral bulb   The expanded portion of the urethra at the bladder.

urethral opening   The opening in the urethra, through which urine is expelled.

urethritis   Inflammation of the urethra.

urophilia   A paraphilia in which a person gets sexual pleasure from contact with urine.

uterus   A hollow, thick-walled, muscular organ held in the pelvic cavity by flexible ligaments and supported by several muscles. Also known as womb.

vacuum aspiration   A first-trimester form of abortion using vacuum suction to remove the conceptus and other tissue from the uterus.

vagina   In females, a flexible, muscular organ that begins between the legs and extends diagonally toward the small of the back. It encompasses the penis during sexual intercourse and is the pathway (birth canal) through which an infant is born.

vaginal ring   A vaginal form of reversible, hormonal birth control. Commonly referred to as NuvaRing®.

vaginismus   A sexual difficulty characterized by muscle spasms around the vaginal entrance, preventing the insertion of a penis.

vaginitis   Any of several kinds of vaginal infection.

value judgment   An evaluation as "good" or "bad" based on moral or ethical standards rather than objective ones.

variable   An aspect or factor that can be manipulated in an experiment.

varicocele   A varicose vein above the testicle that may cause lowered fertility in men.

vas deferens (plural, *vasa deferentia*)   One of two tubes that transport sperm from the epididymis to the ejaculatory duct within the prostate gland.

vasectomy   A form of surgical sterilization in which each vas deferens is severed, thereby preventing sperm from entering the seminal fluid.

vasocongestion   Blood engorgement of body tissues.

vernix   The waxy substance that sometimes covers an infant at birth.

vestibule   The area enclosed by the labia minora.

Viagra   The first effective and safe oral drug for the treatment of male erectile disorder.

viral load test   A blood test that measures the amount of HIV in the bloodstream and serves as an indicator for determining the risk of progressing to AIDS.

virus   A protein-coated package of genes that invades a cell and alters the way in which the cell reproduces itself.

voyeurism   A paraphilia involving recurrent, intense urges to view nonconsenting others while they are engaged in sexual activities.

vulva   The collective term for the external female genitals.

wasting syndrome   Severe weight loss, usually accompanied by weakness and persistent diarrhea; a condition linked to AIDS.

Western blot   A test to determine whether antibodies are specific to HIV.

yolk sac   The producer of the embryo's first blood cells and the germ cells that will develop into gonads.

zoophilia   A paraphilia involving recurrent, intense urges to engage in sexual activities with animals.

Bibliography

Abbey, A. (1991). "Acquaintance Rape and Alcohol Consumption on College Campuses: How Are They Linked?" *Journal of American College Health, 39*(4), 165–169.

Abbey, A., & Harnish, R. J. (1995). "Perception of Sexual Intent: The Role of Gender, Alcohol Consumption, and Rape Supportive Attitudes." *Sex Roles, 32*(5–6), 297–313.

Abel, G. (1989). "Paraphilias." In H. I. Kaplan & B. Sadock (Eds.), *Comprehensive Textbook of Psychiatry, Vol. I* (5th ed.), Baltimore: Williams & Wilkins.

Abma, J. C., Chandra, A., Mosher, W. D., Peterson, L., & Piccinino, L. (1997). "Fertility, Family Planning & Women's Health: New Data from the 1995 National Survey of Family Growth." National Center for Health Statistics. *Vital Health Statistics, 23*(19).

Abma, J. C., & Sonenstein, F. L. (2001). "Sexual Activity and Contraceptive Practices Among Teenagers in the United States, 1988 and 1995." *Vital Health Statistics, 23*(21).

Abrahams, M. F. (1994). "Perceiving Flirtatious Communication." *The Journal of Sex Research, 31*(4), 283–292.

Abramson, P. J., & Mosher, D. L. (1975). "The Development of a Measure of Negative Attitudes Toward Masturbation." *Journal of Consulting and Clinical Psychology, 43*, 485–490.

Absi-Semaan, N., Crombie, G., & Freeman, C. (1993). "Masculinity and Femininity in Middle Childhood: Developmental and Factor Analyses." *Sex Roles, 28*(3–4), 187–202.

Action on Smoking and Health. (1999). Fact Sheet #7: Smoking and Reproduction. Available: http://www.ash.org.uk/papers/fact07.htm (Last visited 5/30/03).

Adler, N., Hendrick, S., & Hendrick, C. (1989). "Male Sexual Preference and Attitudes Toward Love and Sexuality." *Journal of Sex Education and Therapy, 12*(2), 27–30.

Adler, N. A., & Schultz, J. (1995). "Sibling Incest Offenders." *Child Abuse & Neglect, 19*(7), 811–819.

Afifi, W. A., & Faulkner, S. T. (2000). "On Being 'Just Friends': The Frequency and Impact of Sexual Activity in Cross-Sex Friendships." *Journal of Social and Personal Relationships, 17*, 205–222.

Ahn, H. N., & Gilbert, N. (1992). "Cultural Diversity and Sexual Abuse Prevention." *Social Service Review, 66*(3), 410–428.

Aho, M., Koivisto, A. M., Tammela, T. L., & Auvinen, A. (2000). "Is the Incidence of Hypospadias Increasing? Analysis of Finnish Hospital Discharge Data 1970–1994." *Environmental Health Perspectives, 108*, 463–465.

Ahrendt, D. (2001). "Ergogenic Aids: Counseling the Athlete." *American Family Physician, 63*(5), 913–1013.

"AIDS Test for Pregnant Women." (1995, February 23). *San Francisco Chronicle.*

Ainsworth, M., et al. (1978). *Patterns of Attachment: A Psychological Study of the Strange Situation.* Hillsdale, NJ: Erlbaum.

Alan Guttmacher Institute. (1999a). Facts in Brief: Contraceptive Use. Available: http://www.agi-usa.org/pubs_contr_use.html (Last visited 8/22/03).

Alan Guttmacher Institute. (1999b). *Teen Sex and Pregnancy.* New York: Author.

Alan Guttmacher Institute. (2000). *Special Tabulations from the 1995 National Survey of Family Growth.* New York: Author.

Alan Guttmacher Institute. (2001). "Can More Progress Be Made? Teenage Sexual and Reproductive Behavior in Developed Countries." New York: Author.

Alan Guttmacher Institute. (2002a). Sexual and Reproductive Health: Women and Men. Available: http://www.agi-usa.org/pubs/fb_10-02.html (Last visited 12/30/02).

Alan Guttmacher Institute. (2002b). "Teen Pregnancy: Trends and Lessons Learned." *Issues in Brief, 2002 Series,* No. 1. New York: Author.

Alan Guttmacher Institute. (2002c). *In Their Own Right: Addressing the Sexual and Reproductive Health Needs of American Men.* New York: Author.

Alan Guttmacher Institute. (2002d). Contraception Counts. Available: http://guttmacher.org/pubs/state_data/states/california.html (Last visited 12/30/02).

Alan Guttmacher Institute. (2003). Trends in Abortion in the United States, 1973–2000. Available: http://www.agi-usa.org (Last visited 4/7/03).

Alapack, R. (1991). "The Adolescent First Kiss." *Humanistic Psychologist, 19*(1), 48–67.

Albert, A. E., Warner, D. L., Hatcher, R. A., Trussell, J., & Bennett, C. (1995, March 21). "Condom Use Among Female Commercial Sex Workers in Nevada's Legal Brothels." Paper available from Family Planning Program, Emory University School of Medicine, Atlanta.

Alcott, W. (1868). *The Physiology of Marriage.* Boston: Jewett.

Allen, M., Emmers, T., Gebhardt, L., & Giery, M. A. (1995). "Exposure to Pornography and Acceptance of Rape Myths." *Journal of Communication, 45*(1), 5–26.

Allport, G. (1958). *The Nature of Prejudice.* Garden City, NY: Doubleday.

Altman, D. (1985). *AIDS in the Mind of America.* Garden City, NY: Doubleday.

Alzubaidi, N. H., Chapin, H. L., Vanderhoof, V. H., Calis, K. A., & Nelson, L. M. (2002, May). "Meeting the Needs of Young Women with Secondary Amenorrhea and Spontaneous Premature Ovarian Failure." *Obstetrics and Gynecology, 99*(5), 720–725.

Amaro, H. (1988). "Considerations for Prevention of HIV Infection Among Hispanic Women." *Psychology of Women Quarterly, 12*(4), 429–443.

Amato, P. R. (2000). "The Consequences of Divorce for Adults and Children." *Journal of Marriage and the Family, 62*, 1269–1287.

American Academy of Pediatrics. (2000). "Evaluation of the Newborn with Developmental Anomalies of the External Genitalia." *Pediatrics, 106*(1), 138–142.

American Academy of Pediatrics. (2001). "Sexuality, Contraception, and the Media." *Pediatrics, 107*(1), 191–194.

American Academy of Pediatrics. (2002). "Coparent or Second Parent Adoption by Same-Sex Parents." *Pediatrics, 109*(2), 339–341.

American Association of Retired People/*Modern Maturity*. (1999, March). Sexuality Survey. Available: http://research.aarp .org/health/mmsexsurvey_1.html (Last visited 3/11/00).

American Association of University Women Educational Foundation. (2001). *Hostile Hallways: The AAUW Survey on Sexual Harassment in America's Schools*. Washington, DC: Author.

American Cancer Society. (2001). Breast Cancer Facts and Figures, 2001–2002. Available: http://www.cancer.org (Last visited 5/3/03).

American Cancer Society. (2003a). All About Breast Cancer. Available: http://www.cancer.org/docroot/CRI/CRI_2_3x .asp?dt=5 (Last visited 5/3/03).

American Cancer Society. (2003b). All About Cervical Cancer. Available: http://www.cancer.org/docroot/CRI/CRI_2_3x .asp?dt=8 (Last visited 5/3/03).

American Cancer Society. (2003c). All About Ovarian Cancer. Available: http://www.cancer.org/docroot/CRI/CRI_2_3x .asp?dt=33 (Last visited 5/3/03).

American Cancer Society. (2003d). All About Uterine Cancer. Available: http://www.cancer.org/docroot/CRI/CRI_2_3x .asp?dt=63 (Last visited 5/3/03).

American Cancer Society. (2003e). All About Vaginal Cancer. Available: http://www.cancer.org/docroot/CRI/CRI_2_3x .asp?dt=55 (Last visited 5/3/03).

American Cancer Society. (2003f). All About Prostate Cancer. Available: http://www.cancer.org/docroot/CRI/CRI_2_3x .asp?dt=36 (Last visited 5/3/03).

American Cancer Society. (2003g). All About Testicular Cancer. Available: http://www.cancer.org/docroot/CRI/CRI_2_3x .asp?dt=44 (Last visited 5/3/03).

American Cancer Society. (2003h). All About Penile Cancer. Available: http://www.cancer.org/docroot/CRI/CRI_2_3x .asp?dt=35 (Last visited 5/3/03).

American Cancer Society. (2003i). All About Male Breast Cancer. Available: http://www.cancer.org/docroot/CRI/CRI_2_3x .asp?dt=28 (Last visited 5/3/03).

American Diabetes Association. (2001). A Guide for Women with Diabetes. Available: http://www.diabetes.org (Last visited 5/2/03).

American Diabetes Association. (n.d.). Basic Diabetes Information. Available: http://www.diabetes.org (Last visited 5/2/03).

American Psychiatric Association. (2000). *Diagnostic and Statistical Manual of Mental Disorders* (4th ed., text revision). Washington, DC: Author.

American Psychological Association. (1994). *Interim Report of the APA Working Group on Investigation of Memories of Childhood Abuse*. Washington, DC: Author.

American Social Health Association (ASHA). (1996). Hepatitis B. Available: http://sunsite.unc.edu/ASHA/std/hepb. html#why (Last visited 2/14/98).

American Social Health Association (ASHA). (1998a). STD Statistics. Available: http://www.ashastd.org/std/stats/html (Last visited 12/5/00).

American Social Health Association (ASHA). (1998b). *Sexually Transmitted Diseases in America: How Many Cases and at What Cost?* Menlo Park, CA: Kaiser Family Foundation.

American Social Health Association (ASHA). (1998c). Chlamydia: What You Should Know. Available: http://sunsite.unc.edu/ ASHA/std/chlam.html#intro (Last visited 2/14/98).

American Society of Plastic Surgeons. (2003). 2000/2001/2002 National Plastic Surgery Statistics. Available: http://www .plasticsurgery.org (Last visited 5/3/03).

Amnesty International. (1998). Female Genital Mutilation—a Human Rights Information Packet. Available: http://www .amnesty.org/ailib/intcam/femgen/fgm2.htm (Last visited 5/16/03).

Andersen, D. A., Lustig, M. W., & Andersen, J. F. (1987). "Regional Patterns of Communication in the United States: A Theoretical Perspective." *Communication Monographs, 54*, 128–144.

Anderson, C. (1995). "Childhood Sexually Transmitted Diseases: One Consequence of Sexual Abuse." *Public Health Nursing, 12*(1), 41–46.

Andrews, S. (1992, November 2). "The Naked Truth." *San Jose Mercury News*, pp. 1, 4.

Ann, C. C. (1997). "A Proposal for a Radical New Sex Therapy Technique for the Management of Vasocongestive and Orgasmic Dysfunction in Women: The AFE Zone Stimulation Technique." *Sexual and Marital Therapy, 12*, 357–370.

Annon, J. (1974). *The Behavioral Treatment of Sexual Problems*. Honolulu: Enabling Systems.

Annon, J. (1976). *Behavioral Treatment of Sexual Problems: Brief Therapy*. New York: Harper & Row.

"Aphrodisiacs: Do They Ever Work?" (1996). *Sex over Forty, 15*(7), 1–5.

Aral, S. O. (1994). "Sexual Behavior in Sexually Transmitted Disease Research: An Overview." *Sexually Transmitted Diseases, 21*, S59–S64.

Arey, D. (1995). "Gay Males and Sexual Child Abuse." In L. A. Fontes (Ed.), *Sexual Abuse in Nine North American Cultures: Treatment and Prevention*. Thousand Oaks, CA: Sage.

Arndt, W. B., Jr. (1991). *Gender Disorders and the Paraphilias*. Madison, CT: International Universities Press.

Aron, A., & Aron, E. (1991). "Love and Sexuality." In K. McKinney & S. Sprecher (Eds.), *Sexuality in Close Relationships*. Hillsdale, NJ: Erlbaum.

Aron, A., Dutton, D. G., & Aron, E. N. (1989). "Experiences of Falling in Love." *Journal of Social and Personal Relationships, 6*, 243–257.

"Asia: Child Prostitution in Cambodia." (1996). *The Economist, 338*.

Asian American and Pacific Islander Women's Health. (2000). National Women's Health Information Center. Available: http://www.4women.gov/faq/Asian-Pacific.htm (Last visited 6/1/2000).

Athey, J. L. (1991). "HIV Infection and Homeless Adolescents." *Child Welfare, 70*(5), 517–528.

Atwood, J. D., & Dershowitz, S. (1992). "Constructing a Sex and Marital Therapy Frame: Ways to Help Couples Deconstruct Sexual Problems." *Journal of Sex and Marital Therapy, 18*(3), 196–218.

Atwood, J. D., & Gagnon, J. (1987). "Masturbatory Behavior in College Youth." *Journal of Sex Education and Therapy, 13*, 35–42.

Audet, M. C., Moreau, M., Koltun, W. D., et al. (2001). "Evaluation of Contraceptive Efficacy and Cycle Control of a Transdermal Contraceptive Patch vs. an Oral Contraceptive: A Randomized Controlled Trial." *Journal of the American Medical Association, 285*, 2347–2354.

Baca-Zinn, M. (1994). "Feminist Rethinking from Racial-Ethnic Families." In M. Baca-Zinn & B. Thorton-Dill (Eds.), *Women of Color in U.S. Society*. Philadelphia: Temple University Press.

Bachu, A., & O'Connell, M. (2001). "Fertility of American Women: June 2000." *Current Population Reports,* Series P20-543RV. Washington, DC: U.S. Government Printing Office.

Bailey, J. M., & Pillard, R. C. (1991). "A Genetic Study of Male Sexual Orientation." *Archives of General Psychiatry, 48*(12), 1089–1096.

Bailey, J. M., Pillard, R. C., Neale, M. C., & Agyei, Y. (1993). "Heritable Factors Influence Sexual Orientation in Women." *Archives of General Psychiatry, 50*(3), 217–223.

Bajracharya, S., Sarvela, P., & Isberner, F. R. (1995). "A Retrospective Study of First Sex Intercourse Experiences Among Undergraduates." *Journal of American College Health, 43*(4), 169–177.

Baker, C. P. (1995). "Child Chattel: Future Tourists for Sex." *Insight on the News, 11,* 11.

Bakken, R. J., & Winter, M. (2002). "Family Characteristics and Sexual Risk Behaviors Among Black Men in the United States." *Perspectives on Sexual and Reproductive Health, 34,* 252–258.

Baldwin, J. D., Whitely, S., & Baldwin, J. I. (1993). "The Effect of Ethnic Group on Sexual Activities Related to Contraception and STDs." *The Journal of Sex Research, 29*(2), 189–206.

Bancroft, J. (1984). "Hormones and Human Sexual Behavior." *Journal of Sex and Marital Therapy, 10,* 3–21.

Bancroft, J. (2002). "The Medicalization of Female Sexual Dysfunction: The Need for Caution." *Archives of Sexual Behavior, 31,* 451–455.

Bancroft, J., Herbenick, D., & Reynolds, M. (2003). "Masturbation as a Marker of Sexual Development." In J. Bancroft (Ed.), *Sexual Development in Childhood.* Bloomington: Indiana University Press.

Bancroft, J., Loftus, J., & Long, S. (2003). "Distress About Sex: A National Survey of Women in Heterosexual Relationships." *Archives of Sexual Behavior, 32,* 193–208.

Ban on Female Circumcision Reinstated in Egypt. (1997). Available: http://www.ama-assn.org/special/womh/newsline/reuters/12301825.htm (Last visited 1/27/98).

Barak, A., Fisher, W. A., Belfry, S., & Lashambe, D. R. (1999). "Sex, Guys, and Cyberspace: Effects of Internet Pornography and Individual Differences in Men's Attitudes Towards Women." *Journal of Psychology and Human Sexuality, 11,* 63–91.

Barbach, L. (1982). *For Each Other: Sharing Sexual Intimacy.* Garden City, NY: Doubleday.

Barker-Benfield, G. J. (1976). *The Horrors of the Half-Known Life: Male Attitudes Toward Women and Sexuality in Nineteenth-Century America.* New York: Harper & Row.

Barrow, G., & Smith, P. (1992). *Aging, Ageism, and Society.* St. Paul, MN: West.

Barry, K. (1995). *The Prostitution of Sexuality: The Global Exploitation of Women.* New York: University Press.

Barth, R. J., & Kinder, B. N. (1987). "The Mislabeling of Sexual Impulsivity." *Journal of Sex and Marital Therapy, 13,* 15–23.

Bass, E., & Davis, L. (1988). *The Courage to Heal.* New York: Harper Perennial.

Basson, R., Berman, J., Burnett, A., Derogatis, L., Ferguson, D., Fourcroy, J., et al. (2001). "Report of the International Consensus Development Conference on Female Sexual Dysfunction: Definitions and Classifications." *Journal of Sex and Marital Therapy, 27,* 83–94.

Baumeister, R., Wotman, S. R., & Stillwell, A. M. (1993). "Unrequited Love: On Heartbreak, Anger, Guilt, Scriptlessness, and Humiliation." *The Journal of Personality and Social Psychology, 64,* 377–394.

Bauserman, R. (1998). "Egalitarian, Sexist, and Aggressive Sexual Materials: Attitude Effects and Viewer Responses." *The Journal of Sex Research, 35*(3), 244–253.

Bayles, F. (2003, November 20). "Gay-marriage ruling gives little time to prepare." *USA Today,* p. 8A.

Bean, F., & Tienda, M. (1987). *The Hispanic Population of the United States.* New York: Russell Sage Foundation.

Becerra, R. (1988). "The Mexican American Family." In C. Mindel et al. (Eds.), *Ethnic Families in America: Patterns and Variations* (3rd ed.). New York: Elsevier North Holland.

Bechhofer, L., & Parrot, A. (1991). "What Is Acquaintance Rape?" In A. Parrot & L. Bechhofer (Eds.), *Acquaintance Rape: The Hidden Crime.* New York: Wiley.

Beck, J. G., & Bozman, A. W. (1995). "Gender Differences in Sexual Desire: The Effects of Anger and Anxiety." *Journal of Sex and Marital Therapy, 18,* 273–284.

Beck, M. (1992, May 25). "Menopause." *Newsweek,* pp. 71–79.

Begley, S. (1997, February 24). "The Mammogram War." *Newsweek,* pp. 55–60.

Beier, S. R. (2000, April). "The Potential Role of an Adult Mentor in Influencing High-Risk Behaviors in Adolescents." *Archives of Pediatrics and Adolescent Medicine, 154,* 327–331.

Beitchman, J. H., Zucker, K. J., Hood, J. E., daCosta, G. A., Akman, D., & Cassavia, E. (1992). "A Review of the Long-Term Effects of Child Sexual Abuse." *Child Abuse and Neglect, 16*(1), 101–128.

Belanger, C., Laughrea, K., & Lafontaine, M. F. (2001). "The Impact of Anger on Sexual Satisfaction in Marriage." *The Canadian Journal of Human Sexuality, 10*(3–4), 91–99.

Belcastro, P. (1985). "Sexual Behavior Differences Between Black and White Students." *The Journal of Sex Research, 21*(1), 56–67.

Belk, R. (1991). "The Ineluctable Mysteries of Possessions." *Journal of Social Behavior and Personality, 6*(6), 17–55.

Bell, A., Weinberg, M., & Hammersmith, S. (1981). *Sexual Preference: Its Development in Men and Women.* Bloomington: Indiana University Press.

Belzer, E. G. (1984). "A Review of Female Ejaculation and the Grafenberg Spot." *Women and Health, 9,* 5–16.

Bem, S. L. (1975). "Androgyny vs. the Tight Little Lives of Fluffy Women and Chesty Men." *Psychology Today, 9*(4), 58–59ff.

Bem, S. L. (1983). "Gender Schema Theory and Its Implications for Child Development: Raising Gender-Aschematic Children in a Gender-Schematic Society." *Signs, 8*(4), 598–616.

Bem, S. L. (1995). "Dismantling Gender Polarization and Compulsory Heterosexuality: Should We Turn the Volume Up or Down?" *The Journal of Sex Research 32*(4), 329–332.

Benotsch, E. G., Kalichman, S., Lawrence, A., & Nordling, N. (2002). "Men Who Have Met Sex Partners via the Internet: Prevalence, Predictors, and Implications for HIV Prevention." *Archives of Sexual Behavior, 31,* 177–183.

Berger, A. A. (1991). "Of Mice and Men: An Introduction to Mouseology; or Anal Eroticism and Disney." *Journal of Homosexuality, 21*(1–2), 155–165.

Berger, R. M. (1982). "The Unseen Minority: Older Gays and Lesbians." *Social Work, 27,* 236–242.

Berrick, J. D., & Barth, R. P. (1992). "Child Sexual Abuse Prevention—Research Review and Recommendations." *Social Work Research and Abstracts, 28,* 6–15.

Bieber, I. (1962). *Homosexuality: A Psychoanalytic Study.* New York: Basic Books.

Billy, J. O., Tanfer, K., Grady, W. R., & Klepinger, D. H. (1993). "The Sexual Behavior of Men in the United States." *Family Planning Perspectives, 25*(2), 52–60.

Biskupic, J. (2002, April 17). "'Virtual' Porn Ruling Hinged on Threat to Art." *USA Today,* p. A3.

Biskupic, J. (2003a, March 4). "Case Tests Congress's Ability to Make Libraries Block Porn." *USA Today,* p. A3.

Biskupic, J. (2003b, June 27). "Gay Sex Ban Struck Down." *USA Today,* p. A1.

Biskupic, J. (2003c, June 27). "Decision Represents an Enormous Turn in the Law." *USA Today,* p. A5.

Blackless, M., Charuvastra, A., Derryck, A., Fausto-Sterling, A., Lauzanne, K., & Lee, E. (2000). "How Sexually Dimorphic Are We? Review and Synthesis." *American Journal of Human Biology, 12,* 151–166.

Blackwood, E. (1984). "Sexuality and Gender in Certain Native American Tribes: The Case of Cross-Gender Females." *Signs, 10,* 27–42.

Blake, S. M., Simkin, L., Ledsky, R., Perkins, C., & Calabrese, J. M. (2001). "Effects of Parent-Child Communications Intervention on Young Adolescents' Risk for Early Onset of Sexual Intercourse." *Family Planning Perspective, 33,* 52–61.

Blanchard, R. (1993, March). "The She-Male Phenomena and the Concept of Partial Autogynephilia." *Journal of Sex and Marital Therapy, 19*(1), 69–76.

Blanchard, R., & Hucker, S. (1991). "Age, Transvestism, Bondage, and Concurrent Paraphilic Activities in 117 Fatal Cases of Autoerotic Asphyxia." *British Journal of Psychiatry, 159,* 371–377.

Blechman, E. A. (1990). *Emotions and the Family: For Better or for Worse.* Hillsdale, NJ: Erlbaum.

Blee, K., & Tickamyer, A. (1995). "Racial Differences in Men's Attitudes About Women's Gender Roles." *Journal of Marriage and the Family, 57,* 21–30.

Blum, D. (1997). *Sex on the Brain.* New York: Viking Press.

Blumenfeld, W., & Raymond, D. (1989). *Looking at Gay and Lesbian Life.* Boston: Beacon Press.

Blumstein, P., & Schwartz, P. (1983). *American Couples.* New York: McGraw-Hill.

Boakes, J. (1995). "False Memory Syndrome" [Commentary]. *The Lancet, 346*(8982), 1048–1050.

Bockting, W. O. (1997). "Transgender Coming Out: A Psychological Paradigm Shift." In B. Bullough, V. Bullough, & J. Elias (Eds.), *Gender Bending.* New York: Prometheus Books.

Bogaert, A. F. (1993). *The Sexual Media: The Role of Individual Differences.* Unpublished doctoral dissertation, University of Western Ontario, London, Ontario, Canada.

Bogaert, A. F. (2001). "Personality, Individual Differences, and Preferences for the Sexual Media." *Archives of Sexual Behavior, 30,* 29–53.

Bolan, G., Ehrhardt, A. A., & Wasserheit, J. N. (1999). "Gender Perspectives and STDs." In K. K. Holmes et al. (Eds.), *Sexually Transmitted Diseases.* New York: McGraw-Hill.

Boles, J., & Elifson, E. W. (1994, July). "The Social Organization of Transvestite Prostitution and AIDS." *Social Science and Medicine, 39*(2), 85–93.

Bolin, A. (1997). "Transforming Transvestism and Transsexualism: Polarity, Politics, and Gender." In B. Bullough, V. L. Bullough, & J. Elias (Eds.), *Gender Bending.* New York: Prometheus Books.

Bone Loss in Depo-Provera Users Largely Reversible. (2002). National Institutes of Health. Available: http://www.nih.gov/news/pr/sep2002/nichd-06.htm (Last visited 11/30/02).

Bonner, K. (2001). "Male Circumcision as an HIV Control Strategy: Not a 'Natural Condom.'" *Reproductive Health Matters, 9,* 143–155.

Borneman, E. (1983). "Progress in Empirical Research on Children's Sexuality." *SIECUS Report,* 1–5.

Borrello, G., & Thompson, B. (1990). "A Note Regarding the Validity of Lee's Typology of Love." *Journal of Psychology, 124*(6), 639–644.

Boston Women's Health Book Collective. (1996). *The New Our Bodies, Ourselves.* New York: Simon & Schuster.

Bostwick, H. (1860). *A Treatise on the Nature and Treatment of Seminal Disease, Impotency, and Other Kindred Afflictions* (12th ed.). New York: Burgess, Stringer.

Bower, B. (1996, August 10). "From Exotic to Erotic: Roots of Sexual Orientation Found in Personality, Childhood Friendships." *Science News, 150,* 88–89.

Bowman, C. G. (1993). "Street Harassment and the Informal Ghettoization of Women." *Harvard Law Review, 106*(3), 517–580.

Boyer, C. B., Shafer, M., Wibbelsman, C. J., Seeberg, D., Teitle, E., & Lovell, N. (2000). "Associations of Sociodemographic, Psychosocial, and Behavioral Factors with Sexual Risk and Sexually Transmitted Diseases in Teen Clinic Patients." *Journal of Adolescent Health, 27,* 102–111.

Bozett, F. W. (1987). "Children of Gay Fathers." In F. W. Bozett (Ed.), *Gay and Lesbian Parents.* New York: Praeger.

Brady, E. C., Chrisler, J. C., Hosdale, D. C., & Osowiecki, D. M. (1991). "Date Rape: Expectations, Avoidance, Strategies, and Attitudes Toward Victims." *Journal of Social Psychology, 131*(3), 427–429.

Braverman, P., & Strasburger, V. (1994, January). "Sexually Transmitted Diseases." *Clinical Pediatrics,* 26–37.

"Breast Cancer Studies Find Radiation Helps." (1997, October 2). *San Francisco Chronicle,* p. A4.

Brennan, K., & Shaver, P. R. (1995). "Dimensions of Adult Attachment, Affect Regulation, and Romantic Relationship Functioning." *Personality and Social Psychology Bulletin, 21*(3), 267–283.

Brenton, M. (1990, July–August). "The Importance of Touch." *Bridal Guide,* pp. 134, 136.

Breslow, N. (1989). "Sources of Confusion in the Study and Treatment of Sadomasochism." *Journal of Social Behavior and Personality, 4*(3), 263–274.

Breslow, N., Evans, L., & Langley, J. (1985). "On the Prevalence and Roles of Females in the Sadomasochistic Subculture: Report on an Empirical Investigation." *Archives of Sexual Behavior, 14,* 303–317.

Bridgeland, W. M., Duane, E. A., & Stewart, C. S. (1995). "Sexual Victimization Among Undergraduates." *College Student Journal 29*(1), 16–25.

Briere, J. N., & Elliott, D. M. (1994). "Immediate and Long-Term Impacts of Child Sexual Abuse." *The Future of Children, 4,* 54–69.

Bringle, R., & Buunk, B. (1991). "Extradyadic Relationships and Sexual Jealousy." In K. McKinney & S. Sprecher (Eds.), *Sexuality in Close Relationships.* Hillsdale, NJ: Erlbaum.

Brochman, S. (1991, July 30). "Silent Victims: Bringing Male Rape Out of the Closet." *The Advocate,* pp. 38–43.

Brody, J. E. (1992). "Estrogen Is Found to Improve Mood, Not Just Menopause Symptoms." *The New York Times,* p. 141.

Brody, J. E. (1993, February 24). "Don't Panic. Before Worrying About All the Medical Studies, Take a Close Look at the Evidence." *The New York Times,* p. B7.

Brown, G. R. (1995). "Cross-Dressing Men Often Lead Double Lives." *Menninger Letter*, pp. 4–5.

Brown, G. R., & Collier, Z. (1989). "Transvestites' Women Revisited: A Nonpatient Sample." *Archives of Sexual Behavior, 18,* 73–83.

Brown, J. D. (2002). "Mass Media Influences on Sexuality." *The Journal of Sex Research, 39*(1), 42–46.

Brown, J. D., & Keller, S. N. (2000). "Can the Mass Media Be Healthy Sex Educators?" *Family Planning Perspectives, 32*(5), 255–257.

Browne, A., & Finkelhor, D. (1986). "Initial and Long-Term Effects: A Review of the Research." In D. Finkelhor (Ed.), *Sourcebook on Child Sexual Abuse*. Beverly Hills, CA: Sage.

Bruch, H. (1978). *The Golden Cage: The Enigma of Anorexia Nervosa*. Cambridge, MA: Harvard University Press.

Bullough, B., & Bullough, V. L. (1996). "Female Prostitution: Current Research and Changing Interpretations." *Annual Review of Sex Research, 7,* 158–180.

Bullough, V. (1976). *Sexual Variance in Society and History*. New York: Wiley.

Bullough, V. (1991). "Transvestism: A Reexamination." *Journal of Psychology and Human Sexuality, 4*(2), 53–67.

Bullough, V. L., & Bullough, B. (1993). *Cross Dressing, Sex and Gender*. Philadelphia: University of Pennsylvania Press.

Bullough, V., & Weinberg, J. S. (1988). "Women Married to Transvestites: Problems and Adjustments." *Journal of Psychology and Human Sexuality, 1,* 83–104.

Burcky, W., Reuterman, N., & Kopsky, S. (1988). "Dating Violence Among High School Students." *School Counselor, 35*(5), 353–358.

Burke, M. (1995). "Lesbians and Sexual Child Abuse." In L. A. Fontes (Ed.), *Sexual Abuse in Nine North American Cultures: Treatment and Prevention*. Thousand Oaks, CA: Sage.

Buss, D. (1999). *Evolutionary Psychology*. Boston: Allyn & Bacon.

Buss, D. (2000). *Dangerous Passion: Why Jealousy Is as Necessary as Love and Sex*. New York: Simon & Schuster.

Buss, D. M. (1994). "The Strategies of Human Mating." *American Scientist, 82*(3), 238–249.

Buss, D. M., Larsen, R. J., & Westen, D. (1996). "Sex Differences in Jealousy: Not Gone, Not Forgotten, and Not Explained by Alternative Hypotheses." *Psychological Science, 7,* 373–375.

Buss, D. M., Shackelford, T. D., Kirkpatrick, L. A., & Larsen, R. J. (2001). "A Half Century of Mate Preferences: The Cultural Evolution of Values." *Journal of Marriage and Family, 63,* 491–503.

Bussey, K., & Bandura, A. (1999). "Social Cognitive Theory of Gender Development and Differentiation." *Psychological Review, 106,* 676–713.

Butts, J. D. (1992). "The Relationship Between Sexual Addiction and Sexual Dysfunction." *Journal of Health Care for the Poor and Underserved, 3*(1), 128–135.

Buunk, B., & van Driel, B. (1989). *Variant Lifestyles and Relationships*. Newbury Park, CA: Sage.

Buxton, A. P. (1999). "The Best Interests of Children of Gay and Lesbian Parents." In R. M. Galatzer-Levy & L. Kraus (Eds.), *The Scientific Basis of Child Custody Decisions*. New York: Wiley.

Byers, E. S., & Demmons, S. (1999). "Sexual Satisfaction and Sexual Disclosure Within Dating Relationships." *Journal of Sex Research, 36,* 180–189.

Byers, E. S., & Eno, R. J. (1991). "Predicting Men's Sexual Coercion and Aggression from Attitudes, Dating History, and Sexual Response." *The Journal of Psychology and Human Sexuality, 4*(3), 55–70.

Byne, W., Tobet, S., Mattiace, L. A., Lasco, M. S., Kemether, E., Edgar, M. A., Morgello, S., Buchsbaum, M. S., & Jones, L. B. (2001). "The Interstitial Nuclei of the Human Anterior Hypothalamus: An Investigation of Variation with Sex, Sexual Orientation, and HIV Status." *Hormones and Behavior, 409,* 86–92.

Cado, S., & Leitenberg, H. (1990). "Guilt Reactions to Sexual Fantasies During Intercourse." *Archives of Sexual Behavior, 19*(1), 49–63.

Cahoon, D., Edmonds, E. M., Spaulding, R. M., & Dickens, J. C. (1995). "A Comparison of the Opinions of Black and White Males and Females Concerning the Occurrence of Rape." *Journal of Social Behavior and Personality, 10*(1), 91–100.

Calderone, M. S. (1983). "Childhood Sexuality: Approaching the Prevention of Sexual Disease." In G. Albee et al. (Eds.), *Promoting Sexual Responsibility and Preventing Sexual Problems*. Hanover, NH: University Press of New England.

Califia, P. (1979). "Lesbian Sexuality." *Journal of Homosexuality, 4,* 255–266.

"California Governor Signs Gay Rights Measure into Law." (2003, September 20). *The Herald Times*, p. A2.

Campos-Outcalt, D., & Hurwitz, S. (2002). "Female-to-Female Transmission of Syphilis: A Case Report." *Sexually Transmitted Diseases, 29,* 119–120.

Canavan, M. M., Myers, W. J., & Higgs, D. C. (1992). "The Female Experience of Sibling Incest." *Journal of Marital and Family Therapy, 18,* 129–142.

Cann, A., Mangum, J. L., & Wells, M. (2001). "Distress in Response to Relationship Infidelity: The Roles of Gender and Attitudes About Relationships." *Journal of Sex Research, 38*(3), 185–190.

Caplan, A. L. (1992). "Twenty Years After: The Legacy of the Tuskegee Syphilis Study. When Evil Intrudes." *Hastings Center Report, 22*(6), 29–32.

Carelli, R. (1998, February 24). "High Court Turns Down Megan's Law Challenges." *San Francisco Chronicle*, p. A1.

Carl, D. (1986). "Acquired Immune Deficiency Syndrome: A Preliminary Examination of the Effects on Gay Couples and Coupling." *Journal of Marital and Family Therapy, 12*(3), 241–247.

Carnes, P. (1983). *Out of Shadows*. Minneapolis: CompCare.

Carnes, P. (1991). "Progress in Sex Addiction: An Addiction Perspective." In R. T. Francoeur (Ed.), *Taking Sides: Clashing Views on Controversial Issues in Human Sexuality* (3rd ed.). Guilford, CT: Dushkin.

Carr, P. (1992, February 16). "Sexual Harassment Pushes Its Way into the Schoolyard." *San Jose Mercury News*, pp. L1, L8.

Carrier, J. (1992). "Miguel: Sexual Life History of a Gay Mexican American." In G. Herdt (Ed.), *Gay Culture in America: Essays from the Field*. Boston: Beacon Press.

Carroll, J., Volk, K. D., & Hyde, J. J. (1985). "Differences in Males and Females in Motives for Engaging in Sexual Intercourse." *Archives of Sexual Behavior, 14,* 131–139.

Carroll, R. (1999). "Outcomes of Treatment for Gender Dysphoria." *Journal of Sex Education and Therapy, 24,* 128–136.

Carroll, S. T., Riffenburgh, R. H., Roberts, T. A., & Myhre, E. B. (2002). "Tattoos and Body Piercings as Indicators of Adolescent Risk-Taking Behaviors." *Pediatrics, 109,* 1021–1028.

Cassell, C. (1984). *Swept Away*. New York: Simon & Schuster.

Cassidy, L., & Hurrell, R. M. (1995). "The Influence of Victim's Attire on Adolescents' Judgments of Date Rape." *Adolescence, 30*(118), 319–404.

Cate, R. M., & Lloyd, S. A. (1992). *Courtship.* Newbury Park, CA: Sage.

Cates, J. A., & Markley, J. (1992). "Demographic, Clinical, and Personality Variables Associated with Male Prostitution by Choice." *Adolescence, 27,* 695–706.

Cates, W., Chesney, M. A., & Cohen, M. S. (1997). "Primary HIV Infection—a Public Health Opportunity." *American Journal of Public Health, 87*(12), 1928–1930.

Cautela, J. E. (1986). "Behavioral Analysis of a Fetish: First Interview." *Journal of Behavior Therapy and Experimental Psychiatry, 17*(3), 161–165.

Ceci, S., Loftus, E., Leichtman, M., & Bruck, M. (1994). "The Role of Source Misattributions in the Creation of False Beliefs in Preschoolers." *International Journal of Clinical and Experimental Hypnosis, 42,* 304–320.

Centers for Disease Control. (1982). "Update on Acquired Immune Deficiency Syndrome (AIDS)—United States." *Morbidity and Mortality Weekly Report, 31*(507).

Centers for Disease Control and Prevention. (1992). "1993 Revised Classification System for HIV Infection and Expanded Surveillance Case Definition for AIDS Among Adolescents and Adults." *Mortality and Morbidity Weekly Report, 41,* 961–962.

Centers for Disease Control and Prevention. (1996a). "Ten Leading Nationally Notifiable Diseases—United States, 1995." *Morbidity and Mortality Weekly Report, 45,* 883–884.

Centers for Disease Control and Prevention. (1996b). "Surveillance Report: U.S. AIDS Cases Reported Through December 1995." *HIV/AIDS Surveillance Report, 7*(2), 1–10.

Centers for Disease Control and Prevention. (1997). Sexually Transmitted Disease Surveillance Report, 1996. Available: http://wonder.cdc.gov/wonder/STD/STDD007.PCW.html (Last visited 2/19/98).

Centers for Disease Control and Prevention. (1998a). "1998 Guidelines for Treatment of STDs." *Morbidity and Mortality Weekly Report, 47* (No. RR-1).

Centers for Disease Control and Prevention. (1998b). CDC AIDS Information. Available: http://www.cdc.gov/nchstp/hiv_aids/hivinfo/vfax/ (Last visited 4/11/98).

Centers for Disease Control and Prevention. (1998c). How Safe Is the Blood Supply in the United States? Available: http://www.cdc.gov/hiv/pubs/faq/faq15.htm (Last visited 2/24/03).

Centers for Disease Control and Prevention. (1999a). Fact sheet: HIV/AIDS and U.S. Women Who Have Sex with Women (WSW). Available: http://www.cdc.gov/hiv/pubs/facts/wsw.htm (Last visited 11/22/00).

Centers for Disease Control and Prevention. (1999b). *HIV/AIDS Surveillance Report, 1999, 11*(2).

Centers for Disease Control and Prevention. (2000a). Fact sheet: Some Facts About Chlamydia. Available: http://www.cdc.gov/nchstp/dstd/Fact_Sheets/chlamydia_facts.htm (Last visited 11/15/00).

Centers for Disease Control and Prevention. (2000b). Bacterial Vaginosis (BV). Available: http://www.cdc.gov/nchstp/dstd/Fact_Sheets/FactsBV.htm (Last visited 12/12/01).

Centers for Disease Control and Prevention. (2000c). "HIV/AIDS Among Racial/Ethnic Minority Men Who Have Sex with Men." *Mortality and Morbidity Weekly Report, 49,* 4–11.

Centers for Disease Control and Prevention. (2000d). HIV Prevention: Now More Than Ever. Available: http://www.cdc.gov/hiv/pubs/brochure.htm (Last visited 12/14/00).

Centers for Disease Control and Prevention. (2001a). Chlamydia Disease Information. Available: http://www.cdc.gov/nchstp/dstd/Fact_Sheets/Factschlamydiainfo.htm (Last visited 12/12/01).

Centers for Disease Control and Prevention. (2001b).

Centers for Disease Control and Prevention. (2001c). Genital HPV Infection. Available: http://www.cdc.gov/nchstp/dstd/Fact_SheetsHPV.htm (Last visited 12/12/01).

Centers for Disease Control and Prevention. (2001d). *HIV/AIDS Surveillance Report, 2000.* Atlanta: U.S. Department of Health and Human Services.

Centers for Disease Control and Prevention. (2001e). Primary HIV Infection Associated with Oral Transmission. Available: http://www.cdc.gov/hiv/pubs/facts/oralsexqa.htm (Last visited 2/24/03).

Centers for Disease Control and Prevention. (2001f). Compendium of HIV Prevention Interventions with Evidence of Effectiveness. Available: http://www.cdc.gov/hiv/pubs/hivcompendium/hivcompendium.htm (Last visited 2/3/03).

Centers for Disease Control and Prevention. (2002a). "Youth Risk Behavior Surveillance—United States, 2001." *Morbidity and Mortality Weekly Report, 51,* 1–64.

Centers for Disease Control and Prevention. (2002b). *Sexually Transmitted Disease Surveillance, 2001.* Atlanta: U.S. Department of Health and Human Services.

Centers for Disease Control and Prevention. (2002c). Women Are Having More Children, New Report Shows. Available: http://www.hhs.gov/news/press/2002pres/20020212.htm (Last visited 11/30/02).

Centers for Disease Control and Prevention. (2002d). "Sexually Transmitted Diseases Treatment Guidelines 2002." *Mortality and Morbidity Weekly Report, 51,* 1–80.

Centers for Disease Control and Prevention. (2002e). "Nonoxynol-9 Spermicide Contraception Use—United States, 1999." *Mortality and Morbidity Weekly Report, 51,* 389–392.

Centers for Disease Control and Prevention. (2002f). "Primary and Secondary Syphilis—United States, 2000–2001." *Mortality and Morbidity Weekly Report, 51,* 971–973.

Centers for Disease Control and Prevention. (2002g). Drug-Associated HIV Transmission Continues in the United States. Available: http://www.cdc.gov/hiv/pubs/facts/idu.htm (Last visited 2/21/03).

Centers for Disease Control and Prevention. (2003a). Estimated Percent Distribution of AIDS Cases in Male Adults and Adolescents, by Exposure Category and Race/Ethnicity, Diagnosed Through December 2001, United States. Available: http://www.cdc.gov/nchs/data/statab/lf71_95.pdf (Last visited 5/30/03).

Centers for Disease Control and Prevention. (2003b). *HIV/AIDS Surveillance—General Epidemiology: L138 Slide Series Through 2001.* Available: http://www.cdc.gov/hiv/graphics/surveill.htm (Last visited 2/22/03).

Centers for Disease Control and Prevention. (2003c). *HIV/AIDS Surveillance by Race/Ethnicity: L238 Slide Series Through 2001.* Available: http://www.cdc.gov/hiv/graphics/surveill.htm (Last visited 2/22/03).

Centers for Disease Control and Prevention (CDC), American Society for Reproductive Medicine (ASRM), & Resolve. (1997, December). *1995 Assisted Reproductive Success Rates.* Hyattsville, MD: U.S. Department of Health and Human Services.

Charney, D., & Russell, R. (1994). "An Overview of Sexual Harassment." *American Journal of Psychiatry, 151*, 10–17.

Chelala, C. (2000, November 28). "The Unrelenting Scourge of Child Prostitution." *San Francisco Chronicle*, p. A27.

Cho, C., Bunch, D. O., Faure, J., Goulding, E. H., Eddy, E. M., Primakoff, P., & Myles, D. G. (1998). "Fertilization Defects in Sperm from Mice Lacking in Fertilin B." *Science, 281*, 1857–1859.

Chojnacki, J. T., & Walsh, W. B. (1990). "Reliability and Concurrent Validity of the Sternberg Triangular Love Scale." *Psychological Reports, 67*(1), 219–224.

Christopher, F. S., & Frandsen, M. M. (1990). "Strategies of Influence in Sex and Dating." *Journal of Social and Personal Relationships, 7*, 89–105.

Christopher, F. S., & Sprecher, S. (2000). "Sexuality in Marriage, Dating, and Other Relationships: A Decade Review." *Journal of Marriage and the Family, 62*, 999–1017.

Cloud, J. (1998, July 20). "Trans Across America." *Time*, pp. 48–49.

CNN. (2003). New AIDS Drug Wins FDA Approval. Available: http://www.cnn.com/2003/health/conditions/03/14/aids.drug/index.htm (Last visited 3/14/03).

CNN.com/Law Center. (2003, March 5). Supreme Court Upholds Sex Offender Registration Laws. Available: http://www.cnn.com/2003/law/03/05/scotus.sex.offenders.ap/index (Last visited 3/5/03).

Cochran, S. D., Mays, V. M., Bowen, D., Gage, S., Bybee, D., Roberts, S. J., Goldstein, R. S., Robison, A., Rankow, E. J., & White, J. (2001). "Cancer-Related Risk Indicators and Preventive Screening Behaviors Among Lesbians and Bisexual Women." *American Journal of Public Health, 91*, 591–597.

Cochran, S. D., Mays, V. M., & Leung, L. (1991). "Sexual Practices of Heterosexual Asian-American Young Adults: Implications for Risk of HIV Infection." *Archives of Sexual Behavior, 20*(4), 381–394.

Cohen, A. B., & Tannenbaum, H. J. (2001). "Lesbian and Bisexual Women's Judgments of the Attractiveness of Different Body Types." *The Journal of Sex Research, 38*, 226–232.

Coleman, E. (1991). "Compulsive Sexual Behavior: New Concepts and Treatments." *Journal of Psychology and Human Sexuality, 4*, 37–52.

Coleman, E. (1996). *What Sexual Scientists Know About . . . Compulsive Sexual Behavior.* Allentown, PA: Society for the Scientific Study of Sexuality.

Coleman, E., Colgan, P., & Gooren, L. (1992). "Male Cross-Gender Behavior in Myanmar (Burma): A Description of the Acault." *Archives of Sexual Behavior, 21*(3), 313–321.

Coleman, E., Rosser, B. R., & Strapko, N. (1992). "Sexual and Intimacy Dysfunction Among Homosexual Men and Women." *Psychiatric Medicine, 10*(2), 257–271.

Collins, P. H. (1991). "The Meaning of Motherhood in Black Culture." In R. Staples (Ed.), *The Black Family* (4th ed.). Belmont, CA: Wadsworth.

"Community Study Traces Bulimia's Origins." (1997, July 5). *Science News, 152*, 7.

Condy, S., Templer, D. E., Brown, R., & Veaco, L. (1987). Parameters of Sexual Contact of Boys with Women." *Archives of Sexual Behavior, 16*(5), 379–394.

Contraception Report. (2001). Adolescent Issues: Sexual Behavior and Contraception Use. Available: http://www.contraceptiononline.org/contrareport/ (Last visited 12/30/02).

Cooper, A. (1985). "Sexual Enhancement Programs: An Examination of Their Current Status and Directions for Future Research." *Archives of Sexual Behavior, 21*(4), 387–404.

Cooper, A., Delmonico, D., & Burg, R. (2000). "Cybersex Users, Abusers, and Compulsives: New Findings and Implications." In A. Cooper (Ed.), *Cybersex: The Dark Side of the Force.* Philadelphia: Brunner/Routledge, pp. 5–29.

Cooper, A., Scherer, C. R., Bois, S. C., & Gordon, B. I. (1999). "Sexuality on the Internet: From Sexual Exploration to Pathological Expression." *Professional Psychology: Research and Practice, 30*, 154–164.

Cooper, A. J., Swaminath, S., Baxter, D., & Poulin, C. (1990). "A Female Sex Offender with Multiple Paraphilias." *Canadian Journal of Psychiatry, 35*(4), 334–337.

Cooper, C. (2000, June–July). "Abortion: Take Back the Right." *Ms.*, pp. 17–21.

Copenhaver, S., & Gauerholz, E. (1991). "Sexual Victimization Among Sorority Women: Exploring the Link Between Sexual Violence and Institutional Practices." *Sex Roles, 24*, 31–41.

Corley, M. D. (1994). "The Question of Research into Sexual Addiction." *Contemporary Sexuality, 28*(8), 8.

Cortese, A. (1989). "Subcultural Differences in Human Sexuality: Race, Ethnicity, and Social Class." In K. McKinney & S. Sprecher (Eds.), *Human Sexuality: The Societal and Interpersonal Context.* Norwood, NJ: Ablex.

Cosby, B. (1968, December). "The Regular Way." *Playboy*, pp. 288–289.

Couthino, E. M., & Segal, S. J. (1999). *Is Menstruation Obsolete?* New York: Oxford University Press.

Cowan, G. (2000). "Beliefs About the Causes of Four Types of Rape." *Sex Roles, 42*, 807–823.

Cowley, G. (1996, September 16). "Attention Aging Men." *Newsweek*, pp. 68–75.

Crews, F. (1994, November 17). "Revenge of the Repressed." *The New York Review of Books*, pp. 54–60.

Crooks R., & Baur, K. (2002). *Our Sexuality* (8th ed.). Pacific Grove, CA: Wadsworth.

Crosby, J. (Ed.). (1985). *Reply to Myth: Perspectives on Intimacy.* New York: Wiley.

Crosby, R. A., Sanders, S. A., Yarber, W. L., Graham, C. A., & Dodge, B. (2002). "Condom Use Errors and Problems Among College Men." *Sexually Transmitted Diseases, 29*, 552–557.

Crosby, R. A., & Yarber, W. L. (2001). "Perceived Versus Actual Knowledge About Correct Condom Use Among U.S. Adolescents: Results from a National Study." *Journal of Adolescent Health, 28*, 415–420.

Cross, S. E., & Madson, L. (1997). "Models of the Self: Self-Construals and Gender." *Psychological Bulletin, 122*, 5–37.

Cross, S. E., & Markus, H. R. (1993). "Gender in Thought, Belief, and Action: A Cognitive Approach." In A. E. Beall & R. J. Sternberg (Eds.), *The Psychology of Gender.* New York: Guilford Press.

Crowe, M. (1995). "Couple Therapy and Sexual Dysfunction." *Interpersonal View of Psychiatry, 7*(2), 195–204.

Cummings, J. (1987, June 8). "Disabled Model Defies Sexual Stereotypes." *The New York Times*, p. 17.

Cupach, W. R., & Comstock, J. (1990). "Satisfaction with Sexual Communication in Marriage." *Journal of Social and Personal Relationships, 7*, 179–186.

Cupach, W. R., & Metts, S. (1991). "Sexuality and Communication in Close Relationships." In K. McKinney & S. Sprecher (Eds.), *Sexuality in Close Relationships.* Hillsdale, NJ: Erlbaum.

Curtin, S. C., & Martin, J. A. (2000, August 8). "Birth: Preliminary Data for 1999." Washington, DC: National Vital Statistics Reports.

Cutler, W. (1999). "Human Sex-Attractant Pheromones: Discovery, Research, Development, and Application in Sex Therapy." *Psychiatric Annals, 29*, 54–59.

CyberAtlas. (2002). Search Engines, Browsers Still Confusing Many Web Users. Available: http://cyberatlas.internet.com/big_picture/traffic_patterns/article/0,,5931_588851,00.html (Last visited 1/19/03).

Darling, C. A., & Davidson, J. K. (1986). "Enhancing Relationships: Understanding the Feminine Mystique of Pretending Orgasm." *Journal of Sex and Marital Therapy, 12*, 182–196.

Darling, C. A., Davidson, J. K., & Jennings, D. A. (1991). "The Female Sexual Response Revisited: Understanding the Multiorgasmic Experience in Women." *Archives of Sexual Behavior, 20*, 527–540.

Daro, D. A. (1994). "Prevention of Child Sexual Abuse." *The Future of Children, 4*, 198–223.

Darroch, J. E. (2000). "The Pill and Men's Involvement in Contraception." *Family Planning Perspectives, 32*(2), 90–93.

Darroch, J. E., Landry, D. J., & Oslak, S. (1999). "Age Differences Between Sexual Partners in the United States." *Family Planning Perspectives, 31*(4), 199–207.

Darroch, J. E., Landry, D. J., & Singh, S. (2000). "Changing Emphasis in Sexuality Education in U.S. Public Secondary Schools, 1988–1999." *Family Planning Perspectives, 32*, 204–211, 265.

Darrow, W. W., & Siegel, K. (1990). "Preventive Health Behavior and STDs." In K. K. Holmes et al. (Eds.), *Sexually Transmitted Diseases* (2nd ed.). New York: McGraw-Hill.

Davidson, J. K., & Darling, C. A. (1986). "The Impact of College-Level Sex Education on Sexual Knowledge, Attitudes, and Practices: The Knowledge/Sexual Experimentation Myth Revisited." *Deviant Behavior, 7*, 13–30.

Davies, K. A. (1997). "Voluntary Exposure to Pornography and Men's Attitudes Toward Feminism and Rape." *The Journal of Sex Research, 34*(2), 131–138.

Davies, S., Katz, J., & Jackson, J. L. (1999). "Sexual Desire Discrepancies: Effects on Sexual and Relationship Satisfaction in Heterosexual Dating Couples." *Archives of Sexual Behavior, 28*, 553–567.

Davitz, J. R. (1969). *The Language of Emotion.* New York: Academic Press.

De Cecco, J. P., & Elia, J. P. (1993). "A Critique and Synthesis of Biological Essentialism and Social Constructionist Views of Sexuality and Gender. Introduction." *Journal of Homosexuality, 24*(3–4), 1–26.

DeGenova, M. K. (1997). *Families in Cultural Context: Strengths and Challenges in Diversity.* Mountain View, CA: Mayfield.

De Groot, J. M., Kennedy, S. H., Rodin, G., & McVey, S. (1992). "Correlates of Sexual Abuse in Women with Anorexia Nervosa and Bulimia Nervosa." *Canadian Journal of Psychiatry, 37*(7), 516–581.

De Judicibus, M. A., & McCabe, M. P. (2002). "Psychological Factors and the Sexuality of Pregnant and Postpartum Women." *The Journal of Sex Research, 39*(2), 94–103.

Delaney, J., Lupton, M. J., & Toth, E. (1988). *The Curse: A Cultural History of Menstruation.* New York: Dutton.

Del Carmen, R. (1990). "Assessment of Asian-Americans for Family Therapy." In F. Serafica, A. Schwebel, R. Russell, P. Isaac, & L. Myers (Eds.), *Mental Health of Ethnic Minorities.* New York: Praeger.

Del Romero, J., Marinocovich, B., Castilla, J., Garcia, S., Campo, J., Hernando, V., & Rodriguez, C. (2002). "Evaluating the Risk of HIV Transmission Through Unprotected Orogenital Sex." *AIDS, 16*, 1296–1297.

Demian, A. S. B. (1994). "Relationship Characteristics of American Gay and Lesbian Couples: Findings from a National Survey." *Journal of Gay and Lesbian Social Services, 1*(2), 101–117.

Denny, D. (1997). "Transgender: Some Historical, Cross-Cultural, and Contemporary Models and Methods of Coping and Treatment." In B. Bullough, V. L. Bullough, & J. Elias (Eds.), *Gender Blending.* New York: Prometheus Books.

Derry, F. A., Dinsmore, W. W., Fraser, M., Gardner, B. P., Glass, C. A., Maytom, M. C., & Smith, M. D. (1998). "Efficacy and Safety of Oral Sildenafil (Viagra) in Men with Erectile Dysfunction Caused by Spinal Cord Injury." *Neurology, 51*, 1629–1633.

Des Jarlais, D. C., Paone, D., Milliken, J., Turner, C. F., Miller, H., Gribble, J., Quihu, S., Hagan, H., & Friedman, S. R. (1999). "Audio-Computer Interviewing to Measure Risk Behavior for HIV Among Injecting Drug Users: A Quasi-Randomized Trial." *The Lancet, 353*, 1657–1661.

DeSpelder, L. A., & Strickland, A. (1999). *The Last Dance: Encountering Death and Dying* (6th ed.). Mountain View, CA: Mayfield.

Diamond, L. M., Savin-Williams, R. C., & Dube, E. M. (1999). "Sex, Dating, Passionate Friendships, and Romance: Intimate Peer Relations Among Lesbian, Gay and Bisexual Adolescents." In W. Furman, B. B. Brown, & C. Feiring (Eds.), *The Development of Romantic Relationships During Adolescence.* New York: Cambridge University Press.

Diaz, R. M. (1998). *Latino Gay Men and HIV: Culture, Sexuality and Risk Behavior.* New York: Routledge.

Dickerson, J. (1994, November 21). "Censoring Cyberspace." *Time*, pp. 102–104.

Dick-Read, G. (1972). *Childbirth Without Fear* (4th ed.). New York: Harper & Row.

Di Mauro, Diane. (1995). Executive Summary. Sexuality Research in the United States: An Assessment of the Social and Behavioral Sciences. Social Science Research Council. Available: http://www.indiana.edu/~kinsey/SSRC/sexreas2.html (Last visited 10/8/97).

Dingman, D. J. (1996). "Clients, Not Prostitutes, Seen As Central to AIDS Spread." *AIDS Weekly Plus*, pp. 5–7.

Dion, K. K., Berscheid, E., & Walster, E. (1972). "What Is Beautiful Is Good." *Journal of Personality and Social Psychology, 24*, 285–290.

Division of STD Prevention. (2000). *Sexually Transmitted Disease Surveillance, 1999.* Department of Health and Human Services. Atlanta: Centers for Disease Control and Prevention.

Docter, R. F., & Prince, V. (1997). "Transvestism: A Survey of 1032 Cross-Dressers." *Archives of Sexual Behavior, 26*, 589–606.

Donohue, J., & Gebhard, P. (1995). "The Kinsey Institute/Indiana University Report of Sexuality and Spinal Cord Injury." *Sexuality and Disability, 13*(1), 7–85.

Donovan, P. (1993). *Testing Positive: Sexually Transmitted Disease and the Public Health Response.* New York: Alan Guttmacher Institute.

Dryfoos, J. (1985). "What the United States Can Learn About Prevention of Teenage Pregnancy from Other Developed Countries." *SIECUS Report, 14*(2), 1–7.

Ducharme, S. H., & Gill, K. M. (1997). *Sexuality After Spinal Cord Injury: Answers to Your Questions.* Baltimore: Brookes.

Dunn, M. E., & Trost, J. E. (1989). "Male Multiple Orgasms: A Descriptive Study." *Archives of Sexual Behavior, 18,* 377–387.

Dunne, M. P. (2002). "Sampling Considerations." In M. W. Wiederman & B. E. Whitley (Eds.), *Handbook for Conducting Research on Human Sexuality.* Mahwah, NJ: Erlbaum.

Durkin, K. (1997). "Misuse of the Internet by Pedophiles: Implications for Law Enforcement and Probation Practice." *Federal Probation, 61,* 14–18.

Ecstasy Effects. (1996, May 31). Available: www.columbia.edu/cu/healthwise/0925.html (Last visited 1/29/98).

"Ecstasy: Happiness Is . . . a Pill?" (2000, June 5). *Time,* pp. 64–68.

Edmundson, E. W., Clifford, P., Serrins, D. S., & Wiley, D. (1994). "The Development of a Model to Predict Drinking Behavior from Attitudes of College Students." *Journal of Primary Prevention, 14,* 243–276.

Effects of Marijuana on Libido and Fertility. (1995, October 5). Available: http://www.columbia.edu/cu/healthwise/0682.html (Last visited 1/29/98).

Eisenberg, M. (2001). "Differences in Sexual Risk Behaviors Between College Students with Same-Sex and Opposite-Sex Experience: Results from a National Survey." *Archives of Sexual Behavior, 30,* 575–589.

Eitzen, D., & Zinn, M. (1994). *Social Problems* (6th ed.). Boston: Allyn & Bacon.

Elders, M. J., & Kilgore, B. (1997). The Dreaded "M" Word. Available: http://www.nervemag.com/Elders/mword/mword.shtml (Last visited 10/4/97).

Elias, M. (2003, January 15). "Women's Sex Problems May Be Overstated." *USA Today,* p. A1.

Elifson, K. W., Boles, J., Posey, E., & Sweat, M. (1993). "Male Transvestite Prostitutes and HIV Risk." *American Journal of Public Health, 83*(2), 260–262.

Ellingson, L. A., & Yarber, W. L. (1997). "Breast Self-Examination, the Health Belief Model, and Sexual Orientation in Women." *Journal of Sex Education and Therapy, 22,* 19–24.

Elliot, L., & Brantley, C. (1997). *Sex on Campus: The Naked Truth About the Real Sex Lives of College Students.* New York: Random House.

Elliott, D. M., & Briere, J. (1992). "Sexual Abuse Trauma Among Professional Women: Validating the Trauma Symptom Checklist (TSC-40)." *Child Abuse and Neglect, 16*(3), 391ff.

Ellis, H. (1900). *Studies in the Psychology of Sex.* Philadelphia: Davis.

Ellis, M. (2002, June 10). "Women Leery as Date-Rape Drug Use Soars." *Indianapolis Star,* pp. A1, A6.

Ellison, C. (1985). "Intimacy-Based Sex Therapy." In W. Eicher & G. Kockott (Eds.), *Sexology.* New York: Springer-Verlag.

Ellison, C. (2000). *Women's Sexualities.* Oakland: New Harbinger.

Emergency Contraception. (2002). Available: http://www.agiusa.org/media/supp/ec121702.html (Last visited 12/20/02).

Eng, T. R., & Butler, W. T. (Eds.). (1997). *The Hidden Epidemic: Confronting Sexually Transmitted Diseases.* Washington, DC: National Academy Press.

"Especially for Fathers." (D.U.). American College of Obstetricians and Gynecologists. Education Pamphlet AP032.

Espín, O. M. (1984). "Cultural and Historical Influences on Sexuality in Hispanic/Latin Women: Implications for Psychotherapy." In C. Vance (Ed.), *Pleasure and Danger: Exploring Female Sexuality.* New York: Routledge & Kegan Paul.

Faderman, L. (1991). *Odd Girls and Twilight Lovers.* New York: Penguin Books.

Fagin, D. (1995, February 1). "DES Moms, Gay or Bisexual Daughters: Study Links Exposure to Sexual Orientation." *San Francisco Chronicle.*

Fahey, T., Insel, P., & Roth, W. (2000). *Fit and Well: Core Concepts in Labs in Physical Fitness and Wellness.* Mountain View, CA: Mayfield.

Faludi, S. (1991). *Backlash: The Undeclared War Against American Women.* New York: Crown.

Faludi, S. (1999). *Stiffed: The Betrayal of the American Man.* New York: Morrow.

Farnsworth, C. H. (1992, January 14). "Homosexual Is Granted Refugee Status in Canada." *The New York Times,* p. A5.

Fausto-Sterling, A. (2000). *Sexing the Body: Gender Politics and the Construction of Sexuality.* New York: Basic Books.

Fauci, A. S., Pantaleo, G. Stanley, S., & Weissman, D. (1996). "Immunopathogenic Mechanisms of HIV Infection." *Annals of Internal Medicine, 124:* 654–663.

Fay, R., Turner, C., Klassen, A., & Gagnon, J. (1989). "Prevalence and Patterns of Same-Gender Sexual Contact Among Men." *Science, 243*(4889), 338–348.

"FDA May Soon Consider New Female Sterilization Device." (2002, March). *Contraception Report, 13*(1), 12–15.

Feinberg, L. (1996). *Transgender Warriors: Making History from Joan of Arc to Rupaul.* Boston: Beacon Press.

Feldman, H., Goldstein, I., Hatzichristou, D., Krane, R., & McKinlay, J. (1994). "Impotence and Its Medical and Psychosocial Correlates: Results of the Massachusetts Male Aging Study." *Journal of Urology, 151,* 54–61.

Feray, J. C., & Herzer, M. (1990). "Homosexual Studies and Politics in the 19th Century: Karl Maria Kertbeny." *Journal of Homosexuality, 19*(1), 23–47.

Fergusson, D. M., Swain-Campbell, N. R., & Horwood, L. J. (2002). "Does Sexual Violence Contribute to Elevated Rates of Anxiety and Depression in Females?" *Psychological Medicine, 32,* 991–996.

Fetters, K., Marks, C., Mindel, A., & Estcourt, C. S. (2000). "Sexually Transmitted Infections and Risk Behaviors in Women Who Have Sex with Women." *Sexually Transmitted Infections, 76,* 345–349.

Fields, J., & Casper, L. M. (2001). "America's Families and Living Arrangements; Population Characteristics: 2000." *Current Population Reports,* Series 20-537. Washington, DC: U.S. Government Printing Office.

Finer, L. B., Darroch, J. E., & Singh, S. (1999). "Sexual Partnership Patterns as a Behavioral Risk Factor for Sexually Transmitted Diseases." *Family Planning Perspectives, 31,* 228–236.

Finkelhor, D. (1984). *Child Sexual Abuse: New Theory and Research.* New York: Free Press.

Finkelhor, D. (1986). "Prevention Approaches to Child Sexual Abuse." In M. Lystad (Ed.), *Violence in the Home: Interdisciplinary Perspectives.* New York: Brunner/Mazel.

Finkelhor, D. (1990). "Early and Long-Term Effects of Child Sexual Abuse: An Update." *Professional Psychology: Research and Practice, 21,* 325–330.

Finkelhor, D. (1994). "Current Information on the Scope and Nature of Child Sexual Abuse." *The Future of Children, 4,* 31–53.

Finkelhor, D., & Baron, L. (1986). "High-Risk Children." In D. Finkelhor (Ed.), *Sourcebook on Child Sexual Abuse.* Beverly Hills, CA: Sage.

Finkelhor, D., & Yllo, K. (1985). *License to Rape: The Sexual Abuse of Wives.* New York: Holt, Rinehart & Winston.

Finz, S. (2000, June 12). "Emerging from a Secret." *San Francisco Chronicle*, p. A1.

Firstman, R., & Talan, J. (1997). *The Death of Innocents*. New York: Bantam Books.

Fischer, A. R., & Good, G. E. (1994). "Gender, Self, and Others: Perceptions of the Campus Environment." *Journal of Counseling Psychology, 41*(3), 343–355.

Fisher, B., Anderson, S., Bryant, J., Margolese, R. G., Deutsch, M., Fisher, E. R., Jeong, J., & Wolmark, N. (2002). "Twenty-Year Follow-Up of a Randomized Trial Comparing Total Mastectomy, Lumpectomy, and Lumpectomy Plus Irradiation for the Treatment of Invasive Breast Cancer." *New England Journal of Medicine, 347*, 1233–1242.

Fisher, D., & Howells, K. (1993). "Social Relationships in Sexual Offenders." *Sexual and Marital Therapy, 8*, 123–136.

Fisher, W. (1986). "A Psychological Approach to Human Sexuality." In D. Byrne & K. K. Kelley (Eds.), *Alternative Approaches to Human Sexuality*. Hillsdale, NJ: Erlbaum.

Fisher, W. (1998). "The Sexual Opinion Survey." In C. M. Davis, W. L. Yarber, R. Bauserman, G. Schreer, & S. L. Davis (Eds.), *Handbook of Sexuality-Related Measures*. Thousand Oaks, CA: Sage.

Fisher, W. A., & Barak, A. (2001). "Internet Pornography: A Social Psychological Perspective on Internet Sexuality." *The Journal of Sex Research, 38*, 312–323.

Fitzgerald, L. F., & Ormerod, A. J. (1991). "Perceptions of Sexual Harassment: The Influence of Gender and Academic Context." *Psychology of Women Quarterly, 15*(2), 281–294.

Flaks, D. K., Ficher, I., Masterpasqua, F., & Joseph, G. (1995). "Lesbians Choosing Motherhood: A Comparative Study of Lesbians and Heterosexual Parents and Their Children." *Developmental Psychology, 31*(1), 105–114.

Flaxman, S. M., & Sherman, P. W. (2000). "Morning Sickness: A Mechanism for Protecting Mother and Embryo." *Quarterly Review of Biology, 75*(2), 113.

Fleming, D. T., & Wasserheit, J. N. (1999). "From Epidemiological Synergy to Public Health Policy and Practice: The Contribution of Other Sexually Transmitted Diseases to Sexual Transmission of HIV Infection." *Sexually Transmitted Diseases, 75*, 3–17.

Foa, U. G., Anderson, B., Converse, J., & Urbansky, W. A. (1987). "Gender-Related Sexual Attitudes: Some Cross-Cultural Similarities and Differences." *Sex Roles, 16*(19–20), 511–519.

Foley, L. A., Evancic, C., Karnik, K., & King, J. (1995). "Date Rape: Effects of Race of Assailant and Victim and Gender of Subjects on Perceptions." *Journal of Black Psychology, 21*(1), 6–18.

Follingstad, D. R., Rutledge, L. L., Berg, B. J., & Hause, E. S. (1990). "The Role of Emotional Abuse in Physically Abusive Relationships." *Journal of Family Violence, 5*(2), 107–120.

Fonow, M. M., Richardson, L., & Wemmerus, V. A. (1992). "Feminist Rape Education: Does It Work?" *Gender and Society, 6*(1), 108–121.

Ford, C., & Beach, F. (1951). *Patterns of Sexual Behavior*. New York: Harper & Row.

Fortenberry, J. D., Cecil, H., Zimet, G. D., & Orr, D. P. (1997). "Concordance Between Self-Report Questionnaires and Coital Diaries for Sexual Behaviors of Adolescent Women with Sexually Transmitted Infections." In J. Bancroft (Ed.), *Researching Sexual Behavior*. Bloomington: Indiana University Press.

Fortenberry, J. D., McFarlane, M., Bleakley, A., Bull, S., Fishbein, M., Grimley, D., Malotte, C. K., & Stoner, B. (2002). "Relationship of Stigma and Shame to Gonorrhea and HIV Screening." *American Journal of Public Health, 92*, 378–381.

Foster-Rosales, A., & Stewart, F. H. (2002). "Contraceptive Technology." In G. M. Wingood & R. J. DiClemente (Eds.), *Handbook of Women's Sexual and Reproductive Health*. New York: Kluwer Academic/Plenum.

Foxman, B., Aral, S. O., & Holmes, K. K. (1998). "Interrelationships Among Douching Practices, Risky Sexual Practices, and History of Self-Reported Sexually Transmitted Diseases in an Urban Population." *Sexually Transmitted Diseases, 25*, 90–99.

Frable, D. E. S., Johnson, A. E., & Kellman, H. (1997). "Seeing Masculine Men, Sexy Women, and Gender Differences: Exposure to Pornography and Cognitive Constructions of Gender." *Journal of Personality, 65*(2), 311–355.

Frayser, S. G. (1994). "Anthropology: Influence of Culture on Sex." In V. Bullough & B. B. Bullough (Eds.), *Human Sexuality: An Encyclopedia*. New York: Garland.

Frayser, S. G. (2002). "Discovering the Value of Cross-Cultural Research on Human Sexuality." In M. W. Wiederman & B. E. Whitley (Eds.), *Handbook for Conducting Research on Human Sexuality*. Mahwah, NJ: Erlbaum.

Frazier, P. A. (1991). "Self-Blame as a Mediator of Postrape Depressive Symptoms." *Journal of Social and Clinical Psychology, 10*(1), 47–57.

Frazier, P. A., Cochran, C. C., & Olson, A. M. (1995). "Social Science Research on Lay Definitions of Sexual Harassment." *Journal of Social Issues, 51*(1), 21–37.

Freeman-Longo, R. E., & Blanchard, G. T. (1998). *Sexual Abuse in America: Epidemic of the 21st Century*. Brandon, VT: Safe Society Press.

Frequently Asked Questions About Infertility. (2002). Available: http://www.resolve.org/main/national/trying/whatis/faq.jsp?name+trying&tag=whatis (Last visited 5/21/03).

Freud, S. (1938). "Three Contributions to the Theory of Sex." In A. A. Brill (Ed.), *The Basic Writings of Sigmund Freud*. New York: Modern Library.

Freund, K., Seto, M. C., & Kuban, M. (1997). "Frotteurism: The Theory of Courtship Disorder." In D. R. Laws & W. O'Donohue (Eds.), *Sexual Deviance: Theory, Assessment, and Treatment*. New York: Guilford Press, pp. 111–130.

Freund, K., & Watson, R. J. (1993). "Gender Identity Disorder and Courtship Disorder." *Archives of Sexual Behavior, 22*(1), 13–21.

Freund, M., Lee, N., & Leonard, T. L. (1991). "Sexual Behavior of Clients with Street Prostitutes in Camden, NJ." *The Journal of Sex Research, 28*(4), 579–591.

Friday, N. (1975). *Forbidden Flowers: More Women's Sexual Fantasies*. New York: Simon & Schuster.

Friday, N. (1980). *Men in Love*. New York: Delacorte.

Friedman, R. C. (1991). "Couple Therapy with Gay Couples." *Psychiatric Annals, 21*(8), 485–490.

Fritz, G. S., Stoll, K., & Wagner, N. N. (1981). "A Comparison of Males and Females Who Were Sexually Molested as Children." *Journal of Sex and Marital Therapy, 7*, 54–58.

Fugh-Berman, A. (2003). "Breast Enlargement: Herbal Prescriptions." *Obstetrics and Gynecology, 101*, 1345–1349.

Fujie, X., Schillinger, J. A., Aubin, M. A., St. Louis, M. E., & Markowitz, L. E. (2001). "Sexually Transmitted Diseases of Older Persons in Washington State." *Sexually Transmitted Diseases, 28*, 287–291.

Furstenberg, F. K., Jr., & Cherlin, A. (1991). *Divided Families*. Cambridge, MA: Harvard University Press.

Furstenberg, F. K., Jr., & Spanier, G. (1987). *Recycling the Family: Remarriage After Divorce* (Rev. ed.). Newbury Park, CA: Sage.

Gagnon, J. (1977). *Human Sexualities*. New York: Scott, Foresman.

Gallup Organization. (2003). Six Out of 10 Americans Say Homosexual Relations Should Be Recognized as Legal. Available: http://www.gallup.com/subscription/?m+f&c_id=13472 (Last visited 6/12/03).

Garber, M. (1991). *Vested Interests*. Boston: Little, Brown.

Gay, P. (1986). *The Bourgeois Experience: The Tender Passion*. New York: Oxford University Press.

Gecas, V., & Seff, M. (1991). "Families and Adolescents." In A. Booth (Ed.), *Contemporary Families: Looking Forward, Looking Back*. Minneapolis: National Council on Family Relations.

Gelles, R. J., & Conte, J. R. (1991). "Domestic Violence and Sexual Abuse of Children: A Review of Research in the Eighties." In A. Booth (Ed.), *Contemporary Families: Looking Forward, Looking Back*. Minneapolis: National Council on Family Relations.

Gerstein, L. (2000). "Very Short and Very Long Interpregnancy Intervals Raise Odds of Prematurity." *Family Planning Perspectives, 32*(4), 196–199.

Gidyez, C. A., & Koss, M. P. (1990). "A Comparison of Group and Individual Sexual Assault Victims." *Psychology of Women Quarterly, 14*(3), 325–342.

Gillen, K., & Muncher, S. J. (1995). "Sex Differences in the Perceived Casual Structure of Date Rape: A Preliminary Report." *Aggressive Behavior, 21*(2), 101–112.

Gilliland, F. D., Berhane, K., McConnell, R., Gauderman, W. L., Vora, H., Rap, E. B., Avol, E., & Peters, J. M. (2000). "Maternal Smoking During Pregnancy, Environmental Tobacco Smoke Exposure and Childhood Lung Function." *Thorax, 55*, 271–276.

Gilmore, M. R., Gaylord, J., Hatway, J., Hoppe, M. J., Morrison, D. M., Leigh, B. C., & Rainey, D. T. (2001). "Daily Data Collection of Sexual and Other Health-Related Behaviors." *The Journal of Sex Research, 38*, 35–42.

Global Campaign for Microbicides. (2002). What's Up with Nonoxynol-9? Available: http://www.global-campaign.org (Last visited 4/10/03).

Gochoros, J. S. (1989). *When Husbands Come Out of the Closet*. New York: Harrington Park Press.

Gold, S. R., Balzano, F. F., & Stamey, R. (1991). "Two Studies of Females' Sexual Force Fantasies." *Journal of Sex Education and Therapy, 17*(1), 15–26.

Gold, S. R., & Gold, R. G. (1991). "Gender Differences in First Sexual Fantasies." *Journal of Sex Education and Therapy, 17*(3), 207–216.

Goldberg, C. (1998, September 8). "Getting to the Truth in Child Abuse Cases: New Methods." *The New York Times*, pp. A1, A16.

Goldberg-Ambrose, C. (1992). "Unfinished Business in Rape Law Reform." *Journal of Social Issues, 48*(1), 173–175.

Goldstein, I., Lue, T. F., Padma-Nathan, H., Rosen, R. C., Steers, W. D., & Wicker, P. A. (1998). "Oral Sildenafil in the Treatment of Erectile Dysfunction." *New England Journal of Medicine, 338*, 1397–1404.

Goldman, A., & Carroll, J. L. (1990). "Educational Intervention as an Adjustment to Treatment in Erectile Dysfunction of Older Couples." *Journal of Sex and Marital Therapy, 16*(3), 127–141.

Goldstein, I., & Rosen, R. (2002). "Female Sexuality and Sexual Dysfunction." *Archives of Sexual Behavior, 31*, 391.

Goldstein, I., & Working Group for the Study of Central Mechanisms in Erectile Dysfunction. (2000, August). "Male Sexual Circuitry." *Scientific American*, pp. 70–75.

Gonzales, V., Washienko, K. M., Krone, M. R., Chapman, L. I., Arredondo, E. M., Huckeba, J. J., & Downer, A. (1999). "Sexual and Drug-Use Risk Factors for HIV and STDs: A Comparison of Women with and Without Bisexual Experiences." *International Journal of STD and AIDS, 10*, 32–37.

Goodman, A. (1993). "Diagnosis and Treatment of Sexual Addiction." *Journal of Sex and Marital Therapy, 19*, 225–251.

Goodman, W. (1992, August 4). "TV's Sexual Circus Has a Purpose." *The New York Times*, p. C-16.

Gordon, S. (2001). *How Can You Tell If You're Really in Love?* New York: Avon/Adams Media.

Gottman, J., & Carrere, S. (2000, October). "Welcome to the Love Lab." *Psychology Today*, pp. 42–47.

Graham, C. A., & Bancroft, J. (1997). "A Comparison of Retrospective Interview Assessment Versus Daily Ratings of Sexual Interest and Activity in Women." In J. Bancroft (Ed.), *Researching Sexual Behavior*. Bloomington: Indiana University Press.

Gray, R. H., Wawer, M. J., Brookmeyer, R., Sewankambo, N. K., Serwadda, D., Wabwire-Mangen, F., Lutalo, T., Li, X., van Cott, T., Quinn, T. C., & Rakai Project Team. (2001). "Probability of HIV-1 Transmission per Coital Act in Monogamous, Heterosexual, HIV-1-Discordant Couples in Rakai, Uganda." *The Lancet, 357*, 1149–1153.

Green, B. C. (1998). "Thinking About Students Who Do Not Identify as Gay, Lesbian, or Bisexual, but . . ." *Journal of American College Health, 47*(2), 89–92.

Greenberg, B. S. (1994). "Content Trends in Media Sex." In D. Zillman, J. Bryant, & A. C. Huston (Eds.), *Media, Children, and the Family: Social Scientific, Psychodynamic, and Clinical Perspectives*. Hillsdale, NJ: Erlbaum.

Greenberg, B. S., & Woods, M. G. (1999). "The Soaps: Their Sex, Gratifications, and Outcomes." *The Journal of Sex Research, 36*(3), 150–257.

Greenberg, J. C. (2003, June 27). "Supreme Court Strikes Down Laws Against Homosexual Sex." *Chicago Tribune*, sec. 1, pp. 1, 4.

Greene, B. (1994). "African-American Women." In L. Comas-Diaz & B. Greene (Eds.), *Women of Color*. New York: Guilford Press.

Greenfeld, L. (1997). *Sex Offenses and Offenders: An Analysis of Data on Rape and Sexual Assault*. Washington, DC: U.S. Department of Justice, Bureau of Justice Statistics.

Greenwald, J. (2000, October 30). "What About the Boys?" *Time*, p. 74.

Greenwood, S. (1992). *Menopause Naturally: Preparing for the Second Half of Life*. Volcano, CA: Volcano Press.

Gregersen, E. (1986). "Human Sexuality in Cross-Cultural Perspective." In D. Byrne & K. Kelley (Eds.), *Alternative Approaches to the Study of Sexual Behavior*. Hillsdale, NJ: Erlbaum.

Gressman, G. D., et al. (1992). "Female Awareness of University Sexual Harassment Policy." *Journal of College Student Development, 33*(4), 370–371.

Gribble, J. N., Miller, H. G., Rogers, S. M., & Turner, C. F. (1999). "Interview Mode and Measurement of Sexual Behaviors: Methodological Issues." *The Journal of Sex Research, 36*(1), 16–24.

Griffiths, M. (2001). "Sex on the Internet: Observations and Implications for Internet Sex Addiction." *The Journal of Sex Research, 38*(4), 333–343.

Grimes, D. A. (2002, March). "Questions and Answers." *Contraception Report, 13*(1), 14.

Grimes, T. R. (1999). "In Search of the Truth About History, Sexuality, and Black Women: An Interview with Gail E. Wyatt." *Teaching of Psychology, 26*(1), 66–70.

Groth, A. N. (1979). *Men Who Rape: The Psychology of the Offender*. New York: Plenum.

Groth, A. N., & Birnbaum, H. J. (1978). "Adult Sexual Orientation and Attraction to Underage Persons." *Archives of Sexual Behavior, 7*, 175–181.

Groth, A. N., & Birnbaum, H. J. (1979). *Men Who Rape: The Psychology of the Offender.* New York: Plenum.

Groth, A. N., & Burgess, A. W. (1980). "Male Rape: Offenders and Victims." *American Journal of Psychiatry, 137*(7), 806–810.

Groth, A. N., Burgess, A. W., & Holmstrom, L. L. (1977). "Rape: Power, Anger, and Sexuality." *American Journal of Psychiatry, 104*(11), 1239–1243.

Groth, A. N., Hobson, W. F., & Gary, T. (1982). "Heterosexuality, Homosexuality, and Pedophilia: Sexual Offenses Against Children." In A. Scacco (Ed.), *Male Rape: A Casebook of Sexual Aggression.* New York: AMS Press.

Guerrero Pavich, E. (1986). "A Chicana Perspective on Mexican Culture and Sexuality." In L. Lister (Ed.), *Human Sexuality, Ethnoculture, and Social Work.* New York: Haworth Press.

Guffey, M. E. (1999). *Business Communication: Process and Product* (3rd ed.). Belmont, CA: Wadsworth.

Gunter, B. (2002). *Media Sex: What Are the Issues?* Mahwah, NJ: Erlbaum.

Gunther, A. (1995). "Overrating the X-Rating: The Third Person Perceptions and Support for Censorship of Pornography." *Journal of Communication, 45*(1), 27–38.

Gur, R., Mozley, L., Mozley, P., et al. (1995). "Sex Differences in Regional Cerebral Glucose Metabolism During a Resting State." *Science 267*(5197), 528–531.

Gurian, M. (1999). *The Good Son: Shaping the Moral Development of Our Boys and Young Men.* New York: Putnam.

Haignere, C. S., Gold, R., & McDaniel, H. J. (1999). "Adolescent Abstinence and Condom Use: Are We Sure We Are Really Teaching What Is Safe?" *Health Education and Behavior, 26*, 43–54.

Hales, D. (2000). *An Invitation to Health* (9th ed.). Belmont, CA: Wadsworth/Thomson Learning.

Hamer, D. H., Hu, S., Magnuson, V. L., & Pattatucci, S. (1993). "A Linkage Between DNA Markers on the X-Chromosome and Male Sexual Orientation." *Science, 261*(5119), 321–327.

Harlow, C. W. (1991). *Female Victims of Violent Crime.* Washington, DC: U.S. Department of Justice. (NCJ-126826).

Hart, L. (1994). *Fatal Women: Lesbian Sexuality and the Mark of Aggression.* Princeton, NJ: Princeton University Press.

Hartman, U., Meuleman, E. J. H., Cuzin, B., Emrich, H. M., DeClerco, G. A., Bailey, M. J., Mayton, M. C., Smith, M. D., & Osherloh, I. H. (1999). "Sildenafil Citrate (VIAGRA): Analysis of Preferred Dose in a European, Six-Month, Double-Blind, Placebo-Controlled, Flexible Dose Escalation Study in Patients with Erectile Dysfunction." *International Journal of Clinical Practice, 102*, 27–29.

Harvard's Men's Health Watch. (2000, January). Viagra and Erections: Do the Benefits Persist? Available: http://www.health.harvard.edu (Last visited 6/3/03).

Harvey, S. (1987). "Female Sexual Behavior: Fluctuations During the Menstrual Cycle." *Journal of Psychosomatic Research, 31*, 101–110.

Harvey, S. M., Beckman, L. J., Browner, C. H., & Sherman, C. A. (2002). "Relationship Power, Decision Making, and Sexual Relations: An Exploratory Study with Couples of Mexican Origin." *Journal of Sex Research, 39*(4), 284–291.

Hatcher, R., Trussell, J., Stewart, F., Cates, W., Stewart, G. K., Guest, F., & Kowal, D. (1998). *Contraceptive Technology.* New York: Ardent Media.

Hatcher, R. A., Nelson, A. L., Zieman, M., et al. (2002). *A Pocket Guide to Managing Contraception.* Tiger, GA: Bridging the Gap Communications.

Hatchett, S. J. (1991). "Women and Men." In J. S. Jackson (Ed.), *Life in Black America.* Newbury Park, CA: Sage.

Hatfield, R. (1994). "Touch and Sexuality." In V. Bullough & B. B. Bullough (Eds.), *Human Sexuality: An Encyclopedia.* New York: Garland.

Haugaard, J. J., & Reppucci, N. D. (1998). *The Sexual Abuse of Children: A Comprehensive Guide to Current Knowledge and Intervention Strategies.* San Francisco: Jossey-Bass.

Hays, D., & Samuels, A. (1989). "Heterosexual Women's Perceptions of Their Marriages to Bisexual or Homosexual Men." *Journal of Homosexuality, 18*, 81–100.

Hazan, C., & Shaver, P. (1987). "Romantic Love Conceptualized as an Attachment Process." *Journal of Personality and Social Psychology, 52*(3), 511–524.

Hazelwood, R., Burgess, A., & Dietz, P. (1983). *Autoerotic Fatalities.* Lexington, MA: Heath.

Hecht, M., Collier, M. J., & Ribeau, S. (1993). *African American Communication.* Newbury Park, CA: Sage.

Henderson-King, D. H., & Veroff, J. (1994). "Sexual Satisfaction and Marital Well-Being in the First Years of Marriage." *Journal of Social and Personal Relationships, 11*, 509–534.

Hendrick, C., & Hendrick, S. S. (1988). "Lovers Wear Rose-Colored Glasses." *Journal of Social and Personal Relationships, 5*(2), 161–183.

Henrick, J., & Stange, T. (1991). "Do Actions Speak Louder Than Words? An Effect of the Functional Use of Language on Dominant Sex Role Behavior in Boys and Girls." *Early Childhood Research Quarterly, 6*(4), 565–576.

Henshaw, S. K. (2003). U.S. Teenage Pregnancy Statistics with Comparative Statistics for Women. Available: http://www.agi-usa.org/pubs/teen_stats.htm (Last visited 5/30/03).

Herbert, C. M. H. (1989). *Talking of Silence: The Sexual Harassment of Schoolgirls.* London: Falmer Press.

Herdt, G. (1987). "Transitional Objects in Sambia Initiation." Special issue: Interpretation in Psychoanalytic Anthropology. *Ethos, 15*, 40–57.

Herdt, G., & Boxer, A. (1992). "Introduction: Culture, History, and Life Course of Gay Men." In G. Herdt (Ed.), *Gay Culture in America: Essays from the Field.* Boston: Beacon Press.

Herek, G. M. (1984). "Beyond Homophobia: A Social Psychological Perspective on Attitudes Toward Lesbians and Gay Men." *Journal of Homosexuality, 10*(1–2), 1–21.

Herek, G. M. (1995). "Psychological Heterosexism in the United States." In A. R. D'Augelli & C. J. Patterson (Eds.), *Lesbian, Gay, and Bisexual Identities over the Lifespan: Psychological Perspectives.* New York: Oxford University Press.

Herek, G. M. (1998). "Heterosexuals' Attitudes Toward Lesbians and Gay Men." *The Journal of Sex Research, 24*, 451–477.

Herek, G. M., Capitanio, J. P., & Widaman, K. F. (2002). "HIV-Related Stigma and Knowledge in the United States: Prevalence and Trends, 1991–1999." *American Journal of Public Health, 92*, 371–377.

Herek, G. M., Kimmel, D. C., Amaro, H., & Melton, G. B. (1991). "Avoiding Heterosexist Bias in Psychological Research." *American Psychologist, 46*(9), 957–963.

Hetherington, S. E. (1990). "A Controlled Study of the Effect of Prepared Childbirth Classes on Obstetric Outcomes." *Birth, 17*(2), 86–90.

Hibbard, R. A., & Hartman, G. L. (1992). "Behavioral Problems in Alleged Sexual Abuse Victims." *Child Abuse and Neglect*, 16(5), 755–762.

Hicks, T. V., & Leitenberg, H. (2001). "Sexual Fantasies About One's Partner Versus Someone Else: Gender Differences in Incidence and Frequency." *The Journal of Sex Research*, 38, 43–50.

Hill, C. A. (2002). "Gender, Relationship Stage, and Sexual Behavior: The Importance of Partner Emotional Investment Within Specific Situations." *Journal of Sex Research*, 39(3), 228–240.

Hill, I. (1987). *The Bisexual Spouse*. McLean, VA: Barlina Books.

Himelein, M., Vogel, R., & Wachowiak, D. (1994). "Non-Consensual Sexual Experiences in Precollege Women: Prevalence and Risk Factors." *Journal of Counseling and Development*, 72, 411–415.

Hirschfeld, M. (1991). *Transvestites: The Erotic Drive to Cross Dress*. Buffalo: Prometheus Books.

Hirschfeld, S. J. (2002). 21% of Women Surveyed in the Latest National Poll Report Having Been Sexually Harassed at Work. Available: http://www.fm.employmentlawalliance.com/ela/fmpro?-DB=ela._articles (Last visited 6/11/03).

Hite, S. (1976). *The Hite Report*. New York: Macmillan.

"HIV–Hepatitis C Infection Warning." (1999, December 2). *San Francisco Chronicle*, p. A5.

Hoffman, V., & Cohen, D. (1999). "A Night with Venus: Partner Assessments and High-Risk Encounters." *AIDS Care*, 11, 555–566.

Holcomb, D. R., Holcomb, L. C., Sondag, K., & Williams, N. (1991). "Attitudes About Date Rape: Gender Differences Among College Students." *College Student Journal*, 25(4), 434–439.

Holmberg, L., Bill-Axelson, A., Helgesen, F., Salo, J. O., Fomerz, P., Haggman, M., Andersson, S. O., Spangberg, A., Busch, C., Nordling, S., Palmgren, J., Adami, H. O., Johansson, J. E., Norlen, B. J., & Scandinavian Prostatic Cancer Group Study Number 4. (2002). "A Randomized Trial Comparing Radical Prostatectomy with Watchful Waiting in Early Prostate Cancer." *New England Journal of Medicine*, 347, 781–789.

Holmes, R. M. (1991). *Sex Crimes*. Newbury Park, CA: Sage.

Holtzman, D., Bland, S., Lansky, A., & Mack, K. (2001). "HIV-Related Behaviors and Perceptions Among Adults in 25 States: 1997 Behavioral Risk Factor Surveillance System." *American Journal of Public Health*, 91, 1882–1888.

"Home Access Health Urges Consumer Caution via Internet." (1997). *AIDS Weekly Plus*, p. 14.

"Home-Use HIV Test Kits." (1998, May 14). *FDA Backgrounder*.

Hooker, E. (1957). "The Adjustment of the Overt Male Homosexual." *Journal of Projective Psychology*, 21, 18–31.

HRSA News. (2002). HRSA Study Finds Narrowing Racial Gap in Women's Use of Prenatal Care. Available: http://newsroom.hrsa.gov/releases/2002releases/prenatal.htm (Last visited 11/30/02).

Hudak, M. A. (1993). "Gender Schema Theory Revisited: Men's Stereotypes of American Women." *Sex Roles*, 28(5–6), 279–293.

Hulley, S., Furber, C., Barrett-Connor, E., Cauley, J., Graham, D., Haskell, W., et al. (2002). "Risks and Benefits of Estrogen Plus Progestin in Healthy Postmenopausal Women: Principal Results from the Women's Health Initiative Randomized Controlled Trials." *Journal of the American Medical Association*, 288, 321–333.

Human Rights Campaign Foundation. (2003). Hate Crimes. Available: http://www.hrc.org/familynet/chapter.asp?article=550 (Last visited 6/12/03).

Humphreys, L. (1975). *Tearoom Trade: Impersonal Sex in Public Places*. Chicago: Aldine.

Hunter, A. G., & Davis, J. E. (1992). "Constructing Gender: An Exploration of Afro-American Men's Conceptualization of Manhood." *Gender and Society*, 6(3), 464–479.

Hyde, J. S. (2001). "The Next Decade of Sexual Science: Synergy from Advances in Related Sciences." *The Journal of Sex Research*, 38, 97–101.

Hyde, J. S., & DeLamater, J. D. (2003). *Understanding Human Sexuality*. (8th ed.). New York: McGraw-Hill.

Hyde, J. S., DeLamater, J. D., Plant, E. A., & Byrd, J. M. (1996). "Sexuality During Pregnancy and the Year Postpartum." *The Journal of Sex Research*, 33, 143–151.

Ickovics, J. R., Beren, S. E., Grigorenko, E. L., Morrill, A. C., Druley, J. A., & Rodin, J. (2002). "Pathways of Risk: Race, Social Class, Stress, and Coping as Factors Predicting Heterosexual Risk Behaviors for HIV Among Women." *AIDS and Behavior*, 6, 339–350.

Imperato-McGinley, J. (1974). "Steroid 5'-Reductase Deficiency in Man: An Inherited Form of Male Pseudohermaphroditism." *Science*, 186, 1213–1215.

Imperato-McGinley, J. (1979). "Androgens and the Evolution of Male Gender Identity Among Male Pseudohermaphrodites with 5'-Reductase Deficiency." *New England Journal of Medicine*, 300, 1233–1237.

Inciardi, J. A. (1995). "Crack, Crack House Sex, and HIV Risk." *Archives of Sexual Behavior*, 24(3), 249–269.

Insel, P. M., & Roth, W. T. (1998). *Core Concepts in Health*. Mountain View, CA: Mayfield.

Institute of Medicine. (1999). *Lesbian Health: Current Assessment and Directions for the Future*. Washington, DC: National Academy Press.

Intersex Society of North America. (2000a). Frequently Asked Questions. Available: http://www.isna.org/faq.html (Last visited 7/13/00).

Intersex Society of North America. (2000b). How Common Is Intersexuality? Available: http://www.isna.org/frequency.html (Last visited 7/19/00).

Intersex Society of North America. (2003a). What Is an Intersex Condition? What Do These Diagnoses Mean? Available: http://www.isna.org/faq/faq-medical.html (Last visited 2/23/03).

Intersex Society of North America. (2003b). On the Word "Hermaphrodite." Available: http://www.isna.org/faq/language.html (Last visited 2/24/03).

Intersex Society of North America. (2003c). Suggested Guidelines for Non-Intersex Individuals Writing About Intersexuality and Intersex People. Available: http://www.isna.org/faq/writing-guidelines.html (Last visited 2/24/03).

Intersex Society of North America. (2003d). Frequency: How Common Are Intersex Conditions? Available: http://www.isna.org/faq/frequency.html (Last visited 2/24/03).

In Their Own Right: Addressing the Reproductive Health Needs of American Men. (2001). Alan Guttmacher Institute. Available: http://www.agi-usa.org (Last visited 5/12/03).

Irvine, J. M. (2002). *Talk About Sex: The Battles over Sex Education in the United States*. Berkeley: University of California Press.

Irvine, M. (1998, June 28). "Studies Say C-Sections Can Fight AIDS." *Monterey Herald*, p. A7.

Isensee, R. (1990). *Love Between Men: Enhancing Intimacy and Keeping Your Relationship Alive*. New York: Prentice-Hall.

Ishii-Kuntz, M. (1997a). "Chinese American Families." In M. K. DeGenova (Ed.), *Families in Cultural Context*. Mountain View, CA: Mayfield.

Ishii-Kuntz, M. (1997b). "Japanese American Families." In M. K. DeGenova (Ed.), *Families in Cultural Context*. Mountain View, CA: Mayfield.

Is NuvaRing Right for You? (2003). Planned Parenthood Federation of America. Available: http://www.plannedparenthood .org/BC/030109_NuvaRing.html (Last visited 4/9/03).

Is Ortho Evra Right for You? (2003). Planned Parenthood Federation of America. Available: http://www.plannedparenthood .org/BC/030109_OrthoEvra.html (Last visited 4/9/03).

Jaccard, J., Dittus, P., & Gordon, D. (1998). "Parent-Adolescent Congruency in Reports of Adolescent Sexual Behavior and in Communication About Sexual Behavior." *Child Development, 69*, 247–261.

Jackson, G. (1999). "Erectile Dysfunction and Cardiovascular Disease." *International Journal of Clinical Practices, 53*, 363–368.

Jacobs, A. (2002, January 29). "In Clubs, a Potent Drug Stirs Fear of an Epidemic." *The New York Times*, p. B1.

Jacobs, S. E., Thomas, W., & Lang, S. (1997). *Two-Spirit People*. Chicago: University of Illinois Press.

Jacobson, J. L., & Jacobson, S. W. (1999). "Drinking Moderately and Pregnancy." *Alcohol Research and Health, 23*(1), 25–32.

Jacobson, S. J., Jacobson, D. J., Rohe, D. E., Girman, C. J., Roberts, R. O., & Leiber, M. M. (2003). "Frequency of Sexual Activity and Prostatic Health: Fact or Fairy Tale?" *Urology, 61*, 348–353.

Jacoby, S. (1999). "Great Sex: What's Age Got to Do with It?" *Modern Maturity, 42R*, 43–45, 74–77.

Janowsky, E. C., Kupper, L. L., & Hulka, B. S. (2000). "Meta-Analyses of the Relation Between Silicone Breast Implants and the Risk of Connective-Tissue Diseases." *The New England Journal of Medicine, 342*(11), 781–790.

Janssen, E. (2002). "Psychological Measurement of Sexual Arousal." In M. W. Wiederman & B. E. Whitley (Eds.), *Handbook for Conducting Research on Human Sexuality*. Mahwah, NJ: Erlbaum.

Janus, S., & Janus, C. (1993). *The Janus Report on Sexual Behavior*. New York: Wiley.

Jeffrey, T. B., & Jeffrey, L. K. (1991). "Psychologic Aspects of Sexual Abuse in Adolescence." *Current Opinion in Obstetrics and Gynecology, 3*(6), 825–831.

Jessor, R., Donovan, J., & Costa, F. M. (1994). *Beyond Adolescence: Problem Behavior and Young Adult Development*. New York: Cambridge University Press.

Jimenez, J. A., & Abreu, J. M. (2003). "Race and Sex Effects on Attitudinal Perceptions of Acquaintance Rape." *Journal of Counseling Psychology, 50*, 252–256.

Johnson, C. (1993, June 5). "More Women-Controlled AIDS Prevention Methods Needed—WHO." *San Jose Mercury News*, p. 6.

Johnson, C. B., Stockdale, M. S., & Saal, F. E. (1991). "Persistence of Men's Misperceptions of Friendly Cues Across a Variety of Interpersonal Encounters." *Psychology of Women Quarterly, 15*(3), 463–475.

Johnson, K. (2002). "Time, Patience Needed to Find Right Testosterone Level with HRT." *Family Practice News, 32*(11), 31.

Johnson, L. A. (2000, March 23). "New Risks Seen with Genital Herpes." *Monterey County Herald*, p. A6.

Joint United Nations Programme on AIDS (UNAIDS). (2000). *Report on the Global HIV/AIDS Epidemic—June 2000*. Geneva, Switzerland: World Health Organization.

Joint United Nations Programme on HIV/AIDS and World Health Organization. (2002). AIDS Epidemic Update: December 2002. Available: http://www.unaids.org/worldaidsday/ 2002/press/epiupdate.html (Last visited 12/5/02).

Jones, J. H. (1993). *Bad Blood: The Tuskegee Syphilis Experiment* (Rev. ed.). New York: Free Press.

Jones, L. M., & Finkelhor, D. (2003). "Putting Together Evidence on Declining Trends in Sexual Abuse: A Complex Puzzle." *Child Abuse and Neglect, 27*, 133–136.

Jones, R. K., Darroch, J. E., & Henshaw, S. K. (2002a). "Patterns in the Socioeconomic Characteristics of Women Obtaining Abortions in 2000–2001." *Perspectives on Sexual and Reproductive Health, 34*(5), 226–235.

Jones, R. K., Darroch, J. E., & Henshaw, S. K. (2002b). "Contraceptive Use Among U.S. Women Having Abortions in 2000–2001." *Perspectives on Sexual and Reproductive Health, 34*(6), 294–303.

Jones, T. S., & Remland, M. S. (1992). "Sources of Variability in Perceptions of and Responses to Sexual Harassment." *Sex Roles, 27*(3–4), 121–142.

Jumper, S. A. (1995). "A Meta-Analysis of the Relationship of Child Sexual Abuse to Adult Psychological Adjustment." *Child Abuse and Neglect, 19*(6), 715–728.

Jurich, A., & Polson, C. (1985). "Nonverbal Assessment of Anxiety as a Function of Intimacy of Sexual Attitude Questions." *Psychological Reports, 57*(3, Pt. 2), 1243–1247.

Just the Facts: Circumcision. (2003). American Academy of Pediatrics. Available: http://www.acp.org/mrt/factscir.htm (Last visited 6/3/03).

Kaiser Family Foundation. (1997). Talking with Kids About Tough Issues. Available: http://www.kff.org (Last visited 3/14/03).

Kaiser Family Foundation. (2000). Sex Education in America. A Series of National Surveys of Students, Parents, Teachers, and Principals. Available: http://www.kff.org/content/2000/3048 (Last visited 2/3/03).

Kaiser Family Foundation. (2001). New SexSmarts Study on Teens and Sexually Transmitted Diseases. Available: http://www.kff .org/content/2001/3148 (Last visited 12/14/01).

Kaiser Family Foundation. (2002a). Relationships. Available: http://www.kff.org (Last visited 3/14/03).

Kaiser Family Foundation. (2002b). "SexSmarts: A Series of National Surveys of Teens About Sex." Menlo Park, CA: Author.

Kaiser Family Foundation. (2002c). *Latest Findings on Employer-Based Coverage of Contraception*. Menlo Park, CA: Author.

Kaiser Family Foundation. (2002d). HIV/AIDS and Other Sexually Transmitted Diseases (STDs) in the Southern Region of the United States: Epidemiological Overview. Available: http:// www. kff.org/content/20021113a/final%20Epi%20 Document .pdf (Last visited 11/11/02).

Kaiser Family Foundation. (2003a). Sex on TV3. Available: http://www.kff.org (Last visited 3/14/03).

Kaiser Family Foundation. (2003b). "Fact Sheets: Teen Sexual Activity." Menlo Park, CA: Author.

Kaiser Family Foundation. (n.d.). Inside-Out: A Report on the Experiences of Lesbians, Gays and Bisexuals in America and the Public's Views on Issues and Policies Related to Sexual Orientation. Available: http://www.kff.org (Last visited 6/11/03).

Kaiser Family Foundation/Harvard School of Public Health. (2000, February). Health News Index. Available: http://www .kff.org (Last visited 1/6/01).

Kalb, C. (2003, February 3). "Farewell to 'Aunt Flo.'" *Newsweek*, p. 48.

Kalichman, S. C. (1998). *Preventing AIDS: A Sourcebook for Behavioral Interventions*. Mahwah, NJ: Erlbaum.

Kalof, L., & Wade, B. H. (1995). "Sexual Attitudes and Experiences with Sexual Coercion: Exploring the Influence of Race and Gender." *Journal of Black Psychology, 21*(3), 224–238.

Kamb, M. L., Fishbein, M., Douglas, J. M., Jr., Rhodes, F., Rogers, J., Bolan, G., Zenilman, J., Hoxworth, T., Malotte, C. K., Iatesta, M., Kent, C., Lentz, A., Graniano, S., Byers, R. H., & Peterman, T. A. (1998). "Efficacy of Risk-Reduction Counseling to Prevent Human Immunodeficiency Virus and Sexually Transmitted Diseases: A Randomized Controlled Trial." *Journal of the American Medical Association, 280*, 1161–1167.

Kamen, P. (2003, October 13). "Kobe and the New Currency of 'No.' " *In These Times*, p. 11.

Kaplan, A. (1979). "Clarifying the Concept of Androgyny: Implications for Therapy." *Psychology of Women, 3*, 223–230.

Kaplan, D. L., & Keys, C. B. (1997). "Sex and Relationship Variables as Predictors of Sexual Attraction in Cross-Sex Platonic Friendships Between Young Heterosexual Adults." *Journal of Social and Personal Relationships, 14*, 191–206.

Kaplan, H. S. (1974). *The New Sex Therapy*. New York: Brunner/ Mazel.

Kaplan, H. S. (1979). *Disorders of Desire*. New York: Brunner/ Mazel.

Kaplan, J., Sadock, B., & Grebb, J. (1994). *Synopsis of Psychiatry* (7th ed.). Baltimore: Williams & Wilkins.

Kaplowitz, P. B., & Oberfield, S. E. (1999). "The Reexamination of the Age Limit for Defining When Puberty Is Precocious in Girls in the United States: Implications for Evaluation and Treatment." *Pediatrics, 104*(4), 936.

Kappy, M. S., Blizzard, R. M., & Migeon, C. J. (Eds.). (1994). *The Diagnosis and Treatment of Endocrine Disorders in Childhood and Adolescence* (4th ed.). Baltimore: Thompson.

Kaunitz, A. M. (1999). "Oral Contraceptive Health Benefits: Perception Versus Reality." *Contraception, 59*(1) (Supplement), 295–335.

Kaunitz, A. M. (2000). "Menstruation: Choosing Whether, and When." *Contraception, 62*, 277–284.

Kavich-Sharon, R. (1994). "Response to Sadomasochistic Fantasy Role Play." *Contemporary Sexuality, 28*(4), 4.

Kaye, K., Elkind, L., Goldberg, D., & Tytan, A. (1989). "Birth Outcomes for Infants of Drug Abusing Mothers." *New York State Journal of Medicine, 144*(7), 256–261.

Kegeles, S. M., Hays, R. B., & Coates, T. J. (1996). "The Mpowerment Project: A Community-Level HIV Prevention Intervention for Young Gay Men." *American Journal of Public Health, 86*, 1129–1136.

Kehoe, M. (1988). "Lesbians over 60 Speak for Themselves." *Journal of Homosexuality, 16*, 1–111.

Keintz-Knowles, K. E. (2002). Fall Colors 2001–02. Available: http://www.children-now.org (Last visited 1/17/03).

Kellett, J. M. (1991). "Sexuality of the Elderly." *Sexual and Marital Therapy, 6*(2), 147–155.

Kelley, H. (1983). "Love and Commitment." In H. Kelley et al. (Eds.), *Close Relationships*. New York: Freeman.

Kelly, M. L., & Parsons, B. (2000). "Sexual Harassment in the 1990s: A University-Wide Survey of Female Faculty, Administrators, Staff, and Students." *Journal of Higher Education, 71*, 548–568.

Kelly, M. P., Strassberg, D. S., & Kircher, J. R. (1990). "Attitudinal and Experiential Correlates of Anorgasmia." *Archives of Sexual Behavior, 19*(2), 165–167.

Kennedy, K., & Insel, P. (2000). "What's New in Contraception?" *Healthline, 6–8*.

Kenyon, E. B. (1989). "The Management of Exhibitionism in the Elderly: A Case Study." *Sexual and Marital Therapy, 4*(1), 93–100.

Keshavarz, J., Hillis, S. D., Kieke, B. A., & Marchbanks, P. A. (2002). "Hysterectomy Surveillance—United States, 1994–1999." *Mortality and Morbidity Report, 51*, 1–7.

Kidd, S. A., & Kral, M. J. (2002). "Suicide and Prostitution Among Street Youth: A Qualitative Analysis." *Adolescence, 37*, 411–431.

Kidder, L. H., Lafleur, R. A., & Wells, C. V. (1995). "Recalling Harassment, Reconstructing Experience." *Journal of Social Issues, 52*(1), 69–84.

Kilmarx, P. H., Akbar, A. Z., Thomas, J. C., Nakashima, A. K., St. Louis, M. E., Flock, M. L., & Peterman, T. A. (1997). "Sociodemographic Factors and the Variation in Syphilis Rates Among U.S. Counties, 1984 Through 1993: An Ecological Analysis." *American Journal of Public Health, 87*(12), 1937–1943.

Kilpatrick, D., Edmunds, C., & Seymour, A. (1992). *Rape in America: A Report to the Nation*. Arlington, VA: National Victim Center and the Crime Victims Research and Treatment Center.

Kim, A. A., Kent, C. K., & Klausner, J. D. (2002). "Increased Risk of HIV and Sexually Transmitted Disease Transmission Among Gay and Bisexual Men Who Use Viagra." *AIDS, 16*, 1425–1428.

King, P. A. (1992). "Twenty Years After. The Legacy of the Tuskegee Syphilis Study. The Dangers of Difference." *Hastings Center Report, 22*(6), 35–38.

Kinsey, A., Pomeroy, W., & Martin, C. (1948). *Sexual Behavior in the Human Male*. Philadelphia: Saunders.

Kinsey, A., Pomeroy, W., Martin, C., & Gebhard, P. (1953). *Sexual Behavior in the Human Female*. Philadelphia: Saunders.

Kirby, D. (2000). "School-Based Interventions to Prevent Unprotected Sex and HIV Among Adolescents." In J. L. Peterson & R. J. Di Clemente (Eds.), *Handbook of HIV Prevention*. New York: Kluwer Academic/Plenum.

Kirby, D. (2002). "Effective Approaches to Reducing Adolescent Unprotected Sex, Pregnancy, and Childbearing." *Journal of Sex Research, 39*(7), 51–58.

Kisabeth, R., Pontius, C. A., Statland, B. E., & Galper, C. (1997). "Promises and Pitfalls of Home Test Devices." *Patient Care, (31)*6, 125–137.

Kitano, H. H. (1994, November). "Recent Trends in Japanese Americans' Interracial Marriage." Paper presented at the Center for Family Studies Lecture Series, University of California, Riverside.

Kite, M. (1984). "Sex Differences in Attitudes Toward Homosexuals: A Meta-Analytic Review." *Journal of Homosexuality, 10*(1–2), 69–82.

Kjerulff, K. H., Rhodes, J. C., Langenberg, P. W., & Harvey, L. A. (2000). "Patient Satisfaction with Results of Hysterectomy." *American Journal of Obstetrics and Gynecology, 183*, 1440–1447.

Klein, M. (1991). "Why There's No Such Thing as Sexual Addiction—and Why It Really Matters." In R. T. Francoeur (Ed.), *Taking Sides: Clashing Views on Controversial Issues in Human Sexuality* (3rd ed.). Guilford, CT: Dushkin.

Klinetob, N. A., & Smith, D. A. (1996). "Demand-Withdraw Communication in Marital Interaction: Tests of Interspousal

Contingency and Gender Role Hypotheses." *Journal of Marriage and the Family, 58*(4), 945–957.

Kloner, R. A., & Jarow, J. P. (1999). "Erectile Dysfunction and Sildenafil Citrate and Cardiologists." *American Journal of Cardiology, 83*, 546–552.

Knafo, D., & Jaffe, Y. (1984). "Sexual Fantasizing in Males and Females." *Journal of Research in Personality, 18*, 451–462.

Koch, P. B., Palmer, R. F., Vicary, J. A., & Wood, J. M. (1999). "Mixing Sex and Alcohol in College: Female-Male HIV Risk Model." *Journal of Sex Education and Therapy, 24*, 99–108.

Kolata, G. (1992, March 17). "How AIDS Smolders: Immune System Studies Follow the Tracks of HIV." *The New York Times,* pp. B5, B8.

Kolodny, R., Masters, W., & Johnson, V. (1979). *Textbook of Sexual Medicine.* Boston: Little, Brown.

Konrad, A., & Harris, C. (2002). "Desirability of the Bem Sex-Role Inventory Items for Women and Men: A Comparison Between African Americans and European Americans." *Sex Roles: A Journal of Sex Research,* 259–272.

Koss, M. P., & Dinero, T. E. (1989). "Predictors of Sexual Aggression Among a National Sample of Male College Students." *Annals of the New York Academy of Science, 528*, 133–146.

Krakow, B., Germain, A., Tandberg, D., Koss, M., Schrader, R., Hollifield, M., Cheng, D., & Edmond, T. (2000). "Sleep Breathing and Sleep Movement Disorders Masquerading as Insomnia in Sexual-Assault Survivors." *Comprehensive Psychiatry, 41*, 49–56.

Kruks, G. (1991). "Gay and Lesbian Homeless/Street Youth: Special Issues and Concerns." Special Issue: Homeless Youth. *Journal of Adolescent Health, 12*(7), 515–518.

Kunkel, D., Farinola, W., Cope, K., Donnerstein, E., Biely, E., & Zwarun, L. (1998, September). *An Assessment of the Television Industry's Use of V-Chip Ratings.* Menlo Park, CA: Kaiser Family Foundation.

Kurdek, L. A. (1995). "Lesbian and Gay Couples." In A. R. D'Augelli & C. J. Patterson (Eds.), *Lesbian, Gay and Bisexual Identities over the Lifespan.* New York: Oxford University Press.

LaBrie, J. W., Schiffman, J., & Earleywine, M. (2002). "Expectations Specific to Condom Use Mediate the Alcohol and Sexual Risk Relationship." *The Journal of Sex Research, 39*, 145–152.

Lacey, D. (2002, January 6). "In Kenyan Family, Ritual for Girls Still Divides." *The New York Times,* Sec. 1, p. 4.

"Lack of TV Diversity Hit." (2002). *San Francisco Chronicle,* p. A2.

Ladas, A., Whipple, B., & Perry, J. (1982). *The G Spot.* New York: Holt, Rinehart & Winston.

Lamaze, F. (1970). *Painless Childbirth* (1st ed., 1956). Chicago: Regnery.

Landry, D. J., Singh, S., & Darroch, J. E. (2000). "Sexuality Education in Fifth and Sixth Grades in U.S. Public Schools, 1999." *Family Planning Perspectives, 32*, 212–219.

Landry, V. (Ed.). (2003). *Contraceptive Sterilization: Global Issues and Trends.* New York: EngenderHealth.

Laner, M. R. (1990). "Violence or Its Precipitators: Which Is More Likely to Be Identified as a Dating Problem?" *Deviant Behavior, 11*(4), 319–329.

Lang, R., & Frenzel, R. (1988). "How Sex Offenders Lure Children." *Annals of Sex Research, 1*(2), 303–317.

Laqueur, T. (2003). *Solitary Sex: A Cultural History of Masturbation.* Cambridge, MA: MIT Zone.

Latina Women's Health. (2000). National Women's Health Information Center. Available: http://www.4woman.gov/faq/latina.htm (Last visited 6/1/00).

Lauer, R., & Lauer, J. (2000). *Marriage and the Family: The Quest for Intimacy* (4th ed.). Boston: McGraw-Hill.

Laumann, E., Gagnon, J., Michael, R., & Michaels, S. (1994). *The Social Organization of Sexuality.* Chicago: University of Chicago Press.

Laumann, E. O., & Mahay, J. (2002). "The Social Organization of Women's Sexuality." In G. M. Wingood, & R. J. DiClemente (Eds.), *Handbook of Women's Sexual and Reproductive Health.* New York: Kluwer Academic/Plenum.

Laumann, E. O., Paik, A., & Rosen, R. C. (1999). "Sexual Dysfunction in the United States: Prevalence and Predictors." *Journal of the American Medical Association, 281*, 537–544.

LaVay, S., and Valente, S. M. (2003). *Human Sexuality.* MA: Sinaver Assoc., Inc.

Layman, S. A., Hughes-McLain, C., & Thompson, G. (1998). "'Date-Rape Drugs': A Growing Concern." *Journal of Health Education, 29*, 271–274.

Leavitt, F., & Berger, J. C. (1990). "Clinical Patterns Among Male Transsexual Candidates with Erotic Interest in Males." *Archives of Sexual Behavior, 19*(5), 491–505.

Lee, J. A. (1973). *The Color of Love.* Toronto: New Press.

Lee, J. A. (1988). "Love Styles." In R. Sternberg & M. Barnes (Eds.), *The Psychology of Love.* New Haven, CT: Yale University Press.

Lee, L. & Fleming, P. (2001). "Trends in HIV Diagnoses Among Women in the United States, 1994–1998. *Journal of the American Medical Association, 56*, 94–99.

Lehner, T., & Chiasson, M. A. (1998). "Seroprevalence of Human Immunodeficiency Virus Type I and Sexual Behaviors in Bisexual African-American and Hispanic Men Visiting a Sexually Transmitted Disease Clinic in New York City." *American Journal of Epidemiology, 147*, 269–272.

Leiblum, S. R., & Nathan, S. G. (2001). "Persistent Sexual Arousal Syndrome: A Newly Discovered Pattern of Female Sexuality." *Journal of Sex and Marital Therapy, 27*, 365–380.

Leinwand, D. (2002, September 23). "Ecstasy-Viagra Mix Alarms Doctors." *USA Today,* p. A1.

Leitenberg, H., Detzer, M. J., & Srebnik, D. (1993). "Gender Differences in Masturbation and the Relation of Masturbation Experience in Preadolescence and Early Adolescence to Sexual Behavior and Sexual Adjustment in Young Adulthood." *Archives of Sexual Behavior, 22*(2), 87–98.

Leitenberg, H., & Henning, K. (1995). "Sexual Fantasy." *Psychological Bulletin, 117*(3), 469–496.

Leland, J. (2000, May 29). "The Science of Women and Sex." *Newsweek,* pp. 46–54.

Lemonick, M. D. (2000, October 30). "Teens Before Their Time." *Time,* pp. 68–74.

Lenz, R., & Chaves, B. (1981). "Becoming Active Partners: A Couple's Perspective." In D. Bullard & S. Knight (Eds.), *Sexuality and Disability: Personal Perspectives.* St. Louis: Mosby.

Lerner, H. E. (1993). *The Dance of Deception.* New York: HarperCollins.

LeVay, S. (1991). "A Difference in Hypothalamic Structure Between Heterosexual and Homosexual Men." *Science, 253*, 1034–1037.

Lever, J. (1994, August 23). "Sexual Revelations." *The Advocate,* pp. 17–24.

Levesque, R. J. R. (1994). "Sex Differences in the Experiences of Child Sexual Victimization." *Journal of Family Violence, 9*(4), 357–369.

Levine, L., & Barbach, L. (1983). *The Intimate Male.* New York: Signet Books.

Levine, M. P. (1987). *How Schools Can Help Combat Student Eating Disorders: Anorexia Nervosa and Bulimia.* Washington, DC: National Education Association.

Levine, M. P., & Troiden, R. (1988). "The Myth of Sexual Compulsivity." *Journal of Sex Research, 25*(3), 347–363.

Levine, S. B. (1997). The Role of Psychiatry in Erectile Dysfunction: A Cautionary Essay on Emerging Treatments. Medscape. Available: http://www.medscape.com (Last visited 2/1/98).

Levy, S. (1997, March 31). "U.S. v. the Internet." *Newsweek,* pp. 77–79.

Li, C. K. (1990). "'The Main Thing Is Being Wanted': Some Case Studies in Adult Sexual Experiences with Children." *Journal of Homosexuality, 20*(1–2), 129–143.

Liben, L. S., & Signorella, M. L. (1993). "Gender-Schematic Processing in Children: The Role of Initial Interpretations of Stimuli." *Developmental Psychology, 29*(1), 141–150.

Lindberg, L. D., Boggs, S., Porter, L., & Williams, S. (2000). *Teen Risk-Taking: A Statistical Report.* Washington, DC: Urban Institute.

"Links Between Genetic and Environmental Factors and Prostate Cancer Risk." (1999, July 26). *Impotence and Male Health Weekly Plus.*

Lipman, A. (1986). "Homosexual Relationships." *Generations, 10,* 51–54.

Lippa, R. A. (2000). "Gender-Related Traits in Gay Men, Lesbian Women, and Heterosexual Men and Women: The Virtual Identity of Homosexual-Heterosexual Diagnosticity and Gender Diagnosticity." *Journal of Personality, 68,* 899–925.

Lippa, R. A. (2002). "Gender-Related Traits of Heterosexual and Homosexual Men and Women." *Archives of Sexual Behavior, 31,* 83–98.

Lips, H. (1997). *Sex and Gender* (2nd ed.). Mountain View, CA: Mayfield.

Lips, H. (2001). *A New Psychology of Women: Gender, Culture and Ethnicity* (2nd ed.). Boston: McGraw-Hill.

Lipscomb, G. H., et al. (1992). "Male Victims of Sexual Assault." *Journal of the American Medical Association, 267*(22), 3064–3066.

Locy, T., & Biskupic, J. (2003, June 23). "Requirement for Library Porn Filters Upheld." *USA Today,* p. A1.

Loftus, E., & Ketcham, D. (1994). *The Myth of Repressed Memory: False Memories and Allegations of Sexual Abuse.* New York: St. Martin's Press.

Long, V. E. (2003). "Contraceptive Choices: New Options on the U.S. Market." *SIECUS Report, 31*(2), 13–18.

Lord, L. (1985, December 9). "Mortality." *U.S. News & World Report,* pp. 52–59.

Lucas, V. A. (1992). "An Investigation of the Health Care Preferences of the Lesbian Population." *Health Care for Women International, 13*(2), 221–228.

MacKay, J. (2001). "Global Sex: Sexuality and Sexual Practices Around the World." *Sexual and Relationship Therapy, 16,* 71–82.

Mackey, R. A., & O'Brien, B. A. (1999). "Adaptation in Lasting Marriages." *Families in Society: The Journal of Contemporary Human Services, 80*(6), 587–602.

Mackey, T., Sereika, S. M., Weissfeld, L. A., Hacker, S. S., Zender, J. F., & Heard, S. L. (1992). "Factors Associated with Long-Term Depressive Symptoms of Sexual Assault Victims." *Archives of Psychiatric Nursing, 6*(1), 10–25.

Mah, K., & Binik, Y. M. (2001). "The Nature of Human Orgasm: A Critical Review of Major Trends." *Clinical Psychology Review, 21*(6), 823–856.

Mah, K., & Binik, Y. M. (2002). "Do All Orgasms Feel Alike? Evaluating a Two-Dimensional Model of the Orgasm Experience Across Gender and Sexual Context." *The Journal of Sex Research, 39*(2), 104–113.

Malamuth, N. M. (1996). "Sexually Explicit Media, Gender Differences, and Evolutionary Theory." *Journal of Communication, 46*(3), 8–31.

Malamuth, N. M. (1998). "The Confluence Model as an Organizing Framework for Research on Sexually Aggressive Men: Risk Moderators, Imagined Aggression and Pornography Consumption." In R. Green & E. Donnerstein (Eds.), *Aggression: Theoretical and Empirical Reviews.* New York: Academic Press.

Malamuth, N. M., Addison, T., & Koss, M. (2001). "Pornography and Sexual Aggression: Are There Reliable Effects?" *Annual Review of Sex Research, 11,* 26–91.

Malamuth, N. M., Sockloskie, R. J., Koss, M. P., & Tanaka, J. S. (1991). "Characteristics of Aggressors Against Women: Testing a Model Using a National Sample of College Students." *Journal of Consulting and Clinical Psychology, 59,* 670–781.

Malcolm, S. J. (1994, October). "Was It Good for You?" *Ms.,* pp. 23–25.

Mancini, J., & Bliezner, R. (1991). "Aging Parents and Adult Children Research Themes in Intergenerational Relations." In A. Booth (Ed.), *Contemporary Families: Looking Forward, Looking Back.* Minneapolis: National Council on Family Relations.

Manning, W. D., & Smock, P. J. "First Comes Cohabitation and Then Comes Marriage?" *Journal of Family Issues, 23,* 1065–1078.

Marchbanks, P. A., McDonald, J. A., Wilson, H. G., et al. (2002). "Oral Contraceptives and the Risk of Breast Cancer." *New England Journal of Medicine, 346,* 2025–2032.

Margolies, L., Becher, M., & Jackson-Brewer, K. (1988). "Internalized Homophobia: Identifying and Treating the Oppressor Within." In Boston Lesbian Psychologies Collective (Eds.), *Lesbian Psychologies.* Urbana: University of Illinois Press.

Marieb, E. N. (1995). *Human Anatomy and Physiology* (2nd ed.). Redwood City, CA: Benjamin/Cummings.

Marijuana and Sex. (1996, April 5). Available: http://www.columbia.edu/cu/healthwise/0860.html (Last visited 1/29/98).

Marin, R., Hannah, D., Colin, M., Annin, P., & Gegax, T. T. (1995, February 6). "Turning in the Badges of Rebellion." *Newsweek,* p. 45.

Marmor, J. (Ed.). (1980a). *Homosexual Behavior.* New York: Basic Books.

Marmor, J. (1980b). "The Multiple Roots of Homosexual Behavior." In J. Marmor (Ed.), *Homosexual Behavior.* New York: Basic Books.

Marshall, D. (1971). "Sexual Behavior on Mangaia." In D. Marshall & R. Suggs (Eds.), *Human Sexual Behavior.* New York: Basic Books.

Marshall, W. L. (1993). "The Role of Attachments, Intimacy, and Loneliness in the Etiology and Maintenance of Sexual Offending." *Sexual and Marital Therapy, 8,* 109–121.

Marshall, W. L., Eccles, A., & Barabee, H. E. (1991). "The Treatment of Exhibitionism: A Focus on Sexual Deviance Versus Cognitive and Relationship Features." *Behaviour Research and Therapy, 29*(2), 129–135.

Martin, P. (1981). "Happy Sexless Marriages." *Medical Aspects of Human Sexuality, 15*(1), 25.

Martin, S. J., Martin, J. A., Curtin, S. C., et al. (2001). "Births: Final Data for 1999." *National Vital Statistics Reports, 49*(1).

Marvel, B. (2002, May 5). "Maximum Exposure." *Indianapolis Star*, pp. Dl, D5.

Masters, W. H., & Johnson, V. E. (1966). *Human Sexual Response*. Boston: Little, Brown.

Masters, W. H., & Johnson, V. E. (1970). *Human Sexual Inadequacy*. Boston: Little, Brown.

Masters, W. H., & Johnson, V. E. (1974). *The Pleasure Bond*. Boston: Little, Brown.

Masters, W. H., Johnson, V., & Kolodny, R. C. (1992). *Human Sexuality* (3rd ed.). New York: HarperCollins.

Matek, O. (1988). "Obscene Phone Callers." In D. Dailey (Ed.), *The Sexually Unusual*. New York: Harrington Park Press.

Matteo, S., & Rissman, E. (1984). "Increased Sexual Activity During Midcycle Portion of the Human Menstrual Cycle." *Hormones and Behavior, 18,* 249–255.

Maxmen, J., & Ward, N. (1995). *Essential Psychopathology and Its Treatment* (2nd ed.). New York: Norton.

Mayers, L. B., Judelson, D. A., Moriarty, B. W., & Rundell, K. W. (2002). "Prevalence of Body Art (Body Piercing and Tattooing) in University Undergraduates and Incidence of Medical Complications." *Mayo Clinic Proceedings, 77,* 29–34.

Mays, V. M., Cochran, S. D., Bellinger, G., & Smith, R. G. (1992). "The Language of Black Gay Men's Sexual Behavior: Implications for AIDS Risk Reduction." *The Journal of Sex Research, 29*(3), 425–434.

Mazel, D., & Percival, E. (1989). "Students' Experiences of Sexual Harassment at a Small University." *Sex Roles, 20,* 1–22.

McCabe, M. P. (1994). "Childhood, Adolescent and Current Psychological Factors Associated with Sexual Dysfunction." *Sexual and Marital Therapy, 9*(3), 267–276.

McCarthy, B. W. (1998). "Integrating Viagra into Cognitive-Behavioral Couples Sex Therapy." *Journal of Sex Education and Therapy, 23,* 302–308.

McCollum, V. J. C. (1997). "Evolution of the African American Family Personality: Considerations for Family Therapy." *Journal of Multicultural Counseling and Development, 25,* 219–229.

McConaghy, N. (1998). "Pedophilia: A Review of the Evidence." *Australian and New Zealand Journal of Psychiatry, 32,* 252–265.

McCormick, E., & Zamora, J. H. (2000, February 13). "Slave Trade Still Alive in U.S." *San Francisco Chronicle*, p. A1.

McCormick, N. (1996). "Our Feminist Future: Women Affirming Sexuality Research in the Late Twentieth Century." *The Journal of Sex Research, 33*(2), 99–102.

McCusker, J., Stoddard, A. M., Zapka, J. G., & Lewis, B. F. (1993). "Behavioral Outcomes of AIDS Education Interventions for Drug Users in Short-Term Treatment." *American Journal of Public Health, 82,* 533–540.

McCusker, J., Stoddard, A. M., Zapka, J. G., Morrison, C. S., Zorn, M., & Lewis, B. F. (1992). "AIDS Education for Drug Abusers: Evaluation of Short-Term Effectiveness." *American Journal of Public Health, 82,* 533–540.

McLeer, S. V., Deblinger, E. B., Henry, D., & Ovraschel, H. (1992). "Sexually Abused Children at High Risk for Post-Traumatic Stress Disorder." *Journal of the American Academy of Child and Adolescent Psychiatry, 31*(5), 875–879.

McNeill, B., Prieto, L., Niemann, Y., Pizarro, M., Vera, E., & Gomez, S. (2001). "Current Directions in Chicana/o Psychology." *Counseling Psychologist, 29,* 5–17.

McWhirter, D. (1990). "Prologue." In D. McWhirter, S. A. Sanders, & J. M. Reinisch (Eds.), *Homosexuality/Heterosexuality: Concepts of Sexual Orientation*. New York: Oxford University Press.

Mead, M. (1975). *Male and Female*. New York: Morrow.

Meana, M., Binik, Y. M., Khalife, S., & Cohen, D. (1999). "Psychosocial Correlates of Pain Attributions in Women with Dyspareunia." *Psychosomatics, 40,* 497–502.

Melhuus, A. (1996). "Power, Value and the Ambiguous Meaning of Gender." In A. Melhuus & K. A. Stolen (Eds.), *Machos, Mistresses, Madonnas: Contesting the Power of Latin American Gender Imagery*. London: Verso.

Men Can Stop Rape. (2000). Why Should Men Care About Violence? Available: http://www.mrpp.org/facts/menissue.html (Last visited 1/19/01).

Menopause—Another Change in Life. (2001). Planned Parenthood Federation of America. Available: http://www.plannedparenthood.org/WOMENSHEALTH/magazine (Last visited 10/3/03).

Metts, S., & Cupach, W. (1989). "The Role of Communication in Human Sexuality." In K. McKinney & S. Sprecher (Eds.), *Human Sexuality: The Social and Interpersonal Context*. Norwood, NJ: Ablex.

Meuwissen, I., & Over, R. (1992). "Sexual Arousal Across Phases of the Human Menstrual Cycle." *Archives of Sexual Behavior, 21,* 101–119.

Michael, R., Gagnon, J., Laumann, E., & Kolata, G. (1994). *Sex in America: A Definitive Survey*. Boston: Little, Brown.

Miller, H. G., Cain, V. S., Rogers, S. M., Gribble, J. N., & Turner, C. F. (1999). "Correlates of Sexually Transmitted Bacterial Infections Among U.S. Women in 1995." *Family Planning Perspectives, 31,* 4–10, 23.

Miller, J. (1995). "Gender and Power on the Streets: Street Prostitution in the Era of Crack Cocaine." *Journal of Contemporary Ethnography, 23,* 427–452.

Miller, J., & Schwartz, M. D. (1995). "Rape Myths and Violence Against Street Prostitutes." *Deviant Behavior, 16*(1), 1–23.

Miller, K. S., Clark, L. F., & Moore, J. F. (1997). "Sexual Initiation with Older Male Partners and Subsequent HIV Risk Behavior Among Female Adolescents." *Family Planning Perspectives, 29,* 212–214.

Miller, L. (2000, October 17). "Panel Agrees: Rethink New Porn Laws." *USA Today*, p. D3.

Mills, J. L., & England, K. (2001). "Food Fortification to Prevent Neural Tube Defects." *Journal of the American Medical Association, 285,* 3022.

Mindel, C. H., Haberstein, R. W., & Wright, R., Jr. (Eds.). (1988). *Ethnic Families in America: Patterns and Variations* (3rd ed.). New York: Elsevier North Holland.

Mishra, R. (1998, April 7). "Drug Begs Many Questions." *Monterey County Herald*, p. A10.

Moller, L. C., Hymel, S., & Rubin, K. H. (1992). "Sex Typing in Play and Popularity in Middle Childhood." *Sex Roles, 26*(7–8), 331–335.

"Moms' Cocaine Hurts Kids' IQs." (1998, October 23). *San Francisco Chronicle*, p. A2.

Money, J. (1980). *Love and Love Sickness: The Science of Sex, Gender Difference, and Pair Bonding*. Baltimore: Johns Hopkins University Press.

Money, J. (1981). "Paraphilias: Phyletic Origins of Erotosexual Dysfunction." *International Journal of Mental Health, 10,* 75–109.

Money, J. (1984). "Paraphilias: Phenomenology and Classification." *American Journal of Psychotherapy, 38,* 164–179.

Money, J. (1988). *Gay, Straight, and In-Between*. New York: Oxford University Press.

Money, J. (1990). "Forensic Sexology: Paraphilic Serial Rape (Biastophilia) and Lust Murder (Erotophonophilia)." *American Journal of Psychotherapy, 44*(1), 26–37.

Monroe, J. (1997). "'Roofies': Horror Drug of the '90s." *Current Health, 2*(1), 24–27.

Montagu, A. (1986). *Touching* (3rd ed.). New York: Columbia University Press.

Montgomery, M. J., & Sorell, G. T. (1997, January). "Differences in Love Attitudes Across Family Life Stages." *Family Relations, 46*(1), 55–61.

Monto, M. A. (2001). "Prostitution and Fellatio." *The Journal of Sex Research, 38*, 140–145.

Moore, K., & Smith, K. (2003). "Policies Needed to Increase Awareness of Emergency Contraception." *SIECUS Report, 31*(2), 9–12.

Moore, N. B., & Davidson, J. K. (1999). "Parents as First Sexuality Information Sources: Do They Make a Difference in Daughters' Sexual Attitudes and Behaviors?" *Journal of Sex Education and Therapy, 24*(3), 155–163.

Morgan, R. (2002, November 29). "Bisexual Students Face Tension with Gay Groups." *The Chronicle of Higher Education,* p. A31.

Morrow, M. (2002). "Rational Local Therapy for Breast Cancer." *New England Journal of Medicine, 347*, 1270–1271.

Morse, E. V., Simon, P. M., Balson, P. M., & Osofsky, H. J. (1992). "Sexual Behavior Patterns of Customers of Male Street Prostitutes." *Archives of Sexual Behavior, 21*, 347–357.

Moser, C. (1988). "Sadomasochism." In D. Dailey (Ed.), *The Sexually Unusual.* New York: Harrington Park Press.

Moser, C. (2001). "Paraphilia: A Critique of a Confused Concept." In P. J. Kleinplatz (Ed.), *New Directions in Sex Therapy: Innovations and Alternatives.* Philadelphia: Brunner/Routledge.

Mosher, D. L., & Maclan, P. (1994). "College Men and Women Respond to X-Rated Videos Intended for Male or Female Audiences: Gender and Sexual Scripts." *The Journal of Sex Research, 31*(2), 99–113.

Moultrup, D. J. (1990). *Husbands, Wives, and Lovers: The Emotional System of the Extramarital Affair.* New York: Guilford Press.

Moynihan, R. (2002). "The Making of a Disease: Female Sexual Dysfunction." *British Medical Journal, 326*, 45–47.

Muehlenhard, C. L., & Linton, M. A. (1987). "Date Rape and Sexual Aggression in Dating Situations: Incidence and Risk Factors." *Journal of Consulting Psychology, 34*, 186–196.

Muehlenhard, C. L., & McCoy, M. L. (1991). "Double Standard/Double Bind." *Psychology of Women Quarterly, 15*, 447–461.

Muehlenhard, C. L., Ponch, I. G., Phelps, J. L., & Giusti, L. M. (1992). "Definitions of Rape: Scientific and Political Implications." *Journal of Social Issues, 48*(1), 23–44.

Muehlenhard, C. L., & Rogers, C. S. (1998). "Token Resistance to Sex: New Perspectives on an Old Stereotype." *Psychology of Women Quarterly, 22*, 443–463.

Muehlenhard, C. L., & Schrag, J. (1991). "Nonviolent Sexual Coercion." In A. Parrot & L. Bechhofer (Eds.), *Acquaintance Rape: The Hidden Crime.* New York: Wiley.

Mulligan, T., & Moss, C. R. (1991). "Sexuality and Aging in Male Veterans: A Cross-Sectional Study of Interest, Ability, and Activity." *Archives of Sexual Behavior, 20*(1), 17–25.

Mulligan, T., Retchin, S. M., Chinchilli, V. M., & Bettinger, C. B. (1988). "The Role of Aging and Chronic Disease in Sexual Dysfunction." *Journal of the American Geriatrics Society, 36*(6), 520–524.

Muram, D., Miller, K., & Cutler, A. (1992). "Sexual Assault of the Elderly Victim." *Journal of Interpersonal Violence, 7*(1), 70–76.

Murnen, S. K., Perot, A., & Byrne, D. (1989). "Coping with Unwanted Sexual Activity: Normative Responses, Situational Determinants, and Individual Differences." *The Journal of Sex Research, 26*, 85–106.

Nadelson, C., & Sauzier, M. (1986). "Intervention Programs for Individual Victims and Their Families." In M. Lystad (Ed.), *Violence in the Home: Interdisciplinary Perspectives.* New York: Brunner/Mazel.

Nakano, M. (1990). *Japanese American Women: Three Generations, 1890–1990.* Berkeley, CA: Mina Press.

Nanda, S. (1990). *Neither Man nor Woman: The Hijra of India.* Belmont, CA: Wadsworth.

National Association of People with AIDS. (2002). "Get the Facts on HIV . . . Latinos and HIV and AIDS." Washington, DC: Author.

National Cancer Institute. (2000). Available: http://cancernet .nic.nih.gov (Last visited 3/9/01).

National Cancer Institute. (2002a). Questions and Answers: Use of Hormones After Menopause. Available: http://www .cancer.gov/newscenter/estrogenplus (Last visited 4/29/03).

National Cancer Institute. (2002b). Lifetime Probability of Breast Cancer in American Women. Available: http://cis.nci.nih .gov/fact/5_6.htm (Last visited 5/3/03).

National Cancer Institute. (2002c). What You Need to Know About Cancer of the Cervix. Available: http://cancer.gov/ cancerinfo/wyntk/cervix (Last visited 5/3/03).

National Center for Environmental Health. (1995). "Smoking Men at Risk for Erectile Dysfunction." *Contemporary Sexuality, 29*(2), 8.

National Center for Health Statistics. (2002). *National Vital Statistics Report, 50*(16).

National Coalition of Anti-Violence Programs. (2003). Anti-Lesbian, Gay, Bisexual and Transgendered Violence in 2002. Available: http://www.avp.org/ncavp.htm (Last visited 6/11/03).

National Institute of Allergy and Infectious Diseases. (2002). Fact Sheet: HIV Infection and AIDS: An Overview. Available: http://www.niaid.nih.gov/factsheets/hivinf.htm (Last visited 2/21/03).

National Institute of Child Health and Human Development. (2000). Fast Facts About Endometriosis. Available: http:// www.nichd.nih.gov/publications/pubs/endometriosis/ index/htm (Last visited 5/13/03).

National Institute of Child Health and Human Development. (2003). NICHD Study Finds No Association Between Oral Contraceptive Use and Breast Cancer for Women from 35 to 64. Available: http://www.nichd.nih.gov/new/releases/ contraceptive_use.cfm (Last visited 8/22/03).

National Institute of Diabetes and Digestive and Kidney Diseases. (2000). Prostatitis. Available: http://www.niddk.nih .gov/health/urolog/summary/prostat/prostat.htm (Last visited 5/13/03).

National Institutes of Health. (1997). Arthritis: What We Know Today. Available: http://www.niams.nih.gov/ne/reports/ sci_wrk/1997/lappin.htm (Last visited 5/2/03).

National Institutes of Health. (2002a). News Release: Multiples Born to Older Moms Fare Same As or Better Than Those Born to Younger Moms. Available: http://www.nih.gov/news/ pr/sep2002/nichd10.htm (Last visited 11/30/02).

National Institutes of Health. (2002b). News Release: Undersize Infants Score Higher on IQ Tests If Breast Fed Exclusively. Available: http://www.nih.gov/news/pr/mar2002/ nichd-20.htm (Last visited 11/30/02).

National Institutes of Health. (2002c). Postmenopausal Hormone Therapy: Questions and Answers. Available: http://www.nhlbi.nih.gov/health/women/q_a.htm (Last visited 4/26/03).

National Institutes of Health. (2002d). NIH News Release: Scientific Task Force to Examine Usefulness of Testosterone Replacement Therapy in Older Men. Available: http://www.nia.nih.gov/news/pr/2002/1106/htm (Last visited 5/1/03).

National Organization for Victim Assistance. (1992). *Community Crisis Response Team Training Manual*. Washington, DC: Author.

National Victim Center. (1995). Posttraumatic Stress Disorder (PTSD). Available: http://www.nvc.org/ns-search/infolink/INF...ch-set\35060\s7g.060c7b&NS-doc-offset+=3& (Last visited 3/10/98).

National Victim Center. (1997a). Male Rape. Available: http://www.nvc.org/ns-search/infolink/INF...ch-set=\35060\s7g.060c7b&NS-doc-offset=0& (Last visited 3/10/98).

National Victim Center. (1997b). Incest. Available: http://www.nvc.org/ns-search/infolink/INF...ch-set\35060\s7g.060c7b&NS-doc-offset=1& (Last visited 3/10/98).

National Victim Center and Crime Victims Research and Treatment Center. (1992). *Rape in America: A Report to the Nation*. Charleston, SC: Author.

National Women's Health Information Center. (2000). Health Information for Minority Women. Available: http://www.4women.gov/minority/index.html (Last visited 3/3/00).

Nelson, A. L. (2000). "Whose Pill Is It, Anyway?" *Family Planning Perspectives, 32*, 89–90.

"New $9.5 Million NIH Grant to Support Male Contraception Research Center." (2003). *SIECUS Report, 31*(2), 8.

"New Non-Hormonal Contraceptive Could Prevent HIV, STDs When Used with Microbicide, Manufacturer Says." (2003). Available: http://www.kaisernetwork.org/daily_reports/rep_index.cfm?DR_ID+17345 (Last visited 5/26/03).

Niccolai, L. M., Farley, T. A., Ayoub, M. A., Magnus, M. K., & Kissinger, P. J. (2002). "HIV-Infected Persons' Knowledge of Their Sexual Partners' HIV Status." *AIDS Education and Prevention, 14*, 183–189.

Nichols, M. (1987). "Lesbian Sexuality: Issues and Developing Theory." In Boston Lesbian Psychologies Collective (Ed.), *Lesbian Psychologies: Explorations and Challenges*. Urbana: University of Illinois Press.

Nichols, M. (1988). "Bisexuality in Women: Myths, Realities, and Implications for Therapy." Special issue: Women and Sex Therapy. *Women and Therapy, 7*, 235–252.

Nicolosi, A., Moreiba, E., Shirai, J., Bin Mohd Tambi, M., & Glasser, D. (2003). "Epidemiology of Erectile Dysfunction in Four Countries: Cross-National Study of the Prevalence and Correlates of Erectile Dysfunction." *Urology, 61*, 201–206.

Niebuhr, R. E., & Boyles, W. R. (1991). "Sexual Harassment of Military Personnel: An Examination of Power Differentials." Special issue: Racial, Ethnic, and Gender Issues in the Military. *International Journal of Intercultural Relations, 15*, 445–457.

Noll, J. G., Trickett, P. K., & Putam, F. W. (2003). "A Prospective Investigation of the Impact of Childhood Sexual Abuse on the Development of Sexuality." *Journal of Consulting and Clinical Psychology, 71*, 575–586.

Noller, P., & Fitzpatrick, M. A. (1991). "Marital Communication." In A. Booth (Ed.), *Contemporary Families: Looking Forward, Looking Back*. Minneapolis: National Council on Family Relations.

Nosek, M. A., Howland, C. A., Rintala, D. H., Young, M. E., & Chanpong, G. F. (1997). National Study of Women with Physical Disabilities: Final Report. Center for Research on Women with Disabilities. Available: http://www.bcm.tmc.edu/crowd/national_study/1NSWWPD.html (Last visited 5/2/03).

Oakley, A. (1985). *Sex, Gender, and Society* (Rev. ed.). New York: Harper & Row.

O'Brien, P., Wyatt, K., & Dimmock, P. (2000). "Premenstrual Syndrome Is Real and Treatable." *The Practitioner, 244*, 185–189.

Office of National AIDS Policy. (2000). *Youth and HIV/AIDS 2000: A New American Agenda*. Washington, DC: The White House.

Office of the Surgeon General. (2001). The Surgeon General's Report on Sexual Behavior. Available: http://www.surgeongeneral.gov/library/sexualhealth/ (Last visited 3/1/03).

Okami, P. (1991). "Self-Reports of 'Positive' Childhood and Adolescent Sexual Contacts with Older Persons: An Exploratory Study." *Archives of Sexual Behavior, 20*(5), 437–457.

Okami, P. (2002). "Dear Diary: A Useful but Imperfect Method." In M. W. Wiederman & B. E. Whitley (Eds.), *Handbook for Conducting Research on Human Sexuality*. Mahwah, NJ: Erlbaum.

Okazaki, S. (2002). "Influences of Culture on Asian Americans' Sexuality." *The Journal of Sex Research, 39*(1), 34–41.

Okonofua, F. E., Larsen, U., Oronsaye, F., Snow, R. C., & Slanger, T. E. (2002). "The Association Between Female Genital Cutting and Correlates of Sexual and Gynaecological Morbidity in Edo State, Nigeria." *Journal of Obstetrics and Gynaecology, 109*, 1089–1096.

Olson, B., & Douglas, W. (1997). "The Family on Television: Evolution of Gender Roles in Situation Comedy." *Sex Roles, 36*, 409–427.

Orbach, S. (1982). *Fat Is a Feminist Issue II: A Program to Conquer Compulsive Eating*. New York: Berkley Books.

Ostrow, D. E., et al. "Attitudes Towards Highly Active Antiretroviral Therapy Are Associated with Sexual Risk Taking Among HIV-Infected and Uninfected Homosexual Men." *AIDS, 16*, 775–780.

O'Sullivan, C. S. (1991). "Acquaintance Gang Rape on Campus." In A. Parrot & L. Bechhofer (Eds.), *Acquaintance Rape: The Hidden Crime*. New York: Wiley.

Padilla, E. R., & O'Grady, K. E. (1987). "Sexuality Among Mexican Americans: A Case of Sexual Stereotyping." *Journal of Personality and Social Psychology, 52*, 5–10.

Padma-Nathan, H., Eardley, I., Kloner, R. A., Laties, A. M., & Montorsi, F. (2002). "A 4-Year Update on the Safety of Sidenafil Citrate (Viagra)." *Urology, 60*(S2), 67–90.

Page, S. (2003, July 23). "Gay Rights Tough to Sharpen into Political 'Wedge Issue.'" *USA Today*, p. A10.

Pallas, J., Levine, S. B., Althof, S. E., & Risen, C. B. (2000). "A Study Using Viagra in a Mental Health Practice." *Journal of Sex and Marital Therapy, 26*, 41–50.

Paludi, M. A. (1990). "Sociopsychological and Structural Factors Related to Women's Vocational Development." *Annals of the New York Academy of Sciences, 602*, 157–168.

Parrinder, G. (1980). *Sex in the World's Religions*. New York: Oxford University Press.

Parsons, C. (2003, July 29). "Sexual Consent Measure Is Signed." *Chicago Tribune*, pp. 1, 7.

Patterson, C. J. (1992). "Children of Lesbian and Gay Parents." *Child Development, 63*, 1025–1042.

Patton, M. (1986). "Twentieth-Century Attitudes Toward Masturbation." *Journal of Religion and Health, 25*(4), 291–302.

Paul, L., & Galloway, J. (1994). "Sexual Jealousy: Gender Differences in Response to Partner and Rival." *Aggressive Behavior, 20*(3), 203–211.

Peo, R. (1988). "Transvestism." In D. Dailey (Ed.), *The Sexually Unusual*. New York: Harrington Park Press.

Peplau, L. (1981). "What Homosexuals Want." *Psychology Today, 15*(3), 28–38.

Peplau, L. (1988). "Research on Homosexual Couples." In J. De Cecco (Ed.), *Gay Relationships*. New York: Haworth Press.

Peplau, L., & Cochran, S. (1988). "Value Orientations in the Intimate Relationships of Gay Men." In J. De Cecco (Ed.), *Gay Relationships*. New York: Haworth Press.

Peplau, L., Rubin, Z., & Hill, R. (1977). "Sexual Intimacy in Dating Relationships." *Journal of Social Issues, 33*(2), 86–109.

Perry, J. D., & Whipple, B. (1981). "Pelvic Muscle Strength of Female Ejaculators: Evidence in Support of a New Theory of Orgasm." *The Journal of Sex Research, 17*(1), 22–39.

Peters, K. (1992, October 15). "Gay Activists Denounce NAMBLA, Attempt to Highlight Differences." *Spartan Daily*, p. 1.

Peters, S., et al. (1986). "Prevalence of Child Sexual Abuse." In D. Finkelhor (Ed.), *Sourcebook on Child Sexual Abuse*. Newbury Park, CA: Sage.

Peterson, J. L. (1992). "Black Men and Their Same-Sex Desires and Behaviors." In G. Herdt (Ed.), *Gay Culture in America: Essays from the Field*. Boston: Beacon Press.

Peterson, K. S. (2002, April 8). "Having It All—Except Children." *USA Today*, p. D1.

Pierce, P. (1994). "Sexual Harassment: Frankly, What Is It?" *Journal of Intergroup Relations, 20*, 3–12.

Piercing Exquisite: Aftercare for Navel and Nipple Piercings. (1998). Available: http://www2.ba.best.com/ardvark/ac-body .html (Last visited 1/15/98).

Pinker, S. (1991). *The Way the Mind Works*. New York: Norton.

Pistole, M. C. (1995). "College Students' Ended Love Relationships: Attachment Style and Emotion." *Journal of College Student Development, 36*(1), 53–60.

Pistole, M. C., Clark, E. M., & Tubbs, A. L. (1995). "Love Relationships: Attachment Style and the Investment Model." *Journal of Mental Health Counseling, 17*(2), 199–209.

Planned Parenthood Federation of America. (2003). Women's Health. Available: http://www.plannedparenthood.org/ womenshealth/infertility/html (Last visited 4/9/03).

Pogrebin, L. C. (1983). *Family Politics*. New York: McGraw-Hill.

Pollis, C. A. (1988). "An Assessment of the Impacts of Feminism on Sexual Science." *The Journal of Sex Research, 25*(1), 85–105.

Popovich, P. M., Gehlauf, D. N., Jolton, J. A., & Somers, J. M. (1992). "Perceptions of Sexual Harassment as a Function of Sex of Rater and Incident Form and Consequence." *Sex Roles, 27*(11–12), 609–625.

Portelli, C. J., & Meade, C. W. (1998, October/November). Censorship and the Internet: No Easy Answers. *SIECUS Report*. Available: http://www.siecus.org/pubs/srpt/articles/arti0001 .html (Last visited 11/30/00).

Potterat, J. J., Rothenberg, R. B., Muth, S. Q., Darrow, W. W., & Phillips-Plummer, L. (1998). "Pathways to Prostitution: The Chronology of Sexual and Drug Abuse Milestones." *The Journal of Sex Research, 35*(4), 333–340.

Powell, E. (1996). *Sex on Your Own Terms*. Minneapolis: CompCare.

Price, D. (1993, January 14). "Twin Study Links Genetics, Gayness Closer." *San Jose Mercury News*, p. 2.

Price, J. H., & Miller, P. A. (1984). "Sexual Fantasies of Black and White College Students." *Psychological Reports, 54*, 1007–1014.

"Prostate Screenings Gain Acceptance." (2000, December 4). *USA Today*, p. D8.

Putnam, R. D. (2000). *Bowling Alone: The Collapse and Revival of American Community*, New York: Simon & Schuster.

Quackenbush, D. M., Strassberg, D. S., & Turner, C. (1995). "Gender Effects of Romantic Themes in Erotica." *Archives of Sexual Behavior, 24*(1), 21–35.

Quackenbush, R. L. (1991). "Attitudes of College Men Toward Women and Rape." *Journal of College Student Development, 32*, 376–377.

Quatrella, L., & Wentworth, K. K. (1995). "Students' Perceptions of Unequal Status Dating Relationships in Academia." *Ethics & Behavior, 5*(3), 249–259.

Queen, C. (2000, November 19). "Sex in the City." *San Francisco Chronicle*, pp. 1, 4.

"Questions About HRT Still Confuse Women." (2002, December 12). *USA Today*, p. D11.

Quinn, T. C., Wawer, M. J., Sewankambo, N., Serwadda, D., Chuanjun, L., Wabwire-Mangen, F., Meehan, M. O., Lutalo, T., & Gray, R. H. (2000). "Viral Load and Heterosexual Transmission of Human Immunodeficiency Virus Type 1." *The New England Journal of Medicine, 342*, 921–929.

Raffaelli, M., Bogenschneider, K., & Flood, M. F. (1998). "Parent-Teacher Communication About Sexual Topics." *Journal of Family Issues, 19*, 315–333.

Raffle, A. E., Alden, B., Quinn, M., Babb, P. J., & Brett, M. J. (2003). "Outcomes of Screening to Prevent Cancer: Analysis of Cumulative Incidence of Cervical Abnormality and Modelling of Cases and Deaths Prevented." *British Medical Journal, 326*, 901–906.

Rako, S. (1996). *The Hormone of Desire*. New York: Harmony Books.

Rankow, E. (1997). "Primary Medical Care of the Gay and Lesbian Patient." *North Carolina Medical Journal, 58*, 92–97.

Rao, K., Diclemente, R. J., & Poulton, L. E. (1992). "Child Sexual Abuse of Asians Compared with Other Populations." *Journal of the American Academy of Child and Adolescent Psychiatry, 31*(5), 880–887.

Rape Network. (2000). Rape Is a Crime of Silence. Available: http://www.rapenetwork.com/whatisrape.html (Last visited 11/16/00).

Rapp, S. R., Espeland, M. A., Shumaker, S. A., Henderson, V. W., Brunner, R. L., Manson, J. E., Gass, M. L. S., Stefanick, M. L., Lane, D. S., Hays, J., Johnson, K. C., Coker, L. H., Dailey, M., & Bowen, D. (2003). "Effects of Estrogen plus Progestin on Global Cognitive Function in Postmenopausal Women." *Journal of the American Medical Association, 289*, 2663–2672.

Rathus, S. A., Nevid, J. S., & Fichner-Rathus L. (2002). *Human Sexuality: A World of Diversity*. Boston: Allyn & Bacon.

Ratings for the Week of April 19–23, 1999. (1999). *TV Guide*. Available: http://www.tvguide.com/soaps/ratings/ (Last visited 4/30/99).

Ratner, P. A., Johnson, J. L., Shoveller, J. A., Chan, K., Martindale, S. L., Schilder, A. J., Botnick, M. R., & Hogg, R. S. (2003). "NonConsensual Sex Experienced by Men Who Have Sex with Men: Prevalence and Association with Mental Health." *Patient Education and Counseling, 49*, 67–74.

Rauch, S. L., Shin, L. M., Dougherty, D. D., Alpert, N. M., Orr, S. P., Lasko, M., Macklin, M. L., Fischman, A. J., & Pittman,

R. K. (1999). "Neural Activation During Sexual and Competitive Arousal in Healthy Men." *Psychiatry Research, 91*, 1–10.

Redoute, J., Stoleru, S., Gregoire, M. C., Costes, N., Cinotti, L., Lavenne, F., Le Bars, D., Forest, M. G., & Pujol, J. F. (2000). "Brain Processing of Visual Sexual Stimuli in Human Males." *Human Brain Mapping, 11*, 343–350.

Reece, R. (1988). "Special Issues in the Etiologies and Treatments of Sexual Problems Among Gay Men." *Journal of Homosexuality, 15*, 43–57.

Reeder, H. M. (2000). "I Like You . . . as a Friend: The Role of Attraction in Cross-Sex Friendship." *Journal of Social and Personal Relationships, 17*, 329–348.

Reid, E. (1998). "The Self and the Internet: Variations on the Illusion of One Self." In J. Gackenbach (Ed.), *Psychology and the Internet*. San Diego, CA: Academic Press.

Reilly, M. E., Lott, B., Caldwell, D., & DeLuca, L. (1992). "Tolerance for Sexual Harassment Related to Self-Reported Sexual Victimization." *Gender and Society, 6*(1), 122–138.

Reinholtz, R. K., & Muehlenhard, C. L. (1995). "Genital Perceptions and Sexual Activity in a College Population." *The Journal of Sex Research, 32*(2), 155–165.

Reinisch, J., Ziemba-Davis, M., & Saunders, S. (1991). "Hormonal Contributions to Sexually Dimorphic Behavioral Development in Humans." *Psychoneuroendocrinology, 16*, 213–278.

Reiss, I. (1967). *The Social Context of Premarital Sexual Permissiveness*. New York: Irvington.

Reiss, I. (1980). "A Multivariate Model of the Determinants of Extramarital Sexual Permissiveness." *Journal of Marriage and the Family, 42*, 395–411.

Reiss, I. (1986). *Journey into Sexuality: An Exploratory Voyage*. Englewood Cliffs, NJ: Prentice-Hall.

Reiss, I. (1989). "Society and Sexuality: A Sociological Explanation." In K. McKinney & S. Sprecher (Eds.), *Human Sexuality: The Societal and Interpersonal Context*. Norwood, NJ: Ablex.

Reiss, I. (1990). *An End to Shame: Shaping Our Next Sexual Revolution*. Buffalo: Prometheus Books.

Remafedi, G., Resnick, M., Blum, R., & Harris, L. (1992). "Demography of Sexual Orientation in Adolescents." *Pediatrics, 89*, 714–721.

Rendell, M. S., Rajfer, J., Wicker, P. A., & Smith, M. D. (1999). "Sildenafil for Treatment of Erectile Dysfunction in Men with Diabetes: A Randomized Control Trial." *Journal of the American Medical Association, 281*, 421–426.

Renshaw, D. C. (1988a). "Short-Term Therapy for Sexual Dysfunction: Brief Counseling to Manage Vaginismus." *Clinical Practice in Sexuality, 6*(5), 23–39.

Renshaw, D. C. (1988b). "Young Children's Sex Play: Counseling the Parents." *Medical Aspects of Human Sexuality, 22*(12), 68–72.

Resnick, H. S. (1972). "Eroticized Repetitive Hangings: A Form of Self-Destructive Behavior." *American Journal of Psychotherapy, 26*(1), 4–21.

Resolve. (2002). Infertility Myths and Facts. Available: http://www.resolve.org/main/national/coping/demystify/mythfact.htm (Last visited 5/21/03).

Restrictions on Minors' Access to Abortion. (2001). NARAL Foundation. Available: http://www.naral.org/mediasources/fact/ pdfs/restrictions.pdf (Last visited 5/12/03).

Rhodes, J. C., Kjerulff, K. H., Langenberg, P. A., & Guzinski, G. M. (1999). "Hysterectomy and Sexual Functioning." *Journal of the American Medical Association, 282*, 1934–1941.

Rhynard, J., Krebs, M., & Glover, J. (1997). "Sexual Assault in Dating Relationships." *Journal of School Health, 67*(3), 89–94.

Rich, A. (1983). "Compulsory Heterosexuality and Lesbian Existence." In A. Snitow et al. (Eds.), *Powers of Desire: The Politics of Sexuality*. New York: Monthly Review Press.

Rich, F. (2001, May 20). "Naked Capitalists." *New York Times Magazine*, pp. 50–56, 80, 82, 92.

Richards, K. (1997). "What Is a Transgenderist?" In B. Bullough, V. L. Bullough, & J. Elias (Eds.), *Gender Blending*. New York: Prometheus Books.

Richardson, C. B., Resnick, P. J., Hansen, D. L., Derry, H. A., & Rideout, V. J. (2002). "Does Pornography-Blocking Software Block Access to Health Information on the Internet?" *Journal of the American Medical Association, 288*, 2887–2894.

Riggs, D. S. (1993). "Relationship Problems and Dating Aggression: A Potential Treatment Target." *Journal of Interpersonal Violence, 8*(1), 18–35.

Riggs, N., Houry, D., Long, G., Markovchick, V., & Feldhaus, K. M. (2000). "Analysis of 1,076 Cases of Sexual Assault." *Annals of Emergency Medicine, 35*, 358–362.

Rio, L. M. (1991). "Psychological and Sociological Research and the Decriminalization or Legalization of Prostitution." *Archives of Sexual Behavior, 20*(2), 205–218.

Riscol, L. (2003). "Bigger, Harder, Better: Natural Sex Enhancers or Viagra-Era Snake Oil." *Contemporary Sexuality, 37*, 1, 4–6.

"Risk of Suicide and Past History of Sexual Assault." (1996). *American Family Physician, 54*(5), 1756.

Risky Sex and Non-IV Drugs. (1998). Available: http://www.columbia.edu/cu/healthwise/0399.html (Last visited 1/29/98).

Rivinus, T., & Larimer, M. (1993). "Violence, Alcohol, Other Drugs, and the College Student." *Journal of College Student Psychotherapy, 8* (1–2).

Roberts, E. (1983). "Childhood Sexual Learning: The Unwritten Curriculum." In C. Davis (Ed.), *Challenges in Sexual Science*. Philadelphia: Society for the Scientific Study of Sex.

Robinson, P. (1976). *The Modernization of Sex*. New York: Harper & Row.

Roddy, R. E., Zekeng, L., Ryan, K. A., Tamoufe, U., & Tweedy, K. G. (2002). Effect of Nonoxynol–9 Gel on Urogenital Gonorrhea and Chlamydial Infection. *Journal of the American Medical Association, 287*, 1117–1122.

Roenrich, L., & Kinder, B. N. (1991). "Alcohol Expectancies and Male Sexuality: Review and Implications for Sex Therapy." *Journal of Sex and Marital Therapy, 17*, 45–54.

Rodgers, S. M., & Turner, C. F. (1991). "Male-Male Sexual Contact in the U.S.A.: Findings from Five Sample Surveys, 1970–1990." *The Journal of Sex Research, 28*(4), 491–519.

Rogler, L. H. (1999). "Methodological Sources of Cultural Insensitivity in Mental Health Research." *American Psychologist, 54*, 424–433.

Rome, E. (1992). "Anatomy and Physiology of Sexuality and Reproduction." In Boston Women's Health Book Collective, *The New Our Bodies, Ourselves*. New York: Simon & Schuster.

Roscoe, W. (1991). *The Zuni Man/Woman*. Albuquerque: University of New Mexico Press.

Rose, S., & Sork, V. (1984). "Teaching About Female Sexuality: Putting Women on Top." *Women's Studies Quarterly, 13*(4), 19–20.

Rosman, J., & Resnick, P. J. (1989). "Sexual Attraction to Corpses: A Psychiatric Review of Necrophilia." *Bulletin of the American Academy of Psychiatry and the Law, 17*(2), 153–163.

Ross, J., & Zinn, A. (2000). "Neurodevelopmental and Psychosocial Aspects of Turner Syndrome." *Mental Retardation and Developmental Disabilities Research Reviews, 6,* 135–141.

Rosser, S., Short, B. J., Thurmes, P. J., & Coleman, E. (1998). "Anodyspareunia, the Unacknowledged Sexual Dysfunction: A Validation Study of Painful Receptive Anal Intercourse and Its Psychosexual Concomitants in Homosexual Men." *Journal of Sex and Marital Therapy, 24,* 281–292.

Rothblum, E. D. (1994). "Transforming Lesbian Sexuality." *Psychology of Women Quarterly, 18*(4), 627–641.

Rothenberg, M. (1991, April 30). "Ending Circumcision in the Jewish Community." Syllabus of Abstracts, Second International Symposium on Circumcision, San Francisco.

Rowan, E. L. (1988). "Pedophilia." In D. Dailey (Ed.), *The Sexually Unusual.* New York: Harrington Park Press.

Rowan, E. L. (1989). "Masturbation According to the Boy Scout Handbook." *Journal of Sex Education and Therapy, 15*(2), 77–81.

Rubin, L. (1990). *Erotic Wars.* New York: Farrar, Straus & Giroux.

Rubin, R. (2003a, January 29). "Testosterone Replacement Therapy Faces Scrutiny." *USA Today,* p. D7.

Rubin, R. (2003b, May 16). "Mammograms Fare Well in Study." *USA Today,* p. Al.

Rubin, Z. (1973). *Liking and Loving.* New York: Holt, Rinehart & Winston.

Russell, D. (1984). *Sexual Exploitation: Rape, Child Sexual Abuse, and Workplace Harassment.* Newbury Park, CA: Sage.

Russell, D. E. H. (1986). *The Secret Trauma: Incest in the Lives of Girls and Women.* New York: Basic Books.

Russell, D. E. H. (1990). *Rape in Marriage* (Rev. ed.). Bloomington: Indiana University Press.

Ryan, J. (1997, October 30). "A Painful Statement of Self-Identity." *San Francisco Chronicle,* p. A1.

Sadker, M., & Sadker, D. (1994). *Failing at Fairness: How America's Schools Cheat Girls.* New York: Scribner.

Saewyc, E. M., Bearinger, L. H., Blum, R. W., & Resnick, M. D. (1999). "Sexual Intercourse, Abuse and Pregnancy Among Adolescent Women: Does Sexual Orientation Make a Difference?" *Family Planning Perspectives, 31*(3), 127–142.

Saks, B. (2000). "Sex Receptors: Mechanisms of Drug Action via Biochemical Receptors on Sexual Response of Women." *Journal of Sex Education and Therapy, 25,* 33–35.

Salgado de Snyder, V. N., Cervantes, R., & Padilla, A. (1990). "Gender and Ethnic Differences in Psychosocial Stress and Generalized Distress Among Hispanics." *Sex Roles, 22*(7), 441–453.

Salovey, P., & Rodin, J. (1991). "Provoking Jealousy and Envy: Domain Relevance and Self-Esteem Threat." *Journal of Social and Clinical Psychology, 10*(4), 395–413.

Samuels, M., & Samuels, N. (1996). *The Well Pregnancy Book.* New York: Simon & Schuster.

Sanchez, Y. M. (1997). "Families of Mexican Origin." In M. K. DeGenova (Ed.), *Families in Cultural Context: Strengths and Challenges in Diversity.* Mountain View, CA: Mayfield.

Sanday, P. (1990). *Fraternity Gang Rape: Sex, Brotherhood and Privilege on Campus.* New York: New York University Press.

Sanders, S., & Reinisch, J. (1999). "Would You Say You 'Had Sex' If . . . ?" *Journal of the American Medical Association, 281,* 275–277.

Sanders, S. A., Reinisch, J. M., & McWhirter, D. P. (1990). "Homosexuality/Heterosexuality: An Overview." In D. P. McWhirter, S. A. Sanders, & J. M. Reinisch (Eds.), *Homosexuality/Heterosexuality: Concepts of Sexual Orientation.* New York: Oxford University Press.

Sarrel, P. M., & Masters, W. H. (1982). "Sexual Molestation of Men by Women." *Archives of Sexual Behavior, 11,* 117–131.

Satel, S. L. (1993). "The Diagnostic Limits of 'Addiction.'" *Journal of Clinical Psychiatry, 54*(6), 237.

Saunders, E. B., & Awad, G. (1991). "Male Adolescent Sexual Offenders: Exhibitionism and Obscene Phone Calls." *Child Psychiatry and Human Development, 21*(3), 169–178.

Savin-Williams, R. C. (1995). "Lesbian, Gay Male, and Bisexual Adolescents." In A. R. D'Augelli & C. J. Patterson (Eds.), *Lesbian, Gay, and Bisexual Identities over the Lifespan: Psychological Perspectives.* New York: Oxford University Press.

Sawyer, S., Metz, M. E., Hinds, J. D., & Brucker, R. A. (2001–2002). "Attitudes Toward Prostitution Among Males: A 'Consumers' Report'" *Current Psychology, 20,* 363–376.

Sax, L. (2002). "How Common Is Intersex? A Response to Anne Fausto-Sterling." *The Journal of Sex Research, 39*(3), 174–178.

Schaap, C., Buunk, B., & Kerkstra, A. (1988). "Marital Conflict Resolutions." In P. Noller & M. A. Fitzpatrick (Eds.), *Perspectives on Marital Interaction.* Philadelphia: Multilingual Matters.

Scheer, S., Peterson, I., Page-Shafer, K., Delgado, V., Gleghorn, A., Ruiz, J., Molitor, F., McFarland, W., Klausner, J., & Young Women's Survey Team. (2002). "Sexual and Drug Use Behavior Among Women Who Have Sex with Both Women and Men: Results of a Population-Based Survey." *American Journal of Public Health, 92,* 1110–1112.

Schiavi, R. C., Schreiner-Engle, P., Mandeli, J., Schanzer, J., & Cohen, E. (1990). "Chronic Alcoholism and Male Sexual Dysfunction." *Journal of Sex and Marital Therapy, 16*(1), 23–33.

Schlosser, E. (1997, February 10). "The Business of Pornography." *Newsweek,* pp. 42–52.

Schmitt, E. (1990, September 12). "Two Out of 3 Women in Military Study Report Sexual Harassment Incidents." *The New York Times,* p. A12.

Schnarch, D. (2002). *Resurrecting Sex.* New York: HarperCollins.

Scholes, D., Darling, J. R., Stergachis, A., Weiss, N. S., Wang, S. P., & Grayston, J. T. (1993). "Vaginal Douching as a Risk Factor for Acute Pelvic Inflammatory Diseases." *Obstetric Gynecology, 81,* 601–606.

"School Sex Education Focusing on Abstinence." (2000, February). *Nation's Health,* p. 24.

Schureurs, K. M. (1993). "Sexuality in Lesbian Couples: The Importance of Gender." *Annual Review of Sex Research, 4,* 49–66.

Schwartz, J. L., Creinin, M. D., & Pymar, H. C. (1999). "The Trimonthly Combination Oral Contraceptive Regimen: Is It Cost Effective?" *Contraception, 60,* 263–267.

Schwartz, M. F., & Brasted, W. S. (1985). "Sexual Addiction: Self-Hatred, Guilt, and Passive Rage Contribute to This Deviant Behavior." *Medical Aspects of Human Sexuality, 19,* 103–107.

Schwartz, M. F., & Southern, S. (2000). "Compulsive Cybersex: The New Tea Room." In A. Cooper (Ed.), *Cybersex: The Dark Side of the Force.* Philadelphia: Brunner/Routledge, pp. 127–144.

Schwartz, S. (2000). *Abnormal Psychology: A Discovery Approach.* Mountain View, CA: Mayfield.

"Second Cesarean Still the Safest Option." (2003, May 23). *Monterey County Herald,* p. A2.

Sears, A. E. (1989). "The legal case for restricting pornography." In D. Zillman & J. Bryant (eds.). *Pornography: Research Advances and Policy Considerations.* Hillsdale, NJ: Ehrlbaum Associates.

Sedlack, A. J., & Broadhurst, D. D. (1996). *Executive Summary of the Third National Incidence Study of Child Abuse and Neglect.*

Washington, DC: National Center on Child Abuse and Neglect, National Committee to Prevent Child Abuse.

Seligman, L., & Hardenberg, S. A. (2000). "Assessment and Treatment of Paraphilias." *Journal of Counseling and Development, 78,* 107–113.

Sellers, R. M., & Shelton, J. (2003). "The Role of Racial Identity in Perceived Racial Discrimination." *Journal of Personality & Social Psychology, 84*(5), 1079–1093

"Sensitivity Training." (2002, December 2). *Newsweek,* p. 9.

Servi, G. (1995, July 3). "'Sexy F Seeks Hot M': A Mother's Tale." *Newsweek,* p. 51.

Severson, K. (2003, January 8). "Breast Milk May Help Control Growing Appetite." *San Francisco Chronicle,* p. A8.

"Sexuality and Cancer." (2002, July–August.) *Clinical Journal of Oncology Nursing, 6*(4).

Shaver, P. (1984). *Emotions, Relationships, and Health.* Newbury Park, CA: Sage.

Shaver, P., Hazan, C., & Bradshaw, D. (1988). "Love as Attachment: The Integration of Three Behavioral Systems." In R. Sternberg & M. Barnes (Eds.), *The Psychology of Love.* New Haven, CT: Yale University Press.

Sheehan, W., & Garfinkel, B. (1988). "Adolescent Autoerotic Deaths." *American Academy of Child and Adolescent Psychiatry, 27,* 82–89.

Shepela, S. T., & Levesque, L. L. (1998). "Poisoned Waters: Sexual Harassment and the College Climate." *Sex Roles: A Journal of Research, 38,* 589–611.

Shilts, R. (1987). *And the Band Played On: Politics, People, and the AIDS Epidemic.* New York: St. Martin's Press.

Shon, S., & Ja, D. (1982). "Asian Families." In M. McGoldrick, J. K. Pearce, & J. Giordano (Eds.), *Ethnicity and Family Therapy.* New York: Guilford Press.

Shotland, R. L., & Hunter, B. A. (1995). "Women's 'Token Resistant' and Compliant Sexual Behaviors as Related to Uncertain Sexual Intentions and Rape." *Personality & Social Psychology Bulletin, 21*(3), 226–236.

Shumaker, S. A., Legault, C., Rapp, S. R., Thal, L., Wallace, R. B., Ockene, J. K., Hendrix, S. L., Jones, B. N. III, Assaf, A. R., Jackson, R. D., Kotchen, J. M., Wassertheil-Smoller, S., & Wactawaski-Wende, J. (2003). "Estrogen plus Progestin and the Incidence of Dementia and Mild Cognitive Impairment in Postmenopausal Women." *Journal of the American Medical Association, 289,* 2651–2662.

SIECUS. (2001). "Issues and Answers: Fact Sheet on Sexuality Education." *SIECUS Report, 29*(6).

SIECUS. (2002). Sexuality in Middle and Later Life. Available: http://www.siecus.org/pubs/fact/fact0018.html (Last visited 12/30/02).

SIECUS Looks at States' Sexuality Laws. (1999, January 19). *SIECUS Report.* Available: http://www.siecus.org/policy/Sreport/srep0004.html (Last visited 11/30/00).

Siegal, H. A., Li, L., Leviton, L. C., Cole, P. A., Hook, E. W., Bachmann, L., & Ford, J. A. (1999). "Under the Influence: Risky Sexual Behavior and Substance Abuse Among Driving Under the Influence Offenders." *Sexually Transmitted Diseases, 26,* 87–92.

Simon, P. M., et al. (1992). "Psychological Characteristics of a Sample of Male Street Prostitutes." *Archives of Sexual Behavior, 21*(1), 33–44.

Simons, R. L., & Whitbeck, L. B. (1991). "Sexual Abuse as a Precursor to Prostitution and Victimization Among Adolescent and Adult Homeless Women." *Journal of Family Issues, 12*(3), 361–380.

Simpson, W. S., & Ramberg, J. A. (1992). "Sexual Dysfunction in Married Female Patients with Anorexia and Bulimia Nervosa." *Journal of Sex and Marital Therapy, 18*(1), 44–54.

Sluzki, C. (1982). "The Latin Lover Revisited." In M. McGoldrick et al. (Eds.), *Ethnicity and Family Therapy.* New York: Guilford Press.

Small, M. (1999). "Nosing Out a Mate." *Scientific American Presents, 10,* 52–55.

Small, S. A., & Luster, T. (1994). "Adolescent Sexual Activity: An Ecological Approach." *Journal of Marriage and the Family, 56,* 181–192.

Smith, N., & Reilly, G. (1994). "Sexuality and Body Image: The Challenges Facing Male and Female Cancer Patients." *The Canadian Journal of Human Sexuality, 3*(2), 145–149.

Smith, R. A., & Saslow, D. (2002). "Body Image, Cancer, and Sexuality." In G. M. Wingood & R. J. DiClemente (Eds.), *Handbook of Women's Sexual and Reproductive Health.* New York: Kluwer Academic/Plenum.

Smith, R. A., Saslow, D., Sawyer, K. A., Burke, W., Costanza, M. E., Evans, W. P., Foster, R. S., Hendrick, E., Eyre, H. J., & Sener, S. (2003). "American Cancer Society Guidelines for Breast Cancer Screening: Update 2003." *CA: A Cancer Journal for Clinicians, 53,* 141–169.

Snyder, P. (1974). "Prostitution in Asia." *The Journal of Sex Research, 10,* 119–127.

"Social Evolution Changed Nature of Sodomy." (2003, June 27). *Chicago Tribune,* p. A4.

Solomon, J. (1998, March 16). "An Insurance Policy with Sex Appeal." *Newsweek,* p. 44.

Sorenson, S. B., & Siegel, J. M. (1992). "Gender, Ethnicity, and Sexual Assault: Findings from a Los Angeles Study." *Journal of Social Issues, 48*(1), 93–104.

Soules, M. R. (2001). "Human Reproductive Cloning: Not Ready for Prime Time." *Fertility and Sterility, 76*(2), 232–234.

Southall, D. P. (1997). "Covert Video Recordings of Life-Threatening Child Abuse: Lessons for Child Protection." *Pediatrics, 100*(5), 735ff.

Sowell, R. L., Seals, B. F., Phillips, K. D., & Julious, C. H. (2003). "Disclosure of HIV Infection: How Do Women Decide to Tell?" *Health Education Research, 18,* 32–44.

Spanier, G. B., & Thompson, L. (1987). *Parting: The Aftermath of Separation and Divorce.* Newbury Park, CA: Sage.

Sprecher, S. (1989). "Influences on Choice of a Partner and on Sexual Decision Making in the Relationship." In K. McKinney & S. Sprecher (Eds.), *Human Sexuality: The Social and Interpersonal Context.* Norwood, NJ: Ablex.

Sprecher, S. (2002). "Sexual Satisfaction in Premarital Relationships: Associations with Satisfaction, Love, Commitment, and Stability." *Journal of Sex Research, 39*(3), 190–196.

Sprecher, S., Hatfield, E., Cortese, A., Potapova, E., & Levitskaya, A. (1994). "Token Resistance to Sexual Intercourse and Consent in Unwanted Sexual Intercourse: College Students' Experiences in Three Countries." *The Journal of Sex Research, 31*(2), 125–132.

Sprecher, S., & McKinney, K. (1993). *Sexuality.* Newbury Park, CA: Sage.

SSSS Signs Letter to President Bush Opposing Abstinence-Only Funding. (2002). Available: http://www.sexscience.org/sex_sci43-1.htm (Last visited 3/18/02).

Stack, S., & Gundlach, J. H. (1992). "Divorce and Sex." *Archives of Sexual Behavior, 21*(4), 359–368.

Standards of Care for Gender Identity Disorders, Sixth Version. (2001, February). The Harry Benjamin International Gender Dysphoria Association. Available: http://www.hbigda.org (Last visited 2/21/03).

Stanton, B. F., Li, X., Ricardo, I., Galbraith, J., Feigelman, S., & Kaljee, L. (1996). "A Randomized Controlled Effectiveness Trial of an AIDS Prevention Program for Low-Income African American Youths." *Archives of Pediatrics and Adolescent Medicine, 150*, 363–372.

Staples, R. (1991). "The Sexual Revolution and the Black Middle Class." In R. Staples (Ed.), *The Black Family* (4th ed.). Belmont, CA: Wadsworth.

Staples, R., & Johnson, L. B. (1993). *Black Families at the Crossroads: Challenges and Prospects.* San Francisco: Jossey-Bass.

"Steamy Cable TV Can Air Anytime, High Court Says." (2000, May 23). *San Francisco Chronicle*, p. A3.

Steck, L., Levitan, D., McLane, D., & Kelley, H. H. (1982). "Care, Need, and Conceptions of Love." *Journal of Personality and Social Psychology, 43*, 481–491.

Steers, W. D. (1999). "Viagra—After One Year." *Urology, 54*, 12–17.

Steers, W. D., Guary, A. T., Leriche, A., Gingell, C., Hargreave, T. B., Wright, P. J., Price, D. E., & Feldman, R. A. (2001). "Assessment of the Efficacy and Safety of Viagra (sildenfil citrate) in Men with Erectile Dysfunction During Long-Term Treatment." *International Journal of Impotence Research, 13*, 261–267.

Stein, M., Chamberlin, J. W., Lerner, S. E., & Gladshteyn, M. (1993). "The Evaluation and Treatment of Sexual Dysfunction in the Neurologically Impaired Patient." *Journal of Neurologic Rehabilitation, 7*(2), 63–71.

Stein, M. D., Freedberg, K. A., Sullivan, L. M., Savetsky, J., Levenson, S. M., Hingson, R., & Samet, J. H. (1998). "Sexual Ethics: Disclosure of HIV-Positive Status to Partners." *Archives of Internal Medicine, 158*, 253–257.

Steineck, G., Helgesen, F., Adolfsson, J., Dickman, P. W., Johansson, J. E., Norlen, B. J., Holmberg, L., & Scandinavian Prostatic Cancer Group Study Number 4. (2002). "Quality of Life After Radical Prostatectomy or Watchful Waiting." *New England Journal of Medicine, 347*(11), 790–796.

Stelzer, C., Desmond, S. M., & Price, J. H. (1987). "Physical Attractiveness and Sexual Activity of College Students." *Psychological Reports, 60*, 567–573.

Stern, S. E., & Handel, A. D. (2001). "Sexuality and Mass Media: The Historical Context of Psychology's Reaction to Sexuality on the Internet." *The Journal of Sex Research, 38*(4), 283–292.

Sternberg, R. (1986). "A Triangular Theory of Love." *Psychological Review, 93*, 119–135.

Sternberg, R., & Grajek, S. (1984). "The Nature of Love." *Journal of Personality and Social Psychology, 47*, 312–327.

Sternberg, S. (2003, February 12). "Once Stable, HIV Infection Rates Appear to Be Rising in USA." *USA Today*, p. D9.

Stevenson, M. R. (2002). "Conceptualizing Diversity in Sexuality Research." In M. W. Wiederman & B. E. Whitley (Eds.), *Handbook for Conducting Research on Human Sexuality*. Mahwah, NJ: Erlbaum.

St. Lawrence, J. S., & Madakasira, S. (1992). "Evaluation and Treatment of Premature Ejaculation: A Critical Review." *International Journal of Psychiatry in Medicine, 22*(1), 77–97.

St. Louis, M. E., Wasserheit, J. N., & Gayle, H. D. (1997). "Editorial: Janus Considers the HIV Pandemic—Harnessing Recent Advances to Enhance AIDS Prevention." *American Journal of Public Health, 87*, 1012.

Stock, W. (1985, September 11–12). "The Effect of Pornography on Women." Paper presented at a hearing of the Attorney General's Commission on Pornography, Houston.

Stockdale, M. S. (1993). "The Role of Sexual Misperceptions of Women's Friendliness in an Emerging Theory of Sexual Harassment." *Journal of Vocational Behavior, 42*(1), 84–101.

Stolberg, S. G. (2001, December 18). "Controversy Reignites over Stem Cells and Clones." *New York Times*, p. D1.

Stoller, R. J. (1982). "Transvestism in Women." *Archives of Sexual Behavior, 11*(2), 99–115.

Stoller, R. J. (1991). *Pain & Passion: A Psychoanalyst Explores the World of S&M*. New York: Plenum.

Storms, M. D. (1980). "Theories of Sexual Orientation." *Journal of Personality and Social Psychology, 38*, 783–792.

Storms, M. D. (1981), "A Theory of Erotic Orientation Development." *Psychological Review, 88*, 340–353.

Strage, M. (1980). *The Durable Fig Leaf*. New York: Morrow.

Strassberg, D. S., & Lowe, K. (1995). "Volunteer Bias in Sex Research." *Archives of Sexual Behavior, 24*(3): 369–382.

Strider, W. (1997). "Making Sense of the Pap Test." *Women's Health Digest, 3*(4), 250–251.

Struckman-Johnson, C., Struckman-Johnson, D., & Anderson, P. B. (2003). "Tactics of Sexual Coercion: When Men and Women Won't Take No for an Answer." *The Journal of Sex Research, 40*, 76–86.

"Study Tracks Decline in Male Fertility with Age." (2002, April 29). *Monterey County Herald*, p. A2.

Stueve, A., O'Donnell, L., Duran, R., Doval, A. S., Geier, J., & Community Intervention Trial for Youth Study Team. (2002). "Being High and Taking Sexual Risks: Findings from a Multisite Survey of Urban Young Men Who Have Sex with Men." *AIDS Education and Prevention, 14*, 482–495.

Stumper, S. F. (1997, March 12). "Myths/Realities of Bisexuality." C:/Winword/Triangle.

Suarez-Al-Adam, M., Raffaelli, M., & O'Leary, A. (2000). "Influence of Abuse and Partner Hypermasculinity on the Sexual Behavior of Latinas." *AIDS Education and Prevention, 12*, 263–274.

Sue, D. (1979). "Erotic Fantasies of College Students During Coitus." *The Journal of Sex Research, 15*, 299–305.

Sullivan, A. (2000, April 2). "The He Hormone." *New York Times Magazine*, pp. 46–51, 58–59, 69–70.

Sundt, M. (1994). *Identifying the Attitudes and Beliefs That Accompany Sexual Harassment*. Unpublished doctoral dissertation, UCLA.

"Suppression of Menstruation with Extended OC Regimens." (2002, October). *The Contraception Report, 13*(3), 8–11.

Supreme Court of the United States. (2003a, June 26). "John Geddes Lawrence and Tyron Garner, Petitioners *v.* Texas." Majority opinion.

Supreme Court of the United States. (2003b, June 26). "John Geddes Lawrence and Tyron Garner, Petitioners *v.* Texas." Minority opinon.

Swan, S. H., Elkin, E. P., & Fenster, L. (2000). "The Question of Declining Sperm Density Revisited: An Analysis of 101 Studies Published 1934–1996." *Environmental Health Perspectives, 108*, 961–966.

Sward, S. (1998, June 27). "High Court Widens Employer Liability for Sex Harassment." *San Francisco Chronicle*, pp. A1, A15.

Swensen, C. H., Jr. (1972). "The Behavior of Love." In H. A. Otto (Ed.), *Love Today: A New Exploration.* New York: Association Press.

Swiatek, J. (2002, November 25). "Pfizer Battles Viagra Wannabes." *Indianapolis Star,* p. C1.

Symons, D. (1979). *The Evolution of Human Sexuality.* New York: Oxford University Press.

Taberner, P. V. (1985). *Aphrodisiacs: The Science and the Myth.* Philadelphia: University of Pennsylvania Press.

Tam, L. W. (2001, November–December). "What Is Postpartum Depression?" *The Network News,* pp. 4–5.

Tanfer, K., Cubbins, L. A., & Billy, J. O. G. (1995). "Gender, Race, Class and Self-Reported Sexually Transmitted Disease Incidence." *Family Planning Perspectives, 27,* 196–202.

Tanke, E. D. (1982). "Dimensions of the Physical Attractiveness Stereotype: A Factor/Analytic Study." *Journal of Psychology, 110,* 63–74.

Tannen, D. (1990). *You Just Don't Understand: Women and Men in Conversation.* New York: Ballantine Books.

Tanner, L. (2002, February 4). "Doctors Back Gay Adoptions." *Monterey County Herald,* p. A7.

Templeman, T., & Stinnett, R. (1991). "Patterns of Sexual Arousal and History in a 'Normal' Sample of Young Men." *Archives of Sexual Behavior, 20*(2), 137–150.

Tenore, J. L. (2000). "Ectopic Pregnancy." *American Family Physician, 61*(4), 1080–1086.

Terr, L. (1994). *Unchained Memories: True Stories of Traumatic Memories.* New York: Basic Books.

Testa, R. J., Kinder, B. N., & Ironson, G. (1987). "Heterosexual Bias in the Perception of Loving Relationships of Gay Males and Lesbians." *The Journal of Sex Research, 23*(2), 163–172.

Thables, V. (1997). "A Survey Analysis of Women's Long-Term Postdivorce Adjustment." *Journal of Divorce and Remarriage, 27*(3–4), 163–175.

Thayer, L. (1986). *On Communication.* Norwood, NJ: Ablex.

Thomas, S. B., & Quinn, S. C. (1991). "The Tuskegee Syphilis Study, 1932 to 1972: Implications for HIV Education and AIDS Risk Education Programs in the Black Community." *American Journal of Public Health, 81*(11), 1498–1504.

Thompson, C. E. (1990). "Transition of the Disabled Adolescent to Adulthood." *Pediatrician, 17*(4), 308–313.

Thompson, M. E., Chaffee, S. H., & Oshagan, H. H. (1990). "Regulating Pornography: A Public Dilemma." *Journal of Communication, 40*(3), 73–83.

Thornberry, T. P., Smith, C. A., & Howard, G. J. (1997). "Risk Factors for Teenage Fatherhood." *Journal of Marriage and the Family 59*(3), 505–522.

Tiefer, L. (2001). "A New View of Women's Sexual Problems: Why New? Why Now?" *The Journal of Sex Research, 38*(2), 89–110.

Ting-Toomey, S. (1983). "An Analysis of Verbal Communication Patterns in High and Low Marital Adjustment Groups." *Human Communications Research, 9*(4), 306–319.

Tjaden, P., & Thoennes, N. (1998). *Prevalence, Incidence, and Consequences of Violence Against Women: Findings from the National Violence Against Women Survey.* Washington, DC: National Institute of Justice.

Tolson, J. (2000, March 13). "No Wedding? No Ring? No Problem." *U.S. News & World Report,* p. 48.

Tone, A. (2003). "The Contraceptive Conundrum." *SIECUS Report, 31*(2), 4–8.

Toppari, J., & Kaleva, M. (1999). "Maldescendus Testis." *Hormone Research, 51,* 261–269.

Torabi, M. R., & Yarber, W. L. (1992). "Alternate Forms of the HIV Prevention Attitude Scale for Teenagers." *AIDS Education and Prevention, 4,* 172–82.

Treas, J., & Giesen, D. (2000). "Sexual Infidelity Among Married and Cohabiting Americans." *Journal of Marriage and the Family, 62,* 48–60.

Trippet, S. E., & Bain, J. (1992). "Reasons American Lesbians Fail to Seek Traditional Health Care." *Health Care for Women International, 13*(2), 145–153.

Troiden, R. (1988). *Gay and Lesbian Identity: A Sociological Analysis.* New York: General Hall.

Tucker, R. K., Marvin, M. G., & Vivian, B. (1991). "What Constitutes a Romantic Act?" *Psychological Reports, 89*(2), 651–654.

Tufts University. (2002, December). "Better Sex Life Not Found over the Counter." *Tufts University Health and Nutrition Letter, 20*(10).

Tully, C. T. (1995). "In Sickness and in Health: Forty Years of Research on Lesbians." In C. T. Tully (Ed.), *Lesbian Social Services: Research Issues.* New York: Harrington Park Press/Haworth Press.

TV Parental Guidelines. (2000, May 29). Available: http://www .tvguidelines.org/default.htm (Last visited 12/8/00).

Uba, L. (1994). *Asian Americans: Personality Patterns, Identity, and Mental Health.* New York: Guilford Press.

Uhlenhuth, K. (2003, March 10). "Hormone Attention Turns to Men." *Monterey County Herald,* p. 2.

Ullman, S. E., & Brecklin, L. R. (2002). "Sexual Assault History and Suicidal Behavior in a National Sample of Women." *Suicide and Life-Threatening Behavior, 32,* 117–130.

Ullman, S. E., & Knight, R. A. (1991). "A Multivariate Model for Predicting Rape and Physical Injury Outcomes During Sexual Assaults." *Journal of Consulting and Clinical Psychology, 59*(5), 724–731.

Undersize Infants Score Higher on IQ Tests If Breast Fed Exclusively. (2002). National Institutes of Health. Available: http://www.nih.gov/news/pr/mar2002/nichd_20.htm (Last visited 11/30/02).

Understanding Your Treatment Options. (2002). Resolve. Available: http://www.resolve.org/main/national/treatment/options/index.jsp?name=treatment&tag=options (Last visited 8/22/03).

Urquiza, A., & Goodlin-Jones, B. L. (1994). "Child Sexual Abuse and Adult Revictimization with Women of Color." *Violence and Victims, 9*(3), 223–232.

U.S. Attorney General's Commission on Pornography (AGCOP). (1986). *Final Report.* Washington, DC: U.S. Government Printing Office.

U.S. Bureau of the Census. (2000). *Statistical Abstract of the United States* (120th ed.). Washington, DC: U.S. Government Printing Office.

U.S. Bureau of the Census. (2001). Marital Status of the Population 15 Years and Over by Sex, and Race and Hispanic Origin. Available: http://www.census.gov/population/socdemo/race/black/pp1-142/tab02.txt (Last visited 2/6/03).

U.S. Department of Commerce. (2001). Census Bureau Releases Update on Country's African American Population. Available: http://www.census.gov/Press-Release/www/2001/cb01-34 .html (Last visited 2/6/03).

U.S. Department of Health and Human Services. (2000a). *Vital and Health Statistics: Trends in Pregnancies and Pregnancy Rates by Outcome: Estimates for the United States, 1976–96.* Series 23, No. 56. Washington, DC: Centers for Disease Control and Prevention/National Center for Health Statistics.

U.S. Department of Health and Human Services. (2000b). *Healthy People 2010.* Washington, DC: Author.

U.S. Department of Health and Human Services. (2002). Emergency Department Trends from the Drug Warning Network: Preliminary Estimates January–June 2001 and Revised Estimates 1194–2000. Available: http://www.samhsa.gov (Last visited 6/18/03).

U.S. Department of Health and Human Services. (2003). HHS Extends Use of Rapid HIV Test to New Sites Nationwide. Available: http://www.hhs.gov/news/press.2003pr4es/2003131b.html (Last visited 2/21/03).

U.S. Department of Justice. (2000). *Criminal Victimization 1999: Changes 1998–99 with Trends 1993–99.* Washington, DC: Bureau of Justice Statistics.

U.S. Department of Justice. (2002). *Criminal Victimization 2001: Changes 2000–01 with Trends 1993–2001.* Washington, DC: Bureau of Justice Statistics.

U.S. Equal Employment Opportunity Commission. (2003). Sexual Harassment Charges EEOC and FEPAs Combined: FY 1992–FY 2002. Available: http://www.eeoc.gov/stats/harass.html (Last visited 6/10/03).

U.S. Food and Drug Administration. (2003). New Device Approval: Essure System—P020014). Available: http://www.fda.gov/cdrh/mda/docs/p020014.html (Last visited 8/22/03).

U.S. Merit Systems Protection Board. (1995). *Sexual Harassment in the Federal Workplace: Trends, Progress, Continuing Challenges.* Washington, DC: Author.

U.S. Preventive Services Task Force. (2002a). "Postmenopausal Hormone Replacement Therapy for Primary Prevention of Chronic Conditions: Recommendations and Rationale." *Annals of Internal Medicine, 137,* 834–839.

U.S. Preventive Services Task Force. (2002b). "Screening for Breast Cancer: Recommendations and Rationale." *Annals of Internal Medicine, 137,* 344–346.

U.S. Preventive Services Task Force. (2002c). "Screening for Prostate Cancer: Recommendations and Rationale." *Annals of Internal Medicine, 137,* 915–916.

"Vaginal Births After Cesarean Births—California 1996–2000." (2002, November 8). *Morbidity and Mortality Weekly Report, 51*(44), 996–998.

Valleroy, L. A., MacKellar, D. A., Karon, J. M., Janssen, R. S., & Hayman, C. R. (1998). "HIV Infection in Disadvantaged Out-of-School Youth: Prevalence for U.S. Job Corps Entrants, 1990 Through 1996." *Journal of Acquired Immune Deficiency Syndromes, 19,* 67–73.

Vandeweil, H. B. M., Jaspers, J. P. M., Schultz, W. C. M. W., & Gal, J. (1990). "Treatment of Vaginismus: A Review of Concepts and Treatment Modalities." *Journal of Psychosomatic Obstetrics and Gynecology, 11,* 1–18.

Van Wyk, P. H., & Geist, C. S. (1984). "Psychosocial Development of Heterosexual, Bisexual, and Homosexual Behavior." *Archives of Sexual Behavior, 13,* 505–544.

Vega, W. (1991). "Hispanic Families." In A. Booth (Ed.), *Contemporary Families: Looking Forward, Looking Back.* Minneapolis: National Council on Family Relations.

Ventura, S. J., Matthews, T. J., & Hamilton, B. E. (2001). "Births to Teenagers in the United States, 1940–2000." *National Vital Statistics Report, 49*(10).

Veronesi, U., Cascinelli, N., Mariani, L., Greco, M., Saccozzi, R., Luini, R., Aguilar, M., & Marubini, E. (2002). "Twenty-Year Follow-Up of a Randomized Study Comparing Breast-Conserving Surgery with Radical Mastectomy for Early Breast Cancer." *New England Journal of Medicine, 347,* 1227–1233.

"A Very Sore Spot." (1997, August 25). *Newsweek,* p. 81.

Viewpoint: News Hour Leaves Women Out of the Discussion. (2002, Spring). National Organization of Women. Available: http://www.now.org/nnt/spring-2002/viewpoint.htm (Last visited 2/23/03).

Vine, M., Margolin, B., Morrison, H., & Hulka, B. (1994). "Cigarette Smoking and Sperm Density: A Meta-Analysis." *Fertility and Sterility, 61*(1), 35–43.

Vonk, R., & Ashmore, R. D. (1993). "The Multifaceted Self: Androgyny Reassessed by Open-Ended Self-Descriptions." *Social Psychology Quarterly, 56*(4), 278–287.

Vredeveldt, P. (1994). *Empty Arms: Emotional Support for Those Who Have Suffered Miscarriage and Stillbirth.* Sisters, OR: Questar.

Waldner-Haugrud, L., & Gratch, L. V. (1997). "Sexual Coercion in Gay/Lesbian Relationships: Among Gay and Lesbian Adolescents." *Violence and Victims, 12,* 87–98.

Walker, E. A., Katon, W. J., Hansom, J., & Harrop-Griffiths, J. (1992). "Medical and Psychiatric Symptoms in Women with Childhood Sexual Abuse." *Psychosomatic Medicine, 54*(6), 658–664.

Wallerstein, J. S., Lewis, J., & Blakeslee, S. (2000). *The Unexpected Legacy of Divorce.* New York: Hyperion.

Ward, L. M., Gorvine, B., & Cytron, A. (2002). "Would That Really Happen? Adolescents' Perceptions of Sexual Relationships According to Prime-Time Television." In J. D. Brown, J. R. Steele, & K. W. Childers (Eds.), *Sexual Teens, Sexual Media.* Mahwah, NJ: Erlbaum.

Ward, L. M., & Rivadeneyra, R. (1999). "Contributions of Entertainment Television to Adolescents' Sexual Attitudes and Expectations: The Role of Viewing Amount Versus Viewer Involvement." *The Journal of Sex Research, 36*(3), 237–249.

Wardlow, G. (1997). *Contemporary Nutrition Issues and Insights.* New York: Brown Benchmark.

Wassertheil-Smoller, S., Hendrix, S. L., Limacher, M., Heiss, G., Kooperberg, C., Baird, A., Kotchen, T., Curb, J. D., Black, H., Rossouw, J. E., Safford, M., Stein, E., Laowattana, S., & Mysiw, W. J. (2003). "Effects of Estrogen plus Progestin in Stroke in Menopausal Women." *Journal of the American Medical Association, 289,* 2673–2684.

Webb, G. (2001). "Sex and the Internet." *Yahoo! Internet Life, 7*(5), 88–89.

Webb, P. (1983). *The Erotic Arts.* New York: Farrar, Straus & Giroux.

Wechsler, H., Davenport, A., Dowdell, G., Moeykens, B., & Castillo, S. (1994). "Health and Behavior Consequences of Binge Drinking in College: A National Survey of College Students in 140 Campuses." *Journal of the American Medical Association, 272,* 1672–1677.

Wechsler, H., Mulnar, B. E., Davenport, A. E., & Baer, J. S. (1999). "College Alcohol Use: A Full or Empty Glass?" *Journal of American College Health, 47*(6), 247–251.

Weeks, J. (1986). *Sexuality.* New York: Tavistock/Ellis Horwood.

Weeks, J. (1993, February 11). "Someone Wicked This Way Comes." *San Jose Mercury News,* pp. C1, C6.

Weeks, J. D., & Kozak, I. J. (2001). "Trends in the Use of Episiotomy in the United States: 1980–1998." *Birth, 28*(3), 152–160.

Weinberg, M. S., & Williams, C. J. (1974). *Male Homosexuals: Their Problems and Adaptations*. New York: Oxford University Press.

Weinberg, M. S., Williams, C. J., & Moser, C. (1984). "The Social Constituents of Sadomasochism." *Social Problems, 31,* 379–389.

Weinberg, M., Williams, C., & Pryor, D. (1994). *Dual Attraction: Understanding Bisexuality*. New York: Oxford University Press.

Weinberg, T. S., & Kamel, G. W. L. (Eds.). (1983). *S and M: Studies in Sadomasochism*. Buffalo: Prometheus Books.

Weir, J. (1992, March 29). "Gay-Bashing, Villainy and the Oscars." *The New York Times,* p. 17.

Weis, D. L. (2002). "The Need to Integrate Sexual Theory and Research." In M. W. Wiederman & B. Whitely, Jr. (Eds.), *Handbook on Conducting Research in Human Sexuality*. Mahwah, NJ: Erlbaum.

Weisberg, D. K. (1990). *Children of the Night*. New York: Free Press.

Weiss, J. (1992). "Multiple Sclerosis: Will It Come Between Us? Sexual Concerns of Clients and Their Partners." *Journal of Neuroscience Nursing, 24*(4), 190–193.

Weizman, R., & Hart, J. (1987). "Sexual Behavior in Healthy Married Elderly Men." *Archives of Sexual Behavior, 16*(1), 39–44.

Wells, B. (1986). "Predictors of Female Nocturnal Orgasm." *Journal of Sex Research, 23,* 421–427.

Werking, K. (1997). *We're Just Good Friends: Women and Men in Nonromantic Relationships*. New York: Guilford Press.

What Is Priapism? (1997, March 28). Available: http://www.columbia.edu/cu/healthwise/1133.html (Last visited 1/29/98).

Whipple, B., & Komisaruk, B. (1999). "Beyond the G Spot: Recent Research on Female Sexuality." *Psychiatric Annals, 29,* 34–37.

Whipple, B., Ogden, G., & Komisaruk, B. R. (1992). "Physiological Correlates of Imagery-Induced Orgasm in Women." *Archives of Sexual Behavior, 21*(2), 121–133.

Whitaker, D., & Miller, K. S. (2000). "Parent-Adolescent Discussions About Sex and Condoms: Impact on Peer Influences of Sexual Risk Behaviors." *Journal of Adolescent Research, 15*(2), 251–273.

Whitbourne, S. K. (1990). "Sexuality in the Aging Male." *Generations, 14*(3), 28–30.

Whitcomb, D., et al. (1994). *The Child Victim as a Witness: Research Report*. Washington, DC: U.S. Department of Justice, Office of Juvenile Justice and Delinquency Prevention.

White, G. (1980). "Inducing Jealousy: A Power Perspective." *Personality and Social Psychology Bulletin, 6*(2), 222–227.

White, J., & Parham, T. (1990). *The Psychology of Blacks: An African-American Perspective* (2nd ed.). Englewood Cliffs, NJ: Prentice-Hall.

White, J. W., & Farmer, R. (1992). "Research Methods: How They Shape Views of Sexual Violence." *Journal of Social Issues, 48,* 45–59.

Whitehead, M., & Holland, P. (2003, January 25). "What Puts Children of Lone Parents at a Health Disadvantage?" *Lancet, 361,* 271–272.

Whitley, B. E., & Kite, M. E. (1995). "Sex Differences in Attitudes Toward Homosexuality: A Comment on Oliver and Hyde (1993)." *Psychology Bulletin, 117*(1), 146–154.

Whitney, B. E. (2002). "Group Comparison Research." In M. W. Wiederman & B. E. Whitley (Eds.), *Handbook for Conducting Research on Human Sexuality*. Mahwah, NJ: Erlbaum.

Widom, C. S., & Kuhns, J. B. (1996). "Childhood Victimization and Subsequent Risk for Promiscuity, Prostitution, and Teenage Pregnancy: A Prospective Study." *American Journal of Public Health, 86*(11), 1607–1612.

Wiederman, M. W. (1996). "Women, Sex, and Food: A Review of Research on Eating Disorders and Sexuality." *The Journal of Sex Research, 33,* 301–311.

Wiederman, M. W. (1997). "Extramarital Sex: Prevalence and Correlates in a National Study." *The Journal of Sex Research, 34*(2), 167–175.

Wiederman, M., Maynard, C., & Fretz, A. (1996). "Ethnicity in 25 Years of Published Sexuality Research: 1971–1995." *The Journal of Sex Research, 33*(4), 339–343.

Wiederman, M. W. (1999). "Volunteer Bias in Sexuality Research Using College Student Participation." *Journal of Sex Research, 36,* 59–66.

Wilcox, A. J., Weinberg, C. R., & Baird, D. D. (1996). "Timing of Sexual Intercourse in Relation to Ovulation." *New England Journal of Medicine, 333,* 1563–1565.

Wilkinson, D. Y. (1997). "American Families of African Descent." In M. K. DeGenova (Ed.), *Families in Cultural Context: Strengths and Challenges in Diversity*. Mountain View, CA: Mayfield.

Wilkinson, S., & Kitzinger, C. (Eds.). (1993). *Heterosexuality*. Newbury Park, CA: Sage.

Williams, E. A., Lam, J. A., & Shively, M. (1992). "The Impact of a University Policy on the Sexual Harassment of Female Students." *Journal of Higher Education, 63*(1), 50–64.

Williams, L. (1994). "Recall of Childhood Trauma: A Prospective Study of Women's Memories of Child Sexual Abuse." *Journal of Consulting and Clinical Psychology, 62,* 1167–1176.

Willis, B. M., & Levy, B. S. (2002). "Child Prostitution: Global Health Burden, Research Needs, and Interventions." *The Lancet, 359,* 1417–1421.

Wilson, P. (1986). "Black Culture and Sexuality." *Journal of Social Work and Human Sexuality, 4*(3), 29–46.

Wilson, S., & Delk, J., II. (1994). "A New Treatment for Peyronie's Disease: Modeling the Penis over an Inflatable Penile Prosthesis." *Journal of Urology, 152,* 1121–1123.

Wilson, S. M., & Medora, N. P. (1990). "Gender Comparisons of College Students' Attitudes Toward Sexual Behavior." *Adolescence, 25*(99), 615–627.

Winters, S. J., Brufsky, A., Weissfeld, J., Trump, D. L., Dyky, M. A., & Hadeed, V. (2001). "Testosterone, Sex Hormone–Binding Globulin, and Body Composition in Young Adult African-American and Caucasian Men." *Metabolism: Clinical and Experimental, 50,* 1242–1247.

Wise, T. N., & Meyer, J. K. (1980). "The Border Area Between Transvestism and Gender Dysphoria: Transvestitic Applicants for Sex Reassignment." *Archives of Sexual Behavior, 9,* 327–342.

Wolff, C. (1986). *Magnus Hirschfeld: A Portrait of a Pioneer in Sexology*. London: Quartet Books.

Wolner-Hanssen, P., Eschenbach, D. A., & Paavonen, J. (1990). "Association Between Vaginal Douching and Acute Pelvic Inflammatory Disease." *Journal of the American Medical Association, 273,* 1936–1941.

"Women's Hormones—Testosterone, the Other Female Hormone." (2002, September). *Harvard Women's Health Watch, 10,* 1.

Wood, M. L., & Price, P. (1997). "Machismo and Marianismo: Implications for HIV/AIDS Risk Reduction and Education." *American Journal of Health Sciences, 13*(1), 44–52.

Woods, S. C., & Mansfield, J. G. (1981, February 11). "Ethanol and Disinhibition: Physiological and Behavioral Links." In R. Room & Collins (Eds.), *Proceedings of Alcoholism and Drug Abuse Conference, Berkeley/Oakland*. Washington, DC: U.S. Department of Health and Human Services, pp. 4–22.

Woodworth, T. W. (1996). DEA Congressional Testimony. Available: http://www.usdoj.gov/dea/ (Last visited 2/6/97).

Working Group for a New View of Women's Sexual Problems. (2001). "A New View of Women's Sexual Problems." In E. Kaschak & L. Tiefer (Eds.), *A New View of Women's Sexual Problems*. New York: Haworth Press.

World Health Organization. (1992). *Reproductive Health: A Key to a Brighter Future*. Biennial Report, 1990–1991. Geneva, Switzerland: Author.

World Health Organization. (2002). Gender and Reproductive Rights: Glossary. Available: http://www.who.int/reproductive-health/gender/glossary.html (Last visited 4/23/03).

World Health Organization. (2002, December). AIDS Epidemic Update. Available: http://www.unaids.org/worldaidsday/2002-press/epiupdate.html (Last visited 12/5/02).

Wyatt, G. E. (1992). "The Sociocultural Context of African American and White American Women's Rape." *Journal of Social Issues, 48*(1), 77–91.

Wyatt, G. E., Guthrie, D., & Notgass, C. M. (1992). "Differential Effects of Women's Child Sexual Abuse and Subsequent Sexual Revictimization." *Journal of Consulting and Clinical Psychology, 60*(2), 167–174.

Wyatt, G. E., & Lyons-Rowe, S. (1990). "African American Women's Sexual Satisfaction as a Dimension of Their Sex Roles." *Sex Roles, 22*(7–8), 509–524.

Wyatt, G. E., & Riederle, M. (1994). "Sexual Harassment and Prior Sexual Trauma Among African American and White Women." *Violence and Victims, 9*(3), 233–247.

Xavier, C., Xavier, B. F., Munoz, N., Meijer, C. J. L. M., Shah, K. V., deSanjose, L., Eluf-Neto, J., Ngelangel, C. A., Chichareon, S., Smith, J. S., Herrero, R., Moreno, V., & Franceschi, S. (2002). "Male Circumcision, Penile Human Papillomavirus Infection, and Cervical Cancer in Female Patients." *New England Journal of Medicine, 346*, 1105–1112.

Yap, P. M. (1993). "Koro—a Culture-Bound Depersonalization." In D. N. Suggs & A. W. Miracle (Eds.), *Culture and Human Sexuality*. Pacific Grove, CA: Brooks/Cole.

Yapko, M. D. (1994). *Suggestions of Abuse: True and False Memories of Childhood Sexual Trauma*. New York: Simon & Schuster.

Yarber, W. L. (1996). "Rural Adolescent HIV/STD Health Risk Behavior: The Accuracy of Estimates of Five Groups." *The Health Education Monograph Series, 14*, 41–46.

Yarber, W. L. (2003). *STDs and HIV: A Guide for Today's Teens*. Reston, VA: American Association for Health Education.

Yarber, W. L., Crosby, R. A., & Sanders, S. A. (2000). "Understudied HIV/STD Risk Behaviors Among a Sample of Rural South Carolina Women: A Descriptive Pilot Study." *Health Education Monograph Series, 18*, 1–5.

Yarber, W. L., Milhausen, R., Crosby, R. A., & DiClemente, R. J. (2002). "Selected Risk and Protective Factors Associated with Two or More Lifetime Sexual Intercourse Partners and Non-Condom Use During Last Coitus Among U.S. Rural High School Students." *American Journal of Health Education, 33*, 206–213.

Yarber, W. L., Sanders, S. A., Graham, C., & Dodge, B. (2001, April). "A Comprehensive Assessment of Male Condom Use Errors Among a Midwestern University Sample of Single Heterosexual Males." Paper presented at the meeting of the Rural Center for AIDS/STD Prevention, Indianapolis, IN.

Yarber, W. L., Torabi, M. R., & Haffner, D. W. (1997). "Comprehensive Sexuality Education in Indiana Secondary Schools: Instructional Topics, Importance Ratings and Correlates with Teacher Traits." *American Journal of Health Studies, 13*, 65–73.

Yarber, W. L., Torabi, M. R., & Veenker, C. H. (1989). "Development of a Three-Component Sexually Transmitted Disease Attitude Scale." *Journal of Sex Education and Therapy, 15*, 36–49.

Yates, A., & Wolman, W. (1991). "Aphrodisiacs: Myth and Reality." *Medical Aspects of Human Sexuality, 25*, 58–64.

Yawn, B. P., & Yawn, R. A. (1997). "Adolescent Pregnancy: A Preventable Consequence?" *The Prevention Researcher*. Eugene, OR: Integrated Research Services.

Yoder, J. D., & Aniakudo, P. (1995). "The Responses of African American Women Firefighters to Gender Harassment at Work." *Sex Roles, 32*(4–4), 125–137.

Yohalem, L. (1995). "Why Do People with Mental Retardation Need Sexuality Education?" *SIECUS Report, 23*(4), 14–16.

Young, J. M., Bennett, C., Gilhooly, P., Wessells, H., & Ramos, D. E. (2002). "Efficacy and Safety of Sidenafil Citrate (Viagra) in Black and Hispanic American Men." *Urology, 60*(S2), 39–48.

Young, K. (1998). *Caught in the Net: How to Recognize the Signs of Internet Addiction and a Winning Strategy for Recovery*. New York: Wiley.

Young, K. S., Griffin-Shelley, E., Cooper, A., O'Mara, J., & Buchanan, J. (2000). "Online Infidelity: A New Dimension in Couple Relationships with Implications for Evaluation and Treatment." In A. Cooper (Ed.), *Cybersex: The Dark Side of the Force*. Philadelphia: Brunner/Routledge, pp. 59–74.

Young, L. (1992). "Sexual Abuse and the Problem of Embodiment." *Child Abuse and Neglect, 16*(1), 89–100.

Zack, A., & McDonald, C. (1997). "Satisfaction and Trust in Intimate Relationships: Do Lesbians and Heterosexual Women Differ?" *Psychological Reports, 80*, 904–906.

Zausner, M. (1986). *The Streets: A Factual Portrait of Sex Prostitutes As Told in Their Own Words*. New York: St. Martin's Press.

Zerbe, K. J. (1992). "Why Eating-Disordered Patients Resist Sex Therapy: A Response to Simpson and Ramberg." *Journal of Sex and Marital Therapy, 18*(1), 55–64.

Zilbergeld, B. (1999). *Male Sexuality* (Rev. ed.). Boston: Little, Brown.

Zimmerman, R. (2002, September 25). "Some Makers, Vendors Drop N-9 Spermicide on HIV Risk." *The Wall Street Journal Online*.

Zinn, M. B., & Eitzen, D. S. (1990). *Diversity in Families* (2nd ed.). New York: HarperCollins.

Credits

PHOTO CREDITS

Chapter 1

p. 3, © Bill Aron/PhotoEdit; p. 4, © Christine DeVault; p. 5, © Rudi Von Briel/PhotoEdit; p. 7, © David Young Wolff/PhotoEdit; p. 9, © 20th Century Fox Film Corp. All rights reserved. Courtesy Everett Collection; p. 11, Courtesy Showtime/Everett Collection; p. 12, © AP/Wide World Photos; p. 14, © Showtime/Courtesy Everett Collection; p. 16, © Joel Gordon; p. 19, © Amy Ramey/PhotoEdit; p. 21, © Erich Lessing/Art Resource, NY; p. 23, Smithsonian Institution, National Anthropological Archives. Neg. # 85-8666; p. 26TL, © Donna Binder; p. 26TR, © Cleo/PhotoEdit; p. 26BL, © Richard Lord Ente/The Image Works; p. 26BR, © Alán Gallegos/AG Photograph

Chapter 2

p. 41, © David Ryan/Lonely Planet Images; p. 48, © Irven DeVore/Anthro-Photo; p. 50, © Mary Evans Picture Library; p. 51, © Mary Evans Picture Library/Sigmund Freud Copyrights; p. 52, © Hulton-Deutsch Collection/Corbis; p. 53, © Bettmann/Corbis; p. 55, © John Chiasson/Getty Images; p. 56, © Bruce Powell; p. 63T, © AP/Wide World Photos; p. 63B, Photo of Dr. Evelyn Hooker courtesy of *Changing Our Minds: The Story of Dr. Evelyn Hooker*; p. 64, © 1978 Raymond Depardon/Magnum Photos; p. 65, © Will Hart/PhotoEdit; p. 67, © Bob Daemmrich/Stock Boston/PictureQuest; p. 71, © Jonathan Nourok/PhotoEdit

Chapter 3

p. 79, Photo © Art Resource/© 2004 Judy Chicago/Artists Rights Society (ARS), New York; p. 81, 82, © Susan Lerner 1999/Joel Gordon Photography; p. 88, Photograph by Imogen Cunningham, © 1978, 1998 The Imogen Cunningham Trust; p. 89, © C. Edelmann/La Villete/Photo Researchers, Inc.; p. 102, © Jeff Greenberg/PhotoEdit

Chapter 4

p. 113, © Joel Gordon; p. 116L, © Bachmann/PhotoEdit; p. 116R, © Luca I. Tettoni/Corbis; p. 117, © David Young-Wolff/PhotoEdit; p. 122, © CNRI/Science Photo Library/Photo Researchers, Inc.

Chapter 5

p. 131, Lisa Lyon, 1981 © Copyright The Estate of Robert Mapplethorpe/A+C Anthology; p. 132, © Tom McCarthy/PhotoEdit; p. 134, © Cleo Photography/PhotoEdit; p. 139, © Bob Daemmrich/The Image Works; p. 141, © David Young-Wolff/PhotoEdit; p. 147, © Myrleen Cate/PhotoEdit; p. 151, 156, © Custom Medical Stock Photo

Chapter 6

p. 166, © Lisa Gallegos/AG Photograph; p. 167, © Christine DeVault; p. 172, © David Young-Wolff/PhotoEdit; p. 174, © Bob Daemmrich/Stock Boston; p. 178, © R. Hutchings/PhotoEdit; p. 191, © David Young-Wolff/PhotoEdit; p. 194, © Joel Gordon; p. 200, © Lisa Gallegos/AG Photograph; p. 204, © Cindy Charles/PhotoEdit; p. 205, © Jean Mounicq/ANA, Paris; p. 208, © Rhoda Sidney/PhotoEdit; p. 209, © Myrleen Cate/PhotoEdit

Chapter 7

p. 217, © Barbara Stitzer/PhotoEdit; p. 220, © Michael Newman/PhotoEdit; p. 223, © David Young-Wolff/PhotoEdit; p. 226, © Joel Gordon; p. 232, © Jonathan Nourok/PhotoEdit; p. 233, © Strauss/Curtis/Offshoot Stock; p. 241, © Ghislain & Marie David de Lossy/Getty Images/The Image Bank

Chapter 8

p. 252, © Sonda Dawes/The Image Works; p. 256, © Wojnarowicz/The Image Works; p. 258, © Bill Aron/PhotoEdit; p. 268, © Ron Chapple/Getty Images/Taxi

Chapter 9

p. 279L, © S. Vacariello/Nonstock, Inc.; p. 279R, © Joyce Tenneson/Nonstock, Inc.; p. 285, 291, © Joel Gordon

Chapter 10

p. 324, © Roberto Soncin Gerometta/Lonely Planet Images; p. 325, © Movie Star News; p. 326, © Markus Morianz; p. 328, © J. Greenberg/The Image Works; p. 330, © Columbia/Courtesy Everett Collection ; p. 332, © J. Sohm/The Image Works; p. 339, Everett Collection

Chapter 11

p. 348, 350, © Joel Gordon; p. 355, © Jonathan A. Meyers/JAM Photography; p. 360, 363, © Joel Gordon; p. 364, © Jonathan A. Meyers/JAM Photography; p. 365, 366, © Joel Gordon; p. 369, © Jonathan A. Meyers/JAM Photography; p. 370, © Joel Gordon; p. 375, Courtesy Conceptus Incorporated; p. 378, © Joel Gordon

Chapter 12

p. 395, Photo by Lennart Nillson/Bonnier Alba AB. From *Behold Man*. Little Brown and Company; p. 410, © Mark Richards/PhotoEdit; p. 412, © Custom Medical Stock Photo; p. 418, © M. Siluk/The Image Works; p. 423, © Bob Daemmrich/Stock Boston; p. 426, © Michael Newman/PhotoEdit; p. 427, Huichol People, Nayarit or Jalisco Mexico. *The Husband Assists in the Birth of a Child*, mid-20th century. Yarn, $23^3/_4 \times 23^3/_4$ in. Fine Arts Museums of San Francisco, gift of Peter F. Young, 74.21.14.

Chapter 13

p. 438, Ryan McVay/PhotoDisc/Getty Images; p. 443, © Carlos Henderson/Shooting Star; p. 445, © Christopher Brown/Stock Boston; p. 459, © Spencer Grant/Index Stock Imagery; p. 465T, © Francoise Sauze/Photo Researchers, Inc.; p. 465B, © Custom Medical Stock Photo; p. 467, © 1980 Hella Hammid. All rights reserved; p. 476, © Joel Gordon; p. 479, © Catherine Leroy/Sipa Press

Chapter 14

p. 505, © Michael Newman/PhotoEdit; p. 508, © Bob Bachmann/PhotoEdit; p. 510, © Spencer Platt/Getty Images; p. 521, © Rachel Epstein/PhotoEdit; p. 524, © Elena Dorfman/Offshoot Stock

Chapter 15

p. 539, © Mark Richards/PhotoEdit; p. 544, Courtesy of the Center for Disease Control, Atlanta; p. 545L, © SPL/Photo Researchers, Inc.; p. 545R, 549T, © Custom Medical Stock Photo; p. 549B, © ISM/Phototake; p. 550L, Courtesy of the Center for Disease Control, Atlanta; p. 550R, © Custom Medical Stock Photo; p. 555, Courtesy of the Center for Disease Control, Atlanta; p. 559, © Joel Gordon

Chapter 16

p. 571, © A. Ramey/PhotoEdit; p. 573, © Custom Medical Stock Photo; p. 578, © Donna Binder; p. 586, © Michael Newman/PhotoEdit; p. 589, 595, © AP/Wide World Photos; p. 597, © Jonathan Nourok/PhotoEdit; p. 601, © Mark Phillips/Photo Researchers, Inc.

Chapter 17

p. 610, © Esbin-Anderson/Lonely Planet Images; p. 618, © Scala/Art Resource; p. 619T, © UPI/Bettmann/Corbis; p. 619B, © James D. Wilson/Getty Images; p. 628, © Mark Peterson/SABA/Corbis; p. 635, © Rhoda Sidney/PhotoEdit; p. 637, © Fotex/Shooting Star

Chapter 18

p. 654, © Joel Gordon; p. 655, © AP/Wide World Photos; p. 659, © Michael Wilhoite from Daddy's Roommate, Alyson Wonderland, 1990; p. 665, © John Maher/Stock Boston/PictureQuest; p. 666, © AP/Wide World Photos; p. 667, © Fred Wood/Summer Productions

Index

Salo, J. O., 475
Salovey, P., 236
salpingitis. *See* pelvic inflammatory disease
Sambian people, 22
same-sex marriage, 21, 194, 672
Samet, J. H., 594
sampling, 43–44, 142–143
Samuels, A., 201
Samuels, M., 412
Samuels, N., 412
Sanchez, Y. M., 68, 147
Sanday, P., 632
Sanders, Stephanie A., 186, 188–189, 535, 536, 560
Sapadin, 218
Sarrell, P. M., 634
Sarvela, P., 623
Saslow, D., 462, 463, 468
Satcher, David, 182
Satel, S. L., 335
Sato, S., 234–235
Saturday Night Live, 329
satyriasis, 320–321
Saunders, E. B., 333, 340
Saunders, S., 120
Sauzier, M., 645
Savetsky, J., 594
Savin-Williams, R., 175
Savin-Williams, R. C., 185
Sawyer, K. A., 462, 463
Sawyer, S., 662
Sax, L., 149
scabies, 555
Scalia, Antonin, 671, 672
scat, 325
Schaap, C., 263
Schanzer, J., 444
Scheer, S., 534, 591
schemas, 40
  gender, 141–142
Scherer, C. R., 653
Schiavi, R. C., 444
Schiffman, J., 445
Schillinger, J. A., 592
Schlosser, E., 654
Schmidt, D. P., 221
Schmitt, E., 615
Schnarch, D., 282, 283, 507, 513–514
Scholes, D., 539
Schrader, R., 637
Schrag, J., 630
Schreer, George, 47
Schreiner-Engle, P., 444
Schultz, J., 640
Schultz, W. C., 503
Schureurs, K. M., 222
Schwartz, M. D., 666
Schwartz, M. F., 16, 321
Schwartz, Pepper, 199, 221, 223, 239, 242, 253, 258, 261, 271, 282, 305, 306, 308, 309, 310, 314
Schwartz, S., 319, 327, 341, 498, 501
scientific method, 42
Scott, J., 136
scripts, 143–144
  See also sexual scripts
scrotum, 114
Seals, B. J., 594
Sears, A. E., 660
Seasonale, 354
secondary sex characteristics, 117–120
secretory phase, 94

secure attachment, 233
Sedlack, A. J., 638
Seeberg, D., 535
Seff, M., 141
Segraves, K. B., 522
Segraves, R. T., 522
Seinfeld, 6
self-awareness, 262, 508–511
self-disclosure, 224, 244, 264
self-help, 96, 519
Seligman, A. J., 319, 341
Sellers, R. M., 139
semen (seminal fluid), 122
seminal vesicles, 116
seminiferous tubules, 115
Sener, S., 462, 463
sensate focus exercises, 515, 517, 518
sensory input, 101–102
serial monogamy, 196
Serines, D. S., 444
seroconversion, 575
serostatus, 575
Servi, G., 660
servilism, 325
Serwadda, D., 585
Seto, M. C., 321
Seventeen, 4
Severson, K., 429
Sewankambo, N. K., 585
sex addiction, 334–335, 497
  cybersex and, 15–16
Sex in America: A Definitive Survey (Michael, Gagnon, Laummann, & Kolata), 56
Sex Appeal, 12
sex (biological), 130
  See also gender
Sex and the City, 6, 10
sex education. *See* sexuality education
sex flush, 104
sex information/advice genre, 35–38
sex offender notification laws, 647
sex organs. *See* female anatomy; male anatomy
sex reassignment surgery (SRS), 157, 158
sex research. *See* research
sex roles. *See* gender roles
sex surrogates, 514
sex therapy, 514–525
  choosing assistance, 524–525
  cognitive-behavioral approach, 55, 514–517
  cybertherapy, 17–18
  lesbian/gay/bisexual people, 522–524
  medical approaches, 519–522
  PSLISSIT model, 518–519
  psychosexual, 517–518
  self-help/group therapy, 519
  See also sexual enhancement; sexuality education
sex tourism, 664–665
sex toys, 458, 510–511, 583
sex trafficking, 663
sex work. *See* prostitution
"Sextasy," 448
sexual abuse. *See* abuse; child sexual abuse; rape; sexual aggression
sexual abuse trauma, 643–645
sexual aggression
  adolescence, 177
  and alcohol use, 444, 445
  defined, 622
  fantasies about, 289, 625
  and jealousy, 236–237

media protrayals of, 14
  and prostitution, 666
  research, 57, 58
  and sexually explicit material, 625, 656
  and sexually transmitted infections, 537
  See also abuse; child sexual abuse; rape
sexual assault, 622
  See also rape; sexual aggression
sexual aversion disorder, 497, 518
Sexual Behavior in the Human Female (Kinsey), 53
Sexual Behavior in the Human Male (Kinsey), 53
sexual coercion, 608–609
  defined, 622
  harassment. *See* sexual harassment
  postrefusal sexual persistence, 630, 631
  sexually transmitted infections and, 537
  See also child sexual abuse; rape; sexual aggression
sexual diary, 46
sexual difficulties, as term, 488
  See also sexual dissatisfaction
sexual dissatisfaction, 488–507
  arousal, 497–499, 516
  classification of, 489–491, 492
  desire, 496–497, 518
  medicalization of, 523
  orgasmic, 499–502, 504, 516–517
  pain, 502–503, 504, 517
  physical causes, 492, 503–504
  prevalence of, 491, 493–496
  psychological causes, 492, 504–507
  relationship causes, 507
  relationships and, 492, 497, 507, 513–514
  self-conflict and, 506
  as term, 488–489
  treatment. *See* sex therapy; sexual enhancement
  See also erectile dysfunction
sexual dysfunction, definitions of, 488–489
  See also sexual dissatisfaction
sexual enhancement, 507–514
sexual enslavement, 626
sexual exclusiveness. *See* extrarelational sexual activity; jealousy
sexual expression, 277–314
  attractiveness, 278–284
  autoeroticism, 286–290
  cultural differences, 300–301
  defined, 299, 304–305
  desire. *See* desire
  fantasies during, 289, 290
  kissing. *See* kissing
  sexual scripts, 284–286
  and sexually explicit material, 655–656
  tantric sex, 313
  touching, 302–303
  See also anal eroticism; intercourse; masturbation; oral-genital sex
sexual harassment, 609–616
  child sexual abuse survivors and, 642
  childhood, 612–614
  college, 614
  defined, 609
  vs. flirtation, 611–612
  touch as violation, 253, 610
  workplace, 614–616
sexual health. *See* health
sexual impulses, 18–20
sexual interest disorder (SID), 321–322
sexual masochism, 338–340